GW01339284

Off the Beaten Track

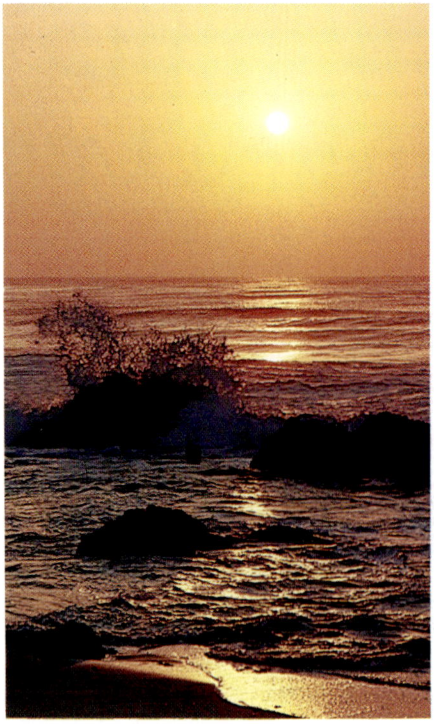

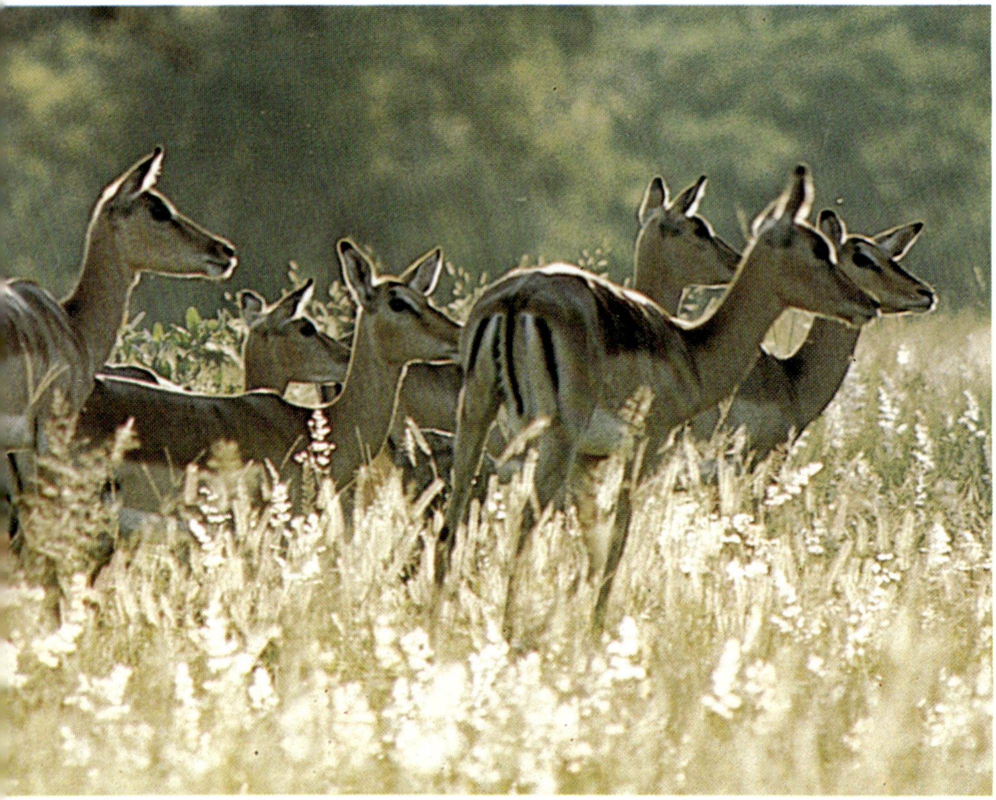

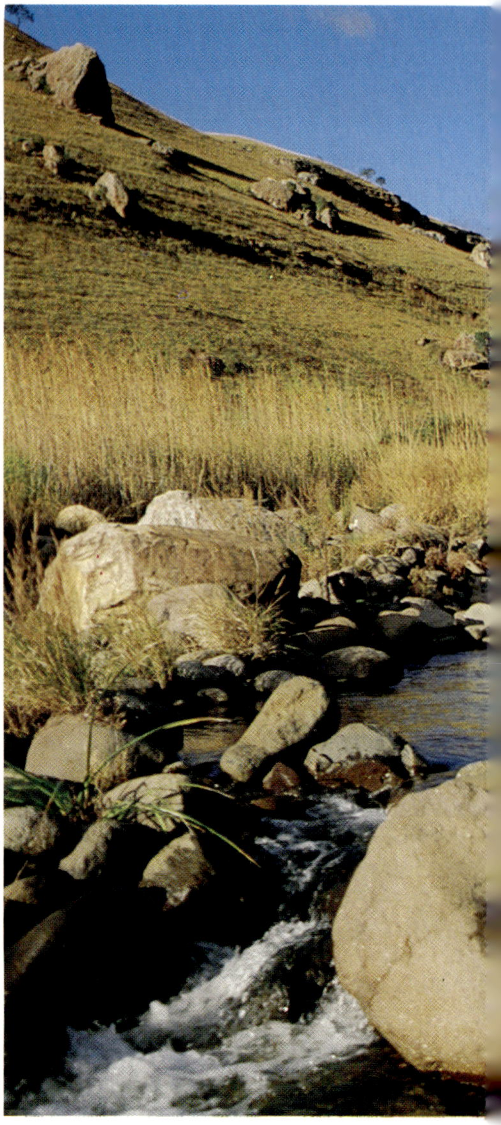

Off the Beaten Track

Selected day drives in southern Africa

Published by AA The Motorist Publications (Pty) Limited for The Automobile Association of South Africa

All rights reserved. No part of this book may be reproduced, translated, stored in a retrieval system, or transmitted in any form or by any means, electronic, electrostatic, magnetic tape, mechanical, photocopying, recording or otherwise, without permission in writing from the publishers.

OFF THE BEATEN TRACK was edited and designed at
AA The Motorist Publications (Pty) Limited, 130 Strand Street, Cape Town 8001.

Information from official maps reproduced under Government Printer's Copyright Authority 8472 of 3 January 1986.

ISBN 1-874912-46-7

Second Edition Copyright © 1996 AA The Motorist Publications (Pty) Limited

Editors Brian Johnson Barker, George Maclay, Alfie Steyn

Art Editor Neville Poulter

Designers Christabel Hardacre, Augusta Prohn

Research Editors Judy Beyer, Frances le Roux

Research Assistants Nazreen Garder, Taryn James, Yana Jardine

Regional and specialist contributors Leo Braack, William Charlton-Perkins, John de Villiers, Alan Duggan, Monica Fairall, Bridget Hilton-Barber, John House, Margaret House, Alan Kircaldy, Rob McCallum, Charles Norman, Tim O'Hagan, Willie Olivier, Sue O'Reilly, Charles Riddle, Charlotte Siebert, Paul Tingay, Anne Turner, Jacqueline Veening

Illustrator Tobie Beele

Project Coordinator Grant Moore

Picture Researchers Rose-Ann Myers, Una Oxche

Indexer Trudie Kettley

Cartographers AA Mapping & Publishing Services (Pty) Ltd; Institute for Cartographic Analysis, University of Stellenbosch; Linda Stevenson Graphic Design

Front cover A trout-filled lake in Kamberg Nature Reserve, KwaZulu-Natal

Back cover Clear waters at Clifton Beach near Cape Town

Title page (Above) A sunset blush of pink on golden sands

(Below) Impala pause in a burst of lowveld sunlight

(Right) The sparkling waters of a Drakensberg stream

Choosing a tour in *Off the Beaten Track*

✳ Take a look at the map on this page. You'll see that we have divided southern Africa into 13 touring regions – usually, but not always, according to provincial or national boundaries.
✳ Now turn to the page number indicated for a more detailed list of drives within a particular region, plus special features and walking tours.
✳ If you want to see a list of the entire contents of this book, please turn the page.
✳ If you want to look up a specific town or place, please use the index at the back of the book.

Zimbabwe (Page 305)
Namibia (Page 335)
Northern & North-West provinces (Page 11)
Gauteng (Page 71)
Mpumalanga & Swaziland (Page 35)
Northern KwaZulu-Natal (Page 105)
Free State & Lesotho (Page 89)
Southern KwaZulu-Natal (Page 125)
Northern Cape (Page 287)
Border & Transkei (Page 159)
Eastern Cape (Page 187)
Western Cape (Page 217)
South-Western Cape (Page 243)

Contents

ABOUT THIS BOOK 8

NORTHERN & NORTH-WEST PROVINCES 10
Louis Trichardt – Wyllie's Poort – Tshipise – Messina 12
Louis Trichardt – Entabeni – Phiphidi Falls – Lake Fundudzi view 14
Venda Traditions: The sacred python dance 16
Historic Soutpansberg: A last, far frontier 18
Tazaneen – Modjadji – Duiwelskloof – Debegeni Falls 20
Tzaneen – New Agatha – Ebenezer Dam – Magoebaskloof 22
Nylstroom – Vaalwater – Thabazimbi – Rankin's Pass 24
Waterberg: The rugged, brooding spaces 26
Magaliesberg: Conservation and recreation combine 28
Pilanesberg National Park: Reserve in a volcano 30
Marico and beyond: Romance of the backveld 32

MPUMALANGA & SWAZILAND 34
Sabie – MacMac Falls – Blyde River Canyon – Bourke's Luck 36
Blyde River Canyon: A waterworn wonderland 38
Sabie – Graskop – Kowyn's Pass – Lisbon Falls – Pilgrim's Rest 40
Pilgrim's Rest: The gold rush lives on 42
Lydenburg – Sudwala Caves – Long Tom Pass – Sabie 44
Long Tom Pass: Gunfire's distant echo 46
Lydenburg – Verraiersnek – Robber's Pass – Burgersfort 48
Nelspruit – De Kaap Valley – Saddleback Pass – Barberton 50
Barberton and De Kaap Valley: A wealth of gold 52
Mbabane – Forbes' Reef – Piggs Peak – Barberton – Badplaas 54
Swazi Traditions: Sacred rites of the New Year 56
Kruger National Park: Introduction and day drives 58

GAUTENG 70
Pretoria (Johannesburg) – Rayton – Middelburg – Fort Merensky 72
Pretoria: Administrative capital in a city of parks 74
Pretoria (Johannesburg) – Hartbeespoort Dam – Breedt's Nek 78
Pretoria (Johannesburg) – Suikersbosrand – Vaal Dam 80
Johannesburg: Exploring *Egoli* – city of gold 82

FREE STATE & LESOTHO 88
Harrismith – The Sentinel – Golden Gate – Clarens 90
Golden Gate National Park: Towering sandstone cliffs 92
Bloemfontein: City at the centre of South Africa 94
Bethlehem – Clarens – Fouriesburg – Ficksburg 96
Maseru – Roma – Bushman's Pass – Ha Khotso 98
Maseru – Teyateyaneng – Thaba Bosiu – Morija 100
Sotho Traditions: Rich store from the past 102

NORTHERN KWAZULU-NATAL 104
Vryheid – Isandlwana – Rorke's Drift – Talana – Blood River 106
Mkuze – Jozini – Ndumo – Tembe Elephant Park – Kosi Bay 108
Ndumo Game Reserve: Wood and water 110
Hluhluwe Game Reserve: Where Zulu kings once hunted 112
Umfolozi Game Reserve: Saving the white rhino 114
Lake St Lucia: Subtropical waterworld 116
Empangeni – Enseleni – Coward's Bush – Eshowe – Mtunzini 118
Greytown – Elandslaagte – Colenso – Weenen – Muden 120
Stanger – Kranskop – Ahrens – Dalton – Fawn Leas – Nsuze 122

SOUTHERN KWAZULU-NATAL 124
Royal Natal National Park: 'Mountain of beginnings' 126
Ladysmith – Winterton – Monk's Cowl – Bergville – Spioenkop 128
Mooi River – Bray Hill – Giant's Castle – Wagendrift Dam – Estcourt 130
Giant's Castle Game Reserve: 'People of the eland' 132
Pietermaritzburg – Hella-Hella – Himeville – Sani Pass – Reichenau 134
Underberg – Coleford – Bushman's Nek – Drakensberg Garden 136
Pietermaritzburg – Howick Falls – Kamberg – Umgeni Valley 138
Pietermaritzburg: Red brick and Imperial echoes 140
Durban – Valley of a Thousand Hills – World's View 142
Zulu Traditions: The people of heaven 144
Durban – Umdloti Beach – Shaka's Rock – Stanger 146
Durban: The heart of the Holiday Coast 148
Durban – Clansthal – Scottburgh – Amanzimtoti 152
Scottburgh – Ixopo – St Faith's – Umzumbe 154
Margate – Uvongo – Oribi Gorge – Port Edward 156

BORDER & TRANSKEI 158
Umtata – Mhlengana – Port St Johns – Umngazi Mouth 160
Kokstad – Flagstaff – Lusikisiki – Port St Johns 162
Xhosa Traditions: People of a land of legend 164
Umtata – Hole-in-the-wall – Coffee Bay – Mtata Mouth 166
Butterworth – Centane – Qolora Mouth – Mazeppa Bay 168
East London – Cefane Mouth – Morgan Bay – Gonubie 170
East London – Igoda Mouth – Hamburg – Buffalo Pass 172
King William's Town: Glamour of an old garrison town 174
Aliwal North – Lady Grey – Barkly East – Rhodes – Maclear 176
Aliwal North – Bethulie – Norvalspont – Venterstad – Burgersdorp 178
Queenstown – Indwe – Otto du Plessis Pass – Dordrecht 180
Fort Beaufort – Alice – Cathcart – Stutterheim – Keiskammahoek 182
Hosgback: Mountaintop wonderland of falls and forests 184

EASTERN CAPE 186

Karoo and Camdeboo: Midlands' roads and roses **188**
Grahamstown – Fort Beaufort – Katberg Pass – Seymour – Alice **190**
Grahamstown – Salem – Port Alfred – Bathurst **192**
Grahamstown: Places of interest in the Settler City **194**
Graaff-Reinet – Nieu Bethesda – Cradock – Pearston **196**
The Owl House: A pilgrim's progress in Nieu Bethesda **198**
Mountain Zebra National Park: Remote mountain sanctuary **200**
Port Elizabeth – Uitenhage – Suurberg Pass – Addo National Park **202**
Port Elizabeth: What to see and do in the Friendly City **204**
Port Elizabeth – Hankey – Grootrivier – Cockscomb **206**
Port Elizabeth – Jeffreys Bay – Cape St Francis – Cockscomb **208**
Port Elizabeth: Walks and wildlife **210**
Graaff-Reinet: A closer look at the Gem of the Karoo **212**
Karoo Nature Reserve: The Valley of Desolation **214**

WESTERN CAPE 216

Plettenberg Bay – Nature's Valley – Tsitsikamma – Storms River **218**
Plettenberg Bay – Noetzie – Spistkop – Diepwalle – Dieprivier **220**
Knysna – Belvidere – Millwood – Wilderness **222**
Steam and scenery: George to Knysna by steam train **224**
George – Oudtshoorn – Cango Caves – Outeniqua Pass **226**
Oudtshoorn – Swartberg Pass – Prince Albert – Meiringspoort **228**
Prince Albert: Gables and a forgotten gold rush **230**
Laingsburg – Seweweekspoort – Zoar – Hoeko – Ladismith **232**
Riversdale – Herbertsdale – Mossel Bay – Gouritsmond **234**
Swellendam – Bonnievale – Montagu – Tradouw Pass **236**
Swellendam – De Hoop Nature Reserve – Malgas – Witsand **238**
Swellendam: An attractive stroll through history **240**

SOUTH-WESTERN CAPE 242

Cape Town: Sampling a wine route **244**
Cape Town – Cape Point – Chapman's Peak – Clifton **246**
Simon's Town: 'Memory Mile' of naval history **248**
Cape Town – Kirstenbosch – Constantia – Hout Bay **250**
Cape Town: Stately beauty of the Mother City **252**
Cape Town: Exploring the city and its lovely setting **254**
The Waterfront: In the steps of sailormen **256**
Robertson – McGregor – Greyton – Genadendal **258**
Hermanus – Elim – Cape Agulhas – Arniston – Bredasdorp **260**
Gordon's Bay – Hermanus – Caledon – Houhoek **262**
Cape Town – Grabouw – Franschhoek – Stellenbosch **264**
Stellenbosch: Historic homes in oak-shaded avenues **266**
Cape Town – Tulbagh – Bain's Kloof – Wellington **268**

Tulbagh: The charm of Church Street **270**
Cape Town – Darling – Yzerfontein – Riebeek West **272**
Saldanha – Langebaan – Velddrif – Cape Columbine **274**
Citrusdal – Prince Alfred Hamlet – Ceres – Tulbagh **276**
Piketberg – Velddrif – Rocher Pan – Elands Bay – Velorevlei **278**
Clanwilliam – Wuppertal – Matjiesrivier **280**
Cederberg: Wilderness of strangely sculpted rock **282**
Van Rhynsdorp – Doornbaai – Lambert's Bay – Klawer **284**

NORTHERN CAPE 286

Springbok – Okiep – Spektakel Pass – Messelpad **288**
Namaqualand: The wildflower wonderland **290**
Upington – Kanoneiland – Keimoes – Kakamas – Augrabies **292**
Augrabies Falls National Park: Mighty waterfall of the desert **294**
Kimberley – Nooitgedacht – Barkly-West – Magersfontein **296**
Kalahari Gemsbok National Park: A wealth of wildlife **298**
Kimberley: Diamond capital of the world **300**
Dorp and byway: Travels through time **302**

ZIMBABWE 304

Harare: Exploring the national capital **306**
Harare – Darwendale – Lake Manyame – Lake Chivero **308**
Harare – Ewanrigg Botanical Garden – Hippo Pools – Mazowe **310**
Mutare – Burma Valley – Bunga Reserve – Leopard Rock **312**
Mutare – Nyanga – Troutbeck – Pungwe – Mutarazi Falls **314**
Nyanga National Park: Enchantment of the Eastern Highlands **316**
Mutare – Hot Springs – Chimanimani – Bridal Veil Falls **318**
Masvingo – Great Zimbabwe – Mutirikwi Game Reserve **320**
Great Zimbabwe: Silent stones tell a story **322**
Bulawayo – Cyrene Mission – Matobos National Park **324**
Bulawayo: Where a king made his home **326**
Victoria Falls – Sinamatella – Hwange National Park **328**
Lake Kariba: Ferry ride on a great manmade lake **330**
Kariba village – Kaburi – Makuti – Chirundu – Otto Beit Bridge **332**

NAMIBIA 334

Keetmanshoop – Fish River Canyon – Ai-Ais **336**
Etosha National Park: Wildlife throngs a vast, shallow lake **338**
Windhoek – Gamsberg Pass – Namib-Naukluft Park **340**
Windhoek: German castles in an African capital **342**
Walvis Bay – Swakopmund – Henties Bay – Cape Cross **344**

INDEX 346

Exploring southern Africa 'off the beaten track'

If you want to discover the real beauty of southern Africa, then you're ready for Off the Beaten Track, a different kind of guidebook that leads you through the most interesting and scenic areas of our countryside, towns and cities. It does this in several ways:

DAY DRIVES The most convenient way to explore is by car – and the bulk of the book consists of drives that can generally be completed in less than a day. Maps and text combine to create a memorable outing.

EXPLORE ON FOOT Every now and then you'll want to leave the car behind and 'explore on foot' historic or scenic towns and special places such as Cape Town's Waterfront or romantic Pilgrim's Rest. Follow the numbered map to find the most fascinating sights.

EXPLORE A SPECIAL AREA These features concentrate on conservation areas and places of natural interest, such as game parks.

PLACES OF INTEREST Learn about our cities and their surroundings, their sights and their special entertainments.

TRADITIONS Read about people and traditions you'll find off the beaten track, such as the snake dance of the Venda, the initiation ceremonies of the Xhosa or the sleepy world of southern Africa's dorps.

Going on a day drive

The day drives in Off the Beaten Track are designed to show you the most beautiful and most interesting places in each region. Each day's outing has been carefully arranged to provide contrast, to bring you to each place at the best time and to create a wonderful adventure-in-one-day. All but a few of the drives are circular, bringing you back to your starting point at the end of the day. A drive may be undertaken as a one-day outing from the city or town that serves as its starting point, or you may link several drives together to create a motoring holiday through a particular part of the country. Here and there, where the natural attractions of the region merit it, a special feature has been included alongside a drive – telling you more about the landscape you are exploring, or perhaps giving you a guided walk through one of the interesting towns in the area.

Remember to start early. Read through the route in advance, prepare the night before (which may include filling the tank with petrol and checking that everything is in working order) then make an early start before the morning traffic fills the roads.

Distances

The distances given in the route instructions are as accurate as possible. You will find discrepancies, because the odometers of different vehicles give slightly varying measurements, and readings are affected by such factors as tyre pressures, and even by your driving style, but almost every distance given is an actual recording. Exceptions may occur where readings are in excess of 15 km, in which case they may be rounded off to the nearest whole kilometre.

Key to maps for day drives

ABOUT THIS BOOK

Throughout the route instructions, the phrase 'note your kms' occurs. If your car does not have a trip odometer that can be reset to zero at the stage referred to, you will need to add the next distance given, to the reading shown on your odometer. Other phrases used are, for example, 'after 10,7 km' or '10,7 km later'. These refer back to the last point at which you were asked to note your kilometres, unless the context clearly indicates some other point of reference. Where a route indicates an opportunity for a short walk, the phrase 'allow 40 – 60 minutes' refers to the total time – there and back.

For further information

The introductory information adjoining the small incidence map in the shaded panel above the start of each set of route instructions tells you briefly about the attractions of the drive. For those who prefer to drive only on tarred roads, it also gives the approximate length of unsurfaced roads on the route.

With each drive, at the end of the route instructions, you will find an information panel containing several valuable addresses and telephone numbers. Use these to inquire into the state of the roads, to get up-to-the-minute information relating to the route, to find out about restaurants, overnight accommodation and generally to answer any further query that you might have.

Many of the drives include scenic mountain or river valley passes that are not suitable for vehicles towing trailers or caravans. If you are towing, contact the AA office listed in the information panel to confirm that the route you plan to take is suitable. Local residents or officials – such as police or local authority employees – are also an invaluable source of information. Remember that untarred roads can be difficult or even impassable after heavy rains. Although the routes were test-driven shortly before publication, ongoing roadworks in a few parts of the country may effect slight changes. Remember also to check what documents are needed before crossing international borders.

Confirm your route in advance

The roads on which you are travelling are being altered continually – gravel surfaces are tarred, old roads are re-routed. With the passage of time, the route instructions will inevitably become incorrect here and there. Where such alterations have occurred, you will need to follow whatever new signs have been erected, and to refer both to the route instructions and to the accompanying map to make the most appropriate adjustment. A sensible precaution, before setting out on a drive, is to contact the AA and ask whether there have been any important alterations to the roads in the area, or whether the route needs to be modified in any other way. (A picnic area might have closed, or a new game reserve might offer an interesting detour.)

The information collected in this volume represents several years of research and over 200 000 km of driving on roads and tracks throughout southern Africa. Great care has been taken to ensure that the information and directions given are correct in every detail. However, the publishers cannot accept responsibility for any loss, inconvenience or damage that might result, either directly or indirectly, from the use of the instructions or the maps provided here.

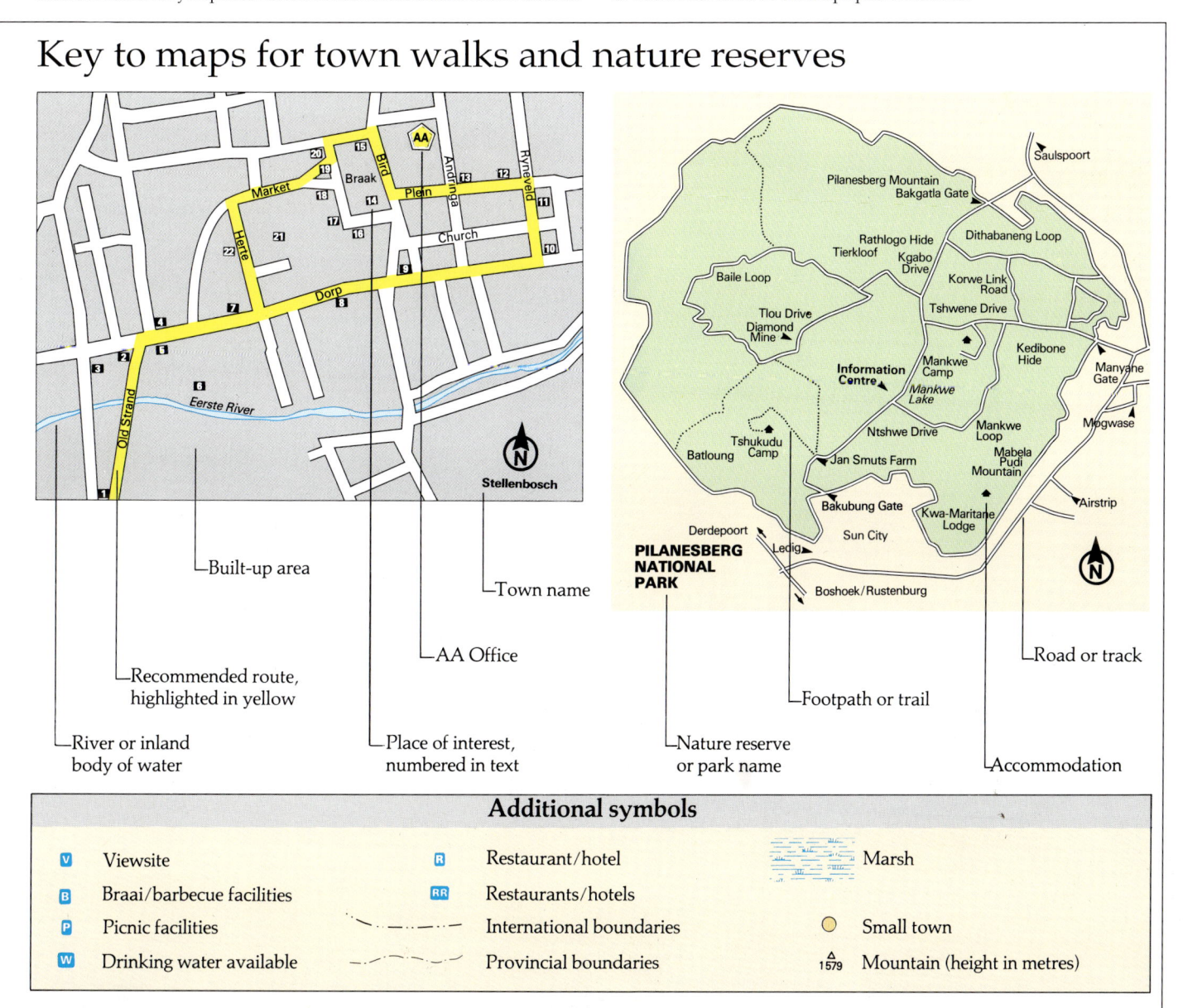

Key to maps for town walks and nature reserves

Additional symbols

V	Viewsite	R	Restaurant/hotel		Marsh
B	Braai/barbecue facilities	RR	Restaurants/hotels		
P	Picnic facilities		International boundaries	○	Small town
W	Drinking water available		Provincial boundaries	▲1579	Mountain (height in metres)

9

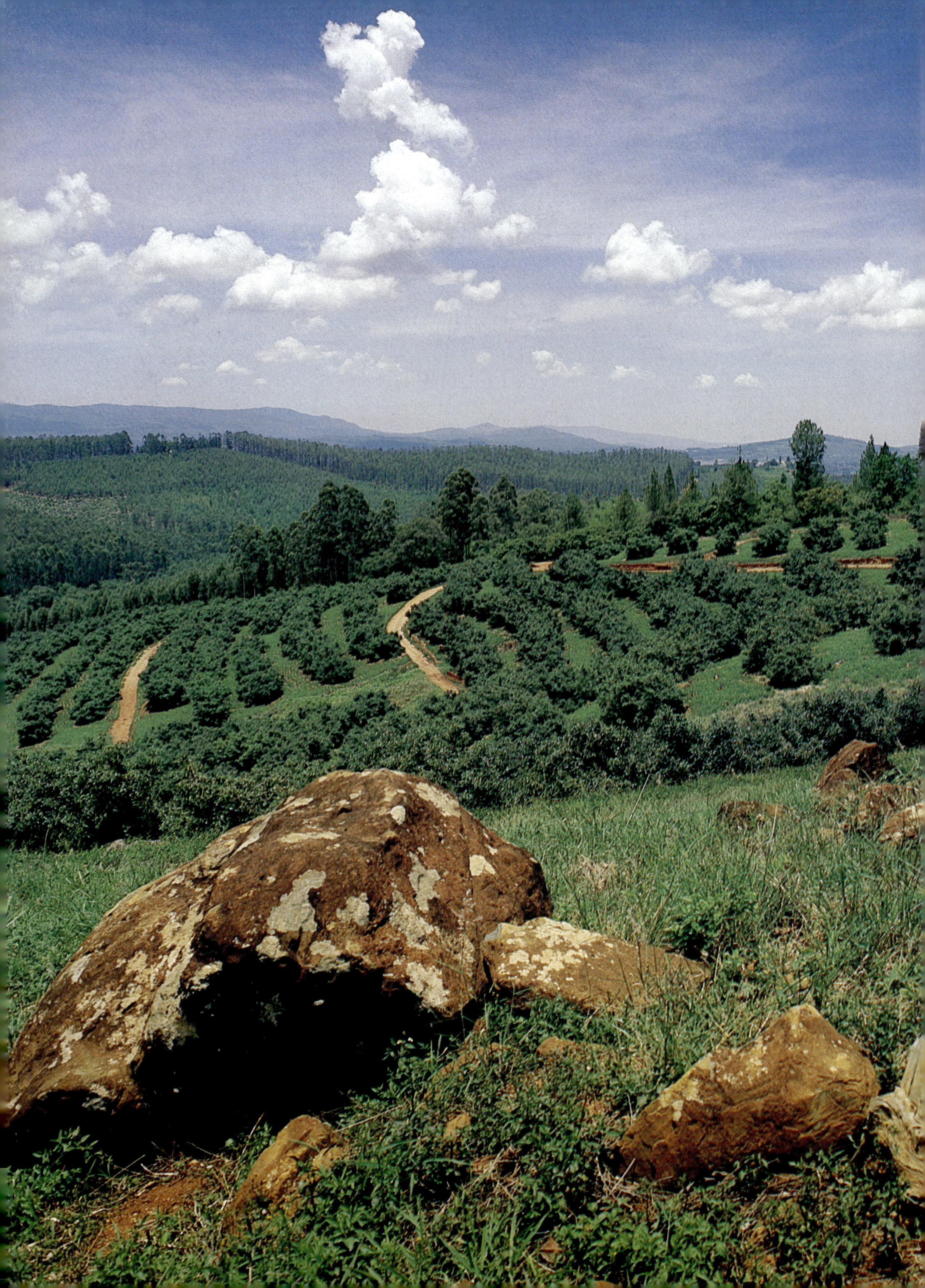

NORTHERN & NORTH-WEST PROVINCES

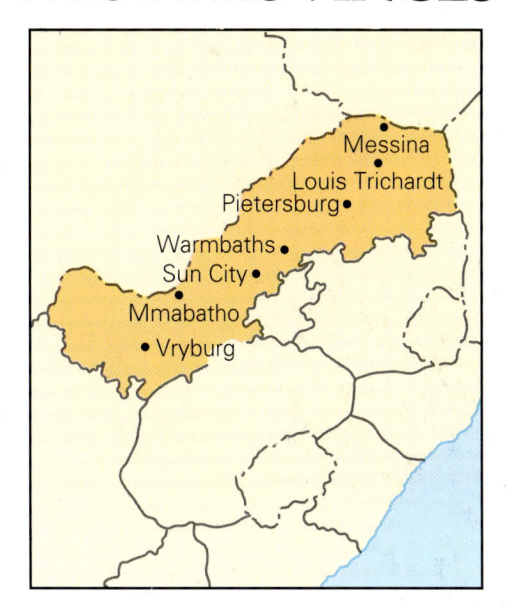

Louis Trichardt – Wyllie's Poort – Tshipise – Messina – Bluegum Poort **12-13**

Louis Trichardt – Entabeni – Phiphidi Falls – Lake Fundudzi view **14-15**

Venda Traditions: The sacred python dance **16-17**

Historic Soutpansberg: A last, far frontier **18-19**

Tzaneen – Modjadji – Duiwelskloof – Debegeni Falls **20-1**

Tzaneen – New Agatha – Ebenezer Dam – Magoebaskloof **22-3**

Nylstroom – Vaalwater – Bakkers Pass – Thabazimbi – Rankin's Pass **24-5**

Waterberg: The rugged, brooding spaces **26-7**

Magaliesberg: Conservation and recreation combine **28-9**

Pilanesberg National Park: Reserve in a volcano **30-1**

Marico and beyond: Romance of the backveld **32-3**

Left: *Subtropical orchards beneath the forested foothills of the Soutpansberg.*

Beyond Capricorn – the far frontiers of the unexplored north

This scenic drive provides a fascinating insight into the relatively unknown northern reaches of South Africa. Follow the Great North Road through the forest-clad slopes of the Soutpansberg and into the arid bushveld, where baobabs stand proud under vast skies and hot springs bubble up from under the earth. Some 45 km of this drive is on gravel.

**Louis Trichardt
Wyllie's Poort
Tshipise
Messina
Bluegum Poort
360 – 380 km**

OUR DRIVE BEGINS AT Voortrekker Square on Krogh Street, Louis Trichardt, where the 1898 Church of the Vow can be seen, as well as Fort Hendrina – one of three such 'portable' steel structures ordered by the republican Transvaal in 1887.

From Krogh Street, drive south for several blocks until you reach a crossroads with the R522. Turn right, into Rissik Street, in the direction of Vivo, and note your kms. After 16 km, turn left onto the gravel road signposted Schoemansdal Museum, the entrance of which is reached after a further 2 km.

From the museum, return via the R522 to Louis Trichardt and drive through the town until you reach the crossroads with the N1. Turn left, in the direction of Zimbabwe, noting your kms. The road begins to ascend almost immediately, climbing up the Soutpansberg through the Hanglip Forest Reserve, which is named after the peak overlooking the town.

Wyllie's Poort to Messina
There is a picnic site on your left after 9,7 km, with a bird's-eye view over Louis Trichardt and the wide plains to the south. After 13 km the road begins its descent into the scenic Wyllie's Poort. About 22 km from Louis Trichardt, you enter the first of two impressive tunnels, completed in 1961. Immediately after this first 400 m tunnel there is a parking area on your left, with a commemorative plaque and an excellent view of the old road through the poort below. North of Wyllie's Poort the vegetation changes to mopane forest with a sprinkling of baobabs. Some 57 km after leaving Louis Trichardt, turn right on the R525 for Tshipise, noting your kms. Keep straight and, after 30 km, turn right into the entrance of the Tshipise Aventura Resort. An entry fee is payable.

With its restaurant, rolling lawns and shaded picnic areas, Tshipise is an attractive lunch stop. The swimming pools and mineral baths afford visitors a welcome opportunity to be soothed and refreshed. Jacaranda, frangipani and flamboyant trees flourish in the area. The resort is adjacent to the Honnet Nature Reserve – home to a variety of game and the well-known Baobab Hiking Trail. Leaving Aventura Tshipise, turn right and after 1 km, turn right again onto the R525 for Messina. This road crosses the Njelele River and winds its way through sparse yet hauntingly beautiful bushveld. After 28,8 km, you cross the Sand River and, at 37 km, reach a T-junction with the N1 that runs through Messina.

Messina to Bluegum Poort
At the T-junction, turn right into the main road of this copper town whose streets are lined with vibrantly colourful trees. On your left you see Messina railway station, which has won awards for many years for South Africa's best kept and most beautiful station. There is an open-air museum alongside the station, which houses a carefully restored Zeederberg mail coach – the original mail coach that used to run between Pretoria and Zimbabwe. There is also an old steam locomotive and an exhibition of photographs and old fire-fighting equipment. Messina's information bureau is also in the main street, with an old steamroller marking the entrance. (Exhibits were temporarily stored in 1996.)

To the north, the N1 continues through Messina, crosses the railway twice and, after 14 km, reaches the Beit Bridge over the lazy Limpopo, the border between South Africa and Zimbabwe. A short drive along this road affords wonderful river views. Drive back south through Messina on the N1. About 2 km from the town, on the left, is an entrance to the Baobab Reserve, which contains more than 1 000 of these ancient trees, all of which have been declared national monuments. The reserve also offers walking trails and picnic spots. Return to the N1 and turn left, noting your kms. You cross the Sand River again after about 6 km; after 33 km, keep straight at the crossroads with the R525. There are regular picnic spots in the shade of baobabs.

Pass through the two road tunnels again and, about 78 km from the Baobab Reserve, turn right onto the gravel road signposted Bluegum Poort, noting your kms as you do so.

Bluegum Poort gets its name from the enormous bluegum trees that line the roadside, at one point forming a shady, aisle-like avenue. This route follows the ridge of the Soutpansberg for about 22,5 km, ending at an attractive picnic site. Bluegum Poort offers spectacular views, imparting a great sense of romantic mystery in the late afternoon light.

From the Bluegum Poort road, return to the N1 and turn right, in the direction of Louis Trichardt town. Turn right at the crossroads with Trichardt Street. Shortly after this, you will see, on your right, the municipal caravan park, which is enclosed in an indigenous tree park where 114 species of tree are preserved. Visitors may also see a number of Voortrekker graves dating as far back as 1864.

Tshipise Aventura Resort PO Box 4, Tshipise 0901 Tel (015539) 624
Schoemansdal Museum Tel (01551) 4237

SCHOEMANSDAL MUSEUM
The pioneering spirit of the region's early Voortrekkers is brought vividly to life in the fascinating open-air Schoemansdal Museum, a reconstruction of the first Voortrekker settlement established here in 1848. Visitors can explore the interiors of the *hartbeeshuisies*, A-frame dwellings of mud and reed. The name, originally *hardbies*, meant 'hard reed'. The furniture, domestic utensils and other objects typical of the Voortrekker lifestyle are displayed. There are also baking ovens, wagon sheds, an authentic laager and an original ox-wagon. A viewing platform offers an excellent overall picture of the museum and its adjacent archaeological excavation site – research is continually being undertaken to unearth more about the early Iron Age and Stone Age people in the area. Guided tours to the site may be arranged by special request. The museum is open from Tuesday to Sunday from 08h00 to 16h00 (entry is free).

Above: *A corner of Schoemansdal's old cemetery.*
Right: *Excavated foundations at Schoemansdal.*

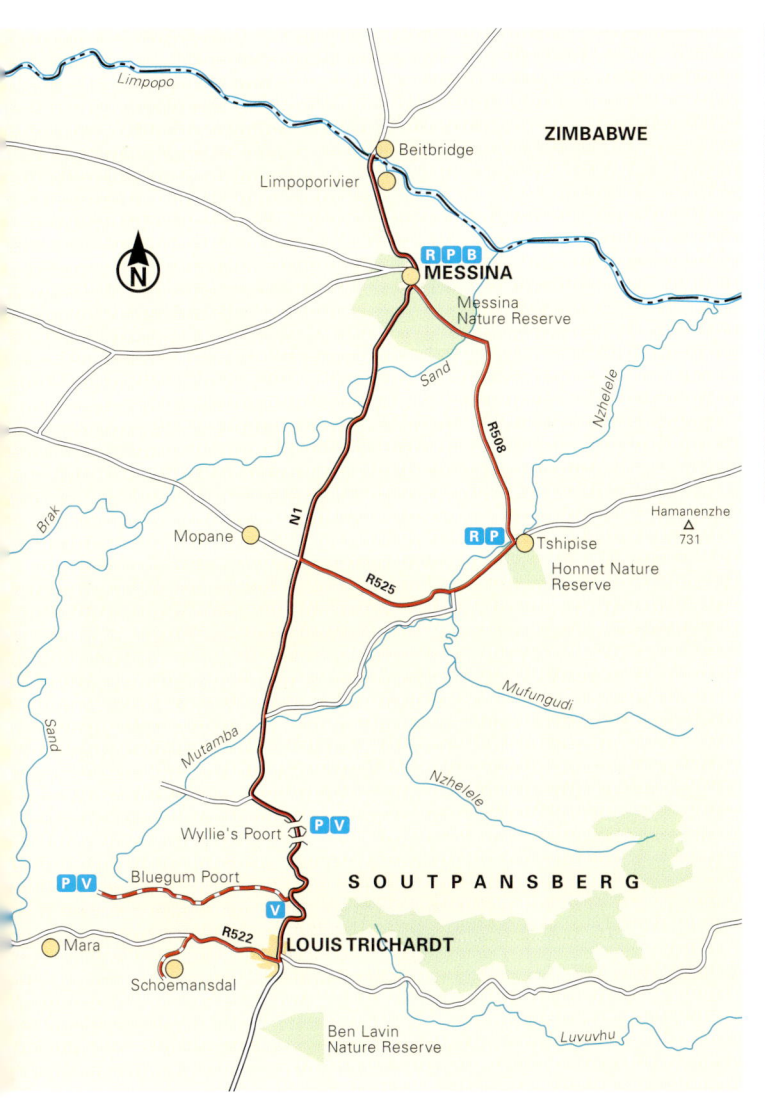

NORTHERN & NORTH-WEST PROVINCES

Winter-flowering impala lilies (Adenium obesum) *brighten Messina streets.*

THE SOUTPANSBERG

South Africa's northernmost mountain range, the Soutpansberg, takes its name from the salt pans that lie at its base near the western end, and have supplied communities with salt from prehistoric times. It rises abruptly from the plains in the west near the village of Vivo and gradually peters out near the northern boundary of the Kruger National Park. The Soutpansberg is made up of an ancient sequence of sedimentary rock and basaltic lava that dates back some 1 900 million years. Because of its geographical position, the range offers an unusually varied spectrum of plants and animals. In the east, it receives some of South Africa's highest rainfall, which decreases to the west. The high rainfall areas support mistbelt-type evergreen forests, which gradually change to deciduous savannah and, finally, to semi-arid scrub in the drier west. The variety of animals includes the thick-tailed bush baby, pangolin, red duiker, rock-elephant shrew, samango monkey and leopard.

WYLLIE'S POORT

Today's travellers heading northwards from Louis Trichardt pass through an impressive pair of tunnels cutting their way through the heart of the Soutpansberg. Taken into use in 1961, the tunnels were built adjacent to the historic Wyllie's Poort, which follows a lower-lying contour. From the parking area at the tunnels, you can see the old road through the poort and savour the history of the first gateway to the far north. Lieutenant Wyllie came to South Africa during the Anglo-Boer War and served in the Corps of Royal Engineers of the British military forces. After the war, in 1904, Wyllie was placed in charge of demobilized British troops recruited to construct this section of the 'great north road', an imperial dream of Cecil Rhodes, later taken up by Lord Milner. In 1907, the first ox-wagon negotiated the pass, which was subsequently named in honour of Wyllie.

Below: *Stubby-branched baobabs near Messina.*

Visitors enjoy an early-morning dip in the naturally heated waters at Tshipise.

TSHIPISE

The name comes from the Venda word that translates as 'is hot' or 'to burn'. Local legend has it that, long ago, a great battle was fought here and ended only when the gods hurled fire at the combatants. Immediately, hot springs burst from the ground. The famous Tshipise koppie still towers protectively over this once-sacred spot, now a bustling resort. At a temperature of around 65°C, 680 000 litres of alkaline water well to the surface daily. Many people believe these waters possess healing properties. Tshipise is adjacent to the Honnet Nature Reserve, home to a number of giraffe, zebra, leopard, hyaena and other game. The reserve is renowned for its 10 km Baobab Hiking Trail, which takes walkers past a number of these mighty trees, one of which is said to be 4 000 years old. Trips to the reserve may be made on foot, on horseback or by bus.

A land of forests – where spirits dwell in lake and waterfall

This drive leads east from Louis Trichardt, passing through lush tropical plantations of fruit, nuts and tea, and climbing the cool forested slopes of the Soutpansberg. We visit the Phiphidi Falls and drive deep into the Thathe Vondo Forest to view – from a respectful distance – the sacred Lake Fundudzi. Roughly half of the route is tarred.

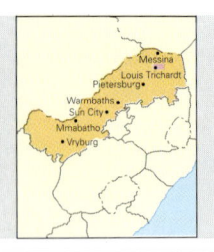

Louis Trichardt
Entabeni Forest
Levubu
Thohoyandou
Phiphidi Falls
Thathe Vondo Forest
170 – 190 km

DRIVE EAST OUT of Louis Trichardt along Trichardt Street. Note your kms at the crossroads with the N1 and proceed straight across onto the R524. The road passes through tropical plantations, including citrus fruit, pecan nuts and mangoes, and gradually approaches the forested slopes of the Soutpansberg.

You cross the Levubu River 17 km from the N1 and, 5,5 km beyond this point, turn right onto a gravel road to visit the Albasini Dam (entrance fee). After 2,4 km on this gravel road, turn right into the area of the dam wall. Opposite this entrance a track leads for some 300 m to a grove of jacaranda trees surrounding the graves of the pioneering family after whom the dam is named.

Return to the R524 and turn right, noting your kms. After 14 km turn left for a short excursion into the Entabeni Forest, this sideroad leading, after 3 km, to the gate to the forestry reserve. A permit is issued here and you may be required to pay a small fee. Turn left at the inclined T-junction 800 m beyond the gate. After a further 3,2 km, take a sharp left turn opposite the Timbadola sawmill on your right. This road winds up the hillside, offering wide views over plantations of pine and eucalyptus to the waters of the Albasini Dam.

Entabeni Forest to Phiphidi Falls

Return to the R524 and turn left, noting your kms. After 500 m turn right for Levubu. The road passes through orchards and a profusion of flowers and trees. Turn left at the first T-junction, pass a road leading right, and turn right at the second T-junction, passing through plantations of bananas. Turn left at the next two T-junctions to rejoin the R524 after a pleasant detour through this extremely fertile tract of country. Note your kms as you turn right onto the R524.

After 19 km you reach, on your left, the brightly painted, traditional-styled buildings of the Ditike Arts and Crafts Centre. It is worthwhile stopping here to view the work on display and to obtain information on the area. (There is a detailed map here, showing the roads in the Thathe Vondo Forest.)

Just under 1 km past the Ditike Centre turn left off the R524 onto the road to Sibasa and Thohoyandou, noting your kms. Follow this road for 4,8 km, passing a large shopping centre on your right, the university on your left, and then a hotel and administrative buildings on your right.

The road climbs until you reach a controlled four-way intersection. Turn left here, noting your kms. The road passes many villages with homes of both traditional and modern design, and there are wide views to your left over the lower-lying countryside and back over Thohoyandou. After 8,9 km, opposite the Phiphidi Centre, turn right and, 100 m later, turn right again to reach the gate to the Phiphidi Falls area.

The road descends to reach a parking area some 400 m further on. From here, a short footpath leads to a sheltered grove where the Phiphidi Falls tumble into a large pool, named Guvhukuvhu. Do not disturb any objects in the area, and do not pick the flowers (see pages 16 – 17). In rainy weather the road to the parking area, and the footpath, are likely to be slippery. Local people venerate the area, especially the falls and the pool below them.

Venda boys fishing in a tranquil stream.

The Dutch Reformed Church, Louis Trichardt.

LOUIS TRICHARDT
The Voortrekker leader, Louis Trichardt, arrived at the foot of the Soutpansberg in 1836 and camped here for some months with his party before setting out on his epic trek to Delagoa Bay – which resulted in the death of Trichardt himself, his wife and many of his followers. The present town, named after this courageous leader, was founded in 1899. During the Anglo-Boer War it was evacuated and was totally destroyed, as nearby Schoemansdal had been several decades earlier (see pages 18 – 19). Large forestry plantations surround the town, and these provide several attractive walks.

The Phiphidi Falls tumble into a sacred pool.

SPIRITS OF THE PHIPHIDI FALLS
Ancestors of the Tshivhase royal family are buried in a sacred grove near the top of these attractive falls, and they are periodically given offerings of beer, left on a rock above the falls. About 2 km above the falls there is a pool said to be the home of the spirits of the VhaNgona, the earliest occupants of this country. People who cross the Mutshindudi River here must obtain the protection of the spirits by making an offering – such as food, beer, clothing or even a strand of hair from one's head – and these tokens are placed in the hollow of a large boulder at the edge of the pool.

Phiphidi Falls to Louis Trichardt

Return to the main road and turn right, noting your kms at the turn. After a short distance you cross the Mutshindudi River. Carry on through large tea plantations to reach the start of the pretty Thathe Vondo Pass. Keep straight through a number of crossroads as the road climbs through forestry plantations. At about 10,4 km you pass a gravel road on your left and, immediately afterwards, a sign reading 'Thathe Vondo Pass 1 077 m' comes into view on the left side of the road. Turn right just before reaching the sign, then turn right again to reach the gate into the Thathe Vondo Forest. An attendant may ask you to record details in a book. Note your kms here.

The gravel road climbs fairly steeply for the first few hundred metres. Keep straight ahead

The lush Entabeni Forest covers the gently rolling slopes of the historic Soutpansberg range.

The mysterious Lake Fundudzi.

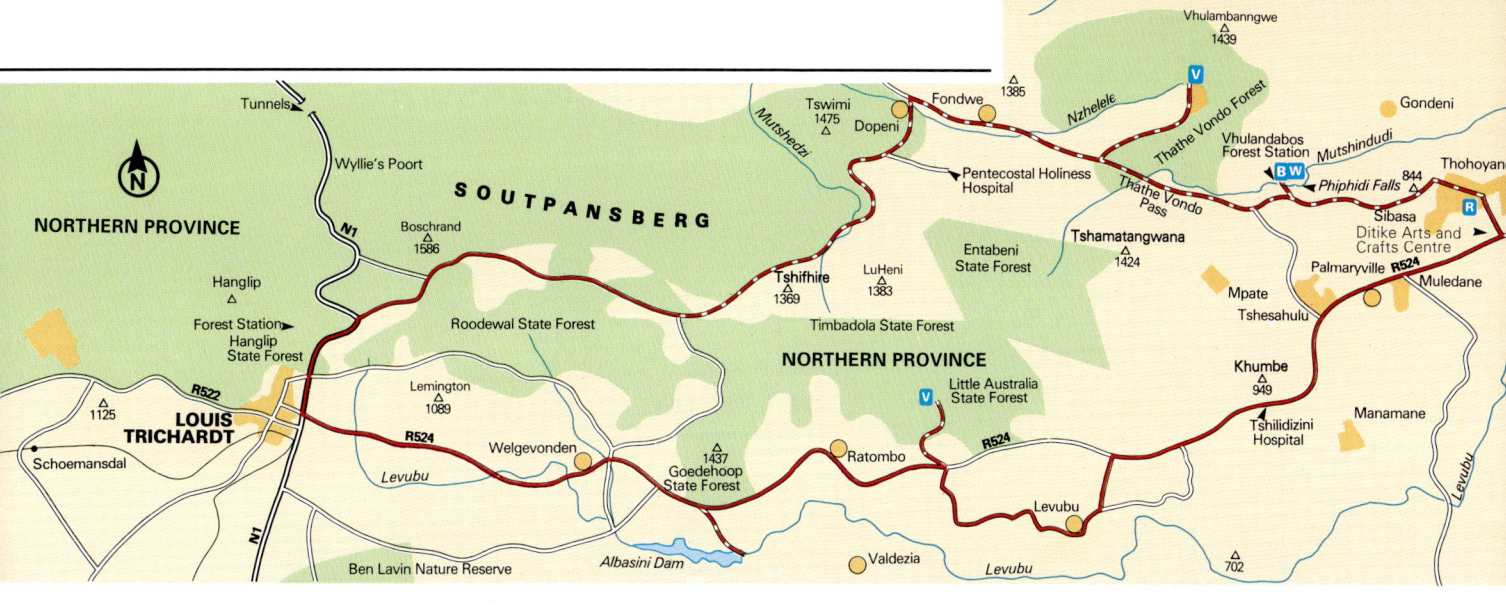

PIONEERING JOÃO ALBASINI

The son of a sea captain, João Albasini was 18 years old when he landed at Delagoa Bay in 1831. Lured by the wildness of Africa he left his ship and became an elephant hunter and a trader and also established a farm at Schoemansdal. He lived there until his death, staying on after the abandonment of the town in 1867. He was widely known as *hoofd-kapitein de Knop-neusen* (paramount chief of the Knob-noses).

Traditional thatch-roofed huts and homesteads decorate the hills.

THE SACRED LAKE FUNDUDZI

This forbidding body of water, encircled by mountains, was created in ancient times, when a landslide blocked the course of the Mutale River. Many legends are connected with the lake, traditionally regarded with veneration by the Venda. It is the home of the great Python God, who is placated annually with gifts of beer poured onto the water. The public may visit the lake only with permission from the local authority.

---

on the widest road. After driving 4,5 km from the entrance gate, park on the side of the road for a good view to your right over the Mukumbani Dam lying among the hills below. About 2,4 km later, a road forks to your right and another road leads left: ignore these and drive straight ahead.

After a further 3,1 km, pass a small building and a sideroad on your right. A little over 700 m later, go right at the fork and, 3,6 km after the fork, the road separates into three – keep straight on the middle road. Just over 1 km later, you drive through a gate and, 400 m beyond this, the road forks – take the road leading right, passing a Zion Christian building on your left. A few metres later you reach a fence in front of a fire-watchers' tower. Go left here, following the fence, then stop.

Ahead of you, and half to your left, you can see the mysterious Lake Fundudzi far below, within its ring of mountains (see above).

Retrace your route down through the forests to return to the tar at the summit of the Thathe Vondo Pass, and note your kms as you turn right onto the tarred road.

Descend slowly, as there may be some patches where the road surface is in poor condition. At 4,3 km you cross the Nzhelele River over a long bridge; at 10,1 km, turn left for Witvlag and Louis Trichardt just after passing a petrol station on your left. About 600 m after the turn, the road crosses the Nzhelele River again.

The tar changes to gravel again soon after you cross the river, and the road enters hilly country where villages clinging to the slopes look out over wide maize fields. Some 19 km after your second crossing of the Nzhelele River the road levels and you drive back onto tar – where you pass a road on your left to Welgevonden; 16,3 km later you reach a T-junction with the N1. Turn left onto the N1, noting your kms. After 6,4 km you reach a four-way stop street. Turn right into Trichardt Street, which leads you back into the town centre of Louis Trichardt.

AA Auto Clinic 52 Church Street
Pietersburg 0700 Tel (0152) 295 3051
Louis Trichardt Public Library Krogh Street
LouisTrichardt 0920 Tel (015) 516 1195
Soutpansberg Marketing & Tourism Association
PO Box 980, Louis Trichardt 0920
Tel (015) 516 0040

• VENDA TRADITIONS •

Young Venda girls weave sinuously in the traditional domba *or python dance, performed by initiates preparing for the responsibilities of adulthood.*

Catch the distant echoes of a vanished, magical drum

NEAR DAWN and sunset, the long ridge of the Soutpansberg may often be shrouded in mist that swirls eerily about bushy and forested slopes. At these times, especially, it seems natural that nature-spirits should play an important part in traditional beliefs – and the Venda have a wealth of tales and legends.

Through their culture and their language, the Venda are closely related to the Shona of Zimbabwe, and both have a common origin that started some 1 000 years ago in the Limpopo region.

There are no Venda ruins comparable in size to those at Great Zimbabwe, but several smaller ones clearly show the connection. Dated to about AD 1450, sites include Makhane and Thula Mela along the Levhuvhu River in the Kruger National Park, as well as Matshemma and Verdun in the western Soutpansberg.

A chief and his city
In the Nzhelele valley lies the ancient capital of the Venda, Dzata, a national monument. Dzata was built around 1700, when the present ruling clan of the Venda, the Singo, settled in the Nzhelele Valley after moving from the centre of Zimbabwe. To assist them on their move, it is said, they had a magical drum, the *Ngoma Lungundu*, and if the chief kept beating the drum while his people were on the move or at war, their enemies would be vanquished. They would arrive safely at their destination and be able to hold the land that they occupied.

Dzata itself was occupied for only about 60 years, which included the rule of the legendary *Thohoyandou* (Head of the Elephant), who is said to have created the Venda nation from the clans already in existence in the Soutpansberg. In about 1760,

The friendly faces of Venda children.

Dzata was burnt to the ground, but the fate of Thohoyandou remains a mystery. Some tales say that he was murdered at Dzata. Others tell of him fleeing over the mountains, taking the Ngoma Lungundu with him, to settle somewhere across the Limpopo. The fate of the Ngoma Lungundu also is uncertain. There is a strong belief that it was hidden in a cave near the village of Netshiendeulu, whose inhabitants were appointed as its keepers.

Phiphidi Falls and their sacred pool.

Most of the traditional villages are to be found nestling under the cliffs, and the legacy of Great Zimbabwe can be seen in stone walls that form terraces and divisions. The typical layout has the chief at the highest part of the village, with his wives and family in front of him. The rest of the villagers occupy the lower areas, protecting the chief and his wives. Mukumbani, the royal residence of the Tshivhase clan, is a good example of such a village.

Sacred sites

Supernatural beings and forces may take up residence almost anywhere – in the human body, in animals, in plants and trees, in caves, pools or waterfalls, in the cattle-enclosure, in small artefacts and in houses. Remember that the local people hold such sites in veneration; unless they are obviously signposted as being open to the public, consult the local department of tourism or a traditional leader in the area before attempting to enter sacred sites.

Lake Funduzi (Fundudzi), in a high valley of the Soutpansberg, is esteemed for its supernatural powers. Being a very large river pool, Funduzi is seen as greater in power and importance than other such pools. It is mentioned in the national domba initiation, which praises it as the place of birth and rebirth, creation and procreation, and describes a python god as the one responsible for the acts of creation. Domba initiation symbolism identifies the wall of the khoro as the python god's body and the courtyard as Lake Funduzi, the place of origin. The initiates, who dance in the *khoro* (public courtyard), are in the womb of the python, ready to be reborn, to graduate as marriageable and respectful members of society.

The myth describes a woman being married to the python without having seen her husband. She flees the country after the horrifying discovery of her husband's identity, and a terrible drought accompanies the mourning of the python over his loss. This drought is broken only when another girl is offered to the python god. The offer is repeated annually to keep the python satisfied.

The python god is not the only inhabitant of the lake. Inside the Great Pool is a village of water-sprites called *zwidudwane*, and local people say that, at night, they can hear their babies cry, their flutes play and their war drums sound. These water-sprites are sometimes described as malignant spiritual beings, sometimes as teachers of arts and crafts. Among the things they have taught human beings are the arts of music, weaving and iron-smelting. Zwidudwane go out at night, helping the surrounding villagers with the stamping of mealies. If the *mutuli* (wooden mortars for stamping grain) are filled in the evening, in the morning they will be found to contain flour, ready for use. Zwidudwane hunt near the lake and game is drawn into the water by invisible hands.

Water-sprites hurl stones at anybody who disturbs their peace. If you should pass by an underwater settlement of zwidudwane, an offering has to be thrown into the water to pacify them. This could be a tuft of hair, some tobacco, a stone, a piece of animal skin or cloth, or even a twig from a nearby tree.

The pool called Gubukuvho, below the Phiphidi Falls, is believed to be the home of zwidudwane, and these sprites can be heard dancing in the falls at night. From time to time, one also hears the sounds of their babies crying, women stamping and the boom of their big war drum.

Sacred groves are the burial sites or ancient living sites of the royal clan of the surrounding area, and are usually situated on a mountain. Entering the grove is forbidden to strangers. In the vicinity of Lake Funduzi lies the Thate Vondo Forest, in which is the Holy Forest, home of the ancestral spirits. Within this forest lies Mount Thate, in which some caves below huge stone boulders are the burial site of local royalty. The caves are also the home of the supernatural sacred lion that protects the graves. Nethathe, one of the ancestral rulers, was a magician who could transform himself into an extremely ferocious lion. This is the very lion that still protects the area, and the forest and its hill are named after him. Visitors are allowed to travel through the Holy Forest but are not allowed to leave the gravel road that runs through it.

Pottery, sculpture and music

From time immemorial, pots have been fired under grass and wood fires and many women still work in the ancient style.

Made of roughish clay without the use of a potter's wheel, pots range considerably in size. Modern cooking pots have a thick band of graphite burnishing just below the lip, while beer pots are usually more heavily decorated with geometrical shapes such as triangles, stars or diamonds. Graphite and ochre provide the traditional colours, but some potters use modern paints.

Until relatively recently, wood sculpture in the area was quite scarce and carving was limited to a few utensils and artefacts made for royal use. Many of these artefacts disappeared during early contact with whites, and missionaries opposed to traditional African religion may also have destroyed a large number of artefacts. Today, there is a lively market in exquisite works of art produced by local sculptors, most of whom – because of traditional divisions of labour – are male. However, in a break with tradition, a female artist has been working in wood for some time. Justifying this move against tradition, she argues that she has the support of the ancestors, who called her to be an artist. Dreams are used by diviners, herbalists and others to justify their calling by ancestral forces. Some carvers also claim that they are called by the ancestors in dreams to be artists and that they receive training and inspiration for their pieces through dreams sent by the ancestors. The work is generally of high quality, mahogany and kiaat being the favourite wood types.

Many musical instruments, styles and performances survive among the Venda and many types of instrument that have disappeared elsewhere in Africa are still regularly used here today.

Ritual drums accompany the domba *dancers as they move around the fire.*

A hillside village near Sibasa.

Grinding mealies – a daily chore – while tobacco dries under the eaves.

THE HISTORIC SOUTPANSBERG

Part of the Soutpansberg range near Schoemansdal, the original capital of the first independent Voortrekker community in the former Northern Transvaal.

Violence and courage on an untamed frontier

THE EARLIEST STORIES of this land are told only through implements of stone, fashioned as long ago as 100 000 years. Paintings by the vanished San people tell a slightly clearer tale, but conventionally recorded history began only early in the 19th century with the arrival of white traders and adventurers. They named the place *Soutpansberg*, after the salt pans, although other people already knew it as Venda. The precise origin of the name is unknown, but it was heard by Coenraad de Buys, one of the first white men to settle here.

De Buys was born near Cogmanskloof, in the Montagu district of the Western Cape, in about 1761. A giant of a man, he courted adventure on the unsettled eastern frontier, and became a popular man with a large following. It is claimed that he was married legally only once, to a black woman recorded only as Elizabeth, but had many unrecorded wives and children. In about 1820, after being declared an outlaw, and with a price on his head after some disputed dealings, Buys trekked away with his families and followers and settled near the salt pan at the western end of the Soutpansberg, far beyond the reach of the old Cape colonial administration.

In 1823, after the death of Elizabeth, De Buys announced that he was going away. His people, he warned, were to stay at the place to which he had brought them. They never saw him again, but were eventually granted rights to the land, and their descendents still live at the old settlement near Mara.

Thirteen years after De Buys' disappearance, in May 1836, a small party of Voortrekkers led by Hans van Rensburg arrived at the Soutpansberg and set up camp. For much of their journey from the Caledon River they had been accompanied by the trek of Louis Trichardt, but the two leaders had quarrelled over wastage of ammunition – a dispute from which *Strydpoort* (quarrel pass) derives its name – and the Van Rensburg trek had continued alone to the Soutpansberg. Early in July they trekked on towards Delagoa Bay, only to be killed in the wilds by unknown assailants.

Fort Hendrina at Louis Trichardt.

The birth of Zoutpansbergdorp

It was the influential Andries Hendrik Potgieter who, desiring to live far beyond the area falling under the jurisdiction of the British government and its representatives at the Cape, decided to establish a permanent white settlement in the Soutpansberg. The independent Voortrekker community (*maatschappij*) of Zoutpansbergdorp was established in 1848. The first public buildings believed to have been erected are the church and the fort, and a site museum shows the styles of other buildings erected there. The commercial life of the town was greatly stimulated by the arrival of traders and transport riders, including the Portuguese trader, João Albasini, (see pages 14 – 15) who transported goods between the new town and Delagoa Bay.

In 1852 Andries Hendrik Potgieter died and his place as leader of the community was taken by his son Piet. Piet died in a raid against the Ndebele Chief Makapan and was succeeded by his brother Hermanus as the joint commandant general with Marthinus Wessel Pretorius.

However, the settlers of Zoutpansbergdorp wanted a free election, and they elected Stephanus Schoeman as their new leader in 1855. He renamed the town Schoemansdal (see map, pages 14 – 15) and married the widow of Piet Potgieter.

Unfortunately, Schoemansdal became host to bands of unsavoury renegades and fortune-seeking ivory-hunters, and the town became an increasingly unhappy place. Eventually the community simply disintegrated and, in 1867, the town was abandoned. What they could not take with them, the citizens of Schoemansdal wantonly destroyed before they trekked south.

the same year, and the women and children were removed to internment camps in Pietersburg while the men went to battle. The new town, like Schoemansdal before it, lay abandoned and derelict. After the war, Louis Trichardt was re-established and today it is a handsome town with wide streets and gardens filled with fragrant flowering trees.

Attractions within the town include the Dutch Reformed Church in the main street, the Indigenous Tree Park at the municipal caravan park, where over 100 species of trees are preserved, and the historic steel structure of Fort Hendrina, which dates from 1887, although it was erected here only in 1969. Fort Hendrina (at one time also known as Fort Edward) served in turn as a base for Boer police and British soldiers and was sited at several places before being brought to Louis Trichardt.

Soutpansberg attractions
Louis Trichardt serves as a convenient base from which to explore the Soutpansberg area. The mountain range is densely wooded with exotic plantations. From the northern end of the town's Krogh Street, Forestry Road leads to the Hanglip Forestry Reserve, named after a peak that overlooks the town. The 90 km Soutpansberg Hiking Trail starts at the forestry office just inside the reserve. The main attractions of this three-day trail, which runs along the ridge of the Soutpansberg range to the Entabeni Forest Station, are the beautiful forests, the wide variety of birds and wild animals, and magical glimpses of Venda villages through the trees and the mists.

The Hanglip Forestry Reserve also contains a variety of shorter walks – several of which lead to points that offer magnificent panoramic views. Excellent views may also be had from the 30 km Bluegumspoort road, which leads west from the N1 north of Louis Trichardt just before the N1 enters the scenic Wyllie's Poort. Between Bluegumspoort and Wyllie's Poort is another scenic drive, the Witvlag road.

Along the length of the Soutpansberg, especially to the east of Louis Trichardt, are vast plantations of subtropical and tropical fruits. The Levubu Experimental Farm, 50 km east of Louis Trichardt on the main road to the Kruger National Park, constantly tries to improve the quality and the yield of local crops, and undertakes experiments on subtropical and tropical fruits such as guavas, bananas, avocados and macadamia nuts. Many hectares of land along the line of the Soutpansberg are also devoted to extensive tea and coffee plantations.

About 6,5 km south-east of the town lies the Ben Lavin Nature Reserve, established in 1976 to preserve wildlife such as giraffe, wildebeest, zebra and ostrich. There are several walking trails here, a few interesting archeological sites, and a game-viewing hide. Accommodation in chalets or at the campsite may be reserved by telephoning the warden at (015) 516 4534.

The cool Hanglip Forestry Reserve.

A new Voortrekker capital
In 1898, some 30 years after the abandonment of Schoemansdal, a Venda uprising in the Soutpansberg under Chief Mpefu was quelled by Commandant General Piet Joubert. The spot where the decisive battle was fought was selected as the site for a church – to be named after the Voortrekker leader Louis Trichardt, who had camped here in 1836 before leaving on his fateful journey to what was then Lourenço Marques.

The new town was proclaimed in February 1899, but had unhappy beginnings. The Anglo-Boer War broke out in October of

Voortrekker graves and the Andries Potgieter memorial at Schoemansdal.

Trekker leader Andries Potgieter.

Traditional Venda homes shelter below the Soutpansberg.

Old and new roads through the scenic Wyllie's Poort.

Debegeni Falls and the land of the mysterious Rain Queen

This route begins with a journey through the Molototsi valley to the sacred cycad forest at Modjadji, hilltop capital of the secretive Rain Queen. Then it leads through Duiwelskloof and the Woodbush Forest – often shrouded in mist – to the smooth-flowing Debegeni Falls. Roughly two-thirds of the route is on gravel and the remainder is on tar.

**Tzaneen
Modjadji
Duiwelskloof
Koedoes Valley
Woodbush Forest
Debegeni Falls
200 – 220 km**

DRIVE OUT OF TZANEEN on the R71 towards Gravelotte and Phalaborwa. Almost immediately, you cross a bridge over the Great Letaba River. Several hundred metres after this, turn left onto the road for Deer Park. Turn left again 5 km later for Modjadji. The road leads through tall eucalyptus plantations to reach a T-junction after 2,5 km. Turn right here and note your kms as you turn.

Roughly 13 km from the T-junction, turn right onto a road that leads along the floor of the Molototsi valley and note your kms.

After 11 km, turn right and follow this sideroad as it climbs the hills on the south-eastern side of the valley, offering spacious views over the surrounding countryside; 3,4 km along this sideroad you reach a fork. Take the road on your right and, when the road forks again several hundred metres later, go left (uphill). After a further 700 m, turn left into the Modjadji Nature Reserve (see opposite). There is a small fee to enter the reserve, which has a refreshment kiosk plus toilets, water and braai places. There are also short walks.

Modjadji to Duiwelskloof
Retrace your route towards Tzaneen, but continue straight past the road on your left on which you came from Tzaneen. Stay on the tarred road, crossing two bridges over the Tzaneen Dam, then turn right onto the R36 at the crossroads and drive north towards Duiwelskloof.

Pass a road on your left after 2,6 km, then pass the Hans Merensky Dam – also on your left. After roughly 10 km on the R36 you reach Duiwelskloof, where there is a hotel that serves lunch, and an attractive picnic site. To reach this site, turn left into Boltman Street at the first stop street in the town, then after 400 m turn right into Mabel Street. A little over 1 km after turning into Mabel Street, turn left at the T-junction onto a gravel road. After 1 km this road swings sharply to the left, uphill.

You pass a road on your left, and reach the picnic area after a further 800 m. There are toilets, and taps that provide drinking water, and a shaded path offers an easy, pleasant five-minute walk into the kloof to a small but very pretty waterfall.

Continue through Duiwelskloof on the main road (R36), passing on your right the municipal offices, which also house the town's library. In front of the municipal offices there are two monuments – one commemorating the inauguration of the Voortrekker Monument in 1949, and another the *Taalfees* (language festival) held in 1975.

Stay on the R36 for roughly 15 km after leaving Duiwelskloof, then, 300 m after crossing the railway line, turn left onto a gravel road for Houtbosdorp – noting your kms. This road leads along the Koedoes River valley. About 5 km along it you pass on your left the prominent hill known as Kranskop. Roughly 4 km after this, also on your left, the bare slopes of Vaalkrans come into view, rising above the forest. The road winds uphill; 26 km after turning onto the gravel, park in a parking area on your right for a fine view back over the Koedoes River valley.

Woodbush Forest and Debegeni Falls
Some 36 km after turning onto the gravel, take the Magoebaskloof/Dap Naudé Dam turn-off on your left, noting your kms. (This intersection is approximately the site of Houtbosdorp – see pages 22 – 23.) The road enters pine plantations, and after 3,6 km you pass a road on your right to Veekraal. Roughly 6 km later, you pass another road on your right from Veekraal.

A little over 14 km from the Houtbosdorp intersection, turn sharp left for the Woodbush state forest.

After 100 m you pass through a gateway into a forest reserve – note your kms here. The road now leads through tall eucalyptus and pines. Roughly 1 km from the gate you pass a small memorial on your right to the pioneer forester

'HAPPY LAND' OR 'LITTLE BASKET'
The origin of the name Tzaneen is uncertain. Tradition has it that the name comes from a Sotho word for a small round basket, *tsana*, and refers to the fact that the town lies in a basket-like circle of hills. In this belief, the town's crest incorporates a basket. More recent research, however, has shown that one of the first European settlers in the valley was told by Chief Magoeba in 1892 that the region was called *tsaneng*, meaning 'the happy land' – Tzaneen being an obvious corruption.

DEVIL'S GORGE
The name *Duiwelskloof* (devil's gorge) was given to this valley by early travellers whose wagons frequently became stuck here in thick mud. The name was taken over by a farm in the valley, and then by the small village that grew up on the farm. Eventually the village was moved to a neighbouring farm called *Skraalhans* (scrawny Hans) to take advantage of a better water supply, but it kept its original name. Duiwelskloof is now an important centre of the timber industry, and it is renowned for the profusion of flowering plants that fill its gardens.

Forest-clad hills reach down to the still waters of the Magoebaskloof Dam.

Mist drifts quietly through the trees.

Alexander O'Connor. About 2,4 km from the gate the road forks – take the right-hand branch for 'Debegeni Falls & Forest Drive'.

The road now passes through large tracts of dense indigenous forest and offers several fine views over the lower slopes of the escarpment to the bright green of distant tea estates; 1,5 km along this road (3,9 km from the gate) you enter De Hoek Forest; 7,5 km from the gate go left at the fork and 1 km later go right at the T-junction. About 1 km from the T-junction, go left at the fork and after a further 1,2 km go right at the T-junction, note your kms, and continue downhill; 2,4 km later, just before a right-hand bend, stop to look back over the upper section of the Debegeni Falls.

After another 300 m, turn sharp left into the recreation area (admission fee) and drive down to the falls. There are braai sites and toilets at the falls. Although the smooth stone gives these falls a friendly appearance, they are dangerous and have claimed many lives. The smooth rocks are especially dangerous when dew or rain has made them wet and slippery. Drive back up the hill to the forest drive and continue in the direction you were travelling. After 3 km you reach the tarred R71 through Magoebaskloof. Turn left here onto the R71 for a 17 km drive back to Tzaneen, passing through neat, fresh-green tea estates.

AA Auto Clinic 52 Church Street
Pietersburg 0699 Tel (0152) 295 3051
Tzaneen Municipal Tourist Office Agatha Street
Tzaneen 0850 Tel (0152) 307 1411
Duiwelskloof Public Library Municipal Building
Botha Street, Duiwelskloof 0835
Tel (0152) 309 9246
SA Tours & Bookings 89A Schoeman Street
Pietersburg 0699 Tel (0152) 297 0816

The mirror-like surface of the Hans Merensky Dam reflects the forested hills of the lower Mabitse valley.

The seemingly gentle Debegeni Falls.

THE RAIN QUEEN

Tradition tells of a chief's daughter who, some 300 years ago, was seduced by her half-brother and bore a son. To escape her angry father, who ruled what is now Zimbabwe, she fled south with her baby and a few followers, and settled where their descendants, the Lovedu, are to be found to this day. With them they brought secret rain charms.

The community flourished, but male succession caused constant strife. Early last century a chief, Mugudo, decided to end this turmoil by instituting a rule of female succession. The chief committed incest with his daughter Modjadji, and when she bore a daughter, he took poison and Modjadji became the first Rain Queen.

Her fame as a rain-maker spread, and supplicants came from great distances to seek her help. Tradition dictates that her successors must live secluded lives and all business is conducted through counsellors. Reverence for the Rain Queen became so great that her people escaped the terrible inter-clan warfare that swept across the former Transvaal, and her territory became a place of refuge. The Rain Queen provided the inspiration for Sir Henry Rider Haggard's novel *She*.

A few of Queen Modjadji's sacred cycads.

SACRED CYCADS OF MODJADJI

Growing on the hilltop in the Modjadji Nature Reserve are the strange trees often referred to as Modjadji palms. In fact they are not even closely related to palms. They are cycads, a primitive type of plant that flourished at about the time when dinosaurs trod the earth. The Modjadji cycads, (*Encephalartos transvenosus*), are among the largest in the world and this species may reach a height of 13 m.

The seeds of the Modjadji cycads are believed to be poisonous, but the pith of the stem, which is rich in starch, has traditionally been used to make a type of bread – hence their common name of 'bread trees'. The many mature specimens in the Modjadji reserve owe their existence to the fact that they are regarded as sacred to the Rain Queen.

Where zebra-drawn stagecoaches carried gold through the kloofs

The forestry station at New Agatha has one of the finest views in the province – over the Letsiteli Valley to the crest of the northern Drakensberg. Today's route climbs to this viewsite, then leads on via the Ebenezer Dam to the Woodbush Forest and Magoebaskloof – with an optional visit to the Debegeni Falls. All but 30 km of the route is on tarred roads.

Tzaneen
Letsiteli Valley
New Agatha
Ebenezer Dam
Woodbush Forest
Magoebaskloof
200 – 220 km

LEAVE TZANEEN BY driving south on the R36 towards Lydenburg. After a little over 14 km, turn right for the Letsiteli Valley, noting your kms. From here the road leads through extensive orchards of tropical fruit – notably mangoes, pawpaws and papinos – and citrus plantations. After 8,7 km on this road, turn right onto a tarred road for New Agatha, noting your kms.

The road now climbs the foothills of the Drakensberg escarpment and soon enters cool plantations of eucalyptus. After 7 km you pass, on your left, a hotel that was formerly a coach house on the old road between Pietersburg and Leydsdorp – in the days when the 'wild west' stagecoaches that travelled this route were sometimes drawn by zebras (see opposite).

Some 2 km after passing the hotel, turn left into the New Agatha Plantation. The avenue of tall eucalyptus trees that lines the left side of the gravel-surfaced road here is believed to date from the old coaching days; 2 km along this road you pass a sideroad on your left and, a few hundred metres after this, you reach the forestry station. From the forester's office you have outstanding views in several directions. (You do not need a permit if you are going no further into the reserve than this.)

New Agatha to Ebenezer Dam

Retrace your route past the avenue of eucalyptus trees back to the tar and turn left as you leave the forest reserve, noting your kms at the turn. You pass a road on your right to Tzaneen after a few hundred metres. Turn right onto a second road to Tzaneen 3,7 km from the turn. This road winds gently down into the Letaba Valley and offers sweeping views over fruit farms and forests.

After travelling on this road for 10,6 km turn left at the T-junction onto the R36 and note your kms. Just over 1 km later exit onto the R528 for George's Valley.

George's Valley is the upper valley of the Great Letaba River and the road is fringed for much of the way by colourful poinsettias and bougainvillea. On both sides stretch wide

Two views from the New Agatha forestry station: south past a coral tree over the magnificent Letsiteli Valley, and west to the forested slopes of the Drakensberg.

HAENERTSBURG

Now a centre of the timber industry and home to a growing number of artists, crafters and writers, Haenertsburg was once the heart of the Woodbush Goldfields. Many prospectors struck gold in the hills, among them the two Haenert brothers, one of whom discovered Ellen's Fortune Reef and the other a reef that he named Haenerton. Which of the two brothers founded the village is uncertain, but it is estimated that it had a population of more than 400 by the late 1890s. The slopes above Haenertsburg are riddled with shallow workings, but most reefs were of poor quality.

GEORGE OF GEORGE'S VALLEY

This scenic drive along the Great Letaba River, with views towards the massive Wolkberg and the Iron Crown, takes its name from George Deneys, a relative of the Zeederberg family that operated the stage-coaches through the area. After being captured and imprisoned by the British during the Anglo-Boer War, Deneys returned to the then colonial Transvaal and applied himself to the construction of roads. He spent many years supervising the building of this road through the valley, and planted many trees and flowering aloes along the route.

The serenely beautiful Ebenezer Dam, viewed from the upper section of George's Valley Road.

GOLD IN THE HILLS

Early settlers found yellowwoods growing in the dense valley-forests between the Great Letaba and the Koedoes rivers. So they named the area *De Houtbosch* (the wood forest). Woodcutters founded the settlement of Houtbosdorp, then prospectors found payable gold in the nearby hills and the hitherto quiet region experienced all the excitement of a goldrush. The Berlin Mission Society established a station nearby in 1878, and this later moved to where the Kratzenstein Mission still operates. In 1901 a running battle took place here between British and Boer forces.

plantations of citrus, mangoes and bananas. Higher up, the landscape becomes wilder. Gorges and ravines come into view on your left, then the cliff-topped peak known as the Iron Crown.

Roughly 30 km after last noting your kms, turn right onto a gravel road for the Ebenezer Dam – noting your kms again. After 2,2 km, pass a road to the boat club. After a further 300 m turn left to picnic sites with views over the dam and part of the dam wall. To reach picnic sites close to the water's edge, turn left after a further 300 m.

Ebenezer Dam to Houtbosdorp

Our route continues past this turn-off, through shady forest, skirting the edge of the dam and offering many fine views across its waters. At all points where the road forks, stay on the larger road. At the T-junction with the tarred Magoebaskloof road (R71), turn right towards Tzaneen and note your kms.

After 1,8 km you pass the Magoebaskloof Hotel on your right (which serves lunch and commands a striking, panoramic view over Magoebaskloof); 2,3 km beyond the hotel, turn left onto a gravel road leading into the Woodbush Forest signposted 'Houtbosdorp', noting your kms at the turn.

This road leads through extensive pine plantations, crosses the small *Helpmekaar* (help each other) River, and reaches a fork after 2,4 km. Go left at the fork, and 4,8 km later you cross a small bridge over the *Broederstroom* (brother stream); 300 m beyond the bridge, go right for Houtbosdorp.

Keep straight at the crossroads 4,6 km later, after which the road begins to wind downhill, offering wide views towards the lowveld over fields and forest.

Some 17 km after turning off the Magoebaskloof road you reach a T-junction with the Koedoes River Valley road. This is the site of the former village of Houtbosdorp (see opposite). Turn left at this T-junction, noting your kms as you turn.

Magoebaskloof and Debegeni Falls

The road surface changes to tar after just over 1 km, and, soon after, you enter drier, higher-lying country dotted with koppies, their slopes sprinkled with huts built in traditional styles. Some 18 km from the Houtbosdorp turn, you pass the town of Turfloop and the University of the North. At 22 km you reach a T-junction with the R71 – this is the Magoebaskloof road.

Turn left here and return to Tzaneen by driving down the full length of Magoebaskloof. (To visit the Debegeni Falls, note your kms as you pass the Magoebaskloof Hotel and turn left 11,7 km beyond the hotel onto a gravel road; 3 km along this road, turn off right and drive downhill to the falls – see pages 20 – 1).

A tea garden on Middelkop Estate, on the right of the R71 and closer to Tzaneen, offers various local teas and a pleasant ending to the day, with splendid views over hills covered with the bright green of tea bushes.

AA Auto Clinic 52 Church Street
Pietersburg 0700 Tel (0152) 295 3051
Tzaneen Municipal Tourist Office Agatha Street
Tzaneen 0850 Tel (0152) 307 1411
Letaba Tourism Information PO Box 129
Haenertsburg 0730 Tel (0152) 276 4307

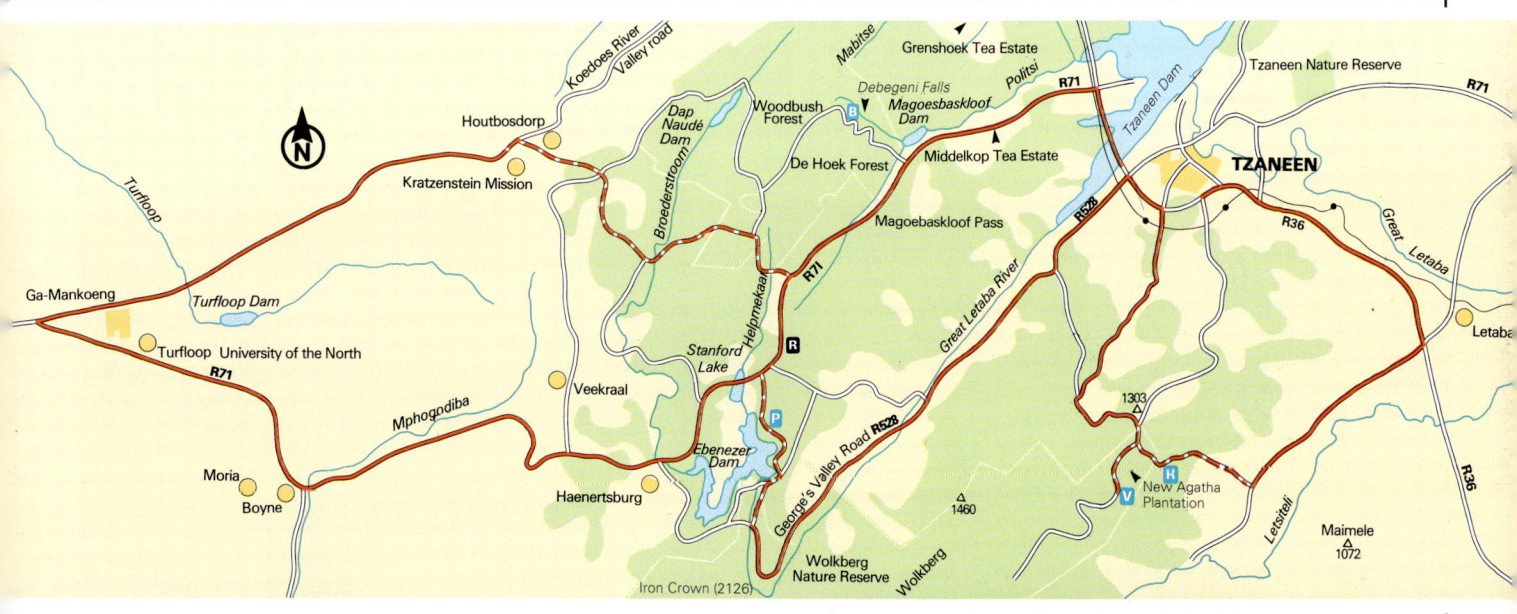

Holiday rondavels in Magoebaskloof.

AGATHA'S ZEBRA-DRAWN COACHES

Late last century a number of small mining companies flourished in the lowveld at the foot of the northern Drakensberg – in an area that was christened Agatha after Agatha Joubert, wife of the South African Republic's mining commissioner. Eventually malaria and bilharzia – and sheer heat – drove the settlers up the slopes to a site that became known as New Agatha. The present hotel at New Agatha was originally a staging post for the Zeederberg Coach Company, which ran a service between Pietersburg and the goldmining town of Leydsdorp. The coachmen had to contend with highwaymen, wet weather that left the roads impassable for days on end and, most worrisome of all, a high death-rate among their horses, caused by the tsetse fly. To solve this last problem the Zeederbergs trained a team of zebras to pull the coaches. The training was fairly successful, and the zebras had a natural immunity to the tsetse-borne horse-sickness, but they lacked the horses' stamina.

Malaria continued to plague the region until well into the 20th century. In 1930 the Dutch specialist, Professor N Swellengrebel, was consulted on the problem. He identified the principal mosquito carriers of the disease and devised a method of combating it. The breeding grounds were sprayed and a research station was established at Tzaneen. It was here that the South African, Dr DS Annecke, worked for 24 years studying the problems of both malaria and bilharzia.

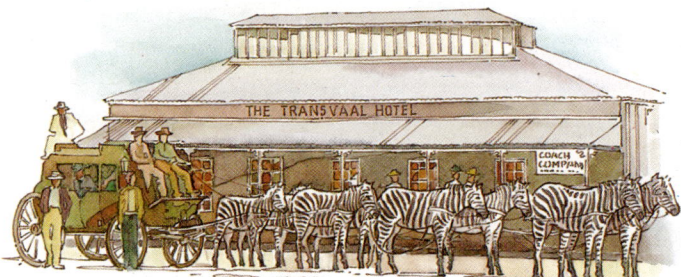

A zebra-drawn stagecoach operated between Pietersburg and Leydsdorp.

In search of the Nile – in the brooding heart of the Waterberg

Over the centuries, the Waterberg range has been a backdrop to the colourful lives of poets, politicians, outlaws and warriors. Our drive follows country roads, passing through small towns steeped in history to rugged heights where vultures soar. The area's unusual history lends great ambience to its unspoilt landscape. About 80 km is on gravel roads.

**Nylstroom
Rankin's Pass
Thabazimbi
Ben Alberts
Nature Reserve
Warmbaths
Buyskop
260 – 280 km**

OUR JOURNEY BEGINS IN Voortrekker Street with a visit to the Nylstroom Concentration Camp Cemetery and its impressive memorial. From Voortrekker Street, travel north for several blocks and turn left into Church Street to reach Strijdom House, the museum that was the residence of the late advocate JG Strijdom.

From Strijdom House retrace your route; turn left into Voortrekker Street and then turn right one block later into Potgieter Street. After several blocks you reach Calvyn Street, where you can see the Hervormde Church – a national monument – built in 1889. Continue along Potgieter Street and turn left into Stasie Street to reach the station, where the old steam locomotive, first used between Pretoria and Nylstroom, is on display.

Nylstroom to Thabazimbi

From Potgieter Street, return though the town and leave on the R33 in the direction of Ellisras. Note your kms at the intersection with Voortrekker Street. The road winds through scenic bushveld and, after 4,8 km, passes a road on your left to Donkerpoort Dam, one of the favourite local angling spots.

After 7,4 km there is a railway crossing and, after 33 km, travellers are confronted by the surprising sight, for this part of the country, of high-trellised grapevines, from which early ripening table grapes are produced. After 40 km, turn left onto the gravel road signposted Alma and note your kms. The high, outlying spurs of the Sand River range loom above you to your right. After 9,8 km, bear left for Alma at the inclined T-junction, crossing a single-lane bridge over the Sand River 600 m later.

Cross another single-lane bridge after some 12,8 km. After 14 km there is a sign to Rankin's Pass, which you reach after 21 km. After 30 km, turn right onto a gravel road signposted Jan Trichardtspas, noting your kms; the road immediately begins a dramatic ascent into the higher reaches of the Sand River Mountains.

After about 12 km the road levels out, affording breathtaking views of the towering cliffs of the Sand River Mountains to your right. Stop and look up after about 35 km to see the so-called Palace of Vultures, an impressive 2 100 m peak that is home to a colony of Cape vultures.

You then descend into Bakkerspas, from where you can look out across seemingly endless plains. After 43 km there is a steep downhill section and, at 47 km, you reach the end of the gravel road. Note your kms here and keep straight on the tarred road to Thabazimbi.

After 14 km you pass a road, on your left, leading into the town. Continue past Thabazimbi on the R510 to reach the Ben Alberts Nature Reserve some 6,5 km later. A right turn into the clearly singposted entrance leads to well-shaded picnic spots and a welcome swimming pool. (Light refreshments and curios are on sale.)

Warmbaths and Buyskop

Leave the Ben Alberts Nature Reserve and turn right onto the R510, noting your kms. After 3,2 km, turn left onto the slip road signposted R511 Brits / R516 Warmbaths.

The Waterberg range is now on your left as you pass through a fertile river valley where fruit orchards, maize fields and cattle ranches abound. After 10,5 km, you cross a bridge over the Sand River and, after 38,5 km, turn left onto the R516 for Warmbaths, noting your kms at the turn. You cross bridges over the Blinkwaterspruit, Tooyspruit, Kareespruit, Swartkloof River and Plats River respectively. After 83 km, you reach a stop street on the outskirts of Warmbaths; turn right into Voortrekker Street to reach the famous hot springs at the Aventura Resort.

Across the road from the resort is the municipal building and behind it in Luna Road is the old Warmbaths cemetery where numerous graves of Voortrekkers are to be found, including that of Christina Pretorius, wife of Andries Pretorius. The British-built blockhouse on Paul Sauer Street, near the railway station, is also of historical interest.

From Voortrekker Street, follow the signs to Nylstroom, noting your kms at the stop street where Voortrekker Street joins Potgieter Street to become the R101. Soon after leaving Warmbaths, you pass a prominent hill on your right, known as Buyskop after the colourful adventurer Coenraad de Buys.

Antique shops, fruit stalls and holiday spots line the road as you pass through the scenic bushveld. After 10,3 km you pass a road on your left leading to *Groot Nylsoog* – the source of a river the early Voortrekkers believed to be the Nile. After 17,5 km a road on your left leads to De Nyl Zyn Oog. The crocodile farm a short distance up this road is a popular tourist attraction. After a further 10 km on the R101 you reach your starting point at Nylstroom.

AA Office AA House, 370 Voortrekker Road
Gezina 0084 Tel (012) 329 1433
Warmbaths Tourist Centre Voortrekker Street
Warmbaths 0484 Tel (014) 736 3694
Nylstroom Municipality Field Street
Nylstroom 1510 Tel (01470) 2755

The Waterberg, seen from the Rankin's Pass road.

A sculpture by Tienie Pritchard at Nylstroom.

BUYSKOP

The legendary hillock of Buyskop stands some 4 km north of Warmbaths and is named after Coenraad de Buys, the rebel of Graaff-Reinet. Declared an outlaw there in the 1790s, he set off to establish his own free republic to the north. Legend has it that De Buys positioned himself at the top of a koppie while under siege from hostile local clans. In the final days of the siege, the warriors, themselves short of water, believed De Buys to be suffering from acute thirst, too. De Buys, however, ostentatiously poured the contents of his waterskin out over the koppie. The impressionable warriors believed this to be a sign that De Buys had resources unavailable to ordinary mortals, and they withdrew. Buyskop was once the halfway point for the stage coaches en route from Pretoria to Pietersburg, and stone was quarried here for the construction of the Union Buildings in Pretoria.

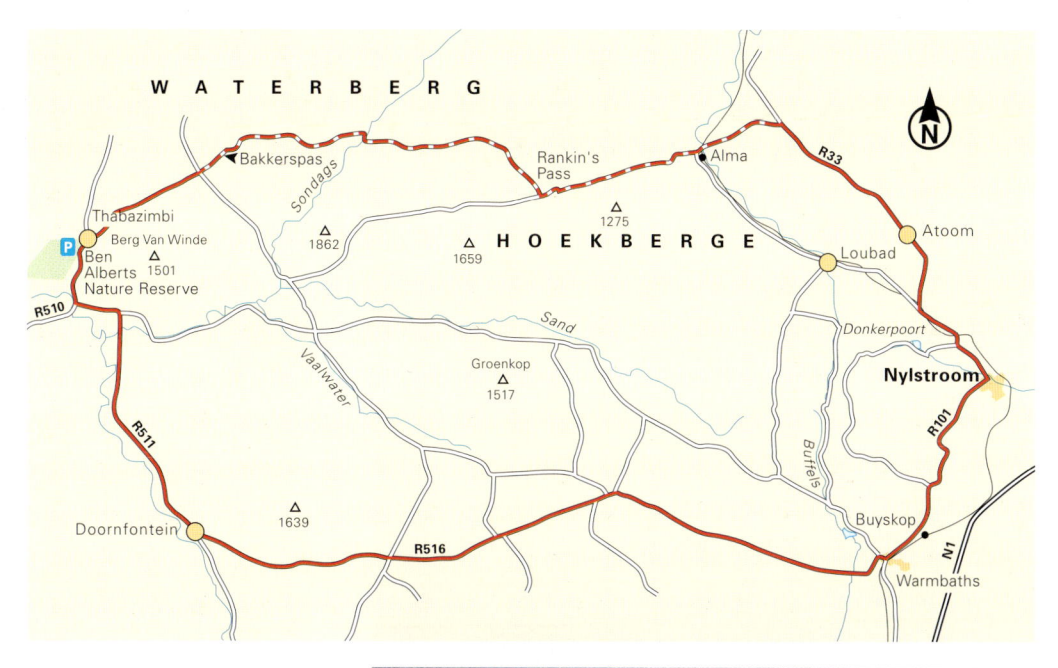

NYLSTROOM

The town takes its name from the *Nyl* (Nile) River, which was named by the *Jerusalemgangers* – a breakaway religious sect of Voortrekkers who were heading for the Holy Land. On seeing a 'pyramid' in the distance and the nearby Mogolakwena River in flood, the Jerusalemgangers thought they had arrived in Egypt at the headwaters of the Nile. The 'pyramid' was actually Kranskop, a lone hill 12 km east of the town. The sect refused to worship with other Voortrekkers, which led to a legal dispute with Commandant General Andries Pretorius. The Jerusalemgangers eventually petered out after the death of their leader.

Nylstroom itself was founded in 1866 and, over the years, has become associated with former Prime Minister JG Strijdom, architect Gerard Moerdijk (designer of the Voortrekker Monument) and the poet Eugene Marais.

EUGENE MARAIS

Outside the public library in Nylstroom stands a bust of Eugene Marais, a human community in the person of one man, to whom the Waterberg district was home, and who farmed here in the early years of the 20th century. He was a poet, drug addict, advocate, journalist, storyteller, psychologist and natural scientist. Settling near a large group of chacma baboons in the Waterberg area, he became the first man to conduct a prolonged study of primates in the wild. This period produced *My Friends the Baboons* and provided the major inspiration for *Soul of the Ape*. The desolation and haunting beauty of the Waterberg also – not surprisingly, perhaps – inspired Marais to write ghost stories. Plagued for many years by ill health and an addiction to morphine, Marais took his own life in 1936.

THE HOT SPRINGS AT WARMBATHS

Many years before the mineral waters at Warmbaths were used therapeutically, they were known as *Biela bela*, the Tswana name for 'water that boils on its own'. The first man believed to have used the water therapeutically was Coenraad de Buys. The R5 million development around the springs was opened in 1979 and, today, the mineral springs at Warmbaths are a popular health and holiday resort. A special pool under glass has massage jets and a central fountain from which the alkaline, mineralized water pours at a temperature of 36°C. The water also flows into an outdoor pool in an enclosed garden. There is a cooler plunge-pool and a hot pool at 41°C for the treatment of rheumatic disease. For the health-conscious there are hydrotherapy baths, saunas, massage cubicles and a beauty clinic, while the more energetic can enjoy cable water-skiing and a supertube at the pool.

Above: *Traditions live on at Thaba Kgatla archaeological site, Nylstroom.*
Below: *Rural refreshment station – a roadside general store and post office.*

The Cape vulture (Gyps coprotheras) finds a refuge in the Waterberg.

• THE WATERBERG'S MOODY MAGNIFICENCE •

Flowing streams and bushveld-covered slopes epitomize the Waterberg range, here seen near its western margin.

Restoring the home and the hunting grounds of earlier man

GAME WAS ABUNDANT, and newcomers watched in awe as the great springbok migrations surged past in herds more than 200 km long by 20 km wide. In later years came the white hunter with his guns, the trekboer with his voracious domesticated flocks and herds, and the commercial farmer with his demands for land and water. The early residents and the game dwindled. That, happily, is not the end of the story, because the Waterberg once again, and on an increasing scale, offers its visitors the opportunity to see wild animals in the wild.

Rebuilding paradise
The name of Springbok Flats, just south of the Waterberg, is a poignant reminder of the great herds that once populated the plain. Today, thanks to the enlightened efforts of conservationists, the natural paradise is rebuilding. Comprising three private reserves – Lapalala Wilderness, Touchstone Ranch and Kwalata – a conservancy of some 50 000 ha has been created along the banks of the Lephalala River in the northern Waterberg. The conservancy protects game such as elephant, hippo, wildebeest, hyaena, jackal and a wide variety of buck in their natural habitats.

The Lapalala Wilderness area made history in 1990 as the first reserve to reintroduce black rhino to the Waterberg after an absence of some 100 years. The Percy Fyfe Nature Reserve, north of Potgietersrus, is noted for its breeding of the rare sable, the roan and the tsessebe.

Other private reserves such as Mabula Game Lodge near Warmbaths, and Welgevonden near Vaalwater, also rank among the country's more rewarding game-viewing destinations.

Day visitors will enjoy the peaceful setting at Naboomspruit's Mosdene Nature Reserve and the abundant bird life at the nearby Doorndraai Dam. A variety of water birds graces the flood plains and banks of the Nylsvley Nature Reserve, which, during the rainy season, is said to be home to the greatest concentration of birds in the southern hemisphere. The Donkerpoort Dam lies 11 km north-west of Nylstroom and, stocked with carp, bream, black bass and catfish, is a favourite destination of freshwater anglers. The Warmbaths and Rust de Winter dams also offer excellent watersports and angling, while the chance to drive through a game reserve is a major attraction at the Ben Alberts Nature Reserve at Thabazimbi.

Nearby, the unspoilt beauty of the Kransberg Mountains was the motivation for the proclamation of the 100 000 ha Marakele National Park. Lying as it does, in the transition zone between wetter and drier regions, it supports an impressive diversity of species, including the world's largest colony of Cape vultures. Trees range from yellowwoods to five-metre-high cycads, and all the large game species are present, from elephant and rhino to the big cats. As an additional bonus, Marakele is in a malaria-free area. At present, access is feasible only in four-wheel-drive vehicles.

Weeping bushes, noisy leaves
Acacias, thorn trees, milkwood, mahogany, cabbage trees and

Right: *Tobacco – a controversial but economically important crop.*

sour-plums are just some of the trees characteristic of the Waterberg vegetation, which is mainly mixed and sour bushveld. Their common names often express a characteristic of the tree; for instance, *huilbos* which is the weeping bush, *lekkerbreek* of which branches break easily; *stamvrug*, a tree bearing fruit on the trunk; and *raasblaar*, which has noisy leaves. The *naboom*, although it may be translated from Afrikaans as 'near tree' or 'almost a tree', really derives its name from the Khoikhoi *gnap*, which means 'vigorous' and refers to the plant's brisk growth pattern.

Man's earliest ancestors made their home here, where, almost within living memory, every ravine and gully was the bed of a perennial stream of crystal-clear water. People named the place *Waterberg* – the mountain of water – and the Waterberg range itself stretches almost due west to east between Thabazimbi and Potgietersrus, with its highest points being the Kransberg (2 085 m) in the west and, to the east, the prominent Hanglip (1 793 m). These heights seem impressive, but peaks are rarely more than 600 m above the surrounding ground level. The central portion of the Waterberg region is the Palala plateau, surrounded by these low mountains.

Changing patterns of nature have seen the high rainfalls recorded by early visitors decline dramatically. Many people gave up their land and, for a while, it seemed that the rain had departed altogether and that the Waterberg would become a desolate place of distinctly coloured mountains around a plain of grass and scrub growing thinly from a hard bed of volcanic rock.

A resort at Warmbaths offers relief from the sometimes fierce tropical heat.

Black stork (Ciconia nigra) nursery on a poorly shaded Waterberg cliff.

Clues to the past
It is in the sedimentary rocks that science reads the records of the past, and archaeological excavations in the Waterberg confirm that the earth is indeed rich with the lives of our kin.

Fossils of early hominids – the Australopithecines – dating back between two and three million years, have been found at Makapansgat Caves near Potgietersrus. About 100 km west of Potgietersrus, excavations in the small, painted rock shelter midway up a low quartzite hill on the farm North Brabant have revealed evidence of Middle Stone Age inhabitants – blades, chisels, scrapers, bone points and beads.

More than a thousand years ago, Iron Age immigrants from the north crossed the Limpopo River, probably in search of grazing for their cattle and of new lands to plough. Their way of life was based on the production of food and metal; they knew how to smelt iron and copper, they made various types of pottery, and grew sorghum and millet.

Stone-walled settlements of the Late Iron Age – dating between 1500 and 1800 AD – can be seen at the Lapalala Wilderness Area. One site consists of an outer boundary wall, a circle of hut floors and middens, and central stock enclosures.

Another site at Lapalala is located at the top of the hill called *Malora* (Sotho for 'ashes', referring to the Iron Age remains at the summit). Here, the surrounding wall is entire and the enclosed area contains a more dense cluster of walled circles, indicating that this was possibly a cattle station and not a village. Like the present towns and villages of the Waterberg, Malora is steeped in the torrid history of successive waves of pioneers and settlers of the old Transvaal.

Pioneers and settlers
The first Afrikaner trekboers probably arrived in the Waterberg in the early 1800s, establishing a series of settlements as they journeyed northwards. One of the biggest cultural-historical collections of their lifestyle can be seen at the Arend Dieperink Museum near Potgietersrus. This illuminating museum contains items as varied as ox-wagons, musical instruments and Bibles, including one that belonged to trekker leader Hendrik Potgieter. The town also has a number of historical sites such as the grave of Piet Potgieter and the Moorddrif Monument. Today, these small towns of the Waterberg are geared primarily to agriculture, with crops that include ground nuts, tobacco and grapes.

The principal town of the region is Nylstroom and an annual grape festival is held here in January, celebrating the rich table-grape industry. The town of Warmbaths is famous for its hot spring, where the first farm was established by Voortrekker Carl van Heerden, who named it *Het Bad* (the bath). Originally known as 'Kauffman se winkel', the town of Naboomspruit lies at the foot of the Swaershoek Mountains, surrounded by nature reserves and hot springs. The naboom itself is a tree euphorbia (*Euphorbia ingens*) that grew abundantly in the vicinity. The steeply sloping town of Thabazimbi is surrounded by mountains rich in iron ore that is extensively mined by Iscor. Every July, the town hosts a Game Festival, with exhibitions and game auctions, while, further north, arid Ellisras overflows with goodwill during an annual three-day Bushveld Festival.

A river valley in the Waterberg.

EXPLORING THE MAGALIESBERG

The weathered rocks of the Magaliesberg glow golden under a summer sky. This is the principal recreation area for the highveld.

Ancient cliffs – where battles raged and vultures soar

IN GEOLOGICAL TERMS the Magaliesberg is no more than a ripple in the earth's crust, but the range has a formidable presence and its own distinctive atmosphere – a huge wall of sunburned rock reaching up into the clear skies of the highveld, rich in memories of human drama.

Magali (or Mohale) was a leader of the people living in the area when the Voortrekkers arrived during the 19th century. *Magaliesberg* means Magali's Mountain, and the range stretches in an almost unbroken line for roughly 125 km, from east of Pretoria to west of Rustenburg. The peaks reach to over 1 800 m above sea level, but this is seldom more than 300 m above the surrounding highveld.

The Magaliesberg region is particularly rich in rock engravings that archeologists have as yet been unable to date. According to one theory, they were completed during the Late Stone Age, but there is still no idea as to who executed them. The tiny settlement of Maanhaarrand lies below the mountains at the centre of an area famous for these engravings, and the remains of many small Iron Age villages have also been discovered in the vicinity.

Early last century the rebel Zulu general, Mzilikazi, settled in the Magaliesberg area after fleeing the wrath of the Zulu king, Shaka. For some years he and his followers enjoyed the area's plentiful water supply and hunted the game, which ranged from the larger antelope to herds of elephant; but clashes with neighbouring clans and with the early white settlers eventually drove Mzilikazi further north – where he founded the Matabele (or Ndebele) nation in what is now southern Zimbabwe. By the time the Voortrekkers settled in the Magaliesberg area, the central highveld was occupied by people under Chief Magali.

Blockhouses
During the Anglo-Boer War, the British built stone blockhouses in the area to watch the movement of Boer commandos, and many of these old blockhouses can still be seen. One of the best-preserved examples is Barton's Folly, a few kilometres south of Hekpoort (see pages 78 – 9). It is clearly visible from the road, but is unfortunately on private property. Many clashes between the Boers and the British took place in the Magaliesberg. Probably the most famous of these was the Battle of Nooitgedacht on

Left: *The lush green of a mountain kloof in the Magaliesberg.*

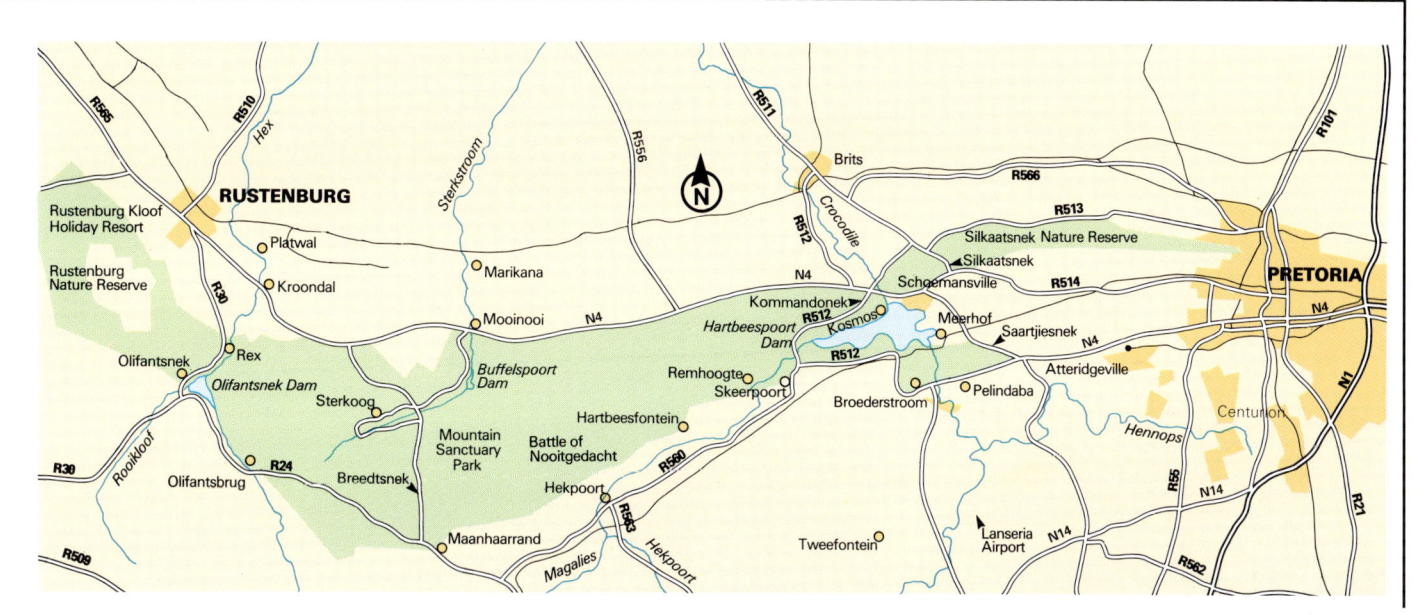

NORTHERN & NORTH-WEST PROVINCES

An unspoilt wilderness only a couple of hours' drive from Johannesburg.

The home of the rare Cape vulture.

13 December 1900, in which a large British force under General Clements was defeated by the Boers under Beyers, Kemp, De la Rey and Smuts. The battle site lies about 10 km north-west of Hekpoort, almost directly beneath the modern communications tower that stands on top of the range. Apart from a memorial to the dead, little evidence remains of the fierce encounter. The Boers surprised the British by climbing Breedt's Nek and moving east along the mountain crest under cover of darkness.

Wild character
Today the Magaliesberg is at peace with its memories. It has also managed to retain a great deal of its original wild character, although encircled by major highways. The large herds of elephant and antelope are gone, but surprising numbers of smaller animals still live in inaccessible wooded ravines – duiker, oribi steenbok, jackal, baboon, monkey, and the rare brown hyena. Cape vultures breed on many of the sheer south-facing cliffs, particularly those to the west of Olifantsnek. Their breeding sites are easily identifiable by their white droppings on the cliff faces. Until recently, the vultures were in danger of extinction, many dying of calcium deficiency caused by the lack of big predators to crush the bones of dead animals on the veld. Such bone fragments, rich in calcium, are a vital part of the vulture's diet. Feeding stations have been established where crushed bone is provided.

With the influx of white settlers on the highveld, several dams were built in the Magaliesberg. Although these are primarily for irrigation purposes, they have also become popular recreation areas. By far the largest is the Hartbeespoort Dam (see pages 78 – 9) where a deep, narrow wall erected more than 70 years ago impounds the Crocodile River. Some 30 km away to the west lies the Buffelspoort Dam on the Sterkstroom, and a further 30 km west the Hex River has been dammed at Olifantsnek.

The best way to absorb the atmosphere of the Magaliesberg is to walk along its slopes. As yet there are no public walking trails, and hikers should obtain prior permission from the owners of land that they intend to cross. There are, however, several private resorts in the area that include short walking trails.

The 4 359 ha Rustenburg Nature Reserve incorporates a farm that once belonged to President Paul Kruger, where the first sable antelope was recorded in 1836. Long since hunted to extinction in the region, sable and a wide variety of other antelope have been reintroduced. The reserve offers the Rustenburg Overnight Trail of 21 km (two days), and the Peglerae Interpretive Trail (named for the rare, endemic *Aloe peglerae*), which takes two to three hours (5 km). Both trails follow a circular route, and there is also a 2 km vlei ramble. Adjoining the Rustenburg Nature Reserve, but entirely separate, is the Rustenburg Kloof Holiday Resort – a recreational area incorporating a well-wooded kloof with a variety of spectacular walks into the mountains.

Right: *Farmland near Hekpoort.*

• EXPLORING PILANESBERG NATIONAL PARK •

At Kwa Maritane, a submerged hide overlooks a waterhole and offers excellent game-viewing, especially during the dry winter months.

The volcano that gave birth to a game reserve

AS YOU DRIVE THROUGH the peaceful bushveld and syenite outcrops of the Pilanesberg National Park, it is hard to imagine the cataclysmic violence that created the area and gave birth to its unique geology some thirteen hundred million years ago.

For the hills of Pilanesberg, a 56 000 ha game sanctuary in North-West Province, situated about 200 km north-west of the Witwatersrand, are actually the crumbling foundations of an ancient volcano – its centre now serving as the beautiful setting for a man-made lake that has become known as *Mankwe*, or 'place of the leopard'.

In the 19th century, Pilanesberg served as a sanctuary of a different kind – Mzilikazi's rebel Ndebele warriors passed through the area as they fled the wrath of Shaka. Not long after this, during the Anglo-Boer War, General Christiaan de Wet's commandos hid from the British amongst these same hills – perhaps prompting the later purchase of a farm in the area by the veteran South African Prime Minister, General Jan Smuts.

During the late 1970s, it was decided to reintroduce wildlife and turn the Pilanesberg area into a game reserve. Cattle farmers who then occupied the area moved to new homes after being compensated, and work began on Operation Genesis, which involved the game-fencing of the entire reserve and the reintroduction of long-vanished species.

The creation of the Pilanesberg National Park was one of the most ambitious programmes of its kind undertaken anywhere in the world. Although initially it suffered somewhat in the public estimation by being considered 'just another attraction' of nearby Sun City, Pilanesberg is a major game reserve in its own right and not an adjunct to this holiday complex on its southern border.

At 560 km^2, Pilanesberg is the third-largest game reserve south of the Limpopo. Since its official opening in 1979, 8 000 large animals of more than 20 species have been reintroduced, so that today the park accommodates virtually every mammal of southern Africa. Lions, too, were brought from Namibia in 1993, by which time the antelope herds were long established. The lions have settled well, their numbers rising satisfactorily from the original 19 to about 35 in three years.

Impala and springbok coexist

Although some animals, including kudu, duiker, leopard and brown hyena, have been in the Pilanesberg area for centuries, others have been brought in from various parts of the subcontinent: eland from Namibia, Burchell's zebra and waterbuck from the former Transvaal, giraffe, black and white rhino and hippo from KwaZulu-Natal, and elephant and buffalo from the Kruger National Park and the Addo Park in the Eastern Cape Province.

Because Pilanesberg lies in a faunal transition zone, a climatic overlap area where animals and plants from both drier and wetter regions can survive equally comfortably, it is one of the few places where one can see both impala and springbok living in the wild. Apart from its population of larger animals, Pilanesberg has an

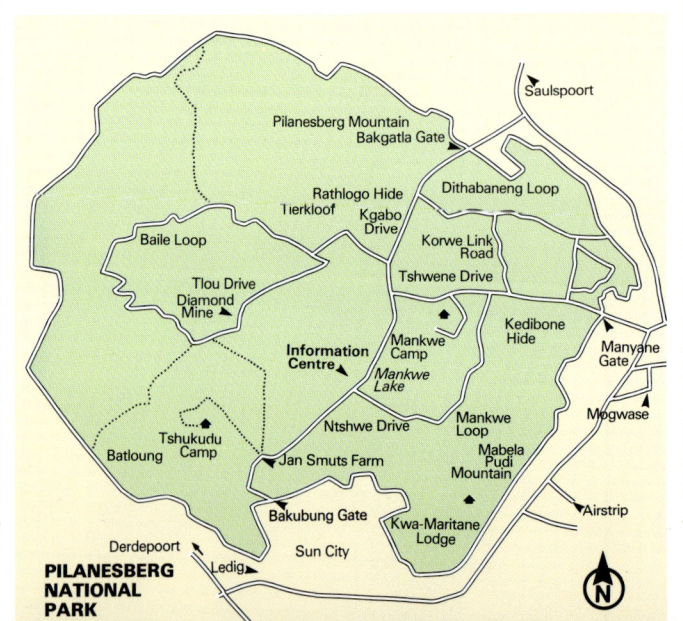

30

The park's vegetation makes it ideal for rhino and giraffe, and provides a beautiful setting for communal eating 'bomas' at the tented camps.

extremely wide range of bird life, with over 200 species recorded, and also a range of plants, shrubs and trees that is unique. (It has several hundred specimens of the rare Transvaal Red Balloon tree – there is only a handful in the rest of the country.)

The animals, birds and plants of Pilanesberg are not the only attractions. The very topography makes the area a feast for the eyes. There are syenite koppies, thickly forested ravines, typical Northern Province bushveld – and also rolling grasslands and lightly wooded areas.

To reach Pilanesberg from Pretoria, take the N4/R27 past the Hartbeespoort Dam. From Johannesburg, you reach the N4/R27 by taking the R512 from Randburg, past Lanseria. Once on the N4/R27, note the prominent hill of Wolhuterskop on your left, and a few kilometres later take Interchange 91 (Pilanesberg/Sun City/Boschfontein) opposite the large settlement of Bapong, to pass over the N4 onto the R556. After about 58 km, turn right onto the R510 for Northam and turn left at Mogwase after another 23 km. Approaching via Rustenburg, take the R510, which is signposted 'Northam'. For Sun City/Lost City or to reach Bakubung Gate, turn left at the intersection (a four-way stop street) with the R556. To reach Mogwase, keep straight on the R510 at this intersection. (There is an entrance fee payable at the park.)

Times for entry and for game viewing

The park is open between 06h00 and 18h30 from April to August, and between 05h30 and 19h00 during the rest of the year. Pilanesberg is free of malaria. Within the park there are about 200 km of good, all-weather gravel roads, including a number of loops and scenic drives.

Although animals can be seen at all times throughout the park, the best viewing is during the cooler hours of early morning and late afternoon. During winter, when animals tend to stay close to dwindling water supplies, the viewing is generally better than in the hot summer season. At the main camp (Manyane), there are two walk-in aviaries well stocked with indigenous birds, and there is also a waterfowl area. In the EEZ (Extensive Education Zone) at Manyane, a self-guided trail of some 8 km has been laid out, providing opportunities for the study of animals both large and small.

The park also has a geological autotrail on which 12 sites of particular interest have been identified and clearly marked.

Most traces of the earlier human presence within the park have been eradicated, but some historical areas have been preserved – such as the site of Jan Smuts' farm, old diamond and fluorite mines, Late Iron Age sites and even an old church.

The beautiful old building that was formerly used as the Pilanesberg Magistrate's Court has also been preserved and has now been put to use as a stop-over point for refreshment.

The shop here, and the larger shop at Manyane on the eastern side of the park, do supply basic requirements, but be sure to take your own food and refreshments if you wish to stop at any of the many picnic and braai sites within the park. There are also three swimming pools, a fully licensed restaurant, miniature golf and trampolines at Manyane. At Mogwase, just outside the park, there are two service stations and a supermarket.

Arranging accommodation

From the start, the philosophy guiding the development of the Pilanesberg National Park has been to create a national and regional asset, and not merely a playground for tourists. Accordingly, emphasis has been placed on the education of the local population. Limited trophy-hunting, professionally controlled, is allowed in the park, and the meat from these surplus animals is sold at reasonable prices to people living nearby. Part of the proceeds from hunting benefits the community through subsidising accommodation of school groups at Bosele Camp.

Daily driving tours of the park are run from nearby Sun City, Bakubung Lodge, Tshukudu Lodge, Kwa Maritane and Manyane gate, but it is also possible to stay overnight within the park itself. In addition, walks are offered in 'big five country'. Accommodation includes a caravan park and campsites at Manyane, where there are also some 60 self-catering and fully equipped chalets.

Mankwe is a rustic camp in the bush, which offers accommodation in 10 tents and 10 wooden cabins. Guests must supply their own food, drink, towels and utensils, and a compact gas cooker is recommended as part of the equipment to be brought along.

Kololo is a place with a view and consists of four tents pitched at the top of a hill. Whereas Metswedi Camp, at the other end of the scale, is a luxurious seven-tented camp with a hostess and a field guide in attendance, Bosele Camp – which has four large dormitories – caters exclusively for schools and for other educational tours.

For reservations in the park, write to the Central Reservations Office, PO Box 937, Lonehill 2062; or tel (011) 465 5423; fax (011) 465 1228. For more information, write to Pilanesberg National Park, PO Box 1201, Mogwase 0302; or tel (01465) 55351; fax (01465) 55525.

A trio of white rhino lumber leisurely away from the shores of Lake Mankwe.

Springbok (Antidorcas marsupialis).

• EXPLORING THE MARICO COUNTRYSIDE •

The old mission, Kuruman, occupied by Moffat and his family for 50 years.

Bosman's bushveld – its places and its people

THE MARICO DISTRICT today – officially it lies in North-West Province – lives in both the present and a gloriously mythical past. This enviable distinction was bestowed by Herman Charles Bosman, one of South Africa's most complex and best-loved authors. As a teacher in 1926 at the school on the Marico farm Heimweeberg, Bosman was awed and inspired by the colourful characters among whom he lived. His warmth, wit and insight have immortalized aspects of life in what was then a rural Afrikaner backwater in which Bosman, himself a city boy, spent no more than six months.

Many people of Marico claim descent from the Voortrekker families who settled on or near the old farm Wonderfontein in the 1840s. But the town of Groot-Marico itself is much younger. In 1900, a British army officer recorded his surprise at the literary quality of the books he had looted from the newly built local parsonage. An urban police post was established in 1903 (apparently a few years too late), and the railway station was built in 1910, when the line was completed between Zeerust and Swartruggens. The Groot-Marico of today, still a small, one-street town along the line of rail and river, is a centre for farming operations, including tobacco, fruit and cattle.

The Marico Bushveld Nature Reserve and Dam are attractions, offering hiking trails, angling, boating, caravanning and picnic sites. There are also game and hunting farms and a homely, fascinating Tobacco Tour. Unique to Groot-Marico is its Mampoer Tour, which, like the Tobacco Tour, starts from the information centre in First Avenue; tel (014252) and ask for 85, or write to PO Box 28, Groot-Marico 2850. It includes a nature tour and an introduction to the many tree types of the Marico bushveld, a visit to the large natural spring of Kaaloog and, in a remote kloof, an opportunity to see how mampoer is distilled, and, of course, to taste it. *Mampoer* is a fiery liquor distilled from almost any fruit except the grape. Peaches and apricots are the favourites, and it was Bosman who, metaphorically, held up a bottle, with 'smoke that is pale and rises in slow curves', for all to savour.

'Mafeking road'

About 6 km west of Groot-Marico, along the N4 or what Bosman knew as the Mafeking road, a roadside monument marks the Anglo-Boer War battlefield of Kleinfontein. Here, in October 1901, a British wagon convoy was seized by the Boers, with heavy losses suffered by both sides. Cut off from sources of supply, the increasingly ragged republicans lived off their enemy and, at Kleinfontein, the booty included 12 wagons of ammunition.

Drive along the N4 for some 30 km past the Kleinfontein monument and you reach the district's largest town, Zeerust. If you arrive on horseback you can tie your reins to the hitching rail outside the elegant magistrate's court. (Distant Pietermaritzburg and Tarkastad also boast hitching rails, but they are a dwindling urban amenity.) The name of Zeerust, far inland, has nothing to do with the sea *(zee)* but was originally Coetzee-rust, after Diederik

Mafikeng Town Hall, now a museum devoted to the siege and to Scouting.

Coetzee who laid out the town in 1867. An earlier, more descriptive name, was *Sebatlani*, which means 'dusty place'. The Church of St John the Baptist is a national monument and is said to be one of the oldest Anglican churches still in use in the former Transvaal.

Drive on along the Mafeking road (now R49) and, about 27 km from Zeerust, a gravel road on the right leads to the site of Mosega. Stop at the railway crossing and look around on your left. Somewhere in this lonely field is buried Jane Wilson, wife of the American medical missionary, Alexander Wilson. She died at the mission station, Sendelingspos, established here in the early 1830s. Within a few years the Matabele of Mzilikazi, in their flight north from the Zulu king, Shaka, arrived at Sendelingspos. They found it congenial, renamed it Mosega, and stayed, but the missionaries soon departed. Next came Voortrekkers, avenging their companions allegedly slain by the Matabele. When the Voortrekkers rode away they drove before them an unknown number of cattle and left behind at least 500 dead Matabele. Like Jane Wilson, they sleep somewhere in this field but, unlike her, they were never lovingly laid to rest. Great diesel trains thunder past and their sirens blow a sad requiem.

The place of stones
On past the tiny villages of Ottoshoop (Otto was a local magistrate) and Slurry (where there is a large cement-works), the Mafeking road comes home to *Mafikeng* – now correctly written thus (place of stones) and a part of Mmabatho, former capital of the 'independent state' of Bophuthatswana and present capital of North-West Province. Modern amenities include boutiques, casinos and hotels, but new Mmabatho has never achieved the renown of old Mafeking, now relegated to suburban status.

Mafeking, for several months of glory, was the focus of Imperial British affection, admiration and anxiety. All this was brought on by an incompetently conducted siege of incomparable emotional impact. A Boer army sat about the veld desultorily firing their artillery into the dusty village. In command of the defence was Colonel Robert Baden-Powell, whose chirpy messages to the

Lily pads and palms where Kuruman's perennial spring reaches the surface.

Bosman gave Marico undying life.

world outside suggested frightful danger being faced with phlegmatic British pluck. Baden-Powell is more worthily remembered as the founder of the Boy Scouts Association, which had its beginnings here, in old-time Mafeking.

A good place to start a visit is the Mafikeng Museum, in the old Town Hall (the entrance is in Carrington Street), where a descriptive map of the town is available. Interesting sites – apart from the museum itself – include Cannon Koppie, Victoria Hospital, Baden-Powell's headquarters, Masonic Lodge, old Mafeking Club, St Joseph's Convent and the old cemetery.

Graves here include that of one of the world's most remarkable fighter pilots, South African Andrew Beauchamp Proctor, who, in the space of just a few months at the front in the First World War, garnered no fewer than five high decorations for bravery, including the rarest of all, the Victoria Cross.

When you've done with history, Mafikeng has its complement of

Right: *Impassive images at a cultural centre outside Mmabatho.*

shops and markets, coffee shops, restaurants and nightclubs, or you can cross town to the brighter lights of Mmabatho. For gamewatchers, there's the Molopo Game Reserve on the outskirts.

Beyond Mmabatho/Mafikeng, distances between towns are greater as you approach the region known for many years as Bushmanland – great arid plains where cattle are raised. Only 16 km south-east of Mafikeng, though, is Rooigrond, the site of what was once the capital of *Het Land Goschen* (the land of Goshen) – one of two tiny republics proclaimed in 1881 by settlers who declined to accept the jurisdiction of either the Cape or the Transvaal. The cattle-ranching centre of Stella – a speck on the vast Gemsbokvlakte – is a reminder of another republic, but the capital was at *Vryburg*, the town of liberty.

The Stellaland flag featured a lone white star on a green background above a coat of arms, and one was sent as a trophy to Queen Victoria, who found a place for it in Windsor Castle. In 1934 King George V generously had it returned to Vryburg and now it hangs in the town's museum. The old stone buildings at Tierkloof – where many prominent South Africans received at least a part of their education – are worth a visit, and the Leon Taljaard Nature Reserve is popular among lovers of the outdoors.

About 140 km south-west of Vryburg you cross the provincial border into the Northern Cape and, almost at once, reach the town of Kuruman, renowned for its unfailing fountain or 'eye' of fresh water. Soon after arriving in the north-western Cape in 1821 Robert Moffat, the missionary, persuaded Mothibi, then chief of the Tlapin people, to move his headquarters to this vicinity, and the mission soon became a busy centre of learning and rare human harmony.

Kuruman's water gushes out of an underground dolomitic cavern, to fill a small lake that is the 'eye', studded with lily pads and set among large willow trees and palms. The spring is so powerful that during even the most severe drought the rate of flow remains constant, with some 10 million litres of water pouring into Kuruman each day.

Moffat's original mission is a popular, if rather remote tourist attraction today. Outside the town, the old church of 1833 and Moffat's house have been preserved, surrounded by a garden planted with a variety of fruit trees, and riverine forests.

The church was for many years the largest building in the Northern Cape and the marriage of Moffat's daughter, Mary, to David Livingstone, took place here. Most of their courting, it is said, was in the shade of the 'Love Garden', still a place of 'peace and holy quiet'.

Bosman to Livingstone, mampoer and missions – the 'Mafeking road' from Groot-Marico leads through an area that is almost entirely unknown to many motorists. It is an area, though, possessing rare charm and a wide variety of attractions.

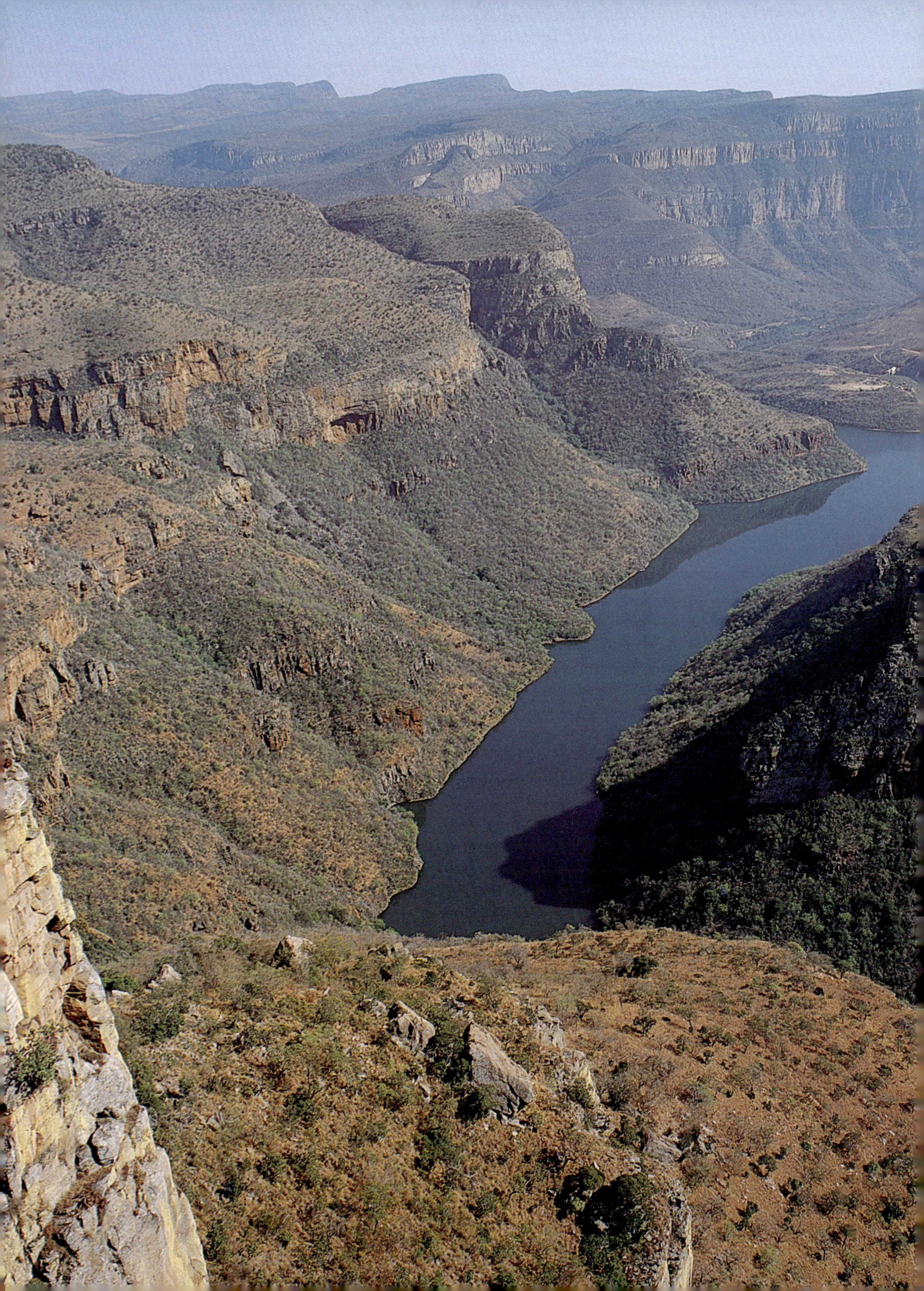

MPUMALANGA & SWAZILAND

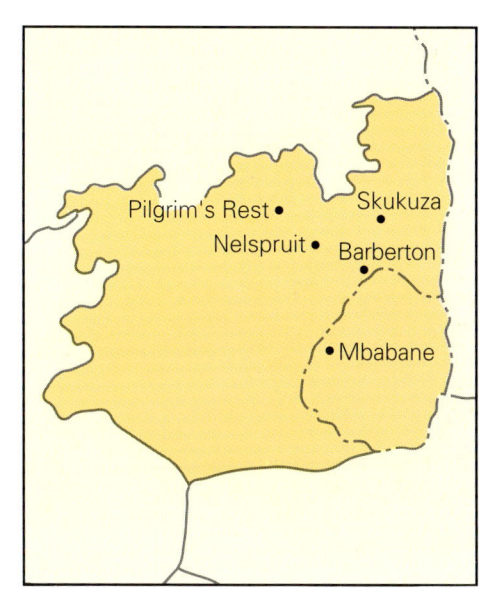

Sabie – MacMac Falls – Blyde River Canyon – Bourke's Luck **36-7**

Blyde River Canyon: A waterworn wonderland **38-9**

Sabie – Hazyview – Graskop – Kowyn's Pass – Lisbon Falls – Pilgrim's Rest **40-1**

Pilgrim's Rest: The gold rush lives on **42-3**

Lydenburg – Sudwala Caves – Montrose Falls – Long Tom Pass – Sabie **44-5**

Long Tom Pass: Gunfire's distant echo **46-7**

Lydenburg – Verraaiersnek – Robber's Pass – Caspersnek – Burgersfort **48-9**

Nelspruit – De Kaap Valley – Saddleback Pass – Barberton – The Cascades **50-1**

Barberton and De Kaap Valley: A wealth of gold **52-3**

Mbabane – Forbes' Reef – Pigg's Peak – Barberton – Badplaas **54-5**

Swazi Traditions: Sacred rites of the New Year **56-7**

Kruger National Park: Introduction and day drives **58-69**

Left: *The Drakensberg escarpment rears over the waters of Blydepoort Dam.*

A bewitching world of soaring cliffs and tumbling crystal waters

Our route leads from the forests of Sabie and the grassy slopes of Graskop down over the scenic Kowyn's Pass. We cross a stretch of lowveld savannah to reach the Blyde River Canyon, climb the Abel Erasmus Pass and return to Graskop and Sabie along the spectacular edge of the escarpment. The entire route is on good tarred roads.

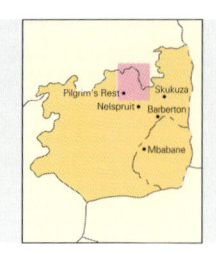

**Sabie
MacMac Falls
Blydepoort Dam
Abel Erasmus Pass
Bourke's Luck
330 – 350 km**

Waterfall and tufa in the Abel Erasmus Pass.

Dawn tinges the lowveld sky above Wonderview.

Water tumbles through the Bourke's Luck potholes.

LEAVE SABIE ON THE R532 for Graskop and note your kms as you cross the Sabie River. The road climbs for 5 km through plantations of eucalyptus and pine trees, then begins a gradual descent. Roughly 11 km beyond the Sabie River, turn right onto a 1,1 km tarred road for the pretty MacMac Pools.

Return to the R532 and turn right, noting your kms. Less than 2 km later the gorge of the MacMac Falls becomes visible on your right (see opposite). Park in the signposted parking area on your right. From here a path leads to several platforms giving uninterrupted views of the falls.

Continue on the R532, noting your kms. After 2,5 km you cross a railway line. Immediately after this there is a picnic area on your right (braai sites, water). On your left, opposite the picnic area and a short distance away from the road, is the small but attractive Maria Shires waterfall. Roughly 10 km later you reach a T-junction below the rocky hillock known as The Bonnet. Turn right here for Graskop. After some 3,5 km you enter Graskop on Pilgrim's Road.

Graskop to Blyde River Canyon
Turn right into Main Street, noting your kms. After 1,5 km you pass a gravel road, on your left, leading to the Panorama Gorge and Falls (see pages 40 – 1). Shortly after this you begin the descent of scenic Kowyn's Pass and, at 5 km, you reach a cairn in a parking area on your right that records the opening of this road. Park here for a fine panoramic view northwards along the steep escarpment.

Driving on from here, you pass under an alpine tunnel – a shelter constructed as a protection against rockslides. At 11 km from Graskop you pass the R535 to Hazyview on your right. Continue straight until, at 34 km, you cross the Nwaritsana River. Slow down for the built-up area just beyond the river and, at the T-junction 4 km after the river, turn left onto the R40 for Klaserie. Note your kms here and, 10,4 km along the R40, pass, on your left, a picnic site sheltered by an enormous tree that overhangs the road. After 34,5 km on the R40 you pass a road, on your right, to Acornhoek, and after a further 6 km you cross the Klaserie River; 500 m later the R40 turns right to Hoedspruit. Keep straight here and note your kms – you are now travelling on the R531.

Immediately you pass, on your left, a road leading to Klaserie. Within 200 m you pass beneath a railway bridge, then cross the Mbezi River, passing through dense indigenous vegetation. After 4,5 km on the R531 you cross the eQunduhlu River (Undothlospruit) and, 15,5 km later, you pass a turn-off left to Mariepskopskool. Some 2,5 km after this, turn left for 'Swadini'.

The road leads towards a jumble of mountains with the towering Swadini Buttress to the right and, after 7,3 km, you reach the entrance to the Blyde River Canyon Nature Reserve. Some 3,5 km later you pass the entrance to the Swadini Resort on your right.

The resort has a restaurant, braai facilities and other amenities, including a swimming pool. (If you propose to eat at the restaurant, the admission fee may be deducted from the restaurant charges.)

Roughly 2,1 km after passing the resort, where the road ahead is closed, turn right and note your kms. Stop at the barrier just after the turn, where the gate attendant will give you an information brochure.

The road now crosses the Blyde River and you pass the Nature Reserve Office on your left. Some 1,8 km from the turn-off you reach a small parking area on your left. Stop here for a fine view of the Blydepoort Dam wall; 1,4 km beyond this parking area the road ends at a second parking site, from which a path leads left to a visitors' information centre, a viewing balcony (see pages 38 – 9) and toilets.

Return to the T-junction with the R531 and turn left, noting your kms. Amid the typical lowveld thornbush that you now pass through, there are great plantations of citrus, bananas, mangoes and pawpaws. After 8 km you pass a tarred road on your right to Hoedspruit and Phalaborwa, and 3,5 km later you reach a T-junction. Turn left here onto the R527/R531, noting your kms.

You cross the well-shaded Blyde River after 2,3 km, and at 17 km you pass a road on your right to Tzaneen (R36). Roughly 6 km later you can see the Abel Erasmus Pass ahead, ascending from left to right, and some 1,5 km after this you reach the start of the pass. After climbing for 1,3 km you reach a small parking area on the right, offering views over the Olifants River; 1,5 km later you reach another small parking area at the entrance to the short JG Strijdom Tunnel.

At the far end of the tunnel there is a parking area offering completely different views. An annually dwindling stream of water can be seen flowing over a tufa formation that it has created in the course of many centuries. Formations such as this one, whether actively forming or inactive, are very rare (see page 39 column 2). Note your kms as you leave this parking area.

Over the Abel Erasmus Pass
You now pass several picnic sites as the road gradually climbs over the Abel Erasmus Pass. At around 16 km there are fine views over cultivated valleys ringed by mountains. After 22 km, turn left onto the R532, noting your kms at the turn. (If you continue straight here, you will reach the gravel turn-off, on your right, to the Echo Caves after 1,1 km.)

After 1,4 km on the R532, you cross the Ohrigstad River, passing tobacco fields and drying sheds on your left. The road winds upwards, with the Ohrigstad River gorge visible on your left, through rolling country with the Drakensberg always in view ahead and to your left. You pass the Blydepoort Resort on your left.

Cross the Kadishi (Kadisi) River after 22 km – it is very small at this point – and 1,8 km later turn left onto a 3 km sideroad to the Three Rondavels viewsite. Return to the R532, driving slowly to appreciate the views on your left over the gorge. The T-junction with the

Lichen colours the Drakensberg rockfaces.

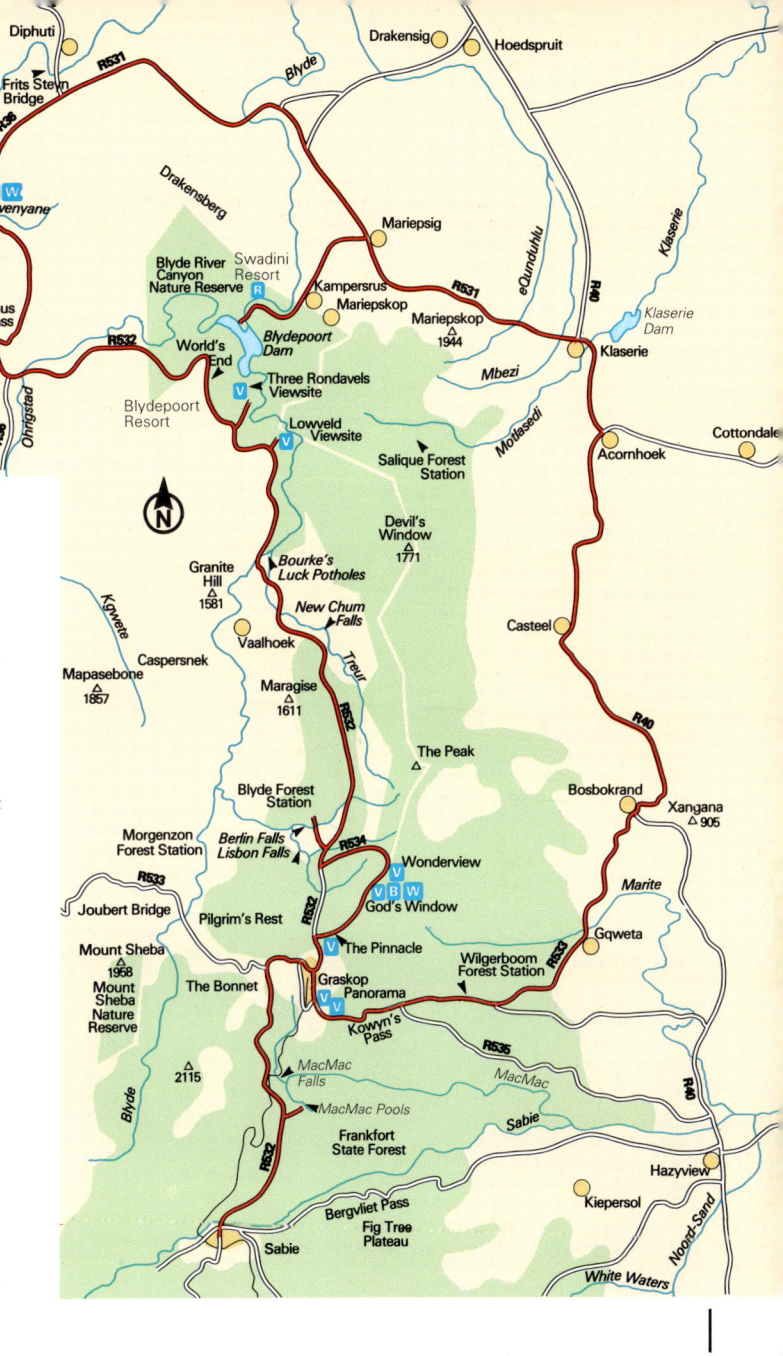

BOURKE'S LUCK
Where the *Blyde* (joyful) River is joined by the *Treur* (sorrow) River, there is a remarkable record of an erosion process that started many thousands of years ago. Minor imperfections in the dolomite rock have been worn away by the swirling water with its load of grit and pebbles, causing 'potholes' to appear. Thomas Bourke, an early owner of the farm on which this feature is situated, discovered gold at the bottom of the holes. The exact amount is unknown, but his farm became known as Bourke's Luck.

ABEL ERASMUS PASS
This magnificent road across the Drakensberg was opened in 1959. For much of its route it follows a wagon track pioneered in the 1840s. Travelling south-west from the lowveld, the road rises 610 m above the Olifants River, then drops 335 m to the level of the Ohrigstad River. The pass is named after Abel Erasmus, who owned the farm Graskop in the 1870s, and who was responsible for keeping the peace between the republican government and the indigenous communities of the former eastern Transvaal.

MACMAC FALLS
Although President Burgers is said to have named the area after the many Scotsmen among the early diggers, another source claims that the name of the falls can be traced to the MacClaughton brothers, who led the rush to this area. The search for gold spread to this scenic waterfall on the Watervalspruit and, particularly, to the pool below its 56 m drop. In an attempt to divert the flow, which was hampering their operations, the miners planted a large charge of gunpowder at the top of the falls. The resultant explosion failed to achieve the desired effect, but it did result in the single stream being split into twin falls.

Morning sun on the MacMac Falls.

R532 appears suddenly at the top of a small rise. Turn left onto the R532, noting your kms.

Turn left after 4,7 km and follow another sideroad for 400 m to reach the lowveld viewsite. Return to the R532 and turn left, noting your kms as you turn. After 9 km turn left into the Bourke's Luck picnic site (entry fee, braai sites, refreshment kiosk, toilets).

A short path leads to the remarkable phenomenon known as Bourke's Luck potholes. None of the fencing in the area is entirely childproof, and small children must be managed with care. (See above.)

Allow about an hour at Bourke's Luck, then return to the R532 and turn left, noting your kms. After 500 m you cross the Blyde River, and at 2,3 km and 5 km you cross and recross the Treur River (see pages 38 – 9).

At just over 9 km you pass a cairn on your left commemorating the Voortrekkers. Cross the Watervalspruit at roughly 22 km and after a further 4,5 km turn right onto a tarred road for the Berlin Falls. After a little less than 2 km, you reach a parking area, from where a path leads to a viewsite near the edge of the gorge.

Return to the R532 and turn right, noting your kms. After 1,2 km turn left onto the R534 for God's Window. Along the R534 there are several clearly marked viewsites on your left, giving vistas of the lowveld (see pages 40 – 1). The first is Wonderview, 7 km from the turn, followed by God's Window and The Pinnacle.

After 16 km on the R534 you rejoin the R532 at a T-junction. Turn left here onto the R532 to enter Graskop on Huguenotestraat. Turn right into Louis Trichardt Street and, 500 m later, turn left into Main Street. Turn right at the stop street into Pilgrim's Road, and retrace your outward route back to Sabie.

Sabie Forestry Museum Ford Street, Sabie 1260 Tel (01315) 41243
Graskop Information Office Louis Trichardt St Graskop 1270 Tel (01315) 71316
Blyde River Information Centre Blyderivierspoort Nature Reserve, PO Bourke's Luck 1272 Tel (01315) 81215

Amid rolling hills – the unexpected Berlin Falls.

THE BLYDE RIVER CANYON

The Blyde River swirls between brightly coloured cliffs at the start of its magnificent canyon.

Ancient, soaring buttresses and a mighty canyon echo the cries of war

As they trekked further into the interior to escape British domination, the 'emigrant Boers' – the Voortrekkers – became increasingly conscious of their need to find access to a seaport that was not under British control.

In 1838, Louis Trichardt had succeeded in reaching the Portuguese town of Lourenço Marques (Maputo) at Delagoa Bay, but the journey was costly: many of Trichardt's party died of fever – probably malaria.

In 1844 Andries Hendrik Potgieter, accompanied only by a few men on horseback, set out on another journey to the coast, and left his party's cumbersome wagons behind at the top of the Drakensberg escarpment – with the women and children, and a few armed men.

This base party outspanned the wagons at a river to await the return of their leader. The time agreed upon for the return passed, but the group stayed on until, eventually, they abandoned hope of ever seeing Potgieter and his companions again. Sadly, they loaded the wagons for the long haul back to Potchefstroom. Before they left, the disconsolate trekkers named the river by which they had camped the *Treurrivier* – the river of sorrow. Later, while they were fording another river some kilometres to the west, they heard distant shots. Looking around, they saw Potgieter and his comrades ride into view, the successful journey having taken much longer than anticipated. There was great rejoicing at the reunion, and the river they were in the process of fording was named the *Blyderivier* – the river of joy.

Blyderiviersport Reserve
Today the Blyde River and the magnificent canyon through which it flows are part of the Blyderiviersport Nature Reserve. The reserve includes all the land surrounding the Blydepoort Dam and extends upstream almost to Graskop.

The Blyde River has its source on Mount Anderson, close to Sabie, and flows through Pilgrim's Rest, being joined by the Treur River at the remarkable Bourke's Luck Potholes, before entering the great canyon that it has helped to create in the course of countless millions of years.

The Blyde River flows strongly throughout the year and has by far the highest run-off of any South African river – some 40 per cent compared with a national average of only nine per cent. This means that 40 per cent of the total rainfall actually appears as stream flow, the remainder being lost to evaporation. The high run-off is due, in part, to the steep terrain of the main catchment area, and also because the porous underground rock stores water, releasing it into the flow as the water table drops.

A great tilting of the land surface, following a massive volcanic disturbance north of Gauteng millions of years ago, produced the mighty northern Drakensberg escarpment. Layers of sand and mud, deposited by long-vanished seas or inland lakes, have become

The Three Rondavels and the higher Mapjaneng dominate the gorge.

compressed to form quartzite and shale. On its long journey to the sea, the Blyde River carried suspended particles ranging from grains of sand to great boulders, and their erosive effect created the formations we see today. At the great Swadini buttress, the harder quartzite forms the vertical cliffs, while softer shales have eroded to form the talus, or sloping sections that are now covered with vegetation. Capping the escarpment is a layer of immensely hard, Black Reef quartzite.

Opposite the buttress, on the road that enters the Swadini resort area, is the peak of Mariepskop, which reaches a height of 1 944 m. Mariepskop is named after Maripi Mashile, a chief of the Mapulana clan who helped the Pedi defeat a force of Swazi invaders here in 1864, in a battle known as *Moholoholo* – the great, great battle. Swadini means the place of the Swazi, although it was actually the home of the Pedi, who lived here throughout the year, except for the very hottest months, when they moved to the top of the cooler escarpment. Swazi raiders would then move in, wreck their settlements and reap their crops. Maripi Mashile's counter-strategy was to scale the mountain with his warriors and taunt the Swazi into attacking them there. As the Swazi climbed after them, they were demolished by an avalanche of boulders hurled down by the Pedi fighters.

Maripi Mashile and his wives

The hills to the right of Mariepskop are known as *Rodille*, or the bundles, because they resemble a file of women carrying bundles on their heads. The striking Three Rondavels, which can be seen best from the top of the escarpment (see pages 36 – 7) are named after three of Maripi's wives. From lowest to highest, they are Magabolle, Mogoladikwe and Maseroto. The peak at the end of the row, which is the highest of all, is *Mapjaneng* – the chief – also named in honour of Maripi Mashile.

As you look across the water of the Blydepoort Dam from the balcony of the Visitors' Centre at Swadini, you see the 1 087m peak of *Thabaneng* at a bend in the dam. Its name means 'the mountain with a shadow that moves' and it is known also as The Sundial. To the right, and beyond a further stretch of water, are the unique Kadishi Falls, the largest active tufa formation in the world. (Tufa is a porous deposit of calcium bicarbonate formed – when the temperature and other factors change – from calcium carbonate carried in solution by a river.)

To the left of the waterfall is a cave that, many years ago, was a part of the river's course – now blocked by the formation of tufa. The dam is at the confluence of the Blyde and Ohrigstad rivers, the latter entering from the west – your right-hand side as you face the Kadishi Falls.

The pools that formed here before the construction of the dam were inhabited by large numbers of hippo and crocodiles, but raising the water level has destroyed much of their suitable environment. A small group of hippo can be seen sometimes on the shoreline to the left of Thabaneng. Few crocodiles remain, and they generally confine themselves to the muddy islands.

Blyderivierspoort Hiking Trail

The bird life in the reserve includes white-breasted cormorants, black eagles and crowned eagles. Buck species include steenbok, klipspringer and kudu, while baboons and samango monkeys – and leopards – inhabit the forests and cool, remote kloofs.

Traversing the reserve – roughly from south to north – is the Blyderivierspoort Hiking Trail, starting at the magnificent viewsite known as God's Window, on the escarpment near Graskop, and ending at the Swadini resort.

The 65 km trail takes five days to complete; it passes the scenically beautiful New Chum Falls, Bourke's Luck Potholes and the Kadishi Falls, and ends with a suspension bridge. There are spectacular views along the entire trail, as well as glimpses of the old coaching road, but the most scenic areas are traversed on the last day, where the route is dominated by the Three Rondavels.

Apart from the Blyderiviers-poort Hiking Trail, hikes within the reserve include the Protea Trail of four days, and the two-day Yellowwood Trail. Obtain permits at the control point just before crossing the Blyde River on the way to the Visitors' Centre.

Boat trips may be undertaken from a jetty near the Visitors' Centre, where all reservations should be made. Swimming pools and other amenities are provided at the Aventura Swadini and Aventura Blydepoort resorts.

The headquarters of the Nature Conservation team is at Bourke's Luck, site of the famous 'potholes', where there is also an interesting Information Centre and a variety of further walks.

Without any warning the highveld gives way to a chasm 700 m deep.

Between highveld and lowveld, a land of gold mines and waterfalls

This route leads from the forest-and-waterfall country of Sabie down to the tropical-fruit plantations of the lowveld, then up over the Drakensberg on Kowyn's Pass. We pass through Graskop, visit God's Window and the Lisbon Falls, then climb still higher over Pilgrim's Pass to Pilgrim's Rest. Almost the entire route is tarred.

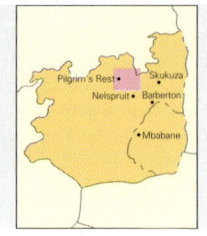

Sabie
Lone Creek
Waterfall
Hazyview
Graskop
Lisbon Falls
Pilgrim's Rest
200 – 220 km

DRIVE DOWN Sabie's Main Street towards Graskop and turn left into Old Lydenburg Road. After 2 km you cross the railway line, then pass a gravel road leading right to the Bridal Veil Falls. Cross the railway line a second time, pass a gravel road leading left to the Horseshoe Falls and, 100 m later, cross the Sabie River.

Keep left where the road divides. Roughly 2,5 km past the river you will see the Lone Creek Waterfall ahead – tumbling over a rock face above the trees. You reach a parking area 300 m later (braai sites, water, toilets). A short, circular walk leads to the foot of the 68 m fall.

Sabie to Hazyview

Retrace your route to Main Street in Sabie and turn right (uphill). Continue straight through town for Hazyview and White River. A few hundred metres after leaving the town, turn right onto the R537 for White River, noting your kms. The road winds through extensive forestry plantations, and after 9 km you see the prominent *Spitskop* (pointed hill) on your right (see opposite).

Some 16 km from Sabie the road descends sharply and 3,2 km later it crosses the *Blinkwaterspruit* (sparkling water stream). At about 28 km from Sabie turn left onto a gravel road for *'Swartfontein'* (black spring). (Drive slowly in wet weather.) This road skirts the wood-fringed Danie Joubert Dam, also known as *Klipkoppie* (stone hill) Dam. The road surface changes to tar at about 3,8 km. After a further 4 km, turn left at the T-junction onto the R40 for Hazyview, noting your kms.

The R40 leads through forest and citrus groves. After 4,8 km you cross the White Waters River and, 600 m later, there is a good view back over the Da Gama Dam before you pass through extensive banana plantations. After roughly 25 km on the R40 you reach a junction with the R538 – take the exit-road to your left and note your kms as you turn onto the R538.

Hazyview to Graskop

Drive through the village of Hazyview, passing the R536 to Skukuza on your right after 3,3 km. About 1 km later you pass the R536 leading left towards Sabie, and you cross the Sabie River. After crossing the river, turn left onto the R535 for Graskop, noting your kms.

The road begins to climb, offering views over forested hills. After 21 km you pass through a crossroads, then plunge again into dense forests. After 25,5 km on the R535, turn left at the T-junction onto the R533 for Graskop, noting your kms.

The road now climbs steeply up the Drakensberg escarpment via Kowyn's Pass. At first, trees may block your view, but later you have fine panoramas of the escarpment unfolding on your right. The road passes through the only alpine tunnel in southern Africa – a shelter built to guard against rockfalls – and soon after this there is a small parking area on your left, with a cairn commemorating the opening of the pass.

After almost 10 km on the R533 you pass the Panorama Gorge and the Panorama Falls on your right. If there has been rain recently, it is worth parking off the road to view the falls – but note that the cliff top is unfenced and children should be held.

About 1 km after passing Panorama Gorge you enter Graskop on Main Street (*Hoofstraat*). Keep straight at the intersection with Pilgrim's

The Pinnacle near Graskop.

Sabie – extensive forestry plantations.

Way and Richardson Avenue, and turn right into Louis Trichardt Avenue. You now pass the Tourist Information Office on your left. Turn left into Hugenote Street, noting your kms.

Graskop to the Lisbon Falls

After 1,9 km turn right onto the R534 and, after a further 1,4 km, turn right into the parking area for The Pinnacle viewsite. There are protective railings at the lower viewsite, but parts of the cliff edge may be inadequately fenced.

Drive back onto the road and turn right. You now pass several parking areas and viewsites on your right and, roughly 5 km later, you reach the parking area for God's Window, also on your right. Here are braai places, water and toilets, and a paved footpath leads to the God's Window viewsite (fenced). The 'window' is the head of a narrow gorge, and the path follows a circular route that includes the Rain Forest.

Continue along the R534 and, after a further 1,3 km, you reach the Wonderview viewsite (fenced, but not entirely safe). You cannot see the escarpment from here because you are standing on the crest of it, but on a clear day you can look far out over the Lowveld. The R534 now swings westwards and away from the escarpment, to join the R532 at a T-junction. Turn left here towards Graskop, then turn right onto a tarred road after just 800 m. This 2,2 km road leads to a parking area alongside the 82,5 m Lisbon Falls and a short footpath leads to a fine viewsite.

Return to the R532 and turn right, noting your kms. You pass through dense pine plantations and cross the Lisbon River to reach the town of Graskop again after 6 km.

Graskop to Pilgrim's Rest

Turn right into Louis Trichardt Avenue, then left into Main Street. At the stop street, turn right into Pilgrim's Way. The road begins to wind through hilly country and, roughly 1 km out of town, there is a parking area on your left next to a small natural rock bridge – a national monument. Roughly 3 km later you reach a Y-junction at the base of the rocky, bush-grown outcrop known as The Bonnet. Go right here onto the R533 towards Pilgrim's Rest.

The R533 climbs Pilgrim's Pass, with views towards Graskop and, as you descend on the western side, you can catch glimpses of the village of Pilgrim's Rest in the valley. Within a few kilometres you pass the outskirts of the village, which extends on both sides of its main road (see pages 42 – 3). Stay on the bypass road if you do not intend to visit Pilgrim's Rest.

Several establishments offer lunch, and there are picnic sites in the town. Amenities are also available at the caravan park – take the lower entrance to the town and turn right at the T-junction. There are braai sites, water and toilets here, firewood is for sale and there is a restaurant and a swimming pool.

From Pilgrim's Rest, retrace your route to The Bonnet, and turn right onto the R532 for Sabie. On your right, just before the level crossing, are the thundering Maria Shires Falls. A 2 km walk leads to Forest Falls from the picnic site on the left of the R532. Nearer Sabie you pass, on your left, first the MacMac Falls, then a road to the MacMac Pools (see pages 36 – 7), both features being on the MacMac River, a tributary of the Sabie River.

Sabie Forestry Museum Ford Steet, Sabie 1260 Tel (01315) 41243
Sondela Tourist Information Centre Sabie 1260 Tel (01315) 43492
Graskop Information Office Louis Trichardt Ave Graskop 1270 Tel (01315) 71316/71126
Pilgrim's Rest Information Office Main Street Pilgrim's Rest 1290 Tel (01315) 81211

Lone Creek Waterfall near Sabie.

THE FORESTRY MUSEUM, SABIE
Sabie's Forestry Museum is the only museum of its kind in South Africa. Its exhibits cover the natural marvels of trees and their wood, and illustrate the ingenious ways in which people have put this wood to use – from violins and matches to the heat-absorbing nose cones of modern intercontinental rockets. Also illustrated is the growth of the South African timber industry, from the earliest days to the highly complex enterprise it is today.

SPITSKOP GOLD
The first payable alluvial gold to be discovered in Mpumalanga (then eastern Transvaal) was found on the slopes of *Spitskop* (pointed hill) early in 1871.

Among the discoverers was Edward Button, who promptly wrote a letter to the landdrost at Lydenburg claiming a reward that had been offered by the Volksraad. No reward was in fact paid, but Button was rewarded in the sense that he was appointed as the Gold Commissioner of the Transvaal – and he went on to initiate gold mining at Eersteling, a site that may be visited near Pietersburg.

Little now remains of the pioneering venture at Spitskop, except for a few shallow workings that have been largely obliterated by extensive pine plantations.

A LUCKY STRIKE THAT CREATED SABIE
The little town of Sabie grew on a farm called Grootfontein, which had been bought by the hunter Henry Glynn in 1880. An earlier owner had paid a mere £7 10s for the same farm, but Glynn had to pay £600 now that gold had been discovered in the area. Glynn's purchase turned out to be highly profitable, however. One day he was taking part in target practice when a bullet chipped off a piece of rock to reveal traces of a gold reef. The mine that resulted, produced gold for the next 70 years. Mining operations required timber for props – and this need gave birth to the extensive forest plantations that now surround the town.

The historic Joubert Bridge across the Blyde River.

Undulating hills and cool forests surround the holiday resort of Graskop.

GRASKOP
The town of Graskop awaits the traveller at the top of the scenic Kowyn's Pass (1 488 m). The name means 'grassy hill', but nobody knows which of the many hills gave the town its name. The town began as a mining camp, established on a farm owned by Abel Erasmus – a prominent figure in the history of the old eastern Transvaal. Graskop serves as a centre for the timber industry, and is the most centrally situated town from which to explore the Drakensberg escarpment, the lowveld and the Kruger National Park.

• EXPLORING PILGRIM'S REST ON FOOT •

Early morning mist curls around the red roofs of Pilgrim's Rest – Leadley's building stands in the foreground.

'Wheelbarrow' Patterson, and furniture made from dynamite boxes

A WALK DOWN the historic main street of Pilgrim's Rest is a walk back in time – to the days when dreamers and desperadoes from around the world converged on this little-known valley in the Drakensberg to scramble for the riches that lay beneath its grassy hillsides.

Pilgrim's Rest owes its name to a group of men who had dug for gold at nearby MacMac. They called themselves 'the Pilgrims'. The group included a crusty old loner named Alec Patterson, also known as 'Wheelbarrow' Patterson from his habit of carrying his meagre worldly goods in a wheelbarrow – it was cheaper than a horse, he said, and it could not die of horse sickness. In 1873 Patterson found MacMac too crowded, so he loaded up his wheelbarrow and wandered away, following a game-trail over the mountains, until he looked down into a valley through which flowed a clear stream on its way to join the Blyde River. Down he went and, even before pitching camp, he panned some of the river gravel. The golden tail in the pan showed a richness beyond his wildest expectations.

Shortly after setting up camp, Patterson was joined by another digger, William Trafford, who had also wandered into 'his' valley. Stunned by the wealth in his pan, Trafford is said to have called out in delight: 'The pilgrim is at rest.' The hills echoed 'pilgrim ... rest ...' and so the first thoroughly profitable goldfield in South Africa received its name.

From Kimberley and from MacMac, from around the world, diggers poured into this rich valley, setting up the main diggings where the river – soon named Pilgrim's Creek – flowed through the farm of Ponieskranz. Within a year there were more than 14 canteens selling liquor to the diggers, with names such as 'Our House' and 'Stent's Cathedral'.

Corrugated iron
As men dug away at the slopes above Pilgrim's Creek, the tent town that had sprung up almost overnight was gradually replaced by more substantial structures, built mainly of corrugated iron on wooden frames.

These were easy to bring in by wagon, quick to erect – and nobody expected the field to last long enough to justify brick and mortar. The diggers also feared that one day, and possibly without warning, they would be ordered out by the republican Transvaal Government: a brick house that had to be left behind would represent a considerable loss to an ordinary prospector.

Probably the oldest surviving stone structure is the little *Anglican Church of St Mary* **(1)**, which is on your left as you enter the long main street from Sabie. It was built in 1884, by which time mining operations had recovered from the setbacks caused by the British annexation of 1877 and the Anglo-Transvaal War that was fought a few years later.

In those days, church functions were held in the corrugated iron *Town Hall* **(2)**, two doors down from St Mary's. Here, on the right side of the road, a plaque records the town's history. (Excavations made by the alluvial-diggers can be seen on the opposite bank of the river, forming numerous shallow depressions in the slope.) The well-restored *Leadley's building* **(3)**, on your left as you travel downhill, is now a hotel annexe. Next on your left are the *Old Print Shop* **(4)** and *Pilgrim's and Sabie News* **(5)**.

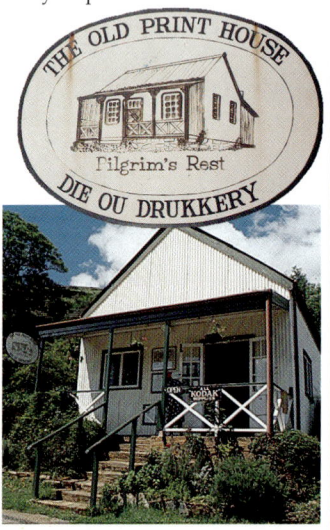

The Old Print House now serves as a tourist gift shop.

The *European Hotel* (6), on your left, with its attractive verandah typical of Pilgrim's Rest, now houses an annexe of the Royal Hotel furnished in a turn-of-the-century style. A little farther down on your right is the wide verandah of *Chaitow* (7), formerly the home of Mr CH Chaitow, one-time hairdresser, tobacconist and stationer in the town. A loop road on your right leads to the *Information Centre* (8), where you should obtain admission tickets to the town's museums before proceeding.

Opposite the Information Centre is the *Royal Hotel* (9), the bar of which once served as a chapel in Lourenço Marques (Maputo) until it was purchased by an enterprising transport-rider heading for Pilgrim's Rest in the 1890s. It now houses fascinating relics of the town's more riotous days, including prospecting pans, helmets, lamps, and numerous liquor bottles drained and discarded by thirsty diggers.

Home-made furniture

Just past the hotel on your right is the *Miner's House Museum* (10) which depicts the home life of a miner during the period 1910–20. Furniture and equipment is robust and simple, and often home-made, as in the case of the paraffin box converted into a chair, the cupboards made from dynamite boxes, and the paraffin-tin baking pans.

Across the road from the Miner's House Museum is the *Post Office* (11), which is still operational. The town's first postmaster (and also the public prosecutor) Mr JE Glinister, was appointed in 1877. After you pass the Victorian Cottage on your right, which serves as an annexe to the hotel, there are public toilets.

Opposite the Victorian Cottage a gravel road leads left to the Methodist Church and climbs steeply to a historic *cemetery* (12), which can also be reached by car along a different road. As you walk to the cemetery, it's easy to appreciate why it was necessary to have relays of bearers at funerals. In the early days of the diggings, although life was robust and rowdy, there was little serious crime. Stealing from the tent of a chum was unforgivable, and a digger, whose name has been forgotten, was once caught in this act, thrashed, and told never again to show his face in the camp. Unwisely, he did return, was seen and recognized in the dusk, and promptly shot. He was buried where he fell, lying along a north-south axis to mark him as unmourned. A day or so later there were two more deaths in the camp, more graves were dug nearby, and so the cemetery – unplanned – grew.

Return to the main road and turn left. The first building you pass on your left is the turn-of-the-century *Dredzen & Company general store* (13). Most of this building is original, including the shelves and counter, and the premises, as was the custom, are divided into two major parts: the commercial section in front, with living quarters in the rear.

The ox-cart was the main form of transport until early this century.

Continuing down the hill, you pass several buildings and an open section before reaching the lower half of the town. Look out on your right for a six-arched cement stage, or ore-bin, where ore was loaded.

War memorial

The first building in the lower half of the town is the *Roman Catholic Church of the Sacred Heart* (14), followed by a number of shops and the Highwayman's Garage (which was established by a man who, allegedly, once held up the gold-carrying stagecoach on Pilgrim's Hill). Turn left after passing the Dutch Reformed Church to visit the *Central Reduction Works* (15), built in 1896. There are a number of attractive old iron buildings on your left. Once inside the works area, note the little monument on the left, where the road leads up to the offices, built in memory of residents who died in World War I.

The works themselves are a forlorn collection of buildings that echo the frenzied activity that once drove their dark and decaying machinery. The buildings include huge stables that housed the mules that dragged countless tons of ore from the various mines, with the adjacent farrier's

Robber's grave in the old cemetery.

and wheelwright's shops still displaying all the tools of these trades. The large carpenter's shop is being used for restoration work, and the smithy itself has been restored, but others, – like the fitter's shop – are deserted except for old tools and machines. Among the old vehicles preserved in the works are an ox-wagon once used to transport goods from Lydenburg, and two Sentinel steam wagons.

Return to the main road and turn left, to pass a cluster of old buildings – mostly shops – before a road on your left leads to the caravan park (see pages 40 – 1). At this point the Blyde River is crossed by the stone *Joubert Bridge* (16), built in 1896 and named after the old Transvaal republic's mining commissioner. The bridge can be taken as marking the limit of the old town, but, after returning to your car, you may, if you wish, visit Alanglade, formerly the fairly palatial residence of the mine manager. Now maintained as a museum, it is a period house of the Art Nouveau and Art Deco eras, dating from 1916 to 1930.

To reach Alanglade, drive across the Joubert Bridge, keep straight where the road left leads to Lydenburg, then turn left shortly afterwards.

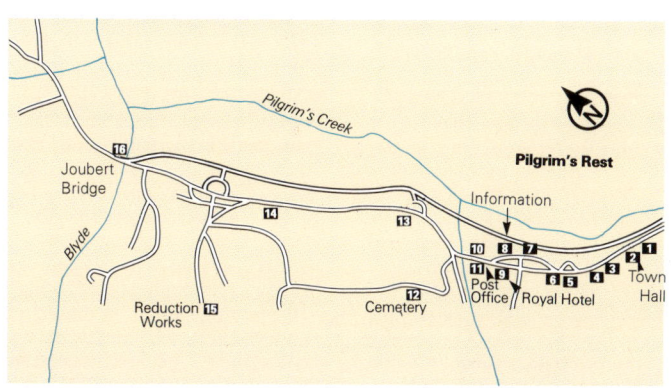

The Chaitow family outside their store.

Mysterious caves and misty memories of Long Tom's thunder

From Nelspruit we drive through forests to visit the ancient Sudwala Caves. Then we cross the Crocodile River, view the Montrose Falls, and wind through the attractive Schoemanskloof and Skaapwagters Pass to Lydenburg. From here we drive over Mauchsberg and then down the magnificent Long Tom Pass. The entire route is tarred.

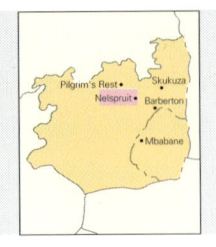

**Nelspruit
Sudwala Caves
Montrose Falls
Schoemanskloof
Lydenburg
Long Tom Pass
Sabie
250 – 270 km**

DRIVE NORTH FROM Nelspruit on the R40 towards White River. Cross the Crocodile River bridge on the outskirts of the town and, 500 m later, turn left onto the R37 and note your kms.

Part of the road is lined with African flame trees *(Spathodea campanulata)*, which form an avenue of bright scarlet blossoms in summer. There are wide views to your right over rolling hills and citrus plantations. You enter an area of pine and eucalyptus plantations, below the ridges of Bossieskop. After 29 km, turn left onto the R539 for Sudwala and note your kms.

The road soon enters dense forests that stretch away to the green hills in the distance. After about 11 km, from where the road begins to descend, there are particularly fine views over the tree-clad hills. After 16 km you cross the *Houtbosloop* (woodbush stream) and reach a T-junction, where the road on the left leads to Nelspruit. Turn right here for Sudwala, noting your kms.

After 1,1 km turn right for the Sudwala Caves and the Dinosaur Park; 400 m later the road forks. (On your left is a hotel with a restaurant and a swimming pool. Picnic sites are available for a small fee.) Go right at the fork, passing, on your right, a large orchard of pecan trees. Trailers and caravans are not permitted on this steep cement road that leads to the caves. After just under 1 km you reach another fork. Go left here, and park where the road ends in a shaded parking area. From here a short flight of steps leads up to the entrance to the cave system.

The caves are open from 08h30 to 16h30 and tours are conducted regularly, the last tour starting at 16h30. The standard tours take approximately one hour, but they can be extended on request. From the entrance to the caves, a path leads to the right to the Dinosaur Park. Among the stones used for lining and paving the paths are some that show fossilized ripple marks and mud cracks. The Dinosaur Park, also known as the Owen Museum, is open during the same hours as the caves. (There are entrance fees for both.)

Sudwala to Montrose Falls
Retrace your route to the tarred road and turn left, noting your kms. After 8,5 km you reach a T-junction with the N4. Turn right onto the N4, noting your kms. After 4,5 km you cross

SUDWALA CAVES
Unmeasured expanses of tunnel and cavern lie undiscovered beneath the bush-clad hill known as *Mankalakele* (crag upon crag). Man lived close to the cave entrance in prehistoric times, but the depths preserve a record of life that dates back over 2 000 million years – in the form of fossilized colonies (known as stromatolites) of the algae Collenia, a primitive single-celled plant.

The dolomite rock in which the caves have formed was laid down by water at the time when the *Collenia* were living. Water flowing into cracks in the dolomite eroded weak regions in the rock, creating a cave system decorated with stalagmites and stalactites, the largest formation of which is the 14 m Rocket Silo.

Early last century, a Swazi king sheltered here from pursuing Zulu impis, who attempted to smoke him out by building a huge fire at the entrance. The caves are named after a Swazi officer who took refuge here after a bloody battle in the valley. Many tales of lost treasure surround the caves, including the legend of the 'Kruger millions'.

Rock formations in the Sudwala Caves.

Tyrannosaurus rex at Sudwala.

LYDENBURG – TOWN OF SUFFERING
This town on the eastern escarpment of the Drakensberg was founded in 1849 by the survivors of the fever-smitten settlement of Ohrigstad, some 50 km to the northeast. In memory of their hardships they named their new town *Lydenburg* (town of suffering). In 1857 it was made the capital of the short-lived Republic of Lydenburg.

The Voortrekker School in Church Street, built in 1851, is the oldest building in the town. The old powder magazine in Viljoen Street was constructed in part from stones taken from nearby Fort Mary, which endured an 84-day siege during the Anglo-Transvaal War of 1880 – 81. History more mysterious and remote is displayed in the Lydenburg Museum, with pride of place going to the Iron Age relics. The museum is situated in the Gustav Klingbiel Nature Reserve 1 km out of town on the road to the Long Tom Pass.

Looking out over the forests of the Long Tom Pass and the Sabie valley.

the Crocodile River. Turn left at the crossroads immediately afterwards, where the road on the right (R539) leads to Bambi.

Pass the hotel, the parking area for shoppers and the petrol station. A visitors' parking area is indicated about 400 m from the N4 – park here to view the Montrose Falls. A path with cement steps leads down to several viewsites from which the two main falls can be seen tumbling into the gorge (entrance fee). It is worth walking further down for a closer view.

Return to the N4, note your kms, and proceed straight across onto the R539 for Bambi. The road climbs for some 3 km, then descends amid forested hills and rocky cliffs. After about 17 km you may see a sparkling waterfall to your right, if there have been good rains recently. The road follows Schoemanskloof and the scenic *Skaapwagters* (shepherds') Pass. After some 46 km turn right onto the R36 for Lydenburg, noting your kms.

After 2,7 km you reach the start of the *Chomse se Hoogte* (Chomse's Heights) Pass. Soon after this the road rounds a right-hand bend to reveal a fine vista of valleys and mountains. At 10 km you pass a road on your right leading to the Kwena Dam, and 2 km later you cross the Crocodile River; for the next few kilometres you have the dam on your right. After 47 km you pass the R540 on your left, cross the *Doringbergspruit* (thorn mountain stream), and enter Lydenburg on Viljoen Street. At the caravan park in Viljoen Street there are braai facilities, toilets and drinking water. Several places in town offer accommodation.

Over the Long Tom Pass

Turn right from Viljoen Street into Voortrekker Street, following the signs for 'R37 Sabie/Nelspruit'. Note your kms as you pass beneath the railway bridge on the outskirts of the town. The road climbs towards the summit of the Long Tom Pass, offering good views on both sides over deep, rugged gorges. Eventually you round Mauchsberg and begin the grand descent of the Long Tom Pass (see pages 46 – 7). Just under 23 km after leaving Lydenburg, you reach a fine viewsite on your left.

After 33 km you pass, on your right, the Long Tom Memorial with its full-scale replica of one of the Boer Creusot siege guns. A few hundred metres beyond the memorial there is a viewsite to your left, from which you can look down onto the road as it loops its way smoothly towards Sabie. After 45 km, keep straight on the R532 where the R37, on your right, leads to Nelspruit. About 8 km beyond this you enter Sabie (see pages 40 – 1).

At the T-junction in the middle of Sabie, turn right (onto the R537) and note your kms. (On your right is the stone church of St Peter, designed by Sir Herbert Baker in 1912.) Some 500 m later, go right to stay on the R537 for White River. After 9,5 km you will see on your right the forested hill known as *Spitskop* (pointed hill) – it was here that the first payable alluvial gold deposits in the Transvaal were discovered in 1871. After about 16 km there are superb views over a sea of forested hills; 44 km from Sabie you reach a T-junction with the R40; turn right here for Nelspruit.

AA Agency Shop 1B2, 43 Brown Street Nelspruit 1200 Tel (01311) 22132
Nelspruit Tourist Information 5 Promenade Centre, Nelspruit 1200 Tel (01311) 55 1988
Lydenburg Museum Voortrekker Street Lydenburg 1120 Tel (01323) 2121
Sabie Forestry Museum PO Box 61, Sabie 1260 Tel (01315) 41243
Sudwala Caves PO Box 48, Schagen 1207 Tel (01311) 64152

The Crocodile River tumbles over the impressive Montrose Falls.

KARL MAUCH AND MAUCHSBERG
Karl Mauch was a German geologist and geographer who arrived in KwaZulu-Natal in 1865. During his travels in southern Africa he discovered gold at three locations – on the Witwatersrand, near Lydenburg and in what is now Zimbabwe. He recorded cartographically the region stretching south as far as Kimberley, north to the Soutpansberg, west to Marico and east as far as Delagoa Bay. He also drew the first accurate geological map of the old Transvaal. Back in Germany, his work was admired, but he could not find a suitable museum post and he lived in poverty. He died after falling out of a window in Blaubeuren in 1875. Mauchsberg, the grass-topped peak near Lydenburg, was named after him.

The attractive Cascades at Nelspruit.

NELSPRUIT
Unlike many lowveld towns, which came into being with a flourish after the discovery of gold, Nelspruit began modestly as a railway station on the Pretoria – Delagoa Bay line, constructed in 1892. The town was named after the stream at which the three Nel brothers used to water their flocks and herds during the winter months.

Today Nelspruit, capital of Mpumalanga, is the centre of a vast citrus-growing region and is the rapidly growing commercial heart of the lowveld. Its attractions include an art gallery (housing some 70 works by South African artists), the Town Hall with its unusual sundial, and the Lowveld Botanic Garden, which preserves more than 500 species indigenous to the Crocodile River valley. The Nelspruit Cascades, also known as the Crocodile Falls, are situated alongside the garden.

• THE STORY OF LONG TOM PASS •

Man-made forests cover the Drakensberg foothills along the Long Tom Pass.

A fighting retreat over the high road to the sea

THE SPECTACULAR tarred road that winds its way over the Drakensberg from Lydenburg in Mpumalanga, follows a route rich in history.

In the 1840s, the Voortrekkers had set up a republic north of the Vaal with Potchefstroom as its emerging capital. But when the British government extended its authority northwards to include Potchefstroom, many of the Voortrekkers, under the leadership of Andries Potgieter, moved away and established a new, rustic capital in a fertile valley just west of the Drakensberg – naming the new settlement Andries-Ohrigstad. Unfortunately this proved a tragic choice. Within a year, the damage caused by floods and the death-rate from malaria were so severe that the site had to be abandoned. So the capital moved to Lydenburg.

All the while, the Voortrekkers had been interested in establishing a route to the east coast – a route that would give them an outlet to a port that was not under the control of the British. Now that the effective centre of the young republic was established on the eastern edge of the highveld, with the Indian Ocean just 210 km away, the advantages of such a route became indisputable – and the obvious point to aim for was Maputo (then Lourenço Marques) on the shores of Delagoa Bay.

Several earlier expeditions had reached Lourenço Marques, but the terrain that had to be crossed was very difficult. The main obstacle was the Drakensberg, running north and south and reaching a height of over 2 000 m.

Replica of the original Long Tom.

It was President Thomas Burgers, a much-maligned man of good intent, who took the decisive steps. He recognized that an easy and reliable route to Lourenço Marques could prove extremely valuable to the young republic, and he managed to wring the equivalent of R3 000 from his *Volksraad* (parliament) to finance its construction.

With this modest sum in hand, work was begun. The contractor was Abraham Espag, and most of the road-building was done with pick and shovel – with occasional help from charges of gunpowder. In mid-1874, the first wagons to use the new road arrived in Lydenburg from Delagoa Bay, but the trip had proved so arduous that the drivers were grateful just to have survived. A report in 1877 mentioned 'the most dreaded part of the road, the Devil's Knuckles... when on top of one of these points the wagon looked as if stuck on the point of a sugar-loaf, and that any attempt to descend must result in a headlong roll down many hundred feet'.

The arrival of the Long Toms

During those early days, this hair-raising roadway over the Drakensberg was known as *Die*

The present road over the Long Tom Pass was opened in 1953.

Ruins at the Devil's Knuckles.

The highest pass in the old Transvaal.

Hawepad (the harbour road). It was only after this route to the sea had played a dramatic part in the Anglo-Boer War that the pass took on a new significance – and acquired a new name.

With war clouds gathering, the two Boer republics of Transvaal and Orange Free State decided in 1896 to update their armaments, and this included the purchase of four 155 mm guns from the firm of Schneider et Cie of Le Creusot in France.

The Boers at first nicknamed the new guns *die Fransmanne* (the Frenchmen), but the British at the siege of Ladysmith called the gun that fired on them 'Long Tom', and this was the name that stuck. Even the Boers eventually adopted the name, despite President Kruger's disapproval.

At the start of the war, the Long Toms outranged any gun the British Army had in South Africa. Large calibre (4,7 inch) guns were dismounted from British warships and fitted to improvised carriages, and a single, massive 9,2 inch (234 mm) harbour defence gun was removed from the fortifications at Cape Town and sent north mounted on a railway carriage. It reached Belfast, but was too late to participate in the battle of Bergendal on 27 August 1900. It was at this battle that all four Long Toms were brought together for the only time, although it is not certain that all were used in the action.

After the battle, the Boer forces split up, and General Louis Botha accompanied the larger group northward to Lydenburg. With them, they took two of their prized Long Toms.

The Boers had proclaimed long before, that their last stand would be made at Lydenburg, so it was a nervous British advance guard that entered the town – and found to their great relief that the Boers had gone. But as the Union Jack was being hoisted, Boer gunners up on Mauchsberg opened up with both Long Toms, dropping shells with lethal effect among the men, animals and vehicles of the British transport column.

The British 4,7 inch guns were soon brought into action, but were unable to locate or silence the deadly Long Toms. And so, on 8 September, infantry advanced under cover of artillery and machine-gun fire. The day ended inconclusively as a thick mist swept over the mountain, and the Boer gunners withdrew to a new position. Casualties for the day's engagement were 19 men of the Gordon Highlanders – all of them victims of the deadly Long Tom.

The Long Tom Pass was tarred in 1964, making the old pass an easy run.

A 'magnificent coup' by the Boers
The British advance resumed the next day, and from the summit of Mauchsberg the Boer wagon train could be seen crossing the Devil's Knuckles. On 10 September, cavalry – Strathcona's Horse and the South African Light Horse – galloped forward, sure that they were about to capture the prized guns. An eyewitness reported:

'When the cavalry were half a mile behind the rear gun, and we regarded its capture as certain, the leading Long Tom deliberately turned and opened fire with case shot (a type of shrapnel) at the pursuers streaming down the hill in single file, over the head of his brother gun. It was a magnificent coup, and perfectly successful. The cavalry had to retire, leaving a few men wounded, and by the time our heavy guns had arrived, both Long Toms had got away.'

The site from which this Long Tom fought off imminent capture is marked today by the memorial. The rearmost gun continued down the slope past its comrade and, at the position signposted as the 'last covering position' of the Long Tom, it was unlimbered in turn and prepared for firing to cover the removal of the gun that had just been in action.

Naming the road over the pass
The present road over the pass, following the old harbour road in places, was officially opened on 22 July 1953. Some of the suggested names were Skyline Road, Trichardtpad, *Oukoetspad* (old coach road) and Long Tom Pass – the last being the name formally given to the road at its opening. The road was tarred in 1964.

Little remains of the original road over the pass, but stretches of it are signposted in several places. Here and there wheel ruts can be seen, ground into the rock by locked wheels as wagons were slid down the terrifying slopes, and travellers who take this high road over the mountains from Lydenburg will pass many other reminders of the old days:

Whiskyspruit (whisky stream) commemorates a theory that the water in the local stream, when mixed with even inferior whisky, produces an excellent drink.

Die Geut (the gutter), also known as 'The Staircase', was a particularly steep section of the old road.

Blyfstaanhoogte (stay-standing height) was the name given to another very difficult stretch where one had to proceed so slowly that one seemed to be standing still.

Old Trading Post – there was a trading post here in the mid-19th century, a site now occupied by a modern motel.

The Devil's Knuckles, a series of hillocks midway along the downhill stretch, were considered the most alarming part of the journey. It is not known precisely how or when they received their name.

Brooklands State Forest was once a farm named *Onverwacht* (unexpected), the starting point for afforestation in the area. At the time of the battle, the farm was occupied by the Shires family, and Florence Shires recorded on 8 September 1900 that 'we have heard cannon since daylight'.

Koffiehoogte (coffee height), some distance south of the present road, was probably where the old transport-riders rested their animals and enjoyed a coffee-break after the first really steep section on the way up the pass.

Olifantsgeraamte was once the name of a local farm on which the skeleton (*geraamte*) of a long-dead elephant was found.

Majestic mountain frontiers that echo the lively past

A series of dramatic passes links the historic towns of Lydenburg, Pilgrim's Rest and Burgersfort. Passing through wide, fertile valleys, our quiet country roads climb to breathtaking heights of ancient mountains, then wend their way down again. These winding gateways tell of a tumultuous history. A short part of the drive is on gravel.

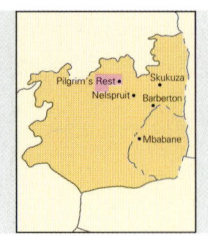

Lydenburg
Verraaiersnek
Robber's Pass
Kaspersnek
Burgersfort
Watervals River Pass
210 – 220 km

At THE HEART OF Lydenburg, on the corner of Church and Kantoor streets, is the Voortrekker School, the oldest existing school building north of the Vaal, dating back to the 1850s. It was restored in 1973 and is a national monument. Across the road is the Voortrekker Church, consecrated in 1894. Travel two blocks north-east along Church Street to see the powder magazine, a relic of the Anglo-Transvaal War of 1880 – 1.

From Church Street, turn right into Viljoen Street and then left into Voortrekker Street, following the signs for the Kruger National Park and Sabie. As the road ascends towards Long Tom Pass, turn left at the clearly marked entrance to the Lydenburg Museum and Gustav Klingbiel Nature Reserve.

After visiting the museum, turn right into Voortrekker Street and, eight blocks later, turn right into De Clerq Street, which becomes the R36. Note your kms as you cross the Klipgat River bridge on the outskirts of town.

Lydenburg to Pilgrim's Rest

After 8 km, turn left onto the gravel road signposted 'Lydenburg Waterfall' and follow this road for 5 km to the dramatic 62 m falls on the Dorps River. Retrace your route to the tarred road and turn left, back onto the R36, noting your kms. After 2 km, you'll see the pair of giant elephant tusks marking the entrance to 'Lunar's Landing' (also signposted 'Jock of the Bushveld'), a locally sculpted world of lifelike concrete animals, with a picnic area.

As you cross the Schalk Burger Bridge over the Spekboom River, note the older bridge next to it, now a national monument, which can be reached from a gravel road ahead.

The magnificently tree-lined road then crosses the Kranskloof River and descends into the winding Verraaiersnek Pass. After 20 km, turn right onto the R533 for Pilgrim's Rest and note your kms. The road passes through a lush and fertile river valley before ascending the magnificent Robber's Pass. There are several clearly marked picnic spots along the way, affording refreshing breaks and panoramic mountain views.

After 18 km you reach the top of Robber's Pass at 1 778 m above sea level. After a further 4,2 km, there is a slip road to your left signposted 'Viewpoint', where a picnic spot looks out onto the dramatic gorges and cliffs of this Drakensberg crest. Descend Robber's Pass with great care – extremely sharp hairpin bends abound and the road is slippery when wet. After roughly 26 km, turn right at the T-junction for Pilgrim's Rest, following the signs to the Old Town where, before enjoying a lunch break, you should buy a ticket for your tour of Alanglade from the well-signposted Information Centre in the main street.

Pilgrim's Rest to Burgersfort

To reach Alanglade from Pilgrim's Rest village, retrace your route to the foot of Robber's Pass, which you now pass as a road on your left. A few hundred metres later, just before the tarred surface changes to gravel, turn left at the small signpost into Alanglade.

On leaving Alanglade, turn sharp left for Kaspersnek Pass. Note your kms as the road becomes gravel and, after 1,7 km, cross the Blyde River Bridge, the first of many single-lane bridges straddling the sparkling, lively rivers that punctuate this pass.

To the right there are wide views of rolling hills, farmlands and abundantly forested areas of the Blyde River Conservancy.

After 18 km, pass a cluster of farmsteads and outbuildings and, 1 km later, turn left for

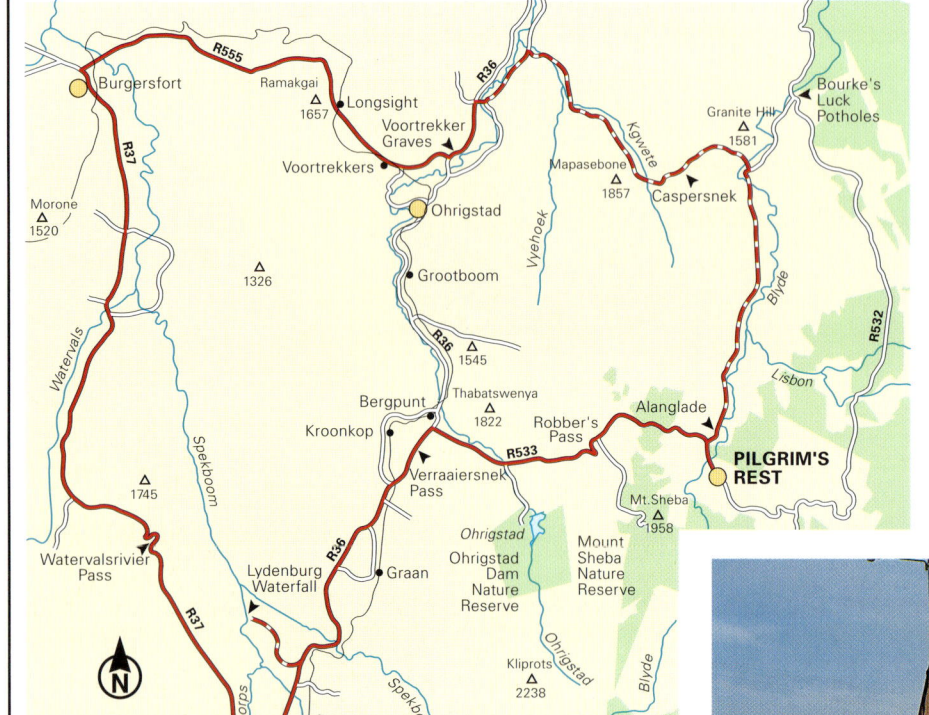

LUNAR'S LANDING

Overlooking the fertile valley of the Spekboom River, some 10 km from Lydenburg, stands an unusual tribute to the animals of the area – Lunar's Landing. This is a lifelike world of concrete creatures. Against a backdrop of rolling hills and distant mountains, this unexpected, silent zoo has beckoned many passing travellers to stop and take a quick holiday snap. Two huge, concrete elephant tusks dominate the entrance, and, across the road, a larger-than-life apeman peers furtively out through the vegetation. Sculpted by locals, the four-legged collection includes giraffe, sable, hyaena, aardvark, lion, monkeys and a lifesize family of elephants. A short climb up a tree-branch ladder leads curious visitors to a sculpted San cave, containing San images and a stone cobra. There is also a picnic site at Lunar's Landing – complete with a notice urging visitors not to feed the animals.

Part of the concrete menagerie near Lydenburg.

Ohrigstad. (The road you've turned off leads to Bourke's Luck.) This tree-lined Ohrigstad road curves its way through mountain foothills for a little more than 10 km to the summit of Kaspersnek and then begins its steep, rather stony descent.

Around 49 km, bear right at a Y-junction for Rietfontein. Soon after this, the road surface changes to tar just before a T-junction with the R36, at which you turn left for Ohrigstad and, 4 km later, turn right onto the R555 for Burgersfort. Note your kms at this turn.

After 1,5 km, there is a parking area on your left at the historic Voortrekker graves. As the road ascends, there are spectacular mountain views in every direction until, at about 33 km, you reach a T-junction with the R37. Turn left, in the direction of Burgersfort, noting your kms. After 2 km you pass the town, dominated by the spire of the Dutch Reformed church high up on the hillside.

After 17 km the R37 crosses the Watervals River and, after 31 km, becomes the scenic Watervals River Pass. This dramatic 15 km approach to Lydenburg affords breathtaking views of the high, outlying spurs of the northern Drakensberg and of distant Mount Anderson. From the end of the pass, drive for a further 12 km to the T-junction with the R36. Turn right to return to Lydenburg.

Lydenburg Museum Sentinel Street, Lydenburg 1120 Tel (01323) 2121
Pilgrim's Rest Information Office Main Street Pilgrim's Rest 1290 Tel (01315) 81211
AA Office Shop 1B2, 43 Brown Street, Nelspruit 1200 Tel (01311) 22132

The Lydenburg Falls on the Dorps River.

HIGHWAY ROBBERY

Twice a week, the coaches of the Zeederberg company transported gold from Pilgrim's Rest to Lydenburg, over what is now known as Robber's Pass. Despite the great quantity of gold carried in some 30 years, only two robberies ever occurred. The first took place in 1899, when two masked and mounted gunmen held up the coach and made off with bullion worth 10 000 pounds sterling. The second robbery, though less successful, was a lot more memorable. Tommy Dennison, the village barber of Pilgrim's Rest, held up the coach on its way *to* the mines. All he got was 129 pounds in half-crown (25-cent) coins. After the robbery he went straight back to Pilgrim's Rest, settled his debts and embarked on a modest spending spree. The coach drivers had recognized him, however, and he was promptly arrested. After five years in Pretoria Central Prison, he returned to Pilgrim's Rest and opened a business that he cheerfully called The Highwayman's Garage.

ALANGLADE DAYS

On the outskirts of Pilgrim's Rest stands the gracious old estate of Alanglade. Former home of Dick Barry, general manager of Transvaal Gold Mining Estates until 1930, Alanglade is now a museum. This great house of gleaming white grandeur was completed in 1916, and the interiors, decor and furniture are preserved almost exactly as they were when the Barry family lived here. Today's visitors find themselves transported to an era grander and gentler than our own. Wandering from the elegant drawing room to the now archaic smoking room, it's easy to imagine the mine manager's lifestyle.

Resplendent with Art Deco fittings and accessories, finely crafted furniture and utensils, Alanglade still feels like a home rather than a museum. Guided tours, lasting about an hour, begin at 10h30 and 14h00 from Mondays to Saturdays. Obtain your ticket at the tourist information office in the village.

The Spekboom River flows north to join the Steelpoort River.

Above: *The tranquil Blyde River.* **Below:** *The Robber's Pass.*

LYDENBURG'S WATERFALL

Some 8 km outside Lydenburg, a single-lane gravel road winds its way to a natural attraction of panoramic proportions – the Lydenburg Waterfall. From the edge of a cliff, visitors have a breathtaking view of the Dorps River as it plunges a dramatic 62 m into the pools below. The steady roar of water fills the air, punctuated by bird calls and the occasional bark of a baboon, ringing out from hideaways in the craggy cliffs. For the adventurous visitor there is a steep and precarious path down to the water's edge, passing majestic aloes, coral trees and mountainous scrub. This spectacular waterfall was used to supply the nearby town with about 40 per cent of its electricity, generated by an on-site hydro-electric scheme. A funicular cableway that used to ferry workers up and down the gorge, although long disused, may still be seen.

To a Valley of Gold through the Crocodile River gorge

East of Nelspruit the Crocodile River winds through a rugged gorge. We follow the river's course, then head south into De Kaap Valley – the 19th century's Valley of Gold, still a place of incomparable scenic beauty. Less than 50 km of the route is untarred. Before starting, check with the Barberton Information Bureau that the Nelshoogte Forest section is open.

Nelspruit
Krokodilpoort
De Kaap Valley
Saddleback Pass
Barberton
The Cascades
Hilltop Pass
220 – 240 km

The boulder-strewn Crocodile River gorge.

DRIVE EAST FROM Nelspruit on Louis Trichardt Street, which becomes the N4 towards Komatipoort. Note your kms as you pass Valencia Road on your left, near the outskirts of the town. For some 8 km the N4 is lined with palms planted in the 1920s, and orange groves extend on both sides of the road. After 20 km the road crosses Gould's Salvation Spruit, named after the Resurrection Hotel that Edward Gould ran on its banks in the early gold-prospecting days. Cross the Crocodile River 200 m beyond this to enter *Krokodilpoort* (Crocodile Gorge).

After 26 km, you pass a rock on the right bearing a plaque commemorating the construction of the road and its re-opening in 1967. Pass a parking area at 27 km and stop at the next one, just after 28 km. This site is marked by a jacaranda tree and a large rock close to the road. From here there are good views down to the river. After 35 km the road crosses the Crocodile River again and you enter more open country. At 37 km, opposite the Kaapmuiden railway junction, turn right onto the R38 for Barberton. Note your kms.

After 8,3 km, you cross Revolver Creek (see pages 52–3) and at 19 km you pass Honeybird Creek. The countryside becomes more mountainous, with successive ridges visible ahead. After 27 km you reach a tarred road on your left that leads to 'Sheba'. Turn here if you wish to visit the old Sheba cemetery that lies some 3,4 km along this road. Park 50 m past the cemetery on the left.

If you have obtained prior permission to explore the remains of Eureka City, continue past the old cemetery and turn right after 1 km at the T-junction. The road reaches Sheba Mine 3 km later. Ask here for directions and information on the private road (see pages 52 – 3).

Return to the tarred R38 and turn left, noting your kms. Pass Noordkaap railway station on your right after 10 km and, 3,6 km later, just after a right-hand bend, note the old thorn tree behind a fence on your left. This is known as Jock's Tree, after the famous canine hero of *Jock of the Bushveld*, and a plaque here commemorates the trek made in 1885 by Jock and his master, Sir Percy Fitzpatrick.

Into nostalgic Barberton

After a further 7 km you enter the outskirts of Barberton on Sheba Road. Turn left at the crossroads onto the R40 for Bulembu. Follow this good tarred road as it climbs to the top of the impressively scenic Saddleback Pass.

Retrace your route down the pass to the junction with the R38 and turn left to enter Barberton on Sheba Road, which eventually swings right and becomes Crown Street. Stop at the Publicity Bureau in the Market Square to obtain a map of the town, showing places of interest. A visit to Belhaven – a late-Victorian gentleman's residence – gives an insight into a life of prosperity that eluded most diggers.

Prospectors' graves in the old Sheba cemetery.

The view over De Kaap Valley from the Saddleback Pass. Many men were lured here by the promise of gold.

VALLEY OF DEATH

The valley called *De Kaap* – the Cape – after the imposing spur of the Drakensberg that dominates it, was originally known to early transport riders as the Valley of Death. This came about because of the diseases of malaria and sleeping sickness that claimed many lives before the causes were isolated and brought under control. Further misery was caused after Bray's discovery of gold in Sheba Reef, when fraudulent companies sold shares in barren mines in the valley, and many men were ruined financially.

However, the 'Valley of Death' has provided some compensation for its hazards by giving garden-lovers throughout the world the handsome Barberton daisy (*Gerbera jamesonii*) and the colourful Pride of De Kaap (*Bauhinia galpinii*).

Barberton to Nelspruit

Before leaving Barberton, check with the Information Bureau about the condition of the road through Nelshoogte Forest. If the road is closed, return to Nelspruit by leaving Barberton on General Street, which becomes the R40. For Nelshoogte Forest, leave Barberton by driving along Crown Street, passing beneath the Havelock Mine's aerial cableway and turning second right into Kruger Street. Note your kms at the turn. The road changes to good gravel after several kilometres and leads through forests and plantations of tobacco and citrus. Where the road forks at 11 km, bear right. At about 15 km, in an area of indigenous bush and trees, stop in the parking area on your right and walk through the gateway to reach the scenic Tegwaans Pools on the Queen's River. (There are no facilities and all contact with the water should be avoided because of the risk of bilharzia.)

Note your kms as you leave the parking site opposite the pools, and continue on the main gravel road, which climbs alongside the impressive river gorge. After 3,5 km you cross a narrow causeway and the road passes through tangled, bushy hills. After 7 km the road enters Nelshoogte Forest and you reach a sawmill on your right. If you have made prior arrangements, either through the Barberton Information Bureau or with the sawmill manager at tel (01314) 25724, you will be allowed to proceed; 300 m later, just beyond the sawmill, go right at the fork and cross another causeway after a further 300 m.

After 11,5 km you cross another narrow causeway and enter a dense pine plantation. Stop about 1,3 km beyond the causeway, just before reaching a fork in an uphill section of the road. Below you, on your left, a fine waterfall – known as 'The Cascades' – tumbles into a rocky gorge.

When you drive on from the waterfall, go right at the fork. The road climbs until, after passing a shop on your right, you reach a T-junction, where the road surface changes

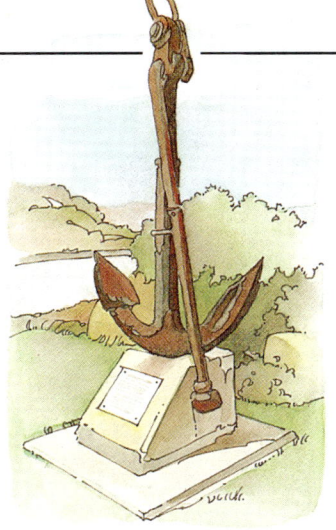

Anchor of the Dorothea, *wrecked at Cape Vidal in 1898 – now in Nelspruit.*

BAPTIZING BARBERTON

After Graham Barber discovered gold in Rimer's Creek in 1884, there was the inevitable rush of fortune-seekers to this corner of De Kaap Valley. The Mining Commissioner, David Wilson, named the new settlement Barberton, and 'christened' it by breaking a bottle of gin on a rock – no bottle of champagne being available at the time. Within a year the town had shot up with amazing speed. In 1885, with the discovery of the Sheba Reef by Yorkshireman Edwin Bray, the nearby town of Eureka City was founded. Two stock exchanges were established in Barberton, and today the facade of the Kaap Gold Fields Stock Exchange Limited still stands in Pilgrim Street, next to the library and museum. Nearby is the former Globe Bar, a typical corrugated iron building of the goldrush era. Contrasts in styles may be seen in the small blockhouse at the end of Judge Street, Belhaven in Lee Street and Stopforth House museum in Bowness Street.

Nature's palette – graceful jacarandas enhance historic Barberton.

Orange groves flourish in Nelspruit's rich soil.

Jock of the Bushveld – the famous canine hero.

JOCK AND HIS MASTER

Outside the Town Hall of Barberton stands the statue of a dog. This is Jock, famed in literature as Jock of the Bushveld. As the runt of the litter and known as 'the rat', the pup was given to a young transport rider, Percy Fitzpatrick. Fitzpatrick, who was born in King William's Town, travelled to the eastern Transvaal as a young man in 1884 and worked at many jobs, including a spell as an editor of Barberton's *Gold Field News*. He later moved to the Witwatersrand, where he was active in the fields of goldmining and public affairs, and he was knighted in 1902. He then moved to the Sundays River Valley and developed citrus farming there. His classic tale of his adventures with Jock during the early days of the Transvaal gold discoveries, has been reprinted many times since it first appeared in 1907.

to tar. Turn left here, and left again after 100 m, and follow this road for 5 km to reach a T-junction with the tarred R38. Turn right onto the R38 and note your kms. The road winds downhill, unveiling grand views over De Kaap Valley. After 26 km, turn left at the T-junction with the R40 which, after crossing the scenic Hilltop Pass, descends gently into Nelspruit some 36 km from the T-junction.

AA Agency Shop 1B2, 43 Brown Street
Nelspruit 1200 Tel (01311) 22132
SA Tourism Board Tarentaal Trading Post
cr N4 and Kaapse Hoop Road, Nelspruit 1200
Tel (01311) 44405/6
Barberton Information Bureau Market Square
Barberton 1300 Tel (01314) 22121
Nelspruit Publicity Association Promenade
Centre, Nelspruit 1200 Tel (01311) 55 1988/9

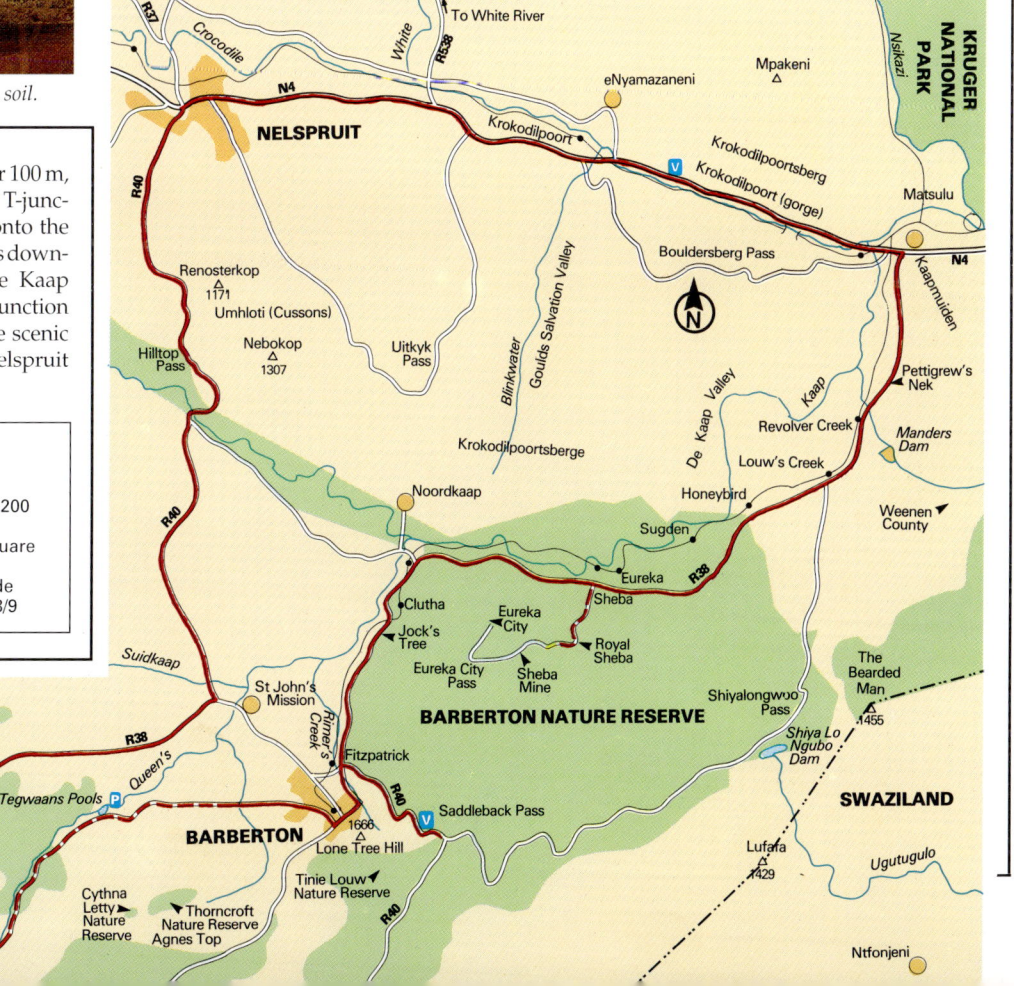

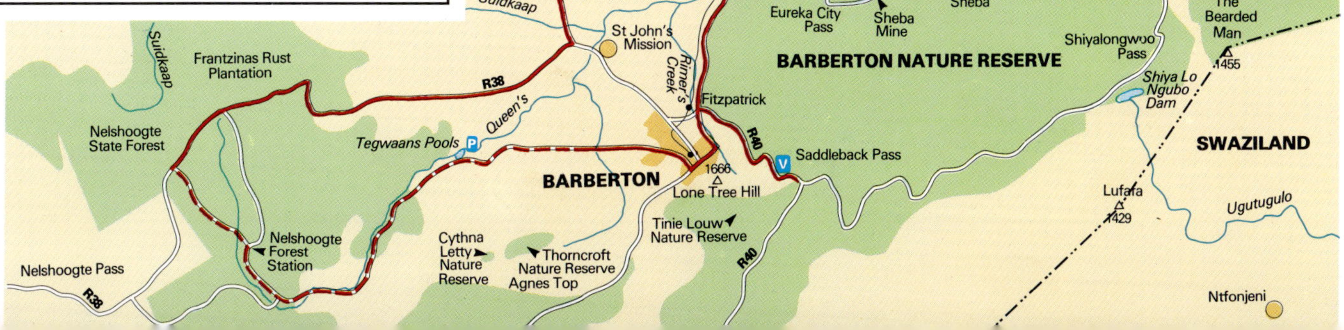

• BARBERTON AND DE KAAP VALLEY •

The dignified facade of the Gold Stock Exchange in Barberton. Established in 1886, this was one of the first stock exchanges to operate in South Africa.

A wealth of gold in the fabled De Kaap Valley

SOME OF THE ROCKS of the mineral-rich De Kaap Valley are among the oldest in the world – the granites having been dated at approximately 4 500 million years. Scattered throughout the strata and rock systems are deposits not only of reef and alluvial gold but also of iron, talc, asbestos and nickel. Early prospectors in the valley searched for gold in its alluvial form – gold that is washed from a reef, carried downstream by rivers and deposited along riverbeds and banks as rare, solid nuggets or as gold dust.

Their basic tools were a shovel and a prospector's pan, the inside of which had been blackened with smoke in order to make the minute specks of gold more visible. The hopeful prospector scooped a shovel of gravel into his pan, added water, and carefully removed the larger stones by hand. He then swirled the water around gently, washing the small particles of gravel over the side of the pan. The gold, having a much greater mass, sank to the bottom, to be revealed as a glistening 'tail' when the water was tipped out.

In 1874 Tom McLachlan, who had found the first gold on Spitskop near Sabie, was the first modern prospector to discover gold in De Kaap Valley – but he decided that the deposits were not payable and moved on. Charles Anderson, known as Charlie the Reefer, was among the next prospectors on the scene, and he found workable gold deposits on the farm Berlyn.

Other reefs were found and the inevitable 'rush' took place. A tent-town arose almost overnight on the edge of the valley, on a plateau named *Duiwelskantoor* (Devil's Office) because of the enormous granite boulders and gloomy shadows that dominated it. The town, however, was christened *Kaapsehoop* (hope of the Cape), and it quickly became a magnet for hopeful prospectors.

In 1883, the Transvaal republican government sold the farm Berlyn to private owners, who then began to charge exorbitant

A 20-kilometre aerial cableway links Barberton with the Havelock Mine.

A prospector in search of a 'tail' of gold.

fees for the right to work on their property. Disgruntled, many diggers left and fanned out across the valley. Auguste Robert, known as French Bob, was the leader of a party that found a good deposit along the Noordkaap River. News of the find leaked out and another rush took place, leading to the establishment of yet another mining camp, named Jamestown after Ingram James, who had originally made the discovery.

George Pigot Moodie, who was the Transvaal Surveyor General, owned several farms in De Kaap Valley, and it was on one of these that French Bob found the Pioneer Reef – the richest gold ore yet. News of the find spread, not only in South Africa but throughout the world. Dazzled by the prospect of wealth, Moodie resigned his government post and raised the capital to establish the Moodie Gold Mining and Exploration Company. The company began to demand high fees from the diggers and, as before, many of them moved off to prospect on cheaper government-owned land.

Barmaids of Barberton

In 1884 a group of prospectors, including Graham Barber from Natal and his cousins Fred and Harry, detected gold in a white quartz reef along the wall of a narrow gully in the valley. Crushed and washed, this proved the richest find to date. As obliged by law, Barber reported his find to the gold commissioner at nearby Kaapsehoop, and the news was out. The commissioner named the site Barberton and christened it by breaking a bottle of gin on the rock – as no champagne was available.

The town mushroomed as prospectors arrived from all over the world to seek their fortunes. These tough characters cursed and gambled and brawled, and Barberton became the scene of much violent crime. Even murder was a relatively common occurrence. Revolver Creek recalls the still-unsolved murder of a lone prospector on the banks of a previously unnamed stream.

It is said that by 1885 the town had one bar or canteen for every 15 residents – most of whom spent their spare time drinking, fighting and carousing. To keep their customers from moving on, the bar owners brought in barmaids. One of these, known as Cockney Liz, achieved notoriety by parading every evening on a billiard table, snapping her garters at the noisy band of drinkers, and auctioning herself to the highest bidder.

Prospecting in the valley was haphazard, but it is estimated that payable gold was found on more than 4 000 claims. Many reefs were discovered by chance. Honeybird Creek was named by a digger who, following a honeybird, was led to a snake. In killing the snake, he exposed a gold reef.

Sheba Reef and Eureka City

The richest find of all was discovered in May 1885 by Edwin Bray, while following his daily route along a narrow trail between tall walls of rock. He knocked his shin on a projecting spur of rock and swung at it angrily with his hammer. In so doing he uncovered the famous Sheba Reef, in what came to be called Bray's Golden Quarry. Sheba Mine today is the world's richest working gold mine.

A former prospector named Sherwood opened a hotel on Sheba Hill overlooking the mine. This was the start of Eureka City, which expanded within a year to include two more hotels, several canteens, a music hall and even a race course. As a mining town, Eureka City was even more violent than Barberton. In 1887 a gang known as the Irish Brigade rampaged through town, wrecking hotels and beating up bystanders. It took the local police and reinforcements from Barberton more than a week to restore order.

In 1899, with the outbreak of the Anglo-Boer War, the mines closed and the people of Eureka City moved to Barberton. Some returned after the war, but the town never flourished again. The buildings were removed and only a few decayed walls now remain.

De Kaap gold mines were so productive that President Paul Kruger came on a special tour of inspection and addressed a crowd of diggers at Barberton. But only six months after his visit the boom collapsed. A number of mines were very profitable, but immense sums of money had been invested in schemes that were never likely to pay dividends. Overnight, Barberton became a shadow of its former brawling, noisy self as many of the prospectors moved on to the Witwatersrand to try their luck all over again. A few years later, a disastrous fire razed much of Barberton to the ground, but the town re-established itself and today is one of the major attractions of Mpumalanga.

Sheba Mine – richest in the world.

From all over the world they came, fortune hunters in pursuit of a dream.

A side verandah of Belhaven House.

Pride of De Kaap (Bauhinia galpinii).

Cockney Liz, a reigning beauty.

The magic of the old mining town – jacarandas in bloom and a cool stoep.

A remote highland world of granite peaks and silent forests

Our route climbs north from Mbabane, to the village of Piggs Peak and the wild mountain scenery of the north-west. We then descend Saddleback Pass to visit Barberton, before returning to Mbabane via the Oshoek/Ngwenya border post. You will need a valid passport. In Barberton, check at the Information Bureau that the Nelshoogte forest road will be open.

Mbabane
Forbes Reef
Piggs Peak
Havelock Mine
Barberton
Cascades
Badplaas
220 – 240 km

A Barberton daisy in bloom.

LEAVE MBABANE BY driving north-west along Gilfillan Street towards the Oshoek/Ngwenya border post. Note your kms at the T-junction where Gilfillan Street joins the main road from Manzini, and turn right onto the main road. After 11 km turn right at the turn-off for Piggs Peak. This tarred road climbs through hills scattered with wattle plantations, outcrops of ancient granite, and small farms and dams.

After 22 km you pass a general dealer's store on your left. Shortly after this a road on the left leads to Forbes Reef, the remains of mine-workings started by Alex Forbes in 1884 and worked sporadically until 1965. (The mine is now inside the Malolotja Nature Reserve, to which an entrance fee is charged.)

Continuing along the tarred road towards Piggs Peak, you pass several roadside stalls selling wood and stone carvings. Note your kms as you pass, on your left, the road leading to the Malolotja Nature Reserve. Park on the shoulder of the road 5,7 km later for a view of the Ngwenya and Silotwane hills. The road now begins a winding descent into a green, forested valley. At around 18 km you reach another good viewsite on your left.

When you enter the village of Piggs Peak, set in the depths of pine and eucalyptus plantations (see opposite), follow the tree-lined main street until you reach the sign for Bulembu/Barberton. Turn left here, noting your kms as you turn. Relatively good in dry conditions, this untarred road can be treacherous in wet weather, and there are hairpin bends that require caution as logging trucks frequently use the route. Some 6,5 km after turning onto this road, stop at a cleared area on your left for a fine view over the forested Drakensberg escarpment.

Forests spread across the Drakensberg hills above the historic town of Barberton.

Piggs Peak to Queen's River

About 15 km from Piggs Peak, the road surface changes to tar again at the Havelock Asbestos Mine at *Bulembu* (place of the spider). When you first catch sight of the mining valley, park in the small area on your left for a view of the multi-coloured houses and headgear; 500 m beyond this point, look up to see the beginning of the 20 km cableway that carries securely bagged asbestos ore over the mountains to Barberton. After a further 2,8 km, around several sharp switchback corners, you reach the Bulembu/Josefsdal border post between Swaziland and Mpumalanga (open from 08h00 to 16h00; travel documents needed).

Note your kms as you leave the border post and follow the main gravel road (now the R40) as it begins its magnificent winding descent over Saddleback Pass into De Kaap Valley (see pages 50 – 1). About 3 km after the tar commences, stop on your left and cross the road for a splendid view across De Kaap Valley.

At the foot of Saddleback Pass you reach a junction with the R38; turn left here and enter Barberton on Sheba Road, which eventually swings right and becomes Crown Street. Stop at the Publicity Bureau in Market Square for a map showing local places of interest. There are several hotels and restaurants in the town that offer lunch and light refreshments.

To leave Barberton, drive along Crown Street (which passes under the cableway) and turn right into Kruger Street (second street after passing under the cableway), noting your kms as you turn. Pass the Barberton airport on your right and drive on past the Correctional Services farm and prison grounds, after which the surface changes to gravel. After about 11 km bear right where the road forks and, after 15 km, you reach a parking area on your right. Park here and walk through the gateway to the lovely Tegwaans Pools on the Queen's River. (Picnic area, but no facilities and the water is unsuitable for swimming or drinking.)

Continue along the main road, noting your kms. The road climbs through attractive scenery with the impressive Queen's River gorge on your right. After 1,2 km bear left at the fork and after 3,5 km cross another causeway. After approximately 7 km you enter the Nelshoogte State Forest. Pass the sawmill on your right here. If the boom here is closed, ask the sawmill manager for permission to proceed. Some 300 m later go right at the fork and, after a further 300 m, cross a narrow causeway. After 13 km you reach a fork in the road. Stop here and look below you to the left to see the impressive Cascades waterfall tumbling into its rocky gorge. Look up to the right and slightly behind you to see the hills known as the *Duiwelskneukels* (Devil's knuckles).

Queen's River to Mbabane

Bear left at the fork, noting your kms as you turn. After about 1,5 km you pass the Queen's River Forest Station. Continue for 10 km until you reach the T-junction with the tarred R38; turn left here for Badplaas, noting your kms as you turn.

After about 24km you pass the R541 for Machadodorp on your right and, after a further 5 km, you enter Badplaas on the R38. Follow the signs to the Aventura mineral springs resort resort on the right-hand side of the road. There are spacious lawns, bunga-

HAVELOCK MINE AND CABLEWAY

The 20 km cableway between the Havelock Mine in Swaziland and Barberton in Mpumalanga was opened in 1938 and, 60 years later, remains an impressive feat of engineering. No fewer than 52 pylons support the cables and carriers, conveying their cargo at a steady 11 km per hour. The suspended pans bring in asbestos (securely bagged and sealed) and return to Havelock loaded with coal and other goods, from groceries to mining equipment. The longest unsupported span of cable is 1 207 m and the greatest cable height is 189 m. The mine itself was started in 1923 and provides employment for hundreds of people, who are housed nearby in an attractive town surrounded by magnificent mountains.

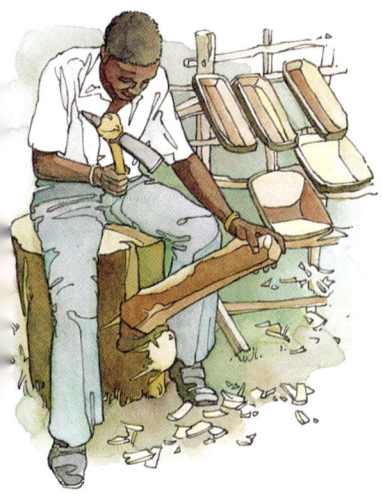

A Swazi wood carver at work.

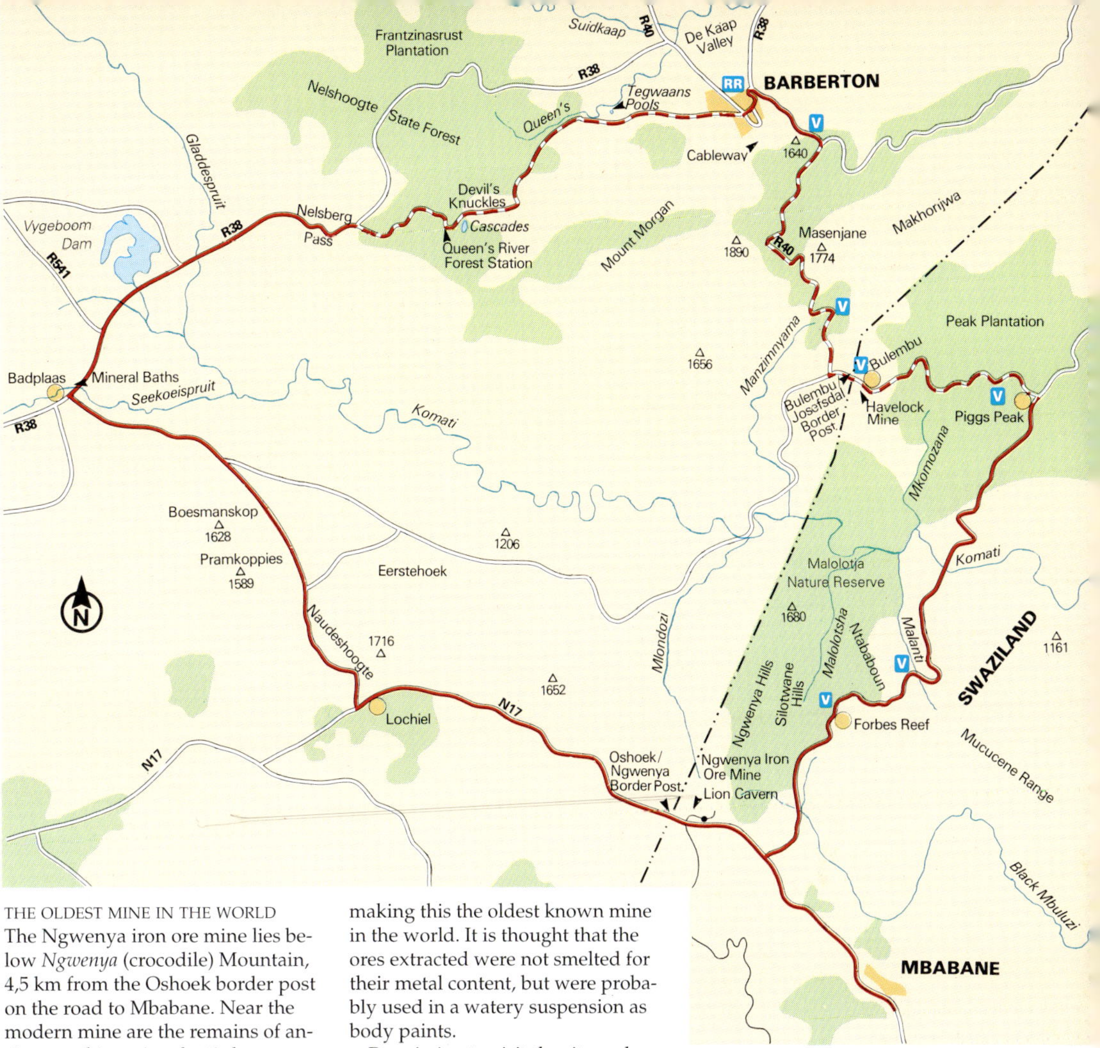

THE OLDEST MINE IN THE WORLD

The Ngwenya iron ore mine lies below *Ngwenya* (crocodile) Mountain, 4,5 km from the Oshoek border post on the road to Mbabane. Near the modern mine are the remains of ancient workings, in what is known as Lion Cavern.

Radiocarbon dating techniques have shown that red oxides and haematite were being mined here between about 41 000 and 36 000 BC, making this the oldest known mine in the world. It is thought that the ores extracted were not smelted for their metal content, but were probably used in a watery suspension as body paints.

Permission to visit the site and the nearby remains of ancient Sotho huts may be obtained from the Swaziland Iron Ore Development Company in Mbabane. This area of Swaziland is still rich in minerals.

PIGGS PEAK

The small village of Piggs Peak is named after the prospector William Pigg, who discovered gold near here in 1884.

The village has become an important forestry centre, with vast plantations of eucalyptus and pine covering the slopes of its magnificent mountain setting. A hotel and casino are situated nearby.

In the village there is a fascinating handcraft market and a famous weaving school – the finely coloured fabrics created here are exported throughout the world.

lows, a caravan park and grand medicinal baths, all surrounded by the mountains known to the Swazi as *Ndlumudlumu* or 'the place of thunder'.

At the T-junction in Badplaas, turn left onto the R541, noting your kms as you turn. After 20 km turn right for Lochiel, and a further 17 km brings you to a junction with the N17/R39. Turn left to the small town of Lochiel.

A further 26 km brings you to the Oshoek/Ngwenya border post (open from 07h00 to 22h00; travel documents needed). Note your kms as you leave the border post.

After about 4,5 km you pass, on your left, the road to Malolotja Nature Reserve, site of Ngwenya iron ore mine, the oldest mine in the world – the Lion Cavern (see above). Soon after, still on the Oshoek – Mbabane road, you reach the Ngwenya glass factory, Endlotane Studios and Phumalanga Tapestries, where visitors are welcome. Continue on the main road, passing the turn-off that you took to Piggs Peak and reaching Mbabane 23 km from the Oshoek/Ngwenya border post.

Barberton Information Bureau Market Square, Barberton 1300 Tel (01314) 22121
Swaziland Tourist Office Swazi Plaza, Allister Miller Street, Mbabane Tel (09268) 42531

Hardy Aloe marlothii on a rocky slope near Barberton.

The forests at Nelshoogte.

SWAZI TRADITIONS

The *Incwala* — sacred rites herald the New Year

Resplendent in their traditional dress, warriors dance during festivities.

Young Swazi women in bright costumes prepare for the reed dance at Lobamba.

THE KINGDOM OF Swaziland, one of the smallest in the world, has a population composed mainly of Nguni and Sotho groups who joined to form the Swazi nation. Their traditions and sacred ceremonies have changed little in spite of the influence of western civilization. Royal succession is still decided according to age-old tradition – and the most recent ceremony was attended by royalty from all over the world. This richness of tradition, combined with the country's scenic attractions and its flora and fauna, has made the small kingdom a popular tourist destination.

A colourful history
Ancestors of the Swazi came to this area from the north during the mid-18th century. The main stream of migrants, under Chief Dlamini, moved on south to the region known today as KwaZulu-Natal, but the Ngwane, named after their leader, settled in the fertile *uSutu* (dark brown) valley in Swaziland. Ngwane conquered small, nearby clans, enlarging his area of control.

His grandson, Sobhuza I, wished to extend the Ngwane area of authority, but clashed with a neighbouring Ndwandwe chief over land along the Pongola River, and was forced to move northwards. He settled near the present-day site of the royal residence at Lobamba, at the entrance to the Ezulwini Valley. Sobhuza developed his kingdom, incorporating the Sotho people who already lived there, and he maintained peace with the Zulu by sending two of his daughters to their all-powerful ruler, Shaka.

Sobhuza's son, Mswati or Mswazi, after whom the Swazi are named, succeeded him in 1840. Mswazi moved his capital to Hhohho (a name derived from the barking noise made by baboons), from where he could closely monitor attacks on the Sotho in the north while at the same time strengthening his army in order to repel the growing number of attacks by *impis* or regiments of the Zulu army.

It was during Mswazi's reign that the first white settlers, missionaries and traders came to Swaziland. Gold was discovered in the hills and the inevitable rush took place, bringing with it attendant swindlers, bandits and riffraff. Mswazi's son, Mbandzeni, granted over 500 land concessions to these newcomers for the building of railways, prospecting and countless other activities in the belief that these concessions expired on the death of their owners. The situation became intolerable when it was realized that almost the entire country was owned by concession-holders whose descendants had merely to continue to pay their dues to ensure ownership of the property.

Mbandzeni's son, Sobhuza II, succeeded to the throne in 1921, and led many delegations to London in attempts to restore the country of his ancestors to national ownership. By the time Swaziland was granted full independence by the British government in 1968, more than 60 per cent of the land had been regained. Sobhuza ruled his beloved country with a fair and

To those who can read them, her beads tell a story.

In Incwala attire, a warrior stands outside a typical beehive-shaped hut.

Local handcrafts at the open-air market, Mbabane.

understanding hand for 62 years, and Swaziland flourished. In 1986 King Mswati III succeeded him.

Although most aspects of western culture are accepted, traditional customs have survived. The king, also known as *Ngwenyama* (the lion), is regarded with adulation and reverence. His fertility and health are taken as a direct reflection of the fertility and prosperity of his country. One of the most sacred of his kingly rituals is the *Incwala*, a lengthy ceremony held during the first new moon every year.

The complex Incwala

Strictly speaking, the Incwala is divided into two parts – the Little Incwala and the Big Incwala. During the Little Incwala (held during the preceding new moon), several special envoys are sent to certain rivers and to the sea to collect water and special herbs, which are then returned to the royal residence at Lobamba. On the following morning the king samples the first fruits of the season in a ceremony accompanied by singing and dancing.

The Big Incwala ceremony lasts for six days and reflects the maturity of the king – the more mature he is, the merrier the festivities. On the first day, Swazi youths gather at the king's residence to sing songs of praise and then march 40 km to Egundwini to collect branches of the lusekwane tree. These are returned to the royal residence on the second day. On the third day a shelter is constructed from these branches, and the king joins his warriors, resplendent in their skins and feathers, to sing sacred songs. A black ox is driven before the king and slaughtered by the youths, who then dismember the carcass. On the fourth day, the king joins the warriors in a great festive dance, with the women of the royal family taking part. No work is done on the fifth day, which is reserved for meditation and peace. The Incwala then ends on the sixth day with a ritual cleansing – a bonfire is lit and all the king's clothes, bedding and the remains of the slaughtered bull are burnt – and the new year is welcomed. (Visitors may watch the proceedings, but must obey the instructions of officials. No photographs may be taken.)

At the end of August, a colourful ceremony takes place at the royal residence of the Queen Mother at Lobamba. During this ritual, known as the reed dance (*uMhlango*), young, unmarried Swazi women bring reeds from all over the kingdom and construct a loose screen around the Queen Mother's home. The highlight of the ceremony is the dance performed by young women in bright costumes of beads, anklets, bracelets and necklaces. On the final day, they dance before the Queen Mother, and dine and sing well into the night.

The Swazi are very particular about their appearance, and their clothes are colourfully ornamented with feathers, skins, cloths and significant beadwork – similar, though not identical, to that of the Zulu (see pages 144 – 145). Combinations of beads in different colours are said to placate ancestral spirits, to bring good luck, or to encourage a loved one. At four months old, babies receive their first strings of white beads – symbolizing goodness and purity – which they wear around their wrists, ankles and waist until they are weaned.

Intricately woven huts

The traditional domed huts in which many Swazi live have been associated with people of Nguni origin throughout the subcontinent. These huts, largely replaced by wattle-and-daub or stone-walled dwellings in other areas, are now built almost exclusively by the Swazi and the Zulu in KwaZulu-Natal. Saplings are woven together into a semicircular framework using grass ropes, forming a beehive shape that is strong and weather resistant.

Swaziland is a predominantly agricultural country and most of the population lives on small farms. The principal crops are maize, sugar, cotton, tobacco, vegetables and subtropical fruit. Cattle provide beef and milk, and pigs and poultry are also kept. Forests cover much of the mountainous western side of the country – where visitors can enjoy many peaceful walks and magnificent scenery.

Right: *The Little Usutu River makes a leisurely meander through the lovely Ezulwini Valley.*

Dawn breaks over the Kruger as a party of tourists prepares for a day's trailing through the park.

Kruger Park: journey through the primeval heart of wild Africa

World famous for its diverse and abundant wildlife, the Kruger National Park is more than just a place to see lions, elephants and an array of other animals. Its magnificent scenery and unique wildness straddling the Tropic of Capricorn make it one of the few remaining areas of South Africa where the old, primeval heart of Africa still throbs.

COVERING MORE THAN 19 000 km² in the Northern Province and in adjacent Mpumalanga, the Kruger is one of the largest national parks in the world, with the greatest diversity of wildlife species: 147 mammals and about 510 birds. It is rightly one of the major tourist attractions in South Africa, with more than 800 000 visitors a year. Although mainly flat with vast grass-filled plains, it also has undulating and mountainous regions, and the southern half of the park especially, is richly covered in a daunting array of plant-forms, including an abundance of gigantic trees. The park is roughly 350 km from north to south and about 60 km wide.

Inevitably, the southern half of the park, being closer to populous Gauteng, receives most visitors. Fortunately, it also has a greater diversity and abundance of wildlife, a more extensive network of tarred and gravel roads, and most tourist camps.

However, the north also has many attractions: a greater abundance of elephant and buffalo, roan antelope, tsessebe, eland and nyala and magnificent baobab trees. Perhaps the greatest attraction of the north is the tremendous atmosphere it generates, a sense of primitive wilderness and isolation; of plains reaching into the distant, hazy horizon, with no sign of human presence.

In the far north, craggy sandstone hills with multicoloured, lichen-covered boulders rear up amid baobabs and other tropical vegetation.

The first steps

It was President Paul Kruger who, in 1884, first suggested that a wildlife conservation area be established in this region. But only in 1898 was the Sabie Game Reserve finally and officially proclaimed, encompassing the area between the Sabie and Crocodile rivers. In 1903 the addition of the Shingwedzi Game Reserve greatly increased the conservation area.

The first warden of the new reserve was Major – later Colonel – James Stevenson-Hamilton, who assumed duty in 1902 and was to play a decisive role in the consolidation of land and the ultimate proclamation of the giant Kruger National Park. There were ceaseless battles with landowning associations who wanted the land for agriculture; and innumerable discussions with politicians to convince them of the need for a national park. In the end, persistence paid off, and the Kruger National Park was formally proclaimed on 31 May 1926.

When to visit

Winter, between May and October, is the best time to visit the park. The days are usually cloudless and warm, with an average maximum temperature of 23°C. It cools down rapidly in the late afternoon and the nights are cold, generally about 8°C during the early hours before sunrise.

In summer, daytime temperatures frequently rise above 40°C, about 30°C being the average. The nights are warm, minimum temperatures hovering around 18°C.

The hottest months in Kruger are December and January, and the coolest are June and July.

Midwinter is the better time to view game, particularly around June, July and August, when all the smaller pools and streams have dried up and animals concentrate around the larger dams and rivers. Most of these are close to tourist roads and, as many trees have shed their leaves and the vegetation cover as a whole is reduced, it is much easier to locate and observe animals.

A winter visit does have certain disadvantages, though: you miss the tremendous scenery of summer, especially in a season of good rain. Luxuriant groves of trees in full bloom complement the rich green fields of revitalized grasses. Many of the larger mammals bear their young during this time, when environmental conditions are most favourable.

Where to stay

Scattered throughout the Kruger are 23 camps, varying in size from small private camps, which accommodate up to eight people and have to be reserved in their entirety, to larger camps such as Skukuza, which has 229 huts, plus guest cottages and a dormitory for school tours. Most camps also have well-tended camping areas for caravans and tents, as well as fuel stations, shops, restaurants and other facilities.

Several types of huts or housing units are available in the park, the most popular being a thatched hut with one room containing two or three beds, air-conditioner or fan, refrigerator, shower, toilet, handbasin and an adjoining verandah, table and chairs. Some camps also have family cottages with two rooms with two or three beds, air conditioner, shower or bath, toilet and handbasin, and a small kitchen with gas stove, refrigerator, washing-up bay, cooking and eating utensils.

Reservations should be made well in advance by writing to The Chief Director, Reservations, National Parks Board, PO Box 787, Pretoria 0001, stating the number of adults and children in the proposed group, your choice of camps, the intended duration of stay in each camp, and the type of accommodation you require. Do not send money with the initial application; this will be requested once accommodation has been reserved.

The reservations office will send you a voucher that must be presented when entering the park and at camps where you have reserved accommodation. At the park entrance gate only, you will be asked to pay a small fee for the car and for all occupants above the age of two years.

Sometimes it may be possible to change your reservation. The reception office in each camp will gladly enquire from other camps if suitable accommodation is available, and reservations may then be transferred to whichever camp you prefer.

There are 900 leopards in the park.

Good gravel and tarred tourist roads cover most areas of the park.

APPROXIMATE NUMBERS OF
THE LARGER ANIMALS IN THE
KRUGER PARK

Lion	1 750
Leopard	900
Cheetah	250
Wild dog	360
Elephant	7 500
Buffalo	17 000
White rhino	2 000
Impala	120 000
Waterbuck	1 500
Zebra	30 000
Blue wildebeest	13 000
Kudu	3 200
Giraffe	4 600
Sable antelope	900

TRAVELLING HOURS

Visitors to the park are allowed out of the camps only during daylight hours. All the camps are fenced and the gates locked at the times listed.

	opening	closing
January	05h00	18h30
February	05h00	18h30
March	05h30	18h00
April	06h00	17h30
May	06h30	17h30
June	06h30	17h30
July	06h30	17h30
August	06h30	17h30
September	06h00	18h00
October	05h30	18h00
November	04h30	18h00
December	04h30	18h30

The park's entrance gates have the same opening and closing times as rest camps, except in November, December, January and February, when they open at 05h30.

GENERAL REGULATIONS

1 No pets are allowed: they may transmit diseases to the animals.
2 Firearms have to be declared on arrival at the park. They will be sealed and the seal removed when you leave.
3 Heed the speed limits indicated (these are generally 50 km/h). Wild animals are unpredictable and may jump into your path, leaving you little time or space in which to react. Concealed speed traps operate in the park at all times.
4 Do not get out of your car except at a camp or designated parking site. Similarly, do not let your head, shoulders or arms protrude from the window: visitors have been bitten by animals that appeared to them to be tame.
5 Do not feed the animals. This misguided kindness makes any wild animals, especially baboons and monkeys, aggressive towards visitors who subsequently do not feed them, and these animals may have to be shot.
6 Don't litter: tins and other refuse are not only unsightly but they could kill animals that eat refuse.
7 Keep to the designated tourist roads. If you break down along a firebreak or other country road, it may be days before park officials locate you.
8 Be considerate to other visitors by not playing a musical instrument, radio or tape deck at a disturbing volume.
9 Never throw a match or cigarette-end out of the window. Extinguish them completely in your vehicle's ash tray, which you can later empty at your leisure.

The tranquil waters of the Sabie River.

SEEING THE PARK IN FIVE DAYS OR FEWER

The next 10 pages contain a five-day tour of the Kruger Park, each double-page spread featuring a day's drive of about 200 km. The routes have been chosen for scenery and game-spotting. The tour begins in the south at Skukuza and ends in the far north at Punda Maria. Visitors with less time should begin their route in the south, exiting at Orpen Gate (two days), Phalaborwa Gate (three days) or Punda Maria Gate (four days without visiting Pafuri). Each day's drive is covered in detail on the pages indicated. The countryside between the Sabie and Olifants rivers is the richest in game, so make sure this area features prominently in your allocated time. If you plan to follow the entire route, you will need to book these camps well in advance (see Where to stay, opposite): 1 Skukuza; 2 Lower Sabie; 3 Satara; 4 Letaba; 5 Punda Maria; 6 Punda Maria.

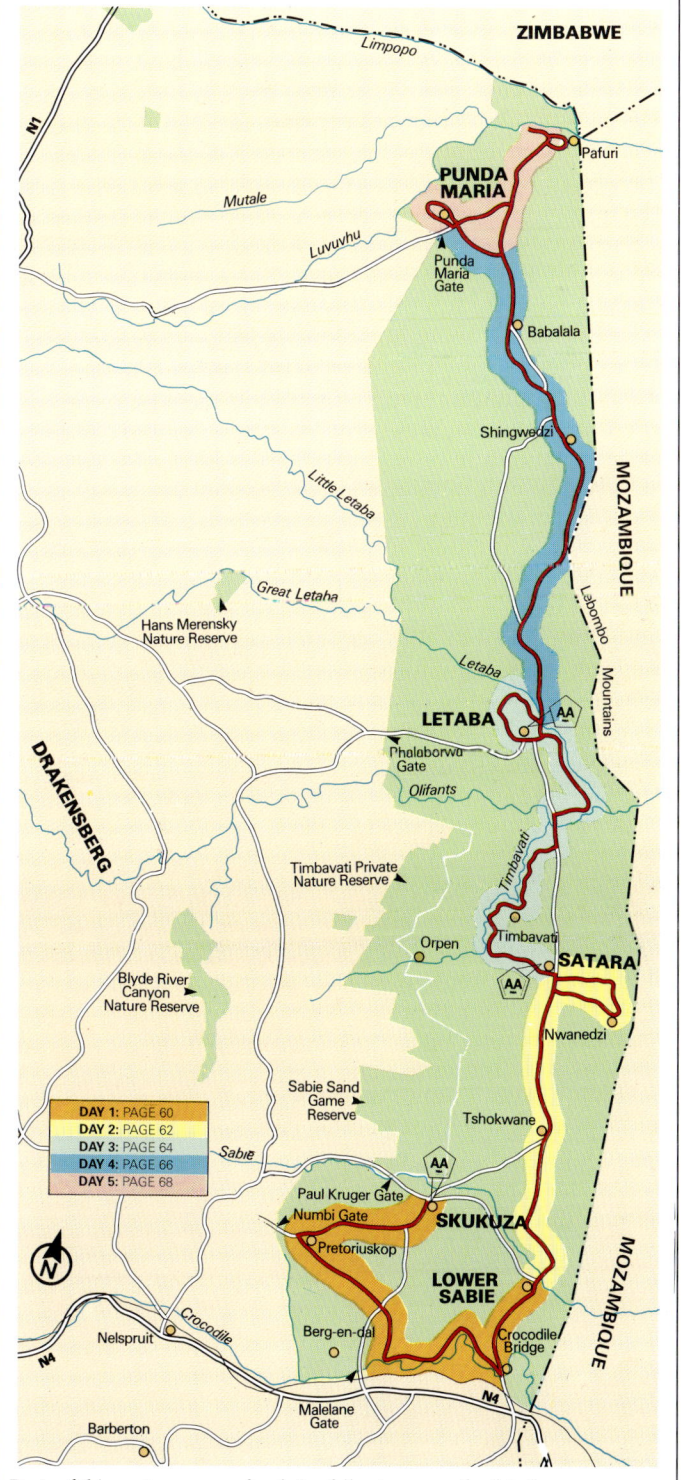

DAY 1: PAGE 60
DAY 2: PAGE 62
DAY 3: PAGE 64
DAY 4: PAGE 66
DAY 5: PAGE 68

Parts of this route are unsurfaced. See following pages for details.

Follow Jock of the Bushveld through the lush south

Our first day takes us through the densely vegetated southern area of the park, dotted with bouldered hills – home of the rare klipspringer antelope and favourite stamping ground of the rhinoceros. Part of the route parallels the path followed by the old transport riders to Delagoa Bay and used by the dog of legend, Jock of the Bushveld.

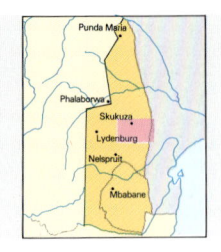

**Skukuza
Pretoriuskop
Afsaal
Crocodile
Bridge
Lower Sabie
200 – 210 km**

LEAVE SKUKUZA EARLY in the morning before breakfast, as soon as possible after the camp gates open, and follow the H1-1 tarred road to Pretoriuskop, ignoring several other roads that branch off within the first 2 km. The road gently winds and dips through fairly dense vegetation much favoured by lions in the early morning. Look out also for nomadic packs of wild dogs.

Five kilometres after leaving the camp, you pass a gravel road on the left to Malelane and Crocodile Bridge. Continue on the tar, turning left some 5 km later on a short gravel road to Granokop, a granite extrusion which provides a magnificent view of the surrounding countryside in all directions. Spend no more than 5 minutes on this hill, then return towards Pretoriuskop.

Some 14 km from Skukuza, the road passes between rocky outcrops where, with a little luck, a rare klipspringer may be seen silhouetted atop the granite boulders. At this point a tarred road branches off to Berg-en-Dal, but you should continue straight on.

Ignore the next turn-off, but at 20 km from Skukuza take a gravel road on the left to the Transport Dam, which is about 2 km from the main road. You should spot some animals gathering for their early drink; but don't stay too long, as a heavy day's driving still lies ahead.

Return to the H1-1 tarred road towards Pretoriuskop for a further 21 km and turn left on a short (1 km) gravel road to Shitlhave Dam. This is another good spot from which to look out for early-morning game. Return to the H1-1 for a further 7 km until you reach a T-junction. Turn left along the tarred road until Pretoriuskop is reached 2 km farther on. Time now for breakfast and, very importantly, to refuel your car if the tank is less than half full.

Pretoriuskop to Afsaal

Try to leave Pretoriuskop by 09h30 at the latest. Less than 0,5 km beyond the gates, turn right onto a gravel road (H2-2) known as the Jock of the Bushveld Road. This scenic drive parallels the route followed by the old transport riders to Delagoa Bay, the same route along which Sir Percy Fitzpatrick and his famous dog Jock shared so many experiences. Keep a lookout for rhinoceros on this road.

Thirteen kilometres out of Pretoriuskop you pass a large mass of boulders on the right known as Ship Mountain, so named because it resembles the inverted hull of a ship.

At 35 km from Pretoriuskop you reach a T-junction with the H3 tarred road and the Afsaal Picnic Site (cool drinks and other light refreshments are available). The road from Pretoriuskop to Afsaal should take no more than two hours.

Afsaal to Crocodile Bridge

From Afsaal, head south on the tarred road over a bridge; then turn left after a few hundred metres onto the gravel H2-2 again. Continue for 8 km until you reach the T-junction with the S114. Turn right and continue south for 9 km, crossing the Mlambane River, until you reach the S25 gravel road on the left. Follow this for 38 km through undulating country dotted with occasional low hills and fairly dense vegetation. Keep your eyes peeled for game – this stretch of road is usually well stocked with animals.

About 42 km from Afsaal there is a well-signposted gravel road to the right leading for 3 km to Hippo Pool in a bend in the Crocodile River. Hippo are usually seen sunning themselves on a sandbank – and an occasional

Lights twinkle in the warm African night as darkness falls at Skukuza.

SKUKUZA

Meaning 'he who turned everything upside down' or 'he who sweeps clean', *Skukuza* was the name his African staff gave Colonel James Stevenson-Hamilton, the first warden of the Sabie Game Reserve. Situated on the banks of the Sabie River, Skukuza is also the operational and administrative headquarters of the park.

By far the largest of the camps, it has lost much of the intimacy that allows visitors to identify with the surrounding wilderness. Nevertheless, Skukuza is popular because of its accessibility, which is greatly enhanced by a nearby landing strip. It is the only camp with a bank (Volkskas, although other cheques may be cashed here), plus a large, modern post office and public telephones. The Stevenson-Hamilton Memorial Library is well worth a visit, and has a wide range of displays on wildlife.

The AA office and the workshop/garage are alongside the petrol station.

The main entrance gate at Skukuza.

KRUGER PARK: DAY ONE

elephant may sometimes wander down for a drink. San paintings adorn the cliff overlooking the pool.

Return to the S25 for the short drive into Crocodile Bridge (cool drinks on sale).

Crocodile Bridge to Lower Sabie
From Crocodile Bridge head north on the H4-2 in the direction of Lower Sabie, which is reached after 35 km. This road is very good for spotting a wide range of antelope species.

AA Emergency Service Centre Skukuza Rest Camp

Always watch for elephants in or near dams and rivers.

Early morning sunlight casts long shadows at Lower Sabie Rest Camp.

LOWER SABIE
A lovely setting, ideal size and great natural beauty make this camp highly popular with visitors at any time of the year. The camp lies on a slight elevation with excellent views of the Sabie River. In the evening, many animals can be seen coming to drink, while buffalo and elephant often feed on the reed-fringed banks of the river. Green, well-tended lawns grace the areas between huts and tall, shady broad-leaved trees help make the camp an oasis for relaxation and enjoyment.

Lower Sabie is located in a prime game-viewing area. The greater part of the surrounding country is made up of flat plains covered with acacia, marula, leadwood, bush-willow and several other trees, with thick grass-cover between, particularly during summer rains.

JOCK OF THE BUSHVELD
Written by Sir Percy Fitzpatrick and published in 1907, this story of a man and his dog in the early Transvaal goldrush days is a classic.

Disillusioned by his job in a Cape Town bank, the young Fitzpatrick opted for a job as a transport rider, carting by ox-wagon supplies for the mining camps from Delagoa Bay to the goldfields of the highveld.

A good dog was an invaluable ally in this harsh environment, and Fitzpatrick was given a crossbred bull terrier pup, the smallest, weakest and ugliest of the litter. But as the dog grew it showed great intelligence, toughness and braveness. Jock, as Fitzpatrick named him, became an inseparable companion.

RHINOCEROS
Once plentiful in the area now covered by the Kruger Park, both black and white rhino were hunted to extinction and have been reintroduced from KwaZulu-Natal and from Zimbabwe. There is no real colour difference between the two species. White rhino are generally larger, with a flattened or square mouth, feeding on grass. Black rhino have a pointed mouth that they use to strip leaves and break twigs. They have a mass of about 1 500 kg. Young black rhino run behind the cow, whereas juvenile white rhino run ahead.

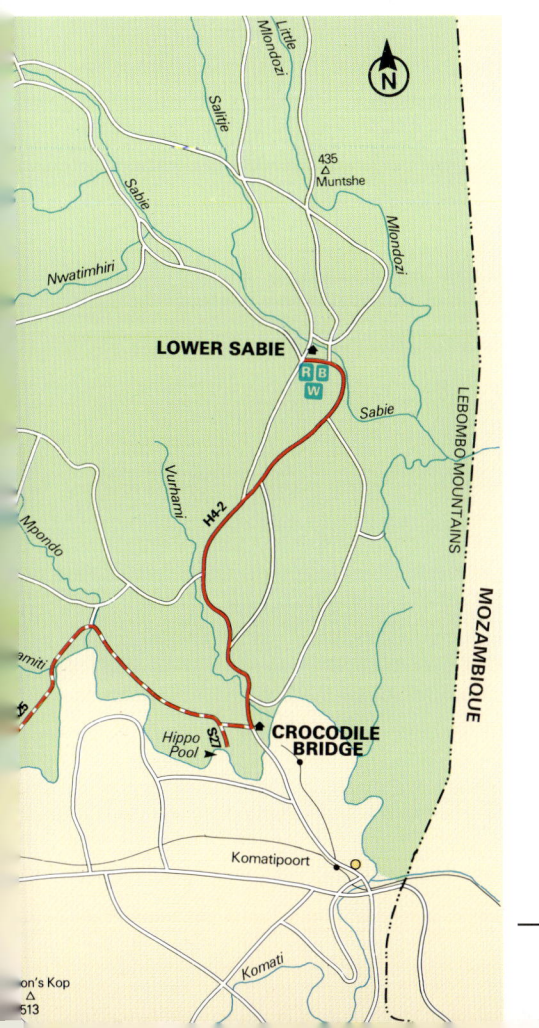

WILD DOG
Sometimes called hunting dogs, wild dogs are generally found in packs of between five and 20. They have long, slender legs and a lean body – advantages to any predator that depends on its running ability to catch its prey. Their large, rounded ears are very distinctive, as is their blotched or mottled colour, generally a mixture of black, orange-brown and white.

Nomadic for much of the year, wild dogs roam over enormous areas, constantly searching for prey to satisfy their almost continuous hunger. Once the pack has chosen its next meal – usually an impala, a zebra, a kudu or other antelope – it hunts down the victim with dogged persistence and stamina. The dogs may rip and snap chunks of flesh from the fleeing animal as it gradually tires and slows. Once down, the unfortunate prey is reduced to a mass of skin and bones within minutes by the milling throng of ravenous dogs – a fearsome and memorable sight for those who witness it.

When pups are born, the pack will cease its nomadic pattern and remain in the same general vicinity. The pups are left in burrows, and adults return after a hunt to regurgitate meat for the youngsters.

The wild dogs in the park – about 360 – tend to favour flat country, but there is no particular area of great abundance.

The distinctive shape of Ship Mountain in southern Kruger.

The 'horn' of the rhino is formed from matted hair and skin.

A good route for game-spotting on the great plains

Our second day takes us through the richest area in the park for animal life. Lions are abundant, together with numerous herds of zebra, wildebeest and giraffe. The road snakes lazily northwards through the enormous plains of the central district that stretch from horizon to horizon and provide a home for the occasional cheetah.

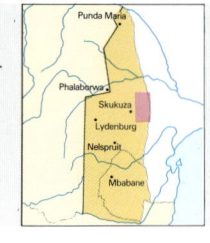

**Lower Sabie
Tshokwane
Satara
Nwanetsi
Satara
150 – 170 km**

AFTER AN EARLY breakfast at Lower Sabie (try to leave by 07h30), cross the Sabie River bridge a short distance outside the camp gates in the direction of Crocodile Bridge. Less than 1 km after crossing the bridge, turn right onto a gravel road (S29). Pass the S122 on your right and, about 14 km from Lower Sabie, turn right onto the S68, which takes you, after about 1 km, to a hilltop observation area with a magnificent view over the Mlondozi Dam and surrounding area.

Hippo and crocodile share the dam with a large number of birds, such as ducks, herons, kingfishers and storks. Kudu, waterbuck, impala and the occasional elephant approach the bank for water or to feed on the nearby vegetation. There are toilets at this lookout point and cool drinks are on sale. Spend no more than about half an hour here.

Return to the S29 and turn right. After 3 km turn right at the crossroads with the H10 tarred road. Stay on this road, travelling north and passing gravel roads on the left, right and left, until you reach the S32, signposted on the right to Eileen Orpen Dam 2 km away. Turn right here. From your hilltop position at the dam, crocodiles are frequently seen lazing on the banks, and elephant occasionally arrive to quench their thirst. There are toilets next to the parking area.

Retrace your route to the H10 and turn right. After 2 km you reach a T-junction with the main H1-2 tarred road; turn right for the short drive into Tshokwane, where snacks, tea and other refreshments can be obtained and enjoyed on the quaint verandah built around the base of a huge sausage tree. Braai facilities are also available.

Tshokwane to Satara
From Tshokwane, drive northwards again on the tarred road (H1-3) which for several kilometres hugs the normally dry Nwaswitsontso stream before sheering away to continue through the grassy plains so characteristic of the central area of the park. Along the way, the Mazithi and Kumana Dams are passed. This whole area between Tshokwane and Satara is filled with numerous herds of zebra, wildebeest, impala, kudu, waterbuck and giraffe. Lion are also frequently seen.

Watch out, too, for ground hornbills strutting in small groups on the roads in their never-ending search for food: insects, reptiles, small mammals and even tortoises. These are the largest of the six species of hornbills in the park, and they can be easily identified by their characteristic large, curved and pointed bill, stark black body and, in the males, brilliant-red bare skin on the throat.

The distance from Tshokwane to Satara along the tarred H1-3 is 50 km, and you should plan your time so that Satara is reached for an early lunch. Before eating, check in at the reception office to find out where your hut is. For lunch you can choose between a self-help restaurant or a cafeteria offering light meals. The reception office, restaurant and cafeteria all conveniently adjoin each other.

Satara to Nwanetsi
After lunch, and possibly a short rest or stroll around camp, you can look forward to a particularly pleasant drive. Take the tarred road (H1-3) out of camp again towards Tshokwane, but take the second left after about 3 km on the tarred road (H6) to Nwanetsi.

Do not be disappointed if you don't see much game on the way to Nwanetsi – it is the return drive that will make the afternoon's trip worthwhile. Even so, the short 20 km trip to Nwanetsi should provide sightings of several herds of zebra, wildebeest, impala and perhaps some ostriches. Nwanetsi camp is out of bounds except to visitors actually staying there, so go straight to the Nwanetsi lookout point. Here you will find a setting so beautiful it will probably be remembered as one of the most pleasant sights of your visit. The thatch-roofed lookout point, with ample seating, stands on the very edge of a sheer cliff that drops to the calm, clear waters of the Sweni River. To the west, flat plains stretch all the way to the horizon, and eastwards loom the rock-littered and craggy heights of the Lebombo Mountains.

Animals can be seen coming in for an afternoon drink and waterbirds are plentiful.

Nwanetsi to Satara
From the Nwanetsi lookout point take the gravel road (S41) northwards for 12 km, then turn left into the gravel S100 that follows the course of the Nwanetsi River back towards Satara. This very pleasant drive provides great scenic views and many animals. Look out for storks, herons and ducks on the tranquil waters of the river; waterbuck, zebra, wildebeest, impala and kudu are common. After 16 km, the tarred road (H1-3) is joined again about 2 km south of Satara. Turn right onto the tarred road to get back to camp to relax for the evening.

AA Patrol Station Satara Rest Camp.

Giraffe are common in the central park.

GIRAFFE
The tallest animals in the world are also the most unusual of all Africa's mammals. Their extraordinarily long legs and necks – the head may be as high as 5,6 m above the ground – allow them to feed on leaves and seed pods of trees at a level where they have no competitors among the other major herbivores.

Apart from calves, several adult giraffe are killed each year by lions. However, a kick from a distraught giraffe can kill or severely injure a careless predator.

Fighting occasionally takes place between males, the contestants arranging themselves side by side and exchanging vicious sweeping blows with their necks and heads.

Giraffe are generally seen in groups of between 3 and 10, and are common in the acacia savannas of the central and southern park.

The cheetah: a daytime hunter.

KRUGER PARK: DAY TWO

Kudu are largely nocturnal, feeding between evening and early morning.

SATARA
Second in size only to Skukuza, this camp lies near the centre of the vast plains between the Sabie and Olifants Rivers. The camp is surrounded by flat, grassy country dominated by tall knobthorn, acacia and marula trees. Despite its size, Satara retains a tranquil and intimate atmosphere with little of the impersonal detachment so often associated with a large camp. Bird life is profuse and large numbers of starlings, buffalo weavers and sparrows fly about among the huts in search of crumbs. Hornbills peer from their tree-top perches, occasionally uttering their mocking, staccato calls.

A small waterhole, where you can watch animals coming in to drink, has been created just off the restaurant side of the camp.

The large self-service restaurant is situated in the building that also houses a cafeteria, a ladies' bar, the reception offices, shop and restrooms. An AA Patrol Station is located at the entrance gate.

Marula and acacia dot the grounds of Satara.

A sausage tree dominates the tearoom at Tshokwane.

LION
With their magnificent, dignified stature, undeniable power and a less-definable aura of wild prowess, these animals are the greatest attraction in the park. Although they occasionally make daylight kills, lions are mainly nocturnal hunters, the males playing only a small part in the hunt. Lions are normally found in prides of from two to six individuals, each pride having a fairly defined area in which it will hunt and live. When ready for mating, a male and female withdraw from the pride for several days, neither hunting nor searching for food. The males especially become irritable and aggressive during this 'honeymoon' stage and need little provocation to attack any intruders. Females give birth to between two and five cubs.

About 1 750 lions are scattered throughout the park, mostly in the central district and around Lower Sabie – the area most abounding in zebra and wildebeest, their favoured prey.

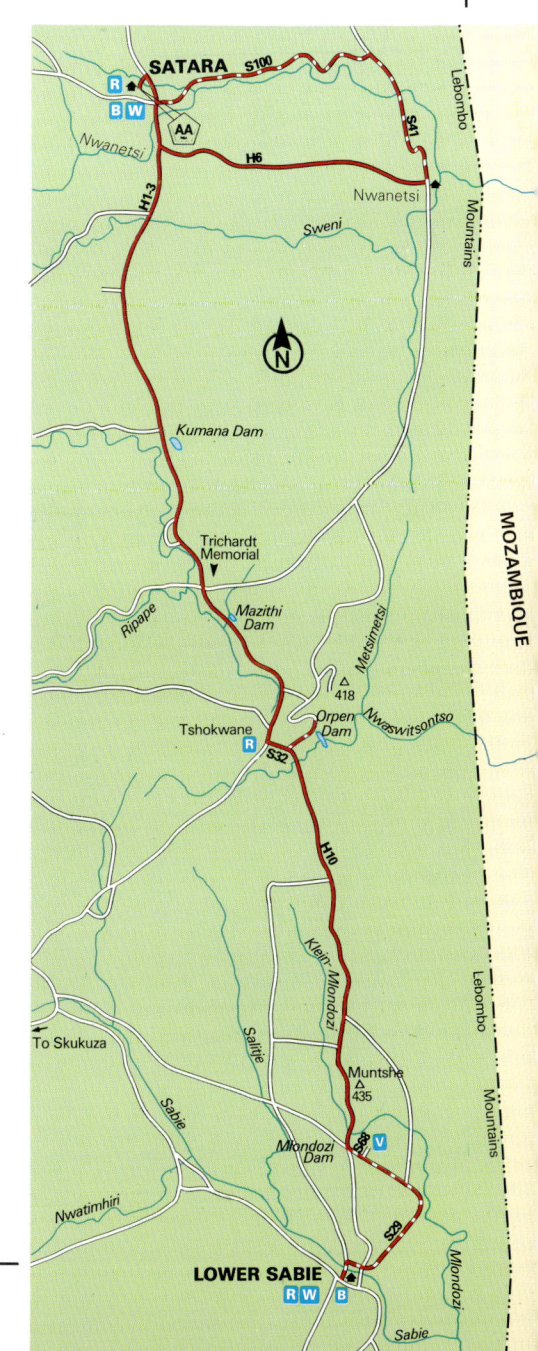

Essentially lazy, lions leave the females to hunt.

WOLHUTER'S LION
A tall, quiet man of few words, Harry Wolhuter was an exceptionally able hunter, respected by all who knew him. Late one evening in 1903, he was on horseback patrol with three assistants about 50 km north of Lower Sabie when he was attacked by two lions. One lion jumped on the horse, and Wolhuter fell onto the other lion, which sank its teeth into his right shoulder.

Feigning death and hanging limply between the lion's legs as he was being dragged off, Wolhuter carefully unsheathed his knife and, in quick succession, plunged it twice into the lion's chest and once in the throat. The lion let go and ran off, to die a short distance away.

In extreme agony, Wolhuter dragged himself up a tree and used his belt to secure himself to a branch in case he lost consciousness. There the second lion found him, and it padded back and forth below the tree, with Wolhuter's dog nearby, barking and worrying.

Several hours later, Wolhuter was found by his assistants, and without dressings and water for the initial part of the trip, they took him to Barberton for medical attention, arriving there four days later. Wolhuter survived.

Elephant, giraffe and lion on the winding road north to Letaba

The third day's drive meanders past a series of watercourses, the first half passing through scenic acacia savannah with an abundance of giraffe, waterbuck and lion. The flat plains eventually give way to rugged hills stubbled with mopane trees and increasing numbers of elephants. Hippopotami can occasionally be seen in the rivers.

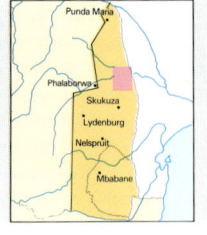

Satara
Timbavati
Olifants
Letaba
170 – 190 km

AFTER AN EARLY breakfast at Satara (try to leave camp by 07h45) take the H7 tarred road towards Orpen Camp. After 7 km a gravel road leads north. Stay on the tar – immediately beyond this junction lies Nsemani Dam, a watering point for many animals and interesting bird species.

Spend a few pleasant minutes at this scenic spot before continuing along the H7, ignoring a gravel road veering north 5 km further.

Some 12 km after Nsemani Dam turn right onto the gravel S39, which parallels the Timbavati River, winding through very interesting bush with much atmosphere and an abundance of animals. Zebra, wildebeest, impala and kudu are common; and giraffe, elephant, buffalo and lion are often seen.

After about 31 km a well-marked short detour leads to the Timbavati picnic site (cool drinks and toilets available). Try not to stay more than half an hour here to stretch your legs. Return to the S39, looking out for a large, solitary baobab tree, one of the very few in the central part of the park.

Timbavati to Olifants

Turn left back on the S39, which continues its winding path beside the Timbavati River. Along the way you will pass some exquisitely shaped umbrella thorns.

You reach the H1-4 tarred road 30 km from the Timbavati picnic site. Turn left and, after heading in a northerly direction for 7 km, cross the Olifants River. The high-water bridge affords an excellent view of the river, where elephant, buffalo and hippo are frequently seen.

Continue along the tarred road (now the H1-5) for another 3 km, then turn right to join the H8 – also a tarred road – which leads directly to Olifants Camp 9 km further. Ignore the gravel roads which turn off first to the right and later to the left near the Olifants Camp.

You should reach camp in time for lunch in the restaurant, otherwise refreshments are

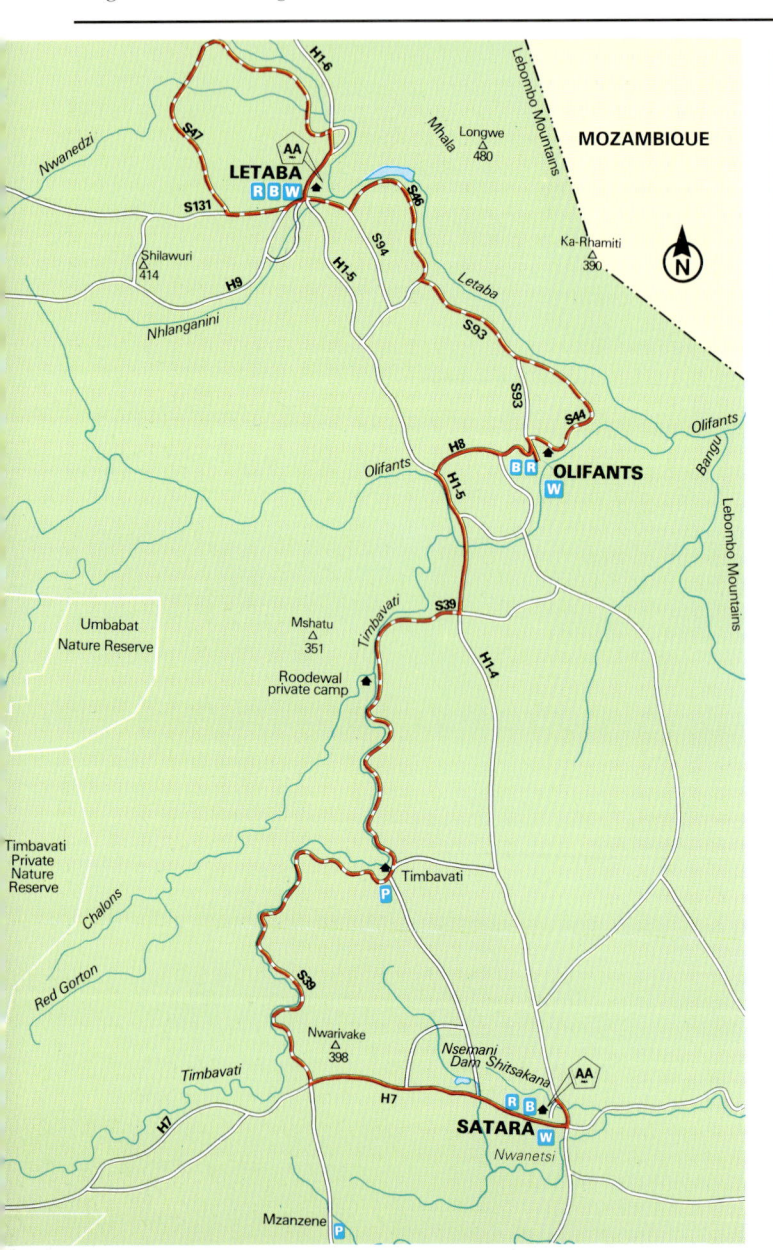

Elephants drink up to 200 litres of water every day.

AFRICAN ELEPHANT

With an adult mass of between 6 000 and 7 000 kg, these are the largest terrestrial animals living today. They feed mainly on grass, roots, bark and leaves, each animal consuming vast quantities each year.

Both males and females have tusks (some have none), although the females' tend to be thinner and smaller. The trunk – really an elongated nose – is useful for feeding, and water is sucked up into it and then squirted either into the mouth for drinking or over the body for cooling and cleaning. Elephants sometimes raise their trunks to sniff the air if danger or any other source of disturbance is suspected.

The African elephant differs most obviously from its Indian counterpart by having larger ears: rounded, flat and thin-skinned, with many blood vessels close to the surface. By gently flapping their ears, they create a breeze that allows heat exchange to take place through the surface blood vessels as excess body heat diffuses out through the thin skin. Elephants generally occur in herds averaging about 14 individuals, but numerous solitary bulls are also found. Most elephant are concentrated in the area north of the Olifants River.

Olifants Rest Camp.

served on the verandah. In front of the restaurant/shop complex is an observation area that offers a magnificent view of the Olifants River and surrounding bush.

Olifants to Letaba

From Olifants Camp take the gravel road (S44) which turns off the S93 about 1 km from the camp. This scenic drive parallels the Olifants River, giving you opportunities to spot many bird species associated with water.

After bearing eastwards for several kilometres, the road veers north, eventually to parallel the Letaba River. As you progress along the S44, the vegetation changes to mixed mopane veld until, about halfway to Letaba, mopane trees vastly outnumber all other species. The rare Sharpe's grysbok is sometimes seen along this drive. Near the junction of the S44 with the S93 the road passes close to a hill covered with large boulders; klipspringer are often seen standing atop these rocks.

At 15 km from the Olifants Camp, the road links up with the gravel S93, which after 9 km joins the S46. Keep right at both junctions. The S93 and S46 closely follow the Letaba River, allowing you to spot animals drinking or feeding along the banks. Lion are also often found in this area. After some 13 km on the S46 the road links up with the S94 (turn right), which ends at Letaba Camp 3 km further.

Letaba to Mingerhout Dam

After an early afternoon tea at Letaba take the H9 tarred road out of the camp towards Phalaborwa. After 2 km, turn right onto the gravel S47 and follow this road for 18 km to the Mingerhout Dam, where hippopotami and crocodiles may usually be seen. Return on the gravel S47, which twists along the course of the Letaba River and offers good sightings of elephant, zebra, waterbuck and several other species. You join the tarred H1-6 after 15 km, where you turn right for the final 5 km drive back to Letaba.

AA Patrol Station Satara Rest Camp.
AA Workshop and Petrol Station Letaba Rest Camp.

The Letaba River from Letaba Rest Camp.

MALARIA

Malaria, caused by microscopic blood parasites transmitted by Anopheles mosquitoes, occurs sporadically during summer throughout the park. Symptoms include vomiting, general body ache and high fever. Although few visitors contract the disease, it is advisable to take preventive tablets which are obtainable at most pharmacies. Doctors recommend that the course be started prior to arrival in the park.

LETABA

One of the larger camps in the park, Letaba is spread along the southern bank of the river from which it takes its name. Many people regard this as their favourite camp because of its relaxed atmosphere.

Tall mlala palms – from which local people derive an intoxicating liquor by allowing the extracted juices of the tree to ferment – add a tropical touch and share the camp grounds with gnarled apple-leaf trees, Natal mahogany and thorny acacias. Short-cropped lawns cover the area between huts, and aloes grace several rock gardens.

Letaba has one of the most beautiful restaurants in the park: a large building with a dining area, bar counter, lounge (where refreshments are served) and a long verandah with a view of the river where you can watch elephants.

Sunset over the Olifants River.

Zebras live in small family groups led by a stallion.

CHEETAH

Cheetahs love the open plains, shunning densely wooded or mountainous regions. They run their prey down in a short burst of very high speed, knocking the animal over and biting into its throat.

Generally encountered in groups of two or three, cheetahs roam over large areas throughout the park. Unlike leopards, they are more active by day and can be distinguished by solid black spots all over the body instead of the leopard's rosette patterns. Also look for the characteristic black 'tear mark' running from the inside of each eye down to the outside of the mouth. Lanky, streamlined animals, they are built for speed, with long thin legs, a relatively elongated thin chest and abdomen, and a head that is less bulky than that of the leopard.

ROLLER

These exquisitely coloured birds are a constant source of delight, their delicate hues blending to produce a beautiful effect. Five species of roller have been recorded in the park.

They can be seen perching singly on dead trees or on projecting branches of living trees, waiting until an insect moves into view. With graceful acrobatic movements they then swoop down to snatch the prey and return to the perch to stun the insect by flicking it against a branch before swallowing it. So intent on their task are these dedicated hunters that they often fly straight into the path of oncoming traffic when in pursuit of some morsel.

All the rollers have a rough, raucous call. They nest in holes in trees, laying up to three white eggs at a time.

CHACMA BABOON

Baboons live in troops of 10 to 30 individuals, with a definite 'pecking order' determining the status of each member in the social hierarchy. Generally a dominant male, known as the alpha male, is the leader and he has the first choice of females and food. Immediately below him follow a number of large, aggressive males, who serve as the protectors of the troop. They feed and roam on the outskirts of the community, always ready to warn or defend the others against danger.

Highly intelligent animals, baboons have a very strong protective instinct towards their young. If an infant has been injured, the members of a troop will rally around and carry it, never leaving it behind.

A baby baboon and family.

When an infant is threatened or held by a predator, the large males will fearlessly charge and make desperate attempts to save it.

Mother baboons are regularly seen carrying babies that have been dead for several days. Baboons are common along the major rivers of the park, where they spend much of their active time looking for insects and other titbits.

Driving north through an endless sea of mopane trees

Our fourth day takes us through a vast expanse of flat plains with only a rare hill breaking through the endless sea of mopane trees. This area is home to numerous herds of buffalo and elephant, and antelope species such as tsessebe, roan, sable and eland. Multicoloured lilac-breasted rollers display their brilliant plumage from treetop perches.

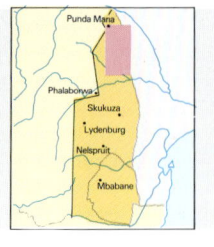

Letaba
Shingwedzi
Babalala
Punda Maria
170 – 190 km

After an early breakfast at Letaba, follow the tarred road (H1-6) north towards Shingwedzi; 6 km after leaving camp you cross the Letaba River, where buffalo and elephant are frequently seen in the reed-dotted riverbed.

The scenery is strikingly different from the southern half of the park. Vast stretches of seemingly endless mopane scrubland roll from horizon to horizon, broken only by herds of zebra, wildebeest, impala, tsessebe and elephant. Stop for a while at Malopenyana and Middelvlei windmills, 20 and 25 km respectively from Letaba, and look out for antelope such as tsessebe. Lions are also regularly seen in the vicinity.

About 33 km from Letaba, turn right onto a gravel road (S50) heading for the Lebombo Mountains. This road will take you past several dams and streams where zebra, impala, tsessebe, elephant and waterbuck are common. You may also see a rare reedbuck.

Tropic of Capricorn

In years with good rainfall Shawu Dam, about 45 km from Letaba, presents a wonderful sight when an abundance of waterbirds perch on the dead trees rearing up from the dam. Shortly after the dam, the road crosses the Tropic of Capricorn, and you enter the tropics.

As you approach the slopes of the Lebombo Mountains the road veers north to parallel the line of rock-strewn hills. These hills, together with the apparently endless mopane plains flowing from them, evoke a quiet sense of desolate timelessness: if you want to feel far removed from city life, this is the place to be. Some 88 km after leaving Letaba, the S50 reaches the Shingwedzi River and veers northwest to follow the river, with many sightings of waterbuck, storks and other animals.

The Kanniedood Dam, nearly 100 km from Letaba, is a magnificent expanse of water that attracts many waterbirds and animals to its vicinity. Darters are abundant, posing breathtakingly on the logs and rocks rising from the water. You are also likely to see buffaloes and elephants.

After a further 20 km you reach Shingwedzi Camp for a much-needed break after the long drive from Letaba. A leisurely lunch and a stroll around camp should stretch the legs and ease any aching backs. A large swimming pool is also available in the south-western corner.

Shingwedzi to Punda Maria

The total distance is about 77 km and you should allow about 2 hours and 30 minutes.

Leave Shingwedzi, turn right after 3 km and cross the river using the high-water bridge on the tarred H1-6. At the bridge the H1-6 changes its designation and becomes the H1-7; continue along this road for 6 km before turning left onto the gravel S56. This road travels beside the Mphongolo River through beautiful groves of tall nyala, jackal berry and apple-leaf trees, which provide a welcome relief from the mopane plains dominating most of the northern half of the park.

There are two points along this 29 km gravel road where you can turn off to the right to rejoin the tarred road, but this is not advised, because more animals can be seen along this riverside road, and it is also more scenic. You rejoin the tarred H1-7 at Babalala picnic site, where you may enjoy a walk and a short rest.

Continue northwards along the H1-7 for another 18 km until just past a lone, rounded hill known as Dzundwini. Turn left here onto a gravel road (S58) for a short 4 km scenic drive near the base of Dzundwini where Sharpe's grysbok are frequently seen.

Turn left at the T-junction with the tarred H13-1 towards the Punda Maria gate. Follow this road westwards for 11 km, before turning right onto the tarred H13-2. Ignore the gravel roads leading off this road at several points and continue to Punda Maria camp. As the camp comes into view, slow down and look out for bushbuck and nyala that regularly feed along the roadside at this point.

AA Workshop and Patrol Station
Letaba Rest Camp

Impala dot the Shingwedzi River bank in the northern Kruger.

The buffalo: even lions are wary.

Martial eagle.

Vervet monkey.

ANTHRAX, A KILLER DISEASE

One of the scourges of the Kruger is anthrax, a bacterial disease probably introduced into southern Africa when the first domesticated cattle entered the area many centuries ago. The disease is now endemic in the northern areas of the park and occasional epidemics occur, especially during very dry seasons, killing more than a thousand large animals in only a few months. Unfortunately some of the rare animal species, such as roan antelope, are very susceptible to anthrax and there is a very real risk that a single outbreak could wipe out the entire population of this and other rare species.

During the early 1970s, park researchers started an immunisation programme to ensure that a significant proportion of roan antelope would survive such an outbreak, and each year more than a hundred are darted from a helicopter with an immunizing bio-bullet.

AFRICAN BUFFALO

About 17 000 buffalo are spread throughout the park, with herds numbering between 10 and 600.

Deceptively docile, these animals are powerful and aggressive – particularly older bulls ejected from the main herd who form small bachelor herds, generally wandering not far from a river or a waterhole. These displaced bulls can be irate and vengeful and, if wounded in a fight, will readily charge any animal that disturbs them. Nevertheless, in spite of their temper, they are regularly preyed upon by lions.

Both males and females have massive curved horns that serve as formidable weapons, although the males' tend to be heavier and wider. Mainly nocturnal, buffalo usually take their daily drink of water at night, and graze mainly on coarser tufts of grass.

A rinderpest outbreak in the late 19th century reduced the number of buffalo in the park to fewer than 100, but concerted conservation efforts have resulted in a resurgence of these powerful creatures.

LEOPARD

These elegant cats generally rest during the day and are active between sunset and sunrise. They

KRUGER PARK: DAY FOUR

Elephants cross the Letaba River. Natural migration routes are now cut off.

The male leopard is essentially a loner.

prefer riverine areas and craggy hills, although occasionally they may also be seen in open bush.

They tend to be solitary, and are most likely to be seen resting on a comfortable branch or in a clump of thick bush. In spite of their size, they are very good and agile climbers, usually dragging their prey high into a tree, out of reach of hyenas and other scavengers.

Leopards are occasionally confused with cheetahs, but have several distinguishing characteristics: they do not have the black 'tear marks' linking the eyes and sides of the mouth; and have rosettes or circular spots along the side and back of the body. Leopards are also more like domestic cats in build, with compact bodies and a large head on a shorter neck.

There are more than 900 leopards in the park, but they are seldom seen because of their nocturnal activities and secretive, typically cat-like habits.

A healthy hippo can live 40-50 years.

WHY CULL?
The need for culling – the removal of certain animals to protect the species and its environment – still remains a controversial subject among conservationists and wildlife enthusiasts.

The root of the problem is simply that, in spite of its size, the park is essentially an artificial, controlled environment.

Fencing began in 1959 and resulted in the Kruger Park becoming an artificial ecosystem in which the animals are confined and unable to migrate along traditional seasonal routes. In 1948 the number of elephants in the park was estimated at between 400 and 500. In 1959 the population had doubled to 986, and by 1964 it had exploded to 2 376. The buffalo population showed a similar upward trend.

Because of the increasing damage being inflicted on trees and other vegetation, especially by elephants, the National Parks Board decided in 1965 that, where a species became a threat to itself, to other animals and the vegetation, that species should be reduced to a level that could be adequately supported by the environment. From 1966, controlled culling was instituted, and the elephant population is still being maintained at between 7 000 and 7 500, and the number of buffalo at about 25 000.

An oasis of water at Shingwedzi Rest Camp.

HIPPOPOTAMUS
In spite of their bulk – hippo reach an adult mass of 2 000 to 3 000 kg – these animals are amazingly graceful, especially in their aquatic environment. They prefer to remain in or near water by day and, if disturbed, will submerge for several minutes, finally breaking surface with a spray of vaporized water.

During the day the males bellow loudly, which may cause several others to respond with similar deep-throated, staccato grunts. They feed at night, leaving the water to forage on grass and shrubs along the river.

Male hippos occasionally become very aggressive, fighting over territory or females. The loser is usually forced to leave the herd. Watch when a hippo yawns – those teeth can inflict severe wounds.

Hippos generally occur in groups of 5 to 10, but may congregate in herds of more than 50.

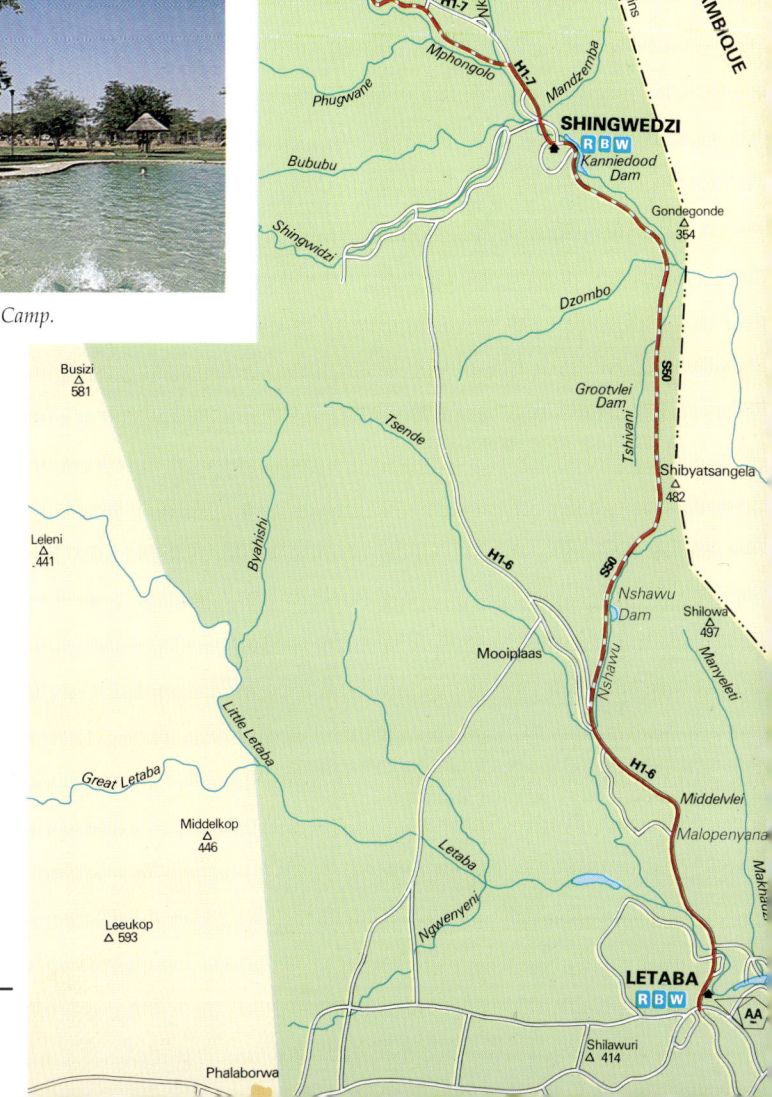

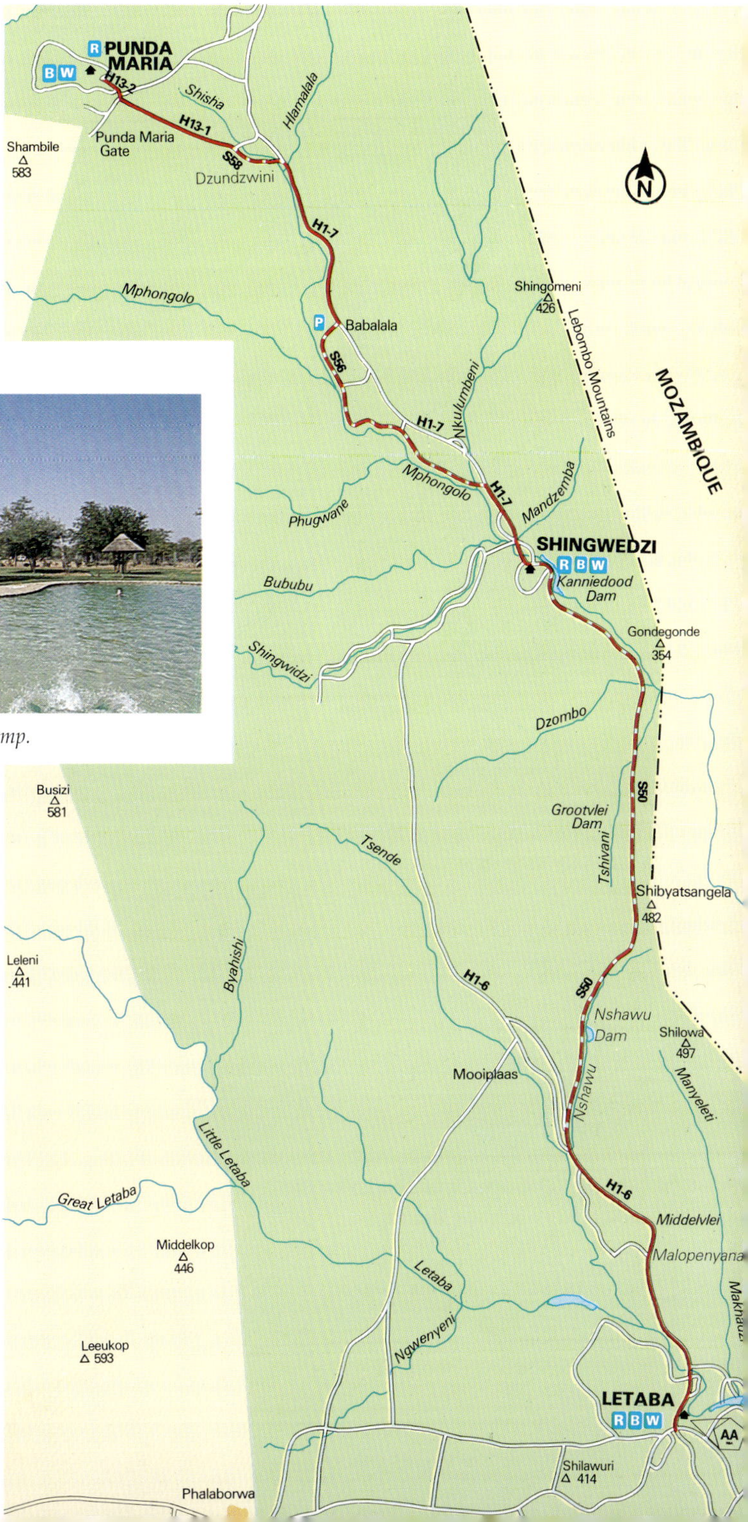

A mysterious, forest-fringed river where crocodiles lie in wait

The last day in the Kruger takes us to the far north of the park through sandstone hills covered in brightly coloured lichens. On the approach to Pafuri, magnificent baobabs dot the landscape, and lush riverine forests fringe the Luvuvhu River, sheltering a large number of nyala and masses of birds. Crocodiles are commonly seen in the river.

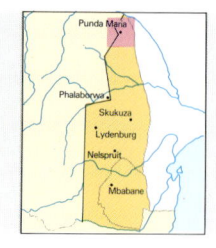

Punda Maria
Mahonie Drive
Luvuvhu River
Pafuri
Punda Maria
150 – 170 km

OUR DRIVE STARTS before breakfast on the Mahonie circular drive around Punda Maria Camp, which should take only about 45 minutes to one hour to complete, including the various stops. Try to leave camp by 06h30, following the tarred H13-2 for about 300 m before turning left onto the gravel S99. Within the first 3 km you pass a waterhole on the left where animals may already be present.

Continuing, you enter the highly diverse vegetation so characteristic of the sandveld north of Punda Maria, with an occasional pod mahogany majestically towering upwards. Halfway along the 20 km drive you reach the Matukwala Dam at the base of a hill, with a convenient off-road clearing under a tree where you can stop for a few minutes. Large numbers of buffalo often congregate around this dam. The final stretch of the S99 takes you through fairly dense bush populated with herds of buffalo before you reach the H13-2 tarred road. Turn left to return, after a further 3 km, to Punda Maria Camp.

Punda Maria to Pafuri

After a leisurely breakfast at Punda Maria, pack a picnic lunch and take the H13-2 out of camp. About 4 km from the camp take the S60 gravel road to the left, passing, after a few kilometres, the elongated and heavily overgrown Gumbandebvu hill on your left. Ignore the gravel turn-off to the right some 12 km along

A lioness surveys her territory.

PUNDA MARIA

Perhaps because of its small size and relative isolation, Punda Maria is one of the gems among the camps in the Kruger. Far from civilization, here you can 'feel' the wildness of the remote bushveld.

The camp began as a ranger's station, established in 1919 by Captain JJ Coetser. His wife apparently had a liking for striped dresses, and he named the station Punda Maria, the Swahili term for 'striped donkey' or zebra, common in the area.

The camp is built in tiers on the slopes of a large hill, looking down on mopane-filled plains dotted with hills. The huts are built on terraces with an appealing rustic appearance. A large and spacious camping area is spread along the base of the hill, complete with ablution blocks and kitchen units.

A small shop at the reception office sells curios, film and food, and there is a small restaurant next door.

NYALA

Occasionally mistaken for kudu or bushbuck – especially the females – there are definite differences in both habit and colour between the species. Bushbuck are almost invariably seen individually or in pairs, whereas nyala and kudu generally occur in small herds. The legs of male nyala are characteristically orange below the knees. When fully grown, the lyre-shaped horns of the male are only about half the length of those of a kudu. Females of all three species lack horns.

Nyala are rare and localized in the park. A small population survives along the Sabie River, while other small, scattered herds live along the eastern half of the Olifants, Letaba, Shingwedzi and Mphongolo rivers and in the tall mopane woodland around Punda Maria. Only in the luxuriant riverine forest adjoining the Luvuvhu and Limpopo rivers in the far north of the park are nyala abundant.

These antelope are usually seen in small groups, although they have been known to gather in herds of up to 30 individuals. They are predominantly browsers, eating the leaves, twigs, flowers and fruit of a wide variety of plants. Bushbuck, nyala and kudu all have an unusual barking sound, like a sharply voiced deep grunt, that they often emit at night.

Terraced huts at Punda Maria.

An impala with her newborn calf.

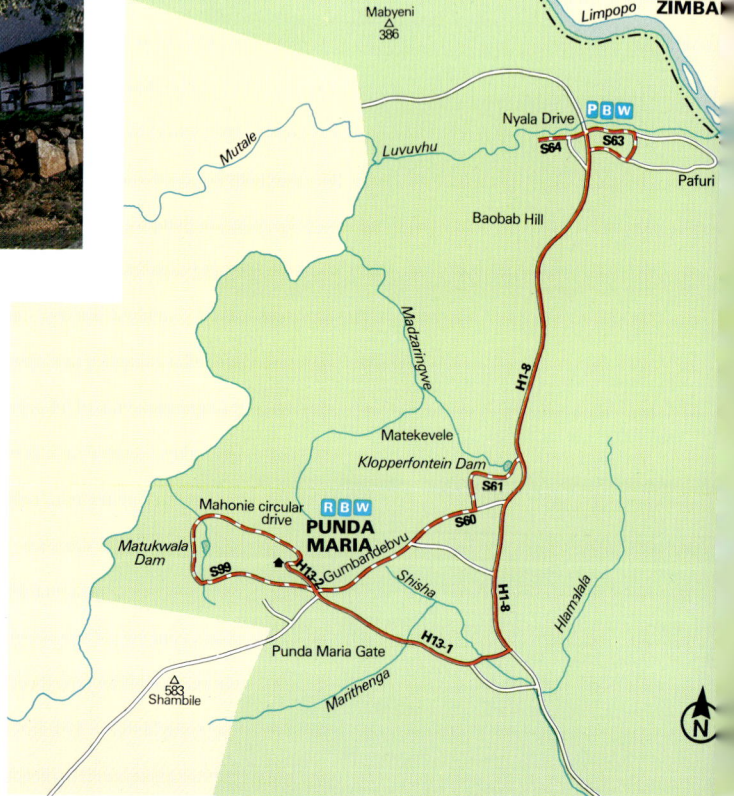

Nyala in the northern riverine forests.

KRUGER PARK: DAY FIVE

the S60, continuing on the S60 for a further 5 km before turning left onto the gravel S61. The tall mopane trees now give way to the more familiar mopane scrub, with baobab trees and low hills making an appearance. Kudus, zebras, impalas, buffaloes and elephants are regularly seen.

After about 7 km on the S61 you reach the Klopperfontein Dam, which is viewed from a short detour off the main road. Spend a few minutes here to enjoy the tranquil setting with its numerous water lilies where plentiful waterbirds trot lightly along the floating leaves. Jacanas and ducks are common, and a hippo occasionally makes this dam its home.

A few hundred metres past Klopperfontein Dam the S61 joins the tarred H1-8. Turn left and follow this road for 28 km until you reach the Luvuvhu River. Stop briefly on the highwater bridge and scan the riverbanks for any crocodiles basking in the sun. With a little luck a fish eagle may be resting in one of the trees.

Turn around and backtrack for about 100 m before turning right onto the gravel S64. This 4 km drive, known as Nyala Drive, parallels the Luvuvhu River, offering some magnificent scenery. Look out for the tall nyala, jackal berry, Natal mahogany and fig trees, and you are almost certain to see several groups of nyala shyly appear among the lush riverine vegetation. Bird life is abundant in this area, and you are likely to hear the eerie, plaintive sound of the trumpeter hornbill. Having completed the Nyala Drive, backtrack along the S64 and cross the tarred road onto the S63, which also follows the Luvuvhu. After 4 km a short turn-off to the left takes you to the Pafuri picnic site overlooking the Luvuvhu River. This is an ideal spot to enjoy your picnic lunch (toilets, braai facilities and boiling water available).

Pafuri to Punda Maria

After lunch continue along the S63, which, after about another 6 km, veers south. The road passes through a dense grove of fever trees with their characteristic yellow-green bark. The road turns westwards to pass through more typical mopane country until it rejoins the tarred H1-8 about 9 km further on.

Travel back towards Punda Maria along the H1-8, but do not turn right until you reach the main H13-1 tarred road near Dzundzwini hill. Depending on your accommodation arrangements, drive on either to Punda Maria Camp or to Punda Maria Gate. If you leave the park, the road from the gate continues past Thohoyandou to Louis Trichardt on the N1, or Great North Road.

AA Workshop and Patrol Station
Letaba Rest Camp

BAOBAB TREE

This giant of African trees is easily recognised by its extreme girth and dominating appearance. Common only in the extreme northern regions of the park, many gigantic specimens dot the mopane landscape and rugged hills in the Pafuri area. Scattered individuals occur as far south as near Tshokwane.

The trees average about 25 m when fully grown, with trunk diameters of up to 10 m. The characteristically thickened trunk ends rather abruptly in a series of twisted branches with rapidly tapering ends. The bark has a fascinating gnarled and flabby appearance, much like the texture of molten wax.

Baobabs are covered in summer with large, glossy leaves, but the foliage falls with the approach of winter, giving the trees a stark and forlorn appearance, like survivors from a forgotten age. Some trees are believed to be up to 4 000 years old.

Baobabs have very soft wood that rapidly disintegrates when the tree dies. Even in life, the central part of the stem is very often hollow with an opening at the top, providing natural and protective nesting and roosting sites for a range of birds, bats and smaller creatures such as centipedes and scorpions.

Baobabs have large white flowers, which are usually borne in November. The fruit is large, vaguely similar to that of the sausage tree, but is light green in colour and covered with a dense layer of fine, velvety fur. Baboons eat the fruit for the pulp and seeds.

Legend has it that, at the beginning of life, the gods provided all animals with seeds and plants to cultivate. Last of all came the hyena, and it received the baobab. In keeping with its supposedly stupid nature, the hyena planted the tree upside down. During winter, when the branches are bare, the baobab certainly does look as though it has been up-ended!

Inquisitive hamerkop at Punda Maria.

Fever trees dot the Luvuvhu River near the Mozambique border.

SCOTCH AND DOGS

Among the memorable characters who pioneered the remote northern Kruger was a Scotsman with 25 years of military service in India, Major Affleck Frazer. Appointed a ranger in 1903, he is said to have had an unequalled ability to consume vast quantities of Scotch whisky without any visible effect.

On one occasion, Harry Wolhuter had to spend a night at Frazer's house. It being winter, he ventured through in the early morning hours to ask Frazer if he had a spare blanket, only to find Frazer snoring on the floor, cosily asleep with his pack of 25 dogs.

The root-like branches of the baobab give it the nickname of 'upside-down tree'.

LEGENDARY POACHER

One of a regular band of cross-border ivory hunters in the northern Kruger, Cecil Barnard was an outlaw for 20 years, defying all attempts by police of three countries to catch him. With a supply base in Crooks' Corner – the infamous junction of South Africa, Mozambique and the old Rhodesia (Zimbabwe) – Barnard roamed a vast area of this truly wild and harsh region in the adventurous days around the turn of the century. He was christened *Bvekenya* by the local people, meaning 'he who swaggers when he walks'.

Of average height, he was powerfully built, with extraordinary reserves of toughness and stamina, attributes sorely needed in rugged bush conditions.

The borders of the three countries met at a beacon on an island in the Limpopo River where outlaws occasionally pitched camp. Depending on which police were in the vicinity, they would shift the beacon so that their camp would be in another country and thus legally out of reach. The adventures of Bvekenya and other fascinating 'bushveld' personalities are related in *The Ivory Trail* by South African author TV Bulpin.

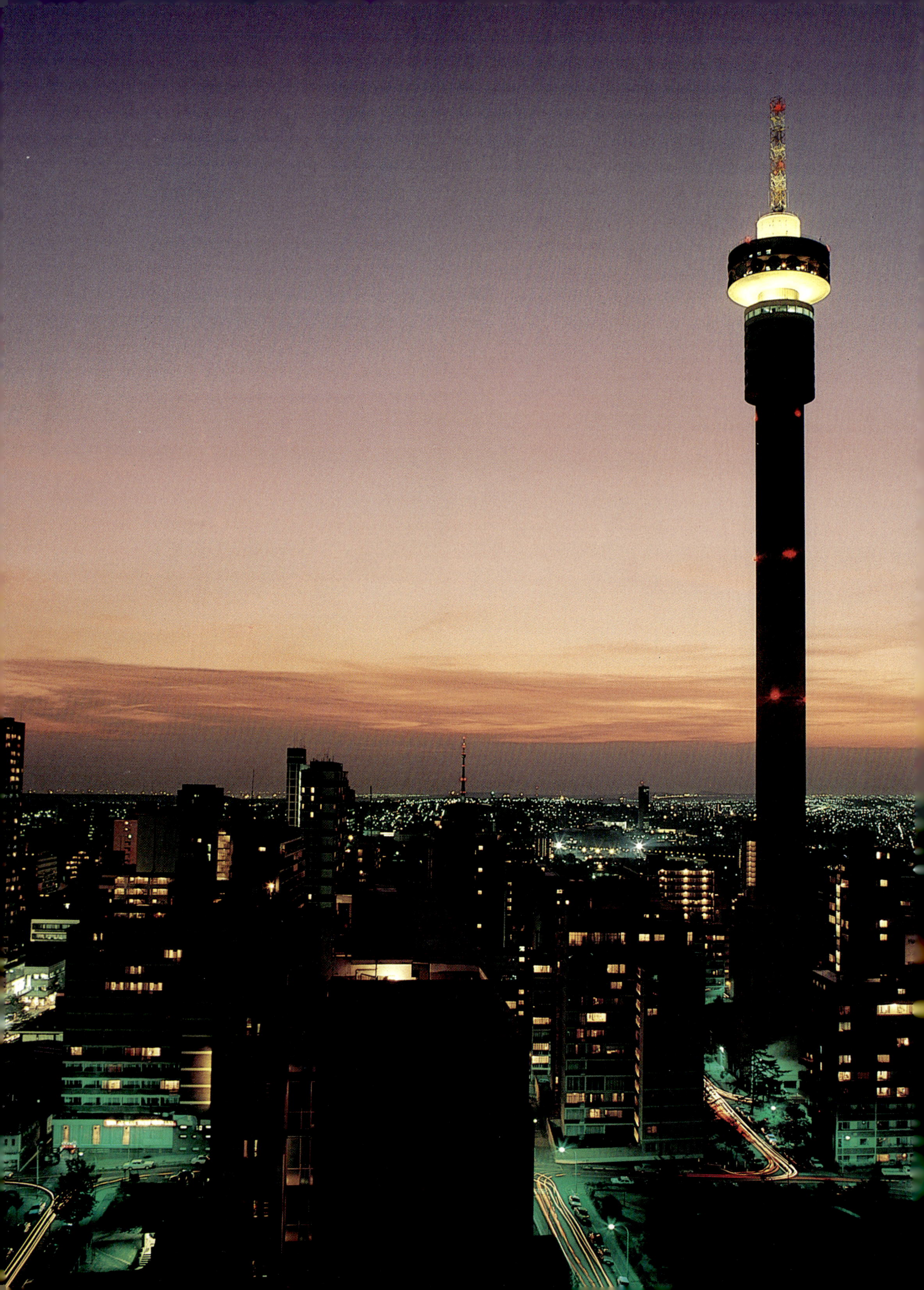

GAUTENG

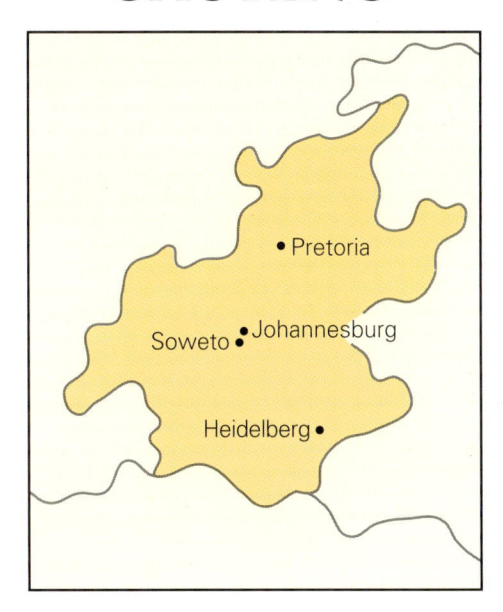

Pretoria (Johannesburg) – Rayton – Middelburg – Botshabelo – Fort Merensky **72-3**

Pretoria: Administrative capital in a city of parks **74-7**

Pretoria (Johannesburg) – Magaliesberg – Hartbeespoort Dam – Breedt's Nek **78-9**

Pretoria (Johannesburg) – Suikerbosrand – Vaal Dam – Heidelberg **80-1**

Johannesburg: Exploring *Egoli* – 'city of gold' **82-7**

Left: *Glittering Johannesburg – modern city with a history steeped in gold.*

Against Sekhukhune's warriors – a German fort on the African veld

This one-day outing is not so much a tour as a visit to two interesting places – first the Willem Prinsloo Agricultural Museum at Rayton, then the rest of the day spent at the old Botshabelo Mission, visiting the colourful Ndebele village nearby and the 19th-century, stone-walled Fort Merensky. Except for minor access roads, the entire route is tarred.

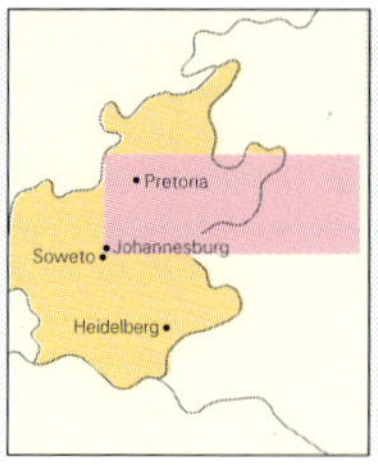

Pretoria 260 – 280 km
Johannesburg 340 – 360 km
Rayton
Middelburg
Botshabelo
Fort Merensky

LEAVE PRETORIA BY driving east along Schoeman Street, which becomes the N4 to Witbank. Stay on the N4 and note your kms as you pass through the N1 interchange. (If you are starting from Johannesburg, drive north on the M1 and N1 towards Pretoria and Pietersburg for roughly 60 km from the city centre, then exit left, following the signs on to the N4 for Witbank. Note your kms at the N4.)

After roughly 26 km on the N4 (from the N1 interchange) take Exit 27 for the R515 to Rayton. At the end of the off-ramp turn left onto the R515; at the four-way stop street turn right onto the R104 for Bronkhorstspruit. The R104 runs almost due east, parallel to the N4, and after travelling roughly 4 km along it, turn left onto the access road into the Willem Prinsloo Agricultural Museum (entrance fee).

The old-established farm, former home of the Prinsloo family, has been developed as a living exhibition of farm life in the former Transvaal during the 19th century (see below).

One of several carriages at the Willem Prinsloo Museum.

FARM BREAD AND PEACH BRANDY
The aim of the Willem Prinsloo Agricultural Museum is to bring the past back to life. The original farm homestead has been fully restored and refurnished as it must have appeared a century ago, and the effect of stepping back through time to a living moment is enhanced by the presence of farm animals and clucking poultry. New buildings have been erected to house a collection of horse-drawn vehicles and a fascinating variety of early farm equipment.

This is a 'living' museum, and it remains a functioning farm, with the old equipment often being used for the farm chores. At weekends, visitors can see the smithy and the leatherworks in action, watch sheep being dipped or bread being baked – or see the fiery 'mampoer' peach brandy being distilled in the traditional manner.

Most of the demonstrations are held on Saturdays.

NAZARETH ON THE HIGHVELD
Roughly 120 years ago the Dutch Reformed Church established a tiny settlement on the south bank of the Klein Olifants River and named it Nazareth. There were objections to this name – for reasons unknown – and a few years later the settlement was renamed Middelburg. Still standing in the town is the so-called white church, dating from 1890. In the early days, when farmers flocked into the town to celebrate *Nagmaal* (Communion) once every three months, the grassy fields around the church became a bustling city of tents and ox-wagons, and the social scene flourished. The church can still be visited, as can the old Meijers Bridge across the river – which also dates back to 1890.

NDEBELE VILLAGE
Some of the descendants of refugees who sheltered at the Botshabelo Mission now live in the brightly painted Ndebele village on the south bank of the Klein Olifants River – just a few hundred metres from the old mission buildings.

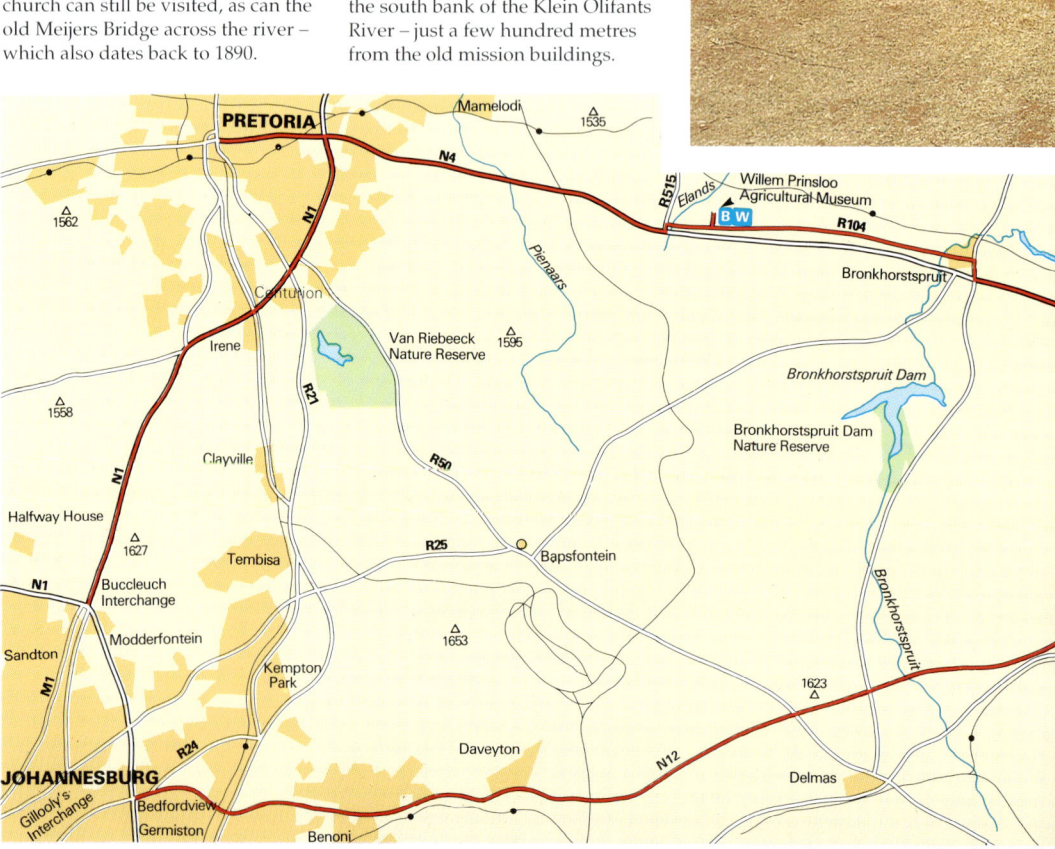

There are shaded braai sites here, a cafeteria, shop and toilets, and there is also a youth hostel and well-used lecture hall.

Return to the tar (R104) and turn left. After roughly 15 km you reach the town of Bronkhorstspruit, near the site of the 1880 Battle of Bronkhorstspruit that marked the start of the First Anglo-Boer War. Drive through the town and, at the stop street on the far side, turn right. Turn left shortly after this to rejoin the N4 towards Witbank and Middelburg, noting your kms as you rejoin the N4.

Bronkhorstspruit to Botshabelo
Continue on the N4 past Witbank. About 68km after rejoining the N4, exit left for Middelburg at the Van Dyksdrift/Middelburg off-ramp. The town owes its name to the fact

72

that in pioneer days it served as the halfway house – a convenient distance for an ox wagon – between Pretoria and Lydenburg.

At the T-junction after 4,5 km, turn right into Kerkstraat and note your kms as you pass Jan van Riebeeck Street (the N11 for Belfast and Nelspruit) on your right. Kerkstraat becomes the N11 for Groblersdal. After 400 m you pass a turn-off on your left to the town's old cemetery, where there are a number of Anglo-Boer War graves, including those of local concentration camp victims. About 200 m after this turn-off you pass the *Witkerk* (white-painted church) on your right. Some 8,5 km after noting your kms, turn left into the Botshabelo Museum and Nature Reserve (entrance fee). A gravel road leads through the reserve for 4 km to the entrance to the old mission station. Just before driving down to the mission, turn right to visit romantic, stone-walled Fort Merensky overlooking the mission (see below).

From the fort, return to the access road that leads, after a few hundred metres, to a parking area opposite the information office (where brochures are available). The mission, on the north bank of the Klein Olifants River, is now the centre of a variety of attractions. The original buildings are now a museum and, along the grassy banks of the river, there are tree-shaded braai sites with water and toilets. A range of accommodation is available. The Ndebele village nearby is notable for its brightly and imaginatively painted houses.

The whole complex lies in the centre of the Botshabelo Nature Reserve, and there are attractive circular trails through the reserve offering hikers walks that range from four hours to two days.

On your return from Botshabelo, retrace your route through Middelburg and join the N4, heading west to bypass Witbank. If you are returning to Pretoria, stay on the N4 for the entire journey. If you are returning to Johannesburg, turn off onto the N12 south-east of Witbank at Interchange 103.

AA Office AA House, 395 Schoeman Street Pretoria 0002 Tel (012) 28 3829
AA Office AA House, 66 De Korte Street Braamfontein, Johannesburg 2001 Tel (011) 403 5700
Willem Prinsloo Agricultural Museum PO Box 677, Rayton 1001 Tel (01213) 44171
Botshabelo Museum and Nature Reserve PO Box 14, Middelburg 1050 Tel (0132) 43 1319

A FORT AGAINST SEKHUKHUNE

Botshabelo means place of refuge, and the mission was established in 1865 by Alexander Merensky of the Berlin Mission Society to serve as a refuge for Christian converts persecuted by King Sekhukhune.

To protect the mission and its inhabitants from further attacks, Merensky built a fort on the hill above the mission. The fort, originally Fort Wilhelm, was a mixture of Sotho stonework and German castle, and it now makes a romantic memorial to the days when the African veld was a frontier of mystery and adventure to some, and a place of profound turmoil to others.

From the fort you can look down over the treetops to the spire of the little church (which you may visit through a side door).

A colourfully dressed Ndebele woman outside her home at Botshabelo.

Fort Merensky retains the flavour of African frontier days.

BOTSHABELO NATURE RESERVE

The reserve surrounds the old mission and is home to eland, blesbok, springbok, wildebeest, hartebeest and many other smaller animals. There are no dangerous predators, and visitors can choose from three walks through the area – two of these take approximately four hours each, and the third is a more substantial hike lasting six hours. There are also short stretches of road through the reserve, allowing visitors to view the game from their cars.

Below: *The old Botshabelo Mission building.*

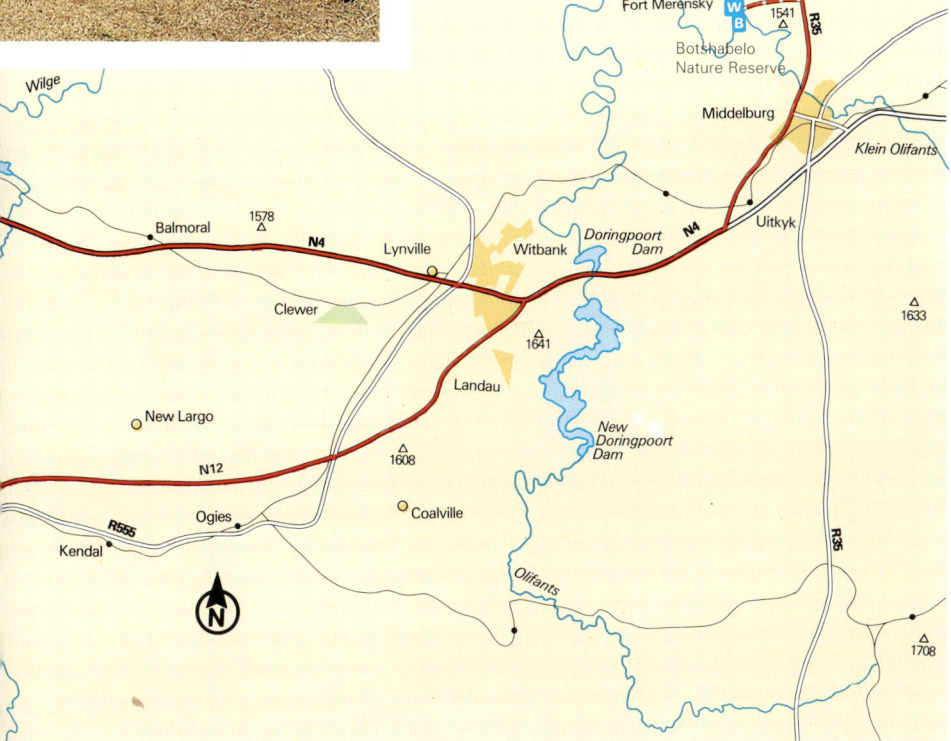

• PLACES OF INTEREST IN PRETORIA •

Manicured lawns surround the stately sandstone Union Buildings – the administrative seat of South Africa's national government.

A mingling of old and new in the Jacaranda City

PRETORIA TODAY is a mix of ultra-modern architecture and stately buildings dating from its days as the capital of republican Transvaal. It is a pretty city – its gardens and trees flourish in the fertile soil of the Apies River valley, and spring brings the spectacle of tens of thousands of flowering jacaranda trees.

This amalgam of modern and historic is also found in the many places of interest in the city. The visitor will find a variety of museums that preserve relics of days gone by, and also fascinating glimpses of up-to-the-minute scientific and industrial developments. Over weekends, residents have easy access to the surrounding countryside, where highveld meets lowveld along the ridge of the Magaliesberg, and rivers and lakes offer lovely settings in which to relax.

Nguni-speaking settlers, who became known as the *Ndebele* (derived from their Sotho nickname of 'refugees'), are thought to have been the first people to recognize the suitability of the Apies River valley as a place to put down roots. They named the river after one of their chiefs, *Tshwane* (little ape), which was later translated into the Afrikaans *Apies*. During the migratory wars in KwaZulu-Natal, another band of refugees arrived here under the leadership of Mzilikazi, but they were forced to abandon their villages in their flight from a regiment of Zulu raiders in 1832.

Voortrekkers were the next people to settle in this lovely valley, and the site was eventually chosen in the 1850s as a central seat of government. They named it Pretoria after Andries Pretorius, the Boer hero at the Battle of Blood River (see pages 106 – 7).

As you approach Pretoria from the south, you see the monolithic, granite *Voortrekker Monument* on Voortrekkerhoogte. Built in 1949, its surrounding wall has been sculpted with 56 wagons representing the laager at Blood River. Inside the monument, marble friezes depict the Great Trek. A museum in the grounds contains furniture, and other Voortrekker relics, and also has a restaurant. Picnic tables nearby offer fine views over the city. Museum and monument open daily except Good Friday and Christmas Day; entrance fee; kiosk open daily; traditional meals Sunday 12h00 – 14h00; tel (012) 323 0682.

Hilltop forts
Nearby are two hilltop forts that formed part of the Boer defence of the city: *Fort Schanskop*, which is reached on the Voortrekker Monument access road, and *Fort Klapperkop*, situated on the scenic Johann Rissik Drive. Built principally to protect the seat of government against armed revolution by the disgruntled foreign gold-seekers *(uitlanders)* of Johannesburg in the 1890s, the forts – after years of neglect – now house military museums; Fort Klapperkop tel (012) 46 3235; Fort Schanskop tel (012) 71 5560.

Johann Rissik Drive winds through part of the *Fountains*

The high-rise skyline of central Pretoria is softened by trees and gardens.

Valley Nature Reserve and offers excellent views of Pretoria, particularly during jacaranda time in October and November. From here you also have fine views of the *Union Buildings* across the valley. This magnificent sandstone administrative centre for the national government was designed by Sir Herbert Baker at the time of Union in 1910. Built on the slopes of Meintjies Kop, the curved main building, colonnaded and flanked by two 55 m domed towers, faces beautiful terraced gardens. Another scenic drive leads between the Union Buildings and the gardens, offering fine city views: a walk up Meintjies Kop reveals panoramic vistas.

'Old lion' remembered

The focal point of the city centre is *Church Square*, at the intersection of Church and Paul Kruger streets. In the central garden stands an imposing statue of President Paul Kruger, sculpted by Anton van Wouw to honour the 'old lion' of the Transvaal, who achieved world fame when his Zuid-Afrikaansche Republiek (ZAR) took on the might of the British Empire in 1899. Several impressive old buildings face onto the square, including the republican *Raadsaal* (council chamber) and the Palace of Justice, which was used as a military hospital during the Anglo-Boer War and now houses the Transvaal Supreme Court. Next to the Raadsaal stands the Gauteng Provincial Building (entrance in Bosman Street), its modern lines contrasting with those of its stately predecessor.

In Church Street, west of the square, you can visit the *Kruger House Museum*, the simple home where President Kruger lived from 1884 until his exile in 1900. Apart from the original furnishings, there are also many of the president's personal possessions, the wagon in which his family trekked to the Transvaal, his state coach and railway carriage, and a collection of mementoes of the ZAR. Open daily except Good Friday and Christmas Day; entrance fee; tel (012) 326 9172.

Across the street is the *Gereformeerde (Kruger) Church*, where the president sometimes delivered the Sunday sermon, and a few blocks further west lies the cemetery known as *Heroes' Acre*, where Kruger is buried.

Delicate jacarandas tint the spring air of Pretoria a hazy mauve.

Another interesting collection of items from the ZAR days is housed in the *National Cultural History and Open Air Museum* in Boom Street. This museum also contains an ethnology section, collections of furniture, costumes, porcelain, ceramics, firearms, Bibles, Anglo-Boer War relics, medals and coins, and an archaeological section where a 2 000-year-old mummy is exhibited. Open daily except holidays; entrance fee; tel (012) 341 1320.

Mammals and birds

The *Transvaal Museum of Natural History* in Paul Kruger Street houses a large display on life's genesis, and exhibits of mammals, reptiles, amphibians and insects. It incorporates the *Austin Roberts Bird Hall* and the *Museum of Geological Survey*. Open daily except New Year's Day, Good Friday, Christmas Day; entrance fee; coffee shop; tel (012) 322 7632.

Pretoria's historic *City Hall* is across the street from the museum. It has an imposing clock tower with a carillon of 32 bells, and the grounds feature a colonnade of fountains, and statues of Andries Pretorius and his son, Marthinus Wessel Pretorius, who became the first ZAR president. Further south along Paul Kruger Street is the *Pretoria Railway Station*, designed by Sir Herbert Baker, where an 1889 locomotive can be seen.

At the close of the Anglo-Boer War, the Treaty of Vereeniging was signed in a beautiful Victorian house in Jacob Maré Street, *Melrose House*. It has been preserved as a period house museum, containing furniture, stained-glass windows, mosaic floors, ceiling mouldings, and a fine doll collection. Open Tuesday to Sunday except public holidays; entrance fee; tel (012) 322 2805.

The house faces onto *Burgers' Park*, laid out in 1882 and named after President Thomas François Burgers, of whom there is a statue in the park. The area was used by early visitors to Pretoria to outspan their wagons. It contains a kiosk (closed Monday) next to the bandstand, and a 'florarium' housing indigenous and exotic plants.

Several blocks from Burgers' Park, in Van Boeschoten Street in Sunnyside, is the *Education Museum*, which portrays the development of education in the former Transvaal since 1837. In the grounds are old-fashioned transport vehicles, a diggers' classroom and a school on wheels. These last two items point to just a few of the problems faced by educationists in the early days: a largely uneducated adult population and, outside the prospecting areas, a population so thinly spread that education, in many cases, literally had to be taken to the pupil's distant doorstep.

The massive Voortrekker Monument.

A view of Church Square, with the old Raadsaal building in the background.

Modern technology is the subject dealt with by the *South African Museum of Science and Technology* on the second floor, Didacta Building, Skinner Street. It has a resource centre for schoolchildren, and exhibitions on such subjects as atoms and nuclear energy, space travel, anatomy and water. Open Monday to Friday and Sunday afternoon, except public holidays; tel (012) 322 6404. The technology of transport is the focus of the *AB Eksteen Museum of Transport Technology* in the Forum Building in Bosman Street, where displays include meteorology, Antarctic expeditions, civil aviation and road safety. Open weekdays; tel (012) 290 2016.

Science and technology are the themes at the *Council for Scientific and Industrial Research*, with its headquarters at Scientia near the N4. The CSIR, which conducts research into almost every aspect of life, offers tours by arrangement (tel (012) 841 2911 and ask for the visitors' office). The *South African Bureau of Standards* in Groenkloof also offers tours of its premises, where it performs a quality-control role for household and industrial goods; tel (012) 341 1311.

Iscor, the iron and steel plant at Wespark, conducts guided tours of its mills, furnaces and smelting and coke ovens once a week. No children under 12; closed shoes essential; tel (012) 298 1111.

At Cullinan, where the Cullinan Diamond of 3 106 carats was discovered in 1905, you can visit the *Premier Diamond Mine*. A tour lasting about two hours takes you to the big hole and shaft, as well as the grease tables and sorting area. Sturdy shoes essential; no children under 10; booking essential; tel (01213) 40081. While you are in the area, visit the mining museum on the road to the mine entrance, and the town of Cullinan, where wood-and-iron buildings date from the early days of the century.

There are also a number of places of interest in and around Johannesburg and the greater Witwatersrand area, all of which are within easy reach of Pretoria – see pages 78 – 87.

Crime comes under the microscope at the *South African Police Museum*, Compol Building, corner Pretorius Street and Volkstem Avenue. Open Monday to Saturday except public holidays; identity document required; no bags or coats; tel (012) 353 6771. In related vein is the *Correctional Services Museum* at Pretoria Central Prison in Potgieter Street. The only museum of its kind in South Africa, it depicts the development of the penal system. Of considerable interest are exhibits of prisoners' hobbies and some of the objects – both lawful and unlawful – manufactured in prisons.

The South African Air Force is the second-oldest in the world; it was founded in February 1920, less than two years after Britain's Royal Air Force and its history is illustrated at Valhalla. Exhibits include aircraft, uniforms, medals, paintings and weapons. Open daily; road access via the R101; tel (012) 351 2111.

Delville Wood Memorial – a tribute to soldiers killed during World War I.

Homes and hearths

Slightly further afield, at the *Pioneer Open-Air Museum* in Pretoria Road, Silverton, you can see an old thatched farmhouse that brings home the simplicity of the lifestyle of some early settlers. Braai and picnic sites overlook the restored old farmyard on the banks of the Moreleta Spruit. On Saturday museum staff bake bread in an outdoor oven and offer it for sale, while during school terms various skills are demonstrated in the mornings, such as soap-making, coffee-roasting and corn-stamping. Open daily; kiosk; tel (012) 803 6086.

Another interesting farm is the old *Doornkloof Farm and Smuts House Museum* at Irene. This unpretentious wood-and-iron farmhouse has been restored to its original state, when South African Prime Minister and international statesman Jan Smuts lived here with his wife, Issie, in sparsely furnished simplicity. There is a tearoom here, and braai and picnic sites on the lovely, wooded hillside. Open daily except religious holidays; small entrance fee; tel (012) 667 1176.

Still almost 'in the country', although on a fairly grand scale, is *Zwartkoppies Hall*, signposted from Exit 11 on the N4 (Witbank Highway) east of the city. Lithuanian-born Sammy Marks, whose home this was, rose from being a pedlar of imitation jewellery to become the leading industrialist of the republican Transvaal. Fairly modest in the beginning, Zwartkoppies represents a prosperous colonial household of the late-Victorian era. Taking refreshments in the tea garden brings substance to the elegant reality. Open daily except Monday; admission on guided tours only; tel (012) 803 6158.

One of the best collections of South African art is housed at the *Pretoria Art Museum* in Arcadia Park. The museum has large holdings of works by Pierneef, Oerder, Van Wouw and Wenning, as well as modern South African artists. The Association of Friends of the Pretoria Art Museum arranges a programme of lectures, films and concerts. Open daily except religious holidays; tel (012) 344 1807.

A more detailed collection of the works of Anton van Wouw can be seen, by appointment, at *Van Wouw House* on the corner of Rupert and Clarke streets in Brooklyn; tel (012) 420 3243. The work of another prominent South African sculptor can be seen at the *Coert Steynberg Museum* in Berg Avenue, Pretoria North. Set on the slopes of the Magaliesberg, the atmospheric house and extensive gardens where Steynberg lived are filled with fine examples of his work. Open Tuesday to Saturday; tel (012) 546 0404.

A 1920s cigarette factory at 218 Vermeulen Street has been converted into the *Pierneef Museum*. Furnished in the style of the 1920s, the double-storey building now houses a collection of Pierneef's paintings, drawings and sketches. Open weekdays except public holidays; tearoom, entrance fee; tel (012) 323 1419.

Historians and collectors alike find a haven in the *Claude V Malan Museum* in Polley's Arcade, where the displays range from militaria to gold and silver, porcelain, jewellery, old timepieces, books and toys. Closed on Sunday; tel (012) 322 0544.

The Performing Arts Council of the Transvaal presents a full programme of theatre, opera and ballet at the ultra-modern *State Theatre* at the corner of Church and Prinsloo streets. Twice-weekly guided tours last 90 minutes.

The Transvaal Museum in Paul Kruger Street houses a fine collection of natural history exhibits.

A statue of Andries Pretorius in front of the imposing City Hall.

The Reformed church that Paul Kruger attended regularly.

Tours include visits to the various auditoriums, and the wardrobes and decor studio. The theatre has a restaurant and a coffee bar. Tel (012) 322 1665 for information; watch local press for programme schedules. Bargain-hunters can visit the regular flea market held outside the theatre on Saturday morning (except long weekends).

Animal kingdom
A favourite with visitors to Pretoria is the famous *National Zoological Garden* in Boom Street. This beautifully landscaped zoo covers 40 ha of hillside, and offers a scenic cable-car ride to the top of the koppie. From here you can stroll down past large enclosures containing big cats, antelope, hippo, camel and rhino. There are also enclosures with owls, eagles and other birds, monkeys and apes – a total of 140 mammal species and 240 bird species. The grounds offer picnic and braai sites on the banks of the Apies River, a restaurant, an information kiosk, and lectures and tours for groups on request. Open daily; entrance fee; carnivores and seals fed daily; tel (012) 328 3268. Outside the zoo, colourful items of craftwork are on sale.

Next to the zoo in Boom Street is the *Aquarium and Reptile Park*, which houses an impressive collection of freshwater and sea fish, snakes, crocodiles, tortoises and lizards. Open daily; entrance fee; tel (012) 328 3268. Further out of town there is another aquarium near Hartbeespoort Dam, as well as a snake and animal park in the village of Schoemansville (see pages 78 – 9).

Also near the dam is *De Wildt Cheetah Research Station*, which is reached off the R513. On the tours by vehicle, offered on Saturday and Sunday, you can see cheetah – including the striped king cheetah – wild dog, brown hyaena and Cape vulture. Advance booking essential; no children under six; tour fee; duration two hours; tel (012) 504 1921.

Central Pretoria is well endowed with parks and nature areas. On the southern edge of the city is the 500 ha *Fountains Valley Nature Reserve* – proclaimed as a game park in 1895. About 60 ha have been set aside as a regional park, amid lawns and trees, tennis courts, a children's playground, a swimming pool and a tearoom. The park is reached from Fountains Circle, along the Johannesburg-Centurion road.

Indigenous trees and shrubs
The *National Botanical Gardens* (entrance in Cussonia Avenue near the CSIR) grows more than half of the South African tree species in its 77 ha of ground. It offers a lovely area for walking amidst the climatically grouped plants. Tours for groups can be arranged; tel (012) 804 3200.)

Faerie Glen Nature Reserve, which forms part of the *Moreleta Spruit Trail*, is one of the most attractive open areas in Pretoria. Many indigenous Transvaal trees, shrubs and aloes have been planted here, and it has a rich variety of birds. The trail also takes you through the *Meyers Park Nature Reserve*, as the paths wind along the banks of the Moreleta Spruit from Menlyn Drive, Garsfontein, to the Pioneer Open-air Museum in Silverton. Further information is available from the Pretoria Parks and Recreation Department, Munitoria Building, corner Van der Walt and Vermeulen streets, tel (012) 313 8820.

Also under the authority of the parks department is the *Wonderboom Nature Reserve* (reached off the R55/M1). The focal point of the reserve is the *wonderboom* (wonder tree) – a wild fig more than 1 000 years old which, with its subsidiary trunks, spreads its branches over 55 m. There are braai and picnic sites, a children's playground and a hiking trail to an Anglo-Boer War fort on top of a nearby koppie. Monkeys, *dassies* (hyrax) and a wide variety of birds make their home here.

The *Austin Roberts Bird Sanctuary* in Boshoff Street, New Muckleneuk, is named after the South African naturalist whose 1940 book of birds is still regarded as a standard work. The fenced sanctuary has a hide overlooking a dam that attracts a fascinating assortment of waterbirds, and you can also see a large number of other species here. (A small museum displays local birds.)

Nearby, at *Magnolia Dell* in Queen Wilhelmina Avenue, a park with beautifully laid-out gardens offers a popular weekend family venue, with a children's playground, a pond for miniature boats, and a refreshment kiosk. Once a month it features Art in the Park – an open-air market for paintings and crafts.

Highveld habitat
A short distance out of the city, *Derdepoort Regional Park* (off the N1 near the R513 intersection) offers a bushveld farm atmosphere for picnics and braais. There is a miniature farmyard with farm animals, playgrounds for children and a hiking trail along the Moreleta and Hartebeest spruits. Open daily; small entrance fee; tel (012) 808 0828.

North of Wonderboom, on the R101 (the Onderstepoort road) is South Africa's first enviro-museum, the *Twaing Museum*, located at the site of a crater lake that was formed some 200 000 years ago when a blazing meteorite slammed into the earth's surface. Open daily; tel (01214) 98730.

The Hennops River valley, Magaliesberg, the Hartbeespoort Dam and Buffelspoort Dam are popular retreats within easy reach of Pretoria, where pleasure resorts and braai and picnic areas attract many visitors over weekends.

For further information on Pretoria and its surroundings, contact the Pretoria Publicity Association, Tourist Rendezvous Centre, corner of Vermeulen and Prinsloo streets, Pretoria 0002. Tel (012) 313 7694/7980.

Melrose House, where the Anglo-Boer War ended.

Dutch Reformed church, Bosman St.

Into the rugged Magaliesberg – to Hartbeespoort and Breedt's Nek

Our route leads first to the Magaliesberg and the Hartbeespoort Dam, then we follow the northern slopes of the Magaliesberg, cut by rugged gorges, and pass through typical northern bushveld to reach the Buffelspoort Dam. Here we turn south and cross the Magaliesberg over the scenic Breedt's Nek. All but a few kilometres of the route is tarred.

Johannesburg
260 – 280 km
Pretoria
240 – 260 km
Magaliesberg
Hartbeespoort Dam
Breedt's Nek

IF YOU ARE STARTING FROM Johannesburg, drive first to Fourways in Sandton – this is a four-way intersection with the R564 running east – west, the M81 running south and the R511 running north. Drive onto the R511, heading north, and note your kms. (If you are starting from Pretoria, leave the city by driving west on the N4 for Rustenburg, and join the route at the intersection of the N4 with the R511/R104, near the Pelindaba Toll Plaza.

After travelling about 15 km from Fourways, turn left to stay on the R511 for Hartbeespoort/Pelindaba. After a further 7,8 km, cross the Hennops River and pass, on your left, the Hennops Pride Pleasure Resort. (This resort has picnic and braai facilities, swimming, water-slides, trampolines, horse-riding and go-karts. Entrance fee.)

Roughly 3,5 km from the Hennops resort, you pass, on your right, a hill covered with aloes. You cross the Hennops River twice more, and pass other resorts on both sides of the river. Some 9 km from Hennops Pride you reach a four-way junction with the R104 and then cross over the Pelindaba/Quagga Toll Road (N4). Travellers on the R104 from Pretoria join our route at this junction, roughly 15 km from Pretoria's outskirts, while those who choose the toll road join the route 2,3 km later. Note your kms at this junction and drive north-west for Schoemansville on what is now the N4/R511; 3,8 km later you crest a hill and see ahead of you the Hartbeespoort Dam and the long summit of the Magaliesberg. Just over 1 km after this you pass, on your right, a stone cross set on top of a small koppie – this commemorates the Anglo-Boer War hero, General Hendrik Schoeman, who farmed nearby.

Some 8,6 km after noting your kms, turn right to visit what is claimed to be the largest freshwater aquarium in Africa. It houses most species of South African freshwater fish, also crocodiles, seals and penguins. (Entrance fee.)

Note your kms at this turn-off to the aquarium, and continue on the R104 towards Schoemansville. After 3 km turn right at the traffic lights and, 900 m later, turn left into the parking area for the Hartbeespoort Cableway. The ride to the summit, from where there are panoramic views, makes a memorable introduction to the Magaliesberg. (There is a refreshment kiosk alongside the upper cableway station; shaded picnic and braai places, water and toilets.)

After descending from the mountain, retrace your route to the R104 and turn right, noting your kms. After 2,2 km, in the centre of Schoemansville, you reach, on your left, the entrance to the large Hartbeespoort Snake and Animal Park (entrance fee, see alongside). Picnicking is allowed in the grounds on terraced lawns overlooking the lake, and short boat trips around the lake are sometimes available. Across the road from the park is a hotel that serves lunches and snacks; other establishments in the town also offer meals.

Kosmos and Breedt's Nek
Continue on the R104 towards Rustenburg; 1,1 km from the Snake and Animal Park you pass through a short tunnel and then drive along the top of the Hartbeespoort Dam wall; 1,8 km later you reach a crossroads where the N4 leads right and straight ahead, and the R512 leads left. If you have already lunched, turn left onto the R512 – noting your kms. If you want to stop now for a picnic lunch, turn right onto the N4. (On your right, after 1,6 km on the R513, is Mount Amanzi, with shaded braai places, water, toilets and a kiosk; 300 m further on, also on your right, is the Crocodile River Picnic Site on the Johan Rissik Estate, with shaded braai places, water and toilets. Both areas charge entrance fees.)

If you choose to picnic at one of these places along the N4, return to the N4/R104/R512 crossroads after lunch and drive straight across onto the R512 – noting your kms. (If you chose not to turn onto the N4, then you will have turned left at the crossroads onto the R512.) The R512 climbs over Commando Nek, then sweeps down into the Magalies River valley, with the dam visible again on your left.

After 1,7 km on the R512, turn left onto the road into Kosmos – a 5 km drive that skirts the shore of the dam. The little settlement of Kosmos is noted for its flower-filled gardens and attractive views over the water.

Retrace your route out of Kosmos and back to the N4/R104/R512 crossroads, then turn left onto the N4/R512 towards Rustenburg – noting your kms. After 5,3 km, where the N4 turns off right to Rustenburg, continue straight ahead on the R104.

You now pass through citrus groves, then typical northern bushveld. On your left are the northern slopes of the Magaliesberg, gashed by river gorges to expose cliffs of red rock. After 35,5 km turn left for Maanhaarrand (immediately after passing the Buffelspoort Holiday Resort) and note your kms again at the turn; 3,1 km later you pass a turn-off left to the Buffelspoort Dam.

Some 6,7 km after this turn-off to the Buffelspoort Dam, turn left onto the Maanhaarrand road, noting your kms again.

Buffelspoort Dam provides 'seaside' entertainments.

TIGERS AND CHIMPS ON THE HIGHVELD
The Hartbeespoort Snake and Animal Park occupies a long stretch of the narrow strip of land lying between the main road and the north-eastern shore of the dam.

The park contains an excellent reptile collection and also lions, tigers, leopards, cheetahs and chimpanzees. Snake and seal demonstrations are held regularly at the park.

Looking south from Breedt's Nek to Buffelspoort.

The tarred surface gives way to gravel almost immediately, and the road begins to wind up the northern slopes of the Magaliesberg towards Breedt's Nek. After 5,1 km, shortly before reaching the summit of Breedt's Nek Pass, park on the shoulder of the road for a panoramic view.

Continue over Breedt's Nek Pass, to reach a T-junction with the tarred R24. Turn left onto the R24 towards Krugersdorp, noting your

GAUTENG

Flowers bloom near Hekpoort in the warm and fertile Magalies valley.

Weekends see Hartbeespoort Dam transformed into a watersport playground.

THE WATERS OF HARTBEESPOORT

The Hartbeespoort Dam was built for irrigation purposes in the 1920s, but it has since become one of the Highveld's principal venues for watersport enthusiasts, and has proved equally popular with innumerable local fishermen.

The dam is fed principally by the Crocodile and Magalies rivers. When full, it covers nearly 12 sq km and reaches a depth of 45 m. On its shores are an assortment of angling and boating clubs, and also numerous holiday houses in Kosmos and Schoemansville. Through a 544 km-long system of canals, the dam irrigates almost 16 000 ha of farmland producing tobacco, wheat, lucerne, flowers and a range of subtropical fruits.

SOARING TO THE MOUNTAIN TOPS

The 1,1 km Hartbeespoort Cableway soars upwards from the lower slopes of the Magaliesberg to a station at the summit. The journey lasts for a thrilling six minutes, and from the top of the mountain there are magnificent views over the surrounding countryside – the Magaliesberg range itself marking a prominent physical division between northern and southern Transvaal. The cable car runs every day of the week from 08h30 to 15h30 (last car ascends at 17h00 at weekends). It is advisable, however, to check on the wind conditions before setting out – tel (01211) 30706.

PREHISTORIC MAANHAARRAND

The village of *Maanhaarrand* (mane ridge) between Breedt's Nek and Hekpoort is named after the steep rocky ridges of the Magaliesberg, which here resemble the *maanhaar* (mane) of a lion. The village lies in the centre of an area rich in prehistoric rock engravings – the precise origins of which are unknown. According to one theory, they date back to the Late Stone Age, but no certain dates have been attached to them. Also found in the area are the remains of Iron Age villages – in which numerous fragments of pottery, bone and human skeletons have been found.

kms. You now pass through Maanhaarrand (see above). After 8,4 km on the R24, turn left onto the R560 for Hekpoort, noting your kms again. The road winds through a picturesque farming area with the craggy spine of the Magaliesberg towering on your left. After 12,5 km you reach a junction with the R563.

If you are returning to Pretoria, continue straight ahead here on the R560 – after about 33,7 km, turn right onto the R104 at the N4/R104/R512 intersection and drive through Schoemansville to rejoin the N4 for Pretoria.

If you are returning to Johannesburg, turn right onto the R563 and note your kms. After 3,5 km you pass Barton's Folly on your left – a small fort built during the Anglo-Boer War by Major-General G Barton. Continue on the R563, merging with the N14 after 24 km and keeping straight for the M47 some 12 km later, where the N14/R28 goes north-east/south-west. Remain on the M47, which leads into the north-western suburbs of Johannesburg and links up with the N1.

AA Office AA House, 66 De Korte Street Braamfontein 2001 Tel (011) 403 5700
AA Office AA House, 395 Schoeman Street Pretoria 0002 Tel (012) 28 3829
Johannesburg Publicity Association
North State Building, cr Market and Kruis streets, Johannesburg 2001 Tel (011) 336 4961

The Highveld as it was – before the arrival of the Voortrekkers

Today's drive begins with a tour of the Suikerbosrand Nature Reserve, which enables the visitor to see what the highveld looked like prior to the arrival of the Voortrekkers and the gold-seekers. We then visit the Vaal Dam and the fine collection of old vehicles housed in Heidelberg's Transport Museum. All but a few kilometres of the route is tarred.

Pretoria (280 – 300 km)
Johannesburg (230 – 250 km)
Suikerbosrand
Vaal Dam
Heidelberg
Museum

FROM CENTRAL JOHANNESBURG, drive south along Eloff Street. On the outskirts of the central city area, take the exit left for the M2. Follow the 'M2 East' signs, and note your kms as you turn onto the M2. After 9 km on the M2, at the Geldenhuis interchange, exit onto the N3 towards Heidelberg, noting your kms. (If you are starting from Pretoria, drive south on the Ben Schoeman Highway (N1). At the Buccleugh interchange, exit left onto the N3 – the Eastern Bypass around Johannesburg – and note your kms as you cross the M2 at the Geldenhuis interchange.)

After 3 km bear left to stay on the N3 and, after travelling 29 km from the Geldenhuis interchange, exit left (Interchange 79) for the R550. Turn right onto the R550, crossing over the N3, and drive a little more than 6,5 km along the R550 before turning left at the sign for 'Suikerbosrand Nature Reserve'. A further 4 km brings you to the gates of the reserve (entry fee; see this page). Shortly after entering the reserve, you reach the Visitors' Centre at Diepkloof. Close to the modern building is one of the first farmhouses built in the territory then known as the Transvaal – dating to 1850.

Suikerbosrand Nature Reserve

The reserve is famous for its 80 km of hiking trails, which offer walks of up to six days' duration. But the Cheetah Interpretive Trail – an easy 4,5 km walk that starts and ends at Diepkloof – is probably of more interest to the day visitor. (Report at the centre if you intend walking this two-hour trail.) A feature of the walk is that it passes the site of a settlement dating back to the Late Stone Age.

From Diepkloof, drive through the reserve on the tarred 'tourist route'; note your kms at the gate and bear left at the junction 2,4 km later. The road winds among rocky ridges and grasslands studded with grazing antelope, and it is easy to imagine yourself back on the highveld of two centuries ago. Roughly 27 km along the route there are attractive picnic sites on your left.

After a further 9,5 km turn left at the crossroads on the western edge of the reserve. The road right leads into Kareekloof Public Resort, which is surrounded by the Suikerbosrand Nature Reserve but is a separate entity.

Suikerbosrand to the Vaal Dam

Drive out of the reserve through the gate on the western boundary, and after roughly 300 m turn left onto the R557. After a further 3,8 km you reach a junction with the R551. If you have lunched and it is now mid-afternoon, turn left onto the R551 for Heidelberg and miss out the Vaal Dam section of the route. (You will enter Heidelberg on the R42, which becomes HF Verwoerd Street. Turn right into Voortrekker Street, then go left into Voortrekker Street Extension where the road forks on the far side of the town. The Transport Museum is on your right after 300 m.) If you toured Suikerbosrand more quickly, drive across the R551 and continue on the R557.

Some 3,6 km further along the R557 you reach the R42, which runs between Vereeniging and Heidelberg. Drive across the R42 and keep straight, noting your kms where the road surface changes to gravel. After 1,3 km go left at the fork for 'Platkoppie'; 7 km later you cross the Suikerbosrand River, and after a further 2,5 km turn right onto the tarred R549 – noting your kms.

After 18,5 km on the R549 you cross the R54, and after a further 6,2 km you pass a picnic area on your left on the banks of the Vaal Dam; 1 km later, turn left into another picnic area (entry fee, braai sites, toilets, water, boat launching areas).

Vaal Dam to Heidelberg

When you leave the picnic area, first turn left onto the R549 and park on your left after 3,2 km for a view of the dam wall and the Vaal River – then note your kms and return along the R549 towards Heidelberg. After some 51 km, as you enter the town, turn left onto the R23/R103; 400 m later turn right, and after a further 1,3 km turn right into Voortrekker Street Extension, to reach the Transport Museum 300 m later (see opposite).

When you leave the museum, drive northwest along Voortrekker Street. This takes you past a number of buildings that date back to pioneer days.

Turn right onto the R42, then follow the signs onto the N3 to return to Johannesburg or Pretoria. (If you turn left onto the R42 and then exit for the R103 about 1 km after that, you will pass the Heidelberg Kloof Resort on your left. There are attractive walks and other facilities. You join the N3 at the Benoni interchange.)

AA Office AA House, 66 De Korte Street Braamfontein 2001 Tel (011) 407 1000
AA Office AA House, 370 Voortrekker Road Gezina 0084 Tel (012) 329 1433
Suikerbosrand Nature Reserve The Officer-in-Charge, Private Bag H616, Heidelberg 2400 Tel (0151) 2181/2/3
Heidelberg Transport Museum Old Railway Station Building, 126 Voortrekker Street Extension, Heidelberg 2400 Tel (0151) 6303

Rolling grasslands of the Suikerbosrand Reserve.

SUIKERBOSRAND NATURE RESERVE
Suikerbosrand (sugarbush ridge) Nature Reserve has been made up out of portions of 65 farms and now comprises 13 337 ha of grassland, rocky ridges and steep, tree-filled kloofs. Many antelope species roam free – including eland, kudu, wildebeest, hartebeest and blesbok, as well as zebra. Also to be found here are leopard, hyaena, jackal and baboon. There are more than 200 bird species in the reserve, and a plant to look out for is the *Aloe davyana*. This is one of the smallest members of the extensive aloe family, reaching barely 50 cm in height; its salmon-pink flowers bring colour to the dry veld in the late winter months.

Kareekloof – a popular family resort.

Hypoxis rigidula brightens the southern highveld.

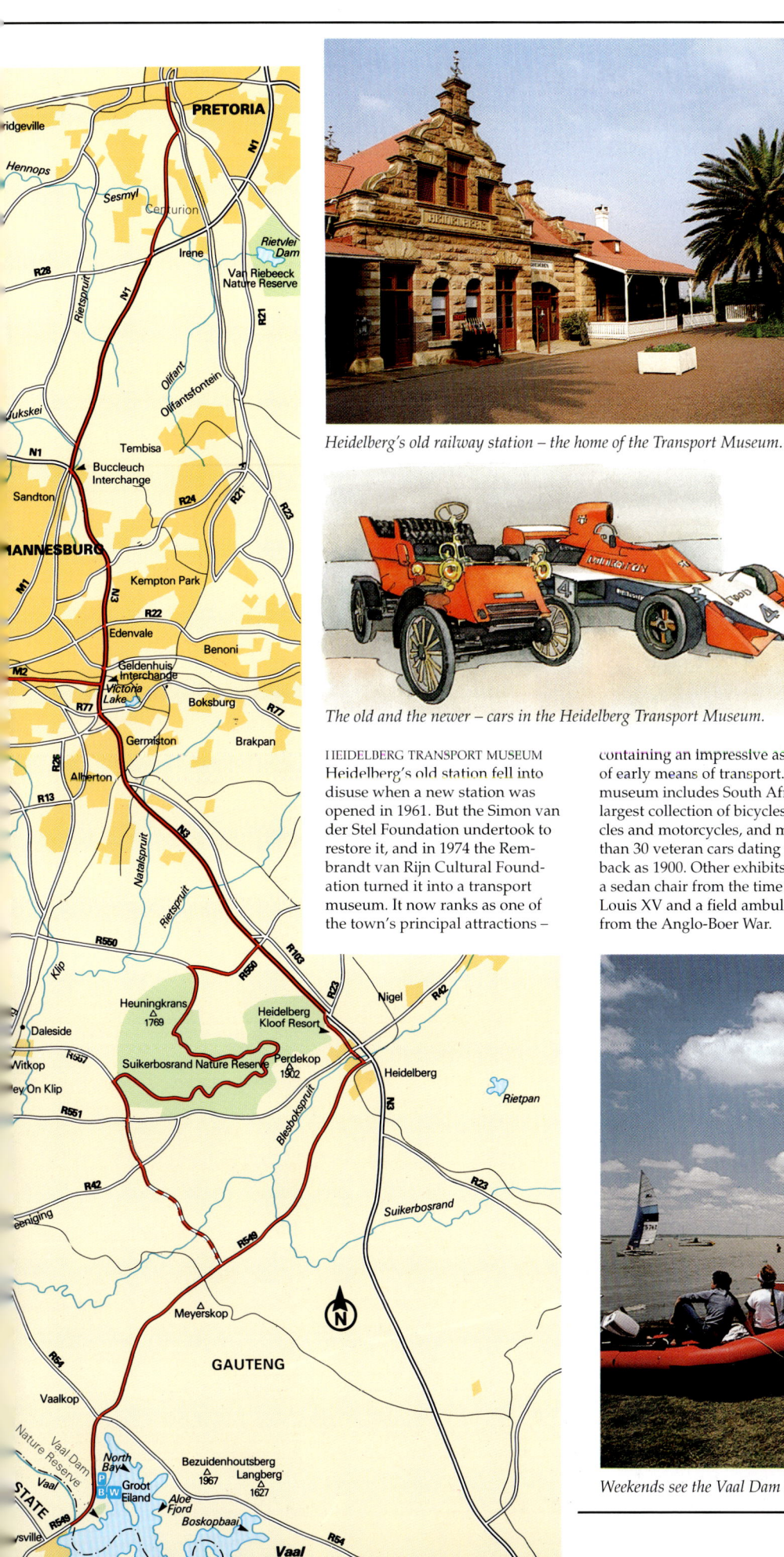

Heidelberg's old railway station – the home of the Transport Museum.

The old and the newer – cars in the Heidelberg Transport Museum.

HEIDELBERG TRANSPORT MUSEUM
Heidelberg's old station fell into disuse when a new station was opened in 1961. But the Simon van der Stel Foundation undertook to restore it, and in 1974 the Rembrandt van Rijn Cultural Foundation turned it into a transport museum. It now ranks as one of the town's principal attractions – containing an impressive assembly of early means of transport. The museum includes South Africa's largest collection of bicycles, tricycles and motorcycles, and more than 30 veteran cars dating as far back as 1900. Other exhibits include a sedan chair from the time of Louis XV and a field ambulance from the Anglo-Boer War.

HEIDELBERG
The historic little town of Heidelberg was born around a crossroads – where the old wagon trails between Pretoria, Potchefstroom, Bloemfontein and Durban all intersected. A German trader named Heinrich Ueckermann established a trading store here in 1860, and he named the area after his old university town in Germany. A town was officially proclaimed here several years later, and soon became the focal point of the region.

During the Witwatersrand goldrush the burgeoning town was able to boast as many as 18 hotels and, for a brief spell of three months during the Anglo-Transvaal War of 1880 – 81, it was the seat of the Transvaal government. The boom days are now past, but the town remains an attractive place and retains much of its original settler character.

THE HIGHVELD'S INLAND SEA
The large and impressive Vaal Dam, built in 1936, serves as Johannesburg's principal source of water. It is also a popular sailing and watersport venue, and has numerous resorts dotted along its several hundred kilometres of shoreline. Though it seems geographically impossible, much of the Vaal Dam's water comes from the KwaZulu-Natal midlands. It is first pumped over the Drakensberg and released into the Sterkfontein Dam. From there it flows into the Wilge River, which eventually runs into the Vaal Dam. (The first phase of the Lesotho Highlands Water Scheme, which will supply the Vaal system with 70 cubic metres of water per second, is due for completion by 2004.) Along the dam's northern shores lies the Vaal Dam Nature Reserve.

Weekends see the Vaal Dam transformed into a moving mosaic of bright sails.

· PLACES OF INTEREST IN JOHANNESBURG ·

The heights of Hillbrow and Berea overlook the busy streets of a part of the city that reputedly never sleeps. In the centre is the Hillbrow Tower.

A tent town that grew into a 'Golden City'

THERE ARE MANY sides to Gauteng's regional capital, and many names, too: the Golden City, *Egoli* and Johannesburg are just a few. The vibrant city centre lies at the heart of vast industrial areas, quiet, leafy suburbs, noisy, dusty suburbs and a network of walks and trails.

The spectacular bird's-eye view from the 50th floor of the Carlton Centre is an ideal visual introduction. Look out from the tallest building in Africa across the city's concrete heart, girded by a green belt of parks and nature reserves that fade into distant hills. The *Carlton Panorama* has telescopes, exhibitions and a cocktail bar and restaurant; the entrance is on the upper level of the Carlton Shopping Centre in Commissioner Street; open daily 09h00 – 23h00; tel (011) 650 7750.

An interesting way to experience the atmosphere of the changing inner city is to take a two-hour walk through central Johannesburg with a guide from *Historical Walks of Johannesburg;* tel (011) 673 8409; booking essential. Highlights include meeting a *sangoma* or traditional diviner (usually female) and visiting the city's oldest pub – the *Guildhall* – where antiques and photographs recall days gone by.

Mining town to metropolis
Johannesburg really is built on gold. Spend time exploring this development, both on the surface and underground, at *Gold Reef City;* open Tuesday to Sunday; tel (011) 496 1600. Built around No 14 Shaft of Crown Mines (once the richest in the world), Gold Reef City is a vibrant reproduction of Johannesburg at the dawn of the 20th century. A lift or 'cage' whisks you 220 m below the surface to see how gold is wrested from the rock, crushed and processed and, finally, poured in

From small beginnings... the rough-and-ready diggers' camp of 1886.

Autumn in Emmarentia Park.

a glowing, molten stream. Gold-pouring takes place on the hour.

Gold Reef City's historic feel transports you back in time. Browse through the curio shops decorated with delicate patterns of cast-iron 'lace' and cool, embossed ceilings. Take a ride in a vintage steam train or a quieter, more leisurely outing in a horse-drawn carriage. Old-style pubs and restaurants offer plenty of refreshments. Mine dancing – formerly almost the only recreation of contracted mine-workers – is demonstrated with energy and enthusiasm every day.

The *Chamber of Mines* arranges tours to active gold mines, but advance booking is essential; tel (011) 498 7100; no persons under 16 years or over 60 years of age are allowed.

The *George Harrison Park* in Baragwanath Road, Langlaagte, is the site where George Harrison is reputed to have stumbled upon a rock outcrop that led to the discovery of the main gold reef on the Witwatersrand in 1886. You can still see the old 10-stamp battery mill that was once used to crush the ore.

The *Roodepoort Museum*, at the Civic Centre, Theatre Street, Roodepoort, is a fine local history museum focusing on the discovery of gold and its dramatic impact on the people who came to settle in the area. It is open Tuesday to Friday, Saturday morning and Sunday afternoon; tel (011) 672 2147.

Catch a glimpse of the glittering history of diamonds at the *Erickson Diamond Centre*. An educational tour takes you through the cutting, manufacturing, design and setting process of these gems. There is also a museum on site but it is essential to make a booking; tel (011) 970 1355.

The gold industry led to the establishment of the *Johannesburg Stock Exchange* as companies were formed to tackle the increasingly expensive process of deep-level mining when the easily worked gold ran out. Twice-daily guided tours of the Stock Exchange, in its modern glass building on the corner of Pritchard and Diagonal streets, take you onto the trading floor. Booking is essential and can be made at tel (011) 337 2200.

Markham's Building, on the corner of Eloff and Pritchard streets, is another, different, downtown landmark. Built in 1897, it was once dubbed 'Markham's Folly', because it was so far away from the centre of town. *St Mary's Cathedral*, in Wanderers Street, is worth a visit to see the chapel that was erected in memory of South African soldiers who fell during the First World War.

A cultural melting pot

Johannesburg has always been a crucible of cultures and peoples. A conducted tour of *Soweto* (the name is derived from SOuth-WEstern TOwnships) provides an insight into the contrasts of Africa's largest black city. The tours are held Monday to Friday, twice a day; booking essential; tel (011) 331 6109 / 933 4177.

In central Johannesburg, traditional *muti* (medicine) shops flourish among the trading stores at the northern end of Diagonal Street. Here, many herbalists still practise their craft, and visitors can come face to face (sometimes literally) with the remedies used for centuries by successive generations of sangomas and *inyangas* (healers). Weekday tours; tel (011) 838 7352. Herbal healing is ancient and universal, and an interesting comparison is to be made at the *Margaret Roberts Herb Garden* in Broederstroom, a little more than 20 km north-west of Johannesburg. Open Wednesdays only; tel (01205) 41729.

Experience several South African cultures under one roof at the *Eskom Village* in Leraatsfontein, Witbank. Day excursions afford visitors the chance to see traditional huts, curios and crafts; tel (0135) 62071. At *Phumangena Zulu Kraal* on DF Malan Drive in Randburg, you can watch a vigorous cultural dancing display while savouring a traditional Zulu meal, and let the sangomas throw the bones for you; Monday to Saturday by appointment; tel (011) 659 0605.

On the corner of Market and Nugget streets in the city centre is a *mosque* with a 30 m minaret, built in 1916 and still used for daily prayers. The *Oriental Plaza* in Fordsburg is crowded with shops, kiosks and stalls that offer visitors a chance to shop for everything from carpets to curios, spices to samoosas, and to dine at authentic curry restaurants.

The history of Jewry in South Africa is traced through exhibits at the *Harry and Friedel Abt Museum* in Sheffield House on the corner of Kruis and Main streets. The museum contains superb examples of Jewish ceremonial art and can be visited on weekdays; tel (011) 331 0331.

People in touch

The *South African Broadcasting Corporation* in Auckland Park is one of the largest and best equipped of its kind in the world. See television and radio studios in action from behind the scenes on a guided tour that also takes you to some of the scenery and wardrobe workshops. Monday to Friday, mornings only; booking essential; tel (011) 714 3744. In the case of the print media, you can see how *The Star* newspaper, one of the country's largest, puts its pages together to meet its daily deadline. Tours are arranged by appointment; Monday to Friday; tel (011) 633 9111.

The internationally renowned arts complex at the *Market Theatre* and *Precinct* was originally a thriving produce market, built in the early 1900s. When 'progress' in 1975 demanded demolition, a small group of dedicated actors insisted on preservation in the form of a theatre centre – and won.

The Market complex is also home to lively jazz and music programmes, art and photographic galleries, shops, and a restaurant offering traditional South African cuisine; tel (011) 832 1641. There are many other theatre venues in Johannesburg – see the local press for listings at current venues.

The *Civic Theatre* in the Civic Centre complex is a successful venue for the performing arts – theatre, ballet and opera. Tours twice a week; tel (011) 403 3408. The City Hall in Rissik Street is a national monument and is one of the venues used by the National Symphony Orchestra for large choral performances. The *City Hall* contains one of the biggest organs in the country, and some parts of the building are used by the Gauteng legislature and

The Oppenheimer Fountain – bronze impala leap gracefully over jets of water.

Bronze group at the City Library.

Making electricity for the city.

provincial government. For more information about the City Hall, tel (011) 836 4672.

One of South Africa's most comprehensive art collections is housed at the *Johannesburg Art Gallery and Sculpture Garden*, Klein Street, Joubert Park; open Tuesday to Sunday; tel (011) 725 3180. The gallery has excellent 19th- and early 20th-century French and English paintings, a 17th-century Dutch collection, more than 2 500 prints dating from the 15th century to the present, and a contemporary international collection. Sculpture is on show in the courtyards and in the gardens of surrounding *Joubert Park*, the city's oldest park.

Host to many exhibitions by local artists is the *Standard Bank Gallery*, Simmonds Street, Johannesburg; tel (011) 636 4231. For a glimpse of African art and displays of African culture from the townships, visit the *Soweto Art Gallery* in Victory House, Harrison Street; tel (011) 836 0252.

The *Gertrude Posel Art Gallery* at the University of the Witwatersrand campus features a wide variety of temporary exhibitions as well as permanent collections of African art; tel (011) 716 3632.

On the last Sunday of the month, take to the *Johannesburg Studio Route* and spend a day watching local crafters and artists at work in their studios; for maps and bookings, tel (011) 646 1170. During the first weekend of the month, there are free, open-air exhibitions at Zoo Lake in Parktown, as *Artists under the sun* display their varied and interesting works; tel (011) 432 1482.

For a delightful outing on the first weekend of every month, take the *Crocodile River Arts and Crafts* ramble. Wander along the riverbanks enjoying the displays of pottery, watercolours, oil painting, handwoven garments and sculpture; tel (01205) 51181.

Sightseeing and leisure
Pioneer Park, on the banks of Wemmer Pan, La Rochelle, offers varied family entertainment and leisure activities. On the northern bank, *Santarama Miniland* displays highly accurate models built to a scale of 1:25, depicting in miniature many historical and modern features of South Africa, as well as working models of trains, a ferry in the mini-harbour and a cable car. There are restaurants and souvenir shops; open daily; tel (011) 435 0543.

For sunset picnics, the *Illuminated Musical Fountains* off the south edge of Wemmer Pan put on an unusual performance – the columns of water rise and fall to the rhythm of popular tunes; Tuesday to Sunday evenings; tel (011) 407 6833.

Alongside Wemmer Pan is the *James Hall Transport Museum*, which features displays of the history of land transport in South Africa; Tuesday to Sunday; tel (011) 435 9718.

The *Randburg Waterfront* has one of the most sophisticated musical fountains in the world, where more than a thousand nozzles weave patterns of light and water high in the air; tel (011) 789 6404.

Children particularly will enjoy the *Rynfield Children's Park and Bunny Park* in Pretoria Road, Rynfield, Benoni, which teems with rabbits, other small farmyard animals and poultry; open daily; tel (011) 845 1650.

Viewed from the air, swimming pools dot the gardens of homes in one of Johannesburg's wealthy northern suburbs.

A fine collection of modern art is displayed in the Johannesburg Art Gallery.

The stately, mellowed elegance of the Johannesburg Public Library building.

In an age before air travel, miners relax outside their tent at Rietfontein in 1877. The main road to the city's international airport passes close by the site today.

In more elegant vein are the displays given on Sunday morning by the national Lippizaner team, trained in the manner of Vienna's Spanish Riding School. See these beautiful white horses performing their graceful high-stepping at the *National Equestrian Centre*, Kyalami. Booking advisable; open every Sunday from 11h00; tel (011) 702 2103.

The one-day wine route on the banks of the Vaal combines the best of the Vaal with a taste of South African wines. Enjoy the route aboard a river raft as it passes through secluded, scenic bushveld; tel (011) 803 9775. For a faster-moving experience, take a steam-train ride from Johannesburg to Magaliesberg on the Magaliesburg Express; tel (011) 888 1154; or Magalies Valley Steamer; tel (011) 773 9238, or take to the skies in the historic tri-motor SAA Junkers Ju52 airliner of the 1930s. Flights take place on the first Sunday of the month and are organized by the South African Airways Museum Society; tel (011) 773 9842.

On the outskirts of Krugersdorp, on top of a dolomite hillock in the Isaac Stegmann Nature Reserve, are the *Sterkfontein Caves*. One of the world's anthropological treasure houses, this is where Dr Robert Broom discovered the fossilized skeleton he nicknamed 'Mrs Ples' and, more formally, *Plesianthropus transvaalensis*. Guided tours may be taken of one of mankind's earliest homesteads, with their dripstone formations and silent, underground lake. There are also attractive picnic grounds and a restaurant. Guided tours of the caves and the museum are held from Tuesday to Sunday; tel (011) 956 6342.

Into the green belt

For excellent views northwards and a profusion of indigenous plants, visit *The Wilds*, the 17 ha park straddling the two hills that flank Houghton Drive. There are four plant-houses and a tea garden. Visitors are advised to view the park in groups or to take a guided tour; open daily 10h00 to 17h00; tel (011) 407 6833.

There are even finer views from the nearby Linksfield Ridge, at the 6 ha *Harvey Nature Reserve*. From here you can see as far as the Magaliesberg to the north, the Hillbrow skyline to the west, and an assortment of mine dumps to the south. It's an easy walk through the nature reserve from the entrance on Linksfield Drive, and the more energetic visitor can climb the koppie from Gillooly's Farm on the eastern side. The 44 ha *Gillooly's Farm* on Boeing Avenue, Bedfordview is a popular site for weekend rambles, picnics and braais. Enjoy its wide-open spaces, dam and streams, and the Gillooly's International Restaurant; tel (011) 453 8066.

Highveld scrub and veldflowers survive in the wild in the city – they characterize the area at *Melville Koppies* on Judith Road, Emmarentia. It was declared a nature reserve in 1959, and of great archaeological interest are relics from the Early Stone Age found here (around 100 000 BC), as well as two furnaces from the Iron Age. More than 150 species of bird have been recorded; open on the first and third Sundays of the month from September to May, but conducted tours may also be arranged at other times; tel (011) 782 7064.

You can walk the slopes of an attractive koppie at the *Kloofendal Nature Reserve* at Galena Avenue, Roodepoort, where several old gold-mining shafts can be inspected. Indigenous vegetation and bird life are prolific. Run by the Roodepoort Parks and Recreation Department, the 100 ha park is open from sunrise to sunset, from September to April; tel (011) 475 1475.

Also in Roodepoort is the *Witwatersrand National Botanical Gardens* on Malcolm Street, Poortview, with the Roodepoort (or Witpoortjie) Falls as the focus of some 220 ha of natural highveld vegetation; open daily from 08h00 to 18h00; tel (011) 958 1750.

An extensive hilly area south of Johannesburg is enclosed in the *Klipriviersberg Nature Reserve*, which has an entrance on Fairway Drive, Kibler Park. Enjoy walking on grassy hills where aloes flourish, or spend time bird-watching.

Slightly further from the city, in a south-easterly direction, is the *Suikerbosrand Nature Reserve*, an attractive area for both walks and drives (see pages 80 – 1).

Many of the parks in Johannesburg are linked by the *Braamfontein Spruit Trail*, a hiking route

The M1 motorway north of the city.

that roughly follows the course of the *spruit* (stream) and its tributary, the Sand River. The first section of the trail takes you through the historic area of *Parktown*, where numerous homes were designed by Sir Herbert Baker around the turn of the century. The Parktown Westcliff Heritage Trust offers mornings-only guided tours aboard topless buses, in conjunction with walking tours; tel (011) 482 3349.

Brochures describing the Braamfontein Spruit Trail may be obtained from the *Johannesburg Publicity Association*; tel (011) 336 4961 or the *Sandton Civic Foundation*; tel (011) 884 1317.

The largest park along the Braamfontein Spruit Trail is *Delta Park*, which abuts Road No 3, Victory Park. This 104 ha park comprises grasslands, shade trees, a number of braai sites and a children's playground. A highlight is the *Florence Bloom Bird Sanctuary*, which has a number of viewing points along its fenced perimeter, from which you can observe many different water birds on the small lake. Near the sanctuary is the charming conservation museum in the headquarters of the South African Nature Conservation Centre and the Wildlife Society of Southern Africa; open Tuesday to Sunday; entrance fee; tel (011) 782 1531.

Another spot for birdwatching is *Melrose Bird Sanctuary*, with more than 120 species recorded. Situated in Melrose Street, it forms part of the larger *James and Ethel Gray Park*, close to the M1.

The Braamfontein *Spruit* (stream) has been dammed on the border of *Jan van Riebeek Park*, creating *Emmarentia Dam* – venue for sailing, boardsailing and rowing, and a haven for many species of duck and goose. On the dam's western shore is the *Johannesburg Botanical Garden*, in Thomas Bowler Street, Roosevelt Park Extension. This popular picnic spot covers 148 ha, and there is a bonsai garden, a herb garden, medical garden and a 4 ha rose garden; tel (011) 782 0517.

A myriad of lakes and dams throughout the Witwatersrand offer attractive settings for walks and picnics. *Florida Lake* in Florida, Roodepoort, has braai facilities, a restaurant, miniature golf, and an Olympic-size swimming pool. Germiston's *Victoria Lake*, home of several watersport clubs, is surrounded by lush lawns and tall trees with braai sites, refreshment facilities and a children's playground. Closer to the city, *Rhodes Park* in Kensington has a restaurant and tea garden overlooking its beautifully landscaped parks and lake, where wedding parties are a regular weekend occurrence.

Zoo Lake and its surrounding *Herman Eckstein Park* in Parkview bustle over weekends. There are rowing boats for hire, children's playgrounds, rolling lawns for picnics, and a restaurant and tea garden. The smaller lakes are rich with bird life. On weekends, artists display here in the open air.

Across Jan Smuts Avenue, also in the Herman Eckstein Park, are the *Johannesburg Zoological Gardens*; open daily, entrance fee, parking on Upper Park Drive; tel (011) 646 2000. The zoo is home to thousands of birds, reptiles and mammals. Other attractions include farmyard animals, donkey rides for children on Sundays and public holidays, refreshment stalls, a restaurant and a small open-air museum containing South African rock art. Take a special 'behind the scenes' tour (last Saturday and Sunday of the month) or fascinating nocturnal tours (Mondays, Wednesdays and Fridays; booking is essential).

On the eastern side of the park in Erlswold Way stands the *Museum of Military History*, which contains relics from World War I and World War II, and the Anglo-Boer War. There are audiovisual presentations on Sunday; (open daily; tel (011) 646 5513).

Wildlife at home
A short distance from the city centre, enjoy a variety of bushveld spots where animals abound in their natural habitat. The *Johannesburg Lion Park* on the old Pretoria-Krugersdorp road offers a 10 km drive, in the course of which you will see many species indigenous to this part of Africa – including lion, black wildebeest, gemsbok, impala, blesbok, zebra and ostrich.

There is a restaurant, a children's corner, a curio shop and a swimming pool; open daily, entrance fee charged per car; tel (011) 460 1814.

West of Krugersdorp between the R24 and N14 lies the 1 400 ha *Krugersdorp Game Reserve*, which also offers a lion camp, amid unspoilt veld inhabited by game species that include giraffe, white rhino, blue wildebeest, eland, kudu, impala and blesbok. The recreation area has two swimming pools, braai facilities and a children's playground; open daily, entrance fee charged per car; tel (011) 953 1770/664 4342.

The *Transvaal Snake Park* on the R101 at Halfway House is home to the world's largest collection of predominantly African snakes. Here, crocodiles, alligators and terrapins are kept in custom-made pools, and crocodile-feeding demonstrations are held on Sunday at 13h00 during summer; as well as daily snake-handling demonstrations. The park is open daily, entrance fee, curio shop; tel (011) 805 3116.

Apart from its rhino, the *Rhino Park* in the *Kromdraai Conservancy* boasts 20 other species of game as well as walking trails, game drives and braai facilities. From the Rhino Park there is an entrance to the *Wonder Caves*, where breathtaking rock formations were created some 2 200 million years ago. The guided tours of the caves start every 90 minutes; tel (011) 957 0106. Booking is essential to ensure a place on the game drives; tel (011) 957 0109.

Capturing a sense of history
Johannesburg's past is beautifully captured by the displays at *Museum Africa* at 121 Bree Street, Newtown; tel (011) 833 5624. Open from Tuesday to Sunday, it

Peaceful waters in the Florence Bloom Bird Sanctuary in Delta Park.

A lily-covered pond in The Wilds, a 17 ha park within sight of busy Hillbrow.

is a treasure house of geological specimens, paintings, prints, photographs and objects relating to the history of the area southwards from the Zambezi to the Cape of Good Hope. Photographs, paintings and memorabilia also offer insight into the often tempestuous history of the city itself.

The captivating history of money comes alive in displays at the *First National Bank Museum* at 90 Market Street, City Centre; open weekdays, Saturday by arrangement; tel (011) 836 5887.

The *South African Transport Museum* in the Station Concourse, De Villiers Street, has a unique collection of model trains explaining the extensive workings of South Africa's transport services – roads, railways, motor services and harbours; open on weekdays; tel (011) 773 9118.

The *Klein-Jukskei Motor Museum* at the corner of Witkoppen and Selborne roads, Randburg, shows a large collection of old cars, motorcycles, photographs and toy cars. There is a picnic area alongside the river, plus swimming pool, restaurant and tea garden; open Tuesday to Sunday, entrance fee; tel (011) 704 1514.

The *South African Air Force Museum* at Lanseria Airport is housed in a hangar and contains memorabilia of the air force as well as several restored old aircraft. You can watch planes take off and land from the cafeteria; open weekdays; tel (011) 659 1041.

The *Benoni Fire Service Museum* has a fascinating collection of fire engines, fire-fighting equipment, old helmets, tunics and other memorabilia. By appointment only at the Ted Barber Fire Station, Pretoria Road, Rynfield; weekdays; tel (011) 422 2222.

The collection of cameras, magic lanterns, photographs and plates at the *Bensusan Museum of Photography* in Raikes Road, Braamfontein delights all visitors; open daily; tel (011) 403 1067. It also houses the photographic section of the Johannesburg Library.

A display of historic clothing is the focus of the *Bernberg Museum of Costume* in Duncombe Street, Parktown. Models are placed in period rooms, and there are collections of fans, buttons, parasols, fobs, pipes and handbags; open daily; tel (011) 646 0716.

A private collection of old furniture – said to be one of the finest in the country – can be seen at the *Ou Kaapse Huis*, Pretoria Avenue, Sandown; tel (011) 884 1054.

A brass band and typical Victorian facade in Gold Reef City.

Inside ivory towers
Take a tour of the *University of Witwatersrand* campus on the first Wednesday of the month from February to November – and visit the reconstructed library of General Jan Smuts, and the Africana collection in the William Cullen Library; tel (011) 716 3162.

Special tours can be arranged to take in any of the other fascinating collections on campus. These include the Bernard Price Institute of Palaeontological Research (valuable fossil remains); the Hunterian Museum (anatomical specimens, and masks made by African people); the Zoology Department Museum; the Moss Herbarium collection; the Bleloch Museum of Geology; the Archaeology Museum and the Social Anthropology Museum. For more information on campus sights, tel (011) 716 3162.

Solve some of the mysteries of the universe at the Planetarium in Yale Road; tel (011) 716 3199.

Another museum administered by the university is the *Adler Museum of the History of Medicine*, at the SA Institute of Medical Research in Hospital Street. Exhibits cover medical and surgical practices, an African herb shop, a traditional doctor's room, and an old pharmacy and operating theatre; open Monday to Friday; tel (011) 725 2846.

Further information about Johannesburg may be obtained from the Johannesburg Publicity Association, 84 President Street, Johannesburg; tel (011) 336 4961.

Shops all a-glitter in Sandton City.

Young prospectors blaze a watery trail on Wild Water Run at Gold Reef City.

High-rise Hillbrow and Berea catch the first light of a winter morning.

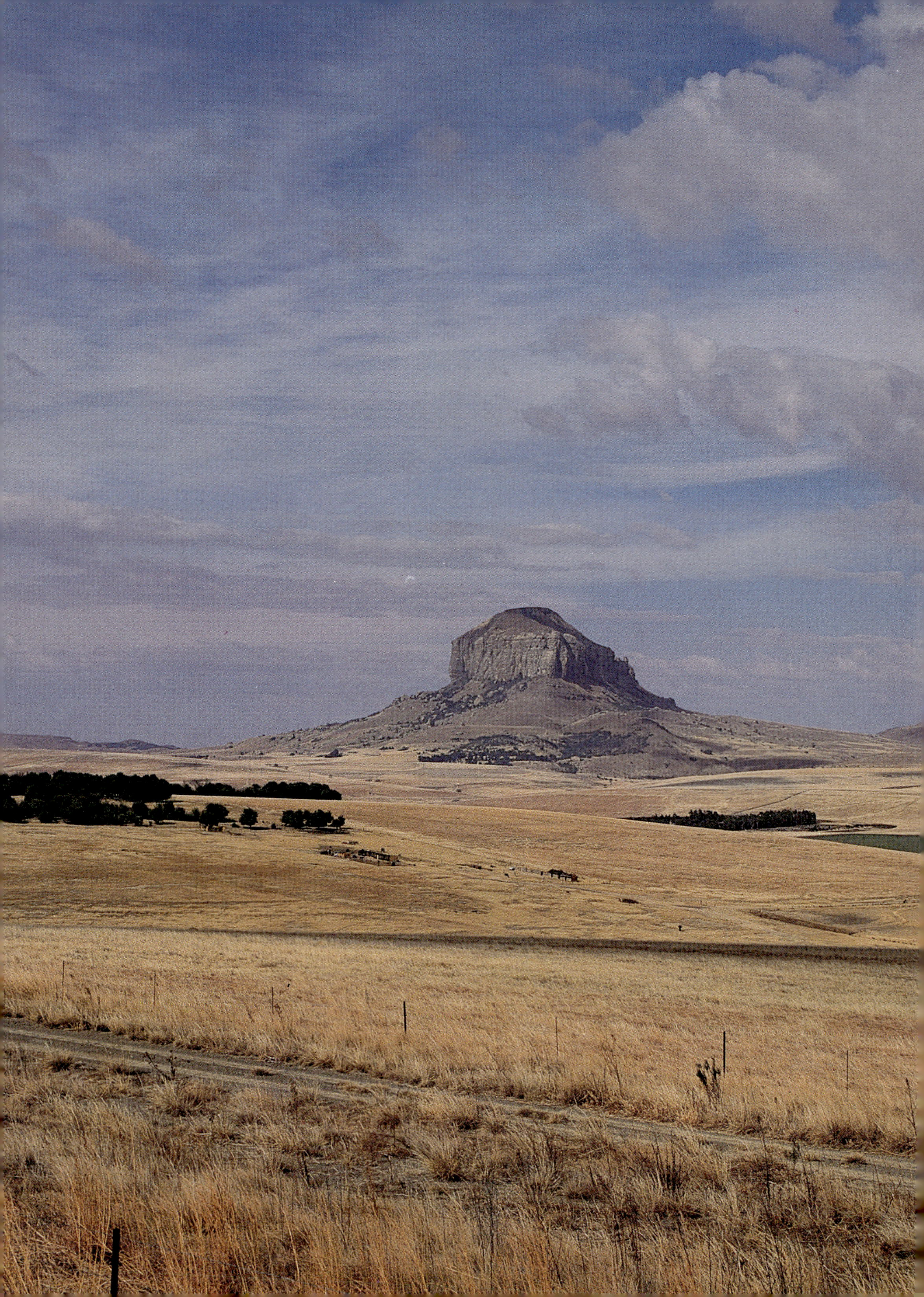

FREE STATE & LESOTHO

Harrismith – Sterkfontein Dam – The Sentinel – Golden Gate – Clarens **90-1**

Golden Gate National Park: Towering sandstone cliffs **92-3**

Bloemfontein: City at the centre of South Africa **94-5**

Bethlehem – Clarens – Fouriesburg – Ficksburg **96-7**

Maseru – Roma – Bushman's Pass – Blue Mountain Pass – Ha Khotso **98-9**

Maseru – Teyateyaneng – Thaba Bosiu – Morija **100-1**

Sotho Traditions: Rich store from the past **102-3**

Left: *A lone rock outcrop stands sentinel over the plains of the Free State.*

Golden Gate's splendour and an eagle's view of the Drakensberg

The eastern Free State is renowned for its magnificent sandstone mountains, and our route winds among the most spectacular of these in the Golden Gate Highlands National Park. On our way there, we stop off at the Sterkfontein Dam, then drive high into the Drakensberg for a view of imposing cliffs towering over the valleys of KwaZulu-Natal.

Harrismith
Sterkfontein Dam
Phuthaditjhaba
The Sentinel
Golden Gate
Clarens
270 – 290 km

LEAVE HARRISMITH by driving south-east along Warden Street, passing the Town Hall on your right. At the T-junction (with traffic circle), turn right into Retief Street and then left into McKechnie Street. Follow the signs for N5/Bethlehem/Bloemfontein to the right into Cloete Street, cross the *Wilge* (willow) River and join the N5, travelling west.

Almost immediately after crossing the *Nuwejaarspruit* (New Year stream) – about 6 km from the Town Hall – turn left on the R74/R712 for Phuthaditjhaba. You now cross attractive farming country, dotted with farmhouses set among tall trees. After 9 km turn left at the foot of Baker's Kop onto the R74 for Bergville, noting your kms.

From this road you soon see the great escarpment of the KwaZulu-Natal Drakensberg ahead of you. After 7 km you pass an entrance on your right to a resort area on the banks of the Sterkfontein Dam. Beyond the turn-off, to your left and ahead of you, lies the imposing sandstone bulk of Kerkenberg, site of Retief Rock (see opposite). Some 12,5 km after noting your kms, turn right onto gravel for a viewsite overlooking the dam.

Sterkfontein Dam to Witsieshoek

Return along the R74 to the T-junction at the foot of Baker's Kop, and turn left onto the R712 for Phuthaditjhaba, noting your kms. Just over 3 km later you pass the dam wall on your left.

Roughly 25 km after rejoining the R712 you can see Qwaqwa Mountain ahead of you, with its sheer sandstone cliffs (see opposite). The basalt heights of the Drakensberg are also visible on your left. At 25,5 km pass a road to Phuthaditjhaba. After 30 km on the R712 turn left onto the off-ramp (the sign reads Qwaqwa) where the road straight ahead goes to Kestell and Golden Gate. Note your kms at this turn.

You now travel alongside Qwaqwa Mountain on your right, passing – after 5 km – a turn-off into the town of *Phuthaditjhaba* (Sotho for 'meeting place of the nations'), and the road continues through an industrial area and straggling settlements towards the Drakensberg. Follow the signs for 'Bergoord' and 'Mountain Resort' which will lead you south-east into the mountains, where the surface changes to gravel. About 25 km from the R712 there is a tollgate at which a small fee per person is payable. A few kilometres past the tollgate, pull off the road under a rock overhang on your right for a view into the attractive valley on your left. Continue from here up the pass – after a few hundred metres a view opens up on your right over Lesotho's spectacular Maluti Mountains stretching away seemingly without end, and you can see the massive basalt buttress of The Sentinel looming to the west of the Amphitheatre.

About 2,5 km from the overhang, go right at the fork (left leads to the Witsieshoek Mountain Resort, which serves teas and lunches and has outstanding views towards the Amphitheatre). Park after a further 8 km, below the Sentinel – a 300 m walk from here brings you to a point from which you have magnificent views over the Royal Natal National Park (see pages 126 – 7), and across to the Eastern Buttress and the Devil's Tooth at the far end of the Amphitheatre. (Allow 30 – 40 minutes. The path continues from here to chain ladders that lead to the mountain top, but time does not allow for the full walk on this outing.)

Witsieshoek to Golden Gate

Return through Phuthaditjhaba towards the R712 and exit left for Golden Gate and Harrismith. At the end of the off-ramp turn right for Golden Gate, noting your kms. After some 3 km you enter the Qwaqwa Highland National Park and travel through countryside characterised by colourful sandstone formations. The Basotho Village Cultural Museum on your left after 7 km is a major attraction – a tour lasts from 30 to 45 minutes.

A little under 9 km from the off-ramp, you pass Silasberg on your left – an excellent example of why Clarens sandstone was formerly known as 'cave sandstone', because of its inclination to erode from below. Roughly 4 km later you can see Rondawelkop on your right alongside a wedge-shaped sandstone formation that juts from the side of the *Rooiberge* (red mountains).

After about 15,5 km you enter Golden Gate National Park – it adjoins Qwaqwa National Park but no signs inform you of the change of name. You cross more flatlands and, after a few kilometres, begin to climb amid beautiful mountain scenery through the first of several short passes. When you reach the top of the first pass, pull onto the shoulder of the road for a fine view back over the countryside through which you have been travelling.

Roughly 25 km after noting your kms you cross the watershed that separates the systems of the Orange and Vaal rivers and, soon afterwards, you enter the colourful valley carved through the sandstone Rooiberge by the Little Caledon River. Soon you can see ahead of you the distinctive cliffs known as Mushroom Rocks. After a further 1 km there is a turn-off on your left to a game-viewing road – a 7 km circular drive across grassy mountain slopes.

Soon afterwards, stop at the Glen Reenen reception area. Cross the road to the parking area at the Glen Reenen campsites (which have braai and picnic places on the banks of the Little Caledon River) for a walk to Mushroom Rocks, a trail that offers an excellent introduction to the geology, flora and birdlife of the park. (The walk starts at the footbridge across the river – allow 40 – 60 minutes.)

Golden Gate to Clarens

From Glen Reenen continue west, noting your kms as you rejoin the tarred road. After 500 m you pass, on your right, the sandstone

Farm cottages against a typical highland backdrop.

CLARENS

Much of the eastern Free State owes its magnificent scenery to Clarens sandstone – weathered over millennia into fantastic shapes. The rock is named after the picturesque little village of Clarens, which in turn was named after the town in Switzerland where Transvaal President Paul Kruger died in exile in 1904. Kruger's connection with the area dates back to the Boer-Basotho War of 1886, when five men of his Transvaal Commando were killed at the Battle of Naauwpoort. A memorial in the town square commemorates their death. The village, now boasting a substantial 'art colony', was founded in 1912 at the foot of sandstone hills and offers grand views of the Maluti Mountains. Nearby, the Highland Route takes a scenic meander among the Maluti slopes to Fouriesburg.

Winter farmland north of the Amphitheatre.

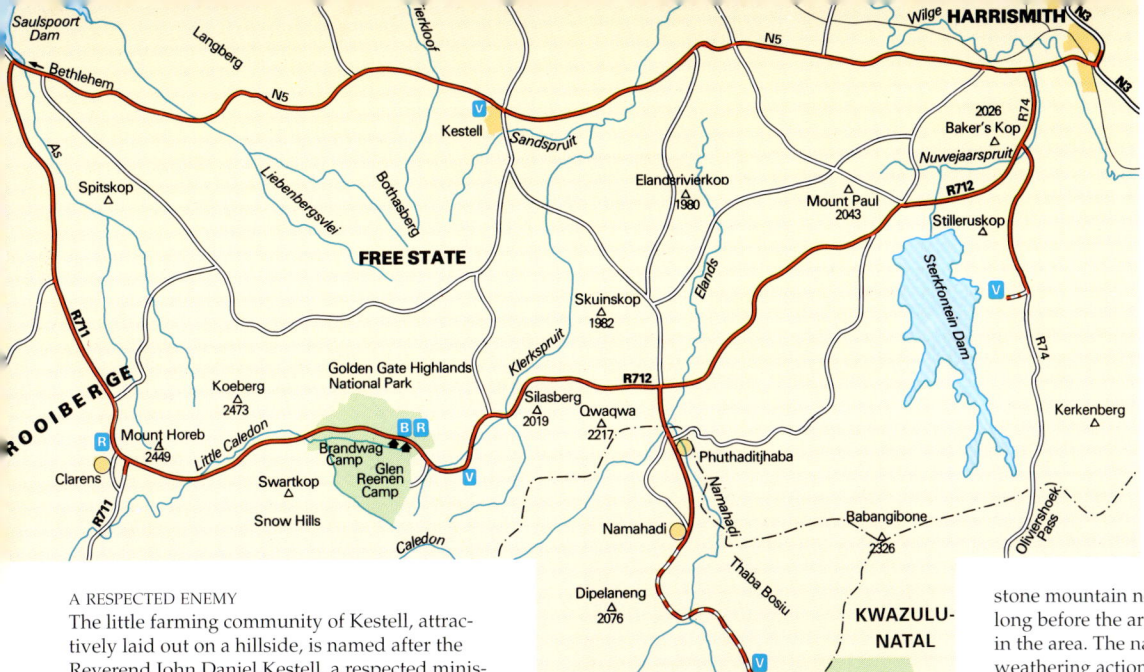

The sheer basalt cliffs of the eastern Amphitheatre.

A RESPECTED ENEMY

The little farming community of Kestell, attractively laid out on a hillside, is named after the Reverend John Daniel Kestell, a respected minister who, among other exploits, travelled with the Harrismith Commando during the Anglo-Boer War. His bravery during the Battle of Wagon Hill outside Ladysmith (see pages 128 – 9) on 6 January 1900, when he ministered to both sides under heavy fire, earned him the admiration of many British soldiers. At their request a small memorial plaque was erected on the hillside where the minister 'brought succour to friend and foe alike'.

KERKENBERG AND RETIEF ROCK

On 11 November 1837, a group of Voortrekkers who had outspanned at *Kerkenberg* (church mountain) near the edge of the Drakensberg escarpment, received the glad news for which they had been waiting; their leader, Pieter Retief, had been assured that the Zulu leadership and British traders in KwaZulu-Natal would welcome them as new settlers. During the celebrations and thanksgiving the next day – which was also Retief's 57th birthday – the leader's daughter, Deborah, painted her father's name and the date in green on a rockface now known as the Retief Rock. Two days later the party of Voortrekkers, their wagons crammed with their possessions, began their extraordinarily arduous journey down the 1 000 m escarpment into the area Piet Retief had described as 'this beautiful land, the most beautiful I've seen in Africa'.

THE 'WHITER THAN WHITE' MOUNTAIN

Qwaqwa, meaning 'whiter than white', was the name the San people gave to this massive sandstone mountain north of the Amphitheatre – long before the arrival of black or white settlers in the area. The name possibly derives from the weathering action on the Molteno sandstone that makes up much of its bulk – the rock is white when freshly exposed, although it later turns a greyish colour.

The name Qwaqwa has now also been given to the area previously known to white settlers as Witsieshoek – based on a corruption of Whêtse, the name of a supposed cattle rustler who was defeated near here when he and his men were trapped in one of the many caves by a commando of Free State farmers in 1856.

Sunlight washes over Mushroom Rocks.

The Sentinel Trail – pathway to an eagle's world.

---

formation known as *Brandwag* (sentinel) and, 600 m later, you pass, on your left, the luxury rest camp also known as Brandwag.

Some 2 km later you pass the small graveyard of the Van Reenen family, on your right alongside Golden Gate Dam, and after a further 200 m you pass between the two sandstone buttresses known as the Golden Gate.

About 17 km beyond Glen Reenen you crest a hill and see the town of Clarens spread across the hillside ahead of you; 2,1 km later you pass a turn-off left for Fouriesburg (the Highland Route) – continue straight on the R712 towards Bethlehem. Just 300 m beyond the turn-off, turn left for Clarens and, after a further 500 m, go left around the town's central square. A number of the town's solid, early buildings still grace its streets.

Clarens to Harrismith

Retrace your route out of Clarens and turn left onto the R712 for Bethlehem, noting your kms. After 1,3 km you pass a turn-off on your left to a hotel (the road also leads to Cinderella Castle, an unusual structure laboriously built from 55 000 beer bottles).

After some 28 km on the R712 turn right at the T-junction onto the N5 for Harrismith, noting your kms again. After roughly 13,5 km on the N5, the aptly named *Langberg* (long mountain) comes into view on your left. After about 37 km on the N5, exit left for Kestell, and, at the end of the off-ramp, turn right at the T-junction; 500 m later, turn right into Kestell and stop after a further 500 m for a look at the imposing church that commands excellent views over the surrounding countryside. Visit the local bookshop for information or return to the N5 for Harrismith.

AA Office AA House, 17 Sanlam Plaza, Maitland Street, Bloemfontein 9301 Tel (051) 47 6191
Harrismith Tourist Information Municipal Offices, Andries Pretorius Street, Harrismith 9880 Tel (05861) 23525
Golden Gate Highlands National Park P/Bag X03, Golden Gate 9708 Tel (058) 256 1471
Basotho Village Cultural Museum PO Box X826 Witsieshoek 9870 Tel (05861) 31794

· EXPLORING GOLDEN GATE PARK ·

Gateway to a mountain paradise – the sandstone cliffs of Golden Gate stand watch over a tranquil park scene.

Where sandstone cliffs tower in blazing gold and burnished copper

BETWEEN THE ROOIBERGE and the Maluti Mountains magnificent sandstone formations, carved by wind and water, create a brilliant display of gold and copper cliffs. Here, in the peaceful seclusion of the Little Caledon River valley, the Golden Gate Highlands National Park provides a spectacular world for walking, horse-riding, bird-watching and game-viewing.

The park, of 11 630 ha, encloses some of the country's finest highland scenery, where many species of game have been reintroduced to their natural habitat and where roughly 160 bird species await the bird-watcher. But it is the geology of the Golden Gate area more than anything else that has established its reputation as a popular holiday resort. Changing light and shadows play on the colourful rock surfaces, creating ever-changing moods, and myriad birds and small mammals make their homes among the rocks.

Fossil remains
Geologists divide the park's rock formations into the Drakensberg lava (the layer of basaltic rock that forms the cliff-tops of the highest peaks); the Clarens sandstone (it was formerly known as 'Cave Sandstone' because of the many hollows in its cliffs); the red and purple Elliot formation; and the coarse-grained Molteno formation with its cream colour streaked with blue and grey shale and mudstone.

Many millions of years before recorded history began, Golden Gate was inhabited by mammal-like reptiles, whose fossil remains have been left behind, preserved in the mudstone and siltstone beds. Prehistoric men left their stone implements as evidence of their sojourn here, and a legacy of magnificent rock art and stone and bone artefacts points to the existence of San people in the area.

The San were lured to the region by its abundant game, which was never threatened by the conservative hunting of these small-statured people. But the early years of the 19th century brought devastation to the wildlife of the area. Trekboer parties, armed with rifles, all but wiped out the vast herds of antelope. Soon after this calamity, the drought, war and deprivation that followed in the wake of the Zulu battle for supremacy in KwaZulu-Natal, rang the death knell for the larger animals of the south-eastern Free State. Clans and families scattered in all directions, placing extra burdens on limited food supplies. It was during this period that the Sotho nation was established under the leadership of Moshoeshoe, who gathered the remnants of clans fleeing from the Zulu army and formed Masada-like settlements on the area's flat-topped mountains to resist attacks by outsiders.

A strife-torn past
In the early history of the nation, their land – known to them as Lesotho (place of the Sotho people) and to white colonists as Basutoland – extended through the Golden Gate area to the summit of the *Rooiberg* (red mountain) range on the northern side of the present park. However, the Sotho people soon clashed with the Voortrekkers over land and cattle and, during the resulting 'Basuto Wars' of 1858–68, the Free State/Lesotho border was moved to its present position along the course of the Caledon River.

Strife again tore through the Golden Gate area during the Anglo-Boer War. A large force of Boers was cornered here by several British brigades, who sealed off the passes. The Boer General Christiaan de Wet talked a small band of men into escaping, and their success persuaded a larger group to attempt a breakout through Golden Gate. At the steep corner just east of the present Glen Reenen camp – still known as *Kanondraai* (cannon corner) – the Boers lost a Krupp field gun down a cliff. About 1 500 Boers surrendered to the British at Klerksvley, a farm east of the park, having first blown up their own ammunition wagons, scattering bullets and cartridge cases in the veld. Even today, hikers sometimes find these relics of distant strife.

Magnificently coloured rock strata form a backdrop to the Brandwag camp.

By the time this war broke out, the area had already been occupied by farmers for a number of years. Many of the Boer women were taken to concentration camps, and farms were burnt in the 'scorched earth' campaign. But one doughty woman, *Ouma* (Granny) Cilliers, hid out in a cave just north of the Golden Gate Dam.

Exploring the riches of Golden Gate can be done either by car or on foot. Two game-viewing drives – both are tarred – wind through the mountains. They offer the best viewing early in the mornings and in the evenings. From a car you are likely to spot any of about 100 species of birds, including the rare bearded vulture (*lammergeyer*), black eagle, Cape vulture and a variety of other raptors. The mammals you are likely to see include oribi, mountain reedbuck, grey rhebuck, springbok, blesbok, black wildebeest, Burchell's zebra and eland. The roads also offer panoramic views of the highlands, the Malutis and the Drakensberg.

Hiking trails
On foot there is even more to be seen. Apart from the larger game, you are also likely to spot smaller mammals such as dassie, mongoose and otter, and a wider variety of birds – up to 160 species. The Langtoon and Golden Gate dams offer good bird-watching.

The camp offices provide maps and information on the many trails in the park. There is a two-day, 28 km hiking trail known as the Rhebok Trail, on which hikers stay overnight in a hut that sleeps 18 people. It includes the climb up Generaalskop and takes you through lovely mountain scenery crossed by streams and waterfalls. The rewards of the Rhebok Trail are not gained easily – it is a strenuous excursion.

There is also a one-day hike, and a number of other shorter walks radiate from the camps at Glen Reenen and Brandwag. Starting from Glen Reenen are the following walks:

Mushroom Rocks This 40 – 60 minute walk takes you under magnificent overhangs of Clarens sandstone. (see pages 90 – 1).

Echo Ravine You walk up a mini-canyon and through a steep-walled ravine onto the top of the sandstone, from where there are fine mountain views. (Allow 60 – 90 minutes.) There is an optional link with the Brandwag Route.

Brandwag Route This steep path takes you through indigenous forest to the top of the Brandwag Buttress, one of the most spectacular formations in the park. (Allow 30 – 45 minutes.)

Langtoon Dam Heading south from Glen Reenen, you walk through a secluded valley to the dam. This 30 – 40 minute walk is good for bird-watching.

From Brandwag camp, there are the following paths:

Brandwag Buttress A steep path leads to the top of this magnificent formation. (Allow at least 30 – 40 minutes.)

Holkrans Route Another good bird-watching walk, this 60 – 90 minute trail leads south along the base of attractive cliffs, then up a series of ladders to the Holkrans caves, famed for their honey-combed sandstone formations.

From the Gladstone Information Centre, where the administrative offices are housed, a number of walks commence. Close to the tarred park road you can take a short walk to Golden Gate Dam and visit the family graveyard of the Van Reenens, who were among the earliest farmers in the area. One of the family members, Mrs SJL van Reenen, named the pair of imposing buttresses that flank the valley 'Golden Gate' when she and her husband first moved here in the 1870s – hence the name of the park.

During peak season, the park offers a programme of guided walks for visitors and, throughout the year, horse-riding trails leave from Gladstone. There is a minimum of three rides every morning lasting an hour each (with more rides laid on during holidays), as well as short pony-rides for children. Or you may choose a two-hour afternoon ride along the Rhebok Spruit, which includes a visit to the historic Noord Brabant homestead, a sandstone building typical of the early architecture of the area.

Park officers warn visitors to steer clear of the upland portions of the park in thunderstorms, and to take warm clothing when walking above the sandstone, as sudden blizzards are a hazard at any time of year. It is wise to avoid solitary eland bulls – their peaceful appearance is deceptive, as they are wild and dangerous.

Accommodation in the park is provided at Brandwag, in luxury chalets or in the main building, which also has a restaurant, ladies' bar, coffee shop and sports facilities. Glen Reenen has more rustic accommodation in huts, as well as a campsite, shop, braai and picnic facilities for day visitors, and a swimming dam.

Enquiries and reservations for accommodation should be made through the National Parks Board offices in Pretoria, tel (012) 343 1991, fax (012) 343 0153; or Cape Town tel (021) 22 2816, fax (021) 24 6211. Enquiries may also be directed to the park at tel (058) 256 1471 or P/Bag X03, Clarens 9707.

The highlands setting offers hiking, bird-watching and game-viewing.

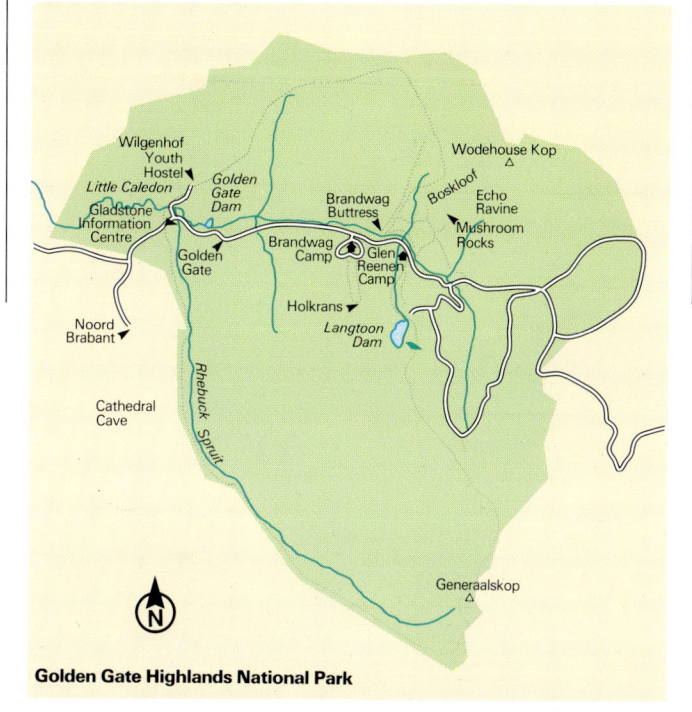

Golden Gate Highlands National Park

The camp at Glen Reenen.

The spectacular Brandwag Buttress.

• PLACES OF INTEREST IN BLOEMFONTEIN •

The Appellate Division of the Supreme Court – South Africa's final court of appeal.

A Voortrekker capital built around a 'spring of flowers'

IT WAS PROLONGED drought that led farmers, in the early years of the 19th century, to seek new grazing far from the settled areas of the Cape. One of these farmers was Rudolph Martinus Brits of Swellendam. In about 1820 Brits crossed the *Gariep* or *Groot* (great) River – officially known as the Orange River – to settle in the territory vaguely referred to at the time as Transorangia.

He found a favourable site next to a clear, perennial spring, and was joined here by his nephew, Johan Nicolaas Brits. The older Brits, moved by the *trekgees* (wanderlust), later wandered away to the south-east to settle on the banks of the *Koringspruit* (corn stream). But his nephew stayed on at the spring with his family and built a house of 'poles and spars, roofed with reed and plastered inside and out'. He dug a furrow from the spring and planted a fruit orchard – of which two pear trees in the grounds of the *Presidency* **(1)** are said to be survivors. His wife laid out a flower garden, and this, in time, gave its name to the spring that had brought them here – *bloemfontein* (spring of flowers) **(2)**. Many people have known Bloemfontein for decades as *Mangaung* – 'the place of the cheetah' – but it is not certain when this name was first used.

As more and more Voortrekkers settled in the territory, which at that time had its 'capital' at Winburg, a British resident or political agent was appointed: Major Henry Douglas Warden, a veteran of the frontier wars and reputedly an illegitimate descendant of Prince Charles Edward Stewart, the Young Pretender.

Warden settled himself at Brits' Bloemfontein farm, and paid Johan Brits £37.10s for the improvements he had made – Brits being considered merely the occupier and not the owner of the land. Warden and his family moved into Brits' house, and clay huts were built for his troops in the vicinity of the *Queen's Fort* **(3)**. This small settlement, when the territory between the Orange and Vaal rivers was annexed as the Orange River Sovereignty in 1848, became the new capital. Major Warden laid out the town himself, naming several streets after members of his family – including Charles, Henry, Douglas and Elizabeth.

A 'prettily situated' village

Within a year or so of its founding, Bloemfontein was described as 'a small village consisting of some half-dozen houses and some huts, prettily situated on the banks of a stream having as its source a bubbling fountain. . .'.

When the Republic of the Orange Free State was declared in 1854, the town expanded across the *Bloemspruit* (flower stream) towards Bloemfonteinberg – which is now known as *Naval Hill* **(4)**. This new name was given during the Anglo-Boer War, when a Naval Brigade was formed to man heavy artillery – some of it removed from the turrets of warships – to oppose Boer gunners.

The statue of General Christiaan de Wet in front of the Raadsaal.

Naval Hill is now the site of the *Franklin Nature Reserve* **(5)**, crossed by a network of roads from which a variety of game can be seen.

Within the reserve is an old astronomical observatory, built by the University of Michigan in the United States, and now used as a theatre **(6)**.

On the slopes of Naval Hill, and visible from Andries Pretorius Street, is the shape of a horse, picked out in whitewashed stones. This was built by men of the Wiltshire Regiment during the Anglo-Boer War, and is a replica of a similar white horse on a hillside in the regiment's home county of Wiltshire.

The site of the original *'Bloemfontein'* **(2)** is off Selborne Street and is marked by a column bearing the city's crest. Although the oldest legible gravestone found in the old cemetery dates from September 1846, the oldest existing building is probably the First *Raadsaal* (council chamber) **(7)** in St George's Street. This was completed in May 1849, and was described as 'a large fine building, nothing very handsome, but it is of good and strong plain work'. Originally it served as church and school, as well as the meeting-place of the Legislative Assembly and the municipal officials.

Although the *Queen's Fort* **(3)** – also known as Bloemfontein Fort – was built some months before the First Raadsaal, it subsequently collapsed in heavy rains, and was entirely rebuilt in 1879. It is now a military museum, with particularly fine collections of regimental badges and of firearms.

A proud old Presidency

Just around the corner from the First Raadsaal, in the continuation of President Brand Street known as Eunice Street, is the imposing old *Presidency* **(1)**. Warden's old house, based as it was on the humble dwelling of Johan Brits, was continually extended to serve as the official residence of Orange Free State presidents, but was eventually described as 'a disgrace to the country'. A new building was erected in 1860, but this, too, was soon judged unsuitable. In 1884, some 27 plans were submitted in a competition to design a new Presidency, the prize of £200 going to a firm of architects in Queenstown. The corner-stone was laid the following year, and within 16 months the building was completed. The Presidency has now been restored, and houses the Cultural History Museum of the Free State.

One of South Africa's most distinctive churches is Bloemfontein's *Tweetoringkerk* (church with two spires) **(8)**, which stands at the head of Church Street. The church was completed in May 1880, but, 55 years later, in April 1935, the western spire collapsed. Fears about the security of the other spire led to its being demolished – down as far as the height of the main roof. A fund was later established for the restoration of the spires in their entirety, which was accomplished in 1943.

From a thatched schoolroom in St George's Street, successive governments moved to two other buildings, since demolished, before meeting for the first time in the *Fourth Raadsaal* **(9)** in President Brand Street, in 1893. Designed by Lennox Canning, architect of the Presidency, the Fourth Raadsaal is regarded as an outstanding example of late-Victorian architecture and as 'the architectural gem of the (Orange) Free State'. The *Old Government Buildings* **(10)** in Maitland Street, begun in 1875, were used as a military hospital during the Anglo-Boer War and today they house the National Afrikaans Literary Museum and Research Centre.

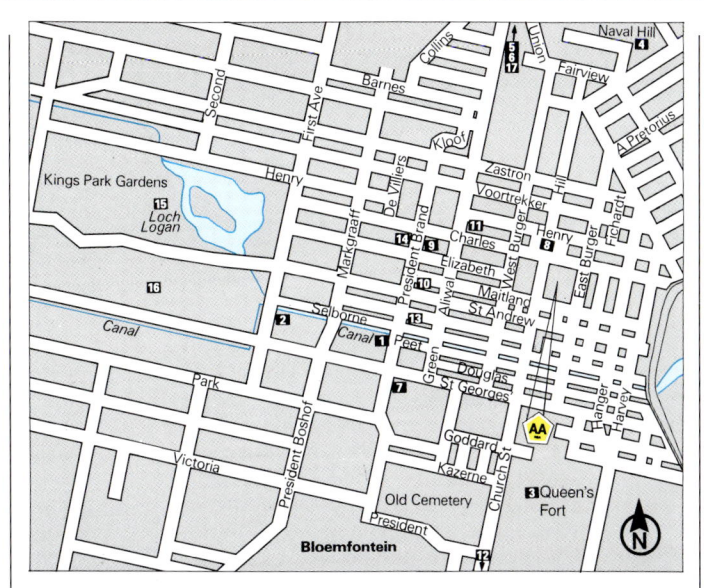

The Presidency in Eunice Street was finally completed in 1887.

The First Raadsaal built in 1849.

The *National Museum* **(11)** in Aliwal Street houses natural history displays, especially of archaeological interest. Here you can see the fossilized skull and a reconstruction of 'Florisbad man' – thought by some scientists to have been an ancestor of the San peoples.

Bloemfontein's best-known monument is probably the *Vrouemonument* **(12)** – the National Women's Memorial. This commemorates the roughly 26 000 Boer women and children who died during the Anglo-Boer War, most of them in concentration camps. The cause of these 'refugees' was championed by an Englishwoman, Emily Hobhouse, whose ashes are buried at the monument – and by other distinguished people, including the guerrilla leader General Christiaan de Wet, of whom there is an equestrian statue in the grounds of the Fourth Raadsaal.

The 'whispering wall'

The tall obelisk of the Women's Memorial is surrounded by a circular 'whispering wall'. The slightest sound made close to the interior of the wall can be heard clearly anywhere along its circumference.

The War Museum of the Boer Republics is in the grounds of the Women's Memorial, and houses many relics of the Anglo-Transvaal War of 1880 – 1 and the Anglo-Boer War of 1899 – 1902. Within the grounds there is an interesting series of statues. One represents a typical Boer fighting man at the start of the war, while another shows him as a hardened *bittereinder* – one who remained in the field to the very end.

Bloemfontein is the judicial capital of South Africa. In addition to having a *Provincial Supreme Court* **(13)** in President Brand Street, it is the home of the highest court in the land – the *Appellate Division of the Supreme Court* **(14)**. Both are panelled in stinkwood.

Apart from all the important official buildings, the city has a number of attractive parks, including the Franklin Nature Reserve on Naval Hill and *King's Park* **(15)**, which contains Loch Logan and the Zoo. Also worth a visit is *President Swart Park* **(16)**, and *Hamilton Park* **(17)** on Naval Hill. In Hamilton Park there is an orchid house containing over 3 000 plants.

Free State highlands and blue mountain vistas

A day in the scenic Free State highlands starts from Bethlehem. We visit the pretty villages of Clarens and Fouriesburg and the border town of Ficksburg – in the heart of cherry country and the Caledon River valley – passing through magnificent sandstone regions with splendid vistas of the Maluti Mountains in nearby Lesotho. The entire route is tarred.

**Bethlehem
Clarens
Fouriesburg
Ficksburg
210 – 230 km**

THE DAY'S DRIVE starts in front of the Bethlehem Municipal Centre, where you note your kms before driving eastwards along Muller Street and out of the town, following the signs for Durban. The road becomes the N5.

After 8 km, turn right onto the R711 for Clarens and note your kms at the turn. The attractive, hilly landscape is dotted with farm dams, and many sandstone homesteads, typical of the area, are to be seen tucked away below the wooded cliffs of rocky ridges and koppies. Clusters of weeping willows grow along the stream banks and long rows of slender Lombardy poplars, superbly golden in autumn, demarcate the extensive cultivated lands and farm boundaries. Clear blue skies are characteristic of this eastern Free State highveld region (as are its inky night skies, sprayed with brilliant stars). Huge, turbulent cloud structures often gather over the mountain horizons in the afternoons and sweep across the pink-coloured plains and the vivid green or flaxen wheatlands. These may be preludes to dramatic summer thunderstorms and often subside into superb sunsets.

After 26,3 km the road passes through a natural gateway of two towering cliffs and you look down onto the picturesque setting of Clarens, nestling among giant boulder formations below the sandstone summits of the Rooiberge. The turn-off to the village is on your right, 2,5 km further on.

When you have explored this scenic village (see opposite), retrace your route to the R711 and note your kms as you turn right, for Fouriesburg. The road passes through a number of secluded valleys overlooked by massive, sphinx-like rock structures typical of this region's topography, before rising to reveal a grand vista of the Maluti Mountains. These stretch away to your left beyond rugged expanses of intermediate lowlands.

Fouriesburg to Bethlehem

After 34,5 km you reach Fouriesburg, lying to the right of the road just before the T-junction where the R711 meets the R26. After exploring the village (see opposite), return to this T-junction and turn left onto the R26, noting your kms. Across the plains in nearby Lesotho, dramatic views of the Malutis continue to unfold on your left as you head south for Ficksburg. Heavy winter snowfalls frequently make this mountain range – it is an off-shoot of the Drakensberg – a dazzling sight, but remember that winter weather conditions can be bitterly cold along this route.

You are now in deciduous fruit country and, in summer, the many roadside fruit stalls tempt motorists to stop along the way. The area is famous for its cherries and visits in spring are particularly rewarding for the magnificent sight of acres of cherry blossoms. After 45 km you reach Ficksburg; turn left off the R26 to visit the town (see opposite).

On leaving Ficksburg, note your kms as you turn right onto the R26 to retrace your route northwards in the direction of Bethlehem. Fine, wide views of the blue Maluti range now appear on your right. Among the fields of maize and wheat, several cherry orchards are visible along the lower slopes below the many koppies flanking the broad valleys of the district. Gum trees, oaks and conifers clustered around homesteads and farm buildings punctuate the landscape.

Some 20 km after leaving Ficksburg, continuous stretches of craggy krantzes and mountain ridges begin to dominate the countryside to the left of your route. These proclaim the beginning of the Witteberge, which stretch northwards towards Bethlehem. After bypassing Fouriesburg (now to the right of the R26) you begin an ascent over a saddle of this range as it curves eastward to join the Rooiberge around Clarens and the Golden Gate Highlands National Park. This climb brings you onto a high, open plateau, where the road straightens out into a long line accompanied by an imposing avenue of tall poplars. Swiftly but subtly the scenery has shifted from dramatic sandstone formations into gently undulating plains and far-flung wheatlands, and soon you reach the outskirts of Bethlehem. Re-entering the town from its south-western approach you pass the entrance to Loch Athlone on your right-hand side and the route becomes a broad, tree-lined suburban street. This leads directly to the town centre. After crossing Church Street (Bethlehem's main thoroughfare), turn right into Muller Street to reach the front of the town's Municipal Centre, where our drive began.

AA Office 17 Sanlam Plaza, Maitland Street Bloemfontein 9301 Tel (051) 47 6191
Bethlehem Publicity Office Civic Centre, Muller Street, Bethlehem 9700 Tel (058) 303 5732
Clarens Local Council Offices Market Street West, Clarens 9707 Tel (058) 256 1380

Its prow-like appearance gives this rock formation near Clarens the names of Titanic *and* The Ship.

CLARENS

Clarens, 'the jewel of the Free State', is a highlight among this route's stopping points. Nestling in the Rooiberge, the village has many graceful willow trees and a wealth of roses that make it a breathtaking sight in spring. The world-famous Golden Gate Highlands National Park (20 km away) augments the village's own aesthetic appeal as an idyllic holiday resort. A hiking and horse-riding paradise, Clarens is also home to many artists and its craft centres and art galleries are well worth visiting. Accommodation ranges from cottages, chalets and bed-and-breakfast lodgings to mountain huts and a wide range of camping options. Pubs, tea gardens, coffee shops and restaurants cater for day visitors who stop here for a meal or to enjoy browsing through the enticing handcrafted ware. A drive through Golden Gate to the Basotho Cultural Village, 40 km away, makes a scenic and interesting outing.

Cinderella's Castle of 50 000 (empty) beer bottles.

FREE STATE & LESOTHO

The fortress-like sandstone Soutkop towers above wheatfields near Ficksburg.

Ficksburg's museum – timber and sandstone.

Cliffs, caves and water await exploration at Meiringskloof.

Modern influences and paint combine with traditional style near Bethlehem.

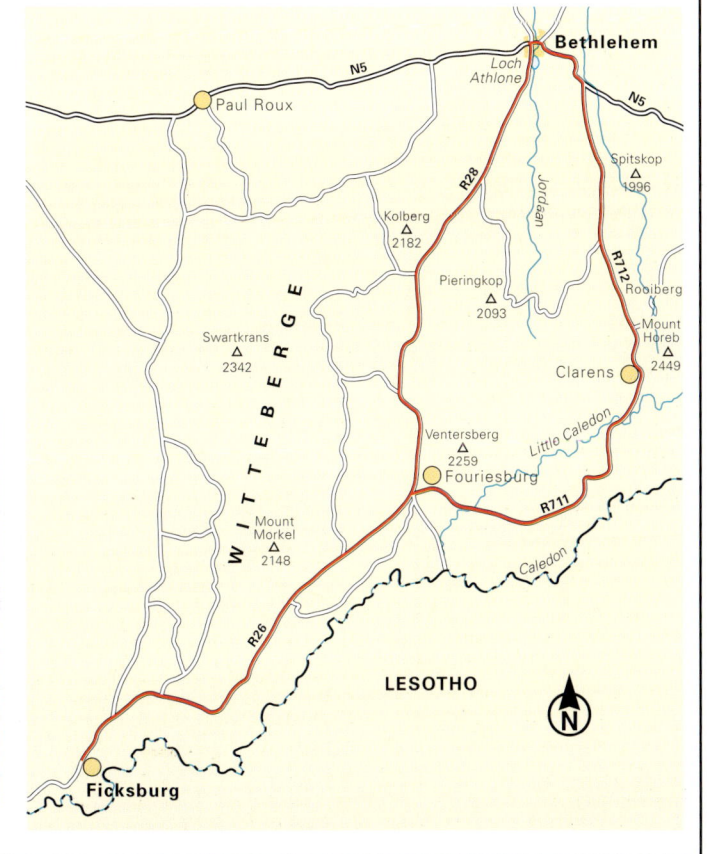

FOURIESBURG

Situated 10 km from the Lesotho border, with magnificent views of the Malutis, this little town has many historic associations and was once the capital of the republican Orange Free State. It received this status during the Anglo-Boer War after the British occupation of Bloemfontein and Bethlehem.

Fouriesburg is noted for its fine sandstone buildings, which include the Dutch Reformed church (over 100 years old and built in the English Gothic Revival style), the First National Bank, President Steyn's house, the Town Hall and the *Ou Residensie* (old residency). Examples of famous Free State country hospitality are to be found in local guesthouses, and a visit to Meiringskloof Nature Resort is also worthwhile. Situated in a beautiful kloof surrounded by sandstone cliffs riddled with interesting crevices and caves, this pretty resort is 1,7 km from the town along a clearly signposted gravel road. Rock art is found on no fewer than 27 farms in the district.

FICKSBURG

This bustling centre between the slopes of the Imperani Mountains and the western banks of the Caledon River is the only town in South Africa situated on the border of a foreign state. Ficksburg is a point of entry into Lesotho; access is through the adjoining residential and industrial centre of Mapoetsoe which is directly across the river.

Founded in 1867, Ficksburg has its own wealth of beautiful and historic sandstone buildings, notably the old post office and the former magistrate's court. Today this attractively laid out and tree-rich town is famous for its Cherry Festival. For the past three decades this has traditionally been held each year during the third week of November. Ficksburg is also noted for the rich crops of asparagus that are grown in the surrounding districts. There are many guest lodges in the district and several organized hiking trails are available.

BETHLEHEM

Today a busy commercial centre, Bethlehem was founded in 1864 on the farm Pretoriuskloof and the old name survives in the nature reserve in the centre of the town. The reserve has pleasant pathways and picnic sites along the Jordaan River. Another scenic attraction is the pleasure resort of Loch Athlone. This is popular for watersports and angling and offers camping facilities and holiday accommodation. A distinctive feature is its restaurant in the form of a replica ocean liner decorated in old Union Castle Line livery. Much of the town's history is reflected in its lovely sandstone buildings, several of which are national monuments. Many of these are public buildings and can be visited: churches, museums (the Nazareth Mission Church and the Baartman Wagon House), coffee shops, restaurants and businesses. Wolhuterskop Game Reserve nearby is a popular destination for nature-lovers who enjoy uninterrupted game-viewing (game species include zebra, eland and red hartebeest), hiking (there is an overnight hut) and horse-riding.

97

Following the mountain road deep into the magic Maluti

We start this route at Maseru and penetrate deep into the heart of Lesotho by driving east on the 'Mountain Road'. We cross four magnificent passes that soar over the majestic Maluti Mountains and we visit the well-preserved San paintings at Ha Khotso. Half the route is on gravel but the roads are continually upgraded; good gravel roads cover 40 km.

**Maseru
Roma
Bushman's Pass
Blue Mountain Pass
Likalaneng Pass
Ha Khotso
250 – 270 km**

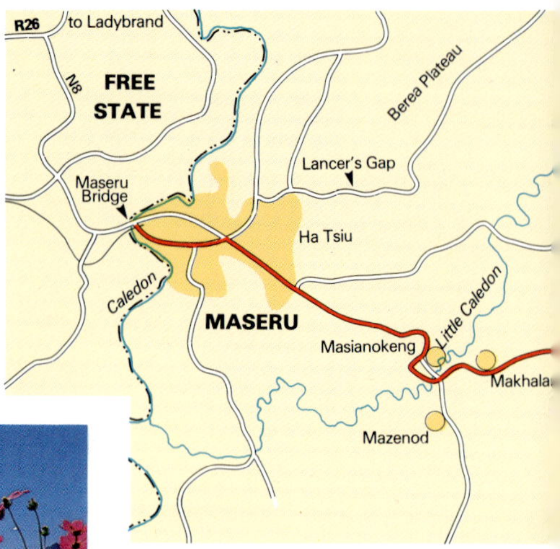

START YOUR DAY WITH a visit to one of Maseru's gift and craft shops. These shops serve as an introduction to the many fascinating works of local craftsmanship that can be found in Lesotho. If you are entering Lesotho from the Maseru Bridge Border Post, note your kms as you leave the post and travel straight along the main road for about 2,4 km to reach Maseru. Turn right at the traffic lights and immediately turn left into the parking area next to the premises of The Basotho Hat.

Return to your car and turn right as you leave the parking area, then turn right onto Kingsway. Travel to the traffic circle at the end of the road which is overlooked by the twin-towered Catholic cathedral, and take the third exit from the traffic circle (Main South 1) onto the road to Mafeteng. After travelling about 14 km from the traffic circle, turn left onto the mountain road for Roma and Thaba Tseka. Note your kms as you turn.

As you drive along this road, you can see the mountains looming mistily in the distance, and the surrounding landscape becomes typical of the lowland farming areas. After 7,4 km you reach the summit of a small hill that offers a magnificent view of the mountains ahead of you. After 11 km you pass a turn-off for Thaba Tseka on your left – note your kms as you pass this road. At this point you can see directly ahead of you a large, triangular rock formation and a small church. Continue straight towards Roma, passing steep cliffs on your left.

After 7 km you enter Roma (see this page), with the entrance to the university on your left and the Roma Business Centre on your right. Continue on the tarred road through this picturesque village, which has many buildings of honey-coloured sandstone, and return to the entrance. Retrace your route back to the turn-off marked Thaba Tseka and turn right here, noting your kms as you turn.

First of the passes

You now begin the ascent of the first of the four passes to be followed across the Maluti Mountains, this stage taking you from the Lesotho lowlands to the foothills zone. After 6 km, park at the side of the road for a fine view back over Roma. From this spot you can also see the impressive Machache Mountain ahead of you. Continue straight and after 10 km you reach the small settlement of Ha Ntsi, where local beer is produced. Shortly after, you reach the settlement of Nazareth and, 15 km later, you pass 'Old Toll Gate', which has a small caravan and camping site and a building from which refreshments are served. Note your kms as you pass the caravan park.

You now begin the long, winding ascent of Bushman's Pass and, after 5 km, you reach a corner protected by a crash barrier. Stop behind this barrier on the right side of the road for a magnificent view over the Lesotho lowlands. You have reached the end of the foothills zone and the beginning of the Maluti front range. Continue up the pass, taking particular care on these winding roads and negotiating blind corners slowly. At the top of the pass there is a sign showing the altitude (2 268 m), before you begin the long descent into the valley. On the valley floor you cross the willow-lined Makhaleng River and, after a further 2,3 km, you reach the Molimo Nthuse Mountain Lodge – a convenient place to stop for refreshments.

Continuing on the same road, you now begin the steep ascent of the *Molimo Nthuse* (God help me) Pass, reaching the summit 3 km after leaving the lodge. Note your kms here. The first of several stretches of gravel-surfaced road begins here and, after a further 100 m, you pass the Pony Trekking Station (see opposite) on your left. Ask here about pony trekking to breathtakingly beautiful destinations, organized on an hourly basis, or you may take part in a longer, one-way outing.

A scenic drive of 2,4 km brings you down onto the valley floor, where you pass the

Wildflowers enliven the roadside fields in the spring.

Sweeping views greet motorists at every turn on Lesotho's mountain roads.

ROMA

The home of the National University of Lesotho, Roma lies 35 km from Maseru. It was founded in 1862, when a Catholic mission was established here by Bishop J Allard and Father Joseph Gerard on ground granted to them by the Basotho ruler, Moshoeshoe. The mission became known as the place of the Ba-Roma or Roman Catholics – hence its modern name. In 1945 the university started here as a Catholic college with five students and four teaching clergy. Today it has over 1 000 students. The campus and the town lie in a beautiful valley surrounded by high mountains that are often snowcapped in winter.

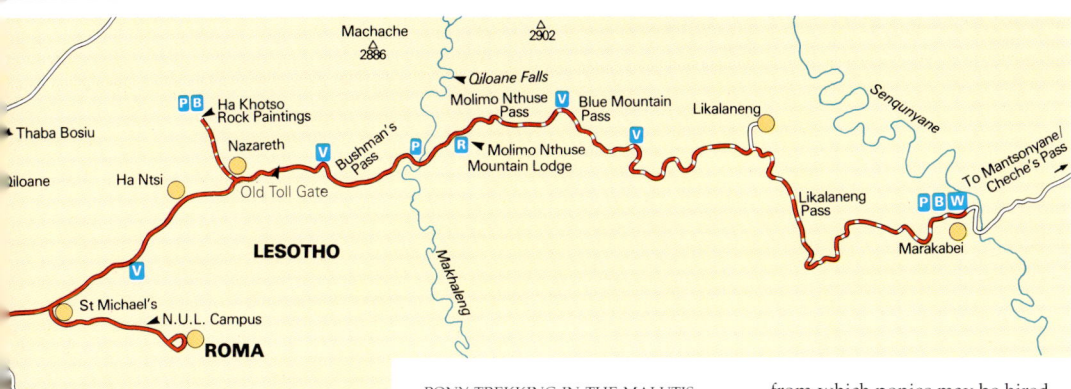

FREE STATE & LESOTHO

ROCK PAINTINGS NEAR HA KHOTSO
The colourful San rock paintings on an ancient overhanging rock shelter at a site called Ha Baroana are among the best-preserved examples of rock art in southern Africa. A footpath leads to the shelter, and the visitor is well rewarded by the quality and quantity of the paintings – representing animals, groups of human figures and hunting scenes. The curator at the shelter charges a small fee to open the gate, and you may picnic on the banks of the small stream that runs alongside the site. The surrounding area is a nature reserve and has remained unchanged since the time when the San artists lived and worked in this part of Africa.

PONY TREKKING IN THE MALUTIS
One of the most exciting ways to cross the rugged Maluti mountain range is on the back of a sure-footed, sweet-tempered Basotho pony. The Basotho people are a nation of horsemen, and their ponies, descended in part from Javanese horses imported into the Cape, are well trained and reliable. After reckless buying during and after the Anglo-Boer War, the breeding stock deteriorated seriously, but the ponies were saved by Irish experts. At the top of the Molimo Nthuse Pass there is a pony-trekking centre from which ponies may be hired and excursions planned. Of particular scenic beauty is the short ride to the Qiloane Falls, where there is a large, natural swimming pool and facilities for picnicking.

For the more adventurous, pony treks of several days are available. This form of travel takes the rider across mountains and through spectacular valleys – an exhilarating experience, offering an opportunity to see parts of Lesotho that cannot be reached by car. For further information contact the Basotho Pony Project, PO Box 107, Maseru.

Ha Baroana, site of San paintings.

A winter scene in Bushman's Pass.

The white, tumbling waters of the Qiloane Falls.

San paintings at Ha Khotso.

remains of an old trading store. You also pass a stream lined with willow trees that makes a convenient picnic spot. After 4,4 km the road surface changes back to tar and you begin the ascent of the next scenic mountain drive – the Blue Mountain Pass (Thaba Putsoa). As you penetrate deeper into the Maluti Mountains, the scenery becomes more and more dramatic, with weathered rocks and soaring peaks that are capped with snow in winter. At the top of the Blue Mountain Pass (2 634 m), where the tarred section ends, park at the side of the road and walk a few metres to your left for a panoramic view over rugged valleys that stretch endlessly into the distance. Continue along the road, which offers more views.

Marakabei and the Senqunyane River
You now begin the descent of the pass and, 10,5 km after noting your kms at the summit of the Molimo Nthuse Pass, the road surface changes back to tar. At this point there is another fine viewsite on your left. The road surface changes to gravel again after 2 km of tar and, several kilometres later, you pass the small settlement of Likalaneng nestling against a steep hillside. After the village you cross a bridge that marks the start of the long Likalaneng Pass.

Some 40 km after the summit of the Molimo Nthuse Pass, stop on the left for good views of the valley. After 47 km you enter the settlement of Marakabei and, after a further 2,8 km, you cross the scenic Senqunyane River. Turn around at this point to start the return journey.

Note your kms as you reach the tar at the summit of the Molimo Nthuse Pass. Roughly 19 km later, in the small mission settlement of Nazareth, turn right onto a gravel road to view a group of San paintings. After 4 km you reach a crossroads. Keep straight on for 1 km to the village of Ha Khotso. A curator will show you the paintings. Retrace your route to the tarred road and turn right for Maseru.

AA Office 17 Sanlam Plaza, Maitland Street
Bloemfontein 9301 Tel (051) 47 6191
Lesotho Tourist Board
PO Box 1379, Maseru, Lesotho
Tel (09266) 31 2896/31 3034

Centuries-old crafts and a majestic mountain-top retreat

This route explores the area north and south of Maseru. The two formidable plateaus of Berea and Qeme are almost constant landmarks in this part of the lowlands, and the visitor to this mountain kingdom is introduced to local handcrafts and history. Over two-thirds of the route is tarred; 40 km are on good gravel roads. Take refreshments with you.

Maseru
Teyateyaneng
Thaba Bosiu
Morija
220 – 280 km

Leave Maseru by driving east along Kingsway. At the traffic circle, before the large twin-towered Cathedral of Our Lady of Victories, take the second exit left. Note your kms as you pass the cathedral. You are now on Main North 1, which leads through the outskirts of the town, and after 1 km you pass the Sebaboleng Dam on your right. After 2,7 km turn right off the main road onto a tarred road that winds up between two large rock formations to Lancer's Gap – where the Radio Lesotho transmitter masts are situated. From the summit there is a fine view looking back over Maseru. Return to the main road and turn right, noting your kms as you turn.

You now pass through farmlands typical of Lesotho's lowlands, with the Berea Plateau a constant presence on your right. After 15,3 km you can see the Tlapaneng Mountain on your right, and often the early morning light will catch the smoke from woodburning fires as it drifts against the backdrop of the plateau. After 29,1 km you pass the settlement of Lekokoaneng, and after 34,5 km you cross the Teyateyaneng River. At 38,3 km from the Lancer's Gap turn-off you reach the hilltop town of Teyateyaneng.

Teyateyaneng to Morija
There are several craft centres that you may like to visit in Teyateyaneng where rugs, tapestries and wall-hangings are made by hand from wool spun on the premises. Visitors may tour the workshops and purchase their products.

From the Setsoto Design Centre, head for the main road. Turn right as if you are returning to Maseru, then immediately left onto a tarred road signposted 'Sefikeng', noting your kms. After 4,4 km turn sharp right onto a gravel sideroad (slightly uphill and not very visible from this direction). Continue along this road, which takes you into the heart of Lesotho.

After 16,2 km you reach a junction – turn left here onto a tarred road. After 18,4 km you pass the small village of Sefikeng, with the mountain of the same name on your left. The road surface changes to gravel 1,3 km beyond the village. Continue straight on this road, which offers fine panoramic views all along its length. After 38 km the hilltop fortress of Thaba Bosiu, the principal feature in the area of Maseru, comes into view on your left. You pass a modern church on your right. The road skirts the base of Thaba Bosiu, the surface changing to tar and, after a short distance, you reach the Thaba Bosiu Tourist Information Office on your right. Stop here for a magnificent view of the historic mountain – Moshoeshoe's natural fortress (see below).

Continue on this road, and 48 km after leaving Teyateyaneng, turn right at the T-junction onto a tarred road – noting your kms at the turn; 6,3 km later you reach another T-junction. Turn left here for Mafeteng (right leads to Maseru). After a further 2,3 km you pass a turn-off leading to the airport.

As you travel south, the large Qeme Plateau looms on your right; 24,2 km after noting your kms you pass the turn-off to Matsieng, and after approximately 32 km you can see the large Masite Mountain that overlooks Morija. Shortly afterwards you cross the Lerato River, noting your kms and, 1 km after crossing the river, turn left to Morija.

Continue for a short distance until you reach the stone Post Office building. Turn right here and stop at the side of the road to view the striking red church in the centre of the village. Next to it is the Maeder House Craft Centre,

Hairpin bend on the steep, winding ascent to Lancer's Gap.

Moshoeshoe I statue in Maseru.

Warm and colourful garments displayed in a shop in Maseru.

LESOTHO CRAFTS
The people of Lesotho are masters of the crafts of weaving, jewellery-making and pottery. Visitors to craft centres in the tiny mountain kingdom are welcome to observe the skill of the craftsmen – and to buy the finished articles. There are several such centres in Teyateyaneng, some 40 km from Maseru on the scenic Main North 1 Highway.

Visitors are invited to tour the workshops to watch craftsmen creating exquisite articles, and these are generally available for sale in an adjoining showroom. Rated as among the finest craft workshops in southern Africa, they are open to the public on weekdays and Saturdays.

MOUNTAIN OF THE NIGHT
Thaba Bosiu (mountain of the night) is a remarkable natural fortress with steep cliffsides rising to over 1 500 m. The mountain stands in the valley of the Phuthiatsana River, and the founder of the Basotho nation, Moshoeshoe established a stronghold here in 1824. From this impregnable position he repulsed attacks by many of the local clans. The ruins of his residence and his grave may be visited on top of the mountain. One emotional feature on the mountain is a footprint carved on a ledge above a steep cliff. This is said to have been carved by one of Moshoeshoe's sons, who leapt to his death from this ledge after being refused permission to marry the girl of his heart.

Soil erosion has begun to mark this steep, hoe-cultivated slope.

FREE STATE & LESOTHO

which displays attractively printed cloth and garments. Approximately 100 m further along this road is the Lesotho Book Centre, behind which is a small museum. If you wish to visit this museum you should enquire about access at the Book Centre.

Morija to Maseru

Turn your car around and leave Morija with the Post Office on your right. Immediately after passing the Post Office building, take the right-hand road at the junction.

The tarred road winds past large sandstone mountains that rise steeply on your right. After just a few kilometres you pass through the Royal village of Matsieng; roughly 600 m later, turn left at the T-junction for Maseru, noting your kms as you turn. After 1 km you pass an attractive stone church set back from the road on your left. The Qeme Plateau is now directly in front of you; 5 km after turning, you enter the small settlement of Mahloenyeng, with attractive views of the Tlouoe Mountains to your right. After 10,5 km you reach a T-junction with the road on which you travelled south. Turn right here and follow this road back to Maseru.

Maseru (place of red sandstones) was selected by Moshoeshoe as a site for the headquarters of the newly established British administration of the small Protectorate of Basutoland in 1869. Commandant James Bowker, agent to the High Commissioner, established his camp there. To the British, the adminstrative posts of Basutoland were 'camps' since it was never expected that they would grow into towns. As a result they did not have the benefit of proper planning. Maseru is atmospheric and cosmopolitan, with a large presence of international aid organizations.

To end the day you might like to visit the statue of Moshoeshoe I in the heart of the capital. When you reach the traffic circle in front of the cathedral, take the first exit left onto Kingsway. Pass the Queen Elizabeth II Hospital, take the third turning to your left with the Post Office on the corner, and park a short distance down this road near a pair of gates. Walk through the gates down to steep steps that lead up to the statue.

AA Office 17 Sanlam Plaza, Maitland Street Bloemfontein 9301 Tel (051) 47 6191
Lesotho Tourist Board PO Box 1378, Maseru Lesotho Tel (09266) 31 2896

Lesotho village against a backdrop of the Maluti Mountains.

MORIJA

Founded in 1833 by pioneer French Protestant missionaries, Morija is still the headquarters of the Lesotho Evangelical Church, and is well known for its excellent mission press and book depot. Behind the depot is a small museum. In the centre of the village is a church with an eye-catching red roof. The roof is supported by octagonal teak columns made from ships' masts, brought by ox wagon from Port Elizabeth in the 1860s. The Thabelang Handcraft Centre just outside Morija produces colourful, locally designed garments.

Left: *A tapestry takes shape.* **Above:** *Church at Morija.*

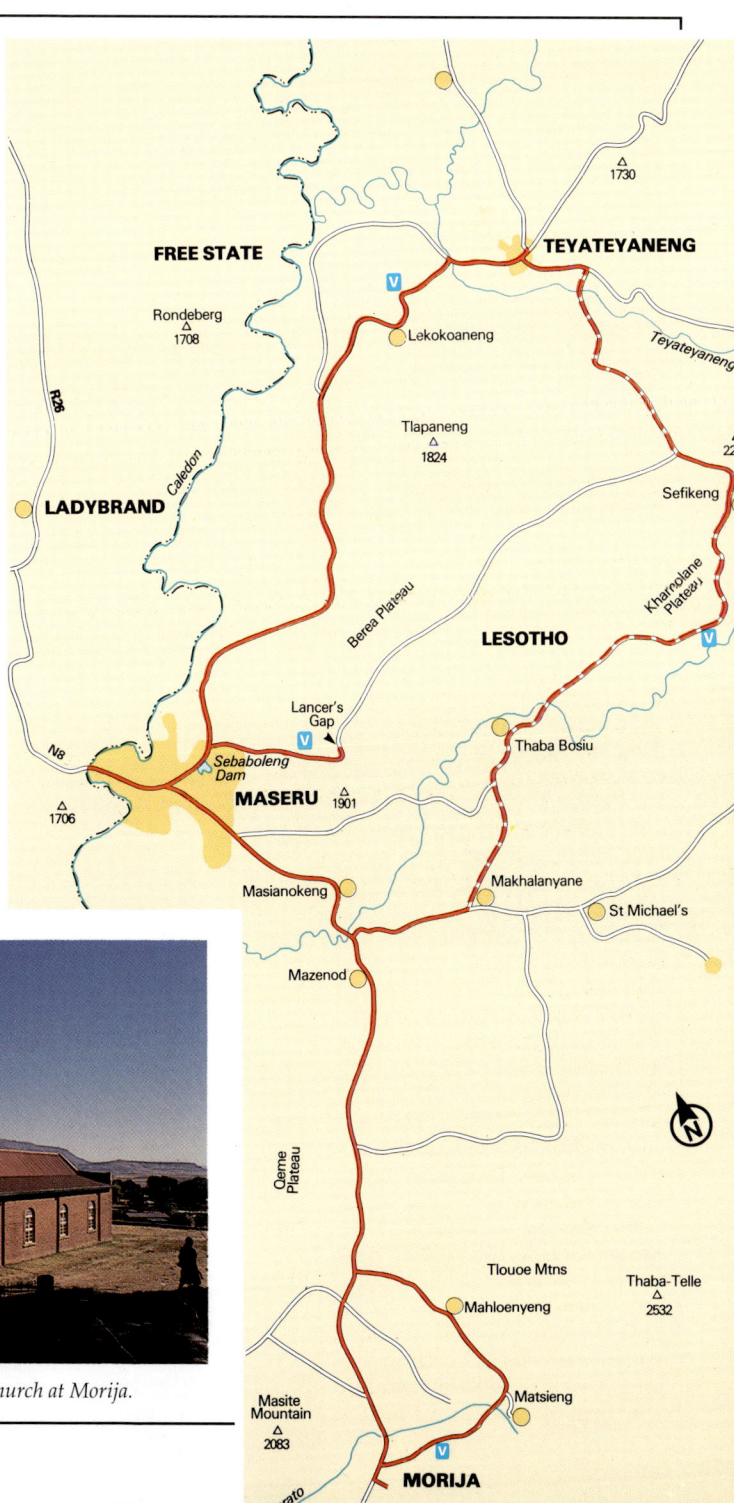

• LESOTHO TRADITIONS •

Most of Lesotho consists of rugged mountains, and the sturdy 'Basuto pony' is often the only reliable means of transport.

One of the richest stores of Africa's ancient traditions

SOME OF THE brooding mystery of this lovely mountain land is expressed in the name of its famous stronghold, *Thaba Bosiu* – Mountain of the Night. It is said that hostile warriors eyed this flat-topped and apparently insignificant outcrop with scorn, promising its defenders a swift and painful death. In a night attack, though, the attackers found the way steep, and the mountain itself seemed to have grown larger and higher. There were few paths to the summit, and these the defenders made impassable by rolling great boulders down on their attackers, smashing and demoralizing them. The enemy withdrew, and the legend of the Mountain of the Night was carefully fostered to discourage future assaults.

Thaba Bosiu is just one of many natural fortresses along the western fringes of Lesotho, all formed by the erosion of sandstone that overlies more resistant ironstone. In weathering, the sandstone has formed precipitous edges, and many of the saucer-like summits can be reached only by a narrow pass, known as a *khoro*. The summits are grassy and usually well watered from springs, and history has shown time and again that a handful of determined warriors established on such a summit, armed only with basic weapons, can hold off vastly superior forces.

The earliest inhabitants of this region are known only through stone implements found in caves and along riverbanks, but later prehistoric people decorated the cave walls with paintings depicting battles, dances and hunting scenes. These were probably San hunters, joined some 400 years ago by the founding clans of the present Basotho people, including the Baphuthi and the Bafokeng. The Basotho – or South Sotho – are

The distinctive design of a Basotho hat – symbol of a proud nation.

part of a larger group that alone managed to remain intact and unconquered during the tremendous upheavals unleashed by Zulu armies.

In addition to the chaos wrought by the Zulus, there was further upheaval when Mma-Nthatisi, fierce queen regent of the Tlokwa people, invaded the region occupied by the Basotho. The latter, however, sought sanctuary on their mountain fortress of Butha-Buthe, and escaped. Their leader was the young chief *Moshoeshoe* – the shaver – a name he earned for a daring cattle raid on the powerful chief Ramonaheng. Moshoeshoe is an onomatopoeic word, signifying the sound made by a razor as it

Colourful blankets are an effective protection against mountain winds.

The unaffected smile of a Basotho girl.

The traditional huts of Lesotho are noted for their simplicity and neatness.

removes a beard; Moshoeshoe's cattle raid was seen figuratively as removing the beard of his rival.

It was in 1824 that Moshoeshoe led his people to Thaba Bosiu, a fortress far more impregnable than Butha-Buthe. And here he repelled attacks by burghers of the Free State, various black warriors – including the AmaNgwane, a breakaway Zulu group – and even the British regular and colonial forces. Lancers' Gap on Berea Mountain recalls the fate of some British lancers who entered the wrong gully during one of the unsuccessful assaults, and who were surrounded and killed by Moshoeshoe's warriors. Finally, threatened by encroachment from the Free State, Moshoeshoe asked Britain to annex his country, so that his people might be as 'the lice in the blanket of the great Queen' – a reference to Queen Victoria and the all-embracing protection of her empire. As a British protectorate, the country became known as Basutoland. This was changed to Lesotho when the country attained independence in 1966, after nearly a century of British rule. In 1996, the nation mourned the accidental death of 57-year-old Moshoeshoe II, who had been king for three decades. He was succeeded by King Letsie III.

The well-known and sturdy 'Basuto pony' is the product of careful breeding with bloodstock captured during wars in the Eastern Cape, mostly by Moorosi of the Baphuthi.

Some claim that among the original breeds were a number of Shetland ponies from Scotland, and that the sure-footed pony of Lesotho is descended from these.

Of their own origins, Basotho tradition tells of man emerging from the reeds of a river in a distant country or, alternatively, at a place called Ntsuanatsatsi.

Winter mornings are dry and cold.

Traditions survive

Christian missionaries have been at work in Lesotho since the 1830s, but traditional religious practices, based on ancestor-worship, survive in various forms – often combined with Christian teachings. *Molimo* is traditionally recognized as a Supreme Being and Creator, and he may be approached only through the intercession of the spirits of the ancestors who, in turn, care for their living descendants. Beer and food are provided for the spirits' sustenance, particularly after good harvests.

Although death is traditionally regarded as birth into the world of the ancestors, it is also the time to perform rituals associated with an old belief that no person merely dies – he has been 'murdered'. If the death has occurred inside a hut, the body might be removed through a hole made in the back of the hut, rather than through the doorway. The body is buried in a crouching or foetal position, to symbolize rebirth, and the face is turned towards the rising sun, symbol of the new life.

The South Sotho say that, after death, the spirit is safe from the schemings of *Moremo* – the evil one – and finds happiness in *Mosimo* – the beautiful place. In the realm of magic and divination, the South Sotho traditionally recognized a variety of specialist practitioners. Most unusual of these was the *ngaka ea balwetse*, a ventriloquist who would visit his clients with his doll, so that the doll could tell them the source of their trouble. The *dilaoli* was skilled at throwing the bones to foretell the future, while the *senohe*, another seer, could see the future in a bowl of clear water. The *moupelli* specialized in protecting houses against lightning, and the *monnesapula* was consulted to bring rain during times of drought.

The traditional Basotho hut is built of stone because, in many areas, there is a shortage of timber and reed. The huts may be round or rectangular, and are usually coated with a mud plaster on the inside and around the entrance. Finger-patterns and paint are applied by the women, though bright commercial paints are now replacing the traditional black and ochre. To protect the hut and its inhabitants, a number of pegs, treated with a magic potion by a diviner, may be hammered into the ground at the entrance.

Domestic centre

The floor of the hut is made from hard, smooth dung, which is also used as a fuel. Attached to the hut may be a semicircular screen of reeds enclosing an open space. This is known as the *lelapa*, and is the centre for domestic activities such as cooking. A birth in the family may be announced by raising one of the reeds of the lelapa high above the others. This custom may be related to the belief that man first emerged from a bed of reeds in a faraway country.

A feature of the small rural village is the *lekhotla*, a sheltered enclosure usually attached to a small hut where elders gather to discuss village affairs and to hear evidence in cases of alleged contraventions of the community code.

Women are excluded from the lekhotla, except when they are required to give evidence. Traditionally, the Basotho show great hospitality to strangers, and a newcomer will receive a hearty welcome and advice at the lekhotla.

Both the boys and girls of the Basotho have traditionally undergone initiation, although decreasing importance is now attached to these rites. Schools for boys may accommodate up to 60 initiates from a fairly wide area, and are usually organized by a chief, who appoints selected men – *mosuoe* – to instruct the boys. The initiation hut is built just before the time of circumcision, which takes place early in the initiation period.

The operation marks the end of childhood and the start of life as a man, and is followed by intensive lessons on the laws and customs the initiate will be expected to follow. Initiates are also taught the traditions of their clan. They are confined to the hut for about a month after circumcision, during which time food is brought to them. Then follows a period when they may wander about to find their own food by almost any way except dishonesty. Those caught stealing are severely thrashed as a reminder that good manners and a sense of community bring surer rewards.

The girls' initiation schools usually have only about 10 *bale* – as the girls are called – and begin at the time of the new moon. The girls then run to a river where they symbolically wash away their girlhood. Initiates cover themselves with dark ash, and later with white clay. During the initiation period the girls hide their identity behind a veil of grass and beads, and wear the traditional costume of a sheepskin apron with plaited grass cords around the waist.

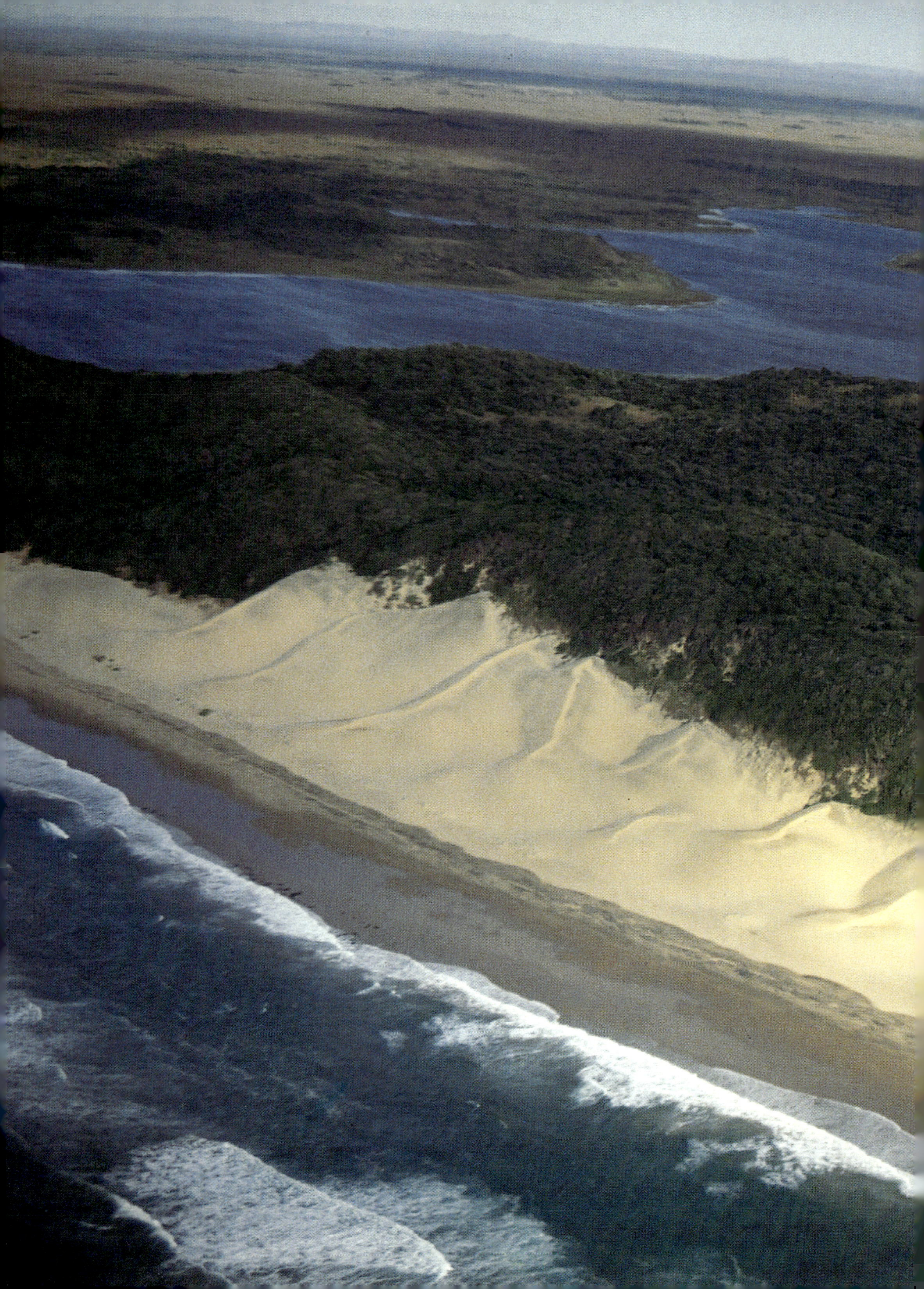

NORTHERN KWAZULU-NATAL

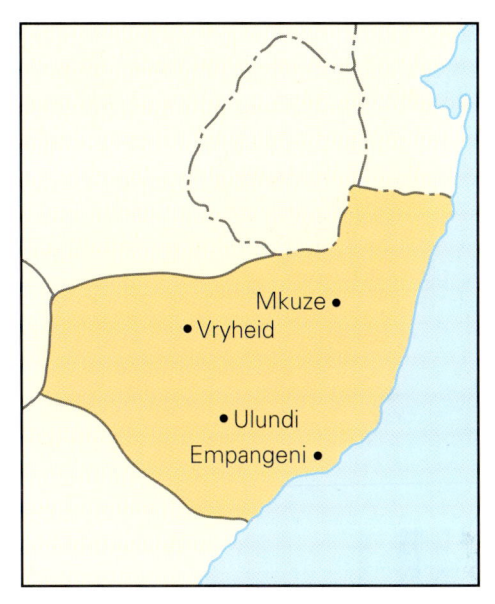

Vryheid – Isandlwana – Rorke's Drift – Talana – Blood River **106-7**

Mkuze – Jozini – Ndumo – Tembe Elephant Park – Kosi Bay **108-9**

Mkuzi Game Reserve: Maputaland magic **110-1**

Hluhluwe-Umfolozi Park: Hluhluwe – Where Zulu kings once hunted **112-3**

Hluhluwe-Umfolozi Park: Umfolozi – Saving the white rhino **114-5**

Lake St Lucia: Subtropical waterworld **116-7**

Empangeni – Enseleni – Coward's Bush – Eshowe – Mtunzini **118-9**

Greytown – Tugela Ferry – Elandslaagte – Colenso – Weenen – Muden **120-1**

Stanger – Kranskop – Ahrens – Sevenoaks – Dalton – Fawn Leas – Nsuze **122-3**

Left: *Typical Maputaland coastline, backed by bush-grown dunes and lakes.*

Assegais and laagers – exploring historic KwaZulu-Natal battlefields

This drive leads from Vryheid on a journey into the past. We visit the Prince Imperial's memorial, then Isandhlwana, Rorke's Drift, Talana and Blood River – scenes of epic battles that shaped South Africa's history. More than half of the route is on gravel, which can become slippery after rains. Take food and drink with you.

Vryheid
Prince Imperial's memorial
Isandhlwana
Rorke's Drift
Talana
Blood River
350 – 370 km

LEAVE VRYHEID by driving west along *Kerkstraat* (Church Street) and note your kms as you pass the stone Dutch Reformed Church on your right. Four blocks later, turn left into West Street. Pass a road to the airfield on your left and cross an old steel bridge over the White Mfolozi River, after which the road surface changes to gravel. After about 16 km you reach a crossroads, where the tarred road on your right leads to eMondlo. Continue on the gravel road, following the sign to Babanango. At about 30 km the road forks – take the road on the right. After 44 km you cross the Mvunyane River and, 2,7 km later, pass the Mhlungwane Store on your right. About 100 m later, turn right at the sign to the Prince Imperial's memorial, noting your kms. The area may be heavily eroded, with a number of shallow gullies and rivulets across the road; they are easily negotiated, but approach them with caution. After 7 km you reach the Jojosi River (Ityotyozi), which you cross on a concrete causeway before turning left to park your car.

The simple memorial about 200 m on the far side of the river was erected by order of Queen Victoria and marks the spot where, revolver in hand, the Prince Imperial died under a hail of spears – 'a miserable death, surely,' according to a writer at the time, 'for he who was once the sun of France.'

Prince Imperial's memorial to Isandhlwana
Retrace your route to the main gravel road and turn right, noting your kms. After 12 km go right at the fork, for Kranskop, and, after a further 27 km, turn right at the T-junction with the tarred R68 and note your kms. After 13,7 km turn left onto the gravel road for Isandhlwana, noting your kms.

Keep straight where a road leads to the left at about 9 km, and to your right is the hill whose shape gave it the name *Isandhlwana* (Zulu for the second stomach of a cow). Follow the signposts and report to the visitors' centre, where there is a model of the battlefield and a small display. On payment of a small entrance fee, you will be given an admission ticket that you must produce to the guard at the gate to the battlefield itself. Profoundly shaken by their defeat here, which claimed the lives of nearly 1 300 regulars and volunteers, the British invasion columns withdrew from the Zulu kingdom and only when they returned several weeks later were the dead buried. Almost all of them were interred where they had fallen, which accounts for the scattered nature of the memorials on the battlefield.

Isandhlwana to Rorke's Drift
Retrace your route to the R68 and turn left, noting your kms. After driving 12 km through a landscape of eroded dongas and scattered Zulu huts you pass through the village of Nqutu. At 31 km you cross a bridge over the *Buffelsrivier* (Buffalo River) at Vant's Drift and, about 1,8 km beyond, turn left onto a gravel road to Rorke's Drift, noting your kms.

After 5 km turn left at the T-junction for Rorke's Drift (where the road to the right leads to Dundee,) and, after 12,2 km, pass a road, on your right, to Helpmekaar. After about 15 km, the buildings of Rorke's Drift are visible on a hill ahead. Some 2 km later, park in the designated area and start your visit at the interpretation centre. A museum in the reconstructed hospital building depicts the sequence of the battle. The Arts and Crafts Centre displays an impressive array of carpets and hangings, pottery and hand-dyed fabrics produced at the mission station here.

Rorke's Drift to Blood River
Follow the gravel road back to the R68 and turn left, noting your kms. At 4,3 km there is a picnic spot. After 26 km you come to a T-junction – turn left onto the R33. About 3 km later, on your right, you come to the Anglo-Boer War battlefield of Talana.

The museum, within shady, parklike surroundings where you may relax in a shady tea-garden, warrants a visit of several hours. It not only displays the Battle of Talana but records earlier wars and local history. In addition, it houses the Consol Glass Collection, the Chamber of Mines' Coal Museum and the Corobrik Heritage Display.

To enter the town of Dundee, where many old and attractive buildings are preserved, continue on the R33. On your return, retrace your route along the R33 towards Vryheid – noting your kms as you pass the Talana battlefield entrance.

After about 21 km, turn right onto a gravel road leading to the Blood River monument – noting your kms. At about 1,2 km you cross a steel bridge over the Buffalo River, and shortly afterwards you come to a junction with the road from Vryheid entering on your left (your return route). Bear right at this junction, and at 19 km the stone ox-wagon monument marking the battlefield is visible on your right.

Drive past the office and after about 200 m stop at the 1938 centenary monument and the Blood River monument, before driving on to the impressive reconstruction of Andries Pretorius's laager. After visiting the laager,

Reconstructed wagons at Blood River.

The calm waters of Blood River today.

SURPRISE AT ISANDHLWANA
On 20 January 1879 a column under Lord Chelmsford, British commander-in-chief, crossed the Buffalo River at Rorke's Drift and set up camp below the hill known as Isandlwana. One of three columns marching on the Zulu King Cetshwayo, they were unaware that a powerful Zulu force of about 20 000 men was hidden in the Nqutu hills just 8 km to the north.

On 22 January, the Zulu army attacked in classic ox-head formation. The British were totally unprepared and the camp was annihilated in half an hour. Afterwards, among the dead – 858 soldiers, 470 black allies of the British and about 1 000 Zulus – most of the British ammunition was found still packed in boxes.

walk 200 m east to Blood River, then 200 m south to see the old hippo pool and the historic donga behind the laager (see opposite).

Retrace your route towards the R33, but note your kms as you leave the Blood River monument. After 17,5 km take the road leading right at the fork – for Vryheid. At 20,5 km you pass over a stone bridge and, 500 m later, turn right onto the tarred R33, which will take you back to Vryheid.

Vryheid Information Bureau PO Box 57
Vryheid 3100 Tel (0381) 81 2133
Talana Museum Private Bag 2024
Dundee 3000 Tel (0341) 22654

LAST OF THE NAPOLEONS

After the Franco-Prussian War of 1870 forced Napoleon III and his family to flee from France, the young Prince Imperial, Eugène Louis Joseph Napoleon Bonaparte, received a military education in England. In search of a successful military career to prove his worth to the French people, he begged to be allowed to go to the war in Zululand. As an observer, he was posted to Colonel Harrison's corps of scouts in Dundee.

On 1 June 1879 the prince was part of a six-man advance party searching for a campsite for the main group near the banks of the Vumankala River. They had offsaddled for coffee at an apparently deserted Zulu homestead when they were attacked by about 50 warriors. The prince's horse bolted before he could mount, and he could only hang on to a saddlebag strap, which broke. He and two soldiers were stabbed to death with assegais.

British redcoats kept up a withering fire against attacking Zulus at Rorke's Drift.

THE DEFENDERS OF RORKE'S DRIFT

Shortly after news of the battle at Isandhlwana reached the military hospital at Rorke's Drift some 16 km to the west, scouts reported that a Zulu impi of about 4 000 men was heading for the drift.

Fewer than 100 men fought off the Zulu warriors from behind makeshift fortifications, retreating room by room as burning assegais were flung onto the hospital roof. The battle continued throughout the night, the defenders being scorched by their red-hot rifle barrels. At dawn, the Zulus finally fell back, and British reinforcements arrived. The British lost 17 men, with 8 wounded, and the Zulus had about 500 dead.

BLOOD RIVER – THE DAY OF THE VOW

After the murders of Boer leader Piet Retief and his followers, a newly elected commander, Andries Pretorius, set out with a 465-strong commando on a punitive expedition against Dingane, the Zulu king. Hearing reports that a large Zulu force was nearby, Pretorius established a tightly defended laager of ox-wagons, with the Ncome Spruit ahead and a deep donga on the right serving as natural barriers. A vow had been made and repeated every night that if they were granted victory, the Boers would hold the day sacred in perpetuity.

When about 12 000 warriors, led by Ndlela Ntuli, attacked on the morning of 16 December 1838, the concentrated Boer firepower was directed onto a narrow front, and 3 000 Zulu warriors died. Only three Boers, including Pretorius, were wounded. In the spirit of a broader-based patriotism, 16 December is still observed as a special day, the Day of Reconciliation.

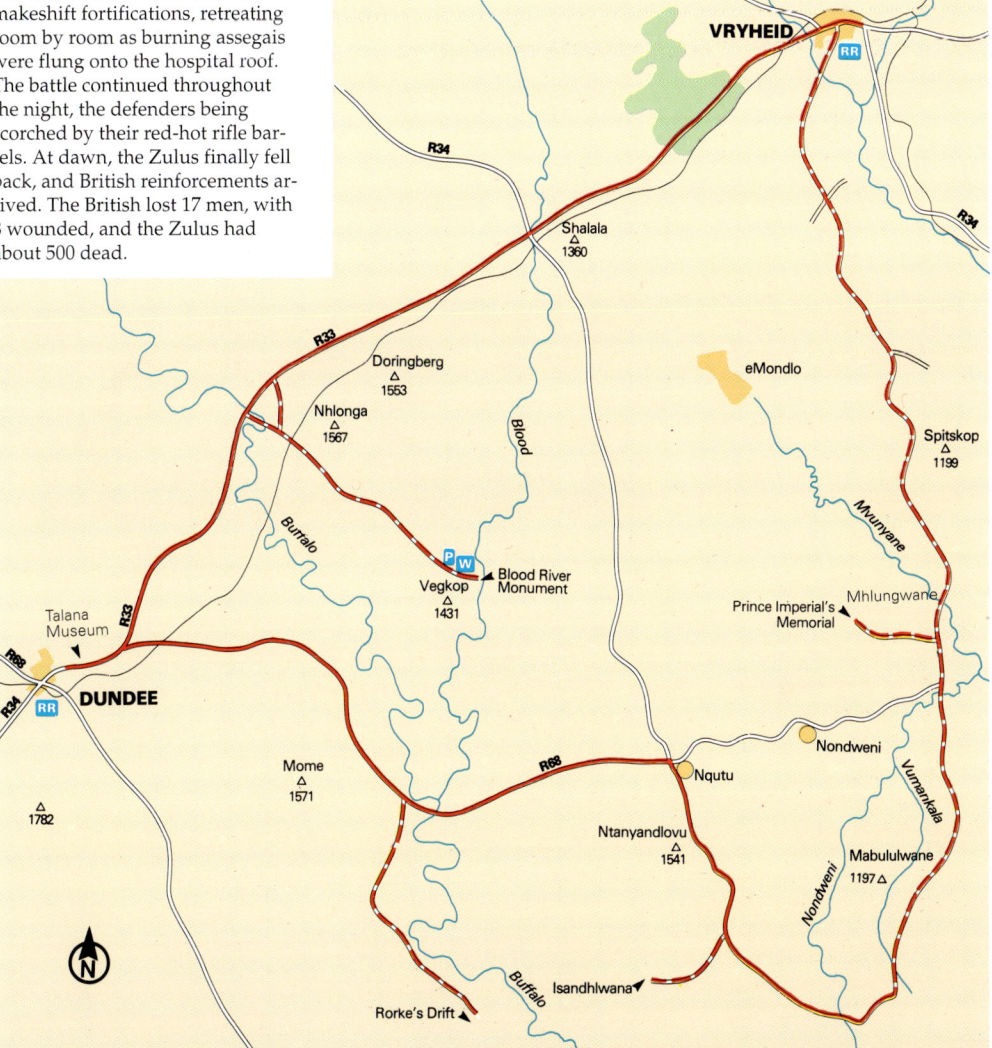

Uniforms of the Anglo-Zulu War: Warrior of the third Undi Regiment; and trooper of the 1st Dragoon Guards.

Exploring the magical mountains and plains of far Maputaland

From Mkuze village we traverse the scenic Ubombo Mountains and skirt the Pongola flood plain, then head east to the ancient dunes and wide waters of Kosi Bay. Ndumo Game Reserve and Tembe Elephant Park are stops along the way. Some 60 km of the route is on sandy or gravel roads that can usually be negotiated in a two-wheel-drive vehicle.

**Mkuze
Pongolapoort Dam
Ndumo
Tembe Elephant Park
Kosi Bay
330 – 350 km**

THE MAPUTALAND TOURISM Information Centre, a small red-brick building in Mkuze village, is the starting point for this drive. Note your kms before setting off and, after crossing the railway bridge, turn right onto the N2, following the sign for Pongola through undulating bushveld terrain. Distinctive among the lush vegetation are hazy clusters of fever trees, *Acacia xanthophloea*, seen along river courses and at the edges of pans. These tall, pale green beauties leave an indelible impression, their ghostly, phosphorescent yellow trunks taking on a luminous appearance in the early morning and late afternoon glow.

Josini to Ndumo

After travelling parallel to the increasingly rugged Ubombo Mountains for 12 km, turn right onto the tarred road to Jozini, noting your kms. The road heads towards the foot of the Ubombo range before curving left in a broad sweep to begin its steep ascent. As you climb, the Pongolapoort (or Jozini) Dam comes into view below you, and the vista becomes increasingly spectacular as the great sheet of water reflects shimmering hills and the skyline of the far western horizon. There are a number of roadside viewsites along the ascent and the picnic site just before the crest of the climb is an ideal spot from which to photograph the magnificent view.

As the road passes along the upper reaches of the range, you will catch frequent glimpses through deep gorges of the dam far below. Gradually the road descends to Jozini, which you reach 19 km after leaving the N2. The road passes through the town, originally built to house workers constructing the Pongolapoort Dam (see opposite). The town's name recalls the legendary Portuguese trader Jose de Silvestre – dubbed 'Jozini' by a local chief – who plied between Delagoa Bay and the once-inaccessible Pongola gorge that is now bridged by the dam wall.

Past Jozini, the road drops steeply for 2 km to cross the Pongola along the top of the dam wall. Ignore the right turn to Sodwana just before the crossing and follow the sign straight ahead to Ndumo Game Reserve. There is a lookout site over the dam on the opposite bank. Note your kms here. The terrain flattens out as you travel north along the Pongola (Phongolo) River flood plain. Take heed of cattle hazard signs – the road passes through rural settlements with children tending animals and playing along the verges. Potholes are another frequent hindrance, especially in the rainy season. After 37,5 km, turn right at the T-junction and note your kms. The tarred road continues north-east for 11 km, at which point you turn left onto a gravel road for Ndumo Game Reserve and note your kms. After a further 5 km, turn left at the T-junction (still following the sign for Ndumo), to drive through subtropical thickets and wooded riverine terrain, past a series of rural settlements. You enter the game reserve 10,7 km after the second T-junction; the security checkpoint is reached after a further 1,1 km. An overnight stop at Ndumo is recommended (see below).

Ndumo to Kosi Bay

After visiting Ndumo, return to the tarred road and turn left, noting your kms. The road skirts the southern boundary of Tembe Elephant Park (see below), to pass its entrance after 18 km. Dense thickets alternate with scrub dotted with wild dates and lala palms. Cattle stray onto the road, so be alert. After 55 km you reach KwaNgwanase and the end of the tarred road. Note your kms at the start of the sandy road ahead. After 5,7 km, turn right to Kosi Bay and cross ancient dune terrain for the final 5,3 km before entering Kosi Bay Nature Reserve. The campsite is on the shore of Lake Nhlange, the largest of the Kosi lakes. To return to Mkuze, retrace your outward route.

Maputaland Tourism Information Centre Main Street, Mkuze Village 3965 Tel (035) 573 1120

NDUMO GAME RESERVE
This 10 000 ha reserve lies just south of the Mozambique border on the Pongola (Phongolo) River flood plain. Heavily wooded, its magnificent pans, lined with reeds and fever trees, attract a wide range of wildlife. The Usutu River marks its northern border and the Pongola runs along its eastern boundary.

The prolific bird life includes many tropical East African species at the southern limit of their range, and a wealth of aquatic birds. Commonly seen are fish eagles, black egret, pygmy geese, white-faced duck, crested guinea fowl, jacanas and the rare fishing owl (*Scotopelia peli*).

Large populations of hippo, crocodile, nyala, bushbuck, impala, grey and red duiker and kudu ensure good game-viewing. Black rhino and white rhino are seen, as well as giraffe and suni.

Visitors may drive through certain areas or take one of several guided Land Rover tours. The rest camp has seven fully equipped, three-bedded 'squaredavels', with a communal ablution block and a (staffed) kitchen.

Fever trees (Acacia xanthophloea) *were once thought to cause malaria.*

An adult male elephant may spend 18 hours daily consuming 170 kg of food.

TEMBE ELEPHANT PARK
Some 100 elusive elephants are the star attractions of this 30 000 ha reserve on the border between South Africa and Mozambique. Having made their way through war-torn territory into the reserve, these giants of the African bush tend to be nervous, but a hide overlooking the pan in the Muzi Swamp offers a fair chance of evening sightings. Situated in a transition zone between tropical and subtropical forms, Tembe has a great diversity of vegetation, predominantly woodland and closed thicket. Game and bird species, comparable to those at Ndumo, offer excellent wildlife experiences for visitors. Access beyond the parking area is limited to four-wheel-drive vehicles and is restricted to one party of day visitors at a time (accompanied by a trail guide). Two established walking trails are available and accommodation is in a tented camp that sleeps eight people at a time. Picnic facilities are available.

KOSI BAY NATURE RESERVE

Bordering on Mozambique in the north and the Indian Ocean in the east, Kosi Bay Nature Reserve is an anglers' and nature-lovers' paradise. The reserve surrounds the Kosi Lake system and its camp is situated on the northern bank of Lake Nhlange, the largest of the Kosi lakes. Three thatched lodges (fully equipped and staffed) house two, five and six visitors respectively and 15 open campsites accommodate seven people each. Angling facilities include a slipway for outboard motorboats and a pier for shore fishing. While the camp area is accessible to all vehicles, sandy terrain makes a four-wheel-drive vehicle essential to reach The Mouth, 5 km from the campsite. The four-day Kosi Bay Hiking Trail offers unforgettable wilderness experiences on the wide, unspoilt beaches at Banga Nek and includes crossing the Sihadla River on a raffia-palm pont and exploring palm and swamp forests.

A grove of native Kosi palms (Raphia Australis).

Kosi Bay – pristine sands and sea.

Once ensnared at low tide within a fence of sticks, fish can be gathered at leisure by net or by spear.

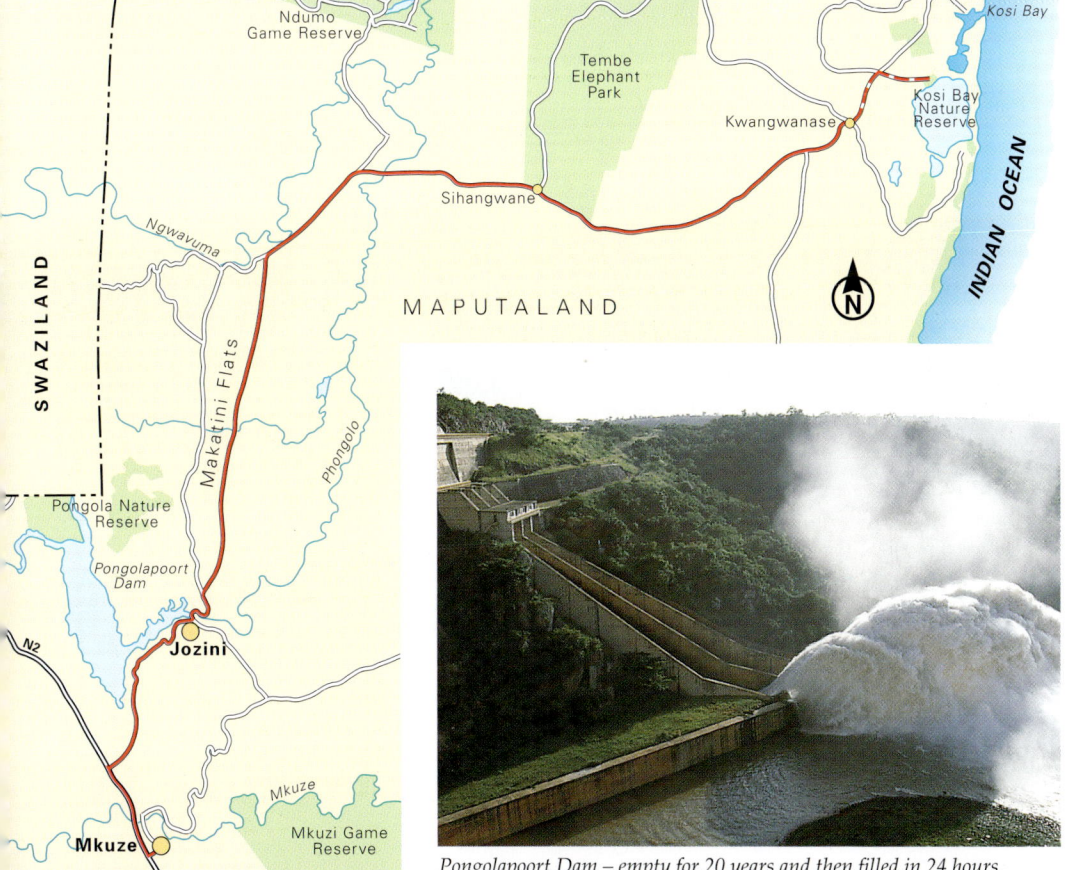

PONGOLAPOORT DAM AND BIOSPHERE RESERVE

Built in the 1960s, the Pongolapoort Dam stood empty for nearly 20 years because of drought. Then, in 1984, the rainfall associated with Cyclone Demoina virtually filled the dam in just 24 hours. Today the dam is surrounded by the Pongolapoort Biosphere Reserve and game-viewing by boat offers sightings of leopard, bushbuck, kudu, giraffe, zebra, wildebeest, rhino, crocodile, hippo and many other species. Bird life is abundant and tiger-fishing is a popular sport. The reserve adjoins Pongolapoort Nature Reserve, a 10 000 ha wilderness area that extends from the Ubombo escarpment down to the water's edge.

First proclaimed in 1894 by President Kruger, it is now proposed as a joint venture with the neighbouring Nyawo clan. Dingane's grave, Hlatikulu Forest Reserve and the archaeologically important Border Caves are situated close by.

Mountain Lake Adventures bush camp, chalets and lodges offer a variety of weekend options. Facilities include sailing, a chartered houseboat, floodlit sundowner cruises, birdwatching and trails.

For more information, tel (035) 572 1054 or write to PO Box 86, Eshowe 3815.

Pongolapoort Dam – empty for 20 years and then filled in 24 hours.

On a trail at Mkuzi, visitors pause to observe pelicans and reflections.

A Maputaland paradise of ever-changing habitats

ONCE VISITED, Mkuzi Game Reserve on Maputaland's coastal plain becomes one of those special destinations that stirs the imagination and takes hold of the affection forever. A proclaimed protected area since 1912, the 40 000 ha reserve now constitutes the north-western spur of the Greater St Lucia Wetland Park to which it has been linked through the acquisition of the Nxwala state land and a number of privately owned properties.

The reserve lies 335 km north of Durban, and access from the N2 is along 16 km of gravel road that passes through a gap in the Ubombo Mountains. A place of beauty and high contrasts, Mkuzi is world renowned as a Mecca for bird-lovers – more than 600 bird species have been recorded here.

Predominantly flat and dry, with sandy red ridges that are ancient dunes, Mkuzi harbours an astonishingly wide diversity of natural habitats. These range from the eastern slopes of the Ubombos, which lie along its western boundary, to broad stretches of gently rolling acacia savannah.

The low-lying hollows adjacent to the red sand dunes harbour attractive groves of *Acacia nilotica*, which grows in clay soils. Of note to ecologists is a substantial – and now rare – sand forest found in the heart of the reserve, a habitat noted for its dark-leafed, wide-spreading sherbet tree, *Dialium*, and *Hymenocardia*, which create a lovely sight in autumn with their pink-winged seeds.

Two beautiful pans, Nhlonhlela and Nsumo (the larger), lie in the north and the east respectively. These shallow expanses of water, lined with water lilies in summer and fringed by a haze of pale green fever trees, are home to communities of hippo and crocodile and attract a magnificent spectacle of aquatic bird life. Nsumo's two elevated bird-viewing platforms provide superb vantage points to see and photograph pinkbacked and white pelicans, as well as a great diversity of duck and large numbers of spurwinged geese that gather here in spring.

Nsumo Pan is fed by the Msunduzi River. This cuts across the southern section of the reserve to join the Mkuze River before it enters the delta area of the Mkuze swamps, which in turn merge into the distant, north-eastern tip of Lake St Lucia.

The Mkuze River curves along the reserve's northern and eastern borders, giving rise to a fine stretch of fig forest growing along its banks near the Nsumo Pan. Fish eagles swoop over the water, snatching prey they have spotted from their hunting perches at the forest edge.

A snug bungalow at Mkuzi in a peaceful woodland setting.

Under the canopy

A self-guided trail through the cool glades takes you into a world far removed from the harsh glare of the surrounding bushveld.

Beneath a dense green canopy, supported by the giant, entwined trunks of ancient sycamore figs, the air is alive with colourful and raucous bird life. Trumpeter hornbills wail like neglected babies; glamorous Narina trogons and purplecrested louries tantalize the eye with brilliant flashes of green and red. Roosting whitebacked vultures take off in startled flight. Other exciting species that add to the forest's allure include African broadbill, little sparrowhawk, Gabar goshawk, forest weaver, the elusive Pel's fishing owl, brownheaded parrots and plump green pigeons.

As always, stealth and an alert responsiveness enhance the experience of being in the wild. Walking along this magical trail, one has the feeling that something momentous has just happened. This may be so, as fresh signs of black rhino and hippo are frequently to be seen (and occasionally those of elephant), together with the spoor of red duiker, bushbuck and leopard.

Besides hippo and crocodile, the wealth of wildlife occurring here includes both black and white rhino, elephant (in 1994 a nucleus herd was reintroduced after years of local extinction), giraffe, leopard, cheetah and a multitude of plains game. Among these are herds of nyala, impala, blue wildebeest and zebra, as well as kudu, eland and the rare suni that can be seen on the red dune terrain. A host of other smaller species includes charmers such as the slinky mongoose and ever-entertaining families of wart hog.

At home in Mkuzi

A wide range of accommodation facilities is available. Not least among these is the new self-catering safari tented camp. This has six two-bed and two four-bed tented units. Each has private ablution facilities (including hot and cold showers) and its own open-plan kitchen. With refrigeration and electricity available, the camp offers a wilderness setting with amenities such as a swimming pool (an essential comfort during the hottest months of summer) and a curio shop.

The shop, in a restful picnic garden adjacent to the main rest camp, houses the camp office and stocks basic food supplies and liquid refreshments. The rest camp has two seven-bed self-catering cottages, four three-bed bungalows, five five-bed bungalows and six three-bed rest huts, all of which are served by a central, staffed kitchen.

The reserve has 100 km of tourist roads for game drives, as well as several picnic sites and six superbly placed hides. Game walks, bird walks and game drives can be booked at the camp office. These include night drives that afford glimpses of the nocturnal species seldom, if ever, seen during the day, such as the thick-tailed bushbaby, leopard, white-tailed mongoose, small-spotted genet, hyaena and porcupine. Nocturnal birds to be seen include nightjars, owls and dikkops.

Mkuzi's caravan park is adjacent to the Emshopi entrance gate and takes up to 60 caravanners or campers. An ablution block with hot and cold running water serves the campsites.

The bird hide at Nsumo Pan gives intimate access to wetland wildlife.

A nyala cow blends into the shade.

Not a yawn, but a noisy challenge.

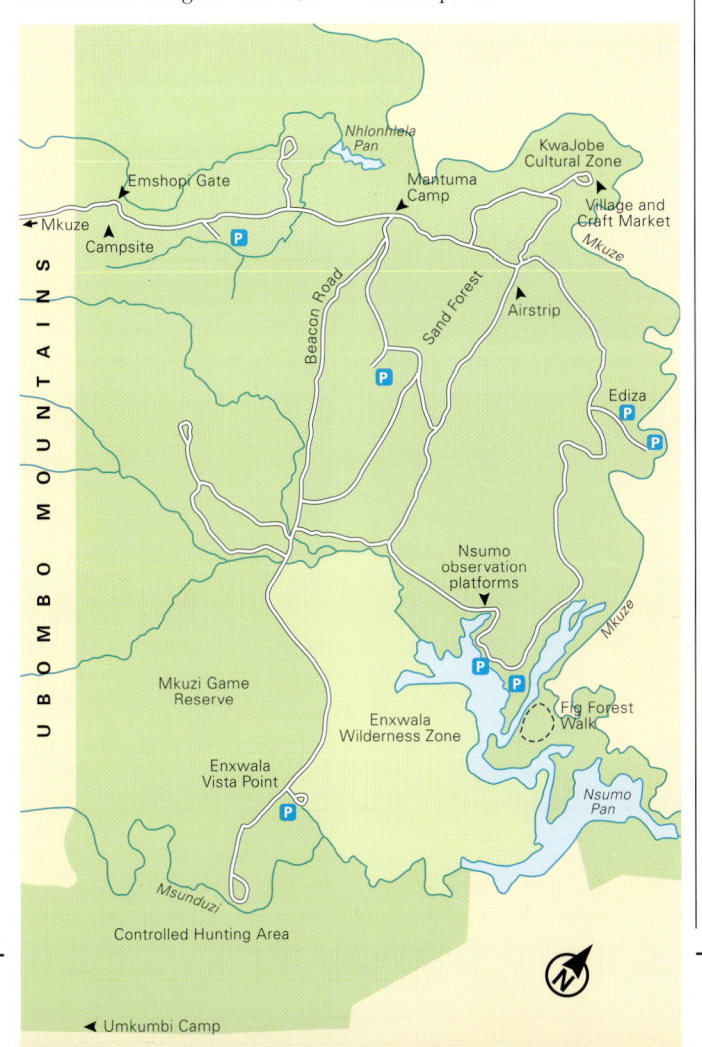

Umkumbi Bush Camp is situated in the controlled hunting area south of the Msunduzi, and is used as a general bush camp from October to March when not in use for hunting parties. Here, accommodation comprises four large, open (furnished and fully equipped) safari tents, each containing two beds. En suite showers, toilets and basins ensure visitors privacy. A thatched wood-and-reed lounge, dining area and bar opposite a natural pan make the most of the typically African bush setting.

Nhlonhlela Bush Lodge is an eight-bed camp overlooking the Nhlonhlela Pan. The distinctive en suite units are of a wood-and-reed design, connected by boardwalks that lead to a central communal lounge and kitchen. A game guard is on hand to take guests on walks and the services of a cook are provided. This camp is available for booking only by a single party of guests at a time. For those who seek a more rugged bushveld experience, Mkuzi's popular trails offer close-up encounters with the reserve's many special attractions. Three nights are spent at the tented trails camp, where amenities include a well-equipped kitchen, a communal shower with hot and cold water on tap and a flush toilet. Full catering and equipment are provided and game walks are conducted from the camp. The hotter part of the day can be spent relaxing and watching wildlife from one of the reserve's hides. Entertainment is often found by watching the pond life, not least the behaviour of terrapins as they slither in and out of the water and clamber atop each other in their attempts to bask in the sun. Also fascinating are the tree frogs whose foam nests hang over the water's edge, ready to dispense their offspring when the time is right. Situated within the boundaries of Mkuzi Game Reserve is a sacred burial site of chiefs of the neighbouring KwaJobe clan who have lived in the region for hundreds of years. The site is not accessible to visitors other than members of the clan, who visit it to commune with the spirits of their ancestors.

Close by, a cultural village in the reserve has been established where members of the community make and sell traditional crafts. This is open to tourists and provides an interesting insight into the traditional lifestyle of a northern Zulu clan. The reserve's management policy includes an active neighbour-relations programme that promotes self-development among the local rural communities. An important part of this programme is devoted to environmental awareness, and a growing number of communities have begun to develop their own conservation areas adjacent to the park. This ever-growing area of privately owned land promotes the conservation of wildlife in the area and enhances ecotourism.

Mkuzi is in the endemic malaria belt and precautions are advised. To book, contact Natal Parks Board Reservations, PO Box 1750, Pietermaritzburg 3200. Tel (0331) 47 1981; fax (0331) 47 1980. For information phone (0331) 47 1891.

EXPLORING HLUHLUWE-UMFOLOZI PARK

The sky turns to pink as dawn edges over the rolling hills of Hluhluwe.

Big game roams fearless where Zulu kings hunted

ON A CLEAR DAY you can see the coastal dunes of St Lucia from Hilltop Camp in the Hluhluwe-Umfolozi Park (HUP). First established in 1933, this award-winning camp was extensively redeveloped in 1992 to meet the demands of burgeoning international tourism. It now accommodates up to 210 guests in a variety of catering and non-catering accommodation ranging from a luxury three-bedroomed lodge to a variety of chalets and bungalows, in a high-lying forest belt dominated by wild palm and white stinkwood trees. Hilltop – HUP's principal camp – commands magnificent views of the surrounding hills and valleys of the old Zulu kingdom. These characterize the topography of the park's 23 000 ha northern sector, formerly the famed Hluhluwe Game Reserve.

Once the hunting preserve of Zulu kings, Hluhluwe is a superb wildlife haven where visitors may view the prolific animal, bird and plant species found in the foothills that rise from the coastal plain in the east. Centred on the Hluhluwe River valley, the partnership of hill and plain in the area offers an unusual combination of forest, woodland, savannah and grassland rarely seen in Africa.

Mbhombe forest
While the wide variety of animal life in the reserve is an obvious drawcard, the Mbhombe semideciduous forest is also a distinctive feature of the area. Hluhluwe is one of the few places in KwaZulu-Natal where a large forest of this type survives.

One of Africa's oldest reserves, Hluhluwe was established in 1895 along with its sister reserves in the same area: Umfolozi (see pages 114–5) and St Lucia (see pages 116–7). The reserve, the nearby village and the river are all named after the monkey rope, *umHluhluwe*, used by the Zulus to muzzle their calves during weaning.

While St Lucia is a separate geographic entity, Hluhluwe and Umfolozi are administered as one park. They are joined by a link road that passes through the central section of the park, formerly known as The Corridor.

It took 12 years to erect the 2,8 m high game-proof fence around the park, which comprises 96 400 ha in total – a task completed in 1979. (The fence includes old mine cable – the only fencing strong enough to contain rhino.) The fenced area, although less than six per cent of the size of the Kruger National Park, boasts 68 per cent of the total number of plant species found in Kruger.

At Hluhluwe the visitor is likely to see both black and white rhino (there is in fact no difference in colour), giraffe, buffalo, zebra, monkey, leopard, cheetah, wildebeest, nyala, the almost comically ugly wart hog, baboon, kudu, impala, bushbuck, crocodile and lion – as recently as 1985 a game guard was eaten by a lion in the reserve.

Elephants were reintroduced from the Kruger National Park to Hluhluwe in 1981 – they had been shot out of the area in the 19th century – and lucky visitors may spot hippo that occasionally wander into the Maphumulo picnic site from the Hluhluwe Dam.

Hluhluwe, 280 km north of Durban, is traversed by more than 80 km of good, all-weather gravel roads, allowing easy access to most of the reserve. The entrance to the Hluhluwe section of the HUP is at Memorial Gate, 17 km from Hluhluwe village. The camp at Hilltop is 12 km from Memorial Gate. All roads in the park are signposted, and every intersection is numbered on a triangular stone marker corresponding with the map handed out at the gate.

Superb views on arrival
Entering from Memorial Gate, you encounter breathtaking views by driving to Hilltop over Magangeni Hill. At the summit you may get out of your car, and there are places to sit and admire the surrounding bushveld that stretches for many kilometres in

A lesser masked weaver and his nest.

A square-lipped (white) rhino and her calf venture into the open to graze.

Zebra and nyala around a waterhole.

every direction. During the afternoon and early morning you may see game on nearby slopes. (At all viewsites and picnic areas in the reserve you leave your vehicle at your own risk.)

Even if you intend spending only a day in the reserve, a short visit to the information centre at Hilltop is worthwhile. The centre has a curio shop at which 'auto trail' pamphlets are available. These describe two easy-to-follow self-guided tours of the park, each taking about three hours. The pamphlets are fascinating tutors, introducing everything from the rhino's social habits to rubbing posts and middens.

Indigenous trees
The centre also provides a booklet on the Mbhombe forest trail, which begins immediately behind the camp. A 30-minute stroll through this indigenous forest will introduce you to trees such as the strangler fig (*Ficus natalensis*), the ruikpeul (*Acacia nilotica*), the Natal milk plum (*Bequaertiodendron natalense*), and the Camdeboo stinkwood (*Celtis africana*), a tree believed by the Zulus to protect one against witchcraft. You will also see specimens of the umHluhluwe climber (*Dalbergia armata*).

Game-viewing
Besides the 'big five' (elephant, rhino, lion, leopard and buffalo), a wealth of game and bird species occurs here, as well as a magnificent kaleidoscope of flora. As it does in all parks and reserves, game-viewing here varies seasonally. In Hluhluwe water shortages are fairly uncommon, so game-viewing opportunities are widespread. Likely places include the area around the Hidli Vlei to the west of Memorial Gate as well as around Munyawaneni and Muntulu, and between Seme and Gunjaneni in the southern section of Hluhluwe.

Elephants are often seen around Magangeni and Maphumulo, while Hlaza near Hilltop generally boasts superb raptor sightings. Crocodile can sometimes be seen at Hippo Pool and near the several river crossings in the park. Both black and white rhino offer exciting viewing, the former in the more wooded areas, the latter in the savannah and grassland. Because it is a grazer, the white rhino prefers short grass and is more likely to be seen.

The black rhino is a browser, living on shrubs and bush, but does come into the open spaces in search of young seedlings. Wildebeest and zebra are quite commonly seen together, both for mutual protection and because they share a liking for open areas and short grass.

Picnic sites
Hluhluwe has five delightful picnic sites. These are signposted at Hilltop Camp, Thiyeni (in the south of Hluhluwe), Hippo Pool on the Nzimane River, and on the Hluhluwe River at Siwasamakhosikazi and Maphumulo.

The picnic site at Maphumulo overlooks a backwater created by the construction of the Hluhluwe Dam, and has trestle tables in a shady, grassed area from which you may see cold-eyed crocodiles basking in the full sunshine on nearby banks.

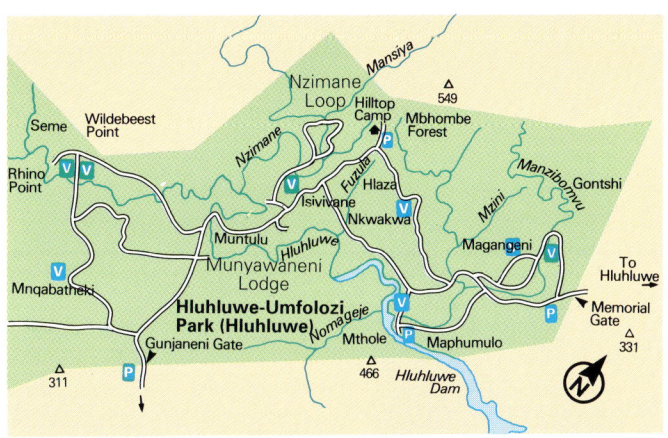

Hluhluwe's bushveld stretches across a succession of hills into the distance.

Bush lodges
Muntulu and Munyawaneni bush lodges overlook secluded spots on the banks of the Hluhluwe River. These offer ideal conditions for game-viewing and birding. Both lodges are constructed of reed, wood and thatch and give visitors a taste of the authentic bushveld atmosphere of Hluhluwe rather than the predominantly forest characteristics of Hilltop. Munyawaneni accommodates eight guests, and Muntulu ten, in en suite units linked by boardwalks to open-plan living areas with viewing decks. A lodge may be booked only by a single party at a time. The services of cooks are included in the tariffs and game guards are available for game walks.

Accommodation may be reserved through the Reservations Office, PO Box 662, Pietermaritzburg 3200, or by telephoning (0331) 47 1981; fax (0331) 47 1980.

You should take precautions against malaria, and take insect repellent with you. Petrol, film, postcards and mementos are sold in the park, as well as basic provisions. It is advisable to check the opening and closing times of the gates before you set off.

The winsome wart hog in profile.

This lion cub's spotted legs show its youth – the spots fade with age.

EXPLORING HLUHLUWE-UMFOLOZI PARK

Nyala are often to be found among trees, where they hide from predators. The reddish ewes are markedly different from the rams – in size and in colour.

Where the battle to save the white rhino was won

ALTHOUGH UMFOLOZI is now well known for the wide variety of game-viewing it offers, there was a time when rangers used to doff their hats to any animal they saw in the area.

The rangers' salute recalled a sad episode in the reserve's history – the slaughter of more than 70 000 head of game during the 1940s in a futile attempt to control the blood-sucking tsetse fly. The fly, responsible for the spread of sleeping sickness, was eventually eradicated by aerial spraying.

Umfolozi (sometimes spelt Mfolozi) has recovered well, and today teems with wildlife. No fewer than 48 species of larger mammal, 37 species of reptile, nine species of amphibian, more than 400 species of bird, and even 130 different butterflies await the keen-eyed visitor.

Set in the heart of KwaZulu-Natal's bush country, the 47 700 ha Umfolozi Game Reserve was established in 1895, and now comprises the southern section of the Hluhluwe-Umfolozi Park (HUP). About 24 000 ha of Umfolozi is a wilderness area accessible only on foot, as there are no artificial structures – not even roads.

Umfolozi is named after the White and Black Mfolozi rivers (*Mfolozi* being Zulu for 'zigzag') that meander through the area before reaching a confluence on the eastern border. It was in the narrow strip of land contained by the meeting of the two rivers that Shaka, king of the Zulus (1816 – 28), organized vast game drives.

Today, Umfolozi is best known for the successful fight to save the white, or square-lipped rhino from extinction. In 1929 only 150 white rhino could be found, and extinction seemed certain. But a determined campaign by the Natal Parks Board has seen Hluhluwe-Umfolozi's square-lipped rhino population rise to about 1 800. In fact, the fight has been so successful that more than 4 000 of the animals have been exported around the world.

The white rhino (whose colour is really no different from that of the black rhino) shares the park with buffalo, blue wildebeest, zebra, giraffe, waterbuck, impala, common and mountain reedbuck, nyala, kudu, bushbuck, steenbok, duiker, warthog, hyaena, leopard,

Assured of survival by rangers' efforts, a white rhino grazes on short grass.

cheetah and jackal. In 1985, elephants were reintroduced to the Umfolozi Game Reserve from the Kruger National Park.

The lion came to stay
Now widely distributed through the Hluhluwe-Umfolozi Park, the lion did not wait for Parks Board officials to reintroduce them to the area. Shot out of Zululand before World War II, 'the king' was considered another casualty of progress. Then a solitary male walked into Umfolozi in 1958 after an epic journey from Mozambique. Greeted by herds of well-fed antelope and zebra, he stayed, and was joined after years of celibacy by a female. Today the two reserves boast about 100 lion.

Wart hog – ugly by most standards – are among the commoner animals in the area, and it is not unusual to find them wandering through the two hutted camps at Mpila and Masinda.

Perhaps the most easily observed birds in the reserve are the fish eagle, the pied and malachite kingfishers, the greenbacked heron and the hamerkop, all of which are associated with water. Among the larger birds of prey that you may see in Umfolozi are the tawny eagle, the jackal buzzard, the blackshouldered kite and the secretary bird.

The lazy course of the Black Mfolozi.

The best tip for aspirant game-watchers is to call in at the office at Mpila camp to consult their latest map, which, as at Hluhluwe, is updated with the latest game sightings. The office will also provide on request an 'auto trail' pamphlet describing a five-hour self-guided tour through the reserve. For a nominal fee one can book a three-hour walk in the company of an armed guard (bookings must be made a day in advance). While at Mpila, it is worth making a short study of the various shapes and spirals of the horn collection mounted at the entrance to the picnic site, as these will help you later to identify game.

Umfolozi, which is traversed by 80 km of good gravel roads, has two entrances: Cengeni Gate in the west, which is reached by travelling south from Vryheid and through Ulundi; and Mambeni Gate in the east, 32 km from Mtubatuba – the reserve's nearest commercial centre.

Visitors may get out of their cars only in the rest camps, or at one of the following places: a viewsite just west of the Sontuli Loop; the rustic hide at the Mphafa water hole; the Bekapanzi hide; and a second viewsite west of Mpila.

The Mphafa water hole, which lies 10 km from the Cengeni Gate on the main road through the reserve, is well signposted. There is a hide 100 m from the car park, built simply of reeds and poles with a few benches. It overlooks a pool set below a small waterfall in the Mphafa stream. Apart from the animals that you may see drinking here, many Cape terrapins sun themselves on the rocks.

The viewsite at Bekapanzi epitomizes Umfolozi for many visitors. Here it is possible to watch animals and birds coming down to the pan to drink. This is a good spot for game-viewing during the hotter months (although for part of the year in winter the pan is dry). Animals may visit the pan at any time, but the most common species, and particularly the wallowing animals such as wart hog, buffalo and rhino, are most likely to be seen between 09h00 and 15h00. (The hide is reached by turning north from the main through-road at intersection 5, towards Sontuli Loop.)

Crocodile haunt

From the Sontuli Loop viewsite, near the intersection marked 8, you overlook the Black Mfolozi River, which came down in flood during Cyclone Demoina in 1984 and washed away magnificent groves of figs that used to grow along the riverbanks. This viewsite is good for seeing white rhino, buffalo and zebra.

The viewsite 2,6 km west of Mpila, marked by a rhino footprint painted in white on a rock, is on the northern boundary of the wilderness area, and gives a superb view of the White Mfolozi River.

About 10 km from the Cengeni Gate, driving north on the Sokhwezele road, you will notice a range of rolling hills on your left known as the Zintunzini Hills (frequented by a number of game species, particularly the common and mountain reedbuck). This entire area, now open acacia savannah, was cleared of bush in the 1930s in an attempt to form a buffer zone against tsetse fly. Stumps from the 3 km wide strip can still be seen, and some of them are used today as rubbing posts by the rhino to rid themselves of troublesome ticks.

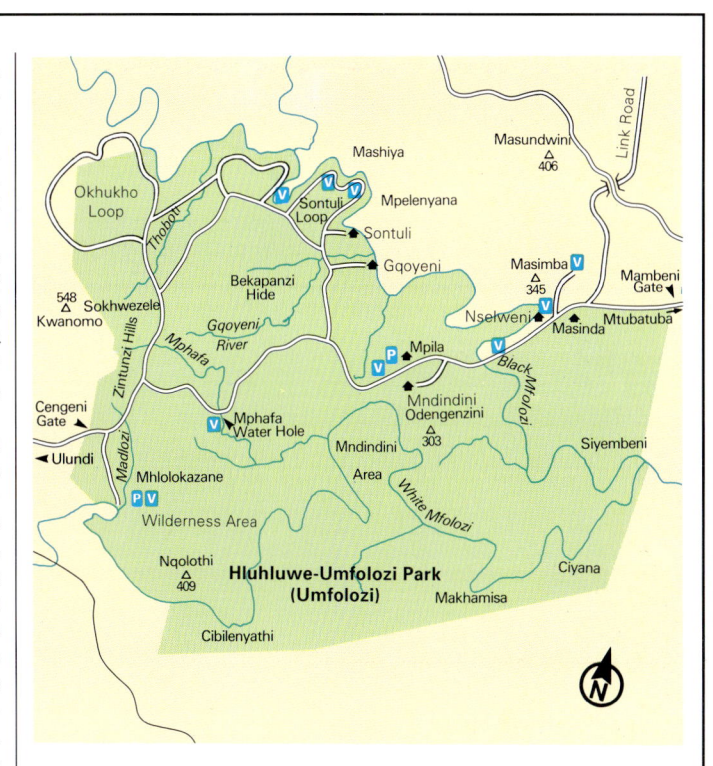

Umfolozi has shady picnic sites at its two rest camps, Mpila and Masinda, one at the Mphafa hide and one on the Sontuli Loop. Hutted accommodation is available at Masinda and Mpila (both named after the hills nearest to the camps). While Mpila has spectacular views of the Black Mfolozi River snaking through the wilderness area, Masinda – 7 km from the Mambeni Gate – is perhaps the more tranquil camp, and boasts rich bird life.

Bedding and utensils are provided, but visitors must bring all food and drink, as these are not sold in the reserve. Petrol is sold at Mpila only, as are postcards, curios and film.

Umfolozi offers bush accommodation at the Sontuli and Nselweni bush camps on the Black Mfolozi and at the slightly more luxurious Gqoyeni bush lodge on the banks of the same river. Each of these is constructed of reed, wood and thatch and accommodates up to eight guests. Each unit may be hired only by a single party at a time. Cooks and game guards are in attendance for the convenience of guests.

There is a tented camp, Mndindini, which is open to the general public in December, January and February, while for the rest of the year it serves as the wilderness trail base. The wilderness hiking trails offer three days on foot with two nights under canvas in the bush. A 'primitive trail' is available on which hikers carry all their requirements with them and sleep in the open.

Anti-malaria precautions and insect repellent are advisable. Bookings for accommodation and the overnight trails should be made through the Reservations Office, Natal Parks Board, PO Box 662, Pietermaritzburg 3200, or telephone (0331) 47 1981; fax (0331) 47 1980.

A kudu with its distinctive stripes.

The zebra – swift and sociable.

• EXPLORING LAKE ST LUCIA •

The sun sets on the subtropical paradise of St Lucia Estuary – and holiday-makers return from a leisurely outing to view the hippos and crocodiles.

A lush waterworld lures anglers and bird-watchers

THE 19TH-CENTURY hunter John Dunn once boasted of a morning's sport shooting 23 hippo in Lake St Lucia before 10 o'clock – a bag that helped his season's tally to 203. Many years later, during the Second World War, Catalina flying boats using the lake as a base for anti-submarine patrols used to 'clear their guns' by shooting up crocodiles basking on sandbanks near the mouth of the Mkuze River.

Today – gunfire a sound of the past – St Lucia is a quiet haven for the nature-lover, bird-watcher, angler and hiker.

The variety of birds at Lake St Lucia is astounding, and the complex is justifiably world famous as an area to see spectacular birdlife. To date more than 520 species of bird have been recorded – one-third of them inhabiting the mud flats, reeds and swamp around the water. Almost half of all the birds recorded in South Africa have been seen at St Lucia.

Caspian terns, spoonbills and greyheaded gulls nest on the islands, and in 1972 – when the lake's salinity was very high – a flamingo breeding colony of 6 000 was recorded.

Comprising more than half the estuarine habitat in South Africa, St Lucia is extremely important to fish life, and a great variety of freshwater, estuarine and marine species occurs here. The lake is also one of the most important prawn habitats in the country.

St Lucia's fishing is deservedly praised and, in the holiday periods, four-wheel-drive vehicles towing ski-boats outnumber more conventional vehicles. The lake is shallow, with an average depth of one metre, and it is home to an estimated 1 500 crocodile and 700 hippo. The crocodiles, whose primary diet is fish, are nevertheless good reason for the Natal Parks Board to ban all paddling and swimming in the lake.

The St Lucia complex consists of a number of separate reserves. The lake itself with its islands – some 36 000 ha in extent, about 60 km long, and shaped roughly like an H (or perhaps a battleaxe) – was proclaimed St Lucia Game Reserve in 1895.

In 1939 an 800 m wide strip of land around the lake was proclaimed St Lucia Park and encompasses the village of St Lucia at the mouth of the estuary.

NORTHERN KWAZULU-NATAL

A flock of flamingoes in flight over an isolated stretch of the lake.

The fearsome Nile crocodile.

False Bay Park, proclaimed in 1944, protects 2 247 ha of northern shoreline on False Bay, between the Hluhluwe and Mzinene rivers. Bird-watchers use the park as a base from which to see terrestrial and wetland birds.

Covering the Ozabeni, Tewati and Mfabeni sections, the coastal strip (proclaimed in 1978) boasts some of the highest forested dunes in the world, reaching a height of 150 m. A marine reserve, three nautical miles wide, stretches from 1 km south of Cape Vidal to the Mozambique border.

Game-viewing

The habitat of the lake shore varies from the wooded western shoreline to the marshy, reed-covered eastern bank. The marshes give way to the grasslands of the Mfabeni section – an ideal environment for the area's 4 500 reedbuck, and grazing ground for hippo and buffalo. The grasslands are specifically managed for these animals, and are so rich that the reedbuck breed all year.

Visitors to the complex may also see monkey, jackal, leopard, zebra, wart hog, buffalo, red duiker, grey duiker, suni, waterbuck, bushbuck, impala, nyala and kudu. The best way to view game in the area is either on foot – on one of the trails offered by the Parks Board – or by boat, as the roads are not designed for game-watching from your car.

The Natal Parks Board operates 10 overnight camps at St Lucia. There are hutted camps at Charter's Creek, Fanies Island, Mapelane and Cape Vidal; three campgrounds at St Lucia Estuary; and campgrounds at Cape Vidal, False Bay, Fanies Island and Mapelane. There is accommodation in St Lucia village, which is a base for the St Lucia area, and also Hluhluwe-Umfolozi Park.

Petrol is available at Fanies Island, Charter's Creek, Cape Vidal and the village, while food and drink are generally available only at the village, although a limited range of provisions is obtainable from the various park shops.

White pelicans are among the 520 bird species recorded around Lake St Lucia.

Places to visit at Lake St Lucia

FALSE BAY PARK
Rustic huts with minimal facilities at the Dugandlovu Camp make an ideal base from which to explore the lake shore and southern side of the park. There is also a pleasant three-hour family walk through the northern reaches of the park, called the Mpophomeni Trail, on which you may see zebra, reedbuck, nyala, duiker and suni. The park has many delightful picnic sites along the shoreline, and there are 40 camping and caravan stands facing the dawn over the lake.
Tel (035) 562 0425.

CHARTER'S CREEK
This camp, set on a rise next to the lake, has excellent views of the water. You may reserve a 90-minute boat tour from here to see wetland inhabitants. Two trails are offered: the Isikhova Walk, which starts in the campground near the jetty and takes the walker through typical western shore coastal forest for three hours, during which you may see vervet monkey, bushbuck, nyala, duiker, wart hog, banded mongoose and forest birds like the Narina trogon. The shorter Umkhumbe Walk starts just outside the camp office.
Tel (035) 550 1513.

FANIES ISLAND
'Fanies', as it is known locally, earned its popularity as a fishing spot. The camp is, in fact, not on an island, but on the western bank of the lake opposite the island. Within a small radius of the camp you can explore open parkland, coastal bush and the remnants of a dune forest by taking the 5 km Umkhiwane Trail, on which there is a possibility of coming face to face with a hippo.
Tel (035) 550 1631.

CAPE VIDAL
At the southern end of the St Lucia Marine Reserve, Cape Vidal offers snorkeling and fishing, while sunbathers can watch the yellowbilled kites, ospreys and fish eagles glide the thermals between sand and sea. The Mvubu three-hour self-guided trail takes the walker through the dune forest and down to the shores of Lake Bhangazi. The Mboma Trail meanders through the wetlands west of this lake. The 30 km gravel road from St Lucia village to Cape Vidal cuts through the Mfabeni Reserve, but is unlikely to offer much game-viewing. The road may be corrugated and potholed in places. On the way to or from Cape Vidal, it is worth turning off to Mission Rocks for a walk along the fascinating marine shelf that reveals itself at low tide. (Tide times are available from all Natal Parks Board offices.) Just north of the Mission Rocks turn-off there is a beautiful, distant view of Catalina Bay on the lake, and a parking area from which there is a short walk to the hides of Mfazana Pans.
Tel (035) 590 1404.

ST LUCIA VILLAGE
The crocodile centre, which has the local Nile crocodile as well as exotic dwarf and long-snouted West African crocodiles in its pool, is well worth a visit. The centre's gift store will also provide information on the many short walks available in the nearby game park, where impala, reedbuck, waterbuck, blue wildebeest and zebra can be seen. Boats may be hired from businesses in town. The *Santa Lucia* boat tour travels up the estuary three times daily.
Tel (035) 590 1340.

MAPELANE
Although close to St Lucia as the crow flies, Mapelane is reached from the Empangeni-Mtubatuba road, and has remained an isolated place with excellent fishing, an abundant birdlife and safe swimming at low tide. There are Swiss-style log cabins and 40 camp and caravan sites. Consult the Parks Board about the condition of the road before you set out on the trip.

All hutted accommodation should be reserved through the reservations officer, Natal Parks Board, PO Box 1750, Pietermaritzburg 3200, or tel (0331) 47 1981. Camping and caravan sites should be reserved through the various camp managers. Tel (035) 590 1407.

The lake yields rewarding catches.

An unspoilt subtropical coast and the heart of Shaka's country

In the wild bushveld beyond KwaZulu-Natal's coastal mountains lies the Mhlatuze valley – an area rich in Zulu history. We follow in the footsteps of the great King Shaka through a landscape dotted with beehive-style huts, then visit Eshowe before heading for the golden beaches. More than half of the route is on tarred roads.

**Empangeni
Enseleni
Coward's Bush
Stewart's Farm/
Kwabhekithunga
Eshowe
Mtunzini
140 – 160 km**

WE BEGIN THE DAY with a visit to Enseleni Nature Reserve. Leave Empangeni on the north-bound N2, noting your kms at the interchange with the R34 (the Melmoth/Richards Bay road). Just over 13 km later you pass an entrance to the nature reserve on your left and, 900 m after this, turn right onto gravel, following a sign to the picnic site, parking area and start/end of the Nkonikini Trail. A shorter walk is also available – allow about 40 minutes. This passes through dense swamp forest on the banks of the Nseleni River.

Enseleni to Stewart's Farm/ Kwabhekithunga

Retrace your route along the N2 to the R34, and exit for Melmoth, noting your kms. The R34 takes you through Empangeni to the hilly country beyond the town. After about 16 km on the R34 turn left onto the P230 for Ndlangubo, noting your kms again. After about 1 km the road gains height, and you can see along the broad valley of the Mhlatuze River that runs parallel to the coastal mountains. You gradually leave behind the more cultivated countryside, and enter a landscape of indigenous bush – including acacias, euphorbia trees and aloes.

After about 5,5 km you cross an attractive stretch of the Mhlatuze River; 1 km later, keep straight where the tar ends, and from here the countryside becomes even more rural. Goats and cattle graze on the hillsides and soon you begin to see beehive huts among the more common mud-and-wattle structures.

About 17 km after turning onto the P230, pull to the side of the road for the magnificent view – on your left over sprawling settlements and across the Mhlatuzana valley towards the Ngoye Mountains, and on your right over the hilly Mhlatuze valley.

Continue west and, after almost 18 km on the P230, stop on your left at the Coward's Bush cairn (see opposite). After a further 700 m, on your right is another cairn, commemorating Shaka's kwaBulawayo kraal.

Some 1,7 km beyond the second cairn turn right at the fork onto the D132 for 'Zoeloekraal', noting your kms. The road begins to drop through dense bush as it winds towards the cultivated valley floor. After about 1,3 km you can see, directly ahead of you, the distant Mandawe hill with its church tower and cross on the summit. After 4 km on the D132, turn right and go through a cattle gate. Just over 1,5 km later, turn right onto the road to Stewart's Farm/Kwabhekithunga.

This sideroad leads, after 1,8 km, to the parking area at Stewart's Farm/Kwabhekithunga, where there is a traditional Zulu village. There is a minimum charge that covers admission only. Lunch may be obtained by prior arrangement – tel (03546) 644.

Stewart's Farm/Kwabhekithunga to Mandawe

Return along the farm road and, at the T-junction, turn right onto the D132. You pass through a stretch of cane fields and citrus groves, and cross the Mhlatuze River on a single-lane bridge. Some 3,5 km after rejoining the D132 you cross the railway line and, 100 m later, turn left at the T-junction onto the tarred R34, noting your kms.

After just over 3,8 km you can see, on your right, a lovely gorge carved through the

A drive through Dlinza Forest.

TOWN OF TALL TREES

Eshowe, with its well-established gardens and tall trees, is the centre of an extensive sugar-farming district. Established as a town only in 1893, it had a long history before that – as headquarters of the Zulu king Cetshwayo; as a Norwegian mission station; as a battlefield during the Anglo-Zulu War. British soldiers stationed in the town after the war created the paths through the Dlinza Forest – now a nature reserve with a rich variety of buck and bird species.

mountain by the Qubuka River; 3,5 km later, turn right at the T-junction with the R68 for Melmoth, noting your kms.

The road begins to ascend a pass. After almost 2 km pull into a viewsite on your left for a view of a softer aspect of the Mhlatuze valley. (Local people may offer a variety of fresh local fruits for sale here.) You can also see the old pass lower down the mountainside.

Retrace your route and, as the road winds downhill, you have excellent views into deep, green valleys with huts and mealie patches clinging to the steep slopes. The views open up as you approach the wide valley floor. At the bottom of the pass, in Nkwalini village, continue on the R68 towards Eshowe, noting your kms.

You cross the Mhlatuze River again after 3,4 km and pass a turn-off right to the Goedetrou Dam. Along this sideroad are two other Zulu villages that offer authentic cultural experiences – Shakaland, tel (03546) 912 and Pobane, tel (03546) 720. Accommodation or meals may be arranged in advance. After 14,4 km on the R68 there is a turn-off left onto the P230.

To visit the Mandawe church, drive along the gravel P230 for 7,4 km, then turn left onto a rough track. This leads, after 2,2 km, to the church, perched atop the hill. This track may be impassable after rain, but when visibility is good and if you don't mind the bumpy ride, the excursion to the little church with its panoramic view is well worth while. Whether or not you visit the church, note your kms at the intersection of the P230 and the R68 before continuing towards Eshowe.

Mandawe to Mtunzini

Some 6,2 km from the intersection, turn right for Eshowe and Nkandla, noting your kms again. After 3,3 km turn left onto a gravel road that takes you through part of Dlinza Forest. At the fork, after about 500 m, go left, and some 300 m beyond that, there is space to park alongside the Bishop's Seat picnic area on your left. After a further 400 m the road emerges from the forest and the surface changes to tar – note your kms here and, 500 m later, turn right at the stop street. After a further 300 m (immediately after the police station) turn right into Windham Street for the Zululand Historical Museum. Just over 800 m later, turn left into Nongqai Road, and follow the tarred road where it curves right into the parking area at the museum at Fort Nongqai.

After your visit to the museum, turn left out of the fort grounds into Nongqai Road. After 200 m turn right into Windham Street and, 800 – 900 m later, turn left at the stop street next to the police station – noting your kms. This road curves to your right and, immediately afterwards (700 m after noting your kms), turn left into the parking area at Vukani – a Zulu handcraft centre.

Turn left out of the Vukani parking area and cross the railway bridge after 100 m. After a further 200 – 300 m turn right for Durban onto John Ross Highway; 1,2 km later, turn left into the viewsite at the gate of Ocean View Game Park. Near here the Zulu king, Cetshwayo, had his last capital, facing the sea across the gently shelving coastal plateau.

Continue down the mountainside and, after a few kilometres, turn right at the T-junction onto the R68 bypass road for Gingindlovu, noting your kms. After just over 9,6 km you pass, on your right, the site of the Battle of Inyezane (see below). About 8 km later you pass, also on your right, a memorial to the 12 red-coated British soldiers and their allies who fell during the Battle of Gingindlovu in the war against the Zulu people in 1879. It has been estimated that about 700 Zulu soldiers died in this battle.

Roughly 18 km after rejoining the R68, turn left at the T-junction onto the R102 (former N2), pass a toll booth and service station on your left and, 3,2 km later, turn right for Umlalazi Nature Reserve.

After a further 1,1 km, you reach the reserve office on your left, where there is a large outdoor map of the area. The reserve offers a choice of walks to end the day – along the beach, through the mangroves that fringe the river, or through the dune forest.

From Mtunzini, your return route to Empangeni is via the N2 toll road or the R102.

Natal Parks Board Box 662, Pietermaritzburg 3200 Tel (0331) 47 1961
Eshowe Tourism and Publicity Association PO Box 37, Eshowe 3815 Tel (0354) 41141
Durban Unlimited 160 Pine Street, Durban 4001 Tel (031) 301 0341

Spearmaking demonstrated at Stewart's Farm/Kwabhekithunga.

COWARD'S BUSH AND SHAKA'S KRAAL
Shaka, the king who consolidated the great Zulu nation, built his second capital on a hillside commanding a grand view over the Mhlatuze River valley. As with his first settlement on the White Mfolozi, he gave his new military headquarters the ominous name of *kwaBulawayo* (the place of killing). The combined town and barracks, with its 5 km circumference, is thought to have housed 12 000 soldiers.

The Kei-apple tree known as Coward's Bush was the scene of many executions at Shaka's command. The name was derived from an incident when Shaka put to death the families, cattle and men of a defeated impi found guilty of cowardice.

MEMORIES OF THE ANGLO-ZULU WAR
At the start of the Anglo-Zulu War in 1879, 4 400 British soldiers invaded Zululand from Fort Pearson on the Tugela River. They were engaged in battle near the Inyezane River by a force of 5 000 Zulus, but defeated their opponents and pressed on for Eshowe. No sooner had they formed a laager at the Kwamondi mission station at Eshowe, than they were besieged by Zulus under Dabulamanzi, who kept up the siege so vigilantly that the British dead had to be buried inside the fort. The force under Lord Chelmsford, who set out to Eshowe, won a battle along the way near *Gingindlovu* (believed to mean 'swallower of the elephant', but which the victors nicknamed 'Gin, gin, I love you'), and ended the siege after ten bitter weeks.

MTUNZINI – THE SHADY PLACE
Mtunzini – meaning 'shady place' in Zulu – lies at the mouth of the *Mlalazi* (grinding stone) River. The town's 908 ha Umlalazi Nature Reserve incorporates a long stretch of golden beach, the sparkling lagoon at the river mouth, a mangrove swamp and the Siyayi dune forest. Crocodiles and sharks may be found in the lagoon. Bird-watching is excellent, and visitors may see fish eagles, or the rare palmnut vultures that breed there.

Intricately woven weaver-bird nests.

The quaint Fort Nongqai, built in 1883, now a museum of history.

The church at Mandawe.

Historic Mvoti, battlefield country and the wilds of Msinga

Travel north from Greytown in timber-clad Mvoti County and cross the Mooi and Tugela rivers in the magnificent wilds of the Msinga region. Heading over the highland plateau through Pomeroy, you drive to Wasbank, then through historic battlefield country, via Colenso, to explore the valleys of Weenen and Muden on the way back to Greytown.

**Greytown
Keate's Drift
Elandslaagte
Weenen
Muden
310 – 330 km**

From the Greytown museum in Scott Street, turn left into Durban Road which leads onto the R33, the tarred route to Dundee, about 1 km later. After 8 km you reach the crest of a long climb and the countryside changes abruptly from timber plantations to wild, mountainous bushveld.

The tortuous descent into the spectacular Mooi River Valley takes you into densely vegetated terrain with high, rocky ridges and towering, red-faced cliffs. Euphorbia, cabbage trees and acacias, interspersed with thousands of aloes, adorn the giant hill slopes.

The tarred surface is generally good but gradients are steep and rockfalls are a potential hazard around sharp corners. Keate's Drift straddles the banks of the Mooi River, where children are seen splashing in the rapids while women do their communal washing. Note your kms as you cross the river over a one-way bridge 30 km from your start at the museum in Greytown.

The road climbs steeply up a rocky hillside and the mountainous terrain between Keate's Drift and Tugela Ferry offers splendid sightseeing. Hundreds of thatched huts dot the landscape of the broad Tugela River basin and you may see a rare beehive hut, once a prominent feature of Zulu rural settlements.

Also of interest is the traditional attire of the local Msinga clan, especially the broad-topped, red headdresses worn by the married women seen bustling around the trading stores at Tugela Ferry. Note your kms as you cross the river over the old steel bridge that you reach 15 km from Keate's Drift.

Pomeroy to Greytown

Around Pomeroy, which is 24,5 km from Tugela Ferry, the countryside changes to grassland. Note your kms as you pass through the village and again as you pass a road on your left, to Wasbank, 9,5 km beyond Pomeroy. Keep heading north towards Dundee onto a plateau commanding distant views of the Biggarsberg. After 5 km you reach a picnic site that makes a pleasant stopping point. Note your kms here.

Some 15 km beyond the picnic site, turn left onto a gravel road signposted Wasbank, and note your kms at the turn. The road winds westwards down Van Tonder's Pass through the Biggarsberg, to reach a T-junction at 12,4 km. Turn right here and note your kms.

The road surface changes to tar after 11,5 km and you reach another T-junction 4 km further on. Turn left here, noting your kms, to bypass Wasbank 5 km later. After a further 4 km, turn left at the crossroads onto the R602 for Elandslaagte, which you bypass 17 km later. At the T-junction with the N11, some 3 km after Elandslaagte, note your kms and turn left for Ladysmith.

Skirting the town, you cross the Klip River after 24 km. Note your kms here and drive on up the hill for 2,2 km before turning left onto the R103 for Colenso.

Bypass Colenso, crossing the Tugela, and turn left at 27 km onto the R74 for Weenen/Greytown, noting your kms. Beautiful views of diaphanous blue hills fade into the distance. After 21 km, turn right onto the Estcourt road to visit Weenen Nature Reserve. The entrance is 500 m from the turn. (See below.)

Return to the R74 and turn right. The road drops into Weenen valley through a dense gorge once called Tierkloof, *tier* (tiger) being a Voortrekker misnomer for leopards found here in bygone days. Take a brief drive around the village (noting its old Voortrekker-built water furrows) and cross the Bushmans River to rejoin the R74.

The road to Muden – some 38 km – passes through successive valleys, surrounded by steep, thornveld-covered hills. You cross the Mooi River as it meanders through the lush Muden valley, well known for its oranges. The road then climbs for 23 km to Greytown, which you enter on Durban Road.

Greytown Museum Scott Street, Greytown 3501 Tel (0334) 31171
Dundee Tourist Information PO Box 76, Dundee 3000 Tel (0341) 22139

WEENEN NATURE RESERVE

Situated 10 km west of Weenen and 28 km north-east of Estcourt, this 4 909 ha thornveld reserve harbours abundant wildlife, including black and square-lipped rhino, Cape clawless otter, giraffe, buffalo, rare roan antelope, python and numerous buck species. The richly vegetated terrain attracts prolific bird life and fishing for bass and tilapia is a pleasant pastime. A superbly designed hide overlooks a dam and vlei, and two self-guided trails, the iMpofu Trail and the Beacon View Trail, are laid out.

The Soil Reclamation Trail provides an encouraging demonstration of human restoration, through conservation techniques, of a formerly damaged environment. You can leave your vehicle at the Mtunzini picnic area and follow a footpath to enjoy a breathtaking view of the Bushmans River and the farms surrounding Weenen. Visitors leaving their vehicles must first sign indemnity forms at the entrance gate. Accommodation facilities include camping and a fully equipped cottage.

Above: *A frieze of prehistoric art outside Muden.*
Below: *The gleaming green of cane fields at Greytown.*

Zulu woman at Msinga – modern fabric; traditional style.

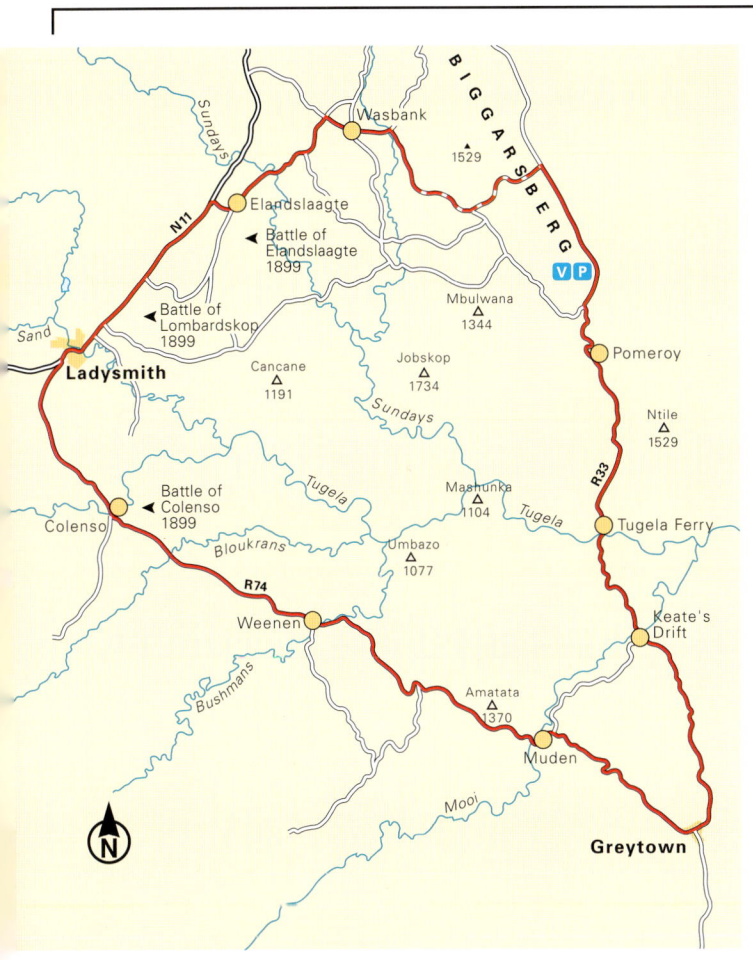

NORTHERN KWAZULU-NATAL

Representative clutter of a cosy Victorian parlour in the Greytown Museum.

GREYTOWN: THE PLACE OF THE LITTLE ELEPHANT

This pretty town, named after Sir George Grey, was established in 1854. It is laid out on the grid system similar to that of Pietermaritzburg, Natal's former colonial capital which was known to Zulus as *Umgungundlovu* (place of the big elephant). Greytown became *Umgungundlovana* (place of the baby elephant). The museum – an old residency and historical monument – has fascinating memorabilia of the Bambatha Rebellion of 1906; military and colonial artefacts; Hindu, Muslim and Zulu cultural exhibits; a coach house, and much more. The district offers hiking trails, scenic excursions and boating on nearby Lake Merthley.

The town boasts fine Victorian architecture, and places of interest include the Shri Vishnu Mandir Temple, St James' Anglican Church, Leuchars Memorial Hall, General Louis Botha's birthplace, the grave of Sarie Marais (celebrated in the famous song of the Anglo-Boer War) and many others.

Beads and bright clothing; Msinga.

MHLOPENI NATURE RESERVE

To sample the life in the great outdoors of Mvoti County, Mhlopeni Nature Reserve between Muden and Greytown offers an authentic bushveld experience. This Natural Heritage Site extends from river valley to craggy hills. The wide-ranging topography supports an extraordinarily rich diversity of bird life and offers exciting sightings, for instance, of black eagle, martial eagle, crowned eagle, blue crane, African broadbill, redthroated wryneck, spotted thrush, longtailed wagtail and plainbacked pipit. Game includes a wide variety of buck and small mammal species. The reserve has several important Iron Age smelting sites that have attracted a number of archaeological digs. Also to be seen are ancient Zulu sites, rock art, Voortrekker wagon trails, a rock-bottomed waterfall that provides safe swimming and a slide down a water chute.

MARIA RATSCHITZ DEVELOPMENT PROJECT

The Maria Ratschitz Mission near Wasbank was established by Trappist monks in 1888 and developed as a thriving centre of education and enterprise. The forced removal of neighbouring communities and a series of financial setbacks led to the mission being abandoned for many years. A multi-faceted rural development project is under way on the 3 200 ha farm to restore the historic and architecturally important buildings as well as the large tracts of productive agricultural land and the scenic, ecologically important slopes and summit of the Biggarsberg.

The introduction of eco-tourism is helping the Diocese of Dundee as well as several conservation and development agencies to fund restoration and to provide training for more than 400 residents of the small estate village of KwaTelaphi, who are partners in this community project.

Tourist trails are already in operation and visits to the monastery are planned once restoration has been completed. Information on the mission and also on the numerous battlefields that can be visited during this drive may be obtained from the Talana Museum in Dundee; tel (0341) 22654.

Above: *An elegant old shopfront at Weenen.*
Below: *Hut roof built in traditional Zulu style.*

Misty hills around the old capital of Shaka's Zulu empire

From Shaka's old capital, Stanger, we climb to scenic Kranskop and to Jameson's Drift on the Tugela. We visit the German mission at Hermannsburg before returning through timberlands around the villages of Sevenoaks, Dalton and Fawn Leas. The road has sharp curves and all but 26 km is tarred. Heavy mists may be experienced during any season.

Stanger
Mapumulo
Kranskop
Hermannsburg
Fawn Leas
260 – 280 km

HEAD NORTH FROM Stanger along the R74 for Kranskop. The road passes through undulating sugar cane fields, punctuated by attractive strips of indigenous forest that line the rivers and streams along the way. After 9,2 km you pass, on your right, the site of the original Kearsney College, a renowned boys' school. This was once the home of Sir James Liege Hulett, founder of the well-known sugar company, and is now St Luke's Home for Healing. The chapel is an interesting example of a turn-of-the-century Wesleyan church. As the R74 climbs inland, the countryside grows increasingly attractive. Panoramic views of cane fields and timber plantations alternate with forest belts and subsistence farming tracts dotted with huts. Heavy mist often occurs and the limited visibility can be hazardous, especially as the gradient of the road is frequently steep and there are several sharp curves. Animals sometimes stray onto the road, so caution is essential.

Mapumulo to Kranskop
About 37 km from Stanger you pass a tarred road, on your left, to Mapumulo, which lies 5,7 km off the R74. Named 'the place of rest' from the Zulu verb, *pumula*, Mapumulo became a focal point of resistance to the payment of poll tax during the Bambatha Rebellion of 1906. Part of the local police station was formerly a small fort, recalling the turbulent past.

Drive on along the R74 and, 24 km past the road to Mapumulo, turn right onto a gravel road for The Kop, where a great spur of the Drakensberg ends precipitously on the southern side of the Tugela. Do not attempt this road in the wet, but in dry weather it is usually easy to negotiate. Along the way, sweeping vistas of cane lands and plantations blend into distant horizons. At the T-junction after 13,3 km, turn right onto a tarred road, for Ntunjambili. The lookout point that you reach after 5 km, on your left, presents a spectacle that is one of the natural wonders of KwaZulu-Natal.

Retrace your route for 5 km to the intersection, where the road becomes tarred. Keep straight at this point (do not turn left) and drive directly into Kranskop 4 km away to explore the village before making an optional detour – adding a total of 70 km of gravel road – up to Jameson's Drift. (See below.)

Kranskop to Fawn Leas
After completing this scenic detour, continue along the R74 in the direction of Ahrens and, after 13 km, turn left onto the D469 for a brief visit to the Hermannsburg Mission House, a total detour of just 4 km. (See opposite page.) Retrace your route to the R74, turn left for Ahrens, noting your kms. Pass a road on the left to Ahrens at 5,5 km and, after 7,6 km, turn left for 'Mizpah/New Hanover/Pietermaritzburg', noting your kms. The route now passes a succession of farm dams on a high plateau characterized by cultivated pastures and stocklands. After a level crossing, turn left at the T-junction at 15,4 km onto the R33 and note your kms.

This is the heart of KwaZulu-Natal's timber country and there are several large sawmills close by. After 9,2 km the road skirts the village of Sevenoaks; 2 km later, turn left onto a secondary road for Dalton, noting your kms. After 6,8 km turn left onto a gravel road for Fawn Leas; after 9,3 km, note the Johanneskirche at Lilienthal on your left side. This attractive cream-and-brown building is in the style of a Bavarian country church. At the four-way intersection, keep straight for Fawn Leas, cross a railway line and turn left at the T-junction at 13,6 km onto the R614.

Fawn Leas to Stanger
You are now on tar and heading back to the coast past Fawn Leas, where you will find a café and a petrol station. After 29 km you pass the village of Nsuze. This section of the route is a good, broad road, but rockfalls have been known to occur in the cuttings where the road drops down onto the coastal plain on the way to Maidstone and Tongaat. After crossing the Wewe River, you can either turn left at the traffic lights to reach Stanger via the R102 or continue to the N2 and turn left there.

Stanger Tourist Information KwaDukuza/Stanger Local Council, 14 Reynold Street, Stanger 4450 Tel (0324) 23091
Kranskop Local Council PO Box 45, Kranskop 3550 Tel (03344) 41167

JAMESON'S DRIFT
Jameson's Drift on the Tugela River is 35 km from Kranskop and is offered as an optional deviation from the main route. After refilling your petrol tank in Kranskop, turn right from Main Street at the sign to Tugela River Rafting: Qudeni and Nkandla.

This becomes a dirt road and the mountainous terrain grows increasingly remote and wild. As the road crosses a ridge and follows a broad curve down to the left, a spectacular vista opens up of the Tugela far below, sweeping back on itself for several kilometres against a backdrop of hazy hills.

The road condition on the descent to the river is usually poor. The detour ends at the narrow bridge that crosses the Tugela at the point once known as Jameson's Drift, named after the engineer who surveyed the road. From here you retrace your route to Kranskop. Note your kms before picking up the route along the R74 in the direction of Ahrens and Greytown.

The rural Bavarian idiom of the Johanneskirche.

Both modern and traditional – a mosque overlooking Stanger.

STANGER

Stanger is situated beside the Mvoti River, which was named by the amaPhumulo tribe for their chief, Mvoti Ncashanga. The town is historically important as the site of Shaka's second great capital, Dukuza. Shaka took up residence in 1826 and lived here until his assassination two years later. Shaka's memorial at the top end of Couper Street in the shopping hub of the town was unveiled in 1932 by his descendant, King Solomon ka Dinizulu, on the supposed site of his grave. The town's English name derives from Dr William Stanger, the first Surveyor General of the colony of Natal. Established around 1850, Stanger became a base for operations during the Anglo-Zulu War of 1879. Today its large Indian contingent makes for a colourful blending of cultures, and there are several outstanding mosques that may be visited by arrangement. Stanger is a centre of KwaZulu-Natal's sugar, pulp and paper-making industries.

Monument to the first Zulu king.

Legend tells of sounds of revelry from within the dome of Kranskop.

KRANSKOP AND THE LEGEND OF NTUNJAMBILI

Called Hopetown when it was laid out in 1894, Kranskop was later renamed after the nearby *kop* or hill, known in Zulu as *iTselika Ntunjambili*, 'the rock with two openings'. A local myth tells of young girls who were weary of carrying water from the river and who asked the mountain to give them relief from their chores. A great cave opened and sounds of revelry tempted them inside. The entrance closed and they were never seen again. Today the district is popular among nature-lovers, who enjoy the excellent birdwatching and hiking trails on several local farms. River rafting down the Tugela Gorge and the annual 'Father and Son' fishing competition in July are popular local events, whereas the hot springs 25 km away across the river are another popular attraction. The village retains a number of old, red-brick colonial houses.

Lamp-lit homeliness of the museum at Hermannsburg Mission.

HERMANNSBURG MISSION HOUSE

This famous old Lutheran mission was founded by Pastor Louis Harms in 1854 and built by German missionaries and colonists from Hermannsburg in Germany. The first pupils were taught here in 1856 and today the centre still comprises a German School as well as an interesting museum housed in the original mission house, surrounded by beautiful old trees and atmospheric gardens. This is now a national monument and is open Monday to Friday from 09h00 – 12h00 and on weekends by appointment; tel (03345) 405/709/714/621/624. The museum has a fascinating collection of antique farming implements and memorabilia from the early days of its existence. It is interesting to note the wide doorways, built to accommodate the crinoline skirts that were fashionable at the time. Typically, the old kitchen is separate from the rest of the buildings to minimize the risk of fire. Woodcraft and pottery are on sale.

Stanger is surrounded by cane fields.

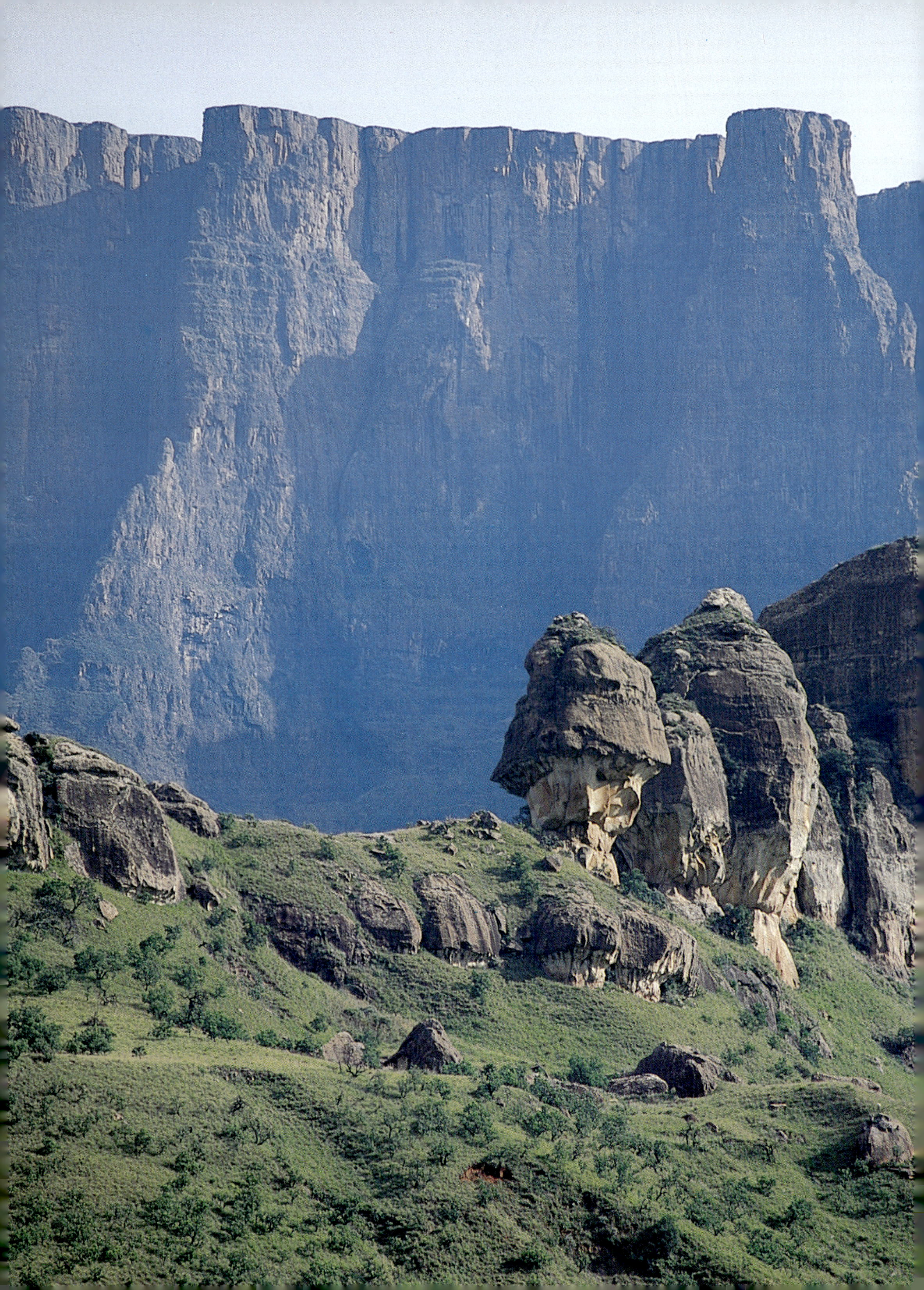

SOUTHERN KWAZULU-NATAL

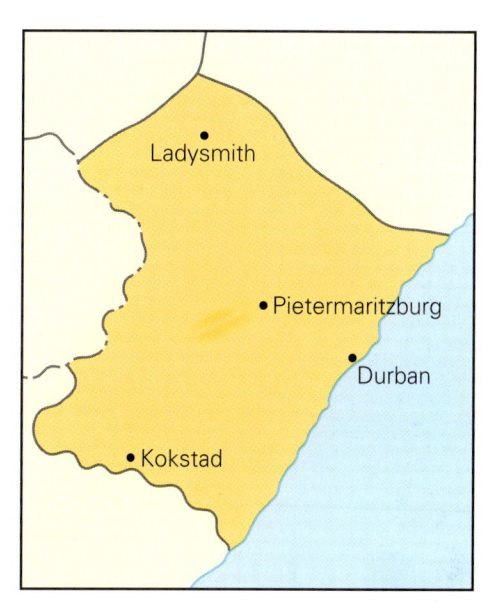

Royal Natal National Park: 'Mountain of beginnings' **126-7**

Ladysmith – Spioenkop Dam – Winterton – Monk's Cowl – Bergville – Spioenkop **128-9**

Mooi River – Bray Hill – Giant's Castle – Wagendrif Dam – Estcourt **130-1**

Giant's Castle Game Reserve: 'People of the eland' **132-3**

Pietermaritzburg – Hella-Hella Pass – Himeville – Sani Pass – Reichenau **134-5**

Underberg – Coleford – Bushman's Nek – Drakensberg Gardens **136-7**

Pietermaritzburg – Howick Falls – Midlands Meander – Kamberg – Umgeni Valley **138-9**

Pietermaritzburg: Red brick and Imperial echoes **140-1**

Durban – Krantzkloof – Valley of a Thousand Hills – Midmar – Pietermaritzburg **142-3**

Zulu Traditions: The people of heaven **144-5**

Durban – Umdloti Beach – Shaka's Rock – Stanger – Umhlanga **146-7**

Durban: The heart of the Holiday Coast **148-51**

Durban – Umgababa – Clansthal – Scottburgh – Amanzimtoti **152-3**

Scottburgh – Ixopo – St Faith's – Umtentweni – Umzumbe **154-5**

Margate – Uvongo – Oribi Gorge – Port Edward – Southbroom **156-7**

Left: *Rugged Drakensberg buttresses in the Royal Natal National Park.*

• EXPLORING ROYAL NATAL NATIONAL PARK •

Fresh streams provide safe swimming.

The inscrutable majesty of Eastern Buttress and Devil's Tooth in an eerie light.

A view over the lip of Tugela Falls.

Jagged cliffs and cascading waters at the 'mountain of beginnings'

IN THE NORTH-WESTERN corner of KwaZulu-Natal a rugged wall of rock drops for more than a kilometre from a plateau as old as Africa. Over a sheer, 4 km-wide, basalt cliff face – known as The Amphitheatre – the waters of several rivers plunge into a landscape exposed by erosion over millions of years.

The Amphitheatre, flanked by the distinctive Sentinel on the right and the Eastern Buttress on the left, forms a backdrop to the 8 800 ha Royal Natal National Park, renowned around the world for its magnificent Drakensberg scenery. Here visitors flock every year to explore the park on foot or on horseback, watch the game and the great variety of birds, fish for trout or simply relax in the exhilarating environment.

The cliffs of the Drakensberg are part of a crust of volcanic rock that formed the surface of the Gondwanaland super-continent when Africa broke away from it roughly 120 million years ago. Since then, rivers have steadily pushed back the cliff edge from the coast to where it is now – a dynamic and continuing process.

Above Royal Natal National Park is the Lesotho plateau, a remnant of the old Gondwanaland surface that now forms the watershed of southern Africa, where five rivers have their source, including the Tugela and the Elands. It was the rising of these rivers that in 1836 inspired the French missionary-explorers Arbousset and Daumas to name the highest point in the park (at 3 282 m) *Mont-aux-Sources* – 'mountain of beginnings'.

Although San hunters followed game here in summer, the area below Mont-aux-Sources was not permanently inhabited until early last century, when the San people sought refuge in its rocky shelters from Nguni-speaking and white settlers. A pair of holidaymakers on honeymoon in this area of the park in 1878 saw a few of these diminutive San – probably the last of them to live here.

Throughout the Drakensberg there are excellent examples of San rock art in the sandstone overhangs below the basalt cliffs. Most of the paintings occur further south (see pages 132 – 3), but a small number can be found in the Royal Natal National Park. The most easily accessible are those in the Sigubudu valley, which can be viewed from a walk that takes less than an hour.

Cannibals and woodcutters
The San were not the only people to hide in these remote mountains. During the *Mfecane*, the migration caused by Shaka's 1818 – 28 territorial wars, food became so scarce that a number of tribes resorted to cannibalism. It is said that some of these desperate men lived in a shelter known as Cannibal Cave. The shelter, which also contains San paintings, can be reached on a hike via Surprise Ridge, which offers excellent views of the Drakensberg.

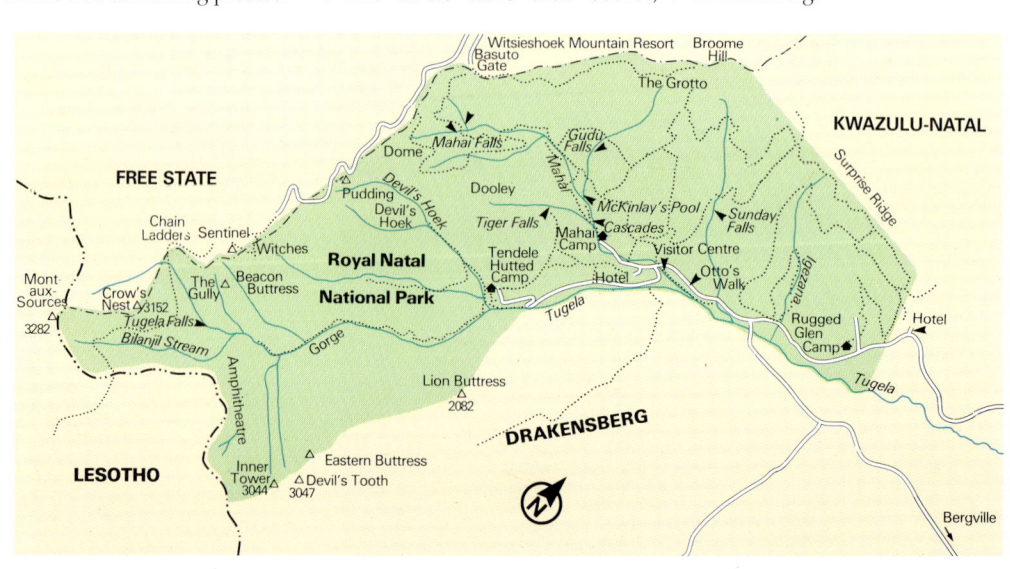

Sandstone cliffs, proteas and forested gorges typify Drakensberg trails.

The rugged Sentinel – aloof in a blue sky as clouds roll in over the park.

The magnificent yellowwood forests that are still a feature of the park's shady gorges brought more men into the area towards the end of the 19th century – woodcutters who were given concessions to chop tons of the beautiful wood. One prominent sandstone mountain bears the name of one of them, an Irishman named Dooley.

The 'Natal National Park' was proclaimed in 1916 – the 'Royal' being added only after the visit, in 1947, by members of the British Royal Family. Today the park offers a choice of 25 walks and hikes along 83 km of well-maintained paths. Described in an excellent guidebook sold in the park, they traverse areas with greatly varying altitude and, therefore, a wide variety of plants, animals and bird life. Many of the paths follow river valleys, where you may swim or paddle in the clear mountain water (except in demarcated water catchment areas).

The Tugela Falls
One of the most breathtaking features of the park is the Tugela Falls. Within a few kilometres of its source on the 3 000 m plateau known as *Phofung* (place of the eland) to the Sotho, the Tugela drops for almost 2 km over a series of falls and cascades, and through a dramatic gorge, to the valley floor. One sheer fall of 614 m is the highest in South Africa, while the combined drop of the Tugela Falls of 948 m makes it the second-highest in the world after the Angel Falls in Venezuela.

The Tugela has also created one of the most popular walks in the park: a six-hour hike up The Gorge to a feature known as The Tunnel, where the river has carved an impressive path through the white sandstone. You then have the choice of boulder-hopping through The Tunnel (when the water is low enough) or of climbing a chain ladder through a steep gorge into the Amphitheatre.

A shorter outing is the Cascades Walk, which takes you to the Queen's Causeway and Cascades on the Mahai River. (Allow 30 minutes – or an hour if you continue to McKinlay's Pool.) If you intend to go trout-fishing, remember that a provincial licence and daily rod permit are required. Both can be obtained from the Natal Parks Board office in the Visitors' Centre.

Mountaineering
The area has long offered challenging climbing to experienced mountaineers and in 1927 the first guidebook was published. Those who wish to climb in the area must be members of a mountain club, or must satisfy the Natal Parks Board that they are experienced enough and properly equipped. A mountain register is kept at the Visitors' Centre and must be signed by anyone venturing above certain altitudes or intending to overnight in the open.

For those who prefer to explore the area on horseback, the Natal Parks Board operates stables at the Rugged Glen camp, from where parties are led by grooms along a number of bridle paths. During peak seasons it is advisable to make reservations.

Birdwatching in the park can be very rewarding. Almost 200 species have been spotted here, including the rare Cape vulture, the bearded vulture (*lammergeyer*) and the black eagle. A number of antelope make their home in the park, and the visitor is likely to see mountain reedbuck on the grassy slopes. On the rocky heights you may see the klipspringer, the agile little buck that was reintroduced after having been hunted out of the area because its hair was so popular for stuffing saddles. More prevalent among the park's mammals are the baboon and the rock hyrax (*dassie*).

Unique protea
Vegetation varies enormously with altitude. In the lowest reaches (the montane belt) you find yellowwood forests and protea savannah, in the sub-alpine belt there is scrub, fynbos and grassland, while the alpine belt on the plateau contains the sparser erica-helichrysum heath. A rare treasure is the little pink *Protea nubigena*, which is found in only one spot in the world – on the steep slopes of The Sentinel.

A valuable aid to the visitor is to be found at the viewsite on your left, 1,7 km after entering the park gate. Here you can match the spectacular view with a sketch that names the prominent landmarks.

Otto's Walk
The Visitors' Centre, which lies 2,4 km from the entrance, is another worthwhile stopping point. It has exhibits on the area, including a model of the mountains, identifying the walks, roads, rivers and other landmarks. A self-guided trail called Otto's Walk starts at the far side of the parking area here.

The roads to the park, and the main internal road to the hotel, are tarred. Visitors (except those eating at the hotel) must bring all their own food and drink.

Hikers should enquire locally about the weather, as sudden thunderstorms, mist or snow make conditions hazardous.

Reservations for accommodation are essential. For the hotel, you may book by telephoning (036) 438 6200, and for campsites, tel (036) 438 6303. Bookings for the hutted camp can be made through the Reservations Office, Natal Parks Board, PO Box 1750, Pietermaritzburg 3200. Tel (0331) 47 1981, fax (0331) 47 1980.

The magnificent Amphitheatre – scenery that draws visitors all year round.

A sortie into the Drakensberg across historic Anglo-Boer War battlefields

West of Ladysmith lie peaceful hills that once echoed the sound of gunfire as Boer and Briton fought to possess the land. We visit Spioenkop, site of one such bitter contest, and drive into the area below Cathkin Peak and Champagne Castle for a walk to a waterfall in a lovely Drakensberg setting. More than two-thirds of the route is tarred.

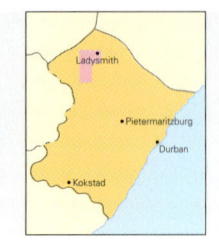

**Ladysmith
Spioenkop
Nature Reserve
Winterton
Monk's Cowl
Bergville
Spioenkop
150 – 170 km**

DRIVE SOUTH along the main road of Ladysmith (Murchison Street) and turn left into Buckingham Street. After 400 m turn right into Forbes Street. The road curves right into Short Street – park here at the footbridge for a visit to the Sufi temple.

Continue from the temple along Short Street and, at the stop street, turn left. Pass Murchison Street on your right, and note your kms soon afterwards as you cross the Klip River (this road forms part of the N11). After 2 km (just before the intersection with the R103), turn left towards the airfield. After a further 250 m, turn left onto gravel for the Burger Monument and, 250 m later, go left at the fork. The road surface changes to tar again 2 km later and, after a further 300 m, you pass the Wagon Hill military cemetery on your left.

About 100 m beyond the cemetery you reach the control gate at the entrance to the historic Platrand/Wagon Hill site, which is controlled by the National Monuments Council. Turn left at the T-junction beyond the gate. (The gravel track on your right here leads, after 1 km, to a number of British memorials and to the grave of the Reverend JD Kestell, who, although he travelled with the Free State Boers, ministered to both sides.) About 600 m beyond the T-junction, park at the Burger Monument. From here you have an excellent view over Ladysmith and the surrounding hills, where many battles were fought (see below).

Wagon Hill to Spioenkop Nature Reserve
Retrace your route to the N11 and turn left onto the R103; 2 km later turn right, back onto the N11 for Bergville, and note your kms. After 8 km, turn left onto the R600 for Winterton, noting your kms again.

The prominent Twin Peaks and Spioenkop soon come into view on your right and, after

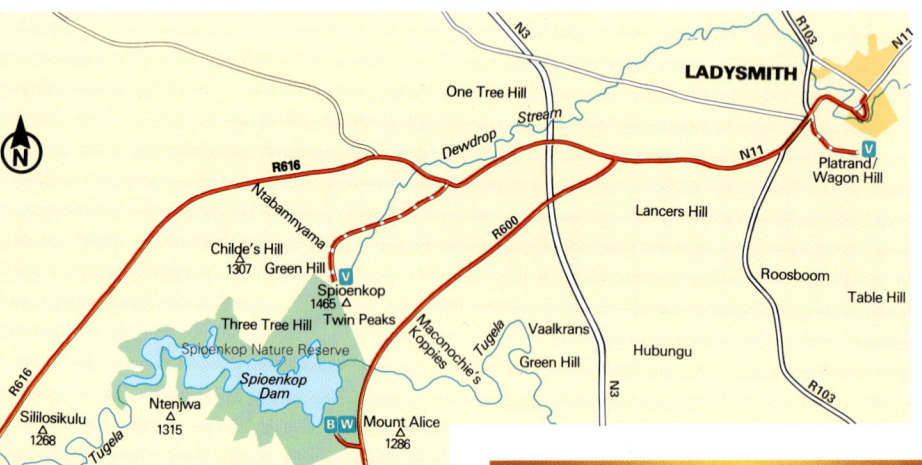

Drakensberg panorama from the Bergville road.

Spioenkop Dam's surrounding hills against the setting sun.

THE SPANISH BEAUTY
Ladysmith, an attractive town set on the *Klip* (stone) River and surrounded by a ring of hills, is an important agricultural centre, an industrial growth point and one of the largest railway marshalling points in South Africa. Many of its interesting historic buildings date from the siege of Ladysmith during the Anglo-Boer War, including the old Town Hall in Murchison Street which was shelled during the siege. Next door is the Siege Museum, which has many fascinating relics from that time. The town's settler past dates back to 1847, when a group of Voortrekkers under Andries Spies formed the Klip River Republic here – but three years later the British annexed the area, naming it after Juana de los Dolores de Leon, the beautiful Spanish wife of the Cape governor, Sir Harry Smith.

A SIEGE THAT HELD THE WORLD
On 2 November 1899 Boer commandos besieged the British and colonial garrison at Ladysmith – a siege that was to last 118 days and capture newspaper headlines around the world. Several attempts were made by the British to relieve the town, leading to heavy losses – most of them British – at places such as Colenso, Spioenkop, Vaalkrans, Hlangwane and *Pietershoogte* (Pieter's Hill). There were also a number of deaths on Wagon Hill (or Platrand, as it was known to the Boers) during a determined attempt to breach the town's defences. Disease and wounds took their toll of the defenders, and daily rations were eventually down to 230 g of bread and about 600 ml of horse extract (known as 'chevril'), but the besieged community tried to keep morale high with a calendar of Shakespeare readings, open-air concerts, picnics and a Christmas party for the 250 children among them. Sir Redvers Buller (known in Ladysmith as Sir Reverse Buller) finally relieved the town on 28 February 1900 – an event celebrated jubilantly in the streets of faraway London.

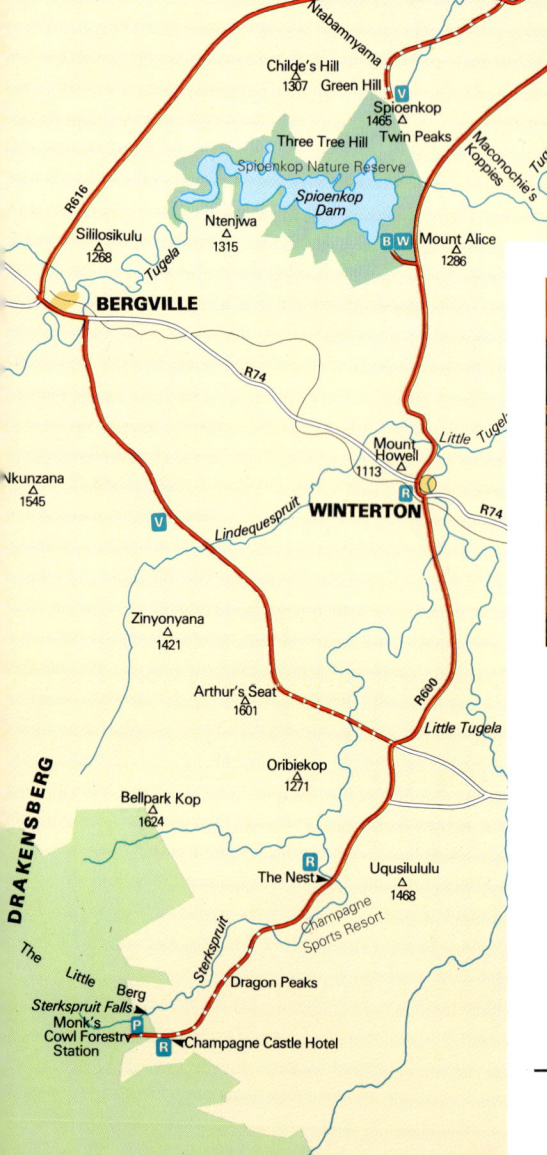

9,5 km, you see Spioenkop Dam shortly before you pass Twin Peaks. Pass a loop of the Tugela River on your left, and pass a turn-off to your right to the dam wall about 2 km later.

Some 21 km after turning off the N11 turn right for Spioenkop Nature Reserve. Soon afterwards you pass through the main gate on your right (where a small entry fee is charged). After a further 300 m turn right at the office for a visit to the Interpretive Centre (the gravel road ahead of you leads to picnic sites at the water's edge). The centre has many fascinating photographs taken during the Anglo-Boer War period, and several models showing the positions during major battles.

Spioenkop Dam to Monk's Cowl
Leaving Spioenkop Nature Reserve, turn right for Winterton, noting your kms. On a clear day you can see the distant wall of the Drakensberg from this road as it winds through the farmlands of the Little Tugela valley. After almost 12 km, turn left at the T-junction onto the R74 for Winterton and Central Berg Resorts, and note your kms. Soon afterwards you pass through the town of Winterton on the banks of the Little Tugela River (a hotel in the town serves lunch).

After a little over 1 km on the R74, turn right onto the R600 for the journey to Cathkin Park, Dragon Peaks and Champagne Castle – and note your kms again.

The road on which you are travelling soon begins to wind closer and closer to the Drakensberg. After 13 km go straight at the crossroads where the gravel road on your right leads to Bergville (your return route later in the day). After a further 7 km, in which you travel through attractive valleys dotted with farmhouses and huts, you have a panoramic view of the Drakensberg.

Some 24,5 km after turning off the R74, turn left into the Champagne Sports Resort for a visit to its attractive little thatched chapel – the large altar window provides an impressive view of Cathkin Peak, Champagne Castle, and the Mount Memory range. You can also walk from the chapel to the MOTH National Shrine, which offers equally splendid views. The shrine, set in the Mount Memory Sanctuary, was built by the ex-servicemen's organisation, the Memorable Order of Tin Hats (MOTH), to honour the dead of World Wars I and II. It is reached along a gravel track that turns off the main road just below the chapel – after 150 m on the sideroad turn right to reach the sanctuary after a further 150 m.

Continue on the main road towards the mountains, noting your kms at the turn-off to the MOTH National Shrine. After 900 m, where a gravel road forks to the right, keep straight for Dragon Peaks and Champagne Castle. The road winds through farmlands with tall stands of trees, overlooked by the sandstone heights of the Little Berg and the more distant basalt cliffs of the Drakensberg.

You pass a turn-off on your right to the Drakensberg Boys' Choir school and Dragon Peaks (a resort with a shop, restaurant and picnic facilities).

About 8,5 km from the MOTH shrine go right (where a road branches off left for Champagne Castle Hotel). Roughly 1,7 km later you reach Monk's Cowl Forestry Station (small entry fee). Enquire at the gate or office for directions to Sterkspruit Falls, a walk of about 60–90 minutes amid magnificent mountain scenery. The stretch of river above the falls makes a lovely spot for a picnic, although there are no facilities.

Monk's Cowl to Spioenkop
Retrace your route for the roughly 22 km from Monk's Cowl to the Bergville/Kelvin Grove turn-off. Turn left, noting your kms. After 100 m the road surface changes to gravel and you wind through mealie fields, sorghum and cattle country, with the wall of the high Drakensberg running almost parallel to the road on your left. The road surface changes to tar at 10 km; pull onto the shoulder of the road after 16 km for a view of the mountains.

After 28 km, turn left onto the R74 for Bergville, noting your kms. You cross the Tugela River, then enter the town of Bergville. After 2,2 km turn right onto the R616 for Ladysmith, noting your kms again.

You now travel parallel to another section of the Drakensberg – the northern extension, noted for its sculpted sandstone formations. After a few kilometres you enter hilly acacia bushveld again.

After 31 km on the R616 turn right for Spioenkop Monument. This gravel road takes you, after roughly 10 km, to the top of Spioenkop (entrance fee), from where you can look out over the former battlefield to a magnificent scene – Spioenkop Dam, the Tugela valley and hills stretching towards the Drakensberg. Retrace your route to the R616, and turn right for Ladysmith.

CATHKIN PEAK AND CHAMPAGNE CASTLE
From afar you notice the distinctive shape of the 3 149 m Cathkin Peak with its flat top and sheer cliffs. Because it is detached from the main Drakensberg wall, it seems to tower above Champagne Castle to its south – at 3 377 m one of the highest points on the escarpment. David Gray, a Scot who moved here in 1858, named the peak after Cathkin Braes near his home town, but for many years it was also called Champagne Castle because of the mysterious disappearance of half a bottle of champagne from the baggage of two explorers. The name Champagne Castle was eventually transferred to the then unnamed height on the main wall.

Above: A hiker is dwarfed by the Sterkspruit Falls.
Below: The exotic Sufi temple in Ladysmith.
Below left: Summer clouds over Cathkin Peak.

Ladysmith Information Bureau Town Hall Murchison Street, Ladysmith 3370
Tel (0361) 22992
Drakensberg Publicity Association PO Box 12 Bergville 3350 Tel (036) 448 1557
Natal Parks Board PO Box 662, Pietermaritzburg 3200 Tel (0331) 47 1961

High mountain splendour and tranquil valleys rich in beauty

From Mooi River we drive through the scenic Little Berg to Giant's Castle. Heading back, we turn towards Estcourt and cross the Bushmans River, visiting Moore Park and Wagendrift Dam and exploring Estcourt. Bridging the Midlands and the Berg, more than two-thirds of the route is tarred and it is rewarding in any season. Summers are misty.

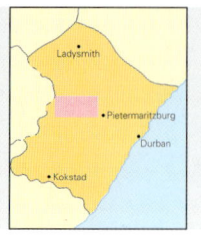

**Mooi River
Giant's Castle
Wagendrift Dam
Estcourt
160 – 180 km**

FROM THE TRAFFIC CIRCLE near the toll plaza, drive out of Mooi River along Lawrence Road, following the signs for Giant's Castle. Note your kms at the circle. The tar ends after 4 km. Approaching the foothills you encounter the willow-lined *Mooi* (beautiful) River as it meanders through the cultivated paddocks and undulating grasslands around you. As the route progresses into the Little Berg, the broadly sweeping landscape becomes increasingly rugged and, after passing through extensive timber plantations, you reach a T-junction some 36 km from Mooi River. Note your kms here and turn right for Giant's Castle.

Giant's Castle and Bushmans River

The route meanders up a scenic valley, running parallel for much of the time to the clear, trout-inhabited upper reaches of the Bushmans River. Enter the Natal Drakensberg Park at the gates to Giant's Castle Reserve after some 20 km, and follow the tarred road through the reserve to the main rest camp. Enjoy the beautiful mountain scenery ahead and the close-up views of sandstone cliffs and rocky outcrops. Here you will find the veld dotted with mountain proteas and Natal bottlebrush (*Greyia sutherlandii*), aflame with scarlet flowers in spring and early summer.

Leave Giant's Castle reserve and retrace your route along the tarred road to the gravel road on which you travelled earlier and turn left, noting your kms. After 12,2 km, turn left for 'Estcourt' and note your kms again. Successive low-lying valley vistas unfold as the road winds gradually out of the foothills of the Drakensberg, and it is fascinating to watch the Bushmans River growing in size as it follows its course away from the mountains towards Estcourt. Cross the river, after 10,8 km, at the one-way Dalton Bridge, a sturdy old iron structure from the days of the Natal colony, 'erected at a cost of £6 000, opened on the 20th day of November 1903 by the Hon H Winter MLA' (Member of the Legislative Assembly). The road climbs steeply and winds around the hillside above the Bushmans as it curves towards the upper reaches of the Wagendrift Dam. Watch your kms carefully at this point as the entrance to Moor Park – at 12,8 km, on your right – is partially concealed on a sharp corner and is not prominently marked for those travelling in this direction.

Moor Park nestles along the river, facing a thickly vegetated thornveld hill overlooking the opposite bank. Picnic sites and toilet facilities are available and the park's wooded river frontage supports a wealth of bird life. It is well worth stopping at this delightful spot, if only to sample its restful atmosphere. Return to the entrance gate and turn right, noting your kms.

Estcourt to Mooi River

Heading towards Estcourt, you now have a fine view of the upper reaches of the Wagendrift Nature Reserve and you pass, on your left after 3 km, Greystones, a national monument that was once the home of Sir Frederick Moore, Prime Minister of Natal. After 8,6 km you reach a T-junction. Note your

When it melts, the winter snow of the Drakensberg will boost the levels of water storage dams.

Caves made cosy homes for pre industrialized society.

EXPLORE THE CREATIVE MIDLANDS

As the 'Gateway to the Midlands' of KwaZulu-Natal, Mooi River has a close tourist association with the Midlands Meander that begins in the district and works its way down-country as far as Hilton, near Pietermaritzburg. This fascinating network of arts and crafts outlets is open to the public, and comprises studios in village homes and on farms and smallholdings. Every imaginable aspect of the arts and crafts industry is represented somewhere along the Meander, from weaving and spinning to furniture-making. An interesting example is the Sharrow Weaving Workshop, started in 1976 to enable Zulu women to meet their financial requirements by exploring their own creative skills. You may feel it is worth your while to extend your stay in the Midlands before or after this present drive, to explore the Meander.

MOOI RIVER

The Voortrekkers so admired the beautiful scenery they found here that they named the local river *Mooi* (beautiful), as much in tribute to the surroundings as to the river itself. Originally known as Lawrenceville, the village was founded by an Irishman, Alexander Lawrence, as a township developed around a railway station on his farm when the railhead reached the river in 1884. Primarily agricultural, the district is also renowned for its racehorse studs, several of which may be visited by appointment.

Places of interest in the vicinity include Craigie Burn Dam for camping (35 km on the Greytown road); St John's Church (on the Weston road) dating back to 1872; and the Rohde Museum (open Monday, Tuesday and Friday 09h30 – 12h30 and on Thursday 13h30 – 16h30). There are several craft centres in the area.

kms and turn left onto the tarred road to Estcourt. After 1,8 km, turn right for a brief detour to Wagendrift Nature Reserve. The 3 km concrete road crosses over the N3 and leads down to the dam, where there are camping sites and picnic facilities, as well as a slipway for boats. From the Wagendrift turn-off it is a short drive – about 5 km – into Estcourt. After exploring the town, particularly St Matthew's Church in Lorne Street and the old civic building around the corner in Harding Street, drive out of Estcourt down Lorne Street and across the Bushmans River.

To pay a visit to Fort Durnford, turn left just past the Eskort bacon factory as the road climbs the hill in the direction of the town of Mooi River. From its prominent vantage point across the Bushmans River the solid, stone-built fort has unimpeded views over the town and its approaches. Its defences were never put to the test of war. (See this page.)

Return to the main road and turn left. The road is clearly marked and heads up the hill past the provincial hospital to join the N3, where you turn left to return to Mooi River.

Estcourt Tourist Information Public Library Victoria Street, Estcourt 3310 Tel (0362) 23000
Gateway Reservations PO Box 174, Mooi River 3300 Tel (0333) 32450
AA Office Shop G23, Brasfort House 191 Commercial Road, Pietermaritzburg 3201 Tel (0331) 42 0571

A typically rugged Drakensberg skyline of (left) Champagne Castle, Monk's Cowl and Cathkin Peak.

ESTCOURT
Estcourt and the township of Wembezi lie at the heart of a rich stock-breeding and agricultural community. The old civic building (1901) in Harding Street, an imposing sandstone structure, served as the agricultural and town hall before the existing town hall was built in 1934. St Matthew's Church in Lorne Street is another attractive stone building. It attained its present size in 1958 with the addition of its Norman tower. The third Anglican church built in the town, it has a fine collection of Victorian and modern stained-glass windows. Interesting outings in the district include a stroll to 'Sheba's Breasts', the twin hillocks overlooking the Bushmans River, so entitled after their association with the famous author, Henry Rider Haggard, who wrote a number of his books in the town.

FORT DURNFORD
Overlooking the town of Estcourt is the austerely imposing Fort Durnford. This stone-built stronghold recalls something of the turbulence that afflicted the history of colonial Natal in the 19th century. The fort was erected in 1874 to protect the townspeople of Estcourt against possible attacks by the Zulus, especially after the Langalibalele Rebellion. It was named after Lt Col AW Durnford, who was killed at the Battle of Isandlwana on 22 January 1879. Its defence mechanisms made it an effective stronghold, and even included patches of broken glass to impede the progress of barefoot enemies. At a later stage it served as a reformatory for girls and subsequently became a school for local children. The water furrow that leads from the Little Bushmans River, a tributary of the Bushmans, can still be seen. Fort Durnford is now a museum with interesting exhibits of local and military history. Outside the fort is an exhibition of a reconstructed ethnic Zulu village.

Boardwalks and bridges on the Giant's Cup Hiking Trail prevent damage to the sensitive environment.

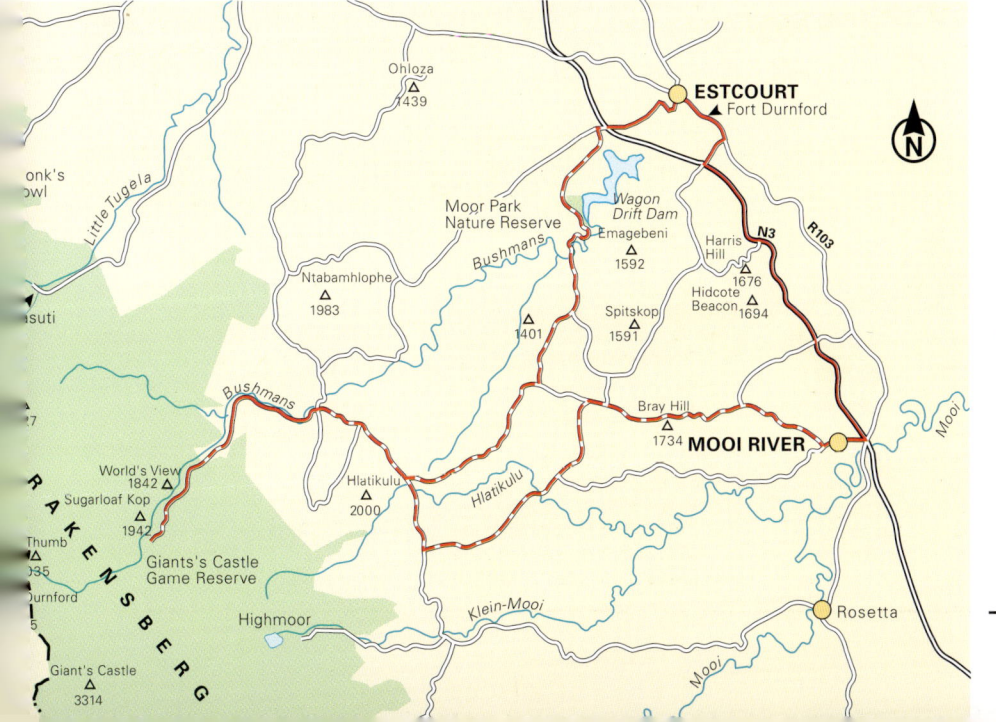

Sunlight will dispel the Mooi River's early mists.

• EXPLORING GIANT'S CASTLE GAME RESERVE •

The Bushmans River winds its way through the rocky hills below Giant's Castle, as the game reserve takes on its golden winter colours.

The mountain kingdom of the 'people of the eland'

ON A RECENT summer's day rangers counted a herd of 250 eland on the grassy slopes of Giant's Castle Game Reserve – a living tribute to the reserve's efforts to save the largest of all antelope from extinction.

When Giant's Castle Game Reserve was established in 1903 to save these handsome beasts from the hunters' guns, there were estimated to be only 27 of them left. Now about 1 200 eland roam freely through the southern Drakensberg, and Giant's Castle has a population of 600 – 800.

The 34 000 ha reserve, overlooked by South Africa's highest peak on the massive basalt wall of the Drakensberg, offers visitors a number of special attractions apart from game and the popular Drakensberg activities of hiking, mountaineering, bird-watching, and trout-fishing. Here you can explore the mountains on overnight horse-riding trails run by the Natal Parks Board; watch from a clifftop hide as vultures feed close by; or discover one of the richest legacies of San rock art.

Unlike the eland, the San people did not survive the arrival of the white man in KwaZulu-Natal early in the 19th century. The diminutive hunter-gatherers – known as the 'people of the eland' because they followed the herds as they migrated – had lived in perfect ecological harmony with their environment for thousands of years. When they saw the vast herds of game cut down by the white men's guns, they launched fierce retaliatory raids. But the San bows and arrows were no match for guns. They were hunted from the area like vermin and all that remains of their occupation of the Drakensberg is a number of artefacts and a collection of paintings in the rock overhangs in which they lived. The reserve and the Ndedema area combined contain more than 40 per cent of all known San rock art in South Africa. Giant's Castle has more than 5 000 paintings, most of which have been recorded and catalogued.

Main Caves Museum
A popular walk in the reserve is through the spectacular mountain scenery to the Main Caves, where there are more than 500 paintings in a single, large shelter. A second shelter houses a site museum with life-size models depicting the traditional San way of life. The caves are reached along a signposted path behind the Giant's Castle hutted camp. The area is fenced to prevent vandalism, and a game guard opens the gate on the hour every hour from 09h00 to 15h00. (There is a small entry fee. Allow two hours for the walk there and back along a gradual-to-steep path, and one hour for the guided tour of the caves.)

Before you set out for the caves, it is worth buying from the Natal Parks Board (for a nominal fee) a brochure on the Bushman's River Trail. The brochure takes visitors on a 'self-guided nature trail' and provides interesting information on the geology, vegetation and some of the history of the area.

The Parks Board also sells an excellent guidebook that describes 20 walks that begin from the main camp, and another 10 that start from the Injasuti hutted camp.

Injasuti is set in the beautiful valley of the *eNjesuthi* (well-fed

Summer thunderstorms contribute to the rich legends of the Drakensberg.

The eland – largest of all antelope.

132

dog) River, from which it takes its name. The area is renowned for ancient indigenous forests with towering yellowwoods, and its magnificent setting below Cathkin Peak, Monk's Cowl and the highest point in South Africa – the eNjesuthi Dome (3 410 m). In the valley lies Battle Cave, a shelter containing superb San paintings that depict a fierce battle between rival armies. The caves may be visited in the company of a game guard, who escorts visitors from the camp.

The main camp and the reserve are named after the 3 314 m peak known as Giant's Castle – or in Zulu as *Bhulihawu* (place of the shield-thrashers) because it was believed that all thunder (called 'thrashing of shields') is born here.

The Langalibalele Rebellion
Several other peaks take their names from an especially sad episode in the history of the area – the Langalibalele Rebellion of the 1870s. Langalibalele, powerful chief of the Hlubi people and a rainmaker and *isangoma* (diviner) of some repute, had come into conflict with the British colonial government in Natal over his refusal to levy taxes on his clansmen, to provide labour gangs for government projects and to hand over his men's guns to the administration for registration.

Annoyed by Langalibalele's resistance, and hearing that he planned to flee over the Bushman's River Pass into Lesotho, the government sent out a force to arrest him. But after a series of disasters aggravated by foul weather and inaccurate maps, the men under Major AW Durnford (later Colonel) who were to head off Langalibalele at the pass arrived too late.

The men who died in the ensuing clash – Robert Henry Erskine, Katana, Edwin Bond, Charles Davie Potterill and Elijah Kambule – and the man who led them have all had peaks named after them.

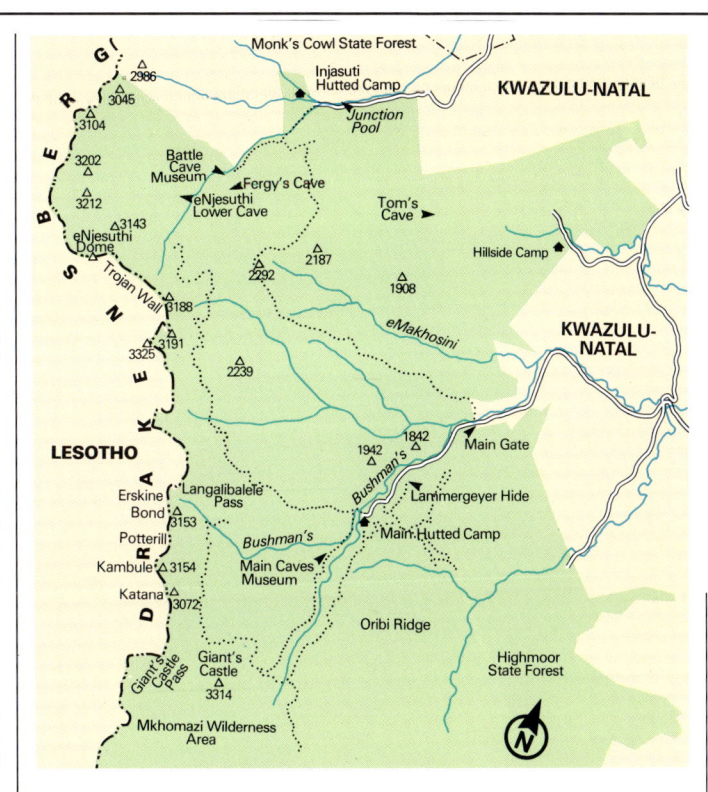

The pass, where the five fallen men are buried in a common grave, has been renamed after Langalibalele (who was later delivered to the British for trial and imprisoned on Robben Island). The pass provides a popular eight-hour hike along the Bushman's River valley into Lesotho. (For hikes above 2 100 m, or overnight trips into the mountains, it is necessary to complete a mountain rescue register at a Natal Parks Board or Department of Forestry office.)

Fauna and flora
While hiking in the reserve, you may see eland, common reedbuck, blesbok, bushbuck, mountain reedbuck, grey rhebuck, the rare oribi, grey duiker, red hartebeest or, in a few rocky areas, the klipspringer. The baboon and rock hyrax (*dassie*) are often seen and the jackal is heard at night, though it is seldom visible.

Giant's Castle, and the Drakensberg in general, is known for its wildflowers. Among the many hundreds of plant species in the region there are more than 60 species of ground orchid, and several plants that occur only in the KwaZulu-Natal Drakensberg – the *Protea dracomontana*, which produces a creamish pink flower on the ground, a heath known as *Erica drakensbergiensis*, and the cycad *Encephalartos ghellinckii*.

For the amateur bird-watcher as well as the ornithologist there are many delights in the reserve, which has a bird list of 140 species. During winter weekends there is the unique opportunity to watch the endangered bearded vulture (*lammergeyer*) through the one-way glass of a hide set high on the edge of a cliff. Here the Parks Board leaves bones for the vultures, to protect them against accidental death from poisoned carcases left out to kill jackals. The ossuary attracts a number of other birds, including the rare Cape vulture, the black eagle, jackal buzzard and Lanner falcon. (The hide must be booked in advance by telephoning the officer-in-charge at (03631) 24616.)

Accommodation in the main hutted camp and the huts at Injasuti should be reserved through the Reservations Office, Natal Parks Board, PO Box 1750, Pietermaritzburg 3200 or tel (0331) 47 1981, fax (0331) 47 1980. There is also a camp site at Injasuti, where sites should be reserved through the camp superintendent at tel (036) 488 1050. Reservations for Hillside camp site should be made through its camp superintendent – tel (0363) 24435. The park also has three overnight huts.

Basic foodstuffs, cooldrinks, charcoal and wood are available at the camp sites, but fresh produce and luxury goods are not sold. Visitors can buy petrol at the main gate.

Snow in winter and thunderstorms or mist in summer can be hazardous to hikers. It is wise to enquire locally about the weather before you set out.

The road from Estcourt to the reserve and from the reserve gate to the main camp is tarred. Gravel roads are sometimes in poor condition after rains. The road to Injasuti should not be tackled in summer without chains, as it becomes very muddy.

The sheer, western eNjesuthi Triplet.

The skilfully camouflaged vulture-hide atop its cliff.

An eagle's view at dawn towards the northern peaks.

The red cliffs of Hella-Hella and the foothills of the Sani Pass

This long drive leads through richly varied landscapes – the farming country around Richmond, the red cliffs of Hella-Hella, and the towering peaks and sparkling trout waters of the Drakensberg. It reaches to the foot of the forbidding Sani Pass, then heads back through grand valleys and forests. More than two-thirds of the route is tarred.

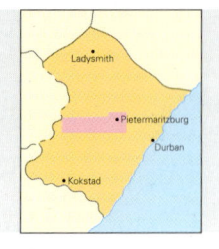

Pietermaritzburg
Richmond
Hella-Hella Pass
Underberg
Himeville
Sani Pass
Reichenau
350 – 370 km

Turn from Pietermaritzburg's Commercial Road into Alexandra Road (R56) for Richmond, noting your kms. The R56 takes you out of the city along a scenic road – after 11,2 km pull onto the shoulder (where a farm road leads left) for a pleasant view back over the hilly countryside towards Table Mountain in the distance.

About 5,5 km later you pass a turn-off on your left to Umlaas Road and Durban. The road winds through the cultivated valleys of the Mlazi (Umlaas) and Lovu (Illovo) rivers. At 20 km from the Umlaas Road/Durban turn-off, exit left for Richmond and, at the T-junction 200 – 300 m later, turn right.

You soon enter Richmond on Shepstone Street, which is lined with a number of attractive old buildings (see below). After just over 1,5 km turn left into Chilley Street, then turn right at the second intersection (Victoria Street) – the Richmond, Byrne and District Museum is on the corner here in a house that served as the Presbyterian manse from 1882 to 1982 (nominal entry fee, opening times vary).

Richmond to Hella-Hella

Return to Shepstone Street and turn left; 1,5 km later, turn left for Hella-Hella, noting your kms. After 600 m you pass a turn-off left to Ndaleni Mission. The road begins to rise immediately after this, giving you ever-changing views over the surrounding hills, with the Byrne Valley, named after the 1850s Byrne settler immigration scheme, on your right.

The tarred surface changes to gravel after 14,4 km and, soon afterwards, you begin a gradual descent into the valley of the Mkomazi (Umkomaas) River and its tributaries. At about 20 km the towering red cliffs of the *Helehele* (buttresses) Mountain come into view ahead of you. After 22,8 km you cross the wide Mkomazi River over the Hella-Hella Bridge. At the far side, park on your right, and walk back to the bridge for a view of the impressive river gorge.

Note your kms as you leave the parking area and begin the steep ascent of the Hella-Hella Pass (not suitable for towing). As you climb, you get ever-wider views of the gorge, the twisting river and the closed-in orchards on the valley floor. After 4,7 km, near the summit

The Mzimkulu River sparkles beneath the Drakensberg foothills.

The Sani Pass begins gently – then becomes a gruelling track over the mountains.

RICHMOND AND THE BYRNE VALLEY

The Byrne Settlers of 1850 occupied the banks of the Lovu (Illovo) River and established a town they named Beaulieu, after their home town in England – the seat of the Duke of Buccleuch in Hampshire. The name proved difficult to pronounce, and the town eventually became known as Richmond.

It is also the main centre for the *amaBhaca* (people who hide), who slowly returned after fleeing south during the Zulu territorial wars early last century. Bhaca women in their colourful traditional dress are often seen in the district.

THE HIGH ROAD OVER THE BERG

The little San hunters were the first people to cross the Drakensberg by the route now known as Sani Pass – today the only road access to Lesotho from the east. Herdsmen followed in their footsteps and the path was eventually upgraded, first to a mule trail and then to a jeep track to carry trade goods between eastern Lesotho and KwaZulu-Natal. The pass follows the upper Mkhomazana River through exceptional mountain scenery to the edge of the escarpment, and the road then continues to the remote settlement of Mokhotlong in Lesotho.

Spectacular walks and hikes abound in the area – including the Giant's Cup Trail (named after the basin between the prominent twins, Hodgson's Peaks), and a number of excursions to San paintings. Many of the walks and hikes are on land owned by State departments and permits may be required.

Left: *Thatched huts near Donnybrook.*

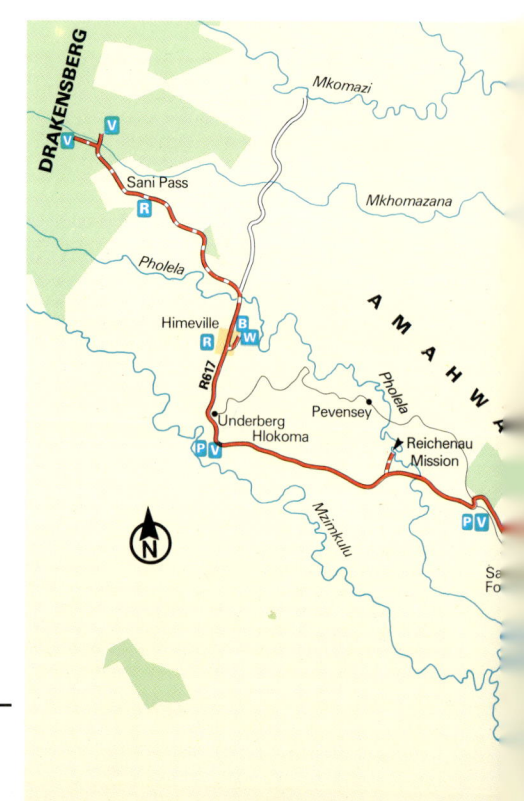

and opposite the Ka Hele Hele Nature Reserve, pull off the road for the grand view.

Hella-Hella to Underberg

Note your kms as you restart and, after 9,5 km, go right at the fork for Eastwolds and Donnybrook. Some 9 km later, turn right at Eastwolds trading centre onto the tarred road (R612) for Donnybrook and Bulwer – noting your kms at the turn.

You travel along the crest of a hill for a while, with views into valleys on both sides – crops and pastures interspersed with forests. Pass a turn-off on your left to Donnybrook after 8,4 km and another soon afterwards. Roughly 2 km later you can see the spire of the red-brick church of Kevelaer Mission on your right.

After about 24 km on the R612 the road begins to wind among the foothills of the mighty Drakensberg range, and you can see the southern end of the distinctive Amahwaqa Mountain looming ahead of you. After 27 km on the R612 turn left at the T-junction onto the R617 for Underberg and Himeville (where right leads to Bulwer – your return route). Note your kms here.

Roughly 7 km later you can see a sweep of the Drakensberg stretching to the west. After 9 km on the R617 turn left into a tree-shaded picnic site that offers a good view across farmlands towards the distant mountains.

Note your kms as you rejoin the R617. After 6 km you cross the Pholela River, and 2 km later on your right you have a glimpse of Reichenau Mission on its banks. After a further 14 km turn left into another shady picnic area that offers a magnificent view over Underberg, the Drakensberg and the fairytale shapes of its foothills. Some 2 km later you enter Underberg. Pass the small traffic circle on your right, and 200 m later turn right for Himeville and Sani Pass, noting your kms.

Underberg to Sani Pass

Only a few kilometres separate Underberg and Himeville. After 5,3 km turn right in Himeville (with the town's museum on the corner) onto a gravel road leading to the nature reserve; 400 m later you enter Himeville Nature Reserve and, after a further 500 m, you reach the office (where a small fee is payable). Some 800 m beyond the office is an attractive, shady picnic site alongside a trout dam – an ideal lunch stop (braai sites, water, toilets).

Retrace your route to the tarred main road, turn right and then turn left 3,6 km later onto gravel for Sani Pass, noting your kms.

The road winds into the Mkhomazana River valley past a number of vleis. After 8,5 km you can see Khanti Ridge directly ahead of you, with balancing rock formations on its summit and, 3 km later, turn right into the Sani Pass Hotel. There is a delightful walk to a waterfall on the Mkhomazana River. (Walk towards the tennis courts, but, 60 m before reaching them, branch off right through a gate and follow the occasional yellow stone markers through an avenue of poplars. Allow 40 – 60 minutes.)

Leaving the hotel, turn right, noting your kms. After 4,3 km turn right at the fork and park near the bridge for a view up the valley towards the Twelve Apostles. Return to the fork and turn right onto the road that becomes Sani Pass. A further 1 km brings you to a good turning point – the road beyond here is steeper and narrower, and, by law, vehicles without four-wheel drive may not proceed further.

Sani Pass to Lundy's Hill

Retrace your route through Himeville to the T-junction in Underberg and turn left onto the R617 for Bulwer. After just over 15 km, turn left onto a gravel track for Reichenau Mission, which you reach after 2 km.

Leaving the mission station, turn left onto the R617, noting your kms. After 18 km you pass the R612 to Donnybrook and Ixopo on your right, and 3 km later you enter Bulwer, nestling below the south-eastern end of the Amahwaqa. After a further 1 km, turn right onto a gravel road that leads, after a short distance, to an unpretentious little chapel built a century ago entirely out of yellowwood.

Return to the tarred main road and turn right, noting your kms. Travel through Bulwer and, after roughly 4 km, the view opens out over a wide section of the Mkomazi valley. You begin the descent into the valley and, 17 km after noting your kms, turn left into a parking area overlooking a horseshoe bend in the river.

Rejoin the R617 and cross the river soon afterwards. Now you start the ascent of Lundy's Hill (from 920 m to 1 390 m), which gives excellent views of the valley. From the summit of the pass the road winds through hilly countryside towards Pietermaritzburg, eventually passing Midmar Dam on your left. Roughly 60 km from the Mkomazi River viewsite turn onto the N3 for Pietermaritzburg. About 5,4 km later exit left for Hilton (Interchange 94) and, at the end of the off-ramp, turn right; 2,7 km later turn left onto the R103 (Old Howick Road) for Pietermaritzburg and, after a further 2 km, turn right for World's View 1and Boesmansrand for the splendid late-afternoon view (see pages 142 – 3).

REICHENAU MISSION
The substantial stone and brick buildings of Reichenau Mission stand as a monument to the missionaries' achievements. Apart from the impressive church with its carved wooden panels, painted murals and stained-glass windows, there is an old monastery, convent, farm buildings (some built of bricks fired at the mission) and a mill on the Pholela River which, until fairly recently, generated electricity. The missionaries also established a teachers' training college and an agricultural college, both of which are now closed, and a school, which still enrols local children. Founded in 1886, the mission was named after the German monastery island of Reichenau.

Left: *A detail from the stone church at Reichenau Mission.*

AA Office G23 Brasfort House, 191 Commercial Road, Pietermaritzburg 3201 Tel (0331) 42 0571
Pietermaritzburg Publicity Association
cr Commercial Road and Longmarket Street Pietermaritzburg 3201 Tel (0331) 45 1348
Richmond, Byrne and District Museum
cr Chilley and Victoria Streets, Richmond 3780 Tel (03322) 3038

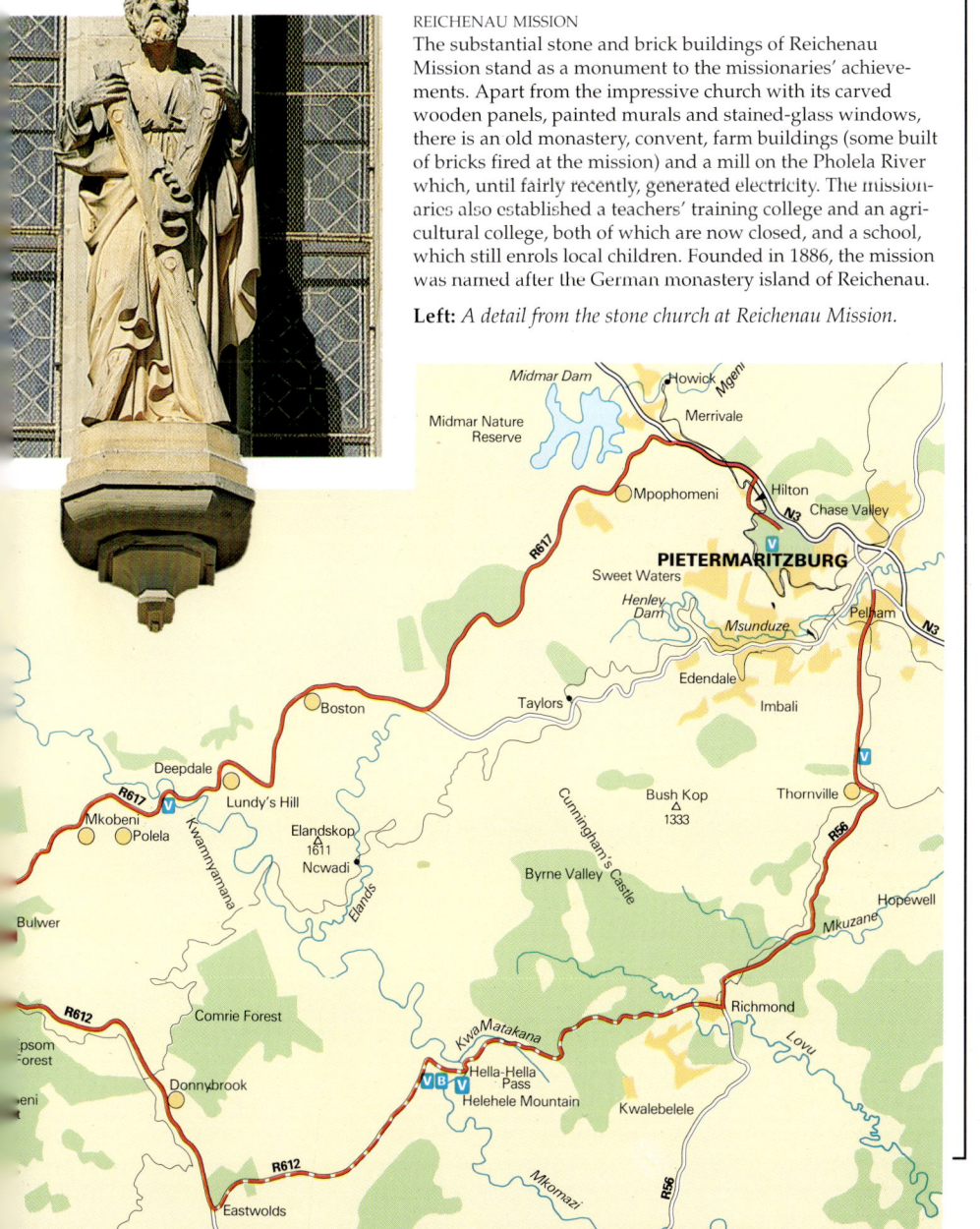

Touching the craggy face of the southern Drakensberg

Around the village of Underberg is a landscape of snowcapped winters and vividly green early summers, when many local gardens are open for viewing. Before setting out, visit the Himeville Museum, 5 km from Underberg, for an insight into the ethnic and colonial history of this area of majestic beauty. Most of the drive is on gravel roads.

Underberg
Himeville
Coleford
Garden Castle
Bushman's Nek
Drakensberg
Gardens
170 – 190 km

From Underberg's clock tower take the R617 towards Bulwer, noting your kms at the start. After 3,3 km, turn right at the Coleford sign onto a gravel road and note your kms. The route winds among the rolling hills as you pass through park-like surroundings with tree-lined pastures offset against the blue backdrop of the southern Drakensberg. After 17,5 km, turn right at the T-junction for Coleford Nature Reserve, to reach the entrance, in the Ngwangwane River valley, some 5 km later.

Coleford's rest camp is on the left of the road, its entrance clearly marked; note your kms here. The route cuts through the reserve, which offers superb trout-fishing and hiking opportunities. Sightings of game such as eland and black wildebeest add to the day's pleasures. While still in the reserve you pass a number of trout dams and turn right at the sign to Underberg/Swartberg. The road is rough and fairly steep, passing a number of old settler homesteads on the ascent out of the valley. As you approach the summit of the hill, another valley sweeps into view, offset once again by the magnificent mountain backdrop which, in winter, is frequently blanketed in snow. From this point you see the distinctive form of Garden Castle.

The first 'Giant's Castle'

This mountain was originally named 'Giant's Castle' by Captain Allen Gardiner in 1835 (and was subsequently renamed to avoid confusion with the better-known Giant's Castle that forms a cornerstone of the 'Berg further north). Set forward from the surrounding range and seen from different angles as you progress, this becomes a pivot around which the rest of the drive revolves. Just short of 12 km from Coleford's camp, turn right at the T-junction with the tarred R617 and note your kms at the turn. You now head down a hill back towards Underberg; at 1,3 km, turn left onto a gravel road that leads to Bushman's Nek and note your kms.

You are now driving directly towards the southern Drakensberg range, passing lush green pastures with large herds of Friesland cattle. After 17,2 km, turn left at the Y-junction onto the D2, which leads to Bushman's Nek mountain resort. The hotel is 6,2 km along this road and is set in sylvan surroundings dominated by poplars, planes and conifers, its gardens abloom in spring with roses, irises and foxgloves. Past the hotel entrance on your left, the route leads into a picturesque valley. Note your kms as you pass the hotel and, after 1 km, pass the Silverstream Trading Store, established in 1915. Pony rides are available here and petrol is sold during business hours. The road then leads past the adjoining Bushman's Nek and Silverstream caravan parks 1 km further on and ends at the mountain border post to Lesotho.

Bushman's Nek to Underberg

Retrace your route to the Y-junction and turn left onto another gravel road, leading to Underberg. This rises and dips from one valley to the next, passing through sedgy wetlands along the way, the higher reaches of the road commanding splendid mountain views. After 25 km, turn left towards Underberg at the T-junction with the R617. You are now briefly back on tar as you cross the Mzimkulu River. Immediately after the bridge, turn left to Drakensberg Gardens, noting your kms as you head towards the mountains along this intermittently tarred road. After 5,4 km you pass the Underberg Trout Hatchery. Much of this section of the route is dotted with craft centres as well as several bed-and-breakfast stopovers that are popular with backpackers and motorists. Curving around Garden Castle on your left, the route again plunges through successive valleys and there is often the illusion of being completely encircled as you watch the nearby peaks glowing in the sunlight.

The Zizi clan who settled in the foothills nearby called this section of the Drakensberg, *Khahlambo*, which means 'mountain barrier'. After 28,3 km you reach Drakensberg Gardens mountain resort. This has a three-star hotel and an 18-hole golf course, and petrol is available. From here, retrace your route back to the R617. At the T-junction, turn left and proceed 2 km into Underberg to complete your drive at the clock tower from which you set out.

Underberg Publicity c/o NUD Sports, Main Street, Underberg Tel (033) 701 1096
Natal Parks Board Main Street, Underberg Tel (033) 701 1471

GARDENS AND GETAWAYS
The southern Drakensberg in spring is a nature-lover's paradise. Apart from the thousands of hectares of nature reserves and mountain wilderness areas, many of the local gardens are open for public viewing. A particularly fine example of these is the Iris Garden at Mount Dragon. This is reached 10 km from Underberg on the Swartberg Road (R617). It is situated on the left of the road heading away from Underberg. The garden's world-class selection of irises is on show between October and November and its commercial nursery offers visitors the chance to purchase selections of the splendid plants they see. XL Farm along the Bushman's Nek road 20 kms from Underberg (heading towards Bushman's Nek, the turn-off is on the left), is a charming example of the many local guest farms. It has a lovely country garden, and homely cottage accommodation is available to guests who can enjoy scenic walks, horse-riding, tennis and swimming.

A boulder-strewn stream bed near Giant's Castle.

The peaks and hill-slopes in Giant's Castle Game Reserve gleam white after a sudden snowfall.

UNDERBERG AND SURROUNDS

This bustling village, with neighbouring Himeville, forms the social and commercial hub of the southern Drakensberg region, an area famous for its wide recreational focus. It is crisscrossed with mountain rivers and dotted with dams and lakes of clear water that offer superb trout fishing. The splendid landscape is also ideal for climbing, hiking and horse-riding and its unspoilt characteristics and great scenic beauty make it one of South Africa's most gratifying aesthetic destinations – for photographers, painters, craftspeople and nature-lovers who revel in the great expanses of nature reserves and wilderness found here. This is the setting for the renowned National Giant's Cup Hiking Trail and vehicle access (four-wheel drive only) to Lesotho is through the historically famous Sani Pass near Himeville. The wide variety of local accommodation includes hotels, guest farms, cottages and Natal Parks Board resorts and camps.

The Mzimkulu River near Underberg.

Clasping the crag – a jackal buzzard surveys its world.

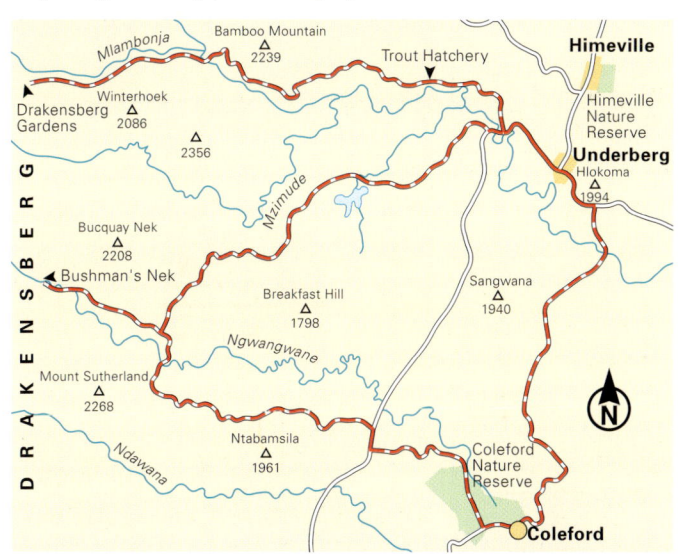

A REST AT COLEFORD

Comfort and simplicity are the keynotes of this scenic southern 'Berg reserve that offers an idyllically peaceful break close to the mountains. Amenities at Coleford's rest camp include seven chalets of varying size and six rustic cabins. The chalets have their own cooking facilities and the cabins have a communal kitchen and ablution block. Each unit has braai facilities.

Alternative accommodation in the reserve is found at Sunnyside Cottage, 5 km from the camp. Sunnyside sleeps seven, with all essentials provided, although visitors do their own cooking.

The Ngwangwane and Ndawana rivers provide superb sport during the trout season and, in addition, there are four dams that are regularly stocked with rainbow trout where you can try your luck.

Anglers try their luck from boat and jetty in the Himeville Nature Reserve.

The stone-and-thatch Bushman's Nek hut on the Giant's Cup Hiking Trail.

HIMEVILLE MUSEUM

Complementing an appreciation of the area's attractions and its background is this fascinating little country museum, originally built as a fort. It was completed in 1900 and was the last of its type to be built in KwaZulu-Natal, serving as the local jail until 1972, when it was converted into a museum. Exhibits include Zulu craft, an overview of the San people, an example of one of the prison cells, a schoolroom, and a military collection representing the Anglo-Boer War and World War I.

Various period pieces of the early pioneers are displayed in what was the warder's cottage. These exhibits include costumes and furnishings and various personal artefacts. There are interesting exhibits of wagons, carts and agricultural implements that offer an insight into the lifestyle of the settlers. The museum also has a Trout Room and a wildlife exhibit that features a range of indigenous fauna. (It is open between 10h00 and 12h00 on Wednesday, Friday, Saturday and Sunday.)

Meander through the Midlands to the grandeur of the Little Berg

Our route through the hilly country of the KwaZulu-Natal Midlands begins with a visit to the imposing Howick Falls, then meanders through well-watered farmlands to the grassy plains below the Little Berg – with sweeping Drakensberg views. We return through forests to the lovely Mgeni River gorge below Howick. Roughly half the route is on tar.

PIETERMARITZBURG
Howick Falls
Midlands Meander
Kamberg Nature Reserve
Umgeni Valley Nature Reserve
280 – 290 km

LEAVE PIETERMARITZBURG on the northbound N3 for Ladysmith and, after roughly 25 km, exit left for Howick and Midmar Dam. At the end of the off-ramp turn right for Howick. After 2 km, turn left at the T-junction for Howick and, 1,3 km later, cross the Mgeni River – immediately afterwards turn right into Falls View Drive, to reach a parking area at the Howick Falls observation point after a further 400 m (see this page).

Return along Falls View Drive and turn right into Howick's Main Street, noting your kms. After 300 m go left where the road curves, following the Mooi River sign. (The quaint old library building is on your right here.)

At the T-junction after roughly 7,7 km turn right onto the R103 for Lions River, Balgowan and Nottingham Road, noting your kms again. The R103 winds through attractive farming country with patches of forest, and follows the course of the railway line. After 3,5 km you enter the sprawling old settlement of Lions River, and 700 m later you cross the river from which it takes its name. (Both were named for the last lion to be shot in the area in 1856.)

After 6,8 km on the R103, turn right onto gravel for Caversham, noting your kms. This pretty country lane winds its way through beautiful surroundings along the Lions River to the site of Caversham Mill, after 5,6 km. The mill was built in 1855 and, for almost a century, its great, wooden wheel was turned by the river which, during floods in 1987, destroyed almost the entire structure.

Caversham to Rosetta

Continue northwards from the site of the mill, noting your kms as you cross the bridge just beyond it. After 1,8 km turn right at the inclined T-junction, and 2,8 km later turn left for Balgowan. After a further 6 km turn right onto the tarred R103, noting your kms.

After 300 m you pass the grounds of the well-known Michaelhouse school on your left, alongside Balgowan railway station. A little more than 10 km later you reach the town of Nottingham Road.

A few hundred metres later, turn left to remain on the R103 for the town centre, Rosetta and Sani Pass – and note your kms. The road takes you under the railway, and after 300 m you pass a turn-off on your left to Fort Nottingham. After a further 300 m you pass the attractive red-brick railway station on your right. After 600 m you pass, on your left, the road on which you will return later.

The R103 winds through rich farmland, then enters the town of Rosetta on the banks of the Mooi (pretty) River. After 7 km turn left in the town for Kamberg, noting your kms.

Rosetta to Kamberg

After 1,6 km you cross the Mooi River on a single-lane bridge, and soon afterwards the road surface changes to gravel. The main feature of this road is the magnificent panorama it soon offers of the high Drakensberg ahead of you. Just after 9,6 km turn right into a parking area for a view over farmlands towards the mountains – from the distinctive Giant's Castle on your left to the buttress of Cathkin Peak in the distance on your right.

After a further 11,7 km, you pass the small stone church of St Peter's, Kamberg, on your left. A turn-off 100 m later leads to an entrance to the church grounds – note your kms opposite this side-road. After roughly 3,5 km the scenery becomes dominated by the sandstone heights of the Little Berg, and you can see the round-topped Kamberg on your left. About 5 km later (8,5 km from the church turn-off), turn left at the foot of Mount Lebanon for 'Kamberg Natuurtuin', noting your kms.

Cross the Mooi River after 5,1 km and, almost immediately, pass a turn-off on your left to Loteni and Nottingham Road (your return route). Just over 1 km later you can see, on your right, the mushroom rock known as Thwalelinye jutting out from the side of Mount Erskine, and roughly 2 km later you enter Kamberg Nature Reserve.

A little over 1 km later you pass a picnic site at the start of the Mooi River Trail on your right – an ideal lunch spot with braai facilities, toilets and water. (Walking even part of the trail makes a superb introduction to the area, but first continue to the office to obtain a booklet on the trail. The road to the camp and office branches off to your left 500 m later.)

Kamberg to Karkloof

Retrace your route from Kamberg and, 3,3 km beyond the gate, turn right for Nottingham Road and Loteni, noting your kms. This road winds below the Little Berg, and after 2,3 km you pass through the Stillerus section of Kamberg Nature Reserve, with the mountain known as Gladstone's Nose on your right. About 8 km after noting your kms, pull over to the side of the road for a view back towards the profile of Gladstone's Nose.

About 5,2 km later, turn left at the T-junction at the foot of Spioenkop for Nottingham Road. The road surface changes to tar.

After 16,5 km along this road pull onto the shoulder for an excellent view back towards

Roaring white waters plunge over Howick Falls.

HOWICK AND THE MGENI RIVER
The Mgeni River plunges roughly 97 m over the Howick Falls into a spectacular gorge below. One may view the falls from the easily accessible observation point in the town of Howick, or from the Mgeni Valley Nature Reserve – on a scenic drive along the edge of the gorge, or from one of the footpaths that crisscross the reserve. Owned by the Wildlife Society of Southern Africa, the Mgeni Valley Nature Reserve has an education centre and offers accommodation, game-viewing, excellent bird-watching, and swimming in the Mgeni River. The town of Howick, named after Howick Hall in Northumberland, the birthplace of Earl Grey, the British Colonial Secretary, grew up around the old river-crossing above the falls. The Howick Museum, in its turn-of-the-century, red-brick house on Morling Street, preserves mementoes of the town's past.

The steep, sunlit plunge of Karkloof Falls.

the Drakensberg and the area through which you have been driving.

About 12 km later, turn right at the T-junction in Nottingham Road for the R103, following the Balgowan sign. After a further 1,1 km turn left at the T-junction onto the road for Mooi River and Pietermaritzburg. Just over 200 m later you pass a turn-off on your left to the hotel and station – after a further 500 m, stop on your left for a visit to the little wood-and-iron building of St John's Gowrie Church, built in 1885 on the farm Gowrie.

Continue on the Mooi River road from the church, and 7,3 km later turn onto the N3 for Pietermaritzburg; 6,7 km later exit left for

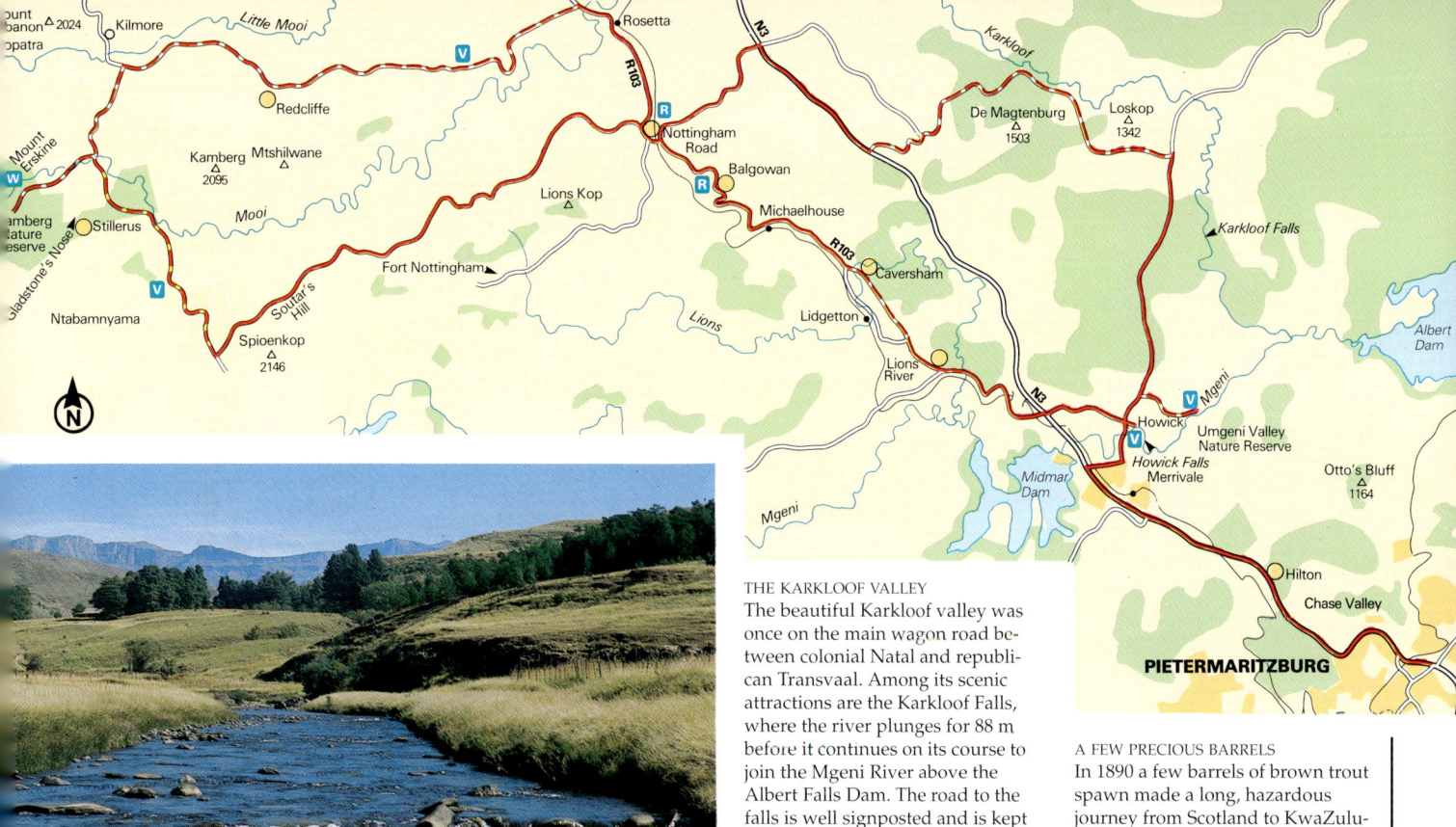

Kamberg Reserve – peaceful trout waters in a magnificent mountain setting.

View from the edge of the Mgeni River gorge towards the distant plains.

THE KARKLOOF VALLEY
The beautiful Karkloof valley was once on the main wagon road between colonial Natal and republican Transvaal. Among its scenic attractions are the Karkloof Falls, where the river plunges for 88 m before it continues on its course to join the Mgeni River above the Albert Falls Dam. The road to the falls is well signposted and is kept in good condition, with some 4 km being on gravel.

The Karkloof district has a renowned polo club, dominated during its early years by a family of Shaw cousins who proved their skills with sticks and balls that they carved from indigenous wood. One member of the family – Campbell Shaw – developed such an excellent rapport with his pony that he could ride and play without a bridle.

A FEW PRECIOUS BARRELS
In 1890 a few barrels of brown trout spawn made a long, hazardous journey from Scotland to KwaZulu-Natal. The eggs were hatched at Balgowan, from where the fingerlings were introduced to the Mooi River. Today, trout-fishing is one of the attractions of the province, and Kamberg Nature Reserve – which now has its own hatchery on the banks of the Mooi River – is renowned for the size of its trout. Natal Parks Board hatcheries provide stock for rivers throughout the Drakensberg and for farm dams.

Kamberg farmlands stretch towards the faraway Drakensberg.

Balgowan and Currys Post, and at the end of the off-ramp 500 m later turn left for Currys Post, noting your kms.

The road surface changes to gravel after 50 m. Just short of 4,8 km later, turn right at the T-junction for Currys Post and Howick. After 300 m turn left onto the D293, noting your kms. Soon, you enter some of the forests that typify this section of the drive. After 6,4 km you round a bend in the road at the summit of a delightful pass that overlooks the densely wooded Karkloof valley, below the attractive Karkloof mountains. At the foot of the pass you skirt *Loskop* ('fanciful' or 'loose hill') and drive across the valley floor.

Continue straight through the crossroads where right leads to 'Currys Post/Howick' and, after 17,3 km on the D293, turn right at the T-junction for Howick, noting your kms.

After 5 km you pass a turn-off on your left to the magnificent Karkloof Falls. Some 2,2 km beyond the turn-off to the falls, you glimpse Albert Falls Dam on your left. After just over 12,6 km on tar, turn left into the Umgeni Valley Nature Reserve and follow the gravel road that leads past Cascade Falls and Shelter Falls, then along the edge of the cliff of the Mgeni River gorge, giving you magnificent late-afternoon views of Howick Falls, dense indigenous vegetation and the opening of the valley with Albert Falls Dam in the distance. (The scenic road stretches 6,5 km from the entrance, but turn around after 4,7 km if the road is poor.)

Return to the tarred road, and turn left for Howick. Once in Howick, follow the signs onto the N3 to Pietermaritzburg.

AA Office Shop G23, Brasfort House 191 Commercial Road, Pietermaritzburg 3201 Tel (0331) 42 0571
Pietermaritzburg Publicity Association cr Commercial Road and Longmarket Street Pietermaritzburg 3201 Tel (0331) 45 1348
Natal Parks Board PO Box 662, Pietermaritzburg 3200 Tel (0331) 47 1971
Howick Publicity Association PO Box 881 Howick 3290 Tel (0332) 30 5305

Memories of the 1890s live on at the old Pavilion and bandstand alongside the Oval at Alexandra Park.

Red-brick splendour of a colonial capital

PIETERMARITZBURG, set amid forested hills and the rolling countryside of the KwaZulu-Natal Midlands, is one of the best-preserved Victorian cities in the world. Started as a well laid-out Voortrekker town in the early 19th century, then expanded during British colonial rule into a grand seat for a new government, Pietermaritzburg retains an old-world flavour alongside its modern development.

The Voortrekkers had made their arduous crossing of the Drakensberg escarpment by ox-wagon in 1837 to establish a new republic. They encountered opposition from the Nguni-speaking inhabitants of this lush land, who a decade earlier had been consolidated into the Zulu nation by the warrior-king Shaka. After bitter fighting, the Boers defeated the Zulus in the Battle of Blood River in 1838, and settled down to establishing their Republic of Natalia. They named their new capital on the banks of the Msunduze River after their leaders Pieter Retief and Gerrit Maritz.

A few years later, in 1843, the British garrisoned the town, establishing their headquarters at Fort Napier, which stands today in the grounds of a hospital. The town duly became the seat of government for the Colony of Natal, and after Union in 1910 it remained the capital of Natal Province. Its continued status – as capital of the present KwaZulu-Natal Province – is undecided.

Links with the sedate past
The historic heart of Pietermaritzburg is dominated by the elaborately decorated, red-brick *City Hall* (1) with its tall clock tower, on the corner of Commercial Road and Church Street. The original building was built in 1895 on the site of the old Voortrekker *Raadsaal* (parliament), then rebuilt in 1901 after being destroyed by fire. Next door to the City Hall is the station built for the Borough Police in 1884.

Across Commercial Road stands the historic *Old Supreme Court* (2), completed in 1871. It is the home of the *Tatham Art Gallery*, which exhibits fine 19th and early 20th century French and English paintings, as well as china, glassware, and clocks. Around the corner in Longmarket Street are the twin edifices of the *Legislative Assembly Building* (3) (inaugurated in 1889) and the *Legislative Council Building* (4) (opened in 1900 after government was passed to a two-house parliament). The dignified interiors of both the Assembly and the Council buildings may be visited by arrangement.

The Carbineer Gardens alongside the City Hall and the gardens of the Old Supreme Court contain a number of interesting statues and memorials commemorating aspects of the city's past.

An interesting collection of Voortrekker relics is to be found in the *Voortrekker Museum* (5) in Church Street, not far from the City Hall. The museum is housed in the original Church of the Vow – built by the Voortrekkers in 1841 in accordance with their vow to build a place of worship to commemorate their victory at Blood River. Welverdient, the historic home of the commander at Blood River, Andries Pretorius, is also part of the museum. Statues of Pieter Retief and Gerrit Maritz stand in front of the new Church of the Vow, built alongside the old.

Another Voortrekker home, that of Petrus Gerhardus Pretorius in Boom Street, has been converted into a museum, known as the *Oldest House in Town* (6). Built in 1846 of local shale, it is the only surviving double-storey Voortrekker house in the city, and still has its original yellowwood floors and ceilings beneath thatch.

The graves of many early inhabitants are at the *Voortrekker Cemetery* (7) in Commercial Road, and parts of the Voortrekker wagon road to the coast survive on the outskirts of the city.

The Oldest House in Town, 1846.

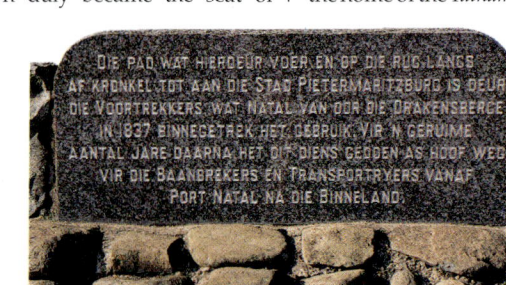

Above: *Plaque at World's View.* **Right:** *The Old Provincial Council Building.*

The City Hall's red-brick splendour.

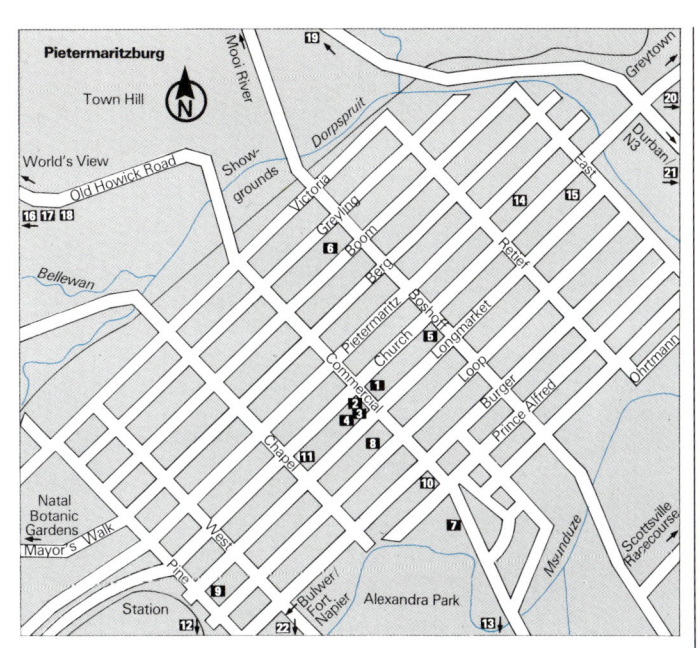

The *Natal Museum* **(8)** in Loop Street, one of five national museums in the country, offers an introduction to the history of the province in its Hall of History, and also contains superb exhibits on mammals, birds, reptiles, fish, insects, geology, palaeontology and ethnology.

A fascinating glimpse into an elegant Victorian lifestyle is offered by the *Macrorie House Museum* **(9)** on the corner of Loop and Pine streets. Built in 1862, it was the home of Bishop William Macrorie, who was sent to Pietermaritzburg after Bishop John Colenso fell out with the church over ecclesiastical issues (and with the colonial government over politics). The charming house museum contains among its exhibits Bishop Macrorie's private chapel.

The city has a number of fine old churches, including *St Mary's* **(10)** on the corner of Commercial Road and Burger Street, which is a replica of Bishop Colenso's original church for Africans; *St Peter's* **(11)** in Church Street (Colenso's new 'cathedral' after his rift with the church); *St George's Garrison Church* **(12)** of 1897, near the historic railway station and Fort Napier; and the little *Italian Church* **(13)** in Golf Road, Mkondeni, built by Italian prisoners during World War II.

The arrival of Indians in Natal from 1860 introduced an Eastern influence on religious life in the province, and in Pietermaritzburg the two main creeds, Islam and Hinduism, are well represented. Visitors are permitted at the largest mosque in the city, the *Islamia Mosque* **(14)** in Church Street. The main Hindu temple, the *Sri Siva Soobramoniar and Marriamen Temple* **(15)** in Longmarket Street, scene of the annual fire-walking ceremony on Good Friday, is also open to the public.

Parks and nature trails

Pietermaritzburg's moist climate and rich soil have seen to it that the city maintains a lush, garden quality, and beautiful parks abound. On the banks of the Msunduze River, start of the annual Duzi Canoe Marathon to Durban, is the 65,6 ha Alexandra Park. The park has lovely gardens, including a rockery known as the Mayor's Garden, sportsfields, a swimming pool, and a tearoom alongside an ornate bandstand (built in 1892) and the chinoiserie pavilion (dating from 1897).

The tearoom in the Botanic Gardens, in its pretty setting alongside a lake, is another favoured retreat from the city bustle. Founded in 1870, the gardens are famed for their lovely avenue of plane trees, and the beautiful, tall trees in the Exotic Garden. In 1970 the Indigenous Garden was started to propagate the many varieties of local plants, and a fine collection of cycads, aloes and trees has been established.

Wylie Park **(16)** in Taunton Road, Wembley, also specializes in indigenous plants, and is particularly attractive when the azaleas (the floral emblem of Pietermaritzburg) are in bloom in spring. *Queen Elizabeth Nature Reserve* **(17)** on the city outskirts (see pages 142 – 3) is the headquarters of the Natal Parks Board, and here visitors can see zebra, blesbok, impala, duiker, bushbuck and rhino amid a dense vegetation. Birdwatching is also rewarding in the reserve, and there are several nature walks and picnic sites in the grounds. The Parks Board shows wildlife films in its theatre from time to time.

For those interested in walking or hiking, there are a number of Green Belt Trails leading through the World's View area (see pages 142 – 3), and the Department of Forestry offers a forest trail, and a shorter trail for the handicapped, at *Cedara State Forest* **(18)** (a permit from the forester is needed). There is a picnic site alongside a small dam in the forest.

Watersport and fishing

Inland watersport enthusiasts have a number of nearby venues to choose from. The Parks Board administers popular boating, fishing and recreational resorts at *Midmar Dam* **(19)**, which also has a fascinating historical village; and at *Albert Falls Dam* **(20)** on the Greytown road. Another attractive fishing and boating venue is *Nagle Dam* **(21)** at the head of the Valley of a Thousand Hills (see pages 142 – 3); and *Henley Dam* **(22)** off the Bulwer road offers fishing and picnicking.

Venturing further afield

Other out-of-town venues popular with people setting out from Pietermaritzburg include the magnificent Howick Falls and Karkloof Falls (see pages 138 – 9); the drive to Otto's Bluff in July/August when the aloes are in bloom; the Natal Lion and Game Park and adjacent Zoological Gardens; and Natal Table Mountain at the head of the Valley of a Thousand Hills.

A number of potters, weavers and other craftspeople in the Midlands also open their studios and workshops to visitors, providing an excuse for lovely drives into the country.

The Pietermaritzburg Publicity Association is in Sanlam Chambers, Church Street; tel (0331) 45 1348. Excellent brochures on the city are available here, including several featuring self-guided trails through the historic centre of the city – notable for its magnificent old commercial buildings, charming lanes, stock exchanges, hitching rails and other memories of the 19th century.

Pietermaritzburg's railway station – a period piece in red brick and cast iron.

Valley of a Thousand Hills and the old Voortrekker wagon road

The breathtaking Kloof Falls set the tone for this drive, which then follows the high road along the edge of the spectacular Valley of a Thousand Hills. We visit the historic village on the shores of Midmar Dam, then meander back through the area traversed by the old Voortrekker route to the coast. All but a few kilometres of the drive is on tar.

Durban
Krantzkloof
Valley of a
Thousand Hills
Midmar
Pietermaritzburg
Nshongweni Dam
260 – 280 km

Leave Durban on the N3 for Pietermaritzburg. Shortly before the start of the Mariannhill toll road, exit at Interchange 17 for the M13 for Pinetown and Pietermaritzburg. Roughly 25 km from Durban, exit left for 'Kloof Station/Old Main Rd'. At the end of the off-ramp, turn right, noting your kms.

After 400 m, turn right at the T-junction, pass Kloof Station on your left and, after a further 200 m, turn left to cross a bridge over the railway line. Immediately afterwards, turn left and pass the station building again on your left. At the stop street 1,1 km from the M13, turn left, then immediately right into Kloof Falls Road.

This attractive, tree-lined road (which becomes Bridle Road) winds down into the valley and, after roughly 3 km, you enter the Krantzkloof Nature Reserve. Note your kms soon afterwards as you pass a gravel road on your right that leads into a picnic area alongside the river.

You cross the river, then begin to climb steeply. After 750 m turn right onto a gravel road that leads to a parking area 100 m later. A walk of a further 100 m brings you close to the edge of the cliff, with magnificent views of Kloof Falls and the rugged clifftop across the forested gorge. (There is no barrier at the edge.)

Return to Bridle Road and turn right. After 100–200 m turn right onto another gravel road. At the end of it, a short walk to the left gives you an excellent view over the gorge where it opens up towards a broad sweep of the Mgeni River. (Again there is no barrier.) There are several self-guided trails in the reserve, ranging in length from 30 minutes to over four hours.

Krantzkloof to Monteseel

About 2 km beyond the second viewsite, turn left out of Bridle Road at the T-junction into Link Road, noting your kms. After 1,5 km, turn left into Inanda Road for Hillcrest and, after a further 6,8 km, turn right onto the Old Main Road (R103) for Botha's Hill and Drummond, noting your kms again.

You enter Botha's Hill and soon afterwards a view into the Valley of a Thousand Hills opens up on your right (see opposite). After 5 km turn right for the Rob Roy Hotel (which serves teas and offers excellent views over the Valley of a Thousand Hills). If you continue along this sideroad for 700 m beyond the hotel, there is a place to stop on your left for an equally attractive view into the valley.

Return to the Old Main Road and turn right. After 1 km turn right into *Phezulu* (meaning 'high up' in Zulu) – an African craft centre and traditional village perched on the edge of the valley. There is a small entry fee for the village, which covers a demonstration of Zulu dancing and a guided tour.

As you leave Phezulu, turn right onto the Old Main Road, noting your kms. The road winds along a line of hills, wandering first to one side of the crest, then to the other side, giving superb views into the valleys on both sides. After 4,8 km there is a large viewsite parking area on your right next to another Zulu village and a curio shop. Note your kms here.

Some 3,5 km later, turn right for Monteseel. At the T-junction after 100 m turn left into Albert Street, then turn right immediately onto gravel (Magdalene Avenue). Where the road forks after 150 m, go left. Park after another 700 m and walk to the edge of this spur of land for a magnificent view. In the wild kloof on your right there are three examples of the extremely rare cycad *Encephalartos natalensis*. The oldest of the three is believed to have rootstock older than 1 000 years and has been declared a national monument.

Monteseel to Midmar

Retrace your route to the Old Main Road, noting your kms as you turn right. After 5,2 km turn right for Cato Ridge and, 6,4 km later, turn right for the N3 to Pietermaritzburg.

After 11 km on the N3 there is a good view to your right of Natal Table Mountain, dominating the head of the Valley of a Thousand Hills. The countryside changes slowly as you venture further inland, with acacia trees becoming a feature of the landscape. Roughly 22 km after joining the N3, you crest a hill and look down on Pietermaritzburg and its surrounding hills.

Note your kms as you pass the exit for Pietermaritzburg, and bypass the city. After 3,3 km you cross the Msunduze River, venue for the annual Duzi Canoe Marathon and, 28 km after the city turn-off, exit at Interchange 103 for Howick and Midmar Dam.

At the end of the off-ramp turn left for Midmar Dam, noting your kms, then curve right for the R103 to Midmar. There is an excellent view of the dam on your left, before the road dips behind the dam wall and crosses a bridge over the Mgeni River. After 2,7 km, pass a turn-off on your left to Midmar Historical Village and, after a further 400 m, turn left into Midmar Resort, to which an entrance fee is charged. (See above. The resort has a restaurant and cafeteria and there are attractive picnic and braai sites along the water's edge.)

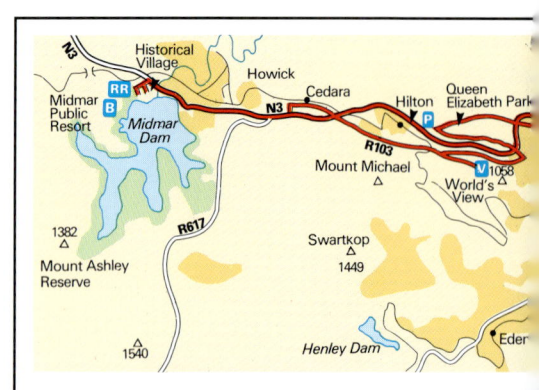

Midmar Dam – a popular venue for watersports.

MIDMAR DAM AND VILLAGE

The 2 831 ha Midmar Public Resort, set in the Mgeni valley among the Inhluzana hills, offers sports (particularly watersports), camping, caravanning, game-viewing – from vehicle or boat tours – and a rich variety of birds. The historical village on the banks of the dam contains several original and reconstructed old buildings, and fine collections of old animal-drawn and motorised vehicles.

A fine vista over the Valley of a Thousand Hills.

Over weekends you can enter the fascinating Midmar Historical Village through a pedestrian gate from the resort. Otherwise, return along the R103 and turn right into the village. (An additional entrance fee may be charged.)

Midmar to Nshongweni Dam

Return to the N3 for Pietermaritzburg. After 7 km on the N3, exit left at Interchange 96 for Mount Michael and Cedara. At the end of the off-ramp, turn right onto the Old Howick Road (R103) for Mount Michael. After 6,1 km on the Old Howick Road turn right for

SOUTHERN KWAZULU-NATAL

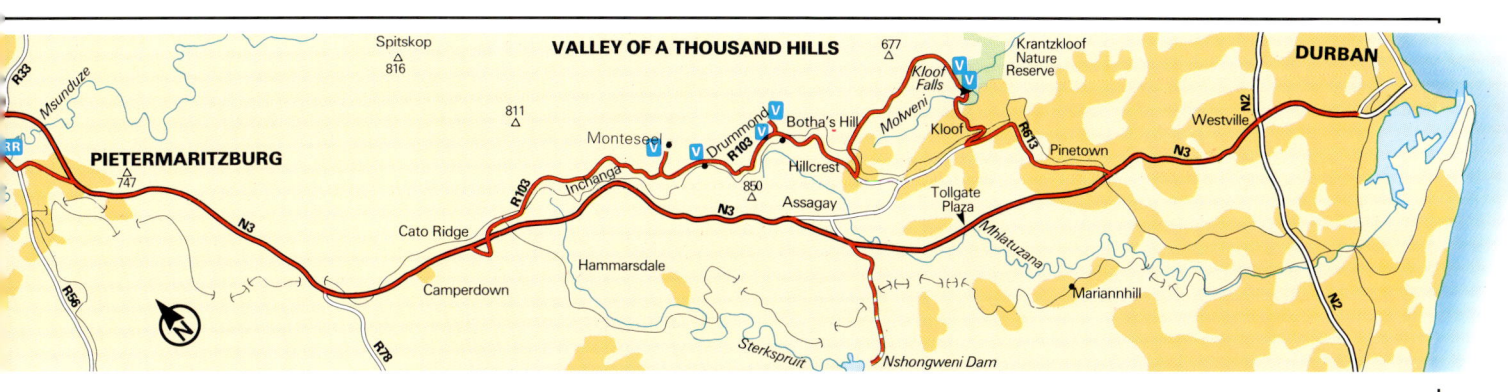

VALLEY OF A THOUSAND HILLS

For the last 64 km of its course, the *Mgeni* River (river of the acacia trees) winds its way through the spectacular, deeply eroded Valley of a Thousand Hills. The scenery in the valley varies from dense bush to farmland and cultivated areas where huts cling to the steep slopes.

The 959 m Natal Table Mountain towers above the scenic Nagle Dam at the head of the valley. The mountain can be climbed along a relatively easy path from the western side. The dam, with its nature reserve and picnic sites, is reached from the east. Both are popular venues for weekend outings from Pietermaritzburg.

Young girls offer a display of Zulu beadwork to passing travellers in the Valley of a Thousand Hills.

Krantzkloof, with its sheer cliff sides and lush bush, is home to many birds.

The rugged, flat-topped Nshongweni hill rises above the dam of the same name.

THE OLD VOORTREKKER WAGON ROAD

North-west of Pietermaritzburg a spur of the *Boesmansrand* (Bushman's ridge) forms a plateau that well deserves its name of World's View. From here you can see the city nestling below in the Msunduze valley, and the extensive surrounding hills. Below the viewsite lies an old wagon road. The Voortrekkers, who crossed the Drakensberg by ox-wagon in 1837, used this road to reach the coast at Port Natal (later Durban). The road has been declared a national monument, and is part of the Green Belt Trails system of Pietermaritzburg.

THE SEEDS OF A THRIVING INDUSTRY

An Englishman of Dutch descent, John Vanderplank, arrived in KwaZulu-Natal early last century with seeds of the Tasmanian black wattle shrub among his belongings. On one of his farms – named Camperdown after a battle in which the British defeated the Dutch – he planted these shrubs as a low windbreak, but to his surprise the seeds grew into large trees. Vanderplank did not benefit from the industry that grew from his accidental discovery – only after his death, wattle bark was found to contain commercially valuable tannic acid.

Boesmansrand and World's View. A further 2 km brings you to the parking area at the viewsite and picnic spot overlooking the old Voortrekker wagon road and the magnificent countryside surrounding Pietermaritzburg (see above and pages 140 – 1).

Rejoin the R103, noting your kms as you turn right. After 2,3 km turn left for Montrose/Queen Elizabeth Park, and after a further 600 m turn left into Duncan McKenzie Drive; 800 m later you enter the park.

You pass the Natal Parks Board head office, then wind through luxuriant vegetation where you may spot buck along the roadside. Go left beyond the park entrance, and, at another fork, 500 m later, go right.

Note your kms again as you leave the park and turn left into Duncan McKenzie Drive. Follow this road as it changes name a few times before merging with the N3 for Durban.

After roughly 45 km on the N3, exit at the Summerveld Interchange (number 32), turn right at the end of the off-ramp and note your kms. Just 1,3 km further, turn left, then, roughly 600 m after that, turn right onto gravel. After a further 1,5 km, go right where a road leads left. Within the next 3 km you can see the dam, set in a richly wooded gorge on your right, with Nshongweni hill rising from it. After almost 6 km on gravel you reach the control gate and the road becomes tarred.

The road leads for 2,7 km to the dam wall and picnic area. Return to the N3 for Durban.

AA Office AA House, 33 St George's Street Durban 4001 Tel (031) 301 0341
AA Office Shop G23, Brasfort House 191 Commercial Road, Pietermaritzburg 3201 Tel (0331) 42 0571
Natal Parks Board Box 662, Pietermaritzburg 3200 Tel (0331) 47 1961
Pietermaritzburg Publicity Association cr Commercial Road and Longmarket Street Pietermaritzburg 3201 Tel (0331) 45 1348

ZULU TRADITIONS

Clustered rondavels with painted mud walls and thatched roofs grace the slopes of the serene hills of KwaZulu-Natal.

Brightly coloured beadwork is the only dress worn by this little girl.

The Zulu: a proud people whose name was once synonymous with war

THE RICH LANDSCAPES of KwaZulu-Natal, a region blessed with some of the world's most splendid scenery, have been given an additional, distinctive character by the colourful traditions of the Zulu. Almost every hillside is dotted with their beehive huts, the valleys are hazy with the scented smoke from their fires, and throughout the region the visitor can see elaborate traditional costumes being worn by a people proud of their cultural heritage.

The Zulu are thought to be descended from several successive waves of settlers who, centuries ago, migrated southwards from central East Africa. The area the migrants penetrated was lush and fertile, with rolling hills as far as the eye could see, and there were few other groups to challenge their occupation of this land. For many generations their descendants have hunted the wild game that thrived here, cultivated an assortment of traditional crops, reared the cattle they had brought with them from the north – and have gradually evolved a rich store of customs and cultural traditions.

The Zulu owe their identity very largely to two of their historic leaders. The early settlers did not call themselves Zulu, but their descendants derived the name, which means 'heaven', from the first of these two leaders. Little else is known about this chief who gave his name to his people, but he is thought to have established his capital in the valley of the Mkhumbane River. The second of these two particularly influential chiefs was Shaka – the warrior leader who came to power early in the 19th century and who introduced successful new military tactics that turned the Zulu into an all but invincible military force. Initially there had probably been little to distinguish this community from many other groups that were closely related, but Shaka's military victories gave the Zulu a strong and lasting identity.

Traditional roles in a rural economy

It has often been claimed that women constitute the economic backbone of the Zulu community. The women have traditionally been responsible for all cultivation of the soil, have fetched the water, prepared the food and cared for the children. The men, meanwhile, have been hunters and warriors, and the boys have traditionally been charged with looking after the cattle.

Cattle have always played an extremely important part in the Zulu way of life. Cow's milk, most often in a curdled form, makes up a large part of the Zulu diet, and hides have been used for making clothes and all-purpose thongs. Cattle are wealth and the measure of a man's social worth. They are traditionally used for the payment

A Zulu woman decorates her upswept hair with elaborate bands of beadwork.

of *lobola* (the compensation paid by a bridegroom to his father-in-law for acquiring his bride) and they have also been used as sacrificial gifts to the spirits. The cattle enclosure has traditionally been regarded as a sacred place, and no women other than daughters of the house are permitted to enter it.

The everyday clothes worn by the Zulu in the early days were extremely simple, consisting mostly of short leather aprons. Skins and feathers were worn for ceremonial occasions, but the warriors on parade adorned themselves more elaborately still, adding furs and feathers. Vestiges of the awe-inspiring dress and ornamentation worn by the warriors can still be seen on ceremonial occasions. In the late 18th and 19th centuries the world of the Zulu was a violent one, characterized by almost constant warfare – against neighbouring clans, against Afrikaner Voortrekkers and against the regiments of the British Empire. The hide shields that the men now carry on ceremonial occasions are derived from that era – when each Zulu regiment was identified by the colour and design of its shield.

A colourful addition to Zulu dress, and to Zulu customs generally, came with the advent of imported beads. These first made their appearance when the communities living along the coast began to trade with sailors journeying to and from the East – bartering gold and ivory for brightly coloured beads and other European goods. As with other indigenous peoples, the Zulu used these beads as personal ornaments, and a highly elaborate beadlore has evolved during the course of many generations.

The meaning of beads

Every stage in the life of the individual is marked by certain traditional styles of dress, including many kinds of ornate beadwork. Beads are also used to send messages. Zulu women are expert in weaving the beads into intricate patterns that spell out love letters *(izincwadi)* for their menfolk. Each colour of bead has a different significance. A red bead represents blood, and denotes tears and longing. A white bead represents bone and signifies love and purity. A blue bead, called *ijuba* (dove), symbolizes faithfulness. Other colours indicate such things as jealousy, wealth, or doubt.

The beads are sewn together in necklaces in such a way that the recipient knows exactly what the message is, whether it is loving ('My heart is full of love and I want to wear the leather skirt of marriage') or admonishing ('You are telling lies about your possessions'). The recipient may then wear the message for all to see, or, as in the latter case, might prefer to hide it in shame.

This poetry in the language of beads is matched by a notably poetic way of speaking. The Zulu have a musical language, rich in metaphor and full of subtle meaning – the substance of remarks being very often implied rather than stated explicitly.

Examples of local Zulu handicrafts.

Echoes of an animated universe

As with many indigenous African peoples, a pre-industrial lifestyle is a relatively recent memory for the Zulu – a fact that has resulted in a wealth of spiritual folklore. Many Zulu beliefs date back to an early period when there were few religious rites. The people who first migrated into this region saw themselves as presided over by *Nkulunkulu* (great, great one), and they were acutely aware in everyday life of the presence of their ancestral spirits. Every pool, every rocky outcrop, every thunderstorm or change in the weather was attributed to a supernatural being or an ancestral spirit.

The early beliefs of the Zulu gave rise to two classes of what Europeans have mistakenly called witchdoctors. In fact, the Zulu have the *nyanga* (doctor) and the *sangoma* (diviner). The nyanga treats the sick, whereas the sangoma copes with such problems as unrequited love and protection from ill-willed spirits. The Zulu traditionally believe that a man possesses, besides his own physical being, the spiritual qualities of breath or air, and a shadow or reflection.

The prestige of a man is thought of as being intimately linked to the strength and length of his shadow. A chief has a very strong shadow, and much of his personal power is believed to derive from this. The shadow and the breath, together constituting what might be called the spirit, depart from people when they die. The socially significant dead, however, become ancestral spirits, and they continue to govern the fate of the living from their graves.

A traditional beehive-shaped hut with its distinctive thatched roof.

Colourfully dressed, a Zulu woman grinds maize on a well-worn stone.

Subtropical beaches lead north to 'the one that startles'

The sugar country north of Durban presents an ocean of green edged with a golden subtropical coast. On our way to the mighty Tugela we stop off at some of the unspoilt beaches and romantic coves that dot the shore – then we make a sortie past rugged hills into the isolated Mvoti valley. All but a few kilometres of the route is on tar.

Durban
Umdloti Beach
Shaka's Rock
Harold Johnson
Nature Reserve
Stanger
Umhlanga
310 – 330 km

LEAVE DURBAN ON THE M4 for the North Coast. Pass the Blue Lagoon on your right and then cross a long bridge over the Mgeni River. At the end of the bridge exit left for Prospect Hall and Riverside (M21). Some 100 m later, turn left at the fork for the M21. After a further 200 m turn left at the T-junction into Riverside Road for the Umgeni River Bird Park, which is on your right 2 km later (entrance fee).

Bird Park to Sheffield Beach

Retrace your route to the northbound M4, noting your kms as you rejoin the M4. Just short of 10 km you pass the resort of Umhlanga on your right. The Natal Sharks Board, which conducts research into shark behaviour and is the only organisation of its type in the world, has its headquarters here. Beyond Umhlanga, the road is flanked by dense coastal forest and, some 13 km after noting your kms, you can see Umhlanga Lagoon on your right.

The lush green of rolling sugar cane soon becomes a feature of the landscape; 17 km after noting your kms (at the interchange with the M27), take the exit for Umdloti, noting your kms again. The road winds through sugar cane down to the beach. Just short of 2 km turn left onto North Beach Road, and after a further 500 m park anywhere on your right for a walk on the beach, with its interesting rocks and natural tidal pool.

Retrace your route inland and, at the interchange with the M4, exit for this northbound coast road for Stanger. Note your kms as you cross the Mdloti River on the outskirts of La Mercy. The road then hugs the coast for a while, giving you glimpses of stretches of unspoilt beach. Near Port Zimbali the road veers inland and, about 18 km from the Mdloti River, intersects with the road linking Ballito with the old national road (R102).

Turn left here, almost immediately passing over the new N2. Turn right onto the N2 and, after just under 2 km, exit for Shaka's Rock, turning right at the end of the off-ramp.

About 2,8 km later, turn right at the T-junction into Ocean Drive; 600 m later, turn left into Rock Lane, and turn left again immediately into a parking area.

A short walk down Rock Lane brings you to a rocky outcrop believed by some to have been a lookout of the Zulu king Shaka and, by others, to have been a place where he executed criminals by having them flung into the sea. There is a good view to your left over Shaka's Rock and Salt Rock beaches, while Thompson's Bay on your right offers a lovely short walk to the Hole-in-the-Wall on its far side beyond the tidal pool (allow 40 minutes).

Turn right from Rock Lane into Ocean Drive, noting your kms. The road takes you through the resorts of Shaka's Rock and Salt Rock (where a number of places provide teas and lunches). After 3 km turn right into Hugh Dent Drive, noting your kms again. This road merges with Sheffield Drive, which winds through the resort of Sheffield Beach. The road attains some height, giving you good views over the sea and beach. After 2 km turn left into Colwyn Drive, go left again 2,1 km later where a road joins from your right, and, 400 m after this, turn right for Umhlali. After a few hundred metres you cross the N2 toll-road – turn right to join its northbound lanes at Interchange 215, for Stanger, and note your kms at the turn.

Sheffield Beach to the Tugela

From here the N2 passes through KwaZulu-Natal's first canefields, which stretch across the coastal hills. Stanger, an important centre for the sugar industry (see opposite), lies on the hillside to your left after about 12 km.

After roughly 36 km on the N2/R102, turn right onto gravel for Fort Pearson, noting your kms again. After 700 m you pass a turn-off on your left to the Harold Johnson Nature Reserve (to which we return later). Soon afterwards there are good views over the mouth of the Tugela River, with the resort of Tugela Mouth on its north bank; 2,6 km from the N2 you pass a turn-off on your right to a number of war graves from the Anglo-Zulu War of 1879. Immediately afterwards turn left for Fort Pearson and 'Naval and military graves'. Park 800 m later at the end of this sideroad for a visit to the site of Fort Pearson, with its magnificent river view (see opposite).

Retrace your route for the 800 m along this sideroad and turn left. Cross over the N2 and, 1,5 km later, turn left onto a track that leads, after 500 m, to the Ultimatum Tree. From here retrace your route for the roughly 4 km to the nature reserve turn-off and turn right. After passing through the gate, you reach a number of shaded braai and picnic sites overlooking the Tugela – an ideal lunch spot (water, toilets).

Tugela to Mvoti valley

Retrace your route to the tarred R102 and turn left; 7,4 km later turn left for Zinkwazi Beach, noting your kms. Cross over the N2 after 4 km and, 3 km later, there is a fine view of a golden beach stretching northwards. Continue on this road (Nkwazi Drive), then, 8,1 km from the R102, turn left onto gravel for the parking area at the beach and lagoon.

Return to the R102 and turn left towards Stanger and Durban, noting your kms. At the interchange 9,6 km later, exit left for the R74 for Stanger and Greytown and, at the end of the off-ramp, turn right onto the R74, noting your kms. The R74 climbs as you pass Stanger on your left. You can see a domed mosque and an impressive white-and-gold Hindu temple next to the road.

After 17,5 km on the R74, turn left for Glendale, noting your kms. The road you are on winds down through ever-changing scenery into the beautiful Mvoti valley, its rocky-crested hills contrasting with the cultivated fields. After 9,5 km you reach Glendale Sugar Mill, which has been operating here since 1881. Tours of the distillery and attractive cellars may be undertaken by prior arrangement. At the mill, the road crosses a bridge over the Mvoti and the tar ends some 700 m later. A road to the left here leads over

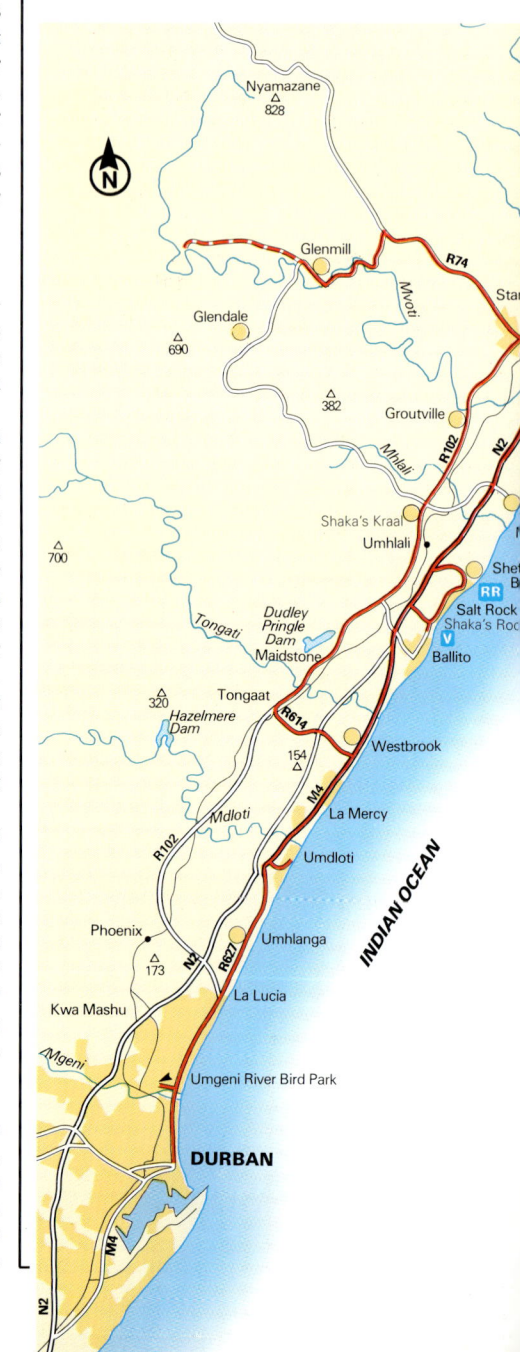

Glendale Heights with beautiful views over the valley. Some 2,3 km beyond this turn-off, the road forks, with the right-hand branch passing extensive irrigated smallholdings. Go left at the fork and continue for a further 3,3 km as far as the single-lane bridge over a tributary of the Mvoti – for views over the valley landscape with its rows of hills stretching inland. On the far side of the bridge a road on your right offers a good turning point.

Mvoti valley to Umhlanga

Return from the valley to the R74, which offers sea views as you descend past Stanger. After 15 km, turn right onto the R102 for Shaka's Kraal. The R102 passes through the settlements of Groutville (where Albert Luthuli, former president of the African National Congress and 1961 winner of the Nobel Peace Prize, was elected chief in 1935) and Shaka's Kraal. After 25 km you pass a turn-off on your right to Esenembi and a road left to Compensation Station – the first sugar mill in South Africa operated near here. A few kilometres later you enter Tongaat, headquarters of a large sugar corporation. After 35 km on the R102, turn left onto the R614 (M43) for Tongaat Beach and Durban and, 6,3 km later, turn right onto the coast road (M4). Remain on the coast road for Umhlanga, and after 17,5 km exit left for 'Umhlanga Rocks'. At the end of the off-ramp turn left, and 200 m later follow the road as it swings left; 500 m later turn left at the stop street into Lagoon Drive.

At the end of Lagoon Drive you enter the Umhlanga Lagoon Nature Reserve (open sunrise to sunset) where you can enjoy a good afternoon walk. There is an equally pleasant walk along the beach promenade.

AA Office AA House, 33 St George's Street
Durban 4001 Tel (031) 301 0341
Durban Unlimited 160 Pine Street
Durban 4001 Tel (031) 304 4934
Umhlanga Publicity Association P/Bag X4
Umhlanga Rocks 4320 Tel (031) 561 4257

The Mvoti River takes a lazy course to the sea.

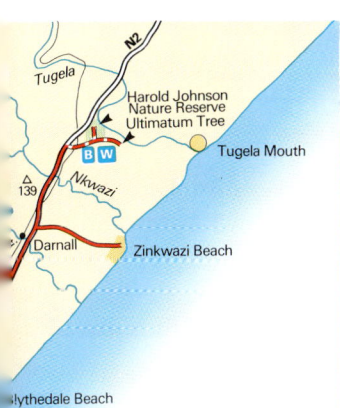

Aloes bloom high above the Tugela River at the site of the historic Fort Pearson.

THE ULTIMATUM TREE
On 11 December 1878 representatives of the British Governor, Sir Bartle Frere, and the Zulu king, Cetshwayo, met under a large fig tree on the banks of the Tugela River alongside a ferry crossing. The British presented their ultimatum to the Zulu delegation – a list of demands that left no option other than war.

When Cetshwayo failed to meet the ultimatum date, the British marched into Zululand on 12 January 1879 from Fort Pearson – the start of the Anglo-Zulu War. Six months later, the British defeated Cetshwayo's army at Ulundi.

NAMES THAT TELL A TALE
Many of the names of towns in this region are corruptions of the original Zulu names for the rivers of the area. We cross, among others, the *Tongati* and *Mhlali* rivers, both named after local varieties of the monkey orange tree. The *Mdloti* is named after a type of wild tobacco that grows on its banks. *Mhlanga* means 'reedy river', and *Nkwazi* is the Zulu name for the white-headed fish eagle. The Tugela (*Thukela*) is named 'the one that startles', possibly because of the awe the river inspires when it is in spate.

KEEPING THE COUNTRY SWEET
Edmund Morewood built a crude sugar mill on his farm, Compensation, in 1851 and this was the start of a lucrative industry that has shaped the landscape, population and fortunes of KwaZulu-Natal.

Vast seas of green canefields cover the coastal area north of Durban, and during the cutting season one often sees the bright orange of cane fires – deliberate burning to facilitate the milling process. The cane provides not only sugar, but a number of by-products such as fuel, paper, wallboard and chemicals.

In the 1860s, large numbers of Indian contract workers were brought to colonial Natal to harvest the sweet crops, and many of their descendants still live in the predominantly Indian communities of Stanger and Tongaat.

Mohandas Gandhi, the Indian lawyer and pacifist whose name became synonymous with passive resistance, worked for 21 years among the early Indian immigrants and founded a communal farm at Phoenix settlement.

Left: *Palms at La Mercy.* **Above:** *Sugar cane covers rolling hills.* **Right:** *Umdloti's beachfront.*

PLACES OF INTEREST IN AND AROUND DURBAN

The start of a perfect day – and early-morning strollers enjoy an uncrowded South Beach.

East meets West in a subtropical holiday city

DURBAN – A GREAT natural harbour that served in centuries past as a temporary refuge to successive bands of refugees, adventurers and traders – has grown into one of South Africa's best-known and most popular coastal resorts. Stretches of safe, sandy beach, an abundance of holiday accommodation and all-year sunshine attract an estimated three and a half million visitors to the city every year.

Most of these visitors content themselves with a lazy lifestyle – encouraged by the subtropical climate – cultivating an east coast suntan and sampling the nightlife. But beyond the facade of carefree tourism, Durban has a great deal more to offer. It is one of the busiest harbours in Africa and a bustling industrial centre, while the blend of African, Asian and European lifestyles makes it an interesting, cosmopolitan city.

Fun at the waterfront

Most holiday-makers head directly for Durban's beachfront, where bathing beaches stretch for some 4 km from Addington in the south to Country Club and Blue Lagoon in the north. (North from here to Umhlanga the coast is ideal for walks, but unprotected by shark nets.) The sea temperature is welcoming in summer, and bracing but not too cold in winter. The Rachel Finlayson saltwater pool alongside North Beach, and nearby children's paddling pools, provide even safer swimming.

For those tired of the beach, the *Marine Parade* area offers a number of other attractions. There are trampolines, a miniature golf course, and a mini pleasure park for children, with fun rides and an aerial cableway. *Sea World* combines aquarium displays, a fascinating shark tank, and lively dolphin and seal performances; tel (031) 37 3536; check feeding and show times.

One of the most memorable experiences is a ride along the beachfront in an extravagantly decorated *ricksha*, powered by a vividly garbed ricksha puller. The ricksha tradition started less ornamentally in the 1890s, as conveyance for cargo as well as passengers. The present-day ricksha pullers are based opposite the Holiday Inn Garden Court, South Beach, and rates are set by time and distance. Zulu women sell traditional handcrafts along the walk beside the Marine Parade.

Opposite the Holiday Inn Garden Court, North Beach, is *Minitown*, a charming city, scaled down to children's eyelevel. It has replicas of Durban buildings and the harbour, models of aircraft and trains, and even a drive-in cinema; tel (031) 37 7892. A minute's walk away is *Fitzsimons Snake Park*, with cages and pits filled with snakes, lizards and tortoises. Informative demonstrations are held several times a day and there is also a well-stocked curio shop; tel (031) 37 6456.

Inland of Country Club Beach lies Durban *Waterworld*, where one entry fee admits you to several rides, water slides and jumps; tel (031) 37 6336. Further afield, at Amanzimtoti Beach, a water chute is open daily during the holiday season and pleasure craft can be hired on the banks of the lagoon (see pages 188 – 9).

The Bluff, the wooded headland that so effectively protects the bay, has inviting beaches and tidal pools at Anstey's and Brighton beaches. For those willing to drive a short distance out of the city, attractive beaches can also be found at Umhlanga and Umdloti (see pages 146 – 7).

Watersport and fishing

Ocean swimmers sometimes have to compete for water space. Durban is a world-famous surfing centre, with the Bay of Plenty a premier venue for the international contest circuit. Vetch's Pier and the expanse of beach stretching from North Pier to Addington is a gathering place for boardsailors, paddle-skiers and skindivers. One of the popular inland watersport venues is *Hazelmere Dam*, near the sugar-producing centre of Verulam.

The coastal waters are a paradise for anglers, particularly during the famous annual marine phenomenon of the sardine run, which occurs in June and July (see pages 154 – 5). Catches along this coast include kob, shad, spotted grunter and Natal stumpnose. For rock and surf fishing, there are the groynes (breakwaters) and piers from Vetch's Pier at the harbour

Golden domes of the Juma Mosque.

148

mouth to Country Club Beach. Also popular for shore fishing is Blue Lagoon. Deep-sea fishing cruises can be booked through the Isle of Capri Cruises (tel (031) 37 7751) on the waterfront at the end of Point Road.

The harbour and Embankment
Durban's harbour is a constant source of interest, and bay cruises offer a sortie into the romantic world of the sea. Sarie Marais launches use the *Gardiner Street Jetty* daily, from where they chug around the harbour or take to the sea – parallel to the shoreline. The harbour ferry leaves from the *New Small Craft Harbour* on Victoria Embankment. Used mainly by harbour folk, the ferry is good fun.

A slow drive south along *Maydon Wharf* will bring you to the *Prince Edward Graving Dock*, where ocean-going ships are brought in and left high and dry for repairs. Driving around the bay edge towards *Salisbury Island*, you will find the *floating dock* where vessels are raised out of the water for repair.

The three *sugar terminals* at the junction of Maydon Wharf and Canal Road store and move large quantities of KwaZulu-Natal's sweetest export. Entire shiploads can be loaded in a day. Public tours operate three days a week; tel (031) 301 0331.

Victoria Embankment, landing site for many an early seaborne settler, has a number of historical features. Graced by the *Old Supreme Court Building*, a national monument, the Embankment is the site of the first railway in South Africa, which was constructed from Durban to the Point in 1859.

On the Embankment, known also as the Esplanade, there is a *statue of Dick King*, commemorating his historic ride of 1 000 km to Grahamstown in 1842 to fetch aid for the British soldiers besieged in the Old Fort by the Boers. Another brave rescue mission, by the young boy John Ross, is honoured by a statue in front of the imposing *John Ross House*. In 1826 Ross walked 1 000 km north to Delagoa Bay to obtain medicines for the fledgling Port Natal settlement.

Stepping back into the past
The *Kwa Muhle Museum* in Ordnance Road houses exhibitions of ethnic and local interest; tel (031) 300 6310; while the *Local History Museum* in Aliwal Street offers a good introduction to Durban's past and its peoples; tel (031) 304 8694. Backing onto the museum is the *City Hall*, pivot of the city's historic centre. The majestic building, resembling the Belfast City Hall in Northern Ireland, was opened in 1910 and houses a first-rate natural science museum (tel (031) 300 6211) and art gallery (tel (031) 300 6231). The entrance to these is in Smith Street.

The City Hall faces *Francis Farewell Square*, named after one of the British naval men who established the first recorded settlement at Port Natal in 1824. The square is believed to be the site of Farewell's camp. Also overlooking the square is the *Post Office*, which started out in 1885 as Durban's town hall. Now a national monument, along with the square and the City Hall, it has a plaque on its eastern steps commemorating a speech made there in 1899 by the young war correspondent – and later British prime minister – Winston Churchill.

Church Street Plaza, next to the Post Office, is the scene of a daily flea market. The underpass from the Plaza brings you out on the former site of Durban's old station, where Victorian railway sheds have been converted into the *Workshop Shopping Complex* and the *Exhibition Centre*. Next to the Workshop, in the ornate entrance to the original station, is *Tourist Junction*; tel (031) 304 4934. This is the home of *Durban Unlimited*, the city's publicity association. Guided historical and 'Oriental' walks set off from here regularly. The original platform section of the old station is now a modern gym and fitness centre.

The *Old House*, 31 St Andrew's Street, was built in 1849 by a former mayor of Durban. The tiny house is crammed with the trappings of early colonial homes; tel (031) 300 6250.

The *Old Fort* on the corner of NMR Avenue and Old Fort Road, tel (031) 307 1776, is the site of the British camp during their 1842 Battle of Congella against the Boers. Some earthworks, a small chapel, and barracks that have been converted into quarters for war pensioners, are surrounded by informal gardens. Military memorabilia are on view at *Warriors' Gate*, a small building modelled on a Norman gatehouse. The building is also headquarters for the ex-servicemen's organization, the Memorable Order of Tin Hats (MOTH).

Golden beaches and the Indian Ocean make up Durban's 'Golden Mile'.

The sparkling jewel of the South Coast reflects its holiday lights on the bay.

A ricksha puller in colourful costume.

Surf fishing offers splendid rewards for anglers with patience and stamina.

Durban's ornate old City Hall is a replica of the City Hall in Belfast.

The *Killie Campbell Africana Museum* may be visited by appointment; tel (031) 207 3432. High up on the ridge known as the Berea, this is a gracious house that belonged to the famous 'sugar baron', Sir Marshall Campbell, and holds an acclaimed Africana library and collections of furniture and Zulu arts and crafts. Medical memorabilia are on display at the *Addington Hospital Centenary Museum*; tel (031) 32 4360.

Photography buffs can focus on the *Whysalls Camera Museum* in Brickhill Road, said to hold the second-largest collection of old and rare cameras in the world; tel (031) 37 1431. The *Natal Maritime Museum* at Maritime Place, Victoria Embankment, is well worth visiting; tel (031) 300 6324. This (and the BAT Centre – see below) is reached through the entrance to the yacht basin.

Orientation and viewsites

Viewing spots reached by bus or car include the *University of Natal*, in King George V Avenue on the crest of a Berea ridge, and a number of points along South and North Ridge roads. A drive around the crown of the Bluff gives views of the city, the bay and the Indian Ocean. A stroll to the end of *North Pier* provides a shoreline panorama – close enough to passing ships to feel you can reach out and touch them.

A more extravagant way to get your bearings is a 20-minute air flip from Virginia Airport, organized by the Natal Flight Centre; tel (031) 84 4720.

Culture and the arts

Several cultural and arts venues are to be found in Durban and its outlying areas. Focus of the performing arts is the *Natal Playhouse*, a multi-theatre complex run by the Playhouse Company; tel (031) 304 3631. This venue for musical theatre, dance, drama, contemporary theatre, supper theatre and recitals is to be found in Smith Street. The complex's two main theatres are in the refurbished shells of two former cinemas – hence the eccentric facade.

Giving 27 symphony concerts each year, the Natal Philharmonic Orchestra performs regularly in the City Hall, and presents several lighter outdoor programmes at the Village Green and in the Botanic Gardens.

The *BAT Centre* at 45 Maritime Place, Victoria Embankment, supports many arts ventures, including visual and performing arts as well as community arts, cultural research, conferences, exhibitions and arts education programmes; tel (031) 32 0451/468/402.

Open-air theatre is staged on the parkland slope of the University of Natal campus. The *Elizabeth Sneddon Theatre*; tel (031) 814 5440, on the campus, features local and touring productions and is the venue for the Durban International Film Festival.

The *Durban Arts Association* in Avondale Road, Morningside, is an excellent source of information on all aspects of the arts, including music in the city parks; tel (031) 23 1236. For the visual arts, the *Durban Art Gallery* in the City Hall offers one of the best-patronized formal galleries in the country. It houses permanent collections of South African and international works, and covers the applied arts; tel (031) 300 6231.

The *Natal Society of Artists (NSA) Gallery*, 166 – 74 Bulwer Road, Glenwood, regularly exhibits works by local and nationally renowned painters and sculptors, as does the *Elizabeth Gordon Gallery*; tel (031) 309 4370, in its Victorian house in Windermere Road. On a smaller scale, the *Grassroots Gallery* in Westville also displays works by KwaZulu-Natal artists in a building that is part of an Islamic religious complex built last century; tel (031) 86 6263. The *African Art Centre* off Gardiner Street has work by black artists and sells beadwork, baskets, woven goods and woodcuts; tel (031) 304 7915.

The *Mariannhill Monastery*, in its rural setting near Pinetown, houses church and religious artefacts, as well as an ethnological collection of art. The mission complex, founded in 1882 by Trappist monks, is equally interesting; tel (031) 700 4288.

Indian settlers have brought much of their culture and tradition to bear on the local environment since the first 341 indentured labourers arrived in Natal in 1860. Their varied creeds have added a number of exquisite buildings to the city landscape. The *Juma Mosque* in Grey Street, said to be the largest in the southern hemisphere, may be visited by arrangement.

Hindu temples adorn the city – eye-catchingly ornate or simple

Catamaran sailors take to the water at the start of a regatta at Vetch's Pier.

Marine Parade – a tourist's paradise and a fun-filled world for children.

Medwood Gardens; a tranquil spot to escape the bustle of the city.

and flower-strewn – and the Hindu religious calendar brings many colourful festivals, including fire-walking, processions and acts of penitence. The most accessible temples are those in the Umgeni Road complex, another in Somtseu Road, and the Bellair temples west of the University of Natal.

Another religious venue open to visitors is the *Hare Krishna Temple of Understanding* in Chatsworth, with its dazzling architecture set in spacious gardens; tel (031) 43 3360.

Nature trails and parks

A number of parks, gardens and protected areas add to the general effect of a lush, green Durban, and provide havens from the city bustle and hot beaches. Closest to the beach are the formally and attractively landscaped *Amphitheatre Gardens* between North Beach and the snake park. *Medwood Gardens* offer a pleasant refuge for strollers and *Albert Park* has a restaurant and roadhouse surrounded by acres of shade and attractive, open expanses.

The *Botanic Gardens*, which started as an agricultural research station in 1849, offer a tranquil setting and a tea kiosk ; tel (031) 21 1303. The gardens are well known for their orchid house and rare collection of cycads, and the *Natal Herbarium* (or Botanical Research Institute) is in the St Thomas Road corner of the gardens; tel (031) 22 4095. A popular family destination is *Mitchell Park* with its playgrounds, displays of animals and birds, and its open-air café. *Jameson Park*, next door, specializes in roses.

The *Metropolitan Open Space System (MOSS)* has established self-guided walking trails not far from the city centre at Pigeon Valley, Burman Bush and Virginia Bush. Excellent guidebooks are available from Durban Unlimited at Tourist Junction in Pine Street or from its beachfront information kiosk opposite the bottom end of West Street (near Sea World).

Also nearby are walking trails and picnic sites at the *Kenneth Stainbank Nature Reserve* in Yellowwood Park; at *Paradise Valley* on the Umbilo River; and at *Krantzkloof Nature Reserve* in Kloof. The *Japanese Gardens* in Durban North, laid out in Oriental fashion, make a popular picnic spot, and the *Umgeni River Bird Park* offers aviaries of exotic and indigenous birds; tel (031) 84 1733 (see pages 146 – 7). *Umhlanga Rustic Village and Animal Farm*, tel (031) 561 4058, caters for birthday parties. With its attractive tea garden, this is a popular venue for family outings seven days a week.

The *Umhlanga Lagoon Nature Reserve* has a lagoon trail through the Hawaan Forest to picnic and barbecue sites. On Umhlanga Rocks Drive is the headquarters of the *Natal Sharks Board*; for guided tours, tel (031) 561 1001.

Shoppers' delight

For those who enjoy shopping for arts, crafts and bargain items, there are sprawling flea markets every Sunday (in addition to the daily flea market in Church Square). These are held in the *Marine Parade Amphitheatre* and at *South Plaza* around the Exhibition Centre, opposite the Workshop. Other popular flea markets are the *Berea Craft Market* in Essenwood Road (held every Saturday from 09h00 to 15h00) and the *Point Waterfront* flea market, to be found in the harbour at the end of Point Road. This operates on weekends and public holidays and offers entertainment, in addition to its wide variety of stalls.

Shoppers unfamiliar with Durban should make a point of exploring the many arcades between Smith and West streets in the city centre. And for shopping – and bargaining – for fish, meat, spices, ornaments, curios and knicknacks in an exotic Afro-Oriental environment, the *Victoria Street Market* near Warwick Avenue is the ideal place to go on weekdays.

Shopping complexes in and around Durban include the Workshop, Berea Centre, Musgrave Centre, The Wheel, La Lucia Mall and Westville's super-shopping complex, The Pavilion.

For further information, contact any of the following sources: Durban Unlimited, Mezzanine Floor, Station Building, 160 Pine Street, Durban 4001; tel (031) 304 4934, fax (031) 304 6196. Beachfront information kiosk, Marine Parade (opposite West Street); tel (031) 32 2608/32 2595. Amanzimtoti Publicity, PO Box 471, Amanzimtoti 4125; tel (031) 903 7493, fax (031) 903 7509. Umhlanga Publicity (Chartwell Drive), Private Bag X4, Umhlanga 4320; tel (031) 561 4237, fax (031) 561 1397.

City skyline above the yacht basin.

Vasco da Gama clock, the Esplanade.

Palms, wild bananas and golden sands adorn the Strelitzia Coast

The wild bananas that grow profusely in the dune forests south of Durban have given this popular holiday area its name: Strelitzia Coast. We make our way to idyllic beaches lapped by the warm Indian Ocean and we also venture inland – to visit the domain of the deadly crocodile and explore a gently winding country road.

Durban
Umgababa
Clansthal
Crocworld
Pennington
Scottburgh
Amanzimtoti
210 – 230 km

LEAVE DURBAN BY travelling south on Victoria Embankment (the Esplanade), passing the yacht basin and harbour on your left. At the end of the embankment, exit left for 'South Coast/M4'. After about 13 km the road merges with the southbound N2 – note your kms here.

After almost 18 km on the N2, exit left at interchange 133 for the R603 to Pietermaritzburg and Winkelspruit. At the end of the off-ramp turn left, then, 100 – 200 m later, turn right at the T-junction for Winkelspruit and Illovo Beach. At the traffic lights 300 – 400 m later, turn right onto the R102, noting your kms.

The R102 runs parallel to the N2 on your right for a short distance, with a large sugar plantation on its far side. After roughly 1,5 km you cross the wide Lovu (Illovo) River. Soon afterwards you pass a turn-off on your left to Illovo Beach. After just over 7 km on the R102, you have a view on your left of the lagoon formed by the *uMgababa* River (Zulu for place of jealousy), with dense bush on its far bank.

Soon afterwards you cross the river and, if you wish, turn into the Umgababa Curio Centre, a market that sells fresh subtropical fruits, baskets, beadwork, pottery, carvings and other curios.

Umgababa to Crocworld

From the curio centre continue south on the R102, noting your kms as you depart. The road closely follows the coastline for a while and, 4,7 km beyond the curio centre, crosses a bridge high above the wide mouth of the Mkomazi River – before entering the town of Umkomaas.

Note your kms as you pass the turn-off to the town on your left soon afterwards (it also leads to the tidal pool, the beach and the river mouth). After 3,8 km turn left for Clansthal Caravan Park; 200 m later you cross the railway line, with Claustal station on your right (see opposite). Go right immediately afterwards onto Green Point Road and, after 400 m, park on your left for a short walk south along the beach towards the aptly named Green Point, with its lighthouse high up on the hill (allow 30 – 40 minutes).

Retrace your route to the R102, turn left and note your kms. After 2 km turn right for Crocworld, which lies a further 400 m along this sideroad. (There is an entry fee, and the centre has a restaurant and a snack bar. Visitors may watch the crocodiles being fed at 11h00 and 15h00; enquire at the gate about enclosures to visit. A shady trail of some 3 km leads through the forest.)

Crocworld to Pennington

Return to the R102, and turn right. After 1,8 km you cross the pretty lagoon of the Mahlongwa River. Soon afterwards you cross the Mpambanyoni River on the outskirts of Scottburgh.

Remain on the R102 through the resort towns of Scottburgh and Park Rynie, and note your kms as you pass a turn-off to the N2 and the R612 to Park Rynie and Umzinto. After 6 km you cross the wide Mzinto River; 2,6 km later, turn left into Pennington Drive, an attractive tree-shaded road that leads to the beach. After 400 m go right at the fork, and 600 – 700 m later go straight where the larger road curves sharply to the left. Cross the railway line and stop in the parking area alongside the shaded picnic spot (which has braai place and toilet). There is a safe tidal pool here, and the beach offers a lovely walk along a stretch of unspoilt coastline backed by thick indigenous bush.

Pennington to Scottburgh

Return to the R102 and continue south. The road winds its way inland through attractive rural scenery; 3,2 km after rejoining the R102 you cross the attractive Mkumbane (or Inkabana) River. You cross the N2 soon afterwards – 200 m later, turn left for Bazley to remain on the R102, and note your kms.

Soon afterwards you cross the Sezela River (named after a legendary man-eating crocodile whose reign of terror over the Malangeni people was ended when Shaka ordered it to be killed for its skin). The road traverses rolling green hills covered with sugar cane, traditional huts, mealie fields, banana trees and patches of forest. You are likely to spot troops of vervet monkeys in the bushes alongside the road.

After 6,2 km on this road you cross the lovely *Fafa* (Zulu for sparkling) River; 1,3 km later turn left onto gravel for Ifafa Beach. After just over 1,8 km turn left for Club Marina, and 1 km later turn right into a viewsite for a view over a bend in the Fafa River with its dense indigenous forest on the far bank.

Return to the tarred R102, and turn left. Very soon you pass a turn-off on your left to the N2, Ifafa Beach and Elysium, then the road begins to descend towards the Mtwalume River. You cross the river over a single-lane steel bridge. (The river is named after a tree whose bark is believed by Zulus to be a cure for dysentry.) Just under 1 km beyond the river turn left for Mtwalume, Scottburgh and Port Shepstone, and after a further 3,3 km turn left onto the N2 for Durban, noting your kms.

After 24,8 km, at Interchange 104, exit left for the R612. At the end of the off-ramp, turn right and, 1,4 km later, turn left onto the R102 for Scottburgh, noting your kms. After 4,2 km turn right into Scottburgh's Airth Street. Turn left into Scott Street (the main road), then right into Gardiner Street. At the T-junction 200 m later, turn left and cross the railway line to reach the parking area at the beach, tidal pool, river mouth and miniature railway.

Scottburgh to Amanzimtoti

Retrace your route to the R102 and turn right. After 1 km you cross the Mpambanyoni River, and 500 m later turn left for Dududu (Dudutu) and the N2 to Durban. After roughly 1,2 km turn right onto the N2.

Roughly 30 km from Scottburgh, you pass the exit for Adams Road. After a further 2 km, exit left (Interchange 141) for 'Amanzimtoti/Umbogintwini/KwaMakutha'. At the end of the off-ramp, turn right and note your kms. At

Crocodiles laze in the sun – safely behind fences.

THE GENTLENESS OF DEADLY JAWS
The Nile crocodile, one of the most ancient creatures surviving, has a powerful jaw that can exert 40 tons of pressure per square centimetre. Yet a mother crocodile can roll an egg between her teeth to gently crack the shell if her hatchling is having difficulty emerging into the world. The first journey the young make to the water is also in the mouth of their mother. This is the safest place for them to travel, because, despite the immense power of adults, the young are extremely vulnerable to predators; out of a clutch of 40 – 80 eggs, a mere one or two crocodiles will survive to adulthood in the wild.

Vervet monkeys abound in the coastal forests.

the T-junction, turn right for Amanzimtoti. Just after 1,4 km, turn left for Inyoni Rocks, then turn left immediately. At the bottom of the hill (1,8 km after noting your kms) turn right into Beach Road; 700 m later park on your left next to the Visitors' Bureau for a late-afternoon stroll along the beach at Inyoni Rocks.

Amanzimtoti to Durban
From the parking area, turn left, noting your kms. After 1,1 km, you pass a parking area on the left alongside the lagoon, where boats may be hired. Some 500 m later, turn left and, after a further 150 m, turn right for 'Durban/Adams Road'. After crossing the N2, turn right again and follow the signs onto the N2 for Durban.

> **AA Office** AA House, 33 St George's Street Durban 4001 Tel (031) 301 0341
> **Durban Unlimited** 160 Pine Street, Durban 4001 Tel (031) 304 4934
> **Amanzimtoti Publicity Association** 93 Beach Road, Amanzimtoti 4126 Tel (031) 903 7493

Colourful Zulu crafts tempt shoppers at Umgababa.

SCOTTBURGH
This popular holiday resort was founded in 1860 and named after the Lieutenant Governor of Natal, Sir John Scott. The little bay known as Scott's Bay was once used as a precarious port for the export of sugar and, at the beginning of last century, Shaka's warriors are believed to have drawn their water supplies from a spot near to where the present water slide has been built next to the river.

Apart from the tidal pool near the river mouth and protected surf swimming, Scottburgh offers rides on a miniature railway, angling and several amusements for children.

WHERE THE WATERS ARE SWEET
The resort and residential area of Amanzimtoti takes its name from a remark attributed to the Zulu King Shaka when he was given water from the river: '*Kanti amanzi mtoti*' (So, the water is sweet). There is a tidal pool at Inyoni Rocks, from where a promenade leads along the beachfront. The lagoon is popular for boating and there is good surf and rock angling. Other attractions in the area include the Ilanda Wilds Nature Reserve and the Amanzimtoti Bird Sanctuary.

The pretty lagoon of the Amanzimtoti River.

CLANSTHAL AND GREEN POINT
The beautiful beach at Clansthal takes its name from the nearby farm Clausthal, which in turn was named after a German town. Although the misspelling is now official, the railway station of Claustal retains a name closer to the original.

Overlooking Clansthal beach is the Green Point lighthouse, built in 1905 to warn seamen against the offshore Aliwal Shoal, on which many a ship has come to grief. Green Point is now a popular surfing spot.

The tranquillity of Clansthal's unspoilt beach belies the danger of this coast for passing ships.

Where endless river valleys reach down to a golden shore

The rivers that rise in the Drakensberg have carved steep valleys that zigzag towards the golden sands of the coast. Our route through this lovely land includes visits to a hilltop nature reserve, a historic mission station, the attractive settler town of Ixopo and several delightful beaches. More than two-thirds of the route is on tar.

Scottburgh
Vernon Crookes
Nature Reserve
Ixopo
St Faith's
Umtentweni
Umzumbe
310 – 330 km

LEAVE SCOTTBURGH BY turning inland from Scott Street (the main road) into Airth Street, between the library and the post office; 750 m later, turn left onto the R102, noting your kms. After 4 km you pass, on your right, the R612 to Umzinto and the N2. Just over 1,8 km later, turn left onto gravel for Rocky Bay Caravan Park. A further 250 m brings you to a parking area alongside Park Rynie's old whaling station jetty (now used as a fishing pier). The unspoilt stretch of beach offers a lovely early morning walk.

Park Rynie to St Michael's

Return to the tar and turn right onto the R102. Retrace your route for the 1,8 km to the R612, and turn left towards Umzinto, noting your kms. Soon afterwards you cross the N2, and after 12 km on the R612, turn right onto the gravel D145 for the Vernon Crookes Nature Reserve, noting your kms. Follow the signs for the reserve as the road climbs steadily through hills covered with sugar cane and forests, to enter the nature reserve 5,6 km from the R612 (entry fee). Ask for a map at the gate and follow the signs to the picnic area at the summit of the hill, beyond the dam wall (6 km from the gate). The road and picnic area offer good views and you may spot zebra and impala.

Retrace your route to the tarred R612 and turn right. The road climbs through sugar cane fields and, after 9 km, you can see, far away on your right, the As-Salaam Islamic seminary with its exotic tower. Just over 6 km further you can see the Himmelberg Mission settlement, also on your right.

The scenery changes gradually to grassy cattle country, dotted with traditional huts and maize patches, and with large tracts of forest in between. Some 32,5 km after rejoining the R612, turn right onto a gravel track for St Michael's Mission and Ndonyane Weaving Centre. (The 3 km road to the churches at St Michael's may be treacherous after heavy rain.) Park near the churches and walk along the 200 m path behind the old church to visit the weaving centre.

St Michael's to Ixopo

Retrace your route to the tarred R612 and turn right, noting your kms. After 3 km you pass through Jolivet, named after CC Jolivet, Catholic Bishop of Natal and co-founder of the Mariannhill Mission near Durban. The road climbs ever higher through magnificent scenery, hugging the course of the old narrow-gauge railway for much of the way.

Some 17 km after noting your kms turn left into the grounds of St James Anglican Church, Highflats. A track of about 200 m leads to the small stone church, from where stone steps lead to pretty falls on the Mtwalume River.

Continue northwards from the church on the R612. After a few kms you enter Highflats, an attractive town founded in 1863, where a few lovely old buildings survive. In the town, you pass a turn-off on your left to St Faith's (our return route).

The beach at Park Rynie curves to the north beyond the old whaling jetty.

'A STRANGE, WEIRD TALE ...'
St Michael's, founded in 1854 as the first Catholic mission in Natal, was soon abandoned because of its lack of success in converting the local people. Two missionaries, who later returned to rebuild the church and make a fresh start, had their daily building work quietly torn down each night while they slept. But now the mission has grown to such an extent that the 1894 stone church has had to be supplemented by a new, bigger building.

The community made world headlines in 1907 with a personal account by Bishop Delalle of a 'strange, weird tale from the depths of darkest Africa', in which he told of an exorcism rite he performed to rid two adolescent African girls – Germana and Monica – of the demon 'Dioar'. They were reported to have had great strength and cognitive powers under his influence.

Today the mission welcomes visitors to its weaving and spinning centre, named Ndonyane after the nearby river.

Beyond Highflats the road climbs even higher in a richly forested area. Roughly 22 km after leaving Highflats, go straight at the crossroads where the R56 leads right to Richmond and Pietermaritzburg and left to Umzimkulu; 1,5 km later, turn left for Ixopo, which you enter on Margaret Street. (Several establishments in the historic town serve lunch.)

Ixopo to Umtentweni

After your visit to Ixopo, return along Margaret Street and the R612 to the R56 and turn left onto the R56 towards Richmond and Pietermaritzburg, noting your kms. After 4,7 km, turn right onto a gravel track that leads, after 200 m, to Mariathal Catholic Church, a stately red-brick building decorated with magnificent paintings, statues and stained-glass windows.

Retrace your route along the R56 to the R612 and turn left onto the R612 for Highflats, noting your kms. After a little over 22 km, turn right for St Faith's, noting your kms again. After 15 km the road surface changes to gravel and soon you can see across the undulating *Mzimkulu* (home of the rivers) valley to the far-away Drakensberg. Shortly afterwards you can also look out over the attractive hills of the Mzumbe valley on your left.

After 28 km on this road, pull onto the wide shoulder on your left for a view over the Mzimkulu valley on your right. You will see the prominent double hump of Nkoneni rising from the valley. Continue from here along the scenic St Faith's road, which roughly follows a ridge of hills between the Mzimkulu and Mzumbe rivers. The mission village of St Faith's lies 40 km from Highflats and commands a lovely view of the cliffs above the Mzimkulu.

From St Faith's the road winds through magnificent countryside, with other views over the cliffs of the Mzimkulu valley on your right. Eventually, after 51 km of gravel, the road surface changes to tar and you begin to glimpse Port Shepstone on your right and the sea ahead of you. Some 83 km from Highflats you reach the N2. Cross over the N2 for Umtentweni, noting your kms, and cross the railway line after 300 m. Immediately afterwards, turn left into Second Avenue and, after 100 m, you reach a parking area with a beach kiosk and change rooms (with toilets). The tidal rocks here offer interesting pool life and safe bathing.

Umtentweni to Scottburgh

Retrace your route to the N2 and turn right onto the N2, noting your kms. The road makes its way through a string of holiday resorts and you cross a number of pretty river mouths. Just after 10 km on the N2 you can see an attractive sweep of unspoilt beach ahead of you, with St Elmo's Convent silhouetted on the hillside above a rocky point. Opposite the convent, after 11,6 km on the N2, turn right for Umzumbe, noting your kms.

After 400 m, turn right into Stiebel Rocks Road and cross the railway line soon afterwards. Pass a parking area on your left and follow the road where it curves to the right; 600 m after leaving the N2, turn left into a parking area and walk onto the outcrop known as Stiebel Rocks for a beautiful view of the coast. The beach here offers a delightful late-afternoon walk.

Leaving the Stiebel Rocks parking area, turn right, noting your kms. After just under 300 m, turn right at the T-junction and, after just over 1,1 km further, turn right for Port Shepstone and Scottburgh. A few hundred metres later, turn left onto the N2 for Scottburgh and Durban, noting your kms.

Some 17,5 km after rejoining the N2 you cross the wide mouth of the Mtwalume River, then enter countryside lush with fields of sugar cane, banana plantations and tracts of dense, indigenous bush. After 28 km exit left (Interchange 93) for Sezela, Pennington and Esperanza and, at the end of the off-ramp, turn right onto the R102 – an attractive country road that winds its way back to Scottburgh.

AA Office Robinson Street, Port Shepstone 4240
Tel (0391) 682 1018
Durban Unlimited 160 Pine Street, Durban 4001
Tel (031) 304 4934

The sparkling blue lagoon at the mouth of the Mpambanyoni River is part of Scottburgh's appeal.

SOUTH COAST SILVER

The waters off the stretch of coast we travel along are the scene of an extraordinary annual event – the sardine run. Every year at the beginning of autumn, hundreds of millions of sardines make their way from the Cape up the Mozambique Current to spawn in the warm East African coastal waters. The current keeps the sardines out to sea for much of the journey, but sweeps them close to the shore for a 250 km stretch from Port St Johns to just south of Durban. Apart from the thousands that people catch along the way – sometimes by the bucketful – the little fish are also prey to larger fish, and the run provides excellent game-fishing in its wake.

IXOPO

The novel *Cry the Beloved Country* by Alan Paton begins in the beautiful hill country of the Ixopo area. Established as a colonial town in 1878, Ixopo was at first named Stuartstown in honour of a local magistrate, but eventually reverted to the original Zulu name for the river and area. Spelt *eXobo* in Zulu, it imitates the noise made when walking through marshy ground. A number of interesting old buildings date from the town's early history. It has become an important centre for timber and dairy farming.

Left: *Burchell's zebra and wildebeest at the Vernon Crookes Nature Reserve.*
Right: *Typical landscape near Ixopo.*

The Mzumbe River makes its way through hilly land to the sea.

The stark beauty of Oribi Gorge and a lush, sun-drenched coast

KwaZulu-Natal's South Coast offers a string of golden beaches, hidden away amid lush forest, sugar-cane fields, and plantations of bananas, mangoes and pawpaws. Our route includes stops at several coastal resorts and leads through the spectacular Oribi Gorge, famed for its magnificent rock shapes. Almost the entire route is tarred.

Margate
Uvongo
Oribi Gorge
Umtamvuna
Nature Reserve
Port Edward
Southbroom
180 – 200 km

LEAVE MARGATE by travelling north along Marine Drive (R620) and turn right onto the R61 coastal road just outside the town. You pass through Manaba and about 2 km from Margate you enter Uvongo. After crossing the Vungu (Uvongo) River, turn right at the first intersection into Forster Street, then right again at the stop street into Uvongo Beach Road. Park 200 m later for an early morning walk on the beach, alongside the lovely lagoon. You may hire boats here, to paddle a short distance upstream to a 23 m waterfall (allow 30-40 minutes). The pool at the foot of the waterfall is 27 m deep, making this the deepest estuary in the province.

Uvongo to Oribi Gorge

Return along Uvongo Beach Road and turn right into Marine Drive, noting your kms. The road passes through St Michael's On Sea and Shelly Beach, offering fine views over the sea and inland hills. After 3,6 km, turn left for Gamalakhe and Izotsha.

After a further 3,6 km, turn right towards Port Shepstone onto a pretty country road that winds through cultivated farmlands and clusters of banana trees. The industrial area of Marburg on the outskirts of Port Shepstone soon comes into view ahead of you.

After 5 km on this road, turn left onto the N2 for Harding and Kokstad, noting your kms. The N2 climbs steadily through hills covered with sugar cane and after 5,2 km you ascend a pass with views left to the coast and right over the valley of the Boboyi River. Soon after the road levels out (after 8,2 km on the N2) turn right for Oribi Gorge, noting your kms.

Almost immediately you have views of rolling hills in the valleys of the Mzimkulwana and Mzimkulu rivers – many of the hillsides intensely cultivated despite their steepness. After 4,2 km the road begins to descend into the Mzimkulwana valley, and 1,3 km later you can see the high Four Men's Hill on your left at the southern end of Oribi Gorge. After a further 1,8 km you cross the river, then begin to climb steeply towards Oribi Gorge Flats; 12 kms after leaving the N2, turn left onto gravel for 'Oribi Gorge/Oribi Gorge Hotel' to reach the viewsites. Some 1,3 km later, pay the entrance fee at the hotel – a map of the viewsites area is obtainable here. The drive along the edge of the gorge for roughly 4 km to the panoramic view of Oribi Heads is particularly worthwhile, and there are a number of spots along the way that offer breathtaking views. (There are picnic and braai sites and the hotel serves lunches and teas.)

Oribi Gorge to Wilson's Cutting

Return to the tarred road and turn left, noting your kms; 5,6 km later, turn right onto the gravel D419. After a further 1,5 km, stop alongside the road and walk to your left for a magnificent view of the cliffs on your left known as the Walls of Jericho, which tower above a classic horseshoe bend in the Mzimkulwana River and locked-in farms far below on the fertile riverbanks. Some 800 m further along the D419 there is another view into the spectacular gorge, with the prominent Gibraltar Rock standing like a sentinel above it.

Return to the tarred road and turn right. After 1,5 km turn left for the Oribi Gorge Nature Reserve. The road descends a steep pass into the gorge amidst dense natural forest and towering sandstone cliffs. Some 5 km from the turn-off, turn left into a parking area alongside the river at the foot of Oribi Heads – this makes an ideal lunch spot (with braai and picnic sites, and toilets); 100 m beyond the parking area you cross the river on a narrow bridge, then begin the steep ascent out of the gorge. After a further 3,7 km you pass a turn-off right to the Natal Parks Board hutted camp; 300 m later, turn right at the T-junction onto the N2 for Izingolweni and Harding, noting your kms.

Roughly 4 km later you pass through the small farming community of Paddock. Beyond the town the views open out over a gentle landscape scattered with huts, with the Transkei mountains in the distance; 11,5 km after rejoining the N2 you begin to descend a pass – 300 m later, turn left into the Wilson's Cutting viewsite, which gives excellent views over the Mbizane River valley and the surrounding countryside.

Wilson's Cutting to the Mtamvuna River

Note your kms at the far side of the viewsite parking area as you continue down the pass on the N2. After 800 m you pass the KwaCele traditional village on your right, and on your left here you can see back towards the rocky mountainside you have just crossed. The road winds amongst the crest of hills, offering fine views over KwaZulu-Natal on both sides.

After 4,8 km – on the outskirts of Izingolweni – turn left, then, 100 m later, turn left again for Port Edward, noting your kms. The road now descends along a spur of land between the Mbizane and Mtamvuna rivers – through beautiful countryside, and offering towards the distant Indian Ocean. Roughly 29 km after noting your kms, turn right into the Umtamvuna Nature Reserve. You reach the gate after 200 m (entry fee), and the parking area after a further 250 m. A short walk to the top of a rocky knoll near the parking area gives excellent views over the nature reserve, with the sea in the distance on your left (allow 30-40 minutes).

Return to the tarred road and turn right, noting your kms. After 6,5 km you pass a turn-off right to Old Pont Road, which leads to the old river crossing and the lower section of the Umtamvuna Nature Reserve; 1,7 km later, turn right onto the R61 for Bizana and 3,9 km later you cross the Mtamvuna River. Park on the far bank and walk back onto the bridge for a view of the river and mouth.

Mtamvuna River to Margate

Return along the R61 and, 3 km beyond the bridge, turn right (where left leads to Banner's Rest Retirement Village), noting your kms. The road leads into the resort of Port Edward. After 1 km turn right into Portsea Avenue and, 200 m later, turn left into Newport Street; 600 m later, where the tar curves left into Gloucester Road, continue straight on gravel, past the lighthouse on your left. Park at the end of the road for a walk at the interesting rocks known as The Gully. Return past the lighthouse, turn right onto tar into Gloucester Road and, 700 m later, turn right into Owen Ellis Drive. Turn right into Beach Road, which leads to a parking area at the foot of Tragedy Hill (see below).

Return along Beach Road and Owen Ellis Drive to the R61, turn right for Margate and Port Shepstone and note your kms. After 9,7 km, turn right for Southbroom, noting your kms as you turn. After 1,5 km you reach a small traffic circle, where you bear left on Imbezana Drive. Follow this road for 1 km until you reach a parking area overlooking a magnificent stretch of beach at the mouth of the Mbizane Lagoon. Drive out of the parking area and turn right along the same route to the R61 coastal road. Turn right onto this main road for the short journey to Margate.

AA Office c/o Publicity Association Office cr Aiken and Robinson streets, Port Shepstone 4240 Tel (0391) 21018
Hibiscus Coast Publicity Association Panorama Parade, Beachfront, Margate 4275 Tel (03931) 22322
Durban Unlimited 160 Pine Road, Durban 4001 Tel (031) 304 4934 Fax (031) 304 3868

The magnificent, forested Oribi Gorge, from the top of Lehr Falls.

ORIBI GORGE

The Mzimkulwana River has carved a 24 km ravine known as Oribi Gorge through KwaZulu-Natal's hilly interior, creating a unique gallery of sculpted sandstone cliffs. From the cliff-top vantage point of the privately owned Fairacres Estate one can view formations such as Baboon's Castle, The Pulpit, The Needle, Overhanging Rock and Oribi Heads, which tower above the river 400 m below. There is also a hotel on the estate laid out along the panoramic drive that leads along the lip of the gorge.

A reserve of 1 800 ha in the gorge preserves dense indigenous forest, where trails and climbs bring visitors close to the bushbuck, blue and grey duiker, monkeys and people-wary leopards that make their homes here. There are picnic and braai sites in this idyllic setting, and the Natal Parks Board has a camp with bungalows overlooking the head of the gorge. Details of walks and climbs in the area are available from the camp superintendent.

A TRAGIC RUMOUR

Tragedy Hill, overlooking Port Edward's main bathing beach, was the scene of a massacre sparked by a false rumour of war. In 1831 the Zulu king, Dingane, received a report that the fledgling British community at Port Natal (now Durban) was about to attack him. A party of settlers led by Frank Fynn, fleeing from Dingane's army, was cornered and killed on this pyramid-shaped hill by a group of Zulus who believed that settlers were stealing Dingane's cattle. When Dingane learnt that the report of the planned attack had been false, he ordered the man who had started the rumour to be shot – an execution performed by one of the settlers.

UMTAMVUNA NATURE RESERVE

The old pont across the Mtamvuna River between KwaZulu-Natal and the Eastern Cape operated just downstream from the border of the present Umtamvuna Nature Reserve – a 3 100 ha sanctuary for wildlife and birds that is also noted for its impressive riverine forest. Endangered Cape vultures make their home in the steep cliffs of the river gorge, and the call of the fish eagle is also heard here. The reserve has a bird list of 80 species, and hikers may see baboon, black jackal, large spotted genet, reedbuck, blue and grey duiker, bushbuck, monkey, oribi, serval and leopard.

A boardsailor makes the most of the end of the day at Southbroom.

The Horseshoe Bend, Oribi Gorge.

Above: *Rock anglers at Uvongo Beach.*
Below: *Umtamvuna Nature Reserve.*

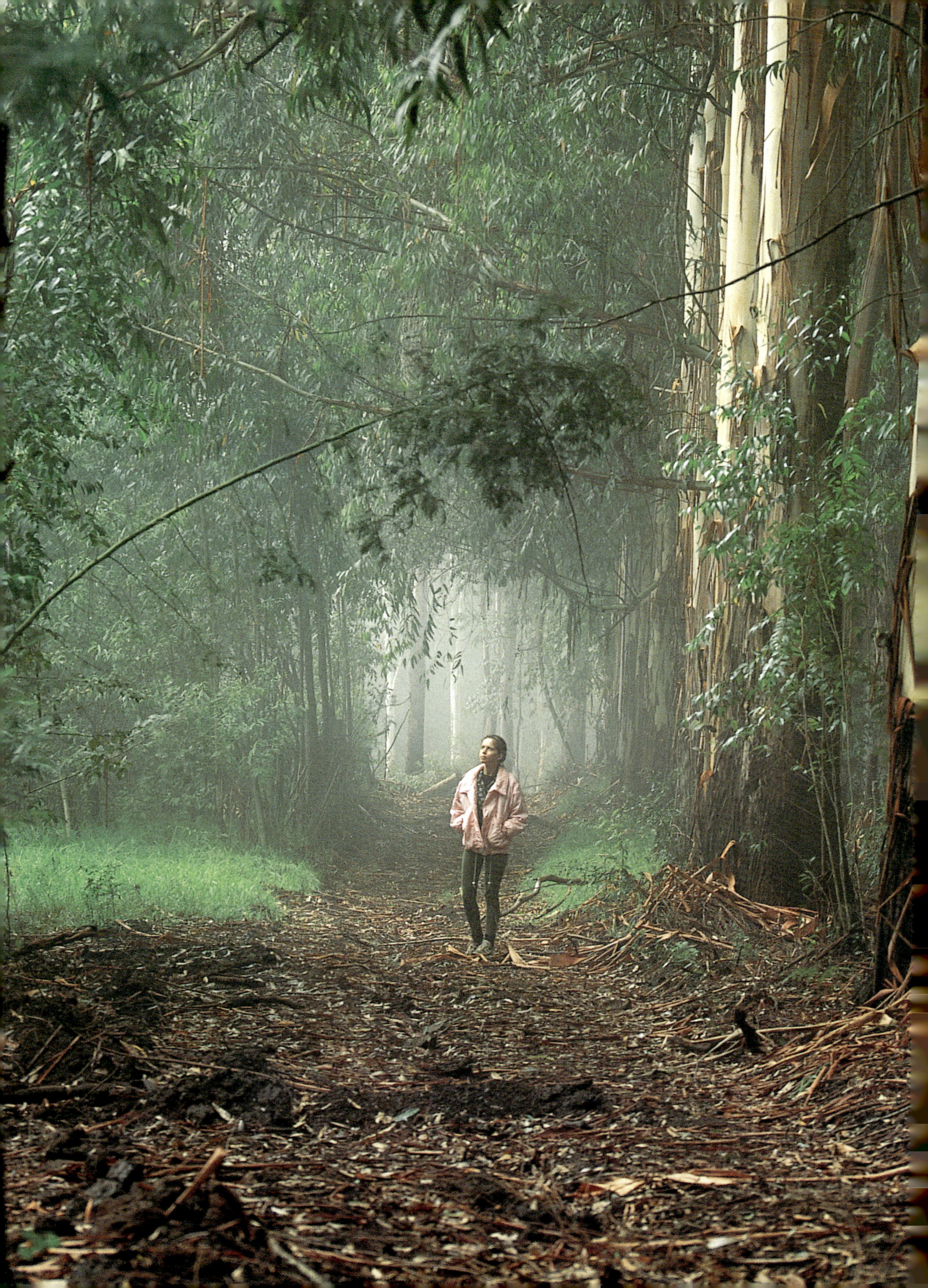

BORDER & TRANSKEI

Umtata – Mhlengana Rock – Port St Johns – Umngazi Mouth **160-1**

Kokstad – Flagstaff – Lusikisiki – Port St Johns **162-3**

Xhosa Traditions: People of a land of legend **164-5**

Umtata – Hole-in-the-wall – Coffee Bay – Mtata Mouth **166-7**

Butterworth – Centane – Qolora Mouth – Mazeppa Bay **168-9**

East London – Cefane Mouth – Morgan Bay – Double Mouth – Gonubie **170-1**

East London – Igoda Mouth – Kidd's Beach – Hamburg – Buffalo Pass **172-3**

King William's Town: Glamour of an old garrison town **174-5**

Aliwal North – Lady Grey – Barkly East – Rhodes – Maclear – Elliot **176-7**

Aliwal North – Bethulie – Norvalspont – Venterstad – Burgersdorp **178-9**

Queenstown – Lady Frere – Indwe – Otto du Plessis Pass – Dordrecht **180-1**

Fort Beaufort – Alice – Cathcart – Stutterheim – Keiskammahoek **182-3**

Hogsback: Mountaintop wonderland of falls and forests **184-5**

Left: *A misty morning on the high-lying, forested slopes of Hogsback.*

The timeless magic of Umngazi Mouth and Port St Johns

This drive from Umtata to Port St Johns leads east through the hills and valleys of central Transkei, passing the ominous bulk of Mhlengana Rock. Almost all of the route is tarred. You may wish to stay the night at Umngazi Mouth. As with all trips through sparsely settled areas, determine conditions before you set out. Avoid travelling at night.

**Umtata
Libode
Mhlengana Rock
Port St Johns
Silaka Nature Reserve
Umngazi Mouth
130 – 150 km**

Huberta the divine hippo.

LEAVE CENTRAL UMTATA by driving east along Sutherland Street. Cross Madeira Street and note your kms immediately after the traffic lights. Continue out of town along Sutherland Street, which becomes the R61. After 2,7 km you cross the Mtata River and enter a restful, undulating landscape of rustic villages, small maize fields and cattle kraals flanking the road. After 13 km, stop on the left shoulder of the road and cross the road for a fine view back the way you have come, over the Mtata Valley.

From here the road leads into progressively greener country, with small stands of eucalyptus and wattle dotted about the grassy hillsides. Cross the Mdlankomo River 27 km after leaving Umtata and, 900 m later, reach a turn-off left into the small town of Libode. The town is worth visiting, especially on a Friday or Saturday, when the local Pondo and Mpondomise people trade beadwork here. Whether or not you drive into the town, note your kms at this junction as you continue on the main road towards Port St Johns.

Libode to Port St Johns

About 18 km from Libode, the road begins the descent through the Mhlengana Cutting into the magnificent Mngazi Valley – the cutting includes some sharp curves and requires slow, careful driving, especially in rainy weather. At 20,5 km from Libode, stop on the shoulder of the road for a good view over the Mngazi Valley and eastwards to the distant Indian Ocean. Stop again, 800 m later, to see in front of you and to your right Mhlengana Rock – where, according to legend, offenders were formerly executed, by pushing them over the side. Looking down from here into the Mngazi Valley, you can see rows of white huts perched above the river as it snakes towards the sea. Another 1,7 km brings you to the base of Mhlengana Rock.

Driving on from here, you pass hillsides thickly covered with aloes. A little over 26 km from Libode, the cutting ends and you drive past picturesque Xhosa settlements. After a further 18 km you reach a parking area on your right, from where there are good views west over the tranquil Mngazana River. Note your kms as you leave this parking area.

Soon the road drops down again into the Mngazi Valley, crosses the Mngazi River (also written as Umngazi), and then climbs out of the valley on the eastern side. After driving almost 12 km from the parking area, keep straight on the R61 past a road on your right signposted to 'Umngazi River Mouth'.

Mhlengana (execution rock) on the road to Port St Johns.

The Mngazi River meanders through rural Transkei.

After 3,7 km the R61 descends quite sharply into a valley blanketed in thick riverine forest, and shortly after this you emerge from the greenery to your first view of the *Mzimvubu* (hippopotamus) River. After 12,5 km, you pass, on your left, the bridge that carries the eastward arm of the R61 over the river to Lusikisiki, Kokstad and Port Edward in southern KwaZulu-Natal.

Follow the course of the river until you enter Port St Johns. Note your kms as you enter the town. After 900 m stop on the left side of the road and walk down onto the beach at the point where the impressive Mzimvubu reaches the sea. Behind you are the famous 'Gates', the two headlands that flank the river mouth – Mount Thesiger to the west and Mount Sullivan to the east.

Port St Johns to Silaka Nature Reserve

Return to your car and retrace your route for 300 m. Take the second turn-off on the left (the road to Second Beach), noting your kms as you turn. This road leads west out of the town. After 2,5 km, turn left onto a dirt track, which twists up and around a steep hillside. Eventually this track leads along a high, narrow ridge, and brings you, after 1,5 km, to a grassy hilltop from where there is a splendid view over the coast. To the west the Indian Ocean thunders down on Second and Third beaches, where dense subtropical vegetation

HIPPO ON THE MOVE

One of the great legends of Port St Johns concerns Huberta the hippo, who strolled into the town one day and found it so much to her liking that she stayed for six months. Huberta's incredible journey started in November 1928, when she left her muddy swamp in northern KwaZulu-Natal, and ended three years and 1 600 km later. She wandered at a leisurely rate along the coast, stopping in Durban, Port St Johns and East London. Some Pondos of the Wild Coast honoured her wherever she went as the reincarnation of a legendary diviner and, in Port St Johns, she was the first hippo to wallow in the Mzimvubu River for almost one hundred years. At night she ambled through the streets, venturing into gardens for food.

From the Wild Coast, Huberta's wanderings took her south to East London, which she reached in March 1931. She was spotted asleep on the main railway line and was gently nudged out of the way by a kindly engine-driver.

Huberta's wanderings ended suddenly and sadly when she was shot while bathing in the Keiskamma River – by three hunters who claimed to know nothing of her special status.

BORDER & TRANSKEI

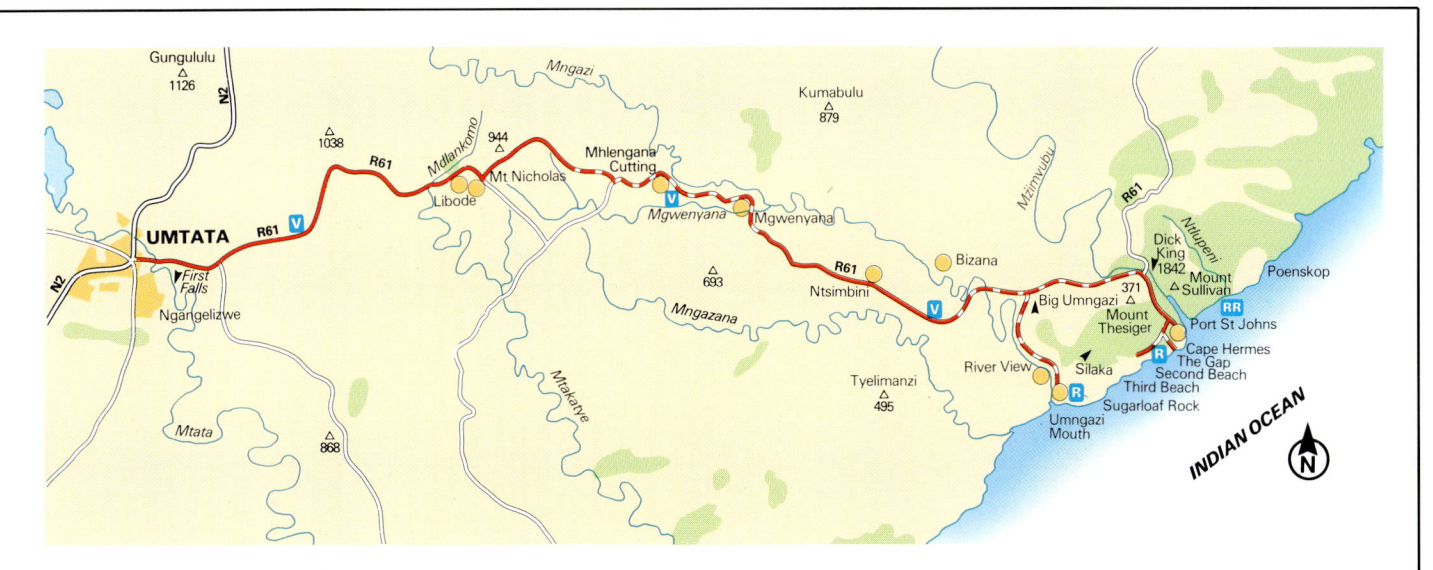

THE ILL-FATED SAO JOÃO

Transkei's shore is littered with wrecks, dating back to the days when the first European navigators edged gingerly along this treacherous, uncharted coast on their way to seek the riches of the Orient. Port St Johns is thought to owe its name to one of the earliest of these wrecked vessels, a Portuguese sailing ship, the *Sao João* (Saint John).

The *Sao João* came to grief on the rocks just south of the Mzimvubu River on 5 June 1552. Miraculously, of the 540 people on board, 440 passengers and crew reached the shore alive – and faced a 700 km walk to Lourenço Marques (Maputo). Hunger and sickness, and hostile locals, all took their toll as the survivors painfully made their way along the coast. After three months of hardship, the straggling party reached Lourenço Marques, only to discover that the annual trading ship to Portugal had just left.

The disappointed band continued their journey northwards, losing many lives, until just 25 survivors eventually reached the island of Mozambique, roughly 1 600 km from the wreck of the *Sao João*.

PORT ST JOHNS

The story of Port St Johns began in 1846, when the British schooner, *Rosebud*, became the first vessel to cross the sandbar at the mouth of the Mzimvubu River – proving that this was a viable harbour. It became a busy trading port, supplying ivory, maize, hides and other goods to the outside world. But the traders who settled here and the soldiers of the British garrison, established in 1882, lived a very isolated existence – albeit surrounded by some of the world's finest scenery. The majestic gates of Mount Thesiger and Mount Sullivan, named after General Thesiger and Commodore Sullivan who hoisted the Union Jack here, bore mute witness to many drinking parties under the wild fig trees.

Life is more orderly today, but the town retains its isolated atmosphere and is a popular retreat for naturalists seeking simpler lifestyles. This stretch of coast has some of the best fishing spots in southern Africa, and the bathing facilities are good. There are numerous walks through beautiful riverine forests and along uncluttered sandy beaches.

Wreck of the Sao João, from an 18th-century pamphlet.

Beadwork in Transkei.

The wide estuary of the Mzimvubu River near Port St Johns.

seems to tumble down the cliffs into the sea. By now you will also have noticed a difference in the climate in the subtropical coastal region.

Return to the tarred road and turn left towards Second Beach, noting your kms. After 2,6 km you pass a turn-off to Second Beach and, a short distance after this, you cross a bridge and reach a sign pointing the way to Third Beach. Turn onto this track to Third Beach, which leads through dense bush and up a hill to the entrance to Silaka Nature Reserve and Third Beach. Drive down the hill towards the beach, cross a small stream, and take the first track leading to your left. After driving 200 m along this track, you reach an attractive picnic site. Blesbok, wildebeest, steenbok and vervet monkeys are protected in the reserve, and more than 200 bird species have been recorded.

Silaka Nature Reserve to Umngazi Mouth

Retrace your route to Port St Johns and leave town on the R61. Keep straight where the eastward arm of the R61 leads right to Lusikisiki, and note your kms. Some 12,5 km later, turn left for Umngazi Mouth.

This narrow sideroad twists and turns as it follows the eastern bank of the river. The river's name means 'place of blood', recalling clan warfare that took place in its valley. You pass through an assortment of banana plantations, patches of dense forest and fields of pumpkins and maize. Just under 12 km after turning, you pass through the gate of Umngazi River Bungalows and a short distance further brings you to a parking area at the river's edge. The views of sea and estuary are outstanding, and surf and river fishing (including fly fishing) are popular pastimes. Park here for an attractive 500 m walk along the banks of the river to the sea. An impressive feature is the great cliff face known as Brazen Head or Ndluzulu, after the thundering sound of the surf.

Transkei Tourism Bureau Umtata Tel (0471) 25344
Umngazi River Bungalows PO Box 75, Port St Johns 4830 Tel (0471) 22370

Where the mighty Mzimvubu flows through rocky gates to the sea

From historic, oak-shaded Kokstad we set out for the coast over the green hills of Pondoland. The terrain offers fascinating glimpses of the lifestyle of Xhosa rural communities, and terraced maize fields, surrounding thousands of neatly built huts, stretch as far as the eye can see. Through Flagstaff and Lusikisiki we drop to the coast. The last 16 km is on gravel roads.

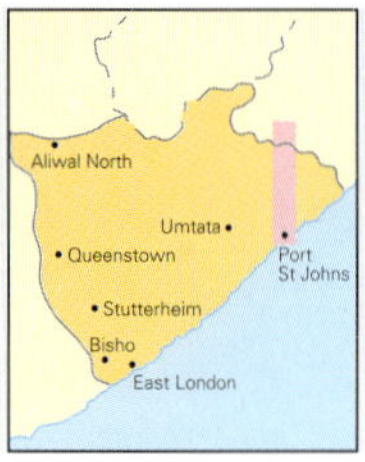

Kokstad
Flagstaff
Lusikisiki
Port St Johns
320 – 340 km

TAKE TIME TO EXPLORE Kokstad before starting this drive in front of the museum, diagonally opposite the Town Hall in Main Street. Note your kms as you set off, driving south down Main Street. Just before the second set of traffic lights, turn right into Barker Street and pass the war memorial on your left and the magistrate's offices on your right. This quaint-looking old building runs the length of the block. Turn left into Hope Street, which leads straight out of town to join the N2 heading in the direction of Mount Ayliff. As the road climbs, the spectacular mountain scenery south-east of Kokstad unfolds, the high hilltops sometimes shrouded in low cloud. This region can be extremely cold in winter, and the mountain grassland type of vegetation is similar to that of the southern Drakensberg of KwaZulu-Natal.

After 10 km the road begins a descent into a world of endless green hills, dotted as far as the eye can see with Xhosa huts. These spread across the landscape in a loose-knit network of straggling villages and rural communities, surrounded by carefully tended, terraced market gardens and maize fields that slope down the steep hillsides. After 16,6 km, turn left onto the tarred road (T4) to Bizana/Flagstaff/Port St Johns. Note your kms here. Sharp curves and steep gradients characterize much of the route now, as the road climbs and drops through successive valleys.

Visibility can be bad in the mist over the mountain passes and moderate speeds are advised. Other traffic hazards in this region are potholes, livestock in the road and the precipitous (often unbarricaded) roadside fall-aways that accompany the steep topography. The eye is constantly attracted by the scenic valley vistas that appear on either side of the road, overlooked by large, round-topped hills that resemble giant puddings.

After 33 km on the T4, keep straight towards Port St Johns at the intersection with the road to Port Edward. At this point your route becomes the R61, which descends over the next 30 km to Flagstaff, a little town that offers poor sightseeing. After leaving Flagstaff, the road continues its descent along the coastal escarpment for a further 46 km to Lusikisiki, where the R61 passes through the town centre, a convenient refuelling point.

The tar ends 21 km after Lusikisiki and the final 16 km stretch to the coast is on a poor-quality gravel surface. The terrain has now become deep, enclosed valleys, heavily covered with sweet-thorns intermingled with wild bananas and thick undergrowth interspersed with huts and maize patches.

The final descent to Port St Johns is through dense forest, giving wonderful views of the magnificent natural gateway to the sea, formed by the Mzimvubu River gorge and its two gigantic cliffs that frame the wide estuary. Steep, rocky cliffs loom over the road on this final section of the route and rocks in the road are an occasional hazard. After crossing the river, turn left at the T-junction. The road runs along the southern bank of the estuary, offering superb views of the continuous cliff face that towers over the northern bank, and is dominated by the corresponding cliff on the southern bank as you enter Port St Johns, a once-famous coastal jewel and potentially still one of southern Africa's loveliest natural beauty spots. It is thought to be named after *Santo João*, a Portuguese galleon wrecked in the vicinity in 1552. The first English name of the town was Rosebud Bay. Explore the town and beaches before embarking on the return route inland to Kokstad. (See pages 160 – 1.)

Kokstad Tourism Information PO Box 475 Kokstad 4700 Tel (037) 727 2083
Port St Johns Local Council PO Box 2 Port St Johns 4830 Tel (047) 44 1206

KOKSTAD

This thriving centre of old East Griqualand is named after Adam Kok, the Griqua leader who led a trek over the Drakensberg of some 2 000 burghers to make their homes here in 1863.

Trout-fishing is popular on many dams in the district, as well as on the Mzintlava River, which flows around the southern and western boundaries. The town has a proud rugby tradition dating back to 1890 and there are excellent facilities for other sports, including an 18-hole golf course, bowls, tennis, cricket and squash at the country club. The museum in Main Street (open weekdays 08h00 – 13h00 and 14h00 – 16h00) is interesting for its exhibits of the town's early history, both Griqua and colonial. Visit the Rocky Ridge Cheese Factory (Kokstad is famous for its cheese), and the Ingeli Weavers to see rugs and carpets being made.

UMNGAZI RIVER BUNGALOWS

Leisure is the keynote at this resort, situated within 20 km of Port St Johns. Described as an 'antidote' to city life, Umngazi River Bungalows has a wilderness setting that combines an unspoilt coastline with a meandering river. An on-site shop stocks fishing tackle and holiday wear. There are five guided walks to mangrove swamps and through indigenous forests (with some 240 bird species). Access to the resort is from the tarred road from Port St Johns to Umtata, and along 11,5 km of good gravel road.

Right: *Long Beach, Port St Johns.*

The twin spires of Kokstad's Catholic cathedral.

The grave of Griqua leader Adam Kok III, who died in 1875.

BORDER & TRANSKEI

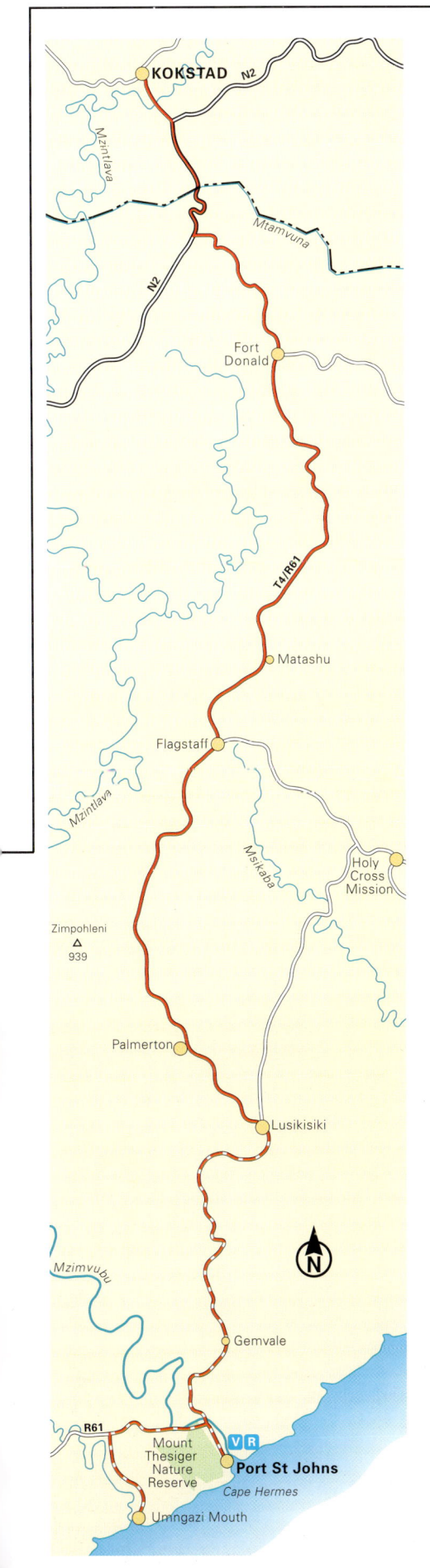

MOUNT CURRIE NATURE RESERVE

This beautiful reserve offers excellent hiking, camping, angling and bird-watching. The bird list exceeds 220 recorded species, ranging from flufftails in the vlei to bearded vultures seen by climbers on Mount Currie. Wildlife is varied and includes grey rhebuck and mountain reedbuck, both commonly seen, as well as oribi, grey duiker, common reedbuck, bushbuck and blesbok. There are several climbs and walks (some along old cattle tracks and paths) and also a self-guided trail around Crystal Dam near the camp. The dam is popular with anglers and is stocked with large-mouth bass and bluegill. Watersports are popular in summer. The camp ground has 10 sites with communal cooking and ablution facilities, and picnic areas are provided. A national monument in the reserve commemorates Adam Kok's laager that he set up for his followers on the southern slopes. Their cemetery is also in the reserve.

PORT ST JOHNS

Two precipitous sandstone cliffs – 'the Port St Johns Gates' – overlook the mouth of the Mzimvubu River and dominate the splendid natural setting of this once-famous Wild Coast resort.

A lack of subsidies, and decades of neglect prior to political reform, led to the town's becoming almost derelict. Now, with funding becoming available again, restoration projects and a revived tourism infra-structure are promised. Second Beach, 5 km south of the town, provides superb surfing and safe bathing during peak seasons, when life-savers are on duty. A view of the bay and headland ('The Gap') has been rated by an influential German tourism magazine as one of the world's five most beautiful coastal vistas. Follow the well-signposted road to the end of the point at Second Beach.

Abundant grazing for a small herd near Port St Johns.

European building styles predominate in this Transkei village.

Shreds of morning mist hang over the Mzimvubu River.

The sand bar is an ominous barrier to shipping at the mouth of the Mzimvubu River at Port St Johns.

• TRANSKEI TRADITIONS •

In the land of *uthikoloshe* and the giant Lightning Bird

An endless succession of grassy hillsides, clusters of thatched huts, friendly people and healthy cattle – ingredients of a Transkei holiday.

White clay masks an initiate's face.

ALTHOUGH OLD-STYLE South African history told of southward-migrating Nguni peoples who clashed with Cape colonists moving north and east in the 18th century, the Transkei – the land beyond the Kei – has been occupied by the Nguni and their ancestors for many centuries. Their presence has been confirmed by archaeologists and was recorded by shipwrecked Portuguese mariners who trudged wearily along the Wild Coast beaches, leaving behind them shattered caravels and broken dreams of the route to the Indies. Inland, had they but known it, lay abundant food in a smiling land of green hills and clear rivers, like the Great *Kei* itself – the 'sand' or 'shining' river of the earlier Khoikhoi.

Although they were doughty opponents in a century of wars of colonial expansion, the people of Transkei did not possess the rigid militarism with which Shaka was to infuse the Zulu nation to the north. Wars between clans were fought by no more than a few dozen warriors, casualties were slight and, by the end of the day, the quarrel was considered as settled. The men went back to admiring their Sanga cattle – a longhorn-zebu cross, now extinct as a result of interbreeding with European strains – and the women returned to tilling the fields. This idyll was ended by the coming of the white man and the *difaqane* – a state of continuous war – unleashed by Shaka.

Early in the 19th century, Transkei was already settled by a number of different tribes, the largest of which was the Xhosa, named after their 16th-century founder, the son of Mnguni. The Xhosa were – and are still – divided into two main groups, stemming from the followers of Gcaleka and his grand-nephew Ngqika (Gaika). Other clans include the Thembu, Mpondo, Mpondomise and Bomvana. Relative newcomers, fleeing from the difaqane, were the Mfengu, made up of numerous destitute clans. The Mfengu were settled by the Cape Government on land belonging to the Gcaleka in the southern part of Transkei – an act that created great resentment and led eventually to the outbreak of 'the last frontier war' in 1877.

'National suicide of the Xhosa'
The coastal strip for some 32 km north of the Mbashe (Bashee) River is known as Bomvanaland, home of a people who had originally sought refuge among the Gcaleka, but who moved to this region in 1856 after refusing to take part in the cattle-killing that was to become known to whites as 'the national suicide' of the Xhosa. The causes were many and complex, and found their trigger in a young girl's vision.

Nongqawuse, the girl, claimed to have been spoken to by ancestral spirits and to have seen visions at a pool on the Gxara River. If the people killed their cattle and destroyed their crops, she said, their warrior ancestors would arise and assist them in driving the whites from the land on an appointed day, believed to have been in February 1857. The people did as she instructed – but then the day passed, and no ancestors appeared, neither did the promised crops nor the cattle miraculously return. As a result, at least 25 000 people are believed to have starved to death.

In about the year 1500 two sons of a chief, Mpondo and Mpondomise, formed two separate clans, which are known today by the names of their founders. Pondoland, the region in which they live, is the section of coast north of the Umtata River. Here high hills sweep down to a shore that has claimed innumerable fine ships.

Uthikoloshe and impundulu
Even today, witchcraft and superstition play a large part in the traditional way of life, and there is widespread belief in the hairy and mischievous goblin known as *uthikoloshe*. As a rule, uthikoloshe can be seen only by children who, unaware of his evil reputation, accept him as a playmate. He becomes a danger only after he has been captured by a witch who makes him the instrument of evil. Hili, as he is also known, may cause disease in human beings and animals, but is said to show mercy sometimes, especially when the intended victim is a young child.

Another creature inspiring fear is *impundulu* – the huge lightning-bird, believed to cause death and disease. Standing, impundulu is as tall as a man and, when the creature flaps its wings, the roar of thunder is heard. When it spits, so the superstition goes, lightning flashes across the sky.

Rivers are believed to be the home of *aBantu bomlambo* – the people of the river. These are kindly creatures, very closely resembling humans, except that they have smooth, flipper-like appendages instead of hands and feet. There should be no mourning for a person who has drowned and whose body is not recovered, because he has been accepted into a family of aBantu bomlambo.

Despite widespread acceptance of Christianity among the *amaXhosa*, traditional religious practices flourish. There is, for example, veneration of a supreme being, who may be *umDali*, *Qamata* or *uThixo* – creator of the world and of life.

An important member of the community is the *igqirha*, or diviner, who mediates between the world of the living and that of the spirits. Failure to satisfy the spirits will inevitably bring misfortune, and professional advice must be obtained on how to placate the dead. Most of the diviners are women who have spent a long period of apprenticeship with an older practitioner.

Outside the towns, life is concentrated in the family settlement unit known as *umzi* – a collection of huts grouped around the cattle enclosure. Typically, those who live here consist of the head of the family, his wife or wives, and children – including the married sons.

Huts were formerly made from grass and reeds plaited around a framework of sticks, but during the past century this style has been replaced by a round, mud-walled hut with a cone-shaped thatch roof. The traditional floor is of cowdung or the crushed soil of an antheap, tightly compressed and easily swept.

A hut with two similar-sized euphorbia trees growing close by is probably the birthplace of twins. Among many clans, twins were once regarded as unlucky and either one or both would be killed. Today in Transkei the birth of twins is welcomed, and the trees are planted to grow up with them. The death of a tree foretells the death of the twin with whom it is associated.

Education and initiation
Traditionally, Transkeian children had no formal education, but would learn from their elders the work that would occupy their adult life. From an early age, boys herded cattle and girls helped their mothers with the chores of housekeeping, cooking, and gathering water and firewood.

Hunting and war games have been regarded as important to a boy's development, and stick-fighting is an advanced art in Transkei. A boy's standing in youthful society is based on his skill with the fighting-sticks – a stout knobkerrie for attack and a stave for defence.

Before boys and girls are accepted as adults they must undergo initiation. With the exception of almost all Mpondo clans, circumcision is regarded as an essential step towards manhood. The youth's departure for the initiation lodge is a significant event, which may be marked by the sacrifice of a goat. Initiation schools may consist of only a few boys, and it is considered important to be a member of a school attended by a chief's son. The school is held in a remotely situated hut, usually near a stream and specially built for the purpose. Initiates are instructed by a 'father', assisted by 'guardians', and, before circumcision, must sit in the stream, ritually cleansing themselves while confessing their misdeeds to the adults. The circumcision itself is expected to be borne unflinchingly.

Throughout the period of initiation, the boys must go naked beneath the particular pattern of blanket of their initiation lodge, with their bodies and faces smeared with white clay to conceal their identities and as protection against evil. For a month after circumcision, while the wound is healing, initiates must remain in their lodge. After this, a goat is slaughtered and initiates may venture from the hut in search of food.

At the end of the initiation period the new adults wash the white clay from their bodies and the lodge is burnt, together with every article used during the initiation period – symbolizing the end of the child-life.

In their colourful traditional garb, the peoples of Transkei make fascinating subjects for the photographer. However, before you photograph an individual or a group, always ask permission, even if you have to do this by means of sign language. A suitable gift to the subject is always greatly appreciated.

A red and gold dawn silhouettes the Hole-in-the-Wall formation, a short distance south-west of Coffee Bay.

Above: *Regional dress varies.*

Right: *White water on the Wild Coast.*

High, green hills sweep down to the cliffs of the Wild Coast

This route leads from bustling Umtata through the rural heartland of Transkei to the sea. We stop to view the Mtata River Valley, take a sideroad to the fascinating Hole-in-the-Wall and continue to the resort of Coffee Bay. As with all trips through sparsely settled areas, determine local conditions before you set out. Avoid travelling at night.

Umtata
Viedgesville
Mqanduli
Hole-in-the-Wall
Coffee Bay
Mapuzi River
Mtata Mouth
140 – 160 km

THIS IS AN ATTRACTIVE drive but the rural nature of the area travelled as well as, on occasion, the rather poor condition of the roads tend to make for a slow but pleasurable outing.

Leave Umtata by driving south on the N2 (towards East London) and note your kms as you pass the Holiday Inn on your right. After 16 km, turn left onto tar at a road signposted 'Mqanduli/Coffee Bay' – and note your kms again as you turn. Drive with care – the road is flanked by many small, unfenced communities, and cattle and other livestock wander freely across the road.

Pass through the small trading centre of Viedgesville, after which the road begins to wind through undulating hills towards the coast – a fine drive, highlighted in early winter by the magnificent crimson blooms of aloes and, in summer, by green fields of maize. After 8 km, you descend into an area of cool eucalyptus plantations and, shortly after this, the sea appears mistily through the green rolling hills. About 6 km later, you cross the Manqondo River and climb to the little town of *Mqanduli* (the maker of grind-stones).

Mqanduli to Hole-in-the-Wall

Continue along the main tarred road, which crosses countryside deeply scarred by soil erosion. After 30 km, there is a cairn erected on the left side of the road to commemorate Dick King's historic ride from Port Natal to Grahamstown in 1842; 1,8 km after this you pass a Xhosa village on the opposite side of the road, then a deep, tree-lined valley.

Pass the Lutubeni Mission (there may be a signpost reading 'Mission Hospital') at just

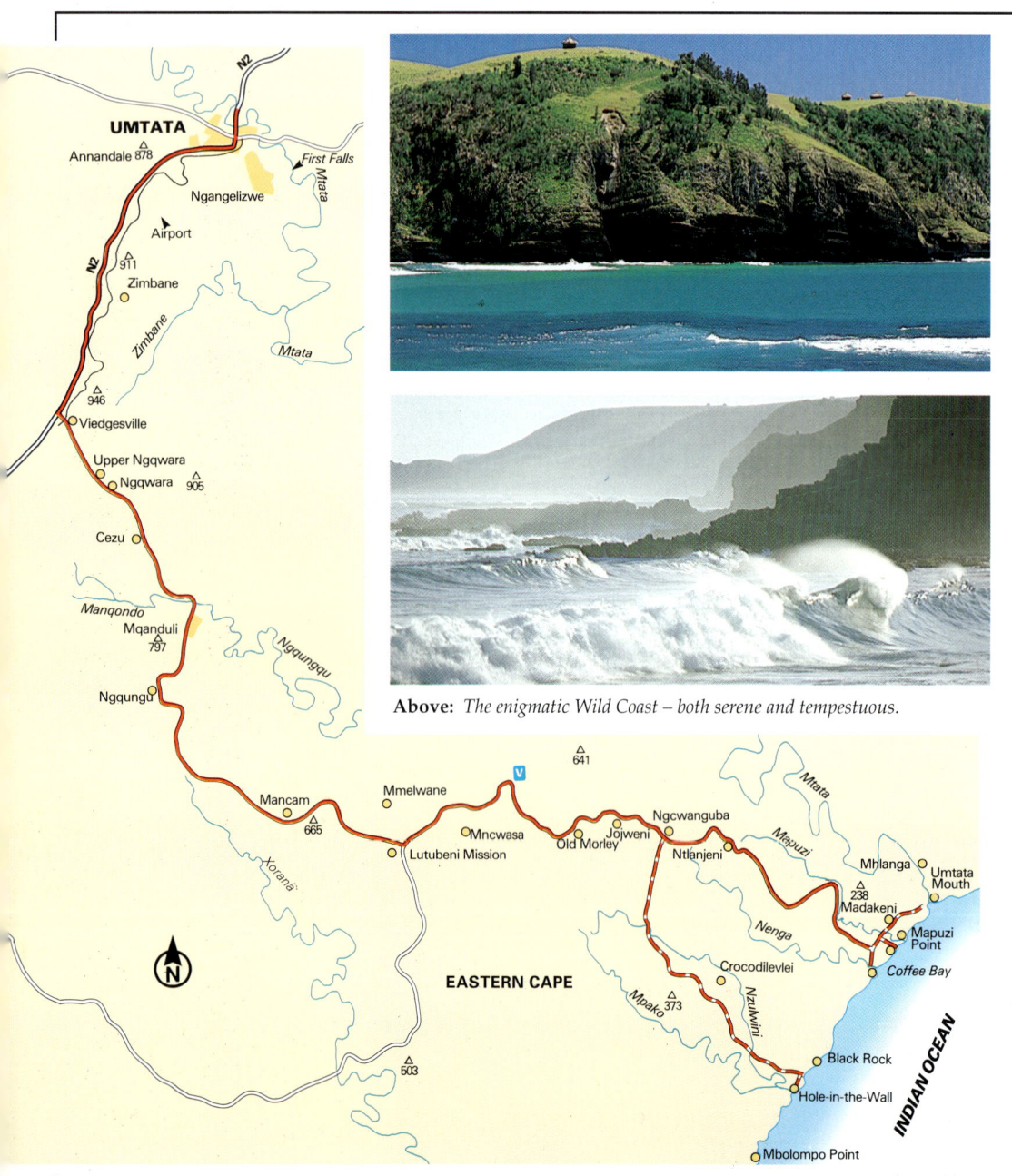

Above: *The enigmatic Wild Coast – both serene and tempestuous.*

HOLE-IN-THE-WALL

One of southern Africa's most interesting natural formations is the massive outcrop of rock that rises from the sea some 8 km south of Coffee Bay. Referred to by local people as *esiKhaleni* (the place of sound), it is more widely known as Hole-in-the-Wall. The huge tunnel through the centre of the cliff has been eroded over millennia by the constant pounding of the waves, and is large enough to accommodate a fair-sized fishing boat. Many people have been tempted to climb the cliff faces, but most have had to be rescued from the grassy top. There are also local tales of people who have drowned or been dashed against the rocks when trying to swim through the tunnel. Fishing in this area is excellent.

WILD COAST SHIPWRECKS

This wild stretch of coast has long proved treacherous to ships, and beneath the restless waves lie the remains of many vessels – plus their cargoes and their passengers. Most of these ships were Portuguese, including the *Sao Bento*, one of the largest ships of the 16th century, which foundered at the mouth of the Mtata River on 21 April 1554 with the loss of 150 lives. The *Santo Alberto*, a merchant ship, was wrecked near the Hole-in-the-Wall on 24 March 1593, losing a valuable treasure and 63 lives. A particularly unfortunate gentleman, Manuel de Castro, survived one shipwreck and the subsequent overland trek to the north, was taken from Lourenço Marques to India, and was then put aboard the *Sao Bento* for Portugal. He died in despair when that ship also perished on the same stretch of coast and he was faced with the prospect of a second overland trek. In 1991, all those aboard the cruise ship *Oceanos* were saved by helicopters. The ship, which had developed a heavy list, sank soon after.

under 40 km. Now the road begins its long and winding descent to the coast through a succession of river valleys densely covered with subtropical vegetation. After 49 km, turn left onto a narrow gravel track that follows the ridge of a steep mountain. Some 200 m along this track, park your car and look east for a magnificent view over the Mtata River valley – a wild, unspoilt landscape.

Return to the main road and turn left to continue your journey, noting your kms as you turn. After 9,2 km turn right onto the gravel road for picturesque Hole-in-the-Wall, noting your kms again.

The road descends gently through thick forest and curls around small settlements of thatch-roofed huts. Some 8 km later you reach a fork; take the road on your left, which leads into the territory of the friendly Bomvana people. After 11 km you descend sharply into a valley and, a few kilometres further on, you reach Hole-in-the-Wall, named thus in 1823 by a passing English ship's captain. The Hole-in-the-Wall Hotel (which offers lunch) is metres from the crashing surf and white sands of the Indian Ocean. The resort consists of hotel and self-catering accommodation.

Pass the hotel and continue up the hill for a beautiful view overlooking the geological formation known as the Hole-in-the-Wall.

Numerous people have attempted to climb the 'wall' containing the hole, which is no easy exercise. A Bomvana man, who had watched a party of experienced mountaineers reach the summit, tried his hand. He climbed to the top but, when he had to get down again, he lost his nerve and sat calling for help for the next three days until news of his plight reached campers who – fortunately – could climb.

Hole-in-the-Wall to Coffee Bay
Retrace your route to the main tarred road and turn right towards Coffee Bay, noting your kms as you turn.

You now descend through a series of loops and bends into a particularly attractive part of Transkei, with huts sprinkled across the rolling hills. After about 14 km, palm trees come into view and shortly after this you cross the Mapuzi River. Pass a road on your left to Umtata Mouth and, a little more than 1 km after, enter the village of Coffee Bay. Drive past the Ocean View Hotel and park near the former Lagoon Hotel. From here, a short, sandy path leads under a canopy of indigenous trees to the wonderfully tranquil beach.

Coffee Bay to Mtata Mouth
Retrace your route out of the village and turn right for Mapuzi and Umtata Mouth. Just after the start of the gravel surface, turn right for Mapuzi Golf Course onto a distinctly rural track to be negotiated slowly and with care. After about 2 km the road drops from the ridge down into the Mapuzi River valley and reaches the lush, subtropical Mapuzi Reserve. There are attractive views from the base of the steep headland and, if you are prepared to climb it, the top offers even grander views east to Mapuzi Point and west to a line of mighty, precipitous cliffs.

Return to your car, retrace your route to the tarred road and turn right. After about 2 km, turn right onto a gravel road at the signpost 'T314 Mdumbi'. This road winds above the bank of the Mtata River for several kilometres and crosses a bridge before reaching a fork. Go right here, onto a road that takes you to the summit of a hill overlooking the Mtata River and its generous expanse of white, sandy beach. You may want to park your car at the side of the road here, and walk down the steep, grassy slopes to the river. There is an unscheduled ferry service that carries passengers to the other side.

Return at your leisure to your choice of accommodation. (This coast is renowned for its beautiful subtropical sunsets.)

Transkei Tourism Bureau Umtata Tel (0471) 25344
Ocean View Hotel Coffee Bay Tel (0471) 37 0252
Hole-in-the-Wall Hotel PO Box 13135, Vincent 5217 Tel (0431) 31 2715

Subtropical aloes dot the hillside above the mouth of the Mapuzi River.

Anglers try their luck at Hole-in-the-Wall.

COFFEE BAY
It is believed that the restful resort of Coffee Bay received its name when a large cargo of coffee beans was washed up at the mouth of the Nenga River after a shipwreck. Many of the beans took root and grew into small coffee plants, but all died and today the only coffee found here is imported. Nestling snugly between the rolling green hills of the Transkei coast, this small village has two hotels, caravan and camping areas, and various sports facilities. The beach is popular with surfers and the lagoon is safe.

Near Coffee Bay, the Mapuzi River reaches the sea in a spectacular curve, passing steep sandbanks and high, wooded hills.

Donkey power in Transkei.

Densely forested valleys and idyllic Wild Coast beaches

Our route leads from Butterworth across fertile hills to the historic village of Centane. From here, we drive to the palm-fringed beaches of Qolora Mouth and to Mazeppa Bay. Almost the entire route is on gravel roads. You may want to stay the night in Mazeppa Bay – or change the order of drives from Centane to end your day at Qolora Mouth.

**Butterworth
Tutura
Centane
Qolora Mouth
Kobonqaba River Valley
Mazeppa Bay
130 – 150 km**

TRAVELLING NORTH on the N2, just after the town centre of Butterworth, turn right for Centane (Kentani) at the traffic lights – roughly 200 m after crossing the Gcuwa River on the outskirts of the town – noting your kms as you turn. The first 2 km of this road takes you through the industrial fringes of Butterworth, the oldest town in Transkei and main trading centre for the southern part of the territory. It grew up around a Wesleyan mission school built in 1827. A few kilometres after the turn, the road surface changes to gravel and you enter typically rural Transkei, with tall grass and dense groves of acacia trees flanking the road.

After 7 km the road descends into a small valley, crosses a bridge and soon passes through farming country, with maize fields, cattle kraals and clusters of huts scattered across the hillsides. After 13 km you drive through the small settlement of Tutura, and after a further 3 km you enter an area that is relatively densely populated – be alert for livestock wandering onto the road. After travelling 22 km from the N2, stop on the left side of the road for a panoramic view of the countryside stretching down to meet the sea. To your right you can see the distant valley of the Great Kei River snaking southwards. This part of Transkei is rich cattle country, with grassland covering the hills. After good rains in spring and summer, the country is emerald green, whereas in autumn and winter – the dry season – the grass fades to a drab brown.

Continue along the main road and, at 24,5 km, stop again for a view left over the mighty valley of the Kobonqaba River. Note your kms as you drive on from this spot.

Just 700 m later you pass the Centane Hills Forest Reserve and from here the landscape becomes greener. After 7,6 km you enter Centane (Kentani). The village contains several shops, as well as being of historical importance (see below).

Centane to Qolora Mouth
Retrace your route out of Centane and, on the outskirts of the village, turn left, following the sign for Qolora Mouth and Kei Mouth. Note your kms at the turn.

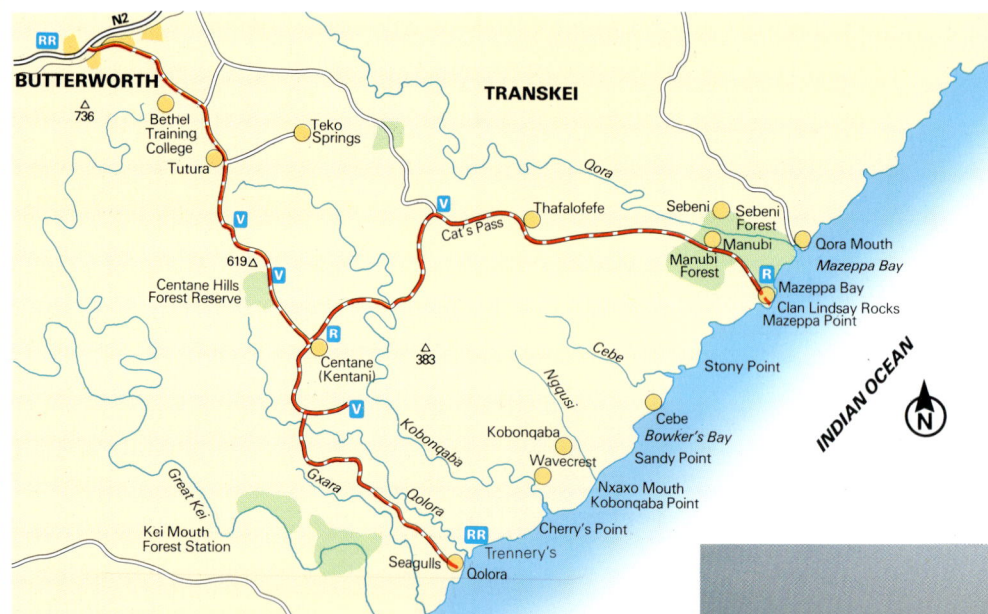

MAZEPPA BAY
If you don't catch a fish at Mazeppa Bay, you won't catch one anywhere – so say the residents of the beautiful resort along this interesting coastline. The fishing here is so good that people come from all over the world hoping to catch 'the big one'. Shark fishing is the main attraction – particularly hammerhead sharks – and every August heralds the arrival of hundreds of fishermen in the grip of 'shark fever'. Great white sharks, ragged-tooth sharks and hammerheads are caught in abundance – the largest of all being a 791 kg great white that was caught in April 1981 off the rocks at the Boiling Pot. The following year a dusky grey, weighing 564 kg, was caught at the same place.

Wave-kissed mouth of the Kobonqaba River near Qolora.

ATTACK ON CENTANE
In February 1878, some 5 000 Xhosa warriors, led by the great chiefs Kreli and Sandile, mounted an attack on the British garrison of 700 men stationed at Centane. Despite assurances from the spirit diviner, Xito, that the white soldiers' bullets would not harm them, 300 warriors lost their lives. Kreli and his soldiers disappeared, hiding in the forests and valleys of Gcalekaland, until eventually they surrendered and went into retirement near Elliotdale. Sandile and his followers fled south to the Kei River.

Wild Coast graveyard: wreck of the Jacaranda *near Qolora.*

The road winds down a small mountain pass – and it is worth stopping after 2,4 km for another good view over the coastal hills. You then begin the steep descent to the coast, passing through grasslands and thick acacia forest. About 6 km after noting your kms, you reach a fork – take the road leading right. (The road to the left leads to Kobonqaba Mouth, and we drive part of the way along it later.) A short distance after this fork you cross the Qolora River and, later, there are views to your right over the valley of the Gxara River (see opposite). Continue straight where a road branches right to Kei Mouth 20 km further.

A little over 27 km from Centane, palm trees appear and you enter Qolora, in an attractive subtropical coastal setting. You come to a sign that points the way to the Trennery's Hotel and the Seagulls Hotel (both of which offer lunch). Continue straight here and, roughly 300 m later, park on the grass overlooking the beach. You can take a short walk eastwards to the Qolora River mouth (allow 30 – 40 minutes).

When you leave Qolora to drive back towards Centane, note your kms at the sign that points the way to the hotels. Some 21 km later you reach the fork where the road to Kobonqaba Mouth leads off to your right. Turn onto the road to Kobonqaba Mouth, but stop after driving 4,4 km along it – for a breathtaking view of the Kobonqaba River Valley with its deep green subtropical forests. Retrace your route to the fork and turn right, to return to the town of Centane.

Centane to Mazeppa Bay

When you reach Centane, drive straight across the main road onto the road for Mazeppa Bay and Nxaxo Mouth – noting your kms. The road leads north-east and descends into the broad Kobonqaba Valley, dotted with rural settlements. After 8 km you cross the Kobonqaba River and, after 10 km, you pass a road on your right that leads to Wavecrest and Nxaxo Mouth. After travelling 20 km from Centane, you begin the descent of Cat's Pass. Stop here at the beginning of the pass for a fine view northwards over the valley of the *Qora* (place of clay) River.

You now penetrate the heart of Gcalekaland and, after 25,6 km, you pass the Dutch Reformed mission hospital of Thafalofefe. A further 14,4 km brings you into the Manubi Forest – noted for its indigenous yellowwood and stinkwood trees and a rich variety of orchids.

Some 48 km after leaving Centane you reach Mazeppa Bay, with one of the most idyllic beaches on the whole of the Wild Coast. Follow the main road down the hill and into the grounds of the Mazeppa Bay Hotel – the only hotel at this resort. Park in front of the reception area and walk 100 m, under a canopy of rustling palm trees, to the gently sloping white sand beach. If you then walk 500 m eastwards along the beach, you will come to a suspension footbridge linking the mainland to a small island, and you can end your day with a walk across the bridge while the Indian Ocean foams beneath your feet.

AA Office 27 Fleet Street, East London 5201
Tel (0431) 21271
Trennery's Hotel PO Box 31, Kei Mouth 5260
Tel (0474) 3293
Seagulls Hotel PO Box 61, Kei Mouth 5260
Tel (0474) 3287
Mazeppa Bay Hotel 9A Dyer Street, East London 5201 Tel (0431) 42 0382

End of the road: suspension bridge at Mazeppa Bay.

Finely chiselled rocks tumble into the sea at Mazeppa Bay.

A Xhosa youth during his initiation period.

SUICIDE OF A NATION

There is a small pool in the Gxara River where a legend was created that led to the tragic deaths of more than 40 000 people. In 1856 a 14-year-old prophetess, Nongqawuse, claimed that she had seen faces of her ancestral spirits in the pool and that they had warned her that the Gcaleka people should destroy their crops and cattle. If they did this, the sun would rise blood red, the white people would be driven from the land, and all the cattle pens and grain bins would be filled. For 10 months the Gcaleka – a dispossessed and desperate people – engaged in a frenzy of cattle killing and crop burning, until the day of deliverance, 18 February 1857, ended without any of the promised omens. They starved to death in their thousands. The girl fled to King William's Town and sought sanctuary with the British there until her death in 1898.

Traditional dress is still very much an important part of rural Transkei.

Exploring a romantic coast of sandy shores and lazy lagoons

East of the Buffalo River, the warm Indian Ocean washes gently into a succession of tranquil lagoons and glittering river estuaries. Inland the rounded hills are dotted with traditional African huts in a peaceful green landscape unexpected so close to a major city. A little more than half of this drive is on tarred roads, the rest is on gravel.

East London
Cintsa Mouth East
Cefane Mouth
Morgan Bay
Double Mouth
Gonubie
210 – 230 km

Leave East London on the North-East Expressway. After crossing the Nahoon River, turn right onto the N2 for Umtata/Gonubie. After 3,9 km, turn to your left for East Coast Resorts/Gonubie. At the T-junction, turn left and immediately afterwards turn right onto the R102 for East Coast Resorts, noting your kms. After 5,4 km, turn right onto the Schafli Road for East Coast Resorts, noting your kms again. You pass a number of turn-offs on your right. After 19 km, turn right for Cefane Mouth/Cintsa Mouth East and note your kms.

This pleasant rural road crosses a single-lane bridge shortly before the surface changes to gravel. You pass a turn-off to Cefane Mouth on your left, and the road descends directly towards the sea, the surface changing to tar; 400 m later turn left at the T-junction within the resort of Cintsa Mouth East and park under the trees. A shady 100 m path leads along the lagoon to the broad, gently shelving beach.

Cintsa Mouth East to Morgan Bay
Retrace your route out of Cintsa Mouth East and, roughly 3 km from the resort, turn right for Cefane Mouth. Within a further 2 km the road leads along the wide and placid Cefane Lagoon, with wooded hills on its far bank. Park at the end of this road – a short walk brings you to the beach and the lagoon mouth.

Return to the tarred Schafli Road and turn right; 7,6 km later, turn right at the T-junction onto the N2 towards Umtata, noting your kms. You pass an intersection with turn-offs to Kei Mouth and Haga Haga, and to Bluewater. After 21 km on the N2, turn right onto gravel towards Kei Mouth; 2,4 km later turn right at the T-junction towards Kei Mouth, noting your kms (the road on the left leads to Komga).

At the fork after 19 km, go left for Kei Mouth/Morgan Bay and turn right 14 km later for Morgan Bay. A further 7 km brings you to Morgan Bay, with its wide beaches and tranquil lagoon. (A hotel in the resort serves lunch – booking is advisable.)

Beyond the hotel you reach a small road – follow this past a beach, across a stream and uphill towards the Double Mouth Reserve. There is a gate across the road (please close it behind you), and beyond it a second fence, from where two sets of tracks lead to the left. Follow either of these and park where convenient. Footpaths crisscross the four headlands between Double Mouth and Morgan Bay, offering magnificent views of the sea and cliffs. The grassy hillside offers a splendid place to picnic, although there are no facilities.

Continue along the road towards the reserve. Just before the reserve entrance there is a white beacon on a low hill – a short walk uphill towards the beacon gives good views of the two broad river channels below.

Beyond the beacon the road descends to the camping and fishing spots at the beach, which offers a pleasant walk along the seashore.

Morgan Bay to Gonubie
Retrace your route, noting your kms as you pass the Morgan Bay Hotel. After 7,3 km, turn left at the oblique T-junction where the road from Kei Mouth joins from the right. After a further 14 km turn left towards East London and Haga Haga, named after the ceaseless murmur of the waves upon the shore.

Continue on this road for 23 km – past a turn-off to Haga Haga, across a number of narrow causeways and through several minor intersections. Opposite the Moria Church and a signpost to Mooiplaas, turn left onto the tarred N2 towards East London, noting your kms.

Shortly after the N2 becomes a double-lane freeway – roughly 30 km after you rejoined it – turn left for Beacon Bay/Gonubie. Turn left at the T-junction, noting your kms. After 7 km, turn left into Riverside Road for Gonubie Mouth Caravan Park. Less than 1 km along this road, turn right outside the caravan park onto the beach parking area for a pleasant late-afternoon walk along the sandy edge of the lagoon. Gonubie, known to Xhosa people as *Gqunube* after the bramble berries growing along the banks of the river, is a popular holiday resort with a safe bathing beach. The river is navigable in small boats for 3 km. Return to East London on the N2.

AA Office AA House, 27 Fleet Street, East London 5201 Tel (0431) 21271
East London Metropolitan Tourism Association 35 Argyll Street, East London 5201 Tel (0431) 26015

The broad sweep of the Nahoon River between low hills near East London.

Cintsa Mouth bay forms a backdrop to rustic farm buildings.

EAST LONDON
The first ship to exchange cargo at the mouth of the Buffalo River was George Rex's brig, *Knysna*, in 1836, and the little anchorage became known as Port Rex. Abandoned by the British for several years, the port was revived later with the creation of British Kaffraria and was named first London, then East London.

It was exposed to storms for many years, and the early name was recalled by some cynics, who suggested that the anchorage should be renamed Port Wrecks!

The headlands at Double Mouth offer superb walks overlooking rivers and sea.

The intimate resort of Morgan Bay nestles at the mouth of restful rivers.

THE RAUCOUS HADEDA

The coastal area east of East London, with its varied habitat and plentiful water, is particularly rich in bird life. At Morgan Bay, almost 200 species have been recorded in a relatively small area. Among the most common of the larger birds in this region is the hadeda, a type of ibis named for the raucous sound it makes when startled, and often also when flying. These short-legged wading birds hatch their chicks in early summer in nests built of platforms of sticks lined with grass, high in trees along the river banks.

MORGAN BAY

The idyllic resort at Morgan Bay, with its hotel, grew up at the spot named after AF Morgan, sailing master of the ship *Barracouta* in which Captain WF Owen surveyed the coastline in 1822. From adjacent Cape Morgan a tall light-tower flashes its message far out to sea. Nearby are the abandoned workings of the Cape Morgan titanium mine, first exploited in 1958.

Four rivers reach the sea within a few kilometres of each other on this stretch of coast. Northernmost is the Great Kei and south of it is the Ntshala River, which forms the lagoon at Morgan Bay. Further south the Gondwane and Quko rivers join to form the lagoon at Double Mouth. Rare shells are often found along these beaches, and fragments of ancient Chinese porcelain are sometimes washed out of forgotten wrecks to lie scattered on the sand.

THE SHIP OF BRIDES

Perhaps the most eagerly awaited ship to cast anchor in the river port of East London was the *Lady Kennaway* in 1857. Her 'cargo' consisted of 157 young Irish girls who had left their homeland to seek a new life – and husbands – on the Cape frontier. The men they came to marry were of the British-German Legion, disbanded after the Crimean War, who had been settled as farmers along the frontier. The severe shortage of eligible women had led the British government to import brides for the men. The *Lady Kennaway* was wrecked, but by then her precious human cargo was safely and happily ashore.

A lazy afternoon on a broad sweep of the Gonubie River.

Glittering river estuaries and the silent sands of an unspoilt coast

West of East London, along the fringes of the Indian Ocean, our route explores a pretty coastline with lagoons, winding rivers and wide sweeps of shining sand. We then swing inland to a rolling countryside of scrubby and forested hills, traditional home to a section of the Xhosa people. More than half the route is tarred, the rest is good gravel.

East London
Igoda Mouth
Kidd's Beach
Hamburg
Buffalo Pass
220 – 240 km

LEAVE EAST LONDON by driving west along Fleet Street. Go right at the fork, following the airport sign onto the R72. The road crosses a bridge over the railway line, then the John Vorster Bridge over the Buffalo River. At the end of the bridge, turn left into Nuffield Road and, a few hundred metres later, turn right at the T-junction. Turn left at the next T-junction into Bank Street and follow the road to the right, into Strand Street, following the sign for 'Coastal Resorts'.

After roughly 3,5 km on Marine Drive follow the larger road to the right – the road ahead leads to a shooting range. This stretch of road is part of the Grand Prix motor racing circuit (see opposite) and you soon pass between the grandstand and control tower, with the pit lane and pits on your left immediately afterwards.

Marine Drive to Igoda Mouth
Continue on this road across two narrow bridges, and follow the main road to the right where, on your left, a smaller road joins from Cove Rock. Within 2 km you reach an intersection with the R72.

Turn left onto the R72 towards Kidd's Beach and Port Elizabeth, noting your kms. You pass Ncera Road on your left and, soon afterwards – after 4,1 km on the R72 – turn left onto tar for Igoda Mouth, Winterstrand and Hlozi Beach, the surface changing to gravel after 1 km.

Pass a road on your right leading over the hill and, after 2 km on the gravel, turn right for Igoda Mouth. Park where the road ends, overlooking the mouth of the lagoon, for a pleasant stroll along the beach or lagoon shores.

Igoda Mouth to Kidd's Beach
Return to the R72 and turn left towards Port Alfred, noting your kms. You soon cross a bridge over the Igoda River, and then a bridge over the Gulu River. After 7,5 km there is a turn-off on your left to Gulu Beach. (To reach the beach along this road, turn right at the T-junction on the river bank, and left after the old bridge. This brings you to a small parking area with change-rooms and toilets next to the lagoon and the wide beach.)

Continuing on the R72, pineapple plantations either side of the road are a reminder that you have arrived in the heartland of pineapple production in South Africa. Pineapples are grown in the subtropical regions of Natal and Mpumalanga but most extensively in the Eastern Cape between the Kei and Bushman's rivers. The start of pineapple farming here is attributed to Charles Purdon, who in 1865 obtained some 30 Queen pineapple tops in the barber's shop of Lindsay Green at Grahamstown, and planted them on his farm Thorndon in the Bathurst district. The Purdon family also introduced the Cayenne variety after successfully cultivating some specimens from the Grahamstown Botanical Garden.

You cross the Mcantsi River 4,5 km beyond the Gulu Beach turn-off. After a further 800 m turn left for Kidd's Beach. The road leads to a parking area near the resort's tidal pool, and there are long stretches of unspoilt beach to walk on.

Kidd's Beach to Hamburg
Return to the R72 and turn left towards Port Elizabeth, noting your kms. You cross the Ncera River and, soon afterwards – 5,3 km after rejoining the R72 – you pass a gravel road on your left leading to Kayser's Beach.

You are now in an area that was formerly part of *Ciskei* (this side of the Kei River), the name given to land between the Keiskamma and the Kei rivers to distinguish it from Transkei, an area north and east of the Kei. Both areas were accorded 'independent republic' status for several years but, in 1994, on the assumption of democratic government in South Africa, were reincorporated into the Eastern Cape Province.

The road passes two turn-offs on your left to the Chalumna (Tyolomnqa) River mouth, then winds through the attractive scenery of the Keiskamma River valley.

You pass a turn-off on your right to Peddie after 41,4 km. Approximately 5 km further, turn left onto the gravel-surfaced R345 to Hamburg. Stop at the parking area at the extensive and magnificent beach, where a hotel and oyster farm add to the interest.

Return to the R72, and turn right for East London. Follow the R72 for 69 km to the Cove Rock/R72 intersection at which you turned onto the R72 in the morning. Turn left here for Buffalo Pass (right leads to Marine Drive); 1,7 km later, turn right for Buffalo Pass and King William's Town. The road passes through indigenous forest and traverses the scenic Buffalo Pass. As you begin the descent into the pass there is a parking area on your left with a view over a classic horseshoe bend in the Buffalo River. Continue through the pass back into East London.

AA Office AA House, 27 Fleet Street, East London 5201 Tel (0431) 21271
East London Metropolitan Publicity Association 35 Argyll Street, East London 5201 Tel (0431) 26015

A coelacanth recovered off the Comoro islands.

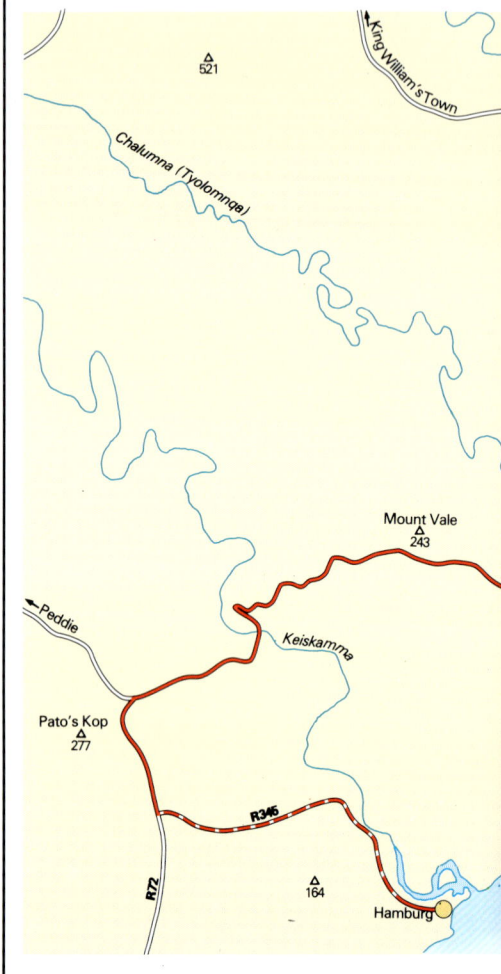

The curve of unspoilt coast at Kidd's Beach.

THE LIVING FOSSIL

Tipped from a trawler net off the mouth of the Chalumna River near East London in 1938 was a fish the likes of which none of the trawlermen had seen before, with fins like stumpy, rudimentary legs and a curious pointed tail. Palaeontologists knew it as the coelacanth – but only from fossil imprints, of which the youngest was about 80 million years old. It was determined that this specimen, about 1,5 m long, had come from the vicinity of the Comoros. The coelacanth continues to live – mostly at great depth – off the east African islands.

GRAND PRIX GLORY

For more than 30 years, East London was the 'capital' of motor-racing in South Africa. In 1934 the track near the Buffalo River was the scene of the first international race in this country – the 'Border Hundred', won by Whitney Straight of the USA. From then until 1967, with a break during World War II, the world's leading drivers were seen here regularly. In 1962 the SA Grand Prix received championship status, but the cost of bringing the stars to East London became prohibitive and, in 1968, Kyalami took over as motor-racing centre.

East London's rocky shore – a lure for anglers.

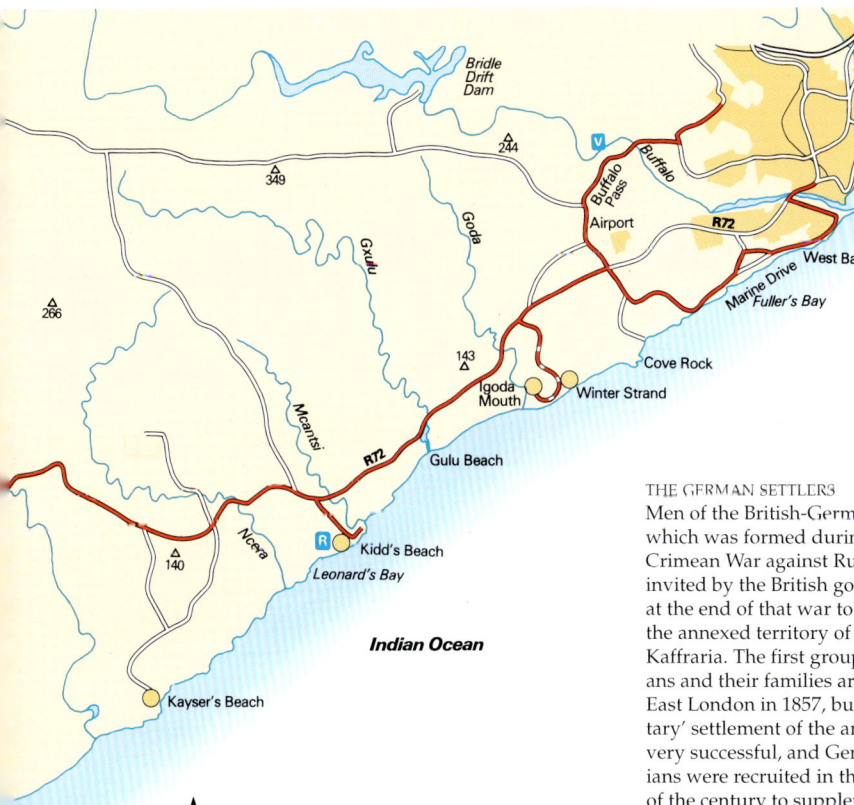

A view over hills and forests from Buffalo Pass.

THE GERMAN SETTLERS

Men of the British-German Legion, which was formed during the Crimean War against Russia, were invited by the British government at the end of that war to settle in the annexed territory of British Kaffraria. The first group of veterans and their families arrived in East London in 1857, but the 'military' settlement of the area was not very successful, and German civilians were recruited in the latter half of the century to supplement dwindling numbers. Many of the towns in this part of the country bear the names of these German settlers' home towns, such as Hamburg, Berlin and Potsdam.

The tranquil charm of the lagoon at Igoda Mouth.

KIDD'S BEACH PHANTOM

The coastal village of Kidd's Beach has long been a popular resort. A shop established here during the last century did good trade with the Xhosa and provided for the needs of summer campers. One day the owner inspanned his oxen and set off for East London to replenish his stocks before the summer 'rush' – and vanished, along with the entire team, wagon and leaders.

Since then, some locals believe, if you visit the beach on the night of the last full moon before Christmas, you can hear the bellowing of oxen and the shouts of men as these lost souls re-enact their futile battle to free themselves from quicksand.

The Gulu River lagoon between Winterstrand and Kidd's Beach is ideal for swimming and for walks along its banks.

• EXPLORING KING WILLIAM'S TOWN ON FOOT •

The Magistrate's Court clock tower with its distinctive weather vane dominates the view along Taylor Street.

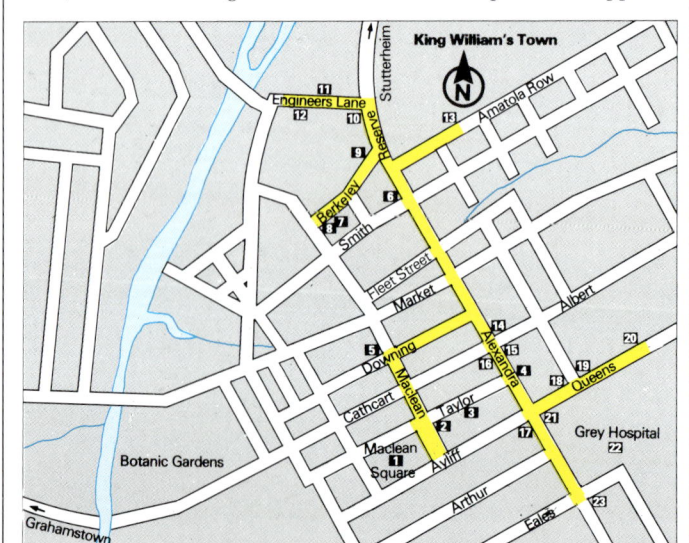

Memorial to the dead of World War I.

Solid stone buildings and mellowed memories

KING WILLIAM'S TOWN, a former garrison town and capital of the short-lived Province of Queen Adelaide, and later of British Kaffraria, is rich in history, much of it reflected in the mellow stonework of its gracious old buildings. This leisurely stroll explores the heart of the old Borough of King William's Town, an area that retains many reminders of its strong colonial and military past.

Our walk begins on the lawned expanse of Maclean Square at the *statue of Queen Victoria* (1), which was unveiled in 1899. A few years later the four smooth-bore, muzzle-loading cannons that stand around the statue were presented to the town, after the obsolete pieces had been found among military stores.

At the northern end of the square, on the corner of Taylor Street, is the ornate building of the former *British Kaffrarian Savings Bank* (2). This bank is one of the few survivors of the many financial institutions established during a boom in the 1860s. If you look past the bank along Taylor Street, you will see the double-storey facade of *Lonsdale Chambers* (3) next door, with the entire street dominated by the tower of the *Magistrate's Court* (4).

The Military Reserve

Walk north-west along Maclean Street until you reach the historic *Town Hall* (5) on your left. Built in 1867, it has the borough arms in relief on the gable. Turn right at this corner into Downing Street, then left into Alexandra Road.

Some distance along Alexandra Road, beyond Smith Street, you will see, on your left, the *Holy Trinity (Anglican) Church* (6) begun in 1850 as a military chapel. Behind it is the old rectory.

Turn left into Berkeley Street. Set into the pavement opposite Alfred Street, on your right, is a large, round-topped grey stone with the letters 'B.O.' and the British Army 'broad arrow' cut into it. This Board of Ordnance beacon is one of several that once marked the bounds of the Military Reserve that the British established in the town.

On your left is the *Missionary Museum* (7), which is housed in a former Methodist Church building of 1855. You also pass the old double-storey Methodist manse, before reaching the town's former *synagogue* (8). This building, originally part of the Methodist complex, was the first venue for the Borough Council. It was converted into a synagogue in 1908 and was closed in 1993.

The Old Residency

Return to Alexandra Road, passing the prominent stone monument to the German Settlers. Turn left into the continuation of Alexandra Road known as Reserve Road.

On your left, set back slightly from the pavement, a stone plinth with a bronze plaque records the history of the *Old Residency* (9), the thatched building behind the plinth. On this site the man dubbed the 'father of King William's Town', the Reverend

174

John Brownlee of the London Missionary Society, built his original mission house in 1826 on the banks of the Buffalo River.

Sir Harry Smith lived at the old Residency 10 years after it was built while he was military governor, and it was here that he announced somewhat melodramatically to thousands of Xhosas that Governor D'Urban had annexed their country as the Province of Queen Adelaide. Seven months later the British Government under Lord Glenelg repealed the proclamation of the province. In 1847, when Sir Harry had been appointed Governor of the Cape, he again annexed the area, this time as British Kaffraria. This time the annexation of the territory was not repealed.

Just beyond the Residency, turn left into the shady, gravel-surfaced avenue known as Engineers Lane. You pass, on your left, the former *Royal Engineers officers' mess* (10) and on your right the old *Military Hospital* (11), both dating from the 1840s.

Workmen's legacy

Beyond the officers' mess on your left is a square building with a curious roof – this was once the *blacksmiths' shop* (12) where the British Army farriers did their sweltering work. The roof rises to a central peak, surmounted by a smaller canopy – the space between the roof and the canopy allowed the hot air of the smithy to escape.

A little further along the lane you will come across neatly built, stone rainwater channels on both sides of the road – these are also the work of the men of the versatile Corps of Royal Engineers. Turn around here, return to Reserve Road and turn right.

Turn left into Amatola Row at the small Dick King Memorial. About 100 m along this road is a pair of grey *gateposts* (13), on your left, which once marked the main entrance to the Military Reserve. Pass through the gate, into what is now a technical college, to examine the bronze cannon under its roofed shelter. As you walk towards the cannon, you pass, on your right, the long stone building of 1849 that was the store of the Commissariat Department.

The little cannon bears the name of Major General Frederick Eardley Wilmot, Superintendent of the Royal Gun Factory at Woolwich, England, where the cannon was cast. Coincidentally, his younger brother, Henry Robert Eardley Wilmot, who was also an artilleryman, was killed in action in the Fish River bush near Peddie during the war of 1850-3. According to rumour current at the time, (Henry was commandant of Fort Peddie,) he was shot in the back by one of his own men. The gun was taken to yet another war in 1877 by the Grahamstown Volunteer Horse Artillery.

The Kaffrarian Museum

Return to Alexandra Road, and turn left. Pass Downing Street on your right, before reaching the *Roman Catholic Church and Presbytery* (14) on your left.

Cross Albert Road to reach, also on your left, the main entrance to the *Kaffrarian Museum* (15) through its Thomas Daines Wing (which was previously the public library). The buildings in the museum complex include the old post office, which lies next to the Thomas Daines Wing on Alexandra Road and houses the museum's Xhosa Gallery, and the 1898 Natural History Museum building around the corner in Albert Road. The Xhosa Gallery contains exceptional exhibits relating to the indigenous peoples of the area, their history and Xhosa cosmology.

Huberta the Hippo

The Kaffrarian Museum also contains a section devoted to the Germans who settled in the area in the middle of the 19th century. There are also many military items on display and a famous natural history section. Among the natural history exhibits is Huberta the hippopotamus, who made headlines around the world from the end of 1928 when she began a journey southwards from KwaZulu-Natal that lasted several years. Huberta turned up in many unusual places, and was once found fast asleep on a busy railway line. She was eventually shot by hunters while she was bathing in the Keiskamma River.

Leave the museum through the Thomas Daines Wing in Alexandra Road. On the opposite corner is the elaborate, *domed building* (16) erected for an insurance company in 1904.

Continue south-west on Alexandra Road. Opposite Taylor Street is the Magistrate's Court, dating from 1877, with its elegant clock tower and brass plaque commemorating the Reverend John Brownlee. The bronze plaque in front of the court building outlines the history of the town, and shows profiles of King William IV and Queen Adelaide.

Across the road, on the corner of Ayliff Street, is a *monument to Sir Henry Timson Lukin* (17), who commanded the South Africans at Delville Wood, France, in 1916.

War memorial

Turn left into Queens Road. On your left you reach the neoclassical *Victoria Drill Hall* (18), built in 1897, *Sutton House* (19), a school property dating from 1877 and the *Convent of the Sacred Heart* (20), also of 1877. Return to Alexandra Road, passing the soaring *memorial to the dead of World War I* (21) on your left as you turn left into Alexandra Road.

Our walk ends at the corner of Eales Road. As you reach the corner, look left at the elegant facade of *Grey Hospital* (22) which was built in 1859. The long, stone building on the corner of Eales Road was originally the town's *railway station* (23) from 1877 to 1933. There was only a single spur line, and trains reversed all the way from the main line outside the town to the station so that they would be facing the right direction for departure.

The charming entrance to Grey Hospital, built by Sir George Grey in 1859.

Huberta – the hippo who won hearts around the world.

Elegance and substance in a turn-of-the-century bank.

The high road over the wild and solitary southern Drakensberg

Eastwards from the old river-crossing of Aliwal North, our route winds through the awesome southern Drakensberg, crossing Naudesnek – at 2 621 m the highest road pass in South Africa – and Barkly Pass. This long drive takes a full day and should be avoided in wet or snowy weather. Roughly two-thirds of the route is on tar, the rest is on gravel.

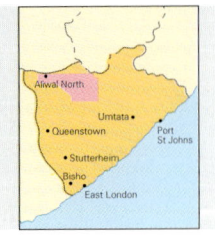

**Aliwal North
Lady Grey
Barkly East
Rhodes
Maclear
Elliot
510 – 530 km**

Turn out of Aliwal North's Somerset Street into Young Street – towards Lady Grey and Barkly East on the R58 – and note your kms. After 47 km you pass a turn-off on your left to Sterkspruit; 4 km after this, turn left for Lady Grey, which you reach about 2,5 km later (see below). Return to the R58, and turn left for Barkly East and Elliot. After 3 km, you pass a turn-off on your right to Jamestown and, roughly 12 km later, you cross the Karnmelkspruit. After a further 5 km, the road begins to wind up the scenic Benjaminshoogte and, within the next 2 km, you pass a turn-off on your right to Dordrecht. Roughly 4 km later you pass, on your left, a turn-off to Lady Grey via Joubert's Pass. Soon afterwards, on your right, you pass the prominent *Motkop* (drizzle hill) and, at its foot, the railway siding known as Drizzly. This apparent description of the prevailing weather is soon reinforced by signs that warn of ice and slippery road surfaces.

After passing a turn-off on your left to New England and Sterkspruit via Lundeansnek, the road soon begins to descend into the Kraai River Pass, which crosses two rivers. The road passes another turn-off to Dordrecht, then continues into Barkly East, which you reach 117 km from Aliwal North.

Barkly East to Naudesnek
Barkly East was proclaimed in 1874 and reached municipality status seven years later. You enter the town on Molteno Street. Turn left into De Villiers Street, then turn right into White Street (onto gravel, this road becoming the R396), noting your kms. There is a very short experimental tarred section before the road surface changes to gravel again. After travelling roughly 14 km, you reach the Rebelshoogte Pass.

After several kilometres more, you pass, on your right, the R393 to Elliot and, 100 m later, you cross a single-lane bridge over the Kraai River. Within the next 1 km the road passes a turn-off on the left (the R393 to Lundin's Nek – the spelling varies) and crosses a narrow girder bridge over the Bell River.

After roughly 43 km on the gravel road, the route traverses a ridge, giving wide views of mountains and valleys on both sides. About 3 km later there is another narrow causeway. At the fork 52 km from Barkly East, go right for Rhodes where the road on the left leads to

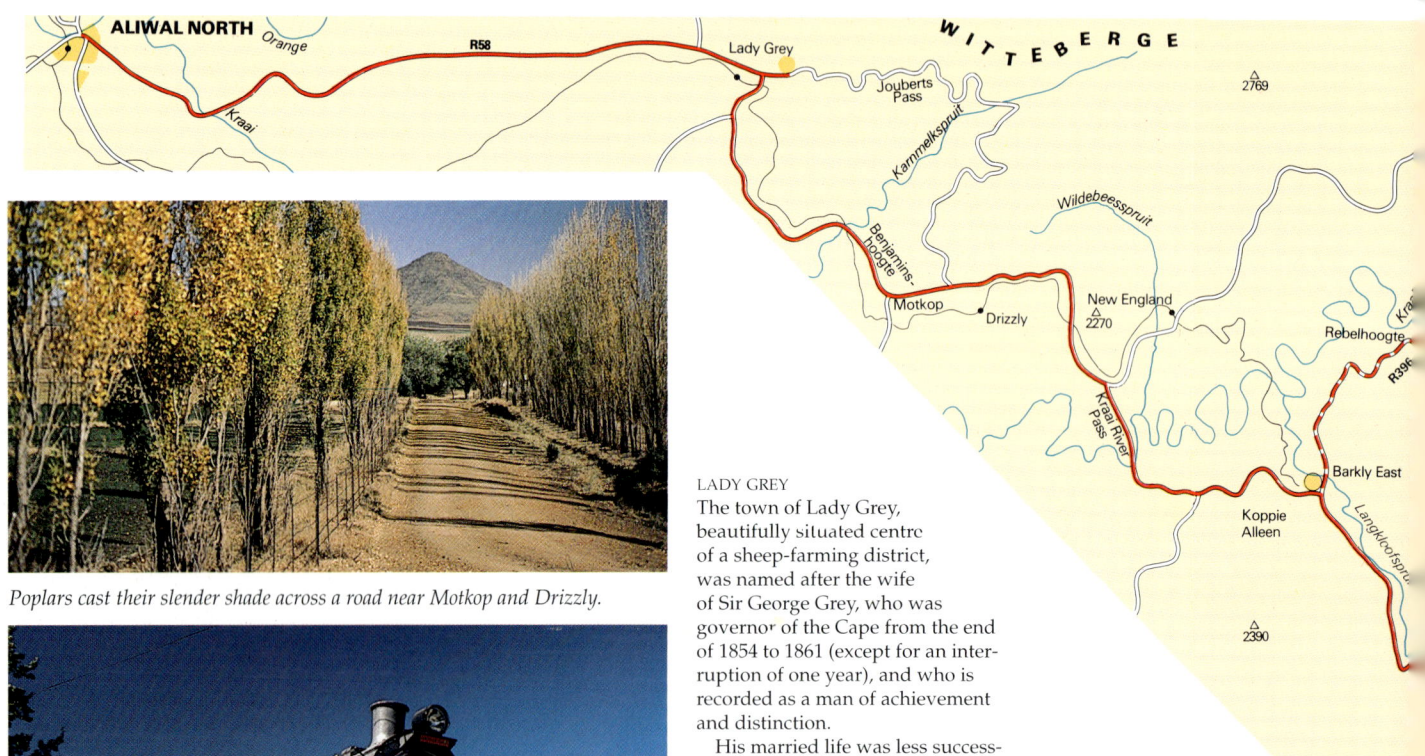

Poplars cast their slender shade across a road near Motkop and Drizzly.

LADY GREY
The town of Lady Grey, beautifully situated centre of a sheep-farming district, was named after the wife of Sir George Grey, who was governor of the Cape from the end of 1854 to 1861 (except for an interruption of one year), and who is recorded as a man of achievement and distinction.

His married life was less successful, however, although it started happily enough when he married in Australia. Unreasonably, Sir George blamed his wife for the early death of their only child. Lady Grey remained loyal but, on a voyage from England to South Africa, Sir George suspected her of committing some indiscretion with a naval officer. She was put ashore in South America, and the two were estranged for 37 years. Well-meaning friends brought them together in their old age, but the attempt at reconciliation failed, and Lady Grey died sad and misunderstood.

A Class 19D steam locomotive stands in the town square of Barkly East.

A TOWN OF CHILLY NIGHTS
Barkly East's temperature drops to below freezing point on an average of one night in four, giving this pretty town the reputation of being one of the coldest in South Africa.

Named after Governor Sir Henry Barkly, the little town at an altitude of 1 800 m presented problems to the railway-builders. They solved them by building a line with an average gradient of 1 in 36, with eight reversing stations. Its museum specializes in early transportation.

BORDER & TRANSKEI

Maartens Hoek. The road crosses a narrow causeway after 400 m and enters the village of Rhodes 6,2 km later.

Turn left for Maclear and Naudesnek at the T-junction, noting your kms. After 12,2 km there is a small riverside picnic area on your left (with braai place) at the foot of the spectacular Naudesnek Pass. A plaque here records that two brothers who farmed nearby, Stefanus and Gabriel Naude, had found a way out of the isolated valley over the mountains in 1896 and that the pass was built along their original route. The road twists upwards from the foot of the pass, which is 1 920 m above sea level, to reach the summit at 2 621 m. After 8 km, the long and gradual descent begins. (If your time is limited, Naudesnek Pass makes a convenient turning point.)

Naudesnek to Maclear

There are a number of causeways to be crossed, and the road passes two turn-offs to the left (the second to Mount Fletcher). Roughly 50 km from the summit of Naudesnek the road reaches the Pot River Pass; the surface changes to tar after a further 30 km. On the outskirts of the town of Maclear, turn left for 'Sakesentrum' at the four-way stop street, follow the road as it bends sharply to the left, then turn right at the T-junction for Elliot. After about 800 m turn right onto the R56 for Ugie, Elliot, Barkly East and Aliwal North.

Maclear to Barkly East

About 19 km later the road enters Ugie, named after a stream in Scotland and overlooked by the *Prentjiesberg* (picture mountain). The route then continues to Elliot.

In Elliot, turn right at the second stop street into Lloyd Street (R58). After 9 km you reach the start of the scenic Barkly Pass. The road passes a turn-off on your right to Rhodes and Sterkspruit after 19 km and reaches Barkly East after a further 40 km.

Turn right into De Villiers Street, then left into Molteno Street and retrace your route on the R58 to Aliwal North.

AA Office AA House, 27 Fleet Street, East London 5201 Tel (0431) 21271
Aliwal North Local Council Barkly Street, Aliwal North 5530 Tel (0551) 2441
Barkly East Local Council 15 De Smidt Street Barkly East 5580 Tel (04542) 73
Rhodes Hotel PO Rhodes 5582 Tel via (04542) 73

The Kraai River cuts a gorge through arid land.

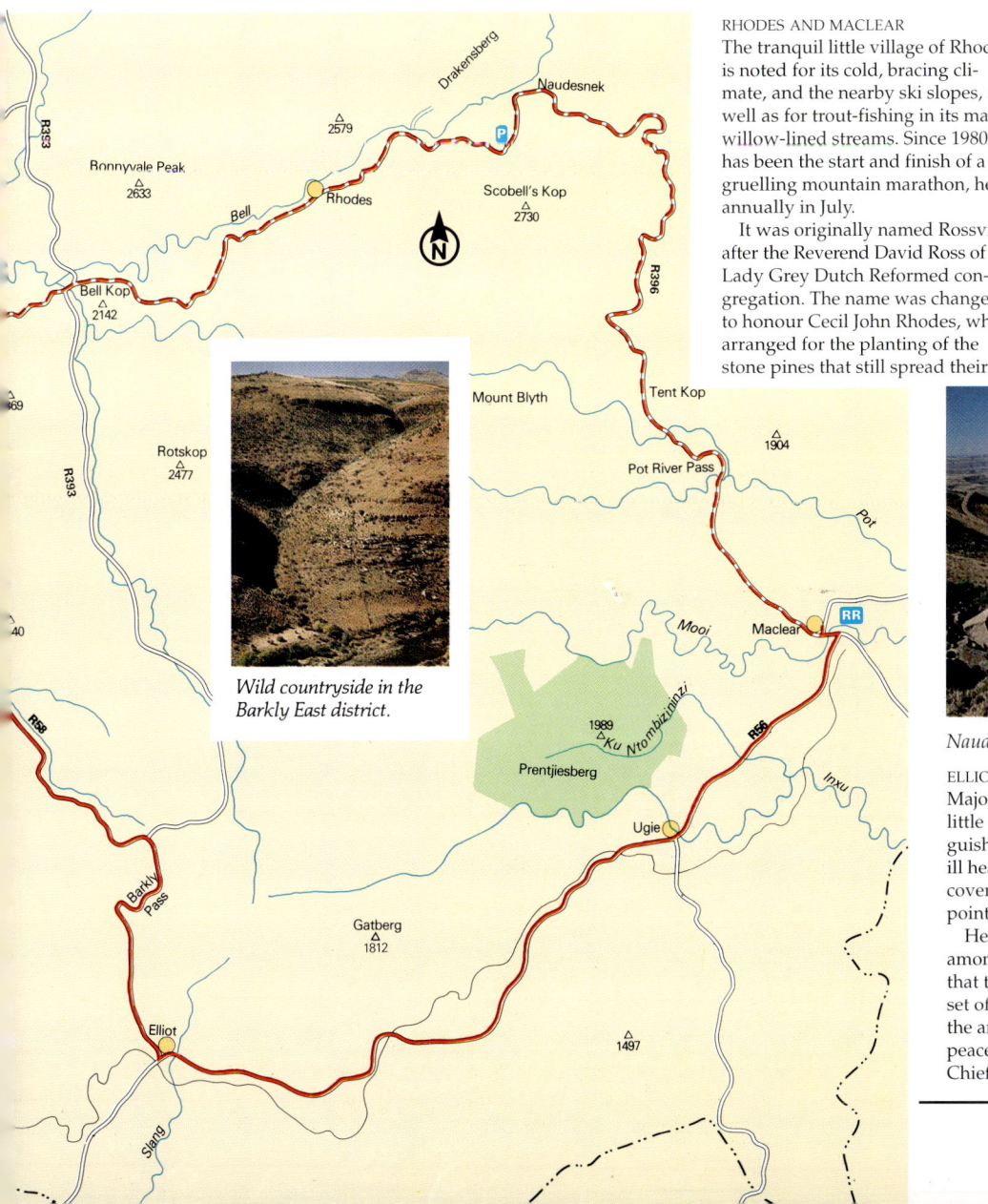

Wild countryside in the Barkly East district.

RHODES AND MACLEAR

The tranquil little village of Rhodes is noted for its cold, bracing climate, and the nearby ski slopes, as well as for trout-fishing in its many willow-lined streams. Since 1980, it has been the start and finish of a gruelling mountain marathon, held annually in July.

It was originally named Rossville, after the Reverend David Ross of the Lady Grey Dutch Reformed congregation. The name was changed to honour Cecil John Rhodes, who arranged for the planting of the stone pines that still spread their generous shade over the town's main road.

Separated from Rhodes by the wild beauty of Naudesnek is Maclear, established in 1876. The town was named after Sir Thomas Maclear, the Queen's Astronomer at the Cape for almost 40 years.

Trained as a medical doctor, Maclear was an amateur but very gifted astronomer who eventually contributed much to the science. Travelling with him to the Cape was his servant, Thomas Bowler, who went on to achieve fame as one of the colony's leading artists.

Naudesnek Pass – the highest road in the country.

ELLIOT

Major Henry Elliot, after whom this attractive little town was named, resigned from a distinguished career with the British army because of ill health. He came to South Africa in 1870 to recover, and was about to return when he was appointed Chief Magistrate of Tembuland.

He had a unique method of keeping the peace among the local communities – when he heard that trouble was about to break out, he would set off with a single black trooper to reason with the antagonists. He gained a reputation as a peacekeeper, and was eventually appointed Chief Magistrate of the whole Transkei.

The waters of the Orange River bring life to a thirsting land

The first sight of the vast expanse of the Gariep Dam comes as a surprise in the arid Karoo landscape. Our route traverses the shores of this impressive man-made lake, passes two nature reserves and the longest bridge in the country and takes in the historic towns of Bethulie and Burgersdorp. All but some 25 km of the drive is on tarred roads.

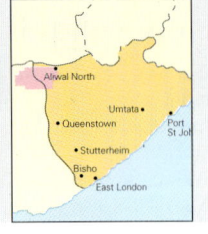

**Aliwal North
Bethulie
Norvalspont
Venterstad
Burgersdorp
320 – 340 km**

Turn west out of Aliwal North's Somerset Street into Barkly Street. Go right at the fork, following the signs for N6/Bloemfontein/Rouxville. Cross the Orange River over the steel General Hertzog Bridge and, 200 m later, turn left for Goedemoed and Bethulie, noting your kms.

After about 25 km the road surface changes to gravel. Continue straight on, crossing the Caledon River about 43 km from Aliwal North. Several kilometres beyond the river, the gravel gives way to tar as you pass the R701 to Smithfield on your right. Continue straight on for Bethulie, turn left at the intersection with the R701 and, about 56 km from Aliwal North, turn left to Bethulie.

At the intersection outside the town (about 90 km from Aliwal North), where the road on the left leads to the railway station and the road on the right to Bethulie, continue straight to visit the DH Steyn Bridge over the Orange River. This is the longest bridge in South Africa, measuring 2 993 m if you include the approaches. The concrete bridge section is 1 121 m long and is supported on 26 arches.

Return to the intersection on the outskirts of the town, and turn left. After 100 m there is a gravel road on your left that leads to the site of the Bethulie concentration camp and of the old cemetery dating from the Anglo-Boer War. Turn right at the four-way stop street 1 km later. After 100 m you will see on your right the Pellissier House Museum, in what is believed to be the oldest settler-built structure north of the Orange River. Continue on this road to reach the caravan park on the shores of the Bethulie Dam (braai places, toilets, water).

Bethulie to Norvalspont
Return to the four-way stop street and turn right, noting your kms. Some 3,2 km later you turn left onto the R701 towards Gariep Dam and Donkerpoort. After a further 47 km, turn left at the T-junction for Gariep Dam and Norvalspont (where the road on the right leads to Donkerpoort and the N1). About 3,5 km later, turn left again onto the R58 towards

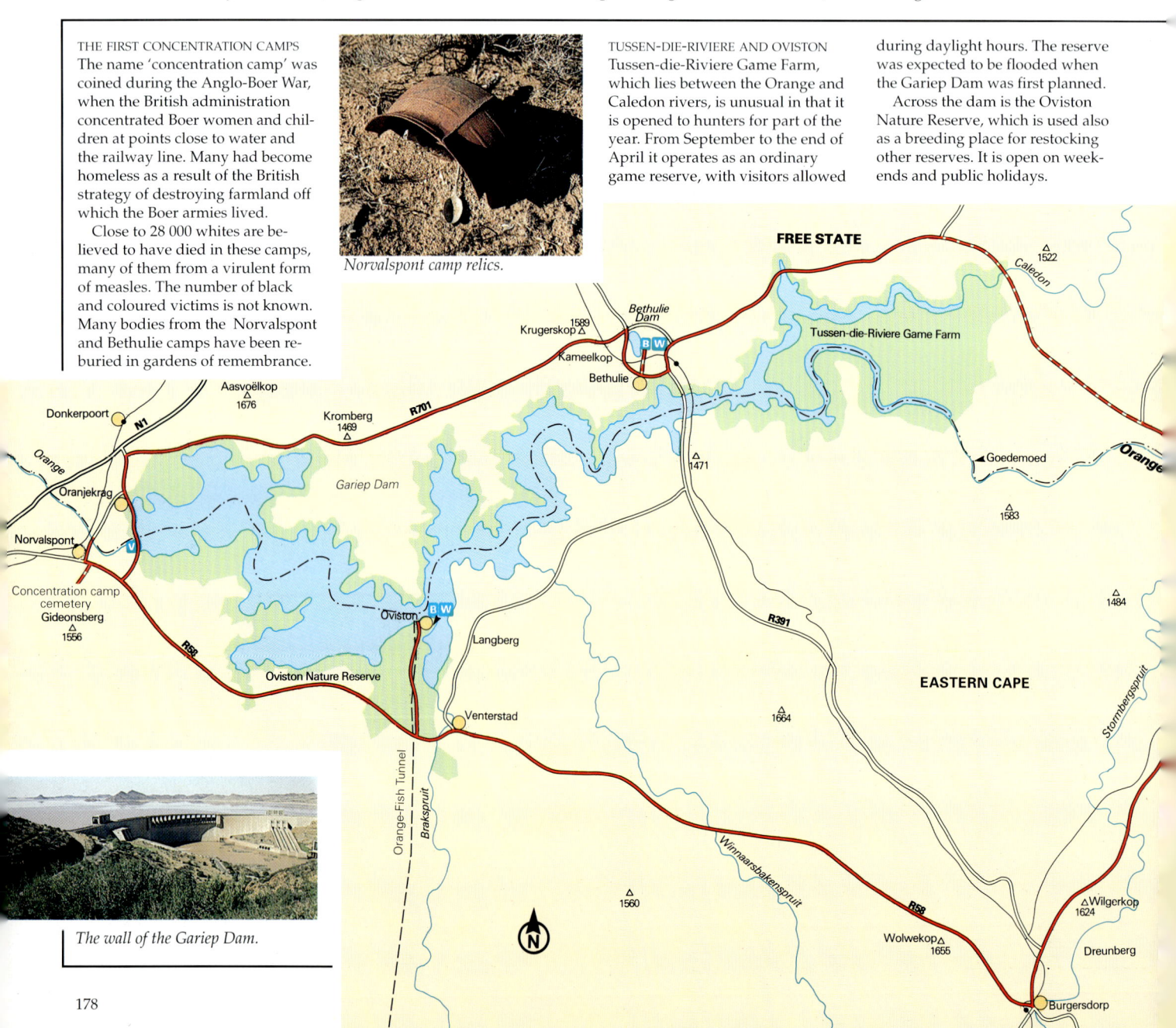

THE FIRST CONCENTRATION CAMPS
The name 'concentration camp' was coined during the Anglo-Boer War, when the British administration concentrated Boer women and children at points close to water and the railway line. Many had become homeless as a result of the British strategy of destroying farmland off which the Boer armies lived.

Close to 28 000 whites are believed to have died in these camps, many of them from a virulent form of measles. The number of black and coloured victims is not known. Many bodies from the Norvalspont and Bethulie camps have been re-buried in gardens of remembrance.

Norvalspont camp relics.

TUSSEN-DIE-RIVIERE AND OVISTON
Tussen-die-Riviere Game Farm, which lies between the Orange and Caledon rivers, is unusual in that it is opened to hunters for part of the year. From September to the end of April it operates as an ordinary game reserve, with visitors allowed during daylight hours. The reserve was expected to be flooded when the Gariep Dam was first planned.

Across the dam is the Oviston Nature Reserve, which is used also as a breeding place for restocking other reserves. It is open on weekends and public holidays.

The wall of the Gariep Dam.

Venterstad via Gariep Dam. The R58 leads past a motel that serves lunch, and, several kilometres later, it runs along the top of the dam wall. (Before the road reaches the wall, there is a fork to the right that leads to the Department of Water Affairs offices, from where there is a good view of the dam wall.)

Cross the dam wall to the south side. Turn right onto a road signposted 'Viewsite', and continue straight for just over 1 km. A footpath of about 100 m leads around a small hillock to the viewsite.

When you leave the viewsite turn right, noting your kms. After 2,6 km, turn right on the R58 towards Colesberg and, 4 km later, turn right onto the R701 towards Norvalspont and Oranjekrag.

The road passes through the village of Norvalspont and, soon afterwards, on your right, a blockhouse dating from the Anglo-Boer War has been converted into a dwelling and is now almost hidden by trees.

Immediately afterwards there is a long, single-lane bridge over the Orange River. A railway bridge runs alongside it. Turn around here, and retrace your route back through Norvalspont to the R58.

Norvalspont to Burgersdorp

Turn left onto the R58 for Venterstad. After 900 m there is a gravel road on your right that leads to the site of the Norvalspont concentration camp and the camp cemetery.

After a further 3,1 km you pass the road on which you arrived earlier from the Gariep Dam wall – note your kms here.

Continue straight and, after 32 km, turn left off the R58 for Oviston (where the road on the right leads to Steynsburg); 3,6 km later, turn left at the T-junction for Oviston. Follow the signs to the right where the road ahead is blocked by the gate to the nature reserve (open weekends and public holidays; entrance fee).

The road passes the offices of the Department of Nature Conservation on your left, and a turn-off to picnic sites on your right (braai places, toilets, water). Continue straight to the edge of the dam, where a parking area overlooks the intake tower of the Oviston tunnel. This tunnel links the Orange and Fish rivers – hence the name, from the Afrikaans *Oranje-Vis Tonnel*. It is the longest tunnel of its kind in the world and runs for 82,8 km from Oviston to Teebus in the south.

Return to the R58 and turn left for Venterstad, first laid out as a town in 1875. Follow the signs through Venterstad for Burgersdorp and East London. The historic town of Burgersdorp, birthplace of one of South Africa's Afrikaans universities and home of the first *Taal* (language) monument, is reached after a further 58 km. A British blockhouse, known as the Sentinel, built in 1901, still keeps watch over the town and is one of several national monuments in the area.

When you leave Burgersdorp, follow the signs for Aliwal North, which lies just over 52 km further along the R58.

> **AA Office** 17 Sanlam Plaza, Maitland Street Bloemfontein 9301 Tel (051) 47 6191
> **Aliwal North Library** PO Box 5, Aliwal North 5530 Tel (0551) 2362
> **Bethulie Municipality** PO Box 7, Bethulie 9992 Tel (051762) 2

A railway bridge arches above the tree-lined road to the Bethulie Dam.

The moon rises over grain silos as sunset tints the Aliwal North sky.

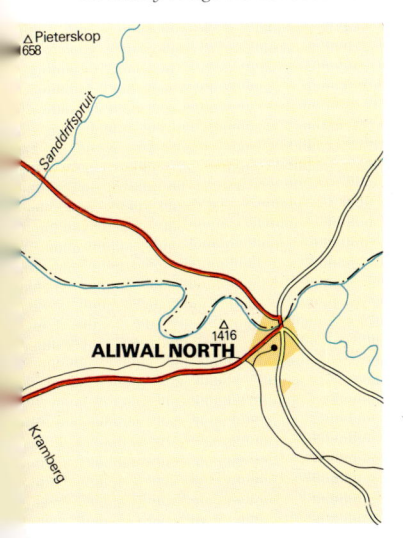

The head of the Oviston Tunnel – 82,8 km from its outlet at Teebus.

THE GARIEP DAM

Covering 374 sq km and with a storage capacity of 5 958 million cubic metres, this dam has harnessed the life-giving waters of the Orange River to the benefit of not only the surrounding arid land, but also of valleys further afield. The dam is part of the Orange River Project and supplements the Fish River via the 82,8 km Oviston Tunnel. Another tunnel feeds the faraway Sundays River with valuable additional water for irrigating the citrus groves and other farms on its banks.

The Gariep and Vanderkloof dams together supply 455 million litres of water per day. The dams also generate 600 000 kilowatts of hydro-electric power.

TOWN OF CITIZENS

Burgersdorp, meaning simply the 'town of citizens', is the chief town of the old Division of Albert. It was the home of the country's first Dutch Reformed theological college, which later moved to Potchefstroom. The original college buildings now house a museum. The town was also the site of the

ALIWAL NORTH

This town on the Orange River was named to honour Sir Harry Smith's victory over the Sikhs at Aliwal in India in 1846. The 'North' was added because Mossel Bay had been renamed Aliwal South.

Two thermal springs at Aliwal North provide more than 3 million litres of water a day at a temperature of 34,4°C. The waters are credited with curative properties and the springs have been visited by invalids for many years.

During the Anglo-Boer War, the town was the site of a concentration camp, and a garden of remembrance has been made on its outskirts at a well-preserved blockhouse dating from the same war.

first *Taal* (language) monument, unveiled in 1893 to commemorate the use of Dutch in the Cape Parliament. It was damaged during the Anglo-Boer War, moved and finally lost. A replica was erected, but about 35 years later the original was found, by accident, buried at King William's Town. Both original and replacement are in Burger Square.

Where traditional villages shelter beneath dramatic peaks

From Queenstown our route enters the rural heartland, passing traditional African villages dotted among rolling hills. The road then crosses the wild southern Drakensberg via the soaring Otto du Plessis Pass, before returning through wooded kloofs to Dordrecht, which serves the surrounding sheep country. Well over half the route is on tarred roads..

**Queenstown
Lady Frere
Indwe
Otto du Plessis Pass
Rossouw
Dordrecht
310 – 330 km**

DRIVE NORTH ALONG Queenstown's Kingsway, which becomes Hangklip Road as it veers left, to the Lawrence de Lange Nature Reserve. Some 2,4 km after the start of the gravel surface, turn left into the reserve and follow the road for 4,8 km to reach a viewsite that offers a splendid panorama.

Retrace your route along Hangklip Road and Kingsway, but turn left out of Kingsway into Livingstone Road, which becomes the main road to Indwe (R359) and Dordrecht (R392). You pass a road to the Bonkolo Dam on your left and, shortly afterwards, turn right onto the R359 for Lady Frere.

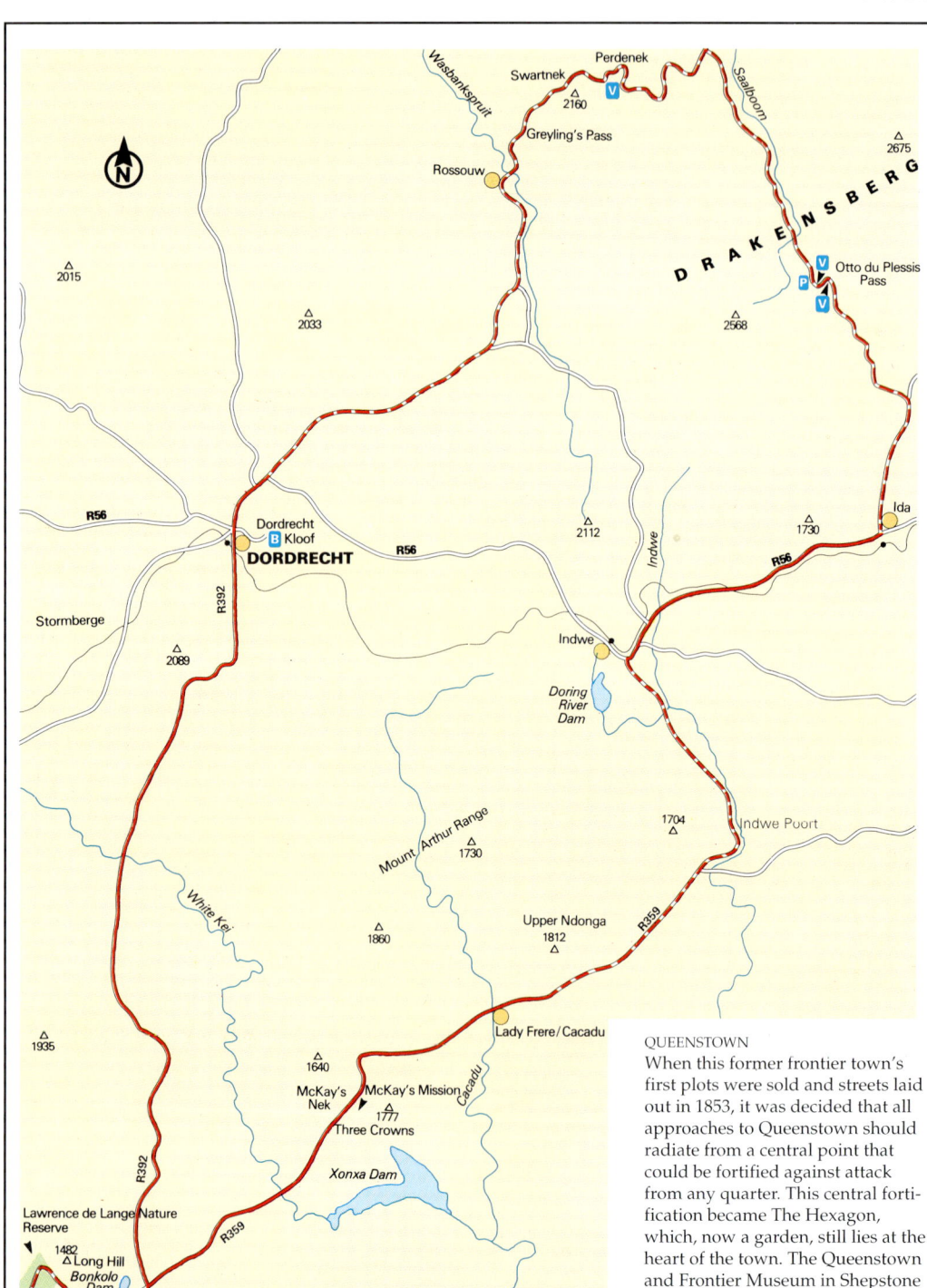

The tranquil Three Crowns setting.

Picturesque McKay's Nek Mission.

LAST REFUGE OF A HUNTED PEOPLE
Deep among the kloofs where the Stormberg and Drakensberg ranges merge, the San people, hunted and harried from the plains, established their last strongholds. Their stone implements and many other artefacts are still to be found throughout the area, and in many places San artists have painted the rocks with enduring scenes from their day-to-day lives.

QUEENSTOWN
When this former frontier town's first plots were sold and streets laid out in 1853, it was decided that all approaches to Queenstown should radiate from a central point that could be fortified against attack from any quarter. This central fortification became The Hexagon, which, now a garden, still lies at the heart of the town. The Queenstown and Frontier Museum in Shepstone Street contains many relics from the days of the wars fought along the bitterly contested frontier in the 19th century.

LADY FRERE
This little town was originally named after the wife of Sir Henry Bartle Frere, the High Commissioner for South Africa who was recalled in 1880 after the disastrous Anglo-Zulu War. Following its incorporation into 'independent' Transkei, the town was officially renamed Cacadu, after the nearby river, but the original name is still much in use. The town serves the Glen Grey farming district and has several old churches as well as a quaint prison building with an ornate plaster harp on its facade.

After about 6 km the Xonxa Dam comes into view on your right and, some 16 km later, you pass a road on your right to McKay's Nek Mission and begin to climb McKay's Nek Pass, with a view eastwards to the peaks known as the Three Crowns.

The road continues through rocky countryside and crosses a bridge before entering Lady Frere, about 48 km from Queenstown. The Xhosa name sometimes applied to the village – Cacadu – is derived from that of the Cacadu River. There is some interesting plasterwork on the facades of a few of the old buildings in the main street. Several kilometres beyond Lady Frere the road surface changes to gravel. Pass a turn-off on your right, to Cala, about 18 km from Lady Frere before the road winds through the picturesque Indwe Poort. Pass several gravel roads on both sides before reaching the T-junction with the R56, just short of 42 km from Lady Frere. Turn right at the T-junction, for Elliot, noting your kms. (The road on your left leads directly into Indwe.)

You pass a turn-off on your left to Barkly East via Barker's Nek and, after 22,5 km on the R56, almost directly opposite the village and railway siding of Ida, turn left onto gravel, noting your kms. You pass a church on your right and then turn left almost immediately at the fork. Pass a turn-off on your right for Elliot, then a turn-off on your left for Tungela, and cross two narrow causeways. The road then climbs fairly steeply, with views back over fields and foothills. Soon afterwards, 12 km after turning off the R56, go left at the fork for Barkly East via Otto du Plessis Pass. (The pass is not suitable for towing caravans or trailers.)

Within the next 21 km the road crosses six causeways, then reaches a signboard on your left reading 'Dr Otto du Plessis Pass'. The road climbs steeply up the pass and crosses a causeway within 1 km. On the steep section roughly 3 km after the sign there is space on your left to pull over and enjoy the view. You can stop again 2 km later on your right for a different view – of a mountain amphitheatre. The picnic site, which is 1 km further along the road, also offers good views. Roughly 300 m later you reach the summit of the pass at 2 254 m.

Otto du Plessis Pass to Dordrecht
The road winds down the pass, crossing the Saalboom River and its tributaries seven times and reaching a T-junction 21 km from the summit. Turn left at the T-junction for Dordrecht, noting your kms. (The road to the right leads to Barkly East.)

A steep ascent soon brings you to the summit of Perdenek, after which the road descends again. After 6,8 km, go right at the fork for Dordrecht (the road on the left leads to Kettingdrift). After a further 5 km, go left at another fork for Dordrecht, where the road on the right goes to Heuningneskloof. Roughly 1,5 km later, just before a sharp left bend, pull off the road for a view back over a large, irrigated valley locked in by mountains.

After 5 km the road begins to descend Swartnek, offering constantly changing views of rugged mountains. The road then descends further, following the old Greyling's Pass.

On the outskirts of the tiny settlement of Rossouw you cross the Jan Schoombee Bridge; 5,2 km beyond the bridge, after crossing two narrow causeways, turn right at the T-junction, noting your kms. Pass roads on your left to Bonthoek and Indwe. After 13,8 km, go right at the fork for Dordrecht, and after a further 19,4 km turn right at the T-junction onto the tarred R56 which brings you to Dordrecht.

Dordrecht to Queenstown
To visit the beautiful picnic and braai sites in Dordrecht Kloof, turn left into Tower Street just past the stone Anglican church. Turn right after roughly 100 m (where a smaller track goes straight up the hillside). Turn left after another 100 m and follow this road for a few kilometres to reach the kloof.

Leave Dordrecht by travelling south on the R392, which soon winds among pleasant hills with hutted villages dotting the cultivated valleys. After a further 60 km, you reach the junction with the R359, into which you turned in the morning from Queenstown for Lady Frere.

Tall shade trees and dappled sunlight combine to make Dordrecht Kloof an idyllic braai and picnic site.

A poplar turns to gold beside the Doring River.

TOWN OF THE BLUE CRANE
In 1896 several companies were formed to exploit coal deposits in and around the Stormberg range, and the town of Indwe came into being near the towering sandstone cliff known as *Xalanga* (place of vultures). The seams proved to be patchy and the coal was of poor quality, so the mines were soon abandoned, but the small town of *Indwe* (the Xhosa name for the blue crane) continues to flourish – as an agricultural centre.

CHILLY SLOPES OF THE STORMBERG
Dordrecht, now the centre of a sheep-farming area, was founded in 1856 and named after the town in Holland where the historic 1618 synod of the Reformed Churches was held. Situated on the northern slopes of the Stormberg range, the town is often hit by snowfalls and bitterly cold weather in winter.

The Anderson Museum, housed in an early 20th century stone-built shop, has varied exhibits relating to the history of the area.

AA Office AA House, 27 Fleet Street, East London 5201 Tel (0431) 21271
Queenstown Publicity Association PO Box 592 Queenstown 5320 Tel (0451) 82233

Forest-clad mountains remain where territorial wars once raged

This drive from Fort Beaufort is as rich in history as it is in scenery. We head north along the fertile Tyume Valley with its orchards and villages, then climb the spectacular Hogsback Pass towards Cathcart. Our return route skirts the Amatole range, passing through picturesque Stutterheim. More than half the route is on tarred roads.

**Fort Beaufort
Alice
Hogsback
Cathcart
Stutterheim
Keiskammahoek
210 – 240 km**

Leave Fort Beaufort on Campbell Street and cross the white-walled bridge dated 1958 on the outskirts of the town. The road (R63) passes through thornbush-covered cattle-country and, as you approach Alice – roughly 22 km from Fort Beaufort – you see the prominent Stewart Memorial on Sandile Kop (see pages 190 – 1). Drive through Alice on McNab Drive for King William's Town, cross a bridge over the Gagha River and pass Fort Hare University on your left.

Alice to Hogsback
About 3 km east of Alice, turn left onto the tarred R345 towards 'Cathcart via Hogsback', noting your kms. You pass crossroads 3 km later, with the village of Dyamala on your left. After a further 11 km you pass a turn-off on your left to Seymour and Queenstown. The road then ascends the easily negotiated Hogsback Pass, offering spectacular views of the Tyume Valley and lush mountain scenery.

After 27 km on the R345, the surface changes to gravel on the edge of the forest plantations at the Stormberg divisional boundary. The road now passes through the straggling settlement of Hogsback (see pages 184 – 5).

Hogsback to Cathcart
Roughly 5 km beyond the police station, which is about the first building you pass in Hogsback, you reach a T-junction. Turn left here towards Seymour and Fort Beaufort via Michel's Pass, noting your kms. After 2,1 km, stop on the left for the magnificent view of the surrounding countryside. Retrace your route, noting your kms as you pass the Hogsback turn-off on your right, and keep straight for Cathcart. On your right here is the prominent Gaika's Kop (see opposite).

After 7 km, turn right at the T-junction for Happy Valley and Cathcart, noting your kms again. You cross several single-lane causeways and, after 18,5 km on this road, you pass a sideroad on your left. Immediately afterwards you cross a narrow bridge and pass a little church and cemetery on your right. Many shady sites along the roadside offer attractive picnic places. About 34 km after turning onto the Happy Valley road, turn right at the T-junction for Cathcart. After a further 6,2 km, turn right at the next T-junction. Soon afterwards turn left at another T-junction onto the N6, which leads into Cathcart.

Cathcart to Keiskammahoek
Leave Cathcart by travelling south on the R30 through green and tranquil countryside to reach Stutterheim after roughly 48 km. In Stutterheim, turn right into Hill Street towards Keiskammahoek and note your kms.

This road becomes the R352, and the surface changes to gravel. Soon afterwards you pass a turn-off on your right to the indigenous Kologha forest and Eagles Ridge resort. You cross a number of single-lane causeways and, 14,6 km from the turn in Stutterheim, you pass a turn-off on your left signposted for Sandile's Grave and Evelyn Valley (this road leads to the chief's grave after roughly 10 km).

Roughly 4 km beyond this turn-off, the Gubu Dam comes into view on your right and, after a further 3 km, you begin to descend through the pine-shaded Dontsa Pass, first built in 1857. A memorial to one of the builders, George Dacre, is at the foot of the pass.

The road passes St Matthew's College and Hospital, with several buildings dating from the 1850s, then passes a large sawmilling complex on your right before you enter the town of Keiskammahoek. The road is tarred in the town and it veers left before it gives way to gravel again. Cross a bridge soon afterwards, then turn right for Middledrift and Alice.

Roughly 7 km beyond Keiskammahoek you cross the wall of the Sandile Dam. Turn left at the far end of the dam wall and, about 4,8 km later (after crossing two narrow causeways), go right at the fork – staying on the main road all the time.

A further 4 km brings you to the village of Burnshill and, after another 7,6 km, turn right onto tar (R63) at the T-junction for Alice. From Alice, retrace your route to Fort Beaufort.

AA Office AA House, 27 Fleet Street East London 5201 Tel (0431) 21271
Contour Fort Beaufort Military Museum, 20 Bell Street, Fort Beaufort 5720 Tel (04634) 31503
Stutterheim Information Office 18 Long Street Stutterheim 4930 Tel (0436) 31433

The famous Ngqika leader, Sandile.

SANDILE
Sandile, son of Ngqika (Gaika) and his senior wife, was born about 1820 and succeeded to the leadership of the Ngqika tribe when he was only 20 years old. His reign was marked by violent clashes with the settlers and the colonial military – for which he was not entirely to blame. The most tragic event of his reign was the 'national suicide' of the Xhosa, the large scale cattle-killing and destruction of crops. The refusal to deliver the man who had stolen an axe from a Fort Beaufort shop led to the War of the Axe during his reign.

The Ngqika tribe, subjected to a white, British-appointed paramount chief, took part in the uprising of 1877. Sandile was fatally wounded the next year in a skirmish with Mfengu troops and died on Isidenge Mountain. The British commander ordered that his body lie in state before being accorded a military funeral. The grave is south of Stutterheim at Mount Kempt.

A finger of land reaches into the waters of the Sandile Dam.

FORT BEAUFORT
This town, now a centre for the citrus farms irrigated by the Kat River, was founded in 1822 as a defence post and named after Governor Lord Charles Somerset's father, the Duke of Beaufort.

The martello tower, built in 1836 to replace the original fort, still stands in Bell Street and is believed to be the only martello tower ever to have been built inland. A short-barrelled cannon is mounted on its flat roof on a wooden turntable that allows it to be rotated to fire through a full circle. The old double-storey building nearby was built as a barracks for the garrison, and houses a military museum. The history museum is in the old officers' mess – a house in Durban Street.

Fort Beaufort's martello tower, built in 1836.

Gaika's Kop dominates this rural scene.

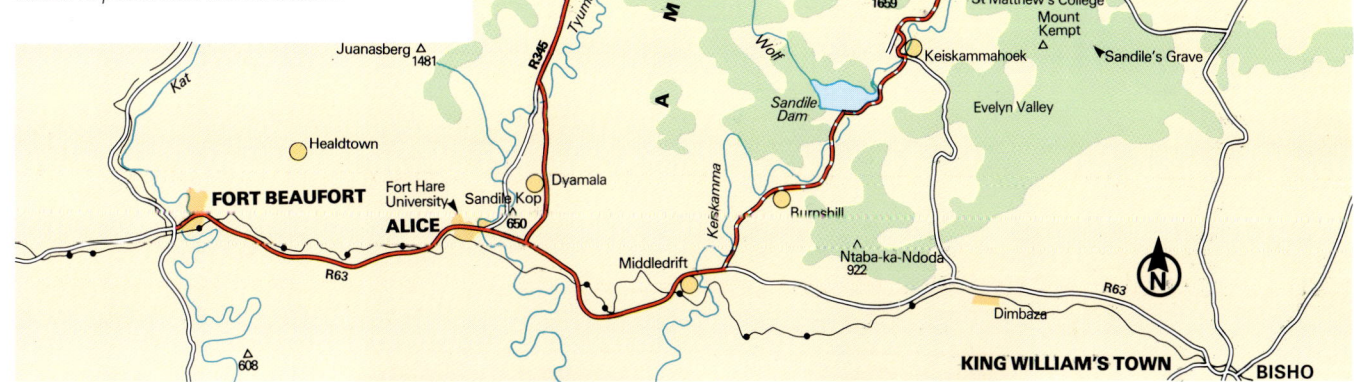

Young pines cast their mottled shade over a track near Stutterheim.

The cannon mounted on the roof of the martello tower in Fort Beaufort.

GAIKA'S KOP

This prominent peak in the Amatole range takes its name from Ngqika (Gaika), the warrior-chief and founder of a Xhosa clan. Legend has it that he made his home under the frowning slopes of Gaika's Kop and that death sentences were carried out by flinging the condemned from the precipitous cliffs near the 1 963 m summit.

Another and more likely legend claims that Gaika's Kop was once the home of a famous *ngqira* or diviner, and that the present name is simply a mispronunciation.

STUTTERHEIM

The richly forested mountainsides around Stutterheim not only support a healthy timber industry, but are also the basis of the area's popularity with holidaymakers. The nearby Kologha State Forest – on a spur of the Amatole range – is a favourite spot for weekend relaxation, and the Kubusi River offers fishing, swimming and boating. The Bethel Mission to the north of Stutterheim was established in 1837 by Berlin missionaries. More German settlers arrived in the area after the disbanding of the British German Legion in 1857 and the town they established was named after their commander, Major General Richard von Stutterheim.

SIR GEORGE CATHCART – MAN OF ACTION

The town of Cathcart, under the slopes of Windvoëlberg, is named after a Cape governor who showed himself to be fearless and incisive in action and who died, disillusioned, far away from the frontier that he had rigorously subdued.

As a young soldier, George Cathcart took part in many battles against Napoleon, including the final slaughter at Waterloo. He was appointed Governor of the Cape in 1852 and, by personal leadership at the war front, ended the most disastrous frontier war to date.

He was immediately appointed to the British army that had just gone to Crimea to fight the Russians. The Crimean War is said to have been the worst-managed war in which Britain ever took part. In protest against gross inefficiencies, Cathcart exposed himself with reckless gallantry at the battle of Inkerman, and the hill on which he died was later named Cathcart Hill.

Cathcart's market bell, which hangs at the municipal building, is inscribed *Orient*. It was the bell of the Russian ship of that name that went aground at East London in 1907, giving Orient Beach its name.

• EXPLORING THE HOGSBACK •

A forested walk and a rustic stone bridge capture the magic of walking in the Hogsback.

Mountain-top wonderland of forests, streams and waterfalls

AT THE WESTERN END of the Amatole range an escarpment falls away to the broad, green Tyume valley. Before reaching the fertile flats, the Tyume and its tributaries fall in showering cascades over silvery rocks in the cool depths of an ancient indigenous forest. This remote mountain resort area has been known for more than a century as the Hogsback.

The village of Hogsback, which lies a short distance from the three Hogsback peaks, straggles along a mountain slope with considerably varying altitudes – from the post office at 1 213 m above sea level, to the T-junction at the top of the village at 1 532 m. It is this high altitude that is largely responsible for the area's wonderfully cool summers, as well as the winter snowfalls that blanket the peaks, and often the village too.

Features of Hogsback are the distinctiveness of the four seasons and the 'Englishness' of many of the avenues and gardens, which flourish under a high annual rainfall of 1 270 mm. A riot of rhododendrons and azaleas in spring, their summer offering includes a profusion of edible berries which, served with cream, are a local delicacy. (The berries and many other plant species were introduced by Thomas Summerton, a market gardener from Oxfordshire, who settled at Hogsback about 100 years ago.) Autumn, too, is a magical time, as the leaves of Japanese maple, liquidambar, dogwood and viburnum turn to shades of red and gleaming gold.

Early visitors
The name 'Hogs Back' – as two words – first appeared in 1848 in the journal of the artist Thomas Baines, applied to the 'Great Amatola Peak'. There are several theories about the name, but the most generally believed explanation is that it comes from the fact that the ridge known as the first Hogsback looks like the back of a hog, with the summit rocks and fissures resembling the bristles on the animal's back.

Xhosa pastoralists probably grazed their cattle here in the lush summer vegetation many years before the first soldiers arrived in the 1830s under Colonel Michel of the Warwickshire Regiment. The soldiers built a fort on the slopes of Tor Doone, where the earthworks still remain. The colonel's name has become corrupted to Mitchell, which is often applied to the fort as well as to the mountain pass that links the Hogsback to Seymour. The Forestry Department started a pine nursery in the area in 1887, and two years later began large-scale planting. By then there were already a few permanent residents, and members of the farming community brought their cattle up the mountain to escape the valley's summer heat. Today the area is reached most easily along the tarred route from Alice via Hogsback Pass (pages 182 – 3) or the gravel road from Cathcart via Happy Valley. The gravel road from Seymour across Michel's Pass is very steep and narrow, and is not recommended, especially when towing or when the surface is wet. The old or original road from Keiskammahoek over Wolf Ridge is no longer passable.

Walking trails
The Hogsback is renowned for its many attractive walks. Several of the trails to the various beauty spots, such as waterfalls and contour paths, are marked with colour-coded hog emblems. These markers are maintained by one of the local hotels, and a key to their destinations is contained in a booklet sold locally and known as the 'piggy book'. Enquire locally before you set out, as some of the routes that cross private property may have been closed since the booklet was published.

A short walk leads along Redcoat Lane (opposite Oak Avenue), past the village library housed in its tiny rondavel, and along one of the paths Colonel Michel's red-jacketed soldiers followed from Fort Hare up to Hogsback in the 19th century. Eventually this pretty lane links up with the Hogsback Pass.

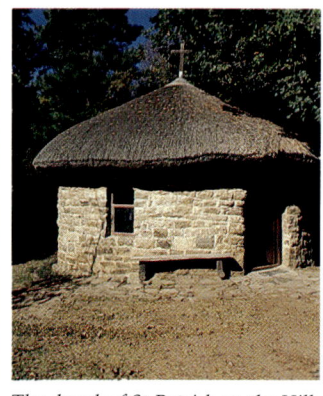

The church of St Patrick-on-the-Hill.

This bird's-eye view captures the English feel of the Hogsback settlement.

The area's waterfalls are among the major attractions. Kettlespout Waterfall is well worth a visit when there has been rain and there is a wind blowing from the valley: this forces the water back, sometimes over the rim of the fall, giving the impression of steam coming from the spout of a kettle. (A number of other pleasant walks also lead from the parking area near the Kettlespout Waterfall.)

The Madonna and Child Waterfall, so named because of the appearance of the rock formation over which the water falls, is reached off the Wolf Ridge road, along a footpath that also leads eventually to an enormous, ancient yellowwood tree known as the Eastern Monarch.

Scenic drives

A footpath from Oak Avenue leads to another waterfall, known as The 39 Steps. Oak Avenue, with its rows of logs placed on both sides of the road, serves as a lofty inter-denominational church at Easter and Christmas, and the road forms the start of a circular drive known as Forest Drive.

Another scenic drive leads for 8 km along the Wolf Ridge road to King's Nek, from where there are superb views over the Amatole range and the Tyume basin.

To the west of the village main road is the road to the Plaatjieskraal plantation. The left fork after the Safcol notice board leads for another 2 km to an area where there are several relatively easy mountain walks with good views.

Travelling north on the village main road, 1 km beyond the Plaatjieskraal turn-off, you reach the little church of St Patrick-on-the-Hill on your left. One of the smallest churches in South Africa, it was built as a private chapel in 1935, and now serves as an Anglican-administered, interdenominational church.

Hiking through the Hogsback forest, you may come across the Knysna lourie, the Cape parrot or the rare Samango monkey, all of which are year-round residents. In the indigenous sections some of the trees are numbered for easy identification. Enormous yellowwoods spread their crowns above the forest canopy, and are often draped with Spanish moss, a beard-like fungus, or the ubiquitous 'monkey rope'. Other indigenous trees you are likely to see include the lemonwood (*Xymalos monospora*), the red-berried forest currant (*Rhus chirindensis*), white ironwood (*Vepris undulata*), assegai-wood (*Curtisia dentata*), and the cabbage trees (*Cussonia spicata* and *C paniculata*).

Lush ground cover

Among notable exotics are the Californian redwoods (*Sequoia sempervirens*) and holy cypress (*Abies religiosa*), which is actually a member of the fir group.

Below the trees, ferns, mosses, berries and bracken include the wild strawberry, and flowers abound – particularly agapanthus, arum lilies and the white blood flower, or *haemanthus*.

The weather patterns of the Hogsback are often described by locals as 'fickle', and it is advisable to take warm as well as rainproof clothing. Late afternoon mists in summer may form quickly and can be a hazard on higher ground. It is wise to ask local opinion on the weather before setting out on any hike, and to let someone know where you plan to go and when you expect to return.

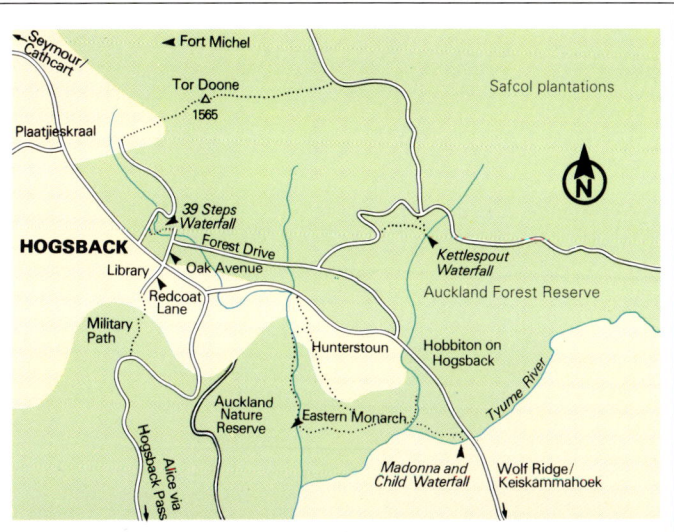

Forest Drive – the beginning of a circular drive through the Hogsback, and popular venue for open-air church services at Christmas and Easter.

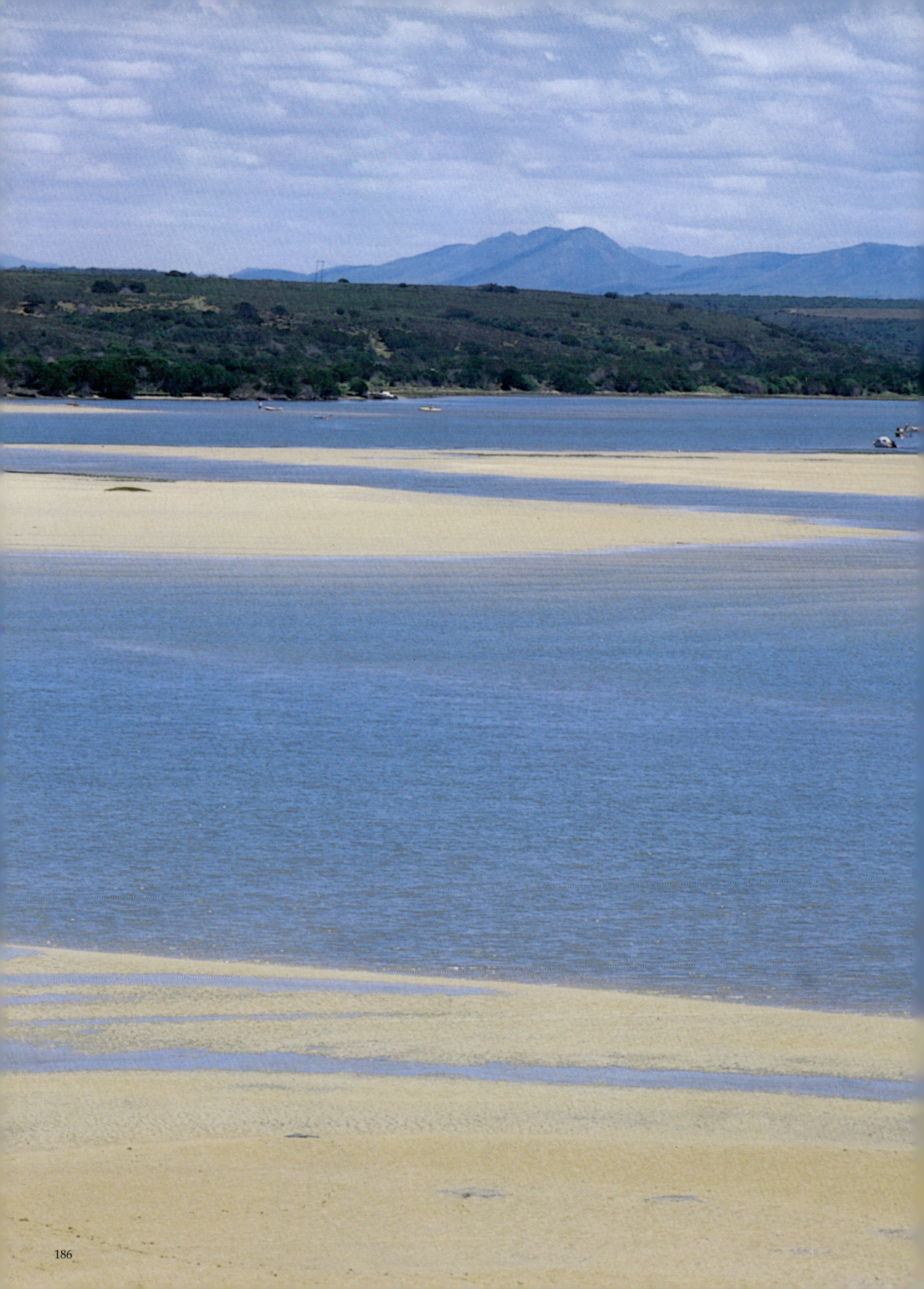

EASTERN CAPE

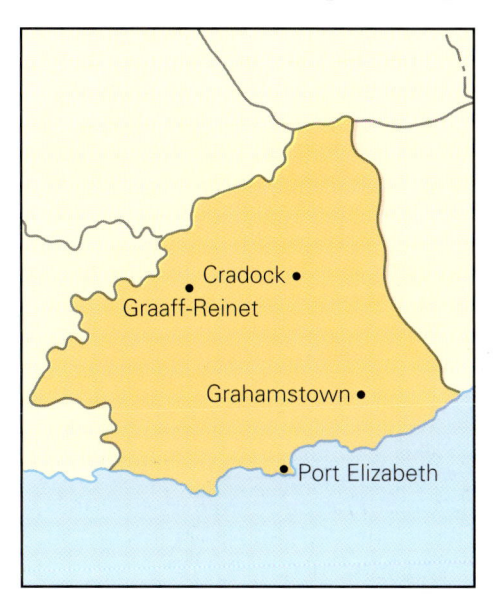

Karoo and Camdeboo: Midlands roads and roses **188-9**

Grahamstown – Fort Beaufort – Katberg Pass – Seymour – Alice **190-1**

Grahamstown – Salem – Bushmans River Mouth – Port Alfred – Bathurst **192-3**

Grahamstown: Places of interest in the Settler City **194-5**

Graaff-Reinet – Nieu Bethesda – Mountain Zebra National Park – Cradock – Pearston **196-7**

The Owl House: A pilgrim's progress in Nieu Bethesda **198-9**

Mountain Zebra National Park: Remote mountain sanctuary **200-1**

Port Elizabeth – Uitenhage – Sundays River Valley – Suurberg Pass – Addo Elephant National Park **202-3**

Port Elizabeth: What to see and do in the Friendly City **204-5**

Port Elizabeth – Van Staden's River Mouth – Hankey – Grootrivier – Cockscomb **206-7**

Port Elizabeth – Jeffreys Bay – Cape St Francis – Cockscomb **208-9**

Port Elizabeth: Walks and wildlife **210-1**

Graaff-Reinet: A closer look at the Gem of the Karoo **212-3**

Karoo Nature Reserve: The Valley of Desolation **214-5**

Left: *The scenic lagoon formed where the Krom River opens into St Francis Bay.*

• EXPLORING A CAPE CORNER •

Green grassland and well-wooded slopes of the Bosberg at Glen Avon, close to the site of the original Somerset Farm.

Some outposts of the Eastern Cape midlands

THIS IS A CORNER of the Eastern Cape where national highways have not yet challenged the wooded heights of mountains prominent in tales of history. Indeed, some of the roads are unsuited to ordinary traffic, and may remain in poor condition for long periods after heavy rains. Rather than a set route, this outing suggests a series of excursions from the main highway linking several small but attractive towns.

Before you leave Somerset East, attractively laid out on the slopes of the Bosberg, take time to look around you. The town was founded in 1825 by governor Lord Charles Somerset on the site of the agricultural station he had established in 1815. Originally it was just 'Somerset' – the 'East' was added much later to avoid confusion with Somerset West nearer Cape Town.

Land in the new town was given to Wesleyan missionaries for a chapel and graveyard. The building and land were later transferred to the Dutch Reformed Church and, in 1835, the chapel was converted into a dwelling. It served as the parsonage for the next 105 years and, in 1975, this distinctive Georgian building took on a new role as a museum. A gracious old structure, it stands serenely among tall indigenous trees, with a magnificent rose garden, a Victorian herb garden and extensive orchards around it.

Walk from these gardens to Paulet Street, named after Lord Charles Somerset's second wife, Lady Mary Paulet. Number 9 is thought by some to have been the home of Louis Trichardt, a leader of the Great Trek, but it is almost certain that it was built by Robert Hart. It has since served as a church and also provided accommodation for visiting circuit court judges. Hart was a soldier and the second superintendent, from 1817, of the government-owned Somerset Farm. His own property, Glen Avon, became a model farm and a popular meeting place. Hart was buried on his farm in 1867 and he is commemorated in the Presbyterian church in town.

The town is rich in historic educational institutions. Bellevue Seminary in Paulet Street was built in 1881 as a school for young ladies, while further down the same street is the Old Hofmeyr School, originally intended for the children of the poor. Gill College High School opened as a college for boys in 1869 and its beautiful school buildings include two national monuments. Dr William Gill was the first district surgeon of the town and, on his death in 1863, left the bulk of his estate to finance an institute for higher learning.

The King of Fook Island

Walter Battiss is one of Somerset East's most celebrated sons, and he lived at 45 Paulet Street, where his parents ran the Battiss Private Hotel between 1911 and 1917. The double-storey house was built in 1816 as an officers' mess, and incorporates yellowwood beams and planks from the Bosberg.

Shortly before his death in 1982, Battiss returned to Somerset East to open the museum created in his honour. He had donated 85 paintings – 58 of his own and 27 by other artists, including his wife Grace, Sydney Khumalo, Maud Sumner and Zakkie Eloff.

The largest collection of Battiss works in the country, the Art Museum provides a view of the full spectrum of his artistic genius and imagination, including the legendary Fook Island currency and stamps. Battiss devised Fook Island in the 1970s as an escape from reality and was the monarch, King Ferd III, or WB Rex, as emblazoned on his multicoloured, hand-knitted jersey. There are stories of travellers, and even Battiss himself, entering and leaving other countries on a Fook Island passport. One tale tells of cashing a Fook Island note for $10 at the international airport in Rome.

Bosberg Nature Reserve

Over 2 000 ha of the Bosberg mountains make up a delightful nature reserve; after good rains, no fewer than 13 waterfalls cascade down the southern kloofs. Patches of indigenous forest shelter a mammal population that includes mountain zebra, baboon, bushbuck, monkey and dassie, more than 80 bird species and 25 different reptiles. Hiking trails, game walks, trout-fishing, two bird hides, five dams and scenic drives are other attractions. There are chalets for hire, and overnight huts on the longest trails. A 10 km scenic drive from Henry Street, past the golf course and Bestershoek recreational area along the summit, gives fine views of the town and district.

Glen Avon

Take the R63 for Cookhouse and, after 7 km, turn left to Glen Avon; the farm is 7 km from the R63. Glen Avon has been in the same family since 1825, when it was granted to Robert Hart, and it remains private property, so keep on for Glen Avon Heights and note your kms here. As you climb from the valley into the foothills of the Bosberg you pass a profusion of wild plumbago and honeysuckle, home to vervet monkeys that give

The Somerset East Museum served as a parsonage for more than 100 years.

great performances in the vegetation by the roadside. After 5,7 km you reach Glen Avon Heights, and successive views of the spectacular horseshoe formation of the mountain buttress unfold. From the top of the escarpment, views south from the upper rolling grasslands seem to extend forever. Beyond the crest of Glen Avon Heights the road is inadequately signposted and is often in very poor condition, particularly beyond Glen Craig House. Your return down Glen Avon Heights gives you more views of the unending vistas.

Cookhouse

Turn left at the R63 and, after some 17 km, you arrive at Cookhouse on the Great Fish River. A military camp was established here, close to the ford, and a small stone shed was built to house the all-important regimental kitchen, or 'cookhouse' in the military jargon of the day. And Cookhouse it has stayed, although sometimes confused with Goodhouse, on the Orange River, which is reputed to be the hottest place in the country.

Golden Valley and Slagters Nek

Drive south from Cookhouse on the R32 for some 7 km to reach a road on your right that leads through Golden Valley, renowned for its citrus orchards. About 2,5 km further, on your left, is the Slagters Nek memorial, erected privately in 1916. (The site was formerly called Van Aardt's Post; Slagters Nek, where rebellion was fomented, lies further north.) It commemorates five frontier farmers who were hanged here for high treason in 1815 and 1816. The bungled hangings raised antigovernment emotions that endured for more than a century.

Hikers pause on the Bosberg Trail.

The historic church at Glen Thorn.

The Walter Battiss Art Museum – a tribute to the only King of Fook Island.

Reminder of a tragic rebellion.

Bedford

Return to Cookhouse, take the N10 north to Cradock and, after 19 km, turn right onto the R63 for Bedford, which you reach after a further 21 km. The town was named after the Duke of Bedford in 1854, and established on the farm, Maasström, of Sir Andries Stockenström, former Lieutenant Governor of the Eastern Cape.

The only Scottish party among the 1820 Settlers, led by poet and writer Thomas Pringle, settled in the Bedford area, where many of their descendants still carry on farming traditions. They were met by Robert Hart, a fellow Scot, who introduced them to their allotted land in the Baviaans River valley. The soft, green hills and undulating grasslands are reminiscent of Scotland and are a lovely background to a little-known attraction of the Bedford district – the outstandingly beautiful gardens that reach a peak of perfection during October and November. All the gardens are privately owned and farm owners welcome visitors by appointment and prior arrangement only.

The big gardens at Maasström, Cavers, Spring Grove and Kelvinside, although attractive enough during autumn and winter, come into full glory in spring and summer. Turn left at the war memorial and, three blocks later, large, white gates mark the entrance to Maasström. For the other farms, continue on the Adelaide road (R63) and, after 7 km, take the left turn marked 'Cowie Valley'. At the T-junction turn left again, to reach Cavers, Spring Grove and Kelvinside in that order. While roses are their common pride, special features such as a mill, a water garden, a white garden, and chunky cycads surrounded by soft lacy shrubs make these lovely gardens quite exceptional.

Adelaide

Drive east from Bedford on the R63, to reach Adelaide some 23 km later. A country town of quiet charm, set on the banks of the Koonap River at the foot of the Winterberg, Adelaide began as a military post in 1834, named in honour of the Queen Consort of King William IV of Great Britain. Now a centre for farmers producing wool, citrus, mohair and grain, it retains its strong links with settler and frontier history.

'Our Heritage' Museum in Queen Street is a pleasing double-storey building that, built in 1860, served as the parsonage for the local Dutch Reformed church until 1964. Sited on the river, the museum has a large garden of roses, shrubs and indigenous trees inviting a picnic during your visit. The museum is reputed to have the largest collection of Wedgwood in the country, including tea sets, plates, jugs and vases. This is complemented by Dresden-ware; Staffordshire dogs and castles; English, German, Viennese, Lalique and Woodstock glass. Shelves of handsome pewter as well as Cape and English silver and a collection of fine English furniture were bequests to the museum from Harry and Margaret Ash.

Harry Ash served in the British Merchant Navy and survived two torpedo attacks during the Second World War. He married Margaret Lomax, only daughter of the founder of the Clock Tower brand of patent medicines that started in Molteno. After the war Harry Ash was able to indulge his passion for collecting beautiful things from all over the world with the help of his wife and the Lomax fortune. He was one of the founders of the Museum and undoubtedly its greatest benefactor.

Glen Thorn Church

Leave Adelaide by crossing the railway line, with the stock pens on your left, and turn right onto the R344 for Tarkastad. The good gravel road passes through park-like country studded with kiepersol trees, and passes Mount Mitchell on your right; just after 27 km, turn left to Glen Thorn Settler Church. Some 5,4 km from the turn-off you will see the little church on the right, commanding a fine view of the hills and the Mankazana River valley. The church was built in 1840 on land granted to John Pringle in 1824. Graves in the tranquil churchyard pay tribute to past worshippers.

To explore further this lovely and little-known corner of South Africa, ask the advice of local residents about roads and their condition. Further information may also be obtained from the following: The Municipality, Market Square, Adelaide 5760; tel (046) 684 0034. The Publicity Association, 58 Charles Street, Somerset East 5850; tel (0424) 31448.

Past forts and forgotten frontiers to the sweeping heights of the Katberg

From Grahamstown the old Queen's Road leads to Fort Beaufort and a magnificent scenic drive over the Katberg range. We return through the tranquil beauty of the Tyume Valley and take the old military road – still dotted with stone forts that once guarded a disputed frontier. Roughly half the route is on tarred roads; the rest is on gravel.

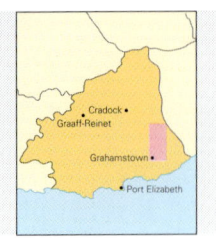

Grahamstown
Ecca Pass
Fort Beaufort
Katberg Pass
Seymour
Alice
300 – 320 km

LEAVE GRAHAMSTOWN on the N2 bypass, following the signs for East London/King William's Town. Just outside the town you pass the tree-crowned hill known as Makana's Kop (see opposite). About 5,5 km from town, turn left onto the R67 for Fort Beaufort, noting your kms.

A little more than 9 km later, you pass a road on your right to Committee's Drift. A few metres beyond this, on your left, is a parking area and a monument to Andrew Geddes Bain, who built the Ecca Pass, which you soon begin to descend (see below).

After 21 km on the R67 you pass, on your right, the turn-off to the Andries Vosloo Kudu Reserve and, 1,5 km later, you reach Fort Brown, also on your right. The fort is now part of a South African Police Service post.

Continue on the R67, which immediately crosses the Great Fish River – note your kms at the start of the bridge. After 50 km, turn right onto the R63 for Fort Beaufort and, 600 m later, turn right again at the T-junction onto the R63/67, which brings you into the town of Fort Beaufort (see pages 182 – 3).

Fort Beaufort to the Katberg Pass

Leave Fort Beaufort on the R67 (signposted Seymour/Queenstown) and note your kms as you pass the R63 on which you entered (signposted for Adelaide/Grahamstown). After 20 km, you pass the former Toll Hotel on your right, on the site of the 19th-century tollhouse known as Tidbury's Toll. Some 8 km later, turn left onto the R531 for Katberg and Balfour.

The road crosses a narrow bridge and passes a turn-off on your left to Post Retief. Continue straight for Katberg Pass at the intersection at a railway level crossing; 2,5 km later, go left at the fork. After 5 km, you pass a road on your left to the Katberg Hotel – established as a mountain resort in 1904 – and reach the offices of the Department of Forestry on your right after a further 1 km – enquiries can be made here about the drives and walks through the local forests. After a further 1 km, go right at the fork for the road over the Katberg Pass (the road on the left is the scenic Forest Drive). Where the road levels at the top of the pass there are places on the side where you can picnic, but no fires are permitted.

Katberg Pass to Alice

Turn back roughly 10 km from the fork, where a road on your left leads to Tarkastad. Return down Katberg Pass and note your kms as you pass the forestry station on your left. After 8,4 km you reach the railway level crossing – turn left at the intersection immediately afterwards.

Roughly 4 km later, turn right at the T-junction with another gravel road. Turn left onto the tarred R67 at the T-junction some 50 m later. The R67 passes a turn-off to the Kat River Dam; 3,2 km after this, turn right into Seymour.

At the stop street in Seymour (with the old town hall on your left) turn right towards Alice and Hogsback. The tarred surface gives way to gravel after 400 m. Note your kms at the start of the bridge immediately afterwards.

You cross a number of cattle grids and, after 23 km, turn right at the T-junction onto the tarred R345 in the Tyume Valley. Some 15 km later, turn right again at the T-junction onto the R63, which leads into Alice.

Alice to Grahamstown

After passing Fort Hare on your right, veer left at the fork at the entrance to Alice. Immediately after passing the railway station on your left, turn left into Temlett Street and cross the railway line. At the Y-junction in front of the hospital, turn right onto the R345, noting your kms. The tar gives way to gravel after 400 m.

Keep straight at the intersection after 15 km (where a small road leads to the right and a fork to the left leads to Junction). After a further 10 km, the road enters Double Drift Nature Reserve – there is no entrance fee, but you may have to wait for the boom to be raised. Some 40 km from the hospital in Alice, turn right where the rambling buildings of the old Breakfast Vlei Hotel now serve as a trading centre.

After a further 16 km, you cross the Great Fish River by a narrow bridge. On your left just after the bridge is a police post that incorporates parts of the old Committee's Drift fortifications. Across the road, a few hundred metres later, is the former Committee's Drift Hotel, now a private residence, and a church of 1888 that was unroofed by a tornado in 1972.

Some 600 m after you pass the road leading to the church, turn left. After a further 20 km you reach a complex of buildings on your left, including a fortified gun-tower, at Trompetter's Drift.

Roughly 2 km later, at the T-junction, turn right onto the N2 for Grahamstown. (A gravel road on your left after 6,7 km on the N2 leads to the remains of the Fraser's Camp signal tower and fort, 2,5 km from the tarred road.)

Grahamstown Publicity Association 63 High Street, Grahamstown 6140 Tel (0461) 23241
Contour Fort Beaufort Military Museum, 20 Bell Street, Fort Beaufort 5720 Tel (04634) 31503
Katberg Hotel PO Box 665, Fort Beaufort 5720 Tel (0404) 31151

A gracious old bandstand in the grounds of Fort Beaufort's Military Museum.

An artist's impression of the 'Blinkwater Monster' and skull found by Bain.

THE BLINKWATER MONSTER

Andrew Geddes Bain is honoured by a cairn on the heights of the Ecca Pass on the Queen's Road which he built from Grahamstown to Fort Beaufort from 1837 to 1845. Bain developed an interest in geology and, in the course of blasting, he worked out the stratigraphy of the Karoo System. Bain discovered the type skull of the fossil reptile group known as the dicynodonts, and also 'the skull of a huge animal with 56 fluted and serrated teeth'. This creature, one of the earliest animals known to have adopted an upright stance (as opposed to crawling), he named the Blinkwater Monster. Bain achieved instant renown in the scientific world for his discovery.

The gentle landscape of the Katberg stretches to a horizon of blue mountains.

St Bartholomew's Church in Alice.

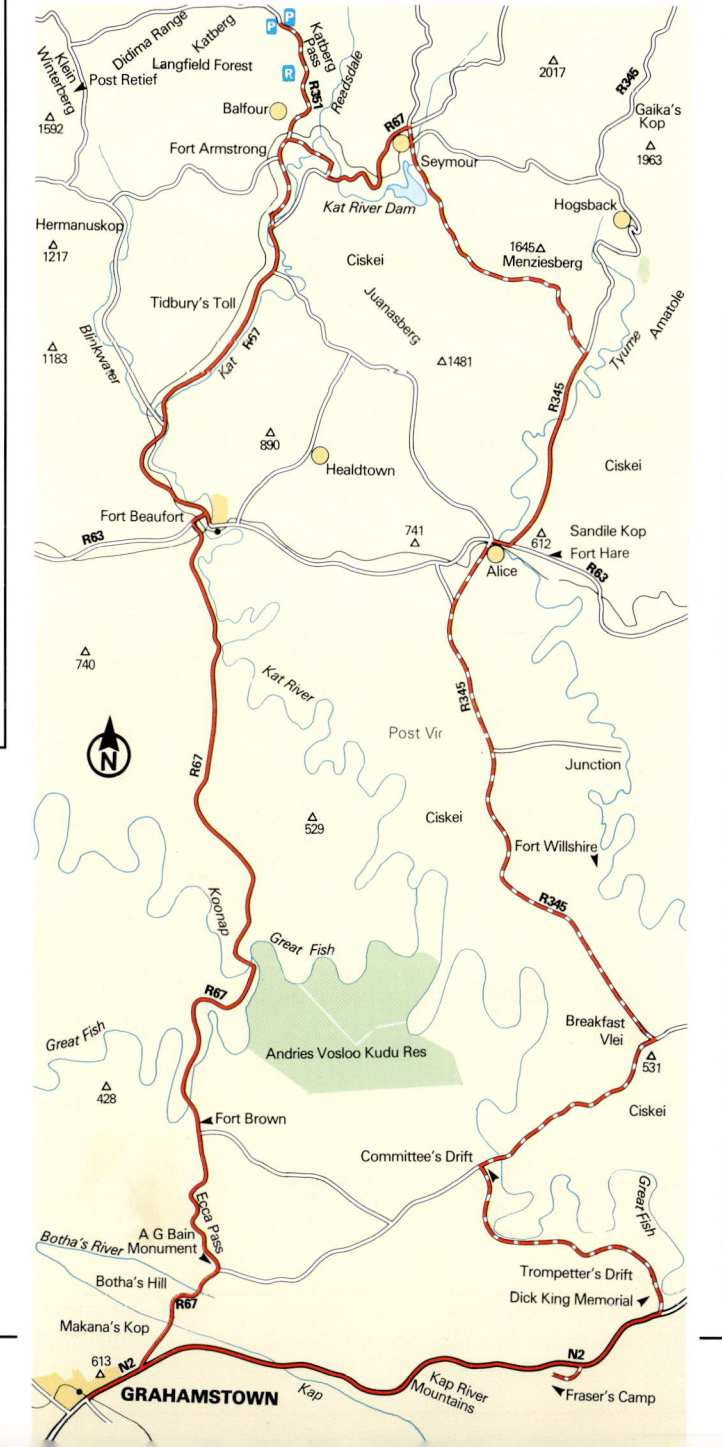

A Roman Catholic mission church in a wide, flat valley near Balfour.

THE 'CAT MOUNTAIN'

The forests and hills of the *Katberg* (cat mountain) make this a popular holiday area for hikers and riders. The range is crossed by the Katberg Pass, a gravel road – of which parts are sometimes in poor condition – that offers spectacular views.

Seymour and the Kat River Valley are distinguished in the history of the development of Afrikaans – Kaatje Kekkelbek, the character created by AG Bain and John Rex in their comic song, came from 'Katrivier'; and one of the earliest published works in Afrikaans, the *Zamenspraak tusschen Klaas Waarzegger en Jan Twyfelaar...* was written by a Seymour magistrate, Louis Henri Meurant. The Kat River Valley saw violent fighting during the frontier wars.

ALICE

Governor Sir Harry Smith really named this town to honour his sister, although he diplomatically claimed to have chosen the name in honour of one of Queen Victoria's daughters. The town started as a mission station of the Glasgow Mission Society in 1824. Today it is home to Lovedale College and the University of Fort Hare. East of the town is Sandile Kop, named after the famous Xhosa ruler and now surmounted by a memorial to the Reverend James Stewart, one of the early Scottish missionaries.

MAKANA'S KOP

In the Battle of Grahamstown in 1819, about 10 000 Xhosa warriors under Makana advanced briskly down this hillside towards the small post defended – along the line of the present York Street – by some 30 civilians and 300 soldiers under Major 'Tiger Tom' Willshire. In spite of the disparity in numbers, the firearms in the hands of professional soldiers proved decisive, and the attackers were driven off.

Shocked by the defeat, Makana later surrendered rather than subject his followers to the risk of further disaster. Makana is often referred to as 'Lynx', a corruption of the Dutch word *Linksch* (left) by which he was known because of his left-handedness.

TROMPETTER'S DRIFT

This drift, one of the oldest crossing places along the Great Fish River, was named not for some 'trumpeter' but after a Khoikhoi adventurer, Hans Trompetter. The Cape Governor, Lord Charles Somerset, established a fortified post here in 1817 as part of his system of frontier defence. During the war of 1835, a large pont was established here under an armed guard to ensure that supplies could reach Grahamstown, but a Xhosa attack captured the entire position.

After this war a more substantial fort was built, and was the scene of fierce fighting in 1846. Today the solid gun tower and some of the perimeter walls are almost all that remain of the original outpost.

Meander across gentle hills to the sparkling sands of the Settler coast

South of Grahamstown our route winds down to wide, sandy beaches and the old harbour of Port Alfred – now an attractive pleasure resort. Then we turn inland again, across hills dotted with Settler buildings that have grown old in a green land where time seems to have stood still. More than half the route is tarred; the rest is on good gravel roads.

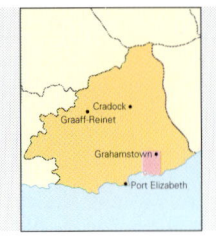

Grahamstown
Salem
Alexandria
Bushman's River Mouth
Port Alfred
Bathurst
180 – 200 km

DRIVE UP GRAHAMSTOWN'S Lucas Avenue to visit the 1820 Settlers' National Monument on Gunfire Hill (see pages 194 – 5 for street map), which offers an excellent view over the town and surrounding countryside. Continue past the monument to the T-junction with the N2 and turn right, noting your kms. The road soon begins a gradual descent through Howison's Poort. After about 10 km, turn left onto the R343 for Alexandria, Kenton on Sea, Thomas Baines Nature Reserve and Salem, and note your kms. You soon pass a gravel road on your left to the nature reserve and Settlers' Dam and, after 12 km on the R343, turn left into Salem to see the old Settler churches that still form the heart of the village.

Salem to Bushman's River
Return to the R343 and turn left for Alexandria. After a few hundred metres the road surface changes to gravel for roughly 16 km. Another 15 km brings you to Alexandria.

At the stop street next to the pharmacy, turn left into Voortrekker Street and, within 200 m, turn right into Karel Landman Street, noting your kms – this becomes the road to Boknes. After 17 km on this road, turn right for Cannon Rocks, then turn left 1,8 km later to reach a parking area on a wide, secluded beach.

Return to the road from which you turned to Cannon Rocks and turn right. (Keeping straight here will take you to Boknes Beach, from where you can walk to the Diaz Cross.) After 700 m, turn left for *Boesmansriviermond* (Bushman's River Mouth). You pass a rough road on your right to Diaz Cross and, 1,7 km later, turn right at the T-junction onto the tarred R72 for Port Alfred. After a further 4,1 km, turn right onto a road signposted 'Boesmansriviermond'. This brings you to a parking area at the mouth of the river. (Both river and beach are safe for bathing. The municipal campsite has braai sites, water and toilets.)

Bushman's River to Port Alfred
Return to the intersection with the R72 and turn right for Port Alfred. You pass turn-offs on your right to Kenton on Sea and Kasouga and reach Port Alfred after 23 km. Keep straight for 'R72/East London' where the road

The simple, puritan lines of the historic Methodist chapel in Salem.

RICHARD GUSH OF SALEM
The name *Salem* means 'peace', yet the village of this name saw much strife during its early years. The little settlement, founded by a party of 1820 Settlers under Hezekiah Sephton, was besieged by Xhosa warriors in the war of 1834. One of those whose wife and children had found precarious refuge in the church was Richard Gush, a Quaker carpenter sternly opposed to the shedding of blood. He offered to go out of the stockade and reason with the warriors, despite the risks. Unarmed, he strode out, followed at some distance by his interpreter Field Cornet Barend Woest. Asked why they were attacking the settlement, the surprised Xhosa could say only that they were hungry. Gush returned to the village for loaves of bread as well as tobacco and distributed them among the warriors who, true to their word, passed on without attacking Salem.

The lagoon at the Bushman's River mouth is a paradise for holiday-makers.

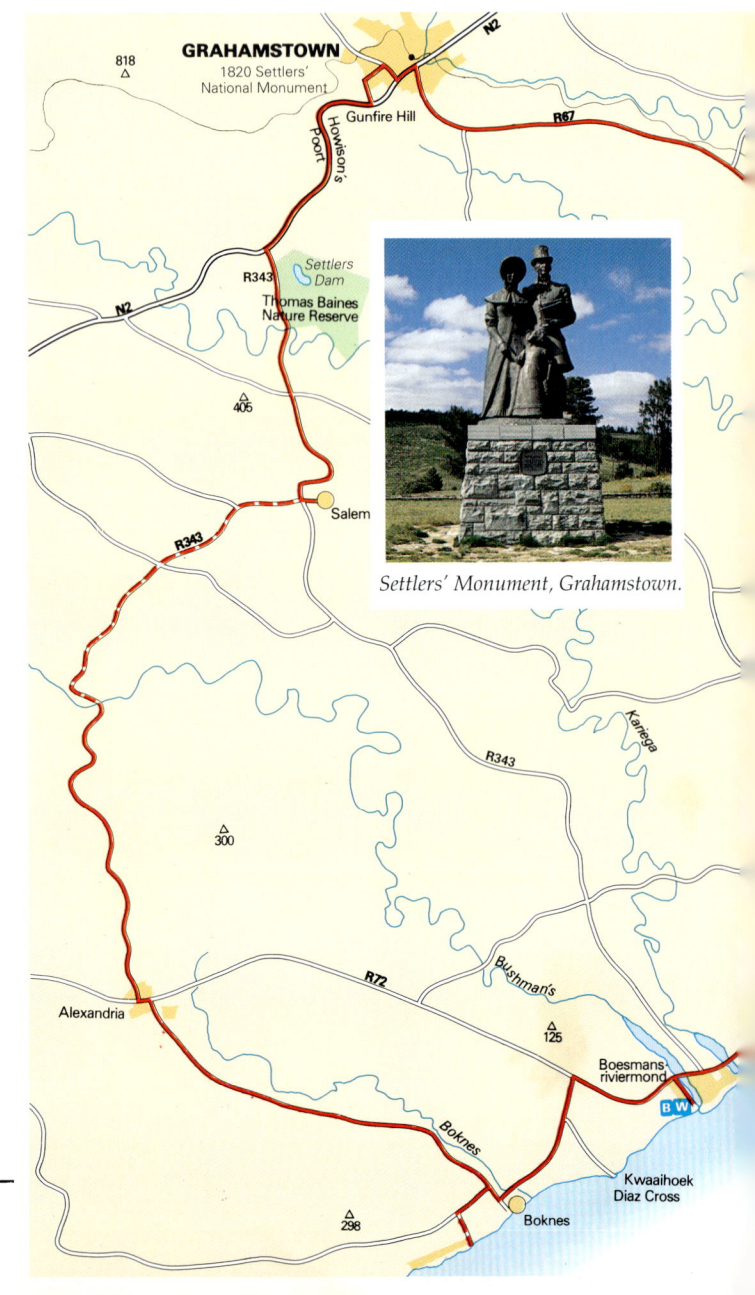

Settlers' Monument, Grahamstown.

forks in the centre of town (the road on the left crosses the Kowie by the Putt Bridge towards Grahamstown).

Turn right at the traffic lights just before the road crosses the modern concrete bowstring-arch bridge, then turn left immediately into Beach Road. This road runs along the west bank of the Kowie River. There is a parking area at the beach, and another road leads off to the right past idyllic bathing and fishing beaches. (A number of establishments in the town provide meals and takeaways.)

Port Alfred to Bathurst
Leave Port Alfred by crossing the Putt Bridge over the river. Turn left into Wharf Street and follow this road across gently rolling countryside to enter Bathurst on Kowie Road.

At the intersection opposite Bathurst's Pig and Whistle Hotel, turn left onto a gravel road for Bradshaw's Mill. Turn right after 400 m, to reach the mill after a further 900 m. Driving back from the mill, turn right at the first T-junction and follow this road for 4 km to an attractive viewsite above a classic horseshoe bend in the Kowie River.

Return to the Pig and Whistle corner and drive uphill on Trappes Road (R67). Follow the sign to your left along a gravel road for 400 m to reach St John's Church on your right.

Turn around, return to Trappes Road and cross it, onto a 2,4 km tarred road that leads to the 1820 Settlers Toposcope. Return to Trappes Road and turn right, noting your kms and, some 3,7 km later, turn right towards Trappes' Valley and Clumber. About 3 km later, you pass a turn-off on your left to Clumber; 6,5 km after this, turn left for 'Kaffir Drift', noting your kms. After 2,7 km, turn right at the crossroads. About 100 m along this road, on your left, are the substantial remains of Cawood's Post, one of the original fortified farmhouses built by the Settlers. Turn around and continue straight at the crossroads.

The road crosses the railway line several times. After 25 km turn right at the T-junction onto the tarred R67 for Grahamstown.

Grahamstown Publicity Association 63 High Street, Grahamstown 6140 Tel (0461) 23241
Port Alfred Publicity Association PO Box 63 Port Alfred 6170 Tel (0464) 41235

EASTERN CAPE

The site of the toposcope atop Thornridge.

1820 SETTLERS' TOPOSCOPE
In 1820 Colonel Jacob Cuyler chose Thornridge near Bathurst – with its wide views over the surrounding coastal countryside – as a base from which to direct the newly arrived Settlers to their allotted farms. In 1968 a toposcope was erected here – using stones from old Settler homes – showing where the Settlers went and the original names of their farms. The view from Thornridge is a wide one and includes the coast.

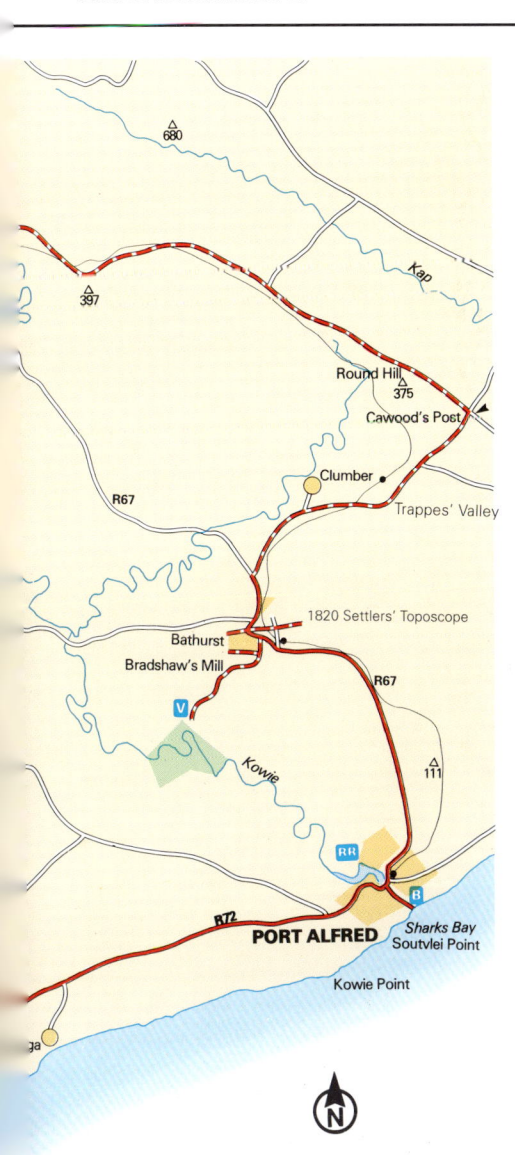

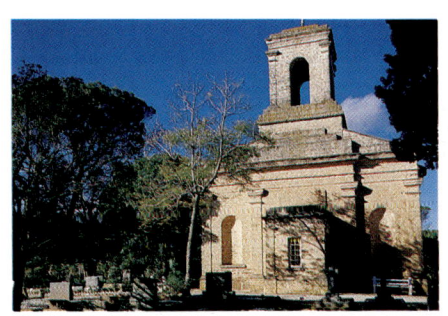

The sturdy little St John's church in Bathurst.

The wool mill Samuel Bradshaw built at Bathurst.

ST JOHN'S CHURCH, BATHURST
This little church, started in 1832, three times did duty as a shelter for Settlers during strife on the frontier – the first time even before the building was completed. St John's was opened for services in 1838 and, during the War of the Axe (1846 – 7) it again served as a shelter, with as many as 300 people sleeping in the church at night. It sheltered the Settlers again, for the last time, during the war of 1850-3.

At the Kowie Museum.

STONE AGE REMAINS
In the hills opposite the hotel on Howison's Poort is a cave that was home to countless families more than 100 000 years ago, during the period known in South Africa as the Middle Stone Age.

Archaeologists have found in the cave a layer some 30 cm deep containing the bones of small animals that had formed the meals of early man – as well as a new phase of stone-implement culture.

THE KOWIE
The resort of Port Alfred lies at the mouth of the Kowie River, exactly midway between Port Elizabeth and East London. It was established as Port Kowie soon after the arrival of the 1820 Settlers, later renamed Port Frances and given its present name after the 1860 visit to the Cape of Queen Victoria's son, Prince Alfred. Faced with all these choices, the locals call their town and the river, simply, 'the Kowie'.

Efforts to turn the Kowie into a port were frustrated by silting, although for 20 years last century, as many as 100 tall sailing ships used the port annually. The Kowie's fortune, however, now seems set to be made as a holiday destination.

Wharf Street in Port Alfred bustles with holiday-makers.

INDIAN OCEAN

EXPLORING GRAHAMSTOWN ON FOOT

A view of Church Square, Grahamstown.

A rough outpost that became 'The City of the Saints'

ONE DAY IN 1812 a weary soldier dismounted from his horse near an abandoned farmhouse on the war-ravaged frontier. He hung his sword on the branch of a thorn tree and looked around. This, he decided, was where he would establish a fortified post. The soldier was Colonel John Graham, and his fortified post was to grow to become Grahamstown, capital city of 1820 Settler country and home to many notable characters in the history of South Africa.

In gratitude for their survival in their new land, many religious denominations built churches in the little town – and a total of close to 40 places of worship gave the place one of its nicknames: 'The City of the Saints.' In spite of the passage of years, Grahamstown retains the dignity of the devotion that raised it, with its soaring stone spires and other historic 19th-century buildings.

Retief's legacy

Our walking tour of historic Grahamstown begins at the south-western end of High Street, facing the *Drostdy Gateway* (1) that leads to the campus of Rhodes University. The gateway was designed by Major Charles Jasper Selwyn of the Royal Engineers, and was completed by men of his corps in 1842. Parts of the original *Drostdy* (magistrate's residence) – which no longer stands – were built by Voortrekker leader Piet Retief, who worked as a building contractor in Grahamstown.

Walk from the gateway along High Street. On the corner of Somerset and High streets is a *double-storey home* (2) that belonged to Andries Stockenström, who became Lieutenant Governor of the then 'Eastern Province'.

On your right, beyond number 120, a single-storey stone house, is *The Yellow House* (3), dating from about 1814 and believed to be Grahamstown's oldest building. Originally built as the town jail, it soon became too small for this purpose, and was later used as a public library and a meeting hall. The north wall of The Yellow House served as the line along which the new town's main thoroughfare, High Street, was laid out. A bas-relief now set into this wall depicts the 1820 Settlers arriving at Algoa Bay.

Continue along High Street. On your right, next to an imposing double-storey stone building, is the distinctly colonial *Albany Club* (4). Beyond this is *Bannerman House* (5) which houses the South African Library for the Blind, founded in 1919. From here you can also view the Supreme Court building with its wooden turret. Shortly before reaching the cathedral, you come to a tall memorial marking the position of a tree under which Colonel John Graham met Captain Andries Stockenström in 1812 to discuss the establishment of the new outpost.

The cathedral

Turn left into Hill Street and cross from here to the *Anglican Cathedral of St Michael and St George* (6). The original church, simply St George's, and the first Anglican church in the country, was started in 1824 on the site of De Rietfontein, the farmhouse that had served as Col Graham's headquarters. When Grahamstown became the seat of a bishop in 1853, the church was elevated to the status of a cathedral and the building was enlarged considerably.

The cathedral contains many monuments and memorial tablets. Among them is a little-known 'horse memorial' recalling the campaign of the 9th SA Mounted Regiment in East Africa during World War I. The inscription from the troopers reads 'with thanksgiving for the help of their patient comrades'.

Walk away from the cathedral along the north side of Church Square – you will see on your left, next to the Publicity Association Building, a daintily designed building erected by an insurance company in 1901 (7). The plasterwork is festooned with flowers and faces, and the building has an ornate tower and a soaring eagle on its roof.

A little further along is the stone *City Hall* (8). Its impressive clock tower originally stood on its own when it was unveiled in 1870 to honour the Settlers, and the halls and chambers were added later. The inaugural meeting of the National Press Union of South Africa – an organisation of newspaper owners – was held here in 1882. The Grahamstown Journal

The Commemoration Church, started 25 years after the Settlers' arrival.

The building in Huntly Street, used as a school for more than a century.

Rhodes University lies behind the gateway that once led to the Drostdy.

The Old Provost in Grahamstown.

(1831) was one of the first newspapers in the country.

If you look across Church Square from the City Hall, you will see a row of *Victorian commercial facades* **(9)** that have been preserved in a group as a national monument.

Where Parliament assembled
Beyond the City Hall on your left, opposite Bathurst Street, is the *Commemoration Methodist Church* **(10)**, the foundation stone of which was laid in 1845. In the centre of the Bathurst Street intersection is a large Anglo-Boer War monument.

Further along High Street, on your right and almost opposite Cawood Street, is *Shaw Hall* **(11)**, where Members of the Cape Parliament assembled before marching to the old military hospital for their 1864 session. This was the only time Parliament met outside Cape Town – to placate 'separatists' who campaigned for a separate administration for the eastern Cape Province.

Return to Bathurst Street and turn left. On your left is the *Observatory Museum* **(12)** (small entry fee). This was the home of jeweller and watchmaker Henry Galpin, who made the first formal identification of a South African diamond here. Chief attraction among the fascinating exhibits is the *camera obscura* Galpin built into the roof and which has been fully restored.

Continue along Bathurst Street, passing the *Baptist Church* **(13)** of 1840 on your left. Turn left into Beaufort Street, and then turn right into West Street. On your right is the *Cathcart Arms Hotel* **(14)** which is on a site that has been occupied by a hotel since the 1820s.

At the end of West Street, facing you on Market Street, is *Merriman House* **(15)**, the home of a former bishop of Grahamstown, where the ill-fated General Gordon of Khartoum spent some nights. Turn right into Market Street. On your left is the *Church of St Bartholomew* **(16)**, built in 1860. Turn right into Bartholomew Street. On your left you pass *Chapel House* **(17)**, built in 1823 as the first Baptist chapel in South Africa.

At the intersection with Cross Street, walk for a short distance to your right to look at the early Settler houses in this area known as Artificers' Square. Turn around, walk along Cross Street to Hill Street and turn right.

On your left is the *Presbyterian Trinity Church* **(18)** of 1842, and on your right is the old, double-storey stone building that now serves as the *First City Regiment's headquarters*, **(19)**. It was built in about 1860 and originally known as Albany Hall. Later this building became the Drill Hall, and was the venue for the Settlers' Jubilee Ball of 1870.

Continue up Hill Street. On your right, on the corner of Dundas Street, is the *Synagogue Hall* **(20)**. On your left is the stone battlemented *St Patrick's (Catholic) Church* **(21)**, in which settler women and children sheltered during the war of 1846. Just beyond it, also on the left, is the *Public Library* **(22)** in a mid-19th century building that once housed a steam mill.

Turn around, walk back downhill to Huntly Street and turn right. On your left you pass the old stone building known as the *Huntly Street School* **(23)**, built in 1844 as a Sunday school for St George's Church.

Turn right into Somerset Street, then turn left into Lucas Avenue between the two buildings of the *Albany Museum* **(24, 25)** – a small entrance fee admits you to both.

About 200 m along Lucas Avenue you reach the *Old Provost Building* **(26)** on your left. Built as a military prison in 1838, its first inmates were mutineers of the Cape Corps, who had shot and killed Ensign Crowe at Fraser's Camp. The mutineers were shot and buried nearby in unmarked graves in what is now the 1820 Wildflower Reserve.

Opposite the reserve, in the grounds of the university, stands the stone building of the *old military hospital* **(27)**. It was here that the working sessions of Parliament took place during the heady three months of its sojourn in Grahamstown in 1864.

Our walk ends at the Wildflower Reserve. If time permits, a short drive along Lucas Street, which becomes Fort Selwyn Drive, will bring you to Fort Selwyn and the 1820 Settlers National Monument on Gunfire Hill. From the historic Fort Selwyn there is a magnificent view down over the steeples of the mellow Settler City.

The striking Observatory Museum.

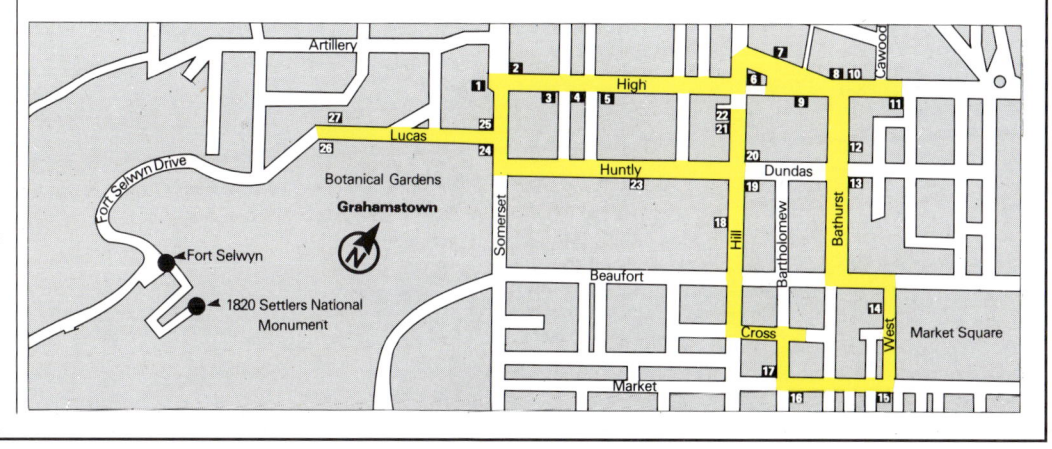

Hidden valleys, majestic mountains and the plains of Camdeboo

From 'the gem of the Karoo' we travel to Nieu-Bethesda to visit the Owl House and its extraordinary sculpture garden. The road leads on to Cradock, former frontier town and home of early feminist writer, Olive Schreiner. The return to Graaff-Reinet is via the beautiful Swaershoek Pass and Pearston. About 180 km of the route is on gravel roads.

Graaff-Reinet
Nieu-Bethesda
Cradock
Swaershoek Pass
Pearston
380 – 400 km

NOTE YOUR KMS IN FRONT OF the grandiose Dutch Reformed church in Church Square and leave Graaff-Reinet on the northbound N9 for Middelburg. After climbing the Goliath's Kraal Heights, turn left at 27 km to Nieu-Bethesda and the Owl House.

A good gravel surface leads through scenic Rubidge Kloof and the Gats River valley; 20 km from the N9, pause at *De Toren* (the tower), a striking and aptly named hill set in a fertile valley in a pretty bend of the river. Some 3 km later the road enters Nieu-Bethesda as Martin Street. (See pages 198 – 9.)

After a stroll through the village and a visit to the Owl House, leave Nieu-Bethesda by turning right into Hudson Street from the Owl House, and then left into Naudé Street. This route returns you, after 27,4 km, to the N9 at Bethesda Road railway station, the nearest rail point to the village.

Turn right onto the N9 and, 600 m later, turn left onto the R61 for Cradock, noting your kms. The road climbs gently up the Wapadsberg Pass, passing pleasant picnic sites and a viewsite on the left at 13 km. It then sweeps along the vast Karoo plain of grasslands studded with thorn trees, against the changing background of flat-topped hills and rugged mountains with peaks that are usually snow covered in winter.

Pass a road on your right, at 80 km, to the Mountain Zebra National Park, which is 12,5 km from this junction. Modest fees are levied for day visitors and good internal roads mean that an hour or so can be well spent there. Some 5,5 km after passing the road to the park, turn right at the T-junction with the N10 to enter Cradock. (See opposite.)

Founded in 1814 on a site chosen for its military and strategic importance, this progressive town keeps pace with the ever-developing agricultural resources around it and now jealously guards its accumulated heritage. (See opposite.) Leave Cradock by driving down Kerk Street towards the railway station and turn left at the Y-junction for 'Somerset East/Pearston via Swaershoek Pass'. Note your kms here. The road follows the railway route for some 2 km before you turn right onto the gravel-surfaced R337.

Swaershoek Pass to Graaff-Reinet

The ascent of Swaershoek Pass starts at around 10 km, and the summit, which offers wide views, is reached at 21 km. Here the Karoo scenery is spectacular, changing from low shrubs to open, rolling grasslands. At Doornbos, at around 52 km, turn right for Pearston and note your kms. After 17 km you reach the steep Buffelshoek Pass, which takes you down between the Coetzeesberge and the Groot Bruintjieshoogte, once the frontier of the Cape Colony, and brings you into the main street of the little town of Pearston. There is a museum of local history in the old Drostdy. Local farmers raise sheep and Angora goats, and hand-spinning and weaving can be seen at many farms where the products of the loom can be purchased.

The municipality has information on rock paintings and fossils occurring on a number of private farms in the area. These may be viewed by appointment only.

Leave Pearston for Graaff-Reinet and Jansenville by driving along Voortrekker Street, which becomes the R63, and note your kms. Turn right at the T-junction with the R75 after 51 km. On your right rises the well-named *Tandjiesberg* (mountain of teeth). One molar appears first and then a jawful of jagged teeth serrate the skyline. Ahead is the distinctive, twin-domed summit of Spandaukop, watching over Graaff-Reinet.

Turn right at the T-junction with the N9, 23 km from the last T-junction, and enter Graaff-Reinet on College Road, which becomes Church Street as it approaches the splendid confection of a church from which you set off in the morning.

Graaff-Reinet Publicity Association cr Church and Somerset streets, Graaff-Reinet 6280 Tel (0491) 24248
Cradock Tourism Association Municipal Office Market Square, Cradock 5880 Tel (0481) 2382

FOSSILS OF THE SUPERGROUP

Dry and dusty though it seems today, the Karoo was once a steaming swamp in which dinosaurs – the terrible lizards – lived, died and, over millions of years, gradually evolved mammal-like tendencies. They stalked the site of Graaff-Reinet, which is part of a great geological system called the Karoo Supergroup. Some 200 million years ago, rocks of this system were formed from mud, sand and clay and were washed into the low-lying marshy Karoo basin. A general uplift of southern Africa, millions of years after the Karoo period came to an end, caused rivers and streams to carve into the relatively soft Karoo sandstone and shales.

Fossilized bones of strange creatures were exposed along the slopes of Karoo koppies. These were the long-extinct dinosaurs of the Karoo marshlands. After death, their bodies were rapidly covered in mud that has hardened to become the Karoo shale of today. In the Graaff-Reinet area fossil bones have been exposed after an entombment of up to 230 million years. Fossils, released from their surrounding rock matrix, are on display in the Graaff-Reinet Museum under the curatorial control of the South African Museum in Cape Town. If you have a genuine scientific interest in fossils, the information centre at the museum can arrange an appointment for a visit to one of the outstanding private collections in the area.

OLIVE SCHREINER HOUSE

The literary career of one of South Africa's most distinguished writers, Olive Schreiner, began when she was in her early teens and living in the modest house at 9 Cross Street in Cradock. Here, too, her religious and philosophical convictions were developed and she formed strong friendships that were to influence her later years.

Although Schreiner House is one of the oldest dwellings in town, there is no evidence of its exact age or original appearance, but a map of 1853 shows a building already on the site. Olive was 11 years old when her brother Theo, who was the headmaster of the local public school, rented the house in 1866. She lived here until 1870, when she took the post of governess to the Orpen family in Barkly East. She returned to the Cradock area in 1875 and by 1880 had completed her *Story of an African Farm*. Her ties with Cradock were strengthened in 1894 when she married Samuel Cronwright, a local farmer. A year after her death in 1920, her body – in accordance with her wishes – was reinterred in a vault on top of Buffelskop, south of Cradock.

The almost severely plain house in Cross Street has been restored and donated to the National English Literary Museum. Open on weekdays from 08h00 to 12h45 and from 14h00 to 16h30, it is a modest, small-town dwelling of the mid-19th century and has an absorbing photographic display that leads from room to room, illustrating the life story of Olive Schreiner.

Karoo kitchen – the simple interior of Olive Schreiner House in Cradock.

Graaff-Reinet, overlooked by Spandaukop and the old gunpowder store.

With increasing numbers of visitors, commerce flourishes in Nieu-Bethesda.

Curled as though sleeping, a small dinosaur is exposed in a rock matrix.

Cradock's Dutch Reformed church – an English image for a homesick wife?

CRADOCK

Named after governor Sir John Cradock, who later took the surname of Caradoc, this former garrison village on the Fish River rewards careful, leisurely exploration. In Stockenström Street is the classically elegant Dutch Reformed church, designed after the style of St Martin in the Field in London (it is said this was commissioned to alleviate the homesickness of the dominee's English wife). Across the road are the municipal and information offices. The Great Fish River Museum is behind the municipal complex, in a parsonage built in the 1820s. In Bree Street, one of the oldest in Cradock, are the Anglican and Methodist churches and a house, number 38, which is a national monument and has a rare, decoratively painted ceiling.

The Cradock Library is one of the oldest in South Africa and houses a large collection of Olive Schreiner's books. Market Street is gaining fame because of some 14 *tuishuise* – Victorian Karoo houses (literally 'home-houses') that have been beautifully restored, in an area steeped in historical tradition where saddlers, shopkeepers, harness makers and wainwrights used to live. The tuishuise are carefully furnished with appropriate period pieces and offer accommodation for the traveller. In Frere Street another Victorian Karoo house is used by the local printing works, while a cast-iron drinking trough commemorating the coronation of King Edward VII in 1902 stands in front of the Baptist church.

The Cradock Club in Dundas Street was built around 1850, and was used as a mess by officers of the Nottinghamshire Regiment (known as the Sherwood Foresters) during the Anglo-Boer War. Two ilex oak trees in the garden are reputed to be among the world's largest. A new and booming cottage industry produces wire-made working models of windmills, cars and helicopters, proudly displayed, demonstrated and sold outside the town on the Port Elizabeth road.

• A VISIT TO NIEU-BETHESDA •

Pilgrims in the Camel Yard on their way to 'the East' raise their arms – perhaps as they receive the precious blessings of light and warmth.

One woman's work draws visitors to a peaceful Karoo hamlet

Kompasberg, at more than 2 500 m the highest peak in the massive Sneeuberg range, dominates the skyline north of Nieu-Bethesda. Like the trembling needle of governor Joachim van Plettenberg's compass in 1778, *Kompasberg* (compass mountain) points the way for those who need direction. Helen Martins, who lived almost her whole life within sight of Kompasberg, chose her own direction and, years after her death, her legacy draws increasing numbers of pilgrims to the silent figures that throng the grounds of her Owl House.

It was nearly a century after Van Plettenberg's visit that the Reverend Charles Murray of Graaff-Reinet saw the beautiful valley with fertile soil and abundant water at the foot of the Sneeuberg. He wanted to name it Bethesda, after the healing biblical pool, and to build a church there. The church was built, but somehow the Dutch expression *nu*, meaning 'now', was confused into meaning 'new', hence the name of the village today.

Pear trees line Martin Street, the main thoroughfare, and bloom delicately in spring. Quince hedges mark the boundaries of allotments and poplar trees along the water furrows add new colours to the changing seasons.

An owl, bright eyed and inscrutable, against panels of amber glass bottles.

Having been so carefully established, Nieu-Bethesda was soon largely forgotten and, but for the extraordinary industry and talent of a strange and lonely woman, it might have been entirely abandoned by the 20th century.

Because of the life and work of Helen Martins and her birthplace and home being opened as the Owl House Museum in 1992, the growing number of visitors to Nieu-Bethesda has meant new amenities for the village. A petrol station is a recent innovation. Electricity has been installed and the availability of guesthouses, light refreshments and evening meals makes a visit to the museum an easy option.

But the village is little changed; there are still no traffic lights or tarred roads, and water from the Gats River, a tributary of the Sundays River, still irrigates fruit and vegetable gardens from a system of furrows. And still the tranquillity and scenic beauty of endless days follow nights of clear and unpolluted Karoo skies with stars clustered closer and brighter than anywhere else.

Guardians and pilgrims

Helen Martins was born in her parents' house in River Street in 1898, the youngest of six children. After basic schooling in the village she went to a teachers' training college in Graaff-Reinet, where she was an exceptional student. A brief marriage to a Karoo farmer, her work as a teacher of English after her divorce, and her return

A genial sun, primary source of the light that was Miss Helen's inspiration.

Kitchen walls and even the ceiling glitter with grains of bright ground glass.

to Nieu-Bethesda to care for her ailing parents seem an unlikely background for the explosion of her artistry and vision.

A dusty street fronts the Owl House, separating it from the stony riverbed on the outskirts of the village. The long verandah is cordoned off to make a wire cage for cement owls of various sizes. One glares balefully from over the front door, guarding the house. More guardian owls, some with two faces, sit on the garden fence, looking both outwards and inwards. On the cement floor of the stoep a wavy shoreline of sea sand runs along the wall of the house.

The shutters and doors opening onto the stoep are covered with a layer of crushed glass mixed with cement. Village children used to collect empty bottles for Helen Martins to crush in an old coffee grinder – a careless practice that gradually destroyed her eyesight. Almost the whole interior of the house – walls, ceilings and some of the furniture – is covered in the same medium. Extravagant and colourful murals of suns, moons and stars are emblazoned on the ceilings. Panes of clear tinted glass in place of ordinary windows make vivid patterns of shifting light. Large, upturned, coloured glass vases suspended from the ceilings make effective shiny lights by day, and enormous mirrors in all the rooms reflect a series of dazzling impressions.

Candlesticks, table lamps, standard lamps and an entire wall cupboard lined with oil lamps of all shapes and sizes tell of the transformation of the Owl House at night during the tenure of 'Miss Helen'. Large sheets of coloured glass instead of conventional window panes gave both the house and the garden an aura of enchantment when she lit her lamps. And when the walls and ceilings glittered and sparkled as they caught the light, the shabbiness of the house melted into the kindly shadows.

But it is outside, in what used to be the vegetable garden, that Helen Martins' creativity takes her from the merely eccentric to the memorable. Over 300 cement sculptures crowd haphazardly into a small space bounded by a wire fence. The first glimpse of them is through the kitchen window, when the urgency of myriads of beckoning arms and hands compels the visitor out of the back door, past a shady grape arbour, through narrow, twin brick pillars and into her wonderful 'Camel Yard'.

Church spires, arches, towers, camels, sphinxes, pyramids, tall bottle-skirted hostesses, giant birds and peacocks, hooded shepherds, Buddhas, sheep, goats, giraffes, dancing girls, lithe men, athletic sun-worshippers and many more owls join zealous pilgrims on their joyful journey to what Helen Martins called 'East/Oos' – even though it isn't east at all. There is a strong sense of urgency and purpose.

Invitation to pause

In sharp contrast is the tranquillity of the relief figures and statues around the water tank, Miss Helen's own pool of Bethesda. Mermaids sit at the corners, inviting weary travellers to pause, while the faces on the tank are reminiscent of the Mona Lisa. Small pools or *dammetjies*, as Miss Helen called them, each with resident mermaid, were kept filled for wild Egyptian geese and other birds that lived in the garden during her lifetime.

Modest controversy surrounds the role played by her helper, Koos Malgas, in the creation of the Camel Yard and the decoration of the house. He maintains that Miss Helen's was the creative spirit and that he was her hands. All the work he did was guided by her and she never actually made any statues herself. This has been contradicted by local residents, who say they actually saw Miss Helen making statues. What is certain is that, because of her small stature and frailness, she would have needed physical help with much of the construction; wet cement is not easy to handle.

Although Koos Malgas left Nieu-Bethesda after Helen Martins' death, he has since returned and is involved in the maintenance of the statues and as a self-appointed guide. He has produced no original work since his return, just copies of owls, that are on sale.

The death of Helen Martins in a Graaff-Reinet hospital, three days after drinking caustic soda, is generally regarded as suicide because it was linked to her fear of losing her sight. She was not prepared to live without her beloved light. Miss Helen was cremated. Her ashes, after years in a box on the mantelpiece of her sitting room, were scattered in her Camel Yard.

Playwright Athol Fugard, who has a home in Nieu-Bethesda, based his award-winning play and subsequent film, *The Road to Mecca*, on the life of Helen Martins. He used the setting and many facts known about her, but declared that his work is not a biographical play about the real Helen Martins.

She, perhaps, will remain an enigma.

Light and brightness reflect off almost every surface within the Owl House.

An attendant at Bethesda pool.

· THE MOUNTAIN ZEBRA NATIONAL PARK ·

An unspoilt wilderness where the dry Karoo plains meet the mountains of the Eastern Cape.

A remote mountain sanctuary for one of the world's rarest animals

THE COOL, HIGH plateaux of the Mountain Zebra National Park, and the rugged Bankberg, rise abruptly and unexpectedly out of the surrounding Karoo landscape. The 6 536 ha park is in many ways an area of striking contrasts. Stretches of grey Karoo scrub are splashed with the brilliant blue of the Karoo wild tulip (*Moraea* species). Four-metre long earthworms move slowly through the soil as fleet-footed buck streak over the veld above. Soaring summer temperatures give way to snow-capped peaks in winter.

The park lies a short distance south-west of Cradock and, in addition to bracing mountain air, it offers a chance to view one of the rarest animals in the world: the once threatened Cape mountain zebra (*Equus zebra zebra*).

These distinctive animals, an easy target for hunters, narrowly escaped extinction in the first decades of the 20th century. At one stage they were dismissed by a cabinet minister as merely 'donkeys in football jerseys', and it took a concerted fight by conservationists before the zebra were granted the safety of a park – established on the farm Babylons Toren in 1937. There are now over 200 zebra in the park, roughly the maximum population that the area can support, and a number of animals have been moved to the Karoo National Park outside Beaufort West and to the Karoo Nature Reserve at Graaff-Reinet. The mountain zebra is easily distinguished from other zebra species by its conspicuous dewlap, white belly, orange-brown muzzle and sharply defined stripes that cover the entire leg down to the hoof. Standing only about 1,25 m, it is also the smallest of the zebra family.

Mountain zebra
Equus zebra zebra.

Variety of scenery and wildlife

The park created to protect these animals offers fine scenery and superb game-viewing for both the hiker and the motorist. Deep ravines cut into the mountains – like the Grootkloof, which is clearly visible from the rest camp and park headquarters.

The park lies in a transition zone between the Karoo shrublands and the better-watered grasslands to the east, and the vegetation is accordingly varied – including shrubby *renosterbos* (rhinoceros bush), sweet-thorn, Cape beech, wild olive, white stinkwood, mountain cabbage tree, Cape mistletoe and the interestingly named bastard shepherd's tree.

The sweet grass covering the Rooiplaat plateau attracts the great majority of the grazing animals that live in the park and this is a particularly good game-viewing area. The plateau is easily reached by taking a steep but well-maintained gravel road that leads from the rest camp and completes a 14,5 km circuit of the plateau summit. From the top there are clear views in all directions as far as the eye can see.

It is here that the visitor is most likely to see the zebra, as well as eland, red hartebeest, kudu, black wildebeest and blesbok. Also found here are the smaller springbok, klipspringer, duiker,

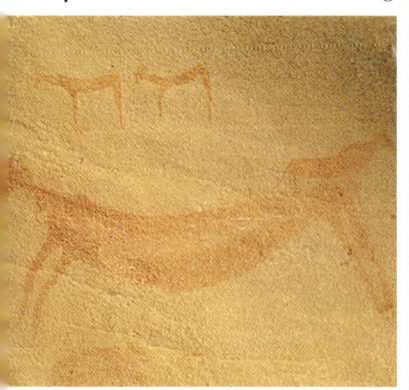

The San paintings are easily reached.

Seemingly lost in the wide African landscape, the administrative headquarters of the Mountain Zebra National Park and two of the park's important residents.

steenbok, mountain reedbuck, and the ubiquitous sunloving *dassie* (rock hyrax). The mountain reedbuck and the dassies form much of the diet of the park's largest predator, the caracal (seldom seen by visitors because it is essentially a night prowler).

The dassies are also preyed upon by the magnificent black eagles that nest in the park, just one of the 200 bird species that will interest the birdwatcher. Also to be seen are martial eagles, tawny eagles and the migratory booted eagle – which flies in from Angola every August and stays until April. At the reception office, visitors can obtain a checklist of all the bird species in the park. The list includes the blue crane, cardinal woodpecker, Cape eagle owl, malachite kingfisher, the African hoopoe and the hamerkop.

The rest camp in the park is modern and well maintained. Its facilities include 20 fully equipped two-bedroom cottages, a camping and caravan park with ablution facilities, a swimming pool, petrol and diesel pumps, an à la carte restaurant and a shop where basic foodstuffs, film and souvenirs may be bought. Doornhoek, which is one of the original farmhouses in the area and has been meticulously restored, is also available for hire. Conference facilities – for up to 60 people – are available.

Hikes, drives and San paintings

From the rest camp, a number of short walks lead into the mountains, and the popular three-day Mountain Zebra Trail also starts here. This is a 31,5 km hike that climbs the slopes of the Grootkloof, descends into the valley formed by the Fonteinkloof stream, then climbs again to the high summit of the Bankberg before returning to the camp. Two picturesque stone huts with fireplaces and water provide hikers with overnight accommodation.

For those who prefer to view nature from the comfort of a car, there are some 40 km of good gravel roads, and two particularly attractive drives are recommended. The first leads to the top of the Rooiplaat plateau, as previously described, and the second leads from the crest of the plateau along the Wilgeboom River, eventually arriving back at the rest camp. There are three well-marked picnic sites along this drive, each provided with tables and benches.

Although the modern rest camp and the roads suggest that man is new in the area, 30 archeological sites in the park prove the contrary. Primitive artefacts have been found, dating back to the *Upper Pleistocene* (38 000 to 10 000 years ago), and, in a cave up on the Rooiplaat plateau, visitors can see San paintings – featuring antelope, baboons, and what appears to be a leopard. Follow the road over the crest of the plateau, then watch carefully for the stylised sign on your left. The paintings are just a short walk from the road.

How to get there

The route to the Mountain Zebra National Park is clearly signposted from Cradock. Drive roughly 5 km out of town along the N10 towards Middelburg, then turn onto the R61 towards Graaff-Reinet. After 7 km on the R61, turn left onto the 16 km access road into the park.

An entry fee is payable when you reach the gate. The park is open to day visitors in the summer (1 October to 30 April) from 07h00 to 19h00 and in the winter (1 May to 30 September) from 07h00 to 18h00.

To book accommodation in the park, contact the National Parks Board at either of the following addresses: National Parks Board, 44 Long Street, Cape Town 8001. Tel (021) 22 2810, fax (021) 24 6211; or The Chief Director, National Parks Board, PO Box 787, Pretoria 0001. Tel (012) 343 0905, or fax (012) 343 1991. Staff at the park can accept bookings only a day or two in advance.

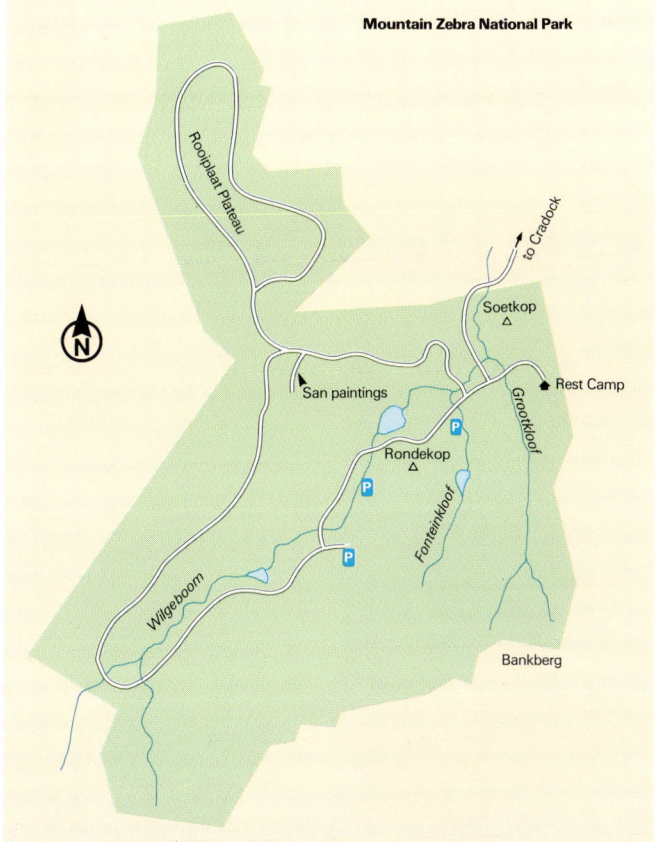

Adventure into elephant country from the shores of St Francis Bay

In the course of this drive we savour a variety of Eastern Cape experiences – a barefoot walk on the golden sands of St Francis Bay; a visit to a historic Uitenhage manor house; a tour through the scented Sundays River Valley and, finally, an afternoon among the elephants in the Addo Park. Over four-fifths of the route is on tarred roads.

**Port Elizabeth
Maitland Mouth
Uitenhage
Sundays Valley
Suurberg Pass
Addo Elephant
National Park
300 – 320 km**

LEAVE PORT ELIZABETH on the N2, heading towards Cape Town. At Intersection 730, take the exit for R102 (Greenbushes, Seaview) and, at the end of the off-ramp, turn left on the M15 for Seaview. Follow the M15 south, passing several sideroads until, eventually, your road sweeps down towards the sea, leading through The Island Forest Reserve, then passing the Seaview Game Park.

At the bottom of the hill, turn right, following the sign to 'Maitland Mouth/Beach View'. The road winds along the rocky shore, begins to climb after passing Beach View Caravan Park, then descends to Maitland River Mouth. Turn left off the main road to reach a small parking area. This is a perfect place for a walk along the beach, but aim to leave by 09h30.

Maitland Mouth to Uitenhage
Continue on the tarred road, passing the Maitland Nature Reserve on your left. The road climbs through a valley blanketed with dense indigenous forest and eventually reaches a T-junction. Turn left here, noting your kms. After 3 km, turn left towards Van Staden's Mouth. After a further 3,6 km you come to a crossroads – continue straight, following the sign to 'Old Cape Road', and note your kms.

After 1,8 km the road crosses over the N2 and, 1,4 km later, you cross a railway line. Immediately after this, turn right at the T-junction onto the R102 (the Old Cape Road). Almost 3 km later, where the R102 widens, turn left towards Rocklands, noting your kms. After 5, 8 km you come to an oblique junction – turn right here for the town of Uitenhage, noting your kms.

After 4,5 km there are views to your left over the Swartkops River Valley and, about 8,5 km later, you cross the Swartkops River and enter Uitenhage (see below). Continue straight ahead on Cuyler Street until you come to Caledon Street (second set of traffic lights). Turn right into Caledon Street, following the sign for Port Elizabeth (R333/M6). Continue on Caledon Street, which changes its name to Union Avenue, then becomes the R333. Note your kms as you pass under the M6 on the outskirts of the town and, 2 km later, turn right, following the sign to 'Uitenhage Historiese Museum'. This short gravel road leads into the grounds of Cuyler Manor. The manor house is open weekdays 10h00 – 13h00, 14h00 – 17h00, but may be closed at weekends and on public holidays (entrance fee).

Uitenhage to Kirkwood
Return to the R333/M6 and turn left to retrace your route for roughly 2 km. Immediately after passing under the M6, turn left to drive onto the R75, following the sign for Graaff-Reinet. A little over 3 km later you pass under the R334 – note your kms here. Stay on the R75 for a further 30 km, then turn right, following the sign to Kirkwood. The road now leads through dense, fenced-in bush and, after 12 km, you reach a T-junction. Turn left for Kirkwood and, almost immediately, you cross the Sundays River (see opposite).

The road leads past citrus groves and rose plantations and, about 2 km after crossing the river, you enter Kirkwood. The main street is lined with colourful bougainvillea and golden shower (in full bloom during May – June) and several establishments offer lunch.

Kirkwood to Addo
Retrace your route out of Kirkwood and re-cross the Sundays River – then continue on this road (R336), noting your kms as you pass, on your right, the road on which you arrived earlier. After a little more then 17 km you enter the village of Summerville and about 700 m later you pass, on your left, a quaint country church surrounded by trees. After a further 1,9 km you cross the Sundays River again – note your kms at the far end of the bridge.

The Maitland River broadens into a lagoon before emptying itself into the Indian Ocean.

A SANCTUARY FOR THE ADDO ELEPHANT
There are about 200 elephants in the 54 000 ha of mountain and evergreen bush that form the Addo Elephant National Park, and visitors are allowed to drive through the park, following a route map issued at the gate. (Ask at which waterholes elephants have been seen earlier in the day.)

The Addo elephants are reddish in colour, smaller than equatorial elephants and they have shorter tusks. In the past they had a fearsome reputation for raiding farms, and this led to their being hunted almost to extinction. The park was proclaimed in 1931 to save the few that remained.

Although the elephants are the main attraction, the park is home to eland, bushbuck, kudu, steenbok, duiker, grey rhebok, oribi, grysbok, red hartebeest, buffalo and bushpig and there are some seldom-seen black rhino. More than 170 bird species have been recorded and there is an observation point at a dam near the entrance.

Accommodation is in self-contained thatched huts and there are caravan and camping sites.

UITENHAGE
Set at the foot of the Great Winterhoek Mountains, Uitenhage is an industrial town with a difference. Its streets are lined with jacarandas and oaks, and it is famed for its beautiful gardens. Near the town's centre is Cuyler Manor, the restored homestead of Jacob Glen Cuyler, a British officer who made Uitenhage his headquarters during the frontier wars. The Railway Museum includes the old station building and is one of the most attractive to be seen anywhere. The Drostdy Museum includes the Africana Museum and the Volkswagen Museum of motor vehicles.

An Addo elephant prepares to drink. Only the bulls have tusks.

After 700 m you cross the railway line. Turn left immediately after this, towards Slagboom and Tregaron. After 2,5 km you cross a small bridge and the road surface changes to gravel. Ignore the road to your right signposted 'Cemetery' and continue on the gravel for a further 1,3 km until a sign reading 'Lookout' indicates a track to your left. Park at the end of this track and walk through the white gates. Sir Percy Fitzpatrick and members of his family are buried here (see below) and there is a fine view over the fertile valley.

Retrace your route to the R336 and turn left. You now pass through the citrus and rose-growing centre of Sunland. A few kilometres later you cross the Coerney River and then pass through the small settlement of Selborne. After this, as the road sweeps downhill, there are good views to your right over the valley, with farmhouses among the orange groves.

About 2 km after crossing the Coerney River, you pass through the settlement of Hermitage and, at the T-junction soon after this, turn left onto the R335 towards the Addo Elephant National Park, noting your kms. After about 10 km you reach a crossroads with the road on your right leading to the Addo Elephant National Park. Turn left onto the gravel road for 'Zuurberg Hotel 16 km'. The road dips as you approach the Suurberg and, roughly 7 km after turning, you reach the start of the Suurberg Pass.

The pass includes a number of sharp bends that need to be taken at low speeds. Roughly 4 km after the start of the pass you can park off the road and look back over the Sundays Valley. A further 5 km brings you to the top of the pass.

Suurberg National Park
At the top of the pass, on your right, you will see the Zuurberg Inn (which offers refreshments and lunches). Immediately opposite the entrance to the inn, turn left onto a narrow gravel track that leads for 750 m to a National Parks Board office. Park here and walk through the gate into the Suurberg section of the Addo Elephant National Park. A few metres after walking through the gate you come to a sign indicating 'circular walks' of one and four hours' duration. Just a few hundred metres along the indicated path will bring you to a fine viewsite. (Two very rare plants that grow in the park are the Suurberg cushion bush and the Suurberg cycad.)

Retrace your route to the main gravel road and down the Suurberg Pass. After 16 km, keep straight through the crossroads onto the access road into the Addo Park. Note that it takes roughly 45 minutes to drive back to Port Elizabeth. When you leave the park, turn left onto the R335 and, after some 50 km on the R335, turn right onto the N2 for Port Elizabeth.

AA Office 1A Greenacres Shopping Centre Cape Road, Newton Park, Port Elizabeth 6001 Tel (041) 34 1313.
Port Elizabeth Publicity Association Belmont Terrace, Donkin Reserve, Port Elizabeth 6001 Tel (041) 55 2564.
Uitenhage Information Centre Indoor Sports Stadium, Park Avenue, Uitenhage 6230 Tel (041) 994 1330.

The Sundays River Valley is also tortoise country.

VALLEY OF FRUIT AND FLOWERS
The Sundays River rises in the Sneeuberge, then flows through the Suurberg range. Its waters are captured in the Darlington Dam, which makes it possible to irrigate the lower reaches of the valley – filling the air with the scent of orange groves, and supporting a profusion of sub-tropical flowers. The town of Kirkwood was named after an early pioneer of irrigation, James Somers Kirkwood, who settled in the valley in 1877. The creation of Lake Mentz (now Darlington Dam) in 1922 was largely the work of Sir Percy Fitzpatrick, author of the classic *Jock of the Bushveld*. Sir Percy settled in the valley after a successful career in the gold-mining industry. He and his wife and two sons are buried at The Lookout.

Below: *Green carpet of the Addo forest.*

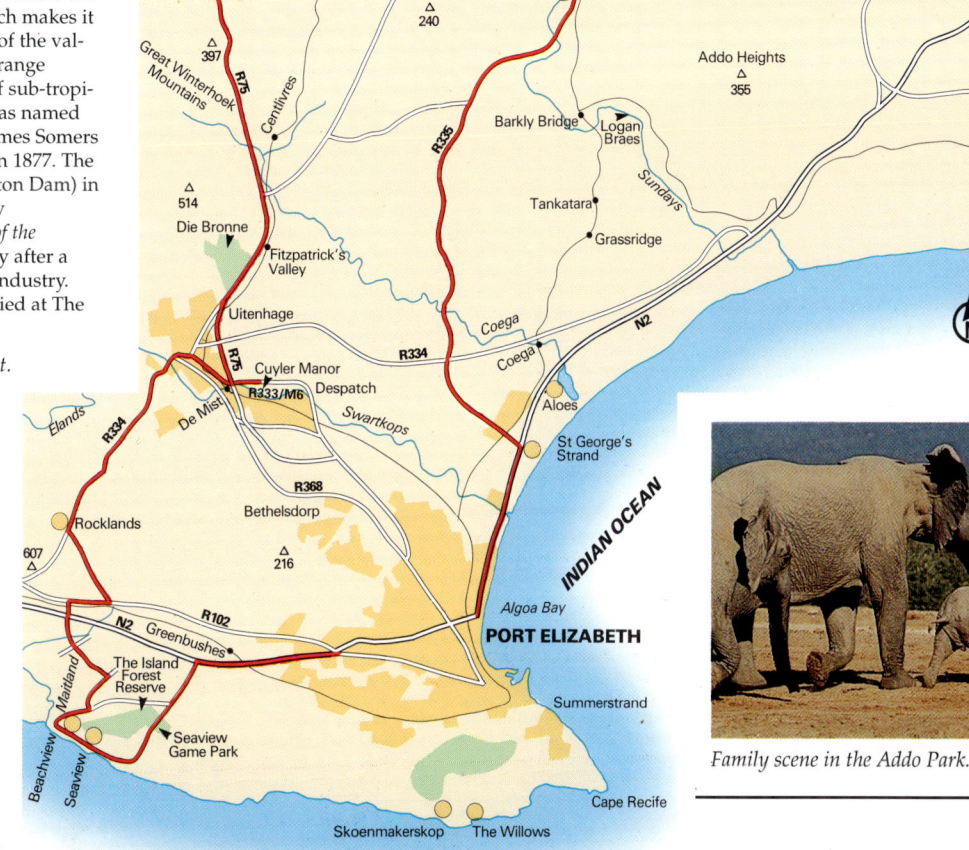

Family scene in the Addo Park.

Terraced houses on the steep slopes rising from the sea, recalling the heyday of Queen Victoria's empire.

A cluster of settler cottages on the coastal hills of Algoa Bay

IN 1576 THE STRETCH of coast where Port Elizabeth now stands was given the name *Bahia de Lagoa* (bay of the lagoon) by Portuguese navigators, but for generations it remained on the navigational charts as merely a 'landing place with fresh water'.

The story of Port Elizabeth began in 1799. The British had occupied the Cape, and they decided to protect their 'Algoa Bay' landing place by constructing a small stone fort – just 24 m square – on a commanding hilltop. It was named Fort Frederick, after the Duke of York, who was commander-in-chief of the British army at the time. A garrison was stationed here and, later, barracks and a military hospital were built. The old fort ranks as the oldest stone building in the Eastern Cape, and it still offers a fine view over the harbour and along the coast.

After the landing of the 1820 Settlers under the supervision of the garrison's commander, Captain Francis Evatt (whose grave is at the fort), the acting Governor of the Cape, Sir Rufane Donkin, visited the growing settlement and named it Port Elizabeth in memory of his wife. The original settlement grew into a substantial town as more and more settlers built their homes on the slopes near the fort – and the slopes were quite steep, with the result that anyone now wishing to explore the old part of the city must be prepared for a few fairly stiff uphill stretches.

If you have come into the city centre by car, park near the fort in Fort Street or Belmont Terrace, and begin your walk by exploring the *Fort* (1). When you leave the fort, walk along Belmont Terrace for several blocks. After crossing White's Road you have the Donkin Reserve on your right and, on your left, the *Edward Hotel* (2), built in 1903. Next on your left, one block further along, you will see the *Old Grey Institute* (3), a Gothic-style building dating back to 1859 and named after Sir George Grey, who established an educational foundation here. By 1915, the Grey High School had grown so large that it was moved to Mill Park. The old building is now a national monument.

Continue along Belmont Terrace and cross over Donkin Street to reach Alfred Terrace – on the corner to your left is the Port Elizabeth *Presbyterian Church* (4), consecrated in 1865. Turn left and walk up Alfred Terrace into the Upper Hill Street area. Many of the houses here have been extensively renovated and the area has again become a fashionable place in which to live. At the top of Alfred Terrace, turn sharp right down Ivy Terrace and, after passing a few houses, turn left into George Street. On the corner of Upper Hill Street and George Street is the Sir Rufane Donkin Rooms restaurant, housed in a restored cottage.

In Upper Hill Street, on an exterior wall, you can see a mural depicting the landing of the 1820 Settlers, and also a very old postbox still in use. Directly opposite the Sir Rufane Donkin Rooms are cottages built from the 1860s, notable for their attractive balconies that are now adorned with trailing bougainvillea. Walk downhill along Upper Hill Street, passing more restored cottages, until you reach Belmont Terrace again.

Terraced houses

Turn right into Belmont Terrace, and walk past the Presbyterian Church again on your right. As you cross over Donkin Street, you will see, down to your left, a *row of terraced houses* (5) that date from the mid-1860s.

Follow one of the footpaths leading half left into the Donkin Reserve, and walk through the small reserve to the *pyramid and lighthouse* (6). From here you can see the bay over the tops of the buildings in the city centre. A few days after he had named the town in memory of his wife, who had died in India, Sir Rufane Donkin visited this hill overlooking the town and marked the spot where the memorial pyramid now stands. The lighthouse was built in 1861 and later increased in height. No longer used as a beacon for ships in the bay, it serves as the offices of the Port Elizabeth Publicity Association. (An extended city walk, the Donkin Heritage Trail, can be followed with the aid of an informative booklet available here.)

Leave the Donkin Reserve by walking back towards the fort, but turn left down White's Road. After about 200 m you pass the *Opera House* (7) on your left. Built in 1892, this is the oldest functioning opera house in South Africa and the country's only

The city's landmark: the Campanile.

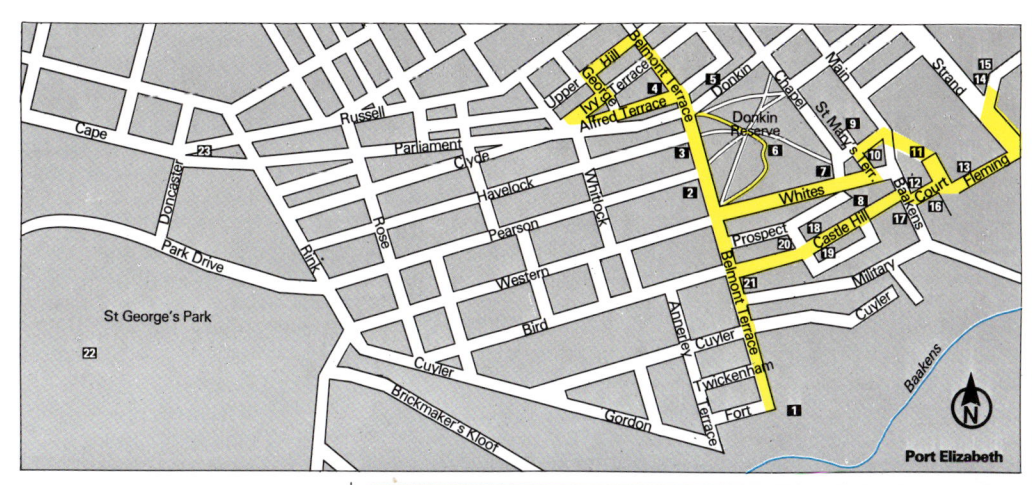

Historic Fort Frederick: oldest stone building in the Eastern Cape.

The steep climb up Castle Hill is dotted with historic buildings.

surviving example of a Victorian theatre. Opposite Chapel Street (which turns off to your left at the side of the Opera House) you can see *St Augustine's Roman Catholic Cathedral* (8), slightly obscured by trees. The cathedral was completed in 1866 under the direction of the parish priest, Father Murphy.

Continue down White's Road until you reach an alley on your left. (There is no street sign, but it is called St Mary's Terrace.) Walk into the alley and take the first turn right. On your left you pass *St Mary's Anglican Church* (9), and on your right the old *Library Building* (10).

St Mary's Anglican Church was begun in 1825, was destroyed by fire in 1895 and rebuilt. The present Library Building, a good example of Victorian Gothic, dates from 1902 and stands on the site of the Commercial Hall (completed in 1848). Its terracotta facade was manufactured in England and sent out in numbered pieces to be assembled here. From Main Street, at the bottom of the hill, you can view the front of the library, and a statue of Queen Victoria erected in 1903. Cross over Main Street, and walk onto the *Market Square* (11), the old commercial heart of the city. At one time a bell was rung to signal the start of the market's activities. (The same bell also served as the town's fire alarm.) The *City Hall* (12) stands on the southern side of Market Square. The original building was completed in 1862, but it was destroyed by fire in 1977 and has since been restored.

To reach the Campanile, walk down the steps to the left of the City Hall, then, after a few paces, turn left and walk along Fleming Street. On the corner of Fleming and Strand streets you pass the *Old Harbour Board Offices* (13) on your left. The building dates from 1904, and is a fine example of Art Nouveau architecture.

From Fleming Street, turn left into Strand Street and walk under the flyovers. From here you can see the brick, 51,8 m *Campanile* (14), built in 1923 to commemorate the landing of the 1820 Settlers on a nearby beach (the beach no longer exists). The Campanile has a staircase of 204 steps leading up to a viewing platform, and a carillon of 23 bells. Just north of the Campanile is the *Railway Station* (15), dated 1875.

Castle Hill

Retrace your route along Strand Street and Fleming Street, then walk along Court Street between the back of the City Hall and the *General Post Office* (16) of 1900.

Cross Baakens Street and walk up Castle Hill, which runs roughly parallel to White's Road. Immediately on your left is the *Feather Market Centre* (17), built in 1885 to accommodate auction sales of the ostrich feathers that were fashionable at the time – and also sales of wool, hides, skins and fruit. The produce market has been converted into a fine concert hall and conference centre.

As you climb the steep hill, you step into another era. On both sides of the road are charming settler cottages, and on your right is *Castle Hill No 7* (18), one of the two oldest dwellings in Port Elizabeth. It was built in about 1830 by the Reverend Francis McCleland, the first rector of St Mary's Church. The house is open to the public and is furnished in the style of that elegant but pioneering period.

Across the road are the two *Sterley Cottages* (19), also built in the 1830s. As you reach the top of Castle Hill Street you pass, on your right, the *Drill Hall* (20), opened in 1882 as headquarters of the distinguished Prince Alfred's Guard Regiment and now serving as a regimental museum.

On the corner of Castle Hill and Belmont Terrace you pass on your left the *Athenaeum Club* (21) – formerly the Athenaeum Institute, founded in the early days to promote cultural activities. Turn left here and walk along Belmont Terrace to return to the fort.

To visit two further places of interest, drive along Fort Street away from the fort, turn right into Annerley Terrace, then, after a short distance, turn left into Bird Street. Continue along Bird Street until you reach St George's Park (see map), where you can visit the *Pearson Conservatory* (22), dating from 1882. The conservatory was named after Henry Pearson, 16 times mayor of the city, and it houses a magnificent collection of exotic plants.

From the conservatory, drive along Doncaster Road (see map). Park in Doncaster Road and walk towards Cape Road to see the famous *Horse Memorial* (23), erected in 1905 and moved to its present site in 1957. During the Anglo-Boer War, Port Elizabeth was the main port of entry for 'remounts' – replacement horses used by the British forces. A resident of the city, Mrs Harriet Meyer, started a fund to commemorate the many horses that died in the course of the war.

The inscription on this unique memorial reads: 'The greatness of a nation consists not so much in the number of its people or the extent of its territory as in the extent and justice of its compassion.'

Follow a river 'wily as a lion' to the Mountain of the Clouds

From Port Elizabeth we take a coastal road to picturesque Van Staden's River Mouth, then explore the Gamtoos River Valley and the scenic Groot River gorge. Finally, we climb the valley wall to confront T'Numkwa, the towering 'Mountain of the Clouds'. Roughly two thirds of the route is tarred, the rest is gravel. (Take food and drink with you.)

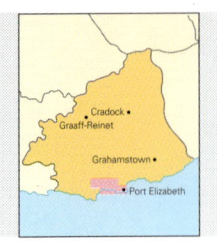

Port Elizabeth
Van Staden's
River Mouth
Hankey
Groot River
Cockscomb
Mountain
310 – 330 km

LEAVE PORT ELIZABETH by driving south on Beach Road (M4). As the road winds through the coastal bush, it becomes Marine Drive and it soon offers attractive views of the rocky coast on your left. Follow this coastal road until it ends on a low bluff known as *Skoenmakerskop* (shoemaker's hill), where you can park and look out along an unspoilt shore towards Sardinia Bay.

Retrace your route for 1,2 km, turn left up the hill and, just over 3,5 km later, turn left again for Sardinia Bay. After a further 4 km, turn right; 700 m later, turn left at the T-junction for Seaview/Beachview, noting your kms.

After about 16 km the road turns inland and begins to climb. On the crest of the hill you pass, on your right, the Seaview Game Park and, 1,5 km later, the entrance to The Island Forest Reserve (see pages 210 – 1). When you come to a crossroads, continue straight ahead for Greenbushes/Maitland Mouth – but 100 m later, turn left towards Maitland Mouth, noting your kms.

After a little over 5 km later, you pass, on your left, a turn-off to Maitland River Mouth. After a further 3 km, turn left for Van Staden's River Mouth and, at the crossroads 3,5 km later, turn left again. The road now descends through high hills to the beautiful estuary of the Van Staden's River (see opposite; entrance fee per car, per day).

Van Staden's River to Hankey

Retrace your route for 13 km to the crossroads and turn left for 'Old Cape Road'. After 1,8 km you cross the N2 and, 1,4 km later, you cross an unfenced railway line. Immediately after this you come to a T-junction – turn left onto the R102 (Old Cape Road), noting your kms. After about 8 km on the R102 you pass under the N2 and, 1 km later, you pass the Van Staden's Wildflower Reserve on your right (see pages 210 – 1). Immediately after this, you come to a fork – go right to stay on the R102, and note your kms. You now negotiate the old Van Staden's River Pass. After 10 km, turn right onto the R331 for Hankey/Patensie, noting your kms again as you cross the N2.

The R331 sweeps over a succession of hilltops, offering views reminiscent of KwaZulu-Natal's Valley of a Thousand Hills. You pass the little town of Loerie and, 26 km after crossing over the N2, you enter Hankey (see below). As you drive downhill into the town, there is a sign on your left that reads 'Enjoy View'; turn off the road here and park. A path leads to the top of the koppie known as *Vergaderingskop* (meeting-place hill), from where there is a fine view over the Gamtoos River Valley.

If the time is right for your picnic, turn right on the far side of Hankey for Yellowwoods and, 1,2 km later, turn left into the shady Yellowwoods picnic area – there are braai places, water and toilets. (To complete the drive, leave here not later than 14h00.)

Hankey to Groot River Gorge

Leave Hankey by continuing on the R331 towards Patensie and note your kms at the point where the road to Yellowwoods joins the R331. After 1,1 km turn left for Philip Tunnel. Park on the side of this road after a further 1 km, just before descending into the valley. From here you can see *Die Bergvenster* (the mountain

The Groot River snakes through the magnificent, richly coloured gorge.

The Gamtoos River Valley from Die Bergvenster – a rewarding climb for the fit.

A MISSION IN THE VALLEY

The little town of Hankey on the Gamtoos River dates from 1822. It was founded by the London Missionary Society and was named after the Society's treasurer.

William Philip, son of the missionary Dr John Philip, saw the valley's potential riches if only the flat alluvial floor of the valley could be properly irrigated. He employed Khoikhoi workers from the mission village to dig a tunnel from a high point in the river to lower-lying fields. Tragically, on the day the tunnel was officially put into operation in 1845, William was drowned in the 'wily river' he had dared to tame when one of the unpredictable flash floods, for which it is notorious, occurred. A pioneering venture in irrigation engineering, the Philip Tunnel is a national monument.

LAND OF THE KHOIKHOI

Before white or Xhosa people encroached on the Eastern Cape, the Gamtoos River Valley belonged to the Khoikhoi. *Gamtoos* is said to mean 'wily as a lion' and it was also the name of the people who lived beside it. There is another echo of Khoikhoi in *Patensie*, thought to mean 'a resting place for cattle'. The distinctive peak that Europeans were to dub Cockscomb Mountain was known to the Khoikhoi as *T'Numkwa*, meaning 'mountain of the clouds'. At 1 759 m this is the highest peak in the Eastern Cape, and it dominates both the Gamtoos and Elands river valleys.

Distant view of Cockscomb Mountain.

window), a natural arch on the crest of the ridge ahead of you. Drive on across the river and follow the gravel road leading to the Philip Tunnel (see opposite). A path near the tunnel leads up to Die Bergvenster, but much of this route this is a steep scramble over loose earth and stones.

Retrace your route to the R331 and turn left for Patensie – noting your kms. After 12 km you pass Patensie on your left. Note your kms again as you cross the small bridge on the far side of the town and, 2 km later, turn left onto gravel towards Humansdorp. Note your kms as you cross the Gamtoos River and, 600 m later, turn right towards Humansdorp; 2,6 km after crossing the river, go left at the fork. Some 7,9 km after the river, turn right at the T-junction onto the R332 towards Willowmore. As you approach the river again the road forks – keep right and recross the river. At the T-junction, turn left onto the tarred road towards Willowmore (still R332), noting your kms.

The road leads up the Gamtoos River Valley. After 4 km you pass, on your left, a turn-off for the Kouga Dam. The road surface changes to gravel here and you continue for 11 km before turning around at the low ford across the Groot River. This excursion gives you a good view of the magnificent Groot River Gorge.

Cockscomb Mountain and the Elands River Valley

Retrace your route from the ford on the R332 and note your kms as you pass, on your right, the turn-off to the Kouga Dam (just after driving back onto the tar). Continue on the tar, passing, on your right, the gravel road on which you arrived earlier. About 19,5 km after noting your kms, turn left onto a gravel road leading to the Elands River Valley – noting your kms at the turn.

The road climbs steadily, and you can look back over the Gamtoos River Valley to St Francis Bay sparkling in the distance. After 15,7 km on this gravel road, at one of its highest points, a road leads off to your left. Pass this turn-off, but after a further 150 m take the next road on your left – this road usually has a better surface. Drive about 1 km along this sideroad for a panoramic view across the green valley to T'Numkwa or the Cockscomb Mountain (see opposite).

Turn around where the road is widest, and return to the main gravel road. Turn left, to drive down the full length of the Elands River Valley. At Rocklands, drive across the X-shaped intersection onto the diagonally opposite arm of the X. Roughly 6 km later, you reach a stop sign – turn left here onto the R102. From here you can take any of the turns signposted 'National Road' or 'N2' to join the N2 to Port Elizabeth.

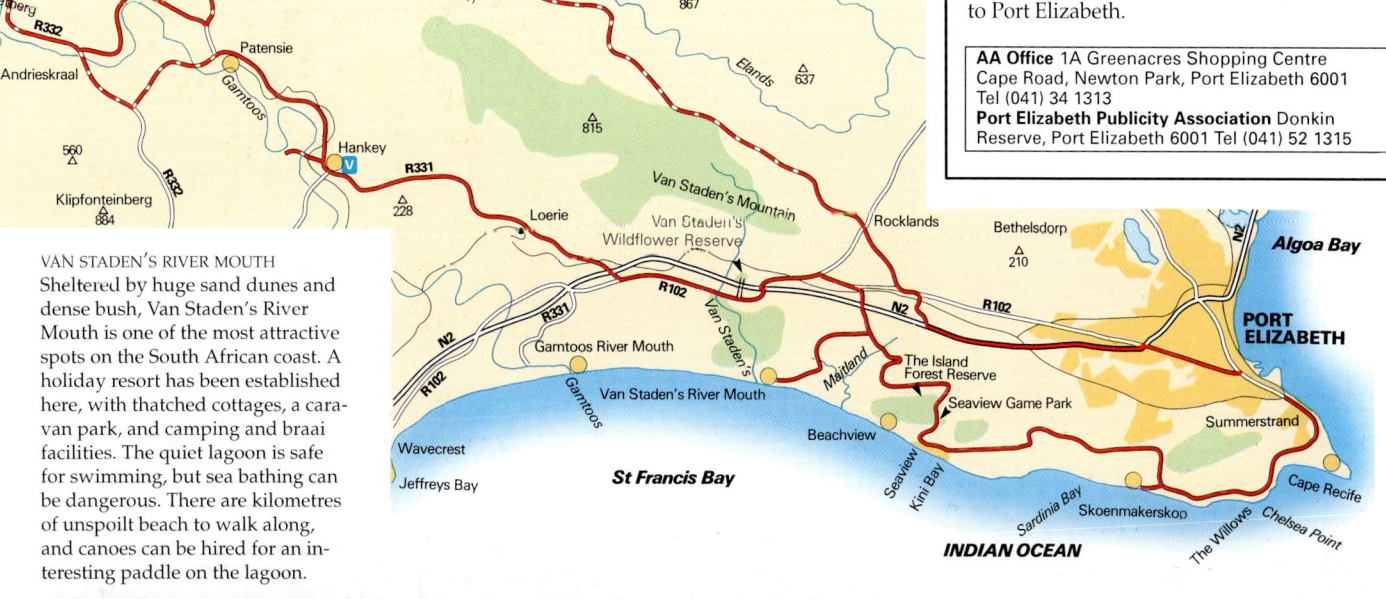

AA Office 1A Greenacres Shopping Centre Cape Road, Newton Park, Port Elizabeth 6001 Tel (041) 34 1313
Port Elizabeth Publicity Association Donkin Reserve, Port Elizabeth 6001 Tel (041) 52 1315

VAN STADEN'S RIVER MOUTH
Sheltered by huge sand dunes and dense bush, Van Staden's River Mouth is one of the most attractive spots on the South African coast. A holiday resort has been established here, with thatched cottages, a caravan park, and camping and braai facilities. The quiet lagoon is safe for swimming, but sea bathing can be dangerous. There are kilometres of unspoilt beach to walk along, and canoes can be hired for an interesting paddle on the lagoon.

Above: *Sea and sand at Van Staden's River Mouth.*   **Right:** *The coast at Skoenmakerskop.*

A sweep of white sand where surfers await the perfect wave

This drive explores the western shores of St Francis Bay – a great curve of gently sloping white-sand beaches, famous among surfers throughout the world as the coast of the perfect wave. We then drive inland to the Groot River gorge and Cockscomb Mountain on our way back to Port Elizabeth. About 50 km of the route is not tarred.

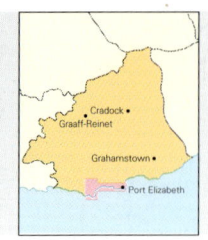

Port Elizabeth
Jeffreys Bay
Cape St Francis
Hankey
Groot River Gorge
Cockscomb Mtn
390 – 410 km

DRIVE WEST OUT OF Port Elizabeth on the N2 highway (towards Cape Town) and note your kms as you pass the exit for 'Greenbushes/Seaview'. Some 6,3 km later you pass the 'Van Staden's River/St Albans' turn-off and, immediately after this, you pass under a flyover. At 17,3 km take the exit for 'Uitenhage R102/Van Staden's Pass' and, at the end of the off-ramp, turn left for Van Staden's Pass.

After a little over 1 km you pass the entrance to the Van Staden's Wildflower Reserve on your right – note your kms as you pass it. A short distance after this you come to a fork – take the road leading right, to stay on the R102 (the Old Cape Road).

Drive slowly as you follow this road through the old Van Staden's River Pass; the road surface is poor and, after heavy rains, there may be places where washaways permit only one car through at a time. (As you cross the old bridge you can see the newer Van Staden's River Bridge towering high above you.)

Roughly 10 km after passing the Van Staden's Wildflower Reserve you reach a major turn-off right to Hankey and Patensie – continue straight ahead here on the R102. Soon after this the road passes under the N2, descends through cuttings to the old bridge over the Gamtoos River, then strikes out across the river's flood plain. Note your kms as you pass under the N2 once again. About 2,5 km later, as the road climbs the hills, park on the shoulder of the road for a good view to your left over the great lagoon at the river's mouth. After a further 7,5 km across the low hillsides you look down onto the much smaller lagoon of the Kabeljous River.

Note your kms as you cross the small Kabeljous River and, 1,2 km later, turn left for Aston Bay/Paradise Beach/Jeffreys Bay. Roughly 700 m later, turn left again and follow the road that leads left between the holiday houses until you reach a parking area alongside the Kabeljous River's lagoon – an attractive place for a short exercise stroll along the beach.

Note your kms as you leave the parking area and continue along the road you arrived on, for a drive along the shores of Kabeljous Bay. After 1 km turn left at the stop street into Da Gama Road, which will take you into the village of Wavecrest. About 2 km after passing through Wavecrest you may see a sign reading 'Supertubes', indicating one of the world's most famous surfing spots. In the course of the next 2 km you cross through three stop streets. Note the third of these, because we return to it later. Immediately after crossing through this third stop street you enter Jeffreys Bay.

Jeffreys Bay to Cape St Francis

Retrace your route to the stop street you noted and turn left (uphill) into De Reygers Street. When De Reygers Street ends at a T-junction, turn right for Humansdorp, noting your kms; 3 km later, turn left at the crossroads onto the R102 for Humansdorp. After driving a short distance through rolling countryside you pass a road on your left leading to *Paradysstrand* (Paradise Beach) and, 6 km later, you enter the town of Humansdorp on Voortrekker Road (see opposite). As you reach the central area of the town, turn left into *Hoofstraat* (Main Street) and continue on Hoofstraat through three four-way stop streets to reach a T-junction. At the T-junction, turn left into Park Street for St Francis Bay via Krom River Bridge. This tarred road later becomes the R330.

After travelling roughly 13,5 km on the R330, you cross the Kromme River on a long, low bridge; continue straight ahead on the main road, passing several sideroads. The road leads through coastal bush for roughly 10 km, and eventually emerges amid the cluster of holiday houses that make up the village of Cape St Francis. Continue on the main road, which gradually swings to the left and becomes Seal Point Boulevard. Turn left when you reach a sign pointing left to 'Beach parking'. This short sideroad leads to a parking area next to a small, pretty beach, known locally as 'Seals' and popular with surfers. (There are toilets near the parking area.)

Cape St Francis to the Groot River gorge

When you leave this parking area, note your kms and retrace your route for a fraction over 7 km, then turn right into Homestead Road. This leads down the hill into the attractive holiday resort of St Francis Bay – formerly known as Sea Vista – notable for its whitewashed houses with thatched roofs (see below). Follow the signs to the beach, where you can park and

Smoothly breaking rollers welcome surfers to St Francis Bay.

ST FRANCIS BAY

In 1575, when Portuguese navigator Manuel de Mesquita Perestrelo named St Francis Bay after the patron saint of sailors, he could not have imagined that, 400 years later, the beaches along the bay's west coast would have become internationally famous for their majestic rollers – regarded by the sportsmen who ride on them as some of the finest waves in the world.

Seal Point, just to the south of Cape St Francis, is the site of a 28 m lighthouse, built in 1876, and a short distance from the cape along the shores of the bay lies the particularly attractive St Francis Bay village – all its houses have whitewashed walls and thatched or dark-tiled roofs. This theme has been continued at the marina nearby on the Kromme River estuary.

SEA SHELLS AND SUPERTUBES

The popular holiday resort of Jeffreys Bay took its name from a trading store that was built on the coast in 1849 by a Mr JA Jeffrey. In those days no railway served the area, and cargo was loaded from and landed onto the beach in front of Jeffrey's store. When holidaymakers discovered how sheltered and safe the beaches were along this stretch of coast, the little settlement blossomed into a popular place to build a holiday shack or a retirement home. Now the name has become synonymous with surfing, and Supertubes and other well-known sites draw enthusiasts from all over the world – especially during the winter months from May to September.

The rollers that put Jeffreys Bay onto the world surfing map also sweep in rich harvests of shells, and a collection of beautiful and rare specimens can be seen in the Charlotte Kritzinger Shell Museum.

Luxury homes line the marina at Kromme River.

walk along a short footpath to a 3 km stretch of white sand, similar in form to the 'Seals' beach but on a larger scale.

When you leave the beach, drive northwards along St Francis Drive to explore the marina where grand holiday villas have been set on the banks of canals – then retrace your route along St Francis Drive and follow the signs back onto the R330 for Humansdorp.

Drive back through the centre of Humansdorp on Hoofstraat and cross Voortrekker Road, following the sign for 'Hankey R330'. After 3 km you cross over the N2. Continue straight ahead on the R330 for Hankey. As you leave the coast and drive further inland the vegetation changes. The road descends from a line of low hills into the Gamtoos Valley and, in the distance to your left, you can see the towering crest of Cockscomb Mountain.

Roughly 25 km after leaving Humansdorp you cross the Gamtoos River on a low causeway and, 2 km later, you enter the small farming centre of Hankey (see pages 206 – 7). At the stop street in the centre of the town, turn left onto the R331 for Patensie. On the town's outskirts you pass a road leading right to the Yellowwoods picnic area, and, 1,1 km later, you pass a road on your left leading to the Philip Tunnel (see pages 206 – 7). Note your kms here. The road leads upriver and, 7,6 km after passing the turn-off to the Philip Tunnel, you have a fine view over the fertile floor of the valley. Roughly 4,5 km later you pass through the outskirts of the small village of Patensie. Continue on this road (R331), passing a number of sideroads and staying close to the river. Roughly 19 km from Patensie you pass the R332 to Humansdorp on your left and, 4 km later, you pass, on your left, a gravel road leading to the Kouga Dam. Immediately after this the road surface changes to gravel – note your kms here. Continue on this gravel road for 11 km, then turn at the low causeway across the Groot River – this 22 km there-and-back trip will give you excellent views of the colourful Groot River gorge.

Groot River gorge to Port Elizabeth

When you return from the Groot River gorge, note your kms as you pass the turn-off (now on your right) to the Kouga Dam – just after driving back onto the tar. After 4,2 km you pass the road leading right to Humansdorp and, after a further 15,5 km, turn left onto a gravel road leading to the Elands River Valley, noting your kms.

Follow this road as it climbs higher and higher, but stop periodically for fine views back over the Gamtoos Valley. After 15,7 km you reach a road leading off to your left. Pass this, but turn left 150 m later – this becomes the same road but has a better surface. Drive roughly 1 km along this sideroad and park for a fine view across the valley to the Cockscomb, known to the Khoikhoi as the 'Mountain of the Clouds' (see pages 206 – 7).

Retrace your route down into the Gamtoos Valley and turn left onto the tarred R331. You now retrace your earlier route past Patensie to Hankey, but drive straight through Hankey, staying on the R331. The road then leads along the crest of a line of hills, offering fine views to your right as far as St Francis Bay and to your left over a scene reminiscent of KwaZulu-Natal's Valley of a Thousand Hills. Roughly 16 km after leaving Hankey you pass, on your right, the small farming centre of Loerie, the site of an important water storage dams for the Port Elizabeth area. The Apple Express, a fun excursion from Port Eliabeth by narrow-gauge railway, ends its outward run at Loerie. About 11 km from Loerie, turn left, following the signs onto the N2 for Port Elizabeth.

AA Office 1A Greenacres Shopping Centre Cape Road, Newton Park, Port Elizabeth 6001 Tel (041) 34 1313
Port Eiizabeth Publicity Association Donkin Reserve, Port Elizabeth 6001 Tel (041) 52 1315

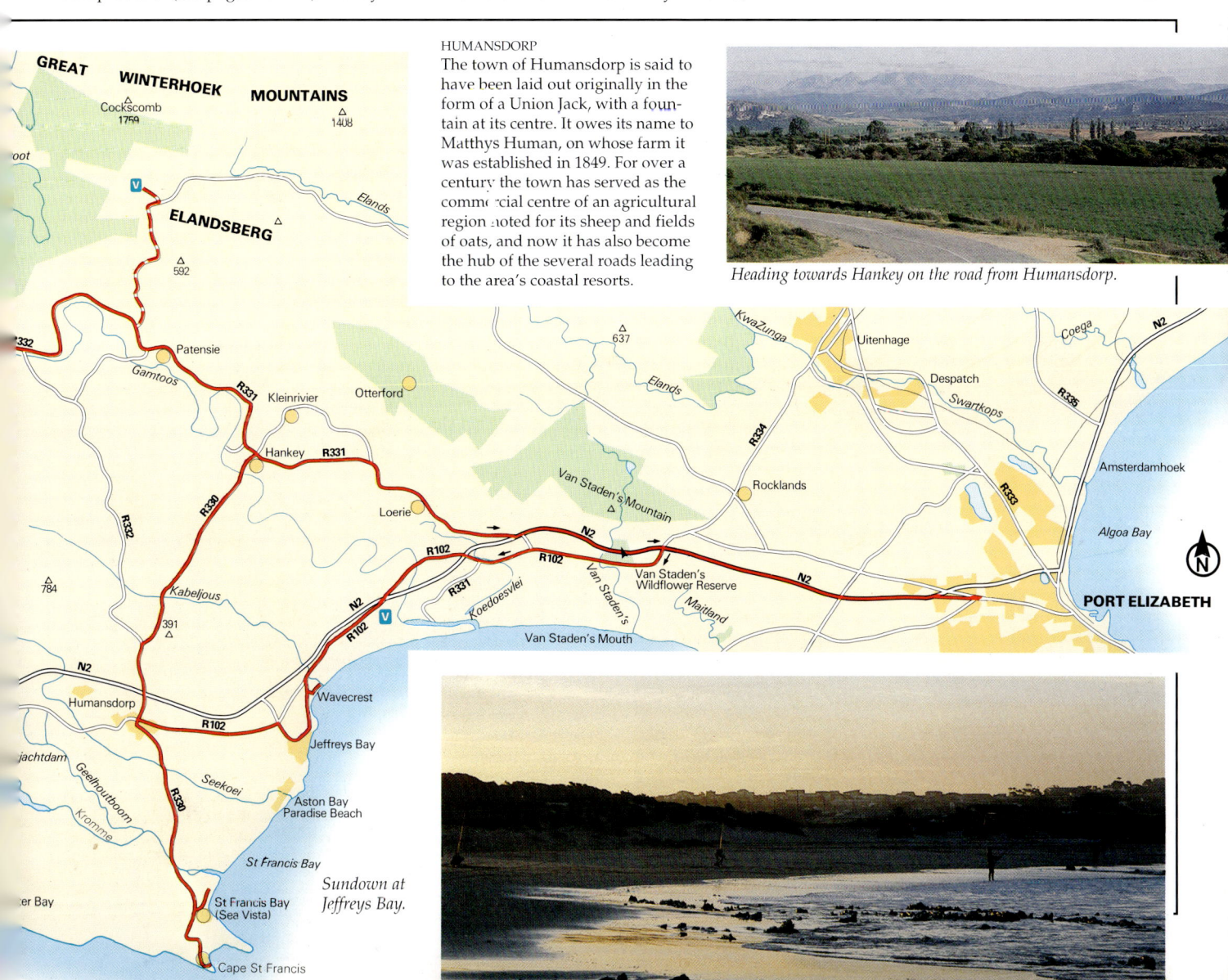

HUMANSDORP

The town of Humansdorp is said to have been laid out originally in the form of a Union Jack, with a fountain at its centre. It owes its name to Matthys Human, on whose farm it was established in 1849. For over a century the town has served as the commercial centre of an agricultural region noted for its sheep and fields of oats, and now it has also become the hub of the several roads leading to the area's coastal resorts.

Heading towards Hankey on the road from Humansdorp.

Sundown at Jeffreys Bay.

– PORT ELIZABETH WALKS AND WILDLIFE –

Port Elizabeth rises above the sparkling waters of the Indian Ocean. A view from Bird Rock.

Wild forests and unspoilt beaches surround the friendly city

THERE ARE MANY places within easy reach of Port Elizabeth that offer exhilarating outings through unspoilt natural surroundings. The city's publicity association has information and maps detailing more than twenty 'eco-walks'.

Even within the boundaries of the city, those who take to the *Guinea Fowl Trail* through Settlers Park will be surprised by the wildness of the area and the variety of its vegetation and bird life. Also common are *dassies* (hyrax), tortoises and leguans. The Guinea Fowl Trail takes two to three hours to walk, but is relatively easy. Many shorter walks through the park are also possible, and the park is easily accessible from almost any part of the city. No permits are required, but hikers should take their own water and are advised not to drink from the Baakens River.

The *Sacramento Trail*, which takes its name from a Portuguese ship that foundered off the shore in 1647, is an 8 km coastal walk from Skoenmakerskop through Sardinia Bay Nature Reserve. An ancient cannon that you pass along the way is a pointer to historical associations, and the vistas of land and sea are unforgettable.

The *Trail of the Roseate Tern*, within Cape Recife Nature Reserve, is another varied and well-known outing. Its 9 km route includes an old lighthouse, a World War II harbour defence installation, a bird hide and a penguin sanctuary and, in addition, it's one of the best sites in the Eastern Cape for bird-watching. A permit for cars to enter the reserve is obtainable from the Beach Manager's office at Happy Valley on the beachfront at Humewood – tel (041) 56 1040.

Bushbuck Trail

A circular 16 km path has been established in the Island Forest Reserve (see pages 206 – 7) and is known as the *Bushbuck Trail*. The reserve itself forms part of an immense sand dune covered with indigenous subtropical coastal forest that is home to bushbuck, blue and grey duikers, bush pig, vervet monkeys and, among the bird population, the rare Knysna loerie (sometimes also *lourie*). Apart from exploring the depths of the forest, you will have some fine views over the great sweep of St Francis Bay.

Just a few kilometres further west is the *Sir Peregrine Maitland Trail*, a shorter forest trail through the Maitland Nature Reserve (see pages 202 – 3). The trail is a little over 3 km or two hours long, and for part of its route it follows an old wagon road through the area. A slightly longer trail in the same reserve is *De Stades Trail*. The forest is noted for its rich bird life and a special feature of both trails is the comprehensive information boxes found along the routes.

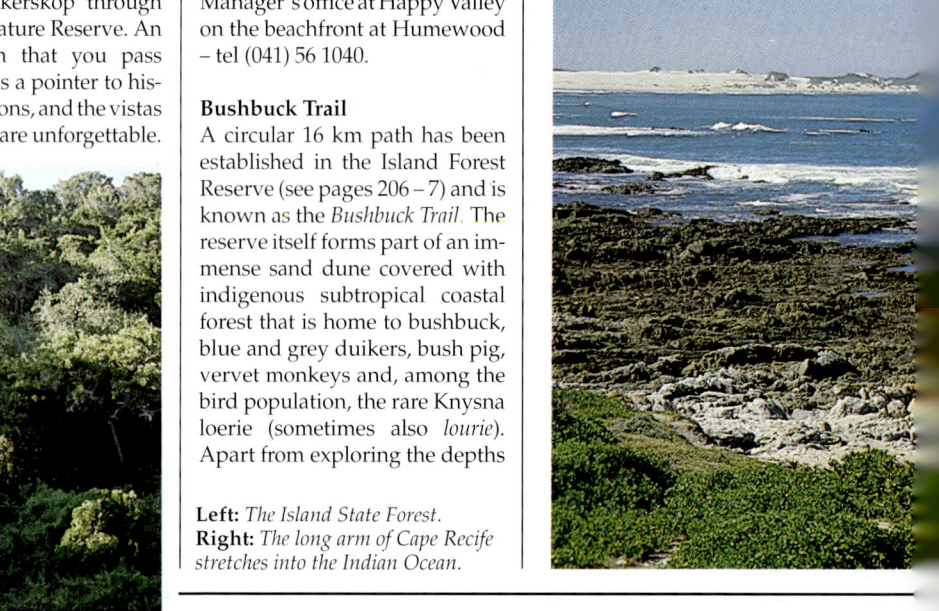

Left: *The Island State Forest.*
Right: *The long arm of Cape Recife stretches into the Indian Ocean.*

Flowers and forests

Inland and slightly further west is the *Van Stadens Wildflower Reserve*. This 400 ha area offers attractive river-gorge scenery and a profusion of indigenous flowering plants. There are two short walking trails and a mountain bike trail through the reserve, and numerous picnic sites – but there is no water, except near the main gate. Entry permits are not usually required, but arrangements should be made if the party is to consist of more than 10 people – tel (041) 955 5649.

A completely different kind of inland vegetation can be found at *Die Bronne* (the springs), in the Uitenhage Nature Reserve about 8 km north of Uitenhage. The reserve is centred on the 'eyes' (source springs) of the Uitenhage Artesian Basin, and it offers several walks (from 40 minutes to three hours) through a landscape of interestingly mixed vegetation, from aloes and other Karoo-type succulents to thick valley bushveld. Entry permits must be obtained from the supervisor of the Springs Holiday Resort – tel (041) 992 6011.

Still further north, some 80 km from Port Elizabeth, the slopes of the Zuurberg range lie within the *Zuurberg National Park* (entrance fee) – offering interesting walks (four hours and one hour) with panoramic views over the Zuurberg Mountains. The scenery in this area is attractive, including large expanses of indigenous forest and mountain tops covered with fynbos and grass. Rare plants include the Zuurberg cycad and among the larger mammals are kudu, grysbok, blue duiker and bushbuck. (See pages 202 – 3 for directions on how to get there.) The Park Warden may be contacted at tel (0426) 40 0581.

Alexandria Forest

Slightly further from Port Elizabeth, eastwards along the coast, is the *Alexandria Forest Nature Reserve*. The reserve comprises roughly 60 km of coastline from the Sundays River mouth past Cape Padrone to Cannon Rocks, plus a broad belt of land lying behind the coast. Part of this area is covered by the Alexandria Forest, a subtropical coastal forest reminiscent of the indigenous forests of the Garden Route, and quite distinct from the surrounding countryside. For details, contact The Nature Conservation Officer, Alexandria State Forest, PO Box 50, Alexandria 6185 – tel (046) 653 0601.

The wildest tract of country that is most easily accessible from Port Elizabeth is *Groendal Wilderness Area* – nearly 22 000 ha of mountain slopes and forested valleys, lying at the foot of the Great Winterhoek Mountains and surrounding the Groendal Dam. The forests here include fine specimens of Outeniqua yellowwood, real yellowwood and white stinkwood, and are home to bushpig, bushbuck and duikers – also leopard and caracal. These remote valleys were among the last parts of the Eastern Cape to be inhabited by the San, and many rock overhangs and caves in the area contain San paintings. The fairly easy *Blindekloof Walk* of 16 km takes roughly six hours. For a full description of the walk and of the other attractions of Groendal, contact The Nature Conservation Officer, Groendal Wilderness Area, PO Box 445, Uitenhage 6230 – tel (041) 992 5418.

Lions and dolphins

Lovers of animal life have several other fascinating places to visit. The most obvious of these is the *Addo Elephant National Park* (see pages 202 – 3). Here, the Addo elephants can be seen living in their natural habitat and, if you are fortunate, you may spot black rhino, buffalo and eland. Here too, you find the *Spekboom Trail*, named for *Portulacaria afra*, a favourite food of the elephant which, with buffalo, black rhino and other larger mammals, do not have access to the trail area. Mainly because of the spekboom – which provides cover as well as nourishment – this area has one of the densest concentrations of game in Africa, so you're likely to encounter kudu, bushbuck, duiker and some of the smaller mammals, as well as abundant bird life.

West of the city, very close to the entrance to the Island Forest Reserve, is the *Seaview Game Park* (for instructions on how to get there, see pages 202 – 3 or 206 – 7). The game park is in a scenically attractive countryside overlooking the coast, and in this natural environment you can see lion, cheetah, giraffe, rhino, and several rare antelope, such as nyala and lechwe.

A particular attraction is the catwalk that takes you through the cheetah enclosure, and there are also walk-through aviaries. For additional information, write to Seaview Game Park, PO Box 27173, Greenacres 6057.

One of the most interesting places to visit is right in the heart of the city – at the Oceanarium complex in Beach Road. The Oceanarium is best known for its dolphin and marine displays, but next to the Oceanarium is the city's principal museum, a tropical house, a night house, and a snake park. The tropical house contains a lush jungle of exotic plants, inhabited by equally unusual birds. The night house is home to many species of nocturnal animals. Here, day and night are artificially reversed, so that the animals can be viewed when they are active instead of asleep.

Dolphins show their paces at the Oceanarium.

Peering into the depths of the tropical house at the Port Elizabeth Museum.

• EXPLORING GRAAFF-REINET ON FOOT •

The 19th-century workers' cottages in Stretch's Court – beautifully spruced up for luxury hotel accommodation.

'Gem of the Karoo' in a spacious mountain setting

LYING IN A LOOP of the Sundays River, beneath the distinctive dome of Spandau Kop, the old town of Graaff-Reinet is progressively being restored to the glory that earned it the title 'Gem of the Karoo'. Another title, conferred by a Cape Town newspaper last century, was 'Athens of the Eastern Cape' – a reflection of the town's enviable reputation as a cultural centre.

The citizens of Graaff-Reinet took some time to attain this status – their town was first no more than a straggling lane of mud huts. These nevertheless constituted one of the capital cities of the world when Graaff-Reinet confidently declared itself to be an independent 'republic' only 10 years after its founding.

The town was founded in 1786 on instructions from the Governor of the Cape, Cornelis van de Graaff, and named after him and his wife, Hester Cornelia Reinet. A frontier spirit prevailed in the new town, and the hardy pioneers took little notice of the regulations posted by the *landdrost* (magistrate). The Dutch East India Company, on the verge of bankruptcy, was unable to enforce its laws in this remote community, and could not spare a garrison to protect or restrain them in the matter of cross-border raids.

Matters came to a head in 1795 when a band of citizens and local farmers formed a committee, dismissed the landdrost and officials who opposed them, and then proclaimed a Burger Government. They appointed their own officials, including a new landdrost, Dawid Gerotz, who was also head of the National Assembly. Thus was born South Africa's first republic, which lasted only a few months until the burgers reluctantly but inevitably submitted to the new British rulers at the Cape of Good Hope.

The gracious old Drostdy

Our walk through old Graaff-Reinet begins at the historic official residence of the landdrost, the *Drostdy* **(1)**, near the northern end of Church *(Kerk)* Street. The building was completed in 1806 to a design by Louis Thibault, although, as always seemed to happen when the architect was absent from the works, local artisans departed from his original plans to some extent.

By 1847 it was decided that the Drostdy had become too dilapidated to be worth repairing, so it was sold. But not only did the building not fall down, it withstood the stress of the addition of a second storey, and had served as a hotel for almost a century when restoration began in 1975.

Accommodation at the Drostdy Hotel is in the attractive and historic cottages in Drostdy Hof, also known as *Stretch's Court* **(2)**, after Captain Charles Lennox Stretch, the surveyor who bought the land in 1855. The land was subdivided for houses for workers, possibly, it is thought, former slaves.

From the back door of the Drostdy, look through the softly lit interior and the elegant front doorway to the serene facade of *Reinet House Museum* **(3)** at the far end of Parsonage *(Pastorie)* Street.

Walk along Parsonage Street on the southern (right-hand) side. The *John Rupert Theatre* **(4)** on your right was once the church of the London Missionary Society, and later the Congregational Church. It was known as *die groot Londen kerk* (the big London church) to distinguish it from its smaller sister in Middel Street. The adjacent rectory, built in about 1840, has been reconverted into a home after serving many years as a school.

Next on your right is a row of houses now used as a home for the aged. The best of the group is number 17, *Williams House*, although the addition of an iron roof has resulted in the clipping of the front and end gables. Much of the external woodwork is believed to date from when the house was built – around 1860.

Firearms through the years

At the corner of Murray Street, on your right, is the old *Residency* **(5)**, probably built in the 1820s. The irrigation furrows in front of the building are a relic of a system laid out in the 1820s by Andries Stockenström, who succeeded his father as landdrost of Graaff-Reinet in 1815.

The Residency, an impressive thatched and gabled house typical of the Cape Dutch style, has an unusually ornate fanlight. The building now houses the Jan Felix Lategan memorial collection of historic firearms which traces the development of firearms used in South Africa. (As with a number of the places that we visit, there is a small entrance fee here.)

Leave the Residency and cross Murray Street to visit Reinet House, which, as the Dutch Reformed parsonage, was occupied for 82 years by the Murray

A lamppost of bygone days still serves historic houses on Parsonage Street.

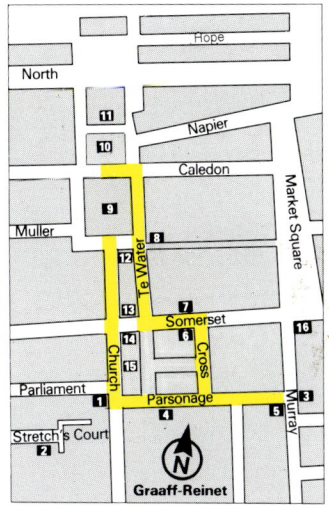

An aerial view of the pretty town that lies in a loop of the Sundays River.

The stately Dutch Reformed Church.

family. The Reverend Andrew Murray served as minister from 1822 until his death in 1866, and was succeeded by one of his sons, Charles, who died, still in service, in 1904.

The building, completed in about 1812, was altered dramatically though. After the Murray family's departure, it became a girls' hostel. The gables were removed and, by 1950, the old parsonage was unrecognisable. Meticulous restoration was started in 1953, based on old photographs and a careful study of old building techniques. Stone steps with their original iron railing sweep up to the stoep, above which the gable bears a winged hourglass to remind passers-by that 'time flies'. Tragically, in 1980, the building was partially destroyed by fire but it has subsequently been rebuilt.

Reinet House is now a superb period house museum, containing some of the personal possessions of the Murrays and many fascinating domestic items. There is also a display of the town's Reinet dolls. These were first made during the years of World War I, when many imports classed as luxuries, including dolls, could not be obtained.

In the back yard of Reinet House there is a reconstructed water mill, which can be operated by inserting a coin, and nearby is the old Black Acorn vine planted in 1870 by Charles Murray and believed to have been the thickest vine in the world until dead wood was removed in 1983.

From the front door of Reinet House you can see the classic facade of the old Drostdy with the mountain – a spur of the towering *Sneeuberg* (snow mountain) – behind it. On the corner of Market Square, to your right, is *Urquhart House* **(16)**, a part of the museum complex. Unusual features are the large anchor in its ornate gable, placed by the builder in 1800 in honour of a seafaring ancestor, and the kitchen floor of peach pips. From the front of this building, look up Market Square to see the old gunpowder store on Magazine Hill, which was carefully and judiciously sited outside the town limits in 1831.

Return to Parsonage Street and walk along its northern side, where most of the little houses as far as Cross Street date from the mid-19th century. Number 18, at the corner of Cross Street, has a curiously 'detached' gable, and small-paned windows with old glass that produces distorted reflections.

Turn right into Cross Street, which contains a number of simple, old buildings. On the corner of Somerset Street, on your left, is the *St James (Anglican) Church* **(6)**, consecrated in 1850. The original church forms the nave of the present building, and is the portion under the higher section of the roof. The church contains much beautiful woodwork and many memorials dating from the Anglo-Boer War.

Victorian beauties

Turn left into Somerset Street. Next to the church is the rectory, which has something of a doll's house quality to its appearance and dates from 1895. Opposite is a long, *two-gabled building* **(7)** with a verandah framed by ornately fretted woodwork.

Cross Somerset Street towards numbers 22 and 24, which form a single unit with three doors and rounded windows on the street frontage. Number 26 shows fretted wooden railings and pillars, with much tracery work below the eaves, while number 28, on the corner of Te Water Street, is a much-altered double storey of the mid- to late-Victorian period.

Turn right into Te Water Street, a short street of small cottages. At the end of the street you emerge onto Church Square, passing the building of the *Graaff-Reinet Club* **(8)** on your right. This rather grand building was erected in 1881 as a social club after the town authorities – apparently somewhat ahead of their time – refused permission to a group of gentlemen to open a 'smoking parlour' in Parsonage Street.

About 3 m before you reach Caledon Street, you can see, to your left, the chimney protruding from the *Dutch Reformed Church* **(9)** between the main and end sections. Chimneys rarely form part of ecclesiastical architecture, but the church elders required a fireplace in their consistory.

Before crossing to the church, walk north towards the *Mayor's Garden* **(10)**, with its war memorial, and beyond it the *Town Hall* **(11)**, built in 1910 and known as the Victoria Hall.

The Dutch Reformed Church is open to visitors during normal business hours. In the consistory there are portraits of all the clergymen who have served the congregation, starting in 1792 with the Reverend Van Manger. The church, consecrated in 1887, was built in the Gothic Revival style, and is known as the *Groot Kerk* (big church) to distinguish it from the *Nuwe Kerk* (new church).

Leave the church and walk along the left (eastern) side of Church Street. You pass a *bank* **(12)** on your left, that was originally the Standard Bank of British South Africa in 1874. Beyond this is a long row of newspaper offices, from which the sound of printing machinery can often be heard.

Karoo fossils and San art

On the corner of Somerset Street, also on your left, is *Te Water House* **(13)**, built in 1818. It was formerly thatched, but now has an iron roof and clipped gables. It is one of the few old South African houses with an underground wine cellar, and was once the homestead of a wine estate.

Cross Somerset Street and pass on your left the *Information Office and Museum* **(14)**, housed in the town's first library of 1847. On display are collections of period costume, fossil remains of Karoo reptiles of 200 million years ago, an exhibition of photographic equipment and prints recording much of the town's progress, and carefully executed reproductions of San rock art.

Also on your left in Church Street is the *Hester Rupert Art Gallery* **(15)**, in a cruciform building of 1821, built as a school and mission church. Like the similar institution in Swellendam, it was known as *die oefeningshuis* – the house of (religious) practice or service – to comply with a regulation that stated that, in certain of the country districts, no church should be built within three days' ride of an existing church of the same faith.

Cross Church Street and, before returning to your starting point, pause to look along Parliament Street, where a number of houses are national monuments.

EXPLORING THE KAROO NATURE RESERVE

Pillars of rock tower above the Valley of Desolation near Graaff-Reinet.

A desolate valley perched high in a thirsty mountain wilderness

Looking out over the dry Karoo.

THE KAROO NATURE RESERVE all but surrounds the historic Karoo town of Graaff-Reinet (see pages 212–3), and the town serves as the ideal centre from which to visit the reserve. The reserve was established in 1975 by the South African Nature Foundation, and it encompasses 16 000 ha of Karoo plains and mountains, including the Van Ryneveld Pass Dam. This great tract of countryside, once fertile and covered with vegetation, had become badly overgrazed and had begun to show signs of consequent erosion, but today it is recognised in South Africa as a model of conservation and correct land management.

The reserve is effectively split into two sections by the roads to Middelburg and Aberdeen/Port Elizabeth. The western section is more accessible, and is by far the most visited. The eastern section is maintained as a natural wilderness – rough tracks do exist, but no good roads, and visitors who wish to hike through this part of the reserve must apply for a permit to do so.

Between the eastern and western sections lies the Van Ryneveld Pass Dam, which constitutes virtually a third section. This is a restricted area accessible only by boat or at various points at the southern end of the dam. The rich bird life makes it well worth visiting. Among the birds to be seen are large numbers of South African shelduck, Cape teal, yellowbilled duck, grey herons, Egyptian geese, spurwinged geese, whitebreasted cormorants and flamingos.

There is a 19 km game-viewing circuit that offers excellent prospects of sighting large species, including kudu, black wildebeest and blesbok. This circuit is reached from the R63, about 4 km beyond the turn-off to the valley.

Butterflies seek life-giving nectar.

Valley of Desolation
The western section of the reserve contains the most spectacular area – known as the 'Valley of Desolation'. Unexpectedly for a valley, this lies high above Graaff-Reinet. To reach the valley, drive out of Graaff-Reinet on the R63 towards Murraysburg, pass the Van Ryneveld Pass Dam on your right, then turn left to enter the reserve. A good tarred road leads up the steep mountainside.

Shortly before reaching the valley you pass a toposcope set on the summit of a small koppie known as 'The Lookout'. From here there is a magnificent view over Graaff-Reinet, and you can clearly see the ox-bow formed by the Sundays River as it curls lazily around the picturesque town.

The Valley of Desolation itself, noted for its grotesque and bizarre dolerite formations, offers a vivid illustration of the slow processes of erosion. Jumbled dolerite pillars, weathering more slowly than the sedimentary rock that surrounds them, now rise to heights of up to 120 m above the boulder-strewn valley floor. Cobbled paths lead to the edges of the valley, where convenient safety walls enable visitors to lean over and admire the confusion of rocks below – thought to be the product of some 200 million years of erosion.

You can also look across from here to Spandau Kop, standing guard over Graaff-Reinet rather like a towering fortress. (Spandau Kop is said to have been given this name by an early Prussian settler, who found that the mountain reminded him of Spandau Castle, a fortress situated near Berlin.)

Flora and fauna
It is interesting to note the changes in vegetation that you pass through as the road to the Valley of Desolation climbs up from the plains. The reserve contains several distinct vegetation zones – the plains are covered with thorny succulents and aromatic shrubs. The lower slopes of the mountains are sprinkled with *spekboom*, also known as 'elephant's food' (*Portulacaria afra*) – a fleshy, grey-green shrub that is a major source of food for browsing animals such as the kudu. Higher up the slopes the spekboom is gradually replaced by mountain veld or grassland – the home of klipspringer and mountain reedbuck. Finally, at the highest level, there is savannah grassland, dotted with stinkwood and karee trees.

This last type of vegetation covers much of the eastern section of the reserve, and is the favoured habitat of the Cape mountain zebra (*Equus zebra zebra*), reintroduced into this area from the Mountain Zebra National Park near Cradock (see pages 200 – 1).

In addition to offering a safe home to mountain zebra, kudu, klipspringers and mountain reedbuck, the reserve contains gemsbok, red hartebeest, buffalo, black wildebeest, blesbok, springbok, steenbok and the common duiker – and there are many smaller mammals, including the caracal, the silver jackal and the bat-eared fox. Large leopard tortoises can often be seen in the summer months.

The reserve also supports a wide variety of birds – quite apart from the waterbirds to be seen on the dam.

On the plains there are ostriches, blue cranes, bustards and secretary birds. High in the mountains, the black eagles build their nests on the towering cliffs and feed on the plump, ever-present rock hyraxes, or 'dassies'.

There are three trails that can be undertaken in the reserve by visitors. The Valley Trail is a 90 minute walk at the top end of the valley, and no permit is required. The Eerstefontein Trail in the western section may be walked from the Berg-en-Dal gate as a 5, 11 or 14 km option. Self-serve (free) permits are available at the gate. Booking is essential for the two-day (optional three-day) Driekoppe Trail in the eastern section of the reserve.

A distant view across the Karoo to the waters of the Van Ryneveld Pass Dam.

If you are planning any of these walks, make a point of taking an adequate supply of drinking water with you. The Karoo takes its ancient name from a Khoikhoi word meaning 'dry' or 'barren', and the area, which is classed as semi-desert, becomes extremely hot in the summer. If you are visiting the reserve in summer, you should confine any walking you do to the early morning and late afternoon – not only will you find the walk more pleasant, but the animals are also more active during these cooler periods.

A rich storehouse of fossils
This region was not always the semi-desert that it is today. The soil and the rock strata that have been exposed by erosion are rich in fossil reptiles – evidence that the area was once an extensive marsh, probably very hot and humid. These fossils, some of them transitional between mammal and reptile, are of the greatest importance, and there is an excellent collection to be seen in the museum in Graaff-Reinet.

The reserve has picnic sites and toilets, but offers no general overnight accommodation, and no camping is allowed within its boundaries. However, there is a caravan park outside the town on the banks of the Sundays River, with a number of bungalows that can be rented, and there are several fine hotels in the town.

The reserve is open to visitors every day from sunrise to sunset. Anyone wishing to take part in a hike through the wilderness areas of the reserve should contact the Officer-in-Charge, Karoo Nature Reserve, PO Box 349, Graaff-Reinet 6280; tel (0491) 23 453.

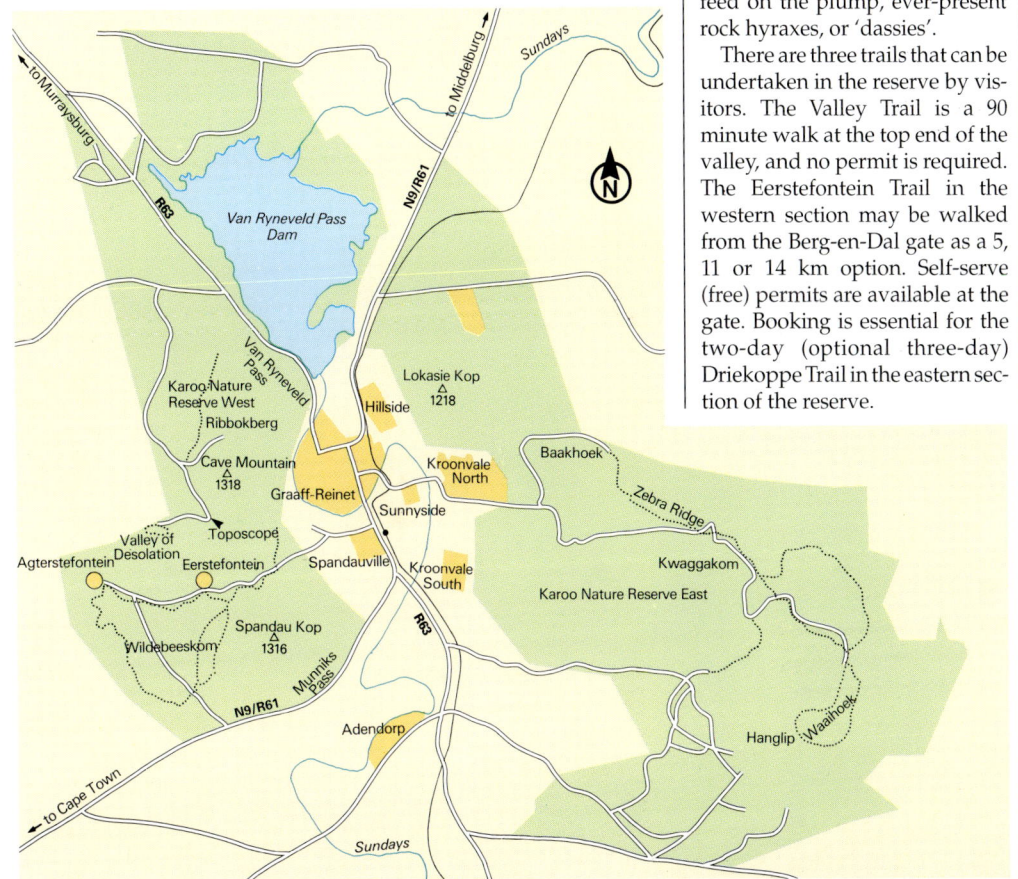

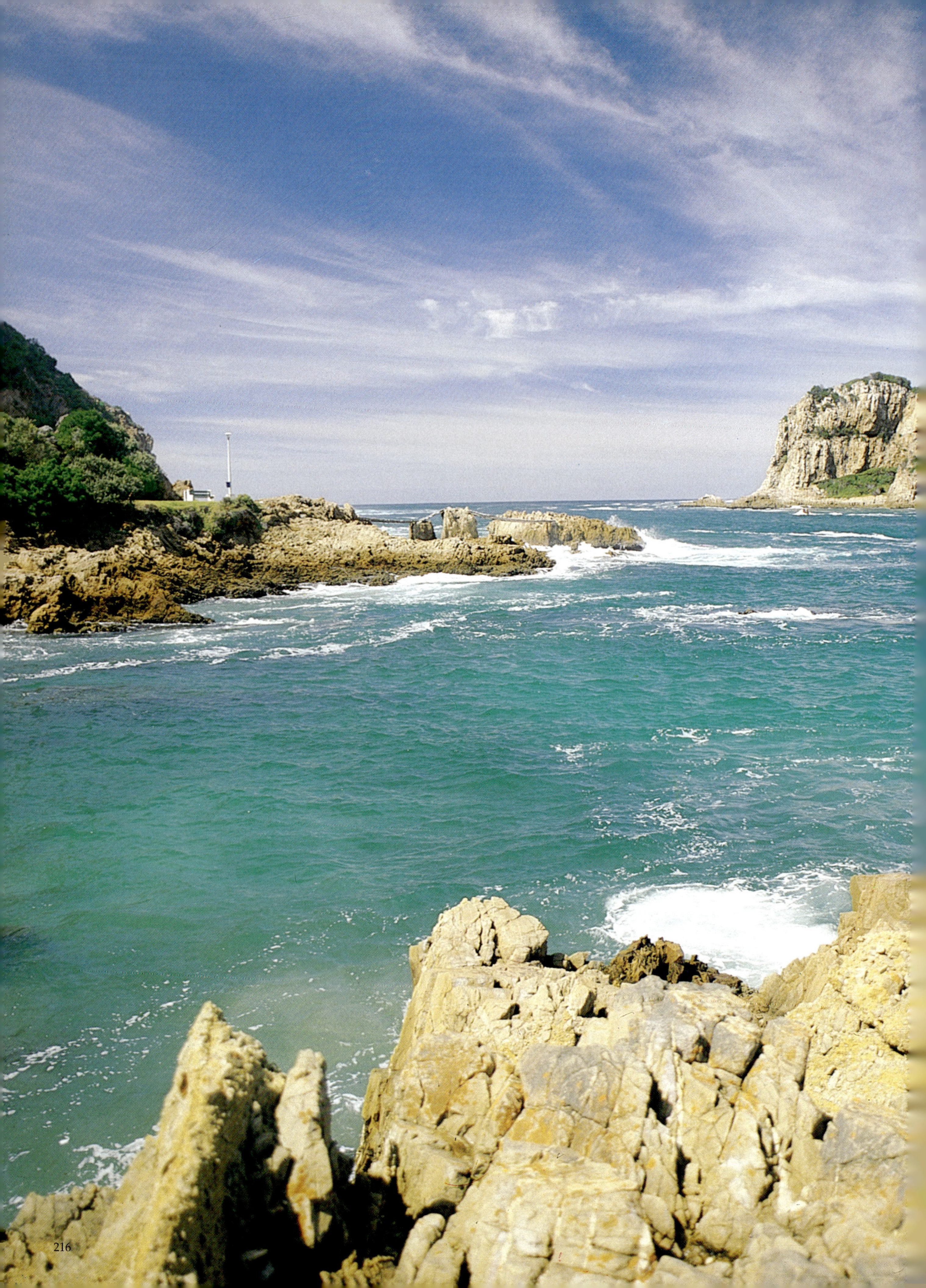

WESTERN CAPE

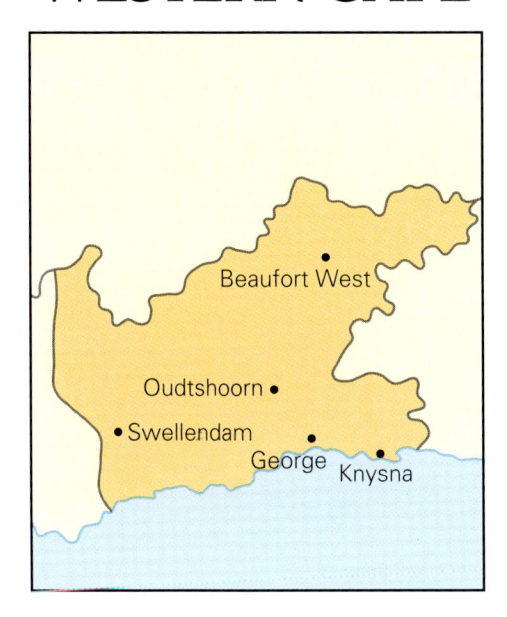

Plettenberg Bay – Nature's Valley – Tsitsikamma – Storms River **218-9**

Plettenberg Bay – Noetzie – Spitskop – Diepwalle – Dieprivier **220-1**

Knysna – Belvidere – Brenton on Sea – Millwood – Wilderness **222-3**

Steam and scenery: George to Knysna by steam train **224-5**

George – Robinson Pass – Oudtshoorn – Cango Caves – Outeniqua Pass **226-7**

Oudtshoorn – Swartberg Pass – Prince Albert – Meiringspoort **228-9**

Prince Albert: Gables and a forgotten gold rush **230-1**

Laingsburg – Seweweekspoort – Zoar – Hoeko – Ladismith **232-3**

Riversdale – Garcia's Pass – Herbertsdale – Mossel Bay – Gouritsmond **234-5**

Swellendam – Bonnievale – Montagu – Tradouw Pass **236-7**

Swellendam – De Hoop Nature Reserve – Malgas – Witsand **238-9**

Swellendam: An enchanting stroll through history **240-1**

Left: *Two sandstone bluffs – The Heads – mark the beautiful Knysna Lagoon.*

Through a giant's garden of dense forests and precipitous gorges

East of Plettenberg Bay the Tsitsikamma (sparkling waters) Mountains crowd in towards the sea, ensuring a rich rainfall throughout the year. Our route leads along the coastal plateau at the foot of the mountains, through a quiet world of primeval high forest, and deep gorges rushing clear mountain streams to the sea.

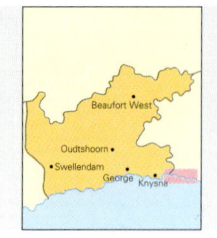

Plettenberg Bay
Keurbooms River
Nature's Valley
Tsitsikamma
National Park
Storms River
180 – 200 km

Leave Plettenberg Bay by driving west past the beach and across the Piesang River, then turn right into Piesang Valley Road. Turn left after 200 m into Robberg Drive – noting your kms. After 3,4 km turn left and follow this sideroad to the parking area at the beginning of the Robberg peninsula.

Walk 100 m along the path on the southern side of the peninsula for a view of the coast below. Then walk from the car park just 25 m through the fynbos to the northern side of the peninsula for a grand vista over the entire Plettenberg Bay region to the Tsitsikamma Mountains in the far distance – the beautiful stretch of country that you are about to explore.

Robberg to Nature's Valley

Drive back towards the town, but turn left into Piesang Valley Road. Pass by the road to the Country Club, then turn right onto the N2 at the T-junction. The N2 offers fine views over the Keurbooms River lagoon.

Cross the Bietou River, then the Keurbooms River, and turn left at the far end of the Keurbooms River bridge into the Keurbooms River Nature Reserve. An old track leads upriver, offering a pleasant walk (allow 45 min). From Keurbooms River the road climbs fairly steeply and turns inland. Several parking areas along the route offer attractive views back over the bay and the lagoon. Turn right onto the R102 for Nature's Valley (there is a huge sign), avoiding the N2 toll road.

The R102 winds down through indigenous forest to the Groot River lagoon. At the bottom of the downhill stretch, turn right for Nature's Valley. After 1 km the road forks – take the left road to a large parking area. From here it is a short walk to the gently shelving beach and along the side of the lagoon. (Strong currents make it unsafe to swim near the river mouth.)

Nature's Valley to Storms River Mouth

Return to the R102 and turn right. There are shaded picnic sites where the road crosses the Groot River. After this the road climbs steeply out of the Groot River valley. At the top of the

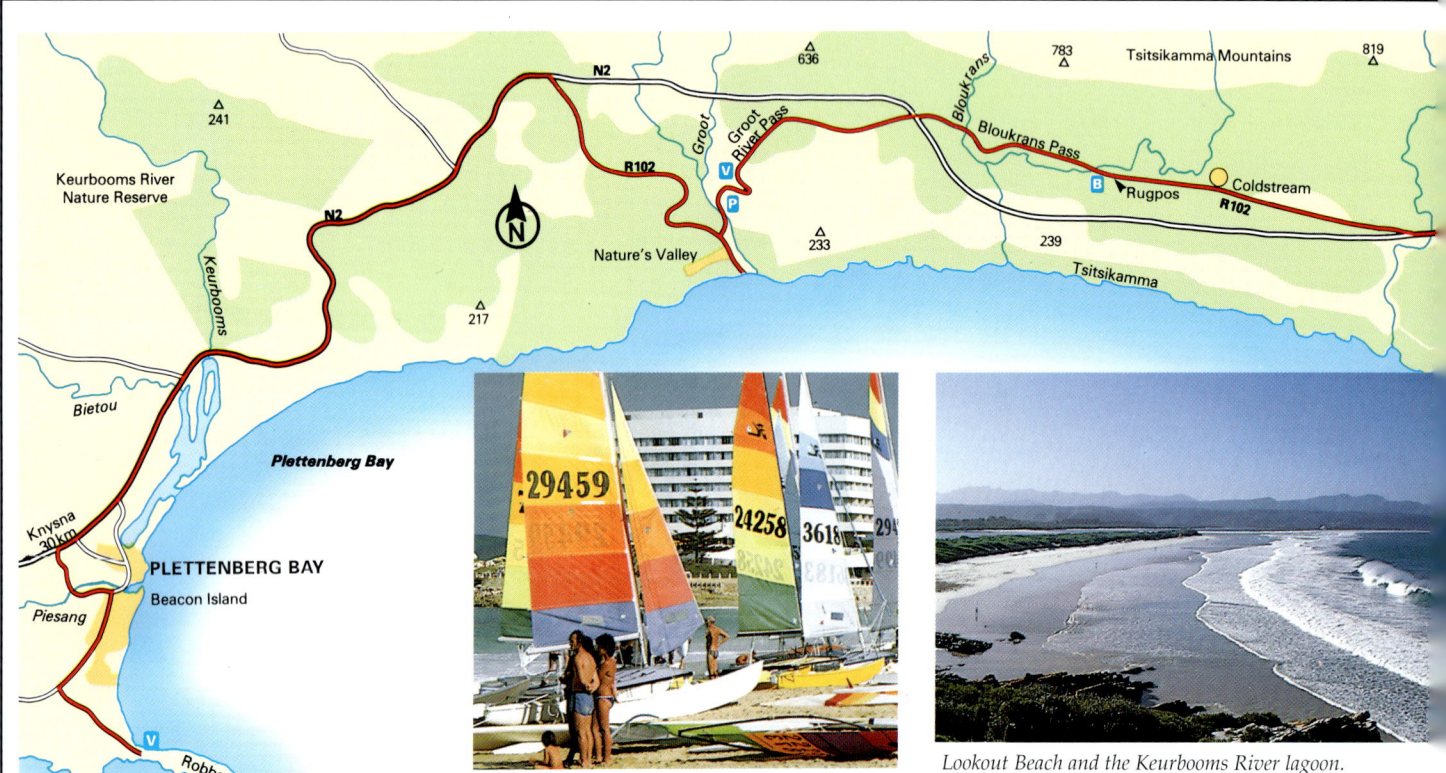

SEAL MOUNTAIN

Robberg or *Robbe Berg* (seal mountain) took its name from the many seals that once basked on its shores. The peninsula is now a nature reserve, noted for its varied coastal vegetation, its rich inter-tidal life and its many bird species.

Archeological excavations in a large cave on the southern side of the peninsula have revealed that this was once the home of prehistoric shore-dwellers.

Fishing from the rocks is permitted in the reserve, and generations of fishermen have criss-crossed the peninsula with footpaths that hikers can use to reach numerous viewsites.

Watersports at Plettenberg Bay's Central Beach.

Die Eiland (the island) juts out into the sea from the southern shore of the Robberg peninsula.

Lookout Beach and the Keurbooms River lagoon.

PLETTENBERG BAY

Baia das Alagoas (bay of the lagoons) and *Baia Formosa* (beautiful bay) were among the names the Portuguese gave to this bay that Governor Joachim van Plettenberg subsequently renamed after himself. This was the site of the first European settlement – unintended though it was – in South Africa. A Portuguese vessel, the *São Gonzales*, was wrecked here during a gale in 1630. The survivors lived here for six months, building two small boats out of the wreckage. One boat reached Mozambique, and eventually Portugal. The other was picked up by a Portuguese vessel, the *St Ignatius Loyola*. Ironically, the *St Ignatius Loyola* was wrecked in the river Tagus, within sight of Lisbon, and most of the *São Gonzales* survivors were drowned.

uphill stretch, as the road swings to the right, park in the small area on your left for a view back over the valley and lagoon.

Continue on the R102, passing over the N2 toll road, down into the Bloukrans Pass. The road is narrow and twists through dense indigenous forest. Looking up from the bottom of the pass, you will see the Bloukrans Bridge (a part of the toll road) high in the sky above you. On the final pull up out of the pass, soon after the white-walled hairpin bend, a road on your right leads to the shady Rugpos picnic site on the forest's edge. There are braai places here and short forest walks.

The R102 continues past the sawmilling centre of Coldstream, which has a shop and a petrol station. About 7 km after the R102 rejoins the N2, turn right for Storms River Mouth and the Tsitsikamma National Park. This sideroad leads through plantations and into the National Park (small entrance fee), then winds through indigenous coastal forest to Storms River Mouth. The road ends alongside a restaurant noted for its seafood. There is a short walk from the restaurant along the shore and through indigenous forest to a suspension footbridge across the river mouth, where the lookout point on the eastern headland gives an impressive sea-view all the way to Plettenberg Bay (allow 1 hr 30 min).

Storms River Mouth to Paul Sauer Bridge

Return to the N2 and turn right, noting your kms. After 5,2 km park off the road on your left at the sign to the 'Big Tree'. There is a parking area near the road, and an interesting 15 minute stroll – along a constructed boardwalk called the Big Tree Trail – leads to the Big Tree, an Outeniqua yellowwood.

About 1 km further east, a disused track leads off the N2 to the original Storms River Pass road, built by Thomas Bain more than a century ago. It winds down through dense indigenous forest to a low bridge across the Storms River, and next to this is the shady *Oubrug* (old bridge) picnic site. No vehicles are allowed on the Oubrug road, but a walking trail has been established along the route. Entry permits must be obtained at Storms River village. Continue driving eastwards along the N2.

After roughly 2 km, as you approach the Paul Sauer Bridge, park in the large parking area on your left. There is a restaurant here, and also a shop and a petrol station. Photographs in the restaurant show the innovative construction method used in spanning the Storms River gorge in the 1950s. Sections of the Italian-designed bridge were hinged to platforms on both sides of the gorge and lowered to meet in the centre, 130 m above the river. The bridge was widened by several metres in 1984.

Return towards Plettenberg Bay on the N2. Take the toll road if you are in a hurry, or follow the signs onto the R102 if you have the time to retrace your outgoing route through the Bloukrans Pass and past Nature's Valley. If time allows, return to your first stop of the day, the Robberg peninsula, and walk to the north-facing viewsite to look out over the bay in its evening colours.

Plettenberg Bay Publicity Bureau Main Street
Plettenberg Bay 6600 Tel (04457) 34065
Tsitsikamma National Park
Tel (042) 541 1651; Fax (042) 541 1629

Surf pounds the rocky shore of the Tsitsikamma National Park – scene of the Tsitsikamma Underwater Trail.

Knysna lourie (Tauraco corythaix).

THE TSITSIKAMMA NATIONAL PARK
The Tsitsikamma National Park stretches for roughly 75 km along the southern Cape coast. It comprises a wild, unspoilt and rugged belt of land, much of it blanketed in dense indigenous forest, and fragmented by winding river valleys.

There are numerous walks and trails through the park, ranging from a strenuous five-day hike (the well-known Otter Trail) to easy one-hour strolls. A particular attraction is the Tsitsikamma Underwater Trail designed for snorkellers and scuba divers. The boundary of the reserve lies 5,6 km offshore and this marine segment is notable for its rich variety of both warmwater and coldwater species.

The forest section of the park lies mainly in the ravines and on the cliffs, and in De Vaselot Nature Reserve at the western end of the park. The forests are noted for their fine yellowwoods, stinkwoods and many impressive ironwoods. Both the Knysna lourie and the relatively rare Narina trogon may be seen.

STORMS RIVER MOUTH REST CAMP
The Storms River divides the Tsitsikamma National Park in half, and the principal access road into the park brings visitors to a point within a few hundred metres of the river's mouth. Several pleasant paths lead off from here, the most scenic one leading to a suspension footbridge (a fairly rare structure in South Africa) over the river and to a small cave that was occupied in prehistoric times by shore-dwelling people.

A mighty yellowwood in the Groot River valley.

The suspension bridge at Storms River Mouth.

A wild, rocky coast and quiet forests of mighty trees

Between Plettenberg Bay and Knysna the N2 winds through pine and gum plantations and patches of indigenous forest. Today's drive, much of it on gravel, follows several sideroads, two of which lead to the coast. Then it turns inland to explore the depths of the primeval forest where for centuries the Knysna elephants have lived their secret lives.

Plettenberg Bay
Kranshoek
Noetzie
Spitskop
Diepwalle
Dieprivier
140 – 160 km

LEAVE PLETTENBERG BAY on the N2 towards Knysna, and note your kms as you pass Stromboli's Inn on your left. After a further 3,7 km turn left onto a good gravel road signposted 'Kranshoek' and 'Harkerville'. Go left after a few hundred metres and then right to reach the boom at the entrance to the Kranshoek Reserve. The reserve is open from sunrise to sunset every day and an entrance fee is payable.

The road passes an indigenous tree, shrub and fern nursery, where braai wood is available, and eventually emerges from the forest onto high cliffs covered with fynbos. There are two large, lawned picnic areas, the first by the Kranshoek River (with toilets), and the second a few hundred metres further on the edge of the cliffs, with a magnificent view over the rocky coastline. Both have braai sites and fresh water and they are linked by a circular drive. From the first site there is a short walk to a point from where the Kranshoek River can be seen falling over the rock face in an almost sheer drop. Post-and-rail fencing and wire mesh have been spanned along the more precipitous sections, but lively children may need restraint.

Kranshoek to Noetzie
Return to the N2 and turn left. After 7,5 km on the N2, turn left and left again onto the adjacent, original national road and then right onto gravel at the signpost 'Large Gum Tree'. The largest of several towering gum trees is 68 m tall, and a notice supplies other statistics.

Keep right at the fork to reach the Bracken Hill Falls viewsite (with toilets). Here the Witels River takes a spectacular tumble into a bushy gorge.

Return to the N2 and turn left. Turn left again onto the gravel road to Noetzie. This road offers outstanding views of the Knysna lagoon, then descends past rocky cliffs to a parking area above the sea at Noetzie, 5 km from the N2.

From the parking area, walk down the concrete strip road towards the river mouth. When the strip road forks, keep right. Near the bottom, walk down the stone steps on your left. The Noetzie River has a small lagoon and a wide sandy beach at its mouth. There are no refreshments available on the beach, but there is a small toilet block tucked away in the bush near the lagoon, and water is available here.

Noetzie to Dieprivier
Return to the N2 and drive across it onto the tarred road to Prince Alfred's Pass – the R339 to Uniondale. For about 1,5 km this road passes informal settlements, so keep a look-out for children and straying animals. The tar ends after roughly 5 km. There are several picnic sites along the road, located at or near 'Big Trees'. Some sites have water and toilets. All have tables and benches. The first picnic site is at Ysterhoutrug on your left, just over 15 km from the N2. Across the road there is a 600 m path to a giant Outeniqua yellowwood, 620 years old and 38 m high.

One of the most interesting sites is near the King Edward VII Tree at Diepwalle. A boom across the road operates from sunrise to sunset and a small fee is charge for people proceeding further into the forest. At Diepwalle are the overnight huts for the start and finish of the Elephant Walk, a tourist information centre, a depot for indigenous timber, and a plant and tree nursery.

Soon after leaving Diepwalle, you pass a road on your left known as Kom-se-pad, which is a scenic 28 km drive to Knysna. Go left at a fork for Buffelsnek, where the road on the right leads to Kransbos, pass two well-surfaced viewsites to reach, 5,6 km from the fork, a narrow road on your left, signposted 'Viewsite'. This 1,5 km road should be driven with special caution – it is steep, narrow and rough, and you cannot turn until you reach the top. There are also enormous drops over the unprotected edge. Park and walk if you prefer. The trip to the top will reward you with a wonderful 360 degree view and is highly recommended.

Return to the main road towards Avontuur and drive on, noting your kms. Pass the pretty *Dal van Varings* (dale of ferns), Buffelsnek forest station and Kruisvallei. After 15 km you reach the Dieprivier picnic site, with braai places, water and toilets, a pleasantly shady expanse of lawn, and the river flowing past. A stone cairn and plaque commemorate Thomas Bain, who built the road on which you have been travelling.

(Adventurous drivers may continue north over the precipitous but spectacular Prince Alfred's Pass to Avontuur, returning to the Dieprivier picnic site by the same route. However, this should not be attempted unless the weather is completely clear and you have at least two hours of daylight. This pass must never be attempted if you are towing.)

Dieprivier to Plettenberg Bay
Retrace your route from Dieprivier but, at the fork at Kruisvallei, turn left for Plettenberg Bay on the R340. (The road to the right is the R339 on which you travelled earlier from the N2.)

The delightful and unspoilt beach at Noetzie.

NOETZIE
Noted for its modern 'castles', Noetzie is one of the prettiest little places on this scenically magnificent southern coast. It was also the scene of an unsolved mystery. In 1881 a three-masted schooner, the *Phoenix*, was washed onto the rocks near the river mouth. No trace was ever found of her crew, and the last entry in her cargo book had been made five years earlier.

A rare photograph of one of Knysna's elephants.

The R340 passes through farmlands and forests, with the rugged gorges of the Keurbooms River on your left. About 7 km after Kruisvallei, the road passes below Perdekop, closely following the route of a track built almost two centuries ago. As you reach the summit about 9 km from Kruisvallei there are fine views on all sides.

A little over 18 km from Kruisvallei you reach the tarred road; 8 km later you pass a turn-off on the right to Wittedrif; 5 km further on, after passing the wide flats of the Bietou River on your right, you reach the N2 at Keurbooms River mouth. Turn right for a short drive back to Plettenberg Bay on the N2.

George Tourism Association 124 York Street
George 6530 Tel (0441) 74 4000
Plettenberg Bay Tourism Association
Kloof St, Plettenberg Bay 6600 Tel (04457) 34 065
Knysna Publicity Association 40 Main Street
Knysna 6570 Tel (0445) 21610

ELEPHANTS OF THE FOREST
The extensive forests of the southern Cape were originally the home of large herds of elephant, but persistent hunting throughout the 18th and 19th centuries greatly reduced their numbers. The hunting has also made them very wary of mankind, with the result that it is now difficult to locate and count the few that survive. Three young elephants from the Kruger National Park were introduced into the forests in 1994, but one died soon afterwards. The survival of the world's most southerly herd is by no means assured, and a survey in 1995 revealed that there are no bulls alive. One of the most celebrated elephant hunters to pass this way was Queen Victoria's second son, Prince Alfred, after whom Prince Alfred's Pass was named. Another renowned hunter by the name of Marais is said to have accounted for exactly 99 elephants. He boasted that before killing his hundredth he would first pluck a hair from its tail. He did indeed pluck the hair, but No 100 killed him in the process. Occasionally the elephants have attacked people other than their hunters. The last instance was in 1963 when an angry cow elephant caught and killed a worker in the forest near Veldmanspad.

THOMAS BAIN AND PRINCE ALFRED'S PASS
From our turning point at the Dieprivier picnic site, the road to Avontuur continues north over Prince Alfred's Pass. This is a narrow pass and dangerous in bad weather, but it offers magnificent views over some of the wildest scenery in southern Africa. The pass and the landscape have changed little since the building of the road was completed in May 1867. The route was originally worked out in 1856 by the Scottish-born road builder Andrew Geddes Bain. However, it was left to his son Thomas to complete the building of the road, with a workforce of 270 convicts. During the building, Bain lived with his family in the farmhouse known as Die Vlug – which you pass on the way, on the left side of the road.

MONARCH OF THE FORESTS
The grandest of the many species of indigenous trees that grow in these southern forests is unquestionably the almost mystic Outeniqua yellowwood (*Podocarpus falcatus*).

The magnificent coastal vista – looking west from the second Kranshoek picnic area.

Many of the giants were felled by woodcutters before controls were introduced in the 1920s, but some fine specimens were left standing. One of these is the King Edward VII Tree that you pass on this route, standing 46 m high and with a girth of 9,5 m – and estimated to be at least 700 years old.

The yellowwood was a boon to the early colonists. Its timber is as light as Oregon pine but far stronger, which made it ideal for furniture, ceiling beams and floorboards. Early yellowwood furniture is now much sought after by collectors, and fetches very high prices. But not too long ago, countless yellowwood trees were being shipped from Knysna as railway sleepers, soaked in creosote.

The massive trunk of an Outeniqua yellowwood, undisputed monarch of the southern forests.

Jewel-like lakes, and gold hidden in the forest's streams

This drive explores one of the most romantic regions in southern Africa – the emerald-green landscape of Knysna, the old gold mines that can still be visited in the forests nearby and the string of glittering lakes that stretches eastwards from Wilderness. More than half of the route is tarred and the rest is good gravel.

Knysna
Brenton-on-Sea
Millwood
Wilderness
Sedgefield
200 - 220 km

NEAR THE EASTERN END of Knysna, turn off the N2 onto George Rex Drive towards the Knysna Heads. As you approach the Heads, take the left fork, uphill, following the sign to 'Coney Glen/Viewpoint'. This road climbs for 1 km to a car park on top of the eastern headland. There is a viewsite a few metres downhill from the car park, but young children must be held, as the cliff edge is only partially fenced.

Knysna Heads to Millwood
Return to the N2, turn left and drive through Knysna. The road skirts the lagoon, then crosses a concrete bridge. At the far end of the bridge turn right and take the road towards Brenton, which swings around and passes under the bridge; 1,6 km after the bridge, turn left and follow the signs downhill for 'Old Belvidere' to reach the picturesque Holy Trinity Church (see opposite).

Return to the road for Brenton and turn left. Note your kms as you cross the railway line. After 1,5 km, park in a well-marked, gravel-surfaced viewsite on your left. From here there is a splendid view over the whole Knysna region.

Drive on to Brenton-on-Sea. There is a hotel here, and you can walk down wooden steps for a short stroll along the beautiful beach.

Return to the N2 and turn right towards George. After 2 km on the N2, turn off right for Rheenendal.

Pass through the little settlement of Rheenendal, then turn right onto a gravel road for 'Millwood/Goldfields'. Stop at the Information Centre in front of the forestry office for a self-issuing permit. Spend some time here to digest the maps and other information.

Soon after, at Krisjan se Nek, there is a Big Tree picnic site on your left (braai places, water, toilets). Keep right here, following signs to Jubilee Creek. Where the road divides into three, keep left for 'Millwood/Jubilee Creek'. At the next fork keep left again, and follow the road down into Jubilee Creek to the picnic area (toilets, braai places, water from the river).

Driving back from Jubilee Creek, turn left at the fork for Millwood; 3,7 km along this road you pass a turn-off to the old town's cemetery on your right. Just after this, the road forks. The left road used to be Millwood's main street, but nothing of the town remains, except for a few fruit trees and flowers.

Unless you're going to explore the site of the town, take the road to the right, then at the next fork go right again. Follow this road, formerly St Patrick Street, to reach a large, landscaped area of the former Bendigo Mine property on your left. Park here and walk down to the open shed housing the steam engine, boiler and other machinery of the mining days. The accessible mine shafts are clearly signposted. The

The unspoilt stretch of sandy beach at Wilderness makes a memorable walk

MILLWOOD GOLD AND JUBILEE CREEK
In 1876 gold was discovered in the Knysna forests. Fortune-hunters began pouring into the area and the mining town of Millwood sprang up amid the many claims. In its heyday, Millwood could boast a post office, a periodic court, three competing newspapers, numerous shops and six hotels. Most of the houses in the town were built of corrugated iron, erected on a stone foundation.

The gold reefs proved thin and were difficult to work, so the miners gradually drifted away, many to the goldfields in the Transvaal. By 1900 only a few diehards remained and the goldfield was deproclaimed in 1924. All that is left are the cemetery, the Bendigo Mine tourist area and traces of old workings scattered about the forest.

Jubilee Creek is one of several sites where alluvial gold was panned. As you approach the picnic site, to the right of the causeway across the river, a pleasant footpath leads to an abandoned gold mine. The mine consists of just a single adit, but you will need a torch to explore it. A few hundred metres beyond the mine there is an impressive waterfall and a deep pool.

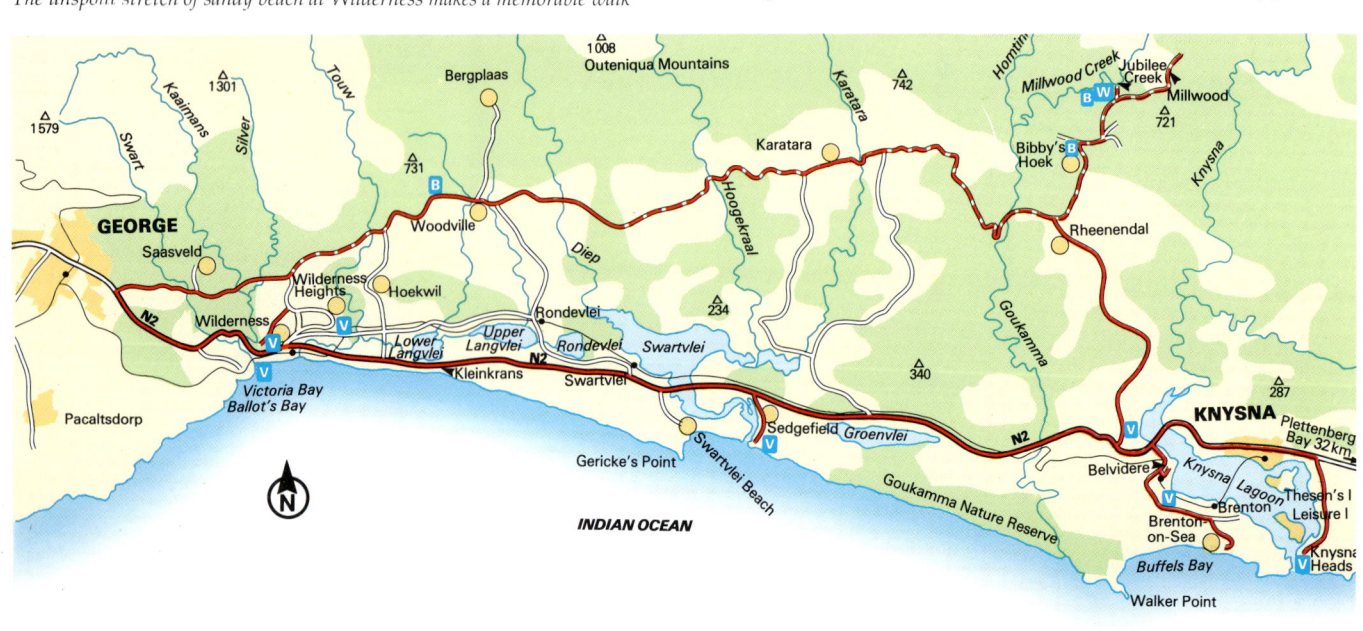

222

main Bendigo Tunnel reaches 200 m into the hillside and now houses a large bat population. (It can be reached by car – retrace your route and take the first left turn.)

From Millwood through the passes
Retrace your route past the forestry station and turn right onto the tarred road. The tar soon gives way to gravel and the road winds down to an iron girder bridge spanning the Homtini River. Beyond the bridge, the road climbs out of the gorge, leads through farmlands, then drops again to the Karatara River.

After crossing the bridge over the Karatara River, the road skirts the Karatara forestry settlement. The next pass leads through the gorge of the Hoogekraal River, and the one after this – with the only modern concrete bridge on the Passes Road – takes you across the Diep River.

The tar starts again soon after the second Ruigtevlei turn-off and, after this, you reach the small settlement of Woodville. Turn right onto the gravel road signposted 'Big Tree and Picnic Spot'. The picnic site to which this leads has braai places and toilets. From the car park, a short path leads across a wooden bridge to the Woodville Big Tree, an Outeniqua yellow-wood roughly 800 years old.

Return to the tarred road and turn right, noting your kms. After a little over 3 km, turn right onto a gravel road signposted 'George via Forest Rd'. The road now negotiates three more river-valley passes. Note your kms as you cross the Touw River; 4,6 km later, keep straight, onto the tar, for 'George'. You then cross the Silver River and, after this, the Kaaimans River. The entire Passes Road and the bridges over the Kaaimans and Silver rivers, have been proclaimed a national monument.

After climbing out of the Kaaimans valley, you pass Saasveld on your right: this is the Faculty of Forestry of the Port Elizabeth Technikon and the country's only training school for foresters. It is worth driving into the grounds to appreciate its beautiful setting. Some 5 km after Saasveld you reach the N2, shortly before entering George. Unless you want to stop in George, turn left onto the N2 towards Knysna.

The N2 crosses the Swart River and, immediately afterwards, the Kaaimans River. It then swings around the hillside overlooking the Kaaimans River mouth, presenting a splendid view of wild beaches and lakes stretching far into the distance. Stop in the designated parking area on the left at Dolphins Point and follow the footprints under the roadway to the viewsite.

Return to the carpark and drive on down the hill. At the bottom of the hill, turn left into the village of Wilderness. After passing the Wilderness Hotel, turn left at the circle and follow the signs for 'Heights Road'. This steep, tarred road leads to the plateau of Wilderness Heights after some 2,2 km. Just past the school, follow the sign on the left for 'Map of Africa' – this sideroad leads to a viewsite overlooking the Kaaimans River. A twist in the river encloses an area of wooded land that resembles fairly closely the map of Africa. Retrace your route to Wilderness and turn left for Knysna at the N2 intersection.

When you reach Sedgefield, turn right at the traffic lights. Drive around the traffic circle and continue straight towards the sea. From the parking area next to the lagoon mouth, a gently inclined boardwalk leads over the dunes to the beach. A short flight of concrete steps leads to a weathered bluff that was a favourite gathering-place of *Strandlopers* ('beach walkers', or pre-industrial, indigenous people who, for at least part of the year, lived by fishing and scavenging along the shore).

Return to the N2 and turn right for Knysna.

George Tourism Information 124 York Street
George 6530 Tel (0441) 74 4000
Knysna Publicity Association
40 Main St, Knysna 6570
Tel (0445) 82 5510

A tranquil evening vista typical of the country to the west of Sedgefield.

BELVIDERE CHURCH
'The little church dreams on in quietness,
Its ancient peace more vocal than a Psalm.'
– from *Memories of Belvidere* by OR Bridgman ca 1935.

In 1833, Captain Thomas Henry Duthie of the Seaforth Highlanders married Caroline, daughter of George Rex, and purchased from his father-in-law a large tract of land on the western shore of the Knysna Lagoon. On a gentle slope a few paces from the lagoon, Duthie built this church, with the help of several other families living in the region.

The church took five years to build, and is a faithfully reproduced miniature in the Norman style of the 11th and 12th centuries.

Belvidere church at Knysna.

THE STRAIGHT DOWN PLACE
The name *Knysna* is believed by some authorities to be a Khoikhoi word meaning 'straight down' – a reference to the sheer cliffs known as The Heads.

Knysna's most celebrated settler was George Rex, who arrived in 1804 and worked hard to develop Knysna as a port. Legend has made him an illegitimate son of George III of England, but this has never been proved. In 1817 the brig *Emu* struck a rock as she entered The Heads, but the *Podargus*, sent to salvage the *Emu*, entered and left the lagoon successfully. From then on, Knysna served as a port for small to medium-sized vessels, including Rex's own boat, the 127 ton *Knysna*.

Scene of the loss of the Emu *– the Knysna Heads watch over the dangerous but navigable channel leading into the sheltered lagoon.*

Pleasure boats laze at their moorings in Knysna Lagoon.

• GEORGE TO KNYSNA BY STEAM TRAIN •

A ride through the Lake District on the 'Outeniqua Choo-choo'

WHEN THE RAILWAY AGE reached George in 1907 after years of delay, the entire town turned out to watch the first train puff into the station. During the festivities, the archdeacon observed that its arrival would be like the kiss of the handsome prince that woke the Sleeping Beauty. Perhaps he was right – there is certainly a fairy-tale quality in a journey by steam train through this fascinating part of the Cape Garden Route.

The lakes route between George and Knysna is the last stretch of rail in the country still traversed regularly by steam locomotives, and the Outeniqua Choo-choo that works this line is known to steam enthusiasts worldwide. The locomotives used regularly are SAR Class 24 and 19D. Other classes used are 7A, GB, 14CRB, 19C and GO, while Class 32 diesels sometimes work the heavy goods trains. The passenger coaches are of the side-door, suburban type dating from 1893 to 1950.

The Choo-choo makes no special concessions for visitors – it is a goods train with usually just a single passenger coach attached at the end. The train leaves George daily (except Sundays and some public holidays) at 09h30 and 13h00, arriving in Knysna after a memorable journey of some two-and-a-half hours – stopping on the way at a host of quaint little places such as *Bleshoender* (bald chicken or the red-knobbed coot) and *Mielierug* (mealie ridge). Passengers may board and disembark at any of the stations (some no more than barren platforms) along the line.

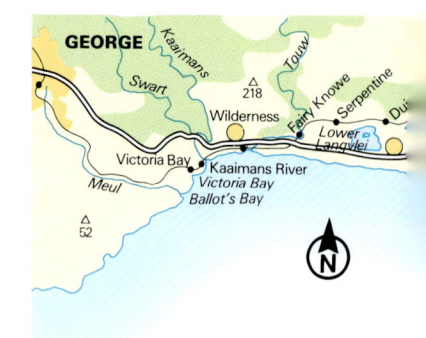

A hidden treasure chest

From George station, the line runs along the valley of the *Meul* (mill) River, with views down to the sea at Ballot's Bay – where a treasure chest is said to lie wedged in the rocks awaiting recovery. The first stop is Victoria Bay, immediately above the tiny beach. This is a popular surfing spot, with a small fishing jetty and children's paddling pool.

Soon after Victoria Bay the train enters a pair of tunnels, then emerges onto a bridge across the mouth of the Kaaimans River. The railings on the bridge are below the height of the carriage windows, and the train seems to be floating high above the river. From the bridge there are superb views, both up the river and out to sea. Soon afterwards there is a magnificent view on your right

Emerging from the second tunnel to cross the Kaaimans River mouth.

WESTERN CAPE

The Choo-choo steams out onto the long bridge over Knysna's lagoon.

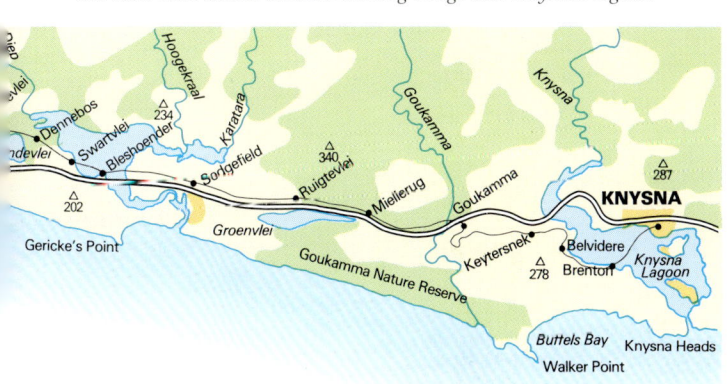

Meandering among the lakes
A narrow canal links Lower Langvlei to Upper Langvlei, which is linked in its turn to Rondevlei by yet another canal. The line passes along the northern shores of these lakes, offering tranquil views of small-scale farming operations, then turns south-east through pine forest and runs between Rondevlei and Swartvlei.

Swartvlei is by far the largest of the lakes in the region. The line runs along its shore, then crosses it at its southern end, shortly before arriving at Sedgefield. After Sedgefield, you travel the full length of Groenvlei, the only freshwater lake in the region, then climb through forest and wind down steeply into the vivid green of the Goukamma valley.

The climb up and out of the Goukamma valley involves a series of loops leading to Keytersnek. After this you begin to catch glimpses of Knysna Lagoon. The train stops at Belvidere, and again on the very edge of the lagoon at Brenton. After skirting the western shore, it swings out over the water and crosses the lagoon on a long wooden bridge, with Knysna station waiting at the far end.

Light basic refreshments are available on the train and at Knysna station. The licensed restaurant at George station opens at 10h00 daily, but is closed on Mondays out of season. To make enquiries or reservations (essential during the season), contact the Transnet Heritage Foundation in George, tel (0441) 73 8288 or in Knysna, tel (0445) 21361. For general enquiries, contact George Tourist Information, tel (0441) 74 4000.

Huffing and puffing out of Wilderness station in a blaze of early morning sun.

over the curving white sands of Wilderness beach, stretching away far into the distance.

Island of the camel's hump
The line descends gradually to the pretty Wilderness station, then crosses the mouth of the Touw River on an iron bridge. Soon after this it crosses the Touw a second time and passes (on your right) a small, rounded hill known as Fairy Knowe.

The line crosses the Touw River a third time, on a combined road and rail bridge, then travels alongside the Serpentine – a meandering waterway that links the Touw River to Lower Langvlei or Island Lake. As you pass the lake you see the island that gives it its name, known as *Drommedaris eiland* (dromedary island) because of its likeness to a camel's hump.

Across the Touw River a second time – the third will be on a narrow bridge where cars must share the roadway.

225

Over the Outeniqua Mountains to the Little Karoo and Cango Caves

Heading west from George, our route leads through the lush coastal terrace of the Garden Route to the sandy shores of Mossel Bay, then turns inland, over the Outeniqua Mountains to the Little Karoo – a dry land of ostriches and scattered whitewashed farmhouses – and the wonderland of the Cango Caves. All but some 35 km of the route is tarred.

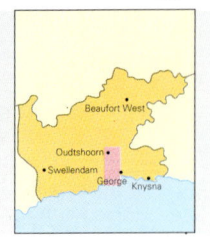

**George
Great Brak River
Robinson Pass
Oudtshoorn
Rus-en-Vrede
Cango Caves
Outeniqua Pass
250 – 270 km**

Leave George on CJ Langenhoven Street, heading towards Oudtshoorn. After passing the golf course on your left, turn left into Witfontein Road (signposted Heather Park/Blanco/Fancourt) and follow the road where it dips to the right to cross the Malgas River, with an old stone bridge to your left. Note your kms as you pass Fancourt Hotel entrance on your left, pass hop gardens and, after 2,3 km, go left at the fork for 'George Airport'.

Drive straight across the R102 and, after skirting the George Airport, turn right onto the N2 towards Mossel Bay. The N2 sweeps down across the coastal hills, offering splendid views over the sea to Mossel Bay and Cape St Blaize.

As the N2 descends to sea level, it crosses a bridge over the Great Brak River. At the far end of the bridge, turn left for 'R102/Great Brak River', and immediately turn left again. Drive back over the river on the old bridge, then turn right and cross the railway line. Pass the station, then turn right to reach 'The Island' by driving across one channel of the lagoon on a single-lane bridge. Park where convenient on the island (or park on the mainland and walk across the bridge). Several lanes between the holiday houses lead down to the beach – an attractive 30 – 40 minute walk. (If the water level is too high for this, drive around the lagoon to the western side.)

Great Brak River to Robinson Pass
Retrace your route across the old bridge to the western side of the Great Brak River, noting your kms at the end of the bridge. Do not turn right onto the N2, but continue straight on the R102 towards Little Brak River.

After almost 9 km, turn right and cross over the N2, then at the T-junction turn right again, for Oudtshoorn; 1,3 km after the T-junction the road forks – take the left-hand (tarred) road here, the other is signposted Riverside. Drive past a road on your right to Gonnakraal 2,2 km later and turn at the Oudtshoorn signpost, keeping to the tar. After another 200 m the tar ends – note your kms here. The road continues to climb, offering views of the Little Brak River and its green valley.

The road now winds among hills and farmlands, and offers increasingly spectacular views as it approaches the Outeniqua Mountains. After 13 km on the gravel there is a road on your right to Leeukloof – drive some 200 m along it, just over the hill, for the view, then return to the junction and continue on the main gravel road.

About 3 km later, turn right onto the tarred R328. After 2,5 km on the R328 you reach the Eight Bells Mountain Inn – the official entry point for the Ruitersbos Forest (see below).

From the Eight Bells Mountain Inn, continue on the R328 over the Robinson Pass. Viewsites and picnic spots dot the roadside, and it is interesting to note how the fynbos changes in character as the road climbs higher. This present Robinson Pass road follows the original Attaquas Kloof road built by Thomas Bain in 1869, and climbs to 860 m above sea level.

Robinson Pass to the Cango Caves
From the summit of the pass the road descends steeply into the Little Karoo, and the landscape becomes drier, with aloes dotting the hills; 1,5 km after the summit there is a picnic site on your right with fine views. As you descend into the Little Karoo, you can see the Groot Swartberg range shimmering on the horizon.

You are now in ostrich country, and it is possible to visit an ostrich show farm. You pass two (Safari and Highgate) as you drive towards Oudtshoorn and another (Cango) on the road between Oudtshoorn and the Cango Caves.

Shortly after the turn-off to Safari Farm you reach a T-junction – turn right for Oudtshoorn (see pages 228 - 9). At the second set of traffic lights turn left into Baron van Reede Street. As you turn, you see on your left a gracious old stone building that now houses the CP Nel Museum – noted for its ostrich exhibits. Park nearby to visit the museum. (Several establishments in Oudtshoorn offer lunch.)

Continue out of town on Baron van Reede Street, which becomes the main road to the Cango Caves. Note your kms as you leave Oudtshoorn. The road passes a crocodile ranch and cheetah park, an ostrich show farm and an angora rabbit show farm, then leads through Schoemanspoort, along the shady banks of the Grobbelaars River, where there are picnic sites on your left.

For an especially attractive picnic spot, turn right onto a road (tarred for 2,3 km) roughly 20 km after leaving Oudtshoorn; 10 km along this road you reach the Rus-en-Vrede picnic area (small entry fee, braai places, water, toilets). From the picnic area, a 2,5 km road and then a short footpath, lead to the Rus-en-Vrede waterfall, which plunges 80 m into a series of pools. (The path includes steps and narrow bridges, and is not recommended for small children.)

Retrace your route to the tarred road and turn right for the Cango Caves. The road leads directly into the parking area for the Cango Caves after roughly 6 km. Tours of the caves are conducted hourly, on the hour, daily except Christmas Day. You may choose from the two-chamber tour (30 minutes), the eight-chamber tour (about one hour) or the Full Adventure, which lasts some two hours. Leave Oudtshoorn an hour before your tour is due to start. For the latest information, contact the Klein Karoo Marketing Association; tel (0443) 22 6643, fax (0443) 22 5007, or the Cango Caves, tel (0443) 22 7410.

Cango Caves to George
Retrace your route through Schoemanspoort to Oudtshoorn. Drive the full length of Baron van Reede Street and continue along this same street where it veers left slightly and changes its name to Langenhoven Street, which eventually becomes the N12/R62 to George.

Some 31 km after leaving Oudtshoorn, turn right for George (the road to the left leads to Uniondale and Port Elizabeth). As you approach the Outeniqua Pass, the road again leads through hop gardens, and also numerous orchards of apples and pears.

The road rises steeply to the summit of the Outeniqua Pass (799 m), then winds down the southern slopes to the coastal plateau and George. There are beautiful vistas over the whole George area and the sea shimmering in the distance. Several parking areas along the route offer opportunities to enjoy the view.

Oudtshoorn Publicity Office
Voortrekker Road, Oudtshoorn 6620
Tel (0443) 22 2221
George Tourist Information
124 York Street, George 6530 Tel (0441) 74 4000

'The N2 sweeps down across the coastal hills...'.

EIGHT BELLS AND WALKING TRAILS
The Eight Bells Mountain Inn on the southern side of the Robinson Pass is the official start and finish of the Ruitersbos Forest Walk, laid out by the Department of Forestry. Entry is permitted between 08h00 and 16h00 (no dogs, vehicles, smoking or fires) and visitors must sign at the reception desk, where maps are available, before starting the walk. Information is also available on six 'Rooster Trails' that start and finish in the inn's garden and which range in duration from 30 minutes to two hours. These include Protea Hill and rambles through lush forest along the banks of mountain streams. Details and maps are available from the reception office at the inn. Outside the main building of the inn is an enormous oak tree reputed to have been planted in 1817, when the original title deed was granted by Lord Charles Somerset.

WESTERN CAPE

Visitors are dwarfed by the crystal wonderland lying hidden in the Cango Caves.

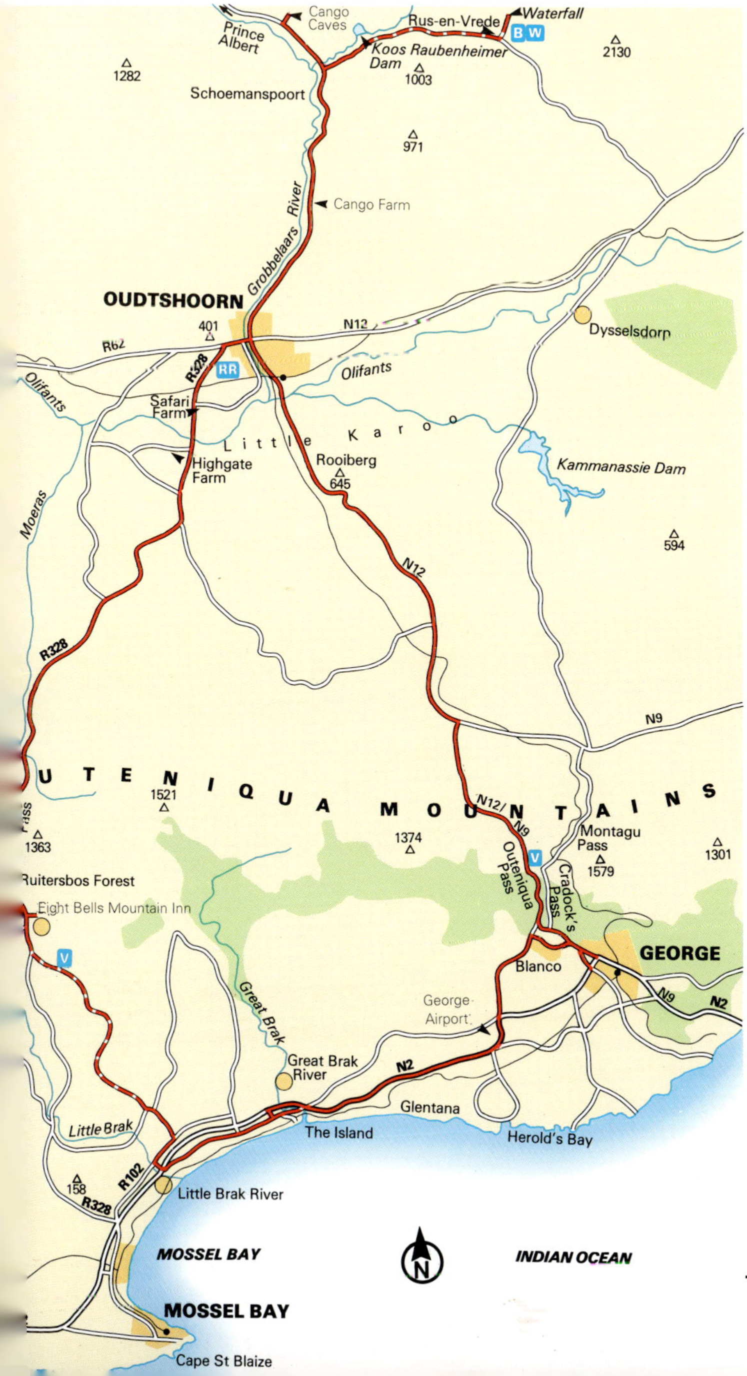

THE CAVES OF THE CANGO MOUNTAINS
The Cango Caves are regarded as one of South Africa's natural wonders. They owe their origin to a geological fault in the Swartberg mountains (which were known to the San as the Cango).

Water seeping through the limestone rock, over hundreds of thousands of years, created the present display of grand caverns ornamented with dripstone formations – stalagmites reaching up from the floor and stalactites hanging from the ceiling.

The cave sequence known as Cango One was discovered by a herdsman in 1780. Two large extensions of this original sequence were discovered relatively recently.

Looking east from the Outeniqua Pass, you can see the Montagu Pass of 1847.

BIRDS OF A FEATHER
Standing 2,4 m high and weighing up to 135 kg when fully grown, the commercially bred ostriches around Oudtshoorn are reminders of the great ostrich-feather boom around late 19th and early 20th centuries. At its height, there were more than 750 000 domesticated ostriches in the Little Karoo.

The boom lasted from 1870 until the start of World War I, when the wearing of ostrich feathers did not fit the austere image of the war years. Many farmers went bankrupt, although ostrich-farming did revive somewhat with a demand for ostrich skin, biltong, eggs and feathers. More recently, ostrich meat has become popular because of its minimal cholesterol content.

Ostrich 'derby' in the Little Karoo.

GEORGE
George is a holiday town with a history. The visitors who crowd it every summer follow in the steps of officials who established the settlement on St George's Day (23 April) 1811, and named it after the reigning King of England, George III.

The George Museum, in the old Drostdy, includes a splendid collection of Victorian bric-a-brac, sections on timber and forestry, mechanical musical instruments and a collection of intriguing fantasy paintings. About 100 m from the museum is a huge oak known as 'the slave oak'. Embedded in its trunk is a length of stout chain and an antique padlock. Legend has it that slaves were chained to the tree to be sold, but the happier truth is that chain and padlock were used to secure the tennis club's roller.

Harvesting hops in the Blanco district.

227

Across the Swartberg and through the brightly coloured Meiringspoort

The Grootrivier (great river) has sculpted colourful Meiringspoort gorge through the barrier of the Swartberg range, and our route follows the road that now winds along this river's bank. First, however, we cross the mountains from south to north by means of the soaring Swartberg Pass. Four-fifths of the route is tarred, the rest is gravel.

**Oudtshoorn
Swartberg Pass
Prince Albert
Meiringspoort
De Rust
180 – 200 km**

IF YOU ARE CONSIDERING this drive in winter, first check with the police in Oudtshoorn or Prince Albert that the Swartberg Pass has not been blocked by snow.

Drive along Oudtshoorn's Baron van Reede Street, following the signs towards the Cango Caves. A number of houses in this street, particularly on the left-hand side, are relics of the ostrich feather boom, and show ornate cast-ironwork, turrets and balconies.

The road out of town is lined by jacaranda and bluegum trees, and on both sides there are tobacco-drying sheds, loosely built of reeds to allow for ventilation. A little further, the road runs alongside the winding, willow-shaded Grobbelaars River through Schoemanspoort.

The Grobbelaars River bridge marks the end of Schoemanspoort; 3,4 km beyond the bridge, turn left onto the R328 for 'Prince Albert/ Swartberg Pass'. Once on the pass, the narrow road, steep gradients and many sharp corners make the route unsuitable for towing.

Soon the road passes De Hoek caravan park and holiday resort, and after a further 9,5 km the tarred road ends. The steep gradients and sharp turns of the pass dictate low speeds, but the gravel surface is almost always in excellent condition.

Swartberg Pass to Prince Albert

Some 1,5 km after the start of the gravel you pass the barely visible ruins of two buildings on your right, and soon after this you reach the first picnic site on the pass, in a cluster of pine trees. About 1 km after the picnic site, the road approaches a left-hand bend beyond which you can see a steep ascent marked by a dry-stone wall. At the apex of the bend, a built-up section carries the road across a ravine. As you approach the bend you can see the date 1887 chiselled into a rock on the culvert. (The date 1886 may be seen about 3,7 km further on, where the road crosses another ravine – showing that the pass was built from north to south.)

THE SWARTBERG PASS

This is one of the most spectacular of South Africa's mountain passes, climbing over the Swartberg range in wide loops and reaching a height of 1 585 m. The pass was completed by Thomas Bain in 1887 after years of difficult work and numerous stoppages in the winter months due to heavy falls of snow and hail.

The appearance of the pass has changed little since its construction, and the mountain slopes along which it makes its way are richly covered in indigenous wildflowers.

Before attempting the pass during winter weather, inquire locally in case the road has been closed.

Fields and fynbos form a rural patchwork amid the foothills of the Swartberg.

The road snakes over the Swartberg Pass.

OSTRICH CAPITAL OF THE WORLD

Oudtshoorn was founded in 1847 and named after Baron Pieter van Rheede van Oudtshoorn, who had been appointed governor of the Cape in the 18th century but who had died on the way to take up his appointment. The town is the principal centre of the Little Karoo – the 250 km long sunburned plain that lies between the Swartberg in the north and the Langeberg and Outeniqua ranges in the south.

Oudtshoorn is also the unrivalled ostrich capital of the world, and many grandiose houses – the so-called ostrich feather palaces – date from the days of the ostrich feather boom. The CP Nel Museum in the heart of the town is noted for its many ostrich-related exhibits.

Ostriches are a familiar sight in the countryside near De Rust and Oudtshoorn.

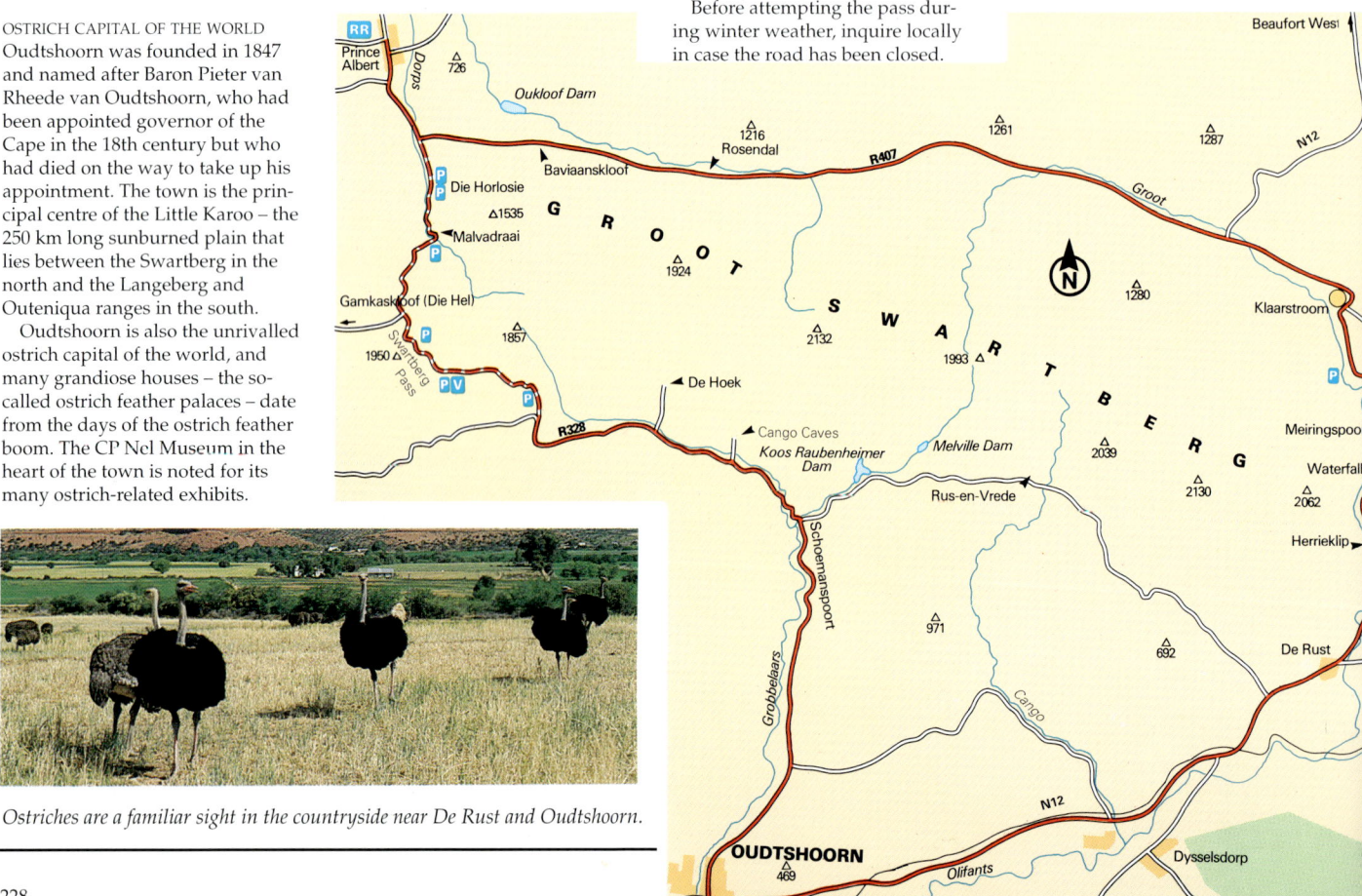

After another 2 km you come to picnic sites with magnificent views over the rolling fields of the Cango Valley.

As you reach the summit of the pass, notice on the left side of the road a stone cairn surmounted by a bronze plaque. This records the story of the construction of the pass (see opposite). The views from here are endless.

About 1 km beyond the summit are clumps of pine trees and the ruins of fairly large buildings. These served as a convict station, and later as the tollhouse and the tollkeeper's residence. There are also picnic sites here.

At 2,7 km from the summit you pass the turn-off to Gamkaskloof, also known as The Hell. (This is a daunting road of 57 km and is not recommended unless you are determined to explore more deeply into the mountains.) A picnic spot on the right, at Malvadraai, is named for the *Abutilon sonneratianum* (wildemalva; butter-and-cheese) which puts out its bright orange and yellow flowers in early spring. The road passes stone quarries, then runs along the foot of towering cliffs to reach a picnic site near the *Tweedewater* (second water) causeway. After a further 600 m you come to a second picnic site at *Eerstewater* (first water). If you study the rocks to the right of the road you will see, just below the highest point, the feature known as *Die Horlosie*, or the clock face. It's unmistakable once you find it.

At the T-junction with the tarred R407, turn left for Prince Albert, a particularly attractive country village (see pages 230 – 1). The Hotel Swartberg and other establishments, all in Church Street, offer meals. The hotel and a handful of guest-houses offer accommodation if you decide to stay overnight.

Prince Albert to Oudtshoorn
Retrace your route out of Prince Albert, but drive past the road from the Swartberg Pass on which you arrived, and note your kms. Follow the tarred road for 'R407/Klaarstroom'. Among other old buildings you pass are the farmhouse and cemetery of Baviaanskloof. The date on the gable reads 1837, but the house is believed to be even older.

At the T-junction with the N12/R23, turn right. Just over 1 km after passing the village of Klaarstroom on the right, the road enters Meiringspoort, where there are frequent picnic sites (with toilets); 8,2 km into the pass there is a parking area with shady picnic sites on your left, signposted as a waterfall. The waterfall (with rock pools) is reached after an easy 300 m walk from the parking area.

At 2,5 km beyond this parking area, on the right side of the road, you can see the 'Herrieklip', on which CJ Langenhoven chiselled the name of his famous elephant – joking at the time (1929) that this rock would be its memorial.

After leaving Meiringspoort the road passes through De Rust, and 34,5 km further you enter Oudtshoorn on Voortrekker Street.

Oudtshoorn Publicity Office Civic Centre
Voortrekker Road, Oudtshoorn 6620
Tel (0443) 22 2221
George Tourist Information 124 York Street
George 6530 Tel (0441) 74 4000

On a country road near Klaarstroom – a 19th-century pace of progress.

The brilliantly coloured and fiercely twisted rock strata of the Swartberg.

MEIRINGSPOORT
It was Petrus Meiring of the farm De Rust who, in 1854, followed the Grootrivier gorge through the colourful Swartberg range to emerge eventually on the southern edge of the Great Karoo.

For many years this remained the sole link between Prince Albert and the Little Karoo – a rough track through the gorge that forded the river some 30 times and was often washed away. The present tarred road was constructed only recently.

A feature of the Swartberg range is the dramatic folding of its sandstone strata – clearly visible both in Meiringspoort and along the Swartberg Pass.

*The **Herrieklip** in Meiringspoort, neatly carved by Langenhoven himself.*

HERRIEKLIP
In his book *Sonde met die Bure* ('Trouble with the Neighbours'), CJ Langenhoven wrote of the bizarre exploit of Herrie the elephant pulling an old tramcar from Oudtshoorn to Meiringspoort.

In a gentle tilt at councillors he described a confrontation between the mayor on the one hand and the elephant plus tramcar on the other.

Herrie is commemorated at both the start and the finish of his immortal journey – in Oudtshoorn's main street by a statue of him, and in Meiringspoort by the Herrieklip, a sandstone rock on which Langenhoven himself carved the elephant's name.

• EXPLORING PRINCE ALBERT ON FOOT •

Typical Prince Albert gables grace 52 Church Street (left) and 4 De Beer Street.

The 1850 watermill of the Alberts family – millers for more than a century.

A town of quaint gables and a forgotten gold rush

ON THE SOUTHERN edge of the thirsty land of the Great Karoo lies Prince Albert – an enchanting little oasis watered by mountain streams from the Swartberg range. Here the peaceful atmosphere of the 19th century lingers on, preserved along with the town's unique and quaint architecture.

Settlement in the area dates back as far as 1762, when a few loan farms were granted at what was described as *agter de Roggelandsberg in de Koup*. (*Koup*, also spelt *gouph*, is a Khoikhoi word believed to mean 'flat, open plain'). In that year, Zacharias de Beer settled on the farm Kweekvallei. He was born in 1719 and farmed at Drakenstein before trekking to this remote valley. A congregation of the Dutch Reformed Church was formed in 1842, and the settlement became known as Albertsburg, changing in 1845 to Prince Albert, in honour of Queen Victoria's consort.

A convenient place to begin a walk through the town is the *Hotel Swartberg* **(1)** in Church (*Kerk*) Street, where there are shady trees under which to park. The hotel dining room contains an enormous, ornate Victorian sideboard that dates from the great Prince Albert gold rush of 1890 – 1.

Two coach lines – the Welcome Line and the Fuller & Coetzee's Line – brought eager diggers from the railhead at Fraserburg Road. There was a butchery and a few buildings, and there was even a newspaper – the *Gouph Gold News*. But the settlement was just a tent town that sprang up on the veld north of the village. The gold was soon worked out, and most of the adventurers drifted away. A few persevered with steam-driven drills, but the reef eluded them, and peace returned.

The Prince Albert gable
Opposite the hotel is *56 Church Street* **(2)**, set unusually far back from the road. Its pedimented gable is dated 1841 – the year before the town was officially established – and the design of the end gables is not typical of Prince Albert.

A feature of the town is the great number of gabled houses that have survived, including a number with so-called Prince Albert gables. These *holbol* (convex-concave) gables, sometimes supported on short pilasters and with characteristic horizontal mouldings, are thought to be the work of Carel Lotz, an artisan who had worked in Tulbagh.

Head south along Church Street to find, on the corner of Deurdrif Street, *number 52* **(3)**, which has a typical example of the Prince Albert gable, dated 1850 and bearing the letters ACT. These are the initials of a member of the Theron family.

Cross Deurdrif Street and pass Chaplin Street on your right. The *Fransie Pienaar Museum* **(4)** is at 42 Church Street. This building was once the home of the Haak family, and also served for a while as the town's hospital. The museum (small admission fee) contains relics of the Prince Albert gold rush, a collection of family bibles, Cape furniture, domestic items, firearms, old vehicles and farm implements.

Diagonally opposite the museum there is an interesting *group of old houses* **(5)**, starting with 53 Church Street. This building has no front gables, but it has end gables with little waisted pediments. Number 51, dated 1858, is linked to number 49 and to number 47, which is thatched and has a gable dated 1852.

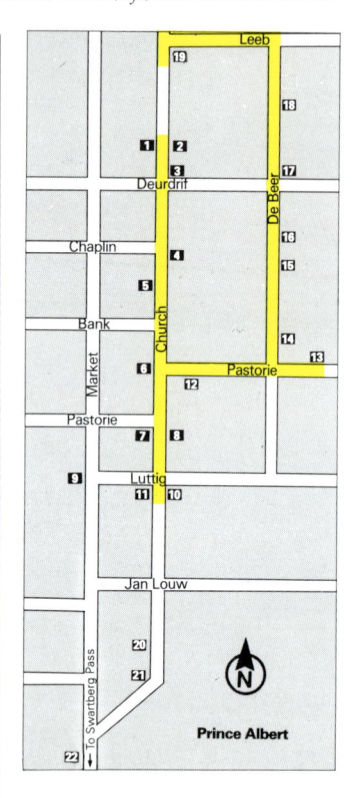

Pass Bank Street on your right to reach the handsome *Dutch Reformed Church* **(6)**, also on your right and facing Pastorie Street. Built in 1865 in the form of a Greek

De Beer Street, with the old cinema and gabled 19th-century homes.

230

cross, it has castellated gables and tower, and originally may have had a thatched roof. During the Anglo-Boer War a sandbag fort was built in its grounds.

End-seats and fanlights

Continue along Church Street to *number 23* **(7)**, on your right. This building has retained its two typical Prince Albert gables. Opposite is *number 24* **(8)**, a double-storey Georgian building known as Huis Krige. The stoep has end seats, and a fine fanlight surmounts the front door. It is thought that this was originally a single-storey building, but since the 'new' floors and ceilings are of yellowwood, it was probably converted at an early date.

As you reach Luttig Street, look right to see the old double-storey *watermill* **(9)** in Market Street. Across Luttig Street, on your left, is *20 Church Street* **(10)**, a fairly plain double-storey Victorian home of 1885. *Number 15* **(11)**, on the opposite side of Church Street, dates from 1858, and is known locally as *die doktershuis* (the doctor's house). Each of the three doors facing the street has an attractive fanlight, and the gable is quite unlike any other in the town, although it still has traces of the Prince Albert elements.

Victorian parsonage

Turn around here, return to Pastorie Street, and turn right. The first house on your right is the *Dutch Reformed parsonage* **(12)**, a late-Victorian building dated 1892, with three tall chimneys of red facebrick. Ornamentation is of wood rather than iron, and it shows the vogue for rustication – 'the imitation of rough rustic work' – in the projections cut in the plaster to resemble massive stonework at the corners and around the doors and windows.

Cross De Beer Street to reach, on your left, a fine example of the smaller *Victorian house* **(13)**. It has retained all its original cast iron, including ornamentation along the ridge line of the roof, which was intended to discourage birds from perching.

Return along Pastorie Street to De Beer Street and turn right. *Number 4* **(14)** has a gable dated 1854 and has retained its thatch – but this is now covered by an iron roof. The house was formerly occupied by a man known to his fellow townspeople as *Swartbaard* (Blackbeard) le Grange. *Number 8* **(15)** has a typical Prince Albert gable (dated 1860), as does *number 12* **(16)**, which dates from about 1850. The verandahs of these houses are all later additions. The little building adjoining number 12 served as the town's first (and no doubt cramped) cinema.

Cross Deurdrif Street to reach, on your right, *a double-T shaped house* **(17)** which, unlike most of the houses in the town, does not face the street. Instead it faces north, with its back to Deurdrif Street. Its gable with the date 1851 and the letters WJG, can be seen clearly from De Beer Street.

Number 22 **(18)**, also on your right, is just one room deep, and has a tall gable that seems to owe nothing to the influence of Carel Lotz. Houses like this one frequently had a lean-to addition (*afdak*) built at the front or back.

Turn left into Leeb Street, passing two old thatched cottages on your right, then turn left into Church Street. You pass *number 68* **(19)** on your left, a charming cottage with elaborate fretwork on its verandah.

If time permits, continue your exploration of Prince Albert's historic buildings by car, driving south along Church Street past a number of other interesting houses. Particularly worth noting is *number 5* **(20)**, on your right, which has been described as having 'one of the purest examples of the Prince Albert gable'. It was once the parsonage of the Dutch Reformed mission church.

Number 1 **(21)**, also on your right, has an unusually complex Prince Albert gable dated 1856. It was one of a number of houses built by Jan Luttig, a Member of the old Cape Parliament who campaigned for the right to use Dutch in the House, and whose name has been recorded on the old Taal Monument at Burgersdorp (see pages 178 – 9).

Where Church Street meets Market Street, turn left into Christina de Wit Street. On your right is *29 Market Street* **(22)**, which was the home of the miller. It formerly had a thatched roof, and retains its *brandsolder* (fireproof attic) formed by a ceiling of reeds and clay which, it was hoped, would be a fireproof layer if the thatch caught fire.

The mill

Prince Albert's best-known landmark is its watermill, to the left of the road on the outskirts of the town, on the way to the Swartberg Pass. The millhouse is open daily during ordinary business hours. Built in 1850, the mill was owned by the Alberts family for more than 100 years. The mill's wheel, 2,4 m in diameter, is of the overshot type – turned by the action of water falling onto it. To save wear on the restored machinery, the water is led to a point just beyond the wheel. The millstones were brought by ox-wagon all the way from the George district.

A Victorian double storey of 1885.

The lovely Dutch Reformed parsonage with its late-Victorian embellishments.

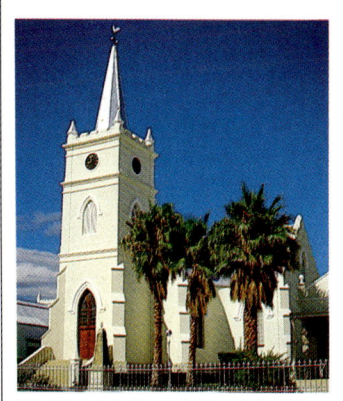

The Dutch Reformed Church building.

The museum's cool, tranquil interior.

The building that is now Prince Albert's museum was once the town hospital.

To the magic mountain through the Seven Weeks' Pass

South of the Great Karoo plains around Laingsburg, rolling hills swell into the sandstone peaks of the Klein Swartberg range. Rivers have etched their way through the seemingly impenetrable rock and the slow erosion has exposed contorted strata that tower high above our winding route into the Little Karoo. About half the route is tarred.

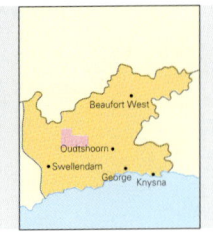

**Laingsburg
Seweweekspoort
Amalienstein
Zoar
Hoeko
Ladismith
200 – 220 km**

Turn south out of Laingsburg's main street between the buildings of the Standard Bank and the Co-operative and note your kms. Some 700 m out of town, you pass under the railway bridge.

At 13 km you pass a turn-off on your left to Floriskraal Dam (the entrance is reached after 7,5 km along this gravel road) and, later, pass a gravel road on your right to Ladismith. Soon afterwards the road crosses a river.

The road surface changes to gravel about 30 km from Laingsburg and soon emerges from among the hills, giving clear views of the Klein Swartberg range. After a further 23 km the hills and mountains close in again. Just short of 2 km later there are some spectacular rocky outcrops on the left.

Some 71 km from Laingsburg the road forks: go right here for Seweweekspoort and Ladismith. The ruins of the original tollhouse are on the left at the fork. Traffic through this poort was infrequent, and the ghost of a lonely toll-keeper is said to haunt the spot.

Seweweekspoort to Hoeko

Immediately after the fork, the road enters *Seweweekspoort* (seven weeks' pass). This follows the river between towering walls of sandstone that in many places almost shut out the sun. On the left, after 2 km, are the ruins of one of the convict stations that housed the labourers who built the original road.

After a further 1,7 km, on the right, is a picnic site (with toilets). On the left 2,2 km later there are braai sites and, 400 m beyond, also on the left, there is another picnic site in front of a large rock overhang. More picnic sites dot the roadside throughout the poort. Passing traffic – what there is of it – tends to make them rather dusty places.

Shortly after the road emerges from the poort, you pass a number of ruined buildings. At the T-junction opposite the old mission village of Amalienstein, turn right onto tar (R62),

Laingsburg's handsome Dutch Reformed Church – unscathed by floods.

SURVIVOR OF THE FLOODWATERS

Laingsburg was laid out on the farm Vischkuil along the banks of the Buffalo River in 1881 and named after John Laing, Commissioner for Crown Lands at the Cape. Growth has never been great in Laingsburg and much of the town was devastated by a flood during its centenary year, but here and there in the side streets are clusters of quaint Victorian buildings with much curved corrugated iron and ornamental cast-iron work.

The original Dutch Reformed Church dates from the earliest years of the town, as does the Lutheran Mission Church. There is a small private museum of local history in Laingsburg's public library.

An isolated cottage among fantastic rock strata typical of the route.

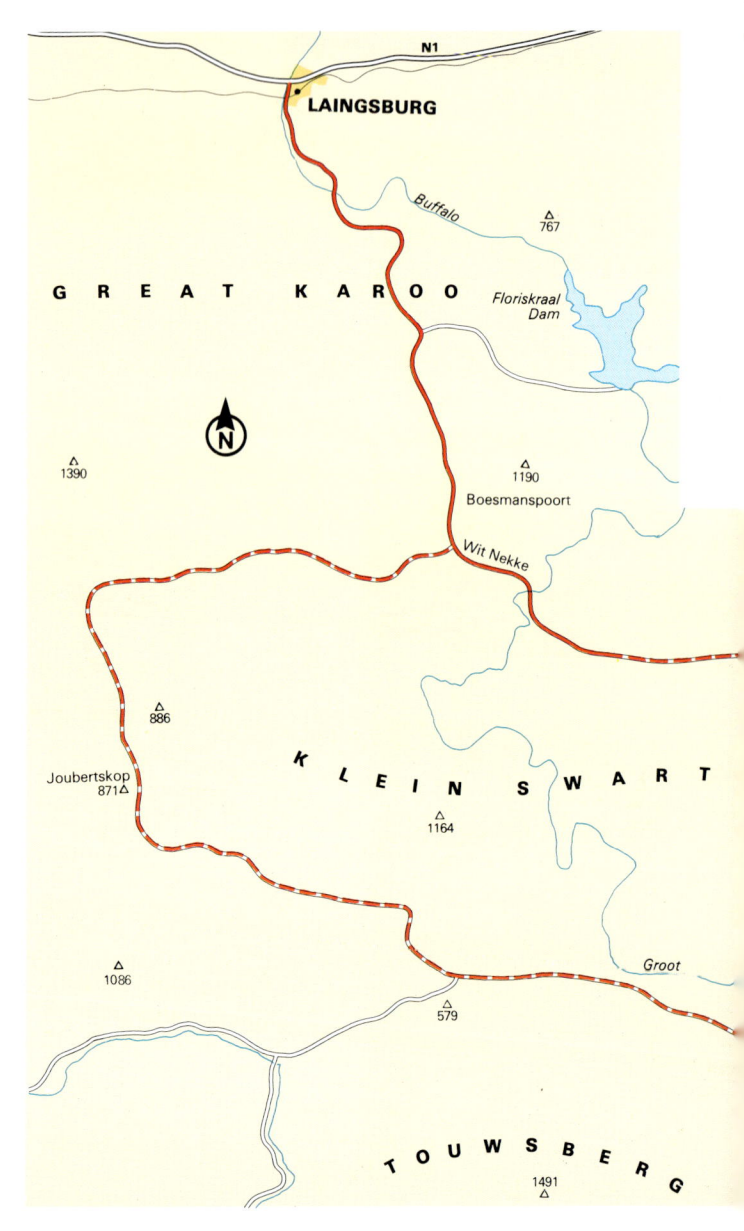

noting your kms. A few kilometres further you come to the still older mission village of Zoar on your left (see below).

Some 9,3 km after the Amalienstein T-junction, turn right for Hoeko; 2,2 km later, on your right, is the house in which the author and poet CJ Langenhoven was born. The T-shaped farmhouse on your right 500 m beyond is believed to have been the original Hoeko homestead, dating from about 1810.

Hoeko to Laingsburg

The road changes to gravel 16 km after you last noted your kms, and, after passing a reconstructed water-seepage tunnel and an old crane, enters Ladismith roughly 9 km later. (There are hotels and guest houses in the town, and a public swimming pool.)

Note the attractive old buildings of the Rhenish Mission before you turn right into Van Riebeeck Street, and drive west out of the town. After about 100 m, on your right is the old synagogue – a reminder of the role Jewish immigrants played in developing the country districts. Note your kms here. The road passes vineyards and irrigated fields before entering an area of rocky, scrub-covered hills, with the cleft summit of *Towerkop* (enchanted peak) on your right at the edge of the Klein Swartberg mountain range.

After some 18,5 km, cross a bridge over the Groot River, the road surface changing to gravel 7,5 km later. Continue on this road, past a turn-off on your left to Montagu, through a number of cattle grids and sharp left and right turns. The road eventually enters a gorge in which the rock strata are almost vertical on your right, yet horizontal in other places.

After about 48 km, turn left for Laingsburg at the T-junction with the tarred road on which you travelled south when starting out.

Captour Rendezvous Centre, 3 Adderley Street Cape Town 8001 Tel (021) 418 5202
AA Office AA House, 7 Martin Hammerschlag Way, Cape Town 8001 Tel (021) 21 1550
Ladismith Municipality Church Street Ladismith 6885 Tel (028) 551 1023

Seweweekspoort – a geological showcase.

A tree-lined lane leads up to the church in Amalienstein mission village.

The attractive Protea aristata.

ZOAR AND AMALIENSTEIN

Zoar, named after the Biblical city of palms, was founded in 1817 by the South African Missionary Society. It was taken over for a while by the Berlin Missionary Society in 1843, but many members of the congregation protested about, among other things, the introduction of crucifix and candles, so the Berlin Missionary Society established another mission at a nearby site. The new mission and village were named Amalienstein in honour of their chief patron, Baroness Amalie von Stein. The mission at Zoar eventually came under the control of the Dutch Reformed Mission Church.

THE SEVEN WEEKS' PASS

There are several explanations of the name of *Seweweekspoort* (seven weeks' pass), including the quaint notion that brandy smugglers used the route to evade revenue collectors – the detour taking them seven weeks to negotiate by ox-wagon.

The likeliest theory is that the name is a corruption of *Zerwick se poort*, after the Reverend Zerwick, one of the founders of the mission at Amalienstein.

The rocky gorge is overlooked by the 2 325 m Seweweekspoort Peak, highest in the Swartberg ranges, and the road is lined by fantastically curved and broken rock strata that tower high above.

A RARE BEAUTY

The *Protea aristata*, discovered only in 1928, was later believed to be extinct, as no further specimens were found for 25 years. But then a clump of five of the plants was found close to the road in Seweweekspoort, and others have now been sighted higher up the mountain slopes.

LADISMITH AND ITS MAGIC PEAK

Dominating the Little Karoo town of Ladismith are the twin pinnacles of *Towerkop* (enchanted peak). Legend has it that one night a *heks* (witch) cleft the towering rock in two with her magic wand when she found to her fury that she was unable to cross the mountain top.

Ladismith was the second town to bear the name of the wife of Governor Sir Harry Smith. Ladysmith in KwaZulu-Natal was founded two years earlier, in 1850, and the spelling of the Cape town was later changed to its present form to distinguish between the two. There are many quaint and beautiful old buildings in the town, particularly in Church Street.

A Sleeping Beauty trail through Kannaland to the Cowherds' River

From tranquil Riversdale, two old passes bring you to Herbertsdale, and the bustling N2 leads on into Mossel Bay, known for its museums and its lovely beaches. The return is via a coastal road that loops down to attractive resorts and a new nature reserve, and the breathtaking activities at the Gourits River bridges. About 90 km of the route is on gravel roads.

Riversdale
Garcia's Pass
Cloete's Pass
Herbertsdale
Mossel Bay
Gouritsmond
350 – 370 km

SET OFF ON THE Garcia's Pass road (R323), for Ladismith, which leaves Riversdale between the showgrounds and the grain silos on your left and Oakdale Agricultural College on your right soon after. Ahead of you is the Langeberg range with its famous Sleeping Beauty, an unusual mountain profile suggesting the fairytale princess who slept for 100 years. The road rises gently into the Langeberg through the Garcia State Forest and Garcia's Pass.

Some 19 km from the town is the old Tollhouse, built in 1877, operational until 1918 and now a national monument. Note your kms here and turn right at 6,2 km, opposite the farm Muiskraal, onto a gravel road for Herbertsdale and Van Wyksdorp.

Muiskraal to Mossel Bay

Features of this road are the numerous cattle grids and the sturdy stone fence and gate posts. Keep straight for Herbertsdale at 22 km, where a road on the left leads to Van Wyksdorp. Keep straight at the intersection at 33 km, after which fields appear more developed and include one with a fine vineyard. At 51 km a sign warns motorists to engage lowest gear and, immediately after, the road descends dramatically to the Groot River and a single-lane bridge.

Some 13 km further on, the road improves and winds into the protea-covered hills of Cloete's Pass, where there are the remains of a stone fort on your left and two more forts on the hill on your right. These forts were built by men of the Mossel Bay District Mounted Troops during the Anglo-Boer War in 1901; 6 km south of the mountains you reach the hamlet of Herbertsdale. Follow the tarred R327 for 38 km to the N2 and turn left, to reach Mossel Bay some 12 km later.

Mossel Bay to Riversdale

When you leave Mossel Bay, note your kms at the intersection of Church and Marsh streets (Marsh Street leads to the westbound N2). After 17 km, turn left for Vleesbaai, Fransmanshoek, Gouritsriviermond and Boggomsbaai. Note your kms and turn left again after 11,5 km for Boggomsbaai, reached after a further 3 km. A paved path leads to the wide, sandy beach on the west-curving bay. Return to the main road and turn left.

Other sideroads lead to the attractive resorts of Vleesbaai and Fransmanshoek (considered to be one of the finest fishing spots on the entire South African coast), and Kanonpunt. Although it is private property, Kanonpunt is interesting for three cannons, salvaged from the wreck of the French warship, *Le Fortune*, and mounted inside the main gate. The safe landing of her crew of 440 men in 1763 led to the naming of Fransmanshoek.

Some 2 km after the road to Kanonpunt, turn left for Gouritsmond. Portuguese sailors of the 15th century named this estuary *Rio dos Vaqueiros* or 'river of the cowherds'. Cross the Gourits River causeway and, 6,5 km further, turn left at the crossroads for Gouritsmond on the R325. You reach this little resort 8 km later. Swimming is dangerous at the mouth of the river, but there is an easily accessible, large tidal pool; long beaches and exciting angling prospects make for good coastal holidays here.

Return to the crossroads, turn left for Stilbaai and turn left again, 7,5 km later, at a sign indicating 'Gouriqua', to reach the entrance to the Rein's Nature Reserve of 3 550 ha with 7,5 km of coast. The pristine lowland fynbos encompassing a variety of habitats presents a perfect picture of an unspoilt coastline. There is a wide range of flora and fauna, even including rare and endangered butterflies. An unequalled diversity of edible fish as well as harmless sharks and skates are found along the coast. A daily fee is charged per car, a selection of self-catering accommodation is available and an attractive restaurant and bar overlook spectacular rocks and seascape.

Leave the reserve and return to the R325, turning left for the N2 and 'Albertinia' at the crossroads. Views over the winding Gourits River are splendid as it gouges its way through rich agricultural lands to the sea. Some 27 km from the reserve you reach the N2.

Turn right, to reach the Gourits River bridges some 7 km later. The spectacular sports of bungee jumping and bridge jumping are well established here and weekends are especially busy. Park on the Mossel Bay side of the new (1977) bridge and you will see the 1892 Victorian road bridge, 65 m above the riverbed, from which daring young people hurl themselves, attached by a harness to elastic ropes in the case of the bungee jumpers, or a trapeze that swings between the two bridges, for bridge jumping.

Recross the new Gourits River bridge for an easy 46 km drive back to Riversdale along the N2. If you have time, stop along the way to explore the little town of Albertinia.

Riversdale Municipality Van den Berg Street Riversdale 6770 Tel (02933) 32418
Mossel Bay Marketing Association cr Church and Market streets, Mossel Bay 6500 Tel (0444) 91 2202

MOSSEL BAY

The town's modern history dates back to 3 February 1488, when Bartolomeu Dias anchored his caravel in a cove now known as Munro's Bay. A replica of the caravel is in the Maritime Museum; the Shell Museum has displays illustrating the history and use of shells by man, while the local history museum deals with cultural and civic affairs. The Post Office Tree is an ancient milkwood in the branches of which a 15th-century ship's commander left a letter in a sea boot. A year later it was found by a captain en route to India and delivered, and so Africa's first postal service started. But people lived here as long as 80 000 years ago; their relics and artefacts have been identified by archaeologists at the cave below St Blaize lighthouse at the Point. The busy harbour serves both commercial and leisure marine interests.

Fine beaches add to the town's attractions. Munro's Bay is always calm, the wide sands of Santos Beach provide sheltered swimming and a replica of the Brighton Pavilion dominates the beach. *De Bakke*, named after the drinking troughs used by old transport riders' oxen and horses, is now a modern accommodation complex fronted by neat lawns, while Pansy Beach and Dias Beach lead on round the curve of the magnificent bay. The dark blob of Seal Island provides a focal point for sailing and boat trips.

The Julius Gordon Africana Centre in Riversdale.

RIVERSDALE'S AFRICANA CENTRE

Julius Gordon and Theodore Versveld were friends who were proud to call Riversdale their home town. They have left it a heritage any town would envy. Gordon was an attorney who, over the years, built up a fine collection of furniture and South African artworks. When Gordon mentioned that he proposed leaving his collections to the people of his town, Versveld decided to bequeath his home, an attractive Georgian-style dwelling, for use as an Africana centre. The two friends combined their bequests and the result is that valuable and fascinating collections are successfully housed and displayed at the present Africana Centre.

Among the South African artists represented are Thomas Bowler, Terence McCaw, Gregoire Boonzaaier, Jan Volschenk, Pieter Wenning, Irma Stern and Maggie Laubser.

A previous curator, Japie Dekenah, was an enthusiastic photographer, botanist and archaeologist, and added his own collection of arrowheads, Khoikhoi pottery, hand-axes and other artefacts that form a compelling display. The Centre is open from 10h00 to 13h00 on weekdays and at other times by appointment through the Riversdale Municipality.

WESTERN CAPE

A replica caravel that has braved the open ocean.

To those with the eyes (and imagination) to see her, the Langeberg discloses Sleeping Beauty.

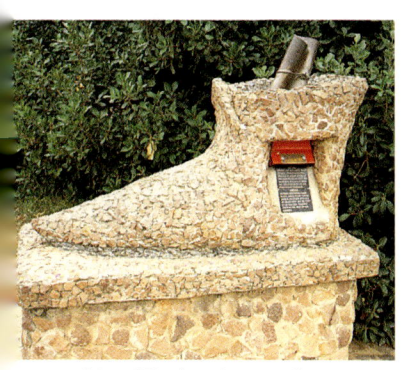

Mossel Bay's unique postbox.

MOSES GARCIA,
INDEPENDENT SETTLER

Maurice Garcia, born Moses Rodrigues Garcia in London in 1800, was a Jewish 1820 settler who paid his own passage to South Africa. From Algoa Bay he came to George and, starting as a magistrate's interpreter, became postmaster. His wife bore him 11 children; after his request for better remuneration to support his large family, he was appointed Civil Commissioner and Resident Magistrate at Richmond, Cape. In 1864 he was transferred to Riversdale, where he held office until his retirement in 1877. Garcia was instrumental in having a pass constructed through the Langeberg to link Riversdale with Ladismith. In 1875 it was opened and named in his honour. He died in 1884 and, although born a Sephardic Jew, he was buried in St Matthew's churchyard and rests together with his beloved wife, Anna Niepoth, in a modest tomb.

An important archaeological site surrounds the lighthouse at Cape St Blaize.

RURAL RIVERSDALE

This small town of gentle beauty and charm, set among fragrant, rolling hills with the 'Sleeping Beauty mountain' as backdrop, serves as a gateway to the Little Karoo and a centre for a thriving agricultural community. Founded in 1848 and named after Harry Rivers, a former magistrate and, later, Cape Colonial Treasurer, the town boasts an Anglican church designed by Sophie Gray, wife of the first Bishop of Cape Town, Robert Gray. St Matthew's Church was completed in 1856, built of hand-dressed local stone and has recently been fully restored.

The church and its peaceful churchyard and garden are a pleasant oasis in a bustling town. Nearby is the Jurisch Wild Flower Garden with many local aloe species and unusual trees, while just outside the town is the Werner Frehse Game Reserve with several species of antelope and local fynbos and flora.

Tomb of Anna and Maurice Garcia.

235

Two ancient and colourful passes through the Langeberg

The Langeberg range forms a natural barrier between the fertile farmlands of the Breede River valley and the sunburned rock garden of the Little Karoo. Our route straddles this rocky divide, passing through two rugged gorges, closely following ancient paths of the San and Khoikhoi. Almost the entire route is on good tarred roads.

Swellendam
Bonnievale
Cogmanskloof
Montagu
Tradouw Pass
200 – 220 km

FOR A VIEW OVER Swellendam and the rolling countryside to the south, turn out of Voortrek Street into Andrew Whyte Street, driving towards the mountain (see pages 240-1 for a town map). After 1 km, turn right for 'Swellendam State Forest'. Go right at the fork, then turn right towards the concrete dome of the reservoir. Park at the reservoir and walk around the fence to the south side, where the view is uninterrupted.

Return to Voortrek Street and turn right. At the end of the town, turn right out of Voortrek Street onto the N15/R60 for Ashton and Montagu, noting your kms. About 5 km later, on your right there is an old water mill. Soon afterwards the road begins to ascend *Bakoondshoogte* (oven heights).

Roughly 20 km from the turn out of Voortrek Street, turn left onto gravel for Middelrivier and Drew, then 2,3 km after that, turn left at the T-junction. Keep straight, passing through the settlement of Drew and crossing the railway within the next 1 km.

Cross the Breede River and turn right at the T-junction onto tar – noting your kms. After a few hundred metres, stop for a view back of the river and bridge.

After 9,4 km, turn right at the T-junction. Continue into Bonnievale and turn left at the T-junction. Call at the municipal offices (opposite the hotel on your left) to collect the key to the Myrtle Rigg Memorial Church. After hours, during weekends and holidays, it may be obtained from the Avalon Hotel.

Turn right out of the main road into Forrest Street. After about 1 km, you turn right into Myrtle Rigg Avenue. The church is on your right after 100 m (see opposite).

Bonnievale to Montagu
Return via Forrest Street to Main Road and turn left, remembering to return the key. At the first road past the municipal offices, turn left for Montagu and Ashton. Go left around the church, and continue straight. Note your kms as you cross the railway and, roughly 7 km beyond, turn left at the T-junction onto the N15/R60. A little over 5 km later, turn right at the T-junction for Montagu.

As you approach Cogmanskloof, about 1 km after the T-junction, there is a shady picnic spot on your left near the river. Close to Bain's Tunnel it is possible to see the Anglo-Boer War blockhouse, Sidney Fort, on the hill – to the left of the top of the tunnel. It's difficult to spot because it is built out of the local sandstone. From the bridge approaching the tunnel mouth you can also see the old road on your right.

Just past the tunnel there is a picnic site on your right (no facilities), with a bronze plaque attributing the building of this road to the engineering skills of Thomas Bain. It was opened in February 1877.

About 2 km beyond the picnic site, the road crosses a bridge and enters the popular country haven of Montagu; 1 km past the bridge, turn left into Barry Street, then turn right into Bath Street (the information office is on your right after 100 m; a number of establishments in the town serve lunch). Continue on Bath Street for roughly 3,5 km, then turn left at the 'hot springs' sign, and immediately turn right into Uitvlugt Street.

There is an attractive 2,5 km 'lover's walk' from the springs along Badkloof to an old mill (Eyssenhuis). While some members of the party walk, one person can drive the car around to meet them – drive back along Bath Street, right into Barry Street, left into Meulstraat, past a suspension footbridge over the river, then right into Tanner Street. The road ends at the old mill.

A CHILD'S LAST WISH
Early this century, goldseeker-turned-farmer Christopher Forrest Rigg bought a tract of land in the Breede River valley known as Bosjemansdrif. He transformed it by building a canal to bring water from the river, and he renamed his acquisition Bonnievale.

The Riggs' daughter, Myrtle, who is said to have been a considerate and deeply religious child, was only seven years old when she became ill with meningitis. Realising that she was going to die, she asked her father to build her a little church. Myrtle died in 1911, and work on the church extended over several years, with only the best materials being used, including imported Italian marble.

Consecrated in 1921, it was initially used regularly by the Bonnievale community, but eventually it fell into disuse. The municipality of Bonnievale restored it in 1978. Mystery surrounds the locked safe in the porch. The key was lost many years ago and the contents – if any – are unknown.

The old Sidney Fort above Bain's Tunnel in Cogmanskloof.

Now a museum, this little church in Bonnievale stands as a memorial to seven-year-old Myrtle Rigg.

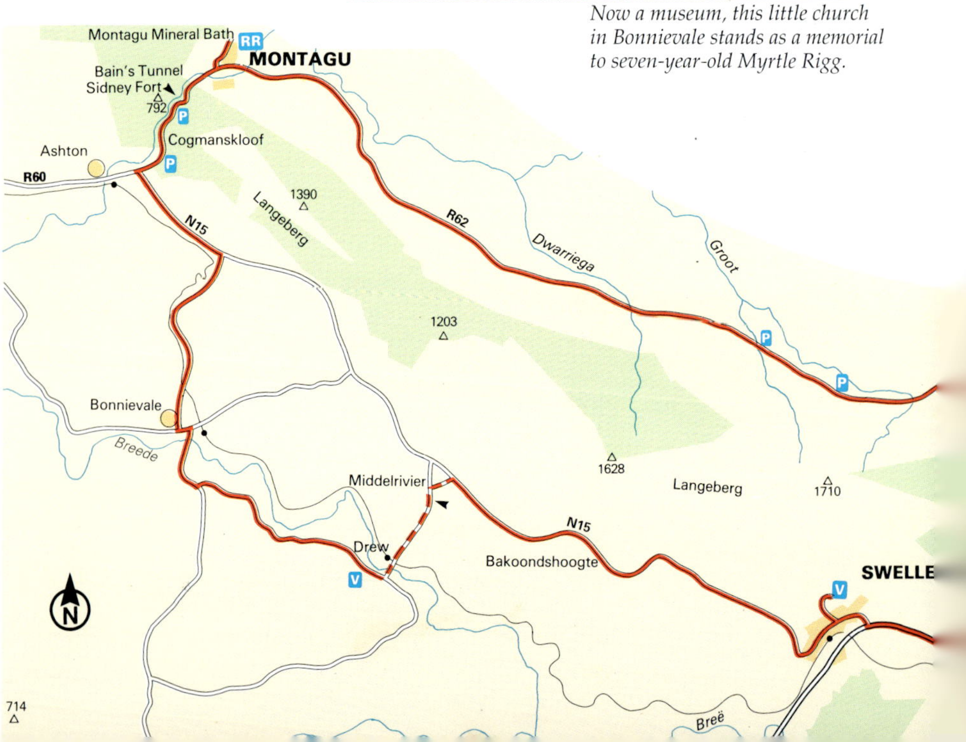

WESTERN CAPE

If it is springtime, visit the Centenary Nature Garden – turn from Badstraat into Kerkstraat, cross Langstraat (the through road) and turn left into Van Riebeeck Street. The entrance to the garden is on your right 700 m from the turn.

Montagu to Swellendam
Drive east out of Montagu on Long Street and follow this road (R62) towards Barrydale. The rugged and apparently impenetrable chain of the Langeberg lies close on your right. On the left, before the Swartberg range closes in, the plains extend clear to the Great Karoo.

On the outskirts of Barrydale, about 60 km from Montagu, turn right onto the R324 for the Tradouw Pass – noting your kms as you turn; 4,6 km from the turn, stop at a large picnic site set back from the road, next to a small stream that flows under the road. There are braai places here, and on the far bank of the stream a steep path leads up to a rock shelter containing San paintings. (Some of the paintings have been damaged.)

About 4 km beyond this picnic site, two loops of the old road can be seen on your left. There are braai sites here near the water. Roughly 3 km past the summit of the pass the road crosses the Andries Uys bridge. To your left you can also see the old Letty's Bridge.

At the T-junction at the end of the pass, turn right; 4 km later the road enters the London Missionary Society mission village of *Suurbraak* (Afrikaans for 'sour march'), which stretches along the roadside for 2,1 km.

A further 2,1 km after leaving Suurbraak, on your right, is the entrance to the farm Rooipoort; 400 m beyond, also on your right, is a small cement campanile set in a field about 10 m from the roadside. A plaque records that this was the site of an outpost established in 1734 by the Dutch East India Company as a protection against attacks by displaced Khoikhoi and San. The fort itself was close to the solitary house in the middle distance as you look directly past the campanile towards the mountain.

Roughly 5 km beyond the campanile, turn right at the T-junction onto the N2 for Swellendam.

AA Office AA House, 7 Martin Hammerschlag Way Cape Town 8001 Tel (021) 21 1550
Montagu Information Bureau Bath Street Montagu 6720 Tel (0234) 42471
Swellendam Publicity Association PO Box 369 Swellendam 6740 Tel (0291) 42770
Captour Tourism Rendezvous Centre, 3 Adderley Street, Cape Town 8001 Tel (021) 418 5202

COGMANSKLOOF'S SUNSET COLOURS
This kloof takes its name from one of the Khoikhoi clans of the area. The Cogmanskloof road, with its tunnel driven through the russet-coloured rocks, is an example of the work of Thomas Bain. His road, opened in 1877, was replaced by the present one only in 1952, and during the floods of 1981 it was Bain's road that remained passable while the modern route was unusable. Sidney Fort, built during the Anglo-Boer War, was named after the district commandant and, no doubt to the relief of its garrison, saw no action. It offers a superb view.

MISSION VILLAGE AT SUURBRAAK
Hans Moos, leader of a clan of the Attaqua Khoikhoi, asked to have a missionary sent to his people at their settlement in a tranquil valley east of Swellendam. In 1812 Mr Seidenfaden of the London Missionary Society arrived, and the village began to grow from that date – virtually all of it along a single main street that stretches more than 2 km.

A feature of the Suurbraak cottages is that a number of them are double-storeyed, with tiny upper windows. The church, which was taken over by the Dutch Reformed Mission Church in 1857, is believed to date from around 1835.

THE PATH OF WOMEN
The Tradouw Pass through the *Langeberg* (long mountains) was given its name, meaning 'the path of the women', by the Hessequa Khoikhoi. A roadway that closely followed the gorge cut by the Buffeljags River was built by Thomas Bain between 1869 and 1873. This new road was officially named Southey's Pass, but it soon reverted to its old name. Letty's Bridge, built of teak in 1879, still stands, in good condition, beside the modern tarred road. The name commemorates a member of the Barry family.

CAPITAL OF THE LANGEBERG VALLEY
Montagu, founded in 1851, was named after John Montagu, the Colonial Secretary who did much to advance the building of good roads at the Cape. Today it is a centre for wine and fruit production.

There are many beautiful and historic houses in Long Street, including the museum and its annexe. The Dutch Reformed Church parsonage, said to resemble a miniature Groote Schuur, was built in 1911 for the Reverend D F Malan, who became South Africa's Prime Minister in 1948.

The Montagu hot springs are situated in an impressive kloof overlooked by walls of rugged rock. A 'lover's walk' leads from here into Badkloof. Other walks can be taken in the Centenary Nature Garden and in the Montagu Mountain Reserve. A memorable ride by tractor and trailer is offered to the summit of the Langeberg – contact the information bureau at tel (0234) 42471.

RIVER WITHOUT END
Riviersonderend, the town that bears the name of the 'river without end', was established in 1925 to serve the farming community of the river valley – which produces mainly fruit, wool and wheat. The river itself was named by the earliest explorers – some say because it seemed to wind on without end. A more likely explanation for the name arises from the impression which the traveller has of endless streams feeding into the river.

Spring blossoms colour the hills of Swellendam.

Farmlands near Bonnievale.

One of Montagu's historic cottages.

An outside stairway adds charm to this attractive old homestead in Montagu.

237

Through rolling hills to the Cape's wild, southern shores

Like the Breede River that winds its way south from Swellendam, this route meanders through the rolling countryside of the Rûens and Duineveld to the sea. It includes the Bontebok National Park and De Hoop Nature Reserve, and a crossing of the Breede River by pont. Most of the route is on well-maintained gravel roads.

**Swellendam
Bontebok
National Park
De Hoop
Malgas
Witsand
200 – 220 km**

THE RESERVOIR ABOVE Swellendam makes an ideal starting point, as it offers a good view south towards the countryside through which this drive leads (see pages 236–7 for directions). From the reservoir, drive down to Voortrek Street and turn left. Turn right at the fork into Swellengrebel Street.

Cross the N2 for the Bontebok National Park (the road surface changes to gravel within 100 m); 3,7 km from the start of the gravel, the road bends sharply to the right and, 1,2 km beyond, you reach the entrance to the park (see below; entrance fee).

Bontebok Park to De Hoop

After your visit to the park, return to the N2 and turn left. The road crosses the Breede River after about 7 km; 1,4 km beyond the bridge, turn left for Malgas and Infanta, noting your kms (the surface changes to gravel within 100 m).

The route now passes through rolling wheatlands, with particularly broad vistas as you crest the appropriately named *Aalwynkop* (aloe hill) 16 km after turning off the N2. About 5 km further, you pass the equally appropriately named *Witklipkop* (white stone hill) on your left. Roughly 22 km after turning off the N2, turn right for Ouplaas and De Hoop. About 13 km further, turn right at the T-junction, pass the tiny settlement of Ouplaas on your left, then, 2,1 km further on, turn left for De Hoop Nature Reserve.

After 1,5 km, as the road crosses the cattle grid, you pass an immense and laboriously constructed stone farm-wall stretching away over the hill ahead of you – a relic of the days before fencing wire reached the country around the middle of the 19th century. You reach the entrance to De Hoop Nature Reserve just short of 5 km further (entrance fee).

Follow the main road into the reserve. Turn right after 4,3 km, following the signs to the administrative office. The administration of the reserve is housed in the old De Hoop homestead overlooking De Hoopvlei.

There is an attractive walk leading from the homestead along the vlei towards the sea (this outing allows time to walk only a short distance along it). Another walk leads along the beach for 5 km on both sides of Koppie Alleen – a 14 km drive from the homestead. Near the homestead there are picnic sites (braai places, toilets, water).

De Hoop to Witsand

Drive out of the reserve and turn right at the T-junction. A short distance beyond Ouplaas you pass on your left the road on which you entered from Swellendam – note your kms here. After 2,3 km, turn left for Malgas and Infanta. (The road from which you have turned reaches the old homestead and environment centre of Potberg after some 9 km.) After a further 11,9 km turn right at the T-junction, and 1,4 km later turn left for Malgas.

A herd of bontebok graze beneath the grandeur of the Langeberg range.

Lesser flamingoes add a dash of pink to the tranquil stretch of De Hoopvlei.

A FIGHT FOR SURVIVAL

The bontebok (*Damaliscus dorcas dorcas*) came close to suffering the same fate as the little bluebuck (*Hippotragus leucophaeus*), which was hunted to extinction almost 200 years ago. But a group of Bredasdorp farmers banded together in 1850 to ensure the bontebok's survival. The Bontebok National Park outside Swellendam, opened in 1961, is in the natural home of the bontebok and bluebuck – a strip of coastal plateau from Bot River to Mossel Bay. Bontebok tend to remain near their waterholes, and are usually easy to spot.

COASTAL SANCTUARY FOR WILDLIFE

De Hoop Nature Reserve is sited in an area rich in coastal fynbos. Well over 200 bird species have been observed in the reserve and the Potberg area has the southernmost breeding colony of the endangered Cape vulture. The major game species are bontebok, zebra, eland and daintier buck such as the klipspringer.

The *Sout* (Salt) River is blocked on its course to the sea to form a lake in the midst of the reserve. Known as De Hoopvlei, it is roughly 14 km long, and there is a beautiful walk along its edge.

Saved from extinction – two Cape mountain zebras enjoy De Hoop's fynbos.

WESTERN CAPE

The road that winds down the short distance to the pont at Malgas is tarred. You should cross the river on the pont (small fee); sound your hooter if the operators are not visible.

On the east bank, after just under 3 km, turn right for Heidelberg. Note your kms as you turn and, after 3,7 km, turn right again. At the inclined T-junction with the main Swellendam – Witsand road, turn right again.

Keep straight on this road for almost 25 km through several intersections until you reach a parking area at Witsand beach. (To reach the old jetties and hotel, drive back from the beach for about 3 km and, after passing the lone-standing church, turn left towards the river.)

Retrace your route to the junction just under 3 km from the pont, and turn right, away from the pont, towards Swellendam. Note your kms as you turn. Pass a road to Michielskraal on your left and keep straight past a number of other turn-offs. After 28 km turn right at the T-junction. Soon after crossing the railway, turn left onto the N2 for Swellendam.

AA Office AA House, 7 Martin Hammerschlag Way Cape Town 8001 Tel (021) 21 1550
Swellendam Publicity Association PO Box 369 Swellendam 6740 Tel (0291) 42770
De Hoop Nature Reserve Private Bag X16 Bredasdorp 7280 Tel (028) 542 1126
Captour Tourism Rendezvous Centre, 3 Adderley St Cape Town 8001 Tel (021) 418 5202

Limitless wheatfields turn Swellendam's rolling hills to gold.

The wool merino – pride of the southern districts.

The hand-pulled pont over the Breede River at Malgas is the only regularly operated pont in South Africa.

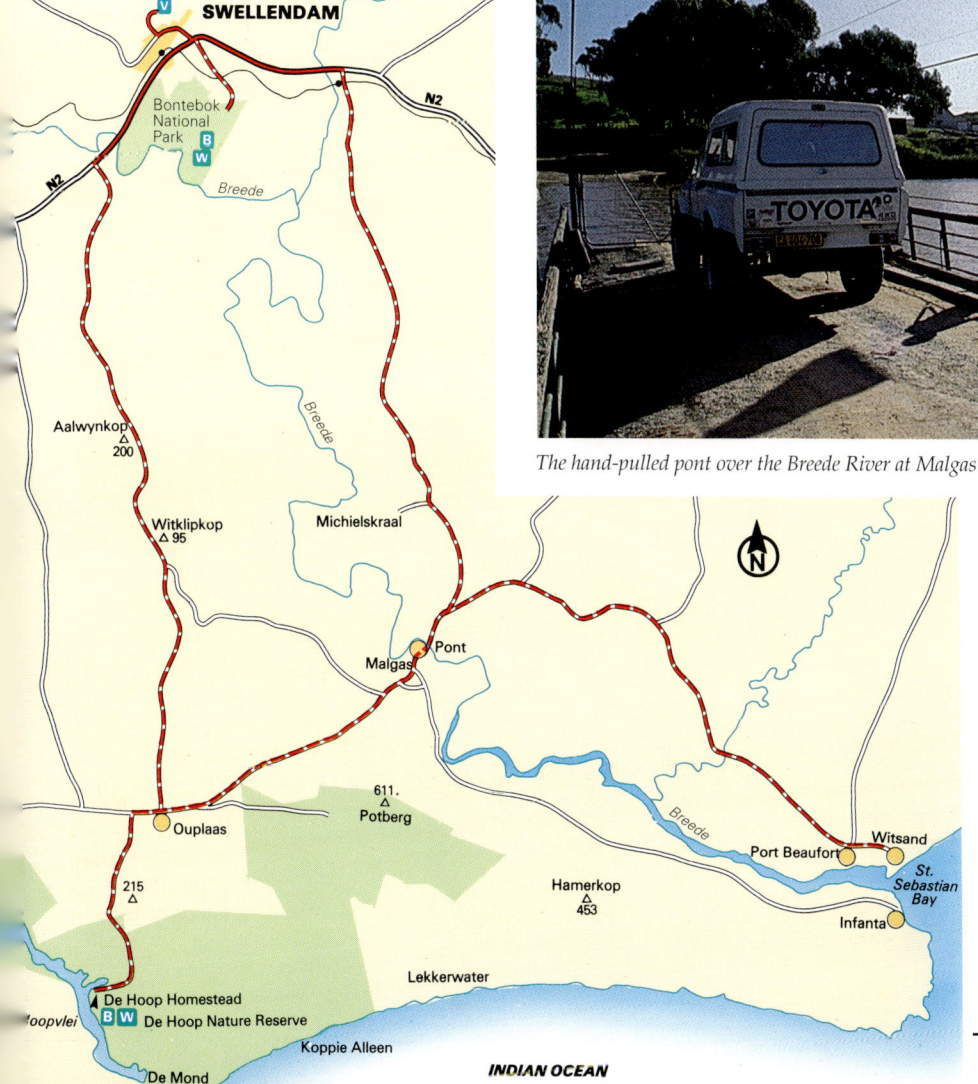

SWELLENDAM'S MERINO COUNTRY

The foundations of South Africa's merino industry were firmly laid on farms to the south of Swellendam. The first merinos were imported from the Netherlands in 1789, and this stock was later successfully crossed with the indigenous fat-tailed Cape sheep. Today the sheep of this district produce the country's highest yield of high-quality wool.

New grazing crops have increased the carrying capacity of the land. Some winter crops shed highly nutritious pods and seeds which the animals eat in summer – the sight of sheep apparently devouring stones in what seem to be barren fields has puzzled many visitors.

MALGAS – RELIC OF A RIVERBOAT ERA

The little river port of Malgas was founded in the middle of the 19th century to alleviate the laborious trek of more than 60 km across the hilly *Rûens* (ridges) from Swellendam to Port Beaufort.

On the west bank of the Breede River, on the farm then known as Mallegaskraal, there is a deep channel where ships could draw alongside a convenient stretch of level ground. A jetty was built there just upstream of the site of the present pont crossing.

WITSAND AND PORT BEAUFORT

Long stretches of sparkling sand gave their name to the little fishing settlement that grew up early in the last century at the wide mouth of the Breede River. The enterprising Swellendam firm of Barry & Nephews established a harbour just inland on the east bank, and named it Port Beaufort in honour of the Cape Governor at the time.

At first, only sailing vessels negotiated the tricky entrance channel. Then, in 1859, the 158 ton auxiliary steamship *Kadie* began to navigate the river as far as Malgas. After well over 200 successful crossings of the treacherous sand bar at the river mouth, *Kadie* was wrecked there in 1865 – a blow from which Malgas never recovered, although Port Beaufort continued to operate for a number of years.

The Barry wool store on your right as you enter Witsand has gables similar to those of the Oefeningshuis in Swellendam. The nearby church, built in 1849, is a national monument.

EXPLORING SWELLENDAM ON FOOT

For ninety-one days a rebellious colony

LYING ALONG THE banks of the Cornlands River at the foot of the Langeberg Mountains, Swellendam is one of the oldest and most gracious of South Africa's historic towns. The site is perhaps the prettiest in the whole of the *Overberg* – the name given by the Dutch settlers at the Cape to the wide coastal plain lying to the east of the Hottentots Holland Mountains.

A dignitary of the Dutch East India Company, visiting the Cape in 1743, chose this tranquil site for the establishment of a new *drostdy* (magisterial district), and the new settlement was called Swellendam in honour of the Governor of the Cape, Hendrik Swellengrebel, and his wife, Helena ten Damme. Work on the Drostdy building began in 1746, and the town grew slowly around this centre of authority.

By 1795, the burghers of Swellendam had become disenchanted with the Company, and they formed their own National Convention, electing one of their number, Hermanus Steyn, president of the convention. (The burghers did not claim complete independence. They rejected the Company's authority, but chose to remain under the Dutch flag. Just 91 days later, however, British forces occupied the Cape, and the days of independent government in Swellendam were over.)

Three years after the burghers' rebellion, in 1798, a congregation of the Dutch Reformed Church was established in the town, with services being held in the Drostdy until the first church was built in 1802. It was the church that was responsible for building the picturesque little Oefeningshuis in Voortrek Street.

Our walk through the old heart of the town starts here, at the *Oefeningshuis* **(1)**. Built in 1838 as a church for the education of freed slaves, its name was derived from the fact that religious instruction (*godsdiensoefening*) was practised there. The plaster clock-face in the west gable had a real clock set in the wall just below it. It is believed that when the real hands matched those of the plaster clock, it was time to assemble. Like many of Swellendam's old buildings, the Oefeningshuis seems to lie well below the road. In fact, the road has been raised to a height far above its original level by repeated reconstructions.

Diagonally across Voortrek Street from the Oefeningshuis is the quaint double-storey shop built by *Buirski and Co* in about 1880 **(2)**. The attractive little *Church of St Luke* **(3)**, sited directly opposite Buirski's shop, retains the precise form in which it was built in 1865.

Cross the road and enter the grounds of the *Dutch Reformed Church* **(4)**. The old gateway on your right once formed part of the original church wall of 1840, while the present ornate building dates from 1910. A side door is usually left open for visitors from 09h00 to 17h00 on weekdays. The original pulpit is still in use, but has been considerably altered.

Turn left as you leave the church grounds. You reach the oak-shaded Church Square on your left at the next intersection, with its row of simple *double-storey houses* **(5)**. This square was where farmers outspanned their wagons and carts when they trekked into the town for the periodic *Nagmaal* (communion) services, and these *tuishuisies* – little townhouses – were built for their use.

In front of the *tuishuisies*, facing onto Voortrek Street, is a thatched house now known as *The Cottage* **(6)**, which was built in about 1832. Next to it, standing well back from the road, is a little house that appears on a map of Swellendam of 1808 as the *'house of Constable Oomse'* **(7)**.

The Barry empire
Across Voortrek Street from The Cottage is *The Auld House* **(8)**, built in about 1802. It was bought in 1826 by Joseph Barry, founder of the firm Barry and Nephews. This was the dominant commercial enterprise in the Overberg for some 50 years, vastly improving the trade-routes with Cape Town and even issuing its own banknotes. Barry's ocean-going vessels sailed far up the Breede River.

The Auld House was enlarged after a fire in 1834, and retains the appearance it was given then. For many years it belonged to Barry descendants, and contained many relics of their 'empire', including the dining table and benches from their steamship *Kadie* – wrecked at the mouth of the Breede River.

The main road, which pre-dates the town and is part of the early Cape Wagon Road, still bends to the south past the Drostdy, just as it did in 1776 when the artist Johannes Schumacher set up his easel somewhere near the Cornlands River to record the scene. Where the road forks, continue straight, slightly uphill, into Van Oudtshoorn Road.

On your left, set back from the road, is *number 23* **(9)**, one of the few houses to have retained its original small-paned casements and wooden shutters. It dates from 1820, the same period as *number 21* **(10)**, which was remodelled in the Georgian style in about 1855.

Turn right into Swellengrebel Street, passing on your left the double-storey *Schoone Oordt* **(11)**, built in 1853 in the Cape Georgian style. The elaborate cast-ironwork was added in the Victorian period.

Across the river on your left is *number 18* **(12)**, which houses the offices of the Drostdy Museum. This was originally a single-storey thatched house, but was converted in the mid-19th century to the Cape Georgian style.

The historic Oefeningshuis with its quaint plaster clock in the end gable.

Buirski and Co's shopfront features an attractive cast-iron verandah.

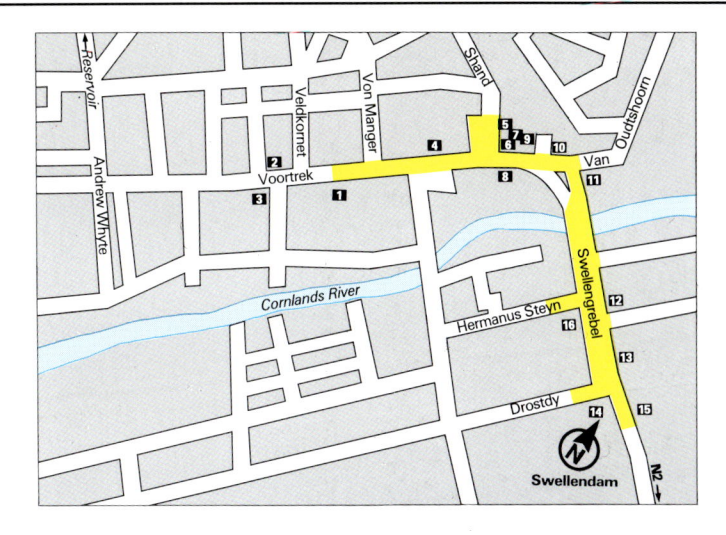

WESTERN CAPE

Lacy cast-ironwork has turned Schoone Oordt into a Victorian beauty.

The Langeberg range forms a majestic backdrop for Swellendam's old jail.

Wintry sunshine casts long shadows over the entrance to the old Drostdy.

Swellendam's museums

A little further, also on your left, is a starkly simple but very attractive row of buildings that can be seen in the Schumacher drawing of 1776. This was the *Swellendam jail* **(13)**, and also the home of the jailer and other Drostdy officials. It is now part of the Drostdy Museum. (There is a small fee at the entrance. Keep your admission ticket, as it will admit you to the two other museum buildings open to the public. The Drostdy and Mayville are open daily, while the *ambagswerf* – see below – is closed on Sundays. All of them are closed on Good Friday, 25 and 26 December and on 1 January.)

In a wing of the old jail building are the cells – including a 'black hole' with no windows. Behind the jail an *ambagswerf* (trades yard) has been built. Around a grassy square with a charcoal kiln there are small buildings in the local style, each containing the tools and products of a particular trade.

The coppersmith, miller, leatherworker, cooper, cobbler, blacksmith, wagon-builder and wheelwright are represented – also nearby are a horse-operated mill, a threshing floor and a replica of the water-mill sketched by Schumacher.

Cross Swellengrebel Street (in which many of the oaks are national monuments) to the *Drostdy* **(14)**. Before entering, look back across Swellengrebel Street at the handsome farmhouse of *Zanddrift* **(15)**, dating from 1768. This farmhouse was originally built near Drew, in the Bonnievale district, and, after standing empty for a number of years, was carefully moved to its present site, where it serves as a restaurant.

A Victorian treasure

The Drostdy, which served as court and residence for the magistrate for 100 years until 1846, was originally a T-shaped building. Later it was enlarged and turned into an H-plan with two short wings.

At the same time the main entrance was moved from Drostdy Street to where it is today. The charming little wine cellar, with its plaster oak leaves and vines, is thought to have been added around 1825.

In the foyer of the Drostdy are large reproductions of paintings of Swellendam and Breede River scenes painted by Thomas Bowler in 1860 – the original paintings are carefully stored in the museum's conservation facility.

A display case holds oriental ceramics made for the Swellengrebel family and the impressive seals of authority of early officials. As you follow their footsteps you'll notice that the Drostdy floors vary considerably in composition. However, all are traditional – from the cow-dung finish of the kitchen floor to the peach pips laid in clay in another part of the building.

The glory of the many exhibits is undoubtedly the outstanding collection of Cape furniture of the late 18th and early 19th centuries. As a whole, the Drostdy represents the period of occupation of the last Resident Magistrate – the anglicised title of the Cape term *Landdrost*.

In an outbuilding of the Drostdy is a small collection of animal-drawn vehicles, including a hearse, an old ox-wagon and a replica of a Zeederberg mail coach, a form of transport once celebrated as the 'veld express'.

A garden with gazebo

When you leave the Drostdy, cross Drostdy Street and walk downhill along Swellengrebel Street. Turn left into Hermanus Steyn Street and enter number 4, on your left. Known as *Mayville* **(16)**, it was built as a private home in 1853 and now houses another section of the museum.

Mayville was built on land cut off from the Drostdy, and the house formerly stood on a plot that extended to the Cornlands River. The mouldering stumps of the oaks that lined the walk to the river are still to be seen in the garden on the opposite side of Hermanus Steyn Street.

Perhaps the most charming feature of Mayville is its garden, laid out in formal Victorian style, complete with gazebo. Only old strains of flowers are grown here, and a slow stroll through this quiet garden of yesteryear is an experience appropriate to a town that preserves so much of a more gracious and leisurely era.

241

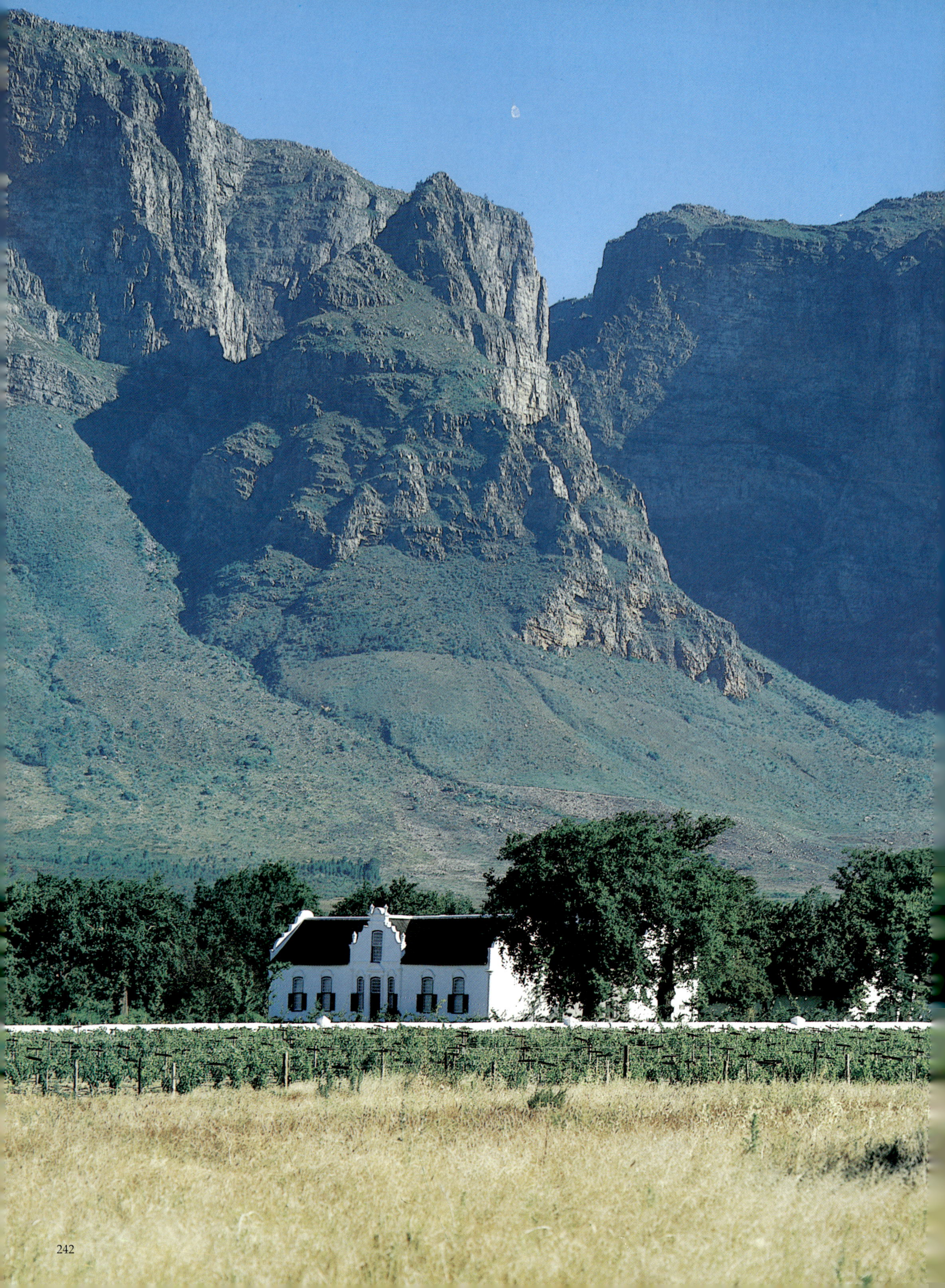

SOUTH-WESTERN CAPE

Cape Town: Sampling a wine route **244-5**

Cape Town – Simon's Town – Cape Point – Chapman's Peak – Clifton **246-7**

Simon's Town: 'Memory Mile' of naval history **248-9**

Cape Town – Kirstenbosch – Constantia – Silvermine – Hout Bay **250-1**

Cape Town: Stately beauty of the Mother City **252-3**

Cape Town: Exploring the city and its lovely setting **254-5**

The Waterfront: In the steps of sailormen **256-7**

Robertson – McGregor – Greyton – Genadendal – Villiersdorp **258-9**

Hermanus – Elim – Cape Agulhas – Arniston – Bredasdorp **260-1**

Gordon's Bay – Kleinmond – Hermanus – Caledon – Houhoek **262-3**

Cape Town – Grabouw – Franschhoek – Stellenbosch **264-5**

Stellenbosch: Historic homes in oak-shaded avenues **266-7**

Cape Town – Malmesbury – Tulbagh – Bain's Kloof – Wellington **268-9**

Tulbagh: The charm of Church Street **270-1**

Cape Town – Mamre – Darling – Yzerfontein – Riebeek West **272-3**

Saldanha – Langebaan – Postberg – Velddrif – Cape Columbine **274-5**

Citrusdal – Prince Alfred Hamlet – Ceres – Tulbagh – Porterville **276-7**

Piketberg – Velddrif – Rocher Pan – Elands Bay – Verlorevlei **278-9**

Clanwilliam – Wuppertal – Matjiesrivier **280-1**

Cederberg: Wilderness of strangely sculpted rock **282-3**

Van Rhynsdorp – Gifberg – Doornbaai – Lambert's Bay – Klawer **284-5**

Left: *Historic Boschendal farmstead below the Groot Drakenstein Mountains.*

Sip fine wines under ornate gables and rugged peaks

The fertile soils of the Eerste and Berg river valleys were first cultivated 300 years ago when pioneer farmers planted vines and fruit orchards. Today many of these historic farms are open to the public, and we visit several on this drive, to admire their fine farmhouses and sample their wines. The entire route is tarred, except for short access roads.

Cape Town
Muratie
Stellenbosch
Blaauwklippen
Helshoogte Pass
Boschendal
Taal Monument
170 – 190 km

FROM CAPE TOWN'S FORESHORE, drive towards Paarl on the N1, noting your kms as you pass, on your left, the exit for the R27 to Paarden Eiland and Milnerton. After passing through extensive built-up areas, you enter a stretch of attractive undulating countryside, with the Slanghoek, Du Toit's and Drakenstein ranges in the distance.

About 35 km after passing the exit to the R27, leave the N1 at Interchange 39 (Klipheuwel/Stellenbosch), then turn right at the T-junction onto the R304 towards Stellenbosch. Note your kms as you cross over the N1. After 1,2 km turn left onto the tarred road towards Paarl. You are now travelling on the R101, the old Great North Road from Cape to Cairo. Just 3,3 km along it, turn right onto the Muldersvlei Road; you soon pass the small settlement of Muldersvlei, on your right, and shortly after this you pass, on your left, the Elsenburg Agricultural College campus. At the T-junction with the R44, turn right towards Stellenbosch – noting your kms. After 2,3 km turn left onto the tarred Knorhoek Road. Follow this road to reach the Muratie and Delheim estates (see below).

Muratie to Spier
Retrace your route to the R44 and turn left towards Stellenbosch. As you enter Stellenbosch, continue straight ahead through two sets of traffic lights and stay on this same road as it runs parallel to the railway line. When the road swings away from the railway line, turn right to follow the signs for the R310 to Eerste River and Cape Town, and continue travelling parallel to the railway line. Note your kms as you pass the massive white-painted cellars of the Stellenbosch Farmers' Winery on your left.

After 2,6 km turn left, to stay on the R310 (towards Muizenberg/N2) and, 2,2 km later, pass the road to the Van Ryn Brandy Cellars on your left. These are open to the public, and offer morning and afternoon tours on weekdays. Some 1,5 km later you pass the Spier wine centre on your left. Spier is one of the largest and oldest wine farms in South Africa

MURATIE – AGE AND ELEGANCE
Muratie (the name means 'ruins' in Dutch and is pronounced 'murasie',) ranks as the oldest privately owned estate in South Africa, having been established in 1685, when the virgin land was granted to Lorenz Kamfer. After changing hands many times, it was purchased early this century by the artist Georg Canitz, and became the first estate on which Pinot Noir vines were planted.

The charming old buildings are surrounded by tall oaks, palms and cypresses, and a plaque near the main homestead lists some of the estate's previous owners. (It was acquired by its present owners – the Melck family – in 1988 and extensive replanting is under way.)

Although Muratie is best known for its port, fine red wines are made not only from Pinot Noir but also from Merlot, Shiraz and Cabernet Sauvignon. Visitors may taste the estate's wines, which may be bought on the estate during normal business hours. Cellar tours may be arranged by appointment.

Tall trees cast welcome shade on the lawns around Boschendal.

A GRAND ESTATE
The Boschendal estate was originally granted to one of the first Huguenot settlers assigned to the Franschhoek Valley. In 1715 it was acquired by Abraham de Villiers, whose descendants ran the farm for nearly two centuries – until it was bought by Cecil Rhodes in 1896. The main house interior is elegant, with beautiful antique furniture and Oriental porcelain, and the farmyard buildings house a restaurant that specialises in Cape Dutch and French Huguenot cooking (booking is advisable). The wine cellars are a short distance from the main farm buildings, and wines from the estate may be purchased here during business hours.

One of the goat towers at Fairview.

SOME WINE ROUTES OF THE SOUTH-WESTERN CAPE
Over 40 wine estates in the Eerste River and Berg River valleys are open to the public. For detailed information about these estates, contact the following:
Stellenbosch Wine Route
36 Market Street, Stellenbosch 7600
Tel (021) 886 4310
Paarl Wine Route
cnr Main and Auret Streets
Paarl 7646
Tel (021) 872 3605
Franschhoek Wine Route
Huguenot Road, Franschhoek 7690
Tel (02212) 3062

Shuttered windows add to the charm of Muratie.

Stark lines of the Afrikaans Taal Monument.

and its old buildings are decorated with an impressive and varied display of gables. The farm buildings house restaurants and other amenities.

Spier to Boschendal

When you leave Spier, turn left onto the R310 and note your kms. After 1,5 km turn left and follow Annandale Road (R44 to Somerset West and Strand) for 5,4 km through farmlands to a T-junction with the R44. Turn left onto the R44 towards Stellenbosch – noting your kms.

After 3,5 km, turn right across the right half of the freeway, onto the access road to the Blaauwklippen estate. The farm buildings include a coach house containing a collection of old horse-drawn and motor vehicles, and a museum. There is also a small shop selling farm produce, and the wines of the estate may be bought during normal business hours on weekdays. In the summer, an open-air restaurant provides a pleasant 'coachman's lunch', and tours of the vineyards may be taken by horse-drawn wagon or carriage. Drive out of Blaauwklippen and turn right onto the R44 towards Stellenbosch, noting your kms. As you enter Stellenbosch, keep straight until you reach Adam Tas Street at an inclined T-junction next to the railway line. Follow the road to the right here, pass Merriman Avenue and, 5 km from Blaauwklippen, turn right into Molteno Road. After a further 1,8 km, turn right at the T-junction into Helshoogte Road (R310), leading out of Stellenbosch and winding up the Helshoogte Pass towards the Drakenstein Valley and Franschhoek. (Unlike the extensive KwaZulu-Natal Drakensberg, Drakenstein was not named after local dragons, but commemorates one of the titles of an early Dutch nobleman.) As the road climbs, you have lovely views, on your left, to the slopes of Simonsberg – over a landscape of farms, forest plantations and dams.

Over the summit of the pass, the road winds down into the Drakenstein Valley. You eventually pass through the small hamlet of Johannesdal, then the old mission settlement of Pniel – dating back to 1843 and centred on a graceful, white-painted church. Note your kms as you pass through Pniel and, a little over 1 km later, turn right into the Boschendal estate (see opposite) which you approach through the farmyard, towards the rear of the main building.

Boschendal to the Taal Monument

Drive out of the Boschendal estate and turn right onto the R310. After 1,5 km you cross two sets of railway lines. Immediately after this, turn left onto the R45 towards Simondium and Paarl – noting your kms. After 10 km, immediately after passing under a railway bridge, turn left onto the R101 towards Klapmuts – then, after 700 m, turn right towards Suid Agter-Paarl, cross over the N1 and, after a further 2,2 km, turn right through the gate-posts into the Fairview estate. In addition to making wines, Fairview specialises in the making of goat's milk cheeses. Visitors are welcome at the cheese factory and at the goat enclosure, and tours of the cellars may be arranged.

When you leave Fairview, turn left – back the way you came. Immediately after crossing over the N1, turn left, back onto the R101 and, 900 m along the R101, turn left and recross the N1. Follow the sharp bend to the right and then turn left into Gabbema Doordrift Road at the Taal Monument sign. The road now climbs the lower slopes of Paarl Mountain to reach a large parking area. Before visiting the monument (see opposite), walk to the edge of the parking area for a splendid view over the Berg River and Drakenstein valleys.

From the monument, retrace your route down the mountain, turning right at the T-junction at the bottom, left at the sharp bend (almost a T-junction from this direction,) and crossing over the N1. Turn left when you reach the R101, and after just 400 m turn left for the N1 – heading back to Cape Town.

AA Office AA House, 7 Martin Hammerschlag Way, Cape Town 8001 Tel (021) 21 1550
Captour Tourism Rendezvous Centre 3 Adderley Street, Cape Town 8001 Tel (021) 418 5202
Stellenbosch Publicity Association 36 Market Street, Stellenbosch 7600 Tel (021) 883 9633, 883 3584

Mountains of the south-western Cape form a backdrop to the Wine Route.

MONUMENT TO A NEW LANGUAGE
Dominating the southern slopes of Paarl Mountain is the Afrikaans Language *(Taal)* Monument, inaugurated in 1975. Afrikaans is the home language of almost 20 per cent of South Africans. The three columns on the west side of the structure symbolise the contribution of Western languages and cultures to Afrikaans, the three rounded shapes on a podium represent the African influence, and the wall flanking the steps represents the Malayan tradition. The main column in the centre represents the Afrikaans language and soars 57 m over a fountain symbolizing growth and new ideas. The smaller column to the right is a symbol of the Republic of South Africa – many cultures but one nation.

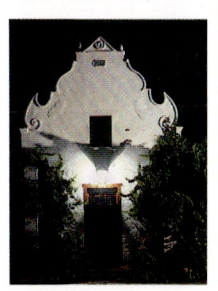

A floodlit gable at Spier.

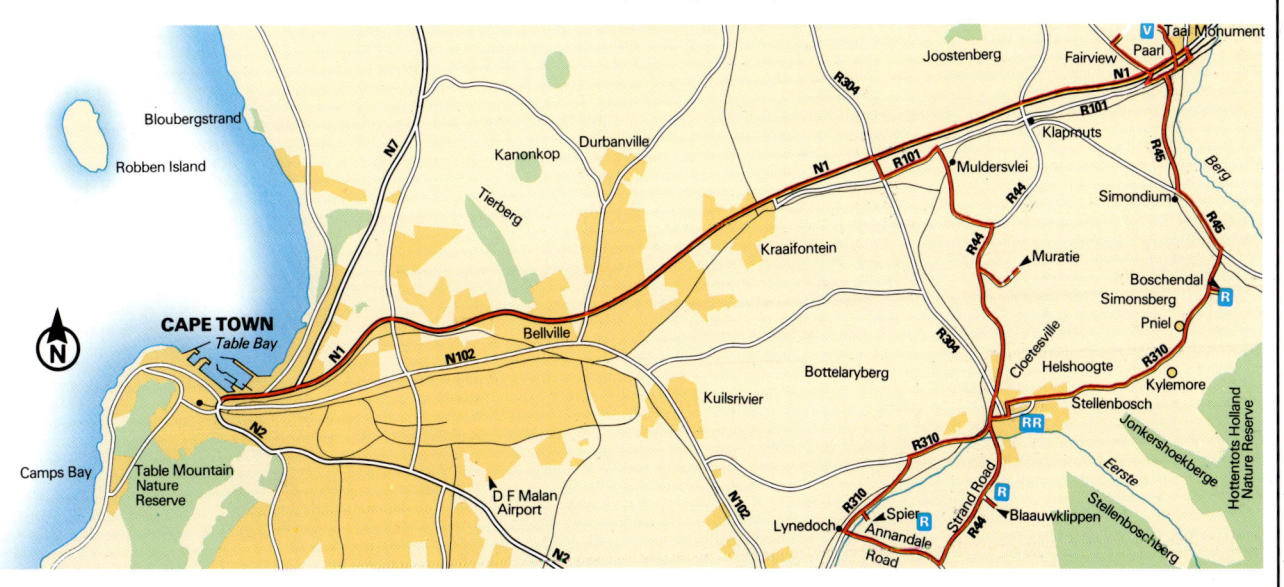

The Cape Peninsula – sand-fringed spine rising from a mighty ocean

The Cape Peninsula is much like an island – a ridge of high mountains jutting into the sea, linked to the African mainland only by the sandy, low-lying Cape Flats. This drive explores the peninsula's scenic shores, close to where the waters of the Indian and Atlantic oceans meet, creating gentle bays, beautiful beaches and wild, wave-pounded headlands.

**Cape Town
Fish Hoek
Simon's Town
Cape Point
Chapman's Peak
Clifton
150 – 160 km**

Leave Cape Town's city centre on the N2/M3. As the road dips to the left, behind Groote Schuur Hospital, move to a right-hand lane for Muizenberg (M3). Soon you pass Mostert's Mill on your left – note your kms as you pass. You next pass the University of Cape Town on the slopes of Devil's Peak to your right; 1,5 km after Mostert's Mill, exit left for Rhodes Memorial, then turn right, under the highway, and drive up the pine-shaded mountainside road (see opposite).

Rhodes Memorial to Kalk Bay
Return to the M3 (turn right immediately after passing under the bridge) and continue towards Muizenberg. When the M3 ends 12,5 km later, turn left at the top of the off-ramp. At the robot-controlled T-junction turn right onto Main Road (M4 – also known as the coast road); 600 m later, turn right onto Boyes' Drive. Park after 2,1 km for the view (see opposite).

Drive on for 2,2 km, then park in a small parking area on the right. Cross the road for a view over False Bay to Cape Hangklip (left) and Cape Point (right). A small iron gate and stone steps lead down to the grave of the financier and mining magnate Sir Abe Bailey.

Drive on until Boyes' Drive dips to the left into Kalk Bay. At the T-junction with Main Road, turn right.

Kalk Bay to The Boulders
Drive past Kalk Bay harbour, around the headland and into Fish Hoek. At the traffic island at the far end of Fish Hoek's Main Road, turn left, then park. Walk down any of several short paths to Jager's Walk, an attractive path along the rocks from Fish Hoek beach to Sunny Cove (allow 40 – 60 minutes).

Return to your vehicle and drive on along the coast road, passing Glencairn. Just before entering Simon's Town, turn right onto Red Hill Road (M66), which zigzags to the crest of the mountains. Park at the top for a magnificent view over Simon's Town harbour and across False Bay.

Drive back to the Main Road, and through Simon's Town. As you leave Simon's Town, turn left into Bellevue Road. At the bottom of Bellevue Road, turn left into a parking area; from here a path leads back towards the town, skirting the pretty Boulders Beach. Admire from a distance, but don't disturb the mainland-based colony of jackass penguins.

Cape of Good Hope Nature Reserve
Return to the coast road and drive on past the large picnic area at Miller's Point. The road climbs, then turns inland. Take the first turn left to enter the Cape of Good Hope Nature Reserve (entrance fee).

Some 7,4 km along the main road through the reserve, turn left for Buffels Bay – an attractive lunchtime picnic area with braai places, water, toilets and a tidal swimming pool. The reserve also has a restaurant (see map), refreshment kiosk and other picnic sites.

Return to the main road, turn left, and drive to the parking area at Cape Point. There is a steep path up to Cape Point Peak. You may walk up, or take the funicular coach, *The Flying Dutchman* (allow 60 – 80 minutes).

Cape Point to Hout Bay
Returning from Cape Point, turn left after 2,5 km. Follow this sideroad along the coast to a small parking area behind Cape Maclear and the Cape of Good Hope. A path leads up the back of Cape Maclear to the cliffs overlooking Diaz Beach (allow 40 minutes).

Return to the main road and head for the entrance. On leaving the reserve, turn left. Turn left again 8 km later where the road forks. Drive through Scarborough (note the 'camel rock' on your left) and the village of Kommetjie. At the intersection with the M6, turn left, then left again after 900 m, for Chapman's Peak.

The road leads through Noordhoek, then hugs the cliffs as it rounds Chapman's Peak. Park in the parking area at the highest point in this stretch of road, where it bends sharply to the right and Hout Bay comes into view. A short path leads to a magnificent viewsite.

Drive on into Hout Bay village and turn left into Princess Street. At the T-junction, turn right into Victoria Avenue. (A left turn leads to the harbour, see pages 250 – 1.)

Hout Bay to Cape Town
Victoria Avenue climbs the side of Little Lion's Head to Hout Bay Nek; 800 m after driving over the Nek, park in the parking area on your left for a view over Llandudno.

Drive on along the coast road beneath the Twelve Apostles, through Bakoven and Camps Bay, then park again where the road swings to the right into Clifton. Walk down any of the several flights of steps leading to the beach, to stroll along in the evening light, before driving on through Sea Point into the city.

AA Office AA House, 7 Martin Hammerschlag Way, Cape Town 8001 Tel (021) 21 1550
Captour Tourism Rendezvous Centre 3 Adderley Street, Cape Town 8001 Tel (021) 418 5202

The setting sun bathes Clifton Beach in a soft pink light.

Lion's Head as seen from below the Twelve Apostles.

CHAPMAN'S PEAK AND HOUT BAY
The road around Chapman's Peak is cut into cliffs overlooking the sea, creating one of the most spectacular sea-cliff drives in the world. All the Cape mountains are composed of strata of colourful sandstone laid on top of a granite base, and the Chapman's Peak drive, for much of its length, follows the natural join between these two rock formations.

From the recommended viewsite you can look out over the whole of Hout Bay, from the impressive Sentinel on your left, jutting forward from the Karbonkelberg peninsula, to the steep slopes of the Constantiaberg on your right. Further along the route, immediately before entering Hout Bay village, you can see, perched on one of the boulders overlooking the beach, a 295 kg bronze leopard – the work of the sculptor Ivan Mitford-Barberton.

Fishing boats at their moorings in Hout Bay harbour.

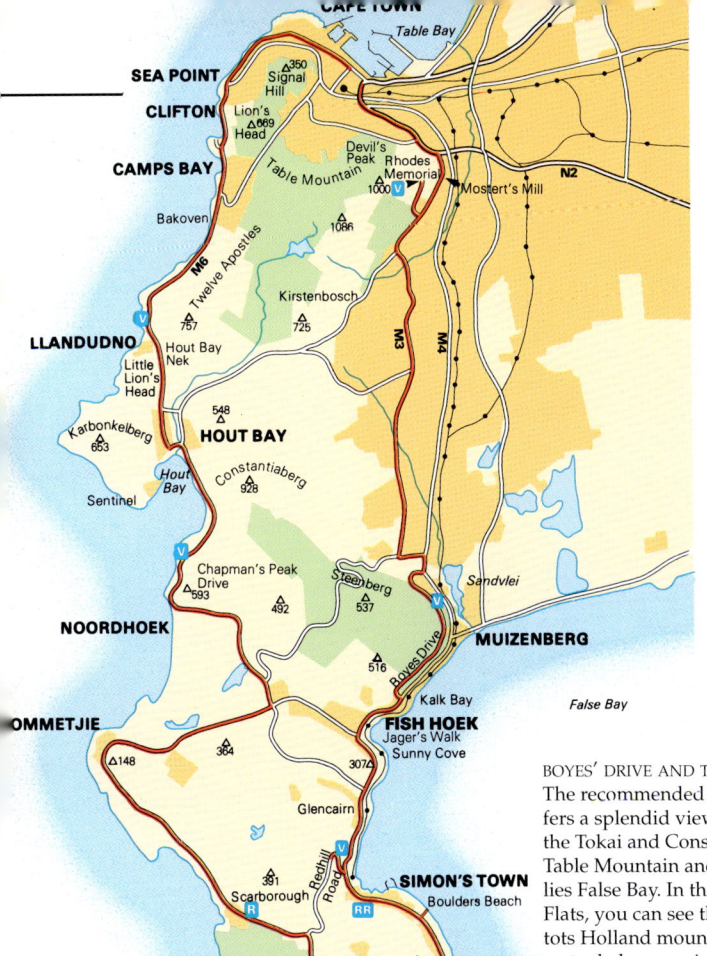

SOUTH-WESTERN CAPE

The impressive memorial to CJ Rhodes on the slopes of Devil's Peak.

REMEMBERING AN EMPIRE
Rhodes Memorial is set amid clusters of umbrella pines on the eastern slopes of Devil's Peak, and commemorates one of the most colourful personalities in South Africa's history, Cecil John Rhodes (1853 – 1902). Rhodes often enjoyed the view from here. The focus of the neo-classical granite structure, designed by Sir Herbert Baker and Francis Masey, is the equestrian bronze statue, 'Energy', by GF Watts. From the stone-paved apron in front of the statue you can look out, as Rhodes did, to the enticing mountains of the interior – the Groot Winterhoek range away to your left, the Slanghoek and Drakenstein ranges and Simonsberg in the centre, then the Helderberg, and the Hottentots Holland range away to your right. According to some, it is also possible to look out from here over two oceans at the same time. On your left is Table Bay (Atlantic) and far away to your right is False Bay (Indian).

BOYES' DRIVE AND THE BATTLE OF MUIZENBERG
The recommended first stop on Boyes' Drive offers a splendid view. To your left you look over the Tokai and Constantia valleys to the backs of Table Mountain and Devil's Peak. To your right lies False Bay. In the distance, beyond the Cape Flats, you can see the Drakenstein and Hottentots Holland mountain ranges. The stretch of water below you is Sandvlei, now a popular weekend venue for sailboard enthusiasts and dinghy sailors, but in 1795 it was the scene of the Battle of Muizenberg. Dutch forces had established themselves on the northern side of the vlei, down to your left, and were firing cannon across at the British, who were advancing around the foot of the mountain to your right. Superior numbers (and leadership) led eventually to a British victory.

Fishing and pleasure craft shelter in Kalk Bay harbour, with Simon's Town in the distance.

A chacma baboon – Papio ursinus.

CAPE OF GOOD HOPE NATURE RESERVE
Established in 1939, the reserve is home to eland, Hartmann's mountain zebra, bontebok, springbok, baboon and porcupine. Many bird species can also be seen, including ostrich, fish eagle and several species of albatross. The low-lying *fynbos* (flowering evergreen shrubs of the Cape floral kingdom) is rich in proteas and ericas – the total number of indigenous plant species in the reserve exceeds that of the entire British Isles.

WHERE DO THE OCEANS MEET?
Geographers regard Cape Agulhas, the most southerly point on the African continent, as marking the division between the Indian and Atlantic oceans. However, there is some commonsense support for the popular notion that the two oceans meet off the rocky cliffs of Cape Point. For much of the year the strong Mozambique Current sends its warm Indian Ocean waters around the southern tip of the continent and into False Bay. Eventually this great mass of warm water meets the cold South Atlantic. The results are dramatic. The fish populations are quite different on the two sides of the peninsula, and the two distinct masses of water often have a totally different colour. Of the greatest importance to most holiday-makers is that, along the eastern shores, they have decidedly warmer water in which to swim.

The wild and rocky promontory of Cape Point.

• EXPLORING SIMON'S TOWN ON FOOT •

Winter sunshine highlights the old facades of St George's Street.

St George's Street – memory mile of a naval town

THE BUILDINGS that rise in their steep terraces above Simon's Bay look down on a harbour that sheltered square-rigged warships armed with muzzle-loading guns and today protects the deadly submarines of the South African Navy.

Between the houses and the sea runs St George's Street – the main thoroughfare of Simon's Town that has echoed to the tramp of marching feet for many generations. Countless sailors from throughout the world have a memory-filled corner of their hearts reserved for what is known today as 'the historic mile' – the central section of St George's Street and heart of the old town.

The navy's here
From the railway station (the train ride from Muizenberg is memorable), walk towards the town centre on the sea side of the road to get the best view of the town's historic features. This side of the road also offers more shade, especially in the morning. There are restaurants and cafeterias along the route. Allow at least two hours for the complete walk.

The beginning of your walk is slightly uphill, and you pass on your right a fine double-storey building with a central pediment. This is known as *Palace Barracks* **(1)** and is now naval property. Built early in the 19th century by John Osmond, it was originally named Mount Curtis, but soon became known as 'The Palace' in tribute to Osmond, known in his day as 'the king of Simon's Town'. Some 400 m further, on the left, is *Admiralty House* **(2)**, which dates back to about 1740 and is used by the Chief of the Navy when he visits the Western Cape. The 40-roomed building was acquired by the Royal Navy in 1814 and housed successive British admirals until 1957 when, with the naval base, it was handed over to the South African Navy.

After passing the gates of Admiralty House, you see on your right an old building known as *Studland* **(3)**, built in about 1800 as a wine house and later converted into a residence for the manager of the old brewery that stands alongside it (dated 1830).

Turn left into Court Road, at the corner of which stands the *Church of St Francis of Assisi* (Anglican) **(4)**. Simon's Town is the oldest Anglican parish in South Africa, dating from the first British landings in 1795. The present church, consecrated in 1837, houses some very fine memorials, including one to the men of HMS *Boadicea*, listing names such as Tom Cockroach, Jack Ropeyarn, Bottle of Beer and Blackwhale. These were among the black West African 'kroomen' who served with the Royal Navy and whose proper names were unpronounceable to the British sailors. The kroomen's 'naval names' stayed with them throughout their service, and were even used in official documents.

Grog and a slave-ship gun
Some 100 m down Court Road is *The Residency* **(5)**, which now houses the Simon's Town Museum. Built in 1777 to accommodate the Governor on his visits to Simon's Town, it later served as a home, a school and a post office, before being bought by the Cape Government in 1814. Since then it has been a customs house, a port office, a prison – with slave quarters below serving as cells – and a magistrate's court. Museum exhibits include a grog barrel donated by the Royal Navy, a model of Lord Nelson's HMS *Victory* (Nelson visited Simon's Town as a young lieutenant) and a rare brass-barrelled flintlock swivel gun taken from a slave ship in the early 1800s. A corner of the museum is devoted to Able Seaman Just Nuisance, the Royal Navy's canine mascot during World War II. A gate at the side of The Residency leads into the Dockyard itself, where the *South African Navy Museum* **(6)** is housed

The figurehead of HMS Flora.

Admiralty House, a reminder of two-and-a-half centuries of imperial history.

248

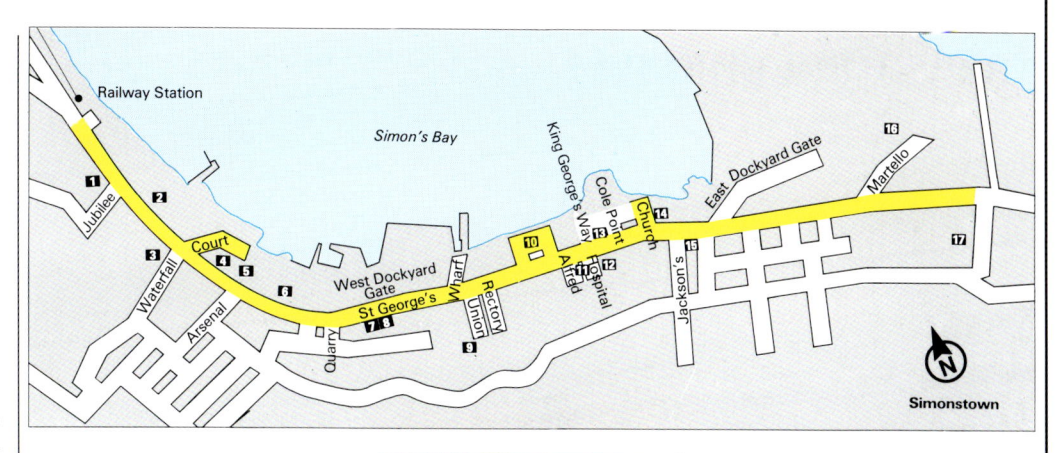

in the historic sail loft. Here are uniforms and medals, models and weapons, all evoking memories of a long and proud tradition. Hands-on exhibits are especially popular with younger visitors. Her seafaring days over, the attractive figurehead of HMS *Flora*, a frigate that served as the Simon's Town guardship for 20 years until 1891, has found a permanent haven here.

Retrace your steps to St George's Street and turn left, looking out for a number of plaques set in the white-painted wall on your left that record the history of various buildings in the dockyard. Notice the old Dockyard Church, or sail loft, known since 1801 as St George's Church and now the Navy Museum, the building being easily recognised by its clock tower.

You now pass, on your right, a number of the short, steep streets that are so typical of central Simon's Town. After a short distance you come to a small stone building on your right **(7)** that was designed by Sir Herbert Baker for Cecil John Rhodes. Immediately after this is the *British Hotel* **(8)**, a three-storey building with elaborate cast ironwork – originally built in 1819 and modified in 1898.

On the left side of St George's Street you now come to the West Dockyard Gate, where a plaque records the building of the first slipway in 1859 over a granite outcrop known as Sober Island. (The public may enter the harbour area at Wharf Road, a few metres farther along on the left, but no dogs are allowed.)

Outside the Post Office, on the corner of Wharf Road, are a blubber pot from whaling days and two large cannons. Opposite the second cannon is Union Lane, from where you can see a small whitewashed building, originally the *Union Tavern* **(9)**, that dates back to 1806.

Near to the Post Office, on the left, is a small stone cairn commemorating the many people uprooted from their homes in Simon's Town in 1967 by the Group Areas Act. Opposite this is Rectory Lane, with an ancient flight of steps leading to the site of the town's first Anglican church.

From Jubilee Square to Black Town

Jubilee Square **(10)**, on the left, commemorates King George V's Silver Jubilee in 1935. By coincidence, the drinking fountain in the square commemorates an earlier jubilee – that of Queen Victoria in 1897. A statue of Able Seaman Just Nuisance was unveiled nearby in 1985.

About 50 m beyond Jubilee Square you see Alfred Lane to your right. A short way along the lane you can glimpse a mosque, originally a private house, in which religious services were first held in 1888. (Opposite Alfred Lane, in St George's Street, there is a toilet.)

On your right, after passing Alfred Lane, you will see *Bayview House* **(11)**, which once served as a tavern and lodging house for sailors. A former resident of the house papered some of the walls with postage stamps, including rare Cape of Good Hope triangulars. A little farther on, behind the stone wall on the right, is the *Old Hospital Terrace* **(12)**, built in 1812–13. Used until 1915 as a hospital, it is now a naval residence.

On the left side of the road, after crossing King George's Way, you come to the imposing *Phoenix Hall* **(13)**. Dated 1860, its street gable features a phoenix rising from the flames, and a Masonic emblem. You are now entering Black Town, as this part of the town was known over a century ago. It was here that African men, women and children, freed from slavers by the Royal Navy, awaited resettlement.

Anthems and emblems

Cross Church Street to the Dutch Reformed Church (1856) and the adjacent parsonage, built in 1899 and known as the *Stempastorie* **(14)** (now the Museum for National Symbols), where the Rev M L de Villiers composed the music for Langenhoven's *Die Stem van Suid-Afrika*. De Villiers was born in Paarl in 1885 and studied at the Theological College, Stellenbosch, moving to Simon's Town in 1918, where he stayed until his retirement in 1930. Die Stem is incorporated in the present South African national anthem, while the country's striking new flag, although well representing its peoples in unity, owes nothing to earlier designs. Lively exhibits bring the story of flag and anthem up to date.

In the Stempastorie, the sitting room has been arranged as in De Villiers' day, including the piano on which *Die Stem* was first played. Upstairs, the study where he composed the music has also been preserved. Also of interest

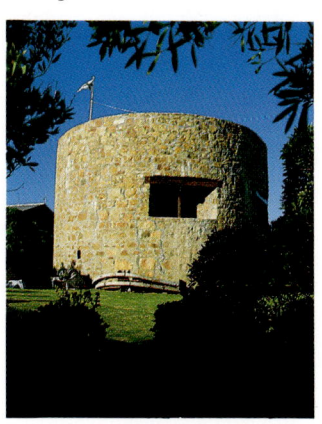

'Pub corner' in Simon's Town Museum.

are the flag room, with examples of all the flags that have flown over South Africa, and the heraldry room, where the country's various coats of arms are displayed. The flag room has a collection of some 200 designs, some of them bizarre in the extreme, submitted during competitions to find a new and acceptable national flag.

Walking on a short distance from the Dutch Reformed Church, you will see the *Catholic Church of Simon and Jude* **(15)** on your right, a handsome stone building with adjoining presbytery dating from 1855. The bell, dated 1871, was cast in the dockyard, complete with silver coins thrown into the molten metal to sweeten the bell's tone. The large St Joseph's Convent, adjoining the church, is now a boarding house.

Lost ships and sailormen

Pass the East Dockyard Gate on your left and, after walking a short distance farther, you can see, down on your left, the historic *Martello tower* **(16)** – a classic coastal defence position of two centuries ago. The tower was built during the Napoleonic Wars to protect the town and harbour from a feared French landing.

Cross St George's Street to the *old burying ground* **(17)**. Among the graves is a monument to the men of HMS *Nerbudda*, which put out from Port Elizabeth in 1855 and was never seen again. An enormous stone near the St George's Street boundary commemorates Adriaan de Nys, 'onder Coopman en Hooft van de Baay Fals' (junior merchant and head of False Bay), the Dutch East India Company's 'postholder' at Simon's Bay, who died in 1761.

To return to the railway station, walk back along St George's Street, stopping for a new look at whatever caught your interest.

The formidable Martello tower.

Through the historic heart of the Cape Peninsula

The Cape Peninsula has a rich history. Here is a short drive that allows time to savour it. Our route leads through avenues of ancient oaks, past vineyards cultivated for three centuries, to places that share a peaceful, old-world charm – from the cool of Groot Constantia's cellars to the romance of small fishing boats in Hout Bay's harbour.

Cape Town
Mostert's Mill
Kirstenbosch
Groot Constantia
Silvermine
Hout Bay
70 – 80 km

Cape Town, the Twelve Apostles and Lion's Head.

THE LOW RIDGE OF land between Table Mountain and Lion's Head is known as Kloof Nek. You reach it from the city centre by driving along Adderley Street towards the mountain, turning right into Wale Street, then taking the 6th left turn, into Buitengracht, which becomes Kloof Nek Road.

Driving around the Kloof Nek traffic islands, take the 4th exit (uphill). Follow this road along the 'lion's back' to Signal Hill, from where there are fine views in all directions.

Return to the city centre and turn from Heerengracht (the lower extension of Adderley Street) into Hertzog Boulevard for the N2. After the downhill left-hand bend behind Groote Schuur Hospital, move into the second-from-right lane. The two right lanes veer right and become the M3 towards Muizenberg. Take the first exit left (Mowbray), to reach Mostert's Mill (see opposite).

On leaving Mostert's Mill, drive downhill along Rhodes Avenue and turn right at the traffic lights into Main Road. After 600 m turn right, uphill, into Woolsack Drive, then follow the signs back onto the M3 towards Muizenberg. You pass the University of Cape Town on your right and, after 1,2 km, pass Groote Schuur estate on your left.

The road runs along the edge of Newlands Forest, then dips to the left. Turn right for Kirstenbosch at the first traffic lights into another Rhodes Avenue; 1,7 km later, turn right into Kirstenbosch (small entrance fee).

Kirstenbosch to Silvermine Reserve

Leaving Kirstenbosch, turn right into Rhodes Avenue, then right 700 m later at the T-junction. The road winds up the mountainside to Constantia Nek. At the traffic circle, turn left into Constantia Main Road (first exit) and note your kms. After 3,3 km turn right and follow this side road into the Groot Constantia estate. (A restaurant here offers lunch.)

Leave Groot Constantia and turn right into Constantia Main Road – noting your kms. After 900 m, turn right into Ladies Mile Road Extension. After 1 km, turn right at the traffic lights into Spaanschemat River Road, noting your kms. Follow this road for 7 km (it changes name a few times) then turn right onto the *Ou Kaapse Weg* (old Cape road), which leads up the Steenberg mountainside.

There is a straight stretch of road at the top of the pass. If you have already lunched, turn right at the end of this stretch into a large parking area (signposted 'To picnic spots'). There is a splendid view from here over the Tokai and Constantia valleys, and the backs of Table Mountain and Devil's Peak. If you plan to picnic, ignore this turn and take the first left turn, 600 m further, into the southern section of the Silvermine Nature Reserve (free entry). In the reserve, follow the road for about 600 m to the parking area. (Don't leave valuables in your car and note that no fires are allowed.) The northern section of the reserve (small entry fee) has picnic and braai sites, water and toilets, as well as walks with splendid views.

Silvermine to Hout Bay

Retrace your route to Constantia Nek, then drive straight on past the traffic island, noting your kms. The road winds down into the Hout Bay valley through cool green tunnels of oaks. After 5,6 km you pass the old Kronendal homestead on your left; 1,1 km after this, turn right into Princess Street. (To continue straight will bring you, after 5,7 km, to a magnificent viewsite at the highest point on Chapman's Peak Drive – see pages 246 – 7. Turn left at the T-junction into Hout Bay Harbour Road. The road ends near the harbour entrance after a few hundred metres, having passed Fisherman's Wharf on the left.

Drive back along Hout Bay Harbour Road and follow this road, now called Victoria Avenue, as it climbs up the side of Little Lion's Head and over Hout Bay Nek. Some 800 m after driving over the Nek there is an attractive view from a parking area on your left.

Drive along the coast road beneath the peaks of the Twelve Apostles. As you enter Bakoven (the first built-up area you reach) turn right into Houghton Road. When this ends in a T-junction, turn right into Camps Bay Drive, which leads you back to Kloof Nek. At the Kloof Nek traffic islands turn right (uphill) onto Table Mountain Road. Note your kms as you pass the cableway station. After 2,3 km, park on the left for a fine view of the face of Table Mountain, Kloof Nek and Lion's Head, and the city spread out below.

Drive back to Kloof Nek, and now take the second exit left (Kloof Road). After 2,1 km turn right at the T-junction and follow the road as it winds behind Clifton; 1,2 km later, just before rounding the headland and leaving Clifton, park in the narrow area on your right. Cross the road for a splendid evening vista – before driving on into the city via Bantry Bay, Sea Point and Green Point.

AA Office AA House, 7 Martin Hammerschlag Way, Cape Town 8001 Tel (021) 21 1550
Captour Tourism Rendezvous Centre 3 Adderley Street, Cape Town 8001
Tel (021) 418 5202

SIGNAL HILL

This 350 m hill abutting Lion's Head is also known as *Vlaeberg* (Flag Mountain) and it has been used as a signal station since the earliest days of European settlement at the Cape.

On its eastern slopes stands the Lion Battery. Gun salutes are fired from here on ceremonial occasions, and the gun is also fired automatically at noon every day except Sunday.

Along the road to Signal Hill you pass, on your left, the domed *mazar* or *karamat* (shrine) of Mohammad Hassan Ghaibi Shah – one of several Muslim shrines that encircle Cape Town and protect it from natural catastrophe.

Fishing boats in Hout Bay harbour.

The high, whitewashed walls of Groot Constantia.

RELIC OF AN OLD CAPE INDUSTRY

Built in 1796 for the farm Welgelegen, Mostert's Mill, on the lower slopes of Devil's Peak, was one of the first windmills in the country. The owner of the farm, Gysbert van Reenen, subsequently sold both the farm and the mill to his son-in-law, Sybrandt Mostert – hence the name. Wheat-milling, using horse-driven apparatus, was one of the first industries to be established in South Africa, and Mostert's ancestors were the first millers at the Cape.

Cecil John Rhodes bought the farm in 1891, but the mill was almost derelict. It was fully restored in 1936, and the mill and its adjoining threshing floor were proclaimed a historical monument four years later. The latest restoration was commenced in 1995.

The farm was included in Rhodes's bequest to the nation, and part of it is now the site of University of Cape Town residences and administrative buildings.

Mostert's Mill, restored after two centuries.

KIRSTENBOSCH BOTANICAL GARDEN

The National Botanical Garden at Kirstenbosch covers 560 ha of land, stretching up the slopes of Table Mountain to its highest point – Maclear's Beacon. There are several walks that lead through the garden, where staff cultivate 4 000 of the 22 000 southern African flowering plants in a setting of mountain streams, pools and rolling lawns.

The land was a bequest from Cecil John Rhodes, who had bought it in 1895. In 1911 the site was chosen for a national botanical garden, and this was proclaimed two years later.

Remains of Jan van Riebeeck's wild almond hedge around the first Dutch settlement can still be seen in the garden, and another relic from the past is a sunken bath at one of the springs of the Liesbeek River. This quaint, bird-shaped structure is popularly known as Lady Anne Barnard's bath, but it was built by Colonel Christopher Bird early in the 19th century.

The grounds also contain a lecture theatre and exhibition hall, the Compton Herbarium (housing more than 250 000 specimens), the offices of the Botanical Society of South Africa, a nursery, a curio shop and a popular restaurant. Summer concerts – orchestral evenings, recitals and African music – are held on the lawn on Sundays from December to the end of March.

A pool in the Kirstenbosch Botanical Garden.

GROOT CONSTANTIA ESTATE

In 1685 Governor Simon van der Stel could choose almost any part of the Cape on which to develop his own private estate. He chose the site of Groot Constantia – fertile, well watered, with beautiful views over False Bay and what is now Tokai, and still wider vistas towards the mountains of Stellenbosch and Paarl.

Van der Stel's original homestead was no doubt impressive for its time, but it was not the classic Cape Dutch manor house that we see today. The present manor house and the old wine cellar date from the 18th century and were the work of architect Louis Thibault and sculptor Anton Anreith – employed by Hendrik Cloete, who had bought the farm in 1778.

By the late 18th century the wines of Constantia had achieved world fame. The farm was bought by the Cape Government in 1885 and it is now run as a model wine estate.

A view east over the Cape Flats from Silvermine.

ON THE SPINE OF THE PENINSULA

The 2 151 ha Silvermine Nature Reserve on the mountain spine of the peninsula extends from the boundary of Muizenberg in the east to Noordhoek Peak in the west. It provides numerous walks through wild mountain scenery and countless magnificent views – in the east over the Cape Flats and False Bay, in the west over Chapman's Bay, Hout Bay and the Sentinel. The reserve owes its name to an unsuccessful attempt to mine silver here in 1687.

The vegetation in the reserve consists of fynbos, including colourful species of protea, erica and leucadendron; pine plantations and areas of indigenous forest with yellowwood, rooiels, sagewood and boekenhout trees. Bird life includes the long-tailed Cape sugarbird, the Cape robin, and the orange-breasted and malachite sunbirds. The mammals in the reserve include grysbok, porcupines, genet and civet.

• EXPLORING CAPE TOWN ON FOOT •

The Great Synagogue towers above Sydney Harpley's controversial statue of JC Smuts in the Company's Garden.

A morning flea market on the Grand Parade – Wednesdays and Saturdays.

The imposing Houses of Parliament.

Grace and stately beauty of the Mother City

CAPE TOWN, THE oldest city in South Africa, has retained many features of its historic past amid all the bustle of modern development. Efficient skyscrapers rub shoulders with elegant, centuries-old buildings.

In a leisurely stroll through the heart of the city, you can trace its gradual growth and development. Our walk starts at the *Castle of Good Hope* (1) which lies to the east of the Grand Parade. The Castle was built by the Dutch between 1666 and 1679 to replace their original mud-walled fortress. The Castle's main entrance at first faced the sea, which in those days almost lapped at its walls. The present main gateway with its elaborate stonework was built by Governor Simon van der Stel.

Tours begin daily (closed on New Year's Day, Christmas Day, Good Friday and Easter Sunday) on the hour from 10h00 to 15h00 and the colourful ceremony of changing the guard takes place at noon from Monday to Friday. A small admission fee is charged. The buildings contain a museum depicting the military history of the Cape of Good Hope from pre-colonial times and of Cape-based regiments, and part of the William Fehr Collection of antiques and pictorial Africana.

As you leave the Castle, turn right and cross the road at the traffic lights to reach the *Grand Parade* (2). Walk diagonally across the Parade to the north-western end (towards Plein Street).

The impressive Bath stone building on your left on Darling Street is the old *City Hall* (3). It is the venue for the Cape Town Symphony Orchestra's performances, and now houses a municipal lending library.

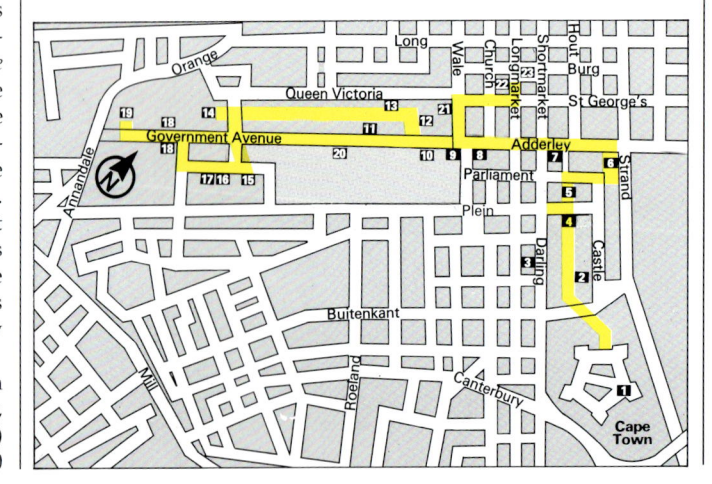

At the north-western end of the Parade there are green-roofed fruit and refreshment *kiosks* (4) – these stand on the site of the settlers' original fort.

Cross Plein Street at the intersection with Darling Street. On your right is the granite *General Post Office* (5). Walk through the first entrance on the Plein Street side, which takes you through the lofty central hall to Parliament Street.

Turn right, pass the flower sellers in Trafalgar Place, and enter the Golden Acre shopping centre. On the lowest level is *Wagenaer's Dam* (6), which was built by Zacharias Wagenaer, second commander of the colony, on what was then the beach of Table Bay. Walk up the steps next to the dam – on the landing is a display showing Table Bay as it was in the earliest colonial period.

Walk out of the Golden Acre into Adderley Street and turn left. Pass the flower sellers again, and then the imposing *Standard Bank building* (7), a high-Victorian edifice built in 1882.

Stately old church

Cross Darling Street and continue up Adderley Street. On the left, on the corner of Bureau Street, is the stately *Groote Kerk* (8). with its impressive vaulted ceiling and 18th-century pulpit by Anton Anreith. Consecrated in 1704, the church was altered a number of times until 1840, but the tower and much of the east wall are part of the original structure.

The next building on your left in Adderley Street is the *Cultural History Museum* (9). The building started out as a slave lodge in 1680, and later housed the Supreme Court. Its overall appearance dates from about 1810, when Louis Thibault and Anton Anreith remodelled it. Today, the building houses the cultural and Africana sections of the South African Museum.

Beyond the museum is the Ivan Mitford-Barberton statue of General JC Smuts. Behind the statue you can see the imposing *Houses of Parliament* (10), which were opened in 1885.

Enter the *Company's Garden* (11) via Government Avenue to the right of Parliament. The establishment of a garden was the main reason for the existence of the European settlement at the Cape, although over the years the emphasis has changed, and the vegetable garden for scurvy-stricken sailors has become a botanical haven for indigenous and exotic plants.

Away from the bustle

After about 150 m, walk half-right through the entrance gate to the gardens. The white building on the right here is the *South African Library* (12), a national reference library containing some 400 000 books. It is also a 'copyright library' and a copy of every work published in South Africa must be lodged here. (The library is open to the public, and displays are held in the exhibition room.)

The *restaurant* (13) further along the path into the Garden offers an idyllic setting for lunch or tea. Nearby are aviaries, a statue of Cecil John Rhodes, a reconstructed slave bell, a fountain set in a fish pond and public toilets.

From the restaurant, walk towards the mountain. Go up the steps beyond the rose garden to the Delville Wood Memorial Garden above. On your right is a statue of General Sir Henry Lukin, who commanded the South Africans at the Battle of Delville Wood in 1916. On your left a howitzer of that era serves as a memorial to the men of the South African artillery regiments.

Walk up the steps beyond the memorial garden to the *South African Museum* (14). The museum has displays of reconstructed dinosaurs, lifelike dioramas of San people, and extensive natural history collections of mammals, reptiles, birds, fish, insects and whales. It operates a planetarium and is an important centre of research. (Open 10h00 – 17h00 daily, except Good Friday and Christmas Day; small fee.)

Leave the museum through the front gates, turn right and cross Government Avenue. You will see another statue here of General JC Smuts – this one by Sydney Harpley. Its unveiling in May 1964 caused a public controversy that led to the commissioning of the statue by Mitford-Barberton at the foot of Government Avenue.

At the far end of the lily ponds, walk up the steps to the *South African National Art Gallery* (15). The gallery houses the works of many local and foreign artists, and includes works by Romney and Gainsborough. (Open 10h00 – 17h00 daily except Monday (13h00 – 17h00), Good Friday and Christmas Day; small entry fee; café; gift shop).

Leaving the gallery, turn left, walk up Paddock Avenue and pass the white arch and wall on your left. The next building on the left is the *Jewish Museum* (16), housed in South Africa's oldest synagogue, which was opened in 1861. The imposing *Great Synagogue* (17) next door, built in 1905, dwarfs its tiny predecessor.

Beyond the synagogues is an attractive terrace of double-storey houses dating from the 1890s, which are now part of a school. Turn right at the T-junction then left into Government Avenue.

Georgian grace

A few hundred metres later, you reach a pair of *gateways* (18) flanking the avenue. These once led to the paddocks of a zoo. On the left is the Lion Gateway, originally sculpted by Anreith but later replaced. On the right is the Lioness Gateway (although Anreith may have intended these animals to represent leopards).

Continue up the avenue, and turn right through a small gate at the sign for *Bertram House Museum* (19). This Georgian brick townhouse of about 1820 is run by the Cultural History Museum as a Regency period display. Several interesting buildings of the Orange Street campus of the University of Cape Town surround Bertram House, including the pillared Egyptian Building of 1841,

A tranquil avenue of oaks in the Company's Garden.

which was the first building in South Africa built for the purpose of higher education; the Little Theatre, built in 1881 as a chemistry laboratory; and six buildings designed by Sir Herbert Baker around the beginning of the 20th century.

Return to Government Avenue and turn left. On your way back to Adderley Street you pass, on your right, a gateway to *Tuynhuys* (20), the residence and offices of the President during sessions of Parliament. Governor WA van der Stel built a lodge here in 1700 for housing important guests. This was gradually extended until Tuynhuys became the official residence of the governors.

At the foot of Government Avenue turn left. On your left is *St George's Anglican Cathedral* (21). Work on the present cathedral, designed by Sir Herbert Baker, began in 1901. The building replaced the 'old' St George's, the copper cross of which still remains – now standing above the old steps.

Turn right into St George's Mall, cross Church Street, and turn left into Longmarket Street. On the left, with its steps jutting out into the street, is the *Old Town House* (22), also known as the Burgher Wachthuis. Built in 1755, it was used by Cape Town's earliest police force and the Burgher Senate, and later by the Cape Town Municipality. Today it houses the Michaelis Collection of old Dutch and Flemish paintings.

The Old Town House faces onto *Greenmarket Square* (23), where, weather permitting, a busy and colourful open-air market is held daily (except Sundays).

(For an exploration of The Waterfront, see pages 256 – 7.)

Wagenaer's 17th-century dam, Golden Acre.

Flower sellers ply their colourful trade in Trafalgar Place.

PLACES OF INTEREST AROUND CAPE TOWN

Visitors to the top of Table Mountain have magnificent views from the cable car over the Mother City and Lion's Head.

A cable car ride to the mountain top and the romance of the 'penny ferry'

Cape Town is famous throughout the world for its majestic mountain setting, and the many places and sights that both the city and the Cape Peninsula offer the tourist. Over the centuries, visitors have marvelled not only at the peninsula's natural splendour but also at the cultural diversity of the Mother City – the blending of Eastern, African and Western ways of life, which is constantly evident in architecture, dress and local customs.

Many interesting and scenically impressive parts of the peninsula have been mentioned in the preceding pages (pages 246 – 53, and see also Discovering the Waterfront, pages 256 – 7). Here are a number of further attractions to tempt the holidaymaker – a rich assortment of mountain walks, glittering beaches and various artistic and cultural venues.

Nature reserves and mountain walks

The whole of Table Mountain is a nature reserve and there are countless footpaths leading up and along its slopes. An alternative to climbing is to take the cable car, which sweeps visitors to the mountain top from the *cableway station* **(1)** on Table Mountain Road. There is a tearoom at the top, and footpaths crisscross the summit, leading to various viewsites. The cable car operates every day of the week, but is closed in bad weather.

Lion's Head, connected to Table Mountain by the saddle of land known as Kloof Nek, has a path spiralling to the summit – with chains to help the walker over the steeper parts. Devil's Peak, at the eastern end of Table Mountain, offers several walks.

Newlands Forest offers a number of pleasantly shaded walks, as does *Cecilia Forest*, close to *Kirstenbosch Botanical Gardens*. From Constantia Nek there is a long but easy walk to the top of Table Mountain. Further south there are shaded walks (and picnic sites) in *Tokai Forest*, and the *Silvermine Nature Reserve* offers high mountain walks with splendid vistas (see pages 250 – 1). On the western side of the peninsula there are walks along the mountain slopes above Camps Bay and Hout Bay. These walks will take you through scenery far wilder than you would expect to find so near a major city.

The nature reserves on the peninsula contain baboon, porcupine, and various antelope – but none of the larger game animals that tourists come to Africa to view. A greater variety of animals can be seen at *Tygerberg Zoo*, which can be reached by driving out of the city on the N1 and taking the Klipheuwel exit (number 39). Here are over 60 mammal, 200 bird and 60 reptile species. Lion and chimpanzee are the favourites, while kangaroo are probably the most unusual.

For bird-lovers the Cape has several places of note. The *Rondevlei Bird Sanctuary* near Zeekoevlei is one of South Africa's leading ornithological research stations, and visitors are free to use several observation platforms and waterside hides. (Hippopotami have also been successfully reintroduced here.) Many bird species can be viewed at the *Rietvlei Bird Sanctuary* in Milnerton, while the *World of Birds* **(2)** in Valley Road, Hout Bay, a world renowned bird sanctuary, contains a huge collection of birds from throughout the world – many housed in enclosures through which visitors may walk.

A chain of beautiful beaches

The peninsula is edged on both its eastern and western shores with numerous superb beaches – but if you are planning to swim, note that the water on the False Bay coast is many degrees warmer than that on the western or Atlantic seaboard.

There are several small beaches alongside the Sea Point promenade, used more for sunbathing than swimming. More swimmers will be found in the large seawater swimming pool at the *Sea Point Pavilion* **(3)**. Moving south along the Atlantic coast, you come to the *Clifton beaches* (particularly photogenic), the small *Glen Beach* (popular with surfers), and the grand white-sand sweep of *Camps Bay beach*. Several small beaches can be found tucked away along the coast before you come to the scenic beaches of *Llandudno* and *Hout Bay*. South of Chapman's Peak stretches *Noordhoek beach*, a favourite with walkers, and this eventually runs into Long Beach at *Kommetjie*, which is recognised as one of the finest surfing spots in South Africa.

North of the city, but also on the cold Atlantic coast, there is the

A leisurely trip in the 'penny ferry' across the entrance to the Alfred Basin.

The slopes above Camps Bay.

SOUTH-WESTERN CAPE

The Baxter Theatre in Rondebosch.

popular *Bloubergstrand*, with its classic, world-famous view across Table Bay to Table Mountain. Between Bloubergstrand and the city lies the wild stretch of *Milnerton beach*, a place for walks and shell-collecting.

The False Bay coast has a string of popular beaches, preferred by many bathers because of the warmer water. Muizenberg has *Sunrise Beach* and *Surfer's Corner* – where many a young Capetonian first learned to ride the waves. Here too there is the *Muizenberg Pavilion* **(4)** and amusement park. Another favourite swimming spot on this side of the peninsula is *Fish Hoek beach*. At *Miller's Point* **(5)**, *St James* **(6)** and *Dalebrook* **(7)** there are natural seawater swimming pools suitable for children, and a small, well-sheltered beach can be found among the rocks at *Boulders* (see pages 246 – 7).

Places of cultural interest
Three hundred years of history have left Cape Town richly endowed with elegant old buildings. Many of these interesting places are included in the city walk described on pages 252 – 3, but there is far more than can be visited in a single day.

One of the oldest thoroughfares in the city is *Strand* (beach) Street, and it contains several important buildings. At the upper (western) end there is the *Lutheran Church* **(A)** of 1776, which has many carvings by Anton Anreith. Adjoining the church is the *Martin Melck House* **(B)**, which was the church's original parsonage. Also in Strand Street, a short distance down the hill, is the *Koopmans De Wet House* **(C)**. This dates from 1701 and houses a priceless collection of Cape Dutch furniture.

On the slopes of Signal Hill, the heart of the *Bo-Kaap* (upper Cape Town) or *Malay Quarter* **(D)** now has national monument status – an area bounded by Rose, Wale, Chiappini and Shortmarket streets – and in Wale Street is the *Bo-Kaap Museum* **(E)**, preserved as a typical 19th-century Cape Muslim house. Two other buildings of interest are the *SA Sendinggestig* (mission) *Museum* **(F)** in Long Street, and *Rust-en-Vreugd* **(G)** in the Buitenkant. Rust-en-Vreugd houses part of the William Fehr Collection of watercolours and prints – the rest of the collection is held at the Castle.

A number of other places of historical and cultural interest can be found in the city's outlying suburbs. On the coast road between Muizenberg and Kalk Bay, Rhodes' Cottage and the old Post Huys are both open to the public. The small and simple Post Huys dates from 1673 – a year earlier than the first occupation of the Castle. A contrast in building styles is provided by the elegant old double-storey dwelling, *The Fort* **(8)**, now administered by the SA Cultural History Museum. In Cecil Road, Rosebank, is the *Irma Stern Museum* **(9)**.

Of the several cultural venues that merit mention, perhaps the foremost is the *Nico Malan complex* **(H)** on the foreshore – comprising opera house, theatre and restaurant. In Rondebosch there is the *Baxter Theatre* **(10)**, with a concert hall and two theatres. In Wynberg there is the open-air *Maynardville Theatre* **(11)**, renowned for its summer-evening performances of Shakespeare plays. The *Theatre on the Bay* in Camps Bay and at the *Masque Theatre* in Muizenberg also offer live shows.

Boat trips large and small
Several trips may be taken from *Hout Bay Harbour*. One trip visits the seal colony on Duiker Island. Another is a sunset cruise to Table Bay Harbour – offering magnificent views of the Twelve Apostles. From Kalk Bay there are launch trips to Seal Island.

More extravagant is a helicopter tour of the peninsula which leaves from the *heliport* **(12)** in the Waterfront. But perhaps the quaintest outing is a ride on the 'penny ferry' **(13)** in the heart of the *Waterfront* (see pages 256 – 7).

Additional information on places and events may be obtained from Captour (see below).

Captour Tourism Rendezvous Centre, 3 Adderley Street, Cape Town 8001 Tel (021) 418 5202

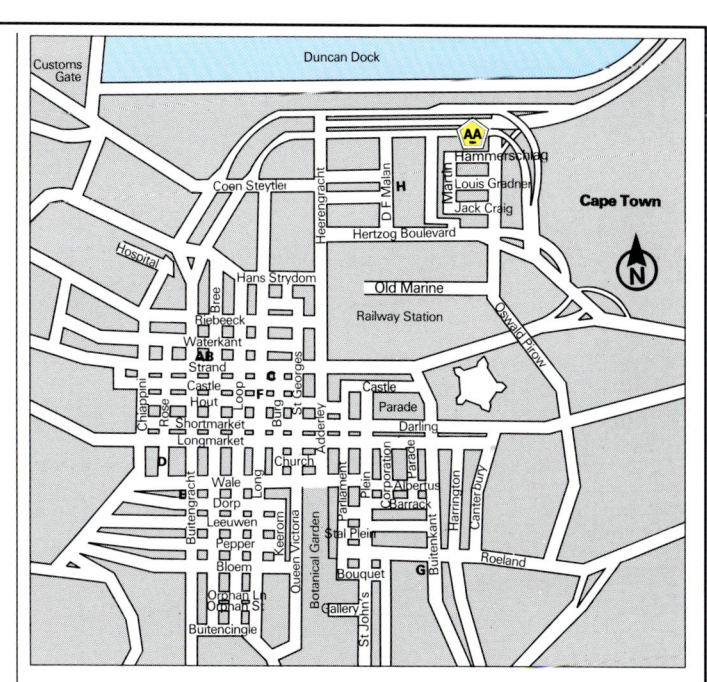

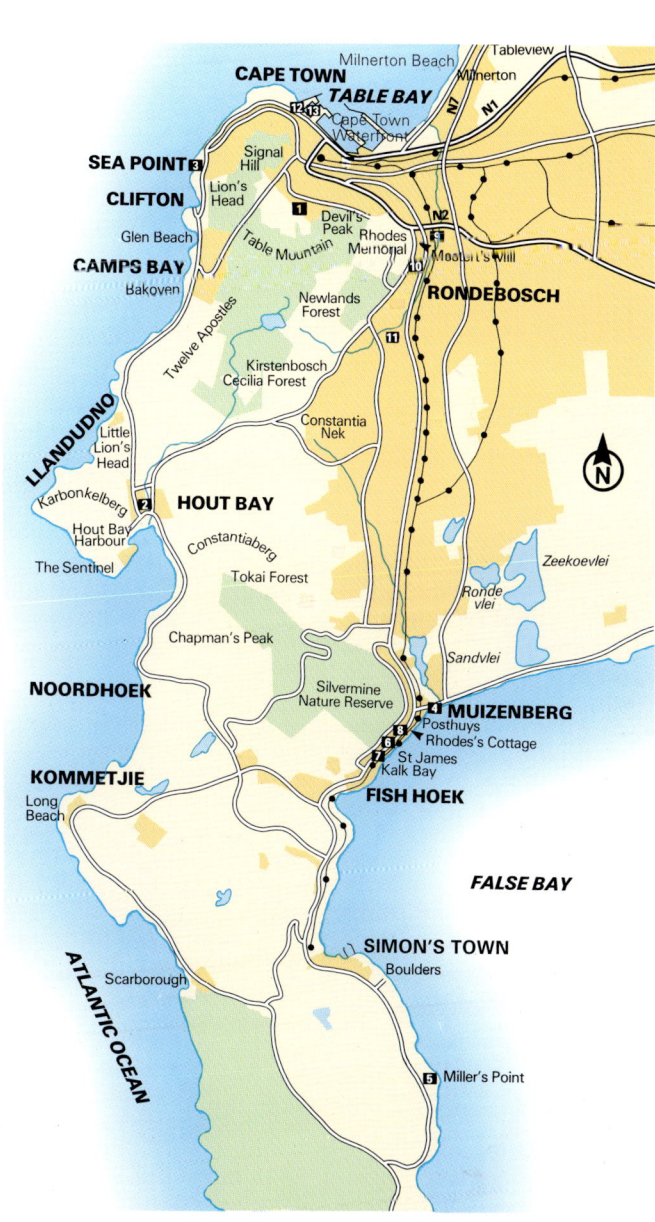

· EXPLORING CAPE TOWN'S WATERFRONT ·

The comforting bulk of Table Mountain shelters a rejuvenated Waterfront.

From dilapidated dockland to premier tourist attraction

For more than 70 years it was the very heart of the Tavern of the Seas. Then, after the Duncan Dock was taken into service in 1945, the old Victoria and Alfred basins – the original dockland – gave shelter only to Cape Town's fishing fleet and occasional other small craft. Decline and dilapidation set in, until, in 1988, it was decided to redevelop the area as a prime asset of the Mother City.

The transformation has been remarkable and, today, the Victoria and Alfred Waterfront again throngs with people. In 1995 some 16,4 million visitors came to enjoy the relaxed atmosphere and to browse through craft markets, watch an open-air concert, enjoy a meal at establishments that range from takeaways to sophisticated restaurants, or simply to sit on a bench admiring the spectacular view of Table Mountain and take in all the activities of a working harbour.

The first harbour basin

Make your way to the *Visitors' Centre* **(1)**, which is situated near the centre of the Waterfront. Here you can see a scale model of the development, ask questions, collect some helpful brochures and find your bearings.

From the Visitors' Centre, walk towards the *Victoria and Alfred Hotel* **(2)**, formerly the North Quay Warehouse built in 1904. Walk all the way through the Alfred Shopping Mall till you reach the wharfside – this is the original harbour basin, the *Alfred Basin* **(3)**. Before it was built, ships simply had to anchor out in the bay and shipwrecks were commonplace, especially during winter gales. After years of wrangling over finance, construction work was begun in 1860 when Prince Alfred, second son of Queen Victoria, ceremonially tipped the first truckload of stones into the water. A plaque that marks the exact spot can be seen later on the walk.

Years of hard, backbreaking labour followed as the basin was excavated out of solid rock, the rock being used to build the breakwater. In 1870, Prince Alfred, now the Duke of Edinburgh, officially opened the Alfred Basin. Look carefully at the workmanship that, more than 100 years ago, produced structures that are still in excellent condition.

Lying at the quay is one of two museum ships – the *SAS Somerset* **(4)**, a boom defence vessel that may be explored from bridge to bilges (entrance fee).

Walk along the wharf in the direction of Table Mountain, passing, on your right, a small square and the modern sculpture called *Still Life Ice Cream Cone and Blue Cheese* **(5)**. Farther along, on the right, is the old *Electric Power Station* **(6)**, now ingeniously converted into a bistro, restaurant, functions venue and theatre. Some of the original machines, as well as the original brickwork, have been incorporated into the design. The first electricity in South Africa was generated at this station when, on 25 April 1882, power was switched on to provide lighting for the harbour area.

Next to the old power station building is the *SA Maritime Museum* **(7)**, which exhibits sailing history and has a fine collection of model ships on display. The

A popular meeting-place is watched over by the fussily formal old clock tower.

Watch and be watched – cuttlefish at the Two Oceans Aquarium.

Robinson Graving Dock **(8)**, opposite the Maritime Museum, is impressively large when pumped dry. The foundation stone was laid in 1867 by Prince Alfred, and work was completed in 1882. It was named after the governor, Sir Hercules Robinson, and is one of the oldest operational dry docks in the world.

Beyond the museum, in the same building, is an extensive *Art and Craft Market* **(9)**, open on holidays, Sundays and every day over the Christmas season. Here you can buy anything from lampshades to belts, slippers and T-shirts, or you can simply spend time browsing among the stalls admiring the crafts.

The last building on this section is the *Two Oceans Aquarium* **(10)**, overlooking the New Basin. Bulk storage tanks for oil products were erected decades ago in this large excavated area, which was flooded in 1996 for use as a marina and yacht basin. Look across the road to the old *Breakwater Prison building* **(11)**, now the Breakwater Lodge, on top of Portswood Ridge. In its day it ranked as one of the most dreaded prisons in the world, and was the cheerless home of the convicts – many of them imprisoned for illicit diamond dealing – whose unwilling labour built the old harbour.

Time for ships in the bay

Cross the road, climb the stairs to the top of the Ridge and walk down to the *Scratch Patch* **(12)**. Here, for a fee, you can scratch around in a huge pile of polished semi-precious stones and fill a packet of your favourite kind to take away as a souvenir. Leave the Scratch Patch and make your way between the restored buildings, now business premises, to the end of the Ridge where, in front of the former *Harbour Master's Residence* **(13)**, built in 1860, the old Dragon Tree and the Time Ball Tower stand. The Dragon Tree, *(Dracaeno draco)* is a native of the Canary Islands and is said to have been planted over 100 years ago by a passing sailor. Its resin, commonly known as 'dragon's blood', has given the tree its name. The Time Ball Tower played an important role in days gone by as ships in the harbour set their chronometers when the time ball dropped precisely at noon every day. There is a delightful view of the Waterfront from this point. Turn towards Green Point and cross Portswood Road to the ultra-modern *BMW Pavilion* **(14)** that houses the IMAX cinema, with its cinema screen showing images up to seven storeys high.

Turn back towards the sea and cross the road. Descend the steps and walk past *Mitchell's Brewery* and *Ferryman's Tavern* **(15)**. Outside is a childrens' shipwreck playground. Opposite Mitchell's Brewery is the entrance to the *Red Shed* **(16)**, a craft market that is open all week. Walk through the market into the *King's Warehouse* **(17)** and on into *Victoria Wharf* **(18)**. This international award-winning centre is a favourite Cape Town spot for shopping and socializing over a cup of coffee. Among the wide range of shops here are a supermarket, book shops, antique shops, and clothing stores. The centre also has 11 cinemas. More than 100 new shops were added in 1996.

As you leave Victoria Wharf, walk past the open-air Agfa Amphitheatre and stop by the plaque **(19)** that marks the spot where Prince Alfred inaugurated the building of the Alfred Basin. Spurred on by the discovery of gold on the Witwatersrand, construction work began on the Victoria Basin in 1889. The stone for the additional breakwaters and docks came from the tank farm site. The Victoria Basin was completed in 1899 – just in time to cope with some of the troopships bringing soldiers to fight in the Anglo-Boer War.

Boat trips around the harbour leave from Quay Five. Walk right to the end of this quay and, beyond, at Quay 6, you'll find the *Victoria* **(20)**, a replica of an East Indiaman dating from about 1770.

A trip on the Penny Ferry

Return to Quay Five and walk round the square past the *Quay Four Restaurant,* **(21)** (formerly boatbuilding sheds), the *NSRI office and boat shed* **(22)** on the left and

Handicrafts preserve old techniques.

the *Union Castle Building* **(23)** on the right. The Union Line and the Castle Line amalgamated in 1900 to form the Union Castle Company – a name associated with sea travel for almost 80 years. The Union Castle Building was built in 1919 and the upper floor is now the home of the Telkom Exploratorium – a wonderful display of modern interactive experiments and telephonic history.

Walk on past Hildebrand's, which was the *old Harbour Cafe* **(24)**, originally a Victorian tearoom and now a modern restaurant, to the *Pierhead* **(25)**. A second museum ship, a coal-fired steam tug, may be boarded here. You can take the Penny Ferry (although the fare is no longer a penny) across *The Cut* **(26)** to *Berties' Landing* **(27)** with its seal-viewing platform, and the Gothic-style little *Clock Tower* **(28)**. The Clock Tower, or Time and Gauge House, was built in 1882 as the Port Captain's office. The tide gauge gave an accurate reading of the state of the tide in the harbour. It is difficult to believe this was once the most prominent structure in the harbour. In 1904 the Port Captain moved across The Cut to the Victorian building that stands at the Pierhead and now houses the V&A Waterfront head offices and a charter and boat-trip office.

Finally, walk around the quayside in the direction of the Victoria and Alfred Hotel and make your way back to your starting point.

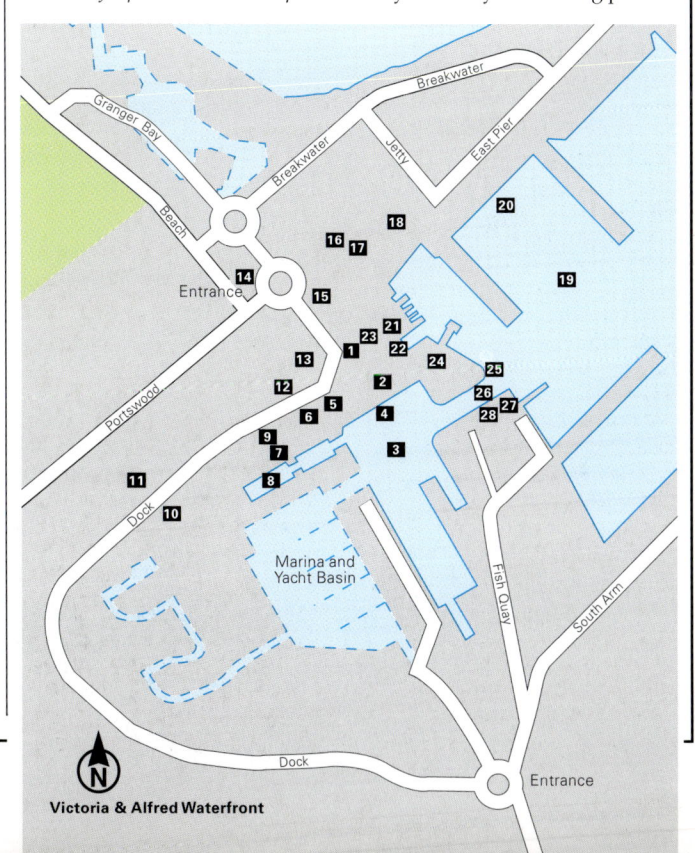

Victoria & Alfred Waterfront

Land of timeless villages and the 'river without end'

This route leads through a landscape of wild mountains and remote river valleys that have been bypassed by the clamour of commerce. Villages have retained their appearance of a century or more ago, except perhaps their oak trees which have grown larger and more noble. About half of this route is on good gravel roads – the rest is on tar.

**Robertson
McGregor
Stormsvlei
Riviersonderend
Greyton
Genadendal
Villiersdorp
230 – 250 km**

At the south-east end of Robertson's railway station, turn south out of Voortrekker Street towards McGregor. After about 2 km, the road crosses the Breede River over the Victoria Bridge. Turn left immediately after crossing the bridge.

This road passes the Vrolijkheid Nature Reserve on your left. Also on your left is the McGregor Co-operative Winery, which is open to the public during the week for tasting and sales, and makes an interesting stop. Beyond the winery, the road crosses a bridge before entering McGregor, 18 km from Robertson. The picturesque architecture of the town merits a short walk through its streets (see opposite).

To leave McGregor, turn left from Voortrekker Street into Van Reenen Street and, 200 m later, turn right at the stop street. After about 2 km the road takes a sharp left bend, and on the right here is the old Rhebokskraal homestead, with a gable dating from 1874.

At the T-junction 1,6 km later, turn right, noting your kms; 18,5 km further on, turn right for Stormsvlei, then turn right 6 km later at the T-junction. After a further 3,5 km, turn right for Stormsvlei at the T-junction with the R317.

The road winds down through the scenic Stormsvleipoort. Towards the end of the pass, broad vistas suddenly open out before you – pull to the side of the road for the view over the fertile valley of the Riviersonderend.

Continue through the poort, cross a narrow bridge over the *Riviersonderend* (river without end), and enter the tiny settlement of Stormsvlei, where there is a hotel and a guest house.

Stormsvlei to Greyton

At the T-junction 1,3 km beyond the river, turn right onto the N2. Continue on the N2 for some 20 km to the town of Riviersonderend. Roughly 2 km beyond the town, turn right from the N2 onto gravel for 'Lindeshof, Greyton, Genadendal', and note your kms as you turn.

After 5,3 km go left at the fork where the road to the right leads to Lindeshof School. Pass another road to Lindeshof School on your right and, 16,5 km from the N2, go right at the fork, immediately passing a road (to Schuitsberg farm) on your right.

As you crest a hill just over 2 km further, there is a sign on your right, reading *'Het Ziekenhuis'* (hospital), erected by the National Monuments Council. When clear of the hill, pull off the road. Next to the signboard there is a small brick pillar with a plaque describing the cave that provided shelter for invalids on the old road to the interior. Among the initials carved on the rock are 'OB', believed to be those of the late-17th-century Swedish explorer Oloff Bergh.

Turn right for Greyton at the T-junction about 500 m later. After a further 1,6 km, in which you cross three narrow bridges, turn left at the T-junction. About 3,5 km further is the homestead of The Oaks, dating from 1792.

Roughly 10 km later you cross a bridge on the outskirts of Greyton; 400 – 500 m later, turn right at the fork into High Street. Turn right onto the tarred main street at the Greyton Hotel. (The hotel and a few other establishments serve lunch.) Where the tar ends, turn left, following the sign for the 'nature reserve', and turn right at the T-junction. Continue to the gate of the nature reserve and park under the oaks. There is an attractive walk into *Noupoort* (narrow gorge) – allow 40 – 60 minutes and you can picnic at the entrance to the park, but there are no facilities.

The historic bell tower in Genadendal – built in 1798.

'THE VALE OF MERCY'

Genadendal was the first mission station in South Africa, established in 1737 by Georg Schmidt of the Moravian Mission Society. However, his baptism of his Hessequa Khoi-khoi converts annoyed the church, as Schmidt was not ordained. He returned to Germany in 1744, and work lapsed for almost 50 years until other missionaries from the society arrived.

A village soon grew up, with school, church, mill and a small factory for making sheath knives. The name Genadendal – it became official in 1806 – also was given to the President's Cape Town residence, formerly Westbrooke, in 1995.

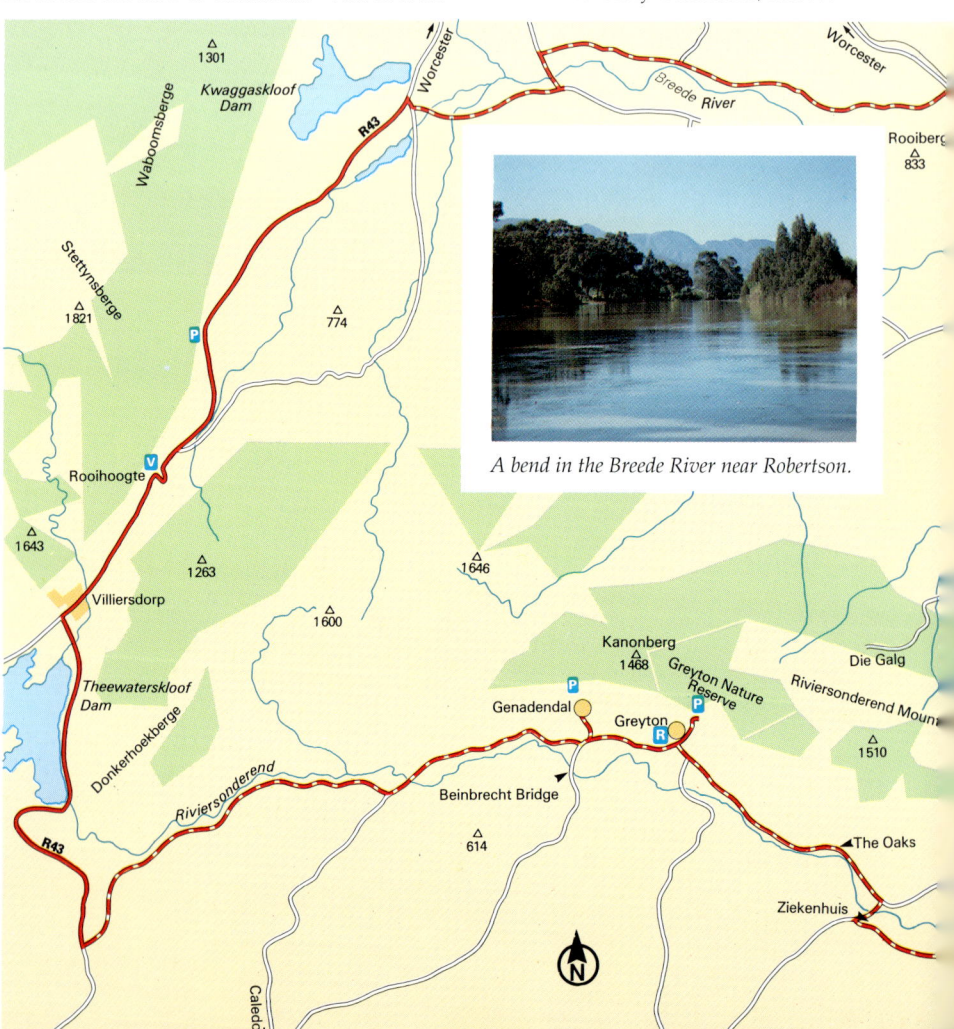

A bend in the Breede River near Robertson.

SOUTH-WESTERN CAPE

Greyton to Villiersdorp
Return to the main street and drive towards the south-west end of town. Note your kms as you pass the hotel and, after almost 5 km, turn right for Genadendal. A few hundred metres further on, you pass the police station on your left and, 1 km later, you pass the post office, also on your left. Turn left 100 m later and, after a further 300 – 400 m, turn right to park near the church for a stroll around the historic mission complex and to visit the museum.

Retrace your route and 1 km beyond the post office turn right, next to the police station. Turn left after 200 m and, after a further 600 m, turn right at the T-junction – noting your kms. After 11,2 km (after crossing the Riviersonderend) turn right for Villiersdorp. The route runs alongside the Riviersonderend and passes the entrance to the large Helderstroom prison complex on your right. After 21 km on this road, turn right at the T-junction onto tar (R43). The road climbs for 3 km, then descends Floorshoogte to cross the wall of the Theewaterskloof Dam.

After 19 km on the R43, turn right at the T-junction with Main Street in Villiersdorp, noting your kms. After 1,6 km (at the road that leads, on your left, to the Co-operative) there is a large, old-fashioned steam engine on the corner. Roughly 6,5 km later you reach the crest of the *Rooihoogte* (red heights) Pass, and as you descend there are good views ahead over the Breede River valley. After a further 9 km, there is a large picnic site under oaks on your left.

Some 15 km later, turn right onto tar for Doornrivier and Scherpenheuwel and, 500 m further, turn left, noting your kms; 7,5 km later, turn left for Worcester. A few hundred metres beyond the turn, the road crosses the Breede River over a long causeway. After a further 1,4 km, at an intersection rather like a reverse fork, turn right for Eilandia.

About 21 km later, turn right at the T-junction onto the N15. After about 12 km, a road on your right leads to the resort of Silver Strand – laid out on the banks of the Breede River – on the outskirts of Robertson.

AA Office AA House, 7 Martin Hammerschlag Way, Cape Town 8001 Tel (021) 21 1550
Robertson Publicity Association PO Box 52 Robertson 6705 Tel (02351) 3167/8
Captour Tourism Rendezvous Centre 3 Adderley St, Cape Town 8001 Tel (021) 418 5202

THE VILLAGE OF McGREGOR

Time seems to have stood still in McGregor, which was founded in 1861 to benefit from the passing trade that was expected to stream over the new pass linking the Breede River valley to the coastal plain. But the road was never finished – although you can drive for some 16 km south to the point where the roadmakers finally downed tools when bureaucratic bungling lost them their jobs.

McGregor is one of the best-preserved 19th-century villages in South Africa, without the later-Victorian embellishments. Several guest houses and self-catering establishments offer accommodation.

Rich farmlands lie tucked away beneath the Riviersonderend Mountains.

THE MUSCADEL CAPITAL

The peaceful town of Robertson – the muscadel capital of the wine world – is also renowned for its enormous brandy distillery and its jacaranda-lined streets.

Some 27 wineries in the vicinity form the Robertson Valley Wine Route, and the KWV brandy distillery here, with its 128 potstills under one roof, is believed to be the biggest in the world.

There is a large cactus garden 8 km out of town off the N15 to Ashton, and a smaller one – the Malherbe Memorial Garden – at the Ashton end of Voortrekker Street. The river resort of Silver Strand is just 600 m out of town on the N15.

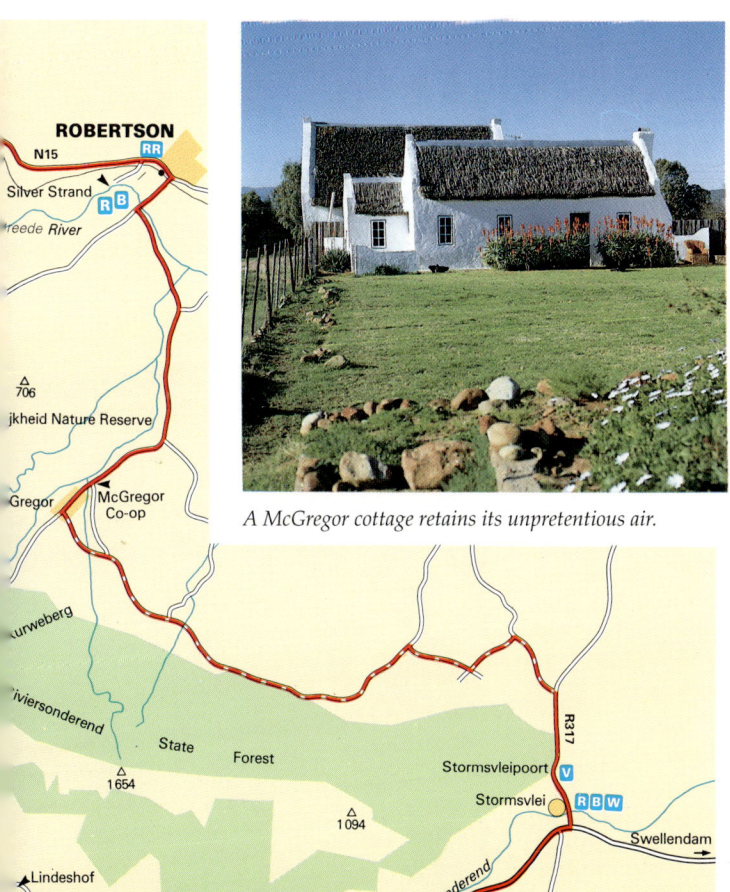

A McGregor cottage retains its unpretentious air.

The village of Greyton preserves the tranquillity of a bygone era.

RIVER WITHOUT END

Riviersonderend, the town that bears the name of the 'river without end', was established in 1925 to serve the farming community of the river valley – which produces mainly fruit, wool and wheat.

The river itself was named by the earliest explorers – some people say because it seemed to wind on without end. In fact, it joins the Breede River just south-west of the present town of Swellendam, on a route well known to the early travellers. A more likely explanation for the name arises from the impression that the traveller forms of endless streams feeding into the river.

259

The Strandveld – exploring the southernmost shores of Africa

Lying at the southernmost tip of Africa, the Strandveld is an isolated land of sun-bleached sand dunes and beautiful bays. Popular holiday resorts now mark a coastline feared by generations of sailors and littered by the shattered remains of countless shipwrecks. About two-thirds of this route is tarred and the remainder is good gravel.

**Hermanus
Elim
Cape Agulhas
Waenhuiskrans/
Arniston
Bredasdorp
260 – 280 km**

AA Office AA House, 7 Martin Hammerschlag Way, Cape Town 8001 Tel (021) 211 550
Hermanus Publicity Association Main Road Hermanus 7200 Tel (0283) 22629
Bredasdorp Museum 6 Independent Street Bredasdorp 7280 Tel (02841) 41240

AT THE WESTERN END of Hermanus, turn inland from Main Road into Rotary Way and follow this scenic mountain drive for some 3,7 km to the point where it forks. Park near the benches on the right, from where there is a fine view over the town and the full sweep of the Walker Bay coastline.

Return to Main Road, turn left, and follow this road (R43) through the town towards Stanford and Gansbaai. After passing the Hermanus Lagoon or Kleinriviervlei on your right, cross a bridge over the Klein River and enter Stanford 300 m beyond.

Keep straight on for just over 17 km, then turn right for *Die Kelders* (the cellars). After 400 m, park outside the hotel to enquire about admission to the caves. An underground stream forms deep pools as it flows through caverns below the cliff. (In 1995 the caves were closed to the public, but may be re-opened.)

Return to the T-junction with the R43 and turn right. The road enters Gansbaai after some 2,6 km; 100 m after passing the Gansbaai sign on your left, turn right out of Hoofstraat. After a further 300 m turn right at the T-junction with Park Street – this becomes Coast Road as it bends left towards the sea, and the surface soon changes to gravel.

The road passes a tidal bathing pool with change-rooms on your right. Turn right immediately after the pool to stay on the shore, and pass the entrance to the harbour. Return to Hoofstraat (R43) and turn right.

Gansbaai to Agulhas
Note your kms 700 m out of Gansbaai as you pass the road on your right leading to Danger Point. Keep straight for 18 km, then turn left onto gravel at the intersection where the road on the right leads to Pearly Beach (after some 2,2 km). Note your kms as you turn.

The road climbs Groenkloof, an area noted for its proteas, then reaches a T-junction almost 10 km after leaving the tarred road. Turn right, and go right at the fork 6 km later. After a further 9,6 km the road enters Elim (see opposite). A monument built in 1938 near the Elim church commemorates the centenary of the liberation of slaves at the Cape. Drive along the right side of the church to a grassy clearing just beyond to visit the old water mill.

Drive back past the church and turn right towards Bredasdorp, noting your kms. The road surface changes to gravel soon after.

Continue on this road, passing a number of sideroads. Clumps of milkwood trees become a feature of the landscape after roughly 20 km. About 10 km later you pass, on your left, the entrance to the farm Soetendals Vallei, with a homestead dating from around 1816.

Some 34 km after noting your kms, turn right onto the R319 at the T-junction. Pass the residential area of *Molshoop* (mole hill) on your left, and then the fishermen's cottages of *Hotagterklip* (left-rear stone) about 1 km beyond. As you enter Struisbaai, turn left at the four-way stop street, follow the road along the coast, past the harbour and rejoin the main road (Marine Drive). Stop roughly 7 km later, after passing the Cape Agulhas lighthouse (also a museum), near the southernmost tip of the continent, which is marked – several hundred metres further on – by a large plaque.

Agulhas to Waenhuiskrans
Drive back through Struisbaai and note your kms as you pass the last cottage on your right in Hotagterklip. Pass, on your left, the road on which you arrived from Elim.

After 15 km turn right onto gravel for Waenhuiskrans/Arniston; 7 km later, turn left at the T-junction. Cross a cattle grid after 300 m and immediately turn right for Waenhuiskrans/Arniston. After 6,5 km turn right onto tar, and enter Waenhuiskrans/Arniston 5,5 km later.

At the four-way stop street, the road on your left leads to the slipway, hotel (which serves lunch), old fishing village, and the *Arniston* memorial. Turn right here for Waenhuiskrans cave, passing a number of cottages that have been proclaimed national monuments. This road reaches the parking area near the cave after about 1,5 km. The mouth of the cave faces the sea, and can be reached at low tide by walking across some 200 m of sand and rocks – in which there are many fascinating pools – and turning right when you reach the shore.

Waenhuiskrans to Stanford
Return to the four-way stop street, and retrace your route out of Waenhuiskrans/Arniston. Pass the Struisbaai road on your left and continue straight; 15 km from the four-way stop, the road passes a turn-off on your right to the farm Nachtwacht, with a homestead dating from around 1835. Immediately afterwards you cross the Kars River.

Enter Bredasdorp on Kerkstraat and continue straight to the T-junction. Turn right and park as soon as possible to visit the Bredasdorp Shipwreck Museum on your left. Continue down the hill on Independent Street to the traffic lights, and turn left. This tarred road will bring you to Napier after about 14 km. Drive straight through, passing the Dutch Reformed Church on your left. Note your kms as you pass the sign to 'Kleinhoewes', at the intersection with Wesstraat, and keep straight on.

After 27 km turn left on tar for Stanford (R326). This road leads through the *Akkedisberg* (lizard mountain) Pass, which follows the valley of the Klein River. At Stanford, turn right for Hermanus.

Early morning washes over weathered fishing boats at the Old Harbour in Hermanus.

A street scene in the old mission village of Elim – almost unchanged in 100 years.

A rocky outcrop at Gansbaai, battered by waves.

SOUTH-WESTERN CAPE

Cape Agulhas lighthouse in 1986.

ELIM MISSION
The main street of this Moravian mission village has been described as 'one of the finest historic streetscapes in the Cape', lined as it is by ancient whitewashed cottages with black thatched roofs.

The parsonage, just below and to the left of the church, is dated 1796, and the church itself dates from 1834. The clock mechanism is over 200 years old and was installed in 1914.

The watermill building has been restored and still houses the mill machinery, much of which was replaced in 1881 and continued in use until 1972.

THE SOUTHERNMOST TIP OF AFRICA
The name *L'Agulhas*, meaning 'needles' in Portuguese, is said to have been given to this far tip of Africa because here, in about 1500, the needle of the compass pointed true north with no deviation.

The lighthouse at Agulhas was designed by Colonel Charles Michell in the middle of the 19th century and originally looked like a fortress when seen from the sea. The old light served faithfully for more than a century until its task was taken over by a more modern (and much less picturesque) light in 1962. But the old light, after years of restoration and repair, once more sends its beam across the waters. The building serves as a detached extension of the Bredasdorp Museum.

A VILLAGE WITH TWO NAMES
A gaping cavern in a cliff gave *Waenhuiskrans* (wagon house cliff) its official name – the shape reminding early visitors of a wagon shed. The cave is easy to reach at low tide, and may yield exciting discoveries cast up by the sea.

The little resort is also known as Arniston, from the troopship that ran aground on its way from Ceylon (Sri Lanka) to England in 1815 (the year of the Battle of Waterloo) with the loss of 372 lives.

Struisbaai fishermen row in to the beach after a day out at sea.

A pair of historic fishermen's cottages at Waenhuiskrans.

Waenhuiskrans cave – gouged out of the rock by pounding waves.

BREDASDORP SHIPWRECK MUSEUM
The Bredasdorp Shipwreck Museum in Independent Street has as its theme the shipwrecks of this southern Cape coast. The fascinating relics date from the wreck of the *Haarlem* in 1647 and include elaborately carved figureheads, gold and silver coins and handsome shipboard furniture. The restful garden of the museum contains a number of ancient cannons, including a rare bronze mortar, and the coach house shelters a display of old vehicles.

The Bredasdorp Nature Reserve is reached via Van Riebeeck Street, which leads off Independent Street, and preserves local fynbos – including many proteas and ericas. The hill in the reserve offers good views over the town and surrounding countryside.

261

Salt spray and wildflowers where the Cape mountains meet the sea

This drive leads east from Gordon's Bay, along a magnificent moody coastline where the colourful Cape mountains, blanketed in wildflowers, run directly into the sea. It then reaches inland and returns to Gordon's Bay through the rolling wheatfields of Caledon and past the orchards of Elgin and Grabouw. Only about 35 km of the route is not tarred.

**Gordon's Bay
Kleinmond
Hermanus
Caledon
Houhoek Pass
170 – 180 km**

START FROM GORDON'S BAY, 53 km from Cape Town on the N2. Drive along the beachfront towards the nearest mountains. Pass the harbour entrance and turn right at the T-junction onto Faure Marine Drive; 1,5 km after the T-junction, turn left onto the tarred road to Steenbras Dam. This road climbs the mountainside and offers outstanding views over Gordon's Bay, Strand and Somerset West, and across False Bay to the mountains of the Cape Peninsula. Turn back at the entrance to the dam area, 3,6 km from the turn-off.

Drive back to Faure Marine Drive and turn left. After 3 km you pass a holiday resort with accommodation, swimming, braai area and tearoom; 300 m after this the road crosses the Steenbras River, with a view to your right of the rocky river mouth. There is a picnic area on the right just after the bridge; from here the road (R44) is known as Clarence Drive.

Steenbras River Mouth to Kleinmond

More picnic and braai sites dot the side of the road as it leads to Koeëlbaai, a long white beach with rows of breaking waves. Nearly 2 km beyond the beach a gravel road on your right leads to Sparks Bay, where there are more braai sites (no water, no dogs, no camping). Ahead of you now is the prominent outcrop of Klein Hangklip, overlooking tiny Rooiels village which you reach after crossing the Rooiels River. Bathing in the river is safe.

Continue inland past Pringle Bay and Betty's Bay, which has shops and a petrol station on the road. Immediately after Betty's Bay, turn left to enter the picturesque Harold Porter Botanic Garden, where there is an indigenous plant nursery (you can picnic on the lawn; no dogs or fires).

Continue on the R44 for Kleinmond, noting your kms as you turn left out of the Harold Porter Garden. After 6 km stop on the side of the road and look up the mountainside to see the rock formation known as 'the elephant'. After another 6 km you pass the Kleinmond Coastal Nature Reserve (the entrance is on the right). There are picnic sites along the road, which crosses the Palmiet River before entering Kleinmond, where there are several restaurants and a lawned picnic area with toilets, water and braai places.

Kleinmond to Hermanus

Some 11 km beyond Kleinmond, turn right towards Hermanus at the T-junction with the R43. The road crosses the Bot and Afdaks rivers and passes roads to Hawston, Vermont and Onrus, before entering Hermanus. About 800 m after entering the built-up area, turn left onto a tarred scenic drive called Rotary Way, which leads for 3,7 km through unspoilt fynbos and offers excellent views over the town and coast.

Return to the main road, turn left, and drive into the town, passing the road to the New Harbour. Continue straight through the town centre until you reach Marine Drive on your left. (Entry into the road opposite you is forbidden from this end.) Turn left into Marine Drive, then turn right and park in the Market Square, across the road from the war memorial (flanked by two 12-pounder guns).

To the left of the war memorial a short path leads down to the Old Harbour and its museum. (A little further to the left of the memorial is the start of a pleasant 'cliff walk' of many kilometres along the seashore.)

After exploring the Old Harbour, drive back to the traffic lights, with Marine Drive now on your right, and turn right, noting your kms. After 3,4 km turn left and follow the signs to Fernkloof Nature Reserve. Here you can take your time strolling through fine expanses of coastal fynbos, including roughly 50 species of erica, and you can visit the herbarium, which has over 700 specimens.

Hermanus to Caledon

Retrace your route out of Hermanus and turn right onto the R320 towards Caledon. This is a gravel road, but it is usually kept in fair condition. The R320 passes through the Hemel-en-Aarde Valley which has the southernmost vineyards in Africa – lying some 35 km further south than those at Groot Constantia in the Cape Peninsula.

The gravel gives way to tar after 24 km, at the start of Shaw's Mountain Pass. Pause at the summit of the pass for panoramic views over rolling wheatfields and sparkling dams backed by blue mountains.

Continue past a turn-off to the right for Bredasdorp and Napier, then turn left in front of a cluster of silos onto the R316 for Caledon. (These silos, of some interest to beer-drinkers, are part of the largest malting plant in the southern hemisphere and annually produce 138 000 tons of malt from local barley.)

Follow this road into Caledon (where it becomes Plein Street) until the intersection with Prince Alfred Road/Mill Street in the centre of the town. To visit the Victorian house museum, turn right here and then left to reach 11 Constitution Street. There are many interesting old buildings in the town, with the greatest concentration in Mill Street. In Prince Alfred Road, which you follow to reach the N2, you pass on your right the small sandstone Anglican Church of the Holy Trinity, consecrated in 1855.

At the T-junction with the N2 turn right for the Caledon Wildflower Garden, 1,3 km along the road on the left side. About 1 km further along the N2, on the right-hand side, is the road to a mineral hot springs resort, famous for three centuries.

Caledon to Sir Lowry's Pass

Follow the signs towards Cape Town on the N2. After 23 km, you take the exit left and cross the N2 towards Bot River on the R43 for a short detour through this picturesque town, the centre of an onion-growing district. Follow the main road past the hotel and rejoin the N2.

Some 2,5 km beyond the summit of the pass there is a crossroads, with the Houhoek Inn on your right. Continue on the N2, passing the R321 to Grabouw. The road winds to the 450 m Sir Lowry's Pass. At the summit, turn into the parking area on your left to enjoy the view (picnic site; no fires, no water).

GORDON'S BAY
Gordon's Bay was first known as Visch Hoek Baay, after a fishing station was erected there in the early 1700s. The town's current name was given in honour of Colonel Robert Jacob Gordon, a soldier of Scots-Dutch descent who was the last commander of the Dutch East India Company garrison at the Cape. (He committed suicide after the Dutch capitulated to the British in 1795.) On the slopes above the town are the letters GB and an anchor, picked out in white-painted stones.

Gently shelving beaches makes it a safe bathing resort. The coastline from here to Cape Hangklip offers excellent angling, but many anglers have been swept to their deaths by exceptionally large waves. The sheltered harbour has launching facilities.

A lazy late afternoon in Gordon's Bay harbour.

AA Office AA House, 7 Martin Hammerschlag Way, Cape Town 8001 Tel (021) 21 1550
Hermanus Publicity Association Main Road Hermanus 7200 Tel (0283) 22629
Caledon Museum & Information Centre 14 Constitution St, Caledon 7230 Tel (0281) 21511
Captour Rendezvous Centre, 3 Adderley Street Cape Town 8001 Tel (021) 418 5202

Gentle colours, gentle textures, where the pretty Rooiels River meets the sea.

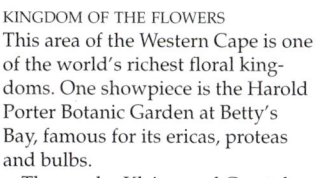

The Houw Hoek Inn – 160 years of history.

Caledon's velvety fields.

KINGDOM OF THE FLOWERS
This area of the Western Cape is one of the world's richest floral kingdoms. One showpiece is the Harold Porter Botanic Garden at Betty's Bay, famous for its ericas, proteas and bulbs.

The nearby Kleinmond Coastal Nature Reserve contains a rich mixture of riverine, kloof-living and seashore plants, many indigenous trees, and over 1 200 different wildflower species. An 8 km coastal walk leads past rock pools and inlets. The Fernkloof Nature Reserve at Hermanus ranges in altitude from 63 m to 842 m, with a wide variety of flora to match.

The Caledon Wildflower Garden owes its existence to three young men who in 1892 held a wildflower show, with prizes worth £60. It became an annual event, leading in 1927 to the establishment of the Wildflower Garden.

WHALES BY THE WAYSIDE
'Living in Hermanus,' according to a British journalist writing in 1994, 'is about as close as you can get to having whales in your back garden.' Acknowledged as offering the best land-based whale watching in the world, Hermanus boasts the world's only official whale-crier who announces the new arrivals – whose calls as they approach the coastline are also amplified by the sonar buoy (another first) in the Old Harbour. Hermanus' southern right whales are a source of delight to locals and visitors alike.

The Old Harbour – replaced almost 50 years ago after nearly a century of service – now has a museum housed in a row of fishermen's cottages. Long before tourism, the people of Hermanus lived from the sea, as many do to this day. The museum also contains numerous relics of the bad old days of whaling.

LAST OF THE COACHING INNS
The original name of the Houhoek Pass, a route 'much dreaded by those who have to pass it in wagons', is thought to have been *Hout Hoek* (wood corner). Alternatively, *Hou* or *Houw* (hold) may refer to the marked steepness and awkward twisting route of the old road.

There have been four earlier passes, all passing close to the Houw Hoek Inn which, dating from 1834, is claimed to be the oldest coaching inn in the country.

The Old Harbour at Hermanus, with the Kleinriviersberge in the distance.

Four passes that link together the pastoral patchwork of the Boland

The Boland mountains, long an obstruction to pioneer travellers, are crossed today by several easy, scenic passes. The passes overlook fertile valleys blanketed with vineyards, fields and orchards, where gracious homesteads nestle beneath craggy peaks. Our route through this region is on good tarred roads and includes a number of attractive picnic sites.

**Cape Town
Sir Lowry's Pass
Grabouw
Franschhoek
Stellenbosch
250 – 260 km**

BEGIN THIS DRIVE AT Rhodes Memorial on the slopes of Devil's Peak. The access road leads from the M3 (Rhodes Drive) just south of the University of Cape Town. From here you have a view across the Cape Flats towards the distant mountains through which your route meanders.

Drive down to the M3 and head towards Muizenberg. At the end of the M3 after about 14 km, exit left, and at the end of the off-ramp 600 m later turn left. At the T-junction, turn right onto the Main Road.

After 3,4 km turn left at the robot-controlled intersection into Atlantic Road, Muizenberg. Follow this road past the pavilion and amusement area on your right, and turn right across the bridge over the Sandvlei mouth.

Drive around the traffic circle and continue straight for Strandfontein and Mitchell's Plain (R310). Known as Baden-Powell Drive, this road runs along the sandy coast of False Bay, offering splendid views, then veers inland. After roughly 25 km on this road, turn right onto the N2 towards Somerset West.

Continue on the N2 up Sir Lowry's Pass. As you approach the top of the pass, move into the central lane and, at the crest, turn right into the parking area. From here you look over the Lourens River Valley to your right, and across False Bay to the Peninsula mountains.

(Across the road from the viewsite entrance is the start of the Boland Hiking Trail that leads past the old Gandou Pass – see alongside.)

Sir Lowry's Pass to Purgatory

Return to the N2, and after 8 km turn left for Grabouw and Elgin (R321). Keep straight through the village, cross the bridge over the Palmiet River (with a stop at the Apple Museum on your left immediately after), then turn left at the sign for Villiersdorp and Franschhoek (R321).

The start of Viljoen's Pass is reached about 5 km later. Where the road begins to descend, there are wide views of tree-bordered fields in the valleys below.

About 6 km from the start of the pass there is a hairpin bend to the right. Stop here in the parking area on your left to enjoy the view over the fertile upper reaches of the *Riviersonderend* (river without end).

From here the road descends into the valley, and you pass through the settlement of Vyeboom. Soon there are good views over the Theewaterskloof Dam, with the Franschhoek Mountains on its far side.

Cross the bridge over the dam and immediately turn left for Franschhoek (R45). About 2,8 km later, on a right hand bend, park on the left side of the road for a view of the dam and the road bridge. After a further 7,6 km you reach the tree-shaded Purgatory picnic site (braai places, toilets, drinking water).

THE FRUIT OF DRAKENSTEIN

Until 1892, Cape fruit farmers were prevented by the lack of refrigerated cargo holds from exporting their surplus fruit. But in that year the ship *Drummond Castle* safely delivered delicate peaches to London, changing the fruit farmers' fortunes.

A few years later, CJ Rhodes bought up a number of Drakenstein farms. These formed the basis of Rhodes Fruit Farms, today run by a large corporation.

GANDOU PASS AND FAR-SIGHTED SIR LOWRY COLE

The Khoikhoi and San people knew the animal track over the Hottentots Holland Mountains as *Gandou* (path of the eland). Early European settlers used this same steep track to haul their wagons over the mountains – until the traffic to and from the farms became so heavy that pressure mounted for the building of a properly graded pass. Sir Lowry Cole, Governor at the Cape in the early 19th century, invoked the displeasure of the British Government – but the gratitude of the farmers – when he authorized the use of local funds to build the new pass that bears his name.

Shortly after the picnic site, the road begins to ascend the Franschhoek Pass and crosses a bridge over the Du Toit's River. A few hundred metres past the bridge you can see traces of the old pass marked by a row of stones on the hillside to your right.

Over the Franschhoek Pass

Immediately after crossing the Jan Joubertsgat Bridge, stop at a parking area on your right. Steps lead down to the river on the mountain side of the road on both sides of the bridge. This allows you to examine the construction of the bridge – the oldest road bridge still in use in South Africa.

Continue up the pass, stopping just after the first hairpin bend at a parking area on your left, for a view back down the pass into the valley with its rocky walls and deep kloof.

From the lower slopes of Sir Lowry's Pass, the Hottentots Holland Mountains stretch to the east.

Springtime sees Elgin apple country in blossom.

Luxuriant pastoral scene alongside the Theewaterskloof Dam.

As the road begins to descend, turn left into a parking area. From here there are magnificent views of the Franschhoek Valley with its farmlands, vineyards, forests, shimmering dams and ribbons of road.

The road winds down the mountainside into Franschhoek, reaching the Huguenot Monument on your left as you approach the town. Park here to visit the monument and the adjoining Huguenot Museum. (Franschhoek has several restaurants offering lunches and teas.)

Franschhoek to Boschendal

About 100 m beyond the main museum building, turn right into Huguenot Road for Paarl, Stellenbosch and Cape Town. Drive along this road, passing the historic Dutch Reformed Church and the Town Hall on your right. Follow this main road (R45) through the town. The road passes through the village of *Groendal* (green dale), crosses the railway, then leads through the vineyards of many of the original farms established by the first French Huguenot settlers.

After passing a forested picnic area on your left, the road crosses the railway again, then crosses the Berg River twice. (This section was under reconstruction in 1996, but the main features will remain unaltered.) About 5 km later, turn left for Pniel and Stellenbosch (R310). Immediately after the turn, cross a double set of railway tracks; 1,5 km later, turn left to visit Boschendal homestead (see pages 244 – 5).

Boschendal to Cape Town

After leaving the Boschendal estate, the road leads through the tree-shaded mission village of Pniel, with its picturesque church on your right, then winds gently uphill through the adjoining village of Johannesdal. Continue on the R310 as it winds over the Helshoogte Pass, and down through Ida's Valley on the outskirts of Stellenbosch.

At the traffic lights, you may choose to turn left into Cluver Road to reach the centre of town, or to turn later into Hammanshand Road and then right into Bird Street. Continue straight on Bird Street (R304) for 15 km, then turn left onto the N1 towards Cape Town.

AA Office AA House 7 Martin Hammerschlag Way, Cape Town 8001 Tel (021) 21 1550
Stellenbosch Publicity Association 36 Market Street, Stellenbosch 7600 Tel (021) 883 9633
Franschhoek Publicity Association PO Box 178 Franschhoek 7690 Tel (02212) 3603
Captour Tourism Rendezvous Centre, 3 Adderley Street, Cape Town 8001 Tel (021) 418 5202

The view west from the Franschhoek Pass over the fertile Berg River Valley.

Huguenot Monument, Franschhoek.

THE PARADISE THEY CALLED PURGATORY

The Franschhoek Pass, among the highlights of this scenic drive, replaces a number of earlier roadways. One of these was built in 1822 by the 'irregular and desperate' men of the Royal African Corps. Toiling in the alternating heat and cold on the Villiersdorp side, they named the place Purgatory. Lord Charles Somerset had sent them there not only to build a road but also so that they could 'be prevented from committing violence and depredation' on innocent citizens. The road they built replaced one made by a local farmer, SJ Cats of Ida's Valley.

The Jan Joubertsgat Bridge, believed to be named after an early traveller who drowned in the river that it crosses, was built in 1823.

APPLE COUNTRY

The lucrative Elgin apple industry is relatively young – it was started only after World War I on the initiative of medical man and member of the Cape Legislative Council, Sir Antonie Viljoen, after whom the pass was named. Viljoen planted the first apple trees in the area, but died before his dreams of a large apple-growing venture became a reality. Although the apple capital is actually Grabouw, the industry has become known by the name of the nearest railway despatching point, Elgin, built on Glen Elgin farm.

HUGUENOT MONUMENT AND MUSEUM

This complex, commemorating the Huguenot settlers who fled persecution in 17th-century France, is laid out among lawns and flower beds in the fertile bowl of the mountains. The main building, Saasveld, is loosely modelled on a Cape Town dwelling designed by Louis Thibault.

The museum houses fine collections of Cape silver, old crockery and furniture, and relics of the early fruit and wine industries. Staff members specialize in tracing Huguenot ancestry.

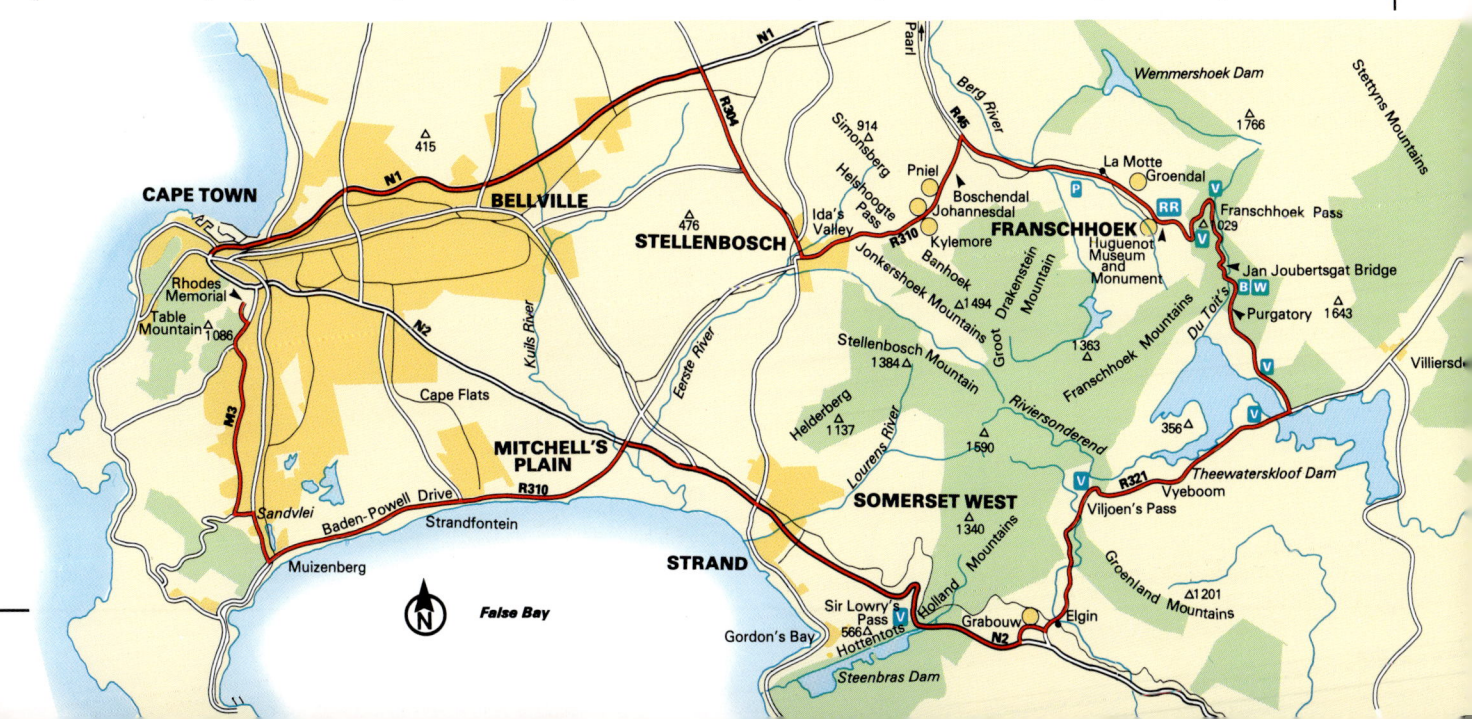

Elegant buildings and stately old oaks line Stellenbosch's Dorp Street.

Oak-shaded avenues and historic homes

IN THE SPRING of 1679 Simon van der Stel, governor of the Dutch settlement at the Cape, set out on a 'venture into the wilderness', to explore the settlement's immediate hinterland and assess its usefulness. In his journal he recorded his discovery of the Eerste River Valley:

'... a level valley comprising several thousand morgen of beautiful pasturage. It is also ideal for agriculture, being drained by a particularly fine, clear river, along whose banks grow handsome, tall trees, suitable for timber and also for firewood.'

Van der Stel's encampment on an island in the Eerste River was referred to as *Stellenbosch* (Van der Stel's wood) and this became the name of the village that subsequently grew here when settlers arrived and established farms.

The older part of the town lies close to the river, and in a leisurely exploration on foot it is possible to visit many well-preserved homes and other buildings of interest, dating from various periods in the town's 300 years of mostly tranquil history.

Arriving in Stellenbosch by car, turn into Old Strand Road at the western end of Dorp Street. Cross the small bridge over the Eerste River and park on the left.

Across the road from where you have parked, there is a group of whitewashed *cottages* **(1)**, thought to have been designed by Sir Herbert Baker as 'model dwellings' for workers on one of Cecil Rhodes' farms, *Vredenburg*. The cottages now make an attractive setting for a restaurant.

Walk back along Old Strand Road, crossing the bridge over the river. Looking up-river from the bridge, imagine the scene three centuries ago, as the first few European settlers began erecting their simple cottages within convenient water-carrying distance of this lively and sparkling mountain stream.

Where Old Strand Road meets Dorp Street there are several interesting buildings. On your left is *Libertas Parva* **(2)**, which now houses the Rembrandt van Rijn art collection, and its adjacent wine cellar, now the *Stellenryck Wine Museum* **(3)** (both open to the public). Across the road is *50 Dorp Street* **(4)**, formerly owned by a Mrs Ackermann, where Jan Smuts boarded while studying at Victoria College (now the University of Stellenbosch).

Workers' cottages designed by Sir Herbert Baker, in Old Strand Road.

Living in Libertas Parva at that time were a Mr and Mrs Krige, with their daughter Sybella. Jan Smuts and Sybella met, in the vicinity of this crossroads, eventually married, and went forward to a destiny that was to hold them in the international spotlight.

Rich rows of historic buildings

As you walk east along Dorp Street, you pass through one of South Africa's richest collections of interesting old buildings.

Opposite the Ackermann house there are the *Krige cottages* **(5)**, built by Mr Willie Krige in a Victorianized Cape style. A short distance further along, set back from the street, is the old farmhouse *Vredelust* **(6)**, now a restaurant. In earlier days Vredelust was known as Libertas Oos, and the farm was originally granted to a Jan Cornelisz in 1689. Cornelisz must have been quite a character, for he was generally known as Jan Bombam, and was even referred to by this name in official documents.

At 84 Dorp Street, on the left side of the street, is *Oom Samie se Winkel* **(7)**, a village shop that retains the charm of a more leisurely way of life. At 95 Dorp Street, on the right, we come to *La Gratitude* **(8)**, with a fine Cape Dutch facade.

La Gratitude was built in 1798 by the Rev Meent Borcherds. It is still possible to see from the street the 'all-seeing eye of God' that Borcherds had carved above the front gable window.

Further along the street, on the left, there is the old *Lutheran Church* **(9)** of 1851 – its modest space now housing the University of Stellenbosch Art Gallery.

Exploring the Village Museum

Continue along Dorp Street, then turn left into Ryneveld Street.

A 'fine, clear river along whose banks grow handsome, tall trees...'

White-walled Burgherhuis, adjoining the Braak, dates from 1797.

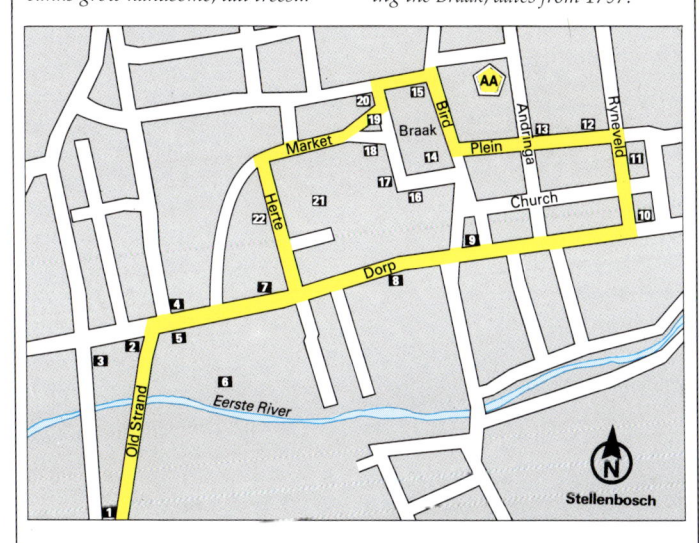

The very simple but warm interior of the early 18th century Schreuderhuis.

You now pass on your right the *Kolonieshuis* **(10)** (the official residence erected in each new drostdy, or magisterial district). The present building incorporates parts of the original house of 1694. The new congregation's first permanent minister, Hercules van Loon, lived here for four years from 1700, until he committed suicide by 'cutting his own throat with a pocket knife'. Nobody could discover 'the cause of his profound despair', but it may have had something to do with the serious social problems then plaguing the new congregation.

Cross Church Street and enter the *Village Museum* on your right at 18 Ryneveld Street **(11)** (small entrance fee). The Village Museum incorporates a section of the old town, and includes several distinct houses representing various periods in the town's history.

One of these, *Schreuderhuis*, is probably the oldest restored townhouse in South Africa. It is clearly recognisable in the oldest known drawing of Stellenbosch, dated 15 February 1710. The interior is striking in its simplicity. Even much later in the 18th century only the wealthy could have glass panes in their windows and use wooden planks for their floors and ceilings. Here the window frames are covered with cotton rubbed with beeswax, the ceilings are made of sticks and reeds and the floors are simply compacted earth.

Next in the complex is *Blettermanhuis*, built in the last quarter of the 18th century and furnished in the style favoured by a wealthy burgher of about 1780. A third house in the complex is *Grosvenor House*, furnished in a style characteristic of the early 19th century, while a fourth is *Berghhuis*, former home of Oloff Bergh, now furnished in the style of affluent townsfolk at about the middle of the 19th century.

Leave the museum complex through the Ryneveld Street entrance, turn right, then turn left into Plein Street. In Plein Street, on your right, is *De Witt House* **(12)**, dating from the second quarter of the 19th century, and named after a dentist who practised from here.

The Braak and the Kruithuis

From De Witt House, continue along Plein Street. In front of the City Hall complex on your right you will see the old furrow of the *mill stream* **(13)**, believed to date back to the founding of the town.

Cross Andringa and Bird streets to reach the *Braak* **(14)**, or the village green. Over the centuries this has served as fairground, sports venue and military parade ground.

To your right, at the north end of the Braak, there is the thatch-roofed *St Mary's Anglican Church* **(15)**. Along the southern and western sides of the Braak you can see the handsome collection of buildings known as the *Rhenish complex*, including the elegant *Rhenish Church* **(16)**, the *Rhenish Institute* **(17)**, now an arts centre, and the *1905 building* **(18)** that housed the Rhenish High School and the Rhenish Primary School. Today, *36 Market Street* houses the Stellenbosch Visitors' Bureau and the Stellenbosch Wine Route office, and both organizations provide the latest information.

Cross from the Braak to the small triangular traffic island at the head of Market Street. Here you can see the old *VOC Kruithuis* (arsenal) of 1777 **(19)**. It now houses a collection of weapons and military uniforms, including examples of the heavy matchlock weapons with which Van Riebeeck's men were armed.

Across the northern arm of Market Street from the Kruithuis you can see the *Burgherhuis* **(20)**, built in 1797. Part of this building is now open to the public as a museum and houses displays of furniture, glassware and ceramics. It is also the head office of Historical Homes of South Africa, an organization concerned with the restoration of historically important buildings.

Walk along Market Street away from the Braak, passing on your left several more buildings of the Rhenish complex, including the *old parsonage* **(21)** dating back to 1815. Today it houses a toy museum and a fine display of miniature furniture. Turn left into Herte Street. Along the right side of Herte Street, behind a line of oaks, you will see a row of *cottages* **(22)** believed to have been built in 1834 as homes for some of the town's newly freed slaves.

Continue along Herte Street, then turn right into Dorp Street. Turn left into Old Strand Road to arrive back at the point where you parked your car.

The 'Land van Waveren' and the wild beauty of Bain's Kloof

This drive starts with the famous view of Table Mountain from across Table Bay, then heads north in the footsteps of early seekers after the fabled treasure of Monomotapa. The wealth they found was in the soil – rich farmlands flank our route to the 'Land van Waveren' beyond the mountains. The entire route is on good tarred roads.

Cape Town
Bloubergstrand
Malmesbury
Nuwekloof Pass
Tulbagh
Bain's Kloof
Wellington
260 – 280 km

Turn off Table Bay Boulevard (N1) onto Marine Drive (R27). Drive through Milnerton, with the lagoon on your left. Soon after passing Rietvlei on your right, turn left for Bloubergstrand, noting your kms. There are a number of parking areas along the beachfront that afford magnificent views of the sweep of the bay and Table Mountain.

After 3,6 km turn left into Sir David Baird Drive, then turn left into Stadler Road to reach a parking area where the wide beach offers a pleasant walk – and at low tide it is possible to walk across a sand bar to an outcrop of rocks.

Bloubergstrand to Tulbagh

Leave the parking lot, and turn left at the T-junction onto Sir David Baird Drive – then turn left again at the next T-junction towards Melkbosstrand. Continue on this road as it turns inland, and cross the R27. After a further 9 km turn left at the T-junction onto the N7, noting your kms. After 34 km turn off the N7 for the R315/R46, and follow the signs into Malmesbury. Turn left into Voortrekker Street at the four-way stop. After 100 m, turn right into Rainier Street, then turn right into Piet Retief Street at the three-way stop. After a further 3,9 km turn left onto the R46 for Riebeek-Kasteel and Hermon, noting your kms.

Roughly 11 km later, the road reaches the summit of the Bothmaskloof Pass. A short distance down the pass, turn left to reach a parking area from where there is a splendid view over the town of Riebeek-Kasteel and the surrounding countryside. A monument here records the passage of explorers sent out by Jan van Riebeeck in 1661 (see below). Return to the R46, noting your kms as you turn left.

Pass roads on your left to Riebeek-Kasteel and Hermon. After 12,5 km, turn left at the T-junction onto the R44. Pass a road on your right to Voëlvlei Dam after a further 11,5 km.

About 8,5 km later the road crosses the Klein Berg River in the Nuwekloof Pass, built by Thomas Bain in 1873. An older road, which led to the valley known then as the 'Land van Waveren', can be seen clearly on the right. Roughly 4,5 km after entering the Nuwekloof Pass, turn left to reach the town of Tulbagh.

There is not enough time on this drive to explore fully the historic area of the town, but a drive along Church Street gives a glimpse of Tulbagh's beautifully restored 18th- and 19th-century buildings (see pages 270 – 1). Several

The best-known view of Table Mountain – from the flower-covered dunes at Bloubergstrand across Table Bay.

BAIN'S KLOOF PASS
This picturesque road above the *Wit* (white) River, winding through rugged peaks of eroded sandstone and granite, was built by convict labourers under Andrew Geddes Bain. In places the pass is carried on dry-packed stone walls more than 12 m high. More than half its 30 km length had to be blasted from solid rock with gunpowder, as this was before the invention of dynamite. Bridges have been reinforced and the road has been tarred, but otherwise it remains as it was built by Bain. On the Wellington side of the summit, several features of the original pass, such as the old tunnel, have been signposted.

CAPITAL OF THE SWARTLAND
Malmesbury is the chief town of the wheat-rich *Swartland* (black country), so named not for the colour of its soil – which is reddish brown – but probably for the dark *renosterbos* (rhino bush) that formerly covered the area.

A warm sulphur spring was discovered in the region in 1744, and a few people settled nearby. The place became the venue for periodic *Nagmaal* (Communion) services, and three wells were sunk for water. One of these may be seen inside the furniture store on the corner of Hill and Piet Retief streets. Malmesbury was named by Governor Sir Lowry Cole in 1829 in honour of his wife's family.

SEARCHING FOR MONOMOTAPA
Pieter Cruythoff led an expedition from the Castle in Cape Town early in 1661, under orders from Commander Jan van Riebeek, to find a route to the legendary and fabulously wealthy kingdom of Monomotapa. They failed in this objective, but they did discover a way to the north as far as the edge of Namaqualand – and they made contact with new trading partners, the Nama.

On the way they encountered a great isolated ridge that Cruythoff loyally named Riebeek-Kasteel. Today the name applies only to the village at its foot, and the mountain is known as *Kasteelberg* (castle mountain).

In this vicinity the party found many hippopotamus, rhinoceros, lion and herds of buck. Lions attacked them near the present Bothmaskloof Pass, which winds downhill towards Riebeek-Kasteel.

WELLINGTON – COLONIAL LIMIT
Limiet Vallei was one of the earliest names given to the Wellington district, when it marked the limit of settler expansion. The town of Wellington, founded in 1837, is the home of the Huguenot Seminary started by the Rev Andrew Murray, and of South Africa's first teachers' college. Among many diversions – apart from its magnificent scenic surroundings – Wellington offers hikes and scenic drives, berry-picking and a wine route, as well as an absorbing museum and several old and interesting buildings. Ouma Granny's House in Fountain Street is a smaller Victorian townhouse that keeps alive the homely atmosphere of 'the good old days'. Dried fruit and leather products may be bought direct from the respective factories, and tours may also be arranged. The town is named after the first Duke of Wellington, victor of Waterloo (1815).

The view from Bothmaskloof Pass near Riebeek-Kasteel.

Cool, clear mountain streams tumble through the rocky Bain's Kloof.

SOUTH-WESTERN CAPE

establishments in Tulbagh offer lunch. On the corner of Church Street and Twee Jonge Gezellen Road there is a municipal picnic site (braai places, toilets, water), and on the banks of the Klip River there is the Tulbagh municipal holiday resort, which has a swimming pool as well as braai and picnic facilities – the entrance is on Van der Stel Street.

Tulbagh to Bain's Kloof

Leave Tulbagh by travelling south along Van der Stel Street for Wolseley. Note your kms as you pass the road on your right to Gouda and Cape Town. The peaks of the Witsenberg range on your left and of the Watervalsberg and Elandskloofberg ranges on your right are frequently snow-clad in winter.

After 13,2 km turn right for Wolseley and Worcester. Continue straight through the town of Wolseley. About 3,3 km beyond the town, on your right there is a stone blockhouse dating from the Anglo-Boer War. With the better preserved blockhouse on your left 400 m beyond, it was built to guard the railway bridges.

Turn right (towards Worcester) at the T-junction 900 m later, noting your kms. Pass the R43 to Worcester on your left after 7 km. Cross a single-lane bridge over the Breede River some 500 m later at the beginning of Bain's Kloof, and another single-lane bridge within 200 m, followed by a sharp left bend.

After a further 5,5 km there are picnic places on both sides of the road next to a small stream (no facilities). Cross a single-lane bridge after a further 2,2 km, and turn right 100 m later into the *Tweede Tol* (second toll) camp and picnic site (closed during winter; entry fee, braai places, toilets, water). About 2,4 km beyond Tweede Tol the road is overhung by a mass of rock known as Dacres' Pulpit, after a clergyman who was a member of a party that explored the kloof. Pass the Bishop's Arch rock formation on your left l,5 km later and stop at the parking area 400 m beyond it to enjoy some excellent views along the gorge.

At the crest of the pass, 2,8 km later, is the site of the former tollgate known as *Eerste Tol* (first toll). A plaque on the right records the construction of the pass in 1853. Park at the viewsite on the right 1,5 km later for magnificent views over the town of Wellington and the Berg River Valley.

Bain's Kloof to Cape Town

From the viewsite the road winds down the pass to Wellington, which you enter on Church Street. Look out for the museum, with its many fascinating collections, on your right. At the T-junction with Main Street, opposite the fine old Dutch Reformed Church, notice the statue of the much-loved clergyman, Andrew Murray.

To return directly to Cape Town, turn left at the T-junction and follow the R44 to the N1 at Klapmuts.

If you wish to travel through Durbanville, after about 15 km turn right from the R44 onto the R312. Continue straight at the intersection with the Paarl – Malmesbury road. After a little more than 12 km, turn left for Durbanville (R312), and roughly 6 km later turn left onto the R302. The road enters Durbanville 5 km after this. Turn left into Main Road, and follow the signs onto the N1 for Cape Town.

AA Office AA House, 7 Martin Hammerschlag Way, Cape Town 8001 Tel (021) 211 550
Captour Tourism Rendezvous Centre 3 Adderley St, Cape Town 8001 Tel (021) 418 5202
Wellington Information Centre Main Road Wellington 7655 Tel (02211) 34 604

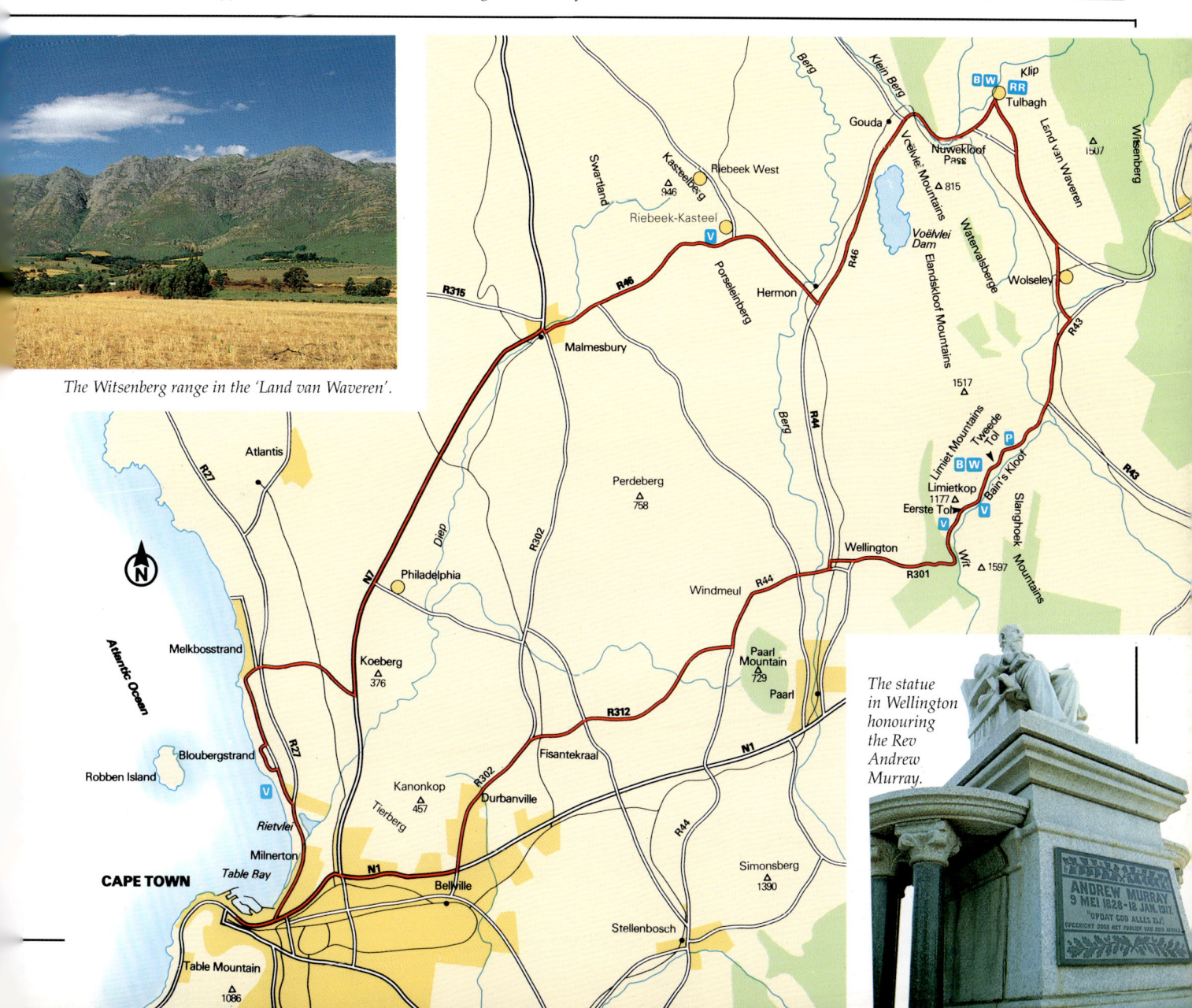

The Witsenberg range in the 'Land van Waveren'.

The statue in Wellington honouring the Rev Andrew Murray.

• EXPLORING TULBAGH ON FOOT •

The shock that restored Church Street to splendour

Unspoilt by later development, the row of perfectly restored buildings on Tulbagh's Church Street preserves the gracious atmosphere of the late 18th century.

TULBAGH LIES IN a valley sheltered by the Witsenberg and Winterhoek ranges, yet it is exposed to perhaps the most unusual of all natural hazards in South Africa – earthquake. On the night of 29 September 1969, a shift in the nearby Worcester geological fault brought widespread destruction to this peaceful town.

Ironically, it was this threat of oblivion that mobilized efforts to restore Church Street – representing an almost perfect village of the late 18th century. Meticulous research and modern rebuilding techniques have combined to preserve a unique architectural treasure – one of the largest concentrations of national monuments in South Africa.

Tulbagh once had the quaint nickname of *Tulpiesdorp* (tulip town) because of the profusion of Cape wild tulips that grew in the area. The soil is intensively cultivated now, but the upper slopes of the mountains are still rich in wildflowers.

The existence of the valley was reported to Commander Jan van Riebeeck as early as 1658. In 1699 Governor WA van der Stel looked down on the valley and named it the 'Land van Waveren' after a wealthy Amsterdam family. Farmers were at once dispatched to the valley, where poor roads kept them isolated from the main Cape settlement for many years.

Work on a church was started in 1743 and lasted until 1748. This building is now the *Oude Kerk Volksmuseum* **(1)** – old church folk museum – one of four buildings forming the museum complex. Our walk begins here at the Oude Kerk, at the southern end of Church Street.

A sexton's prophecy

The entrance to the church originally faced the old wagon road on the west side, but was changed to its present position during alterations in 1795, at the time that Church Street was built in a straight line to the parsonage.

For many years the church had an earth floor and, as burials took place within the building, collapses of the floor were fairly frequent. The sexton nonchalantly filled them in. There were no pews, and, as was the custom, the members of the congregation brought their own chairs – or rather, the chairs were carried to the church by slaves.

One of the sextons, Leendert Haasbroek, was stabbed to death by a slave whom he had rebuked for failing to clean the church to his satisfaction. As he lay dying, Haasbroek prophesied that the slave would be brought to justice because 'even the crows would tell the story'. The killer escaped and remained at liberty for a long time, until one day he awoke beneath a tree and heard the crows chattering above. Convinced that they were proclaiming his guilt, he surrendered, was tried, and was publicly hanged on Tulbagh's Gallows Hill.

The Oude Kerk Volksmuseum contains fine examples of early Cape chairs and other furniture, musical instruments, Cape silver, brass and copper articles, weapons, toys, porcelain and costumes.

Restoration photographs

When you leave the museum, cross the street diagonally to an *old house* **(2)** with a high stoep and an iron verandah painted in red and white stripes. This building, which also serves as an information centre for the town, houses a large collection of photographs that show Church Street – originally known as *Onderstraat* (lower street) – during various periods, including 'before-and-after' pictures of the restorations following earthquake damage.

Walk north along Church Street, away from the Oude Kerk. *Number 12* **(3)** is believed to be

Behind the elegant lines of the Oude Kerk's entrance lies a fine museum.

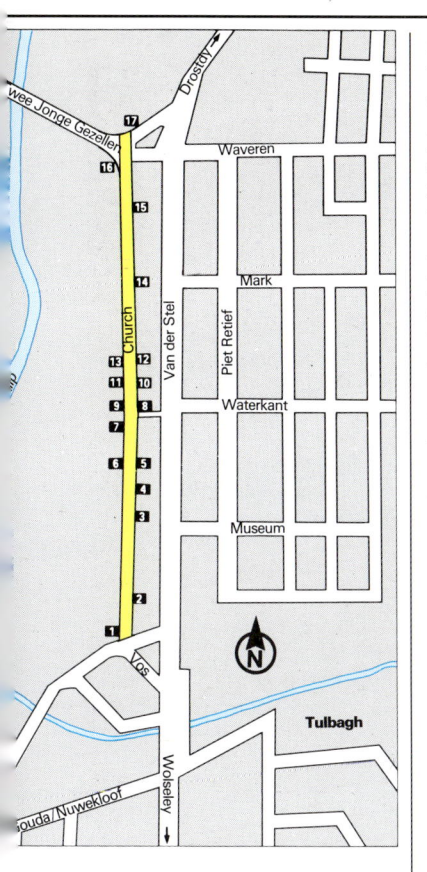

A wine press at De Oude Drostdy.

The Witsenberg makes a wintry backdrop to Tulbagh and the Land van Waveren.

the oldest house in Tulbagh. It was built in about 1754 – roughly 40 years before the street was made, which explains why its frontage is out of line with the street. The house became church property, and was gradually extended to serve as both school and house. Its pointed gable is typical of the Tulbagh district, and the house has been restored to its appearance of about 1861. The little garden saw the creation of a new variety of rose that, in honour of its breeder – who lived here – was named 'Marie Blanc'.

Next on your right is *number 14* **(4)**, a late-Victorian village house in which the museum stages periodic exhibitions.

Number 16 **(5)** is thought to have been an old wagon house, which had already been converted to a home by 1861. Its present yellow-ochre colour matches a shade found beneath layers of lime-wash, and the two front doors make an unusual arrangement. Across the street is *number 17* **(6)**, probably built in 1852 by a bachelor Van der Merwe for himself and his mother.

A feature of Church Street is the narrow street frontage of the houses, typical of the time when street frontage, together with windows, formed the basis for determining property taxes.

Another unusual feature is that there are so few buildings on the west side of the street. This came about because all the original Church Street plots stretched down to the Klip River, allowing each occupant to irrigate his garden. On the west side of the street there is a stone-lined canal with steel sluices – a direct descendant of the early irrigation system.

Danie Theron's home
Among the first settlers at Tulbagh were members of the Theron family, and many Therons still live in the town, much as one finds many De Villiers families in Paarl. Just past number 18 on the right is *number 21* **(7)** on the left, which was bought in 1877 by WW Theron – the father of the famous Boer scout, Commandant Danie Theron, who fought to the death against overwhelming odds at Gatsrand near Potchefstroom. Cmdt Theron, born in 1872, lived here for much of his youth. Earlier, the family had lived in number 12, where the future hero was probably born.

Number 22 **(8)**, now a museum annexe, was built in about 1803. It is furnished in the style of a modest house of over a century ago, and contains many of the surprisingly ingenious little implements and accessories that our ancestors used for making their lives a little more comfortable.

Across the street is the entrance to *Paddagang* **(9)** (frog passage). This was either a store or slave quarters, and is now run as a restaurant. (There are other eating places in Tulbagh, and municipal picnic sites. One picnic site is on the corner of Church Street and the Twee Jonge Gezellen road – with braai places, toilets and water. The other picnic site, in the Tulbagh Holiday Resort on the Klip River, where permits for both sites are obtainable, has its entrance on Van der Stel Street and has a swimming pool, braai places, toilets and water.)

H is for home
Continuing north along Church Street, you pass *number 24* **(10)**, one of the few old H-shaped houses in Tulbagh, probably built before 1815, and occupied for many years by the local postmaster. The house across the street **(11)** was built at about the same time.

Number 26 **(12)** was once the mission parsonage, and *number 27* **(13)** across the street from it served as its stables and coach house. Stand in front of number 28, and you can see a tree-shrouded hill across the little valley – this was once Gallows Hill.

So far as is known, only two people were ever hanged here in law-abiding Tulbagh. Impressive and unusual in a street of gables and unpretentious single storeys is the double-storeyed Georgian appearance of number 36, known as *Monbijou* **(14)**. The design of the house is attributed to Thibault, and it is thought to have been built before 1815.

Personal differences and fiery clergy led to the establishment of two parishes in the tiny settlement, a situation that lasted from 1843 until 1935. *Number 42* **(15)** was the parsonage of the rival *Kruisvallei* (cross valley) congregation, and the clergyman of the Oude Kerk therefore had to pass his rival's door on his way to his church from his own parsonage at the northern end of Church Street.

The last house on the left is *Ballotina* **(16)**, thought to have been built to a design of Thibault on land granted to the widow of the Reverend HW Ballot. The *Dutch Reformed Church parsonage of 1765* **(17)** occupies its original position at the northern end of the street.

If time permits, drive along Van der Stel Street, which contains a few interesting old buildings, for some 3 km to reach, on your right, De Oude Drostdy. This building was planned after it was decided in 1804 to make Tulbagh a *drostdy* (magisterial district or the magistrate's official residence) separate from Stellenbosch, of which it was then a part.

After much controversy relating to cost, the Drostdy was formally opened in 1806. By then the British had already taken over at the Cape. (The new district was named after Ryk Tulbagh, a genial and much-loved governor of the 18th century.)

Today the Drostdy serves as a museum, particularly rich in furniture and porcelain. Some 500 m beyond it, on your left, are the Drostdy Wine Cellars, which offer tours and wine-tastings twice a day (except Sundays).

A statesman's birthplace in the wheatlands of the Cape

Our route is through wheatlands and wildflower country – where our first stops are at hamlets that owe their origins to religion. We visit Darling, with a diversion to the coast at Yzerfontein and then on to Moorreesburg, Riebeek West and Malmesbury, before returning to Cape Town via Kalbaskraal. About 40 km of the route is on good gravel roads.

**Cape Town
Darling
Yzerfontein
Moorreesburg
Riebeek West
Malmesbury
260 – 270 km**

Leave the city on the N1, passing Table Bay harbour on your left. About 11 km later, turn left for the N7 for Malmesbury/Goodwood West (Interchange 13), noting your kms. After about 13 km on the N7 you pass, on your right, the West Coast Ostrich Ranch. Soon after, you pass Koeberg Hill, the highest point in the area at 376 m, also on your right. Look left here, towards the sea, and you will see the Koeberg Nuclear Power Station in the distance.

At 25,5 km turn right at the crossroads onto the R304 for Philadelphia, which lies 3 km down this narrow tarred road. The Dutch Reformed Church is still the centre of the village that grew around it from the 1860s.

Philadelphia to Moorreesburg

Retrace your route, noting your kms as you cross the N7; 4,6 km later, turn right at the T-junction onto the bluegum-lined road to Atlantis and Mamre (R304). At 16 km, turn right at the T-junction and, some 3 km later, turn left at another T-junction and keep a lookout for the Mamre turn-off about 2 km further on. Turn sharp left into Mamre, pass residential areas and turn left at the traffic circle to enter the Moravian Mission Station.

Retrace your route to the road from which you entered Mamre, and turn left for Darling. On your left you pass the farm Oudepost, which has the largest orchid nursery in the southern hemisphere and holds an annual orchid show in September – the same time as the Darling wildflower show.

Enter Darling (which has a fascinating museum in Pastorie Street) and follow Main Street (*Hoofstraat*) through the town. Note your kms where Main Street turns sharp right for Yzerfontein. About 10 km beyond the town, on your left, is the Tienie Versveld Flower Reserve, entered by mounting a stile over the boundary fence. Keep straight at the intersection with the R27 some 3 km later. After a further 2,3 km you pass a reconstructed lime kiln on your left and, 4,7 km beyond the kiln, enter Yzerfontein, well known for its 27 km long beach and excellent surfing and fishing.

Drive back to Darling and, just as you reach the town, turn left onto a gravel road for the Hildebrand Memorial. About 5 km later, just before the road crosses the railway line, turn right onto a good but narrow track into the wheatfields to reach the tall monument.

Return to Darling and turn left onto the road on which you travelled to and from Yzerfontein. This becomes Main Street. Turn left out of Main Street into Church Street (R307) for Moorreesburg/Hopefield and note your kms. The surface soon changes to gravel.

About 23 km from Darling, keep straight at the crossroads with the R45 and, at 36 km, turn left at the T-junction at the foot of Neulfontein se Berg (335 m). After a few kilometres you reach the town of Moorreesburg, centre of the area's wheat industry and dominated by huge grain silos. Moorreesburg is the home of the Wheat Museum.

Moorreesburg to Cape Town

After visiting Moorreesburg, turn right onto the road to Malmesbury, but, after less than 2 km, turn sharp left onto the R311 for Riebeek West. Directly ahead in the distance lies the 946 m high Kasteelberg, and you reach the foot of it about 26 km from Moorreesburg. Look out for the sign on the left that reads 'PPC/W Cape'. Turn left here to see the reconstructed house in which Jan Smuts, a former Boer general and Prime Minister of South Africa, was born. The house stands just inside the main gate and there are delightful picnic spots in the garden surroundings.

Drive on through Riebeek West, passing a number of wine cellars along the short distance to the neighbouring village of Riebeek

Furrows still lead water – the motive power – to Mamre's old mill.

THE HIDDEN, GREEN VALLEY

The site of the Mamre mission station, with its plentiful supply of water, was originally called *Groene Kloof* (green ravine). A military post was established here in 1701, but abandoned by 1791. The neighbouring area was reserved for remnants of the Khoikhoi people for whom, in 1808, the German Moravian Mission Society established a mission, building a church, a school and a watermill. The old nucleus of the mission station has been restored and seven of the old buildings are national monuments; the watermill is a museum. Although surrounding areas have become urbanized, the original little valley with its sound of running water, its tall, green oaks and whitewashed buildings, remains unspoilt.

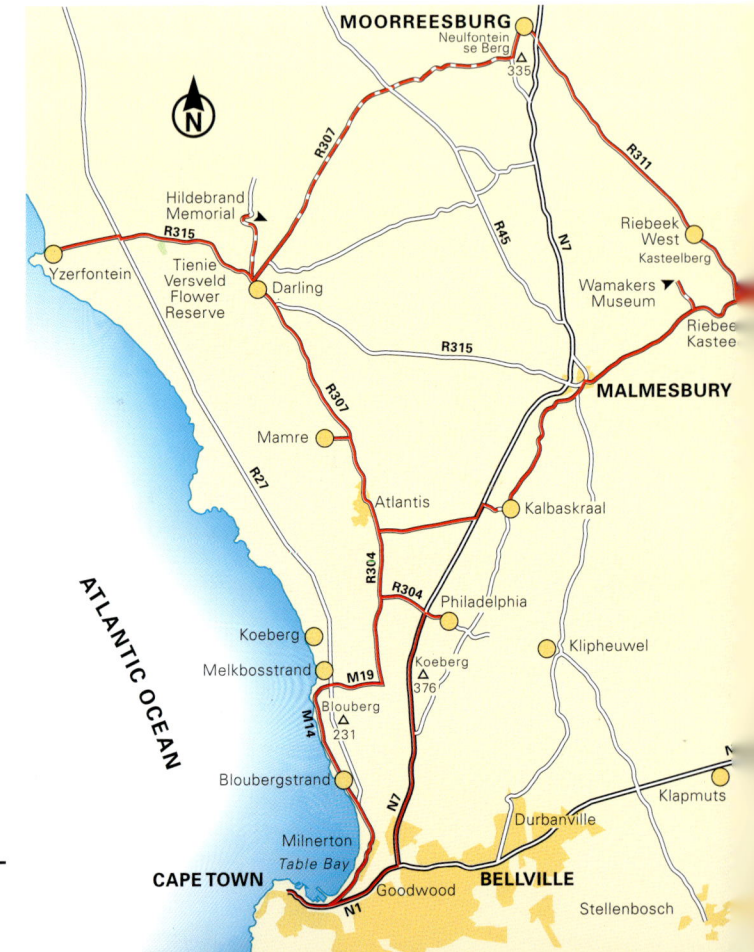

Kasteel. After admiring the pretty houses and, in the town square, South Africa's biggest statue of an ox (a monument to the oxen that drew the Voortrekker wagons), turn right for Malmesbury at the T-junction with the R46.

Drive over the not-very-steep Bothmaskloof Pass with its monument to a group of explorers who passed this way in 1661. After about 7,8 km on the R46 there is a road, on your right, to the *Wamakers* (wagon-makers) Museum where one Le Fébre Relihán worked from 1885 to 1918. The museum, on a farm a few kilometres along the road, displays more than 700 items.

Return to the R46 and turn right, to enter Malmesbury several kilometres later. This town received its name in 1829 when the governor, Sir Lowry Cole, visited the hot spring here and named the place after his father-in-law, the Earl of Malmesbury. Leave the town by driving south along the main street (Voortrekker Road), which becomes the R302 for Durbanville. After only a few kilometres turn right for Kalbaskraal, an important railway junction. At Kalbaskraal, turn right onto a gravel road and, 3 km later, at the T-junction with the N7, turn left for Cape Town. Less than a kilometre further, turn right for Atlantis and, 13 km later, turn left onto the shady R304 on which you travelled earlier. After about 15 km on the R304, turn right onto the M19 for Melkbosstrand. From Melkbosstrand the road continues south along the coast, to join the N1.

| **AA Office** 7 Martin Hammerschlag Way Cape Town 8001 Tel (021) 21 1550 |
| **Captour** Tourism Rendezvous Centre 3 Adderley Street, Cape Town 8001 Tel (021) 418 5202 |

A red sky at night holds no threat to neatly stacked bales on a Malmesbury wheatfield.

GOLDEN HARVEST FROM THE SWARTLAND
Moorreesburg, which, with Malmesbury and Piketberg, forms part of the Swartland, is a major wheat-growing centre, where the first wheat was planted in 1752. Today the countryside is covered with wheatfields and the skylines of the towns are dominated by grain silos. The Wheat Museum in Moorreesburg is devoted to the wheat industry in South Africa. The town was founded in 1882 and named after the Swartland Dutch Reformed minister, the Rev JC le Fébre Moorrees (1834 – 81). The origin of the term *Swartland* (black land) is uncertain, since the soil is actually reddish. It is generally accepted that the term refers to the dark leaves of a local bush, the renosterbos (*Elytropappus rhinocerotis*).

BIRTHPLACE OF A WORLD STATESMAN
The birthplace of Jan Christiaan Smuts, Anglo-Boer War general, prime minister, statesman and philosopher, lies on Bovenplaas, at the foot of the Kasteelberg just outside Riebeek West. The house, which is owned by a cement company, was restored and furnished in the 1980s to give an impression of what it was like when Smuts was a small boy growing up here. Smuts was born in the house in 1870, the farm having been bought by his great-grandfather in 1813. The gardens have been attractively laid out, with picnic tables under the trees.

White walls and thatch at Yzerfontein are typical of Cape coastal cottages.

A SOUTHERLY SKIRMISH
Situated on a hill in a wheatfield outside Darling, the Hildebrand Monument commands a view of countryside very different to that of the former Transvaal and Orange Free State republics. It was here, far from home, that the republican officer, Field Cornet CP Hildebrand, was killed in a skirmish on 12 November 1902 and was hastily buried in a porcupine hole. Many years later his body was discovered and properly reburied. The monument, which incorporates his tombstone, was unveiled in 1939. It also marks the point closest to Cape Town reached by Boer commandos during the Anglo-Boer War of 1899 – 1902.

The voorkamer of the Smuts home.

Malmesbury's 19th-century church.

A sunburned haven for sea birds and hardy fishermen

Saldanha Bay and Langebaan Lagoon are the focal points of this drive through some outstanding west coast scenery. From Saldanha the route leads around the lagoon to the Postberg Nature Reserve – then heads north to the historic fishing harbours that dot the coast between Laaiplek and Paternoster. More than half the route is tarred.

**Saldanha
Langebaan
Postberg
Velddrif
Cape Columbine
Vredenburg
160 – 180 km**

BEFORE LEAVING SALDANHA, drive inland along Diaz Road. Turn right into Sea Bride Street, then left at the T-junction into Windhoek Street. Some 200 m further turn right into Panorama Drive, and now take all turn-offs leading uphill. This will bring you to a magnificent viewsite 1 km from Windhoek Street. Away to your right is the entrance to the bay. At your feet lies the town, with Hoedjieskop rising among the streets.

Beyond the town stretches the lagoon, an enormous expanse of sheltered water, with the ore-loading quay forming an unnatural, straight line across it. To your left the land stretches away flat and fertile, into a region renowned for its wheat and sheep.

Saldanha to Postberg

Leave Saldanha by driving along Kamp Street, which heads east along the north shore of the bay. You pass a caravan park and holiday resort on your right and, about 6 km after leaving Saldanha, you reach an intersection and a railway level crossing. Keep straight on here, but if the railway crossing is blocked by an ore-train, turn left and use the level crossing a few hundred metres along the road.

Note your kms at the railway crossing on the main road and drive on towards Langebaan. After a little more than 9 km keep straight at the four-way stop street with Club Mykonos on your right; 3,7 km later turn right for Langebaan. Note your kms as you leave Langebaan village, following the brown West Coast National Park signs. About 18 km after the park entrance, turn right at the T-junction for Postberg. You pass close to the cottages of Churchhaven just under 10 km further. After about another 5 km, you reach the Postberg Nature Reserve (entry fee). The main road through the reserve can be followed at any time of the year as far as the SANDF security fence 5 km from the entrance. Even when the reserve is closed, there is a good chance of

CAPE COLUMBINE LIGHTHOUSE

The nine-million candlepower Cape Columbine lighthouse, first switched on in 1936, came none too soon – the area around Cape Columbine has long been a graveyard for unwary mariners.

Soldiers' Bay, one of the indentations on this rockbound coast, is the site of two memorable shipwrecks. The troopship *St Lawrence* struck a reef here, and the Portugese mail steamer *Lisboa* ran aground here in 1910, with a cargo that included large casks of red wine. The *Lisboa* was eventually broken up by a gale, which stained the sea red with wine and washed many barrels safely onto lonely beaches where they were buried by locals – to be retrieved when the customs officials eventually left.

Malgas Island – a favourite roost for many of Saldanha Bay's hundreds of thousands of seabirds.

AN IMPENETRABLE CLOUD OF BIRDS

One of the unforgettable sights of the Saldanha Bay area comes at sunset as thousands upon thousands of birds – seabirds and waders – stream home in long, ragged lines over the water. The French naturalist Le Vaillant, visiting Saldanha two centuries ago, reported seeing an 'impenetrable cloud of birds of every species and all colours'.

Three islands in the bay – Malgas, Jutten and Marcus – are home to thousands of jackass penguins, and Skaap Island holds the largest known breeding colony of kelp gulls in southern Africa.

In the summer months, up to 23 species of wader have been counted in the area near the mouth of the bay, most of them migrants from far to the north, and some coming from as far afield as Greenland and Siberia.

Meeuw (gull) Island was named by the early Dutch explorers for the countless gulls that favoured it as a roosting place. These birds feed on the microfauna of the intertidal zone along the shores of the lagoon – and have left a treasure trove in their droppings, or guano. Malgas Island was 10 m deep in guano when it was first exploited for fertiliser in the 1840s.

'DAAR KOM DIE *ALABAMA*'

Among the many famous ships to have dropped anchor in Saldanha Bay was the Confederate commerce raider, *Alabama*, in 1863, during the American Civil War. Her Captain, Raphael Semmes, wrote: 'There is no finer sheet of landlocked water in the world than Saldanha Bay.' He was surprised that the unsheltered anchorage of Table Bay had been chosen above Saldanha. (It had abundant fresh water, which was lacking at Saldanha.)

When *Alabama* sailed, she left one of her crew, Third Engineer Simeon W Cummings, who was accidentally killed while hunting. His remains were 'taken home' to Elm Springs, Tennessee, in 1994, although his gravestone on the farm, Kliprug, is still to be seen.

Taking advantage of Langebaan's sheltered waters.

A weathered fishing boat on Churchhaven beach.

The sun sets on a flotilla of yachts at Saldanha.

Postberg to Dwarskersbos

Retrace your route through Churchhaven, turn right at the first T-junction, and left, for Velddrif, at the T-junction with the R27. You reach Velddrif some 19 km from this junction. The town is the site of one of the old crossing-places of the Berg River on the road to Namaqualand. Cross the Berg River and enter Velddrif; turn right at the stop street into Voortrekker Road. After 2 km you will see, on your right, a black and white gravestone surmounted by a cross; 100 m after this, turn right into Vyelaan.

This road winds along the river bank, past fisheries and old cottages, with bunches of *bokkems* (dried salted fish) hanging up to dry. Turn right at the first stop street, then turn left at the intersection with Voortrekker Road and drive through the town. At the T-junction with Jameson Street turn left, then turn right into De Villiers Street to reach the entrance to Laaiplek harbour. (There are hotels and restaurants in Velddrif and Laaiplek, which are virtually opposite ends of the same town.)

After visiting Laaiplek harbour, turn left into Jameson Street; you will reach Dwarskersbos after 10 km. Turn left here into Iris Road to reach a parking area on the beach. This is an attractive place for an exploratory walk, a swim, or a picnic lunch.

Dwarskersbos to Cape Columbine

Return to Laaiplek, turning left out of Jameson Street into Voortrekker Street, then turn right in Velddrif to cross the Berg River bridge; 1,5 km later, turn right onto the R399, towards Vredenburg and Saldanha. After 10 km on the R399, turn right towards St Helena Bay.

The road passes close to the sea at St Helena Bay, with views of fishermen's cottages, the harbour, and the first of a succession of fish-processing factories. A sign indicates the way to the Da Gama Monument, a few hundred metres to the right of the road. Immediately after the monument, turn left onto a gravel road towards Vredenburg and Paternoster. After a further 5,7 km turn right at the intersection. (A small sign indicates that the farm on the left is called Rondekop.) After a further 8 km turn right at the T-junction for Paternoster.

The road continues through Paternoster for 4 km, through the Cape Columbine Nature Reserve, past the lighthouse and arrives eventually at the resort of Tietiesbaai.

Return through Paternoster and pass, on your left, the road on which you arrived from St Helena Bay. You reach tar just before Vredenburg, a distance of some 15 km. Drive along Vredenburg's Main Street and turn right at the second four-way stop street into Saldanha Road – a 12 km tarred road that leads back to Saldanha.

AA Office AA House, 7 Martin Hammerschlag Way, Cape Town 8001 Tel (021) 21 1550
West Coast Peninsula Transitional Council P/Bag X12, Vredenburg 7380 Tel (02281) 32231
Captour Rendezvous Centre, 3 Adderley Street Cape Town 8001 Tel (021) 418 5202

Cape Columbine's light warns of a rocky coast.

A MAGIC CARPET OF FLOWERS

Langebaan Lagoon penetrates the rich floral kingdom of Namaqualand, and furnishes its own special kind of wildflower display, with the edge of the lagoon always richly blanketed in salt-marsh succulents.

The annual rainfall here is around 260 mm, and the display of colour is at its brightest in spring. Gazanias, forget-me-nots and buttercups are among the most abundant species, competing for attention with brilliant vygies. In the higher and drier patches, gnarled evergreens stand out among the granite outcrops.

Bright flowers dress the fields near Vredenburg.

Traversing rugged mountains and sheltered, bountiful valleys

A series of scenic passes over stark and rocky mountain ranges forms a natural circuit – eastwards and southwards from the orange-groves of Citrusdal to the varied orchards of the Ceres valley, then west and north through the historic town of Tulbagh and the rolling wheatfields of the fertile Swartland. All but 40 km of the route is on tarred roads.

**Citrusdal
Prince Alfred
Hamlet
Ceres
Tulbagh
Porterville
240 – 250 km**

TURN EAST OUT OF Citrusdal's Voortrekker Street into Paul de Villiers Street, noting your kms. After about 3 km there are fine views back over the town. The tarred surface ends and you pass tangled rock formations.

The road begins the winding approach to Middelberg Pass after a further 3 km. At the fork 12,5 km from Voortrekker Street, go right on the larger road. Stop roughly 3 km later for good views into an isolated valley. The road now climbs steeply through a hairpin bend to reach the summit of the mountain. From here the pass is known as Buffelshoek Pass, and there is a descending hairpin bend some 200 m further along, where the road seems entirely shut in by the mountains.

In the valley below, on your right, you pass the thatched farmhouse of Tuinskloof, then cross a causeway 700 m beyond. Among the rock formations that you pass soon afterwards is one on your right that is said to resemble a weathercock on a steeple.

Some 30 km from Citrusdal, the road crosses a concrete bridge dated both 1968 and 1961 and, 4 km later, the surface is tarred for about 600 m as it climbs a steep hill. From close mountain scenery, the view becomes one of fields dotted with shimmering dams and, 40 km from Citrusdal, the road surface changes to tar.

Dutch Reformed church, Porterville.

THE NARROW PASSAGE
The little Swartland town of Porterville, below the Olifants River Mountains, was founded in 1863 on the farm Willemsvallei and named after William Porter, the Attorney-General of the Cape Colony. The gentle air currents that swirl around these craggy mountains make them ideal for hang-gliding. A favourite venue is the farm *Cardouw*, which takes its name from the old Khoikhoi word for 'narrow passage'. Cardouws (or Kardouws) Kloof was once an important route across the mountains, although it was described by the traveller Thunberg as 'one of the most difficult roads that go across the African mountains'. The old pass can no longer be traversed by vehicle, and has not been used for more than a century. Even that section that is still usable (approaching close to the summit) is not for the nervous motorist.

A land of plenty – the fertile bowl of the Ceres valley below the Gydo Pass.

CERES – VALLEY OF THE GODDESS
The settlement in the Warm Bokkeveld was called Ceres after the Roman goddess of agriculture – an appropriate name for a fertile valley that has become known for its production of wheat and fruit. The first stock-farmers arrived in the *Bokkeveld* (goat or buck country) in 1727. More than a century later, after the discovery of diamonds in the Northern Cape, nearby Michell's Pass became the main highway to the north, and the settlement entered a period of hectic prosperity. The pass collected a greater revenue than any other toll in the country, but this came to an end when the railway lines to the north bypassed Ceres. The *Togryers* (transport riders) Museum on the corner of Munnik and Oranje streets preserves many relics of the town's exciting history.

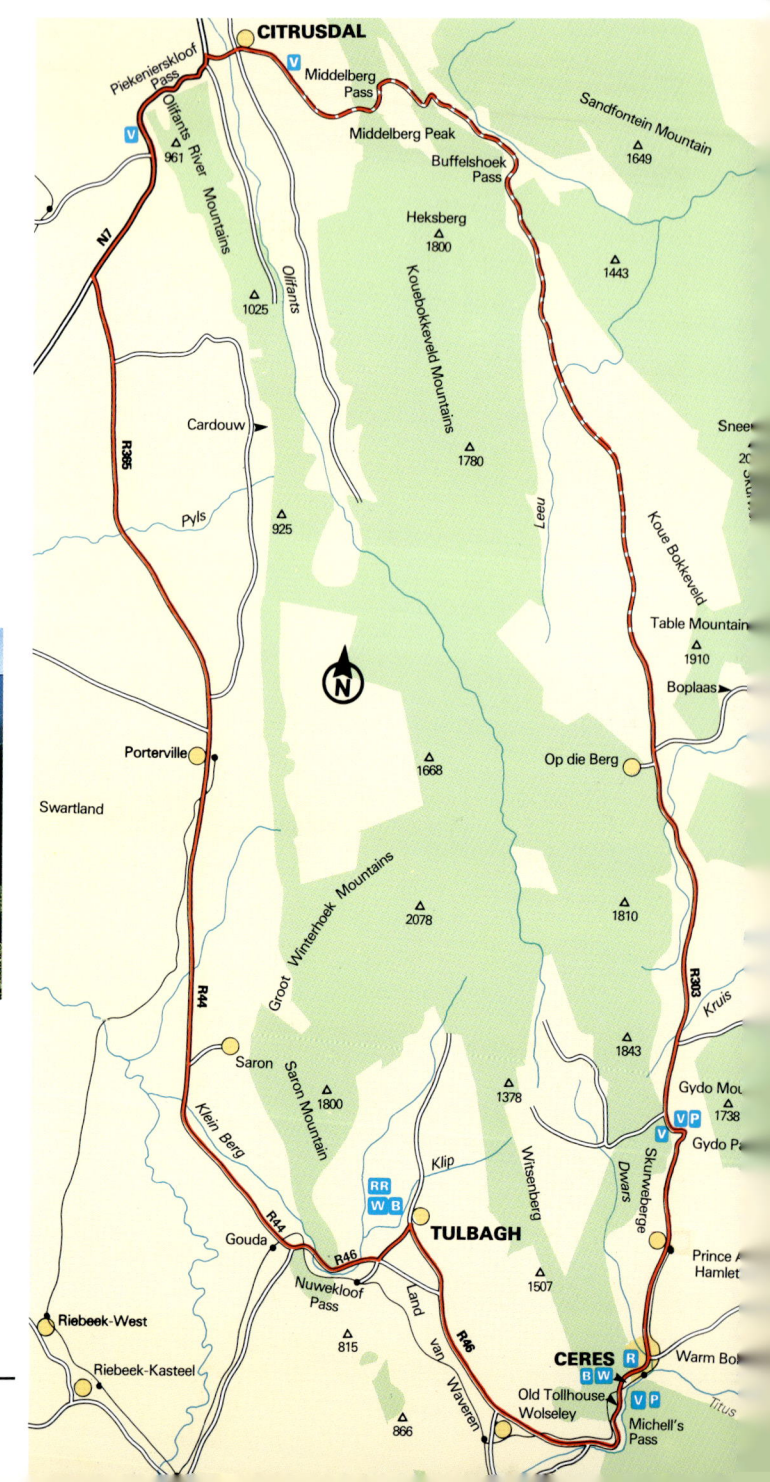

Note your kms as you pass a turn-off on your left to Boplaas, which was formerly the farm Moddervallei – birthplace of the poet Boerneef and historic home of 11 generations of the family Van der Merwe.

Soon afterwards you pass a turn-off on your right to the settlement of *Op die Berg* (on the mountain). After 25 km you reach the start of the easily negotiated Gydo Pass. After 3,2 km on the pass, stop on your left at a picnic site for a splendid view over the fertile Ceres valley (see opposite).

The road descends the pass, then continues through Prince Alfred Hamlet. About 8 km later, you reach the outskirts of Ceres. (A number of establishments in the town provide lunch.) Some 300 m after the start of the dual carriageway in the town, turn right and follow the signs for the Pine Forest Public Resort. (There is an entrance fee to this well-wooded resort, which offers trout-fishing, swimming, braai sites, water and toilets. Overnight facilities are also available.)

Whether you have visited the resort or not, continue along the road on which you entered the town, and turn right at the traffic lights. After 1,4 km turn right and park at the entrance to the small Ceres Nature Reserve, where there is a delightful trail (allow 30 – 40 minutes).

Ceres to Tulbagh
Leaving the nature reserve parking area, turn right. The road immediately enters Michell's Pass. Stop after about 1 km at the tarred loop of road on your left for an excellent view over the Dwars River (which becomes the Breede River after a few kilometres). There are picnic sites here, and on your left a waterfall tumbles down into a dark pool known as *Koffiegat* or Coffee Pot. On your right after a further 1,5 km is the old tollhouse, built in about 1850 on what was then the main road to the mining towns to the north. Beyond the pass you drive past a road on your left to Wellington and Worcester (R43), two roads to Wolseley, and the road to Gouda and Cape Town.

Tulbagh to Citrusdal
You enter Tulbagh on Van der Stel Street, passing a turn-off left into Stasieweg for Gouda and Cape Town (see pages 270 – 1 for a street map and information on picnic sites and restaurants). After visiting the town, return to Stasieweg and turn right for Cape Town and Gouda, noting your kms. After 3 km turn right onto the R46, to enter Nuwekloof Pass 2,5 km later. After a further 5,5 km, turn right onto the R44 for Porterville and Piketberg.

Continue on the R44 through rolling wheatlands to reach Porterville's main street after 35 km. Leave the town by continuing northwards for Citrusdal, and note your kms as you pass the turn-off for Piketberg (R44) on your left. (A gravel road on your right soon afterwards leads to the farm Cardouw – a favourite launching site for hang-gliders.)

After 32 km turn right at the T-junction onto the N7, noting your kms. The road now heads directly towards the mountains, and soon you can see the line of the Piekenierskloof Pass ascending ahead and to the left. Below the present road are the old retaining walls of the original pass – known as Grey's Pass and built by Thomas Bain in 1857. It was the first major construction task he supervised.

After 12,5 km on the N7, stop on your left for good views of the Swartland. Continue over the summit of the pass and turn right for Citrusdal. (A gravel road on your right before you reach the town leads, after 15 km, to the hot springs resort.)

AA Office AA House, 7 Martin Hammerschlag Way, Cape Town 8001 Tel (021) 21 1550
Ceres Publicity Association Owen Street, Ceres 6835 Tel (0233) 61287
Captour Rendezvous Centre, 3 Adderley Street Cape Town 8001 Tel (021) 418 5202

The stark and barren rocks of the Koue Bokkeveld Mountains rise above the bounty of the plains.

DALE OF CITRUS GROVES
Although farms near Citrusdal have been worked for well over two centuries, the town dates only from 1916. The main road north reaches it through *Piekenierskloof* (pikemen's gorge) – a name dating from 1675, when the Dutch East India Company stationed soldiers near here to protect one of their Khoikhoi allies from a rival chief, Gonnema. Encumbered by heavy pikes and breastplates, the soldiers pursued their foes through the mountains in vain.

Citrusdal nestles in a tranquil valley along the banks of the Olifants River, surrounded by the deep green foliage of orange and lemon trees that fill the air with the fragrance of their blossoms in spring. A 200-year-old orange tree on the farm Groot Heksrivier, near Citrusdal, still bears fruit and is a national monument.

The spa south of Citrusdal has been visited for the purported restorative powers of its water since the days of the earliest explorers.

An inquisitive trio on a Ceres valley stud farm.

The Lover's Bridge on Lyell Street in Ceres.

THE ORIGINAL HOME OF THE GRIQUAS
The countryside through which you travel after Porterville was once the home of a Khoikhoi clan called the Griquas, encountered in 1661 by the surgeon Pieter van Meerhoff, who noted that some of them wore copper ornaments. It was a Griqua chief who later guided Governor Simon van der Stel on his expedition to the copper mines of Namaqualand.

One of the leaders of the clan, Adam Kok (born in 1710), is said to have derived his surname from the fact that he worked as a cook (*kok*) to the governor. He later led his people northwards to settle at what became Griquatown. His descendant Adam Kok III, headed the long Griqua trek that ended in the founding of Kokstad, thus creating a Griqualand West and a Griqualand East.

Middelberg Pass crosses wild mountain scenery.

Out of the Swartland bread basket to the 'bokkem' coast

Our route descends the fynbos-covered Piketberg mountains, through the Sandveld to the rugged beauty of the West Coast where bokkems are hung to dry in the sun. We visit a vlei with a stunning diversity of bird life and, after passing a headland with the silhouette of a baboon, we follow Verlorevlei – the 'lost lake' – almost to its source.

Piketberg
Velddrif
Rocher Pan
Elands Bay
Verlorevlei
250 – 270 km

Follow Langstraat north out of Piketberg to a stop street; turn right here, following the sign for 'R365/Versveld Pass/Elandsbaai/Redelinghuys'. Note your kms at the turn and, after 1,2 km, turn left onto the tarred Versveld Pass. A parking area and picnic site 6 km later offer outstanding views over seemingly unending grainfields, especially in the light of early morning. Retrace your route to Piketberg.

Piketberg to Velddrif
Drive south on Langstraat and, about 400 m outside the town, turn right for Aurora, De Hoek and Velddrif, noting your kms. After 2,7 km, turn right onto the R399. After 7 km you see the Berg River and, some 2 km further, turn right on tar for Goedverwacht, (see below), which you reach 5,5 km from the R399. Return to the main road (R399) and turn right, noting your kms. At around 12 km you are aware of the transition from Swartland to Strandveld, the strip of loose, sandy soil just inland from the West Coast. In spring, low-growing *vygies* (Mesembryanthemum) flower brightly next to the road. Near Velddrif, the river divides into channels flowing between dense green reed banks.

Velddrif to Rocher Pan
Note your kms as you enter Velddrif along Voortrekkerweg (about 47 km from the turning to Goedverwacht) and, after 1,7 km, turn left into Vyelaan. At the riverbank, turn right to pass picturesque buildings that are the home of the *bokkem* (salted fish) industry (see opposite). Return via this riverbank road to Voortrekkerweg and, after a few hundred metres, you reach a viewsite on your left with a boardwalk leading to a hide among the reeds. Here you can see the rare little blue heron and redshank as well as the curlew sandpipers and plovers that abound here. Some 600 m later, keep straight at a crossroads and, 1,1 km further on, reach a T-junction in the town of Laaiplek. Turn left into Jameson Street and, after 400 m, right into De Villiers Street. This road is part of a 1,4 km circular route that includes the mouth of the Berg River and the harbour. There is a small entrance fee.

Leave Laaiplek on Jameson Street, which becomes the R535, hugging the barren coastline. About 10 km from Laaiplek, you reach the small resort town of Dwarskersbos which, in 1969, was struck by one of the rarest of local hazards, a tidal wave. Follow the main road through the town for 1,6 km and turn left into Anshovie Street; 200 m further on you reach a parking area at the beach, an attractive place to pause for lunch. Drive north from Dwarskersbos, noting your kms as the road surface changes to gravel that is very slippery after rain. Some 12 km later, pass a gate, on the left-hand side of the road, to Rocher Pan Nature Reserve (see opposite). At the next gate, 500 m further on, turn left, cross a cattle grid and report at the office. After you have signed the visitors' book, return to the first gate to visit the vlei with its great variety of birds.

VERSVELD PASS
The old road, built in 1899 by farmer JPE Versveld, opened up one of the most productive fruit-growing regions of the Western Cape, where, previously, only scanty tobacco crops had been grown. The present road was built in 1958 and bypasses, among others, Deze Hoek homestead where there is a water-wheel that drives a corn-mill, a forage press and a circular saw. The pass winds its way up from the wheatlands through mountain fynbos, offering striking views of the patchwork pattern of fields below. The upper plateau is known as *Die Berg* – the mountain – and, in addition to fruit-growing, supports poultry and dairy farming.

GREAT EXPECTATION
Hidden away in the foothills of the Piketberg mountains is the small village of *Goedverwacht* – good or great expectation. Originally, it was a farm called Burgerskloof that was bequeathed to freed slaves and it was later bought by the Moravian Evangelical Association. The present community has a primary school, a shop and a fine building of the Evangelical Fraternity Church of South Africa, with 2 433 local members. The stone church is approximately 100 years old. Goedverwacht also has an old water-mill which, together with the small gardens of the householders, gives the village a peaceful, old-world atmosphere.

The stone church of the people of Goedverwacht.

Rocher Pan to Elands Bay
From Rocher Pan turn left onto the R535 and note your kms. After 1,7 km you pass over the Sishen-Saldanha railway. (The road to the left, just before the bridge, is a private maintenance road.) At the T-junction 8,7 km from Rocher Pan, turn left towards Elands Bay. Soon, the road veers towards the hills around Verlorevlei, where, at the top of the rise, at about 37 km, an impressive panorama unfolds. The road leads to the shore of the vlei and, because there are few fences, cattle and horses tend to wander onto the road.

The road follows the edge of the vlei, home to countless aquatic birds, and you pass a turn-off, on your right, to Elands Bay. Ignore a second road that is little more than a track, as you approach the great outcrop of Baboon Point. The road hugs the cliffs and immediately below you is a cluster of small crayfish factories with brightly coloured rowing boats drawn up beyond the reach of the tide. Following the sign for 'Jettys', pass under the railway bridge at 44,6 km to reach Baboon Point 47,5 km from Rocher Pan.

Swartland fields unfold below the Versveld Pass.

Out of the reach of the high tide, off-duty fishing boats bask in the sun at Elands Bay.

Baboon Point to Piketberg

Drive back from the point and turn left, crossing the low-water bridge over the vlei. Turn left and left again at an inclined T-junction to reach the hamlet of Elands Bay. From the central tarred square, turn into Hoofstraat and note your kms as you leave town.

After 1,6 km turn left for Lambert's Bay. The road again follows the edge of Velorevlei, passing a turn-off to Lambert's Bay at 3,8 km until, after about 14 km, it curves through the Sandveld hills. Some 27 km from the outskirts of Elands Bay, turn right for Redelinghuys and Aurora, cross the bridge over the vlei and, 900 m further on, reach a T-junction at the small town of Redelinghuys.

Turn left and, 400 m further on, after passing through a stop street, turn right into Van Lille Street, which leads up to a historic Dutch Reformed church. Make your way out of town and turn right towards Piketberg, noting your kms. After about 11 km the road surface changes to tar and, after meandering through the hills, regains the Piketberg basin about 30 km from Redelinghuys.

At 37,5 km you pass a road on your right that leads to Winkelshoek Wine Cellar; 2,5 km after this road, turn left for Eendekuil and Citrusdal to reach Eendekuil after a further 8,4 km. Appointments may be made to visit the cheese factory in the town.

Return to the point where you turned left for Eendekuil, and turn left to reach Piketberg approximately 2 km later.

Piketberg Information Office Library, Municipal Building, Kerkstraat, Piketberg 7320 Tel (0261) 31126
Velddrif Information Office Library, Municipal Building, Hoofstraat, Velddrif 7365 Tel (02288) 31112
Rocher Pan Nature Reserve Tel (02625) 727

Properly salted and sun-dried 'bokkems' require no refrigeration.

The Dutch Reformed church in Piketberg is a national monument.

BOKKEMS

The southern mullet or *harder* is a fish found mainly in the sea, but from October to March it moves in shoals up the Berg River estuary – and those caught in the river are usually of a superior quality. For six months of the year the bokkem fishermen take to the water daily with their boats and floating nets. Back on shore, the fish are washed and placed in brine for two days and nights. Then they are tied together in bundles of 10 and put out to dry on racks in the sun. The popular dried and salted fish or *bokkems* are distributed and sold throughout the country as fish biltong.

ROCHER PAN

A seasonal vlei and adjacent coast provide sanctuary to 183 bird species, of which 70 are waterbirds. White pelican and greater and lesser flamingo are seen here as well as South Africa's second rarest coastal bird, the African black oystercatcher. Thousands of waders and ducks depend on the vlei as their only source of food, especially when the water levels start to drop. Apart from the birds, the reserve is home to springbok, duiker, steenbok, water mongoose and African wildcat. Reptiles and amphibians are also numerous and sightings of Southern Right whales are regularly made from the coast. Between June and September the reserve may be a mass of bright flowers.

Gargoyles and dragons – the magnificent rocks of the Cederberg

A circular drive – almost all on gravel – takes you through the rugged Cederberg. But the section of some 32 km from Wuppertal to Matjiesrivier is a rough track suitable only for a sturdy vehicle with a high ground-clearance. Without such a vehicle this should be treated as two there-and-back day trips from Clanwilliam – as we have described it.

Clanwilliam Wuppertal 140 – 150 km

Clanwilliam Matjiesrivier 180 – 190 km

FOR THE NORTHERN DRIVE from Clanwilliam to Wuppertal, turn right at the northern end of Main Street for Wuppertal and Calvinia, noting your kms. Keep straight past a road to Klawer on the left after 2,4 km. The tar surface ends soon after, and the road begins its gentle ascent amidst tumbled rock formations on both sides of the road – some of the rocks appearing to defy gravity by their top-heaviness.

About 16 km from Clanwilliam, stop at the parking place on your left to visit the grave of Dr C Louis Leipoldt, the poet, author, journalist, physician and authority on Cape cooking. A short path leads through a gate to the simple grave, which is in a rock shelter once occupied by San hunters. There are faded paintings of an elephant and calf, and of human figures, which can be seen slightly to the left of the grave as you face the shelter.

Roughly 500 m further along the main road, on your left, is the entrance to the Rheeboksvlei picnic area (small entry fee, water, toilets). There are a number of attractive walks here – a permit may be obtained from the forester a few hundred metres further along the road.

Continue through rugged countryside and pass a road on your left to Elizabethsfontein. Note your kms as you reach a cement causeway, and stop 5,8 km later, just before a sign that warns of a road to the right. On your right here is the Englishman's grave – almost entirely concealed by a large eucalyptus tree (see opposite).

Some 100 m beyond the grave, turn right for Biedou Valley and Wuppertal, noting your kms. Lonely farms in isolated valleys come unexpectedly into view as the road rises and twists. After 7,7 km the road begins the steep descent of *Uitkyk* (lookout) Pass. Stop after a further 100 m on the left in a parking area that offers magnificent views.

The road crosses two cattle grids within the next 3 km, then crosses a low, narrow causeway. Soon after, on your left, you pass a road to the Biedou Valley and Uitspanskraal. (This road is popular with visitors during the spring flower season.) On your right here is the farm Mertenhof, which has a homestead dating from the beginning of the 19th century and a stone-walled threshing floor that is visible from the road.

After a further 5,5 km the road crosses another narrow causeway, followed within 200 m by another cattle grid. Roughly 3,6 km later, on your right, a waterfall has created a smooth rock face that seems out of character with the ruggedness of the Cederberg.

The final steep descent to Wuppertal down Kleinhoogte begins 3,3 km later, and offers frequent glimpses of thatched and whitewashed buildings in an oasis of soft green. The road passes the old cemetery on your right just before entering the village.

After your visit to Wuppertal, retrace your route back to Clanwilliam. (The rough track that links this route to Matjiesrivier leaves the village on the south side.)

Clanwilliam to Matjiesrivier
For the southern Cederberg drive, turn southwest at the southern end of Clanwilliam's Main Street (opposite the old jail) onto the *Kaapse Weg* (Cape road). Within the first kilometre, pass a road on your right to the dam, wildflower garden and caravan park. The road surface changes to gravel soon after.

For several kms the road runs along the shores of the Clanwilliam Dam, offering many fine views. After 7 km a road on your left, signposted Cederberg, offers a shorter (by 15 km) alternative route to Algeria. The alternative route is often in better condition than the road you are on. Keep straight here and cross a narrow stone bridge 1,1 km later. Stop 700 m past the bridge for wide views over the dam.

Note your kms as you cross a steel-and-concrete bridge over the Rondegat River, pass a picnic site and pull off the road on your left 4,4 km from the bridge, to explore a large rock overhang and a number of smaller shelters containing old ochre hand-prints.

You leave the dam behind a few kilometres later as the road passes citrus groves. At the crossroads roughly 8 km later turn left, for Algeria, away from the river, noting your kms.

The road soon ascends the Kriedouw Kloof Pass, and then rises even higher into the mountains over the Nieuwoudt Pass, offering spectacular views to remote valleys before entering the area known as the Sederberg State Forest after about 16 km.

After a further 500 m turn left for the Algeria campsite and office (entry fee). There are toilets, water and braai places here and firewood is for sale. The Rondegat River offers swimming, and there are walks from the camp.

As you leave Algeria, turn left and note your kms. Pass a road on the left to the Uitkyk Waenhuis at the start of the Cederberg Pass (also known as Uitkyk Pass). After 6,8 km pull off the road for a fine view over the Driehoek River Valley, which stretches ahead.

The road crosses a number of causeways and cattle grids before you reach a fork about 30 km from Algeria. Turn right for Kromrivier at the fork. The road winds down the steep mountainside to reach the entrance of the resort (small entry fee, braai places, toilets, water, swimming). Maps of the area are available here, as well as detailed directions for walks and sightseeing. Obtain a permit here for entering the Stadsaal area, and ask for instructions on how to open the locked gate there.

Return to the fork 4,4 km from Kromrivier and turn right, noting your kms. After 3,5 km turn right towards the locked gate on a minor road. After passing through the gate and locking it, turn right onto a side track about 600 m beyond. Stop before the track forms a loop, to view the excellent group of San paintings of elephants and human figures on the large rock overhang on your right.

Return to the track on which you entered the locked area, and turn right. After about 1 km the road ends among the tumbled rock formations and caves of *Stadsaal* (city hall).

After your visit to Stadsaal, retrace your route to the main road and, after re-locking the gate, turn right. Roughly 2 km later you cross a causeway. Stop on the right, where there is a shady picnic site next to the river. Nearby are the old farm buildings of Matjiesrivier, with the new homestead close by.

Retrace your route from here back to Clanwilliam. (The Jeep track that leads to Wuppertal is reached by turning left at the T-junction 700 m beyond the picnic site.)

AA Office AA House, 7 Martin Hammerschlag Way, CapeTown 8001 Tel (021) 21 1550
Clanwilliam Tourism Association Main Street Clanwilliam 8135 Tel (027) 482 2024
Captour Tourism Rendezvous Centre, 3 Adderley Street, Cape Town 8001 Tel (021) 418 5202
Sederberg State Forest PO Citrusdal 7340 Tel (027) 482 2812

Spring blooms at Clanwilliam Dam.

Lawns and shady trees at the Algeria campsite.

ROOIBOS CAPITAL

Among the attractive old buildings in Clanwilliam (established on the farm Jan Disselsvlei in 1814,) are the Dutch Reformed Church, which was built in 1864 and the Anglican Church, consecrated in 1866. At the southern end of Main Street is the old jail and courthouse – now the museum and tourism office.

The road divides here, with many quaint buildings in the area between its branches. It is not widely known that a party of Irish settlers was placed in Clanwilliam in 1820.

The library in Main Street contains mementoes of C Louis Leipoldt and of Dr P le Fras Nortier, father of the rooibos tea industry, of which Clanwilliam is the centre.

The wildflower garden on the outskirts of the town offers lovely spring displays. The Clanwilliam Dam is a major venue for water sports, and there are camping and picnicking sites along its shores.

Weathered rocks lie scattered across the landscape of the Pakhuis Pass.

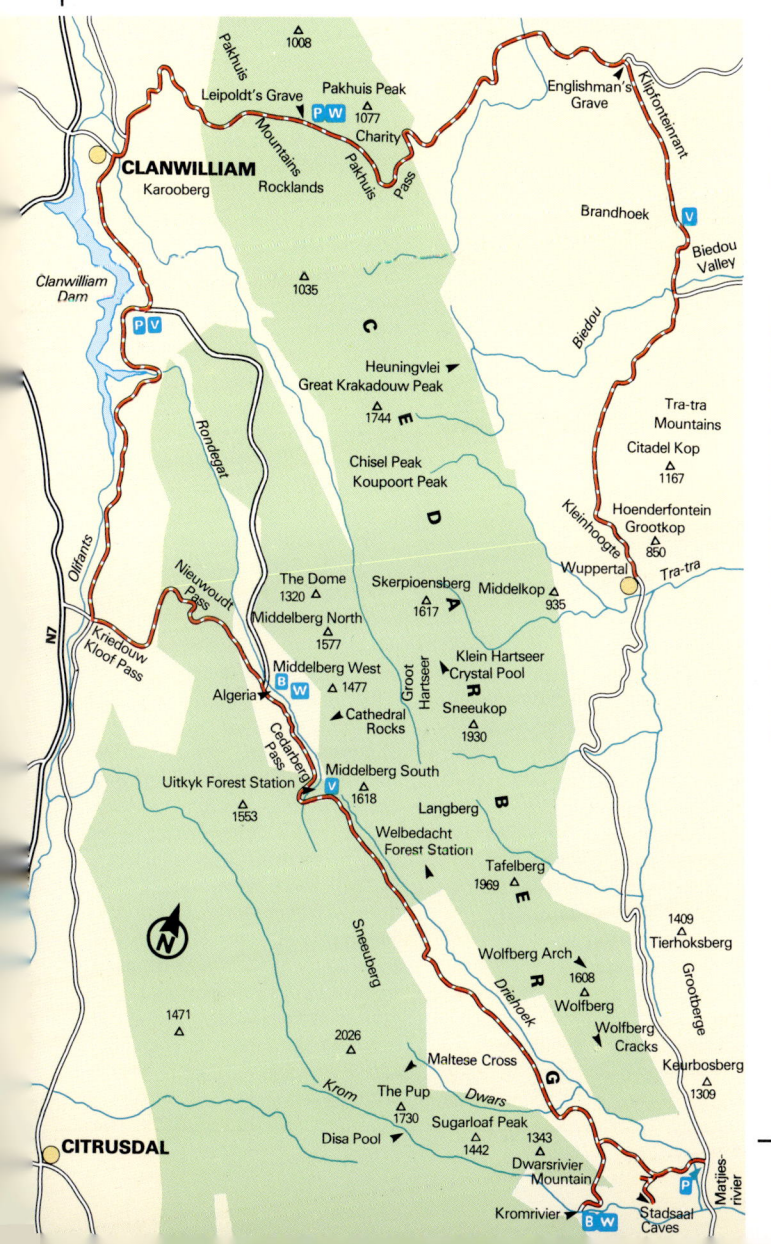

Wuppertal's picturesque church – at the heart of this old-world village.

WUPPERTAL MISSION VILLAGE

This village was established in 1830 on a farm known as *Koudeberg* (cold mountain) – an appropriate name in an area where the peaks are snow-covered in winter. In summer the heat may be equally intense in these tucked-away valleys.

The settlement grew around the Rhenish church on the banks of the Tra-Tra River, and many of the cottages are more than 100 years old. On your right when you enter is the former school, built on a high plinth or *stoep* in about 1830. If you turn right at the end of it, you will reach an old house that is believed to have been built for the first missionaries, Baron von Wurmb and Johann Leipoldt, who was C Louis Leipoldt's grandfather.

The church bells at Wuppertal.

San artists left these enduring mementoes of their sojourn at Stadsaal caves.

THE ENGLISHMAN'S GRAVE

During the Anglo-Boer War, 21-year-old Lieutenant Graham Clowes of the 6th Mounted Infantry set out from Clanwilliam with his batman, Trooper Clark, to ensure that horses could cover the ground towards the Boer headquarters in Calvinia. As they reached the Wuppertal turn-off, there was a flurry of shots and the two men dropped from their horses – Clowes dead and Clark seriously wounded. Clark was taken to Clanwilliam, where he died, and Clowes was buried close to where he had fallen. After the war, Clowes's widowed mother had the present monument erected here – plus a memorial at Eton College, where her son had sung in the choir.

In spring and summer, visitors to this lonely grave may find small bunches of veld flowers laid upon its stones. The identity of the person who places them there - close to a century after the young man's death – is a mystery.

Wolfberg Arch epitomizes Cederberg magic – crisp air, spectacular rock formations and an unspoilt panorama.

The Cederberg – a wilderness of sculpted rock and unspoilt valleys

The Cederberg remained a little-known area for more than a century after the first European settlement was established at Cape Town – a mere 200 km away. Even today, as the range comes under increasing pressure as a resort area for metropolitan Cape Town, there are places among the craggy mountains that are known only to forestry officers or those hardy people who have made their homes here.

The area's dual role as resort and as home is clear in the many names that fill the map of the Cederberg (see pages 280 – 1). There are the names that have been bestowed by the climbers and the visitors – names such as Frustration Peak, Maltese Cross and Machine Gun Ridge. But no matter how descriptive they are, they lack the intimacy of such older names as *Hartseer* (heartache), *Wegwaai* (blow or blown away), and *Filander se Werf* (Filander's farmyard) – the little farm where Filander, whoever he was, tended his crops in a majestic but lonely setting.

The rock wilderness is a superb recreational area – for walkers, climbers, lovers of nature, photographers and artists.

Hiking trails

The Cederberg region covers some 130 000 ha. Just over half the area is State forest land, and, of this, a 71 000 ha portion was proclaimed a wilderness area in 1973. The mountains are criss-crossed with rough trails and pathways, beneath fantastic rock formations among the weathered sandstone peaks. These trails merely provide access to the 'primitive zone' and are intended mainly for use in the unending task of environmental management.

Hikers may set out from the Cederberg campsites on short walks or they may spend a few days exploring the area. A number of primitive huts dot the range – some of them built more than 80 years ago by forestry officer George Bath and still used by forestry staff and, in emergencies only, by hikers. Caves are also used for overnight stays, particularly Sederkop and Welbedacht.

Algeria Forestry Station was founded by Bath who thought the area shared a likeness with the Atlas Mountains of North Africa. From here the hiker has access to the towering Middelberg peaks, Helsekloof with its waterfall, the craggy Cathedral Rock where weather-bleached cedars shelter from fire, and excellent views of the Sneeukop-Langberg massif. The footpath through Wildehoutdrif leads along the Groot Hartseer plateau to the waterhole of Crystal Pool, while the track to Heuningvlei passes a number of the higher peaks – Great Krakadouw, Chisel Peak and Koupoort Peak. These northern areas can also be reached from Pakhuis Pass.

The Clanwilliam cedar tree

In the southern area, there are a number of popular excursions – to Tafelberg, the Wolfberg Arch, the Wolfberg Cracks (which are on private land and may be visited only with the owner's permission), the rock pinnacle known as the Maltese Cross, which lies on the eastern approach to Sneeuberg (at 2 027 m the highest peak in the range), the Disa Pool swimming hole on the Krom River, and the Stadsaal Caves, a series of smooth caverns worn out of the rock (also on private land).

The Clanwilliam cedar tree (*Widdringtonia cedarbergensis*) which grows at the higher levels of the mountain range, and after which the area is named, is not at all like the cedars of Lebanon, but rather like the cypress family. The excellent qualities of the local cedarwood were brought to the attention of Governor Willem van der Stel in 1700, and for more than a century the forests were recklessly exploited – in one instance in 1879 more than 7000 young trees were cut down to provide telegraph poles between Calvinia and Piketberg. Although the trees are now stringently protected, it is estimated that the slow process of restoring the forests to their former splendour will take a number of centuries.

Wind-weathered rock takes on fantastic shapes high up in the Cederberg range.

Bleached 'skeletons' of a cedar tree.

The Maltese Cross dwarfs hikers.

The majestic Wolfberg Cracks frame scenery typical of the wilderness area.

A rare beauty

Another beauty to be found on the highest reaches of the Cederberg is the snow protea *(Protea cryophila)*, among the rarest of all proteas. It has an underground stem, which makes the flowers and leaves appear to sprout directly from the soil. The snow protea flowers between December and February – a bloom that is white and 'woolly' on the outside and red and smooth on the inside. Less rare is the Cederberg, or rocket, pincushion *(Leucospermum reflexum)*, a popular garden plant that grows naturally only in the northern Cederberg.

Two plants that are found in abundance here are rooibos *(Aspalathus linearis)*, from which a tannin-free, tea-like infusion is made, and buchu *(Agathosma betulina)*, which has been renowned for its medicinal properties for many centuries. Both are important commercial crops for the area. The strange elephant's foot plant *(Diascorea elephantipes)*, from which cortisone was orignally obtained, is another species that is common in the Cederberg.

The number of wild animals in the wilderness area has increased in recent years since the introduction of stricter conservation measures. Among the mammals is the spectacled dormouse *(Graphiuris ocularis)*, or *namtap* as the locals call the pretty, bushy-tailed rodent. The namtap has a reputation for rummaging through rucksacks in search of food during the night. The most common antelope are the grey rhebuck *(Pelea capreolus)* and the dainty klipspringer *(Oreotragus oreotragus)*, and baboons *(Papio ursinus)* are often seen.

Leopards *(Panthera pardus)* still prowl the Cederberg but are very rarely seen, and the old stone leopard-trap in the Sederhout Kloof is a relic of wilder days. An old legend from those times tells of a buchu-picker named Hans Moller whose wife died while the two of them were out in a remote kloof. Night fell, and soon Hans realised that leopards were stalking him. All he had with him was his violin, so, in desperation, he began to play. The leopards did not leave, but sat down to listen and, so the story goes, Hans was obliged to play all through the night until the big cats finally left him (and his late wife) at dawn.

Maps are essential if you intend to undertake a long hike. An excellent map is available from the Reserve Manager at Algeria, and permits to walk in the wilderness area may be obtained from the District Manager, Cape Nature Conservation Department, Private Bag X1, Citrusdal 7340, or tel (022) 921 2289. It is important to take warm clothes, as the nights can become very cold, and enough water for your proposed walk. No pets are allowed, nor may fires be made, except in the purpose-built braai places at the Algeria campsite.

The camping ground is enhanced by the Rondegat River which forms a natural swimming pool there. Downriver the road passes through fine scenery for 35 km to Clanwilliam.

The Poison Mountain in a sea of shining quartz pebbles

The Gifberg (Poison Mountain) rises from the arid Knersvlakte like a fantasy island of flowers, clear streams and rock paintings. After visiting the scenic summit, follow the Olifants River through fertile vineyards and a rolling landscape to meet the cold Atlantic Ocean and its stern, rocky coast. Half of the route is on tar and half on gravel.

Vanrhynsdorp
Gifberg
Lutzville
Doornbaai
Lambert's Bay
Graafwater
Klawer
340 – 350 km

Drive east from the museum in Van Riebeeck Street, Vanrhynsdorp, and turn right into Troe-Troe Street. At the next stop street, turn left into Voortrekker Street and then turn right immediately for Gifberg. Note your kms as you cross the Troe-Troe River and keep straight, to begin ascending Matsikamma Mountain 15 km later; pull over at 19 km to admire the view over the plains. Mountain fynbos includes the poison tree (*Hyaenanche globosa*) from which *Gifberg* (poison mountain) derives its name. At the top, at about 22 km, follow the signs for JF Huyshamen/Gifberg Rusoord. You reach the resort area some 7 km later, where accommodation and refreshments are available, and there are walks through the fynbos.

Gifberg to Lutzville
Return to Vanrhynsdorp and leave the town westwards on Van Riebeeck Street which passes under the N7 (note your kms here) and becomes the R27 for Vredendal. Keep straight at the crossroads at 22 km, cross the railway line soon after and reach Vredendal 1,8 km later. At the first traffic lights, turn right into Kerkstraat, where the library, on your left after 300 m, offers local information. Kerkstraat becomes the R363 for Lutzville and, 12 km from Vredendal, you pass under the impressive Sishen-Saldanha railway bridge. A parking area on the left allows you to admire its robust construction. The strange, antennae-like plants growing beside the road in the vicinity include *gifmelkbos* or poison milkbush (*Euphorbia mauritanica*).

Note your kms as you pass a road, on your left, to Strandfontein and Doornbaai and, 3,5 km later, turn left (R362) at a crossroads to enter Lutzville on Stasieweg, which leads on towards Strandfontein.

Lutzville to Strandfontein
Cross the Olifants River and, 700 m later, turn right at the T-junction onto the R362 for Strandfontein and Doornbaai, noting your kms. After about 16 km on this road, as you pass over a rise, you will see the Olifants River mouth far over to your right. Another 11 km on, turn right for Strandfontein. After passing through the town and the camp site you reach the beach and the site for day-campers about 1 km further on. Rejoin the R362 and drive south for Doornbaai.

The road surface changes to gravel after about 2,5 km, with the route hugging the rocky shore to reach the hamlet of Doornbaai after 7 km. Where the road forks in town, the right-hand branch leads to the jetty and that on the left becomes the road for Lambert's Bay.

Doornbaai to Klawer
Leave Strandfontein for Lambert's Bay, noting your kms at the fork. Turn left after 300 m, with the road surface soon changing to gravel, and turn left at the fork after 1,7 km. The road winds inland to the Strandveld, where skilpadbos (*Zygophyllum morgsana*) features regularly along the route. Panoramic views unfold towards Lambert's Bay with the *Koeivlei* (cow lake) mountain jutting out in the east. Some 20 km further on, turn right at the T-junction with the R365 for Lambert's Bay. About 1 km further on, pass a road on the left that leads to Heerenlogement and Graafwater. After 31 km, turn right at the T-junction with the tarred R364, noting your kms.

Lambert's Bay is reached in just over 5 km, presenting a pink-spotted expanse of blue water on your right. This is Jakkalsvlei and the pink spots are countless flamingoes. The Sandveld Museum and information centre is in Kerkstraat. Park at the harbour entrance and follow the signs to reach the bird island. Be careful when walking on the harbour wall; it is uneven and high waves breaking may leave you drenched. Also situated at the parking area is a boat charter company that will take you on an hour-long cruise in search of dolphins and seals. Retrace your route out of Lambert's Bay on the R364.

After 32,5 km turn left into Van der Stel Street in the village of Graafwater; the road surface soon changes to gravel. Some 24 km later, park next to the picnic site at Heerenlogement. Close to the parking site, the interesting structure on the left-hand side is an example of the thatch houses built by early Sandveld settlers. Note your kms as you leave and watch out for tortoises crossing the road. Turn right for Vredendal at the T-junction after 17 km and, after a further 18 km, turn right again, for Klawer, at the T-junction with the tarred R363. A pretty drive of about 14 km past vineyards and fields of lucerne brings you to a bridge over the Olifants River on the outskirts of Klawer. The municipal and information offices are in Valleistraat, on your right. On leaving Klawer, follow the N7 northwards to reach Vanrhynsdorp after about 24 km.

AA Office AA House, 7 Martin Hammerschlag Way, Cape Town 8001 Tel (021) 21 1550
Vanrhynsdorp Publicity Association PO Box 1 Vanrhynsdorp 8170 Tel (02727) 91552
Klawer Publicity Association, PO Box 28, Klawer 8145 Tel (02724) 61504

Old-world graffiti on the rocks at the Heerenlogement.

HEERENLOGEMENT
It is more of an overhang than a cave and is situated in the hills adjacent to the Uitkoms Mountains with a commanding view of the plains below. The milkwood tree (*Sideroxylon inerme*) in a cleft at the back of the overhang was described in 1777, when this place regularly sheltered travellers. It was first recorded by a Swedish adventurer called Oloff Bergh who, while in the service of the Dutch East India Company, called it Dassenbergfontein in 1682. In 1685 Simon van der Stel also visited the Heerenlogement on his copper-prospecting expedition to Namaqualand.

For a few brief weeks in spring, the Knersvlakte is carpeted in flowers.

KNERSVLAKTE
Literally the word means *grinding plains* and apparently it was suggested by the noise of wagon wheels crunching over the quartz pebbles. Many people see the Knersvlakte as no more than a bleak plain when, in reality, it supports a multitude of dwarf succulents and is one of the four distinct floral regions of Namaqualand. Every year after good winter rains this landscape puts out a spectacular profusion of colour as the spring flowers open. It is said that the best way to see the Knersvlakte is to get down on hands and knees, when another world will reveal itself.

BIRD ISLAND
The loud braying noise of Cape gannets and then the strong smell of their guano announce it long before you see it. But they are not the only inhabitants of this island in Lambert's Bay, as Cape cormorants and jackass penguins also breed here. These birds feed on pelagic fish and were considered a threat to the fishing industry until it became clear that they harvest only a small amount of fish compared with the commercial catch. Every year during April, after the breeding season, the nitrogen-rich guano deposited by the gannets and, to a lesser extent, by the cormorants is collected for making fertilizer.

CRAYFISH
The cold Atlantic waters that wash the rocky West Coast support a large population of these spiny scavengers among the shoreline's crevices and kelp. Females produce about 40 000 to 150 000 eggs every year, which they carry for about three months until the eggs hatch in October. The microscopic larvae drift away on the currents; survivors moult and grow and, eventually, swim back inshore to settle among the rocks. Crayfish (*Jasus lalandii*) grow extremely slowly, so that when a female reaches the minimum catch-size limit she is more than 20 years old. Males grow somewhat faster and reach the minimum size limit at 7 to 10 years of age. They are caught mainly for the export market and are packed as frozen tails – mainly for the USA and as whole cooked lobster for Japan and France.

The fishing town of Lambert's Bay with boats at anchor.

*Huge colonies of Cape gannets (*Morus capensis*) breed and nest noisily on Bird Island in Lambert's Bay.*

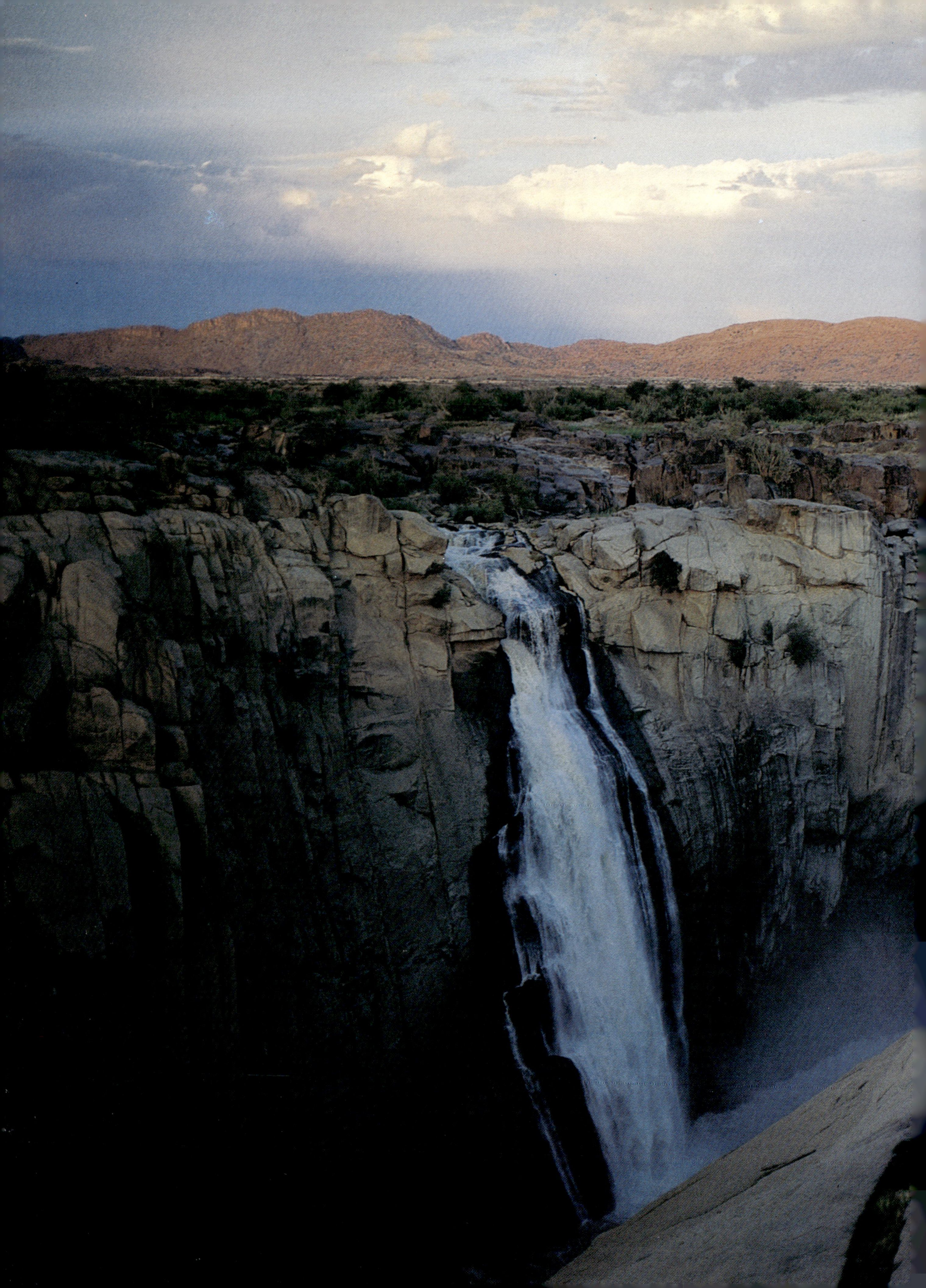

NORTHERN CAPE

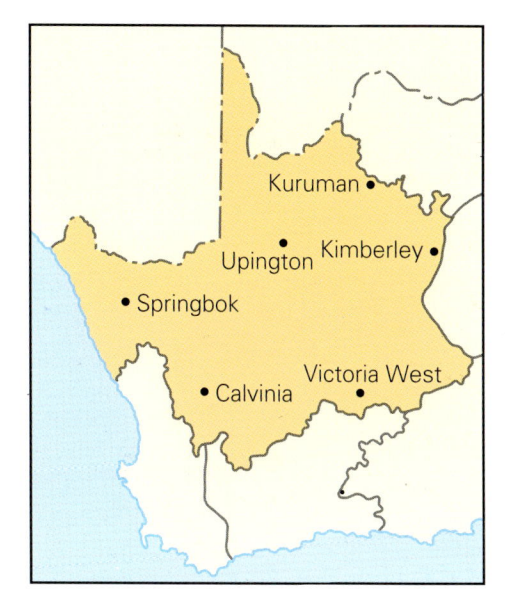

Springbok – Okiep – Nababeep – Spektakel Pass – Messelpad **288-9**

Namaqualand: The wildflower wonderland **290-1**

Upington – Kanoneiland – Keimoes – Kakamas – Augrabies Falls **292-3**

Augrabies Falls National Park: Mighty waterfall of the desert **294-5**

Kimberley – Nooitgedacht – Barkly West – Magersfontein **296-7**

Kalahari Gemsbok National Park: A wealth of wildlife **298-9**

Kimberley: Diamond capital of the world **300-1**

Dorp and byway: Travels through time **302-3**

Left: *Augrabies Falls – a stark landscape softened by the glow of sunset.*

Quiet old roads through the land of the copper mountains

This drive is most rewarding in spring, when the display of wildflowers is at its best. But the panoramic views over Namaqualand and its mountain passes – Spektakel Pass and the Messelpad – are memorable at any time of year. Note that two-thirds of the route is on gravel roads, and that you should take food and drink with you on this journey.

Springbok
Goegap Reserve
Okiep
Nababeep
Spektakel Pass
Messelpad
220 – 230 km

DRIVE NORTH-EAST ALONG Springbok's Voortrekker Street and turn right for Cape Town, noting your kms as you turn. After 1 km, turn right at the T-junction and, after a further 4,3 km, turn left, noting your kms again. You pass the airport on your right soon afterwards, and after 2,7 km you reach the entrance to the Goegap Nature Reserve. The reserve is home to a number of Hartmann's mountain zebra, as well as many smaller mammals, and there is a display of Namaqualand succulents alongside the administrative offices.

Retrace your route into the town and turn right into Voortrekker Street. Note your kms as you pass under the N7 road bridge about 200 m after turning. The N14 on which you are now travelling leads through a harsh granite landscape and, after about 4 km, you will see on your right, the *Koperberg* (copper mountain) with a number of old mines – including the fenced-in shaft dug in 1685 on instructions from the commander of the Cape settlement Simon van der Stel (see this page).

After roughly 6 km you reach Carolusberg. Turn right here, towards this small mining settlement and then turn right onto a gravel road (7,3 km from the N7 road bridge), at the sign to 'Simon van der Stel Mine'. Go left at the fork 200 m later, which brings you to a parking area at the foot of the Koperberg after a further 800 m. A steep path leads from the parking area up to the Van der Stel mine, from where there are wide views over the sun-baked flats and the massive granite outcrops that characterise this region. (Allow 30 – 40 minutes.)

Van der Stel's mine to Nababeep
Return to the N14 and drive straight across it onto the private (mine-owned) road, noting your kms. After about 10 km turn right at the T-junction to enter Okiep (see opposite). On your left, after slightly less than 1 km, is Okiep mine's historic stone chimney-stack, and behind it the stone building housing the steam-powered Cornish pump formerly used to keep the workings dry. Some 100 m after passing the chimney, turn left past the hotel. After a further 2,3 km you reach a T-junction with the N7; turn left onto the N7, noting your kms.

After 2,3 km on the N7, exit left for Okiep/Nababeep, turn right at the crossroads, and cross the bridge over the N7. You pass a huge granite outcrop on your left after 2,5 km, and roughly 7 km later you enter Nababeep, passing great slag heaps and mine workings on your right. After about 1 km you reach a fork with a sign reading 'Mine Museum'. Turn right here, then park in the space on the right after 100 m, just outside the town's museum (see opposite).

After visiting the museum, retrace your route out of town, noting your kms as you pass the 'Mine Museum' sign; 3,7 km later, turn right onto gravel for 'Kleinsee via Spektakel' and, after a further 7,5 km, turn right at the T-junction onto the R355 – noting your kms.

Sandhoogte and Spektakel Pass
The R355 winds down *Sandhoogte* (sand hill) into the valley of the *Eselsfontein* (donkey spring) River, passing huge granite outcrops and boulders that have been split apart by the daily extremes of temperature. After a while the scene changes to one of bushy koppies and scrubby valleys.

After 17,6 km on the R355 you reach the start of the Spektakel Pass. A further 2 km along there are fine views over the plains far below, and at 21,2 km, there is space to pull off the road at a good viewsite. Some 10 km after this, after descending from the pass, turn left for Komaggas, noting your kms as you turn. (The Spektakel mine and its slag heaps are visible further along the R355.)

The first few kilometres of this road to Komaggas may be corrugated, but the surface soon improves. The road passes between rugged hills and irrigated fields, with a scattering of modern and traditional homes, then begins to wind among the mountains. At 8,5 km from the turn-off you cross a riverbed, then the road narrows and climbs steeply. Copper salts and lichens give a range of subtle, sombre shades to the rocks in this area.

Komaggas to the Messelpad
At about 20 km from the turn-off the road passes through *Komaggas* (the name is believed to mean 'brown clay') where you can watch spinning and the weaving of carpets. In front of the community centre building, the road forks – take the road on your right and, 5 km later, turn left at the crossroads for Soebatsfontein – noting your kms.

The road you are now on has a good surface, but was constructed without any deep road-cuttings and it undulates over the hills. There may be farm gates along the route to be opened and closed, and signs that prohibit the removal of wood – an indication of its scarcity in these parts. After 27 km turn left at the

VAN DER STEL'S JOURNEY
In an elegant coach drawn by six horses, Commander Simon van der Stel set out from the Castle in Cape Town on an exploratory expedition to the Copper Mountains of the Nama people. The party took 57 days to reach its destination. On their arrival at the Copper Mountains, an apparently rich vein of copper ore was discovered almost immediately. The return proved to be disappointing and, in addition, the shortage of firewood made smelting difficult. Eventually the mine had to be abandoned. Copper is still mined nearby.

Cultivated fields near the Messelpad *(masonry road).*

Spring covers the Namaqualand veld with wildflowers.

A TOWN WITH A WILD PAST
Springbok is the largest town in Namaqualand, and serves as the commercial centre for a vast region. The town began life as the small settlement of Springbokfontein on the site of a copper mine that began operating in the early 1850s. It gained a reputation as a rough mining town, and one of the first acts of the local magistrate was to order a set of stocks for the detention of prisoners. A prison was built in 1856 and, from the day of completion, was usually full – the mining town having attracted a population of tough adventurers, few of whom knew anything about mining. The town has outgrown its wild youth, but many relics from the old days are preserved in its museum, a former synagogue built in 1930.

crossroads (the road on the right leads to Koingnaas, and on the left to Springbok) – noting your kms.

You can now see the road rising ahead of you, as it climbs towards the summit of the *Wildeperdehoek* (wild horses corner) Pass. After 8 km you reach an inclined T-junction. Turn left here for Springbok, and you begin the ascent of the pass 100 m beyond this.

This road has a good surface, but is steep and narrow – extremely narrow in places. As you climb you have a succession of grand views on your right over the plains and low hills of Namaqualand far below. As you round the bends, you can glimpse ahead of you the dry-stone support walls that gave this road the name *Messelpad* (masonry road).

Just over 9 km after beginning the ascent of the pass you reach a viewsite marked 'Historic Prison'. Far below are the extensive stone ruins of the Koringhuis outspan (see below).

The Messelpad eventually emerges from the hills and you find yourself in a gentler landscape. Continue on this road for some 25 km until you reach the tarred N7. Turn left onto the N7 and, after 7,6 km, turn left again – to reach Springbok after a further 3 km.

AA Office AA House, 7 Martin Hammerschlag Way, Cape Town 8001 Tel (021) 21 1550
Tourist Information Old Anglican Church Namakwa Street, Springbok 8240 Tel (0251) 22011
Captour Rendezvous Centre, 3 Adderley Street Cape Town 8001 Tel (021) 418 5202

The historic chimney stack of the Okiep mine.

MULE-POWERED RAILWAY TRAINS

The town of *Okiep* takes its name from a Khoikhoi word meaning 'large brackish place'. When the area was surveyed as a mine in 1856, there was just a single shaft, 3 m deep. Within a few years it had grown into the most important mine in the region, worked largely by skilled Cornish miners.

When the railway was built to Port Nolloth, replacing the old Messelpad to Hondeklipbaai, it turned out that there was insufficient water to operate the steam engines, so teams of mules were used to pull the carriages. Eventually the water-supply problem was solved, and *Clara*, on display at Nababeep, is an example of the mountain-type locomotives that were put to work on this route.

The old stone pump-house at Okiep.

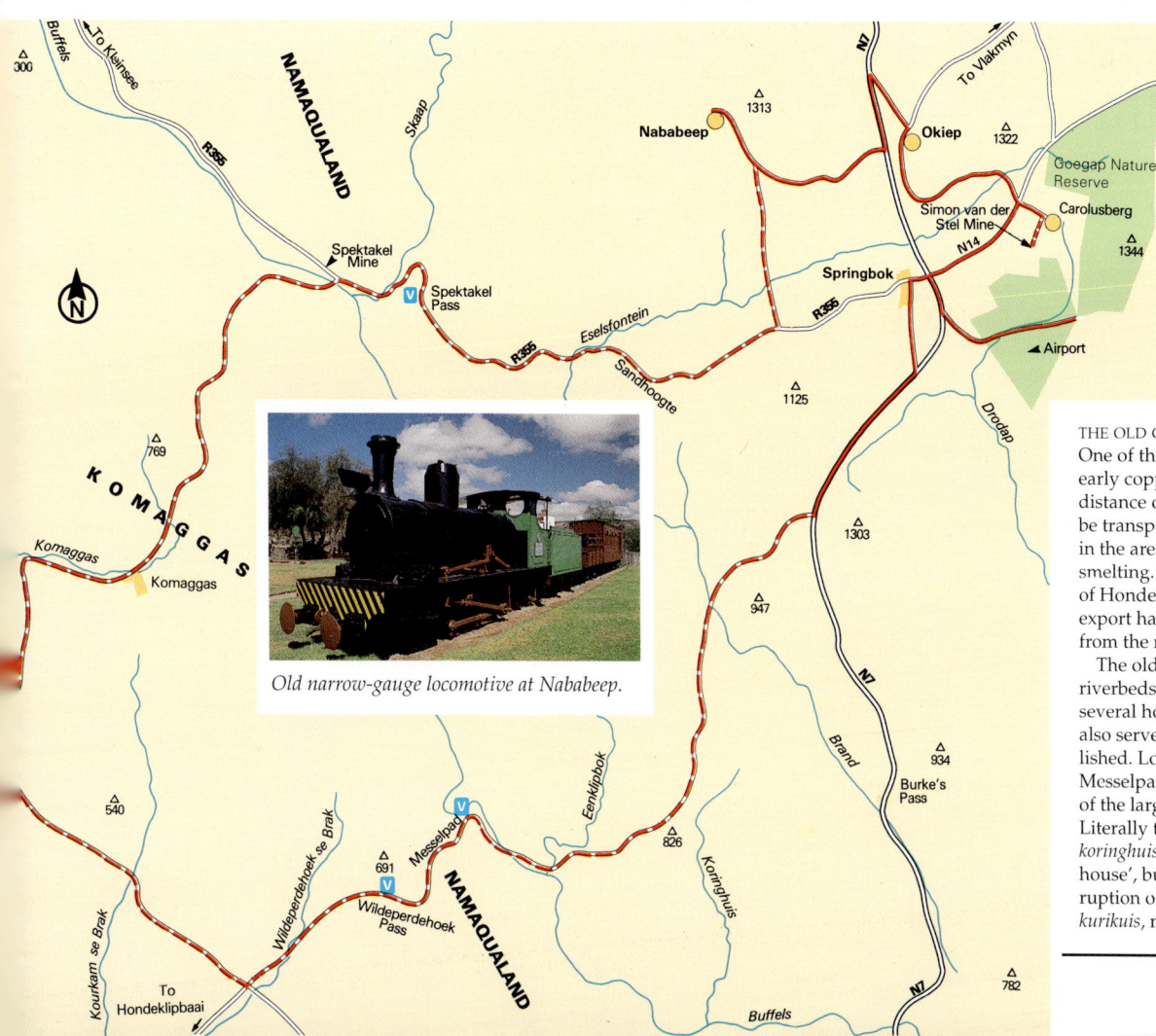

Old narrow-gauge locomotive at Nababeep.

THE OLD COPPER ROAD

One of the problems affecting the early copper mines was the great distance over which the ore had to be transported. The shortage of fuel in the area also prevented local smelting. Eventually the small inlet of Hondeklipbaai was chosen as an export harbour, and ore was carried from the mines in ox-wagons.

The old road followed dry riverbeds for much of the way, and several hostelries – some of which also served as prisons – were established. Looking down from the Messelpad, you can see the remains of the largest of these – Koringhuis. Literally translated from Afrikaans, *koringhuis* would mean 'wheat house', but in fact the name is a corruption of a Khoikhoi word *kurikuis*, meaning 'white quartz'.

· NAMAQUALAND'S WILDFLOWER WONDERLAND ·

A sea of yellow Pentzia grandiflora *washes over the veld near Lambert's Bay.*

Where Nature paints the world with wildflowers

Swirling up from the frozen South Atlantic, the Benguela Current chills a shore where the remains of dead ships loom ghostlike in the mist, and diamonds sparkle on lonely beaches. There is little evaporation from these icy waters, and few winds sweep the fragile clouds inland to the great plains of Namaqualand. This is a world of dry riverbeds threading their way through huge outcrops of granite that have been stained by the percolation of copper salts and glitter with fragments of quartz and mica. On the plains beneath the mountains, sheep and goats range far in their search for grazing across sandy, arid landscapes.

But if there has been rain, a miracle occurs with the coming of spring. Millions upon millions of brightly coloured flowers appear, seemingly from the very rocks, to spread their petals wide beneath the sun. Namaqualand is in flower.

It is said that more South Africans have visited Europe than have ever been to Namaqualand. But a visit to this wonderland during a good flowering season is an experience never forgotten.

The flower-rich area – although not all of it can properly be called Namaqualand – stretches roughly from the Darling district in the south to the Orange River in the north, and inland to include Calvinia and Aggeneys. The region can be divided into many districts, each with its own character and particular mix of flora.

Splendours of the Sandveld

In the south, one area that is particularly rich in flowers is the Sandveld, a 30 km wide strip of low-lying, sandy country along the coast in the region of Lambert's Bay. The flora here consists mainly of semi-succulent scrub, the plants obtaining moisture from the mists that roll in from the sea. Here too you can see large patches of shimmering yellow *Grielum*, or flat thorn, and wild flax (*Heliophila*) – the last forming chains of azure lakes among the sands. A good route

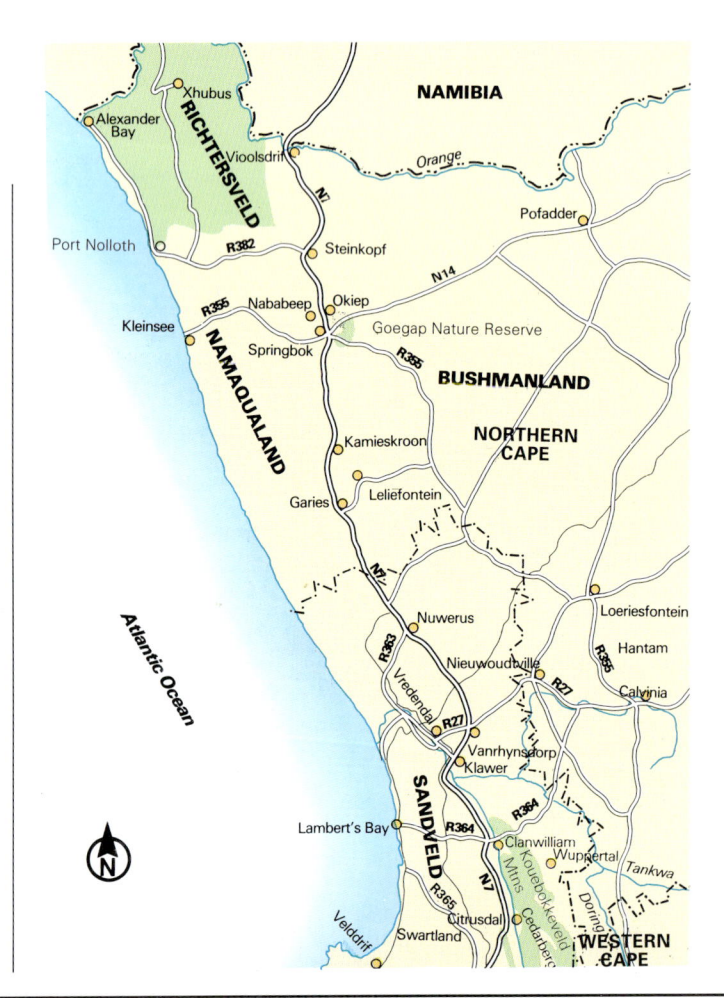

The flower-lined N7 near Steinkopf.  *A kokerboom sprouts from the rocks.*  Ruschia extensa *forms brilliant mauve cushions among the granite boulders.*

through this region leads from Clanwilliam to Lambert's Bay, then along the coast to Doringbaai and Strandfontein, and back to Clanwilliam via Lutzville, Vredendal and Klawer. The section of this road that runs along the coast is sometimes in poor condition, but the flower displays at their best are splendid.

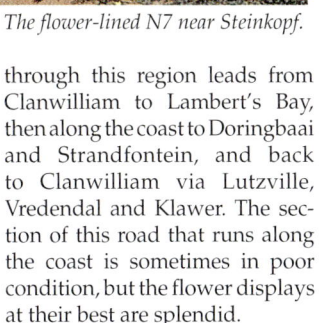

Inland from here, but still south of Namaqualand proper, lie the richly flowered landscapes of the Clanwilliam district and the Biedou Valley (see pages 280 – 1), and slightly further north there is the countryside around Nieuwoudtville. In these areas the various daisy species appear in great numbers and in a profusion of brilliant colours.

Kamiesberg and Springbok

North from here we enter the region properly called Namaqualand, where the land rises to form the Kamiesberg range. The mountainsides support an evergreen fynbos flora, including Namaqualand's only protea species *(Protea sulphurea)*. Several rare wildflower varieties are to be found here, including the large-flowered, blazing orange *Gladiolus equitans*. The mission village *Leliefontein* (lily spring) takes its name from the *Androcymbium*, a ground-hugging plant with a deeply buried corm, whose white blossoms can be seen scattered thickly over the veld.

North of the Kamiesberg lies the boulder-mountain country around Springbok. The rainfall is higher here, and supports a greater variety of species. Springbok is one of the best bases from which to take short flower-viewing trips and it lies amid hills that are thickly clothed with blooms. Alternatives are nearby Okiep or Nababeep – all three towns offer accommodation. The day-drive from Springbok described on pages 288 – 9 will take you past many excellent displays in a good season, in addition to providing outstanding panoramas from the Spektakel Pass and the rugged Messelpad.

North of Springbok, and especially beyond Steinkopf, the quantity of wildflowers diminishes, but taking their place there are strange plants such as the *Puchypodium namaquanum*, or *halfmens* (half man). The plant does resemble a man when seen from a distance or in poor light, and it is the subject of many legends among the Nama. It has a single trunk, swollen towards the base, and the head, which is always turned towards the north, is crowned by leaves that are shed during the scorching summer months. The tubular flowers are a delicate yellow tipped with red. Home for many of these *halfmense* is the Richtersveld, stretching north from Steinkopf to the Orange River, and lying west of the N7 from the Cape to Namibia. This is an extremely arid region where only the hardiest of succulents can survive.

Desert displays surprise the traveller

East of the N7, sandy flats stretch away to Pofadder, and south from here as far as Loeriesfontein. The wildflower show is restricted in these regions by the low rainfall, but fine displays are occasionally encountered. Some fortunate travellers may be greeted by huge expanses of pastel-shaded *Arctotis canescens*, or they may see the formerly scorched veld tightly blanketed in the blue flowers of the low-growing Karoo violet *(Aptosimum)*.

For anyone planning a springtime trip through the flower country, several practical tips may prove valuable. One is to book your accommodation early – a year or more ahead of your visit. Another is to find out in advance where the rains have been good and where fine displays are expected. (For sources of information, see the information panels on pages 288 – 9.) A third point to keep in mind is that many of the flowering species present their petals to the sun – sometimes, especially when you are driving northwards, you must remember to stop and look behind you to see the flowers at their best.

The quintessential Namaqualand vista – a carpet of flowers stretches into the distance as far as the eye can see.

Following the Orange River to the 'Place of Great Noise'

Augrabies is a place of striking contrast. In a land of little rain, the surging waters of the Orange River create a ribbon of life, then thunder over one of the world's mightiest waterfalls. This drive leads from Upington to the Augrabies Falls National Park, passing through Keimoes and Kakamas. All but a few kilometres of the route is tarred.

**Upington
Kanoneiland
Keimoes
Kakamas
Augrabies Falls
National Park
250 – 270 km**

OUR FIRST STOP of the day is Upington's famous avenue of palms at the *Eiland* (island) holiday resort. To get there, drive south-west along Schröder Street from the old mission complex, now the town's museum with a marvellously evocative Donkey Monument. Turn left at the stop sign. After some 200 m you pass, on your left, an irrigation canal and then cross a bridge over the northern channel of the Orange River. A few hundred metres further, turn left to reach the entrance to the resort area (an entrance fee may be charged at weekends and during holiday seasons). The well-shaded main thoroughfare through the resort is said to be the longest palm avenue in the world, and has been declared a national monument.

When you drive out of the resort area, turn left and note your kms. Cross the southern arm of the Orange, and at 1,2 km turn right for Louisvale. The road soon leads through irrigated fields and vineyards – this is the northernmost wine-making region of the Cape provinces. After a little over 14 km you pass through the small farming settlement of Louisvale.

Some 27 km after leaving the resort, turn right, staying on the tar. (The road ahead leads to Neilersdrif, and its surface changes to gravel.) You now pass, on your left, a Voortrekker Centenary monument and a Roman Catholic mission, then cross the 400 m single-lane *Eendragbrug* (unity bridge) to Kanoneiland (see opposite). As you cross the bridge, you can see the river tumbling over a prominent weir on your right.

Kanoneiland to Augrabies

At 28 km you reach a road on your left that leads to the village on the island. Unless you wish to call in at the village, drive on past this turn-off, crossing the Manie Conradie Bridge over the northern arm of the river and then two sets of railway lines. When you reach the T-junction with the N14, turn left for Keimoes – which you reach after a further 13 km.

As you enter Keimoes, turn right into Hoofstraat. On your left you pass a waterwheel at work in an irrigation canal, and on the opposite side of the road, just a few metres back, you can see the Dutch Reformed Mission Church that dates from 1889. The local waterwheels, which raise water from one channel and transfer it to another at a higher level, are mechanized forms of the ancient Egyptian shadoof, still in use along the lower Nile.

Continue along Hoofstraat, which becomes the N14 to Springbok. Roughly 5 km from Keimoes you pass a road on your right that leads to the Kalahari Gemsbok National Park. After this the road moves away from the river, the irrigated fields are left behind, and the country takes on a desolate appearance.

About 33 km from Keimoes the road draws close to the river again, as you approach Kakamas. Watch for a large sign indicating the 'Water Tunnels' (the access road is easy to follow) and a small sign to 'The German War Graves 1914 – 18'. (If you pass a small cemetery on your left, set back from the road, you've overshot the track to the graves by a few hundred metres.) To visit the war graves and a monument commemorating the 1915 Battle of Kakamas, follow the sign onto a narrow gravel road on the right of the N14 and drive straight, crossing the cattle grid and following the main track. The monument soon becomes visible ahead of you, and you reach it after 1 km on the gravel road. There is a good view over the Kakamas Valley from the top of the hill.

Return to the N14 and turn right, noting your kms. After 700 m you pass a road on your right that leads to Namibia and the Kalahari Gemsbok National Park. Shortly after this you cross a bridge over the Orange River and enter Kakamas (see opposite); 2,9 km after rejoining the tar you come to a crossroads. Turn left here to see, in the course of roughly 2,5 km, a number of the old-fashioned waterwheels still at work supplying the irrigation canals. The association of the waterwheel with the Egyptian shadoof probably inspired the design of the building – now a national monument – housing the transformer that first distributed electricity to Kakamas in 1914.

Return to the crossroads and turn left to continue your journey on the N14, noting your kms as you turn. After 8,2 km turn right for Augrabies Falls National Park; 4,5 km along this road you pass the small town of Marchand on your right. Here and there you will see some of the sloping cement 'floors' that are common in this region. They are used for drying fruit in the sun – mainly sultanas and raisins.

About 9 km beyond the turn-off into Marchand you pass Augrabies village on your right. Roughly 11 km later, turn right and, after a further 4,6 km, in the course of which you cross one of the channels of the Orange River, you reach the entrance to the Augrabies Falls National Park (entrance fee; no animals and no motor cycles allowed).

Augrabies Falls National Park

Close to the entrance there is an information centre where you can obtain a free booklet on the park. There is also a shop that sells basic foodstuffs (including frozen meat), firewood, wine and beer. There is also a restaurant, and there are picnic places nearby – set among trees along one of the river's channels. There are braai sites here, with water and toilets. (No drinking water is available elsewhere in the park.) There are also swimming pools, and a play pool for younger children.

There are several roads in the park leading to out-of-the-way corners (see pages 294 – 5). Among these are Ararat and Oranjekom, and

A waterwheel on an irrigation canal at Keimoes.

CHRISTIAAN SCHRÖDER'S LEGACY

One of the main crossing points on the Orange River became known to early European explorers as *Olyvenhoutsdrif* (olive-wood drift), and Christiaan Schröder, a missionary, established a mission station here in 1871. In 1884 the name of the small settlement that had grown around the mission was changed to Upington, honouring the new Prime Minister of the Cape Colony, Sir Thomas Upington,

One year before the name change, the first of an intricate system of irrigation canals had been constructed, and Upington now serves as the centre of a rich farming district – thanks to the abundant waters of the Orange. Fruit, vegetables, cotton and wine are produced here.

The shady avenue of palms on Die Eiland.

NORTHERN CAPE

Augrabies – one of the world's most awesome waterfalls when in flood.

The Orange River gorge cuts through the Augrabies Falls National Park.

A BATTLE IN THE DESERT
World War I began in August 1914, and in September the government of the Union of South Africa decided to invade German South West Africa (Namibia). An invasion force was assembled, with 6 000 men encamped south of Kakamas.

The German commander, Major Francke, decided to attack rather than wait to be invaded. At that time the Orange River was crossed by means of two ponts that were heavily guarded by the South African forces. These ponts were the target of the leader of the German expedition, Major Ritter.

Shortly after dawn on 4 Feburary 1915, four German field guns opened fire, at a range of over 1 km, from a position near the site of the present monument. The rest of Ritter's forces, who had advanced closer to the river, opened fire on the troops at the ponts. The battle lasted six hours – the Germans being forced eventually to withdraw, with the loss of seven lives.

The simple monument was erected in 1960 by the *Volksbund Deutschen Kriegs-gräberfürsorge*, and the remains of the six soldiers whose graves could be found were reinterred here.

KANONEILAND
This is probably the best known of the many islands in the Orange River, and it has been occupied as an agricultural settlement since 1926. The island received its name during the Second Northern Border War of 1878 – 9, fought between the Cape Colony forces and the Koranna, led by Klaas Pofadder.

It is thought that the island takes its name from a cannon that Pofadder and his men constructed here from a hollowed-out aloe stem. This was loaded with gunpowder and stones, and pointed at the Cape Colony forces. When fired, the cannon exploded, killing several Koranna men.

THE GOLDEN PEACH FROM KAKAMAS
For many years, experts at the Elsenburg Agricultural College near Stellenbosch struggled to find a variety of peach that would be suitable for canning – a potential fortune in fruit lay rotting on the ground unable to be preserved.

Eventually, a former Elsenburg student, AD Collins, found a promising peach tree near Kakamas. Evidently a natural mutation, the peach proved to have all the qualities needed for successful canning. The newly discovered variety was carefully propagated, and from a single tree has come 75 per cent of all the trees now supplying South Africa's giant canning industry.

The mighty Orange River brings life to the desert near Kakamas.

the road to both passes a 1 km sideroad that leads to the bare Moon Rock. At Ararat there are fine views up the rugged gorge, but shade is in short supply. At Oranjekom a roofed shelter – with cement tables and benches – provides some shade for picnickers. From Oranjekom there are wide views over the river *kom* (basin) between towering cliffs.

Augrabies to Upington
Retrace your outgoing route as far as Keimoes but, when you reach the traffic lights in Keimoes, continue straight ahead instead of turning left towards Upington – noting your kms at the lights. After 1,5 km you cross a single-lane bridge and at 2,4 km turn right for the Keimoes Nature Reserve.

Drive slowly from here, as the road may be bumpy and it becomes steep as it approaches *Tierberg* ('tiger' or 'leopard' mountain). From the summit of Tierberg there are superb views over Keimoes and the irrigated lands nearby – the great expanse of green being in sharp contrast with the landscape near the awesome Augrabies Falls, where the river is channelled into a rocky ravine. Return from Tierberg to the traffic lights in Keimoes, and turn right. Stay on this main road (N14) the whole way to Upington, passing, on your right, the road on which you crossed the river at Kanoneiland.

Upington Publicity Association Civic Centre Market Square, Upington 8800 Tel (054) 26911
Tourist Officer, Augrabies Falls National Park Private Bag X1, Augrabies 8874
Tel (054) 451 0050

293

AUGRABIES FALLS NATIONAL PARK

A thundering waterfall in a dry, desert landscape

The Orange River below the falls.

A bungalow in the park.

Known to the wandering Khoikhoi as *Aukoerebis* (place of great noise), the Augrabies Falls thunder over a great granite slash in the barren Orange River broken veld of the Northern Cape. Here, the tumbling waters of the Orange River go mad in a series of deep ravines and dangerous, dizzying cliffs.

The first white man to see the falls was a Swedish-born soldier named Hendrik Wikar. Wikar deserted his post at the Cape in 1775 to escape an accumulation of gambling debts, and for four years he wandered through the uncharted country now known as the Northern Cape, describing in a journal, and sometimes also mapping, many of the places that he visited. Three years after leaving the Cape, he came to the verge of this immense granite gorge, with the full mass of the Orange River surging down over the ancient rocks.

Today, visitors can share in Wikar's experience by viewing the falls from various observation points along the edge of the gorge. (Another viewsite, a suspension footbridge linking the banks just a short distance above the falls, was torn away by raging floodwaters.) From these sites you can see how the river, in the course of many millions of years, has worn through the granite – gneiss base-rock to form a 186 m deep and 18 km long chasm. This erosion of granite by water is considered by many geologists to be the finest example of its kind in the world.

Contrasting scenery

The Augrabies Falls National Park covers a large area of land on both banks of the river, completely surrounding the falls. One of the most striking aspects of the park is the contrast in its scenery. The banks of the river are painted bright green by the lush vegetation, yet only a few metres away there is little but sand and rock, a virtual desert stretching away to the horizon. The falls themselves (see photograph, pages 286 – 7) are, of course, the centrepiece, mighty and harshly beautiful, with the river tumbling 56 m over the edge of a massive granite barrier into a mysterious pool that is 92 m across and believed to be close to 130 m deep.

Striking, though less powerful, this secondary fall plunges into the gorge.

These falls are regarded as one of the six greatest waterfalls in the world. When the Orange River is in flood, up to 405 million litres of water crash over the granite shelf every minute in 19 separate falls. Best known of the secondary falls is the Bridal Veil Falls, which becomes part of the main falls when the river is in flood. The gorge at this time is shrouded in mist and the noise of the water is deafening.

The deep pool into which the falls plunge is surrounded by sheer cliffs, and is reputed to contain a fortune in diamonds – washed down the river and trapped in the gravel at the bottom. The pool is also claimed to be the home of a 'river monster', but sightings of this creature can perhaps be attributed to shoals of giant barbel, which grow to a length of two metres. During a severe drought in the 1930s, a group of thirsty cattle wandered up the dry riverbed to the edge of the pool, in search of water. A strong wind blew them into the pool and they were never seen again – an incident that helped to convince many local people that a monster of some kind does indeed lurk in the depths.

Walks and drives

Augrabies Falls National Park is centred on Klaas Island, just to the West of the main falls. Here is a caravan park with picnic sites and swimming pools, several bungalows that can be hired, and also an information centre, a shop and a restaurant. In front of the restaurant there is a succulent garden containing several species of aloe.

From here there are a number of walks and drives that you can take to outlying viewpoints (see pages 292 – 3). One of the most popular walks is along the 2,5 km path leading to the Arrow Head

Sunset washes the grey boulders of the Orange River chasm with a pink hue.

viewsite. From here you can look out over the rapids that career along the bottom of the gorge far below. For the more energetic there is the Klipspringer Hiking Trail that runs for 26 km along the southern bank of the river. This is a three-day hike and walkers stay overnight in huts along the route. The trail passes Ararat, a granite rock that offers a magnificent view along the gorge, and also Moon Rock, which provides panoramic views over the whole park.

Walking through the park, you will discover that there is a far richer variety of animal and plant life than might be expected in such a barren landscape. Camelthorn trees (*Acacia erioloba*) and *kokerbome* or quiver trees (*Aloe dichotoma*) are the most prominent plants, while the fauna includes the klipspringer, the springbok, a number of smaller mammals and 150 bird species. The park is particularly rich in reptiles. At the edge of the gorge you can often see the beautifully coloured red-tailed rock lizard (*Platysaurus capensis*) and various geckos and agamas scuttling briskly in the heat. In the hot summer months, you will frequently see snakes basking on the rocks – the Cape cobra (*Naja nivea*), the spitting cobra (*Naja mossambica mossambica*) or the widespread puff-adder (*Bitis arietans arietans*).

Treacherous granite walls

As a safety measure, chest-high fences have been erected at most of the popular observation points, but there will always be overeager tourists who tempt fate by climbing over the fence for a slightly closer look. Since the proclamation of the park in 1966, more than 20 people have died after losing their balance on the edge of the gorge and slipping down its steep, erosion-polished granite walls. To slip over the edge spells almost certain death, but occasionally miracles do happen.

In 1979 a Scandinavian visitor lost his footing and slid the whole way down the rock face. The friction was so great that his clothes were ripped from his body. He suffered lacerations and broken bones, but was still able to clamber out of the river onto a rock. From this point he was saved by park wardens. Even his wallet containing R400 was found on a precipitous ledge.

The open nature of the countryside in the park, and the clear light, offer rich opportunities to the photographer, and eager cameramen have tried many stunts to capture the falls from a new angle. One of the first of these photographic adventurers was an acrobat named Lulu Farini, who toured the region with his stepfather Guillermo. He photographed the falls from many angles, but could find no way of capturing the main fall from the bottom of the gorge. Eventually he set his sights on an outcrop of rock about 100 m down the sheer rock face – a point that could be reached only with ropes. After joining some kudu-hide harness straps to the rope they had, the two men lowered the camera equipment, then climbed over the edge. From the outcrop below, Lulu made two exposures of the falls before climbing back 'hand over hand, quicker than we had come down, for we were now sure of the rope's strength'. (The Farini expedition went on to popularize the legend of the 'lost city' of the Kalahari.)

Year-round attractions

The park can be visited at any time of year, and each season has its own particular attractions. Spring and autumn are the best seasons for hiking, as the temperatures in summer and winter are too extreme for comfort. The falls, however, are at their most spectacular in summer, between October and January, when the greatest flood of water rushes down from the highlands of Lesotho and the Eastern Cape. (If you are planning to photograph the falls, note that they are best captured in the afternoon when the sunlight catches them – often creating a bright rainbow in the finely blown spray.)

Combined canoeing, hiking and mountain-biking excursions of a day's duration are available. Participants are taken to a starting point from which they canoe some 3 km on the Orange River, hike for 4 km and then cover the 11 km return to the rest camp by mountain bike. No guides accompany the outings, but the routes are clearly marked and route maps are provided. Life jackets, canoes, paddles and mountain bikes are provided, and groups comprise between two and a maximum of six people.

Other day outings include a river trip by rubber duck (inflatable raft) followed by a safari in an open vehicle with an experienced field guide and tracker, to view – among many other species – the rare black rhino. For bookings and enquiries, contact the Chief Director, National Parks Board, PO Box 787, Pretoria 0001. Tel (012) 44 1191/98. If a booking is needed within 12 days, you can contact the Tourist Officer at the park: Private Bag X1, Augrabies 8874. Tel (054) 451 0050/1/2 or fax (054) 451 0053.

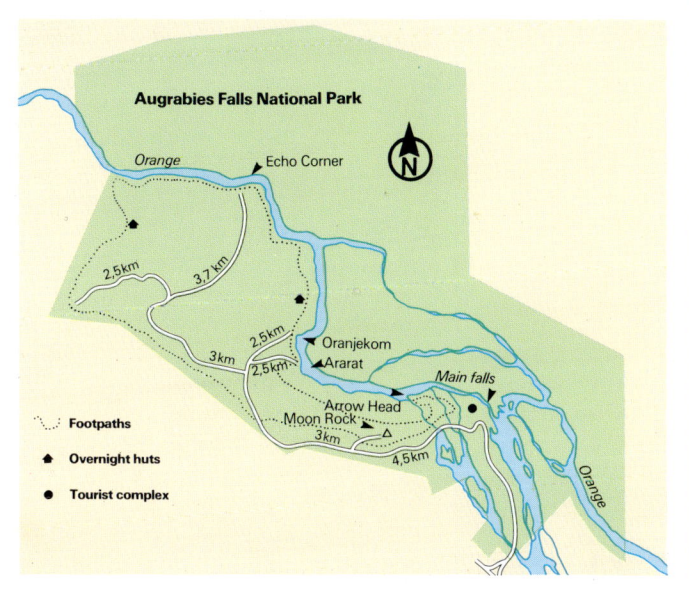

Springbok are easily seen on the bare rocks of the Augrabies Falls National Park.

Granite rock, shaped over millennia by rushing water and extreme temperatures.

Diamond fields, battlefields – and decorated glacial floors

Diamonds brought this region to world attention, and a famous siege ensured its place in history. Soldiers sleep on in their lonely graves while new generations of diggers wash and sift the alluvial gravel. Rivers bring relief and surprising greenness to the area, where people have roamed since prehistoric times. About 60 km of the route is on gravel.

Kimberley
Magersfontein
Nooitgedacht
Riverton
Barkly West
Vaalbos Park
230 – 250 km

DRIVE SOUTH ALONG Kimberley's Bultfontein/Dalham Road and turn right at the traffic lights for Memorial Road/Cape Town/N12, noting your kms. Memorial Road becomes the N12, which runs parallel to the railway line as it enters a countryside dotted with thorn trees that are adorned with the nests of weaverbirds. After 34,5 km on the N12, turn left for Scholtzburg/Magersfontein, cross a bridge over the railway line and immediately turn left for Magersfontein Veld/Field Museum. Note your kms as the road becomes gravel some 300 m later and, after a further 1 km, turn left for Magersfontein. Some 6,5 km after you noted your kms, the Magersfontein Koppie, topped by a tall memorial, appears ahead of you. After 8,3 km on gravel, turn left and go through a gate, following the road as it winds up and around Magersfontein Koppie to reach the museum, observation post and tearoom some 2,3 km later. (Small entry fee.)

Magersfontein to Barkly West
Retrace your route to the gate, turn left for Kimberley and note your kms. After 5,7 km you pass the Magersfontein Burgers Monument on your right and, after 20,5 km on the gravel road, you reach a four-way stop street where the road surface changes to tar. The large building on your right is the Officers' Club of the SA National Defence Force; as the Alexandersfontein Hotel, it was formerly a favourite Kimberley resort.

Turn left into Kenneth van der Spuy Rylaan to reach – some 600 m later – the Pioneers of Aviation Museum where you can see a replica of the 1913 Compton Patterson biplane on which some of South Africa's first pilots learnt to fly. (Entry fee.) Leave the museum and turn left, noting your kms. Pass the Northern Cape Command Headquarters after 2,2 km, cross two railway bridges and, at 6 km, the large, Herbert Baker-designed Honoured Dead Memorial comes into view. Drive past it, taking the exit to the city centre (second exit, Dalham/Bultfontein/Pniel Road).

Continue north along this road on which you travelled earlier and note your kms as you pass the Big Hole on your left. Pass two sets of traffic lights as the road becomes the R31 to Barkly West. After 12,8 km, turn right at the T-junction for Barkly West/R31. Note your kms and, 7,6 km later, turn right onto a gravel road for 'Nooitgedacht Gletservloere'. You cross a number of cattle grids before the Vaal River comes into view on your left and, 5,6 km after turning off, you reach the old Nooitgedacht homestead and an information booth. Park and walk towards the gate behind the homestead, pass through the gate and follow the path as it winds along the glacial pavement, looking carefully for the San etchings.

Note your kms as you leave Nooitgedacht; cross a number of cattle grids and farm roads before crossing a railway line after 7,9 km, taking extra care where the road surface is sandy. Some 15 km after leaving Nooitgedacht you pass the lush, green, tree-lined banks of the Vaal River; at 23 km turn left onto tar at the T-junction for Riverton, entering the pleasure resort after a further 1,7 km. Here you can braai, swim, play tennis, go boating or fishing, and enjoy walks. (Entry fee.)

Leave the resort and, roughly 600 m later, turn left onto tar for Langleg/Barkly West, noting your kms. The road runs beside the Vaal River; go straight at the crossroads after 2,7 km and, at 3,8 km, cross the Vaal on a narrow causeway. At the T-junction 22 km later, turn left for Barkly West, cross the railway bridge and, shortly after, at 26 km, turn right at the T-junction into Barkly West on Transvaal/Campbell Street; 1 km after turning, visit the library for information. The town has an interesting mining museum and the St Mary's Anglican church dates from 1885.

Barkly West to Kimberley
Leave Barkly West along Campbell Street, noting your kms as you pass through a crossroads about 2 km later, with the road becoming the R31 for Kuruman. Some 16,5 km later, turn left onto gravel for Vaalbos Natuur Oord/Sydney on Vaal, noting your kms. After 2,3 km turn right; you soon notice the diamond-digging operations and prospecting equipment along the river bank. After 5,9 km you cross a causeway and then turn left at the fork to reach the entrance to the Vaalbos National Park. There are two circular drives that allow you to observe animals such as rhino, buffalo, zebra and eland in their natural habitat.

Retrace your route to the R31 and turn right for Barkly West. Soon after passing the turn-off to Riverton, you pass Canteen Koppie, site of Africa's first alluvial diamond diggings. Almost immediately after that, turn left through a set of gates to see the old tollbridge. Return to the R31 and turn left to reach Kimberley after a further 34 km.

AA Office AA House, 13 New Main Street Kimberley 8301 Tel (0531) 25207
Tourist Information Office City Hall, cr Old Main Street and Transvaal Road, Kimberley 8301 Tel (0531) 27298/9

The ridge and scrubby plain of Magersfontein.

MAGERSFONTEIN
Contrary to popular belief, the Battle of Magersfontein in 1899 did not see the birth of trench warfare, which can be traced back to much earlier wars. Rather, it was its innovative employment, coupled with British misfortune, that proved so deadly. A British army, on its way to break the Boer siege of Kimberley, had fought three set engagements by the time it arrived within striking distance of the ridge at Magersfontein. Believing that the Boers, as usual, would be dug in along the crest of the ridge, the British commander, Lord Methuen, ordered a heavy bombardment of the upper slopes. The Boers, in the meantime, sat out the bombardment in trenches that they had dug ahead of the ridge, and the deadly shells flew over their heads. A British observation balloon, from which the trenches might have been detected, was not ready for use before the first scheduled advance. The Highland Brigade led a night march across the veld in preparation for a dawn assault on the heights, only to blunder into the Boer trenches and be shot down at once by concentrated rifle-fire or picked off during the long, hot day that followed. After nightfall, the remnants of the Highland Brigade withdrew, and the British army fell back on its base camp at Modder River. The relief of Kimberely had to wait a while longer. (See pages 300 – 1.)

The Honoured Dead Memorial in Kimberley.

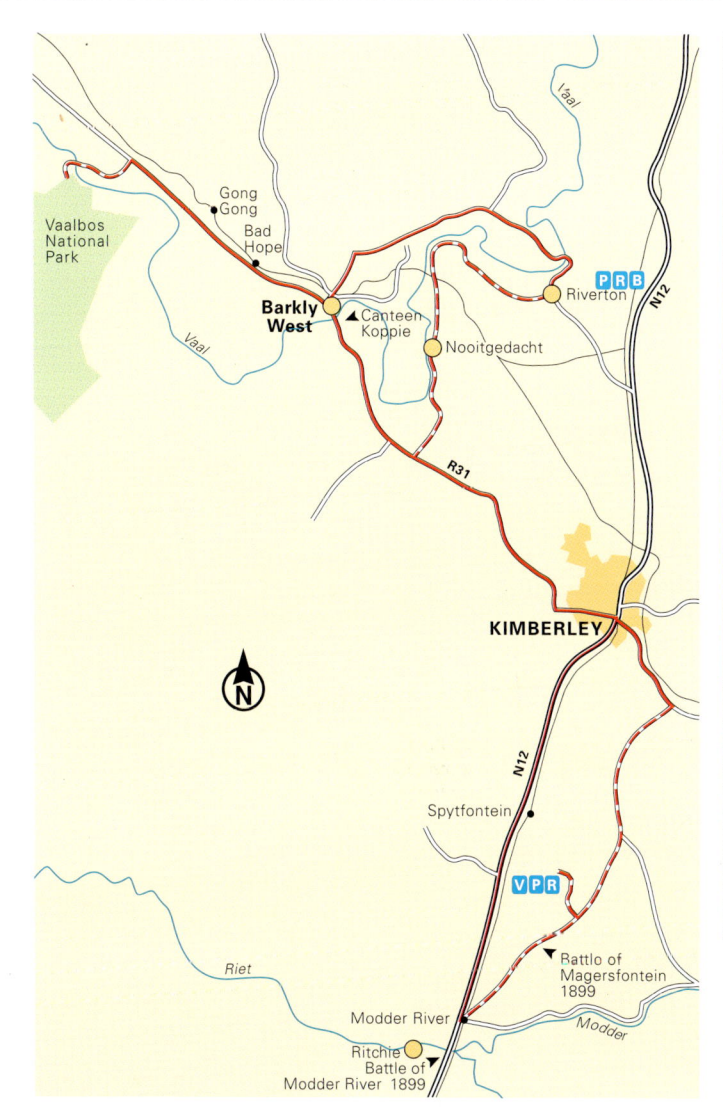

NORTHERN CAPE

Battlefield memorial to the pro-Boer Scandinavian Corps at Magersfontein.

DIAMONDS IN THE DIRT

Piles of sifted earth and gravel bear witness to the frenzied activity that began in 1869 on Canteen Koppie just outside Barkly West. The search for diamonds had truly begun, and Barkly West (then known as Klipdrift) was at its centre. For a short while, in 1870, the diggers even proclaimed their own republic, but a stern magistrate soon brought order (and the present name). The first permanent bridge across the Vaal River – to replace the often-precarious ponts – was built at Barkly West and is now a national monument. It was built by a private company which charged a fee for its use and even established a tollhouse to see that their money was collected. Interestingly named camps that came into being along the river nearby include Gong Gong, Poor Man's Koppie and Moonlight Rush, and diggers are still to be seen patiently at work at these and other sites. Barkly West's representative in the old Cape Parliament was Cecil Rhodes, who had a house here. There is a small museum in the town.

Barkly West's tollbridge.

PAVEMENT ARTISTS

Blazing summer in the Northern Cape is far removed from the Ice Age – by about 250 million years. This is when gravel and boulders, frozen in slow-moving glaciers, scored deep lines in Nooitgedacht's rock pavements, themselves the product of volcanic action and then more than 2 000 million years old.

People of the Stone Age – probably San hunters – found the smoothly polished rock a challenging medium in which to work, and they have left a record of their own occupation and of the many animals that once roamed freely in this area. Their petroglyphs or incised stone carvings show rhino, elephant and many types of antelope, as well as human and stylized figures, the images being scattered over an area of almost 200 ha.

The farm Nooitgedacht was the venue for an important meeting to resolve land claims between the Cape Colony and the Orange Free State Republic in 1870.

San carvings or petroglyphs on the glacial pavement at Nooitgedacht.

297

• EXPLORING KALAHARI GEMSBOK PARK •

A pride of lions keeps a watchful eye on a lone eland in a sandy stretch of the Kalahari Gemsbok National Park.

A wealth of wildlife in a world with little water

THE TRAVELLER IS greeted by an extraordinarily stark and sunburned landscape. Stretching away to a shimmering horizon are great waves of red sand, dotted here and there with camelthorn trees. The climate ranges from dry to very dry, and periods of extreme drought can be measured by the carcasses in the dry riverbeds. Yet there is abundant life in the harsh environment of the Kalahari – a primeval vitality that comes as a surprise in the seemingly inhospitable surroundings. For those who want to see and feel an unspoilt Africa, this is perhaps the most rewarding place to visit. Here it is still possible to experience the wild excitement of a lion-kill or to witness the lightning dash of a hunting cheetah – exactly as if mankind had never appeared on the scene.

A park between two rivers
The Kalahari Gemsbok National Park covers almost 1 000 000 ha of rugged desert country, sandwiched between Namibia in the west and Botswana in the east. An even larger game park adjoins it in Botswana, and animals roam freely between the two reserves– which together form the largest game park in southern Africa.

The boundaries of the South African park are marked by the watercourses of two rivers – in the west the *Auob* ('bitter tasting' in the language of the San people) and in the east the *Nossob* (big water). The rivers rarely flow, but more than 40 boreholes have been sunk along the riverbeds at intervals of several kilometres, and these make a small supply of water available to the game.

The two principal routes in the park follow the courses of these rivers, and are linked by a road that switchbacks its way over the dunes that lie between them. (The roads in the park are untarred, but are usually in good condition.)

Evocative names
Each borehole, with its attendant wind-pump, has an individual and often evocative name, ranging from 'Groot Skrij' and 'Kijkij' to the unexpected 'Montrose', and the no-doubt heartfelt *Lekkerwater* (lovely water). The waterholes offer excellent vantage points for game-viewing, especially in the early mornings and the late afternoons. It is here that cheetah, leopard and lion stalk the antelope that are attracted to the precious water, and few visitors leave the park without sighting one or more of the big cats. Vultures, hyenas and black-backed jackals clean the carcasses that the large predators leave behind – until a pair of horns and a few bones are all that remain of a once proud antelope.

There are more than 10 000 springbok in the park, and visitors may be treated to the amazing sight of enormous herds of these agile animals as they seem to flow effortlessly over the dunes. Also to be seen are smaller herds of gemsbok, with their fearsome, rapier-like horns. Other animals commonly seen are blue wildebeest, eland (large numbers of which occasionally migrate across the park), kudu, red hartebeest, ostrich, bat-eared fox, silver fox and porcupine. Some 170 bird species have been recorded in the park. In addition to the ostriches, you are likely to see kori bustards, secretary birds, martial eagles, bateleur eagles, and various owls.

The most prominent trees in the park are the distinctive, umbrella-shaped camelthorns (*Acacia erioloba*) – often supporting the huge nests of social weaverbirds. The camelthorns provide a small amount of welcome shade, and their seed-pods are a valuable source of food for many species.

Adapt or die
The animals that live in the park have all had to adapt in one way

Sparse vegetation clings to the side of a sand dune.

Springbok drink at one of the few waterholes in the park.

Ostriches seem to float across the harsh horizon of the Kalahari.

or another to an almost waterless world. There are roughly 250 lion in the park, which are able to live for years without water, drawing moisture from the animals they kill. Gemsbok and other desert antelope can survive without water as long as tsamma melons and wild cucumbers are available. There are no elephant, giraffe or zebra in the park; they have not been able to adapt to the extremely dry conditions.

A lot of game can be spotted as you travel between the three rest camps in the park. (Allow for one or two nights at each camp, if possible.) All the camps have fully equipped cottages and pleasant, albeit sandy, campsites. You can buy basic and non-perishable provisions at all three camps, including firewood and liquor, but no fresh produce or camera film is available. The camps have filling stations for petrol and diesel, but no repair facilities.

The largest of the three camps is *Twee Rivieren* (two rivers), situated at the southern entrance gate, where the Auob and the Nossob meet. Twee Rivieren is also the administrative headquarters of the park. This is the only camp that stocks frozen meat, and it also provides simple meals in a 'lapa'. The smallest of the camps is *Mata Mata* (the very pleasant place), which lies on the Auob River at the entrance to the park on the Namibian border.

Guidelines for visitors

In the north-eastern area of the park is the Nossob camp. There is an interesting information centre here (temporarily closed pending upgrading), and this is regarded as the best camp to head for if you want to see lion.

The park is open throughout the year. Summer heat is at its extreme during the months of December, January and February. The days in winter may also be hot, but winter nights can be very cold, with the temperature often falling to below freezing point surprisingly soon after sunset.

There are several access roads leading to the park, all involving fairly long drives on sandy, untarred surfaces. One route leads from Kuruman, another from Upington, and several roads in Namibia converge on the entrance at Mata Mata.

Visitors should start a course of anti-malaria tablets before departure. When driving to and through the park, always carry a plentiful supply of water.

For further information, and for applications for accommodation or for camping sites, write to: The National Parks Board, PO Box 787, Pretoria 0001; tel (012) 343 9770, fax (012) 343 0153; or to The National Parks Board, 44 Long Street, Cape Town 8001; tel (021) 22 2810, fax (021) 24 6211.

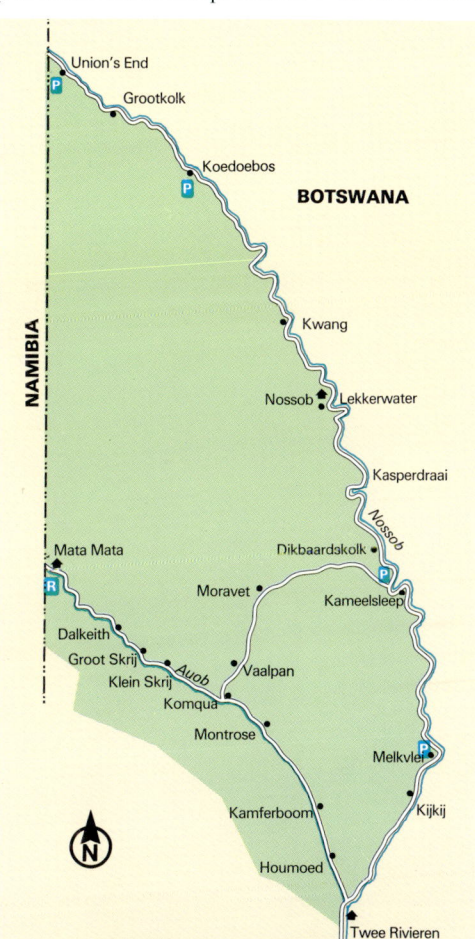

Kalahari Gemsbok National Park

A blue wildebeest strides through the dry landscape.

KIMBERLEY PLACES OF INTEREST

Iron lace fronts the De Beers head office in Stockdale Street, one of the many evocative buildings in the city.

Take a tram ride in the world's diamond capital

WITHOUT THE enthusiastic digging of a cook, whose name is remembered only as Damon, Kimberley might never have existed. It was Damon who first brought to light in July 1871 the riches that lay under a hill known as Colesberg Koppie: three precious diamonds, the tip of an iceberg of glittering stones that within a few years were to be dug out of the biggest man-made hole in the world.

Today the Big Hole, as the mine is known, with the restored diamond village nearby, forms the *Kimberley Mine Museum* **(1)**.

The best way to travel to the museum is by electric tram from the imposing *City Hall* **(2)**. Kimberley – known at first as New Rush and later named after a British Colonial Secretary – was the first town in South Africa to have electric trams. The vehicle now in use dates from about 1910.

The museum is dominated by the great mine headgear, erected in 1892 and used until the mine closed in 1914. Nearby is *Olive*, an old locomotive once used to transport diamondiferous concentrates to the recovery plant, and a reconstruction of a diggings, where visitors can try their luck, and even find a diamond.

Highlight of the museum is the Big Hole itself – and at the entrance to the viewing platform are three fully laden cocopans representing the volume of diamonds (some 14,5 million carats) recovered from the mine. The Big Hole occupies 15,4 ha and has a mean diameter of 457 m. It was worked as an open-cast mine to a depth of 366 m, after which shafts and tunnels carried the depth to 1 096 m. Water now fills the Big Hole to within some 175 m of the surface.

The De Beers Mining Company, which eventually acquired control of the mine, took its name from the De Beer brothers, owners of the farm Vooruitzicht on which the diamond 'pipes' were discovered. (Modern processes may be seen on a tour of the Bultfontein Diamond Mine in Molyneux Road – the only underground diamond tour anywhere in the world.)

The old town

Not far from the Big Hole is a reconstruction of *a Kimberley Street* during the diamond boom. Fronting the street, with its ornate cast-iron lamp standards, are the *St Martini Lutheran Church* of 1875, still with its original fittings and pews, and Kimberley's oldest post-diamond discovery house – a prefabricated structure consisting of little more than a front parlour and bedroom.

A *diamond buyer's office* is furnished with a desk that once belonged to Sir Alfred Beit, one of the founding directors of De Beers. Among the framed shares and photographs on the wall is a diagram of a section through the Kimberley Mine as it was during the height of digging in 1890.

Of particular interest is the *Digger's Rest*, one of the many pubs that opened for business in the early days of the brawling mining camp. Next door is the original *Boxing Academy* run by Barney Barnato, who started his career on the diamond fields selling cigars and went on to become one of the world's richest men.

The nearby *ballroom*, a large, iron building with impressive, pressed metal ceilings, erected in 1901, contains a display of ladies' evening gowns of the period.

At the head of the street is *Transport Hall*, containing a steam-powered locomotive that pulled an earlier version of the present Kimberley tram, and a home-made tricycle, powered by pedal and sail, on which a determined digger made his way from Plettenberg Bay to the diamond fields in about 1880.

Among the motor vehicles on display is Kimberley's first car, a Panhard et Levassor of 1901, purchased for the General Manager of De Beers, and a 1906 Columbia Electric Victoria, which could run for only 13 km before its three 12-volt batteries needed recharging. A 1926 Chevrolet, converted for use as a hearse by the Jewish community, travelled only 2 900 km. Across the street is a very different form of conveyance: a specially built Pullman railway carriage imported for the De Beers directors. This luxurious carriage was equipped with a bathroom (rare on carriages of the time) and a wine store.

Reconstructed shops, including a *pawnbroker's*, which provided an essential service in the uncertain early years of the diggings, form an arcade around an ornate cast-iron bandstand, with a restaurant nearby, close to a reconstruction of the original De Beer homestead. On display in the Diamond Hall is a fabulous collection of diamonds, including the '616' – the largest octahedron ever found – and the 'Eureka', the first recorded diamond found in South Africa.

The Mine Museum is by no means the only attraction in the Diamond City. In Atlas Street the *McGregor Museum* **(3)**, housed in a magnificent late-Victorian building used by Rhodes as his headquarters during the siege, records the development of Kimberley and its numerous volunteer regiments. Rhodes's rooms have been restored to record his occupancy during the siege, with lifelike figures creating his historic meeting with the leader of the relieving force, General French. The Hall of Religions illustrates Kimberley's multicultural origins. The museum also houses displays on the history of Griqualand West,

Religion and commerce mix at the Mine Museum adjacent to the Big Hole.

Inside the Digger's Rest.

Kimberley's famous Big Hole.

Kimberley 'firsts' and the environment of the Northern Cape.

There is a tea garden at the museum, close to the *Duggan-Cronin Ethnographic Gallery* in The Lodge, erected in 1889, which records in photographs and artefacts the cultures of the indigenous people of southern Africa.

In Chapel Street the *Alexander McGregor Memorial Museum* **(4)** details southern Africa's costumes, natural history, geology and prehistory; while in Jan Smuts Boulevard, the *William Humphreys Art Gallery* **(5)** with its statue of Queen Victoria outside, is the only A-graded art gallery in South Africa and houses the city's art collection. Close by is the *Ernest Oppenheimer Memorial Garden*, with a fountain honouring the early diggers. In Loch Road *The Bungalow* **(6)**, which once belonged to a son of CD Rudd, Rhodes's great friend and business partner, is a good example of a mining magnate's home of the late 19th century. Another elegant residence is *Dunluce* **(7)**, in Lodge Road, built for a diamond buyer in 1897 and still containing some of its original furnishings – including a coal scuttle damaged when a Boer shell penetrated the breakfast room during the siege. Arrangements to visit The Bungalow and Dunluce should be made at the McGregor Museum in Atlas Street.

The *Honoured Dead Memorial* **(8)**, designed by Sir Herbert Baker with inspiration from a temple at Xanthos and a Greek tomb at Agrigentum in Sicily, commemorates those who died during the siege. The memorial includes *Long Cecil*, built in the De Beers' workshops in 24 days during the siege by men who had no previous experience of ordnance construction. The 4,1 inch (104 mm) rifled breech-loader was able to fling its 12,7 kg shells 7,3 km. The Boers responded by bringing up one of their Long Tom guns (see pages 46 – 7) and, ironically, the designer of Long Cecil, American engineer George Labram, was killed by a Long Tom shell.

Near the Honoured Dead Memorial, between Memorial Road and Oliver Street, is the MOTH *Garden of Remembrance* **(9)**, a tranquil garden that houses a Stuart (or 'Honey') light tank of World War II vintage, a six-inch howitzer of 1917 and an Impala jet training aircraft.

City of churches

Among Kimberley's churches is a *modest iron structure* **(10)** at the corner of Dyer and Blacking streets in Beaconsfield. This mother church of the Seventh Day Adventists in South Africa was founded in 1885 when a local farmer, Pieter Wessels, left the Dutch Reformed Church after a conflict over which day of the week should be 'kept holy'. *St Cyprian's Anglican Cathedral* **(11)** in Du Toitspan Road contains many interesting memorials, as well as flags – or colours – of diamond fields' regiments. The statue in the grounds, of *Sister Henrietta Stockdale*, is believed to be the world's only portrait statue of a nun in her habit. Sister Henrietta established professional nursing in South Africa at Kimberley's hospital just across the road.

In the town that he described as his 'foster-mother', Cecil Rhodes is honoured by a large *equestrian statue* at the corner of Du Toitspan Road and Regiment Way **(12)**. Opposite this, at the corner formed with Lennox Street, is a *memorial* **(13)** to Kimberley men of the *Cape Corps*: a German field gun captured from Turkish troops by the 1st battalion of the corps at the battle of Square Hill, fought in arid countryside close to Jerusalem in September 1918.

Kimberley's mother congregation of the *Dutch Reformed Church* is in Long Street **(14)**. The church building, dating from 1885, includes a memorial to those who died in the nearby concentration camp during the Anglo-Boer War.

The *old cemeteries*, including Pioneers' Cemetery in Cemetery Road, West End Cemetery in Green Street and Gladstone Cemetery in Kenilworth, contain the remains of early diggers and townsfolk and of many Anglo-Boer War casualties reinterred from nearby battlefields. (The important *Magersfontein battlefield* is only some 40 km from the city.)

Apart from buildings and memorials open to the public, Kimberley contains many old buildings – modest and magnificent – tucked away in quiet streets. In Stockdale Street is the headquarters of the De Beers Consolidated Mines Limited. Tree-shaded *Armagh House* in Memorial Road, with its cast-iron and fretted verandahs, was built and named by an Ulsterman, RH Henderson, who, on the outbreak of the Anglo-Boer War, was Mayor of Kimberley.

Dunluce - hit by a Boer shell during the siege of Kimberley in 1899.

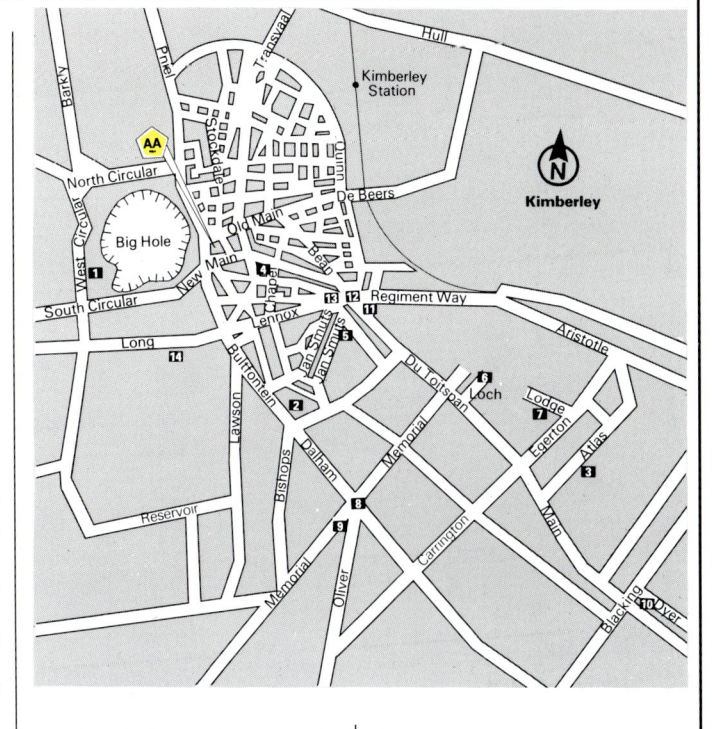

Tourist Information Office
City Hall, Market Square
Kimberley 8301
Tel (0531) 82 7298
AA Office 13 New Main Street
Kimberley 8301
Tel (0531) 25207

• EXPLORING SOME URBAN ORIGINS •

A dwelling and tree (kokerboom or Aloe dichotoma) *typical of Namaqualand.*

Dorp and byway – interwoven fabrics of the veld

A DORP IS NOT MERELY a small South African town. You may have your own definition, but, to many people a dorp is a country town where time – if it hasn't actually stood still – has at least been kind. The dorp retains, in brick and thatch and corrugated iron, as much as in local custom, the spirit of its origins.

How many towns do you see first as a church steeple, sometimes huge and grand out of all proportion to the settlement around it. *Aberdeen* in the Eastern Cape claimed for many years that its Dutch Reformed church had the tallest steeple in the country, at a little over 50 m. Certainly, you see it long before you reach the town, although you'd need special instruments to be able to tell that it's a few degrees off the vertical. Not far away is the massive and lavishly decorated *Groot Kerk* (big church) of *Graaff-Reinet*, well placed as the focus of the long approach on Church Street. There are no lavish decorations in *Kamieskroon*, but the steeple proclaims the town there all the same.

There were two opinions about church steeples; one said that they were raised to the glory of God, while cynics claimed that they merely advertised the prosperity of the congregation. In fairness, they were also useful landmarks when travellers had few roads or signs to point their way.

Squares and homes
The open space around the church – if it hasn't been built on – is or was known as *Kerkplein* (Church Square). This was an area of the town commonage allotted to the Dutch Reformed Church authorities for use as a camping ground on the three or four occasions every year when *Nagmaal* or Holy Communion was celebrated. Farmers streamed into town in their wagons and carts, the wealthier ones staying in their own little *tuishuisies* (see page 240). Most of them, though, outspanned their wagons on Church Square and simply camped right there. *Grahamstown* is interesting for having a Church Square around its Anglican church (now cathedral) rather than, as in almost all other cases, around the Dutch Reformed church. *Beaufort West* too, has a curious distinction – instead of a church serving as the visual focus of its long main street, it has the town jail.

Another common placename is Market Square, where most farmers, hunters and travelling merchants did their trading, the chief exception being the Jewish hawker or *smous*, who conveyed his goods, often on his back, right to his customer's door. (There's a little monument to the smous in Graaff-Reinet's College Road, an extension of Church Street.)

In later years, hotel proprietors provided a 'sample room' in which manufacturers' representatives displayed their wares for inspection by the local merchants. Some hotels still have their sample rooms, but the number is dwindling because of the changing patterns of trading. Now, even in small towns you're likely to find branches of 'city' shops, and the selection of stock is decided at corporate headquarters. Country hotels themselves were individual places, too, and not simply images of others in the same group.

But no dorp will reveal its nature to the motorist who merely

A tall steeple beckons in Campbell, on the wide plains of Griqualand West.

passes along its main street or sees its modest cluster of buildings from a bypass road.

The sidestreets are where most of the townspeople (*dorpsmense*) live. Preservation of vernacular architecture was not always considered a good idea and, with the first flush of prosperity, facades and roof lines were often 'improved' to match the prevailing fashions, and, of course, to emphasize the new-found wealth. Thus, flat roofs acquired a pitch; front facades lost their plain or moulded pediment and received a gable which, however well intended, was usually of poor proportions. Small windows with small panes were discarded in favour of larger ones. If the source of prosperity lasted long enough, 'improvements' would also be seen in the local church buildings, in the school and in the public offices. New corrugated-iron verandahs and ornate cast-iron poles marred the facades of classically proportioned Cape Dutch-style dwellings. In many cases, however, there remains enough of the original style or structure to enable the building to be pictured as it was originally erected.

Rarely, whole groups of original structures have survived, as at *Klaarstroom* at the northern end of scenic Meiringspoort, near Oudtshoorn. The use of local material in the days of irregular transport, combined with economic status and weather conditions, led to the evolution of the style. Similar origins with a different result may be seen in the oldest houses at *Genadendal*. Perhaps the most distinctive of local styles was that which produced the all-stone corbelled houses of the Northern Cape, that you can see from the road (R63) between *Williston* and *Carnarvon* in the Kareeberg Karoo. In Carnarvon you can examine one closely as part of the town's museum. But it is fairly certain that none of these three styles – Klaarstroom, Genadendal and Kareeberg – will ever be built again as 'ordinary' dwellings.

Unpretentious and unambiguous – conveying the message in Bushmanland.

Shopping, before supermarkets – and after – at Baievlei in Namaqualand.

Shelter from the heat at Goodhouse.

Pointing the way
The earliest signposts along the way were the natural ones, such as *de kromme boom* (the bent or twisted tree), still the name of a road in busy suburban *Cape Town*. More than one distinctive summit was known as *Towerkop* – enchanted peak. *Ladismith's* magic mountain has a massively cleft summit, while *Colesberg's* peak seems to recede across the shimmering Karoo plain, never drawing any nearer.

The first officially placed signposts served as proprietary notices rather than as route indicators. Typical examples come from the Garden Route – the Van de Graaff beacon at *George* and Van Plettenberg's beacon at *Bahia Formosa* (the beautiful bay), which the governor renamed after himself. Both beacons, carved in stone in the 18th century, claimed the land for the Dutch East India Company.

Milestones were just that – stones placed at intervals of one mile (about 1,6 km) from a well-known central point in a town. Cape Town probably led the way with its series of carved slate stones erected along the Main Road to *Simon's Town*. They were erected shortly before British settlers of 1820 raised a large boulder on the banks of the Kowie River to mark their safe crossing place. A few old military milestones are to be seen on the road between Grahamstown and Fort Beaufort. Until 1855 the responsibility for placing these lay with the Board of Ordnance which, in that year, changed its name to War Department, so the carved letters 'BO' or 'WD' can be used as a rough chronological guide.

Going places
The country's first roads followed game tracks, and some roads have stuck to their courses for a surprisingly long time. Cape Town's Main Road, which runs most of the length of the Cape Peninsula, still divides at *Rondebosch* as it did more than 300 years ago when loggers turned aside there to enter the forest at *Nieuweland* (new land). On crossing the Hottentots Holland Mountains over Sir Lowry's Pass, though, it's no longer possible to see 'the path of the eland' which dictated the original route and gave it its old name of *Gantouw*.

Roads that have undergone the most dramatic changes are probably the mountain passes, and not because their original routes were badly chosen. Mechanical excavators simply 'eat' their way directly through a mountain slope that, in the old days, would have demanded a laboriously contoured roadway ascending in a series of loops or zigzags. Excellent examples of old roads include the mid-19th century Montagu Pass, near George, and the incomparably scenic Swartberg Pass of the 1880s, between *Oudtshoorn* and *Prince Albert*.

The word 'Road' in a placename usually indicated a railway station. *Prince Albert Road* in the Karoo was originally no more than the rail halt for the town of Prince Albert, some 45 km to the south-east. Most of the old 'Roads', however, have acquired newer names, such as *Wolseley* (Ceres Road), *Bellville* (Durban Road when it was the halt for *Durbanville*), and the busy Karoo junction of *Rosmead* (Middelburg Road).

Road and rail spun interlinked webs of progress across the land, making possible not merely travel but trade. Roads became an index of prosperity on which the seal was set by the arrival of the first train at a makeshift platform decorated with flags and bunting. But there is always the exception.

Gamkaskloof, deep in the Swartberg, was an isolated community in which life changed little in a hundred years. The only way in or out was by donkey-track. Then, in the early 1960s came the road, a steep, rocky and narrow road, not for the faint-hearted motorist. In almost four decades it has seen little traffic, but it has carried the people of Gamkaskloof out of their valley, never to return. Gamkaskloof, which in civic status was barely even a dorp, is a place of empty houses and of fruit trees grown wild in a lost, lonely valley. It is a rare and possibly unique example of a settlement that died, not for lack of a road, but because – with the best of intentions – a road was provided.

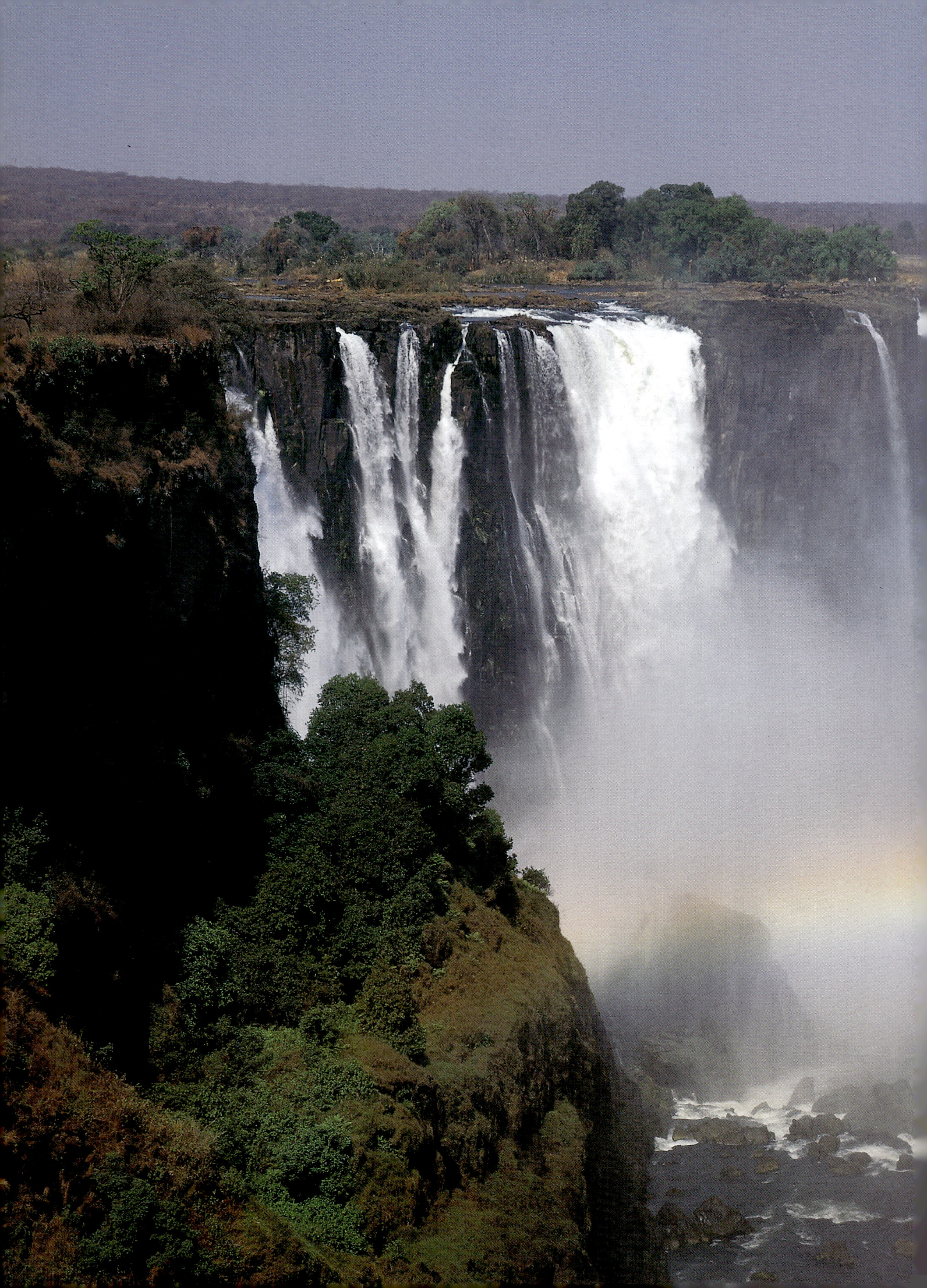

ZIMBABWE

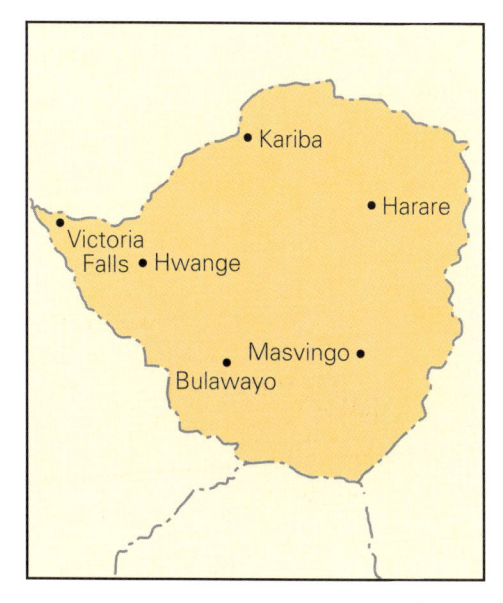

Harare: Exploring the national capital **306-7**

Harare – Darwendale – Lake Manyame – Lake Chivero – Lion Park **308-9**

Harare – Ewanrigg Botanical Garden – Hippo Pools – Mazowe Valley **310-1**

Mutare – Burma Valley – Bunga Botanical Reserve – Leopard Rock **312-3**

Mutare – Juliasdale – Nyanga – Troutbeck – Pungwe – Mutarazi Falls **314-5**

Nyanga National Park: Enchantment of the Eastern Highlands **316-7**

Mutare – Hot Springs – Cashel – Chimanimani – Bridal Veil Falls **318-9**

Masvingo – Great Zimbabwe – Mutirikwi Game Reserve **320-1**

Great Zimbabwe: Silent stones tell a story **322-3**

Bulawayo – Cyrene Mission – Matobos National Park **324-5**

Bulawayo: Where a king made his home **326-7**

Victoria Falls – Sinamatella – Hwange National Park **328-9**

Lake Kariba: Ferry ride on a great man-made lake **330-1**

Kariba Village – Dam Wall – Kaburi – Makuti – Chirundu – Otto Beit Bridge **332-3**

Left: *Victoria Falls – the awesome spectacle of the 'smoke that thunders'.*

• PLACES OF INTEREST IN HARARE •

Typical of the arresting work on show in Harare sculpture gardens and art galleries is Boira Mteki's 'Mother and twins', carved in white dolomite in 1994.

An African heartland in Zimbabwe's capital city

MAUVE JACARANDA TREES, white bauhinias and flowering yellow cassias create shaded arches along Harare's avenues. Leaves and flowers filter the overhead sunlight in this city 1 500 m above the faraway sea, mellowing the bright reflections from pagoda-pointed, steel-and-glass high-rises. The reflections are never brighter, the sun never hotter, than in October, when everyone waits anxiously for the annual rains. Chief *Neharawa* – the one who does not sleep – would recognize only the weather and a few of the trees.

Named now after this 19th-century leader of the Shona people and occupied in 1890 by paramilitary 'pioneering adventurers' financed by Cecil John Rhodes, an area of marshy vlei became a tent town called Salisbury.

Harare has a population of 1,5 million and provides much of the industrial support for a national economy based on agriculture (principally tobacco), mining and tourism. Strolling down First Street, it is difficult to believe you are in Africa, so chic and Western are the boutiques, hotels and flower-banked streets of this neat, grid-pattern city, proud of its parliament, museum, national art gallery and delightful public gardens. Harare's public transport system is relatively undeveloped, but otherwise the city has most of the amenities of metropolitan sophistication.

Markets and memorials

Off the usual visitor-route, but only 10 minutes from Harare Post Office, is *Mbare Musika* **(1)**, the country's largest and noisiest craft and vegetable market. It's also Zimbabwe's busiest bus terminus. Here, Harare bursts into colourful life in a wash of pavement hawkers, piled tomatoes, African masks, soapstone carvings, medicine-man muti, jitjive music and packed country buses. As in crowded places the world over, beware of pickpockets.

Harare is home to the world's largest tobacco auction floors. At the *Tobacco Sales Floor* **(2)**, which is larger than the average sports stadium, each auctioneer sells a 100 kg bale in under 10 seconds. The daily total is close to 17 000 bales during the April – October sales, representing 170 million kg in a year. Buyers follow the singsong auctioneer as he moves up the 40-bale sales lines calling the prices, taking the bids, usually indicated by a nod, a wink or a

The flower market brightens a shady corner of Africa Unity Square.

ZIMBABWE

One of the city's open-air markets.

hardly discernible hand movement. Ten per cent of Zimbabwe's population is dependent on the revenue from tobacco – more than Z$2 billion annually. Zimbabwe is the world's largest tobacco exporter; China is the largest producer. Visitors may tour the floors and enjoy free tea and coffee.

Heroes' Acre **(3)**, 7 km along the Bulawayo road, is completely different. You need a permit from the Public Relations Office of the *Ministry of Information* **(4)** (in Linquenda House, Baker Avenue) to visit this memorial to the *Chimurenga* or war of resistance that brought independence in 1980. Dedicated to the 25 000 people who lost their lives in the 15-year struggle, the 57 ha site is dominated by a 40 m needle-shaped tower topped by an eternal flame, overlooking a bronze statue of three guerrilla fighters – two men and a woman – at the tomb of the Unknown Soldier.

Art and culture

Chapungu, the Shona word for the bateleur eagle, is the name of a large *open-air sculpture garden* **(5)** 8 km west of the city along the Mutare road. Here you can see some of the country's internationally acclaimed sculptors at work on granite, verdite, jasper and

The Anglican cathedral overlooks part of African Unity Square.

Colonial styles have given way to high-rise blocks in the city centre.

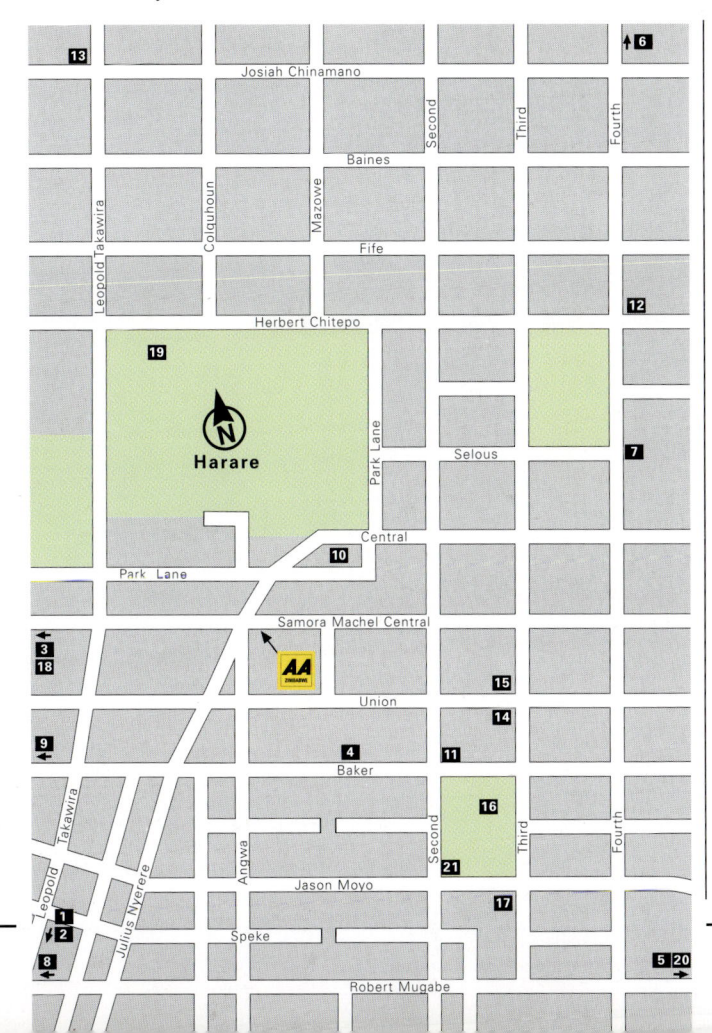

serpentine, creating huge 3 m high works reflecting the soul of Shona cosmology. The resident *Boterekwa* traditional dance group performs here and the music floats across the lawns, shady trees, lake and thatched restaurant of Chapungu, which is open every day.

Extending the ancient tradition of Great Zimbabwe, the country is known for its stone sculpture. There are galleries in several parts of town and the best works are highly priced.

A peaceful hideaway is the *National Archives* **(6)** in a setting of euphorbia and msasa trees on the Borrowdale road 2 km from town. Among its 40 000 books is a collection of Thomas Baines paintings, on display with stamps, maps, uniforms, diaries and the delicate watercolours of Victorian traveller Alice Balfour. The archives are open daily from Monday to Saturday.

Minerals, fossils and rocks can be seen in the little-known *MacGregor Geological Museum* **(7)** (open on weekdays) in Maufe Building, at the corner of Selous Avenue and 4th Street.

Steel, stone and shutters

Relics of the Victorian Salisbury of red, tin-roofed bungalows and frilly cast iron are being steadily replaced by the high-rise Harare of large expanses of glass set in steel and concrete. The *Market Hall of 1894* **(8)** is perhaps the oldest building, situated off Robert Mugabe Road in the old Kopje area of town, where a number of elegant, wood-framed shop fronts still survive. Near the centre are the *Guild Hall* **(9)** in Baker Street and, in Central Avenue near the National Gallery, *Cecil House* **(10)** (built in 1901 and recently restored). The appeal of old-style architecture is depicted in a new office block adjoining Cecil House, where the Victorian idiom, including wooden shutters, is repeated.

The *Anglican Cathedral of St Mary and All Saints* **(11)** is built in massive stone and has what may be the largest all-copper roof in the world. There is also a *Roman Catholic cathedral* **(12)** and a *Greek Orthodox cathedral* **(13)**. Next door to the Anglican cathedral is the *Parliament Building* **(14)**, originally designed as a hotel but admirably suited to the solemn business of government. On the same side of the street is the *Lonhro Building* **(15)** of 1910, and all face the gardens of *Africa Unity Square* **(16)**. Old golden lions still guard (a much-modernized) *Meikle's Hotel* **(17)**, whose fleet of courtesy cars consists of dignified old London taxis, their black paint gleaming.

Sport and recreation

Harare has some 70 restaurants, 14 golf clubs, and hotels ranging from five-star luxury to a satellite of safari lodges within a radius of 100 km. The *National Sports Stadium* **(18)** is on the outskirts of the city and provides facilities for many sports. The many public swimming pools include an Olympic-size pool adjoining *Harare Gardens* **(19)**.

You can safari in Harare at *Mukuvisi Woodlands* **(20)**, only 4 km from town and the headquarters of the Wildlife Society. Elephant, eland, zebra, giraffe, impala and crocodile can be seen from walking trails in this 270 ha game park. Additional information may be obtained from the *Harare Publicity Bureau* **(21)**, Africa Unity Square, cr Second Street and Jason Moyo Avenue, Harare; tel (14) 70 5085.

Lakes, snakes and curio crafts – Harare and round about

Cattle farms flank the Great North Road to Kariba, branching off past the bass-fishing Manyame Dam and then Chivero's lovely lakeside game park. Start early, because the delightful Larvon Bird Garden, the Lion and Cheetah Park and tempting wayside craft stalls will fill the day. About 40 km of the route is on untarred roads.

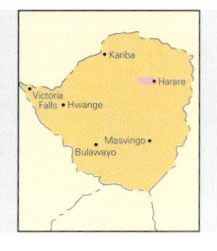

Harare
Darwendale
Manyame
Lake Chivero
Larvon Bird Gardens
190 – 200 km

DRIVE NORTH FROM Harare's Africa Unity Square along Second Street for 5,5 km. At the ninth and last set of traffic lights, turn left into Lomagundi Road (also called Kariba Road), passing, 8 km further on, the new Westgate Shopping Mall and reaching open farmlands. At Stableford Store, some 9 km further, turn left over the railway line to Fambidzanai Training Centre along narrow tar, keeping your left-side wheels on gravel and the right on tar when traffic approaches. After 1 km, turn right into Fambidzanai, sited among msasa trees, where colourful screen prints may be bought. Retrace your route to the main road and turn left. Some 24 km from Fambidzanai (or 46 km from Harare's Africa Unity Square), turn left onto Darwendale Dam Road, also (and more correctly) known as Manyame Dam Road.

Manyame to Lake Chivero

About 3 km to your right, a low range of hills forms part of the Great Dyke, a 500 km treasure trove of minerals stretching across Zimbabwe. The road, which usually carries only a small volume of traffic, crosses the Gwebi River, with its steel girder bridge, at the 18 km peg (black and white roadside markers placed every 500 m along the country's main roads). About 3 km after the river, you pass the village of Darwendale and, after a further 2,5 km, turn left onto a gravel road for the dam. After 13 km on gravel, you reach the entrance to the Manyame Dam Recreation Park on your left (small entrance fee). Although there is no restaurant, there are bushveld camping facilities, thatched picnic rondavels and opportunities for excellent bass fishing. The interconnected manmade lakes of Manyame (Darwendale) and Chivero provide Harare with its water supply and much of its weekend watersport.

Retrace your route out of Manyame Dam Recreation Park and turn left. Turn left at the Norton - Kutama T-junction; 23 km later, turn left again, after passing woodlands, ostrich farms and the quaint Final Inn Motel. The blue-green hills ahead are the Hunyani range. Turn right at the Norton T-junction to reach the main Gwaai - Harare highway 500 m later.

Turn left at the T-junction, towards Harare, passing irrigated wheat fields for some 8 km to reach the Lake Chivero Recreation Park sign and 32,5 km peg, just before the bridge. Turn right to the park (formerly Robert McIllwaine Recreational Park). Go right at the fork, where the left-hand road leads to the spillway and restaurant, cross a railway line and reach the park entrance after 2,5 km. The park is open from 06h00 to 18h00, although you may be admitted later if you have reserved a chalet. Look out for giraffe, impala, rhino, wildebeest and zebra, especially near water, and watch out for the humps that help enforce the speed limit of 40 km/h.

Chivero is 11 km long and up to 8 km wide. The birdlife among the mainly msasa and *munhondo* (Brachestegia) woodland includes Angolan rock thrush, boulder chat, Mashona hyliota and, at the water's edge, cormorants, ducks, herons and geese. Some 320 species of birds have been recorded. There are 70 km of well-maintained, winding gravel roads with names such as Tsessebe Drive, Eland Loop and Bateleur Drive. The National Parks chalets are 10 km from the entrance.

Lake Chivero to Harare

Retrace your route to the Park turn-off (at the 2,5 km peg), turn right for Harare and, 3 km later, turn right at the petrol station onto the Lake Chivero Road, which leads to the gap in the Hunyani hills. After a further 1,5 km turn right at the T-junction for the Hunyani Hills Hotel, which you reach 1 km later. The thatched hotel is in a setting of trees, flowers, children's playground, outdoor chessboard and wide lakeside views. Here too is the National Parks caravan site (no camping), the Lakeside Tea Gardens and the headquarters of the Mazowe Sailing Club.

Retrace your route to the last junction, turn left and, 500 m later, turn right, passing an avenue of hilltop houses for 1 km and then an expanse of woodland, to reach the Lion and Cheetah Park after a further 4,5 km.

After visiting the park, turn right and, after a further 600 m, turn right again, onto the main Harare Road. After 7 km on this road, either turn right for the Larvon Bird Gardens (open daily) or continue for another 1 km to the Snake Park – also on the right and with potteries situated nearby.

Leaving Larvon, return to the main road and turn right again, to reach the city centre after 18 km, passing, on your way, the high eternal flame of Heroes' Acre on your right and the National Stadium on the left. The road becomes Samora Machel Avenue and flanks the Harare Sheraton Hotel. Turn right at Second Street to reach your starting point – Africa Unity Square – after 500 m.

AA Office Fanum House, Samora Machel Avenue, Harare Tel (14) 75 2779
Publicity Bureau Africa Unity Square, cr Second Street and Jason Moyo Avenue, Harare Tel (14) 70 5085
National Parks (Reservations) Botanical Gardens, Sandringham Drive, off Borrowdale Road, Harare Tel (14) 70 6077

A picnic chalet provides wide views and welcome shade near the edge of Lake Manyame.

ROBBIES, BREAM AND BASS

There are 138 species of fish – 122 of them indigenous – in Zimbabwe's rivers and dams, ranging from the fighting tigerfish of Kariba to chessa, nkupe, bream, carp, bottlenose and, in Manyame Dam, bass and the large-mouthed predator, the robbie. The annual robbie competition here attracts fishermen from all over the country. The robbie is caught on artificial lures, especially spinnerbait in bright Chartreuse or white. Look for changes in water depth around submerged anthills, and the steep drop-offs to old riverbeds, for the best sites. Manyame also offers bass of up to 2 kg – aggressive predators with very large mouths, that will go for absolutely anything they consider edible. Signs at Manyame (which has two concrete launching areas, good camping facilities and is only an hour's drive from Harare) exhort fishermen to release the bass they catch.

HEROES' ACRE

A massive bronze statue of guerrilla fighters and a soaring 40 m structure that carries the Eternal Flame dominate the 57 ha amphitheatre surrounding the Tomb of the Unknown Soldier at Heroes' Acre, 7 km west of Harare on the Lake Chivero road. Some 25 000 Zimbabweans died in the 14-year *Chimurenga* (liberation struggle) that led to the birth of Zimbabwe in 1980. The project cost Z$18 million and was partially designed by North Korean artists. State funerals held here are major occasions but, most days, the awesome structure lies sombre and quiet in the gentle winds, with sweeping views across indigenous msasa trees back to Harare. A courteous soldier will show you around if you have a permit from the Ministry of Information's Public Relations Office (in Linquenda House, 5th Floor, Baker Avenue, between First and Second streets).

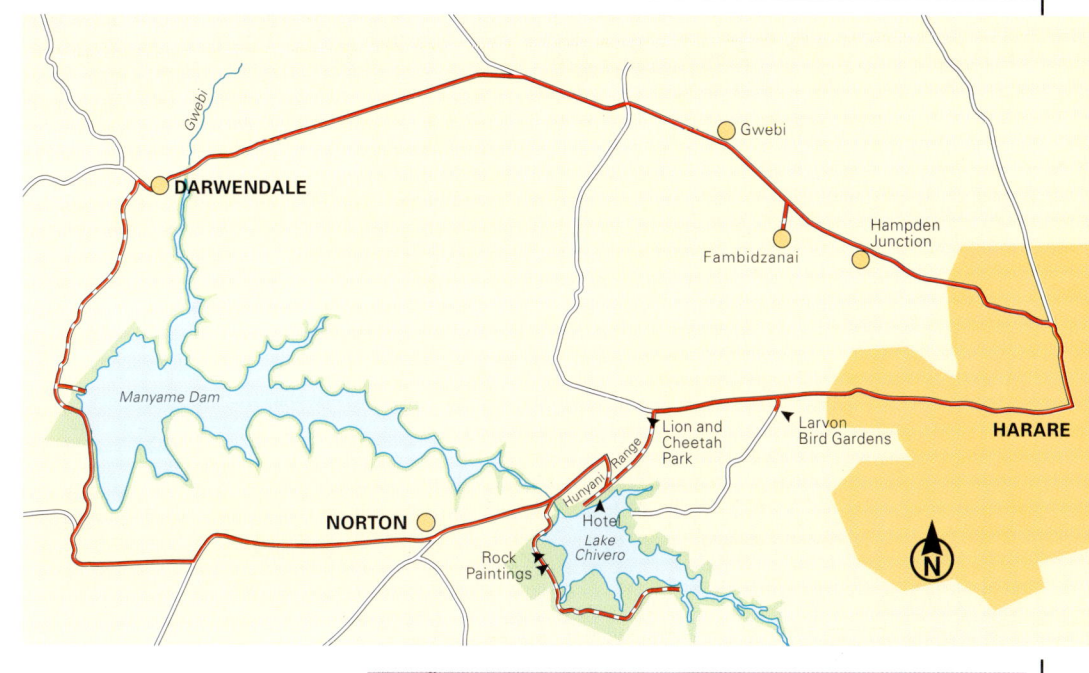

Erosion has produced this complex natural balancing act.

ALL THE BIRDS OF THE AIR

Only 18 km from Harare and set in open woodland around an ornamental lake, one of the highlights of Larvon Bird Gardens is a walk-through aviary which, with its tinkling streams, trees and grasses, suggests a tropical jungle alive with butterflies and tiny, darting birds.

Larvon's soaring aviaries have some 1 200 birds of 250 different species, including sacred ibis, hornbills, parrots, fish eagles, rare wattled cranes, five species of vulture, owls, white-faced ducks, swans and red-billed teals. Clearly labelled in roomy, individual nesting cages, Larvon's birds can be seen close up as you stroll along the shaded walks, making this is an ideal place to study Zimbabwe's bird-life before venturing into the wild. A huge thorn tree by the lake shades the garden's restaurant.

Giraffe – their leggy ancestors once roamed from Greece to China.

Like many predators, lions usually hunt at nightfall and drowse by day.

THE STATELY CAMEL-LEOPARD

Standing 5 m high when fully grown, the giraffe is the tallest animal in the world and can trace its ancestry back 22 million years. They are regularly seen in Lake Chivero Recreational Park, their spots resembling those of a leopard and their deceptively fast pace that of a camel. The Arabic term *xirapha* (one who walks swiftly) is the root of the scientific name *Giraffa camelopardalis*. The female gives birth, after a gestation period of 15 months, in a standing position, the 100 kg baby dropping harmlessly some 2 m to the ground. The long legs are a giraffe's main defence, and a single kick from an adult has been known to kill even a lion.

Gold mines – and the glistening green of citrus trees

There are five game parks on this route north of Harare, starting from Ewanrigg Botanical Garden. We proceed via a wildlife orphanage to Hippo Pools on the Mazowe River, returning via Shamva Gold Mine and Bindura. Check with the Harare Publicity Association whether you need to book for the private game parks in the Mazowe Valley.

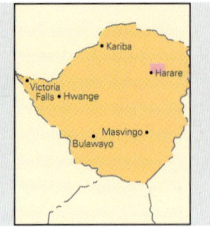

Harare
Ewanrigg
Botanical Garden
Hippo Pools
Mazowe Valley
Bindura
310 – 330 km

DRIVE NORTH ALONG Second Street from the Publicity Bureau on Africa Unity Square, turn right into Samora Machel Avenue and, about 1 km later, turn left at the Enterprise Road crossroads, noting your kms. After 20 km, bear left at the Shamva and Mutoko fork and, after a further 15,5 km, turn right onto gravel at the Ewanrigg Botanical Garden sign, to reach the entrance to the garden 3 km later.

Retrace your route to the main road and turn right. Some 6 km later, turn left onto gravel at the Mermaid's Pool sign near a solitary petrol station. You reach the pool after 2 km on gravel. The long rock slide into Mermaid's Pool was a favourite venue for Harare picnics 50 years ago and is still a delight for children. Retrace your route to the main road and turn left to reach the Bally Vaughan Bird and Animal Orphanage after 1,5 km. Here, in open, wooded paddocks overlooking hills and a dam, are hand-reared lions, crowned cranes and a host of wilderness orphans.

Animal orphanage to Shamva

Retrace your route to the main road and turn left, noting your kms. You pass the red-soil farms of the Umwindzi Valley flanked by 'goose-bump' hills and, 10 km later, begin passing through communal lands (beware of wandering livestock). The road then twists for 37 km through orange groves and a range of wooded pyramid-shaped hills to *Shamva* (friendliness) – originally called Abercorn. Pass Shamva Mine on a road that twists through hills, the tar narrowing then widening, every turn revealing stony hills topped with feathery trees and with small *musha* (homesteads) tucked below, until, at 32 km, you reach the turn-off for Mount Darwin. Ignore this left fork and continue on a bad gravel road for 700 m to Madziwa Mine village. Turn right through the small market and bus terminus, a distance of 300 m, and take the

BEADY-EYED BUFFALO
Zimbabwe has 50 000 buffalo, with herds thousands strong in Hwange, but there were once many more. They were systematically destroyed in several areas because, being carriers of foot-and-mouth disease, they posed a threat to man's cattle. Today, the largest herd of specially reared foot-and-mouth-free buffalo in central Zimbabwe, 42 animals out of a total of a few hundred, is that in Zindele Game Park north of Harare. Conservationists and ranchers now see buffalo as a more valuable asset than cattle and they are protected in game sanctuaries (formerly ranches) throughout the country. The 800 kg buffalo, with powerful head-boss and upturned scimitar horns, is the most dangerous of Africa's animals. Mud-grey, bad-tempered and wily, it will take on lion and will even sneak around behind you, unseen and unheard, to charge. A good climbing tree (and considerable agility as a climber) is then essential as buffalo cannot be 'turned' by a clap or rifle-shot like lion or elephant.

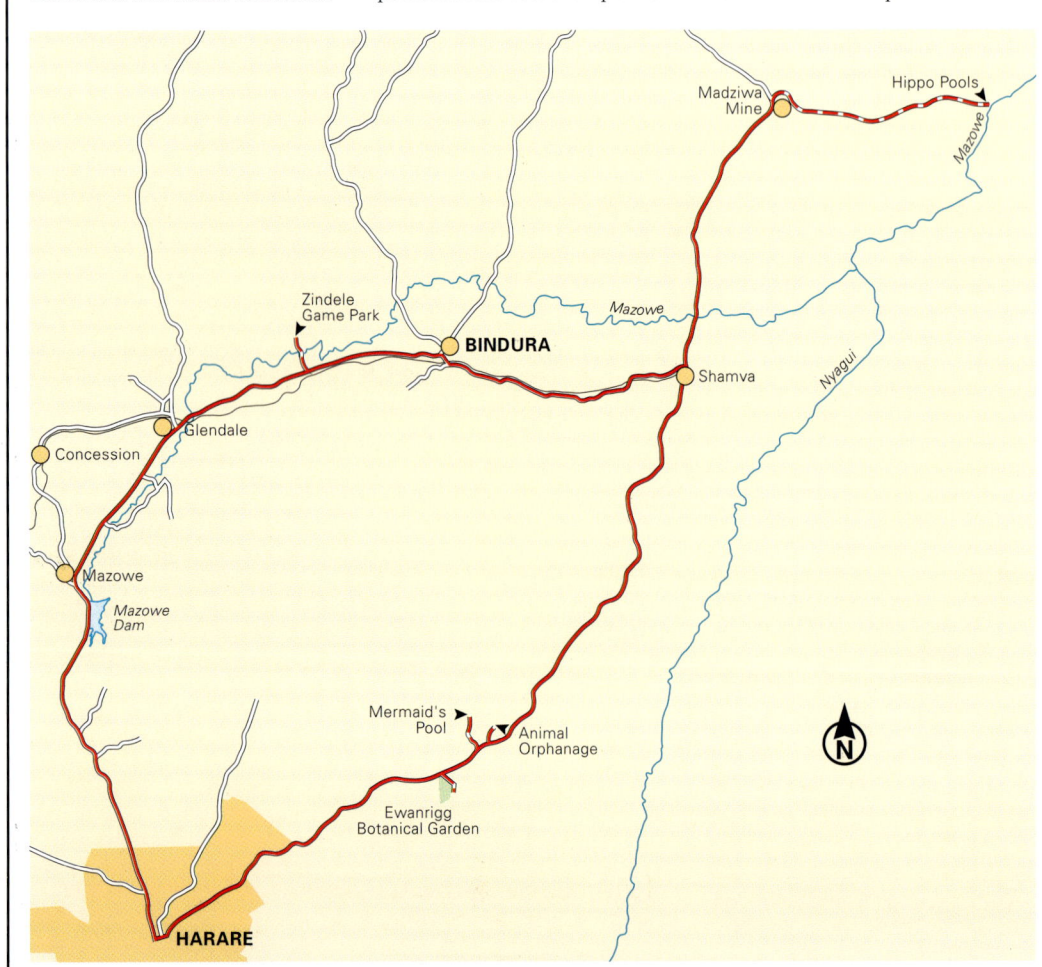

Hippo pools on the Mazowe River.

CROWNED CRANES OF MWANGA
Mahem is the loud, trumpeting call of the crowned crane, often uttered in flight, to be heard at the Mwanga Game Park and the adjoining Bally Vaughan Bird and Animal Orphanage. These big (3,5 kg), gorgeously coloured birds – mainly grey, white and black with red jowls and a gold-spiked helmet – prefer marshy areas, where they congregate in flocks of up to 150 as they search for frogs, insects and the occasional lizard. They breed from November to May, when their call becomes a deep, booming note. The male crowned crane is one of nature's great dancers, performing high-kicking displays of colourful finery, in pairs or groups, to impress the females and to intimidate rivals. The Animal Orphanage has 22 species of wild animal, including elephant, buffalo, sable, wildebeest, eland, lion (in the sanctuary), giraffe, zebra and impala.

second turning to the right at the Hippo Pools and Umfurudzi Safari Area sign. The bumpy gravel road now loops around the perimeter of Madziwa gold and nickel mine on your right for 1,5 km until you reach a T-junction with a rough tarred road. Turn left here for Amm's Mine, which you reach after 6 km, the road surface changing to gravel as you go left around Amm's Mine (ignore all other left turnings) for 500 m to a fork and a National Parks sign. Go right at the fork and, after 5,5 km on this road, go right again at another fork. After a further 1,5 km, you reach the National Parks Warden's Office. Retrace your route to the fork and turn sharp right onto the gravel Hippo Pools road that runs between lovely, wooded hills, crossing several low-level bridges. After 12,5 km on this road you reach the Hippo Pools on the Mazowe River. Cosy chalets of wood and thatch nestle beneath large riverine trees on the bank. Retrace your route via Madziwa Mine to Shamva, where, in front of the mine, you take the third turning to the right, signposted Bindura. Note your kms here.

Shamva to Harare

As you drive along the wide Mazowe Valley there is an unguarded railway crossing after 3,5 km and the road continues for another 24 km to reach the busy commercial and farming centre of Bindura.

In Bindura, follow the Dombawera Game Lodge sign towards Mazowe for 15 km until you reach the sign for Zindele Game Park. At the sign, turn right onto a gravel road which, after 8 km, reaches the entrance to Zindele. (Only two cars at a time are usually allowed in this private 7 000 ha game sanctuary that has lion, buffalo, elephant, giraffe and sable antelope. Day visitors are welcome, but phone ahead from Harare.)

Retrace your route to the main road and turn right to continue driving up the Mazowe Valley flanked by mountains and by citrus groves that produce 'Mazoe', a well-known orange juice. (The large white dish you see along here is part of an earth satellite station.) At 32,5 km pass a road, on your right, to the Mvurwi and Centenary tobacco-growing areas. Continue past this road and past the Mazowe Hotel 1 km later. Another 1 km further, a sign indicates Manzou Game Park (15 km down a sideroad) amid the citrus estates. Just 500 m beyond the sideroad is a fruit kiosk and the Mazowe Dam wall. Keep straight on the main road to reach Africa Unity Square in Harare after a further 35 km.

AA Office Fanum House, Samora Machel Avenue, Harare Tel (14) 75 2779
Harare Publicity Bureau Africa Unity Square, cr Second Street and Jason Moyo Avenue Harare Tel (14) 70 5085

Gold is where you find it. At Shamva, which means 'friendliness' it's far away from the city lights.

'WATER HORSE' WILDERNESS

Towering trees overlook pools of snorting hippo, while for 70 km the Mazowe flows past scenic mountains, granite hillocks, ancient Portuguese loop-holed forts, San paintings and even a tree-hide in which to sleep. Week-long hiking trails start at Hippo Pools along the banks of the Mazowe River in the hilly, 74 000 ha Umfurudzi Safari Area. The game, although not abundant, includes roan antelope, wildebeest, impala, zebra and sable, while hyaena are heard at night. The 300 species of bird include eagles and the rare and restless Livingstone's flycatcher. But the star attractions are the hippo. They have pink, twitching ears, weigh up to 1,5 tons and can stay submerged for six minutes at a time, walking along the riverbed. To the Greeks they were known as the 'water horse'. A hippo may eat as much as 130 kg of green grass during a night, turning riverbanks into neatly cropped lawn.

TO A BROTHER'S MEMORY

The 18 m leaves of the raffia palm are the largest in the plant kingdom and, in Ewanrigg Botanical Garden, they tower over the miniature lakes, banks of flowers, cacti, bamboos, cycads and 57 species of aloe. Farmer Harold Christian started the garden in the 1920s, naming it after his brother, Ewan, who was killed in the First World War. Aloes are often seen in the wild, especially at Great Zimbabwe and among rocky ruins in Nyanga. A member of the lily family, the name 'aloe' comes from the Arabic word for this prickly-leaved succulent with its flaming spears of flowers. Paved paths follow streams among valley woodland, rockeries, trees and banks of flowers in an environment ideal for spotting Zimbabwe's 15 species of brightly coloured sunbirds. The midwinter months are best for aloes, when they flaunt their banners on Ewanrigg's slopes.

Zimbabwe's aloes flaunt some unusual colours.

Tranquil Ewanrigg recalls a soldier-brother's sacrifice.

Bvumba – bananas and mist on the high road above the Burma Valley

The Bvumba, near Mutare, is a high promontory of proteas, mist and forest above the tropical Burma Valley, providing a varied and scenic outing past banana plantations and coffee farms, forest reserves and colourful botanical gardens. The loose-surfaced Burma Valley section must be driven with extreme caution in wet weather.

Mutare
Burma Valley
Bunga Botanical Reserve
Leopard Rock
120 – 140 km

At 140 km the shortest of the Mutare drives, this route starts outside the Information Bureau. Drive south along Herbert Chitepo Street, take the right fork in front of the colonial-style Custom House and, 1,5 km further, turn left into the Bvumba Road. You immediately start climbing, with the Mozambique lowlands and Beira road stretching into the distance on your left until, after 8 km, you turn left onto the Prince of Wales Viewpoint, facing the western flank of the Bvumba promontory. From here you go downhill for 3 km and then up until you reach the roadside map at the 11 km peg; turn right at the fork to the Burma Valley. You will descend rapidly into the populated Zimunya communal lands, with the Himalaya Mountains (2 211 m) in the distance. Here, women carry water buckets on their heads, goats skitter across the road and children steer homemade wire toys.

Some 15 km down this road you drive between the bald, 1 500 m peaks of Chishakwe and Hwangura. You then ascend a steep little pass for a further 3 km, closed in by msasa trees (*Brachystegia spiciformis*), and descend into lush banana and mango plantations in the steep-sided Burma Valley.

Drive 5 km along the valley floor until, at the 47 km peg (measured from the other end of the road), you reach a thatched farm kiosk and lawns where cooling light refreshments, and earrings made from seedpods, are on sale.

Burma Valley to Bvumba

Drive on for a further 17 km through the hot, low-lying valley where bright blue bags cover and protect bananas growing along the Nyamataka River. Of the many small streams that you cross, some flow eventually into Mozambique's Chikamba Reial Dam, 15 km to the east. In this lush valley you pass farms that produce macadamia nuts, mangoes (the smaller trees flanking the bananas), pawpaws and lichees, while almost every dwelling seems to be set in a colourful riot of bougainvillea. Double-storey, slatted burley tobacco barns are also much in evidence.

At the 30 km peg (40 km from the Burma Valley turn-off), the road veers left up into hills covered with lovely msasa trees. You are soon within 200 m of the (unmarked) Mozambique border. Drive on for another 3 km and on the left there is a picnic spot signposted Mia Falls, overlooking this little waterfall in the Chinakatori range.

Keep winding upwards for another 2 km, to the point where the 25,4 km gravel road (now called Essex Road) up into the Bvumba begins. Be alert for heavy timber lorries on this section. There is a sweeping viewsite some 4 km further on as you approach the Crake Valley farm store, on your left, where you can buy delicious Vumba cheeses. Some 2,5 km further you pass Blue Mountain Road leading to the Ardroys Guest House. You now climb a really narrow, steep road for 15,5 km, through avenues of indigenous trees and towering giant gums, terraces of coffee, and the final 2,5 km (on tar) back to the Bvumba Road.

Bvumba to Mutare

Turn sharp left at the reverse fork onto the Bvumba Road and within 1 km you will be on the 'cloudlands saddle' (1 590 m) with its panoramic views. There is a picnic spot 2 km further on amid banks of flowering wattle and, 1 km beyond this, you pass a simple structure describing itself as the Bvumba Dawn Drive-in Hyper Kiosk, where you may buy local handwork.

Continue along this road on the narrow ridge of the Bvumba promontory for another 1,5 km and stop at the picnic site on your left where signs announce the Bunga Botanical Reserve. Paths lead into this primeval montane forest that has its own miniclimate on the mist-cocooned cliff edge. Some 2,5 km further, you pass a gravel sideroad that leads to a nursery. About 5 km beyond this road a sharp turn to the left and a detour of 2 km will bring you to the Bvumba Botanical Garden Nursery (signposted at the corner). Refreshments include light lunches, and a small entrance fee is charged to enter these delightful gardens of azaleas, indigenous trees, massive banks of flowers, lily ponds and stunning views over the Mozambique lowlands 1 000 m below. Retrace your route to the main road and turn left to reach, after 500 m, a footpath on your right to the Leopard Rock summit. Colourfully dressed local women sell embroidered work here, a Bvumba speciality.

After a further 1,5 km, a road on your right leads for 2,5 km to the Leopard Rock Resort, where a magnificent 18-hole golf course is overlooked by pink, turreted towers suggestive of a fantastic Disney-like castle. Retrace your route to the Bvumba Road and turn left to return to Mutare, a distance of some 30 km.

AA Office Fanum House, cr Robert Mugabe Avenue/Fourth Street, Mutare Tel (120) 64422
Manicaland Publicity Association Market Square, cr Robert Mugabe Avenue/Herbert Chitepo Street, Mutare Tel (120) 64711

Children seek shade in a banana plantation.

MIX AND MATCH

Hawk moths sometimes sound like humming birds as they circle you at night, while their Death's Head cousins actually squeak. There are some 500 types of butterfly in Zimbabwe, but thousands more moth varieties, many of which find the Bvumba's lush greenery to their taste. Not all moths are nocturnal and dull coloured; some luxuriate in daylight, can be exceptionally beautiful and, to protect themselves, mimic the appearance of butterflies that secrete an unpalatable fluid. The swallowtail butterfly, with its distinctive hindwing aerials, is everyone's favourite, but there are hundreds of others, including foxy charaxes, the striped policeman, the paradise skipper, the male diadem and the orangey acraceas that languidly open and close their wings as they feed. The frosted emperor moth, with a wingspan of 18 cm, is the largest winged insect in southern Africa.

Indigenous trees cast shade on the Essex Road.

SWEET BANANAS

Zimbabwe is almost synonymous with tobacco, but bananas (which originated in Africa) are the more profitable crop. Some are no larger than your finger, others are 450 mm long, while one variety has a bright red skin. Bananas cannot tolerate frost and cold, so they flourish in the hot Burma Valley below the Bvumba mountains, where most of Zimbabwe's bananas are grown. The locally favoured variety is Dwarf Cavendish from the Canary Islands, rather than the less-tasty 'gros Michel' Caribbean variety of Europe's supermarkets. The average trees in Burma Valley's 2 km-long plantations are 3 m high, but they grow to three times that height; from planting to fruiting takes one year. The stalks are used for cattle feed and on Africa's offshore islands the shiny fronds are used as beach tablecloths and food wrappers. Wild bananas and the related strelitzias with their beak-like flowers grow in the Bvumba's rain forests and forested gorges.

Cows in lush pasture – an early stage in producing Vumba cheeses.

The police in Mutare have one of the country's most elegant headquarters.

VUMBA CHEESE

Along a dusty Bvumba road flanking the mountains of Mozambique is a farm in a green valley shaded by giant albizia trees and indigenous forest. Here, mottled black and white Holstein (Friesian) cows graze on the lush pastures, producing a creamy milk that, in accordance with tradition, is never pasteurized but turned into Vumba cheese, one of the few soft, French-style farmhouse cheeses to be perfected in Africa. Cheese has delighted the heart and palate of man for 6 000 years; the Persians made it in goatskin bladders, while the ancient Greeks of Homer's *Odyssey* marvelled at the enormous roundels in the Cyclops' gigantic cave. France, with 750 varieties, is the world leader, and it is to France that the Vumba cheese-making family regularly goes to update their 'savoir' of the delicate art, and to reacquaint storybook Anatole, their jaunty beret-capped mouse mascot, with his illustrious relations.

FIREBOXES AND FLASH FLOODS

The 1903 Ivel tractor with iron-rimmed wheels in Mutare Museum may be the second oldest tractor in existence. It is the focus of the museum's display of vintage cars that includes a Nash Metropolitan, America's first 'modern' small car and a 1909 Schacht. Standing proudly at the museum entrance in Aerodrome Road is a Bow McLachlan traction engine of 1897. This monster's wheels were made 2,5 m high, so that its wood-burning firebox would not be doused while crossing swollen rivers. The museum also features a fine and fearsome collection of ancient pistols, firearms, swords and bayonets. There are also displays of the birds, animals, snakes and insects (including a working beehive) of the Eastern Highlands and of the area's intriguing and extensive Stone Age and Iron Age industries.

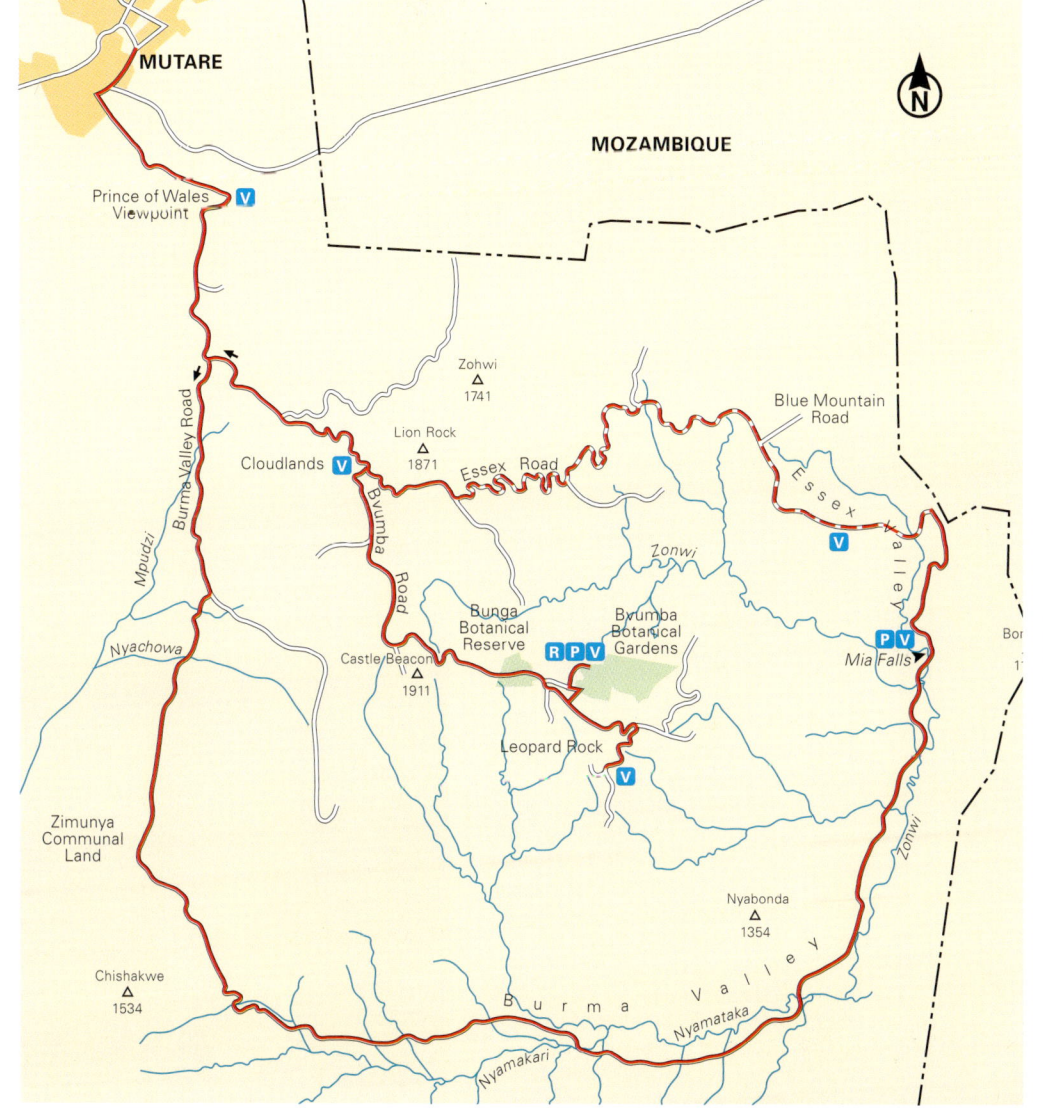

Prince of Wales View before the rain.

Zimbabwe's highest mountain, trout streams and sparkling waterfalls

Distant misty mountains and green valleys shadowed by moving cloud greet the motorist in the Nyanga highlands. Trout-fishing, cream teas and delightful picnic vistas are features of this drive including tropical Honde Valley. The gravel road surfaces may be rutted or waterlogged during the rainy season.

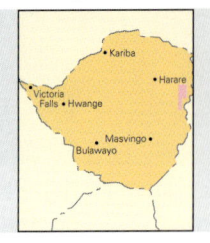

**Mutare
Nyanga
Honde Valley
Inyangani
Penhalonga
290 – 310 km**

From the publicity bureau in Mutare, note your kms and take Robert Mugabe Avenue west up and over Christmas Pass. Pass a road on your right to Penhalonga and, at 10,5 km, turn right onto the Juliasdale Road. Along this road you pass the Africa Methodist University after 5 km and, after a further 2 km, the exotically named L'Amour Store and Hands On Ethnic Prints.

You then climb gently for 25 km past communal farmlands set against rugged boulder country with dramatic bare rock *gomos*, the small hills so typical of boulder-strewn Zimbabwe. Note your kms as you pass a turn-off on your right to Odzi and Penhalonga at Watsomba village and, some 13 km further on, you enter typical highlands countryside with forest plantations covering the encircling hills.

About 18 km from Watsomba village, pass the turn-off to the tropical Honde Valley and Pungwe Scenic View. The road now twists and turns across the Odzi River for 10 km until, at the 60,5 km roadside peg, you reach the Nyakupinga River, where a shady kiosk offers jams and frozen trout for sale. Some 1,5 km past the Nyakupinga River, pass a road, on your right, which leads to the Nyakupinga-Brackenridge fruit-growing valley and drive on up a long, lonely road to reach the Rusape-Nyanga junction after a further 11 km. A helpful feature of the Nyanga area is the roadside maps, and there is one at this junction.

Turn right at the Rusape-Nyanga junction for Juliasdale village, which you reach after 1 km, and where there is a tourist information office, a petrol station, the Montclair Casino Hotel and the pretty Church of the Good Samaritan, used by various Christian communities in turn. Note your kms as you drive through Juliasdale, where the sweep of the Inyangani massif immediately opens on your right and Claremont apple orchards and lakes unfold in the valley below. After 9 km you pass a fruit kiosk and, 2 km later, you enter the Nyanga National Park. Pass the turn-offs to Rhodes Dam, Udu Dam and Troutbeck and, 19 km from Juliasdale, turn right into Nyanga village, where, at Kashmir Store, you can buy trout flies and, in nearby Nyamhuka village, *gudza* mats. Made of woven bark and measuring about 1,5 x 1,0 m, these are the traditional sleeping blankets of the rural Shona.

Mountains and champagne air

Retrace your route for 4 km to the Troutbeck turn-off and turn left. From here, a 15 km climb with panoramic views brings you to Troutbeck village, where the lakeside hotel has an attractive golf course through which winds the mountain road to World's View. Retrace your route for 3,5 km and turn left onto the gravel-surfaced Kwarangusa Road, where the surroundings soon open into a stunning vista of the whole Nyanga Park. The altitude here is more than 2 000 m, and wildflowers abound on the open hills and along tiny streams.

Continue along this road for 15 km to reach the eastern gate of the Nyanga National Park, which is open daily from 07h00 until 17h00. Pay the entrance fee here. Two kilometres further, go left at the inclined T-junction, to reach, after 800 m, the foot of Inyangani, Zimbabwe's highest mountain at 2 593 m above sea level.

Retrace your route, passing, after 800 m, the Troutbeck-Kwarangusa road on which you came. After a further 400 m, turn left at the junction onto the gravel road for Nyangwe (Mare) and Nyanga (Rhodes) dams, where the right-hand fork leads to Nyamziwa Falls. Note your kms at the turn. You reach Nyangwe Dam after 8 km. Drive past the chalets, over the dam bridge; 800 m further up the hill, you pass a road on your left that leads, after a further 1 km, to Nyangwe Fort (in reality a 16th-century walled Shona homestead).

Retrace your route to the Nyangwe Fort turn-off and turn left. After about 6 km you pass Nyanga (Rhodes) Dam, 25 m off the road on your left, and the entrance to the park's headquarters. Some 500 m past the entrance, turn left at the T-junction and, after a further 800 m, right onto tar. Go left at the main Nyanga-Juliasdale Road after another 800 m.

After 9 km on this road, go left at the fork onto the gravel-surfaced Placefell Road and, 6 km later, turn right onto the Pungwe Scenic Road, noting your kms. A word of warning; parts of the route negotiate very sharp bends and the surface may be badly rutted.

Pungwe Falls to La Rochelle Gardens

After 4 km the road leaves the forest to reveal the Inyangani massif looming above valley and downs, and after a further 8 km, a road on your left leads for 800 m to Pungwe View, with its deep forested gorge and waterfall. Return to the main scenic road and turn left, noting your kms. After about 2,5 km, turn left for Honde, following this road for some 5 km to the Honde viewsite – looking over a precipitous valley and the mountains of Mozambique – and then driving on for another 2 km to the parking area 800 m from Mutarazi Falls. An easy walk brings you to their impressive 762 m drop. Retrace your route to the main road and turn left, noting your kms. After 14,5 km, turn right onto tar and, 1,5 km later, turn left, to reach Watsomba village after a further 18 km. At Watsomba, turn left, onto gravel, for Penhalonga, noting your kms.

The road rises over rugged slopes to the Odzani Road and forestry plantations. At 10 km turn right, onto tar, then cross a bridge, pass Odzani Dam and the Odzani Falls turn-off, to reach a picnic site opposite Kadzamu Fort after a further 4,3 km.

Continue along this road for 16,5 km to reach the historic mining town of Penhalonga, with its Pioneer Nursing Memorial on the outskirts. (Turn left 2,2 km further on for lovely La Rochelle, reached after a further 3 km along

---

THE MSASAS ARE OUT

The mopane is the tree of the lowveld, but the photogenic msasa (*Brachystegia spiciformis*), with its filigreed twisty branches, is the quintessential tree of Zimbabwe's high savannah. Often seen in conjunction with the munondo (*Julbernardia globiflora*), which is similar in appearance, it grows as high as 15 m. The small-leafed or dwarf variety (*Brachystegia microphylla*), exposed to the chill winds of the mountains, trails long wisps of old man's beard from its grey, flaky branches. The woody pods of the msasa look like dried twists of pastry and split open with a resounding crack to disperse their seeds.

Like the daisies on the plains of Namaqualand, Zimbabwe's springtime mountains are a major attraction when the delicate colours of the young msasa leaves explode in a rainbow from honey gold to crimson, creating a lacy coat of many colours across the hills.

MOUNTAIN WILDFLOWERS

There is a little dell halfway up the path to the 2 593 m summit of Inyangani, Zimbabwe's highest mountain. Beside a wind-feathered cascade of pure mountain water and protected by a rugged bluff, this bower shelters a dozen different wildflowers. Undisturbed, the Nyanga Mountains host a lovely variety of the country's 5 000 flowering plants and herbs. They include the blushing Manica daisy, mountain hibiscus, forest flame creeper, purple Inyanga selago, and fairy everlastings. The flowers of Africa are often tiny, some less than 1 cm across, so you may have to bend down to see them delicately fluttering at your feet. In the vast emptiness of the Nyanga Park, these little ones – forest stars, groundbells and suteras – are the hidden jewels in the crown. Stop, park and – even by the roadside – you will see much to delight you.

Common Pentanisia is a bright, wayside flower.

this sideroad.) Retrace your route to the main road from where, after turning left, it is about 6 km to the main Harare – Mutare road near Christmas Pass. Turn left here, to reach Mutare after a further 8 km.

AA Office Fanum House, cr Robert Mugabe Avenue/Fourth Street, Mutare Tel (120) 64422
Nyanga Tourist Association The Library, Village Green, Nyanga or PO Box 110, Nyanga.
Manicaland Publicity Association Market Square, cr Robert Mugabe Avenue/Herbert Chitepo Street, Mutare Tel (120) 64711
National Parks (Reservations) Botanical Gardens, Sandringham Drive, off Borrowdale Road, Harare Tel (14) 70 6077

Flowertime at La Rochelle Gardens.

THE GREAT ESCAPE
A dozen mountain rivers and well-stocked dams offer fly-fishing for rainbow trout in Nyanga. Those caught in rivers are considered tastier. Trout were introduced into Nyanga's mountains in 1905 and may reach a mass of 4,5 kg. Fly-fishing has long been associated with mountains, silence and splendid isolation, but the art can be learned by anyone with a fibreglass rod of 2,6 m, a No 7 double paper floating line, a 9 cm diameter reel, a net, a 'priest' (club) and a minimum of three Walker's Killer flies.

And if the gentle casting back and forth to send your line looping across the tranquil water seems impossible at first, revel in the wattled cranes, redbilled teals, blackheaded herons, dabchicks, coots, giant kingfishers, creamy augur buzzards and black eagles among the 300 or so bird species that will share your seeming solitude.

The Pungwe River's waterfall.

This view of World's View is across Nyanga's Cumberland Valley.

ANCESTORS OF IRON AND STONE
Many visit Nyanga and never realise that, Great Zimbabwe excepted, the most extensive archaeological ruins in the country lie in the dusty lowlands along a gravel road 30 km north-west of the mountains. The Ziwa (formerly Van Niekerk) stone terracing, enclosures, platforms, stock pens and walls cover an area of 52 square kilometres and date back 350 years to when the Nyanga population, threatened by deteriorating soil fertility and worsening weather conditions, retreated to the low country. Pyramid-like *Ziwa* ('place of offerings'), looms over an informative site museum and picnic shelters. Pottery and iron implements excavated in the Ziwa area show that man was living here as far back as AD 300. The most dramatic ruin, probably a chief's settlement of iron-smelting specialists, lies halfway up beautiful Nyahokwe Mountain, 8 km back along the road to Nyanga village. A massive stone enclosure flanks a walled platform or *dare* that offers panoramic views of the mountains.

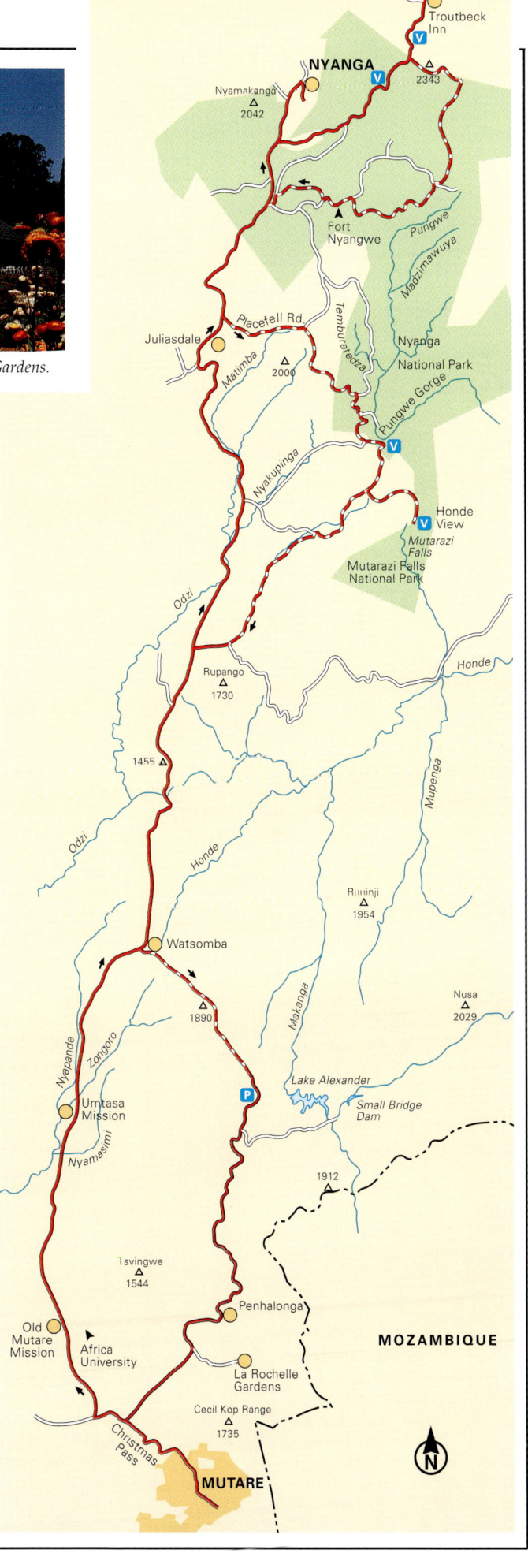

315

EXPLORING NYANGA NATIONAL PARK

Early morning mist – a frequent occurrence in the highlands – lends a metallic sheen to the unruffled waters of the Mare Dam.

Misty moorlands and high mountain forests where trout streams flow past silent, ancient ruins

UPLAND WINDS – scented by heather and ferns – cool the range of blue mountain that divides the high Zimbabwe plateau from the tropical lowlands of Mozambique, that lie some 1 200 m lower down. Dominating every horizon, the Inyangani massif, the country's highest mountain (2 592 m), provides from its mist-swept summit a full panorama of trout streams, lakes, ancient walled ruins and rolling downlands in the west, and precipitous cliffs, waterfalls and montane forest down to the Honde Valley in the east.

The mountains incorporate the Nyanga National Park, which, with its lakeshore cottages, icy rivers and open moorland, is reminiscent of highland Scotland, and not Africa. Light blankets of cloud creep over the heights, quilting the open slopes where wildebeest graze and sinking into forested gorges rich in flowers.

The park covers 47 000 ha and stretches from the 762 m high Mtarazi Falls in the south, to Troutbeck, which, with Juliasdale and Nyanga, is one of the area's villages well provided with holiday accommodation. Memorable places include Pungwe's deep green gorge, the Honde View, Rhodes Nyanga Museum and Ziwa's Iron Age ruins, the trout lakes surrounding the park's headquarters and a necklace of lovely waterfalls on the dozen rivers that rise in the park. But the mountains, both in the park and along the access routes, have hidden secrets worth exploring.

Set in the centre of emerald circles of tea estates, Aberfoyle lies in the northern culvert of the Honde Valley, with the steep flanks of Inyangani Mountain rising sheer above its golf course. The approach route, 63 km of tarred road, falls in coils down from the mountains, passing plantations of mango and banana. From Aberfoyle, walks can be arranged in the shade of nearby Gleneagles Mountain Reserve.

Its tropical forest hides rare bird species such as the marsh tchagra *(Tchagra minuta)*, which also occurs in Mozambique, and the elusive red and green Narina trogon *(Apaloderma narina)*.

A more adventurous dry-season route starts 22 km east of Troutbeck on the gravel-surfaced Nyamaropa Road. It winds for some 65 km past sweet-tasting mzanje wild fruit trees and tiny

Most of Zimbabwe's trout start life in the breeding dam at Nyanga Park.

An Iron Age site at Nyanga.

Seen from the main road, the Honde Valley is one of the delights of Zimbabwe.

mountain-hugging huts, each with its patch of pineapples. Some 43 km from the Troutbeck road turn-off and beyond Nyafaru School, at the bridge over the Jora River, tree ferns and purple everlastings mark the river's escape through a gorge of descending pools, 800 m from the road.

Inyangani Mountain is an initially stiff, but only a four-hour return climb from the car park 9 km east of Nyangwe (Mare) Dam. Start early on this well-marked route and you may see kudu grazing on the slopes among wind-ruffled proteas. Stop at a natural wildflower haven halfway up to the saddle and, right by the path along the ridge, you can drink pure mountain water from the stream. This is the home of the Nyanga aloe (*Aloe inyangensis*), found almost exclusively on the higher-lying ground, while woodlands of msasa grow densely on the west-facing slopes. The msasa (*Brachystegia spiciformis*), is one of the dominant and most widespread trees of Zimbabwe, the upward and outward thrust of its branches, often curved and twisted, presenting a pleasing appearance. The msasa may grow from 8 to 15 m in height and has a pale grey bark that becomes cracked and deeply fissured with age.

Another of Nyanga's lofty perches, 25 km to the north, is Rukotso Mountain (2 405 m), where red-hot pokers and wild fig trees grow in lichen-covered rock terraces built and then abandoned by Nyanga's Iron Age cultivators 350 years ago. Rukotso overlooks the dusty plains of Nyanga's lowlands, where the same farmers settled and built other sophisticated stone structures for themselves and their livestock. The terraces, each one supported by a stone wall up to 1,5 m high, may have been built to combat soil erosion and to enable crops to be grown on otherwise unsuitable ground. Most of the terraces are found on steep slopes, although others occur on lower-lying land; some of the structures may also have been used as water furrows. This culture of stone construction goes back some 800 years, to Great Zimbabwe.

A gravel road takes you almost to the top of Rukotso (please shut the farm gates that you find closed along the route) from the Ezulwini Cottages turn-off, 11 km east of Troutbeck. If this lonely Nyangui Forest road seems daunting, pause at Nyamoro farm, 1,5 km from the main road, where, overlooking fields of daffodils in spring and a large dam, you can buy homemade cheese, butter and blueberry jam and watch the Jersey herd being milked.

There's a no-entry sign on the access road to Nyazengu Nature Reserve, 500 m from Inyangani car park. Drive past and pay the small entrance fee 5 km further down this road at Stonechat Cottage's trout pools. You may then explore the well laid out trail of 12 km through this 1 250 ha private reserve tucked into Inyangani's flank. With the mountain always above you, there is a lovely walk past mist-swept montane forest, open grasslands, the cliff-edge Nyazengu Falls and a series of cascades along the Matenderere River. Lions have occasionally been seen and, from October to April, there are also leopards in Nyazengu. One of Nyanga's rare snowfalls was reported here in 1993.

The Matenderere eventually joins the Pungwe and Temburatedza rivers in a series of large, clear pools and waterfalls 10 km south-west of Nyazengu Reserve. They are reached, by those with stout boots, down a narrow path 2,5 km north of the Pungwe Cottages and Drift turn-off from the Scenic Route. Most people approach Nyanga via Mutare or Harare-Rusape but the Nyanga North dry-season routes include one, 14 km east of Murewa; another, 8 km east of Mutoko via All Souls' Mission (where there is a lovely Italian church); and a third, from Nyamapanda Border Post to the Rwenya River. The three routes converge at the tarred Nyamaropa Valley Road at Ruwangwe, the eastern approach to Troutbeck village.

Tea-picking in the Honde Valley.

Nyanga Tourist Association
Dilly Crafts, Nyanga Village
Tel (129-8) 341 (enquire at Camp and Cabin in Juliasdale for local sub-branch)
Manicaland Publicity Association Market Square cr Robert Mugabe Avenue/ Herbert Chitepo Street, Mutare
Tel (120) 64711
National Parks (Reservations)
Botanical Gardens,
Sandringham Drive, off
Borrowdale Road, Harare
Tel (14) 70 6077

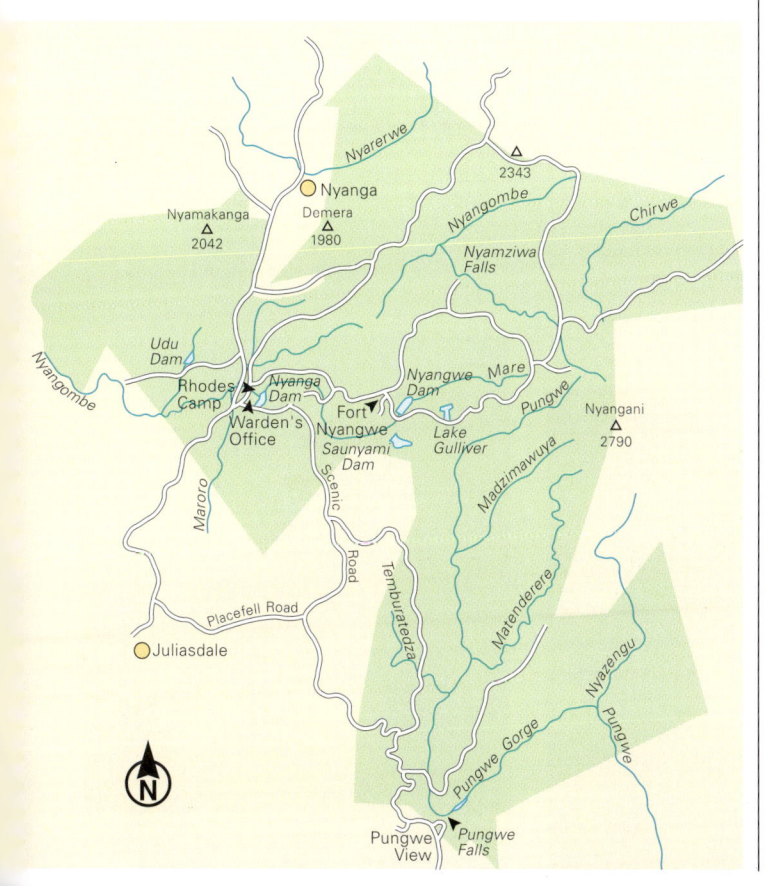

A great mountain divide, hot springs and baobabs

Perhaps the grandest drive in the mountains that divide Zimbabwe from Mozambique, this route runs close to the wild Chimanimani Mountains and then passes through cool eucalyptus forests to the lush coffee farms near Chipinge. It drops down to the Save River, where dusty baobabs stand sentinel, and on to Birchenough Bridge and Hot Springs Resort.

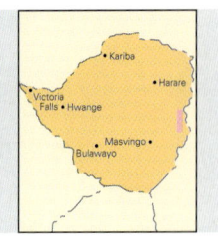

**Mutare
Chimanimani
Skyline Junction
Chipinge
Birchenough
Bridge
Hot Springs
400 – 420 km**

From the Manicaland Publicity Office in Mutare, head south along Herbert Chitepo Street and go right at the fork after 800 m. After 5 km you reach the outskirts of town, facing a pyramid-shaped hill, and soon descend into communal farmlands. Beware of livestock on the road. The mountains you pass far to your left at the 44,5 km peg are the Himalayas. Some 66,5 km from Mutare, turn left at the fork just before Wengezi Junction village and note your kms.

You now climb, following the Umvumvumvu River, named for the noise it makes as it hurtles down the ravines. The road forks after 13 km. Ignore the direct route to Chimanimani and go left here past vegetable farms to Cashel Valley, another 16 km on. Turn sharp right 2 km beyond the last little building in Cashel and cross the Umvumvumvu River onto gravel.

Chimanimani scenic route

(This section should not be attempted soon after heavy rain. Corrugated and dusty in parts, this scenic mountain section continues for some 66 km from Cashel to Chimanimani.) Stop after 15 km from Cashel, especially in late August, to admire the multicoloured msasa trees carpeting the slopes. Traffic along this road is usually only slight and the dust-filtered views over waves of purple mountains, especially in the late afternoon, may be enjoyed from many sites. Continue for another 5 km, passing the unmarked right fork to Moodie's Nek and negotiate the pass for a further 9 km up hairpin bends and past gullies of indigenous montane forest frequented by butterflies and birds. You know you are at the top, about 1 900 m high, when you can see, in the distance, straight ahead, the hazy massif of the Chimanimani National Park.

The road descends by the glacier-like cut in the mountains for 12 km until, on the valley floor, a sign reads, simply, 'cheese'. Turn right here, 43 km from Cashel, onto the farm road for 500 m, to reach a Cape Dutch farmstead in the shelter of a remote bowl of hills where, over a drink of homemade pineapple juice, you may make your cheese selection.

Return to the main road and turn right. Ignore all left turns as you pass through tall plantations. The twisting climb flanks the soaring bulk of Chimanimani with increasingly dramatic views across the divide. Because of the risk of fire in the forestry plantations, 'no smoking' signs – rare in tobacco-growing Zimbabwe – are frequent along the last 22 km to Chimanimani village.

Skyline Junction to the lowveld

Chimanimani village, with its venerable hotel in the Indian hill-country style, offers a panoramic view of the mountains. Bear in mind that it is a tough three-hour climb up to the Chimanimani Plateau, so if you need to make arrangements to stay overnight, ask at the A-frame tourist office. Follow the stony road opposite the petrol station for 3,5 km to visit Bridal Veil Falls, a stepped cascade with moss-covered rocks, pool, ferns, strelitzias and a grassed picnic site.

Retrace your route to the village and, at the tarred T-junction 100 m past the hotel, turn right for Skyline Junction, which you reach after 19 km. At Skyline Junction you can opt for the direct route back to Mutare (132 km) or turn left to continue the drive.

After turning left, you drive through tall gum and wattle plantations. At 30 km, just past an open picnic site, a pocket of indigenous forest near a sharp U-bend picks out a wayside plaque on the right informing you that this Ponte Italia culvert was built by Italian prisoners of war in 1944. Some 6 km beyond the culvert you pass the roadside grave of pioneer trekker Thomas Moodie (1839 – 1894) just before you reach the T-junction to Chipinge, 36 km from Skyline Junction.

Turn right at this T-junction, passing mountain slopes covered with coffee plantations; 14,5 km along this road, in splendid mountain isolation, is Buffelsdrift Holiday Cottage. Continue for a further 34 km until you reach dry baobab country and the T-junction with the main road back to Mutare. Turn left and drive for 3,5 km to see the 330 m steel arch Birchenough Bridge across the sandy Save River – an incongruous but impressive sight on the African veld. Retrace your route back to the Chipinge-Mutare junction and take the Mutare road. For the first 25 km you pass wayside craftsmen and their baobab bark rugs; then donkey carts, goats, open plains of baobab trees and the mangoes of Nyanyadzi irrigation scheme (where you can buy woven hats on the right-hand side of the village). Turn left at Hot Springs, 42 km from the bridge, to the pleasant resort with its thatched chalets and therapeutic waters. The bird life in the surrounding bush is extremely busy. From Hot Springs, your road follows the final 86 km through Wengezi Junction village back to Mutare.

AA Office Fanum House, cr Robert Mugabe Avenue and Fourth Street, Mutare
Tel (120) 64422
AA Consul Chipinge Diesel and Agricultural Services, Chipinge Tel (127) 2233
Manicaland Publicity Association Market Square, cr Robert Mugabe Avenue and Herbert Chitepo Street, Mutare Tel (120) 64711
Chimanimani Tourist Association A-frame building near village shops, Chimanimani Tel (126) 2294

HONEY THAT SMELLS OF TOBACCO

The best honey in Zimbabwe, it is said, and certainly the cheapest, comes from Chimanimani. Long before commercial farming began, hunter-gatherers used wooden pegs to climb up baobabs (you still see the scars in these 1 000-year-old trees) and rob hives of the delicious, almost white, honey. Although only a few do it today, a decade ago Save River peasant farmers would remove hives from logs and wedge them high in trees. Using smoky fires to distract the bees, daring young men would scoop out the honey at night. Wild bees forage anywhere, so in Zimbabwe – inevitably – their honey, at times, even smells of tobacco. Walking in this hot bushveld you sometimes hear a noise like the flight of distant aircraft – a swarm of bees is passing. Stay still until it passes – African bees, especially those inhabiting rock clefts, are aggressive. To remove a bee sting, don't pull it out. Use a penknife blade between flesh and sting and quickly scrape it out.

Above: *Msasa trees clothe much of the Zimbabwe countryside.* **Left:** *The lacy Bridal Veil Falls.*

KURUKURU

Kurukuru is the name the Shona give to the Livingstone lourie, the large ruby-and-emerald coloured touraco, one of six varieties in southern Africa that swoop secretively from tree to tree in the dark, evergreen forests of the Eastern Highlands. Its strident call is very like its name, although experts describe its noisy emanations in a variety of whoops, kerks, hurrs, kok-koks and rorrs. Easy to hear but difficult to see, this variant of the Knysna lourie has a longer green-and-white helmet and deeper blue upper parts. Often you will need to be on a ridge overlooking dense forest to catch the Livingstone in flight, a sight of soaring beauty on its rounded red-and-green wings. Landing, it runs along branches, jumping heavily from one to another. David Livingstone first saw the lourie in Malawi's Manganja Mountains; ironically, the Victoria Falls species is named after another explorer.

HOT SPRINGS

There are 91 minerals dissolved or suspended in the comforting water of Hot Springs Resort in the Chimanimani lowveld. Rising high in the mountains, the water seeps down towards the earth's fiery core to a depth of 3 353 m before granite channels allow it to bubble up as the 'eye' of a spring, the subterranean journey taking as long as 40 years. The water at the eye reaches temperatures of 42°C in summer and a mere 6°C in winter. Today the shady lake and trees of this oasis in the dry lowveld attract both bee-eaters and bird-lovers, but in the old days legend had it that the waters were protected by ancestral spirits, old men whose chopping of wood to keep the magic fires burning could be heard by anyone brave enough to approach.

There are 30 hot springs in Zimbabwe, many of them in the Kariba-to-Hwange area. Some, now submerged, are still active beneath Lake Kariba.

Rustic A-frame chalets line the quiet pool at the Hot Springs Resort.

WALK ON THE WILD SIDE

'Milkmaps' available from the information office in the A-frame building in Chimanimani, may tempt you to explore on foot. The 10 km southern ridge route along the crest of Greenmount, flanking the village, takes five hours. Allow two hours for the 4 km northern ridge walk past the Frog and Fern guesthouse along the Eland Sanctuary perimeter. Or drive to the parking area atop *Nyamzure* (Pork Pie) Mountain and then walk up to the steep, rough summit. An hour's stroll down Tilbury Road past the arboretum and Heaven Lodge will bring you back along the Cashel-Chimanimani scenic route. Serious climbers will head for the mountain park itself, 19 km from the village, with its wild mountain plateau, a wilderness of cracked strata, trout lakes, lichens, mists, banana-like trees, proteas, butterflies, rare birds, rivers, peaks reaching to 2 437 m, and mysterious, deep caves.

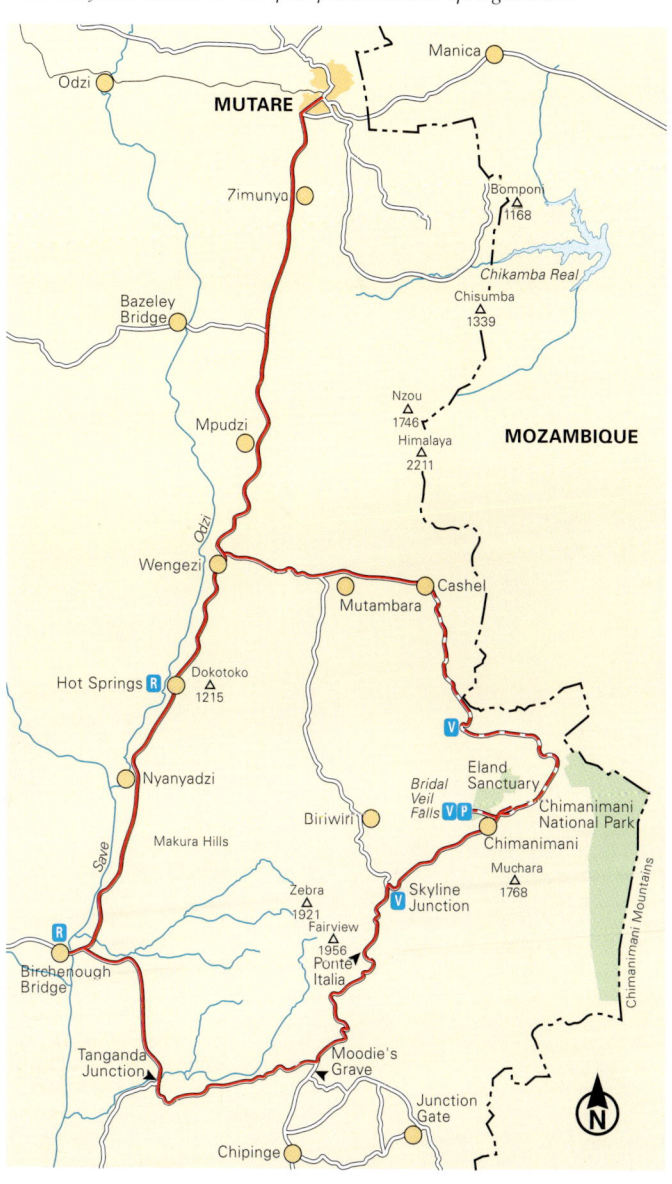

Above: *Cloud on the Chimanimani Mountains.* **Below:** *Hard-wearing mats are woven from strips of bark of the baobab tree.*

Mountains, missions and houses of stone – the way to Great Zimbabwe

The ancient structure of Great Zimbabwe is the focal point of the area. Modern artists in stone and wood are still to be seen on this route that goes north to the Driefontein and Serima missions, then swings south around Lake Mutirikwi to Great Zimbabwe and back to the historic town of Masvingo. Many of the gravel roads are impassable in the wet.

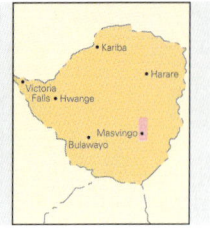

Masvingo
Serima
Gutu
Mutirikwi Dam
Great Zimbabwe
340 – 360 km

DRIVE NORTH FROM the Post Office along palm-lined Robert Mugabe Street in Masvingo. Cross the road to Harare and take the right-hand fork after 400 m. Turn left after 3,5 km and turn left again 200 m later to reach, after a further 100 m, the army barracks and the chapel of St Francis. Decorated with frescoes, the chapel was built during World War II by Italian prisoners of war.

Retrace your route to Masvingo – formerly Fort Victoria and the oldest town in Zimbabwe – and turn right at the crossroads into Josiah Tongogara Street towards Harare.

Some 72 km from Masvingo, you reach the Golden Spiderweb thatched resort, crochet shop and reconstructed 1890 Pioneer Column settlement; 3 km later, turn right onto a gravel road just before the Nyamatiki River, noting your kms.

After a further 11 km you reach Driefontein Mission, known for its exquisite jacaranda-wood carvings. The brick church was built in 1908, its interior rich with carved wooden panels and beams. Retrace your route for 800 m to the crossroads marking the edge of the mission and turn left on gravel, noting your kms.

You'll find 60 km/h a comfortable speed at which to travel through this open country of thorn trees and cattle ranches. After 15 km, turn right at the crossroads marked by a lone building adorned with a pair of kudu horns and a yellow Serima Mission sign. Some 8 km later turn left at the next Serima signpost, passing woodlands to reach a crossroads, after a further 4,5 km, where there is a white Serima sign. Keep straight here but reduce speed to about 40 km/h on this rough road; 3,5 km later you pass a dam and turn right, to reach the mission church 500 m off the road. The exquisite Driefontein-style doors and altar stools to be seen here are outstanding examples of their type.

Retrace your route for 0,5 km to the T-junction, note your kms and turn right. After a further 2 km there is another T-junction. Turn left here and, 8 km further, at the next T-junction – with a tarred road – turn right to reach the Gutu crossroads 30 km later.

Gutu to Mutirikwi Dam

Keep straight at the crossroads, noting your kms. Refuel, if necessary, and then drive south through koppie-sprinkled farmlands and

European visitors were slow to see Great Zimbabwe as an African creation.

SUGAR CANE LAKE

Hippos and crocodiles bask in the hot sun of Mutirikwi, or Kyle Dam, as it was originally called, the 15 km-long, V-shaped recreational lake in the lee of Glenlivet's forested hills that divide Great Zimbabwe from the game park on the northern shore. Fed by the Shagashe and Mutirikwi rivers, it was built in 1961 to supply water for the burgeoning citrus and sugar estates of Chiredzi, in the lowveld 168 km to the south-east. The 'blend' petroleum used throughout Zimbabwe is distilled from this sugar cane. Recurrent droughts have blighted the lake's potential, but it is still a popular venue for sailing, boating and, above all, bass-fishing. Largemouth bass reach 4 kg, the best fishing spots being the flooded points where the rivers enter the lake.

Lake Mutiriki is really a dam, supplying water to citrus and sugar estates.

THE GREAT ZIMBABWE MYSTERY

Great Zimbabwe (see pages 322 – 3) was never King Solomon's mines, the biblical Land of Ophir or Indiana Jones' Temple of Doom. Scientific evidence shows that it was built during a flourishing period of history by the ancestors of today's Shona-speaking Zimbabweans. Despite the earlier and correct attribution by Arab and Portuguese explorers, the German geologist, Karl Mauch, declared in 1871 that Great Zimbabwe was the work of Phoenicians, Indians, ancient Hebrews, Arabs or perhaps even the biblical Queen of Sheba. During Rhodesia's UDI years, it was politically reckless to state otherwise. Publicists, polemicists and awed visitors conspired to make the origins of Great Zimbabwe the most meticulously maintained 'mystery' in history. It is a mystery that a visit to the site, its museum and bookshop quickly solves, but the more one learns of this quiet, brooding site, the greater is its fascination.

Above: *A sheep farmer and his flock near Masvingo.* **Left:** *Carvings in the church at Serima Mission.*

increasingly mountainous views of msasa and euphorbias as you approach the hills surrounding Lake Mutirikwi. After some 55 km turn right at the T-junction with the main Masvingo-Birchenough Bridge road, to reach the Popoteke River Gorge turn-off 21 km later. Turn left here and, 2,5 km further on, you reach a remote picnic spot usually shared only with some resident Egyptian geese. There are braai places and rustic toilets.

Retrace your route to the main road and note your kms. Turn right and, 6,5 km later, just before the Mutirikwi River bridge, turn right again onto the scenic Glenlivet Hotel Road. After 11 km you reach the access road to the hotel on your left, and the hotel itself – in a grandly scenic setting – some 800 m later.

Retrace your route for 800 m to the Glenlivet Hotel entrance and note your kms as you turn left for Great Zimbabwe (to which the road sign gives the distance as 54 km). For the first 2,5 km the road hugs the wooded slopes, offering fine views down onto Lake Mutirikwi. Turn left at the T-junction at 2,5 km and, 7,5 km later, turn right at the inclined T-junction. The road surface changes to tar (and is known from here on as Murray MacDougall Drive) 18 km from the Glenlivet Hotel; 800 m later, the Chamavara Cave and rock paintings are signposted, but you will need a local guide to find them. A picnic site overlooks the mountain view 6,5 km after the start of the tar, but there are more attractive ones at the far end of Mutirikwi Dam wall, which you reach some 12 km further on.

Mutirikwi Dam to Great Zimbabwe

Drive slowly down to the dam via the single-lane 309 m span of the bridge. Pass flamboyant trees before turning sharp right 500 m beyond the dam, and drive 500 m further to spectacular picnic sites overlooking the wall. At the top, among aloes and euphorbias, is Zimbabwe's smallest chapel, St Andrew's, which accommodates just 12 worshippers. Children here will probably offer to sell you seed necklaces and other trinkets.

Return to the main road and turn right, noting your kms. As the road climbs high above the dam wall, new and spectacular vistas unfold. A sign 3 km along this road indicates rock paintings on the right; local children will direct you to them. The colourful gardens of Norma Jeane's chalets are passed 3 km later, followed by Mutirikwi Lakeshore Lodges and Kyle View Lodges. The road then moves inland for a further 7 km to reach the approach to Great Zimbabwe. Turn left here to reach the entrance gate (open 06h00 – 18h00) after 1 km. At the inclined T-junction 300 m later, turn left to reach the shaded car park and camping sites. Allow yourself at least two hours to explore Great Zimbabwe.

Great Zimbabwe to Masvingo

Return to the entrance gate, note your kms and turn left. You pass the entrance to the Great Zimbabwe Hotel (meals, drinks and fuel available) after 800 m and reach the main road after a further 500 m. Note your kms here and turn left, reaching the main Masvingo-Beitbridge road 21 km later. Turn right to reach the Post Office in Masvingo 5 km later.

AA Office c/o Magic (Pvt) Ltd, Shop 5, Robert Mugabe Street, Masvingo. Tel (139) 62563
Masvingo Publicity Association Immediately south of the railway on the Beitbridge Road edge of town. Tel (139) 6249
Mutirikwi Recreational Park (Reservations) National Parks Board, PO Box CY826 Causeway, Harare. Tel (14) 70 6077

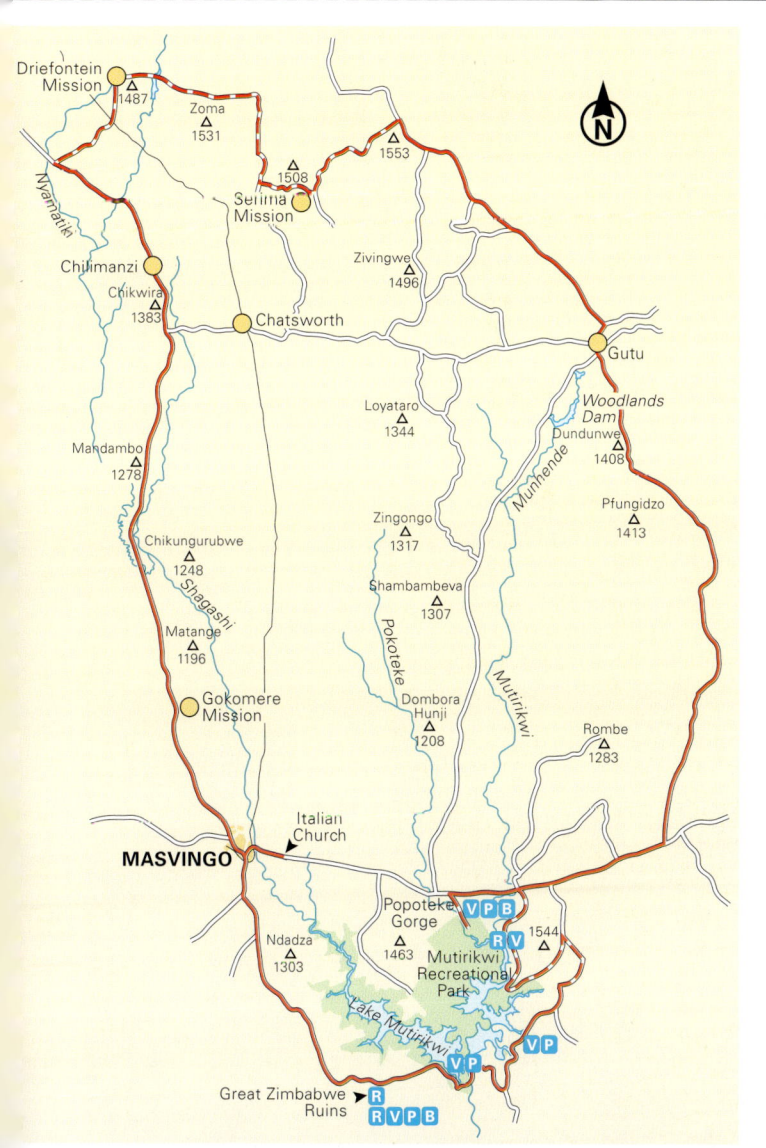

The Golden Spiderweb resort includes a reconstructed settler home of 1890.

GIRAFFE FROM HORSEBACK

Game-viewing on horseback, arranged daily by the National Park authorities, is the ideal way of seeing Lake Mutirikwi Game Park's rich selection of wildlife that includes square-lipped white rhino, whose forebears were introduced from KwaZulu-Natal in South Africa. In addition, there are giraffe, wildebeest, impala, zebra and ever-present leopard – a total of 40 mammal species.

The colourful checklist of birds includes eagles and falcons in the 4 856 ha of well-watered grasslands, miombo woodlands and acacia thorn scrub. Accompanied by a trained ranger, you are able to get exceptionally close to game in areas not normally accessible from the park's 64 km of roads. For non-riders, there are numerous bush and lakeshore walking trails and a wildlife interpretive centre. Chalets have been built near an area of 150 species of trees and plants set aside as an arboretum.

ELDORADO TO THE NORTH

'We think of it, dream of it, sigh for it', *The Nugget*, Fort Victoria's first newspaper, wistfully declared 100 years ago. Gold was the reason Cecil Rhodes' Pioneer Column invaded Zimbabwe, the 1 000-year-old land of the Shona, in 1890. Despite 140 claims, however, not much was found. The site of the invaders' first military camp, Fort Victoria, can still be visited 8 km south of their second settlement, Masvingo, and a replica of their spartan mud and thatch settlements is to be seen at the Golden Spiderweb 69 km north of town. *Masvingo*, the old name for the area, means 'walled-in enclosure', a reference to nearby Great Zimbabwe. Situated halfway between Beitbridge and Harare, the small town retains the fort's original bell tower, a handsome three-storey structure overlooking the high palms, a cannon-topped war memorial and attractive civic gardens in Robert Mugabe Street.

In many ways a 'sphinx without a secret', the mighty remains of Great Zimbabwe continue to fascinate visitors and to exercise their romantic imagination.

Under the African sun – an air of mystery about ancient 'houses of stone'

LONG BEFORE Portuguese mariners sailed around the southern coast of Africa in the 15th century, Great Zimbabwe was a flourishing town of 18 000 people and at least two centuries old. The Shona-speaking rulers, rich in cattle and trade and united in a powerful spirituality, controlled a confederation stretching across 100 000 sq km between the Zambezi and Limpopo rivers.

The word *zimbabwe* comes from the Shona words *dzimba dza mabwe*, meaning 'houses of stone'. There are many smaller such 'houses' *(madzimbabwe)* throughout south central Africa, of which Great Zimbabwe is believed to have been the commercial and political capital. European adventurers who rediscovered (and looted) the site in the late 19th century made fanciful biblical associations with King Solomon and the Queen of Sheba, and the mines of Ophir. Despite contrary proof, many people remain convinced that the origins of Great Zimbabwe do lie with some foreign invader or lost civilization, rather than with its real builders – the ancestors of the Shona.

Settlement on this hill at the headwaters of the Muturikwi River began in the early phase of the Iron Age, in about the 4th century AD. The place was healthy, fertile and easy to defend, so the settlement grew, gradually spreading down into the valley.

To the visitor the layout may seem confusing, so start at the museum's miniature layout of the ruins, then cross to the Great Enclosure or *Imba Huru*. This massive Colosseum-like structure, 225 m in circumference, stands 11 m high and has walls up to 5 m thick in a construction believed to contain some 900 000 hand-trimmed granite blocks interlocked without mortar. One of its uses may have been as a pre-marital initiation school where young men and women spent up to a year learning the decorum and the responsibilities of Shona married life. Archaeologists have

The sheer mass of an external wall.

deduced this from the 'snake of fertility' chevron pattern on the rear wall and other symbols covering the four categories of Shona adulthood, similar to those found on Shona *hakata* or divining dice. One wall of the Great Enclosure has recently been rebuilt by archaeologists because it was bulging and in danger of collapse.

From below the lichen-grey curvature of the Great Enclosure you can look across the grassy valley with its phalanxes of ruins and flaming aloes to the hill opposite, crowned also with granite walls.

Ivory and gold

Before Zimbabwe achieved its greatness, Mapungubwe – close to where Botswana, South Africa and Zimbabwe meet – was the southern African capital of the rich gold and ivory trade with distant Arabia and India. But Mapungubwe, the first settlement of what historians call the Zimbabwe culture, was displaced by the Shona of Great Zimbabwe, this pleasant yet powerful place of silent stones.

Although all the people of Great Zimbabwe lived in huts made from thatch and *dagha* (Shona for 'clay' or 'mud'), the rulers surrounded their own dwellings and places of importance with huge circles of stone. This may have been done because there was so much sun-fractured granite available, to maintain royal prestige or simply because they had the cattle-wealth to do it. Defence was probably not a major consideration, either at Great Zimbabwe or at the 150 lesser madzimbabwe that were eventually built.

The valley in front of the Great Enclosure was probably occupied solely by the royal wives, with their children and attendants. Ordinary citizens appear to have lived outside Great Zimbabwe's royal perimeter altogether. The first wife or *vahozi* supervised this area and she probably lived in the oldest enclosure, known as the 'royal treasury', one of her functions being to safeguard the iron gongs, ivory, brass wire, hoes and ceremonial spearheads of the king which, together with a few Chinese and mid-Eastern trade goods, are now in the museum.

Messengers of the gods

The king or *Mambo* lived in ritual seclusion according to Shona custom, on the hill. Many Shona praise-songs refer to chiefs as 'mountains' and this central hill is traditionally the only part of Great Zimbabwe known as *dzimbabwe*, 'the chief's court or house'. It is a stiff walk from the curio shop up the ancient stairway to the Western Enclosure, the king's residence. It was first occupied in about AD 320 and again around 1270 – the golden age – when the first stone walls were built. Surrounding the king were the residences of the royal messenger, the diviner and the senior 'sister' of the ruling line.

The Eastern Enclosure at the other end of the hill is where six of Zimbabwe's ceremonial soapstone birds, ancestral 'messengers of the gods', were found. They were usually placed on upright plinths along the walls. It was the main religious centre, and spirit mediums may have lived there. Great Zimbabwe stretched for four kilometres and there was high-density housing outside the walls, rather like the clusters of buildings around medieval European castles. It was built between 1250 and 1450, growing rich on its cattle herds in this lush summer and winter grazing area and on its control of the gold and ivory trade. Tin, iron bells, copper, salt and soapstone also formed part of a tribute system that supported Great Zimbabwe.

The final abandonment of Zimbabwe was rapid and took place at the close of the 15th century. Oral tradition puts it down to a shortage of salt. Depletion of firewood and trees to make bark nets and sleeping blankets, together with decreasing soil fertility and perhaps a failure of central economic control, were probably important contributory factors. The stone-building tradition, however, continued at Kame, in the west, while the breakaway Mutapa dynasty flourished for a while in the north.

The structures relied for their stability on sheer massiveness and, only recently (in 1995) did archaeologists find it necessary to dismantle and rebuild one of the walls of the Great Enclosure that was bulging and in danger of collapse. The only ancient African structures that can compare in size and grandeur with Great Zimbabwe are the Pyramids of Egypt, themselves built by descendants of black Africans who migrated east from the Sahara when that lush plateau became a desert some 6 000 years ago. The ruins of Great Zimbabwe cover an area of some 720 ha and have been proclaimed a UNESCO World Heritage Site (see pages 320 – 1).

For more information on Great Zimbabwe, contact the AA Office, c/o Magic (Pvt) Ltd, Shop 5, Robert Mugabe Street, Masvingo, tel (139) 62563; the Masvingo Publicity Association (immediately south of the railway on the Beitbridge road edge of town), tel (139) 62643; National Museums and Monuments, PO Box 1060, Masvingo, tel (139) 62080.

Stone wall blends with the rock.

Decorative stonework in a chevron pattern is a recurring feature.

Great Zimbabwe was the creation of the ancestors of modern Zimbabweans.

The impressive 'Great Enclosure'.

Nature's architecture and an imperialist's view of the world

Rhodes Matopos National Park is an area of such outstanding beauty and historical interest that it may be listed as a World Heritage Site. On the way there, we visit one of the finest decorated churches in southern Africa. Overnight stays in the national park must be booked and you may need to obtain tickets to visit Nswatugi Cave.

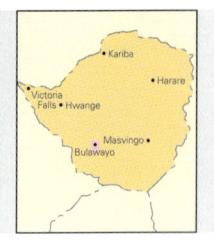

Bulawayo
Cyrene Mission
Whovi Game Park
Nswatugi Cave
World's View
160 – 180 km

LEAVE BULAWAYO BY driving south on Main Street and check your kms as you pass the Post Office on the corner of 8th Avenue. Follow the signs to Plumtree through the light industrial area; 6 km out of town the Plumtree road is crossed by *Si Ye Pamili* (let us go forward) Drive, its name taken from the motto of the City of Bulawayo. The rapidly extending informal settlements give way to thorny scrub and then to ranching country.

At the 28,5 km peg from Bulawayo, turn left into the gravel-surfaced Cyrene road (on which cattle are regularly encountered) and, 2,5 km later, turn left again through the well-marked gateway to Cyrene Mission. A driveway shaded by gum trees leads to the chapel.

Cyrene to Nswatugi Cave

As you leave Cyrene, turn left; 11 km later you reach the main road between Bulawayo and Kezi. Turn right here and note the km pegs along the edge of the road (35 km, on your left). The granite koppies of the Matobo Hills begin to appear all round. The word *Matobo* means 'the bald ones' and refers to the many bare, rocky domes. As you drive southwards, watch out for wild animals; private game farms spread out on both sides of the road and include paddocks for ostrich-breeding. You might be lucky enough to see Nkone cattle, the local indigenous breed, with their white line along the back, white belly and rich red or black flanks, their hides formerly considered ideal for shield-making.

At the 41,5 km peg are the scanty ruins of Fort Inungu, one of the many reminders of the battles that took place between the Matabele and the settlers in 1896. Only a low, weathered earth wall remains.

From now on you can begin to study the amazing shapes of many of the koppies with their balancing rocks. As you pass the 48,5 km peg, you enter the Rhodes Matopos National Park. This is part of Cecil Rhodes' original estate that was bequeathed to the nation. All flora and fauna within the park are protected. Notice the profusion of candelabra trees of two species: *ingens* and *cooperi*.

At the 49 km peg there is a turn-off to Bambata Cave, one of the many that contain large spreads of rock paintings. A walk of some 4 km is necessary to view it, so you may prefer to wait for a cave nearer the road.

At the 56 km peg, turn right to the Whovi Game Park entrance gate. When you pay your entry fee, ask for a map and for advice about the best animal-viewing areas. If you want just a short drive, the 10 km to Mpopoma Dam and back is recommended. There are picnic sites, fishing is permitted and white rhino are seen regularly in this area.

As you leave the game park, turn right onto the main road and immediately left through the National Park entrance gate, heading for Maleme Dam. After about 400 m take the left turn to Maleme via Nswatugi. If you are towing a trailer, you will have to take the shorter route straight on. Note your kms at the turn.

Again you enter an area of granite hills; watch out for tree orchids, game animals and black eagles. The black eagle population of the Matobo Hills is one of the most concentrated in all Africa. Try to spot the many nesting sites on ledges high up on the vertical cliff walls. April to August is the main nesting season. Klipspringers *(Oreotragus oreotragus)* are also fairly common in these hills.

After 4,5 km you reach Musilume Dam with its camping and picnic sites. Its permanent water attracts many animals, including the elusive reedbuck and sizeable herds of wildebeest. At 6 km the road rises very steeply. When you reach the top, look out for the interesting rock bridge on the left. The descent is equally steep and requires the use of a low gear.

Some 7,5 km from the park entrance gate, turn right for Nswatugi Cave; 2 km of this rough road takes you to a parking point from which the cave is a short, well-marked walk. This cave contains some of the best rock art in the area, including wonderfully accurate depictions of kudu and giraffe.

Nswatugi Cave to World's View

Note your kms as you leave the parking area at the caves, drive back to the main route and turn right. At the inclined T-junction 5, 4 km from the caves, take the road left to Maleme Dam. After 1 km, a very steep descent to the dam requires the use of low gear; you reach the dam 2 km from the T-junction. Maleme Dam is a delightful place hemmed in by precipitous rock walls. Waterfowl are common on the lake and the grassy banks attract wart hogs and other grazers. Dassies, klipspringers and eagles inhabit the mountainsides. There are picnic and camping sites on both sides of the water and fishing is permitted.

Note your kms as you drive across the dam wall, from which passengers will enjoy the sight of the jumble of massive, dark grey boulders crammed into the riverbed. A steep ascent, on tar, leads to the rest-camp entrance 2 km from the dam. The lodges and chalets here must be booked in advance at the National Parks office in Bulawayo.

CYRENE
The Cyrene Mission School was started in January 1940 by Canon Ned Paterson and has always concentrated on teaching art and the revival of art as a means of African expression. The paintings on the chapel walls, both inside and out, depict biblical stories and scenes of Christian devotion as seen through the eyes of Africans, most of them students. The murals inside the chapel are even more brilliant and inspirational than those on the outer walls.

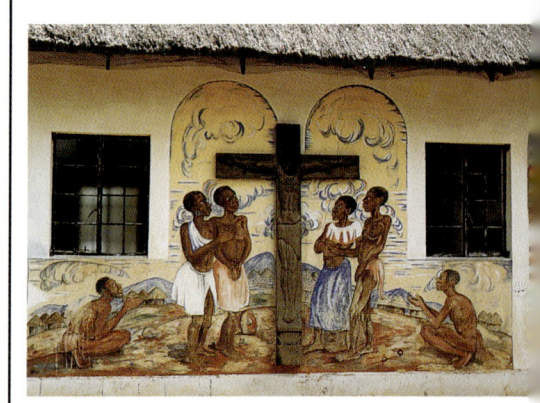

One of the stirring wall-paintings at Cyrene Mission, which was founded in 1940.

A young klipspringer in Matopos National Park.

Beyond the rest camp the road ascends another steep rise through dense vegetation, where glimpses of birds and animals can often be caught. At 3 km from the camp entrance a turn-off on your left leads for 800 m to the Pomongwe Cave and site museum. This huge cave is only 100 m from the car park, but unfortunately the paintings are in poor condition. The site museum depicts aspects of Stone Age culture and paintings.

Some 12 km from Maleme Dam, turn right at the T-junction and, almost immediately, turn left, following the signs to Rhodes' grave, which you reach 4 km later. If you need to brush up on your history, you will find an excellent set of photographs and notes under a

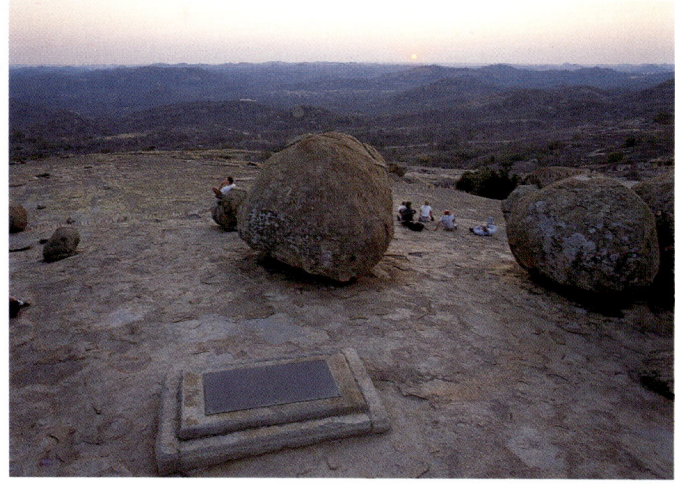

Zimbabweans of untold generations have watched sunsets from World's View.

WORLD'S VIEW

Cecil Rhodes was impressed by the grandeur of the Matobo Hills and, on one of his infrequent visits to this country, he chose this wonderful rocky dome as the place where he wished to be buried.

He called it 'one of the views of the world'; to the Ndebele people the hill is known as *Malindidzimu*, or 'the dwelling place of the benevolent spirits'.

In addition to CJ Rhodes, his great friend LS Jameson, the first Premier of Southern Rhodesia (Charles Coghlan), Allan Wilson and the members of his Shangani Patrol are buried on the hill.

Matobo's rock paintings depict a blend of animals and mystical half-humans.

AN EXCEPTIONAL LANDSCAPE

The unusual and even startling shapes of the granite Matobo Hills fascinate visitors, many of whom imagine that this tumbled landscape might have been formed by some sudden volcanic action. In fact, the enormous domes and the precariously balanced fragments were produced by millions of years of exposure to alternating heat, cold and running water – the basic elements of geological weathering.

A close look at some of the koppies will show that fig trees have sent their roots into the tiniest of cracks, which, as the tree has grown, have been forced further apart. This has merely furthered the work of nature, which has already cracked the rocks along planes of weakness. In time, great slabs have peeled from the domes like the skin off an onion, and continued weathering has created the final bizarre sculptures.

A Matobo's balancing rock formation known as the Mother and Child.

shelter in the car park. The walk up to the grave site is less than 1 km and is not steep.

Retrace your route for 4 km from the car park to the main road and turn left. The road passes the White Rhino Shelter, an overhang with a clear outline of a white rhinoceros. Next on the right (after 8 km on the main road) is the MOTH Shrine, a tranquil, walled garden established by members of the ex-servicemen's organization (Memorable Order of Tin Hats) to commemorate their comrades-in-arms who died in battle. At the T-junction with the Circular Drive, turn right, within site of the exit gate from the national park.

On leaving the park, follow the signs for Bulawayo; 5 km from the park gate a rich spread of Cape Dutch buildings stands on the hillside in front of you. These belong to Rhodes Estate Preparatory School. On this site you will also find the well-preserved Rhodes stables and summerhouse dating from the time when Rhodes used to visit his Matopos Estate. You approach these buildings by following the Bulawayo road and turning left into Charles Murray Drive. The estate now serves as an agricultural research station.

As you continue your journey northwards along the main road, you pass Matopos Dam. This recreational area is noted for its boating and fishing, and was bequeathed in terms of Rhodes' will for the people of Bulawayo to enjoy in perpetuity.

At the 10,5 km peg from the city (the peg is on your right-hand side) you reach the entrance to Tshabalala Game Sanctuary. This small game park offers excellent sightings of many types of antelope, zebra, wart hog and other herbivores. It specializes in wildlife education; there are picnic sites and game walks are available. The main road brings you back into Bulawayo along Robert Mugabe Way.

AA of Zimbabwe Fanum House, cr Leopold Takawira Avenue and Jason Tongogara Street
Bulawayo Tel (19) 70063
Bulawayo Publicity Association PO Box 861
Bulawayo Tel (19) 60867
National Parks (Reservations) 140a Fife Street
Bulawayo Tel (19) 63646

PLACES OF INTEREST IN BULAWAYO

A quiet day on broad, jacaranda-shaded Leopold Takawira Avenue, one of the city's main thoroughfares.

Bulawayo, a king's choice

THE SECOND-LARGEST CITY in Zimbabwe, Bulawayo is set on the highveld in the south-west of the country. Here, in 1893, white settler-soldiers entered the still-smouldering ruins of the principal town of the last Matabele king, the ailing Lobengula, who, having set fire to his capital, withdrew northwards to die as a fugitive.

The city's past
The Matabele people were part of the Ndebele (Zulu) nation of KwaZulu-Natal until their leader, Mzilikazi, quarrelled with King Shaka and fled from his wrath. Mzilikazi and his followers acquired the name *Matabele* (the people who use shields) and, when they settled here in about 1840, this area became known as Matabeleland. Mzilikazi died in 1868 and was succeeded by his son, Lobengula, two years later. Lobengula built his royal town 20 km south of the present city and named it *GuBulawayo*, 'the place of slaughter' – a reference to the civil warfare that preceded his succession. This site is now named Old Bulawayo and there are plans to reconstruct it.

By 1881 the royal town had moved and Lobengula's house occupied the site where State House now stands, 5 km north of the city centre. The Indaba Tree under which the king sat at important meetings is close by, as is the rondavel built for CJ Rhodes on his infrequent visits.

Rhodes arrived a month after the destruction of Lobengula's Bulawayo, and, with LS Jameson, decided that a new town, with the same name as the old, should rise from the ashes.

A spacious design
It was to be laid out as a grid of one square mile, surrounded by parkland. The width of the streets, still a remarkable feature of Bulawayo, was determined by the space required to turn a full span of oxen pulling a wagon. In 1895 the Hillside Dams were constructed to supply the town with water, but by 1896 war had broken out and the townspeople were in laager. A well had to be dug and it is preserved in front of the *City Hall* **(1)**, which was built in Fife Street in 1939 on the site of the laager. An imposing building set in neat gardens, the City Hall houses many items of historical value and has a library for use by serious students of history. Across the car park are the offices of the *Bulawayo Publicity Association* **(4)**, where the staff will help you to plan your visit.

The first train arrived in November 1897 and, in time, Bulawayo became the railway headquarters of the country. The present *railway station* **(2)**, with its notably long platform, was built in 1913 and is not far from the *Railway Museum* **(3)** in Prospect Avenue. The entrance to the museum is the old Shamva railway station, where office equipment of yesteryear is on display. Outside, locomotives and rolling stock that date from the early 1900s make a picturesque contrast to more modern diesel engines. The museum is closed on Monday and Thursday.

Colonial architecture
An attractive old colonial building is to be seen in Main Street on the corner of Leopold Takawira Avenue. *Douslin House* **(5)** was built in 1900 with neo-classical facades ornamented in the Art Nouveau style with delicate cast-iron tracery, balustrades and timberwork. Reconstruction and renovation began in 1991 and were completed in 1994, in time for the building's official opening, during the city's centenary year, as a branch of the National Art Gallery of Zimbabwe. The gallery (which is closed on Monday) has exhibitions of contemporary art and sculpture, a gallery shop and a courtyard café.

Another version of the neo-classical style is the copper-domed *High Court building* of 1935 **(6)** that you see when you walk westwards along 8th Avenue from the City Hall. Designed by the then Director of Public Works, it set standards for many government buildings, both large and small.

Volunteering or part-time soldiering was a popular pursuit of British manhood both at 'Home' (in Britain) and in the colonies. In Bulawayo it is represented by the *Drill Hall* **(8)** at the corner of 10th Avenue and Basch Street. The foundation stone was laid by Cecil Rhodes in 1901 and, in April 1902, his body lay in state in the partially completed building prior to interment in the Matobo Hills. Here, men of the Southern Rhodesia Volunteers and of later units spent their spare evenings practising their parade drill. Since 1967 the old Drill Hall has been the city's

Ornate Douslin House is part of the National Art Gallery of Zimbabwe.

ZIMBABWE

An old steam engine at the museum.

The cool facade of Bulawayo's High Court building retains its dignity.

police headquarters – ask permission before attempting to photograph the building.

Bulawayo is doubly a cathedral city. First, there is the Roman Catholic *Cathedral of St Mary* **(7)**, built in stone in 1903 at the end of 9th Avenue in Lobengula Street. The first Anglican *Church of St John the Baptist* **(9)** was built in March 1895 and it is now the chapel of St Gabriel's Home, between 3rd and 4th Avenues on Jason Moyo Street. The present Anglican *Cathedral of St John* **(10)** dates from 1910 and can be seen on George Silundika Street and 6th Avenue.

Parks and gardens

In addition to the gardens at the City Hall, *Centenary* **(12)** and Central parks are within easy walking distance along Leopold Takawira Avenue. *Central Park* **(11)** has large trees and picturesque walks beyond the fountain close to the road. In Centenary Park a modern building houses the *Museum of Natural History* **(13)**. Exhibits of Zimbabwean wildlife include the second-largest mounted elephant in the world. Other exhibits depict the history and the mineral wealth of the country. In the grounds is an open

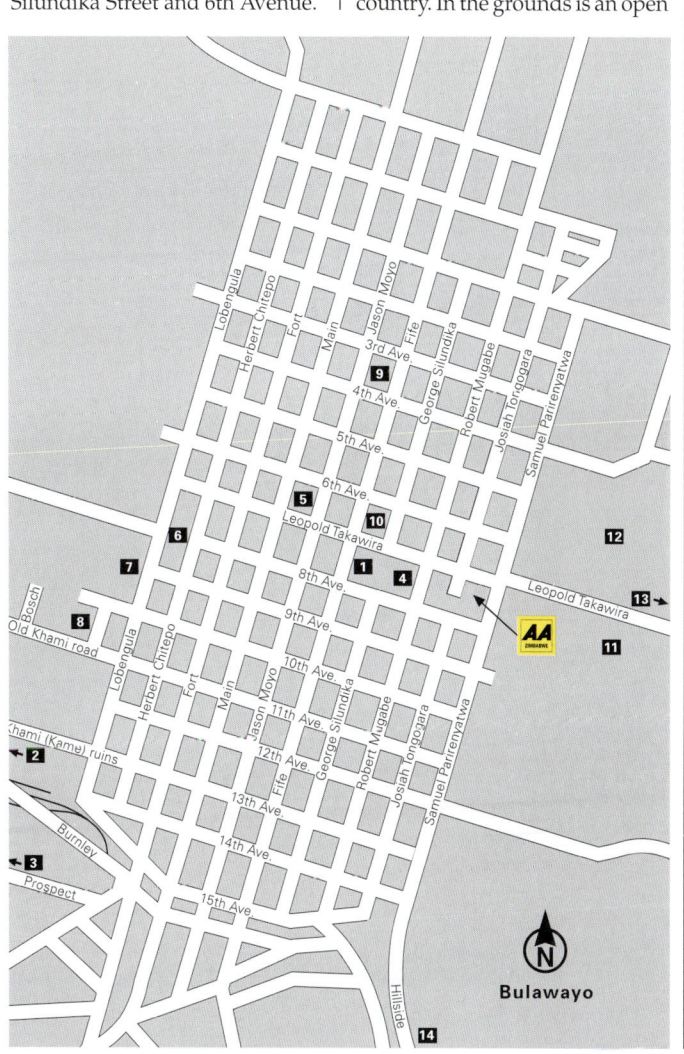

The old colonial-style Drill Hall.

display of mining equipment of the 19th and 20th centuries. The museum is open every day.

The Hillside Dams are a nature reserve and bird sanctuary, with pleasant walks and a tea garden. From the City Hall, go eastwards along Leopold Takawira Avenue and turn right into Samuel Parirenyatwa Street, which becomes Hillside Road, along which the route is well signposted. At the beginning of Hillside Road, you will notice the *Trade Fair and Agricultural Showground* **(14)** on your left; the busy Zimbabwe International Trade Fair is an important annual event held at the end of April.

Arts and crafts

In the City Hall grounds, close to the Publicity Association offices, is the Jairos Jiri Craft Shop, named for its founder and run by an organization concerned with rehabilitating and providing sheltered employment for the disabled. Here you can see a wide variety of rural and traditional crafts on sale. On the pavement in front of the City Hall, an open-air market for curio sellers almost obscures the historic well. Among many items on offer are carved wooden animals, walking sticks, chairs and stools, basketware, beadwork and crochet work.

At the Mzilikazi Art and Crafts Centre on the Old Falls Road, some 3,5 km from the City Hall, you can see hand-thrown pottery of a very high standard. The centre is open from Monday to Friday. (From the City Hall, turn left into Robert Mugabe Way and left again at Masotsha Ndlovu Avenue, which becomes the Old Falls Road.) Close by is the Bulawayo Home Industries Centre, which produces batiks and hand-woven items.

In the same area is the cultural centre called Township Square – full details of the wide variety of activities that take place here may be obtained at the Publicity Association offices.

Outside the city

To visit the Khami (Kame) Ruins – a UNESCO World Heritage Site 22 km west of Bulawayo – leave the city along 13th Avenue (not along 11th Avenue as shown on older maps) through an industrial area devoted to steel. At the 9,5 km peg you pass the Matabeleland Provincial Heroes' Acre on the left. At 15 km a right turn to Khami Prison also leads to the Mazwi Nature Reserve (12 km away). Continue along the Khami Road, taking great care at the narrow bridge over the Khami River (16,5 km). At 19 km, turn right through a brick gateway to Green Gables. It is well signposted. A rough gravel road through the farm leads to the parking area beside the site museum, which houses artefacts discovered at the ruins. Guidebooks are obtainable here. The Passage ruins are as attractive as the Hill ruins. After your visit, retrace your route to 13th Avenue.

Wildlife

If you enjoy seeing wild animals at close quarters you will appreciate the Chipangali Wild Life Orphanage and Research Centre, which is 23 km from the city. Chipangali cares for sick, abandoned and orphaned wild animals. From the City Hall, drive eastwards along Leopold Takawira Avenue. This is the road towards Beit Bridge and Chipangali is clearly signposted. The orphanage is closed on Monday and on Christmas Day.

Mguza Nature Reserve, 15 km from the city along the Victoria Falls road, is 650 ha in extent and has picnic spots, picturesque walks and drives that offer opportunities to see small animals and birds.

327

From the place of thunder to the empire of the mighty elephant

This drive starts from the town of Victoria Falls, but the Zambezi is soon left behind for the relatively dry plains of Hwange National Park. Here, no fewer than 107 animal species – including 30 000 elephant and 15 000 buffalo – and the wilderness of mopane and teak forests are sustained by water from boreholes that feed Hwange's manmade dams and pans.

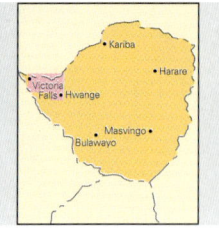

Victoria Falls
Hwange
Sinamatella
Mandavu Dam
Lukosi Mission
Dekadrum
340 – 360 km

VICTORIA FALLS IS A vision of power and splendour unparalleled in Africa. When you have seen Devil's Cataract, strolled through the Rain Forest and braved the white-water rapids in a raft, head south on the Bulawayo Road.

For the first 20 km you pass wayside craft stalls shaded by huge indigenous trees, including mottled black and brown bastard mopane. Gradually the road climbs out of the Zambezi Valley until, 80 km later, you reach the turn-off to Hwange town marked by an old green steam locomotive. Take the right-hand fork and drive 1 km to the town, the roadway divided by banks of flowering bougainvillea.

Retrace your route to the main road, turn right at the junction and, after 500 m, turn left up Baobab Hill; 1 km later, turn left again to reach the Baobab Hotel after a further 1 km. Retrace your route to the main Victoria Falls road and turn left, noting your kms. After 4,6 km, turn right onto the Sinamatella Camp road. The road surface changes to gravel after 8 km and weaves among hillocks and then dense stands of mopane trees until, at 46 km, you arrive at the park entrance (and at Sinamatella Camp), where fuel is available. One of four camps in Hwange (all with chalets), Sinamatella is named after the river that meanders across a vast, dusty plain, best seen from the bluff near the camp's Elephant and Dassie Restaurant. You will need binoculars to spot the elephant, giraffe, wildebeest, zebra and impala far below.

Sinamatella to Hwange dams

From Sinamatella, drive for 13 km to Mandavu Dam – adhering to the 40 km/h speed limit. At the Mandavu Dam sign turn right onto the dam wall and, 1 km later, you arrive at the thatched viewing platform where, if you have booked, it is possible to camp. You should spend at least an hour overlooking this broad sweep of water with its immensely varied life of birds and mammals. Retrace your route for 1 km to the Mandavu Dam turn-off and turn right, noting your kms. Keep straight on this road for some 13 km to reach the smaller Masuma Dam.

Retrace your route from Masuma Dam for 6,1 km and turn left. At the Detema Dam turn-off 19 km later, turn right to reach this peaceful stretch of open water surrounded by thick woodland after a further 2 km. Retrace your route for approximately 36 km to Sinamatella and, from there, for another 45 km to the Victoria Falls road.

Victoria Falls road to Dekadrum

Note your kms and turn right. After 10 km, just before you reach the long bridge over the Lukosi River, you will see, on your left, the silver-domed tower of the 60-year-old missionary church of St Mary. Turn left up the gravel road and, after 800 m, park beneath a large baobab tree. The Spanish missionaries will be happy to show you their church with its fine views over the river, and the chapel mural in which Adam and Eve beam up at a long-bearded God. Retrace your route to Hwange town, a distance of 14 km (refuel if necessary); 1,7 km beyond the town turn right for Dekadrum, which is where the *Deka* (flat) River joins the Zambezi. The tarred road is fairly narrow, with low-level bridges in the passes as it twists downhill, flanked by lovely trees that drop pods like pink confetti in the dry season. The large pipe that follows much of the route supplies water to Hwange Colliery. After some 47 km turn left to reach Tiger Mile fishing resort, its rustic chalets and swimming pool set among large riverine trees a further 2 km on. Retrace your route from Dekadrum for 6 km, where you have a choice of taking the shorter, scenic, gravel road of 103 km (for four-wheel drive vehicles only) back to the Victoria Falls road with a further 13 km to Victoria Falls, or retracing the longer, tarred route of 145 km via the junction approximately 2 km to the west of Hwange town.

AA Office Avis Rent-a-car, cr Livingstone Way and Mellet Drive, Victoria Falls Tel (113) 4532
AA Office Manica Travel, Coronation Drive Hwange Tel (181) 3441
Victoria Falls Publicity Association
cr Livingstone Road/Parkway, Victoria Falls Tel (113) 4202
National Parks Central Reservations
PO Box CY826, Causeway, Harare
Tel (14) 70 6077/8

ELEPHANT CHARGE

You come very close to elephants along Hwange's roads. The park has the world's greatest concentration of these tusked giants, more than is probably ecologically sustainable, as each adult eats 170 kg of grass and leaves and needs 160 litres of water daily – and drops 100 kg of straw-like dung. Not noted as bad-tempered, elephant may nevertheless show aggression, so never hoot at them or get out of your vehicle to take photographs. If an old bull, or a female with young, trumpets, paws the ground or even, ears flapping, makes a mock charge, you are too close. Keep quiet and back off slowly, or switch off your engine and sit still. When an elephant charges with its trunk tucked down between its tusks and its ears held out wide, it will almost certainly carry the movement through to contact. Elephant move exceptionally fast on their large, cushioned pads of feet and 'contact' is inevitably violent and destructive.

Victoria Falls, also known as Mosi-oa-tunya – *'the smoke that thunders'.*

Above: *Elephants, sociably engaged in the shallows at Hwange.*
Right: *A skilled woodcarver at work at Victoria Falls.*

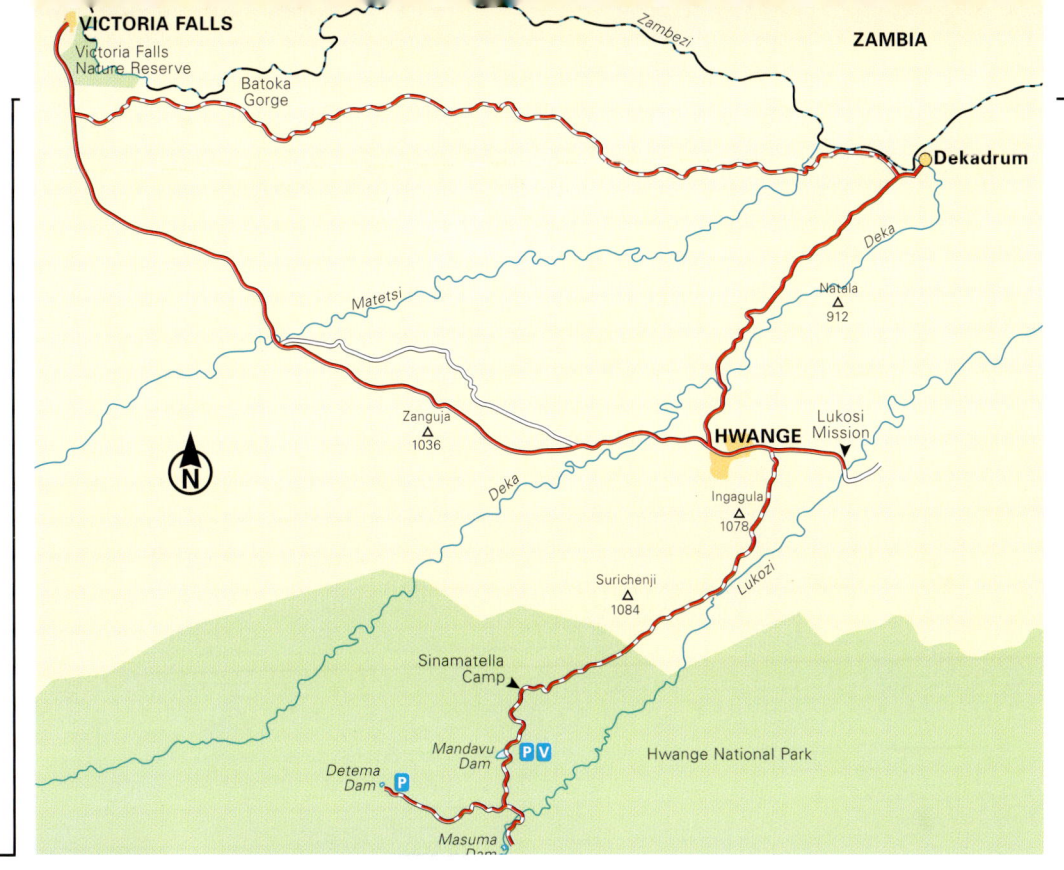

ZIMBABWE

Wildlife conservation at work.

HUNTERS OF THE WILD
Beautiful teamwork characterizes a hunting pack of wild dogs or 'painted dogs', as they are coming to be called because of their mottled dark brown, white and honey colouring. Working in open country, 12 to 15 in a pack, these long-legged hunters with large, rounded ears will run down an impala or even a bulky wildebeest, maintaining a relentless 50 km/h. As the leaders tire, they are replaced by others, snapping and tearing until their panic-stricken prey turns, buckles and is overwhelmed by the yelping pack. And then occurs one of those magic moments of the wild: the ravenous dogs, instead of tearing into their kill, lope back a few metres and allow their pups to feed first – and will ruthlessly savage any opportunistic hyaena that dares to approach. Signs on the Hwange-Victoria Falls road announce 'Beware: Wild dogs crossing' – an event you may be privileged to witness as they sniff excitedly around your car.

THUNDER AND RAINBOWS
It was the Zambezi River approach, with its baobabs, hippo and graceful ilala palms, rather than the Victoria Falls, that explorer David Livingstone described as 'scenes so lovely ... gazed upon by angels in their flight'. But, peering over the edge on 16 November 1855, with Devil's Cataract on his right and the 'thundering smoke' of *Mosi-oa-tunya* rising in billowing updrafts from the tumbling water, the description would have been equally apt. The Victoria Falls is neither the largest, nor the highest, nor the widest waterfall in the world. Its distinction lies in its panoramic 'mile-long' visibility and its breathtaking proximity from grandstand viewpoints in the Rain Forest only 60 m away across the black basalt gorge. As the spray rises to your face, it seems you can reach out and touch the great white curtain of water. A rainbow (sometimes a ghostly version at full moon) frequently graces its awesome splendour.

During the flood season in April and May, some 340 million litres per minute flow over the falls.

The first 'rest huts' of 1898 once stood on the site of the present Craft Village at Victoria Falls.

329

• TAKING A CRUISE ON LAKE KARIBA •

Even to those who have seen it before, the wide, watery sunset over Kariba is a surprising spectacle to encounter in central Africa.

The ingredients for a romantically adventurous sea cruise – on an African lake

SEVERAL TIMES A WEEK the *Sea Lion* and *Sea Horse* car ferries ply the 282 km length of Lake Kariba between Mlibizi, near Victoria Falls, and Kariba. It's a 22-hour adventure-picnic rather than a luxury cruise and offers breezy, open decks for relaxation and opportunities for game-viewing. Sunsets are spectacular, the meals are large and there's even the chance to swim in mid-lake far from curious crocodiles.

From Victoria Falls it is 252 km by road to west Kariba Lake, but many passengers choose to spend their night at the safari-style Mlibizi Hotel in a setting of tropical trees, patio dining, lawns and lakeside bar. Petrol is available at the nearby Mlibizi Zambezi Resort, known too for its bream and tiger-fishing. After a relaxing night, passengers are in good time for the 08h00 check-in at the ferry slipway. Cars line up in the already hot sun as you reverse down the concrete slipway, then onto the steel ramp and into the bowels of the tightly packed *Sea Horse*, which resembles a twin-deck version of an old-fashioned wartime landing craft. Passengers watch from the sun deck as the mooring ropes are released, the ferry's 160 horsepower twin Daf 825 engines reverse their thrust and you are soon being carried smoothly through the 500 m wide exit from Mlibizi creek. Fish eagles, calling from cliff-hanging trees, are clearly audible above the slight mechanical noise and the sound of the water.

The area covered by Lake Kariba is some 5 180 sq km. When the dam was completed in 1959, Kariba was the world's largest manmade lake, but it has been exceeded in water-surface area by Ghana's Lake Volta, which, formed by the Asokombo Dam, reached 8 482 sq km in 1969. As a reservoir, though, Kariba has a greater capacity and, at its deepest, measures some 116 m. The movements of this immensely heavy mass of water cause small earth tremors from time to time.

Coffee is served as the ship's hostess conducts lifeboat drill. The 20 m *Sea Horse* has a large lounge-saloon and a smaller sun deck, divided by a gangway of showers (ladies to port, gentlemen to starboard). It carries nine vehicles and up to 40 passengers,

Sea Horse takes on cargo and passengers at the west ferry terminal, Mlibizi.

while its sister ship, the *Sea Lion*, takes nearly twice this number. A cooling breeze blows through the ferry as it reaches its cruising speed of 7,5 knots (about 22 km/h; note that knots are measured 'per hour' only as a rate of acceleration, not when cruising). To ensure that it has the maximum depth of water beneath the keel, the ferry's course takes it along the

Free from the cares of navigation, passengers enjoy the sun and the scenery.

Caribbea Bay is an appropriate name for a busy inlet of sparkling blue water.

Early morning and Sea Horse *is in.*

Elephants in a houseboat's garden.

With its net swung outboard, a kapenta *rig goes after sardines at sunset.*

underwater channel of the Zambezi (which is the Zimbabwe-Zambia border) out into the lake.

Devil's Gorge to Binga

The crew of a small craft nearby, a rusting iron replica of a whaleboat, paddles furiously to cut across the *Sea Horse's* path, laughing at their dexterity. In the wheelhouse, the skipper disapproves and comments that the traditional *mekoros* or dugouts are rarely seen today. Two hours later, the ferry navigates the Sebungwe narrows, actually about 1 km wide and named after the river that rises high on the Chizarira National Park massif, 50 km inland. Lush green after the December rains, the water-lapped boulder cliffs of Sebungwe stand parched and brown in the summer heat. Ever hunting or hopeful, a pair of grey-headed gulls follow the ferry's wake and a brown-and-white African skimmer flies low over waves freshened by the north-easterly breeze.

The steel monohull ferry carries the latest navigational and radar equipment and a crew of between 12 and 15, ever attentive to their passengers' demands – especially for iced lagers. The ferry will occasionally stop to off-load cargo if the demand is there and – once – even transported live buffalo during a game relocation exercise. A buffet lunch is served as you approach the long bluffs of Binga village, where a 15 km lagoon is fed by the Logola River. Thatched lodges come into view at this fast-growing fishing resort and a Lake Navigation craft speeds briefly alongside to hand over mail for Kariba. Binga's origins go back some 35 years to when the lake flooded and some 50 000 Gwembe Tonga were moved from their ancestral homes along the Zambezi.

Chete to Kariba

Having sailed 90 km by mid-afternoon, the ferry approaches Kariba's largest island, *Chete*. The name means 'that's it' and was given by Tonga fishermen, frustrated and finally philosophical on finding that the swirling rapids in the narrow 800 m gorge prevented them from venturing further. A group of elephant are spotted on a sandy beach and, a little further in Chete Bay, kudu and buffalo are seen at the water's edge. A speedboat races past, everyone waving. Because of droughts, Kariba's water level has dropped several metres in recent years and floodmarks are clearly visible on the rocky banks. Reaching Sengwa Basin, one of the deepest parts of the lake – here 25 km wide – the *Sea Horse* slows, and most of the passengers, having been reassured that no crocodiles have ever been seen so far from land, take a welcome dip from the grid platform at the stern.

As the *Sea Horse* heads for Sibilobilo Lagoon, the sun burns its way down into the lake, creating a fiery pathway across the waters. In the saloon, supper is ready and, soon after, reclining chairs or deck mattresses are selected for the night. Deck mattresses are not always a wise choice – if the lake becomes choppy, a sudden burst of spray wakes the sleeper. The lights of *kapenta* rigs or 'sardine boats' twinkle like fairy lanterns all around and a spotlight catches the eyes of crocodiles as the *Sea Horse* picks its way through the islands of the Kota Kota Narrows and Tigerfish Gap. During the night, the *Sea Horse* chugs on, passing the distant mountains of the Matusadona National Park to arrive after breakfast before the blue hills of Kariba and Andora Harbour.

Kariba town, 367 km northwest of Harare and 490 m above sea level, is whimsically referred to as Zimbabwe's hot spot – temperatures may rise above 40°C during the hottest season. The town was built during the 1950s to house the 10 000 people involved in building the dam and has become one of Zimbabwe's major tourist resorts.

For further information, contact the AA Office, c/o FJ Burdett, Tamarind Lodges, Nzou Road, Kariba, tel (161) 2697; Kariba Ferries (Reservations), PO Box 578, Harare; or Kariba Publicity Association, View Point, Kariba Dam Wall, tel (161) 2328.

A central African riviera shares its waters with hippo and crocodile

Vistas of a shimmering 'sea' greet you at every hairpin turn of the road that winds around the hills of Kariba Village, close to where the massive arch of the dam has tamed the Zambezi that courses below. The return from Kariba to Makuti through the rugged Kaburi wilderness brings you back to lakeside views of game, wading birds and crocodiles.

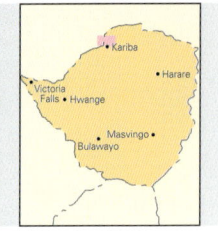

**Kariba Dam
Kariba Heights
Santa Barbara
Church
Makuti
Chawara Harbour
220 – 260 km**

As you leave Kariba Ferries slipway exit, turn left into Leopard Close and immediately turn left again, into Buffalo Drive. After 500 m, turn right into Sable Drive and, after a further 500 m, turn right again at the main Kariba road or Lake Drive. At the Shell service station 500 m further on, turn left and follow the road uphill for some 400 m before turning right to the Observation Point and Information Bureau, which are reached after a further 100 m.

Frangipani trees shade the view down to the dam wall that holds back a lake some 282 km long. The wall contains 1 million cubic metres of concrete and 11 000 tons of reinforced steel. Retrace your route downhill and, at the service station, turn left into Lake Drive; 800 m later, turn left up Kariba Heights Drive and, after a further 1,9 km, on the level saddle near the hospital, turn left up Nature Reserve Drive. This road winds for 1,8 km up to The Peak, with a grand view of Kariba's Andora harbour and the lake spreading into the distance. Turn around and descend about 300 m to another (unmarked) viewsite on the left overlooking the churning Zambezi and ranges of hills. Retrace your route 1,5 km back to the junction, turn left onto the circular Kariba Heights Drive (where, fairly recently, elephants have been known to browse at night), to reach Kariba Village Square after a further 1,8 km.

Kariba Heights to Cloud's End

Surrounding the Square are little shops, the bowling greens of the Kariba Country Club (visitors welcome any day and especially to Sunday games and braais) and the church of Santa Barbara, built by off-duty Italian dam-workers 35 years ago. Lovely stained-glass windows adorn the chapel, which has a plan like that of a circular coffer-dam. Now, with the church on your right, continue for 200 m to where a viewsite opens onto a magnificent panorama of the lake and the blue mountains of Matusadona National Park beyond it. Pause to read the monument to Operation Noah, listing the thousands of animals rescued while 5 000 sq km of the Zambezi Valley was being inundated by the rising waters. Continue downhill for 1,3 km and turn left at the reverse fork; 2,4 km further on turn left onto the main road at the inclined T-junction.

If already feeling the heat, you may want to stop 4 km further on at the service station and Polly's Ice Cream Parlour or follow the signs downhill for 1 km to the lakeside Kariba Breezes Hotel for a dip in their pool. Back at the service station turn right, reaching the Wildlife Society's thatched information centre 9 km later. Here you will learn that Kariba is a protected game corridor facilitating access to the lake for elephant, leopard and buffalo. Watch your speed as you wind along the precipitous road up the Zambezi Valley escarpment for 60 km through the harsh Kaburi Wilderness that links the Hurungwe and Charara safari areas to Makuti and Cloud's End Hotel.

Cloud's End to Mahombekombe

Cloud's End Hotel perches on a hill overlooking the Zambezi Valley crossroads to both Kariba and the Chirundu border post with Zambia. Note your kms at Makuti and retrace your route, travelling at no more than 60 – 70 km/h. This road, incidentally, follows the elephant migration route to the Zambezi. Some 57 km from Makuti turn left at the Nyanyana sign onto a poorly maintained gravel road and, after about 3 km, cross a narrow, low-level bridge. Turn left 800 m beyond the bridge and left again after another 500 m to reach the Lake Crocodile Ranch after a further 1,5 km. Here you can view these chillingly prehistoric creatures basking in long pools according to their age-groups.

KABURI WILDERNESS

Kariba's surprises might include a leopard by the roadside as you turn into your hotel, or an elephant browsing in your driveway. Over 5 000 animals, including 6 anteaters, 10 lions, and one bushbaby, were rescued from islands in the Zambezi Valley when the dam's water level rose. The Operation Noah tradition of preservation is continued by Zimbabwe's Wildlife Society at Kaburi Wilderness. An area of 37 700 ha of lakeshore and wooded sun-blasted hills close to the town now receives its special protection. Even the airport and a banana farm are included in this rugged outback cut by a dozen, often dry, riverbeds. Animals at Kaburi include elephant, lion, the ferocious little honey badger, 33 reptile species and 357 bird types. An ecological school caters for parties of young adventurers.

The crocodile survives on its thick skin and sharp teeth, rather than its brains.

Nyaminyami, the Zambezi river god, gazes down at the captive stream.

POWER AND THE GLORY

At Kariba, the 2 700 km-long Zambezi River is confined in a narrow gorge just 100 m wide. In 1955, or a century after Dr Livingstone visited the Victoria Falls upriver, an Italian construction team sought to block its escape to the Indian Ocean. Ignoring the anger of Nyaminyami, the River God, the first coffer-dam, a concrete circle in the river, was sufficiently advanced to withstand the floods of 1957. But the next year brought near disaster when unprecedented rains caused the river to rise 35 m. A leak in the main coffer-dam, behind which the ramparts of the wall were being laid, collapsed the road bridge and ripped away the high suspension bridge. But work doggedly continued in the relentless 50°C heat, forcing workmen to carry their tools in buckets of water. By 1959 the wall was complete, a soaring crescent 128 m high and 500 m wide. A granite memorial in Santa Barbara Church records the names of the 86 people who died during the period of its construction.

Note your kms as you retrace your route for 1,5 km, turn left at the reverse fork and left again after 300 m. You then drive between high mopane trees for 1,5 km to reach Kaburi Wilderness headquarters and camp site on the lake shore. Note your kms and retrace your route; pass the entrance to the Crocodile Ranch after 1,8 km and turn left 700 m later. At the crossroads 1,7 km later, turn left again for Chawara harbour buildings, 500 m ahead.

Keep to the right of the buildings and follow this dirt track for another 2 km to a wide plain where the lake has receded. Here you will be able to see zebra, impala, hippo and buffalo grazing not far from where the Mississippi-style paddle steamer, *Southern Belle*, is moored. Kapenta rigs – noisy, diesel-driven, steel-hulled fishing boats – leave from here in the late afternoon, trailed by flights of swooping terns.

Retrace your route to the crossroads (2,1 km), note your kms and turn left; follow the power lines for 5 km and then turn right onto the tarred Cutty Sark Hotel road. After 1 km turn left at the junction onto the main road back to Kariba and, 5 km later, turn left again at the Mahombekombe township turn-off. Take the left fork after 500 m, to reach the Kariba Ferries turn-off at the Hudson's taxidermy sign after a final 1,5 km.

AA Office c/o FJ Burdett, Tamarind Lodges Nzou Road, Kariba Tel (161) 2697
Kariba Publicity Association View Point, Kariba Dam Wall Tel (161) 2328
Wildlife Society PO Box 275, Kariba Tel (161) 2705
Zambezi Society PO Box HG996, Highlands Harare Tel (14) 71 3596

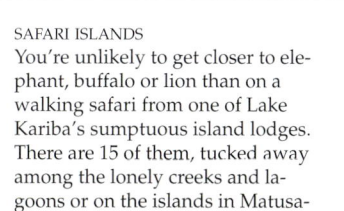

An idyllic Kariba day comes to a colourful end.

A sheltering canopy of ana trees (Acacia albida).

Close-up game-viewing from a canoe is one of Kariba's delights.

SAFARI ISLANDS

You're unlikely to get closer to elephant, buffalo or lion than on a walking safari from one of Lake Kariba's sumptuous island lodges. There are 15 of them, tucked away among the lonely creeks and lagoons or on the islands in Matusadona's mountainous park. Reached by light aircraft or speedboat, they support abundant game that feeds on the green panicum grass of the shores. Because of their aquatic environment, the islands also offer an extravagant mix of bird life. Boat excursions among the drowned trees of the shoreline provide unparalleled opportunities to photograph fisheagle, hippo and crocodile. You may decide on tigerfishing at Mlibizi, in the west, or opt for the luxury of a sailing safari aboard a catamaran. Each of the resorts has its own special appeal.

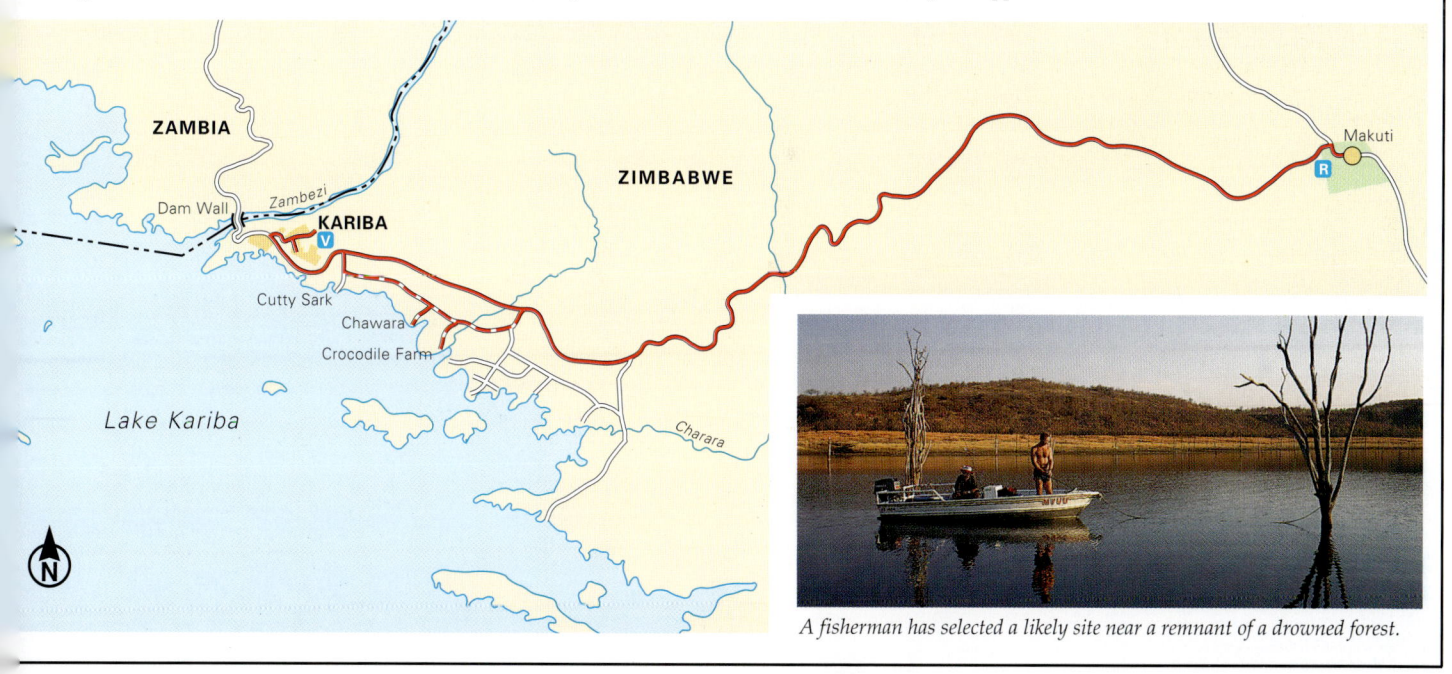

FISHING FOR TIGERS

The world's largest freshwater angling competition is reputed to be the Zimbabwe Tigerfish Tournament, held annually on Lake Kariba. It takes place in October, when the temperature has been known to soar to 57°C, making Kariba the hottest holiday resort on earth, at least for a day or two. Some 500 boats and 1 500 fishermen laden with rods, tackle boxes, bait and mountains of iced beer descend on Kariba's silvery sea to do battle with the tiger. The record catch is 15,8 kg. This striped orange and silver predator-fighter lunges with interlocking, razor-like teeth at spoon, spinner and swivel in violent zigzag rushes, twisting lines around sunken trees and leaping clear out of the water to throw the hook. The bony tiger is not really good to eat, but the lake's bream are delicious and the kapenta sardines, deep fried, make an excellent snack at the cocktail hour.

A fisherman has selected a likely site near a remnant of a drowned forest.

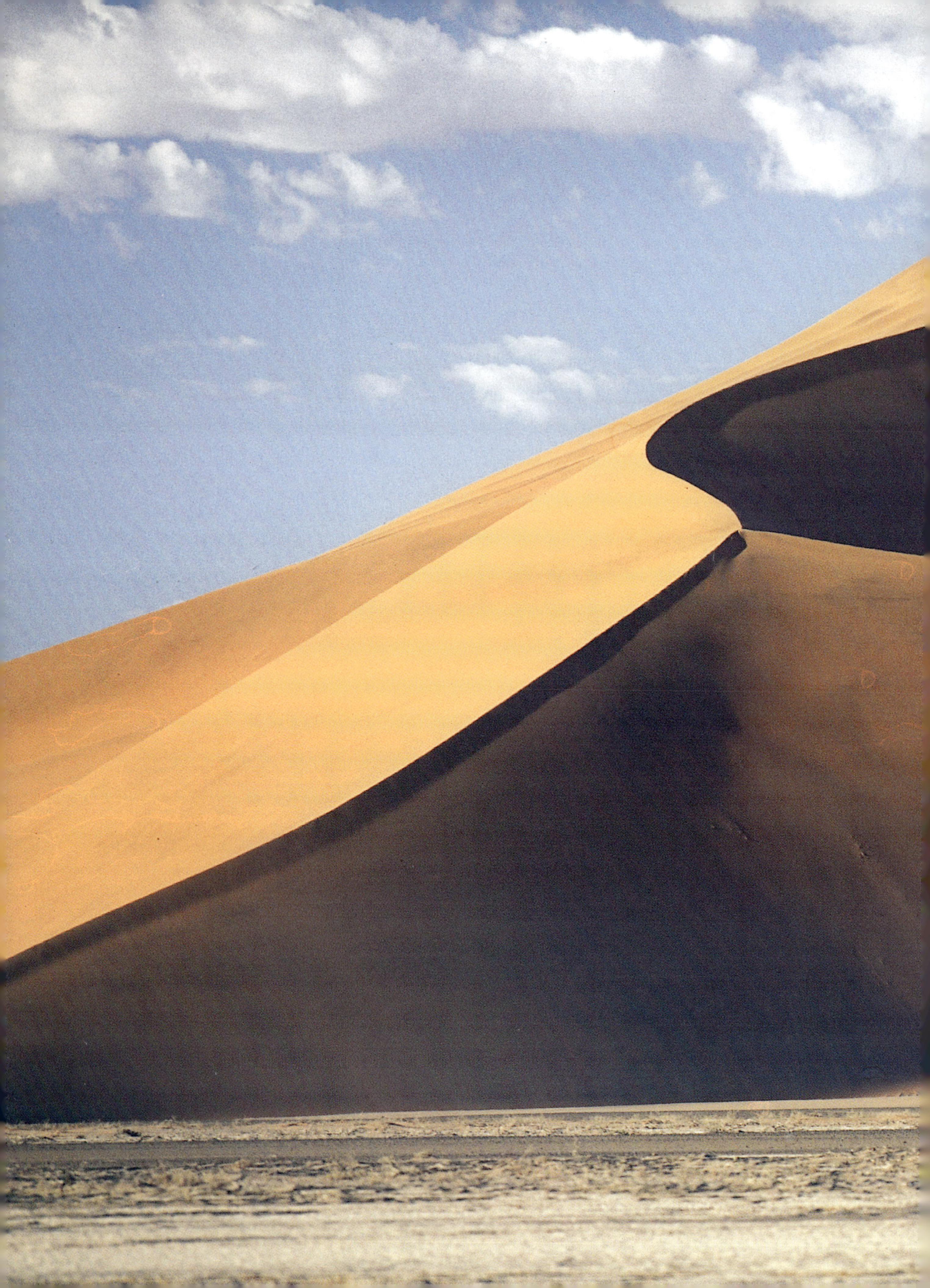

NAMIBIA

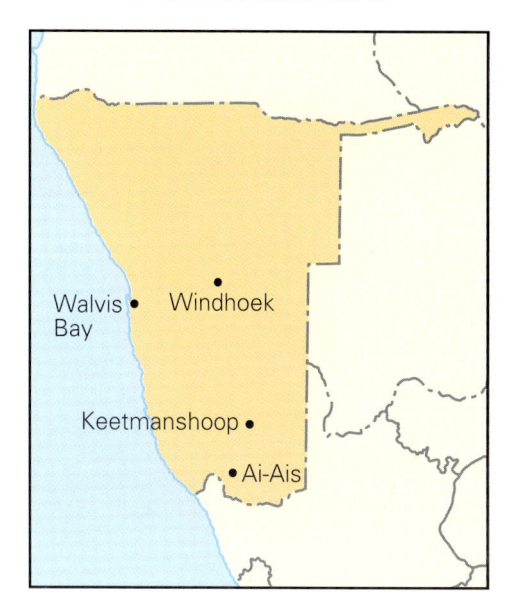

Keetmanshoop – Fish River Canyon – Ai-Ais **336-7**

Etosha National Park: Wildlife throngs a vast, shallow lake **338-9**

Windhoek – Gamsberg Pass – Namib-Naukluft Park **340-1**

Windhoek: German castles in an African capital **342-3**

Walvis Bay – Swakopmund – Henties Bay – Cape Cross **344-5**

Left: The shifting sand dunes of Sossusvlei are the highest in the world.

Lonely graves on the road to one of Nature's remarkable excavations

This two-day drive includes the awesomely vast and lonely Fish River Canyon. In summer, temperatures of 50°C are not uncommon and the route is best tackled between mid-March and 31 October when the long drive can be broken overnight at Ai-Ais. The return journey includes the Quiver Tree Forest. Well over half the drive is on gravel roads.

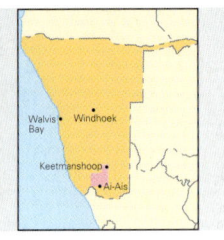

Keetmanshoop
Naute Dam
Fish River
Canyon
Ai-Ais
Quiver Tree
Forest
565 – 585 km

LEAVE THE CENTRE of Keetmanshoop by driving south along Fifth Avenue, noting your kms. After 1,5 km, turn right onto the B1. Keep straight after 700 m (you are now on the B4) where the B1 splits off to the left. Among scenery dominated by flat-topped ridges, the dolerite-capped Kaiserkrone is a prominent landmark on your right. At 34,3 km, turn left onto the D545, noting your kms; 16,5 km later you reach the turn-off to the Naute Dam's Water Purification Works. To visit the dam (open daily from 08h00 to 18h00), turn left here and drive for about 600 m to reach the Purification Works and collect the key to the viewpoint overlooking the dam.

Retrace your route for 600 m and bear left when you rejoin the D545, continuing for 1 km to the turn-off for the dam. The entrance gate is reached about 250 m further on and the viewpoint is a short distance past the gate. Built on the *Löwen* (lions) River, the Naute Dam nestles among black dolerite koppies and has one of the most scenic settings in Namibia, where many 'rivers' are rivers of sand.

Naute Dam to Fish River Canyon

After visiting the dam, return the keys and note your kms as you rejoin the D545. At 1,7 km the road crosses the Löwen River and at 17,6 km you cross a railway line and, about 100 m further on, turn left onto the C12. Your view here is bounded on the left by the Little Karas Mountains. At 58,5 km you reach the railway siding of Holoog on the northern bank of the Gaub River, a major tributary of the Fish River. Pull off the road just before crossing the river, to view the graves of two German soldiers killed in the war against the Namas in 1906. The graves are shaded by a camelthorn tree.

Continuing south, you recross the railway line at 66,4 km and, some 800 m further on, turn right onto the D601, noting your kms. At 18,3 km you cross a cattle grid marking the northern boundary of the Ai-Ais Nature Reserve that forms part of the 346 117 ha Fish River Canyon Conservation Area. At 26 km a deep valley on your right is the first indication that you are approaching the canyon. Ignore the turn-off to Ai-Ais at 30,8 km, driving straight ahead for 2,6 km to the gate at Hobas, where entry fees are payable to visit the

FISH RIVER CANYON

Second in size only to the Grand Canyon in the United States of America, the Fish River Canyon is one of the world's great natural wonders. It meanders for 160 km through the barren landscape of southern Namibia, reaching a depth of 547 m and a width of 27 km and is really a canyon within a canyon. The upper canyon was formed some 500 million years ago when part of the floor was thrust upwards to form the eastern and western rims, while the lower canyon was carved through the rock over countless aeons by the Fish River. Animal life is scarce, but includes a few troops of baboons, the sure-footed Hartmann's mountain zebra, klipspringer, leopard and smaller animals such as dassie, dassie rat and ground squirrel. The backpacking route from the northernmost viewpoint to Ai-Ais is one of the most popular in southern Africa and, between May and September each year, thousands of hikers set off on this gruelling 85 km trail.

Sand, wind and water have carved the deep and sinuous Fish River Canyon.

AI-AIS

Situated in the lower reaches of the Fish River Canyon, the resort at Ai-Ais owes its existence to the thermal spring that surfaces here. The early Khoikhoi inhabitants of the area named the spring *Ai-Ais*, a Nama name translated as 'fire water' – a reference to the water which has a temperature of 60°C when it surfaces. The mineral-rich water has been exploited for recreational purposes since after World War I.

The modern rest camp offers accommodation ranging from luxury flats to huts and campsites. In addition to the outdoor thermal pool there is a modern indoor spa, restaurant, shop, tennis courts and a petrol station. Because of the extreme summer temperatures, the resort is closed from 1 November until the second Thursday in March. The surrealistic moonscape surroundings were created over millions of years by the many tributaries of the Fish River that have carved the landscape into a maze of valleys and ridges.

Above: *A giant's playground of boulders.* **Right:** *The indoor pool at Ai-Ais.*

viewsites on the edge of the canyon. Hobas is conveniently situated close to the viewsites, and amenities include shady campsites, a swimming pool, kiosk and communal ablution blocks. Note your kms as you leave the office and, after travelling west for 10 km, pass a turn-off to the Sulphur Springs and several other viewsites to reach, 1,5 km later, the Main Viewsite, where there are picnic places with braai facilities and toilets. You can find other views by following the rather rocky track that winds northwards from the Main Viewsite for about 2 km to Hikers' Point, start of the Fish River Canyon Backpacking Trail. Alternatively, you can take the track to the Sulphur Springs viewsite, but the views are not as spectacular and the road is rather bumpy.

Fish River Canyon to Ai-Ais

From the Main Viewsite, retrace your route for 14,3 km and turn right onto the D324, noting your kms. After initially heading across plains dotted with clumps of euphorbias and the occasional quiver tree, and with distant views of the canyon, the road winds among granite koppies and at 43,6 km you join the C10. If you are travelling through the area during the period when Ai-Ais is closed, turn left here and continue for 52 km to the B1. However, if you are headed for Ai-Ais, turn right; pass the turn-off to the D316 after 12,6 km and continue straight on the C10, which follows a river valley carved through the ancient rocks. At 64 km you pass through a narrow poort to reach the entrance gate to the Ai-Ais Hot Springs some 3 km further on.

Ai-Ais to Keetmanshoop

After a night at Ai-Ais, follow the C10 for 75 km to its junction with the B1 (a tarred road) where you turn left, noting your kms. At 32 km you pass the small farming settlement of Grünau and at 58 km the road meanders through the western outliers of the Great Karas Mountains. Further north, the road traverses the sparsely vegetated plains of the Karas region and, at 149 km, you cross the Löwen River, reaching the junction with the B4 at 196 km. Turn right to stay on the B1, bypassing Keetmanshoop, to reach the turn-off onto the C16, just north of the town. Turn right, noting your kms, and, after about 800 m, turn left onto a gravel road that leads to the turn-off for the Quiver Tree Forest, reached at 13,1 km. Turn left here and continue for 500 m to the farmhouse where an entry fee is payable, and another 700 m to the parking area.

After visiting the Quiver Tree Forest, return to the main gravel road (C17), turn left and continue towards Koës for 4,2 km to the turn-off for the Giant's Playground. Turn right, pass through the gate and drive about 300 m to the parking area. A well-marked circular walk of about 10 minutes winds among the mad jumble of dolerite boulders, balanced precariously on top of one another and creating the impression of a giant's abandoned playthings.

To return to Keetmanshoop, retrace your route for 17,3 km to the B1 and turn left, continuing for 1,6 km to the northern entrance to the town. Turn right here, to reach the town centre after 1,5 km.

Ministry of Environment and Tourism
(Reservations) Private Bag 13267, Windhoek
Namibia Tel (061) 23 6975
Southern Tourist Forum Private Bag 2125
Keetmanshoop, Namibia Tel (0631) 22905/4

KEETMANSHOOP

Situated on the banks of the Swartmodder River, Keetmanshoop developed around the Rhenish mission station established in 1866. The town was named after the chairman of the Rhenish Mission Society, Johann Keetman. In 1890 the Swartmodder River came down in flood and swept away the church built 22 years earlier by the first missionary, Johan Schröder. A new church, built from dressed stone, was inaugurated in 1895 and now serves as a museum that depicts the early history of Keetmanshoop and its surroundings. Other historic buildings include the Old Post Office with its pointed gable and rectangular tower (opposite the park in the centre of town), Schutzenhaus in Gibeon Street and the old hospital, known as the Johanniter House, in Second Avenue. Keetmanshoop is the largest town in the south of Namibia and administrative centre of the Karas Region, southernmost of the country's 13 regions.

Above: *The old Rhenish church in Keetmanshoop.* **Below:** *A rare forest of quiver trees, of the aloe family.*

THE QUIVER TREE FOREST

The quiver tree or *kokerboom* (*Aloe dichotoma*), a plant characteristic of arid areas north of Namaqualand, usually grows singly or in small groups. However, on the farm Gariganus, near Keetmanshoop, some 250 of these tree aloes grow closely together to create the effect of a forest. Young trees have smooth, pearl-grey stems, but as they age the bark peels off in large flakes, forming light, yellowish patterns. Large specimens can grow up to 9 m high, with a diameter of 1 m at ground level, and the estimated lifespan is between 200 and 300 years. The first bright yellow flowers bloom when the trees are between 20 and 30 years old, and many birds are attracted to the nectar – mostly in June and July. The fibrous branches were hollowed out by the San who used them as quivers (*kokers* in Afrikaans) for their poisoned arrows – hence the name.

THE WILDERNESS HAVEN OF ETOSHA

Visitors to eastern Etosha sleep secure in Fort Namutoni, once the headquarters of schutztruppen *(colonial troops) of imperial Germany.*

Exploring the grandness of 'the great white place'

CENTRED ON THE WHITE expanses of Etosha Pan, the Etosha National Park in northern Namibia is a world of shimmering mirages and seemingly endless stretches of mopane veld. It is also one of Africa's great game reserves.

The heart of the park, the Etosha Pan stretches 125 km from east to west and 55 km from north to south, with a variation in height of only 13 m. Until about 80 000 years ago it was a vast inland lake, fed by the waters of the Kunene River. But when the river changed its course, the lake dried. Today, large areas of the pan's sun-baked clay floor are inundated only during years of exceptional rainfall that covers it in a brine between 20 and 50 cm deep.

The early San inhabitants of Etosha, the Heikum, attributed the origins of this massive saline desert to the tears of a mother who mourned the death of her baby following a battle in which all except the women were killed. As she wept inconsolably, her tears formed a huge lake and when the sun dried the tears only the salt-encrusted ground was left behind. Harsh though it seems, this environment supports no fewer than 114 mammal species, some 390 bird species and a rich diversity of reptiles and amphibians.

Wildlife haven

The park has been a refuge for large herds of game and other animals ever since an area of 93 240 sq km was set aside as Game Reserve Two by the German administration in 1907. During the next 63 years the park's boundaries were redrawn several times, until it was finally reduced from 99 526 sq km to the 22 270 sq km of today.

One of Etosha's attractions is the relative ease with which large herds of game can be seen at the waterholes fringing the pan. Game-viewing is especially rewarding during the dry winter months, when most trees are bare – improving visibility – and when the animals are reluctant to venture far from the perennial waterholes.

The animals of Etosha are typical of the southern savannah plains of Africa. The lively springbok is the commonest large animal, and there are large herds of Burchell's zebra; the ungainly blue wildebeest is also seen, as are giraffe and elephant. Kudu are abundant, and so are gemsbok, and seeing one of these hardy antelope walking purposefully across the vast expanse of the pan is an unforgettable sight. Two other antelope species, the red hartebeest and eland, are less frequently seen.

Etosha is renowned for its large population of lions (numbering between 180 and 220) and visitors seldom leave the park without seeing 'the king'. Although common, leopard are shy and your chances of seeing this largely nocturnal creature and the spotted hyaena, the most abundant large predator in the park, are best during the early morning hours. Cheetah also occur, but because of the relatively small population – estimated at between 70 and 100, you would be fortunate to see one. Among the smaller predators are the black-backed jackal, bat-eared fox and African wildcat.

Rewards of a night watch

In addition to its large numbers of game, Etosha is a sanctuary for several species that are classified as rare or endangered in Namibia. Among these are the black-faced impala, which is endemic to north-western Namibia and south-western Angola, and the diminutive Damara dik-dik, a firm favourite with visitors. Also occurring is the roan, reintroduced in 1970 from north-eastern Namibia, but this antelope is seen only in the vicinity of Ozonjuitji m'bari in the west. Hartmann's mountain zebra, a close relative of the Cape mountain zebra, is found only in the extreme west of the park, in the rocky terrain of Otjovasandu.

Etosha protects one of the world's largest populations of the endangered black rhino. Despite their size, they are difficult to spot because they usually rest in the shade of thickets during the day. However, a night watch of a few hours at Okaukuejo's floodlit waterhole is usually rewarded with good sightings.

White rhino were reintroduced in 1995 when 10 animals from the Kruger National Park were released in the Halali area. Indications are that they have adapted well to their new

Left: *A suspicious springbok looks up as zebra and wildebeest drink.*

The dainty, diminutive dik-dik.

environment and, although they range widely, sightings are occasionally reported by tourists.

The only member of the Big Five that does not occur in Etosha is the buffalo, a species that became locally extinct in the late 1950s. Another such species is the wild dog – attempts to reintroduce this endangered predator have unfortunately not succeeded.

Birds in the bush
Bird life is prolific and the checklist exceeds 390 species. Conspicuous birds include the ostrich, secretary bird, kori bustard, black korhaan, the showy lilacbreasted roller and the noisy scimitarbilled woodhoopoe. Among the raptors are whitebacked, whiteheaded and lappetfaced vultures, martial eagle, bateleur, pale chanting goshawk and the pygmy falcon.

Fischer's Pan, north-east of Namutoni, supports a variety of birds after the summer rains, and among them are marabou storks, flamingoes, more than 10 species of duck and several summer migrants. Good rainy seasons, when large areas of the pan are inundated, attract over a million flamingoes, large numbers of white pelicans and a rich variety of other waterbirds.

The park's vegetation ranges from mopane woodland and savannah (the mopane accounts for 80 per cent of all Etosha's trees), dense tamboti and terminalia woodlands to the almost barren, saline pan. Fringing the pan are halophytic (salt-loving) grasses and small shrubs that give way to the highly nutritious sweet grassveld.

One of Etosha's best-known attractions is the Haunted or Moringa Forest with its dense concentration of strangely shaped moringa trees. It has been suggested that the trees owe their grotesque shapes to extensive browsing by game. The moringa usually favours rocky mountain slopes and hillsides, but here – quite atypically – several hundred trees grow on the plains, a phenomenon that botanists have not been able to explain. The Heikum San attributed the weird growth forms to the fact that the trees were cast from heaven by the God of Nature and landed upside down with their twisted roots pointing skywards.

Rest camps and amenities
A network of roads covering over 700 km traverses the grassveld along the edge of the pan and the woodlands, linking the park's three tourist camps to about 30 waterholes. Because of the danger posed by wild animals, visitors may alight from their vehicles only in the rest camps and at a number of enclosures where toilets and limited, basic picnic facilities are provided. Except for the 12 km access road between Von Lindequist Gate and Namutoni and the 17 km stretch of road between Andersson Gate and Okaukuejo, all roads are gravel-surfaced, but are generally well maintained.

Visitors are well catered for in the rest camps – Namutoni in the east, Okaukuejo in the west and Halali, situated more or less equidistant from Namutoni and Okaukuejo. Accommodation ranges from rooms in the historic Fort Namutoni to self-catering bungalows and caravan/camp sites. Each camp has a shop stocked with groceries, frozen meat, liquor and curios, a restaurant that serves buffet breakfasts, lunches and dinners, a swimming pool and a petrol station. The rest camps have floodlit waterholes. A natural viewsite among the dolomitic rocks of Tsumasa Koppie at Halali looks down onto the Moringa waterhole. At Namutoni a viewing platform overlooks the waterhole.

Regal and unafraid, a lion near Halali watches the camera.

An elephant feeds on arid thornveld.

Namutoni
For many tourists a visit to the Etosha National Park is not complete without seeing Fort Namutoni. Construction of the first fort, a six-roomed building, was begun in 1899, but it was destroyed five years later in an attack by Ovambo warriors. In 1906 a second fort, an irregular quadrangle with four turrets, was completed, but six years later the fort was closed. During World War I it was briefly occupied by German soldiers and it was later periodically used as a police station. It was opened as tourist accommodation in 1958.

The area to the west of Ozonjuitji m'bari is currently open only to tour operators registered with Namibia's Ministry of Environment and Tourism. Plans are afoot to create a fourth rest camp in the Otjovasandu area in the extreme west of the park, which will be built and managed by private enterprise.

How to get there
There are two entry points – Andersson Gate in the east, which provides access to Namutoni and Galton Gate, conveniently situated near Okaukuejo rest camp.

Namutoni rest camp, 533 km north of Windhoek, is reached by following the B1 through Okahandja, Otjiwarongo, Otavi and Tsumeb. About 82 km north of Tsumeb, turn left onto the C38 and continue for 24 km to Andersson Gate. The rest camp is reached 12 km further along a tarred road. Okaukuejo rest camp, 435 km north of Windhoek, is reached by following the B1 through Okahandja and Otjiwarongo. Follow the C38 from Otjiwarongo to reach Galton Gate about 100 km after passing through Outjo. Okaukuejo rest camp is reached 18 km further.

Address requests concerning reservations to the Director of Tourism (Reservations), Private Bag 13267, Windhoek, Namibia. Tel (061) 23 6975, fax (061) 22 4900.

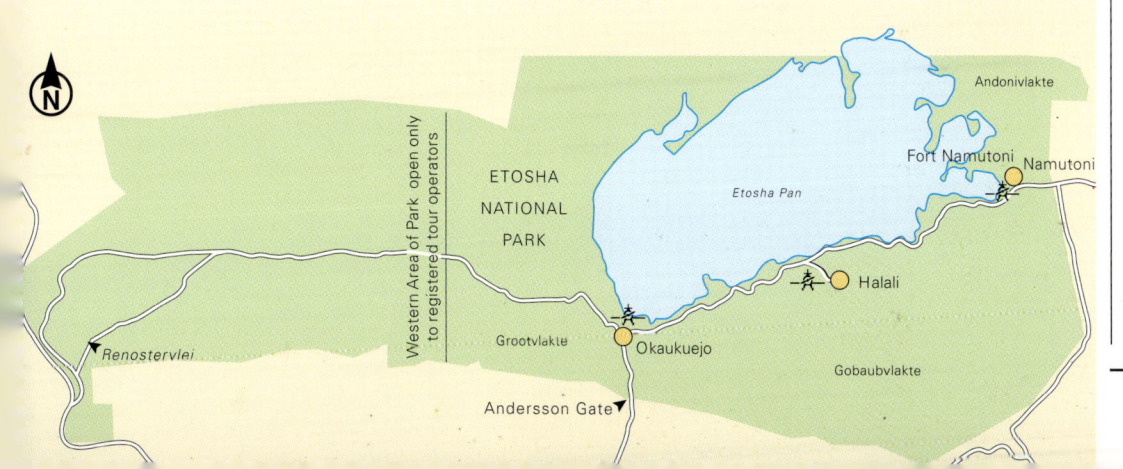

From the Khomas Hochland to the sand sea of the Namib

We descend from the Khomas Hochland down the Gamsberg Pass to the plains of the Namib and to Sesriem, where we explore the Sesriem Canyon and then pass through an endless sea of dunes to reach Elim Dune by sunset. Early next morning we leave for Sossusvlei and head back for Windhoek via the Remhoogte Pass. Almost the entire route is on gravel roads.

**Windhoek
Gamsberg Pass
Sesriem
Sossusvlei
820 – 840 km**

LEAVE WINDHOEK by driving south along Independence Avenue, noting your kms at the main post office. After 300 m turn right into Peter Müller Street and, 200 m further on, turn left into Mandume Ndemufayo Avenue, which you follow to its junction with the Western Bypass at 6,9 km. Note your kms as you continue straight on the C26. At 4,9 km the tar ends and, after 3 km, you reach the start of the Kupferberg Pass that winds for about 10,7 km to the Khomas Hochland plateau.

The road now meanders across the undulating hills of the Khomas Hochland, a cattle-farming region. At 29,9 km turn left, noting your kms, and continue on the C26. At the major junction at 71 km bear right and continue along the C26, which heads towards the Gamsberg – a tabletop mountain rising 600 m above the Khomas Hochland. At 93 km you reach the start of the Gamsberg Pass, and reach the summit 1 km further on. Pull off the road here to enjoy the spectacular view of the deeply dissected valleys of the escarpment giving way to the Namib plains.

Gamsberg Pass to Sesriem

As the road descends, many tight corners require careful driving as there are no safety barriers; 8 km from the summit the road begins to wind along the river valleys at the foot of the escarpment. Heed the warnings about the dangers of river crossings (the rivers flow only after rain) and sharp bends and be alert for cattle on the road. At 157 km turn left at the junction with the C14, noting your kms. The road continues across the sparsely vegetated Namib plains and at 17 km you reach the start of the Gaub Pass; 3 km further on there is a delightful picnic spot on the right-hand side of the road. Immediately after crossing the low-level bridge over the Gaub River, the road climbs out of the rugged valley, continuing across the Namib plains.

After travelling on the C14 for 73 km, turn right onto Route 36, noting your kms; about 300 m later you pass the turn-off to Solitaire, a farm where you can stop for a cup of tea, stock up with cool drinks and refuel. Continuing along Route 36, you pass a picnic site on your right, just before you cross the Tsondab River at 8,4 km.

The road twists around granite hills and at 41 km you enter the corridor connecting the Naukluft section of the Namib-Naukluft Park to the dune sea. Small herds of springbok and gemsbok and flocks of ostriches are frequently seen here. At 44 km you pass a picnic site at Middelpos and 18 km later you reach another picnic spot.

After travelling along Route 36 for 71 km, turn right onto the D826, noting your kms. At 6,9 km you pass a picnic spot and, 5 km later, the entrance to Sesriem, the gateway to Sossusvlei. Facilities at Sesriem consist of the state-owned campsite, a swimming pool, a shop that stocks non-perishable groceries, and a filling station. Alternatively, you can stay at the adjacent Karos Sossusvlei Lodge, situated just outside the park. Follow the signposted road from the Sesriem office for some 4 km to reach the interesting Sesriem Canyon; a late

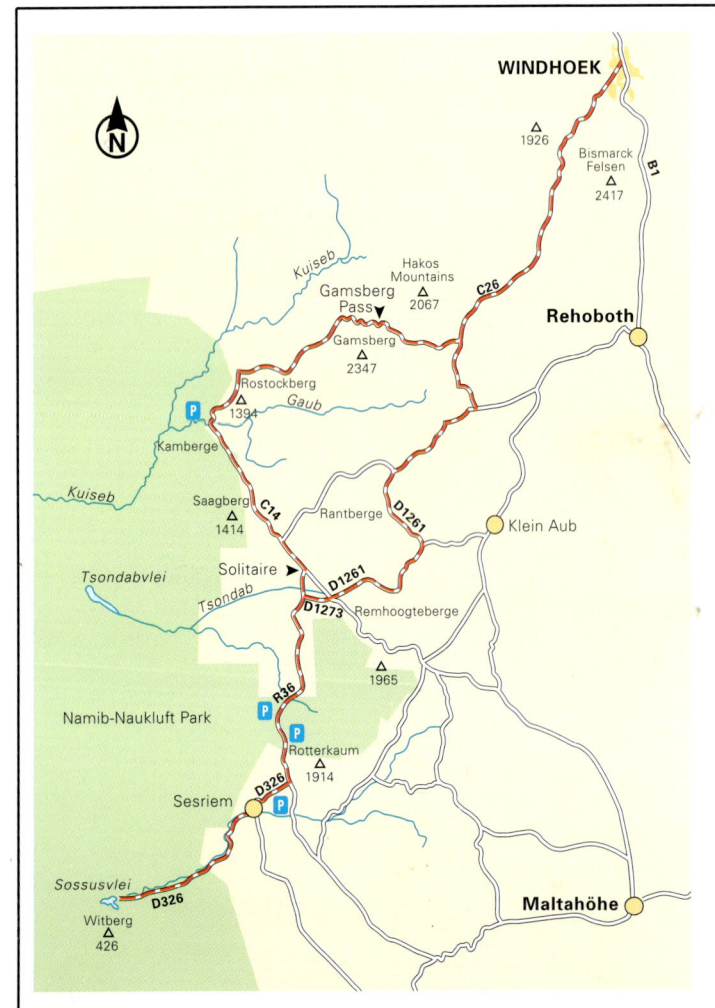

Like stiffly moving waves, the slow creep of dunes changes the landscape.

NAMIB-NAUKLUFT PARK
Covering nearly five million hectares of desert, the Namib-Naukluft Park is one of the largest conservation areas in Africa. It stretches from Lüderitz northwards along the Namib coast to Swakopmund, a harsh tract of desert that is home to the gemsbok with its rapier-sharp horns, the sprawling *Welwitschia mirabilis* and a multitude of *toktokkie* (tenebrionid) beetles and other creatures that are found nowhere else in the world. The scenery varies from vast gravel plains interrupted by occasional granite *inselbergen* (island mountains) between the Swakop and Kuiseb rivers, to the seemingly endless dune sea that is accessible only from Sesriem. In the east, the park links up with the rugged Naukluft Mountains, sanctuary to the rare Hartmann's mountain zebra. Also forming part of the park is Sandwich, a wetland of international importance, south of Walvis Bay. The first step towards protecting this fascinating desert was taken in 1907 when the gravel plains between the Kuiseb and the Swakop rivers were set aside as a conservation area by the German colonial government.

afternoon drive to Elim Dune, renowned for its spectacular sunsets, is not to be missed.

Sesriem to Sossusvlei and back
This is another long day, so you should be ready to set off when the gate opens – usually an hour before sunrise. Guests of the Karos Sossusvlei Lodge can enter the park only when the gate opens at sunrise. Note your kms as you head westwards across the gravel plains north of the Tsauchab River until you cross the river at 25 km, continuing along a valley flanked by towering orange dunes. At 46 km you pass the turn-off to Dune 45 and reach the parking area for sedans 15,3 km later. The last 5 km to the vlei is accessible only by four-wheel-drive vehicle or on foot; allow about 90 minutes each way if walking.

At the vlei you will need about an hour to appreciate its splendour and to climb the dune on its northern edge for a bird's-eye view. Retrace your route to Sesriem and be sure to get back by mid-morning, which will allow you time to have a quick swim before returning to Windhoek.

Sesriem to Windhoek
Note your kms at the Sesriem entrance gate, and retrace your main route for 73 km, to turn right onto the D1273 just before the Tsondab River; you can enjoy fine views of the Naukluft Mountains along this stretch of road. After 10,6 km turn left onto the C14, cross the Tsondab River after 800 m and, very soon after, turn right onto the D1261, noting your kms. After driving some 19 km through the foothills of the escarpment you reach the start of the Remhoogte Pass, which winds up the slopes of the Remhoogte Mountains for about 4 km. At 42 km bear left, continuing along the D1261. Over the next 8 km there are several road signs warning of sharp bends, but once you reach the Khomas Hochland, the driving becomes easier.

At 71 km you reach Nauchas farm, where you can stop for refreshments before completing the journey to Windhoek. Driving on, you join the C26 to Windhoek 53 km beyond Nauchas and, for the remaining 108 km, you retrace the previous day's outward route.

AA Namibia Carl List Haus, cr Independence Avenue and Peter Müller Street, Windhoek Tel (061) 22 4201

Gamsberg Pass descends from the green highlands to the arid Namib plains.

Every clump of grass on this wind-rippled dune is a micro-ecosystem.

SOSSUSVLEI
Surrounded by towering, wavy-crested dunes of reddish-orange sand, Sossusvlei is especially breathtaking in the early morning, when the dunes are transformed into explosions of colour by the first rays of the sun.

The *vlei* (small lake) lies in the Tsauchab River that once flowed all the way to the sea, but the river lost its battle against the shifting dunes that eventually smothered it completely, about 55 km from the coast. Only occasionally does the Tsauchab River flow strongly enough to reach the clay pan of Sossusvlei and, once this water has dried, it could take a decade, or even longer, before water is held here again.

Sossusvlei is the best known of several pans in the area. After exceptionally good rains the Naravlei receives the overflow of Sossusvlei, while the Hiddenvlei and the Deadvlei have been cut off completely from the Tsauchab River and stay dry. The dunes in the Sossusvlei area reach heights of up to 325 m above the surrounding land surface, and are among the highest in the world.

Shade and water in Sesriem Canyon.

SESRIEM
Rising on the escarpment, the Tsauchab River flows across the arid Namib plains until, at Sesriem, it plunges unexpectedly into a narrow canyon. The canyon, up to 10 m deep in places and about 2 km long, was carved through layers of conglomerate between two and four million years ago.

After the Tsauchab River has come down in flood, pools of water remain in the canyon for several months. To use this source of water, the local pioneering farmers and early travellers lowered a bucket tied to six oxhide thongs to the pools, hence the name *Sesriem* or 'six thongs'.

From the car park above the canyon, a path leads down to the canyon floor, enabling visitors to explore this marvel of nature and perhaps to have a refreshing dip. As you walk down into the canyon, the various layers of gravel that were deposited on the Namib plains some 15 million years ago can be seen clearly.

Sossusvlei – where a life-giving river dies in the sands.

Bachelor gemsbok move about in small groups.

341

• PLACES OF INTEREST IN WINDHOEK •

Lights are bright on Independence Avenue as nightlife swings into gear.

Of Europe and of Africa – explore a city of contrasts

ON THE HIGH-LYING PLAINS of the Khomas Hochland, the protective arms of the Eros and the Auas ranges offer shelter to a city of contrasts where the very differences between stately German colonial and modern building styles have become an easy, African blend.

The copious hot-water springs of Windhoek (they are no longer a feature) attracted people for hundreds of thousands of years and what is today the city centre was once a marshy area where San hunters trapped elephants. Herero pastoralists grazing their herds of cattle in the valleys referred to the springs as *Otjomuise* (Place of Smoke) and the Khoikhoi people named the area *Ai-Gams* (Fire Water). The name Windhoek appears to have been used for the first time in 1844 by the Oorlams leader, Jonker Afrikaner, who established his headquarters in the Klein Windhoek Valley in 1840.

Germany's interest in Namibia initially focused on the coastal areas around Lüderitz, but in 1890 Major Curt von Francois established the headquarters of the colonial administration in Windhoek. Today, the German influence is still strongly reflected not only in German colonial buildings, but also by war memorials and German cuisine, as well as the annual *WIKA* or Windhoek Karneval – a carnival in the true German tradition, held around the end of April or early May. Contrasting sharply with the city's Continental atmosphere are Herero women in their Victorian-style dresses, and the craft markets in the Post Street Mall and on the corner of Peter Müller Street and Independence Avenue.

One of Windhoek's familiar landmarks is the *Clock Tower* **(1)** at the upper end of the Post Street Mall. Situated diagonally across from the main post office in Independence Avenue, the tower is a replica of one that graced the Deutsche-Afrika-Bank of 1908, which has since been demolished.

An unusual feature of the mall is the *Meteorite Fountain* **(2)**, where 32 meteorites are displayed, including one that has been cut in half to reveal its high iron content. The meteorites were brought to Windhoek between 1911 and 1913 from the south of the country around Gibeon – the site of one of the world's largest meteorite 'showers'.

Situated alongside Independence Avenue is *Zoo Park* **(3)**, a place of lawns, palm trees and ponds. The name recalls the late 1920s when a zoo was developed here, featuring marble fountains, birdbaths and a tearoom. The zoo closed in 1932 and, over the years, the park has unfortunately lost some of its original charm.

The *archaeological site* **(4)** in Zoo Park, where Stone Age tools and the bones of elephants, dating back some 5 000 years, were uncovered in 1962, is marked by a wonderstone carving. Near the southern end of the park is the *Schutztruppe Memorial* **(5)** – a golden eagle mounted on an iron obelisk. It was erected in 1897 to honour the German *Schutztruppe* (colonial troops) who died in the 1893-4 war against the Namas under Kaptein Hendrik Witbooi.

Looking westwards from Zoo Park across Independence Avenue are three well-preserved German colonial buildings, designed by the renowned architect Willi Sander. The striking, dressed sandstone building on the right, *Erkrath Building* **(6)**, dates back to 1910 and its style is echoed in the adjacent *Gathemann House* **(7)** (built in 1913) with its steeply pitched roof designed, as in the Fatherland, to prevent a heavy build-up of snow – a situation quite unknown in Windhoek. To the left of Gathemann House is the old *Hotel Kronprinz* **(8)**, which was converted into business premises in 1920.

Herero women in Victorian style.

One of the city's most prominent landmarks is the elegant *Christuskirche* **(9)**, or Christ Church, at the top end of Peter Müller Street. Built of local sandstone, its design is based on that of a basilica, with neo-Gothic and Art Nouveau influences. The close links between Germany and its colony at the time are reflected in the stained-glass altar window and the altar Bible, gifts of Kaiser Wilhelm II and his wife, Augusta.

Behind the church and across Robert Mugabe Avenue is the imposing *National Assembly building* **(10)**. Formerly known as the *Tintenpalast* or Ink Palace, it dates back to 1912-13, when it was built as administrative offices for the colonial government. Following independence in 1990, it became the seat of the Republic of Namibia's National Assembly.

Another reminder of the conflict between Namibia's people and the German colonial government is the *Equestrian Memorial* **(11)** to the south of the Christuskirche. The bronze statue of a mounted soldier was unveiled in 1912 in honour of German soldiers killed in wars against the Nama and Herero people in 1903-7.

Stately dignity of the National Assembly building, formerly the Tintenpalast.

A short way further south, in Robert Mugabe Avenue, is the *Alte Feste* **(12)**, Windhoek's oldest building, with its commanding views over the city. Construction of the 'old fort', with its four observation towers and courtyard, began in October 1890, shortly after Major Curt von Francois arrived in Windhoek, but it has seen no military action. The fortress now houses the historical section of the State Museum, which includes permanent displays of the country's national symbols and of the liberation struggle from the earliest times and the movement to independence.

On the corner of Robert Mugabe Avenue and Sam Nujoma Drive is the ornate *Officers' House* **(13)**, completed in 1907, with its red brickwork around the windows. Originally built to house government officials, it serves today as the Office of the Ombudsman.

Romantic castles
The three castles in Windhoek, *Schwerinsburg* **(14)**, *Heinitzburg* **(15)** and *Sanderburg* **(16)**, are situated on the ridge that separates the city centre from Klein Windhoek. They were designed by Willi Sander, architect of the famous Duwisib Castle near Maltahöhe, and were built between 1914 and 1917. Two of the castles are private residences, while Heinitzburg has been converted into a hotel; none are open to the general public.

In front of Windhoek's municipal offices, on the corner of Independence Avenue and Sam Nujoma Drive, is the statue of *Curt von Francois* **(17)**.

A stork on the weather vane of *Elizabeth House* **(18)**, at the end of Storch Street, on the western outskirts of the central business district, is the only clue that this imposing building once served as a maternity home. It opened in 1908 and more than 12 000 babies were delivered here before it closed in 1981.

Windhoek's double-storey *Railway Station* **(19)** has been in use since 1912, when the first standard-gauge locomotive steamed into the station after a 14-hour journey from Swakopmund. The upper level of the station building houses the TransNamib Railway Museum, which depicts the development of railways in Namibia. A focus of attention at the front of the station building is 'Poor Old Joe', one of the few survivors of more than 100 steam locomotives that wheezed along the country's narrow-gauge tracks at the turn of the century.

The life-size bronze *Kudu Statue* **(20)** on the corner of John Meinert Street and Independence Avenue was unveiled in 1960 as a reminder of the rinderpest epidemic of 1896, which killed thousands of head of game and cattle. Almost immediately opposite the Kudu Statue, on the corner of Moltke and John Meinert streets, is the *Oude Voorpost* **(21)** completed in 1902 as the survey offices and now the reservations office of the Ministry of Environment and Tourism.

While the State Museum in the Alte Feste focuses on the country's history, the *Owela Museum* **(22)** houses displays that are concerned with Namibia's environment and its people.

Art and culture
Namibia's dramatic landscapes, wildlife and people have inspired artists for centuries and a fine collection of paintings by prominent Namibian artists can be viewed at the *National Art Gallery of Namibia* **(23)**, on the corner of John Meinert Street and Robert Mugabe Avenue. In addition to the permanent collection, exhibitions of paintings and photographs, as well as indigenous crafts, are held periodically.

Adjacent to the gallery in Robert Mugabe Avenue is the *National Theatre of Namibia* **(24)**, where drama productions, symphony concerts and performances by visiting cultural groups are staged. A regular event on the city's cultural calendar is the monthly Sunday evening concert, featuring local and visiting musicians and presented by the *College of Arts* **(25)** on Peter Müller Street. Housed in an old brewery, the *Warehouse Theatre* **(26)** in Tal Street is characterized by its informal atmosphere that lends itself so well to cabarets and performances by music groups.

Locally made crafts are sold at the *Namibia Crafts Centre* **(27)**, situated next to the old brewery on Tal Street. Goods range from traditional woodcarvings and handwoven karakul rugs to embroidery with colourful indigenous designs and skilfully handcrafted furniture.

Walks and trails
Wide views of the city can be enjoyed along the Hofmeyer Walk, a short ramble along the ridge between the city centre and the Klein Windhoek Valley. East lies the Klein Windhoek Valley, while to the west, the central business district and the western suburbs merge with the rolling hills of the Khomas Hochland – the country's central highlands.

The Daan Viljoen Game Reserve, about 18 km west of the city, offers visitors a choice of two day-walks – the 3 km Wag 'n Bietjie Trail or the more demanding 9 km Rooibos Trail. Game such as kudu, gemsbok, blue wildebeest, red hartebeest, springbok, impala and Hartmann's mountain zebra is often encountered.

The reserve's rest camp is perched on the edge of a dam and amenities include rondavels and camp sites for overnight visitors, picnic sites for day visitors, a swimming pool and a restaurant (reservations essential – tel [061] 22 6806).

For additional information on Windhoek and its surroundings, you could contact the following: AA of Namibia, 15 Carl List House, Peter Müller Street, Windhoek (tel [061] 22 4201), or the Windhoek Information Office, cr Peter Müller Street and Independence Avenue, Windhoek (tel [061] 290 2058). The international code is 09264.

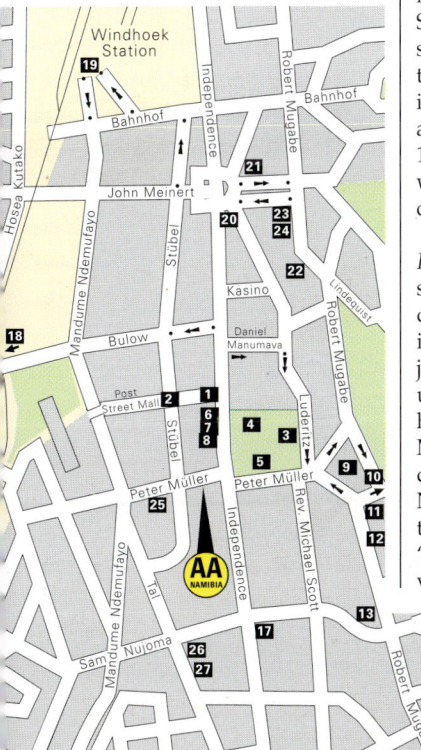

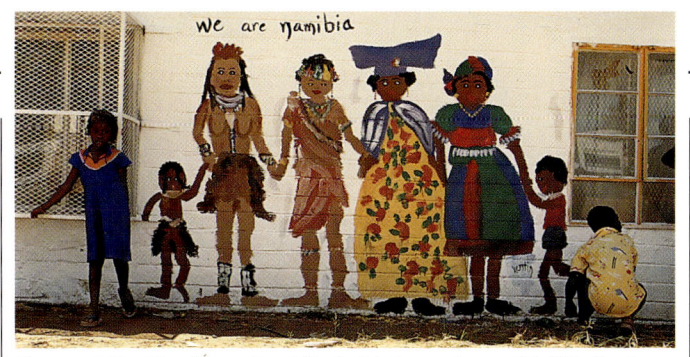

Representative Namibians cheerfully depicted on a shop wall in Windhoek.

The face of the bronze cavalryman is turned to the lovely Christuskirche.

Where the great Namib desert meets the misty Skeleton Coast

This is a long day's drive along the barren but fascinating Namib coast to Cape Cross, with its large seal colony. We end the excursion by exploring the Welwitschia Drive that reveals many unsuspected aspects of life in the Namib Desert. The longer distance includes the Welwitschia Plains. Almost the entire route is on salt or gravel roads.

**Walvis Bay
Swakopmund
Henties Bay
Cape Cross
Welwitschia Plains
315 – 445 km**

DRIVE ALONG Union Street in Walvis Bay and, from the traffic circle, continue north on the B2, noting your kms. The road traverses the narrow coastal strip, flanked by low, orange-coloured dunes on your right and the Atlantic Ocean on your left. Dense banks of fog blanket the coast overnight, usually lingering until mid-morning and demanding cautious driving. At 8,5 km a guano platform in the sea comes into view, a roosting place for tens of thousands of Cape cormorants. About 5,6 km further on, you pass the Dolphin Park resort and, after a further 2,5 km, the popular and well-named resort of *Langstrand* (Long Beach).

Further north you pass several popular angling spots and, at 32 km, cross the Swakop River. Swakopmund's main street, Kaiser Wilhelm Street, is reached 1,7 km further on. Be sure to obtain a brochure and permit for the Welwitschia Drive from the Ministry of Environment and Tourism (weekdays only) or from Hans Kriess Motors (weekends and after hours), both in Kaiser Wilhelm Street, before continuing to Cape Cross.

Swakopmund to Henties Bay

Drive east along Kaiser Wilhelm Street to the traffic lights at the junction with Nordring Street and turn left, noting your kms. The road surface soon changes to one of salt, made by mixing gravel with salt water, which becomes extremely slippery in misty weather. Continuing along this road, you join the C34 and, from the outskirts of Swakopmund, the road heads north across the featureless landscape of the Namib coast.

Many years ago, fishing spots along the coast became known by their distance from Swakopmund. These names have survived the advent of metrication and as you head along the coast, the saltworks north of Mile 4 (oysters are cultivated here) come into view. At 25 km you pass the turn-off to Mile 14 campsite, the southernmost of four state-owned camp sites along the coast.

At 32 km you pass the quaint holiday village of Wlotzkasbaken. The orange *Teloschistes* lichen fields, passed about 6 km north of Wlotzkasbaken to the right of the road, are unlikely to escape your attention and it is worth pulling to the side of the road to have a closer, more leisurely look.

At 69 km you reach the turn-off to Henties Bay, one of the most popular coastal resorts in Namibia. A quiet place for most of the year, it is packed with holidaymakers during the summer school holidays.

Henties Bay to Cape Cross

Return to the main coastal road (C34) and turn left, noting your kms as you head north again. At 36 km the plains give way to Laguneberg – a series of low hills east of the road. The road crosses the edge of the White Lady Salt Pan before the turn-off to the Cape Cross Seal Reserve is reached at 54 km. Turn left and continue for 4 km to the reserve office, where an entrance fee is payable. Immediately beyond the office, bear left and you will pass a picnic site among the rocks on your left. About 700 m further on you pass the turn-off to a picnic site just off the beach and, 2,5 km from the office, the road ends at the parking area that provides access to the seal colony and the Diogo Cão monument.

Welwitschia Drive and Walvis Bay

Retrace your route for 125 km to Swakopmund; if you started out by 08h00, you should be back in time for lunch at one of the town's many restaurants that offer seafood and Continental fare. From the centre of town, travel east along Kaiser Wilhelm Street, noting your kms at the intersection with Nordring Street. At 2,2 km you pass an old steam traction engine nicknamed Martin Luther. Some 800 m further on, turn right onto the C28, a gravel road, which you should follow for 15,2 km to the turn-off onto the Welwitschia Drive. Thirteen points of botanical, historical and geological interest are marked along the route, and among those passed within the first kilometres are wind-blown lichens, drought-resistant shrubs and an old ox-wagon route. At 15,6 km you reach a viewpoint overlooking the spectacular Moon landscape and just over 2 km later you pass another viewsite.

Continuing further, the road descends through spectacular scenery to the Swakop

---

SWAKOPMUND

Situated on the barren Namib coast, Swakopmund developed around the site selected as a port in 1892 to enable Germany to establish control over territory it claimed in the interior. Although German rule ended a mere 23 years later, Swakopmund has a distinctly Continental atmosphere with numerous turn-of-the-century buildings. Among its most striking German colonial buildings are the ornate Woermann House (1905) and Hohenzollernhaus (1906), undoubtedly the finest example of the town's romantic Art Nouveau architecture. Another fine example of this architectural style is the station building of the old State railways (1901) in Bahnhof Street (now the reception area of a hotel). Other historic buildings include the lighthouse (1902), the *Kaserne* or Barracks (1905), the old magistrate's court or *Kaiserliches Bezirksgericht* (1905) and the Prison (1909). The pier, started in 1911 but still unfinished, is a popular spot at sunset and was intended to link the shore to the relatively deep anchorage offshore.

Elegant Hohenzollernhaus in Swakopmund.

Swakopmund's long pier was an attempt to compensate for the shallowness of the inshore anchorage.

River, where there is a delightful picnic spot on the northern bank – an ideal stop for a mid-afternoon break. On leaving the Swakop River valley, the road winds across gravel plains dotted with hundreds of welwitschias; 12,3 km beyond the Swakop River picnic spot you reach another highlight of the drive, the giant Husab Welwitschia.

Note your kms, retrace your route for 18 km and then continue for another 9 km to the C28. Turn right and after about 300 m you will reach the last beacon of the Welwitschia Drive – the Von Stryk Mine, a disused iron-ore mine dating back to the 1950s. Continuing westward along the C28, you reach the park boundary at 52 km; from here you retrace your route for 18,4 km to Swakopmund and another 35 km to Walvis Bay.

You should reach Walvis Bay just in time to watch a flaming sun setting over the lagoon as flocks of pink and white flamingoes swirl elegantly into the air and head home.

Ministry of Environment and Tourism Kaiser Wilhelm Street, Swakopmund Tel (064) 40 2172
Namib Publicity and Tourism Association 28 Kaiser Wilhelm Street, Swakopmund Tel (064) 40 2224

WALVIS BAY

Namibia's main port, Walvis Bay, has been an anchorage for over 500 years. It is the centre of the country's lucrative fishing industry and is Africa's largest producer of salt. The port and surrounding desert were formally annexed by a Cape magistrate and proclaimed British territory in 1878. The 1 124 sq km enclave was subsequently administered by South Africa until its reintegration with Namibia on 1 March 1994. The Walvis Bay wetlands, comprising the lagoon and the saltworks, are one of the 10 most important coastal wetlands in Africa, supporting up to 88 000 birds. In summer, the wetlands become home to thousands of Palaearctic waders, including curlew sandpiper, sanderling, turnstone and little stint. Also attracted are large numbers of greater and lesser flamingoes, as well as the white pelican, avocet, kelp gull, blacknecked grebe and whitefronted plover. It is also an important habitat of the southern African population of the chestnutbanded plover.

Flamingoes are mainly summer migrants, favouring the shallows of lagoons or inland lakes.

CAPE CROSS

Rocky Cape Cross is one of several Namibian mainland breeding colonies of the Cape fur seal and is home to tens of thousands of these marine mammals. The colony is inhabited throughout the year, but is most active from around mid-October, when the bulls establish territories for harems of up to 25 cows. Most of the pups are born between mid-November and mid-December, and mating may take place again within a week of the cows' having given birth.

Shoaling fish such as maasbankers and pilchards account for about half of the seals' diet, while octopus, squid and cuttlefish constitute about 37 per cent and rock lobsters and crustaceans about 13 per cent. Also of interest at Cape Cross is the replica of the limestone padrão or cross erected here in 1486 by the Portuguese navigator, Diogo Cão, the first European to set foot on the Namibian coast.

Above: *Replica of a padrão at Cape Cross.* **Below:** *The Welwitschia.*

THE WONDERFUL WELWITSCHIA

One of the world's botanical curiosities, the strange-looking *Welwitschia mirabilis* is endemic to the Namib Desert, occurring from the Kuiseb River northwards to south-western Angola. It is especially common on the Welwitschia Plains, north of the Swakop River, where several hundred plants grow in river washes. Although it does not resemble a tree, the welwitschia is nevertheless classified as one, and much of its stem is underground. Only two leathery leaves of up to 8 m long and 1,5 m wide are produced on opposite sides of the gnarled stem, but the leaves are shredded by searing winds and extreme temperatures into a tangled mass, creating the impression of a multitude of leaves. Another interesting feature of the welwitschia is that it is unisexual. Female plants bear salmon-coloured cones, while the elongated orange male cones are smaller than those of the female. Despite their inhospitable habitat, they have an incredibly long lifespan and the age of the giant Husab Welwitschia has been estimated to be over 1 500 years.

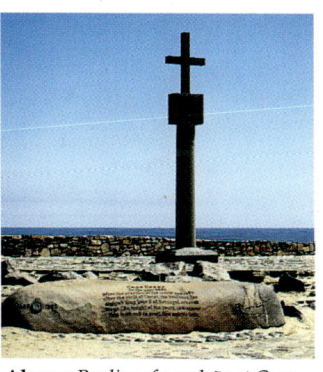

Index

A

Aalwynkop 238
Abel Erasmus Pass 36, 37
Aberdeen 302
Aberfoyle 316
Adansonia digitata see: baobab tree
Addington Hospital Centenary Museum 150
Addo Elephant National Park 202, 203, 211
Adelaide 189
Adler Museum of the History of Medicine 87
Admiralty House 248
Afdaks River 262
Africa Methodist University 314
Africa Unity Square 306, 307
African Art Centre 150
Africana Centre 234
Afrikaans language monuments
  Burgersdorp 179
  Duiwelskloof 20
  Paarl 244, 245
Afrikaner, Jonker 342
Afsaal 60
Agatha 23
Agathosma betulina 283
Agfa Amphitheatre 257
Aggeneys 290
Agulhas 247, 260, 261
Ai-Ais Hot Springs 336, 337
Akkedisberg Pass 260
Alabama (ship) 274
Alanglade 43, 48, 49
Albany Museum 195
Albasini, João 15, 18
Albasini Dam 14
Albert Falls 139
Albert Falls Dam 141
Albert Park 151
Albertinia 234
Albertsburg 230
Alexander McGregor Museum 301
Alexandra Park 140, 141
Alexandria 192
Alexandria Forest Reserve 211
Alfred Basin 254, 256, 257
Algeria, Cederberg 280, 282, 283
Algoa Bay 204
Alice 182, 184, 190, 191
Aliwal North 176, 178, 179
Allard, *Bishop* J 98
Aloe dichotoma 295, 337
Aloe peglerae 29
aloes 311, 317
Alte Feste 343
Amahwaqa Mountain 135
Amalienstein 232, 233
Amanzimtoti 148, 152, 153
Amatole range 182, 183, 184, 185
Amm's Mine 311
Amphitheatre, Drakensberg 90, 91, 126, 127
Amphitheatre Gardens, Durban 151
Anderson, Charles 52
Anderson Memorial Museum 181
Andora Harbour 331, 332
Andries Uys Bridge 237
Andries Vosloo Kudu Reserve 190
Anglican churches see *under* churches
Anglo-Boer War, First 44, 48, 72
  relics 95

Anglo-Boer War, Second 19, 28, 46-7, 91, 106
  graves 24, 73, 128, 179, 214, 273
  memorials 45, 47, 95, 128, 296
  Cape 195, 213, 273, 301
  relics 95
  start of 72
  Treaty of Vereeniging 75
  see also battles; cemeteries; concentration camps; fortifications
Anglo-Zulu War 106, 107, 119, 123, 146, 147
animal orphanage, Harare 310
Anreith, Anton 253, 255
Ansteys Beach 148
anthrax 66
Apies River valley 74
Apple Express 209
apple farming and industry 264, 265
Apple Museum 264
aquariums 77, 78, 257
Ararat 292, 293, 295
Arbouset, (Jean) Thomas 126
architectural styles 303
Arend Dieperink Museum 27
Arniston/Waenhuiskrans 260, 261
art galleries
  African Art Centre 150
  Elizabeth Gordon 150
  Gertrude Posel 84
  Grassroots 150
  Hester Rupert 213
  Johannesburg 83, 84
  Market 83
  Natal Society of Artists 150
  National, of Namibia 343
  Pretoria 76
  Rembrandt van Rijn 266
  Somerset East 188, 189
  South African National 253
  Soweto 84
  Tatham 140
  William Humphreys 301
  Zimbabwe National 326
art routes, Johannesburg 84
art traditions, Venda 17
As-Salaam Islamic Seminary 154
asbestos mine 52, 54, 55
Ash, Harry and Margaret 189
Atlantic coast 254
Atlantic Ocean 247, 254
Attaqua Khoikhoi 237
Attaquas Kloof 226
Auas range 342
Augrabies Falls National Park 292, 293, 294-5
Auob River 298, 299
Austin Roberts Bird Hall 75
Austin Roberts Bird Sanctuary 77
Australopithecines 27
aviation museum 296
Avontuur 220, 221

B

Baakens River 210
Babalala 66
Baboon Point 278, 279
baboons, chacma 25, 65, 247
Baboons' Castle 157
Baden-Powell, Robert 33
Badkloof 236
Badplaas 54
Bafokeng 102
Bahia de Lagoa 204
Bahia Formosa 303
Bailey, *Sir* Abe (grave) 246

Bain, AG 190, 191, 221, 268
Bain, Thomas 220, 221, 236
  passes and roads 219, 220, 221, 226, 228, 236,237, 268, 277
Bain's Kloof 268, 269
Baines, Thomas 184, 307
Baker, *Sir* Herbert 45, 75, 86, 247, 249, 253, 266, 296, 301
Bakkerspas 24
Bakoondshoogte 236
Bakoven 246, 250
Balfour 307
Balgowan 139
Ballot's Bay 224
Bally Vaughan Bird and Animal Orphanage 310
Bambata Cave 324
Bambatha Rebellion 121, 122
bananas 312, 313
Banga Nek 109
Bankberg 200, 201
Baobab Hiking Trail 12, 13
Baobab Hill 328
Baobab Reserve 12
baobab tree 69, 318
Baphuthi 102, 103
Barber, Graham 51, 53
Barberton 50, 51, 52-3, 54, 55
Barberton daisy 50
Barkly, *Sir* Henry 176
Barkly East 176, 177
Barkly Pass 177
Barkly West 296, 297
Barnard, Cecil 69
Barnato, Barney 300
Barracouta (ship) 171
Barry, Dick 49
Barry, Joseph 240
Barrydale 237
Barton's Folly 28, 79
Basotho Village Cultural Museum 90, 96
Basotho-Boer War (1886) 90, 92
Basuto pony 102, 103
Bath, George 282
Bathurst 192, 193
Battiss, Walter 188
Battle Cave 133
battlefields 106, 119, 121, 128, 161
battles
  Bergendal 47
  Blood River 74, 106, 107
  Bronkhorstspruit 72
  Congella 149
  Eshowe 119
  Gingindlovu 119
  Grahamstown 191
  Inyezane 119
  Isandhlwana 106
  Kakamas 292, 293
  Kleinfontein 32
  Magersfontein 296, 301
  Muizenberg 247
  Naauwpoort 90
  Nooitgedacht 28
  Rorke's Drift 107
  Square Hill 301
  Talana 106
  Wagon Hill 91
Bauhinia galpinii 50, 53
Baviaans River Valley 189
Baviaanskloof 229
Baxter Theatre 255
Bay of Plenty 148
Bayview House 249
Beaufort West 302
Bedford 189
bees 318
beetles, *toktokkie* 340
Beit, *Sir* Alfred 300

Beit Bridge 12
Bekapanzi Hide 115
Belvidere 225
Belvidere Church 222, 223
Ben Alberts Nature Reserve 24, 26
Ben Lavin Nature Reserve 19
Bendigo Mine 222, 223
Benjaminshoogte 176, 177
Benoni Fire Service Museum 87
Bensusan Museum of Photography 87
Berea, The 150
Berea Plateau, Lesotho 100
Berg River 275, 278, 279
Berg River Valley 245, 269
Bergendal, Battle of 47
Bergh, Marthinus Oloff 267
Bergh, Oloff 258, 284
Berghhuis 267
Bergvenster, Die 206, 207
Bergville 128, 129
Berlin Falls 37
Bernberg Museum of Costume 87
Bertram House Museum 253
Bestershoek 188
Bethel Mission 183
Bethesda 198
Bethlehem 96, 97
Bethulie 178
Betty's Bay 262, 263
Bhaca 134
Biedou Valley 280, 291
Big Hole, Kimberley 300, 301
Big Tree 219, 220, 221, 223
Big Tree Trail 219
Biggarsberg 120
Bindura 311
Binga (village) 331
Birchenough Bridge 318
Bird Island 285
Bird Rock 210
bird sanctuaries and parks
  Amanzimtoti 153
  Austin Roberts Bird Sanctuary 77
  Bally Vaughan Bird and Animal Orphanage 310
  Florence Bloom Bird Sanctuary 86
  Johannesburg 86
  Larvon 308, 309
  Melrose 86
  Rietvlei 254
  Rondevlei 254
  Umgeni River 146, 151
  World of Birds 254
Bishop's Arch 269
Bishop's Seat 119
Blaauwklippen Estate 244, 245
Black Mfolozi River 114, 115
Black Town 249
Blanco 227
Blanco Nature Reserve 189
Bleshoender 224
Blettermanhuis 267
Blindekloof Walk 211
Blinkwater Monster 190
Blinkwaterspruit 40
blockhouses see fortifications
Bloemfontein 94-5
Bloemspruit 94
Blood River 74, 106, 107
Bloubergstrand 255, 268
Bloukrans Pass 219
Blue Lagoon 149
Blue Mountain Pass 99
bluebuck 238
Bluegum Poort 12
Bluff, The 148, 150
Blyde River 37, 38, 39, 41

346

Blyde River Canyon 38-9
Blyde River Canyon Nature
    Reserve 36
Blydepoort Dam 36, 38
Blyderivierspoort Hiking Trail 39
Blyfstaanhoogte 47
Bo-Kaap Museum 255
Boadicea (ship) 248
boat trips
    Cape Peninsula 255
    Durban 149
Boboyi River valley 156
Boer-Basotho War (1886) 90
Boerneef (IW van der Merwe) 277
Boesmansrand 143
Boggomsbaai 234
bokkem industry 278
Bokkeveld 276
Boknes Beach 192
Boland Hiking Trail 264
Bomvanaland 164
Bond, Edwin 133
Bonnet, The 36, 41
Bonnievale 236, 237
Bontebok National Park 238
Bophuthatswana 33
Boplaas 277
Border Caves 109
Bosberg Nature Reserve 188
Bosberg Trail 189
Boschendal 244, 245, 265
Bosjemansdrif 236
Bosman, Herman Charles 32
Bot River 262
botanical gardens
    Bunga 312
    Bvumba 312
    Durban 151
    Ewanrigg 310, 311
    Harold Porter 262, 263
    Johannesburg 86
    Kirstenbosch 250, 251
    Lowveld 45
    Pretoria 77
    Witwatersrand 85
Botanical Society of South Africa
    287
Botha, Louis 47, 121
Botha's Hill 142
Bothmaskloof Pass 268, 273
Botshabelo Mission 72, 73
Botshabelo Museum and Nature
    Reserve 73
Boulders Beach 246, 255
Bourke, Thomas 37
Bourke's Luck potholes 36, 37
Bovenplaas 273
Bowker, James 101
Bowler, Thomas 177, 241
Boy Scouts Association 33
Boyes' Drive 246, 247
Braak, The, Stellenbosch 267
Braamfontein Spruit Trail 85, 86
Bracken Hill Falls 220
Bradshaw's Mill 193
Brandwag, Golden Gate 91, 93
Bray, Edwin 51, 53
Bray's Golden Quarry 53
Brazen Head 161
bread trees (cycads) 211
Bredasdorp 260, 261
Bredasdorp Shipwreck Museum
    261
Breede River 236, 239, 258, 259,
    269, 277
Breede River Valley 259
Breedt's Nek 29, 78
Brenton 225
Brenton on Sea 222
Bridal Veil Falls 40, 294, 318

bridge jumping 234
Brighton Beach 148
British-German Legion 171, 173
British Kaffraria 173, 174, 175
Brits, Johan Nicolaas 94, 95
Brits, Rudolph Martinus 94
Bronkhorstspruit 72
Bronne, Die 211
Brooklands State Forest 47
Broom, Robert 85
Brownlee, John 174, 175
Buchu 283
buffalo 66, 310
Buffalo Pass 172, 173
Buffalo River 172, 232
Buffalo River Mouth 170
Buffeljags River 237
Buffels Bay 246
Buffelsdrift 318
Buffelshoek Pass 196, 276
Buffelskop 197
Buffelspoort Dam 29, 78
Bulawayo 324, 326-7
Bulembo 54
Buller, Sir Redvers 128
Bultfontein Diamond Mine 300
Bulwer 135
Bunga Botanical Reserve 312
bungee jumping 234
Bunny Park 84
Burgers, Thomas Francois 46, 75
Burgers' Park 75
Burgersdorp 179
Burgersfort 48, 49
Burgher Wachthuis 253
Burgherhuis 267
Burma Valley 312, 313
Burnshill 182
Bushbuck Trail 210
Bushmanland 33
Bushman's Nek Mountain Resort
    136
Bushman's Pass 98, 99
Bushman's River 120, 130, 132
Bushman's River Mouth 192
Bushman's River Trail 132
Bushmen see San
Bushpig Trail 219
Bushveld 32-3, 60
Bushveld Festival 27
Butha-Buthe 102
butterflies 234, 312
Butterworth 168
Button, Edward 41
Buyskop 24
Bvumba 312, 313
Byrne settlers 134
Byrne Valley 134

C

CP Nel Museum 226, 228
Cacadu/Lady Frere 180, 181
cactus garden 259
Caledon 262, 263
Calvinia 290
Camdeboo 196
'camel rock' 246
camel-thorn trees 295, 298
Campanile 205
Campbell 302
Campbell, Sir Marshall 150
Camps Bay 246, 254
Cango Caves 226, 227
Canitz, Georg 244
Cannibal Cave 126
cannibalism 126
Canning, Lennox 95
Cannon Koppie 33
Cannon Rocks 192, 211

cannons, ancient 261
Canteen Koppie 296, 297
Cão, Diogo (monument) 344, 345
Cape Agulhas 247, 260, 261
Cape Columbine 274, 275
Cape Corps Memorial 301
Cape Cross 344, 345
Cape Cross Seal Reserve 344, 345
Cape Flats 247, 264
Cape Hangklip 246
Cape Maclear 246
Cape of Good Hope
    Nature Reserve 246, 247
Cape Peninsula 246-51
Cape Point 246, 247
Cape Recife Nature Reserve 210
Cape St Blaize 234, 235
Cape St Francis 208
Cape to Cairo road 244
Cape Town 244, 246, 247, 250,
    252-7, 264, 268, 272
Cape Vidal 117
Cape wagon road 240
Carbineer Gardens 140
Cardouws Kloof 276
Caribbea Bay 331
Carlton Centre 82
Carnarvon 303
Carolusberg 288
Cascade Falls 139
Cascades
    Crocodile River 45
    Mahai River 127
    Queen's River 50, 54
Cashel Valley 318
Cashel-Chimanimani
    Scenic Route 319
Castle Hill 205
Castle of Good Hope 252
castles, Windhoek 343
Castro, Manuel de 166
Catalina Bay 117
Cathcart 182, 184
Cathcart, Sir George 183
Cathedral Cave 93
Cathedral of Our Lady of
    Victories 98, 100
Cathedral Rock 282
Cathkin Peak 129, 133, 138
Cats, SJ 265
Cat's Pass 169
Cavers 189
Caversham Mill 138
caves
    Bambata 324
    Battle 133
    Cango 226, 227
    Cathedral 93
    Cederberg 282
    Chamavara 321
    Echo 36
    Giant's Castle 132, 133
    Kelders, Die 260
    Nswatugi 324
    Pomongwe 324
    Stadsaal 280, 281, 282
    Sterkfontein 85
    Sudwala 44
    Waenhuiskrans 260, 261
    Wonder 86
Cawood's Post 193
Cecilia Forest 254
cedar trees 282, 283
Cedara State Forest 141
Cedarberg, see Cederberg
Cederberg 280, 282-3
Cederberg Pass 280
Cefane Mouth and Lagoon 170
cemeteries, historic
    Bethulie 17

Kimberley 301
Kokstad 163
Mafikeng 33
Norvalspont 179
Nylstroom Concentration
    Camp 24
Pietermaritzburg Voortrekker
    140
Pilgrim's Rest 43
Pretoria, Heroes' Acre 75
Schoemansdal 12
Sheba 50
Wagon Hill 128
Warmbaths 24
see also graves
Cengeni Gate, Umfolozi 115
Centane 168, 169
Centane Hills Forest Reserve 168
Centenary Nature Garden 237
Ceres 276, 277
Cetshwayo 106, 118, 119, 147
Chalumna River 173
Chamavara Cave 321
Chamber of Mines' Coal Museum
    106
Champagne Castle 129
chapel, smallest in Zimbabwe 321
Chapman's Peak 246, 250, 254
Chapungu 307
Charara safari area 332
Charlotte Kritzinger Shell
    Museum 208
Charter's Creek 117
cheese, farmhouse 313, 318
cheetah 65, 77
Cheetah Interpretive Trail 80
Cheetah Research Station 77
Chelmsford, Lord 106, 119
Chete Island 331
Chikamba Real Dam 312
Chimanimani Mountains 319
Chimanimani National Park 318
Chimanimani Scenic Route 318,
    319
Chimanimani village 318
Chinakaturi range 312
Chipangali Wild Life Orphanage
    327
Chipinge 318
Chiredzi 320
Chishakwe peak 312
Chivero, Lake 308
Chomse se Hoogte Pass 45
Christmas Pass 314
Christuskirche 342
Church of the Vow
    Louis Trichardt 12
    Pietermaritzburg 140
churches 302
    see also mosques; synagogues
    Anglican
        Barkly West 296
        Bathurst 193
        Belvidere 222, 223
        Bulawayo 327
        Caledon 262
        Cape Town 253
        Clanwilliam 281
        Cradock 197
        Dockyard 249
        Estcourt 131
        Graaff-Reinet 213
        Grahamstown 194, 195, 302
        Harare 307
        Highflats 154
        Hogsback 184, 185
        Johannesburg 83
        Kimberley 301
        King William's Town 174
        Pietermaritzburg 141

347

churches *continued*
  Pilgrim's Rest 42
  Port Elizabeth 205
  Riversdale 235
  Sabie 45
  Simon's Town 248, 249
  Stellenbosch 267
  Swellendam 240
  Tulbagh 270
  Zeerust 33
Baptist
  Cradock 197
  Grahamstown 195
Dutch Reformed
  Aberdeen 302
  Bloemfontein 95
  Campbell 302
  Cape Town 252
  Clanwilliam 281
  Cradock 197
  Fouriesburg 97
  Franschhoek 265
  Graaff-Reinet 196, 213, 302
  Kamieskroon 302
  Kimberley 301
  Laingsburg 232
  Louis Trichardt 14, 19
  Malmesbury 273
  Middelburg, Mpumalanga 72, 73
  Nylstroom (Hervormde) 24
  Philadelphia 272
  Pietermaritzburg 140
  Piketberg 279
  Porterville 276
  Pretoria 77
  Prince Albert 230
  Redelinghuys 279
  Simon's Town 249
  Swellendam 240
  Vryheid 106
  Wellington 269
Dutch Reformed Mission
  Keimoes 292
Greek Orthodox 307
interdenominational
  Hogsback open-air 185
  St Martini 300
Lutheran
  Cape Town 255
  Laingsburg 232
  Stellenbosch 267
Methodist
  Cradock 197
  Grahamstown 194,195
  King William's Town 174
  Pilgrim's Rest 43
  Salem 192
mission
  Graaff-Reinet 212
  Kuruman 33
  Morija 101
Nazareth Mission
  Bethlehem 97
Presbyterian
  Grahamstown 195
  Port Elizabeth 204
  Somerset East 188
Reformed
  Pretoria (Kruger) 75, 77
Rhenish
  Keetmanshoop 337
  Stellenbosch 267
  Wuppertal 281
Roman Catholic
  Bulawayo 327
  Grahamstown 195
  Harare 307
  Kokstad 162
  Mariathal 155

Maseru 98, 100
  Pilgrim's Rest 43
  Port Elizabeth 205
  Simon's Town 249
Seventh Day Adventists
  Kimberley 301
Wesleyan
  Stanger 122
Churchhaven 274, 275
Churchill, *Sir* Winston 149
Cilliers, Ouma 93
Cinderella's Castle 91, 96
Cintsa Mouth East 170
Ciskei 172
Citrusdal 276, 277
Clansthal 152, 153
Clanwilliam 280, 281, 291
Clanwilliam cedar tree 282
Claremont, Zimbabwe 314
Clarens 90, 91, 96
Claustal (railway station) 153
Clifton 246, 250, 254
clock tower 256, 342
Cloete, Hendrik 251
Cloete's Pass 234
Cloud's End 332
Clowes, Graham 281
Cockney Liz 53
Cockscomb Mountain 206, 207, 209
coelacanth 172, 173
Coerney River 203
Coetzee, Diederick 32
Coetzeeberge 196
Coffee Bay 165, 167
Coghlan, Charles 325
Cogmanskloof 236, 237
Coldstream 219
Cole, *Sir* Galbraith Lowry 264, 268, 273
Coleford Nature Reserve 136, 137
Colenso 128
Colenso, *Bishop* John 141
Colesberg Koppie 300
Commando Nek 78
Commemoration Church 194, 195
Committee's Drift 190
Company's Garden 252, 253
Compensation (place) 147
concentration camps 95
Coney Glen 222
conservation museum 86
Constantia Nek 254
Constantia Valley 247, 250
Constantiaberg 246
Cookhouse 189
copper mining 288, 289
Copper Mountains 288
copper road 289
Cornelisz, Jan 267
Cornlands River 240
Correctional Services Museum 76
costume museum 87
Council for Scientific and Industrial Research 76
Country Club Beach 149
Coward's Bush 118, 119
Cradock 196, 197
craft traditions, Venda 17
craft centres and markets
  Free State and Lesotho 96, 100, 101,
  Gauteng 84
  Namibia 343
  Northern and North-West Provinces 14
  Northern Cape 288

Northern KwaZulu-Natal 106, 111, 119
South-Western Cape 257
Southern KwaZulu-Natal 130, 136, 141, 142, 151, 153, 154
Mpumalanga and Swaziland 54, 55, 57
Zimbabwe 306, 312, 327, 329, 342
Craigie Burn Dam 130
crane, crowned 310
crayfish 285
Crocodile Bridge 60, 61
Crocodile Centre, St Lucia 117
Crocodile Falls 45
crocodile farms 24
Crocodile River
  Kruger Park 60
  Magaliesberg 29, 78
  Nelspruit 45
Crocodile River Arts and Crafts Ramble 84
Crocodile River Gorge 50
crocodiles 332
  Nile 117, 152
  West African 117
Crocworld 152
Cronwright-Schreiner, Samuel 197
Cruytoff, Pieter 268
Crystal Dam 163
Crystal Pool 282
Cullinan 76
culling of wild animals 67
Cultural History Museum 253
Cultural History Museum of the Free State 95
Cumberland Valley 315
Cummings, Simeon W 274
Curry's Post 139
Cuyler, Jacob Glen 193, 202
Cuyler Manor 202
cycads 21, 133, 142, 203, 211
Cyrene Mission 324

D

DH Steyn Bridge 178
Da Gama, Vasco (monument) 275
Da Gama Dam 40
Daan Viljoen Game Reserve 343
Dabulamanzi 119
Dacre, George 182
Dacre's Pulpit 269
Dalebrook 255
Danie Joubert Dam 40
Darling 272, 290
Darlington Dam 203
Darwendale 308
Dassenbergfontein 284
Daumas, Francois 126
Day of Reconciliation 107
Day of the Vow 107
De Bakke 234
De Beer, Zacharias 230
De Beers Company 300, 301
De Buys, Coenraad 18, 24, 25
De Hoek Forest 21
De Hoop Nature Reserve 238
De Kaap Valley 50, 51, 52-3, 54
De Nys, Adriaan 249
De Rust 228, 229
De Stades Trail 210
De Toren 196
De Vasselot Nature Reserve 219
De Villiers, Abraham 244
De Villiers, ML 249
De Wet, Christiaan 30, 92, 94, 95
De Wildt Cheetah Research Station 77

Deadvlei 341
Debegeni Falls 20, 21, 23
Deka River 328
Dekadrum 328
Dekenah, Japie 234
Delta Park, Johannesburg 86
Deneys, George 22
Derdepoort Regional Park 77
Detema Dam 328
Devil's Gorge 331
Devil's Knuckles 46, 47, 54
Devil's Peak 247, 254
Devil's Tooth 90, 126
Deze Hoek 278
Diagonal Street 83
diamond mining and industry 76, 83, 300
Dias, Bartolomeu 234
Dias Beach
  Cape Point 246
  Mossel Bay 234
Dias Cross 192
Diascorea elephantipes 283
Die Berg *see* Berg, Die
Diep River (near Knysna) 223
Diepkloof 80
Dieprivier 220, 221
Diepwalle 220
difaqane 164
Digger's Rest 300, 301
dik-dik, Damara 338, 339
Dingane 107, 157 109
Dinosaur Park 44
dinosaurs 196, 197
Ditike Arts and Crafts Centre 14
Dlamini, *Chief* 56
Dlinza Forest 118
Dockyard Church 249
dolls, Reinet
Dolphin Park resort 344
Domba initiation 17
Dombawera Game Lodge 311
Donkerpoort Dam 24, 26
Donkey Monument 292
Donkin, *Sir* Rufane 204
Donkin Reserve 204
Dontsa Pass 182
Dooley Mountain 127
Doornbaai 284
Doorndraai Dam 26
Dordrecht 180, 181
Dordrecht Kloof 181
Doring River 181
Doringbaai 291
Doringbergspruit 45
Dorothea (ship) 51
Dorps River 48, 49
Double Drift Nature Reserve 190
Double Mouth Reserve 170, 171
Dragon Peaks 129
Dragon Tree, 257
Drakensberg
  KwaZulu-Natal 90, 130, 132-3, 135, 136-7, 138
  Mpumalanga 38
  Northern Province 22, 23
  southern 176
Drakensberg Boys' Choir School 129
Drakensberg Gardens Mountain Resort 136
Drakenstein 245, 264
Drakenstein range 247
Drew 236
Driefontein Mission 320
Driehoek River Valley 280
Driekoppe Trail 215
Drizzly 176
Drommedaris Eiland 225
Drostdy gateway, 194

Drostdy Museum
   Swellendam 240, 241
   Uitenhage 202
Dugandlovu Camp 117
Duiker Island 255
Duiwelskantoor 52
Duiwelskloof 20
Duiwelskneukels 46, 47, 54
Duncan Dock 256
Dundee 121
dune forest, Siyayi 119
Dunluce 301
Dunn, John 116
D'Urban, Benjamin 175
Durban 142, 146, 148-51, 152
Durbanville 269
Durnford, AW 133
Dutch East India Company
   Kruithuis 267
   Outpost 237
Dutch Reformed churches
   see under churches
Duthie, Thomas Henry 223
Duzi Canoe Marathon 141
Dwars River 277
Dwarskersbos 275, 278
Dyamala 182
Dzata 16
Dzundwini 66

E

eagles 201, 324
earthquake 270
East London 170, 172, 173
Eastern Buttress, Drakensberg 126
Eastern Monarch (tree) 185
Ebenezer Dam 22, 23
Ecca Pass 190
Echo Caves 36
Echo Ravine 93
Education Museum 75
Eendekuil 279
Eendragbrug 292
Eerste River Valley 266
Eerstefontein Trail 215
Eersteling 41
Egundwini 57
Eight Bells Mountain Inn 226
1820 Settlers 189, 192, 194, 204
1820 Settlers' National Monument 192, 195
1820 Settlers' Toposcope 193
1820 Wildflower Reserve 195
Eiland Holiday Resort 292
Eileen Orpen Dam 62
eland 132
Eland Sanctuary 319
Elands Bay 278, 279
Elands River 126
Elands River Valley 206, 207
Elandskloofberg 269
Elandslaagte 120
elephant hunters 221
Elephant Walk 220
elephants 64, 67, 108, 202, 211, 220, 221, 328
elephant's foot plant 283
Elgin 264, 265
Elim 260
Elim Dune 341
Elizabeth Gordon Gallery 150
Elizabeth Sneddon Theatre 150
Ellen's Fortune Reef 22
Elliot 177
Elliot, *Major* Henry 177
Ellisras 27
Elsenburg Agricultural College 244

Emmarentia Dam 86
Empangeni 118
Emu (ship) 223
Encephalartos transvenosus 21
Energy (statue) 247
Englishman's grave 280, 281
eNjesuthi Dome 133
eNjesuthi River 132, 133
Enseleni Nature Reserve 118
Entabeni State Forest 14, 15, 19
Environmental Museum 77
equestrian displays, Kyalami 85
Erasmus, Abel 37, 41
Ernest Oppenheimer Memorial Garden 301
Eros range 342
Erskine, Robert Henry 133
Eselsfontein River 288
Eshowe 118, 119
Eskom village 83
Espag, Abraham 46
Esplanade 149
Estcourt 131
Ethnographic Gallery 301
Etosha National Park 338-9
Eureka City 50, 51, 53
Eureka diamond 300
Evatt, Francis 204
Ewanrigg Botanical Garden 310, 311
Eyssenhuis 236
Ezulwini Valley 56

F

Faerie Glen Nature Reserve 77
Fafa River 152
Fairview Estate 244, 245
Fairy Knowe 225
False Bay 246, 247, 254, 255, 262, 264
False Bay Park 117
Fambidzanai Training Centre 308
Fanies Island 117
Farewell, Francis 149
Fawn Leas 122
Feather Market Centre 205
Fernkloof Nature Reserve 262, 263
Ficksburg 97
fire-walking ceremony 141, 151
firearms display 212
Fischer's Pan 339
Fish Hoek 246, 255
Fish River 179
Fish River Canyon 336, 337
Fisherman's Wharf 250
fishing
   Border and Transkei 162, 163, 166, 173, 183
   Free State and Lesotho 97
   KwaZulu-Natal 109, 137, 141, 148, 150, 155
   Lake St Lucia 116, 117
   Namibia 344
   Northern and North-West Provinces 26
   South-Western Cape 262, 272, 285
   Western Cape 218, 234
   Zimbabwe 308, 320, 328, 330, 333
Fitzpatrick, *Sir* Percy 50, 51, 60, 61, 203
Fitzsimons Snake Park 148
Flagstaff 162
Floorshoogte 259
Flora (ship) 248, 249
Florence Bloom Bird Sanctuary 86
Florida Lake 86

Florisbad man 95
Floriskraal Dam 232
flower regions *see* wildflower regions
Flynn, Frank 157
Forbes, Alex 54
Forbes Reef 54
Forest Falls 41
Forestry Museum, Sabie 41
Formosa *see* Plettenberg Bay
Fort, The, Muizenberg 255
Fort Beaufort 182, 183, 190
Fort Brown 190
Fort Durnford 131
Fort Edward 19
Fort Frederick 204, 205
Fort Hare 184
Fort Hare University 182, 191
Fort Hendrina 12, 18, 19
Fort Inungu 324
Fort Klapperkop 74
Fort Mary 44
Fort Merensky 72, 73
Fort Namutoni 338, 339
Fort Napier 140, 141
Fort Nongqai 119
Fort Nottingham 138
Fort Pearson 119, 146, 147
Fort Schanskop 74
Fort Selwyn 195
Fort Victoria (now Masvingo) 320, 321
Fort Wilhelm 73
fortifications
   Aliwal North 179
   Barberton 51
   Bloemfontein 94, 95
   Botshabelo 72, 73
   Burgersdorp 179
   Cogmanskloof 236, 237
   Committee's Drift 190
   Durban 149
   Fraser's Camp 190
   Grahamstown 195
   Himeville 137
   Hogsback 184
   Louis Trichardt 12, 18, 19
   Lydenburg 44
   Magaliesberg 28, 79
   Midlands, KwaZulu-Natal 138
   Mossel Bay district 234
   Norvalspont 179
   Port Elizabeth 204, 205
   Pretoria 74
   Suurbraak 237
   Trompetter's Drift 191
   Warmbaths 24
   Windhoek 343
fossils 87
   Bloemfontein 95
   Golden Gate 92
   Karoo 190, 196, 197, 213, 215
   Pearston 196
   Sterkfontein 85
   Sudwala 44
   Waterberg 27
   Wolseley 269
fountain, illuminated musical 84
Fountains Valley Nature Reserve 74, 77
Four Men's Hill 156
Fouriesburg 96, 97
Francis Farewell Square 149
Francois, *Major* Curt von 342, 343
Franklin Nature Reserve 95
Franschhoek 244, 264, 265
Fransie Pienaar Museum 230
Fransmanshoek 234
Fraser's Camp 190, 195
Frazer, Affleck 69

French *see* Huguenot settlers
Frere, *Sir* Henry Bartle 147, 180
frontier wars 164, 191, 192, 193
fruit farming, Cape 264
Fundudzi, Lake 15
Fynn, Frank 157

G

Gaika (Ngqika) 164, 182, 183
Gaika's Kop 182, 183
Gallows Hill 271
Galpin, Henry 195
Game Festival 27
game parks and reserves
   Daan Viljoen 343
   Dombawera 311
   Giant's Castle 130, 132-3
   Hluhluwe 112-3
   Krugersdorp 86
   Lake Chivero 308, 309
   Lake Mutirikwi 321
   Mabula Lodge 26
   Manzou Park 311
   Mfolozi 112, 114-5
   Mkuzi 110-11
   Molopo 33
   Mosdene 26
   Mukuvisi Woodlands 307
   Mwanga 310
   Natal Lion 141
   Ndumo 108, 110-1
   Ocean View 119
   Sabie 58
   St Lucia 116
   Seaview Park 202, 211
   Shingwedzi 58
   Tshabalala Sanctuary 325
   Tussen-die-Riviere 178
   Umfolozi 112, 114-5
   Umfurudzi 311
   Welgevonden 26
   Werner Frehse 235
   Whovi 324
   Wolhuterskop 97
   Zindele 311
   see also national parks; nature reserves
Gamkaskloof 229, 303
Gamsberg 340
Gamsberg Pass 340, 341
Gamtoos River 206, 208, 209
Gamtoos River Valley 206, 207, 209
Gandhi, Mohandas 147
Gandou Pass 264
Gansbaai 260
Garcia, Maurice 235
Garcia State Forest 234
Garcia's Pass 234
Garden, Company's 252
Garden Castle 136
Garden Route (railway) 224-5
Gardiner, Allen 136
Gariep Dam 178, 179
Gats River valley 196
Gatsrand 271
Gaub Pass 340
Gaub River 336, 340
Gcaleka (people) 164
Gcalekaland 168, 169
Gem of the Karoo 212
gemsbok 340, 341
Genadendal (presidential residence) 258
Genadendal Mission 258, 259, 303
Generaalskop 93
General Hertzog Bridge 178
Geological Survey, Museum of 75
George 223, 224, 226, 227

George V, *King* (memorial) 249
George Harrison Park 83
George-Knysna train route 224-5
George's Valley 22
Gerard, Joseph 98
German-Nama War 336, 342
German settlers 171, 173, 174, 183
German settlers' monument 174
Gerotz, Dawid 212
Gertrude Posel Art Gallery 84
Geut, Die 47
ghost towns
    Eureka City 50, 51, 53
    Millwood 222
Giant's Castle 136, 138
Giant's Castle Game Reserve 130, 132-3
Giant's Cup Hiking Trail 134
Giant's Playground 336, 337
Gibeon 342
Gibraltar Rock 156
Gifberg 284
Gill, William 188
Gillooly's Farm 85
Gingindlovu 119
giraffe 62, 309
glacial pavement 296, 297
Gladiolus equitans 291
Gladstone's Nose (rocks) 138
Glen Avon Heights 188, 189
Glen Beach 254
Glen Reenen 90, 91, 92, 93
Glen Thorn Settler Church 189
Glendale Heights 147
Gleneagles Mountain Reserve 316
Glenelg, *Lord* 175
Glenlivet 320, 321
Glynn, Henry 41
goat towers 244
God's Window 37, 39, 41
Goedetrou Dam 119
Goedverwacht 278
Goegap Nature Reserve 288
gold mining and prospecting
    Mpumalanga 41, 42, 45, 50, 51, 52, 53, 82
    Northern Province 22
    Western Cape 222
Gold Reef City 82, 83, 87
Golden Acre 252, 253
Golden Gate 91
Golden Gate Dam 91, 93
Golden Gate Highlands National Park 90, 91, 92-3
Golden Spiderweb Resort 320, 321
Golden Valley 189
Goliath's Kraal Heights 196
Gonarezhou Park 310
Gondwanaland 126
Gondwane River 171
Gonubie 170
Gonubie River 171
Goodhouse 303
Gordon, Robert Jacob 262
Gordon Highlanders 47
Gordon's Bay 262
Goshen (republic) 33
Gouda 277
Goukamma Valley 225
Gould's Salvation Spruit 50
Gourits River 234
Gouritsmond 234
Government Avenue 253
Gowrie, St John's church 138
Gqoyeni Bush Lodge 115
Graaff-Reinet 196, 212-3, 214, 215, 302
Graafwater 284
Grabouw 265

Graham, *Colonel* John 194
Grahamstown 190, 191, 192, 193, 194-5
Grand Parade 252
Granokop 60
grape festival 27
Graskop 36, 39, 40, 41
graves
    Boyes Drive 246
    Holoog 336
    Kakamas 292
    Louis Trichardt 12
    Middelburg, Mpumalanga 73
    Sheba 50
Gray, Robert 235
Gray, Sophie 235
Great Brak River 226
Great Dyke 308
Great Fish River 190, 191
Great Fish River Museum 197
Great Karas Mountains 337
Great Karoo 230, 232
Great Kei River 164, 168, 171
Great Letaba River 22
Great Synagogue 252, 253
Great Winterhoek Mountains 211
Great Zimbabwe 320, 321, 322-3
Green Gables 327
Green Point, KwaZulu-Natal 152, 153
Greenmarket Square 253
Greenmount 319
Grey, *Sir* George 121, 175, 176, 204
Grey Hospital 175
Grey's Pass 277
Greyling's Pass 181
Greyton 258, 259
Greytown 121
Griqua people 162, 163, 277
Griqualand East 277
Griqualand West 277, 300
Griquatown 277
Grobbelaars River 226, 228
Groendal
    Franschhoek 265
    Wilderness Area 211
Groendal Dam 211
Groene Kloof (Mamre) 272
Groenkloof 260
Groenvlei 225
Groot Bruintjieshoogte 196
Groot Constantia Estate 250, 251
Groot Hartseer plateau 282
Groot Kerk 302
Groot Marico 32-3
Groot Nylsoog 24
Groot River 206, 207, 209, 218, 228, 234
Groot River Gorge 206, 207, 208, 209
Groot River lagoon 218
Groot Swartberg range 226
Groot Winterhoek range 247
Groote Kerk 253
Groote Schuur Estate 250
Grootkloof 200, 201
Group Areas Memorial 249
Groutville 147
Grünau 337
guano islands 285
Gubu Dam 182
Gubukuvho 14, 17
Guinea Fowl Trail 210
Gully, The 157
Gulu Beach 172
Gulu River lagoon 173
Gunfire Hill 192, 195
Gunjaneni 113
Gush, Richard 192

Gustav Klingbiel Nature Reserve 44, 48
Gutu 320
Guvhukuvhu 14, 17
Gwebi River 308
Gxara River 164, 169
Gydo Pass 276, 277

H

Ha Baroana 99
Ha Khotso 99
Ha Ntsi 98
Haarlem (ship) 261
Haasbroek, Leendert 270
Hadedas 171
Haenertsburg 22
Haggard, *Sir* Henry Rider 131
Halali 338, 339
halfmens (plant) 291
Hamburg 172, 173
Hamilton Park 95
Hang-gliding 276
Hangklip 246, 262
Hanglip (peak) 27
Hanglip Forest Reserve 12, 19
Hankey 206, 209
Hans Merensky Dam 20, 21
Happy Valley 184, 210
Harare 306-7, 308, 310
Hare Krishna Temple of Understanding 151
Harold Porter Botanic Garden 262, 263
Harpley, Sydney 252, 253
Harrismith 90, 91
Harrison, George 83
Hart, Robert 188, 189
hartbeeshuisies 12
Hartbeespoort Cableway 78, 79
Hartbeespoort Dam 78, 79
Hartbeespoort Snake and Animal Park 78
Harvey Nature Reserve 85
Haunted Forest 339
Havelock Mine 52, 54, 55
Hawepad (Long Tom Pass) 46
Hazelmere Dam 148
Hazyview 40
Heads, The, Knysna 222, 223
Heerenlogement 284
Heidelberg, Gauteng 80, 81
Heikum San 338, 339
Heinitzburg 343
Hekpoort 29, 79
Hel, Die (Gamkaskloof) 229
Helehele butresses 134
Hella-Hella Pass 134, 135
Helsekloof 282
Helshoogte Pass 245, 265
Hemel-en-Aarde Valley 262
Henley Dam 141
Hennops Pride Pleasure Resort 78
Hennops River Valley 77
Henties Bay 344
herbalists 83
Herbertsdale 234
Herero 342
Herman Eckstein Park 86
Hermannsburg Mission House 122, 123
Hermanus 260, 262
Hermitage 203
Herrieklip 229
Hessequa Khoikhoi 237
Hester Rupert Art Gallery 213
Heuningvlei 282
Hex River 29
Hiddenvlei 341
Hidli Vlei 113

highest point in SA 133
highest road in SA 177
Highflats 154
Highland Brigade 296
Highland Route 90, 91
Highveld 80-1
Hildebrand Memorial 272, 273
Hillbrow 82
Hillside Dams, Bulawayo 327
Hilltop, Hluhluwe 112, 113
Hilltop Pass 51
Himalaya Mountains 312, 318
Himeville 135, 136, 137
Himmelberg Mission 154
Hindu festivals 151
Hindu temples 121, 141, 146, 150
Hippopotami 67, 254, 311
    Huberta 160, 175
Hlangwane 128
Hlatikulu Forest Reserve 109
Hlaza 113
Hluhluwe Game Reserve 112-3
Hluhluwe-Umfolozi Park 112-5, 117
Hobas 336, 337
Hobhouse, Emily 95
Hodgson's Peaks 134
Hoedjieskop 274
Hoeko 232, 233
Hogsback 182, 184-5
Hohenzollernhaus 344
Hole-in-the-Wall,
    KwaZulu-Natal 146
    Transkei 166, 167
Holkrans Walk 93
Holoog 336
Homtini River 223
Honde View 314, 316
Hondeklipbaai 289
honey 318
Honeybird Creek 50, 53
Honnet Nature Reserve 12, 13
Honoured Dead Memorial 296, 301
Hoogekraal River 223
Horse Memorial
    Grahamstown 194
    Port Elizabeth 205
Horseshoe Falls 40
hot springs
    Ai-Ais 336, 337
    Aliwal North 179
    Badplaas 54
    Bronne, Die 211
    Caledon 262
    Chimanimani 318, 319
    Citrusdal 277
    KwaZulu-Natal 123
    Montagu 237
    Tshipise 12, 13
    Waterberg 24, 25, 27
    Windhoek 342
    Zimbabwe 319
Hotagterklip 260
Hottentots Holland Mountains 240, 247, 264
Houhoek Pass 263
Houses of Parliament 252, 253
Hout Bay 246, 250, 254, 255
Hout Bay Nek 246, 250
Houtbosdorp 20, 22, 23
Houw Hoek Inn 262, 263
Howick 138
Howick Falls 138, 139
Howison's Poort 192, 193
Huberta the hippo 160, 175
Huguenot Monument and Museum 265
Huguenot settlers 244, 265
Humansdorp 209

Hunyani range 308
Hurungwe Safari Area 332
Husab Welwitschia 345
Hwange 310, 328
Hwangura 312
Hypoxis rigidula 80

I

Ida's Valley 265
Ifafa Beach 152
Igoda Mouth 172, 173
Ilanda Wilds Nature Reserve 153
impala, black-faced 338
impundulu 164, 165
Incwala 57
Indian Ocean 247
Indian settlers 147
Indigenous Tree Park 12, 19
indigenous trees, Hluhluwe 113
Indwe 180, 181
Infanta 238
Inhluzana hills 142
initiation rites
  Lesotho 103
  Transkei 164, 169
  Venda 16, 17
Injasuti 132, 133
Inyanga 317
Inyangani Mountain 314, 316, 317
Inyezane River 119
Inyoni Rocks 153
Irish Brigade 53
Irish settlers 281
Irma Stern Museum 255
Iron Age 27, 313
Iron Age sites 12, 28, 31, 79, 85, 121, 315, 316, 317, 322-3
Iron Crown 22, 23
iron-ore mines 55, 345
iron-ore reduction works 43
Isaac Stegmann Nature Reserve 85
Isandhlwana 106
Iscor 76
Isidenge Mountain 182
Isikhova Walk 117
Islamia Mosque 141
Island, The, Great Brak River 226
Island Forest Reserve 202, 210
island mountains 340
Italian prisoners of war 318
  churches built by 141, 320, 332
Ixopo 154, 155
Izingolweni 156

J

Jacaranda (shipwreck) 168
Jager's Walk 246
Jakkalsvlei 284
James, Ingram 53
James and Ethel Gray Park 86
James Hall Transport Museum 84
Jameson, Leander Starr 325, 326
Jameson Park 151
Jameson's Drift 122
Jamestown 53
Jan Joubertsgat Bridge 264, 265
Jan van Riebeek Park 86
Japanese Gardens, Durban 151
Jeffreys Bay 208
Jerusalemgangers 25
Jewish Museums
  Cape Town 253
  Johannesburg 83
Jock of the Bushveld 50, 51, 60, 61
Johan Rissik Estate 78
Johannesburg 78, 80, 82-7
Johannesburg Art Gallery 83, 84

Johannesburg Botanic Garden 186
Johannesburg Lion Park 86
Johannesburg Public Library 84
Johannesburg Stock Exchange 83
Johannesburg Zoological Gardens 86
Johannesdal 245, 265
Johanneskirche 122
Johanniter House 337
John Ross House 149
Jojosi River 106
Jolivet 154
Jora River 317
Jordaan River 97
Josefsdal border post 54
Josini 108
Joubert, Piet 19
Joubert Bridge 41, 43
Joubert Park 84
Jubilee Creek 222
Jubilee Square 249
Juliasdale (village) 314, 316
Julius Gordon Africana Centre 234
Juma Mosque 148, 150
Jurisch Wild Flower Garden 235
Just Nuisance 248, 249
Jutten Island 274

K

Ka Hele Hele Nature Reserve 135
Kaaimans River 223
Kaaimans River mouth 224
Kaaloog 32
Kaapsehoop 52
Kabeljous Bay 208
Kabeljous River 208
Kaburi Wilderness 332, 333
Kadie (ship) 239, 240
Kadishi Falls 39
Kadzamu Fort 314
Kaffraria, British 173, 174, 175
Kaffrarian Museum 175
Kaiserkrone 336
Kakamas 292, 293
Kalahari Gemsbok National Park 292, 293, 298-9
Kalbaskraal 273
Kalk Bay 246, 247, 255
Kamberg Nature Reserve 138, 139
Kambule, Elijah 133
Kame Ruins 323
Kamfer, Lorenz 244
Kamiesberg 291
Kamieskroon 302
Kanniedood Dam 66
Kanondraai 92
Kanoneiland 292, 293
Kanonpunt 234
Karamat, Signal Hill 250
Karas region 337
Karatara River 223
Karbonkelberg peninsula 246
Kareeberg Karoo 303
Kareekloof Public Resort 80
Kariba Dam *see* Lake Kariba
Kariba (town) 331, 332
Kariba Dam *see* Lake Kariba
Karkloof Falls 138, 139
Karkloof Valley 139
Karnmelkspruit 176
Karoo 196, 200-1, 212-5, 230-1, 232-3
  flora 211
  fossils 190, 213
Karoo geological system 196
Karoo Nature Reserve 197, 214-5
Kaspersnek Pass 48, 49
Kasteelberg 268, 272, 273
Kat River 182

Kat River Valley 191
Katana 133
Katberg Pass 190, 191
Kayser's Beach 172
Keate's Drift 120
Keetmanshoop 336, 337
Kei Mouth 170
Kei River, Great 164, 168, 171
Keimoes 292, 293
Keiskamma River valley 172
Keiskammahoek 182, 184
Kelders, Die 260
Kelvinside 189
Kenneth Stainbank Reserve Nature 151
Kerkenberg 90, 91
Kestell 91
Kestell, *Rev* John Daniel 91, 128
Kettlespout Waterfall 185
Keurbooms River 218
Kevelaer Mission 135
Keytersnek 225
Khami (Kame) Ruins 327
Khoikhoi 206, 237, 258, 264, 272, 277
Khomas Hochland 340, 342
Kidd's Beach 172, 173
Killie Campbell Africana Museum 150
Kimberley 296, 300-1
Kimberley Mine Museum 300
King, Dick 149, 166, 175
King Edward VII Tree 220, 221
King William's Town 174-5
King's Nek 185
King's Park 95
Kirkwood 202, 203
Kirkwood, James Somers 203
Kirstenbosch 250, 251, 254
Klaarstroom 229, 303
Klaas Island 294
Klawer 284, 291
Klein Berg River 268
Klein Hangklip 262
Klein Jukskei Motor Museum 87
Klein Olifants River 72, 73
Klein River 260
Klein Swartberg range 232, 233
Klein Windhoek Valley 342
Kleinfontein 32
Kleinhoogte 280
Kleinmond 262, 263
Kleinmond Coastal Nature Reserve 263
Kleinriviersberge 263
Klip River 128, 269, 271
Klip River Republic 128
Klipdrift 297
Klipkoppie Dam 40
Klipriviersberg Nature Reserve 85
klipspringer 127
Klipspringer Trail 295
Kloof, KwaZulu-Natal 142
Kloof Falls 142
Kloof Nek 250, 254
Kloofendal Nature Reserve 85
Klopperfontein Dam 69
Knersvlakte 285
Knysna 222, 223
Knysna-George steam train 224-5
Knysna Lagoon 220, 223, 225
Knysna (ship) 170
Kobonqaba River Valley 168, 169
Koeberg Hill 272
Koeberg Nuclear Power Station 272
Koedoes River Valley 20
Koeëlbaai 262
Koeivlei Mountain 284

Koffiegat 277
Koffiehoogte 47
Kok, Adam 162, 163, 277
kokerboom 295, 337
Kokstad 162, 277
Kologha State Forest 182, 183
Kolonieshuis 267
Komaggas 288
Kommetjie 246, 254
Kompasberg 198
Koonap River 189
Koopmans De Wet House 255
Koperberg 288
Koppie Alleen 238
Koranna 293
Koringhuis 289
Kosi Bay Nature Reserve 108, 109
Kosmos (settlement) 78, 79
Koue Bokkeveld Mountains 277
Kowie Museum 193
Kowie River 193, 303
Kowyn's Pass 36, 40, 41
Kraai River 177
Kraai River Pass 176
Kransberg Mountains 26, 27
Kranshoek Reserve 220
Kranshoek River 220
Kranskop 25, 122, 123
Krantzkloof Nature Reserve 142, 151
Kratzenstein Mission 22
Kreli 168
Krokodilpoort 50
Kromme River 208
Kromrivier 280, 282
Kronendal homestead 250
Kruger, Paul 29, 53, 58, 75, 90
Kruger House Museum 75
Kruger millions 44
Kruger National Park 58-69
Krugersdorp Game Reserve 86
Kruisvallei 271
Kruithuis, Stellenbosch 267
Kubusi River 183
kudu statue 343
Kuiseb River 340
Kunene River 338
Kupferberg Pass 340
Kuruman 32, 33
Kwa Muhle Museum 149
Kwabhekithunga 118, 119
KwaCele traditional village 156
KwaJobe clan 111
Kwalata 26
Kwamondi Mission 119
KwaTelaphi 121
Kyle (Mutirikwi) Dam 320, 321

L

La Mercy 146, 147
La Rochelle Gardens 314, 315
Laaiplek 275, 278
Ladismith 232, 233
Lady Frere/Cacadu 180, 181
Lady Grey 176
Lady Kennaway (ship) 171
Ladysmith 128
Laguneberg 344
Laing, John 232
Laingsburg 232
Lake Bhangazi 117
Lake Chivero Recreation Park 308, 309
Lake Funduzi (Fundudzi) 15, 17
Lake Kariba 330-1, 332, 333
  ferry cruise 330-1
Lake Manyame 308
Lake Mentz (now Darlington Dam) 203

351

Lake Merthley 121
Lake Mutirikwi 320, 321
Lake Mutirikwi Game Park 321
Lake Nhlange 108, 109
Lake St Lucia 110, 116-7
Lambert's Bay 284, 285, 290, 291
lammergeyer 93, 133
Lancer's Gap 100, 103
Land van Waveren 268, 269, 270, 271
Langalibalele Pass 133
Langalibalele Rebellion 131, 133
Langebaan 274
Langeberg Mountains 234, 235, 236, 237, 240, 241
Langenhoven, CJ 229, 233
Langstrand 344
Langtoon Dam 93
Langvlei 225
Lapalala Wilderness 26, 27
Larvon Bird Gardens 308, 309
Lategan, Jan Felix 212
Lawrence de Lange Nature Reserve 180
Le Fortune (shipwreck) 234
Le Vaillant, Francois 274
Lebombo Mountains 66
Lehr Falls 157
Leipoldt, C Louis 280, 281
Lekokoaneng 100
Leliefontein 291
Leon Taljaard Nature Reserve 33
Leopard Rock Resort 312
leopards 66, 67
Lephalala River 26
Lesotho 98-103
Lesotho Highlands Water Scheme 81
Lesotho plateau 126
Lesotho traditions 102-3
Letaba 65, 66
Letaba River 49, 66
Letaba Valley 22
Letsiteli Valley 22
Letty's Bridge 237
Leucospermum reflexum 283
Leydsdorp 22, 23
liberation struggle memorials 309
Libertas (farm) 266
Libertas Parva 267
Libode 160
lichens 344
lighthouses
 Agulhas 260, 261
 Cape Columbine 274, 275
 Cape St Blaize 234
 Green Point, KwaZulu-Natal 152, 153
 Port Elizabeth 204
 Seal Point 208
 Swakopmund 344
lightning bird (Transkei myth) 164, 165
Likalaneng Pass 99
Limiet Vallei 268
Limpopo River 12, 68
Lion Battery 250
Lion Cavern 55
Lion Gateway 253
Lion Park, Johannesburg 86
lions 63, 113, 114
Lion's Head 246, 250, 254
Lions River 138
Lisboa (ship) 274
Lisbon Falls 41
Little Berg 130, 138
Little Brak River 226
Little Caledon River valley 92
Litte Karoo 226-9, 235
Little Lion's Head 246, 250

Little Theatre 253
Little Tugela River 129
Livingstone, David 33, 329
Llandudno 246, 254
Lobamba 56, 57
lobengula 326
lobola 145
Loch Athlone 96, 97
Loch Logan 95
Lochiel 55
loerie (bird)
 Knysna 185, 210, 219
 Livingstone's 319
Loerie (town) 209
Loeriesfontein 291
Logola River 331
Lone Creek Waterfall 40, 41
Long Beach 254
Long Cecil (cannon) 301
Long Tom Memorial 45, 46, 47
Long Tom Pass 44, 45, 46-7
Lookout Beach 218
Loskop 139
Louis Trichardt 12, 13, 14, 19
Louisvale 292
Lourens River Valley 264
Lovedale College 191
Lovedu 21
Lover's Bridge, Ceres 277
Lovu River 134, 152
Löwen River 336, 337
Lower Sabie 61, 62, 63
Lowveld Botanic Garden 45
Lüderitz 340
Lukin, *Sir* Henry Timson 175, 253
Lukosi River 328
Lunar's Landing 48
Lundy's Hill 135
Lusikisiki 162
Luthuli, Albert 147
Luttig, Jan 231
Lutubeni Mission 166
Lutzville 284, 291
Luvuvhu River 68, 69
Lydenburg 44, 47, 48
Lydenburg Waterfall 48, 49

M

Maanhaarrand 28, 78, 79
Maasström 189
Mabitse Valley 21
Mabula Game Lodge 26
MacGregor Geological Museum 307
Machache Mountain 98
McCleland, *Reverend* Francis 205
McGregor, (town) 258, 259
McGregor Memorial Museum, Kimberley 300
McKay's Nek Mission 180, 181
McKinlay's Pool 127
McLachlan, Tom 52
Maclear (town) 177
MacMac Falls and Pools 36, 37, 41
Macrorie House Museum 141
Madonna and Child Waterfall 185
Madziwa Mine Village 310, 311
Maeder House Craft Centre 100
Mafeking road, the 32, 33
Mafikeng (formerly Mafeking) 32, 33
Magali 28
Magalies River 78, 79
Magaliesberg 28-9, 78, 79, 85
Magangeni Hill 112
Magazine Hill 213
Magersfontein 296
Magersfontein battlefield 301

Magersfontein Field Museum 296
Magersfontein Koppie Memorial 298
Magnolia Dell 77
Magoeba, *Chief* 20
Magoebaskloof 21, 23
Magoebaskloof Dam 20
Mahai River 127
Mahloenyeng 101
Mahlongwa River 152
Mahombekombe 332, 333
Mahonie Drive 68
Main Caves, Giant's Castle 132
Main Road, Cape Town 303
Maitland Nature Reserve 202, 210
Maitland River Mouth 202
Makana's Kop 190, 191
Makapan 18
Makapansgat Caves 27
Makhane 16
Makuti 332
Malan, *Reverend* DF 237
malaria 23, 65
Malay Quarter 255
Malelane 60
Maleme Dam 324
Malgas 238, 239
Malgas Island 274
Malherbe Memorial Garden 259
Malmesbury 268, 273
Malolotja Nature Reserve 54
Malora Hill 27
Maltese Cross (rock) 282, 283
Maluti Mountains 90, 96, 98-9, 101
Malvadraai 229
Mambeni Gate, Umfolozi 115
mampoer 32
Mampoer Tour 32
Mamre 272
Mandavu Dam 328
Mandawe 118
Mandawe church 119
Manganeni Hill 112, 113
Mankalakele 44
Mankazana River valley 189
Mankwe, Lake 31
Manubi Forest 169
Manyama Dam Recreation Park 308
Manzou Game Park 311
Map of Africa (view) 223
Mapelane 117
Maphumulo 112, 113
Mapjaneng 39
Mapulana clan 39
Mapumulo 122
Mapungubwe 32,3
Maputaland 108-9, 110-11
Mapuzi Reserve 167
Mara 18
Marais, Eugene 25
Marais, Sarie 121
Marakabei 99
Marakele National Park 26
Marchand 292
Marcus Island 274
Mare/Nyangwe Dam 314, 316, 317
Margate 156
Maria Ratschitz Mission 121
Maria Shires waterfall 36, 41
Marianhill Monastery 150
Mariathal Catholic church 155
Marico 32-3
Mariepskop 39
Marine Drive, East London 172
Marine Parade 148, 151
Marine Reserve, St Lucia 117
Maritz, Gerrit 140

market square 302
Market Theatre complex 83
martello tower 182, 183, 249
Martin Melck House 255
Martins, Helen 198-9
Maseru 98, 100, 101
Masey, Francis 247
Mashile, Maripi 39
Masinda Camp 114, 115
Masite Mountain 100
Masque Theatre 255
Masuma Dam 328
Masvingo 320, 321
Mata Mata Camp 299
Matabele (people) 33. 324, 326
Matenderere River 317
Matjiesrivier 280
Matobo Hills 324, 325
Matopos Dam 325
Matshemma 16
Matsieng 101
Matsikamma Mountain 284
Matukwala Dam 68
Matusadona National Park 331, 332, 333
Mauchsberg 45, 47
Maydon Wharf 149
Maynardville Theatre 255
Mayville, Swellendam 241
Mazeppa Bay 168, 169
Mazowe Dam 311
Mazowe River 310
Mazowe Valley 311
Mazwi Nature Reserve 327
Mbabane 54, 55
Mbandzeni 56
Mbare Musika 306
Mbhombe Forest 112
Mbhombe Forest Trail 113
Mbizane Lagoon 157
Mbizane River valley 156
Mcantsi River 172
Mdindini 115
Mdloti River 147
medicine, history of: museum 87
Medwood Gardens 151
Meeuw Island 274
Meijers Bridge 72
Meintjies Kop 75
Meiringskloof Nature Resort 97
Meiringspoort 228, 229
Melck family 244
Melkbosstrand 273
Melrose Bird Sanctuary 86
Melrose House 75, 77
Melville Koppies 85
Memorial Gate, Hluhluwe 112
Merensky, Alexander 73
merino sheep 239
Mermaid's Pool 310
Merriman House 195
Messelpad 288, 289, 291
Messina 12, 13
Meteorite Fountain 342
Methuen, *Lord* 296
Meul River 224
Meurant, Louis Henri 191
Meyers Park Nature Reserve 77
Mfabeni Reserve 117
Mfazana Pans 117
Mfecane 126
Mfengu 164
Mfolozi Game Reserve 112, 114-5
Mgeni River 138, 139, 142, 143
Mgeni Valley Nature Reserve 138
Mguza Nature Reserve 327
Mhlali River 147
Mhlanga River 147
Mhlatuze valley 118, 119
Mhlengana (Execution Rock) 160

Mhlopeni Nature Reserve 121
Mia Falls 312
Michaelis Collection 253
Michel, *Colonel* 184
Michel's Pass 182, 184
Michell, *Colonel* Charles 261
Michell's Pass 276, 277
Middelberg, Cederberg 282
Middelberg Pass 276
Middelburg, Mpumalanga 72
Middelpos 340
Midlands Meander 130
Midmar Dam 138, 141, 142
Midmar Historical Village 142
Mielierug 224
milestones 303
Military History, Museum of 86
Miller's Point 246, 255
Millwood 222
Milnerton Beach 255
Miner's House Museum 43
Minitown 148
mining and mines
   oldest mine in the world 55
   see also gold mining and prospecting
Mingerhout Dam 65
Mission Rocks 117
missionary museums
   Cape Town 255
   King William's Town 174
Mitchell Park 151
Mitford-Barberton, Ivan 246, 253
Mkhomazana River 134, 135
Mkhumbane River 144, 152
Mkomazi River 134, 152
Mkomazi Valley 135
Mkuze River 110
Mkuze village 108
Mkuzi Game Reserve 110
Mlalazi River 119
Mlazi River 134
Mlibizi Zambezi Resort 330, 333
Mlondozi Dam 62
Mmabatho 33
Mngazi River and Valley 160
Mnguni 164
Modjadji (village) 20, 21
Modjadji (Rain Queen) 21
Modjadji Nature Reserve 20
Moerdijk, Gerard 25
Moffat, Robert 33
Mogolakwena River 25
Mogwase 31
Mohale *see* Magali
Moholoholo 39
Mokhotlong 134
Molimo Nthuse Pass 98, 99
Molopo Game Reserve 33
Molototsi valley 20
Molshoop 260
monkey, Samango 185
monkey rope 112
Monk's Cowl 129, 133
Monomotapa 268
Mont-aux-Sources 126
Montagu 236, 237
Montagu Pass 227, 303
Montrose Falls 44, 45
Moodie, George Pigot 53
Moodie, Thomas 318
Mooi River 120, 130, 138
Mooi River Trail 138
Moon landscape 344
Moon Rock 293, 295
Moor Park 130
Moorddrif Monument 27
Moorreesburg 272, 273
Moos, Hans 237
Moravian Mission, Elim 261

Moreleta Spruit 76
Moreleta Spruit Trail 77
Morgan Bay 170, 171
Morija 100, 101
Moringa Forest 339
Mosega 33
Moshoeshoe 100, 102, 103
   statue 100, 101
mosques
   Durban 148, 150
   Johannesburg 83
   Pietermaritzburg 141
   Simon's Town 249
   Stanger 122, 123, 146, 147
Mossel Bay 234, 235
Mostert's Mill 250
MOTH Garden of Remembrance 301
MOTH shrines 129, 325
Mothibi 33
moths 312
Motkop 176
Motor Museum, Klein Jukskei 87
Mount Anderson 38
Mount Currie Nature Reserve 163
Mount Dragon 136
Mount Kempt 182
Mount Lebanon 138
Mount Memory range 129
Mount Sullivan 160, 161
Mount Thate 17
Mount Thesiger 160, 161
Mountain Lake Adventures 109
mountain passes 303
Mountain Zebra National Park 196, 200-1
Mountain Zebra Trail 201
mountaineering, Drakensberg 127
Mpambanyoni River 152, 155
Mpcfu, *Chief* 19
Mphafa stream 115
Mphongolo River 66
Mpila Camp 114, 115
Mpondo 164
Mpondomise 160, 164
Mpophomeni Trail 117
Mpopoma Dam 324
Mqanduli 166
msasa tree 314, 317
Msinga clan 120
Msunduze River 110, 140, 141
Mswati (Mswazi) 56
Mswati III 57
Mtamvuna River 156, 157
Mtarazi Falls 316
Mtata River 160, 167
Mtubatuba 115
Mtunzini 119
Mtwalume River 152, 154, 155
Muden Valley 120
Mugudo 21
Muiskraal 234
Muizenberg 247, 255, 264
Mukumbani 16
Mukumbani Dam 15
Mukuvisi Woodlands 307
mule-powered trains 289
Munro's Bay 234
Muntulu 113
Munyawaneni 113
Muratie 244
Murray, *Rev* Andrew 212, 268
   statue 269
Murray, *Rev* Charles 198, 2136
museum ships, Table Bay 256, 257
museums
   Addington Hospital Centenary 150
   Adler History of Medicine 87
   Africa 86

Albany 195
Alexander McGregor 301
Anderson Memorial 181
Apple 264
Arend Dieperink 27
Art, Pretoria 76
Art, Somerset East 188, 189
Basotho Village Cultural 90, 96
Bensusan Museum of Photography 87
Bernberg Museum of Costume 87
Bertram House 253
Bo-Kaap 255
Botshabelo 73
Bredasdorp Shipwreck 261
Bulawayo Natural History 327
CP Nel 226, 228
Chamber of Mines' Coal 106
Charlotte Kritzinger Shell 208
Coal, Talana 106
Conservation 86
Correctional Services 76
Costume 87
Cultural History
   Bloemfontein 95
   Cape Town 253
Darling 272
Doornkloof Farm and Smuts House 76
Drostdy, Swellendam 240
Drostdy, Uitenhage 202
Durban Local History 149
Education 75
Environmental 77
Fire Service, Benoni 87
Firearms 212
Forestry 41
Fransie Pienaar 230
Geological Survey 75
George 227
Graaff-Reinet 196, 213
Great Fish River 197
Harry and Friedl Abt 83
Heidelberg 80, 81
Himeville 137
History of Medicine 87
Huguenot 265
James Hall Transport 84
Jewish 83, 253
Kaffrarian 175
Keetmanshoop 337
Killie Campbell Africana 150
Kimberley Mine 300
Klein Jukskei Motor 87
Kowie 193
Kruger House 75
Kwa Muhle 149
Lydenburg 48
MacGregor Geological 307
McGregor Memorial 300
Macrorie House 141
Mafikeng 32, 33
Magersfontein 296
Main Caves, Giant's Castle 132
Maritime, Cape Town 256
Maritime, Mossel Bay 234
Medicine, History of 87
Military History 86
Mining 296
Missionary 174, 255
Muslim House 255
Mutare 313
Natal 141
Natal Maritime 150
National 95
National Afrikaans Literary 95
National Cultural History and Open Air 75
National Symbols 249

Naval 248, 249
Observatory 195
Old Harbour 263
Oude Kerk Volksmuseum 270
Our Heritage 189
Owela 343
Owen 44
Owl House 198
Pearston 196
Pellissier House 178
Photography 87
Pioneer Open Air 76
Pioneers of Aviation 296
Queenstown and Frontier 180
Railway 202, 326
Reinet House 212
Rhodes Nyanga 316
Riversdale Africana Centre 234
Rock Art 86
Roodepoort 83
SA Sendinggestig 255
San 132
Sandveld 284
Schoemansdal 12
Science and Technology 76
Shells 208, 234
Ships, Table Bay 256, 257
Shipwreck 260, 261
Siege, Ladysmith 128
Smuts House 76
Somerset East 188
South African 253
South African Air Force 76, 87
South African Maritime 256
South African Navy 248, 249
South African Police 76
State 343
Stellenbosch 267
Stellenryck Wine 266
Talana 106
Togryers 276
TransNamib Railway 343
Transport 76, 80, 81, 84, 87, 176, 300, 313
Transvaal Natural History 75
Twaing 77
Uitenhage Historiese 202
Village, Stellenbosch 267
Voortrekker 74, 140
Wamakers 273
War Museum of the Boer Republics 95
Wellington 269
Wheat 272, 273
Whysalls Camera 150
Willem Prinsloo 72
Wine 266
Zululand Historical 119
Mushroom Rocks 90, 91, 93
musical fountains 84
Musilume Dam 324
Muslim House Museum 255
Muslim shrine, Cape Town 250
Mutapa dynasty 323
Mutarazi Falls 314
Mutare 312, 313, 314, 318
Mutirikwi (Kyle) Dam 320, 321
Mutirikwi River 320, 322
Mutshindudi River 14
Muzi Swamp 108
Mvoti River 123, 146, 147
Mvunyane River 106
Mwanga Game Park 310
Myrtle Rigg Memorial Church 236
Mzilikazi 28, 30, 33, 74, 326
Mzimkulu River 134, 137
Mzimkulu Valley 155
Mzimkulwana River and Valley 156, 157

353

Mzimvubu River 160, 161, 162, 163
Mzinto River 152
Mzumbe River and Valley 155

N

Nababeep 288, 289, 291
naboom (tree) 27
Naboomspruit 26, 27
Nachtwacht 260
Nagle Dam 141, 143
Nahoon River 170
Nama 268
  see also German-Nama War
Namaqualand 268, 277, 285, 288-91
Namib Desert 344
Namib plains 340, 341
Namib-Naukluft Park 340
Namibia 334-45
Namutoni, Fort 338, 339
Napier 260
Napoleon, *Prince* Eugène 107
Naravlei 341
Narina trogon 117, 219, 316
Natal Drakensberg Park 130
Natal Herbarium 151
Natal Lion and Game Park 141
Natal Maritime Museum 150
Natal Museum 150
Natal National Park *see* Royal Natal National Park
Natal Playhouse 150
National Afrikaans Literary Museum 95
national anthem 249
National Botanic Gardens of South Africa 250, 251
National Botanical Garden 77
National Cultural History and Open Air Museum 75
National Museum 95
national parks
  Addo Elephant 202, 203, 211
  Augrabies Falls 292, 293, 294-5
  Bontebok 238
  Chimanimani 318
  Etosha 338-9
  Golden Gate Highlands 90, 91, 92-3
  Hwange 328-9
  Kalahari Gemsbok 292, 298-9
  Kruger 58-69
  Marakele 26
  Matusadona 331, 332, 333
  Mountain Zebra 200
  Namib-Naukluft 340
  Nyanga 314, 316-7
  Pilanesberg 30-1
  QwaQwa Highland 90
  Rhodes Matopos 324, 325
  Royal Natal 90, 126-7
  Tsitsikamma 219
  West Coast 274
  Zuurberg 203, 211
  see also game parks and reserves; nature reserves
'national suicide' of Xhosa 164, 169, 182
National Symbols, Museum of 249
National Theatre of Namibia 343
National Zoological Gardens 77
nature reserves
  Baobab 12
  Ben Alberts 24, 26
  Ben Lavin 19

Blyde River Canyon 36
Bosberg 188
Botshabelo 73
Bredasdorp 261
Cape Columbine 275
Cape Cross Seal 345
Cape of Good Hope 246
Cape Recife 210
Ceres 277
Coleford 136, 137
De Hoop 238
De Vasselot 219
Double Drift 190
Enseleni 118
Faerie Glen 77
Fernkloof 263
Fountains Valley 74, 77
Franklin 95
Gleneagles Mountain 316
Goegap 288
Gustav Klingbiel 44, 48
Harvey 85
Himeville 135
Honnet 12, 13
Ilanda Wilds 153
Isaac Stegmann 85
Island Forest 202, 210
Kaburi Wilderness 332
Ka Hele Hele 135
Kamberg 138, 139
Karoo 197, 214-5
Keimoes 293
Kenneth Stainbank 151
Keurbooms River 218
Kleinmond Coastal 263
Klipriviersberg 85
Kloofendal 85
Kosi Bay 108, 109
Krantzkloof 142
Lawrence de Lange 180
Leon Taljaard 33
Maitland 202, 210
Malolotja 54
Marico Bushveld 32
Mazwi 327
Meiringskloof 97
Mgeni Valley 138
Mguza 327
Mhlopeni 121
Modjadji 20
Montagu Mountain 237
Mount Currie 163
Nyazengu 317
Nylsvley 26
Oviston 178
Percy Fyfe 26
Pongolapoort 109
Postberg 274
Pretoriuskloof 97
Queen Elizabeth 141
Rein's 234
Rocher Pan 278
Rustenburg 29
Sardinia Bay 210
Silaka 160, 161
Silvermine 250
Spioenkop 129
Suikerbosrand 80, 85
Table Mountain 254
Tembe Elephant Park 108
Uitenhage 211
Umgeni Valley 139
Umhlanga Lagoon 147, 151
Umlalazi 119
Umtamvuna 157
Vaal Dam 81
Vernon Crookes 154, 155
Vrolikheid 258
Wagendrift 130, 131
Weenen 120

Wonderboom 77
  see also game parks and reserves; national parks
Nature's Valley 218
Nauchas Farm 341
Naudesnek Pass 176, 177
Naukluft 340
Naukluft Mountains 341
Naute Dam 336
Naval Hill, Bloemfontein 94, 95
Nazareth, Lesotho 98
Ndaleni Mission 134
Ndawana River 137
Ndebele (people) 30, 74, 326
Ndebele village 72, 73
Ndluzulu 161
Ndonyane Centre 154
Ndumo Game Reserve 108, 110-1
Needle, The 157
Neharawa (*Chief*) 306
Nelshoogte State Forest 50, 54, 55
Nelson, *Lord* 248
Nelspruit 44, 45, 50, 51
Nenga River 167
Nerbudda (ship) 249
Netshiendeulu 16
Neulfontein se Berg 272
New Agatha Forestry Station 22
New Chum Falls 39
New Rush 300
Newlands Forest 250, 254
Ngoma Lungundu 16
Ngqika (Gaika) 164, 182, 183
Ngqika (people) 182
Nguni (people) 164
Ngwane 56
Ngwangwane River 136, 137
Ngwenya iron-ore mine 55
Ngwenya Mountain 54, 55
Nhlonhlela Pan 110, 111
Nico Malan complex 255
Nieu-Bethesda 196, 197, 198-9
Nieuweland 303
Nieuwoudt Pass 280
Njelele River 12
Nkone cattle 324
Nkonikini Trail 118
Nkunzaneni 118
Nkwalini village 119
Nkwazi River 147
Noetzie 220
Noetzie River 220
Nongqai, Fort 119
Nongqawuse 164, 169
Nooitgedacht 296
  Battle of 28
  glacial pavement 296, 297
Noord Brabant 93
Noordhoek 246, 254
Northern Border War 293
Nortier, P le Fras 281
Norvalspont 178, 179
Nossob Camp 299
Nossob River 298
Nottingham Road (town) 138
Nottinghamshire Regiment 197
Noupoort 258
Nseleni River 118
Nsclweni camp 115
Nsemani Dam 64
Nshongweni Dam 142, 143
Nshongweni Hill 143
Nsumo Pan 110, 111
Nswatugi Cave 324
Ntshala River 171
Ntuli, Ndlela 107
Nuwekloof Pass 268, 277
Nwanetsi 62
Nyabokwe Mountain 315
Nyakupinga River 314

nyala 68, 114
Nyala Drive 69
Nyamapanda Border Post 317
Nyamataka River 312
Nyamhuka village 314
Nyamziwa Falls 314
Nyamzure Mountain 319
nyanga (healer) 145
Nyanga, Zimbabwe 314, 315, 316
Nyanga Mountains 314, 316
Nyanga National Park 314, 316-7
Nyangwe/Mare Dam 314, 316, 317
Nyanyadzi irrigation scheme 318
Nyazengu Nature Reserve 317
Nylstroom 24, 25, 27
Nylsvley Nature Reserve 26
Nzhelele River 15
Nzimane River 113

O

Observatory, Bloemfontein 95
Observatory Museum, Grahamstown 195
Ocean View Game Park 119
Oceanarium, Port Elizabeth 211
Oceanos (ship) 166
O'Connor, Alexander 21
Odzani Dam and Falls 314
Odzi River 314
Oefeningshuis
  Graaff-Reinet 213
  Swellendam 239, 240
Ohrigstad 44, 46
Ohrigstad River 36, 39
Okaukuejo 339
Okiep 288, 289, 291
Old Fort, Durban 149
Old Harbour, Hermanus 262, 263
Old House Museum, Durban 149
Old Provost, Grahamstown 195
Old Toll Gate 98
Old Town House 253
Old Trading Post, Pilgrim's Rest 43
Olifants River 64, 65, 277, 284
Olifantsgeraamte 47
Olifantsnek 29
Olive Schreiner House 197
Olyvenhoutsdrif 292
Op die Berg 277
Opera House, Port Elizabeth 204
Operation Genesis 30
Operation Noah 332
Oppenheimer Fountain 83
Orange River 178, 179, 292, 293, 294
Orange River gorge 293
orange tree (national monument) 277
Orange-Fish River Tunnel 179
Oranjekom 292, 293
Oribi Gorge 156, 157
Orient (ship) 183
Orient Beach 183
Oriental Plaza, Johannesburg 83
Osmond, John 248
ostriches 226, 227, 228
  West Coast 272
Otjovasandu 338, 339
Otter Trail 219
Otto du Plessis Pass 181
Otto's Bluff 141
Otto's Walk 127
Ottoshoop 33
Ou Kaapse Huis, Johannesburg 87
Ou Kaapse Weg 250
Oude Kerk Volksmuseum 270

354

Oude Voorpost 343
Oudtshoorn 226, 228
Ouplaas 238
Our Heritage Museum 189
Outeniqua choo-choo 224-5
Outeniqua Mountains 226
Outeniqua Pass 226, 227
Overberg 240
Oviston Nature Reserve 178
Oviston tunnel 179
Owela Museum 343
Owen, WF 171
Owen Museum 44
Owl House 196, 198-9
ox monument 273
ox-wagon monument 106
oystercatcher, African black 270
Ozonjuitji m'bari 338, 339

P

Paarl Mountain 245
Pachypodium namaquanum 291
Paddagang 271
paddle steamer 333
Paddock (village) 156
Pafuri 68, 69
Pakhuis Pass 281, 282
Palace Barracks 248
Palace of Justice 75
Palace of Vultures 24
Palala plateau 27
Palmiet River 262, 264
Panorama Falls and Gorge 40
Pansy Beach 234
Paradise Valley 151
Park Rynie 154
Parktown 86
parrot, Cape 185
Patensie 206, 207, 209
Paternoster 275
Paterson, *Canon* Ned 324
Patterson, Alec 42
Paul Sauer Bridge 219
Paulet, *Lady* Mary 188
peach, Kakamas 293
Pearly Beach 260
Pearson Conservatory 205
Pearston 196
Pedi 39
Peglerae Trail 29
Pellissier House Museum 178
penguins 210, 246
Penhalonga 314
Pennington 152
'penny ferry', Cape Town 254, 255, 257
Pentzia grandiflora 290
Percy Fyfe Nature Reserve 26
Perdenek 181
Perestrelo, Manuel 208
Phezulu 142
Philadelphia 272
Philip Tunnel 206
Phiphidi Falls 14, 16
Phoenix (ship) 220
Phoenix Hall 249
Phoenix settlement 147
Phofung 127
Pholela River 135
photography museum
  Durban 150
  Johannesburg 87
Phumangena Zulu Kraal 83
Phuthaditjhaba 90
Phuthiatsana River 100
Piekeniersloof 277
Pierneef, JH 76
Piesang River 218

Pietermaritzburg 134, 138, 140-1, 143
Pietershoogte 128
Piggs Peak 54, 55
Piketberg 278
Pilanesberg National Park 30-1
Pilgrim's and Sabie News 42
Pilgrim's Pass 41
Pilgrim's Rest 40, 42-3, 48, 49
pineapple production 172
Pinnacle, The 37, 41
Pioneer Column 320, 321
Pioneer Nursing Memorial 314
Pioneer Open Air Museum 76
Pioneer Park 84
Pioneer Reef 53
planetarium
  Cape Town 253
  Johannesburg 87
Platrand/Wagon Hill 128
Pleistocene, Upper 201
Plesianthropus Transvaalensis 85
Plettenberg, Joachim van 218
Plettenberg Bay 218, 220
  beacon 303
Pniel 245, 265
Pofadder 291
Pofadder, Klaas 293
Pomeroy 120
Pomongwe Cave 324
Pondo 160, 164
Pondoland 164
Pongola River 108
Pongolapoort Biosphere Reserve 109
Pongolapoort Dam 108, 109
Pongolapoort Nature Reserve 109
ponies, Basuto 102, 103
pont, Malgas 239
Ponte Italia culvert 318
pony trekking 98, 99
Popoteke River Gorge 321
Pork Pie *(Nyamzure)* Mountain 319
Port Alfred 192, 193
Port Beaufort 239
Port Edward 157
Port Elizabeth 202, 204-5, 206, 208, 210-11
Port Nolloth 289
Port Rex 170
Port St Johns 160, 161, 162, 163
Porterville 276, 277
Portswood Ridge 257
Portulacaria afra 211
Post Huys 255
Post Office Tree 234
Postberg Nature Reserve 274, 275
Pot River Pass 177
Potberg 238
Potgieter, AH 18, 19, 38, 46
Potgieter, Hendrik 27
Potgieter, Hermanus 18
Potgieter, Piet 18, 27
Potterill, Charles Davie 133
Premier Diamond Mine 76
Prentjiesberg 177
Presidency, Bloemfontein 95
President Swart Park 95
Pretoria 72, 74-7, 78, 80
Pretorius, Andries 24, 25, 74
  at Blood River 106, 107
  home 140
  statue 75, 77
Pretorius, Marthinus 18, 75
Pretorius, Petrus Gerhardus 140
Pretoriuskloof Nature Reserve 97
Pretoriuskop 60
Pride of De Kaap 50, 53
Prince Albert 228, 229, 230-1

Prince Albert Road 303
Prince Alfred Hamlet 277
Prince Alfred's Pass 220, 221
Prince Edward Graving Dock 149
Prince Imperial's Memorial 106, 107
Prince of Wales' Viewpoint 312, 313
Pringle, Thomas 189
Proctor, Andrew Beauchamp 33
Protea Trail 39
proteas, unique 127, 133, 233, 283, 291
Province of Queen Adelaide 174, 175
Punda Maria 66, 68
Pungwe River 317
  falls 314, 315
  gorge 316
Purdon, Charles 172
Purgatory 264, 265
Putt Bridge 193
python dance 16
python god 17

Q

Qeme Plateau 100, 101
Qiloane Falls 99
Qolora 168, 169
Queen Elizabeth Nature Reserve 141
Queen's Causeway 127
Queen's Fort 94, 95
Queen's River 54
Queenstown 180
Queenstown and Frontier Museum 180
quiver tree 295, 337
Quiver Tree Forest 337
Quko River 171
QwaQwa Highland National Park 90
QwaQwa Mountain 90, 91

R

Raadsaal, first in Bloemfontein 75
Railway Museum
  Bulawayo 326
  Uitenhage 202
Rain Forest (near Graskop) 41
Rain Queen 20, 21
Randburg Waterfront 84
Rebelshoogte Pass 176
red balloon tree 31
Red Hill Road 246
Redelinghuys 279
reed dance 56, 57
Reichenau Mission 135
Reinet dolls 213
Reinet House Museum 212
Rein's Nature Reserve 234
Religions, Hall of 300
Rembrandt van Rijn Art Collection 266
Remhoogte Pass 341
Retief, Piet 91, 140, 194
Retief Rock 90, 91
Revolver Creek 50, 53
Rex, George 170, 223
Rex, John 191
Rhebok Trail 93
Rheeboksvlei 280
Rheenendal 222
Rhenish Church complex 267
Rhino Park 86
rhinoceros 31, 61
  black 61, 113, 295, 338
  white 61, 113, 114, 321

Rhodes, Cecil John 177, 297, 306, 326
  estates and buildings 244, 255, 249, 266, 300, 301, 326
  grave 324, 325
  memorial 246, 247, 264
  statue 253
Rhodes (town) 177
Rhodes' Cottage, Muizenberg 255
Rhodes Dam 314
Rhodes Estate, Matopos 325
Rhodes Fruit Farms 264
Rhodes Matopos National Park 324, 325
Rhodes' Memorial, Cape Town 246, 247, 264
Rhodes Nyanga Museum 316
Rhodes Park 86
Richmond 134
Richtersveld 291
rickshas 148, 149
Riebeek West 272
Riebeek-Kasteel 268, 269
Rietvlei Bird Sanctuary 254
Rimer's Creek 51
Rivers, Harry 235
Riversdale 234, 235
Riverton 296
Riviersonderend 237, 258, 259, 264
roan antelope 26
Robberg peninsula 218, 219
Robber's Pass 48, 49
Robert, Auguste 53
Robert McIllwaine Park (now Lake Chivero) 308
Robertson 258, 259
Robertson Valley Wine Route 259
Robinson, *Sir* Hercules 257
Robinson Graving Dock 257
Robinson Pass 226
Rocher Pan Nature Reserve 278
rock art museum 86
roller (bird) 65
Roma 98
Roman Catholic churches
  see under churches
Rondawelkop 90
Rondegat River 280, 283
Rondevlei, Knysna 225
Rondevlei Bird Sanctuary 254
Roodepoort Museum 83
Rooiberge 90, 92, 96
rooibos tea 281, 283
Rooibos Trail 343
Rooiels 262, 263
Rooigrond 33
Rooihoogte 259
Rooiplaat plateau 200, 201
Rorke's Drift 106, 107
Roseate Tern, Trail of the 210
Rosebud (ship) 161
Rosetta 138
Ross, David 177
Ross, John 149
Rossouw (settlement) 181
Royal African Corps 265
Royal Engineers officers' mess 175
Royal Natal National Park 90, 126-7
Rubidge Kloof 196
Rudd, CD 301
Rugged Glen Camp 127
Ruitersbos Forest 226
Rukotso Mountain 317
Rus-en-Vrede waterfall 226
Rust de Winter Dam 26
Rust-en-Vreugd 255

Rustenburg Kloof Holiday Resort 29
Rustenburg Nature Reserve 29
Rustenburg Overnight Trail 29
Ruwangwe 317
Rynfield Children's Park 84

S

Saalboom River 181
Saasveld 223, 265
Sabie 36, 40, 41, 45
Sabie Game Reserve 58
Sabie River 40, 61
sable antelope 26, 29
Sacramento Trail 210
Saddleback Pass 50, 54
Safari Farm 226
St Blaize lighthouse 234
St Cyprian's Cathedral 301
St Faith's Mission Village 155
St Francis Bay 208, 210
  see also Port Elizabeth
St George's Anglican Cathedral 253
St George's Street 248
St Helena Bay 275
St Ignatius Loyola (ship) 218
St James (beach) 255
St John (ship) 162
St Lawrence (ship) 274
St Lucia (village) 117
St Lucia Game Reserve 112, 116
St Lucia Marine Reserve 117
St Lucia Park 116
St Lucia Wetland Park 110
St Mary's Cathedral 83
St Michael's Mission 154
Saldanha 274
Salem 192
Salisbury Island 149
Salt Rock 146
San people 126, 132, 134, 180, 237, 328, 329, 338, 339
  dioramas 253
  museum exhibits 132
Sand River 12, 24, 86
Sand River Mountains 24
Sander, Willi 342, 343
Sanderburg 343
Sandhoogte 288
Sandile 168, 182
Sandile Dam 182
Sandile Kop 182, 191
Sandveld 278, 279
Sandveld Museum 284
Sandvlei 247
  Sandvlei Mouth 264
Sandwich wetland 340
Sanga cattle 164
sangoma 83, 145
Sani Pass 134, 137, 138
Santa Barbara, Church of 332
Santarama Miniland 84
Santo Alberto (ship) 166
Santos Beach 234
São Bento (ship) 166
São Gonzales (ship) 218
São João (ship) 161
sardine run 148, 155
Sardinia Bay 206
Sardinia Bay Nature Reserve 210
Satara 62, 63, 64
Save River 318
Scarborough 246
Schmidt, Georg 258
Schoeman, Hendrik 78
Schoeman, Stephanus 18
Schoemansdal 12, 18, 19
Schoemanskloof 45

Schoemanspoort 226, 228
Schoemansville 78, 79
Schreiner, Olive 197
Schreuderhuis 267
Schröder, Christiaan 292
Schröder, Johan 337
Schumacher, Johannes 240
Schutztruppe Memorial 342
Schwerinsburg 343
Scott, *Sir* John 153
Scottburgh 152, 153, 154
Scott's Bay 153
Sea Point 254
sea shells 171
Sea World 148
seal demonstrations
  Hartbeespoort 78
  Port Elizabeth 211
Seal Island 234, 255
Seal Point 208
Seal Reserve, Cape Cross 344, 345
Seaview Game Park 202, 211
Sebatlani (Zeerust) 32
Sebungwe narrows 331
Sederberg State Forest 280
Sederkop Cave 282
Sedgefield 223, 225
Sefikeng 100
Sekhukhune 73
Selborne 203
Seme 113
Sendelingspos 33
Sengwa Basin 331
Senqunyane River 99
Sentinel, The, Cape 246
Sentinel, The, Drakensberg 90, 91, 126, 127
Sentinel Trail 91
Sephton, Hezekiah 192
Serima Mission 320
Sesriem Canyon 340, 341
Setsoto Design Centre 100
Settler Church 189
Settlers' Monument 192
Settlers Park 210
Seweweekspoort 232, 233
Seymour 190
Sezela River 152
Shagase River 320
Shaka 30, 56, 114, 123, 144, 153, 164, 326
Shaka's Kraal 119, 147
Shaka's Rock 146
Shamva 310, 311, 326
shark fishing 168
shark protection 148
shark research 146
Sharrow Weaving Workshop 130
Shaw, Campbell 139
Shaw Hall 195
Shaw's Mountain Pass 262
Shawu Dam 66
Sheba Reef and Mine 50, 51, 53
Sheba's Breasts 131
Sheffield Beach 146
shells 208, 234
Shelly Beach 156
Shingwedzi Camp 66
Shingwedzi Game Reserve 58
Shingwedzi River 66
Ship Mountain 60, 61
shipwreck Museum, Bredasdorp 260, 261
shipwrecks, Wild Coast 166
Shitlhave Dam 60
Shona-speaking people 306, 320, 322, 323
Sibilobilo Lagoon 331
Sidney Fort 236, 237
Siege Museum, Ladysmith 128

Siege of Kimberley 301
Siege of Ladysmith 128
Siege of Mafeking 33
Signal Hill 250, 255
signposts 303
Sigubudu valley 126
Sihadla River 109
Silaka Nature Reserve 160, 161
Silasberg 90
Silotwane hills 54
Silver River 223
Silver Strand 259
Silvermine Nature Reserve 250, 254
Silvestre, Jose de 108
Simon's Town 246, 247, 248-9
Simonsberg 245, 247
Sinamatella 328
Singo 16
Sir Lowry's Pass 262, 264, 303
Sir Peregrine Maitland Trail 210
Siwasama-khosikazi 113
Siyayi dune forest 119
Skaap Island 274
Skaapwagters Pass 45
Skeleton Coast 344
Skoenmakerskop 206, 207, 210
Skukuza 60
Skyline Junction 318
Slagters Nek Memorial 189
slave lodge, former 253
slaves, 227, 249, 260, 278
Sleeping Beauty 234, 235
Slurry 33
Smith, *Sir* Harry 128, 175, 179, 191, 233
Smith, *Lady* Juana 128, 233
smous (hawker's) monument 302
Smuts, JC 30, 31, 87, 252, 253, 266
  birthplace 272, 273
Smuts House Museum 76
snake parks, 78, 86, 148, 211, 308
snakes, Northern Cape 295
Sneeuberge 203, 282
Sneeukop-Langberg massif 282
snow protea 283
Sobhuza I, *King* 56
Sobhuza II, *King* 56
Soetendals Valley 260
Soil Reclamation Trail 120
Soldiers' Bay 274
Somerset, *Lord* Charles 226, 265
Somerset (ship) 256
Somerset East 188
Somerset West 262
Sontuli Loop 115
Sossusvlei 340, 341
Sotho 56, 92
  traditions 102-3
Sout River 238
South African Air Force Museum 76, 87
South African Broadcasting Corporation 83
South African Bureau of Standards 76
South African Library 253
South African Library for the Blind 194
South African Maritime Museum 256
South African Missionary Museum 255
South African Museum 253
South African National Art Gallery 253
South African Nature Conservation Centre 86
South African Navy Museum 248, 249

South African Police Museum 76
Southbroom 157
southernmost point of Africa 261
Southey's Pass 237
Soutkop 97
Soutpansberg 12, 13, 14, 15, 18-9
Soutpansberg Hiking Trail 19
Soweto 83
Soweto Art Gallery 84
Spandau Kop 196, 197, 212, 215
Sparks Bay 262
Spekboom River 49
Spekboom Trail 211
Spektakel Pass 288, 291
Spier 244, 245
Spies, Andries 128
Spioenkop 128, 129, 138
Spioenkop Nature Reserve 129
Spitskop 40, 41, 45, 52, 220
Spring Grove 189
Spring Valley 189
springbok 30, 31
Springbok (town) 288, 291
Springbok Flats 26
Springbokfontein settlement 288
Stadsaal Caves 280, 281, 282
stagecoaches 22 23
Stanford 260
Stanger 122, 123
State Museum 343
State Theatre, Pretoria 76
steam traction engine 344
steam train journey 224-5
Steelpoort River 49
Steenberg 250
Steenbras River 262
Steinkopf 291
Stellaland 33
Stellenbosch 245, 265, 266-7
Stellenbosch Farmers' Winery 244
Stellenryck Wine Museum 266
Stem van Suid-Afrika 249
Stempastorie 249
Sterkfontein Caves 85
Sterkfontein Dam 81, 90
Sterkspruit Falls 129
Stevenson-Hamilton, James 58, 60
Stewart, *Reverend* James 191
Stewart Memorial 182, 191
Stewart's Farm 118
Steyn, Hermanus 24
Steyn, MT (house of) 97
Steynberg, Coert 76
Stiebel Rocks 155
stinkwood, Camdeboo 113
Stockdale, *Sister* Henrietta 301
Stockenström, A 189, 194, 212
Stone Age industries 313
Stormberg range 180, 181
Storms River 219
Stormsvlei 258
Strand 262
Strandfontein 284, 291
Strandlopers 223
Strandveld 260, 278, 284
Strelitzia Coast 152-3
Stretch, Charles Lennox 212
Strijdom, JG 24, 25
Struisbaai 260, 261
Strydpoort 18
Studland 248
Stutterheim 182, 183
Stutterheim, *Baron* R von 183
succulents 285, 288, 294
Sudwala Caves 44
Sufi temple 128, 129
sugar cane 146, 147
sugar cane petrol 320
Suikerbosrand Nature Reserve 80, 85

Summerstrand 210
Summerton, Thomas 184
Sundays River 202, 212, 215
Sundays River Mouth 211
Sundays River Valley 203
Sundial, The (Thabaneng) 39
Sunland 203
Sunny Cove 246
Sunrise Beach 255
Supertubes (surfing spot) 208
Supreme Court, Bloemfontein 94, 95
Surfer's Corner 255
surfing 148, 254, 255, 272
Surprise Ridge 126
suspension footbridge 219
Suurberg Pass 203
Suurberg range 203
Suurbraak 237
Swadini Resort 36, 39
Swaershoek Mountains 27
Swaershoek Pass 196
Swakop River 340, 344
Swakop River valley 345
Swakopmund 340, 344
Swart River 223
Swartberg Mountains 227, 229, 230, 237
Swartberg Pass 228, 303
Swartfontein 40
Swartkops River and Valley 202
Swartland 268, 273, 277, 278
Swartmodder River 337
Swartnek 181
Swartvlei 225
Swazi traditions 56-7
Swaziland 54-7
Swellendam 236, 237, 238, 239, 240-1
Swellengrebel, Hendrik 240, 249
Synagogue
    Great, Cape Town 252, 253
    Ladismith 233
    oldest in Southern Africa 253

T

Taal Monument
    Burgersdorp 179, 231
    Paarl 245
Taalfees Monument 20
Table Bay Harbour 255, 256-7
Table Mountain
    Cape 250, 254, 268
    KwaZulu-Natal 141, 143
Tafelberg, Cederberg 282
Talana 106
Tandjiesberg 196
Tatham Art Gallery 140
tea eastates 316
Tegwaans Pools 50, 54
Telkom Exploratorium 257
Tembe Elephant Park 108
Temburatedza River 317
Teyateyaneng 100
Thaba Bosiu 100, 102, 103
Thaba Kgatla 25
Thaba Putsoa 99
Thabaneng 39
Thabazimbi 26, 27
Thabelang Handcraft Centre 101
Thafalofefe 169
Thathe Vondo Forest 14, 17
Thathe Vondo Pass 14, 15
Theatre on the Bay 255
Theewaterskloof Dam 259, 264
Theron, Danie 271
Thibault, Louis 212, 253, 265, 271
Thiyeni 113
Thlaping people 33

Thohoyandou 14, 16
Thompson's Bay 146
Thornridge 193
Three Crowns (peaks) 180, 181
Three Rondavels (peaks) 36, 39
Thula Mela 16
Thwalelinye 138
Tidbury's Toll 190
Tienie Versveld Flora Reserve 272
Tierberg 293
Tierkloof 33
Tietiesbaai 275
Tiger Mile Fishing Resort 328
tigerfish tournament 333
Timbavati 64
time ball tower 257
Tintenpalast 342
Titanic Rock 96
Tlapaneng Mountain 100
Tlouoe Mountains 101
T'Numkwa/Cockscomb Mountain 206, 207
tobacco auction 306
Tobacco Tour 32
Togryers (Transport Riders') Museum 276
Tokai Forest 254
toll houses 190, 229, 232, 234, 268, 277
tollbridge 296
Tonga (people) 331
Tongaat 147
Tongati River 147
Tor Doone 184
tortoise country 203
Touchstone Ranch 26
Touw River 225
Towerkop, Colesberg 303
Towerkop, Ladismith 233, 303
Township Square 327
Tra-Tra River 281
Trading Post 47
Tradouw Pass 237
Trafalgar Place 252
Trafford, William 42
Tragedy Hill 157
trails
    Baobab 12, 13
    Big Tree 219
    Blyderivierspoort 39
    Boland 264
    Bosberg 189
    Braamfontein Spruit 85, 86
    Bushbuck 210
    Cascades Walk 127
    Cedara State Forest 141
    Cheetah Interpretive 80
    De Stades 210
    Durban Metropolitan 151
    Fish River Canyon 336, 337
    Giant's Cup 134
    Golden Gate 93
    Guinea Fowl 210
    Klipspringer 295
    Kosi Bay 109
    Lake St Lucia 117
    Mampoer Tour 32
    Mboma 117
    Mooi River 138
    Mountain Zebra 20
    Mvubu 117
    Nkonikini 118
    Otter 219
    Otto's Walk 127
    Peglerae 29
    Pietermaritzburg 141
    Protea 39
    Rooibos 343
    Roseate Tern 210
    Rustenburg Overnight 29

Sacramento 210
Sentinel 91
Sir Peregrine Maitland 210
Soil Reclamation 120
Soutpansberg 19
Spekboom 211
Tobacco Tour 32
Tsitsikamma 219
Umkhiwane 117
Underwater, Tsitsikamma 219
Wag 'n Bietjie 343
Wilderness 115
Yellowwood 39
trams, electric 300
Transkei traditions 164-5
TransNamib Railway Museum 343
Transvaal Snake Park 86
Treaty of Vereeniging 75
Treur River 37, 38
Trichardt, Louis 14, 18, 19, 38, 188
Troe-Troe River 284
Trompetter's Drift 190, 191
Tropic of Capricorn 66
trout 127, 136, 137, 139, 162, 315, 316
Troutbeck 314, 316
Tsauchab River 341
tsessebe 26
tsetse fly 114
Tshabalala Game Sanctuary 325
Tshipise 12, 13
Tshivhase royal family 14, 16
Tshokwane 62, 63
Tshwane 74
Tsitsikamma Mountains 218
Tsitsikamma National Park 219
Tsitsikamma Underwater Trail 219
Tsondab River 340, 341
Tsumasa Koppie 339
tufa formation 36
Tugela Falls 120, 121, 126, 127
Tugela Ferry 120
Tugela Mouth 146
Tugela River 120, 126, 146, 147
tuishuisies 240, 302
Tulbagh 268, 269, 270-1, 277
Tunnel, The, Tugela River 127
Tussen-die-Riviere Game Farm 178
Tutura 20, 168
Tuynhuys 253
Twaing Museum 77
Twee Rivieren camp 299
Tweede Tol 269
Tweetoringkerk, Bloemfontein 95
Twelve Apostles 135, 246, 250, 255
Twin Peaks 128
Two Oceans Aquarium 257
Tygerberg Zoo 254
Tyume River 184
Tyume Valley 182, 190
Tzaneen 20, 22, 23

U

Ubombo Mountains 108, 110
Ueckermann, Heinrich 81
Ugie 177
Uitenhage 202
Uitenhage Nature Reserve 211
Uitkoms Mountains 284
Uitkyk Pass 280
Uitspanskraal 280
Ultimatum Tree 121, 146, 147
Ulundi 115
Umdloti 146, 147

Umfolozi Game Reserve 112, 114-5
Umfurudzi Safari Area 311
Umgababa (town) 152, 153
uMgababa River 152
Umgeni River Bird Park 146, 151
Umgeni Valley Nature Reserve 139
Umgungundlovu 121
Umhlanga 147, 151
Umhlanga Lagoon Nature Reserve 147, 151
Umhlanga Rustic Village and Animal Farm 151
Umkhiwane Trail 117
Umkhumbe Walk 117
Umkomaas 152
Umkumbi Bush Camp 111
Umlaas *see* Mlazi
Umlalazi Nature Reserve 119
Umngazi River 162
Umngazi River Mouth 160, 161
Umtamvuna Nature Reserve 157
Umtata 160, 166, 167
Umtentweni 155
Umvumvumvu River 318
Umwindzi Valley 310
Umzintlava River 162
Umzumbe 155
Underberg 135, 136, 137
Underwater Trail, Tsitsikamma 219
Union Buildings 74, 75
Union Castle Company 257
University of Fort Hare 182, 191
University of the Witwatersrand 87
Upington 292
Upington, *Sir* Thomas 292
Usutu River 108
uthikoloshe 165
Uvongo 156

V

Vaal Dam 80, 81
Vaalbos National Park 296
Vaalkrans 20, 128
Valley of a Thousand Hills 142, 143
Valley of Death 50
Valley of Desolation 214, 215
Van Aardt's Post 189
Van de Graaff, Cornelis 212
Van de Graaff beacon 303
Van der Merwe, IW 277
Van der Merwe family 277
Van der Stel, Simon 252, 266, 277, 284, 288
Van der Stel, WA 253
Van Heerden, Carl 27
Van Loon, Hercules 267
Van Meerhoff, Pieter 277
Van Plettenberg, Joachim 198, 218, 303
Van Reede van Oudtshoorn, *Baron* Pieter 228
Van Reenen family 91, 93
Van Rensburg, Hans 18
Van Riebeeck, Jan 268
Van Ryn Brandy Cellars 244
Van Ryneveld Pass Dam 214, 215
Van Staden's River Mouth 206, 207
Van Staden's River Pass 208
Van Staden's Wildflower Reserve 211
Van Tonder's Pass 120

357

Van Wouw, Anton 75, 76
Vanrhynsdorp 284
Vant's Drift 106
Vasco da Gama clock 151
Velddrif 275, 278
Venda (people) 14, 19
  traditions 14, 16-7
  villages 16, 19
Venterstad 179
Verdun 16
Vergaderingskop 206
Verlorevlei 278, 279
Vernon Crookes Nature Reserve 154, 155
Verraaiersnek Pass 48
Versveld, Theodore 234
Versveld Pass 278
Vetch's Pier 148, 150
Victoria (ship) 257
Victoria and Alfred Waterfront 256-7
Victoria Basin 257
Victoria Bay 224
Victoria Cross 33, 107, 300
Victoria Embankment 149
Victoria Falls 328, 329
Victoria Lake 86
Victoria Wharf 257
Victory (ship) 248
Viedgesville 166
Viljoen's Pass 264, 265
Village Museum, Stellenbosch 267
Villiersdorp 259, 265
vine, thickest in the world 213
Visch Hoek Baay 262
Vlaeberg 250
  see also Signal Hill
Vleesbaai 234
Voëlvlei Dam 268
volcanoes, extinct 30
Von Stryk Mine 345
Voortrekker School 44, 48
Voortrekker Square 12
Voortrekkers 14, 18, 25, 38, 46, 91, 140
  battles 107
  churches 12, 48, 140
  graves 12, 19, 24, 25, 27, 49, 140
  memorials 19, 20, 37, 106
  monuments 20, 74, 292
  museums 12, 74, 140
  settlement, reconstructed 12
  wagon trails 121, 140, 143
Vredelust 267
Vredenburg 266, 275
Vredendal 284, 291
Vrolikheid Nature Reserve 258
Vrouemonument 95
Vryburg 33
Vryheid 106, 115
Vukani 119
Vumba cheese 313
Vungu 156
vultures
  bearded (*lammergeyer*) 133
  Cape 24, 25, 26, 29, 133, 138
Vyeboom 264

W

Waenhuiskrans/Arniston 260, 261
Wag 'n Bietjie Trail 343
Wagenaer's Dam 252
Wagendrift Dam 130
Wagendrift Nature Reserve 130, 131
Wagon Hill/Platrand 128
  Military Cemetery 128
Walker Bay 260
Walls of Jericho (cliffs) 156
Walter Battiss Art Museum 189
Walvis Bay 344, 345
Wamakers Museum 273
Wapadsberg Pass 196
War Museum of Boer Republics, Bloemfontein 95
War of the Axe 182, 193
Warden, Henry Douglas 94
Warehouse Theatre 343
Warmbaths, 24, 26, 27
Warriors' Gate 149
Water Wonderland 148
Waterberg 24, 26-7
waterfalls
  Augrabies 294
  Bridal Veil 294
  Hogsback 185
  Kettlespout 185
  Lehr 157
  Lone Creek 40, 41
  Madonna and Child 185
  Maria Shires 41
  Rus-en-Vrede 226
  The 39 Steps 185
Waterfront *see* Victoria and Alfred
Watervals River Pass 49
Watervalsberg 269
Watervalspruit 37
water-wheels 278, 292
Waterworld 148
Watsomba village 314
wattles 143
Watts, GF 247
Wavecrest 208
Waveren, Land van 270, 271
  see also Tulbagh
Webezi 131
Weenen 120
Weenen Nature Reserve 120
Welbedacht Cave 282
Welgevonden 26
Wellington 268, 269
Welwitschia Drive 344, 345
Welwitschia mirabilis 345
Wemmer Pan 84
Wengezi Junction Village 318
Werner Frehse Game Reserve 235
Wessels, Pieter 301
West Coast National Park 274
West Coast Ostrich Ranch 272
Whales 263, 279
whaling relics 249, 263
Wheat Museum 273
Whiskyspruit 47

White Lady Salt Pan 344
White Mfolozi River 106, 114, 115
White Rhino Shelter 325
Whovi Game Park 324
Whysalls Camera Museum 150
Wikar, Hendrik 294
Wild Coast 166-7, 168-9
wild dogs 61, 329
Wildeperdehoek Pass 289
Wilderness 223, 225
Wilderness Heights 223
wildflower show, Darling 272
Wilds, The 85
Wilge River 81
Willem Prinsloo Agricultural Museum 72
William Fehr Collection 252, 255
William Humphreys Art Gallery 301
Williston 303
Willshire, 'Tiger Tom' 191
Wilson, Allan 325
Wilson, David 51
Wilson, Jane 33
Wilson's Cutting 156
Wiltshire Regiment 95
Windhoek 340, 342-3
Windhoek Karneval 342
Windvoëlberg 183
Wine Museum 266
wine routes, Robertson Valley 259
wine route, Western Cape 244-5
Winterhoek range 270
Winterstrand 173
Winterton 129
Wit River 268
Witbank 72
Witbooi, Hendrik 342
witchcraft 145, 165
Witels River 220
Witkerk (church) 72, 73
Witklipkop 238
Witpoortjie Falls 85
Witsand 238, 239
Witsenberg range 269, 270, 271
Witsieshoek Mountain Resort 90
Witteberge 96
Wlotzkasbaken 344
Woest, Barend 192
Wolf Ridge 184, 185
Wolfberg Arch 282
Wolfberg Cracks 282, 283
Wolhuter, Harry 63, 69
Wolhuterskop 31
Wolhuterskop Game Reserve 97
Wolseley 269
Women's Memorial, Bloemfontein 95
Wonder Caves 86
Wonderboom Nature Reserve 77
Wonderfontein 32
Wonderview 36, 37, 41
Woodbush Forest 20
Woodbush Goldfields 22
Woodville 251
World of Birds 254

World War, First
  battle sites 292, 293
  memorials 43, 83, 174, 175, 293
World's View
  KwaZulu-Natal 140, 143
  Zimbabwe 314, 315, 324, 325
Wuppertal 280, 281
Wurmb, *Baron* von 281
Wylie Park 141
Wyllie's Poort 12, 13, 19

X

Xalanga 181
Xhosa
  museum exhibits 175
  'national suicide' 164, 169, 182
  traditions 164-5
Xonxa Dam 181

Y

yellowwood forests 127
Yellowwood Park 151
Yellowwood Trail 39
yellowwood trees 185, 211, 219, 220, 221
Yzerfontein 272, 273

Z

Zambezi River 329, 332
Zambezi Valley 328, 332
Zanddrif (farmhouse) 241
zebras
  Burchell's 155
  Cape mountain 200-1, 215, 238
  Hartmann's mountain 247, 288, 336, 338, 340
  stage-coaches drawn by 23
Zeederberg coaches 12, 23, 49, 241
Zeerust 32
Ziekenhuis (cave) 258
Zimbabwe 304-5
Zimbabwe ruins *see* Great Zimbabwe
Zimunya communal lands 312
Zindele Game Park 310, 311
Zinkwazi Beach 146
Zintunzini Hills 115
Ziwa Iron Age ruins 315
Zoar 233
Zoo Lake 86
Zoo Park 342
zoological gardens
  Bloemfontein 95
  Johannesburg 86
  Pretoria 77
Zuid-Afrikaansche Republiek 75
Zulu (leader of Zulu people) 144
Zulu Kraal, Phumangena 83
Zulu traditions 144-5
  villages 118, 119, 131, 142, 156
Zulu-Voortrekker battle 107
Zuurberg National Park 203, 211
Zwartkoppies Hall 76

Acknowledgments

Many people assisted in the preparation of this book. The publishers wish to express their thanks to all who helped in any way, especially the staff of local authorities throughout the country, who supplied and checked volumes of information. Special mention is also due to the following:

Carol and Gavin Adams; Julian Ardagh; Denyse Armour; Kevan Aspoas; Lieutenant Colonel OEF Baker; Mike Behr; Elizabeth Biggs; Daphne Carr; Barbara Castle; Keith Cooper; Colin Cochrane; Peter Coston; Petrus de Klerk; Max du Preez; Naas Ferreira; Rhoda Fourie; Jeff Gaisford; Richard Garstang; Sal Gerber; Danie Gouws; Isobel Grobler; Reg Gush; Martin Harvey; Frank Hollier; Bruce Hopwood; Kate Hoy; Lydia Johnson; Dick Jones; Robert King; Bill Leppan; Theo Luzuka; Myles Mander; Guy and Jane Mathews; Corrie Middel; Paul Miles; Adrienne Millet; Theresa Moore; Barney Mostert; Dumisane Ngobese; Colin and Lynn Palmer; Pamela Paton; June Payn; Lena Payne; Derek Petersen; John and Cherise Pledger; Hugh Poulter; Elise Pretorius; Harry Pretorius; Sheryl Raine; Tony Rees; Dr John Rourke; Captain Tommy Ryan; the late Charles O Sayers; Derek Schaefer; Robert Schell; Grant Scholtz; Digby Schutz; Colleen Schwager; Anne Schwegmann; Paddy and Carol Smith; Cynthia Spurr; John and Rose Spurr; JJ Stapelberg; Dr Pierre Swanepoel; Gwyn Taverner-Smith; Sally van Aardt; Erika van Greunen; Cynthia van der Mescht; Hannes van der Merwe; Dr John Vincent; Agnes von Bodenhausen; Ted Walsh; Denver A Webb; Alison Whitfield; Dr WG Winckler; John Wray; Terry and Kim Wray.

Bibliography

The publishers acknowledge their indebtedness to the following books that were used for reference.

African Heritage by Barbara Tyrrell and Peter Jurgens (Macmillan); *Boot and Saddle* by H Morin-Humphreys (George Robertson); *Bowler's Cape Town* by C Pama (Tafelberg); *A Cape Childhood* by Norah Henshilwood (David Philip); *Cape Colony Harbours: Knysna, Mossel Bay* by Sir John Coode (Waterlow and Sons); *Cape Drives and Places of Interest* by Jose Burman (Human and Rousseau); *Cape Town Guide* (Cape Town Directories); *Church Street in the Land of Waveren* by Gawie and Gwen Fagan (Tulbagh Restoration Committee); *Coastal Holiday* by Jose Burman (Human and Rousseau); *Complete Guide to Walks and Trails in Southern Africa* by Jaynee Levy (Struik); *Connolly's Guide to Southern Africa* by Denis Connolly (Connolly Publishers); *Daar is maar net een ... Elim, 1824-1974* deur JJ Ulster (Elim Sendingstasie); *Descriptive and Illustrated Catalogue of the Fossil Reptilia of South Africa in the Collection of the British Museum* by Richard Owen (The Trustees of the British Museum); *Discovering Southern Africa* by TV Bulpin (TV Bulpin Publications); *The Drostdy at Swellendam* by ME and A Rothmann (Drostdy Commission); *Dynamite and Daisies: The Story of Barberton* by PGJ Meiring (Purnell); *The Early Days of George* by DJJ De Villiers (The George and Knysna Herald); *A Field Guide to the Natal Drakensberg* by Pat Irwin, J Ackhurst and D Irwin (Wildlife Society of Southern Africa); *52 Day walks in and around Johannesburg* by Brendan Ryan (Struik); *Gedenkboek Swellendam* deur LL Tomlinson (Swellendam Eeufeeskomitee); *Gleanings in Africa* (James Cundee); *Graaff-Reinet: A Cultural History* by CG Henning (TV Bulpin Publications); *Great Shipwrecks off the Coast of Southern Africa* by Jose Burman (Struik); *Guide to Lesotho* by David Ambrose (Winchester Press); *Guide to the Museums of Southern Africa* by Hans Fransen (Southern African Museums Association); *The Historical Monuments of Southern Africa* by JJ Oberholster (National Monuments Council); *A History of Caledon* by Joy Edwards (Venster Printing Works); *History of Oudtshoorn* (Oudtshoorn Van Riebeeck Festival Committee); *Illustrated Guide to Southern Africa* (Reader's Digest Association South Africa); *Illustrated Guide to the Game Parks and Nature Reserves of Southern Africa* (Reader's Digest Association South Africa); *Illustrated History of South Africa: the True Story* (Reader's Digest Association South Africa 1994); *An Illustrated Social History of South Africa* by Alan Hattersley (Balkema); *Johannesburg Alive* by Heather Johnston and Judy Rowe (Map Studio); *Looking Back on George* by Charles O Sayers (Herald Phoenix); *Myths and Legends of Southern Africa* by Penny Miller (TV Bulpin Publications); *Official South African Municipal Yearbook 1995* (Gaffney Group); *Overberg Outspan* by Edmund Burrows (Maskew Miller); *Pioneer Port: The Illustrated History of East London* by Joseph Denfield (Howard Timmins); *Pioneer Travellers of South Africa* by Vernon Forbes (A A Balkema), *Portrait of Plettenberg Bay* by Patricia Storrar (Centaur Publishers); *Riches of the Sea* by John R Grindley (Caltex); *Shipwrecks of the Southern Cape* by Brian Wexham (Timmins); *So High the Road* by Jose Burman (Human and Rousseau); *South Africa Yearbook 1995* by the South African Communication Service; *South African Commercial Advertiser 1837-1848*; *South African Illustrated News 1884-1885*; *Standard Encyclopedia of Southern Africa* (NASOU); *Stellenbosch Three Centuries* by Francois Smuts (Stellenbosch Town Council); *The Stormy First Twenty Years of Graaff-Reinet* by Robin Blignaut (Graaff-Reinet Publicity Association); *The Story of Hottentots Holland* by Peggy Heap (the Author); *Thomas Bowler of the Cape of Good Hope* by Frank and Edna Bradlow (AA Balkema); *Thornton Cox Travellers Guides: Southern Africa* (Geographia); *Timber and Tides* by Winifred Tapson (Juta); *Veld Express* by Harry Zeederberg (Timmins).

Use was also made of pamphlets from local publicity associations.

Picture credits

Picture credits for each page read from top to bottom, using the top of the picture as the reference point. Where the tops of two or more pictures are on the same level, credits read from left to right.

Abbreviations:
ABPL: Anthony Bannister Photo Library
PA: Photo Access

Front cover Walter Knirr, **Back cover** Jean Morris, **Title page** Gerald Cubitt; Walter Knirr; Anthony Bannister. **10-11** Walter Knirr. **12** Both Walter Knirr. **13** All Walter Knirr. **14** Walter Knirr; Walter Knirr; Jean Morris. **15** All Walter Knirr. **16** Walter Knirr; Jean Morris; Brian Johnson Barker. **17** Walter Knirr; Jean Morris. **18** Walter Knirr; Brian Johnson Barker. **19** All Walter Knirr. **20** Gerald Cubitt; Herman Potgieter. **21** David Steele; David Steele; Brian Johnson Barker. **22** Brian Johnson Barker; Brian Johnson Barker; David Steele. **23** David Steele. **24** Walter Knirr; Andrew Meintjies. **25** Nylstroom Modimolle-Kranskop Tourist Org.; Andrew Meintjies; Roger de la Harpe/ABPL. **26** Both Andrew Meintjies. **27** Hein von Hörsten/ABPL; Warwick Tarboton/ABPL; Anthony Bannister/ABPL. **28** Both Walter Knirr. **29** Both Walter Knirr. **30** Anthony Bannister. **31** All Anthony Bannister. **32** Peter Lawson/PA; John Kramer. **33** David Rogers/Getaway/PA; Reader's Digest; Anneke Kearney. **34-35** Walter Knirr. **36** David Steele; David Steele; Walter Knirr. **37** David Steele; Walter Knirr; Walter Knirr. **38** Both David Steele. **39** David Steele. **40** Brian Johnson Barker; Gerald Cubitt. **41** Walter Knirr; Walter Knirr; Brian Johnson Barker. **42** All David Steele. **43** Transvaal Museum Services; Brian Johnson Barker; Transvaal Museum Services. **44** David Steele; Walter Knirr; Brian Johnson Barker. **45** Walter Knirr; Brian Johnson Barker. **46** David Steele; David Steele; Brian Johnson Barker; Paddy Hartdegen; David Steele. **47** David Steele. **48** Marianne Alexander. **49** Peter Pickford/Focal Point; Zelda Wahl; Bridget Hilton-Barber; Walter Knirr. **50** Both Brian Johnson Barker. **51** Walter Knirr; David Steele; Walter Knirr. **52** Walter Knirr; David Steele. **53** Brian Johnson Barker; Government Archives; Brian Johnson Barker; David Steele; Africana Museum; Walter Knirr. **54** David Steele; Gerald Cubitt. **55** David Steele; Brian Johnson Barker. **56** Both Jean Morris. **57** All Jean Morris. **58** Both Anthony Bannister. **59** Anthony Bannister; David Steele. **60** Anthony Bannister; Gerald Cubitt. **61** David Steele; Leo Braack; David Steele; Anthony Bannister. **62** Both Gerald Cubitt. **63** Gerald Cubitt; Leo Braack; David Steele; Gerald Cubitt. **64** Both Gerald Cubitt. **65** David Steele; Gerald Cubitt; David Steele; Gerald Cubitt. **66** Gerald Cubitt; Gerald Cubitt; Anthony Bannister; Gerald Cubitt. **67** Gerald Cubitt; Leo Braack; Anthony Bannister; Anthony Bannister. **68** Anthony Bannister; Gerald Cubitt; Leo Braack; Anthony Bannister. **69** Gerald Cubitt, Leo Braack; Gerald Cubitt. **70-71** Walter Knirr. **72** Herman Potgieter; Walter Knirr. **73** Walter Knirr; Herman Potgieter. **74** Both Walter Knirr. **75** Walter Knirr; SA Tourism Board; Walter Knirr. **76** Both Walter Knirr. **77** Walter Knirr; Walter Knirr; Mark van Aardt; Walter Knirr. **78**

Both Walter Knirr. **79** Both Walter Knirr. **80** All Walter Knirr. **81** Both Walter Knirr. **82** Both Walter Knirr. **83** Walter Knirr; Walter Knirr; Herman Potgieter; Herman Potgieter. **84** Gerald Cubitt; Walter Knirr; Walter Knirr. **85** Africana Museum; Gerald Cubitt; Gerald Cubitt. **86** Gerald Cubitt; Gerald Cubitt; Walter Knirr. **87** Walter Knirr; Gerald Cubitt; Walter Knirr/PA; Gerald Cubitt. **88-89** Walter Knirr. **90** Both Alfie Steyn. **91** All Walter Knirr. **92** Walter Knirr; Alfie Steyn. **93** All Walter Knirr. **94** Walter Knirr. **95** Both Brian Johnson Barker. **96** Walter Knirr/PA; Walter Knirr. **97** All Walter Knirr. **98** Dirk Schwager; Neville Poulter. **99** Dirk Schwager; Neville Poulter; Dirk Schwager; Neville Poulter. **100** Both Gwynneth Glass. **101** Dirk Schwager; Neville Poulter; Neville Poulter. **102** Both Dirk Schwager. **103** All Dirk Schwager. **104-105** David Steele/Getaway/PA. **106** Both Rob McCallum. **107** Talana Museum, Dundee. **108** Steve McKean; A G Mountain. **109** AG Mountain; Roger de la Harpe; AG Mountain; AG Mountain. **110** Natal Parks Board; AG Mountain. **111** Keith Young; Steve McKean; Roger de la Harpe. **112** Gerald Cubitt; David Steele; David Steele; David Steele. **113** Gerald Cubitt; David Steele; David Steele. **114** David Steele; Gerald Cubitt. **115** David Steele; Gerald Cubitt; David Steele. **116** Felicity Harris. **117** All David Steele. **118** David Steele. **119** Alfie Steyn; David Steele; David Steele; Alfie Steyn. **120** Roger de la Harpe; Barbara Bannister/ABPL; Roger de la Harpe/ABPL. **121** Roger de la Harpe; Lisa Trocchi/ABPL; Patrick Royal; Rick Matthews. **122** Johan van Zijl; Jeremy Edwards. **123** Roger de la Harpe; Johan van Zijl; Johan van Zijl; Jeremy Edwards. **124-125** Walter Knirr. **126** Walter Knirr; Martin Harvey; Martin Harvey. **127** Gerald Cubitt; Walter Knirr; Martin Harvey. **128** Both David Steele. **129** Herman Potgieter; David Steele; Alfie Steyn. **130** Nigel Dennis/ABPL; David Steele/PA. **131** Walter Knirr; Walter Knirr; Roger de la Harpe/ABPL. **132** Marek Patzer; Alfie Steyn. **133** David Steele; Alfie Steyn; Marek Patzer. **134** All Walter Knirr. **135** Walter Knirr. **136** Walter Knirr; Roger de la Harpe/ABPL; Roger de la Harpe. **137** Roger de la Harpe; Roger de la Harpe; Walter Knirr. **138** Walter Knirr; Johan van Zijl. **139** Walter Knirr; Walter Knirr; Alfie Steyn. **140** David Steele; Alfie Steyn; Alfie Steyn; Walter Knirr. **141** Both Alfie Steyn. **142** Both Walter Knirr. **143** Walter Knirr; Gerald Cubitt; Walter Knirr. **144** Both Jean Morris. **145** All Jean Morris. **147** All Walter Knirr. **148** Both Walter Knirr. **149** Both Walter Knirr. **150** Both Walter Knirr. **151** All Walter Knirr. **152** Alfie Steyn; David Steele. **153** Both Pat Evans. **154** Alfie Steyn. **155** Emanuel Maria; Emanuel Maria; Gerald Cubitt; Gerald Cubitt. **157** Emanuel Maria; Emanuel Maria; Alfie Steyn; Alfie Steyn; Alfie Steyn. **158-159** Friedrich von Hörsten. **160** Jean Morris; Tim O'Hagan. **161** Africana Museum; Herman Potgieter; Gerald Cubitt. **162** Mark van Aardt; Mark van Aardt; Wayne Saunder/ABPL. **163** Bobby McLeod; Mark van Aardt; Peter Pickford/Focal Point; Herman Potgieter/ABPL. **164** Both Jean Morris. **165** Herman Potgieter; Jean Morris; Gerald Cubitt. **166** Both Herman Potgieter. **167** Both Herman Potgieter. **168** Both Tim O'Hagan. **169** Tim O'Hagan; Gerald Cubitt; Jean Morris. **170** Walter Knirr; Ethel Rosenstrauch. **171** All Ethel Rosenstrauch. **172** Prof MM Smith; Ethel Rosenstrauch. **173** Gerald Cubitt; Ethel Rosenstrauch; Brian Johnson Barker; Brian Johnson Barker. **174** Both Brian Johnson Barker. **175** All Gerald Cubitt. **176** Both Brian Johnson Barker. **177** All Brian Johnson Barker. **178** Both Brian Johnson Barker. **179** All Brian Johnson Barker. **180** Both Brian Johnson Barker. **181** Both Brian Johnson Barker. **182** Africana Museum; Ethel Rosenstrauch; Brian Johnson Barker. **183** Gerald Cubitt; Brian Johnson Barker. **184** Don Briscoe; Brian Johnson Barker. **185** SA Tourism Board; Gordon Douglas; Gerald Cubitt. **186-187** David Steele. **188** Friedrich von Hörsten; Sue O'Reilly. **189** Zelda Wahl; Sue O'Reilly; Sue O'Reilly; Friedrich von Hörsten. **190** Brian Johnson Barker. **191** Gerald Cubitt; Brian Johnson Barker; Gerald Cubitt. **192** Brian Johnson Barker; Gordon Douglas; Gerald Cubitt. **193** Brian Johnson Barker; Gerald Cubitt; Brian Johnson Barker; Brian Johnson Barker. **194** Both Brian Johnson Barker. **195** Herman Potgieter; Brian Johnson Barker; Brian Johnson Barker; Brian Johnson Barker. **197** Friedrich von Hörsten; Keith Young; Mark van Aardt; Sue O'Reilly; Walter Knirr. **198** Thea Grenfell; E Hosten/Landmarks. **199** Sue O'Reilly; Mark van Aardt; Shaen Adey/ABPL; Marek Patzer. **200** Gerald Cubitt; David Steele. **201** Both Gerald Cubitt. **202** David Steele; Gerald Cubitt. **203** David Steele; Gerald Cubitt; Gerald Cubitt. **204** Herman Potgieter; David Steele. **205** Both David Steele. **206** All David Steele. **207** Both David Steele. **208** Both David Steele. **209** Both David Steele. **210** All David Steele. **211** Both David Steele. **212** David Steele; Brian Johnson Barker. **213** Both Brian Johnson Barker. **214** All David Steele. **215** David Steele. **216-217** Walter Knirr. **218** All David Steele. **219** Anthony Bannister; David Steele; Walter Knirr. **220** David Steele; Wildlife Society of Southern Africa. **221** Herman Potgieter; David Steele. **222** David Steele. **223** Herman Potgieter; David Steele; David Steele. **224** David Steele; Jean Morris. **225** Both David Steele. **226** David Steele. **227** David Steele; Gerald Cubitt; Landbouweekblad. **228** Gerald Cubitt; David Steele; David Steele. **229** David Steele; Jean Morris; Zelda Wahl. **230** All David Steele. **231** All David Steele. **232** Brian Johnson Barker; David Steele. **233** All David Steele. **234** Sue O'Reilly. **235** David Steele/Getaway/PA; Sue O'Reilly; Gwynneth Glass; Thea Grenfell; Sue O'Reilly. **236** David Steele; Anthony Bannister. **237** All David Steele. **238** All Gerald Cubitt. **239** Gerald Cubitt; Ken Gerhardt. **240** Both David Steele. **241** All David Steele. **242-243** Gordon Douglas. **244** Herman Potgieter; Dirk Schwager; Neville Poulter; Neville Poulter. **245** Dirk Schwager. **246** David Steele; Gerald Cubitt; David Steele. **247** David Steele, Gerald Cubitt; David Steele. **248** All Gerald Cubitt. **249** Both Gerald Cubitt. **250** Gerald Cubitt; Herman Potgieter. **251** David Steele; David Steele; Gerald Cubitt. **252** All Gerald Cubitt. **253** Both Gerald Cubitt. **254** Both David Steele. **255** David Steele. **256** Mark Skinner; Walter Knirr. **257** Gerhard Dreyer; Zelda Wahl. **258** Both David Steele. **259** All David Steele. **260** Ken Gerhardt; Herman Potgieter; Ken Gerhardt. **261** David Steele; Herman Potgieter; Herman Potgieter. **262** Jean Morris. **263** Herman Potgieter; Gerald Cubitt; Gerald Cubitt; David Steele. **264** Will Till Inc.; David Steele. **265** Jean Morris; Herman Potgieter. **266** Both Dirk Schwager. **267** All Dirk Schwager. **268** Walter Knirr; Walter Knirr; David Steele; David Steele. **269** Reader's Digest. **270** Gerald Cubitt; David Steele. **271** Walter Knirr. **272** Zelda Wahl. **273** Gerhard Dreyer; Mark van Aardt; Keith Young; Keith Young. **274** Anthony Bannister; Gerald Cubitt; Herman Potgieter; Gerald Cubitt. **275** Both Gerald Cubitt. **276** Brian Johnson Barker; Ethel Rosenstrauch. **277** David Steele; David Steele; Ethel Rosenstrauch. **278** All Adriaan Oosthuizen. **279** Both Adriaan Oosthuizen. **280** Both John Yeld. **281** John Yeld; Ethel Rosenstrauch; David Steele. **282** John Yeld. **283** Gerald Cubitt; Gerald Cubitt; John Yeld; John Yeld. **284** Mark Skinner; Gerhard Dreyer. **285** Both Mark Skinner. **286-287** David Steele. **288** Brian Johnson Barker; David Steele. **289** All Brian Johnson Barker. **290** Walter Knirr. **291** Gordon Douglas; Jean Morris; Jean Morris; David Steele. **292** David Steele; Brian Johnson Barker. **293** Brian Johnson Barker; David Steele; David Steele. **294** David Steele; Gerald Cubitt; David Steele; David Steele. **295** Both Gerald Cubitt. **296** Zelda Wahl; Walter Knirr. **297** Trevor Smith; Rick Matthews; John Kramer. **298** Both David Steele. **299** All David Steele. **300** Brian Johnson Barker; Gerald Cubitt. **301** Gerald Cubitt; Walter Knirr; Brian Johnson Barker. **302** Both John Kramer. **303** All John Kramer. **304-305** Walter Knirr. **306** Both Mark Skinner. **307** Paul Tingay; Paul Tingay; Mark Skinner. **308** Paul Tingay. **309** Mark van Aardt; Friedrich von Hörsten; Mark van Aardt. **310** Paul Tingay. **311** All Paul Tingay. **312** Both Paul Tingay. **313** All Paul Tingay. **314** Paul Tingay. **315** All Paul Tingay. **316** Peter Pickford/Focal Point; Mark van Aardt. **317** Brendan Ryan/ABPL; Paul Tingay; Walter Knirr. **318** Paul Tingay; Colin Paterson-Jones. **319** Paul Tingay; Dewald Reiners/ABPL; Paul Tingay. **320** G Griffiths/PA; Paul Tingay; Paul Tingay; Friedrich von Hörsten. **321** Paul Tingay. **322** Walter Knirr; Mark Skinner. **323** Brendan Ryan/ABPL; Mark Skinner; Peter Steyn/PA; Brendan Ryan/ABPL. **324** M and J House; Friedrich von Hörsten. **325** All Mark Skinner. **326** Friedrich von Hörsten; M and J House. **327** All M and J House. **328** Walter Knirr; Friedrich von Hörsten; Friedrich von Hörsten. **329** Mark Skinner; Roger de la Harpe/ABPL; Mark Skinner. **330** Mark Skinner; Walter Knirr. **331** Walter Knirr; Paul Tingay; Mark Skinner; Mark Skinner. **332** Walter Knirr; Walter Knirr. **333** All Mark Skinner; Friedrich von Hörsten; Phillip Richardson/ABPL; Mark Skinner. **334-335** Johan le Roux/ABPL. **336** Mark van Aardt; Mark Skinner; Mark van Aardt. **337** Willie and Sandra Olivier; Mark Skinner. **338** Both Gwynneth Glass. **339** Roger de la Harpe; Mark van Aardt; Friedrich von Hörsten. **340** Gwynneth Glass. **341** Marianne Alexander; Willie and Sandra Olivier; Gwynneth Glass; Willie and Sandra Olivier; Robert Nunnington/ABPL. **342** Mark Skinner; Mark van Aardt; Mark Skinner. **343** Kerstin Geier/ABPL; Mark Skinner. **344** David Bristow/Getaway/PA; Mark van Aardt. **345** Brendan Ryan/ABPL; Willie and Sandra Olivier; P Blackwell/PA.

Reproduction by CMYK (Pty) Ltd, Cape Town. Printed by Tien Wah Press (Pte) Ltd, Singapore.